Managing Diversity

People Skills for a Multicultural Workplace

by Norma Carr-Ruffino, Ph.D.

CUSTOM EDITION FOR COLUMBIA COLLEGE

MGMT 339

Taken from

Managing Diversity: People Skills for Multicultural Workplace, Eighth Edition
by Norma Carr-Ruffino, Ph.D.

Learning Solutions

New York   Boston   San Francisco
London   Toronto   Sydney   Tokyo   Singapore   Madrid
Mexico City   Munich   Paris   Cape Town   Hong Kong   Montreal

Cover Art: Courtesy of Columbia College.

Taken from:

Managing Diversity: People Skills for a Multicultural Workplace, Eighth Edition
by Norma Carr-Ruffino
Copyright © 2009, 2007, 2006, 2003, 2002, 2000, 1998 by Norma Carr-Ruffino
Published by Pearson Learning Solutions
A Pearson Education Company
Boston, Massachusetts 02116

Printed in the United States of America

1 2 3 4 5 6 7 8 9 10 XXXX 14 13 12 11 10 09

2009160660

CY/HA

www.pearsonhighered.com

ISBN 10: 0-558-49590-7
ISBN 13: 978-0-558-49590-9

To Fredo, who is always there
To Lorene, who saw good qualities in "different" people
And to Jack, who saw through the eyes of unconditional love

Contents

HOW THIS BOOK CAN CHANGE YOUR LIFE

This book can do more for you than just provide information about changes in the multicultural workplace. It provides tools for you to change your life—if you to choose to raise your awareness, change limiting beliefs, and adopt new success strategies. Transformation, or lasting change, can only take place at the level of belief, so this book is designed to help you to open up your worldview—and therefore transform it. Such transformation will open up richer relationships with people who hold quite different worldviews.

Is This Book For You?

This book is for you if you see yourself as a workplace leader—now or in the future—whether you take a leadership role as the new member of a work team, the head of an organization, or somewhere in between. This book is for you if you're ready to develop the people power and people skills you need for managing diversity. In this book you'll get the information you need to make informed choices—as well as the processes for broadening your viewpoints and integrating new success skills into your daily interactions.

People Skills You Will Develop

Managing Diversity provides in-depth information, as well as self-awareness activities, for raising your awareness and building your people skills as follows:

- Raising awareness of your own cultural viewpoints and stereotypes
- Recognizing typical values, habit patterns, and concerns of each major cultural group: the dominant U.S. group Euro-Americans, men and women—who are raised in parallel gender cultures, African Americans, American Indians, Arab Americans, Asian Americans, Latino Americans, gay persons, persons with disabilities, older persons, persons of all sizes and shapes, and persons from diverse religions.
- Recognizing each group's burden of myths (that reflect the stereotypes and prejudices of the dominant culture) versus reality, historical background, current demographic profile, and cultural patterns and issues
- Meeting the leadership challenges and opportunities posed by the range of diverse employees in the workplace
- Finding common ground upon which multicultural employees can build productive, trusting relationships
- Developing strategies you can use to meet challenges and to enhance opportunities for members of each group to contribute to team and organizational excellence
- Building productive relationships among team members, coworkers, customers, suppliers, and other business and personal contacts
- Providing a work environment where all types of people can grow and thrive
- Channeling diverse talents, viewpoints, and experiences toward building synergy, enhancing creativity, and developing innovative approaches and products
- Functioning effectively in multicultural marketplaces—in the U.S. and globally

What's New in This Edition

The big news in this 8th edition of *Managing Diversity* is the addition of a new chapter, *Working with People from Diverse Religions*. Laws concerning freedom of religion and religious expression in the workplace are covered, ranging from the U.S. Constitution to the Civil Right Act to guidelines used in federal workplaces. The seven major religions that are practiced by U.S. residents are explored—Christianity, Judaism, Islam, Confucianism, Taoism, Hinduism, and Buddhism—along with what managers need to know in order to accommodate employees' various religious practices. The goal is to better understand the members of these various religions and to help you manage religious diversity in a fair and effective way in your workplace. Two case studies—Ali's Headscarf and Carol's Uniform: Pants or Skirt?—provide opportunities to apply chapter concepts to workplace situations.

Case studies are now called "case studies" instead of Skill Builders and have a new focus on ferreting out the root problems, as opposed to surface problems. Guidelines for Completing Case Studies is presented in Chapter 3, where first case study occurs.

All chapters have been updated in various ways, including demographic information from ongoing releases of Census 2000 data, legal information from court cases and rulings, data on average disposable income of each group, which can result in profitable market opportunities, and results of new surveys and research studies. More specifically, you'll find the following new materials:

- **Chapter 1 Introduction**—business ownership by women and minorities, new payoffs for managing diversity

- **Chapter 2 Culture**—corporate culture section moved here from Euro-American chapter, with new information on minority networking groups; improved organization of how we communicate culture. A new case regarding ethnic stereotypes.

- **Chapter 3 Euro-Americans**—new facts about the Euro-American culture; new skill builder on matching comments to certain aspects of the Euro-American culture.

- **Chapter 4 Stereotyping**—new surveys of stereotyping and prejudice. A new case study on stereotyping.

- **Chapter 5 Discrimination**—reorganized according to ways of managing diversity from melting pot to legal approach to multicultural approach; new information on hate crimes. A new case study on hiring practices.

- **Chapter 6 Gender**—How younger women are bridging the gender gap; updates on occupational segregation, the pay gap, leadership styles, the pink ghetto, subtle barriers, and career-family issues; new suggestions for removing glass ceiling barriers; and a new case study Jill, a Professor.

- **Chapter 7 African Americans**—updates on African American CEOs, business ownership, and the African American marketplace; two new case I Karla Gets Promoted and Cuba, Junior Consultant.

- **Chapter 8 American Indians**—update of sports team mascots-logos issue, poverty on reservations, two new case studies, Nursing Home Incident and English Only?

- **Chapter 9 Asian Americans**—updates on demographics, model minority issue, Hmong Americans, and Korean Americans.

- **Chapter 10 Arab Americans**—update of demographics, gender differences, and issues; new case study Dagany at FedEx; most information on Muslims within this group has been moved to Chapter 16 Religions.

- **Chapter 11 Latino Americans**—extensive new material on the Mexican American immigrant issues and cultural differences that affect the workplace.

- **Chapter 12 Gay Persons**—updates of demographics, attitudes toward gay rights, research on brain differences, legal protection from discrimination, marriage and family rights, hate crimes, and corporate support

- **Chapter 13 Persons with Disabilities**—updates of demographics, cost of accommodation.

- **Chapter 14 Persons Older & Younger Persons**—updates of demographics, studies of ageism, the various generations, retirement decisions, unemployment, and flexible career options.

- **Chapter 15 Obese Persons**—updates of health statistics.

- **Chapter 16 Religions**—a new chapter on managing religious diversity.

- **Chapter 17 Managing Diversity**—new information on revitalizing the AA program and on creating diverse teams; a new section on overcoming resistance to diversity and providing diversity training.

The People Who Contributed to This Book

I am especially indebted to the following people who gave me feedback and moral support in the long process of developing this book:

- Jane Baack, management professor, San Francisco State University
- Becky Beard, Lansing Community College, Lansing, Michigan
- Nicole Butler, American Indian Studies professor, Sacramento State University
- Joely De La Torre, Native American Studies professor, San Francisco State University
- Lorraine Dong, Asian Studies professor, San Francisco State University
- John Dopp, management professor, San Francisco State University
- Connie Marie Gaglio, management professor, San Francisco State University
- Karen Hossfeld, sociology professor, San Francisco State University
- Olive James, library consultant, San Francisco
- Sherri Norris, California Indian Museum & Cultural Center, Santa Rosa, CA
- Elaine Pogoncheff, Lansing Community College, Lansing Michigan
- Murray Silverman, management professor, San Francisco State University
- Anita Silvers, philosophy professor, San Francisco State University
- Barbara Smith, diversity management consultant, San Francisco
- Students in the seminar, Managing Diverse Workers, San Francisco State University, who have given me feedback on these materials over many semesters.
- Editorial staff of Pearson Custom Publishing.

Many other colleagues, friends, and family members supported me through their willingness to listen, to comment, and to understand when for days on end I was "committed to the computer" as the project grew and developed. It is truly a privilege to do this work. Just doing it has been a powerful source of personal growth for me. May working through the resulting book be similarly powerful for you, the reader.

Norma Carr-Ruffino, Ph.D.
Department of Management, College of Business
San Francisco State University

CHAPTER 1
Succeeding in a Diverse Workplace

*Companies must recognize that diversity is an imperative, not just something nice to do.
The more diverse they are, the more successful they will be.*
Pat Russo, Executive VP, Lucent Technologies

Who are we, the people of the American workplace? To begin with we're a community of people who are quite diverse, yet solidly unified around some core principles.

One nation with liberty and justice for all
Unity in Diversity

We're experiencing more diversity in the workplace—by the day. Are we doing a good job of maintaining our unity while honoring our diversity? And what skills do we need in order to succeed in this diverse workplace? This book is all about answering such basic questions.

Who Are We?

First, we are human beings—members of one species, homo sapiens, and one race, the human race. Our genetic heritage is 98 to 99 percent alike, and the tiny genetic differences must account for our different physical appearance and makeup

Second, we are Americans—all of us who are citizens and residents of the United States. Our Constitution and Bill of Rights established our equality under the law and endowed us with certain freedoms, especially freedom of opportunity. In fact, those freedoms help to define the American culture—the beliefs and attitudes, ways of thinking and feeling, decisions about life, and choices we make moment by moment. These "ways of being" are the cultural glue that binds us. As members of the American culture, we have some very strong ties.

Third, we are each a unique combination of cultural heritage and individual "ways of being." As Americans, we or our ancestors came from other cultures around the world. And those cultures, those "ways of being" learned from family and community, can vary dramatically, amazingly, and delightfully. As individuals, we are each as unique as a snowflake, and we each belong to a particular ethnic group that blends us together into its own type of cultural "snow."

When we meet someone who seems very "different," therefore, we should first note our commonalities—how much we are alike. Then we must learn about our differences—what makes us unique, and how those differences may reflect our cultural heritage and background.

How Will We Handle Our Differences?

When cultural differences are not understood and appreciated, people tend to engage in stereotyping, prejudice, and discrimination. The more powerful groups can exclude the less powerful from the freedom of opportunity that is the heritage of all Americans. Although this condition has been a strong element in American history, we have always aspired to a more open, inclusive, and equitable society.

When cultural differences *are* understood and appreciated, we tend to form cross-cultural relationships that broaden and deepen our worldviews, that stimulate our thinking and creativity, that boost our effectiveness and productivity—and therefore our success in life. Clearly, such powerful cross-cultural relationships enable more effective teams, organizations, and communities—and a more vibrant nation. This is the embodiment of an ideal America symbolized by the Bill of Rights and the Statue of Liberty.

What Skills Do We Need?

You need to develop some specific diversity skills to include in that marketable package of skills you bring to the workplace. That's because the ability to relate well to all types of people is an essential leadership skill these days—and becoming more important all the time. As a leader in the fast-paced, ever-changing American workplace, what do you need to know about diverse workers? What people skills must you develop?

You've heard that the *way* we work is becoming more technologically based and team oriented, and that global markets affect almost all businesses. You're aware that global markets are changing almost daily, and so are such American market segments as the African American, American Indian, Arab American, Asian American, and Latino American markets. These diverse markets and workplaces are increasingly made up of people from various cultures and subcultures.

This all means that our individual and cultural differences offer rich opportunities to move into new markets and to boost bottom-line profits. You can learn how to tap into these diversity opportunities. You start by learning about multicultural people skills.

Think about it. If you were an executive making hiring decisions in this environment, wouldn't you hire the applicant who offers some bonus skills: diversity people skills? Wouldn't you treasure employees who can form productive relationships with diverse business associates? Wouldn't you want people who can help the company gain and keep its share of these diverse markets?

You're about to embark on a fascinating journey of discovering what it's like to be a person from another culture. You'll repeat the process for each of the major cultural groups you'll encounter in the workplace. But first, start your exploration by answering the questions posed in Self-Awareness Activity 1.1.

Self-Awareness Activity 1.1: What Do You Know About Diversity?

Purpose: To see what you know about the issues covered in this chapter.
Instructions: Determine whether you think the following statements are basically true or false—and think about why. The answers will emerge in this chapter, and the summary at the end of the chapter focuses on these issues.

1. The majority of employees entering the workplace are "white men."
2. Women who work fulltime now make almost as much as their male counterparts.
3. Minorities are fairly well represented at all levels of management these days.
4. To relate well to people from diverse groups, I should first look at how they are different.
5. Few people hold biases and stereotypes about minorities these days.
6. The major payoff for managing diversity is contributing to social responsibility.

Back to your career, how is this blossoming diversity affecting workplace relationships? Think of your own relationships. You probably relate best to people you feel comfortable with. And you probably feel most comfortable with people who are most like you. Encountering new and different people can be interesting, stimulating, even exciting. But it can also be stressful, confusing, and frustrating when you don't understand where they're coming from, what they're trying to communicate, and why they do what they do. It can also be uncomfortable when they harbor stereotypes about you—and you harbor stereotypes about them, especially when those stereotypes cause you, or them, to feel and act in prejudiced ways.

Stereotypical thinking, prejudiced feelings, and discriminatory actions are what kept the doors to opportunity closed for so long. Discrimination is a typical outcome of prejudiced thinking, and we all harbor prejudices. It's just the flavor and degree that vary. We are all products of our culture, and virtually all cultures are ethnocentric, believing "our way is the true way" of viewing reality.

Traditionally business has handled diversity by adopting the "Melting Pot Myth," but people of color and women never "melted in" because they don't look or act like the dominant majority, Euro-American men. In recent decades legal action has opened many doors of opportunity, but it has not necessarily changed the beliefs and attitudes, nor the thoughts and feelings, that led to discrimination in the first place. Savvy leaders in forward-thinking companies value diverse employees for the unique contributions they can make to the company's success. They are crafting a multicultural approach to managing diversity, an approach that welcomes all types of employees—and then appreciates and nurtures them.

What do you need to know? As a leader in a diverse workplace, the most important knowledge you can gain is how to build multicultural skills. What skills do you need? You need those skills that will provide the basis for building productive relationships with all types of people, skills for creating a work environment that provides challenge and support for people from all cultural backgrounds.

HOW THE WORKPLACE IS CHANGING

The workplace is changing in most every way. The kinds of people we see in high-powered jobs are more diverse. The way people work together and the tasks they do are changing. And the way business is done throughout the world is changing by the day. Of the 286 million Americans living in 2000, 52 percent were women and 15 percent were "minority" men. Only one-third were Euro-American, or "white," men—but they held the huge majority of powerful career positions in the society. Even within this group, the ones who are gay, disabled, obese, or older tend to face career barriers. But the barriers are being challenged by the increasing numbers of "disadvantaged" employees in the workforce.

New Faces in New Jobs

People with university degrees and technical expertise come from all types of backgrounds these days. Since the 1960s more and more African Americans, Latino Americans, Asian Americans, Arab Americans, American Indians, and women have been entering college programs and technical areas that were formerly dominated by Euro-American men. As a result, these "minorities" have been moving into managerial, executive, technical, and professional careers formerly closed to them.

The workplace is becoming more diverse in other ways, too. For example, persons with disabilities have been finding ways to use the many abilities they do have and to become productive employees. Many gay persons no longer try to hide their sexual orientation and want to be dealt with as employees who have rights equal to those of straight employees. Older employees now have the right to refuse mandatory retirement and can work as long as they are still productive. Obese persons are beginning to expect and gain some rights to be treated fairly and equally in the workplace. And people are becoming aware of the unfairness of "appearance bias" in general, especially when it's not essentially related to job productivity.

These dramatic changes in the workplace are producing some interesting challenges for everyone, from entry-level employees to top management. All must face the misunderstanding, communication breakdown, conflict, and even failure that can result when people from widely diverse backgrounds must pull together as a team or at least complete some sort of business transaction together. But these changes also offer opportunities for new levels of growth, innovation, expansion, and productivity. This book is about successfully meeting the challenges and prospering from the opportunities.

More Women and Immigrants

Since the 1960s more and more women work outside the home for most of their adult lives. Some do this because they want careers, even though they may be wives and mothers; some because their family needs their income; and most for both reasons.

More and more ethnic minorities are in the work force because immigration quotas were expanded in the 1960s allowing more Latinos and Asians to become citizens. In 1940 more than 85 percent of people who had come to the United States as immigrants were European, while in 1995, 75 percent were from non-European countries. Most are from Latin American (47 percent) and Asian (22 percent) countries. These immigrants tend to be younger on average and to have more children than the Euro-American population, further expanding their numbers.

FIGURE 1.1: Ethnic and Gender Segments of the Workforce and of Management, 2007

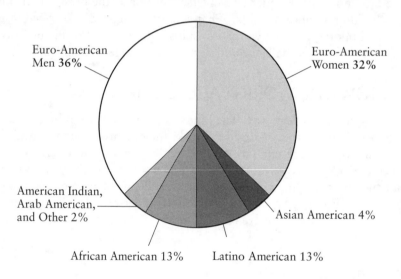

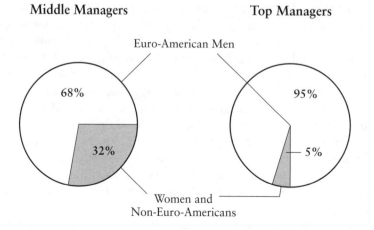

Source: *U.S. Census Bureau, 2000, 2007; U.S. Dept. of Labor, 2000; Pew Research Center 2005.*

The U.S. population of color surpassed the 100 million mark in May 2007, meaning one in every three Americans is a person of color. Total population in July 2007 was 285 million, and the approximate breakdown was

68% - 200 million Euro-Americans
13% - 35 million Latino Americans
13% - 34 million African Americans
4% - 12 million Asian Americans
2% - 4 million other groups

According to the U.S. Department of Commerce, both minority population and purchasing power are going to grow at rates much higher than the population as a whole. From 2000 to 2045, minorities will account for 86 percent of the total U.S. population growth, increasing from 29 to 46 percent of the total population. The total minority population will surpass the non-minority population sometime between 2055 and 2060. Even if current disparities in income persist, minority purchasing power will grow from 20% to 32% of total disposable income. Clearly, the ability to effectively market to ethnic groups will grow increasingly important. Companies that are unable to grab a share of ethnic markets will find themselves catering to the fringes of the consumer population.

Figure 1.1 shows the ethnic makeup of the population and the work force in 2007, as well as the proportions of Euro-Americans and minorities in the better-paying middle- and top-level management jobs (U.S. Census Bureau 2000; U.S. Dept. of Labor, 2000). Euro-American women were nearly one-third of the population, and minorities were nearly one-third, which means that they comprised nearly two-thirds of the workforce. Yet they held only 30 percent of middle management jobs and 5 percent of top management positions. The most powerful positions in corporate American were held by Euro-American men with Euro-American women holding about 4 percent, and ethnic minorities about 1 percent.

This disparity in economic power, as reflected in the workplace, is mirrored by a disparity in political power. In 2001 Congress consisted of 535 members, 435 in the House of Representatives and 100 members in the more powerful Senate. Women and minorities are greatly under-represented in both houses, as shown in Table 1.1. And of course, no women or minorities had ever been elected President or Vice President before 2008.

Table 1.1: Minority Representation Congress

Minority Designation	% of Total Population	House of Representatives		Senate	
		Percent	Number	Percent	Number
Women	52%	14%	61	13%	13
African American	12	9	38	0	0
Latino American	14	5	21	0	0
Asian American	4	1	6	2	2
American Indian	1	.002	1	1	1

A great political turning point occurred in November 2008 with the election of Barack Obama as President of the United States. His primary identification is African American, although he is clearly bi-ethnic, with a Euro-American mother and an African (Kenyan) father. Although Obama did not run on minority issues, minority voters made his election possible. He received the following proportions of votes from various ethnic groups (CNN exit polls 2008)

- Euro-American   43%
- African American   95
- Latino American   67
- Asian American   62
- Other   66

History was also made in 2008 by Hillary Clinton, the first woman presidential candidate to ever come so close to being nominated by one of the two major political parties. And Sarah Palin became the second woman, after Geraldine Ferraro in 1984 to be nominated by a major party as vice presidential candidate.

More Education Leading to Better Jobs and Earnings

The ability of people to get a better education is crucial to the socioeconomic status they are able to attain throughout life. Better education leads to higher levels of employment, more desirable occupations, and higher earnings, as indicated in Table 1.2. Over a lifetime those with a college degree are likely to earn about a million dollars more than those with a high school diploma (U.S. Census 2005). Women and minorities have been using open doors to educational opportunity to boost their career achievement.

Table 1.2: Average yearly salary of workers (age 18+), 2004

Level of Education	Yearly Salary
No high school diploma	$18,734
High school diploma	27,915
Bachelor's degree	51,200
Advanced degree	74,602

U.S. Census Bureau 2005, Pew Research Center 2005.

Ethnic minorities must often struggle to get a better education. For example, Pew's research (Pew 2005) indicates that Latino Americans who manage to attend better secondary schools in turn are more likely to complete a college degree. Likewise, those who get into selective colleges are more likely to complete their degrees than those who enter open-door and nonselective colleges.

Income is affected by educational level and age—as well as "glass ceiling" discrimination. Table 1.3 shows the percentage of persons, age 25 and over, in each major ethnic group that hold high school diplomas and bachelors degrees or higher. It also shows the median age of persons in each group. Education offers entry into the better-paying occupations. The highest-paid are medical doctors, dentists, lawyers, and petroleum engineers—the large majority are Euro-American men. The lowest-paid are dishwashers, child care workers, housekeepers, cafeteria counter attendants, and teacher assistant—the large majority are women and minorities.

Table 1.3: Education and Median Age, 2002

Ethnic Group	High School Diploma*	Bachelors Degree Or Higher*	Median Age by Ethnic Group
Total Population	84%	27%	36
Asian American	87%	47%	32
Arab American	82%	36%	29
Euro-American	89%	29%	39
African American	79%	17%	28
American Indian	n/a**	n/a	30
Latino American	57%	11%	27

*For persons age 25+   **n/a=not available*
Source: U.S. Census Bureau 2003.

Income for these groups reflect the glass ceiling to higher-level jobs still in place in corporate America. Median incomes for full-time male and female workers, as well as household income by ethnic group are shown in Table 1.4. Currently women working full time make 76 percent as much as men who work fulltime.

Table 1.4: Income and Poverty Rates, 2000

	Median Income			Poverty Rates
	Men (f.t)*	Women (f.t)*	Household	
Total	$39,100	$28,800	$42,200	12%
Male-Female Ratio	*100%*	*76%*		
Euro-American	42,200	30,800	46,300	8
Asian American	36.900	27,200	53,600	10
African American	31,000	25,700	29,500	23
American Indian	28,900	22,800	32,100	26
Latino American	25,000	21,000	33,600	22

*f.t.=fulltime
Sources: U.S. Bureau of Labor Statistics, 2001, U.S. Census Bureau 2003

Another indicator of affluence is net worth (totals assets minus total debts). As shown in Table 1.5, the net worth of the average Euro-American household is 15 times that of African Americans and 11 times that of Latino Americans, according to a study based on Census Bureau statistics (Pew 2005). Having more assets enables Euro-Americans to better endure job loss and other crises. African Americans were hit hard in recent years by job losses in the manufacturing industry and professional fields because they often had less seniority than their Euro-American coworkers.

TABLE 1.5: Net Worth of Families by Ethnic Group

Ethnic Group	Net Worth Change, 1996 to 2002*	Families with No Assets or In Debt
Euro-American	+17% to $89,000	11%
Latino American	+14% to $8,000	26%
African American	−16% to $6,000	32%

*accounting for inflation.
Source: Pew Research Center 2005.

Women and minorties are better educated than in the past, but those who work in corporations may be blocked by glass ceilings. Many are leaving to start their own businesses, leading to a virtual explosion in the number of startups, as shown in Table 1.6. The number of businesses begun by women and minorities in the United States between 1997 and 2002 exceeded the national average increase of 10 percent, according to the Census Bureau (Ownership 2005). Overall, those businesses increased their receipts by 22 percent over the five-year period and totaled $22.6 trillion.

TABLE 1.6: Ownership of New Businesses by Women, Minorities

Ethnic Group	Number of New Business Startups in 2002	Increase 1997 - 2002
Men & Women		
Hawaiian/Pacific Islanders	—	67%
Latino American	1.6 million	31%
African American	1.2 million	45%
Asian American	1.1 million	24%
All groups	23.3 million	10%
Women, all groups	6.5 million	20%
Euro-American men	—	5%

Boston Globe 2005

Trends for the Future Workplace

The trend toward a more diverse population and work force is expected to continue. U.S. demographers forecast that women, minorities and immigrants will represent well over 50 percent of all new entrants to the U.S. workforce by 2008 (McCuiston 2004). The proportions of women and ethnic minorities, especially Latino Americans, are expected to grow. Latino American workers are already more numerous than African Americans (Fullerton 2001). Women will account for about four-sixths of new entrants in the workforce, minority men more than one-sixth, and Euro-American men one-sixth, as depicted in Figure 1.2.

Historically, men of European ancestry have run virtually all the major American organizations. They have set the rules of the game in the American culture as well as in corporate cultures. Other types of employees were traditionally kept out of mainstream leadership roles. They worked on the periphery of our organizations as the workers who were told what to do and how to do it, as temporary employees and part-timers. Some were kept out completely—the unemployed and unemployable.

In the past most American businesses functioned primarily within U.S. borders. Now even very small businesses may do much of their business in global markets. Corporate success now depends on building positive, productive relationships with people from many cultures around the planet. Corporate cultures that are open, flexible, appreciative, and savvy about cultural and lifestyle differences have a competitive edge. Having diverse employees at all levels in all functional areas enhances that edge—and is becoming ever more crucial for success and profitability as reliance on global transactions increases.

FIGURE 1.2: New Workers Entering the Workforce, 1990–2010

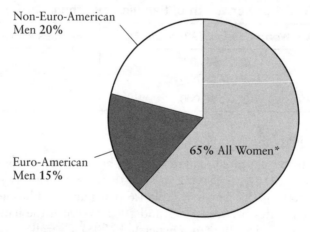

45% Euro-American Women, 20% Non-Euro-American Women
Source: U.S. Bureau of Labor Statistics

New Terms that We Use for People

People are very sensitive about the labels others attach to them. Most prefer no labels at all. Yet how do we discuss the issues of cultures and subcultures, of diverse groups in a pluralistic society, of prejudice and discrimination based on group stereotypes? Obviously, verbal communication requires the use of descriptive terms. Such terms tend to change over time in response to social and cultural changes and interactions. African Americans were properly called "Negroes" during the 1800s, politely called "Colored" during the twentieth century, then took the term "Black" for themselves. Women were politely called "ladies" before the women's movement of the 1960s. When group labels are continually used in a limiting, demeaning, scornful, or hostile way, they eventually are resented by the people they refer to. Therefore, if we want to show respect and appreciation for others, we want to use the terms they prefer. This can be difficult since members of a particular group rarely have unanimous opinions about preferred terms.

The terms used in this book are terms adopted by a multicultural task force in a large university that met weekly for many months to work out terminology and basic policy concerning diverse groups. The terms for the largest ethnic groups are listed below and reflect the preferences of activists and leaders from those groups.

- African Americans
- Arab Americans
- Asian Americans (such as Chinese Americans, Asian Indian Americans)
- Euro-Americans
- Jewish Americans
- Latino Americans (such as Mexican Americans, Puerto Rican Americans)
- American Indians

If you got a sense of equality as you looked at these terms, you're on the right track. The major rationale for these particular terms, rather than some others that may be more commonly used, is that we're all Americans, and most of us are native Americans. If we go back far enough, all of us have ancestors who came from somewhere else. And it doesn't really matter how long we or our ancestors have been here.

If your ancestors were immigrants from Europe, you're a Euro-American, often called *white*, and you're a member of the dominant majority in American culture. The terms *Asian American* and *Latino American* are used for convenience in discussing certain cultural and statistical commonalties. Most Asian Americans don't think of themselves as Asian Americans so much as *Chinese Americans* or *Filipino Americans* or one of the many Asian subcultural groups. The same is true for Latino Americans. These subcultural differences are addressed in the chapters that focus on these groups. The terms used for other diverse groups are based on discussions with various leaders of those groups and on a review of current literature. These groups include:

- Persons with Disabilities
- Gay, lesbian bisexual and transgender persons
- Older persons
- Obese persons

When you're relating one-to-one with people from any of these groups, you rarely need to refer to the group or groups they identify with. You're dealing with the individual. However, when you deal with groups or need to discuss groups with an individual, consider beginning with questions about how the person(s) feel about the various names for the groups. Reach some agreement about appropriate labels. Become sensitive to language that some consider racist and sexist, and weed it out of your vocabulary. Every time we use such terms, we reinforce the prejudicial patterns, whether we intend to or not.

Key Question: What's It Like To Be You?

Whether you are an entry-level trainee, a team leader, or a top manager, your success in and enjoyment of your career increasingly depend on how well you understand and relate to a diverse range of people. If you can mentally slip inside their skin for a time and see the world through their eyes, you'll gain great power in understanding their thinking and feeling and the issues most important to them. **Therefore, the key question that diversity leaders are asking is: *What's it like to be you?*** Here's a brief preview of some of the issues you'll learn about in this book.

Career women often find themselves in catch-22 situations. For example, people expect women to be emotional, indecisive, and vulnerable. But business leaders are expected to be in control of their emotions, decisive, and able to roll with the punches. If women project the typical image, they're not seen as potential leaders. But if they project the "business leader" image, they're often seen as too hard and masculine, even abnormal.

Men are expected to be aggressive, ambitious, and proud. But many corporate cultures are changing in ways that call for leaders who are cooperative and who focus more on challenging and supporting others than on personal achievement. Many men are confused about what companies expect of them, just as they're confused about what the women in their lives expect. The dramatic changes in women's roles have had a major impact on men's lives.

African Americans who have a problem with a "brother or sister" typically take the bull by the horns and confront the issue directly. They go straight to the person, "tell it like it is," and try to work it out immediately. To them this approach is real and honest. But to most other people in a workplace, it may be threatening and may imply anger that might erupt into violence. When Euro-American, Asian American, and Latino American co-workers feel threatened by African Americans' "confrontation, rage, or violence," it's usually because they misinterpret their cultural behavior patterns.

Asian Americans are taught that one of the highest values is to control one's reactions and to become mature enough to put relationships before personal concerns. As a result they may be very indirect about expressing criticism or disagreeing. Often, they don't show or express strong emotion, especially outside the family circle. When Euro-American, Latino American, and African American co-workers conclude that Asian Americans are closed, secretive, inscrutable, and even cold, it's usually because they're unaware of Asian cultural values.

American Indians, according to popular belief, are a vanishing race, either wasting away on remote reservations or raking in big bucks from gambling casinos. Yet many American Indians are part of a vibrant, growing population. Roughly half live on reservations, and the other half work in towns and cities. Only 5 percent benefit from casino money because most reservations are too isolated for success in such an enterprise.

Arab Americans have increasingly been profiled as possible terrorists, who may be members of some violent fundamentalist Muslim sect, and who may represent great danger in our midst. Actually, about three-fourths of Arab Americans are Christians and U.S. citizens. They are devoted to the United States and more concerned than the average American about recent hostilities. Many of them have made and are making significant contributions in the arts, business, and politics.

Latino Americans are often stereotyped by Euro-Americans as having a "manana" (literally "tomorrow") attitude. This stereotype implies that they're not ambitious, productive go-getters, as Americans tend to be. Actually, most Latino Americans are hard workers, but they tend to wait for orders from the boss. Their cultural beliefs include greater respect for authority than most Euro-Americans hold—and greater acceptance of themselves as subordinates to a powerful boss. Also, Latinos tend to be more accepting than Euro-Americans of undesirable circumstances, often seeing such situations as God's will. When Euro-Americans judge Latino Americans as lacking initiative, it's usually because they don't understand these aspects of their cultural background.

Gay persons are sometimes avoided by co-workers on the assumption that gays don't have "normal" relationships. Co-workers have made such comments as, "I just don't feel comfortable socializing with Joe (a gay man). Maybe he'll come on to me sexually," or "Maybe he'll get jealous of my friendship with a guy he's attracted to, when to me we're just hanging out." Joe would probably say, "Hey, I'm *me* first and foremost, just a person. My sexual orientation is just one slice of the whole pie that's me. What's more, I'm very sensitive to the discomforts and fears of straight guys." Studies indicate that people in the gay community have a whole range of relationships, as people in any community do, and that overall they're as likely to have "normal relationships" as people from any cultural group.

Persons with disabilities are thought to be a small minority by most people and are often seen as distinctly "different," even abnormal. Actually, most people have some type of disability, usually fairly minor. Persons classified as "disabled" simply have a disability that affects their ability to perform one or more major life function, such as walking, reading, or hearing. They're not really "different" from the person who limps around occasionally with back trouble, the person who wears contacts, or the person who doesn't hear too well out of one ear. It's just a matter of degree. Even persons with a severe disability, such as paralysis from the neck down, may learn to live and work independently and make significant contributions through their careers.

Obese persons are often as healthy as most adults, depending upon the extent of their obesity and their age. Many cruel myths and stereotypes surround obesity in our culture. The type of discrimination obese employees experience has an element of appearance bias and is related to skin-color discrimination, which is also a form of appearance bias. Obese persons also experience discrimination based on assumptions about what they cannot do, similar to that experienced by persons with disability. Recent court rulings that support the employment rights of obese persons are based on their rights to "reasonable accommodation" under laws that protect the disabled.

Older persons are often assumed to be rigid, dogmatic, and forgetful. Their younger co-workers may avoid them and may wonder why these "old folks" haven't retired or when they're going to retire. Research indicates that aging itself does not cause any significant loss of intelligence, memory, or learning capacity. However, with age one's habits tend to come home to roost. People who abuse or neglect their bodies start paying the price in their later years, while people with good eating and exercise habits tend to remain healthy and vibrant. People who habitually spend much of their time in negative thinking tend to become even more negative with age, while those who work on a positive outlook and self-growth become more delightful to be around.

Every cultural subgroup has its own unique set of values, habits, customs, life circumstances, and issues to resolve. Understanding the key cultural themes and issues of each group can give you great insight and power for building good work relationships and helping other team members do the same.

New Approach = Substance vs. Style

We can see a pattern emerging in the issues of all these diverse groups. Traditional business managers have expected a work style and management style that looked like the Euro-American male style. That's what had become the standard in the American workplace. But this old standard no longer makes sense in today's increasingly diverse workplace. What matters is getting positive answers to key performance questions, such as:

- Does the employee's decision meet the criteria we set?
- Has the employee achieved the goals we set?
- Has the employee maintained the quality standards we set?
- Are the bottom-line results good?

In other words, it's possible that an employee may get just as good results—or even better results—by going about the job in a different way. There is rarely just one good way to get results. In fact, diverse ways of approaching problems and tasks can result in innovative solutions and actions.

Remember: just because a person may seem "too passive, too aggressive, too shy, too excitable, too low-key, too high-key" or any other descriptor of their approach or behavior—that does not necessarily mean that they cannot do an excellent job. These ways of being in the world are a matter of style, often dictated by one's culture. They are not necessarily matters of substance—what the individual employee is actually capable of doing if given the chance. Of course, it's important to give diverse employees proper training and guidance so that they understand the role they are playing and the results that are needed.

As a workplace leader, make it your intention to be open to many styles. Learn to see through the style to the substance—whether it's the substance of an idea, a potential skill, or performance results.

New Ways of Working Together

In the new technologically oriented companies, employees are more highly skilled and educated than ever. Old hierarchies and authoritarian bosses who dictate orders are fading into the archaic past. More common are:

- self-managing work teams
- leaders who facilitate team meetings and help teams to reach consensus
- consultants and technical experts who function more as professionals than as traditional employees.

Relationships with teammates, customers, and suppliers, and the information that flows among them, are the lifeblood of the organization. Corporations are increasingly built upon trust, collaboration, cooperation, and teamwork. In such organizations, it's more obvious than ever that people are the most valuable resource, that how we work together creates energy and innovation or lethargy and demoralization, that our interactions spark the knowledge and information that fuel organizational growth and success.

In summary, key trends that point to the need for multicultural leadership skills are:

- A shortage of qualified, educated workers means companies must be more responsive to workers' needs and expectations.
- The U. S. work force is becoming dramatically more diverse at all levels. Workers expect more accommodation to their needs and identities than in the past. Fewer workers are willing to compromise their unique characteristics for the sake of "fitting in" with corporate cultures built exclusively on traditional Euro-American male values and norms.
- The global marketplace that now affects nearly all American corporations is intensely competitive, making qualified employees more crucial than ever for providing the quality, innovation, and productivity companies need to compete.
- The growth of these subcultural groups means growth of subcultural market segments. Companies need a work force that "looks like America" to project a multicultural company image, contribute to marketing insights, and relate well to customers from all ethnic and lifestyle groups.
- Success in the global marketplace depends on building profitable relationships with people in all the countries where an organization does business. Diverse people skills are as powerful in the global marketplace as they are in the American workplace. Once you develop such skills, you can more easily expand them to include people living in other countries, cultures, and environments.

TEN PAYOFFS FOR MANAGING DIVERSITY WELL

How can you be successful in a global marketplace if you don't understand the various cultures, languages, and ways of doing business that are out there? Virtually all large firms have entered this marketplace, many medium-sized firms are entering, and even some small businesses are plunging in. Business leaders are saying things like, "Aligning corporate culture with a multicultural world helps us overcome the inherent limitations we might place on people, and our ability to fully leverage our intellectual capital. We need to ask ourselves, 'Do our values and our organizational culture allow us to operate effectively in a diverse world?'"

Such business leaders use an active, change-oriented multicultural approach to managing diversity. They are discovering a surprising wealth of payoffs for their organizations. Benefits accrue at all levels: personal, interpersonal, and organizational (Ely 2001). They include the following types of payoffs, all based on published research studies:

1. attracting and retaining the best available human talent
2. reducing costs
3. increasing organizational flexibility
4. attracting and keeping customers and suppliers

5. gaining greater market share
6. improving the quality of management
7. problem-solving and innovating more powerfully
8. increasing productivity
9. contributing to social responsibility
10. bottom line: increased profits

We'll explore briefly why and how each of these payoffs is important.

Payoff #1: Attracting and Retaining the Best People

Attracting and retaining the best people as employees requires that organizations meet potential employees' needs, show respect for them as individuals, and use multicultural skills in working with them.

Attracting Qualified People

As qualified employees become more scarce, employers must become more flexible. Otherwise talented women and minorities will end up working for competitors. Morris (2005) found that women are the largest group still being ignored in talent pools—in spite of research indicating they are just as hardworking and ambitious as men.

Companies can no longer afford to convey the implicit message, "This is what we offer and how we do things. Fit in or leave." Now they must adapt to potential employees who say, "These are my needs and goals. They must be met if I am to stay."

Meeting Employee Needs and Expectations

Nearly five-sixths of new employees will be women and minorities in the coming decade. Most are from a new generation who expect something extra from their careers, namely, meaning and a sense of making a contribution. Most, especially career women, expect to have a personal and family life and are less willing than older generations were to sacrifice all for career success. And most, especially ethnic minorities, are more resistant to fitting into a corporate culture that requires them to squelch important parts of their persona. They need the comfort that comes with a sense of cultural fit.

Many studies speak of the comfort factor. Hariss and Kleiner (1993) found that major advantages accrue when people are comfortable with others who are different and are able to build relationships across gender and cultural lines. Freeman-Evans (1994) concluded that once employees feel comfortable in their work environment, only then are they motivated to work to their fullest potential. Salomon (2003) confirmed that minorities who feel welcomed and valued become more passionate about their work.

These better educated employees want their individual and group needs recognized and met. They want more control over their own destiny, a say in decisions that affect them, and more flexibility in the terms and rewards of employment. They want a fair, open, flexible, responsive, and responsible work environment where they can enjoy the workday as well as be productive. They want to experience the excitement and stimulation of meeting challenging opportunities and problems as well as the security and serenity that come from being appreciated and supported.

Word gets around quickly about how companies treat diverse employees and which companies are the best to work for. People are less likely to stay with employers who don't meet their needs.

Retaining High-Potential Employees

To retain good employees, firms must be truly committed to treating all employees fairly and to valuing diversity. Employers who appear to favor some personal orientations and stifle others risk paying the price of low productivity due to a restricted pool of applicants, employee dissatisfaction, lack of commitment, turnover, and even sabotage. When women or minority employee must persistently work extra hard to have their voices heard and their opinions valued, they eventually become exhausted—physically and emotionally. The work environment seems hostile. These employees are more likely to quit their jobs because they see little hope for their future in the company (Salomon 2003).

No one wants to feel like an outsider. Employees who like the way they are treated are generally friendlier with their coworkers and managers. Patrick Council (2001) found that making sure employees feel comfortable in the work environment is a key factor in retaining them. He said, "A diversified workforce allows people to socialize and relax with coworkers, which leads to higher job satisfaction and less employee turnover."

University of Alabama Professor John Sheridan's research indicates that professionals (both strong and weak performers) stay an average of 14 months longer in firms whose main focus is "interpersonal orientation" values than in firms whose focus is "work task" values. Sheridan estimates that the work task-value firms incurred opportunity losses of $6 to $9 million more, over the six-year period studied, than the interpersonal-value firms. Sheridan concludes that it makes more sense to foster an interpersonal orientation culture rather than to try to find individuals who will fit into a work task culture.

Communicating Respect for Others

One of the basic principles of effective multicultural leadership is to signal respect for the unique characteristics of another's culture. Small gestures can communicate respect, such as greeting persons in their native language, taking time to chat and learn more about a person, and keeping their cultural and personal viewpoints and values in mind as you work together. Doing this effectively requires learning about diverse groups and building skills in relating to group members.

Payoff #2: Reducing Costs

A multicultural approach saves money in the long run and often even in the short run.

Long-Range Costs

A multicultural approach can prevent costly grievances, complaints, and lawsuits. In addition to lost time and legal fees for dealing with such problems, other costs are job-related stress, lowered morale, lowered productivity, and resulting absenteeism and turnover. For example, when companies such as Coca-Cola don't manage diversity effectively, they pay. Recently they paid $8 million in back-pay to African-American executives as part of a discrimination settlement. Then Coke found itself in hot water again for failing to include diverse candidates in their search for corporate board members.

Overall, it is costly to reverse the consequences of miscommunication, ignorance, and disrespect. Organizations must take a proactive approach to appreciating diversity and managing it effectively.

Employee Turnover Costs

Women and minority employees quit their jobs more frequently than Euro-American male employees (Hom 2007). Percentages of employees in various groups who left their jobs during the year 2006 were:

- 3.46% Euro-American men
- 4.07% African American and Latino American men
- 4.61% Euro-American women
- 5.42% African American and Latino American women

Diversity efforts reduce the high turnover rate of nontraditional employees and the costs that go with it. Employee turnover rate is calculated simply by dividing the number of annual terminations by the average number of employees in the workforce. The 2003 median employee turnover rate was about 12 percent for U.S. companies, according to the Bureau of National Affairs (2004).

Estimated costs of employee turnover vary from organization to organization—from as low as a few hundred dollars to as high as four times the annual salary of the employee. On average, it costs a company one-third of a new hire's annual salary to replace an employee. Therefore, at minimum wage, the cost to replace an employee is estimated at $3,700. For an employee hired at $45,000, the average replacement cost would be $15,000 (Musrush 2002).

On the other hand, when a nontraditional manager is included in a development program or gets a promotion, other nontraditional employees at lower levels notice and feel more hopeful and committed to the company. Such companies are more likely to be sought out by nontraditional recruits, which reduces the costs of recruiting.

Payoff #3: Increasing Organizational Flexibility

Companies are teaming up, forming alliances to pool their resources and to tighten relationships with suppliers and customers. An alliance may require that two teams or units from two different companies blend together to act as a link between the firms involved. The most frequently cited source of problems with alliances is "different corporate cultures," according to a Harvard Business Review survey. Multicultural skills can be applied to working in various corporate cultures as well as working with individuals from various ethnic cultures (Kanter 1991).

The Flexibility to Innovate

Another aspect of flexibility is the ability to constantly create game-changing innovations—as current products become commodities and competition intensifies. Diversity breeds innovation; homogeneity does not. In a study conducted in 2003 at Northwestern University, 50 groups were asked to solve a murder mystery. Groups from varied social backgrounds did best. Homogeneous groups were more likely to get it wrong—and were more confident that their answers were right. The researchers concluded that if an organization wants creative ideas that contribute to good problem-solving and decision-making, a diversity of personality types works best (Gill 2005). But how does an organization find the diversity it needs?

The Flexibility to Hire the Best People

Managers are constantly complaining about how hard it is to find talented employees. Yet research indicates that when top managers say of a job candidate, "He'll be a great fit," they may mean, "He's someone who brings a needed talent." But they may also mean, "We like this person because he thinks like we do"; i.e. "He's likely to agree with us." Hiring is one of most difficult tasks a manager faces, and the safest applicant often gets the job. This usually means someone with a background and personality similar to the CEO's or most of the Euro-American managers in the organization. This in turn can lead to a firm full of clones—at least in the main positions. Diversity of personality, sensibility, and work style are important too—and often reflect diverse cultural backgrounds—ethnic, lifestyle, gender (Gill 2005). Managers must focus on chemistry and fit when making an important hire, as well as diversity of ethnicity, gender, and personality type. In an organization of innovative go-getters, what makes a good fit is a person's ambition and drive to change the game.

Game-Changing Flexibility

Many venture capitalists avoid funding firms with a CEO who clones himself. They want to see that management will have people with a diversity of viewpoints and ideas, not a team of yes-persons (Gill 2005). This diversity may mean that meetings are more raucous and consensus is harder to achieve. But arguments often spark new ideas. A certain measure of conflict is healthy, while too much can be destructive, of course. A diverse team is likely to constantly spawn and sculpt new innovations in ways that think-alike teams never can. The old approach may be to let challenges find the management team, and then they "sweat them out." The new approach is to look for ways to change the game, to create challenges and to have fun in finding solutions.

Payoff #4: Attracting and Keeping Customers and Suppliers

Diverse employees understand customers who are like themselves (Overell 2004). To create a global product, an organization must understand its global customers. According to Joan Crockett (1999), "Diversity is about ensuring that a workforce as a whole shares the same experiences, backgrounds and sensitivities as the markets it serves and the communities in which it operates." Diverse employees provide cultural insight as to whether a product or service will be successful or not. This kind of information is more valuable than the information any focus group or survey can provide. The best way to understand a particular culture is to be a part of it (Segal 1997). Bottom line, diverse staff members boost sales revenue and profits because they are able to:

- Clarify diverse target markets
- Identify ways to appropriately represent and portray multicultural images
- Serve as a resource for selling to diverse targeted emergent markets
- Provide the multicultural audience another opportunity to flex its purchasing power
- Broaden the range of ideas and usability of products and services

Attracting the Whole Range of Customers

Having a diverse staff means having employees who can help to attract and retain the whole range of customers. The experiences and perspectives of diverse employees can certainly be valuable in building sales. Such diversity is the best way to be sure the organization remains flexible enough to capture diverse markets and to provide adequate customer service.

Studies indicate that diverse teams are less likely to get trapped in groupthink and more likely to achieve enhanced critical thinking. They are more likely to produce products and services better tailored to diverse customers (Cox and Smolinski 1994). For example, having African American women on the team can motivate management to respond to growing market niches involving such customers. This happened to Avon in the cosmetics market. Also, when experts assessed the problems that led to K-mart's bankruptcy, they concluded that K-mart had lost touch with its customer-base and failed to capitalize on multicultural markets that it once controlled. They suggested that K-mart place more emphasis on wooing consumers of color.

Customers tend to perceive that someone of their own ethnicity or gender is better able to serve their needs, and this can influence them in choosing one service or product over another. Using diversity to improve marketing skills within ethnically diverse domestic markets can help a company to market more effectively internationally, too. Learning how to be responsive to local markets and to project the right image to them will help the company sharpen its skills for the international marketplace.

Diverse employees can prevent many awkward public relations problems. They can also help in those one-on-one provider-customer interactions that are becoming increasingly common, as companies focus on providing services, information, and custom products to customers. It makes sense for a company to employ a workforce that mirrors its customer base. Having African Americans, Asian Americans, Latino Americans, and women on decision-making teams could help prevent these kinds of problems:

- An advertisement for a major telephone company featured a drawing of animals making telephone calls from various continents. A gorilla was making the call from Africa. Many African Americans were incensed.

- An American deodorant commercial shows an octopus putting antiperspirant under each arm. In Japan octopus appendages are called "legs." When the commercial aired in Japan, people were shocked and puzzled to see an octopus applying deodorant under his legs.

- A major bank instructed its tellers, all women, to wear straw hats with a band reading "Free and Easy Banking." The word "Banking" was hidden under the turned-up brims. When women realized why customers were snickering, they were upset.

Banks have come to realize the importance of having a diverse workforce, and also having employees who are fluent in the most common languages of their customers. This eases customer discomfort, makes transactions go more smoothly, and therefore lowers transaction costs and improves customer service (Sudhoff 2004).

Bottom line: a diverse staff provides a better image for an organization, making it a more attractive place to conduct business for a wide range of customers. Organizations that ignore diversity issues in the workforce will ultimate lose the business of a large, diverse customer base (Losey 1993).

Strengthening Supplier Relationships

At times organizations must negotiate with foreign suppliers in their own language and according to their own cultural customs. In fact, the organization that cannot manage such relationships may be unable to conduct business. Some suppliers may even demand to see that the companies they supply have diversity initiatives—because they want to conduct business with diverse teams. One supplier asked a client firm, "How can you explain your diversity program when you send six Euro-American males to meet with us?" (Salomon and Schork 2003).

Payoff #5: Gaining Greater Market Share

Companies that manage diversity effectively are better able to expand their share of markets—locally and globally—and to keep them. For example, the combined purchasing power of the four major minority groups is huge and growing, as shown in Table 1.7 In 2002 it totaled about $1.45 trillion, in 2007 is $2.25 trillion, and in 2010 is expected to reach. $2.70 trillion, representing growth rates of about 100 percent per year. Residents of just one state, California, represent a huge consumer market, and most of them are minorities (MPA 2008).

TABLE 1.7: Purchasing Power of U. S. Minorities

Ethnic Group	2002	2007	2010-Projected
African Americans	$625 billion	$825 billion	$1 trillion
American Indians	25	50	$70 billion
Asian Americans	225	450	580 billion
Latino Americans	575	925	$1 trillion
Total Purchasing Power	**$1.45 trillion**	**$2.25 trillion**	**$2.70 trillion**
Women of all groups	*$5 trillian*	*n/a*	*n/a*

Source: Celent 2003; MPA 2008.

In 2006, the U.S. African American and Latino American consumer markets together were already larger than the entire economies of all the countries in the world—except the economies of the top 9 nations. By 2010, the buying power of African Americans and Latino Americans will exceed the GDP of Canada, the ninth largest economy in the world

The ethnic personal-care market is booming: The combined market for ethnic hair-care, cosmetic and skin-care products is valued at $1.9 billion (Millman 2007). In the telecommunication industry people of color account for one-third of all telecommunications sales. One out of every three dollars spent on telecommunications services in 2009 came from people of color (Insight Research Corporation). In the online retailing industry 31 percent of Asian American consumers make five or more online purchases a year (MPA 2008).

Business travelers are another large market, and about half are now women. In fact, women of all groups spend over $5 trillion a year, over half the U.S. GDP. They are responsible for 85 percent of all consumer purchases—of everything from automobiles to healthcare (PME 2004).

Clearly, such markets have huge financial implications for any organization. If a company wants to understand these markets, it must depend on a diverse staff. It can reach untapped markets only if it has employees with the cultural experiences needed to sell effectively to those markets.

Payoff #6: Improving the Quality of Management

Knowing they must compete with all comers can encourage the more competent Euro-American men to perform even better, while the less competent ones are screened out. Diversity can prod managers to learn fresh approaches to business problems, to see issues from new perspectives, and to add new contacts to their business networks. Exposure to diverse colleagues can help managers develop breadth and openness. Perhaps this explains why Euro-American men who graduate from universities where African American students comprise 8 to 17 percent of the student body earn roughly 15 percent higher wages than whose who graduate from "lily white" schools (Marshall 1995).

Also, much of what an organization learns in trying out a special training program for diversity purposes may later be broadly applied to all employees. For example, we all like to be appreciated for our uniqueness and to be treated with respect.

Payoff #7: Problem-Solving and Innovating More Powerfully

Traditional assembly-line industrial organizations required creative thinking from only a few, but post-industrial organizations with their self-managing work teams require it of many. When organizations expect minorities to adapt to a Euro-Americans corporate culture, they fail to capitalize on the innovative and creative potential of a diverse workforce. A multicultural approach, on the other hand, enhances innovative outcome (Hong 2004).

Diverse groups consist of people with different thoughts, attitudes, personalities, and experiences. Company cultures that are open to differences provide a lush ground for the growth of new ideas. When people feel comfortable communicating diverse viewpoints, the result is a larger pool of ideas, personalities, and experiences. In a truly multicultural environment, people from diverse backgrounds feel respected, supported, and appreciated. They are therefore willing to contribute their ideas to group sessions. This in turn gives the group a broader range of diverse ideas to choose from, increases group synergy, and prevents groupthink (Chatman 2001). Diverse groups are therefore more creative in solving problems (Mayo, 1999).

Research supports the belief that diverse teams enhance problem-solving, decision-making, and innovation. For example, one study concluded that higher-quality decisions are made when different solutions are evaluated and weighted (Mayo 1999). Another showed that great decisions result from the merger of very different ideas (Salomon and Schork, 2003). Chrysler VP James P. Holden said, "Teams become truly effective when they represent the full spectrum of diversity." (Mayo 1999)

The conclusion that creativity is fostered by diversity is supported by research showing that the tolerance of diversity, defined as judging relatively few behaviors as deviant from norms, is a defining characteristic of innovative organizations (Siegel and Kaemmerer 1978). Diverse teams and organizations typically generate more options, especially more creative options and higher quality ideas—because opposing viewpoints are introduced and resolved. Groupthink is less probable. (Nemeth 1986; Nemeth and Wachtler 1983, Cox, Lobel & McLeod 1991; Wanous & Youtz 1986; Watson, Kumar and Michaelson 1993).

For best results, relationships among team members must be predominantly positive. However, a certain amount of conflict is natural and inevitable, and if it is managed well, it can be constructive. Excessive group conflict interferes with productivity, closing down communication, wasting energy, and even causing people to leave. But too little conflict may signal complacency, repression, or old approaches to addressing new problems. The challenge is to stir innovation, manage conflict, and prevent breakdown (Jackson 1991).

Raymond Gilmartin, CEO of Merck, states that "Competitive advantage in a business like ours rests on innovation. To succeed, we must bring together talented and committed people with diverse perspectives" (Salomon 2003).

Payoff #8: Increasing Productivity

All the benefits mentioned so far work together to generally increase organizational productivity. Specifically, an effective approach to managing diversity helps diverse teams and individuals to be more productive (Ely 2001, Carpenter 2002).

First, all team members must learn to move beyond stereotyping others. The team must learn about each member's unique values, abilities, expectations, and goals. Leaders must help members define and assess job objectives, job performance, and career plans. Employees tend to have better job performance and dedication when they feel valued and cared for by their manager, team members, and organization. They are more productive when they enjoy coming to work, feel happy to be working where they're seen as worthy and competent, and can relax into being themselves. Such employees are likely to be more innovative and productive, even without any direct reward or personal recognition.

Research indicates that groups that are diverse in terms of ethnicity, age, values, background and training are more productive and innovative than homogeneous groups (Eisenberger et al 1990). A five-year research program, based on consultation with CEO's, revealed that diversity within a work team, if properly managed, will boost productivity and quality of output. Such diversity positively affects worker behavior, customer attitudes, and ultimately the bottom line (Harvey 2003).

A mixture of genders, ethnic backgrounds, and ages in senior management consistently correlates to superior corporate performance, according to an American Management Association survey (AMA 1999). The survey of more than 1,000 managers evaluated the impact of diversity on such performance measures as annual sales, gross revenues, market share, shareholder value, net operating profit, worker productivity, and total assets. Results echoed the findings from within higher education about the impact of diverse classrooms. The corporate sector sees diversity as a distinct asset.

Smaller companies and service sector companies have more women and ethnic minorities on senior management teams. They also tend to report better organizational outcomes than larger companies and manufacturers. The communications industry, which includes telecommunications providers, broadcasters, and publishers, report senior management teams with more women and younger managers (33 percent compared to overall 21 percent). This industry is also far above average in their report of increased sales, operating profits, and worker productivity (AMA 1999)

Payoff #9: Contributing to Social Responsibility

The organization can become an agent for change, to make the world a better place. If one organization can thrive by creating an environment where diverse people can work effectively together, this can serve as a model for the entire world. A Los Angeles executive said, "In this area the situation is so desperate and so in need of role models, that if we in corporations can't advance minorities so they can turn around and do what needs to be done in their communities, I don't see any of us surviving. The bigger picture we have to deal with is the minority situation in this country."

IBM's Chairman Samuel Palmisano said, "Businesses now operate in an environment in which long-standing concerns—in areas from diversity to equal opportunity, the environment and workforce policies—have been raised to the same level of public expectation as accounting practices and financial performance" (McClenahen 2005). Such indicators of corporate citizenship have become important to the general public.

Payoff #10: Bottom Line—Increased Profits

Bottom line: These various advantages for managing diversity effectively add up for the reason business is in business: making good profits.

Global competition is an established fact of life now. The re-engineering, restructuring, and downsizing of the 1990s reflect the reality that United States business can no longer afford bureaucratic, hierarchical structures with a homogeneous group running the show. We can no longer afford the luxury of paying big salaries to layer upon layer of managers to carry information back and forth between workers, managers, and staff experts, information that all can now access through their computers. We're realizing the potential power of setting up informational networks where many workers can instantly interact

We can no longer afford to pay tiers of high-salaried managers to set goals and make plans for workers and then try to motivate them and keep them productive. We're realizing that work teams and individual workers should be setting their own goals and making their own plans. When they do, they're likely to be self-motivated and work out their own productivity issues.

We can no longer afford to exclude people with the talents and skills we so desperately need for business success. All the benefits they bring to the workplace add up to increased career success and company profits—provided we learn to build productive working relationships with each other.

The need for this approach is reflected in a study from Texas A&M University's Center of Retailing Studies. The conclusion: American retailers must understand the changing ethnic and cultural consumer market in order to survive. In the new millennium, successfully engaging diversity in the marketplace is no longer an option for business. It's the key to economic survival (Stevens 2003).

According to Fortune Magazine, in 1998 the 50 most recognized racially diverse organizations had a total five-year return to shareholders of 201 percent compared to 171 percent for the S&P 500. Other studies show that firms with diverse top management teams get better financial returns (Hartenian 2000). Organizations today have little choice but to diversify in order to remain profitable and sustain a competitive advantage (Harvey 1999, Richard 2000).

MEETING NEW CHALLENGES: GLOBAL, NATIONAL, CORPORATE, AND PERSONAL

The problems we're facing in our business organizations reflect problems we're facing at all levels: personal problems, family problems, national problems, and global problems. As we grow in our understanding of diversity in the workplace, of the major roles of beliefs, values, stereotypes, prejudices, relationships, and access to information, we grow in understanding ourselves, our family dynamics, and our national and global priorities. As we gain skill in establishing and nurturing relationships with the whole spectrum of diverse people in the workplace, we gain skill as a national culture in working out the problems now dividing us: violent crime, ethnic conflict, inner-city decay, failing schools. If we learn how to find greater unity and harmony as a nation, we can bring this knowledge to the arena of global culture, where as a community of nations we can apply it in meeting global challenges and creating global harmony and abundance.

Our diversity can be our greatest source of power, and it can also be the source of our disintegration as a culture. In biology we understand the power of a diverse gene pool, but in organizations we are just beginning to learn the power of a diverse pool of ideas, viewpoints, and talents. When we see the growing crime and violence almost everywhere, and the continued divisiveness and prejudice, we begin to understand the price we must pay when we don't find ways to manage our diversity so that we also have unity and harmony. Unity with diversity has always been an ideal in our nation, along with freedom and equality of opportunity. Our challenge in the workplace today is to make these ideals a reality.

No wonder workplace diversity has become a hot topic! Diversity symbolizes the key to our power in meeting challenges and creating the world we want—at every level of existence. Diversity also symbolizes our hopes for the New Millennium, and the changes we need to make in order to meet its challenges and rise to its opportunities.

CAREER SUCCESS: HOW TO BUILD DIVERSE PEOPLE SKILLS

> *Travel is fatal to prejudice, bigotry and narrow-mindedness. . . .*
> *Broad, wholesome, charitable views cannot be acquired*
> *by vegetating in one's little corner of the earth.*
> Mark Twain

Even if you haven't traveled much, you can take cultural journeys, beginning with the processes given in this book. You can notice that the global marketplace and the American workplace are changing more rapidly every day. Your workplace is becoming more diverse, more technical, more global, and at the same time more dependent than ever on productive working relationships. As a business leader helping to create an inclusive work environment, your success depends more and more on building your multicultural skills. And that's the purpose of this book.

How Do I Build Cross-Cultural Relationships? A 5-Step Process

You establish a strong foundation for building cross-cultural relationships by using the following five-step process.

Step 1. What is culture? How does it affect us? You start by becoming aware of what culture is—its elements, pervasiveness, and impact upon us—as well as the similarities and differences among major cultural groups.

Step 2. How is my own culture different from others? Next, you learn that the beliefs and customs that you accept as reality are only one way of viewing the world, the "ways of being" in your culture.

Step 3. "I'm not biased, but . . ." Then you begin to recognize your own biases, the ways in which you stereotype, assume, judge, and discriminate, so you can own these biases and move beyond them. Self-Awareness Activities help you to do this.

Step 4. What's it like to be you? Perhaps the most important and fascinating step is learning about other cultures—the environments of people you encounter in the workplace, This knowledge helps you to recognize when cultural differences may be at the root of problems. It enables you to appreciate the contributions that people from diverse cultures can make to the work situation.

Step 5. How do I build interaction skills? Finally you practice new behaviors through self-awareness activities, skill builder case studies, interviews, and applying your new understandings to actual people situations at work, school, anywhere you encounter diverse groups.

In chapters 2, 3, 4, and 5 you'll work through steps 1, 2, and 3. In chapter 2 you'll start becoming aware of culture's pervasive influence, and learn some key cultural patterns that will help you recognize cultural similarities and differences. In chapter 3 you'll become more aware of key aspects of the dominant Euro-American culture and of typical corporate cultures. In chapters 4 and 5 you'll begin to recognize your own biases and learn about the nature of prejudice. These chapters lay the groundwork for building your skills; they're the necessary background you'll need.

What's It Like to Be You? And Other Key Questions

The most important question you can ask yourself—and others—about cultural differences is, What's it like to be you? If you really mean it and really care about the answers, you are certain to become highly skilled in building powerful cross-cultural relationships. So ask this question often and open up to any and all answers.

Table 1.8 lists other key questions. You'll find answers to these questions in each of the chapters that focuses on a particular group—chapters 6 through 15.

TABLE 1.8: Finding Out What It's Like to Be You

6 Key Questions	*Chapter Segments: The Answers*
1. What barriers to career success do you face?	1. Stereotypes and myths versus reality
2. How did it get that way?	2. Connections to the past
3. What's going on now?	3. Current profile
4. How do you see the world?	4. Cultural worldviews, values, customs, issues
5. How can I work most effectively with you?	5. Leadership challenges and opportunities
6. How can I apply my new knowledge and practice multicultural skills?	6. Case studies, other skill builders

In chapters 6 through 16 you get to learn about the cultures of others, ranging from the parallel cultural worlds of men and women to various African American, American Indian, Arab American, Asian American, and Latino American subcultures, to the culture-like lifestyles of gay persons, persons with disabilities, older persons, and obese persons. You'll begin building interaction skills and practicing them. Chapter 17 ties the leadership challenges and opportunities together from an organizational viewpoint. You'll focus on how you can influence the organization toward creating an inclusive corporate culture in which all types of employees can be productive and comfortable.

Making Your Skills Count

But what can one person do? Regardless of your position, your skills can make a difference. You can take whatever leadership role your situation allows. To begin with, you can notice the contributions of employees from groups that seem to be excluded in some way, and you can talk up their positive qualities. You can tell the stories of those who succeed, helping to make them stars in the company grapevine of myths and legends. You can visibly support them in any way that seems right. You can unfailingly respect their dignity and speak out against disrespect in the form of wisecracks, jokes, putdowns, exclusion, and similar behavior. If you have the decision-making authority or influence, you can provide training for other employees to help them understand and appreciate people from all groups.

SUMMARY

We are all human beings of the same species and race, 98 to 99 percent genetically alike. We are all Americans—no matter how long we've been here—and it's appropriate that the terms we use for the various cultural groups reflect that fact. And we are each a unique combination of our cultural heritage and our individual "ways of being." How we handle these cultural differences determines how innovative, productive, and vibrant we become. When we meet someone who seems very "different," therefore, we should first note our commonalities—how much we are all alike. Then we must learn about our differences—what makes us unique, and how those differences may reflect our cultural heritage and background.

When cultural differences are not understood and appreciated, people tend to engage in stereotyping, prejudice, and discrimination. The more powerful groups can exclude the less powerful from the freedom of opportunity that is the heritage of all Americans. When cultural differences *are* understood and appreciated, we tend to form cross-cultural relationships that broaden and deepen our worldviews, that stimulate our thinking and creativity, that boost our effectiveness and productivity—and therefore our success in life.

The workplace is changing dramatically, with minorities and women moving into all types of positions, including executive, managerial, technical, and professional jobs. In fact, about 85 percent of new employees are now women and minorities. However, 95 percent of top managers in major corporations are Euro-Americans men, and their income is higher on average. Therefore, equal opportunity and pay have not been achieved yet.

Business relationships are more diverse than ever, and diverse groups have diverse issues that are important to them. Suppliers and customers are ever more international in scope, and they, along with global competition, are changing the way we do business. Self-managing work teams and more highly-educated employees call for leaders and business associates with diverse people skills.

The multicultural approach to managing diversity offers many payoffs for organizations, including attracting and retaining the best available human talent, reducing costs, increasing organizational flexibility, attracting and keeping customers and suppliers, gaining greater market share, improving the quality of management, problem-solving and innovating more powerfully, increasing productivity, and contributing to social responsibility. The bottom line is increased profits

The steps to gaining multicultural skills are to: 1) become aware of culture's impact, 2) recognize your personal biases toward various types of people, 3) learn about your own culture's values and ways, 4) learn about the values and ways of people from other cultures, and 5) build your interaction skills through case studies and on-the-job application of your new knowledge.

What's it like to be you? This is the most important question to ask yourself and others about people from other cultures. Understanding cultural differences can help you to recognize when these differences may be at the root of problems and to appreciate the contributions that people from diverse cultures can make to the work situation.

REFERENCES

AMA, "Diverse Leadership Teams Are More Productive: Findings from the American Management Association," www.diversityweb.org, 1999.

Brislin, Richard and Tomoko Yoshida. *Intercultural Communication Training*. Sage, 1994.

Bureau of National Affairs, www.bna.com, March 2004.

Carpenter, M.S. "The Implications of Strategy and Social Context for the Relationship between Top Management Team Heterogeneity and Firm Performance," *Strategic Management Journal* 23, 3, 275–284, 2002.

Carr-Ruffino, Norma, et al. "Legal Aspects of Women's Advancement" in *Woman Power*. Sage, 1991.

Carr-Ruffino, Norma. "U.S. Women: Breaking Through the Glass Ceiling." *Women in Management Review* 6, 5. 1991.

Carr-Ruffino, Norma. *The Promotable Woman*. Career Press, 1997.

Catalyst, "More Women in Top Management," www.CatalystWomen.Org, November 19, 2002.

Celent Communications, "Ethnic Minorities, Financial Services, and the Web," www.celent.com, January 28, 2003.

Chatman, J.A. and F.J. Flynn, "The Influence of Demographic Heterogeneity on the Emergence and Consequences of Cooperative Norms in Work Teams," *Academy of Management Journal* 44, 5, 956–974, 2001.

Council, Patrick, "Managing Multiculturalism: Valuing Diversity in the Workplace," *Journal of Property Management*, 66, 6, 22–25, Nov/Dec 2001.

Cox, T. Jr. and C. Smolinski, "Managing Diversity and Glass Ceiling Initiatives as National Economic Imperatives" (Working Paper #9410–01). Michigan Business School, 1994.

Cox, T.H., S.A. Lobel and P.L. McLeod, "Effects of Ethnic Group, Cultural Differences, Uncooperative and Competitive Behavior on a Group Task," *Academy of Management Journal* 34, 827–847, 1991.

Crockett, Joan, "Diversity: Winning Competitive Advantage Through a Diverse Workforce," *HR Focus* 76, 5, 9–11, May 1999.

Eisenberger, R., P. Fasolo, and V. Davis-LaMastro. "Perceived Organizational Support and Employee Diligence, Commitment, and Innovation." *Journal of Applied Psychology* 75, 1, 51–59, 1990.

Ely, R.J. and D.A. Thomas, "Cultural Diversity at Work: The Moderating Effects of Work Group Perspectives on Diversity," *Administrative Science Quarterly* 46, 229–273, 2001.

Freeman-Evans, Tia, "The Enriched Association: Benefiting from Multiculturalism, *Association of Management* 46, 2, 52–57, February 1994.

Fullerton, H.N. and M. Toossi, "Employment Outlook: 2000–10," *Monthly Labor Review*, Bureau of Labor Statistics, www.bls.gov November 2001.

Gill, Dee, "Dealing with Diversity," *Inc Magazine*, 37–38, November 2005.

Harisis, Dean and Brian Kleiner, "Managing and Valuing Diversity in the Workplace," *Equal Opportunities International* 12, 4, 6–10, 1993.

Hartenian, Linda and D. Gudmundson, "Cultural Diversity in Small Business: Implications for Firm Performance," *Journal of Developmental Entrepreneurship* 5, 3, 209–220, December 2000.

Harvey, Barron H., "Technology, Diversity and Work Culture—Key Trends in the Next Millennium," *HR Magazine* 44, 11, 58–60, 1999.

Harvey, George, "Program on Redefining Diversity," Wharton, University of Pennsylvania, presented at 4th Annual Summit on Leading Diversity, www.linkageinc.com, 2003.

Hom, Peter, "Women and Minorities' High Quit Rates Make Corporate Diversity Difficult," *Knowledge @ W.P. Carey*. www.knowledge.wpcarey.asu.edu., 2007.

Hong. L. and S.E. Page, "Groups of Diverse Problem Solvers Can Outperform Groups of High-Ability Problem Solvers," Proceedings of the National Academyof Sciences, 101, 46, 16385–16389, 2004.

Jackson, S.E. "Team Composition in Organizational Settings" in *Group Process and Productivity*. Sage, 1991.

Kanter, Rosabeth Moss. *The Change Masters*. Simon and Schuster, 1983.

Kanter, Rosabeth Moss. "Transcending Business Boundaries: 12,000 World Managers View Change." *Harvard Business Review*, 151–164, May/June 1991.

Mannix, E.A. and M. Neale, "What Differences Make a Difference? The Promise and Reality of Diverse Teams in Organizations," *Psychology in the Public Interest*. 2005.

Marshall, Jonathan. "Minority Policy—Gainers, Losers." *San Francisco Chronicle*, July 31, 1995.

Mayo, Margarita. "Capitalizing on a diverse workforce." Ivey Business Journal 64, 1, 20–27, Sep/Oct 1999.

McClenahen, John S. "Manufacturing & Society: Creating Values with Values," *Industry Week*, January 1, 2005.

McCuiston, Velma, B. Wooldridge, C. Pierce. "Leading the diverse workforce: Profit, prospects and progress." *Leadership & Organization Development Journal* 25, 73, 1–2, 2004.

Millman, Jennifer, "Hot New Data: Selig Center Tells You Which Multicultural Markets Are Exploding," *DiversityInc.com*, August 2007.

Morris, Betsy, "How Corporate America Is Betraying Women," *Fortune* 151, 1, 64–71, January 2005.

MPA, *Magazine Publishers of America*, www.magazine.org 2008.

Mushrush, Willis, *Creating Quality Newsletter* 11, 5, www.MissouriBusiness.net, May 2002.

Nemeth, C.J. "Differential Contributions of Majority and Minority Influence," *Psychological Review* 93, 23–32, 1985.

Nemeth, C.J. and J. Wachtler, "Creative Problem Solving as a Result of Majority vs. Minority Influence, *European Journal of Social Psychology* 13, 45–55, 1983.

Overell, Stephen, "Painting Over the Cracks," *Personnel Today*, 10, March 2004.

"Ownership Business Creation Up for Women, Minorities," Boston Globe, August 14, 2005.

Pew Hispanic Center, "Hispanics: A People in Motion," Pew Research Center www.pewhispanic.org January 2005.

PME Enterprises LLC, 216 Main St., Hartford CT 06106, 2004.

Ragins, B. R., Townsend, B. and Mattis, M. "Gender gap in the executive suite" Academy of Management Executive, 12, 1, 28–42, 1998.

Richard, O.C. "Racial Diversity, Business Strategy, and Firm Performance: A Resource-Based View," *Academy of Management Journal* 43, 164–178, 2000.

Salomon, Mary and Joan Schork, "Turn Diversity to Your Advantage," *Research Technology Management* 46, 4, 37, Jul/Aug 2003.

Siegal, S., and W. Kaemmerer. "Measuring the Perceived Support for Innovation in Organizations." *Journal of Applied Psychology* 63, 5, 553–562, 1978.

Simons, G.F., C. Vazquez, and P.R. Harris. *Transcultural Leadership*. Gulf, 1993.

Stevens, Joann, "The Power of Diversity in Corporate America," www.Linkage-Inc.com, March 15, 2003.

Sudhoff, Mollie N., "Can Diversity Be a Strategy?" American Bankers Association, ABA Banking Journal 96, 12, 59–62, December 2004.

U.S. Bureau of Labor Statistics, 2001.

U.S. Census Bureau, 2001, 2002.

U.S. Glass Ceiling Commission. *Good for Business*. U. S. Department of Labor, 1995.

U.S. Glass Ceiling Commission. *A Report on the Glass Ceiling Initiative.* U. S. Department of Labor, 1991.

Wanous, J.P. and M.A. Youtz, "Solution Diversity and the Quality of Group Decisions," *Academy of Management Journal* 29, 149–159, 1986.

Watson, W.E., K. Kumar and L.K. Michaelsen, "Cultural Diversity's Impact on Interaction Process and Performance," *Academy of Management Journal* 36, 590–602, 1993.

Williams, K.Y. and C.A. O'Reilly III, "Demography and Diversity in Organizations: A Review of 40 Years of Research," *Research in Organizational Behavior* 20, 77–140, 1998.

CHAPTER 2

Understanding Cultures: Your Own and Others

*Individuals, sharing the same belief, form a collective consciousness
that can define and shape the world.*
Harry Palmer

Culture is the collective programming of individual's minds that determines how a group of individuals perceives reality. In fact, we the people in a culture collectively agree on what reality is. We agree on the beliefs that form the foundation of the culture, on which beliefs are most important, and on what the culture values the most. We agree on the norms, the do's and don'ts, the rules by which people will live and be judged. And these basic agreements differ from culture to culture. Therefore, if you as a leader want to deal effectively with workers who come from various "realities," you must understand their cultures and your own. Cultural understanding gives you some clues about why people from various cultures and subcultures think and act as they do. It will also help you to maintain your balance and poise when culture clash occurs—and help others to maintain theirs.

Culture clash occurs when an employee's sense of rightness is challenged by conflicting beliefs and values held by someone from another culture. The employee may respond with several emotions, such as confusion, frustration, disgust, and anger, which tend to block the resolution of the conflict. Typical outcomes are communication breakdown and poor working relationships. Moreover, if such emotional responses are frequent and intense and are not adequately handled, they can lead to stress and even illness. Being able to recognize cultural patterns and differences can help you handle such cultural conflict, and the accompanying emotions, with greater ease.

Virtually all Americans could be considered multi-cultural or multi-ethnic in that their ancestors came from several different cultures. However, most Americans' ancestors were all from European cultures. While smaller ethnic groups, such as Latino Americans could be considered bi-cultural or bi-ethnic, most have parents from a Latino culture and they have adapted to the American culture. Increasingly, many Americans have a different cultural background, which we will call "bi-ethnic" or "multi-ethnic." For example, some persons have a Euro-American mother and African American father, or an Asian American father and a Latino American mother. Such persons have a different pattern of experiences and issues than most Americans.

Nearly all U.S. corporations and corporate cultures were founded by Euro-American men, and they are still 95 percent of the top managers who run the larger corporations. Therefore, corporate cultures are also a reflection of Euro-American male values. But corporations are changing because the marketplace is now global and the workplace is culturally diverse. Corporate cultures must become open and flexible enough to profit from that diversity. For example, management researchers such as Taylor Cox and Roosevelt Thomas have discovered that corporate cultures are increasingly moving away from the old attitude: "We're just one big happy family," which usually implies a one-way approach that means, "new employees must adapt to our corporate culture if they want to stay and succeed." They're moving toward a new attitude: "We're learning what it's like to walk in other people's shoes so we can fully appreciate what they need and what they can contribute," which implies a two-way approach that means, "our corporate culture is broad enough and flexible enough to adapt to new employees from a diversity of backgrounds, just as they adapt to us.

You can see that as a leader, you'll do well to move out of your cultural cave, take off your cultural blinders, and enjoy a more universal view of the workplace. That means taking the first step in gaining multicultural skills:

Step 1: Becoming aware of culture and its pervasive influence

In this chapter you'll learn about:

- What we mean by culture and how it affects our lives
- The basic elements of culture
- The eleven basic ways that cultures differ
- Unique issues of bi-ethnic and multi-ethnic Americans
- Corporate culture—how cultural differences affect your company and your job, how corporate acculturation approaches are changing, what works and what does not

First, test your current knowledge by completing Self-Awareness Activity 2.1.

Self-Awareness Activity 2.1: What Do You Know about Cultures?

Purpose: To see what you know about the issues covered in this chapter.
Instructions: Determine whether you think the following statements are basically true or false—and think about why. The answers will emerge in this chapter, and the summary at the end of the chapter focuses on these issues.

1. The most important aspects of culture are those that people don't talk about.
2. A myth is a false belief.
3. People from different cultures experience different realities.
4. People in the United States put families and ingroups above individual desires.
5. Most cultures believe in inequality and status differences, seeing this as normal.
6. Most cultures of the world value achievement over interpersonal relationships.
7. A major issue of bi-ethnic persons is self-identity.
8. Corporate cultures need heroes mainly because people love a good story.
9. Strong corporate cultures are on their way out.

UNDERSTANDING THE BASICS OF CULTURE

The major goal in understanding the basics of culture is to understand that we create it and we learn it and each major cultural group creates it somewhat differently. We'll discuss the key concepts of what culture is; what we mean by the hierarchy of culture, from world culture to corporate culture; and how we learn about our own culture.

What Is Culture?

Culture is like the air we breathe: We take it for granted, rarely think about it, and assume our world viewpoint is merely the human viewpoint. We can work more powerfully with people from other cultures if we understand some key concepts of what culture is all about, how it affects our personal reality, and how we learn the beliefs, values, and rules of our culture. Culture is as pervasive and invisible as the air around us. It's our programmed beliefs, many of them hidden, our mental map, our view of reality.

Culture as Programmed Beliefs

Culture is the collective programming of the mind, the learning process that results in the members of one group of people being different from those of another. Culture is a characteristic, not of individuals, but of people who were conditioned by similar educational and life experiences. A cultural group may refer to a tribe, regional group, minority, majority, or nation. Culture becomes crystallized in the institutions that people build together: family structure, educational structure, religious organizations, associations, forms of government, work organizations, law, literature, settlement patterns, buildings, and even scientific theories. All of these structures reflect common *beliefs* that are rooted in the common culture (Hofstede 1984, 1991, 2001).

Culture is learned, but it is far more than mere habits that can be easily changed from the outside, even though it's always changing and evolving naturally from the inside. Different cultures have different ways of organizing life, of thinking, and of conceiving the underlying assumptions about the family, the state, the economic system, and of humanity itself and its role in the universe, as indicated in Table 2.1. Harvard anthropologist E.T. Hall views culture primarily as a form of communication, the link between people and the means they have of interacting with each other (Hall 1981b, 1982, 1989). Many experts say that culture is very closely related to what has been defined as *mind*, and may be synonymous with it.

TABLE 2.1: Content of Culture

Consensus reality of a group
How we agree to create our reality
Ways of thinking, feeling, speaking, acting
Obvious aspects and hidden aspects
High priority beliefs = values, the roots or foundation of culture
Stories of heroes who exemplify the values told through networks of members
Rituals and symbols that reinforce the values

Culture as Hidden Programming

Beneath the clearly perceived, highly explicit surface culture, there lies a whole other world, a world of hidden beliefs and motives. When we understand this world, we may radically change our view of human nature. Hall says that culture hides much more than it reveals, and what it hides, it hides most effectively from its own members.

Most people strongly believe that their cultural behavior patterns are "human nature," and resist believing that such behavior is learned and can vary from culture to culture. It's quite common to grow up in a culture while gaining little or no knowledge of the basic laws that make the culture work and that differentiate it from all other cultures. That's because people don't talk about most aspects of their culture because they don't realize that so much of their reality is based on cultural beliefs. Therefore, most people are unaware of the extent to which culture is a major influence on behavior. We're socialized in our culture without much conscious awareness of being socialized, even programmed. We normally think about our culture only when it comes into conflict with some aspect of another culture (Brislin and Yoshida 1994).

> *The cultural unconscious, those "hidden" cultural systems that have as yet to be made explicit, probably outnumber the explicit, conscious systems by a factor of a thousand or more to one.*

Lionel Trilling once likened culture to a prison. When we can define the prison, we can begin to plot our own jailbreak. Culture imprisons us in many unknown ways, but the bars that limit our possibilities are woven of our habits and nothing more—habitual beliefs, attitudes, and ways of thinking and feeling, along with customary actions based on long-forgotten decisions we made (Trilling 1955).

Culture as a Mental Map of Reality

As soon as we're born, our parents begin teaching us about consensus reality, helping us build the mental map we need to function in our particular culture. Anthropologists agree on three characteristics of culture:

1. Culture is learned, not innate
2. The various facets of culture are interrelated. If you touch a culture in one place, everything else is affected.
3. Culture is shared, and it defines the boundaries of different groups.

There is not one aspect of human life that is not touched and altered by culture. Culture is the medium or context within which humans live (Hall 1981a).

Culture as Personal Reality

How you view reality, and how you create your own reality, is tied to how you are socialized within your culture. Putting together what many anthropologists and psychologists have discovered about reality, one way of picturing its elements is shown in Figure 2.1. The psychological raw materials from which you create reality are aspects of your mind, such as your beliefs, attitudes, thoughts, feelings, decisions, and action choices. These form a causal chain that determines the reality you experience.

The tools for changing your reality are also aspects of your mind, namely your imagination, desires, and expectancy. Through imagination you picture, vision, and dream new, different aspects of reality. Imagination is your tool for creating new ideas and adopting innovative approaches. Your desires fire your motivation and are the basis for your purposes, intentions, and goals. Your expectancy refers to your trust or confidence that you can change aspects of our reality.

CHANGE A BELIEF

You use these tools on the content or raw materials of your reality, and the most powerful parts to use them on are at each end of the chain, beliefs and the action choices. Beliefs are at the root of every aspect of your reality. Take this belief: *Most people in business are out to get you.* If you believe this, your attitude toward people at work will be cautious and defensive. Your thinking about coworkers will reflect this attitude, and the resulting feelings are likely to be fear-based, such as suspicion and distrust. Therefore key life decisions about relating to people at work will come from caution and fear. *I'll mind my own business, cover my tracks, keep my nose clean.* Or *If I suspect someone's trying to get me, I'll try to get them first.* Such decisions in turn affect your daily action choices as you interact with people at work.

What happens when you shift a key belief? Suppose you recognize that your belief about coworkers is blocking your career progress? You can choose to try out a new belief: *Most people in the workplace have goodwill toward other workers and want to get along.* Clearly your attitude becomes more accepting and outgoing. Your thinking shifts to a more positive stream, triggering goodwill feelings of friendliness, openness, interest. You decide, *I'll assume coworkers have goodwill. If a particular person proves otherwise, I'll then act accordingly to protect myself.* Your daily action choices about dealing with coworkers will be quite different.

CHANGE AN ACTION CHOICE

Shift a key belief and you change your reality. Action choices, at the other end of the chain, are also powerful fulcrum points of change. Actions tend to get immediate results that we can see and experience, so they may change our reality quickly. For example, instead of changing your belief about coworkers, you may change an action choice, a behavior. You make a friendly overture to a coworker and watch what happens. If it turns out well, you may repeat this type of action and then expand it to similar trusting, outgoing behaviors. The resulting experience moves up the chain, changing your key decision, feeling, thinking, attitude, finally changing the belief that's blocking your career progress.

The most powerful change points are at each end of the reality chain—beliefs and action choices. However, change any link in the chain and the results will ripple through all the links, changing your reality and your life.

FIGURE 2.1: Elements of Personal Reality: Mental Map

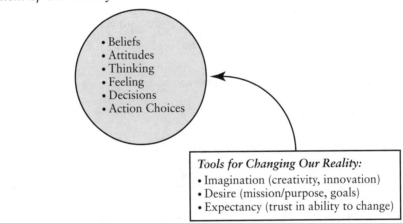

Content of Our Reality:

- Beliefs
- Attitudes
- Thinking
- Feeling
- Decisions
- Action Choices

Tools for Changing Our Reality:
- Imagination (creativity, innovation)
- Desire (mission/purpose, goals)
- Expectancy (trust in ability to change)

When you view another person's actions (or your own), you can't really understand them apart from their cultural meanings. All our beliefs, desires, emotions, and so forth that underlie our actions are in turn affected by our cultural upbringing. Basically we either buy into the beliefs of our culture or we rebel against them. Either way, the better you understand a person's cultural background, the better you understand that person's actions and attitudes.

Cultural Levels—World Culture to Corporate Culture

Cultural groups are found at many levels of society:

- *World culture* = humanity; common values and customs found in all cultures
- *Major culture* = a regional or national group that represents a common culture
- *Subculture* = a cultural group within a major culture
- *Corporate culture* = an organization within a major culture

In the past we thought of a culture as a relatively large group of people within a nation or geographic region who spoke the same language and embraced similar beliefs and practices. Now we recognize a diversity and hierarchy of cultures, ranging in size and scope from the whole world to a small corporation. There are about 6.5 billion people on Earth, living in about 6,000 different cultures, each with its own spoken language. Between 4,000 and 5,000 of those cultures are indigenous tribes, such as the 500 American Indian tribes. They number only about 200 million people, most living as small subcultures within some larger dominant society (World 1993).

Is there really a global culture? Humanity *does* have certain cultural commonalties, so we've always had the potential to become a global culture, but we lacked the necessary frequency and intensity of communication. We are rapidly becoming a global culture in many ways, a trend that's accelerating. Leavitt (1983, 94) states that "a powerful force drives the world toward a converging commonality, and that force is technology." Through advances in communication and transportation, most of us know what's happening in other parts of the world. For example, more than a billion people watch the television news channel, CNN. When the Chinese government clamped down on a student demonstration in Tiananmen Square in 1989, a global audience was watching. People around the world also see the commercials on such stations as MTV and CNN and are more aware than ever of new products becoming available. As a result of such global communication, governments are called upon to be more accountable for their actions. And people in formerly remote, isolated places get in touch with the global marketplace and may want the products and lifestyles it introduces.

Major regions, such as Asia, have many cultural commonalties, a Far East culture, in some ways. Yet within one small nation, Malaysia, there are many subcultures with distinct languages, religious beliefs, customs, and so forth. Likewise, in the United States, although we have a distinct American culture, there are numerous subcultures, such as Vietnamese American.

To complicate matters, we have *corporate* cultures, usually established on the basis of Euro-American male values, norms, and customs, but each having its own flavor and peculiarities. These corporate cultures are changing at an increasingly rapid pace as women and people from various subcultural groups move into positions of power and influence.

Gender as a Cultural Group

Do males essentially live in a different culture from females? Several diversity experts say yes. Evidence indicates that the socialization of people in most societies of the world is greatly influenced by gender, and in each culture the women, as a group, hold a distinctly different worldview from the men (Tannen 1990; Rosener 1990, Cox 1993, Belenky 1986, Fottler 1980). Here are some specific ways their socialization differs: Men and women have different ways of learning and creating knowledge; boys and girls play differently.

- Role modeling behaviors of fathers is different from that of mothers.
- The media portrays men/boys differently from women/girls.

The Content of Culture: Ties That Bind

When you look for culture, what do you look for? The major parts of a culture, the ties that bind us into a unified group, which are:

- **beliefs** that form a worldview, beliefs about why the group exists, what it primarily needs to do, who is included and recognized, how they are rewarded, etc.
- **values** based on the beliefs that people think are most important
- **heroes** and heroines people admire because they personify those values
- **stories**, myths, and legends about them
- **networks** of relationships that connect people who communicate the stories
- **rituals** people engage in, either every day or on special occasions
- **symbols** everyone recognizes as shortcuts for expressing all these other elements.

All these threads of culture form the tapestry that determines how the people in a major culture decide to handle their families, schools, churches, government, housing, business, and science. They're expressed in a culture's art forms, food, dress, play, and every other aspect of life.

Beliefs that are most basic to how people see themselves, their world, and their relationship to people and aspects of that world—these form a culture's worldview.

A value is an enduring belief that one way of acting or being is preferable to another. A value system is an organization of such beliefs along a continuum of relative importance, a prioritizing of beliefs into a set or cluster. Norms are cultural do's and don'ts about how to act. Some values and their related norms may be talked about but most are just understood.

Heroes, heroines serve as role models. They may also be called champions, stars, or big wheels. They're often seen as fearless leaders or courageous adventurers. They personify the core values and the strength of the organization or group. They become symbolic figures whose deeds are out of the ordinary—but not so far out that people can't identify with them. People like to think, "Maybe I can do that too." Such leaders become great motivators, the people everyone will count on for inspiration when things get tough. They tend to know intuitively how to succeed, to envision the future, to experiment, and to appreciate the value of celebrations and ceremonies.

A myth is a story or saying that usually features a hero or heroine, a story that expresses some value important to the cultural group. It may be a legend that symbolizes a central belief of the culture. It's often more symbolic than factual but may be either. Some myths are based on powerful truths; some on manipulative, hurtful lies; still others on harmless little white lies.

Myths often consist of the retelling of an *event* in terms of good versus evil, a morality tale that sets up heroes, villains, and victims. They model the "good and bad" values and norms that the society's leaders want to emphasize. Much or our history is myth to some extent. Real history is complex and messy with many gray areas, but the official versions are often simplified into winners and losers, good guys and bad guys. These "stories we tell ourselves" give coherence and meaning to life's experiences—they help us to make sense of life.

> *A myth is a story or saying whose function is to bind together the thoughts of a group and promote coordinated social action.*

Rituals are the "way we do things around here." They include the customary day-to-day actions people take, their expected actions and responses. Core values would have no impact without ritual and ceremony. The unwritten rules of personal communication, the rituals of social interaction, govern relationships between bosses and workers, professionals and support staff, men and women, old and young, insiders and outsiders.

Work rituals spell out standards of acceptable behavior and how such procedures as strategic planning or budgeting or report writing should be carried out. Recognition rituals. such as awards, are more formal. They acknowledge achievements that are valued and signal that the person belongs to the culture. Rituals meet people's need to belong. They help establish and maintain some common values and goals that connect people in the group. A true ritual is always connected to a myth that represents some basic group value. Otherwise it's just a habit that does nothing but give people a false sense of security.

Networks of relationships, such as the grapevines, are the primary means of communication within an organization. They tie together all parts of the company without respect to the organization chart. They not only transmit information, they also interpret its significance. In most organizations, only about 10 percent of business takes place in formal meetings and events. The real process of making decisions, gathering support, developing opinions, etc., happens before or after the meeting. Of course, formal networks are important too. They include the formal organization chart, task forces, work teams, professional and trade associations, and similar groupings.

Symbols are shortcuts to large packets of cultural meaning. Like an icon on your computer's desktop screen, a symbol can take you directly to an entire program of valued beliefs or customs. Symbols, such as a song, banner, flag, logo, picture, motto, or brand name, quickly remind people of those cultural elements that bind them together. A saying or nickname may recall a heroine or star. A figure of speech may recall a key myth or ritual. A good symbol can serve to trigger communal thoughts and feelings about a common cause or goal.

How Do We Learn Our Culture?

Cultures have specific ways of teaching values and norms. Primary message systems communicate how the culture views the world and does things. Cultures use such techniques as symbols and *myths* within the message systems, most often communicating through networks of relationships and the grapevine. The methods used to pass on cultural values and norms are education, direction, and role modeling.

Primary Message Systems

The primary message systems that communicate cultural values and norms serve to tell people how to do most everything they do. According to Hall (1982) they are:
How we interact with our environment.

- *How we associate with others*, the way we organize our society and its parts, the role of hierarchy, rank, and status.
- *How we meet our survival needs*, including everything from individual food habits to the economy of a country.
- How we learn.
- *How we differentiate male and female behavior.* (Usually when a given behavior pattern becomes associated with one gender, it will be dropped by the other.)
- *How we use space*, our sense of territoriality and personal space.
- *How we use time*, which is tied to life's cycles and rhythms. Whether we focus on a linear, circular, or present-moment approach to time involves how we emphasize the past, present, and future aspects of life.
- *How we play*, relax, enjoy ourselves, and use our leisure time, and what our sense of humor is like.
- *How we defend ourselves* against potentially hostile forces in nature and against destructive forces within ourselves. Defense includes the types of armed forces, law enforcement agencies, religions, and medical practices a culture embraces.
- *How we use things*, including money, transportation, equipment, houses, furniture, clothes, weapons, and all technology.

How we do things communicates to everyone in the culture about our basic beliefs, values, norms, and unspoken rules, as indicated in Table 2.2. The ways we communicate these basics include symbols, slogans, metaphors, and myths and stories, with heroes and heroines. According to an old American Indian saying:

> *The people must tell their stories and sing their songs or the land (and culture) will die*

The media we most often use are networks and the grapevine, and in recent years written and electronic media. Culture has been handed down for millions of years so the traditional way is by word of mouth.

Teaching and Learning

Three major teaching and learning methods were identified by E. T. Hall. Cultures use these methods to convey primary messages and information to succeeding generations:

Education and Training. We educate and train people, beginning in childhood, usually in a very conscious way.

Correction and Direction. We also correct people when they do something the culture considers wrong or improper, and we direct them in the right way to think and act, also primarily in a conscious way.

Role Modeling. When we serve as role models, it's usually not in order to teach children and others how to think and act; we're just "being ourselves." But toddlers watch their parents, and adults watch their heroes or heroines, to learn from them and to emulate them. Role modeling is by far the most powerful teaching mechanism and we're rarely aware that it's going on.

What does this mean for you as a business leader? It means that if you want to create an environment that challenges and supports all types of employees, you must first and foremost be a role model to others. You must hold the beliefs and attitudes that value diversity. Your thinking and feeling, your decisions and day-to-day action choices must reflect your respect for people from all groups. As a leader, it's important to give effective education and training for valuing diversity. It's also important to set up organizational systems that detect and correct discrimination and other diversity problems. But most of all, you must be a role model by "walking your talk."

TABLE 2.2: Essentials of Communicating the Culture

Cultural Category	*Outer Expression of Inner Perceptions*
How we do things:	
Beliefs and values	Family relationships
Norms-do's and don'ts	Behavior
Informal, unspoken rules	Style, Dress
Rituals, customs	Cuisine, food
The ways we communicate:	
Myths, stories about heroes/heroines	Art
Symbols	Music
Slogans	Language
Metaphors	Dialect
The media we use to communicate:	
Networks of relationships	Organizations
The grapevine	Groups
Written and electronic means	Publishing, Internet
The teaching/learning methods we use:	
Education and training	Schools, universities
Connections and direction	Care and nurturing of the young
Role modeling	Showing by example

HOW DO CULTURES DIFFER? ELEVEN MAJOR DIFFERENCES

When we consider all the life forms that we're aware of, it's clear that humans throughout the world are amazingly alike. Yet our differences can make it difficult or impossible to communicate and work together effectively. The purpose of this book is to help you understand where our major differences lie so that you can figure out ways to reconcile and respect differences and to find common ground for working with people from diverse backgrounds. The United States is called the most diverse society in the world. Within our American culture we have many subcultures, each with its own unique set of values and customs. Before exploring some major ways in which cultures differ, do a brief self-analysis about your own cultural orientation by completing Self-Awareness Activity 2.2. Then see how your orientation relates to the 11 types of cultural differences listed in Table 2.3.

Self-Awareness Activity 2.2: What's Your Cultural Orientation?

Purpose: To determine your personal orientation regarding key cultural factors.
Instructions: For each of the following numbered pairs of statements, circle A or B according to which statement *best* reflects your orientation.

1. This is how I feel about what happens to me in life:

    a. I create my life by what I do and by what I allow.

    b. I'm just a cog in the wheel of life. Most of what happens to me is outside my control.

2. If I had to choose among the following priorities, here is how I would choose:

    a. My top priority is to achieve my personal goals.

    b. My top priority is to be a good son/daughter, wife/husband, boss/worker, mother/daughter, that is, to fulfill those roles expected of me.

3. Here is how I feel about my relationships with people:

    a. I'm happiest when I'm ahead or winning.

    b. I'm happiest when I'm working or playing with friends, family, or coworkers.

4. If I had to choose between achievement and relationships at work:

    a. My top priority at work would be getting the job done.

    b. My top priority at work would be maintaining good relationships with people.

5. Here is how I generally relate to people with more power than I have:

    a. If a top manager asked me to discuss my ideas, I'd be comfortable.

    b. If a top manager asked me to discuss my ideas, I'd be nervous and uncomfortable.

6. When it comes to getting ahead in life, my strongest belief is:

    a. People who have talent and work hard can become very successful.

    b. People need the right family background and connections to become very successful.

7. My usual attitude toward risk is:

    a. Nothing risked, nothing gained.

    b. Stick with the tried and true.

8. When it comes to rules and regulations, I'm more likely to believe that:

    a. "the exception makes the rule" and rules were made to be broken occasionally.

    b. We must always stick to the rules of the game or we'll have chaos.

9. When I make a decision, the most important consideration is usually

    a. How it will affect people a few years down the line.

    b. How well it moves me toward my current goals.

Followup: Analyze your responses by reading the answer key at the end of this chapter and the following discussion in this chapter

TABLE 2.3: Eleven Major Cultural Differences

1. Source of Control	1. I'm controlled or I control
2. Collectivism or Individualism	2. Us-first or Me-first
3. Homogeneous or Heterogeneous	3. Tight ties or Loose ties
4. Feminine or Masculine	4. Relationships first or Achievement first
5. Rank-status	5. Class difference or Equality
6. Risk orientation	6. Security-seeking or Risk-taking
7. Decision-making	7. Long-term or Short-term
8. Time use	8. Circular multi-task or Linear single-task
9. Space use	9. Up-close, Arm's length, or Distant
10. Communication style	10. Indirect or Direct
11. Economic system	11. Agricultural, Industrial, Post-Industrial (dependent, independent, interdependent)

How do Euro-American viewpoints compare with those of the large majority of the world's people? Of the world's 6.5 billion people, over 3 billion live in Asian cultures, and over half a billion live in Latino cultures (GeoHIVE.com, 2005). Therefore, a large majority of the world's people live in cultures with these beliefs: I'm controlled, us-first, tight-ties, people first, class differences, play it safe, long-term orientation, and primarily dependent worldview. Arab and African cultures tend to have a similar profile. That means the Euro-American culture differs from the most of the rest of the world on every one of the 11 key cultural differences.

Cultural Difference #1: I'm Controlled or I Control?

The most basic beliefs we have are probably about who or what creates our environment and causes the events within that environment. How much is caused by our own attitudes and actions? How much by a Supreme Being? How much is just chance or coincidence? Beliefs about the cause of life events tend to affect every other aspect of culture. Experts call this cultural aspect locus of control, meaning source of control over life.

I'm Controlled.

People from cultures with a predominantly "I'm-controlled" outlook feel less self-reliant and more dependent on the fates, the whims of a supreme being, or other uncontrollable sources. These people might say, "Things happen to me and I have little control over my life. It depends on my boss, my customer, fate, luck, God's will." Most cultures fall into this camp, including most African, Asian, Arab, and Latino cultures. Women in all cultures are more likely than men to hold this viewpoint. (Tse 1988, Delgado 1981, Asante 1985, Redding 1982, Orpen 1977, Ramirez 1988, Helms 1980, Cote 1989).

I Control

People with an internal source of control believe that they determine their own reality, destiny, and life experiences to a great extent, either by what they do or by what they allow to happen, or both. They are therefore relatively autonomous, independent people. People from I-control cultures might say, "What happens to me is up to me. It depends on what I do or don't do. God helps those who help themselves." Most Western cultures, especially Euro-American, and especially men, hold this viewpoint (Rotter 1966, Spector 1982).

Choices for Control?

Euro-Americans, for example, believe that if they can control a situation, they'll have better results. They believe they should have many options, and they want lots of choices in order to feel in control of what happens in their lives. They're more likely to accept theories that blame the victims of poverty or "bad luck." Since we all have a great deal of control over our lives, those who are "disadvantaged" must be making poor choices.

In contrast, Asian Americans and African Americans are likely to believe that in nature some things are random and out of your control. Most Latinos and Arabs believe that certain things are "God's will" or fate. In these cultures, people say that it's important to recognize the power of random events and have a good attitude about them. You shouldn't blame yourself or others too much. It does no good to blame the reality, because the reality is nature (or God), and nature has its own course. Just because you can make choices does not mean your decisions will pay off.

Asian parents tend to make all the choices for their small children. As a result, Asian children do better on a task if they are told their mothers made preliminary choices for them. In contrast, Euro-American mothers allow their very young children to make many choices for themselves. For example, in grocery stores they allow toddlers to choose their own cereal, peanut butter, jelly, and so forth. As a result, Euro-American children tend to do better on a task if they make the choices themselves.

Inner Problem or Situational Problem?

Euro-Americans tend to explain a person's behavior in terms of internal disposition, while Asian Americans are more likely to see it as a result of the situation the persons finds himself in. Psychologist Kaiping Peng compared reactions to a tragic situation: A Chinese scholar working temporarily in the United States went on a rampage, murdered several people, and then committed suicide. Euro-Americans and Chinese Americans viewed the event quite differently. Most Euro-Americans agreed that a deep-rooted disturbance in the man's personality must have led him to commit the murders and suicide. He must have had a terrible childhood and suffered abuse. The Chinese woman who had dated him must be glad that she didn't marry him because he was clearly a walking time bomb. He might have murdered her too. This explanation reveals a focus on inner causes, such as mental instability or some "dark" features in the person's nature.

Chinese Americans focused on the murderer's situation as a lonely foreigner with few friends in a strange country, a situation that was very stressful for him. The woman who dated him expressed some regret. She speculated that if she had been there to give him the support he needed, he would never have committed such a horrible deed. This explanation reveals a focus on situational causes.

Most Asians have difficulty understanding the concept of evil. They see everything as being part of a state of flux and change, so they tend to explain behavior in terms of situation and context. As a result, they see the "loser" label that's used by Euro-Americans as very cruel. Also, trying to understand people in terms of their personality traits seems very odd to them. And the concept of an "overachiever" or an "underachiever" is strange. The idea that someone "should be achieving something" is bizarre. How do we know that a person is destined to *be* someone or to make good grades or a lot of money? Because nothing is fixed and everything is in a state of change, your score on an aptitude test is just one index of your abilities on a given day.

Cultural Difference #2: Us–First or Me–First?

This is the most important cultural difference for understanding how people interact with others. Cultures that focus on me-first are called individualist cultures because they believe that each individual must first take responsibility for her or his own life and should have the freedom to succeed or fail. Cultures that focus on us-first are called collectivist cultures because individuals are seen first as members of a family or cohesive group. It's similar to looking at a bouquet. Do you focus first on the whole bouquet with the attitude that one flower alone would be out of context and lost? Or do you focus first on each individual flower and then notice how the group forms a bouquet? This cultural aspect is often called collectivism versus individualism.

Us–First

People from an us-first culture may typically make these kinds of comments: "I should first integrate my goals, thoughts, and actions with those of my group. Working within what the group wants and needs, I can try to get what I want and need. People should always stay close to their parents and relatives and never stray far." Hofstede's research indicates that most cultures fall into this camp, including most African, Asian, Arab, and Latino cultures (Hofstede 1980, 1991, 2001).

Me–First

Members of me-first cultures are more likely to make these kinds of statements: "I must first focus on my personal goals. I work toward better things for my family and work team and community, but my personal goals must come first. I'll stay with a group as long as it doesn't block my efforts to meet my own wants and needs. When people grow up, they have to cut the apron strings and make their own way in the world." European cultures fall into this camp, with Euro-Americans being the most individualistic.

Key to People Interactions

Many analysts suggest that the me-first versus us-first aspect of culture is the single most important concept for understanding what goes on when people from different cultures get together. Whether our primary outlook is me-first or us-first greatly influences our goals and priorities. The most important difference between collectivists and individualists is the emphasis they place on the opinions and feelings of group members ("What will they think?") and the psychological closeness between themselves and others (How does this affect our relationship?") (Kagitcibasi 1990, Brislin and Yoshida, 1994, Hofstede 2001, Hui 1990, Kim 1994).

Collectivist or Individualist?

Individualism and collectivism refer to the degree to which people in a culture believe that a person's beliefs and actions should be independent of the group's thought and action. Us-first collectivists believe that individuals should integrate their thoughts and actions with those of a group; for example, the extended family or the work organization.

Me-first individualists are more likely to pursue their own personal goals, while collectivists are more likely to integrate their own goals with those of group members. Certainly, everyone has personal desires and goals they want to pursue and everyone needs to belong to at least one group. The concept revolves around priorities and emphases. What is the relative weight we place on fulfilling the need to belong and the need to do our own thing, especially when these needs conflict?

Euro-Americans, for example, explain human behavior in terms of an individual's experience and disposition, while ignoring the effects of the group situation on behavior. In an experiment Berkeley Professor Kaiping Peng showed people a picture with a single fish that was moving away from a school of fish. He asked people what this fish behavior meant. Most Euro-Americans indicated that the fish was asserting its independence, while most Asian Americans said the fish had been expelled by the school.

Peng showed a picture that included one fish by itself and four fish clustered together. Most Euro-Americans focused their attention on the lone fish, while most Asian Americans focused on the group of fish. Peng asked, "What is the group of fish feeling?" Most Euro-Americans responded by asking, "Which fish?" They found it very difficult to conceive of a group having an emotion. Because they believe that people's feelings should be private and individual, then feelings cannot be expressed by a group.

Happiness?

Euro-Americans tend to feel happy when they're experiencing strong emotions and strong subjective feelings. They're also likely to feel happy when they're experiencing disengaged emotions—feeling different, superior, unique, better, or special. Asian Americans, in contrast, are likely to be happy in relation to their evaluation of social experience. A typical attitude is: "I may feel poorly today and in a bad mood, but my family and society are happy, so I'm happy. If the group around me is happy, my personal mood of the day or hour are not that important." Happiness is likely to involve engaged emotions—getting along with others, feeling connected and bonded and welcomed.

Cut the Apron Strings or Not?

In individualist cultures, members are likely to cut the apron strings when they reach adulthood in a more complete way than do members of collectivist cultures (Hall 1989). For individualists, from birth to death, life is punctuated by separations, many of them painful. Paradoxically, each separation forms a foundation for new stages of integration, identity, and psychic growth. The newborn baby experiences himself and his small universe as one, inseparable. To be truly alive in the Euro-American culture, you must outgrow this state, and the full impact of the process comes when you leave home and establish yourself as an independent person. Conversely, in collectivist cultures, the bonds with the parents, grandparents, and even ancestors are not severed but are maintained and reinforced.

Individual Differences within a Culture

Remember that some people within an individualist culture may have predominantly us-first collectivist values. Women in all cultures tend to be socialized to be collectivist. People in individualist cultures can also adopt collectivist values from their family, their subculture, their religion, or region. For example, in the United States you may be more collectivist if you live in the South or in a New England village than if you live in New York or Los Angeles (Brislin and Yoshida 1994).

Cultural Difference #3: Tight Ties or Loose Ties?

Cultures vary by how much alike people are, how homogeneous or diverse. This in turn helps determine whether people feel bound together by many ties or only loosely connected with few ties. Those cultures in which the fabric of society is tightly woven, such as Japan, are called high-context cultures. Those with a loosely-woven fabric, such as the United States, are called low-context cultures.

Many Ties That Bind = Us–First

People in high-context cultures may say things like this: "I see people first as part of a particular family or organization or community, and they see me that way. If I fail, the others in my group will 'lose face' and feel shame, so I should try to cover up my failure. If I succeed, the glory goes to my group, not to me." This mindset predominates in Eastern cultures and is held by a majority of the world's people.

Such people may say: "As I grew up, I thought of myself as part of 'we' rather than 'I.' It's important to me to protect my family and close friends and to be loyal to them. I expect them to protect and be loyal to me. Who I am is a member of my family, work group, and community. The ideal way to live is in close relationship with them. I belong to several groups and organizations. I depend on those relationships. We make decisions together, and I believe in those decisions. Who my friends are depends a great deal on the groups I belong to. My status and prestige comes from these relationships. The groups I belong to provide what I need—expertise, order, duty, and security. I'm loyal first to my parents and immediate family, then my relatives, and then the clan or nearby community. Success and satisfaction in life comes from living up to those loyalties. If I gain material success, I'll share it with my family and close friends."

When it comes to achievement, these people may make these kinds of comments: "When I was a university student, I studied hard to pass exams in order to acquire the status of a degree. Now I seek the satisfaction of a job well recognized. It's very important for me to preserve "face," or respect from my family and friends, and to avoid shaming them through my failure. My job life and private life are inseparable. It's okay if my boss inquires about my private life, and I expect the boss to help out with family or personal problems. On the job, relationships are even more important to me than getting tasks done. I must develop a relationship with the people I work with and become adopted into the work group before I can do a good job on my tasks."

In more tightly-woven collectivist societies, individuals are viewed in the context of social relationships, such as the family, the organization, the community. They are less differentiated as a self in contrast with others. "We" is usually more important than "I." An individual's failure causes others to "lose face" and results in shame, so it should be covered up and not seen. This mindset predominates in Eastern cultures, and is held by a majority of the world's people.

Key concepts are protection by the ingroup, loyalty to the ingroup, identity that stems from the group and the social system, membership in groups and organizations as the ideal mode, emotional dependence on organizations, belief in group decisions, friendships predetermined by stable social relationships, and need for prestige within these relationships. The organization or group provides expertise, order, duty, and security. Value standards differ for ingroups and outgroups. People are expected to be loyal first to their parents, relatives, and clan; and life achievement and satisfaction consist of living up to those loyalties.

Individuals perceive themselves as belonging to one or more close ingroups from which they cannot detach themselves. The ingroup may be an extended family, clan, or organization, which protects the interests of its members but in turn expects their permanent loyalty. A high quality of life is defined primarily in family and group terms. Children think of themselves as "we" rather than "I." If you gain success and wealth, you're expected to share it with your ingroup.

When they attend a university, people in a collectivist society are motivated to pass their exams in order to acquire the status of a degree. People seek the satisfaction of a job well recognized. Preserving face, or the respect from one's ingroup, and avoiding shame, are important. Job life and private life are inseparable. The company may intrude in the worker's private life and the worker expects the company to help out with family or personal problems. On the job, relationships take precedence over getting tasks done. An essential precondition for achieving a task is developing a relationship with the other person so he or she can become adopted into the ingroup (Hofstede 1984, 2001).

If you're a member of the collective, the ingroup, you will be included, taken in, taken care of, and given much attention by the members of your group. However, as a member of an outside group, you may find it difficult or impossible to get any attention at all. Of course, exceptions are made for the lonely traveler and lone person in need. However, the rules of the game tend to be reserved for people within the collective. If you want to gain entry, you must be introduced and find a way to become accepted.

Earthy or Stylized?

Some anthropologists make a further distinction among tightly woven collectivist groups: the "earthy" cultures and the "stylized" cultures. Earthy cultures include American Indian, African, Latino, Pacific Island, and most Arab cultures. Function and style are one, for they value things that are functional and at the same time express beauty or meaning and honor mythology and nature. Stylized cultures include the Chinese, Japanese, Korean, East Indian, and Thai cultures. They feature many close, irreplaceable connections and are highly structured, with strict expectations, roles, and lifestyles. They're based on the most numerous ties of all and on the closest, most binding relationships.

Loose Ties = Me–First

People who live in a loose-knit society may say things like this: "I'm unique, one of a kind. Growing up means becoming my own person. If I fail in life, it's strictly my fault, and I would probably feel guilty and want to be by myself till I got over it. What I value most are autonomy, self-reliance, self-identity, emotional independence, and individual initiative."

"When I was a university student, I worked hard in order to master the subject matter for my major. It's important to me to maintain my self-respect and avoid guilt. On the job, I value challenges, individual achievement, and personal ambition. I want the satisfaction of a job well done, especially by my own standards. When I come home, I don't want to think about the job, and when I'm at work, I try to forget home problems. At work, it's all about getting the job done, so I don't have much time for getting to know people or hanging out." These are typical views of people from Western cultures. The United States is one of the most loosely knit cultures of modern times.

The United States is one of the most loosely-knit cultures of modern times. In loosely knit individualist societies, the individual is highly differentiated from others. Growing up means becoming an individual who is distinctly separate from others. Failure in life is the "sin" of the individual and may lead to guilt and separation. In such a society the collective goals of the family, ingroup, or community are often subordinated to the needs of individuals. This largely Western mindset is held by a minority of the world's people and is most strongly held among Americans. The mindset tends to be stronger in males than in females. Key values are autonomy, self-reliance, self-identity, emotional independence, and individual initiative. Major workplace values are job challenge, achievement, and ambition (Hofstede 1984, 2001).

In such *self-interest* cultures, people are loosely integrated (low context). Individuals look primarily after their self-interest and the interests of their immediate family. A high-quality life means individual success, achievement, self-actualization, and self-respect. In the workplace people seek the satisfaction of a job well done, especially by their own standards. When they attend a university, people are primarily motivated by a need to master their subject. Preserving self-respect and avoiding guilt are important. Job life and private life are usually sharply separated. Getting tasks done is more important than spending time on work relationships.

Euro-Americans, for example, tend to see themselves as different from others. Most have a strong belief that they're one of "the chosen" and that positive things will happen to them. A typical attitude is: "I'm not similar to others, but others may sometimes be similar to me." They're likely to say proudly that they're not nonconformists, but they do believe that something unique and different is good. In contrast, Asians tend to think that everyone is more or less alike. A typical attitude is: "Others are just like me and I like that idea."

Researcher Kaiping Peng offered people a free pen for participating in his survey. He showed them five pens, four of which were alike and one different. Euro-Americans overwhelmingly chose the "one-of-a-kind" pen, and Asian Americans chose a pen that was part of the group of four.

Cultural Difference #4: Achievement–First or People–First?

Most cultures place greater value on building and maintaining strong interpersonal relationships than on getting things done. Others value most highly a person's (or group's) achievements. People-first values are found most often in us-first cultures, while achievement-first predominates in me-first cultures. Geert Hofstede refers to this aspect of culture as the degree of masculinity or femininity. A people-first orientation reflects feminine values, while an achievement orientation reflects masculine values. However, in both types of cultures men dominate the political and workplace arenas, as research indicates that no country or culture is dominated by women in these areas.

People–First = Connecting, Cooperating = Feminine Aspect

People in a more feminine culture may say things like this: "I focus on building and maintaining positive, personal relationships. The type of life I build is more important than the things I accumulate. I value my hunches and intuition. What motivates me is contributing to my family, workplace, and community. I work in order to live rather than live in order to work."

Relationship-oriented cultures focus on building and maintaining positive interpersonal relationships. They also feature gender equality and quality of life other than the material things in life. Intuition is highly valued, service is the chief motivating drive, and working in order to live is more the case than living for one's work.

The Scandinavian cultures are the most people-focused. Roles and viewpoints of men and women are not as separated as in most cultures. Neither men nor women need be to ambitious, competitive, or focused on material success. Men and women may respect whatever is small, weak, and slow. Values within political and work organizations center around interpersonal relationships and concern for the weak.

Research indicates that while Euro-Americans, especially men, tend to be highly competitive in social interaction and in task performance, Latino Americans, African Americans and Asian Americans favor a more cooperative approach (Cox, Lobel, Mcleod; 1991; Kagan 1971; DeVos 1980).

Achievement–First = Focus on Competition, "Things" = Masculine Aspect

People in more masculine cultures may make these kinds of statements: "I'm very ambitious, and I believe I'm here to work. Hard work will bring me independence. Men should be assertive, ambitious, and competitive. They should work for material success, and respect whatever is big, strong, and fast. Women should serve and care for the intangible qualities of life, for the children, and for the weak."

Achievement-oriented cultures focus on achievement for men. They define very different social roles for men and women. They tend to be patriarchal, materialistic, performance-oriented, and factual. Independence is the ideal, ambition is the motivation, live-in-order-to-work is the viewpoint, and machismo is valued. Men are expected to be assertive, ambitious, and competitive, to strive for material success, and to respect whatever is big, strong, and fast. Women are expected to serve and care for the intangible qualities of life, for the children, and for the weak. Political and corporate values stress material success and assertiveness.

The most masculine culture by far is Japan's, while the United States culture is considered moderately masculine (Hofstede 1984, 2001).

Cultural Difference #5: Equality or Hierarchy?

Some cultures, primarily Western ones, are based on the ideal that all persons have equal value and status as human beings. People are therefore entitled to equal opportunity to achieve and advance in the society. Other cultures accept the idea that some people are naturally more powerful, affluent, and advantaged than others. They therefore accept the inequality of rank and status in a hierarchical or stratified society. In these cultures people from different levels feel a greater sense of "power distance" than do people who live in more egalitarian cultures.

Inequality = Rank/Status Cultures = Large Power Distance

People in cultures that are more accepting of inequalities may make these kinds of statements: "My company's organization chart looks like a pyramid, with a few autocratic leaders at the top and many ordinary workers at the bottom. If my country had an organizational chart, it would look that way too. Our leaders are very strong and powerful. We depend on them to make the right decisions. We expect them to control things. If they asked us what to do, we would assume they were weak and should step down. The leaders we admire are good people, similar to good fathers who take care of things. Of course they live well, with people to take care of menial tasks for them. Such leaders should have the trappings of wealth that go with the territory. I expect my boss to make the decisions, give me clear orders, and to take a personal interest in me and my family. I don't speak up to my boss unless he tells me to. I would never contradict my boss, either at work or elsewhere. My status depends on the status of my boss and my company."

Nearly all so-called under-developed and developing countries have such vertical societies. When people from these cultures move to Western countries to work, they often initially feel lost because their leaders are not so authoritarian and patriarchal. For example, people from Latino and Asian cultures pay more homage to the boss than do people from Western cultures. They may be appalled at the idea of arguing a point with the boss or seeing the boss pitch in to help out in a pinch. They are much less likely to point out potential problems with their manager's decision and may have difficulty speaking up when team decisions need to be made. To them, bosses do the bossing and employees do the work and deviations from that norm imply that one or the other can't do their jobs properly.

In rank/status cultures, power distance is high. Organizations tend to feature hierarchical organizational structures (picture a pyramid), power inequality, autocratic leadership, dependence on leaders, centralized decision making, and the belief that power lies with a few strong leaders. People have strong dependence needs on higher-ups.

While people may aspire to democracy as an impersonal ideal, they expect superiors to behave autocratically and don't expect to be consulted. Ideal superiors are benevolent autocrats or patriarchs, good father types that subordinates can depend on. Superiors are expected to enjoy special privilege and be exempt from certain rules and laws. Status symbols are widely used and contribute to the superiors' authority in the eyes of subordinates. Organizations are identified with one or more powerful individuals. Change comes about by decree from top individuals or by revolution.

Hierarchical cultures are virtually always collectivist cultures. They value deference to authority and sensitivity to status. This is part of going along with the group. Bosses in such cultures may appear arrogant and aloof to individualists, who tend to believe that bosses and employees are basically equal human beings. Such bosses may seem to flaunt the privileges of status, such as fine cars, drivers, and elite dining rooms in contrast to workers who ride the bus and eat from a lunch box (Brislin and Yoshida 1994).

The boss-centered workplace, where the boss calls the shots, is the norm. Workers are not expected to initiate communication with the boss nor to speak up unless called upon to do so. Bosses are respected in and out of the workplace and are not to be publicly contradicted. Employees' status is higher when the status of the boss and the company is higher.

Equality = Democratic Cultures = Small Power Distance

People who live in cultures that focus more on equality may say: "My company's organization chart looks sort of like a low box. The organization chart of my daughter's company looks like a web within a circle with the executive team at the center. I believe that my boss has power because he's worked his way up to boss, not because he's better than me. I appreciate it when my boss consults me about decisions that affect me and my job. I like it even more when he lets me, or the team, make the decisions. I like being independent but I don't mind choosing to be interdependent with my work team."

Equality of power is referred to as small power distance. Key concepts are democratic leadership, independence or interdependence, flat organizational structures, decentralized decision making, and the belief that position power lies in the role, not in the superiority of the person. In general, women are more likely than men to manage in a democratic way (Eagly 1990).

In moderately egalitarian cultures—such as in the United States, Japan, and most European countries—consultation is usually appreciated but not necessarily expected. Participative environments are initiated by the participative leader, not by subordinates. Ideal leaders are pragmatically democratic. Moderate status differences and privileges for leaders are acceptable. Rules and laws are expected to apply to superiors and subordinates alike. Change normally starts with the top leaders, but key people throughout the organization must buy into the change if it is to be effective and lasting.

In very egalitarian cultures—such as in the Scandinavian countries, Israel, and Austria—subjecting yourself to the power of others is seen as undesirable. Everyone should have a say in everything that concerns them. Status differences are suspect. Ideal leaders are democratic and loyally carry out the will of their groups. Change comes about through group consensus. Leaders must persuade and influence the group. Former leaders are usually comfortable with accepting new, less powerful roles, for the power differential is in the roles, not the people who fill them.

Culture Clash

People expect all communication to become public knowledge in group-first cultures, such as Asian and Latino. Among Euro-Americans, if you forward to others a personal, one-on-one email, it may be seen as a breach of etiquette, unless you get permission. However, in group-first cultures, building consensus means everyone stays in the loop. For example, a Euro-American manager sent several e-mails to a manager in an Asian supplier company, asking about a shortage. Finally, not getting a real answer, he sent a one-on-one e-mail to the Asian manager, asking him to identify the cause of the shortage. His e-mail was passed on to the entire group, and the Euro-American came off looking like a finger-pointing American to those who were not aware of his previous inquiries.

Euro-Americans may press Asian or Latino associates for immediate answers by e-mail., but the culture's strong sense of hierarchy often means that an issue may need much consultation with superiors before an answer can be given. Demanding a fast response from people in hierarchy cultures can offend them. You may get instead silence or false promises.

Cultural Difference #6: Take Risks or Play It Safe?

In cultures that value playing it safe, people like to avoid uncertainty. People are not comfortable with unstructured, unclear, or unpredictable situations, so they adopt strict codes of behavior and a belief in absolute truths in order to avoid such uncertainty. This aspect of culture is referred to as the degree of "uncertainty avoidance" that is typical.

Play It Safe

"We keep things under control in my culture. We do it by:

- Making sure that everyone knows the rules and not allowing people to break the rules without punishment.
- Making sure that people know what's expected by designating precise relationships, assignments, and schedules
- Arranging life so that everyone knows what to expect"
- "Since change creates many unknowns and uncertainties, we don't like change and try to prevent it by sticking with tradition."

Cultures that value playing it safe are high in "uncertainty avoidance." This term refers to the extent to which people are comfortable with unstructured, unclear, or unpredictable situations, and the extent to which they try to avoid such situations by adopting strict codes of behavior and a belief in absolute truths. Since change creates many unknowns and uncertainties, people in these cultures resist change more than others. They focus on tradition, and therefore the past, and often become quite rigid in these matters.

People in play-it-safe cultures are also generally more active, aggressive, emotional, security-seeking, and intolerant. Greece is the most certainty-oriented culture, followed by Japan. Most European and Latino cultures fall into this pattern (Hofstede 1984, 2001).

Take Risks

"Nothing ventured, nothing gained' is my motto. Rules have their place but there are exceptions to every rule. I like change and new adventure. I like investing in the future and looking forward to possible payoffs. For a business to be successful, people must come up with new ways of doing things, new products and services, and new technology."

Cultures where people are more comfortable with uncertainty tend to be risk-taking cultures. When people don't fear "reasonable" risks, they are more open to change and more forward-looking, anticipating the payoff from their investment in future changes. New ways of doing things, new products and services, and new technology are highly valued.

People in risk-taking cultures also tend to be more contemplative and tolerant, and less aggressive and emotional than those in play-it-safe cultures. The United States has a moderately risk-taking culture, and Singapore is by far the most risk-taking culture studied by Hofstede (1984, 2001).

Cultural Difference #7: Decisions—Long-Term or Short-Term

In cultures with a long-term orientation, people make decisions based primarily on how the action will affect the person, the organization, and the society in years to come. People in cultures with a short-term orientation are more interested in what the decision will do for them right now.

Long-Term Orientation

"I shouldn't be selfish when I decide what to do. We must take care of what we have and make the best use of it. If we work hard, save, and invest, the future will take care of itself."

Cultures that have the longest-term orientation are American Indian, as well as East Asian countries, such as China and Japan. A long-term orientation is related to collectivist Eastern values of hard work, learning, accountability, self-discipline, and status-obedience relationships.

Short-Term Orientation

"I'm most interested in achieving my current objectives. If I don't, I'll be a loser. My success depends on showing that I've got what it takes, and the powers-that-be won't give me very long to show that I can get results fast."

People in Western countries tend to have a moderately short-term orientation, which is related to individualist Western values of freedom, rights, and thinking for oneself. Hindu India is more short-term oriented. Muslim countries seem to have the shortest-term orientation, perhaps related to a belief that everything is up to Allah, so people have little or no control over what happens in the world.

In Western corporate cultures, especially in the United States, the bottom line is the major concern. Control systems focus on income and profit, and managers are constantly judged by these numbers—using time frames as short as this year, this quarter, and even last month. This over-focus on financial aspects may lead to short-sighted decisions—as well as hasty adoption of new ideas and quick abandonment of them. Table 2.4 shows how decision orientation correlates with such cultural factors as societal norms, work, relationships, and ways of thinking (Hofstede 2001).

TABLE 2.4: How Cultural Factors Relate to Decision Orientation

LONG-TERM DECISION ORIENTATION	*SHORT-TERM DECISION ORIENTATION*
Societal Norms	**Societal Norms**
Deferred gratification of needs expected	Immediate gratification of needs expected
Traditions adaptable to change	Traditions are sacred
Family life guided by shared tasks	Family life guided by imperatives
Frugality, perseverance	Consumerism
Saving, investing	Spending
Building strong market position	The bottom line
Holistic thinking (synthesis)	"Tunnel vision" thinking (analysis)
Structured problem solving	Fuzzy problem solving
Clearly stated, specific goals	Open goals
Work and Relationships	**Work and Relationships**
Build business relationships and market position	Short-term business results, bottom line is most important
Vertical and horizontal coordination, control, adaptiveness in business	Family and business spheres should be kept separate
Prosperity should be distributed so that all have enough	Meritocracy means economic and social life depend on personal achievement
Humility a general human virtue	Humility is a feminine virtue
Daily human relations are satisfying	Daily human relations are less satisfying
Old age coming sooner, that's ok	Old age coming later
Ways of Thinking	**Ways of Thinking**
Either full confidence or no confidence	Probabilistic thinking
What's good-evil depends on situation	Belief in absolute guidelines about good-evil
Opposites complement each other	Need for cognitive consistency
Government by men	Government by law
Synthesis thinking (focus on whole)	Analysis thinking (focus on parts)
Higher performance on basic math tasks	Lower performance on basic math tasks

Many of these factors stem from collectivism vs individualism. For example, research studies of psychologist Richard Nisbett (2004) indicate that Asians focus more on the group context, the whole, than on individual objects, the parts, as discussed in the Asian American chapter. In other experiments Nisbett (2009) showed people a graph with a trend line moving upward and asked what they thought the trend line would do in the future. Euro-Americans tended to expect the trend to continue upward. Most Asians said the trend would continue to a peak and then would go down, decline. The history of most trends is that they increase to a peak and then decline. The Confucian idea that the future will resemble the past is deeply ingrained in the Asian mind; in this case, what has gone up in the past is likely to eventually come down. How might this tendency impact risk-taking, decision-making, and other cultural differences?

Cultural Difference #8: Time—Dive-Right-In or Step-by-Step?

Western cultures see time as a series of points along a line and people doing one task at a time—a linear, single-task use of time. Most other "modern" cultures see time as a circle in which they jump in doing many tasks at one time—a circular, multiple-task use of time. Aboriginal cultures take the circular approach a step further, viewing time as cyclical, seasonal.

Step-by-Step Time

"Time is made up of the past, the present, and an infinite future. I pay most attention to the future. Time can be separated into units or steps with fixed beginnings and endings for events. I measure my time and budget it as I schedule appointments, decide on the starting and ending times for events, get to things on time, meet my deadlines, and plan ahead. The best way to use my time is to focus on one thing at a time."

In Western countries, especially the United States, people tend to view time as separable into quantifiable, discrete units or steps with fixed beginnings and endings for events. They place great emphasis on future events and therefore on planning, scheduling, setting target dates, and being prompt. The segmenting of time leads to focusing on one task, appointment, or event at a time (Graham 1981, Cote 1989, McGrath 1983).

Step-by-step time is linear, like a ribbon or road of time. It's almost tangible because people talk about manipulating it, scheduling it, using it, and borrowing it. Compartmentalizing time in steps or units allows you to concentrate on one thing at a time, but it also denies you much of the context in which events occur. It permits only a limited number of events within a given period. Thus it can limit your possibilities. Your business life, social life, and even sex life, are apt to be completely time dominated. Linear-time people are less likely to see things in a larger context (Hall 1982).

People perceive, as they look backward in time, that the earlier the year, the farther away it is—until it's hard to even imagine people and situations in long years past. The same is true for the future. Many years down the road ahead is difficult to imagine; it's a distant point on the horizon. This perception makes the past seem a remote and foreign place, distancing people from the ancients, and even from their own ancestors.

Dive-Right-In Time

"Time is like a circle, and I use points of time within the circle. Several things may be happening at once in this circle because several people may need my attention at any one time. After all, it's more important to maintain good relationships with others and to complete transactions with others than to do one thing at a time on a preset schedule. Each point in time is sacred but only because I give myself fully to the moment, to the relationships, events, or activities of the moment. An activity simply takes as much time as is needed for its completion, so if the activity is important, the time it takes is irrelevant."

Circular-time cultures include Latino, Middle Eastern, and some Asian and African cultures. In the American workplace, it is likely that many African Americans, Asian Americans, and Latino Americans are circular-time people. While they may necessarily adapt to the Euro-American time orientation when they work in U.S. organizations, they tend to return to their own time orientation for social and family events.

Euro-Americans sometimes feel they don't really have the full attention of a busy circular-time person. They worry that the person may never get around to the most important business at hand. Some feel that nothing seems solid or firm with circular-time people, particularly regarding the future. Often there are changes in the most important plans, right up to the very last minute. In circular-time organizations, systems need a much greater centralization of control because the top person deals continually with many people.

Cyclical, Seasonal Time

Aborigines around the world—and presumably all humans in times past—have a circular view of time that focuses on cycles and seasons. They think in terms of the season, of time moving around from spring to summer to fall to winter and then around again and again. From this view, last spring—and all the springs before it—is just a bit away from this spring. You could almost reach through the thin veil of time and touch it. Related to this, aborigines have an ongoing relationship with the past and are more inclined to honor the ancestors and to understand the contribution that they continue to make in the current world. Ancestors and their way of life seem very real and nearby.

In cultures that are primarily agricultural, the cycles of planting, cultivating, and harvesting are seasonal. People in such cultures do not see time as stretching into the future, but tend to focus on the past and present. This orientation is dominant in Cuban and Mexican rural cultures and African tribal cultures.

Cultural Difference #9: Space—Come Close or Back Off?

Cultures differ in how much personal space individuals expect to occupy, how close they stand or sit to one another, and how much physical contact they have. In the workplace this translates into different perceptions about comfortable office sizes and layout and requirements for privacy in work stations (Hall 1982). Cultures may differ in other aspects of space perception as well. For example, studies show that Asians and Westerners perceive space and objects differently. Asians attend more to the space between objects. Westerners mostly attend to the objects themselves. This difference translates into separate aesthetics in art, architecture, etc. and different ways of solving problems. (Hawkins 2004).

Cultural differences in perception of space probably have the greatest impact on size of the comfort zone between and among people. Arab Americans like the least space and Asian Americans the most, with Westerners somewhere in between.

Come-Close Space

"I'm from the Middle East. When I talk with business associates and friends, we stand close enough to be able to feel each other's breath on our face and to be able to catch each other's scent. We touch each other a great deal as we interact. My male business associates often embrace instead of shaking hands."

Latino and Middle Eastern cultures tend to be high-contact societies, with more touching permitted and expected than in other cultures. Two men will often embrace instead of shaking hands. People in Latino cultures prefer slightly more distance than those in Middle Eastern cultures, but they like to stand closer and to touch more than do people in Western cultures. Asian cultures like the most space and least public touching of all, according to E.T. Hall.

Back-Off Space

"I'm a Euro-American. When I talk with business associates and social acquaintances, it's usually at arm's length, about two or three feet away. Of course, I'm closer to my lover as well as family members and close friends. I notice that I stand farther away when I want to protect myself or to stay uninvolved. If someone moves too close into my space, I usually feel uncomfortable and back up till I feel comfortable. It really bugs me if a person keeps moving in even after I back off."

Western cultures are basically non-contact societies, according to Hall. In most Western cultures we learn to stand about two or three feet away, an arm's length, when we're at business or social events. Only family members, close friends, and lovers are expected to come closer. We may stand farther away when we feel a desire to remain aloof or protect ourselves. When someone moves into our space, we normally feel uncomfortable and back away till we feel comfortable again.

In most Asian cultures, perhaps because of dense populations, people prefer an even greater distance and less touching with all but family and close friends.

Cultural Difference #10: Communicating—Direct or Indirect?

While there are many variations in communication style, two that stem directly from the key cultural patterns we've discussed are directness and indirectness.

Using Go-Betweens and Implied Messages

"I try to maintain harmony and to get along with people, so I never say things that would offend them. Saying no directly would be offensive, so I try to gently let them know that I'm not terribly enthusiastic about something. To make an initial overture or bring up a sensitive topic, I usually ask someone close to the other person to feel them out first."

People in most cultures use an indirect style of communication, especially in those cultures identified as us-first, people-first, rank/status, and play-it-safe. In us-first cultures with many close ties, many messages can be implied because people have been socialized alike and are on "the same wavelength." And in many cultures, go-betweens are used to broach sensitive topics. In all cultures, women are likely to use an indirect style, such as hinting, implying, keeping quiet in order to keep peace, and mentioning problems or desires to associates of the decision-maker in the hope that they'll "put in a good word."

Going to the Person and Getting to the Point

"I try to build trusting relationships based on honesty and sincerity. It's important to be upfront and genuine in my dealings with people. If I have a problem with a person, or want to make a proposal, I go directly to that person first and try to work it out."

The direct style is typical in Western cultures, especially those that focus on I-control, me-first, achievement-first, equality, and risk taking. Within those cultures men are more likely than women to use a direct communication style.

"Did you double check these figures?" Is this directness perceived as business-like or brusque? Asian Americans or Latino Americans may see it as rude and accusatory, while Euro-Americans or African Americans see it as businesslike.

Cultural Difference #11: How We Make Money = Dependence Level

Whether you—and most of the people in your ingroup—are a farmer, an assembly line worker, or a computer programmer will affect your cultural values and customs. Agriculture is the dominant way of making a living in so called undeveloped countries, while most developing countries have become industrialized to some extent. The Western nations are predominantly post-industrial. But many countries have large groups that make their living as farmers and other large groups that work in industry (Nirenberg 1993). In many countries there is a peasant-class value system that's quite different from the ruling-class value system, which may have post-industrial values. This economic-structure approach is directly related to the level of dependence that people in a culture tend to feel. In fact, the 11 cultural differences tend to fall into three distinct patterns of independence, dependence, and interdependence, as shown in Table 2.5. For further detail on how these factors play out in the workplace, see Table 2.9 at the end of this chapter.

Economic and occupational differences may help explain the cultural complexity we find among people in a supposedly homogeneous nation. Within a nation, region or culture, various groups may be operating from the ethos that represents their way of making a living, under-girded to some extent by other traditional cultural values. For example, all workers in the United States share in the cultural

TABLE 2.5: Cultural Differences and Types of Dependence

Dependent Focus	Independent Focus	Interdependent Focus
External source of control: life happens to me **Collectivism**: us-first	**Internal source of control**: I control my life **Individualism**: me-first	**Internal source of control**: I control my life **Combination**: independent persons choose to team up.
Ties: tight, close with ingroup members	**Ties:** loose, few	**Ties**: vary by personal choice
Personal connection first: cooperative, feminine, focus on relationships and intangibles	**Achievement first**: competitive, masculine, focus on material things and tasks	**Combination**: people-first in order to achieve as work teams
Class difference: status, rank, defer to authority	**Equality**: democratic, give-and-take authority	**Equality**
Security-seeking: I must avoid uncertainty; leads to being rigid, rules-oriented, w/focus on tradition, the status quo	**Risk-taking**: I can handle uncertainty; leads to openness, flexibility, focus on future change	**Risk-taking**
Time use: circular, multiple-task	**Time use:** linear, single-task	**Time use:** combination linear and circular; flexible
Space use: close for members **Communication:** indirect **Economic system:** agricultural	**Space use:** distant **Communication:** direct **Economic system:** industrial	**Space use:** flexible combination **Communication:** direct **Economic system:** post-industrial

media—television, film, radio, magazines, and books are readily available to most everyone. Farmers, factory workers, and computer technicians will therefore maintain some common values. But people immigrating from certain Latino, Asian, and African countries may have lacked access to such media and therefore were more segmented and isolated by their economic activities. For example, in China groups in fairly remote areas may be almost entirely involved in agriculture and still adhere to many agriculture-era values. Others, in urban areas, may be focused on manufacturing and therefore on industrial-era values. A few, such as those in Hong Kong, may be focused on post-industrial activities and values.

Agricultural Economy = Dependent Worldview

In many countries that are primarily dependent upon an agricultural economy, the value system of the masses in the peasant class is quite different from that of the elite ruling-class. The masses are quite dependent on the extended family and village groups. They are likely to believe they're controlled, put the group first and have many close ties, focus on cooperative relationships, accept status differences, avoid change and risk, view time as circular, like physically closeness, at least with family, and use an indirect communication style. All this adds up to a worldview that's primarily dependent on external forces, the family, and village groups. The dependent pattern was traditionally typical of most women in all cultures and of men and women in Asian, Latino, and African cultures, in fact of most of the world's peoples.

It seems obvious that putting the group first is good for family and group survival, and it can control personal selfishness and greed. A major disadvantage is the lack of personal choice you're allowed in such cultures. For example, in traditional cultures parents and community leaders determined whom you should marry, where you should live, what work you should do, how you should worship. All the major life decisions were made for you. The effect can be to drain away some of your motivation, passion for life, and ability to make your own decisions and take responsibility for their outcomes. Imagine the difference between living with a husband or wife you were required to marry versus someone you passionately wanted to marry. Or working in an occupation you were expected to follow versus one you knowingly chose once you were clear about what you really wanted to do in life.

Industrial Economy = Independent Worldview

As a culture moves into a manufacturing-based economy, values shift to a more independent focus that's needed for success in that workplace. People are likely to believe they're in control, put their own goals first, have looser ties with others, focus on competitive achievement, demand equality, take calculated risks to bring needed change, view time as points on a line, keep most people at arm's length, and use a direct communication style. An independent worldview is traditionally typical of men in Western cultures. It allows for greater selfishness and greed, and doesn't do as much to encourage concern for others, but it also provides for greater personal power and autonomy. This in turn promotes such skills as taking calculated risks, taking initiative, taking charge, doing independent problem solving and decision making, and taking responsibility for results.

Post–Industrial Economy = Interdependent Worldview

As a culture moves to an information- and service-based economy, it begins to shift to an interdependent focus. Some values and customs seem similar to dependence on the surface. But a major difference is that people are aware of their individuality and independence. They have developed the powerful skills typical of people in an independent culture.

People in post-industrial economies are likely to believe they're in control. They may embrace elements of both the me-first and us-first orientations—as autonomous people they choose to put the work team first in order to achieve greater things together. They focus on cooperative relationships in order to achieve greater success. They're also likely to demand equality, take calculated risks, be flexible in how they use time and physical closeness, and use a direct communication style.

Instead of feeling dependent upon a group for survival, people in interdependent cultures have the power and freedom to either work independently or to team up with others. When they choose to team up or form alliances, it's because they believe that choice will allow them to have more fun, or be more successful, or both.

Key differences between dependence and interdependence:

Group members choose to be part of the group—it's a preference rather than a need—so they bring with them the power of free choice rather than duty or obligation.

- Group members are self-motivated.
- Group members bring the power and skills inherent in an independent lifestyle.

These qualities are especially valuable for the types of work arrangements needed today, such as:

- Self-managing teams
- Entrepreneurial teams
- Project teams
- Business alliances
- Professional networks

Warning: Don't Use Cultural Knowledge to Create New Stereotypes

A little knowledge can be a dangerous thing—or a wonderful thing, if you realize its limitations. Now that you have a little knowledge of cultural differences—and you'll be gaining more detailed knowledge of the largest U.S. subcultures—be sure you use it wisely. When you learn what experts have to say about your own culture, you're sure to think about some aspects, "Oh, no, I don't do that!" Well, that's true for most people. While they live out most of the major beliefs and values of their culture, they'll have their own ideas about some things. There are always some areas where people think independently, or even rebelliously.

Bottom line: Don't use the knowledge you acquire about a culture to create new stereotypes about people from that culture. Focus on each person you meet as an individual, using your knowledge of their cultural background as a sensing device for getting to know the individual, as pictured in Figure 2.2.

Why study cultural differences? Without this knowledge, you'll find that the more diverse your workplace is, the more you get caught in puzzling, conflicting situations without a clue as to how to proceed. You may try to feel your way through the amorphous mass of people's puzzling actions, sometimes engulfed by a swirling ocean of people's mysterious emotions, trying to feel your way through a dense fog of hidden motivations. You feel blocked by the unknowns and can't work your way through to understanding and resolution. Think of your cultural knowledge as threads, lifelines, that you can follow to formulate the

- right questions to ask
- appropriate motivations to explore
- specific feelings to recognize

Used sensitively, cultural knowledge can help you weave together these threads of information to arrive at ways to work with people to resolve problems and conflicts. It can help you figure out how to connect and bond with people and build trusting, productive relationships.

FIGURE 2.2: Focus on the Individual against a Cultural Background

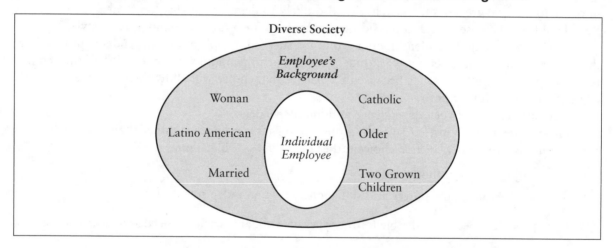

BI-ETHNIC AND MULTI-ETHNIC PERSONS

The 2000 Census was the first time that the U.S. Census Bureau attempted to count the numbers of both mixed-race and mixed-ethnicity, and it was about time. Over 2 percent of all Americans identified themselves as bi-ethnic or multi-ethnic in 2000 (Census 2000). Bi-ethnic people were born of a father from one clearly-defined cultural group, such as African American, and a mother of a different group, such as Euro-American. Multi-ethnic persons have at least one parent who is clearly bi-ethnic and the other parent from a different group. Ultimately we're all multi-ethnic, but most of us clearly identify with one group and are accepted without question by members of that group.

Until 1960 anti-miscegenation laws banned marriage between people of "different races." The Supreme Court ruled such laws unconstitutional in 1960, and since that time such mixed marriages have increased tenfold. This led to the "first generation where it's "OK" to be a bi-ethnic or multi-ethnic child. Many of these persons feel confusion and conflict about who they are and where they belong. Others celebrate their diversity and want to develop a new sense of what it means to be American. This view is the basis for *Mavin*, a multiracial foundation, magazine, and blog (2005).

Many multi-ethnics view pop star Mariah Carey and golf superstar Tiger Woods as heroine and hero who "paved the way for us. They identified themselves as multi-ethnic before that was accepted by society" (Steiner 1999).

Here are some results of Census 2000, which, for the first time in history instructed people to "check off "all that apply" when designating race or ethnicity:

- 2.4% of Americans selected 2 or more categories
- 93% of multi-ethnics selected 2 categories
- 6% selected 3 categories, and 1% selected 4 categories
- 40% live in the West.
- 20% of the San Francisco Bay Area's population is multi-ethnic
- 15% of Honolulu's population is multi-ethnic.
- 54% of native Hawaiian-Pacific Islanders claim 2 or more races
- 40% of American Indians claim 2 or more races
- 14% of Asian Americans, 6% of Latino Americans, 5% of African Americans, and 2.5% of Euro-Americans claim 2 or more categories

Asian American Hapas

In the year 2000, out of 11.9 million Asian Americans, 1.7 million, or 14 percent, were Asian as well as one or more other races—often referred to in the Asian American community by the Hawaiian term "hapa," from the derivative word "half." About 2.1 million Asian Pacific Americans (APAs) are hapas, the second-largest APA subgroup, behind only the Chinese (Dariotis 2008; Fulbeck 2006).

The hapa community is primarily East Asian – Euro-American (especially Chinese and Japanese).

Japanese American – Euro-American

Nearly one third of Japanese Americans are hapa. This number reflects the high out-marriage rate in the post-internment camp era among the Japanese second generation and third generation, but it also includes the children of the so-called Japanese war brides from the 1950s and 1960s. Many Japanese American hapas grew up on U.S. army bases in Japan or the United States, isolated from the larger Japanese American community.

Filipino American – African American

After Japanese Americans, Filipino Americans report the next highest percentage of people of mixed heritage among APAs, at 21.8 percent. But due to their larger numbers, Filipino hapas—more than half a million—rank as the single largest contingent. The U.S.-Philippines War (1899-1902) gave rise to a small but significant population of African American Filipinos, living mostly in the Philippines. Their ancestors were African American soldiers who were convinced to desert during the war, because of their own or their parents' recent status as slaves. Filipino American out-marriage was also encouraged by the limited number of Filipinas immigrating into the United States, relative to the number of Filipino men.

Asian Indian American – Mexican American

Early Sikh immigrants to California often intermarried with Mexican American women; business partners often sought pairs of sisters to marry. This occurred in the early part of the 20th century, particularly in California's Central Valley, where there is a large, fairly-affluent land-owning farming community composed of their descendents. More recent information on Sikh intermarriage is hard to come by. There were 1.9 million Asian Indian Americans counted in the U.S. Census in 2000; of these, about 11.6 percent were Asian Indian hapa.

Major Issues of Bi-Ethnic Groups

Three major issues that multi-ethnic people face are 1) ethnic self-identity, 2) ethnic classification, and 3) whether to "pass" as one ethnicity or another. They may ask themselves, "How do I think of myself? As a white? Black? Euro-American? African American? Mulatto? a mix? just an individual?

who?" The next question might be, "What do I tell others when they ask about my heritage, my ethnic background?" Still other bi-ethnic persons may look Euro-American like their father who has been mostly absent but feel African-American like their mother who raised them. They may ask, "Would it be easier just to let people think I'm Euro-American (i.e. 'pass')?"

The most dramatic choices usually occur when persons are raised by one parent, yet they look like the other parent. For example, Tammy looks more African American than Euro-American, yet she was raised by her Euro-American mother and had little contact with African American relatives. Where does she belong? At age 5, she assumed that she was "white," and was shocked to learn that many others considered her "black." So how does she deal with the ways that others categorize her. If she looked "white," she might make the decision to "pass" as Euro-American because that's really her cultural heritage. Since she can't pass, she must learn to accept her bi-ethnicity and relate to people who can also accept it (Funderburg 1998).

Myra Root (2001) says multi-ethnics have some basic rights, such as the right:

- Not to justify their ethnic legitimacy, nor their existence in this world
- Not to keep their inherent ethnicities separate, but to merge them
- Not to be responsible for people's discomfort with their physical ambiguity
- To identify themselves in the way they want
- To have loyalties to, and identify with, more than one group of people

AMERICAN CORPORATE CULTURES

The evolution from independence to interdependence is reflected in the American business culture generally and in the corporate cultures of leading organizations specifically. *Corporate culture* refers to the values, norms, and principles that underlie an organization's policies and practices. Every organization has its own culture, whether it's a corporation or not, so even if you work in a government agency, a school, or a nonprofit organization, you still work within a "corporate culture," more properly called an organizational culture. A corporate culture is made up of values, symbols, stars and champions, myths and legends, rituals and ceremonies that are often summed up as "what we're all about" and "the way we do things around here" (Deal and Kennedy 1982, 1999). Just as the culture at large ties people together and gives meaning and purpose to their everyday lives, corporate culture is the glue that holds corporations together.

Strong and Weak Corporate Cultures

Some corporate cultures are strong, others weak. Even weak cultures influence almost everything in the organization, from who gets promoted to what decisions are made, from how people dress to what they do when they're off.

Weak Cultures

In weak corporate cultures people adhere primarily to their own culture group's viewpoints, norms, and values. People have more freedom to determine how to act. However, the extreme of weak culture is organizational chaos. Some essential values must be shared by members if an organization is to be able to achieve its goals. To survive and thrive over time, organizations need strong cultures. You can identify a weak-culture firm by looking for the following signs:

- No set of beliefs about how to succeed is delineated by the leaders.
- No rank-ordered priority of values is communicated by the leaders.
- No overriding common values are held by the different subcultures in various parts of the company.
- Role models don't serve the culture well. They may be disruptive, even destructive, or don't reinforce key values and beliefs.

• Rituals of everyday work life are disorganized or contradictory. People do their own thing or work at cross-purposes, undermining each other.

Strong Cultures

In strong corporate cultures leaders clearly define and enforce values and norms, giving more direction to how people should act, more reinforcement about what they should do, and perhaps higher penalties for not conforming. The *actions* of management must be consistent with corporate values, because the inconsistencies will be noticed and magnified out of proportion. When messages and actions are consistent, people get the message. Shared values and expectations act as an informal control system that tells people what's expected of them. The result is that people are more likely to view a situation in the same way, to respond similarly, and to expect similar results. They are marching to the same drumbeat, which impacts organizational performance (Peters 1992). Whether authoritarian or flexible in style, a strong culture typically has these qualities (Carmichael 2009):

• It offers a clear corporate vision or mission
• Corporate beliefs and values are consistent with the mission and objectives of the company
• Employees' personal beliefs and values are aligned with corporate values.

Flexible-style strong cultures can be just as strong as authoritarian-style, while still providing for individual work styles. Management clearly showcases a few core values that people must passionately commit to. Around this clear, hard core all else may be fairly fuzzy. People may decide how to achieve job goals as long as methods are aligned with core values. Strong flexible cultures have the following qualities, in addition to those listed above (Carmichael 2009):

• The culture is adaptable, adjusting to external conditions
• It places a high value on employees at all levels
• The culture is consistent, treating all employees equally and fairly
• It encourages extensive employee interaction across all levels

This type of culture works best with diverse groups because it allows for a greater variety of behaviors.

Authoritarian-style strong cultures are those in which management expects people to conform to values and norms that encompass most of their activities. There is a required company way to do almost everything. See Table 2.8 Comparison of Management Behaviors: High-Conformity and Low-Conformity Corporate Cultures.

The Networked Corporation: Flexible, Open, Diverse

Corporations are evolving—and the ones that are winning are those that are more flexible, open, diverse at all levels, and empower employees to take initiative, think creatively, and make decisions.

SHOWCASE

Southwest Airlines:
Strong Corporate Culture in Action

Southwest Airlines made its first flight from Dallas to Houston in 1971. It was a tiny airline with service limited to Texas and adjoining states. Rather than trying to capture current market share, its strategy was to create a whole new market segment by offering fares that made it cheaper to fly than drive—and a whole new flying experience that reflected a unique corporate culture, strong and flexible (Strategic 2005).

Mission Reflects Beliefs and Values

The Southwest Airlines mission statement expresses the following key beliefs and values:

- *to offer customer service delivered with a sense of warmth, friendliness, individual pride, and company spirit*
- *to provide our employees a stable work environment with equal opportunity for learning and personal growth*
- *to encourage creativity and innovation for improving the effectiveness of Southwest Airlines*
- *to provide employees the same concern, respect, and caring attitude within the organization that they are expected to share externally with every Southwest customer*
- *to value diversity and create an environment that encourages it, both in the workplace and among our supplier base*

On top of the practical value of employee and customer experience, Southwest superimposes the spiritual value of employees' hospitality, warmth, welfare and humor. To achieve this, management tells employees, "Just be yourself. Sing if you like. Tell jokes if you like." So there is an added element of company spirit. For Southwest, it's not enough for customers to fly from Houston to Dallas and get off the plane saying, "Well, I made it." Southwest wants them to get off the plane with big smiles on their faces, saying, "Wow, that was an unusual experience" (Cohan 2005).

Southwest management believes that understanding the mission is important for all the employees because they can then understand how it all fits together with company goals, policies, practices, and spirit—they see the whole process as holistic.

Some reporters have said that putting people first is a Southwest competitive strategy. The founder Herb Kelleher disagrees, saying that treating people right is a matter of morality, not a strategy. It began with management thinking about what is the right thing to do in a business context. They decided they wanted to really take care of employees and customers, to honor them, and to love them as individuals. It turned out that employees and customers responded with trust and a work ethic that made Southwest successful.

Results

Has this type of strong, flexible culture resulted in a successful company? Southwest started in 1971, made a profit in 1973 and has shown a profit ever year since, the only U.S. airline to do so. In the 10-year period 1991-2001 its stock price increased about 30 percent per year. By 2005 it was the fourth largest airline in the USA in terms of domestic passenger miles flown, serving 60 airports in 30 states, and growing.

They are the Apples, Amazons, and Googles, networked to the hilt (Jarvis 2009). Clearly, these types of companies are more likely to appreciate diverse employees and to meet their needs.

The networked corporation is evolving from the demands of a diverse, post-industrial, technological, global economy, especially those with a heavy emphasis on informational technology. Just as virtual reality is a computerized experience that seems real but takes place in cyberspace, a networked corporation may be more virtual than physical. For example, much of the work, the meetings, and communication take place on computer screens, fax machines, car phones, voice mail, and video conferences. Work teams may include company specialists, independent contractors, suppliers, customers, and investors. They may be scattered around the globe, change from month to month, and never meet face to face. Or they may be self-managing teams that meet every day. They may work together to develop the plans, set the standards, identify and solve the problems, make the decisions, and provide the products and services. In any case, the degree of success or failure depends heavily on people's relationships with one another.

Of course, this format affects organizational structure. Old rigid bureaucratic hierarchies are melting into fluid, shifting networks of relationships among employees, customers, suppliers, and allied competitors because a web-shaped structure aids the free flow of communication and collaboration. Table 2.7 shows how manufacturing corporations can fit this model. However, the networked corporation format is also being adopted by all types or organizations. Examples are custom banking, investment services, manufacturers' representatives, wholesale operations, and computer services (Scarso 2008, Davidow 1992).

The networked corporation is built upon trust, collaboration, cooperation, and teamwork, but it also relies on individual achievement and the ability to be entrepreneurial, and therefore competitive, in outlook. In such organizations, it's more obvious than ever that people are the most valuable resource, that how they work together creates energy and innovation or decay and demoralization, that their interactions spark the knowledge and information that fuel organizational growth and success. In these organizations what matters is what you can contribute, not your ethnicity or gender. And the kinds of people moving into these new organizations are more diverse each year.

Table 2.7 Networked and Traditional Corporation Comparisons—Manufacturing Example

Strategies	
Networked Corporation	*Traditional Corporation*
Post-Industrial Economic View: Manufacturing base is essential as customers of services and generator of wealth for employees to purchase services.	*Post-Industrial Economic View:* Buy products from other nations where labor is cheaper.
Result: Develop a complex, rich manufacturing and agricultural base, highly automated, few workers.	*Result:* Hollowed-out economy—manufacturing corporations as mere shells for products made in other countries. Economies of scale.
Targeted market niches.	Engine: The assembly line.
Engine: Information processing.	Large factories, many workers.
Lights-out automated factories.	Many suppliers, few models of products, many customers.
A few long-term suppliers, many customized models—targeted customers.	
Products	
Networked Corporation	*Traditional Corporation*
Virtual products are stored in minds of cooperating teams, in computers, and in flexible product lines.	Products are stored in warehouses and retail stores. Products supplied weeks or months after orders
Virtual products are produced instantly and customized to customer demand.	are placed or plans made—limited, standardized models.
	(Continued)

Structure	
Networked Corporation	**Traditional Corporation**
Fluid, flexible, constantly changing—a web or network of informational relationships. Structure meets unique needs of customers.	Rigid, stable—hierarchical departments filled with job slots, each with a job description and lines of authority.
Structure, planning start with customer needs and desires.	Structure meets needs of corporation—or a broad average (mass) of customers.
Self-managed work teams that may include customers, suppliers, retailers, investors, distributors.	Structure, planning start with what corporation wants to do and can do. Individual workers, some internal task forces and work teams.
Corporation is a vast network of relationships to carry out ever-changing of common activities.	Corporation is a discrete, separate enterprise.

Human Resources	
Networked Corporation	**Traditional Corporation**
Most workers (90%) in knowledge or service jobs.	Most workers in production jobs.
Change focus to targeted production of customized products and services for "niche" customers.	Retain focus on mass production of standardized products and services for mass consumption.
Most jobs require higher education—broad, general knowledge—multicultural and technological.	Most jobs require secondary education—specialized knowledge.
Requires workers to be informed, responsible, adaptable to change, flexible.	Requires workers to be obedient, fit a job slot, specialized.
Free flow of information to managers and workers	Managers have access to information they need; pass along minimal information to workers.
What matters is what you contribute	
Managers as leaders, coaches, facilitator Managers' power lies in people skills	Managers as directors, motivators, evaluators; power lies in the hierarchy.
Worker freedom, power to control work.	Close supervision of workers.
Built on trust, collaboration, mutual cooperation, teamwork.	Built on protecting self-interest, confrontation between managers/workers, adversarial relationships.
Cloud computing connects teams for many functions Rewards leaders for long-term dedication.	Rewards leaders for short-term manipulation.

Undermined Cultures of the New Millennium

Many corporations are on the right track, becoming more diverse, flexible, open, and networked. Many are becoming stronger on core values and objectives, yet allowing more flexibility for how a wide range of employees might go about expressing those values and achieving the objectives.

On the darker side, many people at the top of today's organizations have some major image problems. Greed at the top has undermined the formerly strong corporate cultures of many large corporations and recent scandals in the financial sector nearly toppled the global economy. The culture of any organization is a reflection of the deeply held values and the behaviors of a few people, and in large companies that means the top management team.

Euro–American Management—from Minority Viewpoints

Because the large majority of those top-management teams consist of Euro-American men, we can see this image problem as primarily their problem. Few, if any, Euro-American managers would admit to the following traits as being dominant aspects of the leadership profile:

> *insensitive, bossy, reluctant to share power and wealth*

Yet these are traits assigned to them by many employees from diverse "minority" groups. When "minority" business students in my classes were asked how top management ranks the following corporate goals, what do you suppose they answered?

- Contributions to society
- Change—openness to change, implementation of needed change
- Creativity—encouraging innovative ideas and implementing them
- Profits—short-range primarily and long-range secondarily

Let's start with the last goal. Many minority persons see Euro-American male top management as overly concerned with short-range profits. They see management as open to change that clearly contributes to profits but often unwilling to initiate changes that would broaden the corporate culture, making it more reflective of the cultures of all major employee groups. While many employees perceive that top management values innovation, they say that it doesn't necessarily follow that management views employee diversity as a valuable source of creativity. Finally, many believe that management shows far too little real interest in making a significant and lasting contribution to society, especially to that of future generations.

Greed and Self–Interest at the Top

In the past, nearly all corporate cultures included an unspoken deal between the company and its employees: "You commit to the company and produce for the company, and the company will commit to you." But in the 1980s and 1990s, corporate top management increasingly made decisions driven by greed and self-interest.

Stock option plans became the main source of executive income. This started out as performance-based compensation that gave an executive a stake in the company. But executives soon realized they could earn really big bucks by making decisions that would cause the stock price to jump the most. Quarterly and annual profit statements directly affect stock prices, so leaders began slashing costs to boost stock prices. Downsizing and outsourcing were key cost-cutting measures that were devastating to the long-term employees who lost their jobs or had more work heaped upon them.

By the late 1990s corporations began focusing on mergers as the solution to every corporate problem, often resulting in mergers of very different, even conflicting, corporate cultures. Such incompatible mergers were nightmares for ordinary employees. Next came a whole series of fraudulent practices at the top—ranging from accounting fraud to legal fraud, with reputable accounting and law firms complicit in the actions and cover-ups. This led to the collapse Enron, Worldcom, Tyco, and Madoff, resulting in billions of lost investments and thousands of lost jobs and pensions. Then came 2008 and the collapse of the housing market followed by the near collapse of the financial system and the entire global economy.

Fear and Distrust at the Bottom

A major result of these developments is that the old patriarchal deal between the corporation and its employees is off. Now there's no deal. Employees must look out for themselves. In large corporations a culture of self-interest at the top and fear at the bottom is common now, which has undermined employee loyalty and trust.

Many big corporations in the Fortune 100 will not be around in a few years because they're gutting their cultures so badly that they can't survive: companies like Bank of America, Eastman Kodak, General Motors, and Sears may not be around.

How Corporate Cultures Integrate Newcomers

When we study the research into how companies integrate newcomers into the culture, we find that those that are flexible, low-conformity, and networked are the ones that do the best job of making diverse employees feel comfortable and empowered.

All companies have some sort of orientation process to inform newcomers about the organization's values, goals, and rituals, "the way we do things around here." New employees normally must develop specific work skills, learn role behaviors appropriate to their new job, and adjust to the work group's values and norms. Here's where the unspoken, unwritten, and sometimes most important information about getting along should be learned. The values and norms may be more difficult for culturally different members to learn, because minorities are usually not part of the informal social networks of the dominant group.

Socialization occurs by such formal methods as training, performance appraisal, and promotion decisions, as well as by such informal methods as rituals, stories, jargon, and role modeling. The purpose of orientation, sometimes called organization socialization, is to align employees with the norms of the organization; it is closely linked to acculturation processes.

Acculturation

Acculturation is a process that occurs when new employees join an organization or when two organizations with different cultures merge. Traditionally, acculturation was accomplished through stories that express key values, and norms—stories about role models, rituals, ceremonies, myths, and symbols. Cox describes four modes of acculturation: assimilation, separation, deculturation, and pluralism (Cox and Finley-Nickelson 1991).

Assimilation When the organization's culture is the standard of behavior for all persons, assimilation is the mode of acculturation. The goal is to eliminate cultural differences at work. New employees who are culturally different are expected to reject, or at least repress, their conflicting beliefs, values, norms, and practices. It is a one-way adaptation, similar to the melting-pot approach.

Separation-Clustering Alienation occurs when new employees are unwilling or unable to adapt to the organization culture. They maintain some separation from it. Cultural exchange is minimal. This is possible where a minority group's members are segregated by job category, and they form their own corporate subculture. To a lesser degree, minority groups from various units may cluster together, voluntarily isolating themselves from the dominant group in order to maintain some cultural autonomy. This can lead to a fragmentation rather than consistency of subcultural groups, undermining the goals of all the groups that accept and implement the basic vision and mission of the organization.

Deculturation A lack of enculturation occurs when new employees are not significantly affected by either the organization culture or by their cultural group. The corporate culture is weak. New employees' own cultural identity is ill defined, perhaps because they have severed ties with their original socio-cultural group but haven't formed new ties with the dominant culture. Symptoms may be: very little bonding taking place, very weak loyalty and commitment, and high turnover and absenteeism.

Multiculturalism This is a two-way learning and adaptation process in which both the organization and new employees from various cultures change to some degree to reflect the cultural norms and values of each other. It focuses on mutual appreciation among cultures, the importance of maintaining sub-cultural identity, and interdependence among the corporate culture and the various subcultures. New employees assimilate a limited number of core behaviors and values, but they also maintain important differences.

Acculturation Factors

How well diverse employees are acculturated depends on many factors, especially the culture's tolerance for ambiguity, the degree to which cultural diversity is valued, the extent of conformity that's required, and how well the employees' cultural backgrounds and the corporate culture fit together.

Tolerance for ambiguity This refers to the organization's assumptions about whether ambiguities, uncertainties, and paradoxes are "legitimate and normal" (Meyerson 1992). Organizations with high tolerance exert less pressure on people to conform to rigid "corporate ways," and they are more tolerant or appreciative of diversity. They are more likely to favor multiculturalism as an acculturation mode. Conflict among different ethnic groups is more likely to be viewed as normal and potentially useful as a way to avoid groupthink, rather than as dysfunctional and threatening.

Degree to which cultural diversity is valued Organizations with a strong "valuing diversity" norm tend to welcome the cultural exchange and interaction that is at the core of the multiculturalism mode of acculturation.

Demand for Conformity Cultures vary by the extent and degree of conformity they demand of members. Table 2.8 compares some tendencies of typical managers in high conformity cultures with those in low conformity cultures.

TABLE 2.8: Comparison of Management Behaviors: High Conformity and Low Conformity Corporate Cultures

Managers in High Conformity Cultures:	*Managers in Low Conformity Cultures:*
• Have a narrow view of O.K. behavior. Evaluate, judge, and criticize others	• See many behaviors as O.K. unless they violate a few core values, such as integrity and quality
• Avoid taking risks	• Take calculated risks; encourage others to do so
• Are intolerant of mistakes	• View failure, within limits, as a learning opportunity and part of innovation
• Focus on mistakes	• Pay more attention when people exceed standards than when they don't
• Ignore many positive contributions	• Don't judge ideas until they clearly understand them
• Prescribe the details of how to do things	• React to ideas in ways other than judging them good or bad
• See one right way to do most things	• Encourage people to create new approaches that work

Adapted from Cox, 1993.

Cultural fit Cultural fit refers to the degree of alignment between two or more cultural patterns, and therefore the degree to which subcultures may comfortably exist within the organization culture. Obviously, fit is best where there is a great deal of cultural overlap between the corporate culture and an employee's root culture, where their beliefs, values, and norms are similar (De Anda 1984; Sadri 2001). Some authors have identified types of subcultures according to the their degree of fit with a corporate culture (Siehl 1984). A *reinforcing subculture* is compatible with and strongly reinforces the norms and values of the organization culture. A *refining subculture* shares many of the basic assumptions and values of the organization culture but also holds some that are unique. A *counterculture* embraces basic assumptions and norms that are primarily in conflict with the organization culture and therefore challenges its validity.

When cultural fit is poor, employees must pay the psychological costs of giving up some of their identity and of acting unnaturally. Their choices of how to act become more complex and ambiguous and they tend to experience stress.

Targeted acculturation. Companies can lower turnover rates of diverse employees by targeting acculturation procedures to group and individual needs. Without some special form of orientation, how can women and minorities become properly acculturated?

- Some companies use formal mentoring programs.
- Others try to manage job assignments to ensure a progression of sympathetic and supportive superiors.

- A third strategy is to assign them to a series of problem-solving task forces so they form a series of relationships with their peers that sustain them in their early years with the firm.

How can company leaders influence the culture to accommodate the needs of women and minorities? Some develop explicit guidelines for behavior in situations involving them, and a procedure for making everyone aware of these guidelines. Women and minorities can't become effective members of the culture if they're continually coping with embarrassing situations. Leaders must spell out standards for social behavior in relationships with these new members. They must focus on ritualistic cultural barriers to the acceptance of women and minorities and take specific action to remove these barriers. Leaders must become role models, setting an example of appropriate treatment of minorities and women.

Minority Networking Groups

Acculturation into the organization may be facilitated by minority networking groups. Research indicates that U.S. minority networking groups are flourishing in a growing number of companies (Borchardt 2007). Just a few of the many companies that encourage networking groups include 3M, AT&T, Honeywell, Levi-Strauss, Lockheed Martin, Microsoft, Shell, Siebert, Silicon Graphics, Texas Instruments, and Xerox.

Here is how a typical networking group gets started. A few people from the minority group start talking about the benefits of belonging to such a group. They approach management with the idea of initiating such a group. Management typically supports the idea and requires the group to develop a mission statement and initial goals. Management must approve this document. Normally they want to see that it is geared toward developing a strong, effective group that focuses on the issues important to members of that specific diverse group—and also welcomes supportive employees from any group to join them.

Following are some advantages that minority networking groups can provide.

How Networking Groups Can Help Employees

- Offer members a forum for connecting with others of similar backgrounds, interests, and cultures
- Give members a chance to talk about things that are common to them, to feel included, and to have a sense of belonging to something greater
- Help to remove barriers in order to build a sense of inclusion in the company
- Help create a safe, open work environment where people can contribute to members' full potential
- Offer opportunities for minority employees to grow professionally
- Organize speakers, seminars, and courses that help members to develop their potential
- Provide information to members on educational and development opportunities that are available in the community
- Organize community service projects that also develop leadership skills

How Networking Groups Can Help the Organization

- Help the firm attract new minority employees and customers
- Help in the recruitment, development, and retention of employees from their group
- Support the firm's diversity process
- Provide leadership in resolving diversity issues
- Advise and consult with management on practices and business protocol of other cultures
- Help the firm gain access to markets related to their cultural group, both in the United States and globally

How Management Can Support Networking Groups

- Provide meeting rooms
- Provide time to meet during working hours
- Give access to equipment, such as copy machines and company communications channels to announce meetings
- Arrange use of company videoconferencing facilities so members can communicate between different facilities
- Designate a senior manager to sponsor the group, one who serves as a champion in solving their diversity problems
- Give credit on performance evaluations for achievement within the group

We can see that how an organization integrates new employees into the corporate culture reflects the company's beliefs, values, goals, rituals, and therefore its openness to diversity

SUMMARY

The first step in building multicultural skills is becoming aware of culture and its pervasive influence. Culture is programmed beliefs, hidden programming, our mental map, our consensus reality, and our personal reality. People from different cultures therefore experience different realities. About 1,000 aspects of culture are hidden within our subconscious minds for every element we're consciously aware of Therefore, most aspects of a culture are never discussed by people in the culture.

The major parts of a culture bind its members into a unified group. Parts include the groups major beliefs and values, heroes and heroines that serve as role models who personify important values and norms (do's and don'ts). Myths are stories or sayings that serve to bind together the thoughts and values of a group and promote social action. Rituals and ceremonies indicate to everyone what the culture values and the way people are expected to do things. Networks are the ways people are connected, and grapevines are channels for getting the word around. Cultures use 11 primary message systems that communicate values, norms, rituals, and customs from one generation to the next. The message systems are embedded in the ways adults educate youngsters, direct them, and model appropriate behaviors for them.

Numerous commonalties are found across all cultures. Still, cultures can be quite diverse, and going from one to another can be like going into another world. Even within one culture, girls and boys are raised so differently it's as if they're living in parallel worlds—and gender is said to be one of the most basic differences.

Cultural differences can be categorized into 11 major areas.

1. I'm-controlled or I-Control reflects beliefs about whether I create my situation or it happens to me.
2. Us-first or me-first refers to a focus on the group or the individual.
3. Tight ties or loose ties looks at how tightly-knit the culture is.
4. Achievement-first or people-first refers to whether the culture values most highly getting things done or nurturing relationships.
5. Equality or inequality refers to the importance placed on rank and status.
6. Taking risks or playing it safe relates to needs for security and clarity.
7. Long-term or short-term orientation refers to a basis for decision-making.
8. View of time can range from dive-right-in to step-by-step.
9. How to use personal space may range from come-close to back-off.
10. Communication patterns include directness or indirectness and level of formality.
11. How we make money refers to whether we work in an agricultural, industrial, or post-industrial economy—which affects our degree of dependence, independence, and interdependence.

The Euro-American culture differs from most of the world's people on every one of these key cultural differences. Cultural information provides a background for understanding others. It would be a mistake to use it to form new stereotypes. Get to know individuals in the context of their cultural background.

Over 2 percent of all Americans identified themselves as bi-ethnic or multi-ethnic in 2000. Major issues that multi-ethnic people face are ethnic self-identity, classification, and whether to "pass" as one ethnicity or another. Many say they must establish their rights to resolve these issues in their own way.

Corporate cultures contain the same basic elements as larger cultures—beliefs, values, stories, heroes, symbols, rituals, networks. They can be strong or weak, depending on the leaders at the top. The type of corporate culture that works best in a multicultural workplace is a strong but flexible culture that insists on conformity to only a few core values but gives a great deal of freedom in how to achieve goals.

The networked corporation is evolving from the demands of a diverse, post-industrial, technological, global economy, especially those with a heavy emphasis on informational technology. Just as virtual reality is a computerized experience that seems real but takes place in cyberspace, a networked corporation may be more virtual than physical. These corporations are likely to meet diverse employees' needs.

In recent decades many corporate cultures were undermined by greed and self-interest at the top, resulting in fear and distrust at the bottom. This was a result of executives downsizing and merging workforces to cut costs, boost stock prices, and cash in their stock options—as well fraudulent legal and financial practices.

Newcomers into the corporation may be acculturated or assimilated. When they're not, separation or deculturation may occur. Multiculturalism is a two-way adaptation process that values diversity. How new employees are acculturated depends largely on the flexibility and openness of the corporate culture and its leaders' commitment to a multicultural workplace.

Acculturation may be facilitated by minority networking groups, which are flourishing in a growing number of companies. These groups can provide many benefits to employees as well as to management, and managers in turn can support such groups by providing needed resources.

Preparation for Self–Awareness Activity: What's Your Cultural Identity?

Instructions: Read the information here as preparation for Self-Awareness Activity 2.1.

Your cultural identity consists of the groups you identify with and the strength with which you identify with each group. When we take the time to think about it, we can easily name those aspects of our identity that are most important to us. Most people are quite aware of those aspects that make them different from the dominant majority and are considerably less aware of their other facets. For example, Euro-American women tend to focus on being a woman, expatriates focus on nationality, minority men focus on ethnicity, and nonwhite women focus somewhat equally on gender and ethnicity.

Euro-American males are more likely than any other group to focus on individual identification, according to Cox [1993], even when instructed to refer only to group identifications. As Hofstede [1980, 2001] showed, individuality is a strong cultural norm for Euro-American men. Also, because they are part of the dominant majority group, Euro-American men face the fewest workplace and socioeconomic barriers, and therefore tend to be less aware of group identities than are members of minority groups. [Alderfer 1982]. The ways in which we differ from one include gender, sexual orientation, physical ability, ethnic heritage, occupational or professional influences, educational and socioeconomic background, and religious, spiritual, or philosophical influences. You have a chance to develop your own cultural profile in Self-Awareness Activity 2.1.

The ethnic differences of immigrants tend to recede over time, and each generation born in this country is more Americanized than their parents. However, certain cultural values tend to remain strong. For example, even third-generation Japanese Americans have been found to have relatively high scores on ethnic identification with the Japanese culture, with survey scores virtually unchanged between second- and third-generation respondents. [Matsumoto, Meredith, and Masuda 1970].

Self-Awareness Activity 2.3: Your Cultural Profile

Purpose: To identify key aspects of your cultural heritage and identity.

Step 1. If you have not read the preceding section on Preparation for Self-Awareness Activity, do so now.

Step 2. Complete the second column of table below by completing the statements made in the first column.

Step 3. Complete the third column of the table by determining the importance of each specific category for you. [For example, is being a college graduate a major or minor part of your identity?] Place a number, from 1 to 5, beside each category you've listed, according to its importance, using the following guidelines to assign weights:

     5 = Major, essential aspect of my identity
     4 = Very important aspect of my identity
     3 = Fairly important aspect of my identity
     2 = Somewhat influential aspect of my identity
     1 = Slightly influential aspect of my identity

Step 4. Write a brief paragraph about your cultural profile. Include any thoughts, feelings, surprises, or insights that came to you as you did this Self-Awareness Activity.

Self-Awareness Activity 2.4 Diverse Groups You Need to Learn About

Purpose: To identify those groups of people you need to learn more about, ranging from those you know almost nothing about to those you need no information about.

Aspects of My Identity

Area of Identity or Influence	Specify Categories	Weight 1 to 5
My **gender** is:		
My **sexual orientation** is (heterosexual, homosexual, bisexual):		
My **ethnic group** is (ancestors' country of origin):		
The **nation** where I was born is:		
The **part of the country** I grew up in is:		
The **occupation** I'm in or want is:		
The **company** I work for is:		
My **religion** or philosophy is:		
My **socioeconomic** class is (middle, lower, upper class):		
My **educational** level is:		
My **parents' educational** level is:		
Other groups or aspects that have influenced my identity are:		

Step 1. In the first column of the table below are listed types of groups discussed in this book. In the second column, you may want to set up two categories, men and women, and assign them different weights.

Step 2. The third column of the table refers to the degree to which you lack information on each group listed in the first column. Place a number, from 1 to 5, beside each group you've listed, indicating how much you know about this group, using the following guidelines to assign weights:

5 = I know nothing about this group

4 = I know almost nothing about this group

3 = I know very little about this group

2 = I have a fair amount of information and understanding of this group

1 = I have a great deal of information and understanding about this group and need little or no additional information

Groups I Need to Learn About

Type of Group	More Specific Identity?	Weight: 1 to 5
Arab Americans		
African American		
American Indian		
Asian American (or subgroup)		
Euro-American		
Latino American (or subgroup)		
Persons with Disabilities		
Gay/Lesbian/Bisexual		
Obese persons		
Older persons		
Persons from other religions		
Persons whose mother and father are from different ethnic groups		
Women's issues		
Men's issues		
Other groups:		

Self-Awareness Activity 2.5: Identifying Some Perceptions

Purpose: To learn more about your way of thinking.

Step 1. Relax and focus on the words listed below, one at a time. Notice what mental picture, what words, and what feelings you experience when you focus on the words. Jot down the word and note your reactions and associations with it. Do this for all the words

> *Stranger, Foreigner, Immigrant, Native, People, Family, Home, Work, Nature*

Step 2. Now go back and review your list. For each word, note any judgment, attitude, or belief that came to mind when you first saw the word or that comes to mind now. Do this for all the words.

Step 3. Go back again and review your judgments, attitudes or beliefs. Where do you think each of these originally came from?

Step 4. Write down any thoughts, feelings, and insights that occur to you now that you've completed working with the list of words. What, if anything, did you learn about yourself?

Self-Awareness Activity 2.6: Your Sense of Time

Purpose: To increase your awareness about how you and others view and use time.

Instructions: Describe briefly at least one instance when you and someone from a different cultural background experienced conflict, misunderstanding, or problems about time. Use the following list to help you remember your situation:

• Being on time	• Feeling impatient over others' slowness
• Meeting deadlines	• Focusing on past events, tradition
• Feeling hurried, rushed	• Living for the moment, short-range view
• Using time efficiently	• Focusing on the present moment
• Using time effectively	• Focusing on the future, what might happen
• Being "out of sync"	• Focusing on planning, or long-range view
	• Other issues about time

Self-Awareness Activity 2.7: Your Boundaries

Purpose: To increase your awareness about how you and others view and use personal space.
Instructions: Describe briefly at least one instance when you (or others) experienced conflict, misunderstanding, or problems about personal space, touching, or boundaries. Use the following list to help you remember your situation.

- Invasion of privacy - yours or others
- Discomfort because of lack of privacy
- Invasion of personal body space
- Someone in your face
- Feeling crowded or claustrophobic
- Too much touching
- Invasive touching
- Too much coldness and distance
- Other issues about space, boundaries, or touching

Self-Awareness Activity 2.8: Your Values

Purpose: To learn more about yourself and what you want in life.
Instructions: Before you begin, remember that the purpose of this Self-Awareness Activity is for you to learn more about you. Don't evaluate, judge, or analyze what comes up; just let what wants to come up do so.
Step 1. Brainstorm. Relax, close your eyes for a few moments and think about these questions: What are the aspects of my life that I treasure the most? That I wouldn't want to lose? That I would fight to keep?
What are those aspects of life that I don't yet have and want most to have? That I would work hard to have?
What are my values?
Step 2. Write. Don't try to evaluate or analyze the thoughts that occurred to you. Just write them down in whatever sequence you remember them. As more ideas come up, write them down.
Step 3. Categorize. Look over what you've written. Do the items fall into any patterns or categories, such as:

family	money	intelligence
friends	power	emotions
work	beauty	spirituality
leisure	truth	

You'll find your own categories, not necessarily these. Work with your list till you see some logical categories; then rewrite your list of values by category.
Step 4. Personalize terms. What would you call the items on your list if you didn't call them values? (desires? goals? beliefs? issues? other?)

Self-Awareness Activity 2.9: Cultures You've Known

Purpose: To recognize the hidden aspects of your own and other cultural group.

Instructions: Perhaps reviewing some obvious rites, rituals, heroes, and symbols of the cultures you've belonged to will help you recognize more subtle rites, rituals, etc., in the cultures you encounter. Remember, rites and rituals relate to the need for belonging. A *rite* is any formal practice, custom, or procedure. A *ritual* is any detailed method of procedure that is regularly followed. Be aware that in every organization, the stronger the rules, rituals, symbols, and heroes, the stronger the effect and influence the organization has on its members' lives.

For each category that is relevant to your own life, such as your nation, school, religious community, family, workplace, identify examples of cultural practices, as exemplified in the National Symbols category below.

Step 1: National Symbols

Rites and Rituals: (What rites and rituals gave you a feeling of national unity—an overall community with common purpose? For example, the national anthem.)

Heroes: (What heroes personified key national values?)

Symbols: (What symbols served to unify, to express values? For example, the flag.)

Values: (What values are expressed by the above?)

Step 2: Your life. Pick at least one other area of your life—such as your workplace, school, family, religious community, or social organization—and give examples of important rites, rituals, heroes, symbols, and values.

Case Study 2.1: Problems at Cracker Barrel

Cast of characters:

Hendrick – African American Associate Manager

Joe – Hendrick's former manager

Steve – Hendrick's new manager

Aretha – African American employee

Ken – Aretha's supervisor

Bill – General Manager, who oversees both Steve and Ken

Hendrick Humphries was an African American associate manager at a Cracker Barrel restaurant in Illinois from 1999 to 2001. His performance during his first two-and-a-half years with the company was "generally excellent," according to company records. Hendrick's manager **Joe** often said that Hendrick was "his best associate manager." Hendrick received several bonuses and raises during this period. Then Joe was transferred, and Hendrick got a new **manager, Steve,** who took over as a temporary replacement. That's when Hendrick's problems began.

Steve routinely made racially derogatory remarks, such as stating that all African Americans are "drunk or high on drugs" or that "all Mexicans have a bunch of kids." Euro-American coworkers told Hendrick that **Steve** had stated that he was there "for the white people" and "was going to take care of the white people." During **Steve's** first month on the job, he issued five disciplinary reports on **Hendrick,** alleging a range of misconduct, all of which Hendrick says were groundless and a product of Steve's prejudiced mindset. Hendrick was naturally upset over this and complained about it to **Bill,** the general manager who oversees Steve. But Bill never did a thorough investigation into Hendrick's complaints.

Hendrick's friend **Aretha** worked an earlier shift and reported to **manager Ken.** Aretha complained to Hendrick that Ken was treating her as badly as Steve was treating Hendrick. Shortly thereafter, Ken fired Aretha.

Hendrick again went to **general manager Bill,** saying "I think Ken fired Aretha strictly because she is African American." You know, I am having the same problem with Steve. Do you remember that I reported to you the kinds of things he's been saying and doing?" **Bill** scolded Hendrick for "going outside the management group" and demanded he schedule a meeting with Ken to discuss the Aretha issue. The day before the meeting, Steve confronted Hendrick: "You failed to lock the safe last night. You're fired." Hendrick says he knows he locked the safe.

1. What are the major issues in this case?
2. What do you think of the various managers' behavior?
3. What should Hendrick do next?

REFERENCES

Alderfer, C.P. "Problems of Changing White Male's Behavior and Beliefs Concerning Race Relations," in *Change in Organizations*. Jossey-Bass, 1982.

Asante, M.K. and K. Asante, eds. *African Culture*. Greenwood Press, 1985.

Belenky, M.F., B.M. Clinchy, N.R. Golderberger, and J.M. Tarule. *Women's Ways of Knowing*. Basic Books, 1986.

Borchardt, John F. "Common Ground: Both employer and employees win when minority networking groups succeed." *Graduating Engineer*. www.graduatingengineer.com, September 2007.

Brislin, Richard & Tomoko Yoshida. *Improving Intercultural Interactions*. Sage, 1994.

Carmichael, Evan, "Examples Of Strong Corporate Culture," www.evancarmichael.com 2009.

Census 2000, "The Two or More Races Population: 2000, November 2001.

Cohan, Allen, Watkinson, Boone, "Herb Kelleher Talks about How Southwest Airlines Grew from Entrepreneurial Startup to Industry Leadership," *BabsonInsight.com*, February 2005.

Cote, J.A. and P.S. Tansuhaj, "Culture Bound Assumptions in Behavior Intention Models," *Advances in Consumer Research*, 16, 105–109, 1989.

Cox, T.H. and J. Finley-Nickerson, "Models of Acculturation for Intraorganizational Cultural Diversity," *Canadian Journal of Administrative Sciences* 8, 2, 90–100, 1991.

Cox, T.H., S. Lobel and P. McLeod, "Effects of Ethnic Group Cultural Diufference on Cooperative Versus Competitive Behavior in a Group Task," *Academy of Management Journal* 34, 827–847, 1991.

Cox, Taylor. *Cultural Diversity in Organizations*. Berrett-Koehler, 1993.

Dariotis, Wei Mind. "Hapa: The Word of Power," *Mavin*, www.MixedHeritageCenter.org, 2008

Davidow, W.H. and M.S. Malone. *The Virtual Corporation*. HarperCollins Publishers, 1992.

Deal, T.E. and A.A. Kennedy. The New Corporate Cultures: Revitalizing the Workplace after Downsizing, Mergers & Reengineering. Perseus Books, 1999.

Delgado, M. "Hispanic Cultural Values: Implications for Groups," *Small Group Behavior*, 12, 1, 69–80, 1981.

DeVos, G.A., "Ethnic Adaptation and Minority Status," *Journal of Cross-Cultural Psychology* 11, 1, 101–124, 1980.

Eagly, A.H. and B.T. Johnson, "Gender and Leadership Style," *Psychological Bulletin* 108, 2, 233–256, 1990.

Fottler, M.D. and T. Bain, "Sex Differences in Occupational Aspirations," *Academy of Management Journal* 23, 144–149, 1980.

Fulbeck, Kip, *Part Asian, 100% Hapa*. Chronicle Books, 2006.

Funderburg, Lise, "Black, White, Other: Biracial Americans Talk About Race," *Interracial Voice*, www.webcom.com, 1998.

Graham, R. J. "The Role of Perception of Time in Consumer Behavior," *Journal of Consumer Research*, 7, 335–342, 1981.

Hall, E.T. *The Dance of Life*.: Doubleday, 1983.

Hall, E.T. *The Hidden Dimension*. Doubleday, 1982.

Hall, E.T. *The Silent Language*. Doubleday, 1981b

Hall, E.T. and M.R. Hall. *Understanding Culture Differences*. Intercultural Press, 1989.

Hall. E.T. *Beyond Culture*. Doubleday, 1981a.

Hawkins, Jeff. *On Intelligence*. Henry Holt & Co., 2004.

Helms, J.E. and T.W. Giorgis, "A Comparison of the Locus of Control and Anxiety Level of African, Black American and White American College Students," *Journal of College Student Personnel* 21, 6, 503–509, 1980.

Hofstede, Geert, "The Cultural Relativity of the Quality of Life Concept," *Academy of Management Review*, 9, 3, 389–398, 1984.

Hofstede, Geert, Culture's Consequences: International Differences in Work-Related Values. Sage, 1980.

Hofstede, Geert. Culture's Consequences: Comparing Values, Behaviors, Institutions, and Organizations across Nations, 2d ed. Sage, 2001.

Hofstede, Geert. *Cultures and Organization*. McGraw, 1991.

Hui, C. "Work Attitudes, Leadership Styles, and Managerial Behaviors in Different Cultures" in *Applied Cross-Cultural Psychology*. Sage, 1990.

Jarvis, Jeff. *What Would Google Do?* Collins Business, 2009.

Kagan, K. and M.D. Madsen, "Cooperation and Competition of Mexican, Mexican American, and Anglo-American Children of Two Ages Under Four Instructional Sets," *Developmental Psychology* 5, 1, 32–39 1971.

Kagitcibasi, C. "Family and Home-Based Intervention," in *Applied Cross-Cultural Psychology*. Sage, 1990.

Kim, U., H.C. Triandis, C. Kagitcibasi, S. Choi, and G. Yoon (eds.) *Individualsm and Collectivism*. Sage, 1994.

Leaptrott, Nan. *Rules of the Game*. South-Western, 1996.

Leavitt, T., "The Globalization of Markets," *Harvard Business Review* 83, 3, 91–102, 1983.

Matsumoto, G., G. Meridith and M. Masuda, "Ethnic Identification: Honolulu and Seattle Japanese Americans," *Journal of Cross-Cultural Psychology* 1, 1, 63–76, 1970.

Mavin, foundation, magazine, blog. www.multiracial.com June 2005.

McGrath, J.E. and N.L. Rotchford, "Time and Behavior in Organizations," *Research in Organizational Behavior* 5, 57–101, 1983.

Meyerson, D. and D.S. Lewis, "Cultural Tolerance of Ambiguity," Working paper, University of Michigan, *Behavior 5*, 1983, 57–101.

Morrison, Terri et al. *Kiss, Bow, or Shake Hands*. Bob Adams Inc, 1994.

Nierenberg, John. "Cross-cultural Management Literature May Be Hazardous" *San Francisco State University School of Business Journal*, 47-55, summer 1993.

Nisbett, Richard. *Intelligence and How to Get It: Why Schools and Cultures Count*. WW. Norton & Co., 2009.

Nisbett, Richard. *The Geography of Thought: How Asians and Westerners Think Differently . . . and Why*. Free Press, 2004.

O'Hearn, Claudine C. *Half and Half: Writers on Growing Up Biracial and Bicultural*. Pantheon, 1998.

Orpen, C. and J. Nkohande, "Self-Esteem: Internal Control and Expectancy Beliefs of White and Black Managers in South Africa," *Journal of Management Studies*, 192–199, May 1977.

Peng, Kaiping in *Handbook of Cross-Cultural Psychology*, David Matsumoto, ed. Oxford University Press, 2000.

Peng, Kaiping, as quoted by Timothy Beneke, "The Culture Club" *Express*, 23, 16, 1–14, February 2, 2001.

Peters, Tom. *Liberation Management*. Knopf, 1992.

Ramirez, A. "Racism Toward Hispanics" in *Eliminating Racism*, ed. Phyllis A. Katz and Dalmas A. Taylor. Plenum Press, 1988.

Redding, S.G. "Cultural Effects on the Marketing Process in Southeast Asia, *Journal of Market Research Society*, 24, 19, 98–114, 1982.

Roddick, Anita. *Business as Unusual: My Entrepreneurial Journey, Profits with Principles*. Anita Roddick Books, 2005.

Root, Maria P.P., Bill of Rights for Racially Mixed People," *Interracial Voice*, www.webcom.com, 2001.

Rosener, J.B. "Ways Women Lead," *Harvard Business Review*, 119–125, November-December 1990.

Rotter, J.B. "Generalized Expectancies for Internal Versus External Control of Reinforcement," *Psychological Monographs*, 80, 1-28, 1966.

Sadri, G., Lees, B. "Developing corporate culture as a competitive advantage," *Journal of Management Development* 20, 10, 853, 2001.

Scarso, Enrico and Ettore Bolisani, "Communities of Practice as Structures for Managing Knowledge in Networked Corporations," Journal of Manufacturing Technology Management 19, 3, 374–390, 2008.

Smith, G. "An evaluation of the Corporate Culture of Southwest Airlines," *Measuring Business Excellence* 8, 4, 26-33, 2004.

Spector, P.E., "Behavior in Organizations as a Function of Employee's Locus of Control," *Psychological Bulletin*, 91, 482–497, 1982.

Steiner, Andy, "Birth of a Mavin," *Utne Reader*, 77-78, September 1999.

Strategic Direction, "How corporate culture helped Southwest Airlines become the best: Employees are the No. 1 customer," 21, 4, 16–18, 2005.

Tannen, Deborah. *You Just Don't Understand*. Wm. Morrow, 1990.

Thomas, Roosevelt. *Beyond Race & Gender*. New York: AMACOM, 1992.

Trilling, Lionel. *The Opposing Self*. Viking Press, 1995.

Tse, D.K., K. Lee, I. Vertinsky & D.A. Wehrung. "Does Culture Matter?" *Journal of Marketing*, 52, 81–95, 1988.

Wheatley, Margaret J. *Leadership and the New Science*. Berrett-Koehler Publishing, 1992.

World 1993, State of the. Worldwatch Institute.

RESOURCES

Association of Multi-ethnic Americans, Inc. www.ameaSite.org

Mavin, Mixed Heritage Center, www.MixedHeritageCenter.org,

National Association for the Multiethnic www.nameCentral.org

National Multi-Ethnic Families Association (NaMEFA), 2073 N.Oxnard Blvd, Suite172, Oxnard CA 93030

Feedback on Self-Awareness Activity 2.2: What's Your Cultural Orientation?

1.   a.   Internal source of control, individualism, independent
        b.   External source of control, collectivism, dependent

2.   a.   Me-first, individualism
        b.   Us-first, collectivism

3.   a.   Achievement first, competitive, individualism
        b.   Relationships first, cooperative, collectivism

4.   a.   Achievements and tasks first, linear time orientation
        b.   Relationships first, circular time orientation

5. a.   Focus on equality, democratic orientation, direct communication

    b.   Focus on class differences: status, rank, deference to authority, indirect communication

6. a.   Risk-taking orientation, focus on future change, independence, individualism

    b.   Security-seeking orientation, focus on tradition, hierarchy and the status quo, dependence, collectivism

7. a.   Equality, risk-taking orientation

    b.   Security-seeking, avoid-uncertainty orientation

8. a.   Risk-taking, equality

    b.   Security-seeking, deference to authority

9. a.   Long-term orientation

    b.   Short-term orientation

Table 2.9: The Economic System's Effect on Cultural Values

Values Related to Achievement Vs Relationship:

Agricultural-Era Values—Dependent	*Industrial-Era Values—Independent*	*Post-Industrial-Era Values—Interdependent*
Cooperative - win/win	Competitive (win-lose)	Cooperative (win-win)
Worker as member of a family	Worker as automaton	Worker as dynamic colleague
Static role-based relationships (place-bound)	Mechanistic organizations	Organic organizations
Community	Compartmentalization	Integration
Life is a chore/people must earn redemption	Theory X—people are lazy, must be coerced, directed	Theory Y—people can be self-motivated
Survival focus	Profit centered	Value centered
Traditions/ceremonies	Acquiring material goods for family/self	Experiencing events, life
Work relationships—focus on role	Work relationships—focus on secrecy/need to know	Work relationships—focus on openness
People necessary for family survival	People as means to organizational ends	People as ends in themselves
Feelings channeled through ceremonies	Feeling denied/relationships impersonal	Feelings expressed, relationships personal
Right brain emphasis (intuitive, feeling, holistic)	Left brain emphasis (rational, linear, factual)	Intuitive/rational balance
Role modeling (toward an ideal)	Macho modeling (winning)	Androgyny, masculine/feminine balance
Power over nature	Power over others	Empowerment of self and others
Dominance	Manipulation	Collaboration
Personal/community development	Management development	Organization development
People as necessary components	People as expendable resources, liabilities	People as renewable resource/asset
The spiritual aspects of life most highly valued	Material things most highly valued	Ideas most highly valued
Focus on traditions, values, family	Focus on bottom line	Focus on process/goal/person

Values Related to Me-First or Us-First and to I-Control or I'm-Controlled

Agricultural Economy—Dependent	*Industrial Economy—Independent*	*Post-Industrial Economy—Interdependent*
Family/community focus	Bureaucracy/hierarchy	Flexible teams/networks
Family/clan centered	Organization centered	Organization as part of society
Family/clan centered	Class centered	Lifestyle centered
Extrinsic motivation (expectations)	Extrinsic motivation (incentives)	Intrinsic motivation
Integrated community role	Dependency at work	Autonomy at work
Social norms—universal	Social norms—universal	Social norms—pluralistic

Family/community hold the power	Shareholders/managers hold the power	Stakeholders share the power
Work as a function of life	Work as drudgery	Work as fun
Performance judged by elders, neighbors	Performance judged by boss as control factor	Performance judged by self, others, for growth
Submersion of self in groups	Interpersonal game playing	
Product standard—adequacy	Product standard—planned obsolescence	
Work—rhythmic	Work—routine, often monotonous	Authenticity
Diffuse localization of power and activity	Centralization of power and activity	Product standard—conservation
Diverse chores	Job specialization	Work—creative
Community oriented	Isolated, alienated	Decentralization of power and activity
Risk averse	Risk averse	Job enrichment
Obedience to parent/elder	Obedience to boss	Committed
Workers—role/family centered	Workers—job centered	Entrepreneurial
		Respected associate
		Workers—profession centered

Values Related to Time and Space Orientations

Agricultural-Era Values—Dependent	Industrial Economy—Independent	Post-Industrial Economy—Interdependent
Viewpoint tied to seasonal/life cycle	Viewpoint short-term, narrow, fragmented	Focus on the long term, the holistic
Permanence—social life static	Permanence—social life slow evolving	Transience—instant intimacy
Provincialism	Provincialism	Cosmopolitanism

CHAPTER 3

Understanding The Dominant Culture: Euro–Americans

Many Americans have a great take-charge, can-do attitude,
but it can seem pushy and arrogant in other cultures.
Phillip R. Harris

The American culture was founded by Euro-American men, and their values and customs are still the most dominant. Though it contains many elements of Western culture, meaning European, it has a unique flavor of its own. The pioneering, independent spirit of the founding fathers is an important element, as is the belief in the basic equality of people and their right to be free to pursue the American Dream.

The term "American" as used in this chapter refers to those qualities of the U.S. culture generally agreed upon by such scholars as Gary Althen, R.T. Kohls, P.R. Harris, R.T. Moran, and D.J. Boorstin, who look at American values and customs as compared to those of other national cultures. The cross-cultural research of Geert Hofstede further confirms their work. While American culture is based on the values and customs of the dominant group, Euro-Americans, it also includes some aspects of its subcultures, such as American Indian, African American, Latino American, Asian American, and Arab American. Although culture changes slowly, the American culture *is* changing to reflect more elements of its subcultures as they become greater in number and larger in size and influence.

Euro-Americans are traditionally referred to as "white people." In recent years, "whiteness studies" has emerged at some universities. People in this discipline try to trace the economic and political history behind the invention of "whiteness." They typically challenge the privileges given to so-called "whites" and analyze the cultural practices (in art, music, literature, and popular media) that create and perpetuate the fiction of "whiteness" (Jay 2005).

An important part of gaining diversity skills is understanding your own cultural programming. Assuming that at least part of your cultural background is Euro-American, you need to address the question, How is being an American different from being some other nationality? The better you understand your own culture, the better you can understand people from other cultures. To function well in a diverse workplace and a global marketplace, you need to attain a worldwide perspective. It's similar to climbing the highest mountain you can find, looking around at other cultures, and then looking at the American culture.

In this chapter you may address the second step of the five-step process for becoming a diversity-savvy person:

> *Step 2. Learning about your own culture*

Specifically, you'll learn in this chapter:

- How Euro-Americans view the world and how that differs from other cultures
- What Euro-Americans value the most and how that differs from others
- How Euro-Americans relate to others and how that differs

First, complete Self-Awareness Activities 3.1 and 3.2.

Self-Awareness Activity 3.1: What Do You Believe about Euro-Americans?

Purpose:

- to get in touch with your beliefs and stereotypes about this group of people
- to experience how judgmental beliefs affect your thinking and feeling processes
- to experience the ways in which your beliefs create your reality regarding other persons, even before you have any interaction with them.

Part I. What Do You Believe about Euro–American Women?
Step 1. Associations

- *Relax as deeply as you can.*
- *Close your eyes for a moment and take a few deep breaths.*

Euro-American Man

Courtesy of Digital Vision.

Euro-American Woman

Courtesy of Ken Kaminesky/Corbis Images.

- Now focus on the picture that symbolizes "Euro-American woman"
- Imagine that you are this woman. Be Euro-American woman.
- Notice any resistance to being this person—and any willingness.
- Notice words, images, thoughts, and feelings that come to mind as you are "seeing and being this woman."

Step 2. Negative Associations

- Next, as you focus on the picture, allow negative opinions to come up, perhaps some that you typically hold about Euro-American women.
- Notice your *thoughts* as you see the person in this negative way. What *feelings?*

Step 3. Positive Associations

- Now, still focusing, allow positive opinions to come up, perhaps some that you typically hold about Euro-American women.
- Notice your *thoughts* as you see the person in this negative way. What *feelings?*

Step 4. Insights and Write-up

- Now review this experience and write about it.
- When you first saw the picture, what thoughts and feelings came up? These may reflect your deepest responses to people from this group.
- Think about the differences in your thoughts and feelings when you consciously held a positive opinion versus a negative opinion.
- Write a few sentences about your feelings, thoughts, and insights

Part II. What Do You Believe about Euro–American Men?

Repeat the phases and steps in part I, this time focusing on the image of a Euro-American man.

Self-Awareness Activity 3.2: What Do You Know about the Euro-American Culture?

Purpose: To see what you know about the issues covered in this chapter.
Instructions: Determine whether you think the following statements are basically true or false—and think about why. The answers will emerge in this chapter, and the summary at the end of the chapter focuses on these issues.

1. Euro-Americans are generally fortunate in that they rarely are the brunt of ethnic slurs or hate crimes.
2. Euro-Americans tend to be very aware of their particular ethnicity and how it differs from others.
3. Nearly 90 percent of Americans are Euro-American.
4. A dominant Euro-American value is putting membership in an ingroup ahead of self-interest.
5. Most Euro-Americans tend to see situations in black-or-white terms.
6. Euro-Americans value just "being" even more than doing.
7. The dominant Euro-American view of humans and nature is that we must live in harmony with nature.
8. Euro-Americans in general tend to develop a few deeply committed friendships rather than many friends.

STEREOTYPES AND REALITIES

Since Euro-Americans are the dominant group in the United States, we normally don't think in terms of myths and stereotypes about Euro-Americans. However, all groups hold stereotypes about other groups, and there are a few that Euro-Americans may deal with when they interact with people from the subcultures within American society. The Euro-American culture, especially the public aspects of it that we experience in the workplace, the marketplace, and the political arena, reflects typical Euro-American male orientations rather than female. The strongest stereotypes about Euro-Americans therefore refer more to the men than the women.

Stereotype #1: Whites are homogeneous; they're not ethnic.

The 2000 census showed that Euro-Americans claimed descent from at least twenty-seven countries. It is true that the Melting Pot has worked for Euro-Americans. As waves of immigrants from a particular European country arrived, they had to face stereotypes, prejudice, and discrimination. However, they found it relatively easy to adapt and become accepted. Some say they gave up their ethnicity. Still, the large majority of Euro-Americans today don't need to think much about their ethnicity simply because they are accepted as part of the dominant group that holds most of the power.

Stereotype #2: Whites are more racist than other groups.

Accusations of racism are often tied to the existence of slavery in the South during the early American years. But if we're going to compare groups, we must acknowledge that slavery was common in the world until the 19th century. Europeans also served as slaves in times past. For example, between 750 and 1900 millions of Europeans were enslaved by Arab, Berber, and Turkish Muslims and by Mongolian invaders. They were sold at slave markets throughout North Africa and Asia (Bartlett 1993).

From about 1600 to 1800 the Atlantic Slave Trade resulted in about 10 million Africans being enslaved and brought to the Americas. However, only about 5 percent were brought to North America. About 40 percent went to various Caribbean Islands, 38 percent to Brazil, a Portuguese colony, and the other 17 percent to various Spanish colonies in Latin America (Encarta Newspaper 2001). Virtually all world governments now denounce slavery as a gross violation of basic human rights, but it was certainly not always so.

Prejudice among Euro-Americans covers the entire spectrum from accepting individuals on their merits to intense bigotry. This range applies to people from all major cultures. Studies indicate that since enactment of various Civil Rights laws in the 1960s, Euro-Americans have gradually become better educated about diversity and therefore deal more with realities than stereotypes these days. Most Euro-Americans have come a long way, and some still have a long way to go. Statistics do indicate that Euro-Americans are less likely to commit hate crimes than some of the other American groups. All national, statewide, county, and city statistics about the commission of hate crimes (as opposed to prosecution of hate crimes and publicity about hate crimes) conclusively demonstrate that Euro-Americans perpetrate a smaller share of hate crimes than their share of the population.

Stereotype #3: Whites are rarely victims of ethnic slurs or hate crimes.

In fact, about 30% of all hate crime victims are Euro-Americans. Since they make up 71 percent of the population, they obviously have an advantage here. Still, attacks on Euro-Americans are far from rare.

Probably the slurs that seem most unfair to Euro-Americans who know about them are some Asians' reference to "white devils" and some Muslims' reference to "infidels," meaning anyone who is not a loyal Muslim. Being called "cracker, whitey, or white bread" by African Americans seems relatively harmless but the effect tends to be alienating. Even more alienating is African American mistrust of Euro-Americans. While knowledgeable Euro-Americans understand the mistrust, given our mutual history, it does hold in place old barriers to forming mutually beneficial relationships. A typical comment: "I wish they could learn to see me without bias, as a unique individual, just as I've learned to see them."

I asked university students in my diversity classes to give their immediate responses to seeing pictures symbolizing Euro-American men and women. An analysis and summary of their responses yielded these results:

- Euro-American men were described as *aggressive, competitive, confident, cocky, egocentric, privileged, independent, dominant, controlling, rigid. high achievers, workaholics, educated, and savvy in business.*

- Euro-American women received variations of these same descriptors, as well as *snobby, sophisticated, rich, insecure, moody, boring, and stuffy.*

Stereotype #4: Whites are privileged, so things come easy to them.

Euro-Americans' socioeconomic status ranges from very poor to very wealthy. Among all the people in the United States who live below the poverty line, over half are Euro-Americans. It's true that prior to the 1960s nearly all the better-paying, higher-status positions in business and government were held by Euro-American men, but that picture is changing. This group still dominates at the highest levels of business and government, but other groups are making progress.

To understand Euro-American men, you must realize that most of them don't perceive that just being who they are gives them major advantages. They don't typically think of themselves as being automatically more privileged and powerful than others. Most say they experience high expectations from parents, teachers, and others. They experience a great deal of competition from their male peers. And life often seems to be a tough struggle to either survive or to meet high standards of achievement.

WHO ARE THE EURO-AMERICANS?

Euro-Americans, as the dominant group that founded the United States and is still 70 percent of the population, set the comparative standard for all other groups. In other words, activists representing diverse groups compare their status with the average status of Euro-Americans—whether it's educational achievement, socioeconomic status, percentage holding prestigious positions, or other measures of achievement and affluence.

Where Are They Most Dominant?

Looking at the total U.S. population, Euro-Americans comprise 71 percent. However, they are 98 percent in three New England states. And they're over 90 percent in 14 states: in five of the Midwestern states, in two states that border the South, and in four lightly-populated Western states. They are least dominant in the West Coast states.

New England. Euro-Americans are the most dominant in three New England states, where they are about 98 percent of the population: Vermont, Maine, and New Hampshire

Midwest. Euro-Americans make up 84 percent of people in the Midwest. Their proportion is even greater, over 90 percent, in five states: Iowa, North Dakota, Nebraska, Minnesota, Wisconsin

The South: In five southern states Euro-Americans make up less than 70 percent of the population in the former slave states of Mississippi (61%), Louisiana, Maryland, Georgia, and South Carolina. These states still have relative large African American populations.

On the other hand, only two southern border states have over 90 percent Euro-Americans: West Virginia and Kentucky.

The West. Euro-Americans tend to be least dominant in the West, where they are 68 percent of the population, thanks primarily to California (63%), the most diverse state in the nation. Euro-Americans make up less than 70 percent of the population in New Mexico, which has a relatively large Mexican American population, and Hawaii (31%) with a large native and Asian American population. In contrast, they are over 90 percent in four lightly-populated states: Wyoming, Idaho, Montana, and Utah.

How Educated Are They?

Educational attainment for adults over age 25 in 2000, was as follows:

- 88% had completed high school
- 90% of those who were employed had a high school diploma
- 28% had a bachelor's degree or more
- Educational levels for men and women were almost the same

What's Their Income?

Annual average earnings in 1999 for Euro-American adults 18 and over

- $30,600 for the average man
- $15,900 for the average woman
- 24,572 for all who had completed high school
- $45,678 for all with a bachelor's degree
- Family income average: $44,400

Some Facts about Americans

Because Euro-Americans are the predominant American group, we could say that facts about Americans in general apply also to Euro-Americans. Americans have built the most productive and creative economy in the history of the world. By the 1740s, the Colonies had the highest per capita income in the world. Let's look at some facts comparing the United States with the other 25 wealthy industrialized nations. (Schmitt 2004). For better or worse, we have the

- most religious people—at least twice as many say it's very important in their lives
- greatest gross domestic product at $35,000 per capita
- more autos per household—18% have 3
- largest homes—2330 square-foot average in 2004
- least days of paid vacation—averaging only 10 days a year
- highest divorce rate—6 percent a year in 2000
- greatest credit card debt and lowest savings rate
- most garbage—paying more for garbage bags than the average person in 90 undeveloped nations pay for everything
- greatest military budget—more than all other nations combined

THE EURO-AMERICAN CULTURE: HOW IS IT DIFFERENT?

When we compare Euro-American culture with other major world cultures, using the 11 major types of cultural difference, we see that the Euro-American culture is generally perceived as follows:

- Basic worldview: I control
- Relationship priorities: me-first
- Social fabric: loose ties
- Masculinity: moderately masculine (achievement-first, focus on material things, competitive)
- Equality/Status: democratic
- Risk Orientation: take risks

- Decision Orientation: short term
- Time Orientation: step-by-step time
- Space: moderate, arm's length
- Communication: direct
- Economic: post-industrial, interdependent worldview

Remember, virtually all cultures are assessed primarily by the traits of the men in each culture since men prevail in the workplace, marketplace, and political arena.

Our discussion of Euro-American culture will be more manageable if we focus on three categories, rather than 11. Let's look at 1) the way Euro-Americans view the world, 2) the personal values they hold most important, and 3) the way they handle personal relationships. A summary of these values and customs is shown in Table 3.1. Many other cultures hold some, or even all, of these beliefs. What makes each culture unique is the focus and emphasis they place on them and how they express them in their daily lives.

TABLE 3.1: The American Culture

World View	Personal Values	Relationships
I Control	Individualism, me-first	Friendliness
Conquering nature	Achievement	Generosity
Progress, change	Self-reliance	Many casual friends
Rationalism	Assertiveness	Arm's-length closeness
Scientific method	Work hard—play hard	Competition
Facts, practicality	Material success	Cooperative achievement
Measuring things	Freedom	Fair play
Quantifying things	Equality	Specialized roles
Either-Or thinking	Self-improvement	Directness
Future Oriented	Do it now; stay busy	Informality
Interdependent	Staying young	

WHAT'S THE TRADITIONAL EURO-AMERICAN WORLDVIEW?

Euro-Americans think of themselves as individuals first, the world as basically inanimate, nature as something to be conquered, material success as the major goal, and "doing" as the preferred state. Most value self-improvement and hard work as the way to ensure a better future for themselves and their families. Euro-Americans believe in scientific and technological "progress," viewing the world in rational, linear, cause-and-effect terms. People from European cultures usually see Americans as more pragmatic, factual, and future oriented than the typical European, with a tendency to view things more in either-or terms than the shades between. Europeans also see Euro-Americans as more committed to change and to freedom than they are. The seven aspects of the Euro-American worldview that we'll discuss are:

1. Conquering nature
2. Making progress and welcoming change
3. Using a rational, linear, cause-effect approach
4. Getting the facts and putting them to work
5. Measuring things
6. Thinking in either-or terms
7. Using time to change the future

Worldview #1: Conquering Nature

Making progress often requires conquering nature. Euro-Americans have traditionally gone along with the Western assumption that the external, non-human world is physical, material, like a complex machine with many parts, and therefore does not have a soul or a spirit. Nature, Mother Earth, is not seen as a living entity. Euro-Americans, probably more than any other group, believe the physical environment is there to be used, even exploited, for human purposes, according to P.R. Harris and R.T. Moran (1996). This contrasts with views common in Asia and among American Indians that stress the unity among all forms of life and inanimate objects. They see people as part of nature and the physical world instead of in opposition to them.

Worldview #2: Making Progress, Welcoming Change, Moving Around

Euro-Americans believe in and value progress—scientific and technological developments that improve their material world, according to Gary Althen (1988) and R.L. Kohls (1988). Euro-Americans often use their concept of progress to evaluate themselves and others. This concept is unknown by many in the non-Western world and may be rejected by them. Euro-Americans have traditionally believed that the basic problems of the world are technological and their solution will bring about economic abundance. The final measure of what's good and desirable is how economically feasible or lucrative it is. Progress is usually tied to their struggle to increase their physical comfort, health, material possessions, and standard of living. Also tied to their concept of progress is a feeling of general optimism towards the future, that their efforts can bring about a better future in which there is enough for everyone.

Progress implies change. Euro-Americans have their fair share of resistance to change, yet have pursued institutionalized change to a greater degree than any other society. "New" and "improved" are seen as "better."

This acceptance of change shows up in their willingness to relocate. The U. S. is the most mobile society in the world, changing addresses more often than people in any other nation. That mobility may not apply to countries outside the United States, even for leisure travel. Although Americans are becoming more well-traveled, still only about 20 percent have passports.

Worldview #3: Using a Rational, Linear, Cause–Effect Approach

Euro-Americans believe that everything has a cause-and-effect relationship, as in the operation of a machine. The notion of a natural "happening" has not been familiar or acceptable to most Americans—who see the world as rational in the sense that they believe the events of the world can be explained and the reasons for particular occurrences can be determined. Effective performance in the real world is based on experience and on training and education, which should be practical.

Euro-Americans believe in the scientific method. This means focusing on facts, figures, and techniques as the means to solve problems that represent obstacles to achieving goals. This action orientation leads Americans to look for a simple cause of an event, in order to plug this cause into the problem-solving process and decide on a course of action. Americans like to develop alternative courses of action, anticipate their future effects, compare them, and choose the one that seems best for the purpose at hand. Euro-Americans like action plans that are practical, with results that are visible, measurable, and materialistic. They see action (and the world itself) as a chain of events, a connection of causes and effects projecting into the future. To people from other cultures Americans may seem to sacrifice the end result for the means of getting there, for the scientific method is the only means they trust.

Management scholar Margaret Wheatley (1992) notes that recently some quantum physicists and business leaders have been collaborating to move beyond the traditional scientific method to more holistic approaches to science and management. Based on new discoveries about the interdependence of the web of life, how the mere act of observing a phenomenon can change it, how random events tend to self-organize into coherent patterns, and similar breakthroughs, leaders are focusing more on the importance of intuition, emotional intelligence, human relationships, and similar factors.

Worldview #4: Getting the Facts, Putting Them to Work

Most Euro-Americans don't pay much attention to theories that don't seem to have a practical application. The role of concepts and ideas in American life is to provide direction for purposeful activity.

Theories are judged and tested according to their usefulness in daily life. Americans have not followed in the European tradition of evaluating ideas or systems of thought according to the "intellectual consistency" or "aesthetic appeal" that researcher D.J. Boorstin (1960) identified.

Euro-Americans love facts. Their thinking process generally begins with facts and then proceeds to ideas, an inductive process. How good the ideas are depends on how well they work and whether people can bring them into the way they do business. Euro-Americans are somewhat unique in their insistence on practical applications—the continual need to organize their perceptions of the world into a form than enables them to act. They will accept a certain amount of pure science (research for the sake of curiosity), but expect most research to result in technology or products they can use, something that represents "progress." This operational style of thinking leads to an emphasis on consequences and results. "So much for the hypothetical. What's the bottom line?"

Euro-Americans especially resist systems of thought that lose sight of the individual. For example, despite their many programs of governmental responsibility and care for the individual, Americans resist unifying them into a system of ideology, some sort of modified socialism. Instead, they cling to the ideal of individual enterprise.

Worldview #5: Measuring Things

Euro-Americans prefer qualities that can be measured, and they like to see the world in dimensions that can be quantified. Even quality and experience can be at least partially quantified, if only as first or last, least or most. Or we can assign them arbitrary values, such as "a scale of 1 to 7." In business, government, and academia, Euro-Americans tend to use statistics to measure success and failure, amount of work, ability, intelligence, and overall job performance (Althen 1988).

Euro-Americans have managed to create unparalleled economic abundance with the combined focus on externalized achievement and on exploitation and control of the physical environment. Further, they tend to believe in unlimited physical resources, that there's enough to go around for everyone. This expansive view of achievement in a world of economic abundance contrasts sharply with the perception of limited wealth that prevails throughout most of the world. Only recently have large groups of Euro-Americans, such as environmentalist groups, begun to question the sustainability of their abundance worldview. Now, with satellite television carrying pictures of their abundant lifestyle to every corner of the globe, billions of people are beginning to clamor for similar affluence. If the way of life of 250 million Americans is damaging the planet, what will happen if billions choose this way? Will Euro-Americans have to change their beliefs and their ways? (Wheatley 1992)

Worldview #6: Thinking in Either–Or Terms

When you value the scientific method, objectivity versus subjectivity, and measurable outcomes, this allows you to set a numerical cutoff point for whether something is one way or another. This may be one reason Euro-Americans tend to focus on either-or viewpoints rather than many subtle differences. Euro-Americans draw a clear distinction between the subjective or personal and the objective or impersonal.

Avoiding Paradox

Euro-Americans tend to be very intolerant of contradiction and paradox, according to studies by Kaiping Peng, Berkeley psychologist (Peng 2000). Euro-Americans tend to believe there is one truth in any domain that must be uncovered. That makes them good at science but may cause problems in their personal relationships. Euro-American knowledge theory holds that everything has an identity, a property, and an essence. Everything is in a systematic order and there is a direction to the future and destiny. This line of thinking leads to the belief that one worldview is right and others are wrong. It naturally leads to a religion of a single god and a single truth that's possessed by a church.

Peng contrasts this with the Chinese belief in many truths, which in turn makes paradox, contradictions, and ambiguity more acceptable. This leads to a belief that multiple religious teachings can all have their own truth. In fact, you could have one church that teaches Taoism, Buddhism, Christianity, and other beliefs all together.

When Peng told a story of a mother-daughter conflict, most Euro-Americans said that one was right and the other was wrong—usually that the daughter was right. But most Chinese respondents said that both may be right and wrong in different ways. They were able to accept two contradictory truths at the same time.

Ranking, Comparing, Taking Action

Author Robert Kohls notes that Euro-Americans often ask such questions as, "Who's your best friend?" or "What's your favorite color?" (Kohls 1988). People outside the culture would generally have difficulty answering such questions because the answer would depend on knowing additional factors, such as the friend you most confide in or the friend you have the most fun with, the color you'd pick for a room or for a suit. Euro-Americans often make judgments or justify actions based solely on personal preference. This tendency is related to the tendency to see the world in terms of either this or that, and it's related to a predisposition to action. Euro-Americans set up unequal dichotomies, with one element valued more than the other; for example, right/wrong, good/evil, work/play, peace/war. These polarities simplify their view of the world, prime them for action, and provide them with their typical method of evaluating by means of comparison.

When it comes to evaluating people, however, Americans allow more shades of gray. Most Euro-Americans are unlikely to give much thought to church views that humans are flawed or evil by nature. They're more likely to see humans as a mixture of good and bad or as creatures of their environment and experience. Most important, Euro-Americans stress the ability to change (Kohls 1988).

Worldview #7: Using Time to Change the Future

Euro-Americans see time as an abstract quality, separate from self. "Time moves fast. It's important to cope with time slipping away. You've got to keep up with the times." Time is something to organize, schedule, use, and save. In business, time is money, so being on time and using time efficiently are critical.

Euro-Americans are future oriented, believing they can improve on the present and that action and hard work pay off in creating a better future for themselves. They see any unpleasantness in their work, or any stress due to incessant activity, as necessary intermediate steps for change and as progress toward the future. In contrast, Latinos, who have a present orientation, focus more on immediate events. Chinese, who have a past orientation, focus more on traditions (Harris and Moran 1996; Althen 1988).

EURO-AMERICAN VALUES: HOW DO THEY DIFFER?

Becoming an achieving individual is the name of the American game. As the most individualistic culture on the planet, Americans value responsible, autonomous individuals who make their own decisions and go out and achieve in the world. They admire people who work hard, play hard, get rich, and stay young. The six Euro-American values we'll discuss are:

1. Becoming an individual
2. Making their own decisions
3. Valuing achievement
4. Working hard and playing hard
5. Achieving material success
6. Staying young

Value #1: Becoming an Individual

Euro-Americans love their freedom to be autonomous individuals. Closely related are the values of competition and assertion. They admire people who decide what they want and go for it, who are willing to compete and don't easily give up. They generally don't place as much faith in fate or luck as do people in many other cultures. The meaning of their brand of self-reliance is neither translatable nor self-evident in other cultures (Harris and Moran 1996; Hofstede 1984).

Value #2: Making Their Own Decisions

Euro-Americans encourage their children, from the earliest age, to decide for themselves, to make up their own minds. They encourage children to believe that they're the best judge of what they want and what they should do. Therefore, as adults Euro-Americans are likely to view bankers, teachers, counselors, and other experts as people who can give them advice, not as people who should make decisions for them. Euro-Americans expect to choose their own mates, careers, homes, and to some extent, lifestyles. By contrast, in many other cultures, all or part of these decisions are made by parents.

Euro-Americans believe in democratic processes that are fair, give everyone an equal say, and help groups make action decisions. Most believe in majority rule and that people are capable of helping to make good decisions, although many men still accept the chain of command and autocratic decision making in military, government, and business organizations. In contrast, some Asian cultures, such as Japan, reach group decisions by feeling around or groping for a voice, preferably that of the chairman, that will express the group's consensus. In those cultures it's offensive for any one person to urge the group to accept his own opinion about what to do (Kohls 1988).

Euro-Americans believe that personal motivation should come from within. They don't like it when others, such as managers, impose their motives on them, especially when managers issue orders and threats. Euro-Americans value persuasion as the method of coordinating people in organizations. The subtle threat of failure is always in the background, which empowers the manager's persuasive appeals to self-interest and reason. Euro-Americans want to believe that they decide what they must do.

In rank/status cultures, people accept a personal bond between subordinate and superior, which makes the authority figure an acceptable source of motivation. Direct orders, explicit instructions, and demands for personal conformity may be acceptable, and even desirable, in such cultures. In them, the Euro-American preference for persuasion may be seen as weakness on a leader's part, and employee self-determination may be viewed as egotism and a threat to the organization.

Value #3: Valuing Achievement

Euro-Americans like to think they can achieve just about anything, given enough time, money, and technology. Externalized achievement has traditionally been the dominant motivation of Euro-American men, and they use competition as the primary method for driving themselves and others to achieve. Competition is seen by many as the keystone of American culture (Harris and Moran 1996; Althen 1988).

In many non-Western cultures, and traditionally among Euro-American women, affiliation is the primary motivation and way of relating to others. A communal feeling toward each other excludes the incentive to excel over others, either as a member of a group or individually. Euro-American values seem to be evolving, however. For example, many women are learning to accept their need for individual achievement and success. Some men, who formerly felt compelled to be competitive, are becoming more group-oriented and less autocratic in their behavior, as demonstrated in self-managing work teams and other alliances.

Value #4: Working Hard and Playing Hard

Euro-Americans are known to be work oriented and efficient. They act upon persons, things, or situations. Others may see Americans as living at a fast pace, incessantly active. Euro-Americans are likely to fill their waking hours primarily in a *doing* mode, seldom asking if getting all those things done is really worth it. They like the kind of activity that results in accomplishments that are measurable by standards that the culture says are valuable. Euro-Americans believe hard work is rewarded by success, and failure usually means you didn't know how to do it right, you didn't try hard enough, or you're too lazy to care. In contrast, people in some Asian cultures fill their waking hours with a *being* mode. Their focus is on valuing the spontaneous expression of themselves as humans or on developing all aspects of the self toward a higher-level, integrated, whole person.

Euro-Americans are somewhat unique in categorizing activities as either work activities or play activities. Work is pursued for a living. You may not necessarily enjoy it but you must do it and you put it first. In contrast, many non-Westerners rarely allow work to interfere with the amenities of living. For Euro-Americans, play is relief from the drudgery and monotony of work and is enjoyable in its own right. However, Euro-Americans often pursue play with the same seriousness of purpose as they pursue work. They tend to admire the person who "works hard and plays hard" (Stewart 1992)

Euro-Americans currently in their 30s and 40s are more likely to look to both work and play for personal enlightenment and fulfillment, and are now looking for ways to balance their career goals with family and personal priorities. Those in their 20s are the most insistent on balance, being less willing to sacrifice family and personal life for careers or employers. They're most likely to insist that work be fun—and that play be carefree and to make it whatever they want it to be.

Value #5: Achieving Material Success

Euro-Americans consider it almost a right to be materially well-off and physically comfortable. People should have shelter, clothing, warmth, and all the other necessities for material comfort. An important part of the good life is each household unit having its own house, car, and other physical possessions. Euro-Americans spend great time, effort, and money acquiring such comforts. They expect convenient transportation, preferably under their control, a variety of clean and healthful foods, and comfortable homes equipped with many labor-saving devices, certainly including central heat and hot water. They assume that cleanliness is nearly identical with health, if not with "Godliness" (Kohls 1988).

The Euro-American stress on material things is related to the achievement value and to the Euro-American belief in private property, one that is highly valued and upheld by an entire legal system. It's difficult for many Euro-Americans to imagine, but some cultures don't even have a concept of private property, and some Asian cultures value a person's "state of grace" much more highly than their material wealth. However, Euro-Americans under age 40 are more likely than older Euro-Americans to look to other determinants of status, success and accomplishment; specifically:

- personal satisfaction with their lives
- control of their own lives
- the respect of other people
- a good marriage.

Value #6: Staying Young

America is a youth culture. It often seems that everyone wants to look and act about 25. In most cultures, such as Asian and Latino, older persons are nearly always catered to, honored, and even revered. In the United States they're often ignored, even shunned.

Extensive research by the polling firm Yankelovich Partners, Inc. points to possible changes in this value, based on generational differences. They predict a shift toward these beliefs about youth and beauty:

- Age will be beautiful.
- Comfort will be beautiful—people will be less willing to sacrifice comfort to look stylish.
- Beauty will come in many skin tones and ethnicities

Only time will tell how strong these new value trends will become.

THE EURO-AMERICAN WAY OF RELATING: HOW DOES IT DIFFER?

Americans are seen by those in other cultures as friendly and informal, direct and casual, and having have many easy, casual friendships. Their ideal is equality of all people, but in practice they often violate this ideal. Euro-Americans believe in cooperation and fair play, and they tend to fit people into specialized roles. Six specific values involving relationships are:

1. Making many casual friends
2. Preferring arm's-length space
3. Fitting into specialized roles
4. Seeing people as basically equal
5. Cooperating and playing fair
6. Communicating informally and directly

Relationship Value #1: Making Many Casual Friends

Americans are known to be friendly, informal, and generous. They tend to reject the idea of someone being special or privileged merely because of birth. They're more likely to defer to those who have achieved power and affluence through their own merit. The way they dress and greet each other tends to be informal relative to many cultures. Americans are known to be generous, willing to come to the aid of people, and to embrace a good cause.

To Euro-Americans a "friend" may be a passing acquaintance or a lifetime intimate, but they're likely to have many personal relationships that are friendly and informal and to form few deep and lasting friendships (Harris and Moran 1996; Stewart 1992). In contrast, people from many other cultures are slow to form friendships, but once committed, they're friends for life. They will do almost anything for a *such a* friend, such as loan them money or help them move their household. In these situations Euro-Americans would prefer to hire professional help rather than inconvenience friends (or be inconvenienced, if the situation were reversed). Americans' immediate friendliness, forming of instant friendships, and lack of deep commitment are confusing to people from deep-friendship cultures.

Euro-Americans change friends and membership groups more easily than most. Though they spend a great deal of time in social activities, Euro-Americans generally avoid personal commitments and intense involvement except with one or two "best friends." Their exchange of invitations and gifts is within a loose, informal framework. The quality of their social interactions tends to stress equality, informality, impermanence, and personal detachment. Many Euro-Americans need to express friendship and to be popular in order to feel self-confident. They often judge their personal and social success by popularity, almost literally by the number of people who like them.

Relationship Custom #2: Preferring Arm's–Length Space

Euro-Americans' boundaries are about arm's length. When someone breaks through that boundary, they may feel invaded, and the act often carries sexual or belligerent overtones. The way they use space reflects the desire to have privacy and to maintain some distance in their personal lives. Traditionally, the more space and privacy a person has—both in the workplace and at home—the higher their position probably is. Euro-Americans are more willing than others to sacrifice such benefits as shorter commute time in order to have homes with more floor space and yard space (Stewart 1992; Harris and Moran 1996; Kohls 1988).

Relationship Value #3: Fitting into Specialized Roles

As a primarily industrial economy for the past century, America's workplace roles have been developed and filled with specialists who deal with specific functions and problems. The organizational hierarchy has been like a machine with interchangeable parts; that is, people with specific skills. Until recently, Euro-Americans never thought of an organization as growing out of the unique qualities that people brought to it and their ability to respond to unique opportunities that unfolded in the environment. Instead, they focused on specialized roles in business, the military, and government, particularly where technical skills and complicated equipment are involved. Associates from other cultures often find it difficult to understand the traditional Euro-American insistence on separating planning from implementing. This tendency is changing as America has moved into a post-industrial economy with self-directed teams, which merge these two functions.

Interpersonal relationships have reflected the workplace tendency towards specialization of roles. Euro-American friendships are likely to be based on their role activities, such as work, hobbies, sports, children, charities, games, and political or religious interests. They tend to think of others as co-workers, fellow tennis players, club associates, old school chums, neighborhood friends, PTA parents, etc. This specialization of friends often reflects their reluctance to become deeply involved with more than one or two friends and a wish for privacy. Euro-Americans' separation of occupational and social roles, of work and play, is different from other cultures (Stewart 1992).

Relationship Value #4: Seeing People as Basically Equal

An important theme in Euro-American relationships is equality. Ideally, just the fact of being human gives each person a certain irreducible value, and interpersonal relations are typically horizontal, conducted between presumed equals. However, big business and big government have traditionally been hierarchical and authoritarian, run by able-bodied, straight, Euro-American men, who in practice generally considered themselves the only true equals. When one of them needed to confront another who was a subordinate, he was more likely to establish an atmosphere of equality than are the bosses in rank/status-oriented cultures. However, this value has often not extended to employees who were "too different," such as African Americans or women.

In addition to these contradictions, Euro-Americans have further reservations about total equality: Not everyone is presumed to have equal talent and ability, even though they're entitled to equal rights and obligations. Euro-Americans generally believe, however, that in any group there will be people of ability and leadership potential. They emphasize equality of opportunity more than equality of results or equality of individuals per se. During their history, they've blatantly violated their belief in equality—and they've modified their understanding of it. But the belief remains a pervasive cultural value and the keystone for building an inclusive, profitable workplace (Althen 1988; Harris and Moran 1991; Takaki 1993; Wiebe 1975).

Relationship Value #5: Cooperating and Playing Fair

Although Euro-Americans value competition, they usually compete against a backdrop of cooperation, for competition requires a considerable amount of coordination among individuals and groups. Euro-Americans can do this because they don't commit themselves as wholeheartedly to a group or organization as those from most other cultures. Euro-Americans pursue personal goals while cooperating with others who, likewise, pursue their own. They tend to accept the goals of the group, but if their expectations are unfulfilled, they feel free to leave and join another group. Euro-Americans can adjust their goals to those of other group members for carrying out joint action. This compromise is practical to them, allowing them to achieve a benefit they couldn't attain on their own. Euro-Americans cooperate in order to get things done, but that doesn't imply that they're giving up their personal goals or principles.

Euro-Americans believe you don't have to accept other persons in totality to be able to work well with them. Part of being practical or professional is the ability to work effectively with anyone who can do the job, even if you disapprove of a co-worker's politics, lifestyle, or religious beliefs. It's this trait that allows Euro-Americans to cooperate with a diversity of people in order to achieve specific goals. This is a strength Euro-Americans can build upon to overcome the systemic and subtle discrimination that still exists in the workplace (Harris and Moran 1996; Althen 1988).

Relationship Value #6: Communicating Informally and Directly

The American communication style is known for being informal and direct. Euro-Americans stress a simple vocabulary, a relative disregard for style, and the use of slang to show they (and the other person) are "one of the gang." As a loose-knit, diverse culture, Americans must rely more on the specifics of verbal communication, while tight-knit cultures can rely more on vague, nonverbal signals.

Euro-Americans' informal, direct approach to interacting with others can seem brusque, rude, or confusing to people of other cultures. Compared to others, Americans tend to make fewer discriminations among people—quickly moving to a first-name basis with all and relating with breeziness, humor, and kidding. Their friendly, personal way of treating everyone, even enemies, contributes to a depersonalization.

While Euro-Americans tend to avoid confrontation, once they decide that a situation with another person must be resolved, they're likely to deal directly with the person. This contrasts with the idea of "saving face" and using a go-between or other indirect approaches that are practiced in many other cultures (Harris and Moran 1996; Kohls 1988; Althen 1988).

EURO-AMERICAN MALE IMPACT & ISSUES

Euro-American males, as the dominant powerful group in business and government, have had the strongest and most pervasive impact on American culture and society. Yet they have their own issues to cope with. And some of their typical leadership styles and beliefs are losing favor in the changing workplace as well as blocking changes toward a multicultural approach that includes all types of employees.

Euro-American Male Issues

Even the most powerful group in American society has its challenges and issues. About 20 percent of Euro-American men believe they have been the victim of reverse discrimination, but they did not file a complaint for fear of being labeled racist or sexist (Whitaker 1996). Most people do not think of Euro-American men as a group that needs workplace protection. However, if an organization sets quotas for hiring minorities or women (such quotas are illegal) and blatantly prefer less-qualified minorities over much better-qualified Euro-American men, then a claim of reverse discrimination is valid (Yates 1994, Casio 2003).

Many of these men, especially blue-collar workers, feel they are losing power. Affirmative action did open the doors to better-paying jobs for minorities and women, making them the new competitors for jobs formerly held almost exclusively by Euro-American men. Outsourcing of jobs to overseas employees has further eroded job availability (Schwartz 2003).

Most Euro-American men say they value diversity, but many think some diversity trainers reinforce "white male" stereotypes that lead to further resentment toward them. They worry about the impact of such concepts as white supremacy, white male privilege, and old boy networks. Some say that they resent:

- having to constantly apologize for what their ancestors did.
- coping with minorities' belief that being white male is the reason for their success rather than merit.
- dealing with the perception that they have no valid diversity issues.

Euro-American male support groups are rare in workplaces that may have support groups for African Americans, women, gay persons, etc. Some of these men are saying they need a support group, too. They also have issues in dealing with the changing workplace and society and need a place to bond, discuss, learn, vent, and express themselves (Flynn 1999).

Euro–American Male Leadership Styles & Beliefs

Representing about 95 percent of top management in the most powerful business organizations, Euro-American beliefs, values, and resulting ways of doing business have a huge impact on American corporate cultures and their ability to become multicultural in order to effectively manage diversity. The Euro-American male leadership style generally includes individualism, paternalism, power hoarding, defensiveness, perfectionism/no mistakes, progress means more, quantity vs quality, high sense of decision urgency, either-or thinking, objectivity vs emotions, and reality = the written word.

Individualism, Paternalism, Power Hoarding; Defensiveness

Individualistic leaders put their own interests first. If they view themselves as an authoritarian father figure, such leaders may see little necessity for understanding the viewpoints and experiences of employees who report to them. Conversely, employees experience the impact of leader decisions and yet do not understand how or why the leaders made those decisions.

Such paternalistic leaders may be threatened when employees suggest how things might be done differently because they think such suggestions for change reflect poorly on their leadership ability. Such leaders may assume that they know what's best for the organization and thus that those who want change must be either misled or not capable of producing valid business ideas. These leaders may believe they have a right to certain comforts, and employees who cause them to feel uncomfortable must suffer the consequences.

People in power who feel threatened or uncomfortable by any perceived challenge to their power will naturally turn to various forms of power hoarding. They may harbor a fear of open conflict when an employee raises an issue or problem. Their responses may be to blame the person raising the issue instead of addressing the issue and finding a solution to the problem.

Basically, such leaders fear losing their power, comfort, and privilege. They become defensive, afraid of change, which in turn creates a barrier to the changes that are essential to creating a multicultural workplace that offers equal opportunity for all types of employees.

Leaders can learn to share the decision-making process and to empower teams and individuals to become self-managing. If top management clearly values this approach and uses it as the basis for performance evaluations, managers get the message. Similarly, continuous change and continuous learning can be valued and assessed. At the least, everyone should know who is responsible for which decisions and why they were made.

Dealing with conflict, issues, and problem-solving can result in great learning experiences that boost a leader's confidence in power-sharing. Diversity training can help such leaders to identify with the experiences of all types of employees, a step in learning to effectively manage diversity and thus tap into its many benefits for the organization.

Perfectionism; No Mistakes

Through the lens of perfectionism, managers focus more on employees' mistakes than on their positive contributions, seeing mistakes as an employee problem rather than a problem with the business process or with employee training.

To offset this tendency, leaders can develop a learning organization that focuses on helping employees to learn from their mistakes, and which values a creative process that involves calculated risk-taking and a trial-and-error approach.

Progress Means More; Quantity vs Quality

Seeing progress as achieving more and becoming bigger may mean that the organization is seen as successful when it is able to serve more people, regardless of the quality of the service or product. Things that can be measured are more highly valued than things that cannot. For example, achieving measurable goals that lead to higher profits may be more important than the quality of relationships with employees.

Top management can include process and quality goals in the planning process—to encourage managers and employees to avoid the bigger-is-better syndrome.

High Sense of Decision Urgency; Either–Or Thinking

They want to see results quickly, which can make it difficult to take the time to think long-term, consider alternatives and consequences, and thus make thoughtful decisions. Either/or thinking can create conflicts when people feel that they must make decisions to do either this or that and are therefore not encouraged to consider alternatives.

Leaders can instead work with employees to create realistic goals that can be achieved within a realistic time frame. Such goals can allow employees to consider various alternatives and consequences in the long-term as well as the short-term. They can encourage people to do a deeper analysis and to use a creative approach.

Objectivity vs Emotions

Leaders who highly value objectivity may believe that emotions have no business in the workplace, that they tend to be destructive and irrational and should play no part in decision-making or team processes. Such leaders disapprove of employees who openly express emotion.

Diversity training should include such gender differences as the capacity to fully feel the whole range of emotions and to express them appropriately in a business setting. Euro-American men can learn about the value of certain feminine qualities in the new networked virtual corporation that embraces Generations X and Y, as well as seniors and boomers.

Reality = the Written Word

Some leaders think that if something is not in written form, then it may not really exist. They value employees with strong skills in writing and documentation. They may under-value those with strong people skills. To offset this tendency, leaders can pay more attention to building trusting relationships, which may be more valid in some situations than written documentation.

SUMMARY

Typical stereotypes of Euro-Americans are that they're homogeneous instead of "ethnic," more racist than other groups, rarely victims of ethnic slurs or hate crimes, and so privileged that things come easily to them. Yet their reality is somewhat different from all this. In fact, most new European immigrants have faced discrimination because of their "different" ethnicity. People from all ethnic groups are somewhat ethnocentric, prejudiced, and discriminatory, but Euro-American discrimination is more noticeable because they are the dominant group. Various ethnic groups have their own slurs about Euro-American, and about 30 percent of all hate crimes are against Euro-Americans. Most Euro-Americans males are more likely to focus on the high expectations others have of them and their struggles to succeed rather than their inherent privileges.

Euro-Americans are 71 percent of the U.S. population, yet their proportions range from 98 percent in some New England states to only 31 percent in Hawaii. They are a relatively well-educated and well-paid group.

The Euro-American culture is predominantly a me-first, achievement-first culture that values equality and risk taking. The American way of thinking is predominantly a rational, linear, cause-and-effect approach that relies on measuring things. They believe in getting the facts, preferably measurable ones, and using expertise to conquer nature for a more comfortable, affluent life. Euro-Americans traditionally have thought more in black-or-white terms than in shades of gray. They look toward the future, welcome change and progress, and are beginning to use their individualism in an interdependent way to reach even higher levels of achievement together. Euro-Americans especially value being an individual, making individual decisions, and achieving material success and progress. They therefore believe in keeping busy and in separating work and play. They take a step-by-step, linear view of time and use it by staying busy.

The Euro-American way of relating involves making many casual friends with less intense commitment than in many other cultures. They tend to identify people with specialized roles and to base friendships on specialized activities, such as work, sports, etc. They believe in treating others as equals, cooperating, playing fair, and being direct. In physical terms, their boundary for most colleagues is about arm's length, more distant than Latino and Arab cultures and closer than Asian cultures. Communication tends to be direct and informal.

Euro-American men are dominant in American workplaces, but they have their own issues to cope with. Many think they have suffered reverse discrimination, that they are losing power, that some diversity trainers reinforce negative stereotypes and resentment toward them, and that they need their own support groups just as minorities and women need theirs. Euro-American male beliefs, values, and resulting ways of doing business have a huge impact on American corporate cultures and their ability to become multicultural in order to effectively manage diversity.

The Euro-American male leadership style generally includes individualism, paternalism, power hoarding, defensiveness, perfectionism/no mistakes, progress means more, quantity vs quality, high sense of decision urgency, either-or thinking, objectivity vs emotions, and reality = the written word. All of these tendencies can be balanced with opposing beliefs and values in order to develop a leadership style that is more powerful in today's organizations, which are ever more flexible, fluid, open, virtual, and networked

GUIDELINES FOR COMPLETING CASE STUDIES

Case studies are great opportunities to apply to workplace situations what you learn about managing diversity. They give you chances to build your interactive skills—along with your problem-solving and management skills. The problem-solving process involves recognizing and identifying the surface problems in a situation, uncovering the root problem(s) by asking why? why?, which usually means gathering more information, generating possible solutions, and selecting the best solution.

The surface problems are the easiest ones to identify—they are the ones always mentioned in the written case. In a work situation, they are the communications and actions that are obvious as you talk with people, walk around, look at written materials, etc.—things that you can observe. The difficulty comes in getting beneath the surface problems and figuring out why they are occurring, what is really going on—the root problem(s). Sometimes the root problem could be called "the key issue," and it often is some form of stereotyping, prejudice, or discrimination.

For each case, follow these four steps:

Step 1: Identify surface problems: What problems do I see (listed in written case or observed in actual situation)?

Step 2: Ask Why-Why to get root problem: Why are these problems occurring? What is going on beneath the surface or in the background that is causing them? Do I need to again ask *why* these underlying reasons are occurring (why-why)?

Step 3: Generate Solutions: What are some possible solutions to these problems?

Step 4: Take action or make recommendations: As a manager or consultant, what should I recommend as the best viewpoints and actions to take?

The Support Networks case is a true story (as are all the cases in this text). It demonstrates some typical diversity problems and issues. See if you can ferret out the root problem(s) by asking Why? And perhaps asking Why? Again (the Why-Why technique).

Case Study 3.1: Support Networks

Scott is a manager with Siebert, Inc. He's been with the company for eight years and has been happy with the firm's diversity initiatives, supporting them completely. One of the diversity initiatives is to encourage company support networks for specific diverse groups. So far four successful support networks have emerged: Women's Support Network, African American Support Network, Gay and Lesbian Support Network, and Filipino American Support Network. Siebert Inc. proudly sponsors events that these networks organize, allows members to meet twice a month on company time, and encourages the networks to share their concerns and new ideas with management.

During the past few months several Euro-American male employees have approached Scott asking for permission to start a Euro-American Male Support Network. Membership in this new network would be limited to Euro-American men.

1. What are the key issues (root problems)?
2. If you were Scott, what would you do?

Skill Builder 3.1: Match Comments to Culture

Purpose: To practice applying your knowledge of Euro-American culture to comments made by persons from other cultures.

Instructions: Match each comment below, made by persons from Europe, Latin America, and Asia, to one or more cultural aspects of Euro-Americans found within this chapter.

1. Only Americans smile so often, even at strangers. If we assume the friendliness is special toward us, we may get a rude surprise, finding it hard to establish a real relationship with them. We conclude that Americans are rather insincere.

2. Americans typically look people in the eye and call them by their first names—even when talking with an elder or very important person. This can be a sign of disrespect or trying to dominate in our country.

3. Even though they smile and look very friendly, Americans do not want you to touch U.S; beyond shaking hands.

4. Are American women teases? They wear things like short shorts and low-cut tops, smiling and looking men in they eye, and then become outraged if men make a pass.

5. Americans are not so good at small talk beyond "How are you?" to which they don't expect a real answer, and the weather. We're used to more meaningful small talk about current events.

6. Americans generally refuse to discuss politics or religions at parties. In Europe we love to passionately debate these topics.

7. In business, they are almost rude about being all-business. They get upset when people are late. They want to get right down to business without any niceties or preliminaries. Even a business lunch is nearly all business.

8. They pay almost no attention to business cards, which is rude in my country.

9. Why is their first question so often, "What do you do?" meaning what kind of work do you do?

10. American business people are so business intensive. Yet my American acquaintance seemed shocked when I asked about her income.

11. Americans don't seem to enjoy their food that much, eating just to keep going or to lose weight, often having no formal family dinnertime, eating fast foods, even eating while walking or driving.

12. We know a lot about Americans—through movies and CNN and from studying at school or on our own, but Americans seem to know almost nothing about us.

Sources: Etiquette 101: U.S.A. Conde Nast Traveler; Gary Weaver, American University; Pamela Eyring, Protocol School; Sherry Mueller, National Council for International Visitors.

Skill Builder 3.2: Interviewing Diverse Employees and Their Managers

Purpose: To gain first-hand knowledge about the challenges and opportunities that a particular group of diverse employees is experiencing in today's workplace—and how managers of those employees view the situation. Determine whether to complete this Case Study on your own, with a partner, or as a team member.

Instructions:

1. **Select a diverse group** that you want to know more about.

2. **Interview diverse employees.** Find and interview at least two employees from this diverse group, asking about their challenges, problems, and "horror stories," as well as the opportunities, achievements, and "success stories" they have experienced.

3. **Interview their managers.** Find and interview at least two managers who have significant experience managing people from the diverse group you're studying. Ask them similar types of questions to get their viewpoints of the situation. Ask for tips for managing and working effectively with people from this diverse group.

4. **Gather other information.** Find additional information about the diverse group, and tips for working with them, in library literature and on the Internet.

5. **Write a report.** Organize your research into a report.

6. **Write a case study.** If you got interesting information from the problems and "horror stories" part of your interview, write a case study, similar to the cases you find in this text, concluding with case questions. The case should be written so that it could be used as a case study for others who are studying this topic. In a separate section, write your own case analysis—what you see as the major problems and what you recommend as solutions.

Idea-Starters for Sample Interview Questions

Here are some questions that could be used for many types of interviews regarding workplace diversity.

Questions about Managing Diversity

1. Have you ever had employees from the (Asian American, Gay, Disabled, etc.) group on your work team? If so, what did you learn about meeting the needs and desires of people from this group? The unique kinds of contributions they can make? How to help them make that contribution? Unique problems? Ways of solving those problems?

2. Does the organization have any policies or strategies for *attracting* and *hiring* diverse employees in general? Specifically, for certain groups?

3. Does the organization have any policies or strategies for *retaining* people from these groups?

4. Does the organization have any *policies for promoting* people from these groups?

5. Has the organization adopted any specific *plans or programs* designed to help minorities and/or women to

   - identify their values, priorities, and thus their career goals?
   - identify corporate career paths that fit their career goals
   - gain experience and training needed to be promoted along chosen career paths?

6. Does the organization provide *training opportunities* specially targeted for these groups?

7. Does the organization have some system to *monitor* whether diverse employees have equal or *fair access to training opportunities* at all levels?

8. Has the organization adopted any *plan or strategy to prepare and move* diverse employees *into the highest levels*?

9. Does the organization provide *training programs* specifically designed to help people deal effectively with a culturally diverse work environment?

10. How would you describe the *corporate culture* here? How does it relate to typical values and priorities of key diverse groups?

11. What do you perceive to be the *greatest barriers* to developing and using (within the organization) the *full potential* of members of these groups?

12. What do you think are the *most important problems* that diverse employees face in adapting to the organizational culture here? General problems? Problems specific to each group?

13. Does the organization focus on *work teams*? If so,

    - Are these self-directed teams?
    - Are minorities and women often part of the teams?
    - Is creativity and innovation encouraged?
    - Do you think people are more productive when they work in teams?
    - How successful are the teams in the organization?

14. When these teams are successful, what are the chief factors? In other words, what makes a *successful team* click?

Questions for Employees from a Specific Diverse Group:

1. Has the fact that you're a member of your particular ethnic (or other) group had any effect on your *work experience* in this company? In other companies you've worked with? What success stories? What horror stories? Particular problems? Unique solutions?

2. Are there any *specific problems* you can describe

    - in getting hired?
    - getting adequate and fair pay?
    - getting adequate training?
    - getting good job assignments, projects, appointments to committees, and other opportunities that would groom you for promotion?
    - getting promoted?
    - in being accepted by coworkers, management, customers, others?

3. What specific *encouragement or help* has the company given you in the above areas?
4. How would you describe the *environment* here?
5. Would you *encourage others* from your ethnic (or other) group to go to work for this company? Why or why not?

Skill Builder 3.3: Diversity Audit: Learning More about an Organization's Culture

Purpose: To learn more about a target organization's culture, perhaps the one you work in or one you're thinking about joining, and to place it into a frame of reference for understanding what's going on.
Name of Target Organization: _____
Step 1. Investigate
Visit the organization and observe or ask questions as follows.

1. *Observe the physical setting.*

    - Notice the neighborhood, the physical surroundings, "curb appeal" of the building
    - **Fishbowl Test:** The lobby offers a great "fishbowl" look at the culture.
    - Look for the tone of the place, the people, how they're dressed, how they interact with one another.
    - Get as much of a grand tour as possible, taking notes about all that you see.
    - What's your initial impression?
    - What does the physical layout seem to communicate?
    - Is the image consistent in all divisions? facilities?

2. *Collect and analyze written materials, such as annual reports, newsletters, news releases, manuals.*

    - What does the company say about itself?
    - What type of culture do written materials reflect?
    - Do you see signs of diversity at all levels in the materials?

3. *Observe reception area procedures.*
    - Formal or informal?
    - Relaxed or busy?
    - Elegant or plain?
    - What is the receptionist doing? How does she or he interact with visitors?
    - What procedures or processes are used with visitors?

- Do visitors wait?
- Do you see signs of diversity so far?

4. *Ask employees questions, such as these:*

- Tell me about the history of the company. (Notice what facts seem accurate, what myths surface.)
- What has made the company successful? (Look for company values. Do people generally agree on which company values are most important?)
- What kind of people work here? Who gets ahead? (Look for signs of diverse role models, descriptions of role models; look for clear agreement about how to succeed. Are role models constructive, serve the company well? Do women and minorities often succeed?)
- What's it like to work here? How do things get done? (Look for important rites, rituals, meetings, or bureaucratic procedures; do all departmental or team subcultures have some unifying values? Do rites, rules, and procedures encompass or respect the diversity found within the organization?)
- *Tell me a story. Ask about company values, people's experiences.* Ask for a story that illustrates how the company lives out its values statements—or not. Ask for stories about notable successes or regrettable failures—of problems and solutions. This is a way to get information for your case study, Project 2.
- *Can you take a coffee break?* See if you get your interviewee out of the office and into a coffee shop or restaurant. In a more informal setting, such as coffee or lunch, you have a better chance of getting on a more personal ground and getting more personal stories.

5. *Observe and ask, how do people (really) spend their time?*

6. *Ask about career paths:*

- Who gets ahead? What departments were top people once in? What positions did they hold? Do people from diverse groups get ahead?
- What do people have to do to get promoted?
- What does the company reward? competence in key skills? performance against objective criteria? seniority? loyalty? good team player? other?

7. *Find out how long people usually stay in jobs.*

(Short terms usually mean people are motivated to make their mark quickly and to steer clear of longer-term, slower payback activities. They also can mean people from diverse groups became discouraged, felt they couldn't reach their career goals, and left.)

8. *Find out what people are talking about and writing about.*

- What are memos and reports about - actual content?
- What are meetings about? What is actually discussed, who talks to whom?
- *Put on your spy cap.* Go online to get photographs and biographies of the management team. What kind of diversity do you detect? Check out employee blogs, message boards, and networking sites. Track down lawsuits, especially those regarding discrimination or wrongful termination.

Step 2. Review and Analysis.
Go over the results of your survey to determine how strong or weak, how conformist or flexible, you think the company is. Use it to help identify companies that are in danger of failing. Look for:

1. *Patterns and themes.* Think about patterns that emerged from the stories and anecdotes that people volunteered. What are the key points? Do most stories revolve around customers? political infighting? individual initiative that was rewarded or punished?

2. *Inward focus.* People don't pay much attention to what's going on outside the company with customers, competitors, new trends. They focus on placating the boss, looking good, getting one up on the people around them. They seem to over-emphasize budgets, financial analysis, or sales quotas.

3. *Short-term focus.* If people spend most of their time and energy meeting short-term goals, then sustainable business receives no support and the company is headed for problems.

4. *Declining morale.* Is turnover high or trending upward? Look at the whole company and at subcultures within the company. Look at the track records of employees from diverse groups, such as minorities. Poor morale often begins with a lackadaisical attitude, moving on to loud complaints, and finally people start leaving.

5. *Weak culture.* When a culture is weak or in trouble, people get frightened and anxious. This fright shows up in emotional outbursts in the workplace, such as condemning company policy at a meeting or getting angry with coworkers or bosses. Did you hear any stories that indicate that stress, anger, or other emotions are building up? If so, did you get any clues about the causes?

6. *Fragmentation or inconsistency.* When a division is unhappy about how headquarters is handling things or tells jokes about what goes on there, it's usually a sign that the parts of the culture are not integrated into a coherent whole. Signs that normal variations in different functions of the firm are becoming a problem:

   • Subcultures (within departments, or sometimes within ethnic groups) are becoming ingrown. Regular interaction among subcultures is declining.

   • Subcultures are clashing, publicly trying to undermine each other. The healthy tension among two subcultures has become destructive.

   • Subcultures are becoming exclusive. One or more subculture is acting like an exclusive club. People are feeling left out and resentful, not pulling together toward company goals.

   • Subcultures act as if their values are more important than company values, not giving key overriding company values top priority.

Step 3. Written Report
Write a report giving the results of your diversity audit. Include
   • your analysis of how well the organization is managing diversity
   • the degree to which they have an inclusive multicultural corporate culture
   • how corporate culture, policies, practices, and programs seem to boost or undermine morale for employees from diverse backgrounds
   • any other opinions about the organization's management of diversity

Skill Builder 3.4: Assessing Corporate Culture Fit

Purpose: To raise your awareness about how various corporate cultures fit the needs of diverse employees.

Begin with how a target corporation fits your needs. Select an organization you want to study or to work in. After you have conducted a survey of the corporate culture (Skill Builder 1), complete the following Skill Builder, using this scale.

Step 1. Assessing the organization's values. In the Target Organization column, for each value, assign either an A or B, whichever best represents that organization's value, and a number from *moderately important = 1*   *very important = 2*   *extremely important = 3*

Target Org.	My Root Culture	Values: What's Most Important	
A or B? **1, 2, or 3?**	**A or B?** **1, 2, or 3?**	**A Values**	**B Values**
		Doing the work Living for the present Being aggressive Promoting myself Competing Being unemotional Individual goals Taking risks Other	Building relationships Working for future rewards Being passive Being modest Cooperating Expressing emotions Team goals Avoiding risks Other

1 to 3 that represents moderate to extreme importance placed on that value by the firm. Add any other organization values you think will affect you significantly.

Step 2. Assessing your values. In the My Root Culture column, repeat step 1 for your own values, modifying your root culture's focus, where necessary, to reflect your own values. Add any other workplace values that are important to you.

Step 3. Estimating cultural fit. Compare the target organization's profile of values with your root culture's profile, and write a brief paragraph about what this means in terms of cultural fit between someone from your culture and this organization.

Step 4. Assessing another person's cultural fit. Think of someone from another culture that you know well. Do steps 1-3 substituting that person's profile for your own. In the paragraph write-up in step 3 include comparisons between your own fit and this person's fit and any insights that occur to you regarding cultural fit.

REFERENCES

Althen, Gary. *American Ways*. Intercultural Press, 1988.

Bartlett, Robert. *The Making of Europe*. Princeton University Press, 1993.

Boorstin, D.J. *Americans and the Image of Europe: Reflections on American Thought*. Meridian Books, 1960.

Cascio, Wayne F. *Managing Human Resources: Productivity, Quality of Work Life, Profits*. McGraw-Hill/Irwin, 2003.

Chambers, James. *The Devil's Horsemen: The Mongol Invasion of Europe*. Atheneum, 1979.

Cox, Taylor. *Cultural Diversity in Organizations*. Berrett-Koehler, 1993.

Cox, Taylor. *Developing Competency to Manage Diversity*. Berrett-Koehler, 1997.

De Anda, D., "Bicultural Socialization," *Social Work* 29, 101–107, 1984.

Flynn, Gillian, "White Males See Diversity's Other Side," *Workforce Magazine*, 78, 2, 52–55, February 1999.

Hall, E.T., and M.R. Hall. *Understanding Culture Differences*. Intercultural Press, 1989.

Harris, Philip R., and Robert T. Moran. *Managing Cultural Differences*, 4th ed. Gulf Publishing Co., 1996.

Hofstede, Geert. *Cultures and Organization*. McGraw, 2001.

Jay, Gregory, University of Wisconsin-Milwaukee, *www.uwm.edu~gray/Whiteness*, March 17, 2005

Kohls, Robert L. *The Values Americans Live By*. LinguaTec, 1988.

Kolchin, Peter. "Whiteness Studies: The New History of Race in America." *The Journal of American History*. 89:1, 154–73, 2002.

Pettigrew, Thomas. *A Profile of the Negro American*. Van Nostrand, 1964.

Ramirez, A. "Racism Toward Hispanics" in *Eliminating Racism, ed.* Phyllis A. Katz and Dalmas A. Taylor. Plenum Press, 1988.

Schmitt, Christopher H., "Defining America: A Special Report" *U.S. New & World Report,* 40–46, July 5, 2004.

Schwartz, Joel, "Ninety Percent of Young White Male Workers Now Doing Worse than They Would Have 20 Years Ago," *EurekaAlert.org,* 2002.

Siehl, C. and L. Martin, "The Role of Symbolic Management" in *Leaders and Managers.* Pergamon Press, 1984.

Spector, P.E., "Behavior in Organizations as a Function of Employee's Locus of Control," *Psychological Bulletin,* 91, 482–497, 1982.

Stewart, Edward C. *American Cultural Patterns: A Cross Cultural Perspective.* Intercultural Network, Inc., 1992.

Takaki, Ronald. *A Different Mirror: A History of Multicultural America.* Little, Brown and Company, 1993.

Thomas, Roosevelt. Beyond Race & Gender. AMACOM, 1992.

U.S. Census Bureau, "Census 2000," www.census.gov.

Wheatley, Margaret J. *Leadership and the New Science.* Berrett-Koehler Publishing, 1992.

Whitaker, William A. *White Male Applicant: An Affirmative Action Expose.* Apropos Press, 1996.

Wiebe, Robert H. *Introduction to the Meaning of America.* Oxford University Press, 1975.

Yates, Steven. *Civil Wrongs: What Went Wrong with Affirmative Action.* Institute for Contemporary Studies, 1994.

--------------------------------------CHAPTER 4

Stereotyping & Prejudice: How and Why They Occur

Build bridges, not walls.
Nicole Schapiro

As Americans, we have inherited a legacy of prejudice, but we've also inherited a legacy of belief in equality, and the mainstream has grown to accept more and more people as basically equal and therefore entitled to equal opportunity in the workplace. "Minorities" as a whole will soon outnumber Euro-Americans in some states. Leading-edge businesses know they need people from all the diverse groups—as customers and as talented employees who work in all corporate functions and levels.

But our legacy means that no one grows up without developing some degree of stereotyping and prejudice. They are woven into the very tapestry of our culture, springing up from the grass roots of family; filtering down from the top levels of government, business, and society; and feeding back on themselves at all levels in between. The first step to breaking out of this web is for each of us to quit denying that we're prejudiced. Then we can start rooting out those pockets of prejudice and the specific stereotypes that created them. We can start getting new, valid information, focusing more on the positive aspects of each group. We can deal with people from each group as unique individuals, going beyond the stereotypes to the specific cultural background that provides deeper understanding.

In this chapter you'll work on the third step in building multicultural skills.

> *Step 3: Recognizing your own biases, the ways in which you stereotype, assume, judge, and discriminate.*

You're probably aware that to be a valuable employee or business associate, you must move beyond stereotypes and prejudices that exclude whole groups of people. This involves learning how to bridge the divisive walls of prejudice—and showing others the way. Doing so can bring huge rewards—to you in building success skills and profitable workplace relationships and to your company as you work more productively with people from diverse backgrounds. You'll learn why and how we stereotype, prejudge, discriminate against, and exclude people just because they belong to a particular group. You'll learn how moving beyond assumptions and prejudices can boost success for you and your company. Specifically, you'll learn about:

- Why people avoid and exclude others
- Why we stereotype people
- How you can become aware of your own stereotypes and prejudices
- The connection between the authoritarian personality and prejudice
- How and why people become prejudiced
- How people express prejudices
- How prejudice affects people generally and in the workplace
- How people can move beyond stereotyping to valuing people's differences and building relationships that promote profitable collaboration.

Before you begin your exploration, complete Self-Awareness Activity 4.1.

Self-Awareness Activity 4.1: What Do You Know About Prejudice?

Purpose: To see what you know about the issues covered in this chapter.

Instructions: Determine whether you think the following statements are basically true or false—and think about why. The answers will emerge in this chapter, and the summary at the end of the chapter focuses on these issues.

1. Anthropologists generally agree that there are three major races: caucasoid, negroid, and mongoloid.
2. Most aspects of our culture teach us to appreciate others and not be prejudiced.
3. People who believe in strict categories of right and wrong are unlikely to be prejudiced.
4. Prejudiced beliefs are frequently hidden, not in awareness.
5. Prejudiced beliefs cannot be changed, but discriminatory actions can.

STEREOTYPES, PREJUDICE, DISCRIMINATION— WHAT'S THE DIFFERENCE?

We may exclude whole groups of people because we've bought into a stereotyped belief that people from that group are inferior in some way. This means that we prejudge such persons before we ever get to know them. If we don't give them a fair chance on the job, or if our organization is set up in a way that automatically ignores certain groups of people, then we are participating in discrimination against them.

Workplace prejudice is alive and well. Surveys indicate that stereotypes are still prevalent and that most of the Euro-Americans who dominate the workplace tend to believe that other ethnic groups are less intelligent, less hard working, less likely to be self-supporting, more violence prone, and less patriotic than they. The Executive Leadership Council's study found prejudice to be the most serious career hurdle for African American executives. The research organization Catalyst found prejudice to be the biggest advancement barrier women face today (Morrison 1992; Smith 1990; Baskerville and Tucker 1991; Catalyst 2004).

Three terms are often used to describe the separate but related elements of exclusion: stereotypes, prejudice, and discrimination.

Stereotypes: A Way of Thinking

You're exposed to millions of bits of data every second of your waking life. You couldn't function unless you filtered out most of this data and categorized the rest of it. Categorizing data into groups, giving the groups of information recognizable labels, and fitting them into your current knowledge base—these are some ways that your mind must function. So stereotyping, in this sense, is normal and essential. Problems occur when we allow these labels to become rigid, exaggerated, irrational beliefs about a particular group of people. Such rigid stereotypes about people usually lead to prejudice.

Prejudice: A Way of Feeling

When you view a group of people who are different as somehow deficient, that means you are pre-judging individuals before getting to know them. Prejudice, therefore, means judging a whole category of people as basically better-than or worse-than others. Because individuals within a group have many similarities but also many differences, pre-judging them is obviously unfair to the individuals. Prejudice is a way of feeling because it arises from some of our deepest fear-based emotions and triggers still other problem emotions.

Some prejudice is a matter of blind conformity to prevailing cultural beliefs and customs. However, in most cases prejudice seems to fulfill a specific irrational function for people, such as making them feel superior to others or using others as scapegoats for the prejudiced persons' own resentment or guilt. Prejudice usually is tied to a person's deepest fears, although the connection is normally subconscious and therefore hidden from awareness, according to Harvard psychologist G.W. Allport in his classic work on prejudice (1954).

Discrimination: A Way of Acting

Now we get down to actual actions or practices that result in members of a less-powerful group being treated differently in ways that disadvantage them. Discrimination usually refers to behavior that is prejudiced, and the acts that have an effect on people who are targets of prejudice.

Most discussions of prejudice and discrimination are based on the following assumptions (Ridley 1989):

- Prejudice is reflected in behavior.
- Prejudiced acts can be performed by nonprejudiced as well as prejudiced people.
- Prejudice is found in every ethnic group.
- The criteria for judging whether or not a behavior is prejudiced lies in the consequences, not the causes, of the behavior. (We can't prove someone is prejudiced, but we can prove that their acts have a discriminatory effect.)
- Power is a force that is absolutely essential to perpetuate discrimination.

All this implies that a power imbalance is a key aspect of discrimination. As we've seen, civil rights measures are based on this premise and represent attempts to break the cycle of centuries of discrimination.

Discrimination has been built into American institutions and systems. No one is completely immune to its impact, although people from historically disadvantaged groups tend to suffer the worst effects. Civil rights laws have reduced its pervasiveness and intensity, and activist groups are working against it. But groups are made up of individuals, and change begins within one person and expands person by person. The role you play is important (Ponteretto 1993; Allport 1954; Cox 1993).

Vignettes: How We Stereotype People

Overheard at a restaurant:

> *Sorry I'm late—had to wait in line over 10 minutes at the post office. Most of the clerks seemed to be on a break. Well, what can you expect? Postal employees!*

> *Yeah, really. But they don't bother me—as long as they don't go 'postal' when I'm around!*

In the office:

> *I'm not voting for any of them. They're all a bunch of corrupt crooks.*

> *You're right—and you can't believe any of their promises.*

At a party:

> *Oh, sure, he's good looking and a great dancer, but I probably won't get involved with him. I hear they're all pretty macho when you really get to know them.*

> *Uh huh, and most of them have some kind of Mafia connection.*

If you're like most people, you're improving the quality of your beliefs and attitudes toward people who have traditionally been devalued in our culture—*and* you want to do better at bridging the gaps and connecting in a positive way with people from diverse backgrounds. You want information about how to build rewarding relationships—whether it's with postal employees, politicians, Italian American, African Americans, or others you deal with in your day-to-day activities. You want to link, bond, connect, and ally with people in ways that will build strong relationships.

Moving beyond prejudiced thinking offers many rewards. It can make you a more effective team member, help you give better service to all your customers and associates, and in turn boost your company's profits and success. Clearly, the bottom line reward for moving beyond stereotypes to collaborating with people is the boost to your own career success. A very real bonus is the probability that you'll get more enjoyment from working with people and you'll feel better about yourself.

Why Do We Stereotype People?

The process of stereotyping allows us to manage complex realities by using categories to store new information, to quickly identify things, to handle multi-sensory experiences, and to make sense of things. We may attach strong emotion to these stereotypes, even when they're false, and we often use stereotypes to justify our dislike of someone.

Rigid, limiting stereotypes create barriers to really getting to know people, but you can break free. The first step is to understand how this process of stereotyping works in your everyday life.

Making Complex Reality Manageable

When we stereotype, we form large classes and clusters for guiding our daily adjustments. We must deal with too much complexity in our environment to be completely open-minded. We don't have time to learn all about every new person or situation we encounter. Of necessity, we associate them with old categories in our mind in order to make some sense of the world.

Short-Cutting with Categories

We tend to place as much as we can into each class and cluster. Our minds tend to categorize events in the *grossest* manner compatible with the need for action. We like to solve problems as easily as possible, so we try to fit them rapidly into a satisfactory category and use this category as a means of prejudging the solution.

Quickly Identifying Things

A stereotype enables us to readily identify a related object. Stereotypes have a close and immediate tie with what we see, how we judge, and what actions we take. In fact, their whole purpose is to help us make responses and adjustments to life in a speedy, smooth, and consistent manner.

Incorporating Multi-sensory Experiences

For each of our mental categories, we have a thinking-feeling tone or flavor. Everything in that category takes on that flavor. For example, we not only know what the term *Southern belle* means, we also have a feeling tone of favor or disfavor that goes along with that concept. When we meet someone that we decide is a Southern belle, that feeling tone determines whether we like her more or less than we would if we got to know her on her own merits.

Being Rational—Or Not

Stereotypes may be more or less rational. A rational stereotype starts to grow from a kernel of truth and enlarges and solidifies with each new relevant experience. A rational stereotype can give us information that can help us to predict how someone will behave or what might happen in a situation. An irrational stereotype is one we've formed without adequate evidence or because it met an emotional need. We notice behavior that "proves" the stereotype is true, reinforcing it—for example when the Southern belle bats her eyelashes. As for behavior that refutes the stereotype—for example, when she makes an assertive statement—we either don't notice it at all, or we classify it as a rare exception.

Adding the Emotional Whammy

Our minds are able to form irrational stereotypes as easily as rational ones, and to link intense emotions to them. An irrational idea that is engulfed by an overpowering emotion is more likely to conform to the emotion than to objective evidence. Therefore, once we develop an irrational stereotype that we feel strongly about, it's difficult for us to change that stereotype based on facts alone. We must deal with the emotion and its ties to our deepest fears.

Justifying Dislike

Sometimes we form a stereotype linked to an emotion related to fear—such as hostility, suspicion, dislike, disgust—and set up the framework for prejudice toward an entire group of people based on our experience with one or a few. When people become prejudiced toward a group, they need to justify their dislike, and any justification that fits the immediate conversational situation will do. So we grasp any real or imagined behavior that serves to "prove" the stereotype.

In summary, stereotyping is part of the human need to categorize the massive amounts of information we encounter every day. Categorizing and labeling are ways of making sense of the world and managing the stuff we must do. Stereotyping, when used in this *technical* sense, is a rational thing to do. The problems arise when we make our categories too fixed and our labels too permanent—and what most people call *stereotyping* refers to this fixed, permanent aspect. Rigid stereotyping of groups of people often leads to prejudice and discrimination.

Do Americans Still Stereotype Minorities?

Workplace discrimination has been illegal since the civil rights laws and regulations of the late 1960s— and subsequent amendments, regulations, and laws came into effect. In virtually all large companies, and most small firms, stereotyping, prejudice, and discrimination are considered not acceptable, and resulting actions could even be grounds for discipline or dismissal. On the other hand, a survey of 1200 Americans (NORC 2000) reveals that most people hold stereotyped views of ethnic minorities. Euro-Americans were assessed more highly than African Americans and Latino Americans on every stereotype presented; for example:

- 62% said African Americans are the laziest group and the group most likely to live off welfare; Latino Americans came next.
- 57% said African Americans and Latino Americans are less intelligent than Euro-Americans

The researchers concluded that stereotypes affect attitudes and actions in several key areas of social policy, such as the degree of social distance people wish to maintain from minorities, support for affirmative action programs, and support for government spending on programs perceived to primarily benefit minorities. In other words, most Americans see people from minority groups in a decidedly negative light on a number of important characteristics. Such ethnic stereotypes remain important determinants of attitudes toward minority groups. These images are significant predictors of support for ethnic integration programs and of the desire for social interaction with minority persons.

On the other hand, most Americans are reluctant to admit to such stereotypes, which the NORC survey was designed to ferret out. See the discussion of subtle discrimination that occurs later in this chapter.

Self-Awareness Activity 4.2: Being Tolerated and Being Appreciated

Purpose: To experience the difference between tolerance and appreciation.
Step 1. Being Tolerated

    a. Think of a time when you felt tolerated. Write a few words about it.

    b. How did it feel to be merely tolerated? Write a few words about your feelings.

    c. How did feeling tolerated affect your relationship with the tolerant person(s)?

Step 2. Being Appreciated

    a. Think of a time when you felt appreciated. Write a few words about it.

    b. How did it feel to be truly appreciated? Did you feel respected? Write a few words about your feelings.

    c. How did feeling appreciated affect your relationship with the appreciative person(s)?

Stereotyping, prejudice, and discrimination create gaps between people, as well as major barriers to tapping the full potential of all the members of a diverse work team or any diverse group. They diminish the potential synergy, innovativeness, and success of such groups (Gadamer 1989; Feagin 1978, 2001)

HOW CAN WE PINPOINT OUR PREJUDICES?

Virtually everyone harbors some rigid stereotypes and prejudices. Some prejudice is a matter of blind conformity to prevailing cultural beliefs and customs. However, in most cases prejudice seems to fulfill a specific irrational function for people, such as making them feel superior to others or using others as scapegoats for the prejudiced persons' own resentment or guilt. Prejudice usually is tied to a person's deepest fears, although the connection is normally subconscious and therefore hidden from awareness. Researchers such as G. W. Allport, M.H. Ijzendoorn, and Joseph Ponteretto have uncovered some interesting facts about prejudice:

- Prejudice is found in all types of people and in every ethnic group.
- Prejudice occurs in the mind but can be acted out in ways that exclude others (discrimination).
- Prejudiced acts can be performed by non-prejudiced as well as prejudiced people.

The best way to decide if an action is prejudiced is how it affects another person. You can't prove someone is prejudiced, but you may prove that their acts exclude and disadvantage another person.

Key Aspects of Prejudice/Discrimination

You can discriminate by merely being part of an organization that itself unintentionally discriminates through its traditional business practices. This is because of the power-privilege imbalance that automatically favors a dominant majority and disfavors minorities—unless actions are taken to offset the imbalance. Recent studies indicate that, despite 40 years of such offsetting laws, Euro-Americans still experience a distinct advantage over other ethnic groups (Associated Press 2004).

Power Imbalance

A power imbalance is a key aspect of discrimination. Power is a force that is absolutely essential to perpetuate discrimination. For example, an African American clerk may dislike a Euro-American executive and never try to get to know him as a person. Her actions are not called "discrimination" because she does not have the power to take actions that exclude him in ways that disadvantage his career.

On the other hand, the executive does have the power to discriminate against her, and that type of power differential is not unusual. Euro-American men still hold nearly all the top-level economic and political power in the United States, as mentioned in Chapter 1. They hold 95 percent of the top-level positions in mid- to large-sized businesses and about 80 percent of the seats in Congress, even though they are about 39 percent of the workforce and 35 percent of the population, according to the U.S. Census Bureau and the U. S. Glass Ceiling Commission. Civil rights measures are based on the fact of power imbalance and represent attempts to break the cycle of centuries of discrimination.

Advantage Imbalance

An advantage imbalance goes hand in hand with a power imbalance, meaning there is a powerful group with distinct advantages that other groups don't have. Most Euro-American men and boys are unaware of the hundreds of advantages they enjoy as members of their group, according to research by Peggy McIntosh; for example:

When they leave their family or local community in the morning and go out into the world, they can choose to ignore ethnicity, skin color and other people differences. People from other groups never have that luxury if they want to succeed in the corporate workplace.

When they set their goals and plans for social, professional, or political achievement, they don't ask whether a person from their ethnic group or gender would be accepted in the situation, and what related barriers they must overcome.

When they take a job, co-workers assume they got the job because they're qualified, not because they're a diverse employee. Company expectations are that they will probably succeed.

- They don't have to struggle to be visible, valuable, and important. Educational materials consistently testify to the *existence* of Euro-American men and their *contributions* to the United States
- Anywhere they go in the United States they don't worry about being rejected—just because they're Euro-American men—when they try to join a club, rent an apartment, buy a house, or get a loan. Of course, most rejections are evasive and subtle, but for ethnic minorities they are real.

To better understand the connections between advantage, power, and discrimination, complete Self-Awareness Activity 4.3.

Self Awareness Activity 4.3: How Advantaged Are You?

What are some advantages that you enjoy in life? List a few.

1. How do the advantages affect your life? Do they affect your personal power? Ability to achieve your goals? Your success?

2. Which of these advantages that you enjoy (or that you notice others enjoying) are not available to some people because of the group they belong to? Note them and the names of groups without access to them.

3. If you are not Euro-American, what are some advantages that are *not* available to you that people from this dominant group enjoy? List them.

4. How does this lack of advantage affect your life? Your personal power? Your ability to achieve your goals? Your success?

Some Types of Prejudice

We talk about prejudice in terms of workplace prejudice, sexism, racism, ethnic prejudice, and other ism's.

Sexism

Sexism is prejudice based on gender and is said by some to be the root of all prejudice and discrimination. As children we literally begin learning this form of inequality in the cradle. It doesn't involve a majority and minority, since men and women are relatively equal in number. However, women in all countries are a minority in economic and political arenas and have fewer rights and advantages than men.

Racism: Our Most Dangerous Myth

Racism is typically a problem in societies such as the United States, where there is a predominant majority group and one or more large cultural subgroups. People often use the term racism in discussions of prejudice, which raises the question, "How do I know when I'm dealing with someone of another race, and how can I be sure what race they represent?" This brings us to the myth of race.

Myth: Everyone belongs to one race or another

If your parents came from two different races, then you are bi-racial. Americans tend to believe in three great races—caucasoid, mongoloid, and negroid—a system developed in Europe and North America in the 1700s.

Those who try to distinguish between race and ethnicity say that racial traits are inborn, inherited, and given by nature, while ethnic traits are learned, cultural, and acquired through nurture.

Reality: Scientists view race as a folk myth

"Race as a meaningful criterion within the biological sciences has long been recognized as a fiction," according to Princeton professor Henry Gates (1992). In 1997 the American Anthropological Association asked the U.S. government to drop the term "race" from its census categories and to use "ethnicity," which reflects culture. Anthropologist Ashley Montagu has discussed the fallacies and dangers inherent in the whole concept of race in the many editions of his classic book, *Man's Most Dangerous Myth* [1997]. Race is a myth, but much of the discrimination in society still takes place in the name of race.

We now know that modern humans arose in Africa less than 200,000 years ago, and the great migrations took place less than 100,000 years ago. So we don't even come close to having enough genetic diversity to allow for races or subspecies. The only pattern that shows up consistently is a geographic one. As scientists survey traditional homelands, people look similar to those from nearby geographic areas and different from those who live far away. The greater the distance, the more differences in appearance.

As humans moved into new climates, environmental pressures such as sun, wind, and hot or cold temperatures produced different physical appearances, including slightly different physiques. But the environment literally works only on the surface, changing skin, hair, and facial features a bit. Rather than race, scientists like to discuss "clinal variations" or physical types that may be found in one general area of the world but that fade fairly evenly into other types as one moves across the globe. Even geographic patterns of some sets of genes do not match other sets within the group, showing clearly that human populations have been merging, migrating and intermarrying from the start.

Anthropological work on race has produced these facts:

- As human beings, we are all one species that has one set of common ancestors, all originally out of Africa.
- Genetically, we are 98 to 99 percent alike, according to the Human Genome Project.
- No one belongs to a pure stock, except a very few people found in remote isolated parts of the earth.
- Most of the variable human characteristics ascribed to race are actually due to cultural diversity and should therefore be regarded as ethnic, not racial.

Much of the racism in the United States involves African Americans, viewed as a separate "race." Yet experts estimate that about 75 percent of African Americans are of mixed heritage, usually having some Euro-American ancestors.

Since most of the characteristics that vary from culture to culture are learned, and are not "permanently fixed in our genes," they can theoretically be changed (Allport 1954). "Ethnicity" is much more flexible and changeable than "race."

> *What's in a Name? The terms* race *and* racism *are not biologically meaningful for U.S. subcultures, although racial beliefs are still used by some persons as the basis for discrimination. More realistic and conciliatory terms are* ethnicity *and* ethnic prejudice.

Ethnic Prejudice

Ethnic prejudice leads to ethnic discrimination. Ethnic discrimination against minority subcultures occurs when "minority" status carries with it the exclusion from full participation in the society and the largest subculture holds an undue share of power, influence, and wealth in society (Ponterotto et al 1993, 2001).

Other ism's

Other ism's include ageism, classism or class snobbery, and homophobia, or antigay prejudice. Besides ethnic minorities and women, groups that experience discrimination in the workplace include persons with disabilities, gay persons, older employees, and obese persons. To a lesser extent, persons from lower socioeconomic groups may be targets of prejudice, as symbolized by such derogatory terms as trailer trash and poor white trash. Prejudices know no boundaries, however, and some people believe that all post office employees are deadbeat bureaucrats, all administrators are corrupt political sharks, and on and on.

WHAT IS A PREJUDICE-PRONE PERSONALITY?

While everyone is prejudiced to some extent, the degree of prejudice varies greatly and a large body of psychological investigation explains why. The original work on the authoritarian personality was done in 1950 and was studied by Harvard professor G.W. Allport. Since then more than 1200 well-accepted scientific studies have been conducted on this topic—far more than for any other personality aspect. Many of these studies, such as those by Dutch researcher M.H. Ijzendoorn, indicate that people who score high on an authoritarianism scale also show a consistently high degree of prejudice against all other cultural groups. Now, complete Self-Awareness Activity 4.4.

Self-Awareness Activity 4.4: Twenty Questions About You

Purpose: To learn more about your personal viewpoint.
Instructions: Mark each item true or false.

1. I have little or no difficulty deciding what's right and what's wrong.
2. I thrive on variety and change.
3. I often enjoy being with people that some would call strange or weird.
4. I like my routines.
5. I know how I feel about most situations and don't need to keep thinking about them.
6. I need to know exactly where I'm going and when.
7. I often ask myself why I did certain things, or why I think or feel as I do.
8. I hate it when people change our plans.
9. There is only one right way to do most things.

10. Few actions are totally right or wrong; most actions stem from complex situations and have varying effects.

11. I prefer to focus on a few simple things rather than a wide variety.

12. I can feel comfortable with most situations, even if I'm not sure about what's going on.

13. I don't always agree with people from other groups, but I usually understand why they might think and feel as they do.

14. People basically create the life they have and the sooner they take responsibility for it, the better it will be.

15. I think I know my own strengths and shortcomings pretty well.

16. Most actions can be classified as either proper or improper.

17. People have different ideas about what's proper and improper; that's fine with me.

18. I don't start a job until I know exactly how to do it.

19. I'm comfortable "feeling my way" through a task, if necessary.

20. I need to know what's going on and what to expect at all times.

Followup: To interpret your responses, see the answer key at the end of this chapter and review the discussion in this chapter on the authoritarian personality.

The Highly–Prejudiced Personality

People who are rigid and authoritarian in their beliefs have thinking processes and personality traits that are linked to prejudice. They tend to be more prejudiced than people who are open and flexible. As you begin to understand these key personality traits, you can better understand your own tendencies. Don't be dismayed if you find you're much more authoritarian that you'd like. You can change any belief that you decide doesn't serve you—and you can do it in a heartbeat once you are truly motivated. Understanding the authoritarian personality can also help you to see why some people in your organization are more prejudiced than others. You may be able to help them recognize rigid beliefs and imagine more flexible ones—but the choice to change is up to the individual. Just as no one can make you change, you cannot force change on another.

Thinking Processes

The thinking processes of highly prejudiced people are *in general* different from those of less-prejudiced people. Their prejudice is not likely to be merely a specific attitude toward a specific group—though they may rationalize it that way. More likely, it's a reflection of their whole way of thinking about the world they live in. They're likely to indulge in either-or thinking, such as the following.

- Whenever they think of nature, of law, of morals, of men and women, they think in terms of good/bad, right/wrong, black/white, maleness/femaleness, etc. There's little gray in their thinking.

- They tend to be uncomfortable with categories that encompass variety, and are more comfortable if categories are limited to similar things.

- Their habits of thought are rigid, and they don't change their mental set easily, but persist in their "tried-and-true" ways of reasoning.

- They have a real need for things to be definite and don't cope well with uncertainty in their plans.

- They tend to agree with such statements as "there are only two kinds of people" and "there's only one right way to do something."

- They divide the world into proper and improper.

- They need precise, orderly, clear-cut instructions before proceeding with a task.

- They want social dominance, the basic desire to have your primary ingroup be considered superior to other relevant outgroups (Sidanius et al 1994).

Typical Traits

Highly-prejudiced people have what's known as an *authoritarian personality*. The personality profile includes these typical traits [Ijzendoorn 1989].

- rigid beliefs
- intolerant of weakness in themselves and others; power orientation
- highly punishing; aggressive
- suspicious, cynical
- extremely respectful of authority; a strong commitment to conform to the prevailing authority structure
- politically conservative

The Authoritarian Link to Prejudice

Almost invariably, when the parents of authoritarian people have been studied, they're also highly prejudiced against other subcultural groups (James 2002, Ekehammer 2004). The rigid authoritarian cluster of beliefs and attitudes goes back to early childhood experiences in families with these typical characteristics:

- Parents administered harsh and threatening discipline.
- Parents used love and its withdrawal as their major control mechanism to make the child do as told.
- The child was very insecure and highly dependent on the parents.
- The child feared the parents and felt unconscious hostility toward them.

The child gets a double whammy: the setup for developing an authoritarian personality and role models who specifically teach prejudice.

This set of characteristics usually produces an adult with a high degree of anger and a habit of repressing the anger because of insecurity and fear of expressing it directly. Anger must go somewhere, and in this instance it takes the form of displaced aggression against powerless groups. Meanwhile the authoritarian person maintains an outward respect for law and order.

This person typically dislikes uncertainty more than others. Rigid persons don't easily deal with situations that are unclear or difficult to interpret. They see uncertain situations as threatening, while others may see them as nonthreatening or even as interesting, intriguing or otherwise desirable. Rigidity is also referred to as intolerance of ambiguity. Cultural differences obviously create uncertainty about human behavior, and the behavior of diverse others is less understandable and predictable to us than the behavior of those we grew up with. People with rigid personalities are especially likely to view interactions with diverse others as threatening and undesirable (Cox 1993).

Of course, there are exceptions to this profile. Some persons from authoritarian homes are able to choose an open, flexible approach to life. Others, through personal growth, change their beliefs and attitudes in order to become more open, flexible, and accepting of diversity. But it's difficult. Prejudice is clearly more than an occasional incident for people with rigid, authoritarian personality traits. It's embedded in every facet of their personalities. If and when such persons change their prejudiced viewpoints, it follows that they must change their whole life pattern.

The Less-Prejudiced Personality

Building on the authoritarian personality model, researchers have identified some specific traits that are correlated with the less-prejudiced personality (Barrick 1991).

Agreeable—get along with others in pleasant, satisfying relationships, being courteous, trusting, good-natured, tolerant, kind, helpful (Jackson and Poulsen 2005)

Open to experience—Imaginative, insightful, curious, inventive, creative, and original.

Tolerance of ambiguity—high tolerance of ambiguity is typical in persons who are able and ready to accept situations that are unfamiliar, complex, or provide incomplete information. (Friedland et al 1999)

Self-monitoring—are highly sensitivity to situational norms or behavioral standards (Snyder 1974) and thus high in self-monitoring behavior and sensitive to cues in the social surroundings. They are likely to adapt their responses and attitudes to be consistent with those they perceive as normative of their audiences. As a result, they are sensitive to the viewpoints and emotions of diverse others.

To summarize, less-prejudiced persons have adopted thinking processes that are relatively open and flexible, as follows.

- They rarely see things in black-or-white terms but see many shades of gray.
- They're usually comfortable differentiating among the variety within a category.
- They can be comfortable with people and situations they're uncertain about.
- They often empathize with those who are different—and are sensitive to their way of seeing and feeling.
- They're self-aware and assess the quality and meaning of their thoughts, feelings, and actions.
- They tend to take responsibility for what happens to them in life and for the life they create.
- They know their own strengths and shortcomings pretty well.
- They've built a great deal of inner security, have handled threats to their self-esteem with inner strength, and can be at ease with all sorts of people.
- They handle moral conflict pretty well, and so can be fairly flexible and tolerant with the ethical mistakes people make.
- They can tolerate ambiguity, paradox, and uncertainty.
- They feel safe in saying "I don't know" and in waiting until time brings the information or evidence they need.
- They can feel their way through a task, if necessary

If you're a fairly tolerant person, you're likely to fit the following profile fairly well. You were probably raised in a home with a relatively permissive atmosphere. You felt welcomed, accepted, and loved in an unconditional way. While you were reprimanded for certain behavior, you weren't rejected as a person because of that behavior. You accepted your parents on the whole but weren't afraid to criticize their behaviors or beliefs at times. You generally didn't fear or dread your parents' superior power. Of course, there are exceptions to this profile. Some persons from authoritarian homes are able to overcome their upbringing, reject their parents' approach, and choose an open, flexible approach to life. Some, through personal growth, change their beliefs and attitudes in order to become more open, flexible, and accepting of diversity.

Investigators have failed to discover important relationships between prejudice and such variables as age, gender, or income. People with more education tend to be less prejudiced, but the connection is fairly minimal.

HOW AND WHY DO WE BECOME PREJUDICED?

How we become prejudiced is closely related to why we become prejudiced. Some typical reasons are:

- the need to feel superior to someone
- fear of competition for jobs from the disparaged group's members

- general frustration because of low status and resulting hostility
- lack of education leading to a simplistic, stereotypic view of the world
- difficulty dealing with new, uncertain situations and people
- the need to be approved and included by people from the ingroup, most of whom are prejudiced themselves
- the tendency to conform to dominant beliefs and attitudes

As we explore how people become prejudiced, details of the reasons why will emerge.

Prejudice in the United States is probably rooted in the ethnocentric philosophy that values mainstream dominant cultural beliefs and attitudes more highly than culturally diverse belief systems (Loury 2002). Our history is riddled with many flavors of overt and covert prejudice, ranging from slavery to segregation to ethnic and sexist jokes. Most prejudice today is of the subtle and hidden form. We might view prejudice as both a group disease and an individual disease. People become prejudiced through the following processes and sources:

- being raised in ways that promote such personality traits as rigidity and authoritarianism
- learning from the culture—family, school, church, media, workplace
- stereotyping
- developing an ethnic identity
- forming ingroups
- becoming ethnocentric
- living in a diverse, rapidly changing society

We Learn Prejudice from Our Culture

People learn to be prejudiced first and primarily at home, but regardless of where they first adopt prejudiced beliefs, reinforcement occurs throughout the culture—within the family and in the media, the schools, the churches, the workplace, the government. Prejudice is reinforced when we see the contributions of certain groups being devalued or ignored and when we hear people use negative adjectives and stereotypes for them. It's kept in place when we don't have access to a broad array of factual and suitable information about other groups—and when our contacts with people from other groups are only superficial.

The Society—Attitudes and Actions

"Racial profiling" is a hot topic these days. It usually refers to police officers detaining, harassing, and arresting African Americans and Latino Americans in situations where Euro-Americans are normally left alone. But "racial profiling" occurs throughout society, not just in police departments. It's a form of stereotyping that is acted out in discriminatory ways. Here are some examples of profiling:

- In retail stores, Euro-American who look affluent are eagerly waited on while Asian Americans may be ignored, and African Americans are followed around by store or security personnel to prevent shoplifting.
- In Euro-American neighborhoods, police are apt to detain African Americans just because they seem "out of place," meaning not in their own neighborhoods.
- In airports and at border crossings, Euro-Americans are the least likely to be detained or subjected to baggage or body searches.
- Arab Americans are the group most likely to be detained as possible terrorists.
- Latino American boys are the group most likely to be detained for possible gang activity or illegal immigration status.

Family Beliefs and Attitudes

Children learn about the world first from their families. Let's take ethnic stereotyping. Family environments that influence children toward stereotyping include these factors:

- Parents avoid discussing ethnic issues because they are too touchy.

- Friends who visit regularly are all of the same ethnic group.

- When people (friends, media persons) make prejudicial remarks, parents do not confront them.

- Children remain in segregated schools and play groups.

- Parents don't bother to point out the strengths and contributions of diverse cultures.

The Media

Rigid stereotypes are reinforced by television and radio programs, newspaper and magazine articles, and books by these practices:

- Showing minority group members in stereotypical roles.

- Failing to show minority group members in visible professional positions, such as news anchor, or in positive, leading roles in books, blogs, plays, series, situation comedies, and other programs.

- Allowing imbalanced coverage of minority communities, with more focus on criminal activities and tensions than on positive events and programs. Failing to portray the full range of a community's culture.

Schools

School systems and school cultures reinforce stereotyping, prejudice, and discrimination in these ways:

- Allowing an administration, faculty, or student body that's not as culturally diverse as the community at large.

- Promoting a learning environment that focuses on only one value system, normally middle-class mainstream Euro-American. (For example, promoting competition above cooperation, emphasizing future time emphasis over past or present, emphasizing individual achievement above group or team orientation.)

- Building the curriculum around European history and the dominant Euro-American culture, paying little attention to cultures of other Americans.

- Ignoring the need for education about ethnic and gender prejudice and discrimination.

In recent decades, there have been various initiatives to counter such sources of prejudice in U.S. educational systems, such as the Teaching Tolerance materials used in some K-12 schools (splc.org) and ethnic studies programs offered in some universities. For example, San Francisco State University has an entire College of Ethnic Studies, with departments offering minors and degree programs that focus on perspectives of African Americans, Asian Americans, Latino Americans, and American Indians (sfsu.edu).

The Workplace

The workplace and its corporate cultures reinforce stereotyping, prejudice, and discrimination in these ways:

- Allowing or imposing a glass ceiling that blocks nearly all minorities and women from top positions.

- Encouraging and rewarding only a middle-class and upper-class Euro-American-based value system and organizational culture.
- Tolerating subtle or overt discrimination at the workplace.

Civil rights laws have been somewhat effective in countering the workplace source of discrimination.

The Government

Behavior by the American government that reinforces discrimination includes these practices:

- Not passing, or watering down, equal rights legislation that is needed to promote fairness and equality for diverse groups.
- Halting or undermining affirmative action enforcement before such programs have achieved their purposes.
- Ignoring, minimizing, or downplaying harassment charges.

In some instances minority employees fare better in government jobs than in the private sector. For example, Democratic presidents have frequently issued executive orders designed to alleviate such discrimination. The platform of the Democratic Party in recent decades has strongly supported affirmative action, while the platform of the Republican Party speaks against it (DNC 2008; RNC 2008)

Churches

Research by G.W. Allport and J.M. Ross shows that many people actually equate bigotry with organized religion because religious views have so often been used as the basis for stereotyping and prejudice. Their research also indicates that churchgoers are more likely to be prejudiced.

Of course, not all churchgoers are prejudiced. Churches vary greatly in their beliefs about ethnic groups. Also, bigotry becomes a personal issue when religion becomes the excuse for ingroup superiority and for outgroup denigration. Such bigotry occurs for ego-related reasons.

Allport and Ross were surprised by their research findings, in the 1950s and 1960s, that the greater a Euro-American's commitment to religion, the more prejudiced against African Americans he or she tended to be. Some studies indicated that people with no religious affiliation showed on average less prejudice than did church members. This was puzzling since virtually all denominations are supposedly based upon love of others.

To explore further, Allport [1967] asked, "Why do people go to church in the first place?" His findings revealed two basic motivations: Extrinsically motivated members use their religion, and intrinsically motivated members live their religion.

Extrinsic religious motivation

Some people take a self-serving, manipulative approach to religion that conforms to social conventions. The primary value is to enjoy social acceptance and belonging. Church provides members with security, comfort, status, or social support and may mean belonging to a powerful, superior ingroup. This orientation is associated with prejudice toward outgroups.

Intrinsic religious motivation

Others value religion as a framework that gives meaning to life, a way of understanding all of life, and guidance for day-to-day living. The primary value is to "love thy neighbor," and there's no legitimate place for rejection, contempt, or condescension. The church's basic creed of brotherhood expresses an ideal that these members sincerely believe in. This orientation lends itself to tolerance and acceptance of all groups.

Many church members incorporate elements of both orientations. Some are there primarily for social reasons, but some deeper meaning also motivates them. Others are there for life meaning and guidance but also enjoy the social and supportive aspects. In the 1990s, G.W. Herek's [1994, 2001] analyses confirmed that prejudice or tolerance toward African Americans can be predicted with some accuracy by extrinsic or intrinsic religious motivation.

Herek's studies also indicate that, unlike prejudice toward African Americans, Euro-American prejudice toward gay persons can *not* be predicted on the basis of extrinsic or intrinsic orientation. The major predictor of whether a church member will harbor antigay prejudice is whether or not the church has a fundamentalist orientation. A major aspect of fundamentalism is a literal interpretation of the Bible. For example, when discussing beliefs about gay persons, church leaders and members tend to focus on a few Bible passages that they believe condemn homosexuality.

We Develop an Ethnic Identity

All of us achieve our identity from a period of exploration and experimentation that usually takes place in adolescence and often continues into early adulthood. Working through this exploration, we come to solidify our decisions and commitments regarding our career and occupations, lifestyle, sexual standards, politics, and philosophy of life or religion. We'll review how most Euro-Americans develop their identity as part of the ethnic majority in American culture. We'll also see how a minority person typically develops an ethnic identity. Both are summarized in Table 4.1.

TABLE 4.1: Developing an Ethnic Identity

Euro-Americans	Minority Persons
Little or no ethnic awareness	Identify with Euro-Americans
Ethnic conflict about prejudice	Encounter prejudice, search for own identity
Reaction or retreat from conflict	Attach to own culture
Balance identity to include minorities	Integrate, internalize ethnic identity

How Euro–Americans Develop a Majority Identity

Euro-Americans, or any dominant majority persons, normally experience an ethnic identity process that is different from that of the ethnic minority members. Now assume that you are a young Euro-American and mentally move through the stages of developing an ethnic identity.

Step 1. Before exposure and contact with ethnic differences

Euro-Americans tend to have low levels of ethnic identity development, which leads to acceptance of stereotypes about minority groups. (Thomas, Phillips, Brown 1998) Therefore, in the beginning you don't even think of yourself as an ethnic person. You unconsciously identify with being "a white person" in a culture where most minorities have darker skin coloring, and you accept stereotypes about minorities without questioning them.

Step 2. Ethnic conflict

As you mature, you become acquainted with people from other ethnic groups. You may have noticed that many or all of them don't fit the stereotypes you've held about them. Perhaps you've seen them excluded, castigated, and in many ways treated unfairly. You begin to question the stereotypes and to interact more with members of other groups.

You may experience conflict between wanting to go along with the beliefs and actions of your biased friends and relatives and wanting to treat minorities with respect and fairness, as essentially equal human beings. So you begin to reexamine many of your assumptions and beliefs about Euro-American people, which in turn leads you to challenge your accepted set of beliefs about "being white." You come face to face with minority issues and are challenged to acknowledge the continuing reality of prejudice in American society and your role in perpetuating the status quo. Key emotions that come up during this stage are confusion, guilt, anger, and perhaps even depression, all related to your belief that you have been a part of the prejudiced establishment. Your anger may be directed inward toward yourself as well as outward toward the dominant culture in general.

If you are male, you will deal with being part of a dominant group that discriminates against women as well as ethnic minorities. You'll face contradictions about how your mother, sister, or close friends and other relatives are viewed and treated by men in the culture. If you are female, you'll get in touch with the bifurcated position of being a member of the dominant ethnic group and at the same time a member of the disadvantaged gender group. On one hand, you'll begin to deal with being part of a system where you have the power to exclude others. On the other hand, you'll probably begin to notice commonalties of women's situation with that of other disadvantaged groups.

Step 3. Reaction or retreat

As a member of the dominant majority, you'll probably have one of two reactions to the feelings that came up in step 2.

- *Reaction.* You take a strong stand for minority issues. You begin to fight or resist the prejudice you see around you and to identify with disadvantaged groups. You feel compassion and empathy for them, which somewhat offsets the feelings of confusion and guilt you were experiencing.

- *Retreat.* You avoid situations that cause you to feel confusion and conflict. You back off from any sort of inter-ethnic contact, returning to the comfort, security, and familiarity of your own culture. You decide life is just easier and less complicated that way. You over-identify with "being white" and feel defensive about the dominant culture. You may fear minorities and feel angry about their behavior.

Step 4. Balancing self-identity to include minorities

At some point, you may mature into a more balanced and healthy ethnic identity, especially if you chose the reaction route in step 3. As you develop a positive ethnic self-identity, you are likely to eventually realize the positive attributes of people outside your group (Chrobot-Mason 2004). You acknowledge that as a member of the dominant culture, you share responsibility for maintaining prejudice. At the same time you identify with the larger holistic American culture and with a non-prejudiced Euro-American viewpoint: Not all of us want to perpetuate the status quo. You can see positive and negative beliefs and actions in your own group, as well as in minority groups. You now turn your energy and attention to equality issues and become committed to fighting all forms of oppression. You feel flexible and open to learning more about all cultures, including your own.

How Minority Persons Develop an Ethnic Identity

Members of ethnic minorities are bicultural, having an American cultural identity and also an ethnic subcultural identity. Therefore, their process is different from that of Euro-Americans. Put yourself in the role of a young minority person and follow the typical identity development process through four stages.

Step 1. Identifying with the Euro-American majority

At some point in your life, usually as a young teenager before you've had a turning-point inter-ethnic encounter, you're almost certain to identify primarily with the Euro-American majority culture. You prefer their ways of thinking and acting; that is, their standards, norms, and values. It may be that you simply view your ethnic identity as unimportant. Perhaps your unexamined preferences and commitments are based on your parents' values.

Step 2. Gaining minority awareness, encountering prejudice, searching for identity

Somewhere along the line, you become painfully aware of your status as a minority in a prejudicial society. This awareness may be raised either by a single dramatic encounter with an oppressive or prejudicial experience, or it may grow out of an accumulation of more subtle experiences. This awareness triggers a period when you question your status and the values of the dominant culture. You also begin a search for your own ethnic identity.

You're likely to feel confused, embarrassed, and angry. You begin to develop positive prejudice toward your own ethnic group and negative prejudice toward the Euro-American majority. (This phase is especially difficult for children whose father is from a different ethnic group than the mother.) Your negative prejudice is just forming, so you probably don't act it out in prejudiced behavior yet. But you do become tired of the Euro-American system and you want to strengthen your bonds with your own ethnic group, to really belong and feel a part of that culture. You may feel some confusion about teaming up with members of other minority groups.

Step 3. Identifying with and attaching to your own culture

If you've come into adulthood within the past thirty years, you're especially likely to have entered a phase where you committed yourself to your own ethnic group and immersed yourself in that culture. In this stage you endorse the beliefs, values, norms, and customs of your own group, while completely rejecting values and norms of the Euro-American establishment.

This stage is the most intensely emotional. You're certain to direct anger and even rage toward the majority. You feel intense loyalty and pride toward your own group, so much so that you tend to idealize and romanticize your group. Now you're more likely to act in a prejudiced way toward Euro-Americans than in any stage. You're likely to have a separatist attitude; you may participate in political action that calls attention to minority issues; and you may even act out your rage in a violent manner.

Step 4. Integrating and internalizing your ethnic identity

At this stage you do a more realistic reassessment and reappraisal of your own minority culture, the dominant Euro-American culture, and your role in the scheme of things. Out of this reappraisal, you develop a more balanced bicultural identity that integrates the best of both cultures (your minority culture and the dominant Euro-American culture). You internalize this bicultural identity, making it a part of your belief system. If your mother and father come from different minority cultures, then you must develop a multicultural identity, integrating both minority cultures with the dominant culture.

You've run through the intense emotion of the previous phase. The major characteristic of this stage is the development of a secure ethnic identity along with an appreciation of other cultures. Now you're likely to direct your commitment toward cooperative alliances with committed people from the mainstream culture, from your own minority group, and from other minority groups in order to change discriminatory policies and practices. You're likely to work within the mainstream culture to bring about peaceful change.

How Immigrant Minorities Adapt to the American Culture

Immigrants to the United States typically go through four phases: 1) high-conflict, 2) resolution, 3) marginal, and 4) new identity (Lee 1997).

The high-conflict phase usually lasts about two years, when immigrants are aware of ways in which their native cultural values and practices are in conflict with American ways. They typically must deal with a language barrier, unemployment or underemployment, social isolation, and culture shock.

The resolution phase occurs during the next two to 10 years or more. Immigrants are trying to resolve the culture shock problems they started experiencing in the first phase. They begin to become Americanized to some extent. Immigrant children adapt much more quickly than their parents, and cultural barriers between parents and children may arise.

The marginal phase occurs as immigrants become satisfied with their lives and begin to identify as an American in some regards. However, they still retain many aspects of their native culture and therefore may feel that they do not really belong in either cultural group. They feel socially "marginal."

The new-identity phase occurs when, and if, immigrants develop a sense of new identity. For example, a Vietnamese immigrant becomes comfortable saying, "I am Vietnamese American. I am an American, and I am also of Vietnamese heritage." They become more certain of who they are, where they came from, and what they want in the future. They feel less marginal and more accepted for who they are.

We Form Ingroups

Even before we develop an ethnic identity, we identify with one or more ingroups. Part of the process of developing an ethnic identity is forming ingroups. What we're familiar with tends to become a value. The familiar provides the indispensable basis of our existence. As early as age five, children develop a fierce sense of loyalty to their ingroup. Members of an ingroup all use the term *we* with the same essential significance. Ingroup memberships are not set in concrete. At times people have reason to claim one category of membership, and at other times a different or slightly larger category, depending on their need to look good or be accepted.

No doubt, you've noticed that certain people in your ingroup squabble among themselves all the time. But if one of them is attacked by someone from outside the group, the former squabblers may join together in defending against or attacking the outgroup enemy. Likewise, two groups that formerly fought each other may join together to fight a third group, a common enemy. In this way members may modify their ingroups to fit their needs. When the needs call for hostile action, the purpose of the newly formed ingroup may be action against a hated outgroup.

The term *ingroup* indicates the sheer fact that you're a member of a group, while the term *reference group* indicates whether you cherish that membership or whether you seek to relate yourself with another group. The terms help us to identify two levels of belongingness. A reference group may be either

- an ingroup that you're happy you belong to, or
- another group that you'd like to belong to.

Some people are always comparing themselves with groups which for them are not ingroups. Some minority persons tend to mold their attitudes around those of the dominant majority, which for them may be a reference group. The dominant majority exerts a strong pull on minorities, often forcing them to conform to majority attitudes. This conformity, however, rarely goes so far as a minority rejecting her or his own ingroup. It does explain, however, why women and minorities sometimes echo the opinions of Euro-American men even when such opinions are against the best interests of women and minorities.

Ingroup memberships are vitally important to individual survival. Through memberships we form a web of habits. When we meet outsiders who follow different customs, we tend to unconsciously say, "They break my habits." Habit-breaking is unpleasant because we tend to prefer the familiar. Most of us feel a bit on guard when other people seem to threaten or even question our habits. Attitudes partial to the ingroup, or to the reference group, do not necessarily require that attitudes toward other groups be antagonistic—even though hostility often helps to intensify the ingroup cohesion. Narrow circles can, without conflict, be supplemented by larger circles of loyalty. Allport (1954) noted that this happy condition is not often achieved, but it remains from the psychological viewpoint a hopeful possibility.

We Become Ethnocentric

Ethnocentrism can lead to prejudice, but does not always do so. While prejudice assumes different groups are inferior, ethnocentrism assumes your own group is superior. It's a part of developing an ethnic identity. While ethnocentric attitudes are widespread in human society and seem to reflect a universal tendency, studies indicate that Euro-American managers are more ethnocentric than their counterparts in Britain, Australia, and mainland Europe (Ijzendoorn 1980).

> *Ethnocentrism is the belief that your ethnic group is superior to all others.*

Ethnocentrism is a form of ingroup/outgroup bias. Two related factors stand out:

- Such bias can be based on nearly any group identity, such as blue eyes or brown eyes, and does not necessarily imply a long history of prejudice.
- It's a milder form of ingroup favoritism than the more extreme forms of hostile bigotry that are usually associated with prejudice and discrimination.

In her landmark experiment with school children, Jane Elliott (1985) was able to create the main dimensions of ethnocentric behavior in a matter of hours on the basis of a group separation that was essentially arbitrary—whether a child had blue eyes or brown eyes.

Research provides evidence that dominant group members tend to believe that when outgroup people succeed, it's because they got help or got lucky, but when ingroup members succeed, it's because they deserved it, earned it, and had the right traits and skills. In other words, Euro-American males tend to think that when their own succeed in the workplace, it's because of internal traits, but when others succeed, it's because of external circumstances.

Ethnocentrism in the workplace has made it difficult for people other than Euro-American males to make it to the top. For example, several studies indicate that the major barrier is the tendency for Euro-American males at the top to be more comfortable with their own kind (Morrison, White, and Van Velsor 1987; Carr-Ruffino 1991).

Ethnocentrism is a human tendency that offers several benefits. If you decide to stick with your ingroup:

- You can better predict and understand others' behavior, because they're like you.
- It's easier to figure out why others in the group do what they do.
- It's easier to establish rapport and build a relationship.
- You're more likely to help others, because people are more likely to help others like themselves than to help "strangers."

People who are high in authoritarian and rigid personality traits and low in moral development tend to be more ethnocentric. They tend to be less tolerant toward, and hold less favorable attitudes toward, members of outgroups, especially minority group members (Ijzendoorn 1989; Brewer 1979; Clark 1975; Greenhaus 1991).

People who are more open and flexible enjoy a different set of advantages. When you're comfortable and open to interacting with people from outgroups:

You get to expand your experience and knowledge of other people and cultures.

- You make your work more interesting, exciting, and intriguing.
- You increase your ability to relate to many types of people.
- You boost your social and leadership skills.
- You become more cosmopolitan.

We Are Part of a Diverse, Rapidly Changing Society

We learn prejudice from our culture, and the United States provides the ideal climate for this, simply because of its current situation. Research shows that the following conditions provide fertile ground for prejudice to develop—and can exacerbate or intensify existing prejudice in a culture (Ponteretto and Pedersen 1993).

- The society is heterogeneous.
- Upward mobility is allowed and valued.

- Social change is occurring rapidly.
- Communication barriers and ignorance between groups are common.
- A minority group is large or increasing.
- An increasing minority represents direct competition and a realistic threat.
- Exploitation of minorities sustains important interests.
- Customs regulating aggression are favorable to bigotry.
- Traditional justifications for ethnocentrism are available.
- Neither assimilation nor cultural pluralism is favored

This reads like a current description of American society. We're the most heterogeneous society on earth, and a key value is the opportunity for people to move up if they learn the ropes and work hard. Social change, and every other type of change, is occurring rapidly, especially the family changes caused by women pursuing careers. We've been a segmented society and de facto segregation is still common. Barriers to communication result in ignorance about other groups, which make them easy prey to rumor, suspicion, and stereotype. This process is most likely to occur if the group is also regarded as a potential threat because it is growing and its members are competing with the dominant group in the job market. Internal colonialism has sustained privilege for Euro-Americans, bigotry has been a part of U.S. history, and ethnocentrism is still creating barriers in the workplace. Finally, we're in a state of flux and transition regarding assimilation versus cultural pluralism, both in our corporations and in our communities. Immigrants have found themselves criticized both for maintaining their cultural ways and for pressing for assimilation.

In this section, we've addressed the question, How do we become prejudiced? A review of the processes and influences may leave you wondering, How could we not be prejudiced? The legacy of the patriarchal family teaches us about the inequality and stereotyped roles of men and women just by its very existence. From the cradle, this is part of our enculturation. And the organizations we encounter when we leave our homes have virtually all been founded on the basis of inequality and stereotyped roles. Some psychologists note that prejudice and discrimination at the top level of a society, or an organization, set into motion a continuing cycle of prejudice and discrimination throughout every part (Ponteretto and Pedersen 1993). We can see, then, that prejudice is woven into the very tapestry of our culture. The people with the most influence in sustaining or breaking the cycle are parents in the home and leaders in organizations.

HOW DO PEOPLE EXPRESS PREJUDICE?

When someone is prejudiced, how do you know it? People may express prejudice by denying it or rationalizing it, by acting it out in various ways from mild to devastating, by subtly discriminating, or by using outgroup members as scapegoats.

They Deny and Rationalize

Two common ways of handling the inner conflict that arises when people discriminate against others are:

- *denial*: repressing the conflict by denying the prejudice
- *rationalization*: offering defenses for the prejudice, justifying it

People often choose denial because if they admit prejudice, they admit to being both irrational and unethical. No one wants their conscience to bother them all the time. So it's not unusual to hear the person we perceive as being quite prejudiced saying, "I'm not prejudiced, but. . . ."

The most obvious way for people to defend prejudiced beliefs is to gather evidence in their favor. People may select only that evidence that supports their stereotypes. When we rationalize, we may:

- See only those traits, actions, and events that confirm a decision we've already made, and we simply fail to notice those that don't

- Say it must be true because other people think this way too. "Everybody thinks those people are sneaky" (. . . dirty, stupid, rude), claiming truth by consensus.

- Blame the targets or shift the blame back onto our accusers. "It's their own fault they don't get ahead" (. . . that others shun them, etc.) or "They're just as prejudiced as we are."

- Defend our thinking or action by saying it's the exception to our usual pattern. "Some of my best friends are Platians, but. . . ."

They Act Out

We act out our prejudice toward people from an unfavored group with varying degrees of hostile energy. Talking against such people involves relatively little energy, while actively avoiding them takes more. Stepping up the energy level, we may discriminate against them, physically attack them, or in a rare extreme of hostile energy, participate in exterminating them. While some people would never move to a more intense degree of action, for others activity on one level makes it easier to move to a more intense level.

Talking against

People usually talk against those from outgroups when they're with like-minded friends, and occasionally with strangers. People sometimes disparage an outgroup in order to cement their relationship as part of their ingroup. Talking against includes joking or disparaging comments that express a mild animosity. Name-calling expresses a more intense hostility. The more spontaneous and irrelevant the talking against, the stronger the hostility that lies behind it.

Physically attacking

Actual physical attacks on outgroup members, and other acts of violence or semi-violence, occur far less frequently than the milder expressions of prejudice. However, violent incidents are increasing both in the workplace and in the community, especially against women. They usually occur when people become overwrought and overemotional. However, violence may be calculated to create a reign of terror, to teach others to stay in their place, or to otherwise punish or threaten.

An FBI report cited more than 7,600 hate crimes in 2006. The total falls far short of the full picture because police forces representing 44 percent of the population did not even report hate crimes. Crimes against people accounted for 70 percent of the offenses reported. The most common targets:

African Americans	2,500
Euro-Americans	1,300
Jewish Americans	1,054
Gay persons	777

Offenders were unknown in 42 percent of cases. Of the known offenders, 51 percent were Euro-American and 35 percent African American (FBI.gov).

Although many of the reported incidents occurred at or near the workplace, the actual prevalence of such events is difficult to determine. The U.S. Dept of Labor concluded that homicide is the third-leading cause of fatal occupational injury, and minority groups have a higher risk than majority group members. For example, 32 percent of victims are African Americans and Asian American, although they are less than 17 percent of U.S. population (BLS 2006). Rubenstein's studies (2004) indicate that African Americans, Jews, and gay persons are at higher risk for hate crimes than people from other groups. This study found that 18 gay persons per 100,000 reported hate crimes, compared to 8 African Americans per 100,000.

They Subtly Discriminate

It's not attractive to express prejudice in many social circles, and it can be illegal in the workplace. Therefore, most prejudice today is of the covert and subtle form, sometimes classified as the avoidance prejudice of the liberals and the symbolic prejudice of the conservatives. Psychologically, if you hold your prejudiced beliefs out of conscious awareness, you can hold onto your self-concept as a non-prejudiced, egalitarian person. You can swear you're not prejudiced and define prejudice as an intentional, overt act, the old-fashioned type of prejudice (Blanchard and Crosby 1989).

Avoidance Prejudice among Liberals

A subtle form of prejudice among liberals is called "avoidance prejudice" by some researchers. It refers to avoidance of violating laws, rules, and policies against discrimination. Even though liberals are all for equality and consider themselves unprejudiced, some possess negative feelings and beliefs about minority groups. Because such people hold egalitarian values and see themselves as tolerant, they usually won't discriminate against other ethnic groups in situations where the policies and procedures describing appropriate behavior are clear and unambiguous. To do so would directly threaten their egalitarian self-image. When the rules of the game are weak, ambiguous, or conflicting, or if such persons can justify or rationalize a negative response on the basis of some factor other than ethnicity, many will discriminate, while holding onto their egalitarian self-image. Business leaders can reduce discrimination within the organization, therefore, by developing clear policies and procedures for the treatment of people from diverse groups. At least that portion of discriminatory behavior that is based on avoidance prejudice will be reduced.

Symbolic Prejudice among Conservatives

Subtle prejudice among conservatives is often called "symbolic prejudice." It refers to citing principles or practices that have the effect of indirectly discriminating. These conservatives believe that discrimination no longer exists. They also believe that minority groups are violating our cherished American values and are still making unwarranted demands for changing the status quo. According to symbolic prejudice theory, many Euro-Americans acquire negative feelings toward other ethnic groups early in life. These feelings persist into adulthood but are expressed indirectly and symbolically.

Modern conservatives tend to express their prejudice in such symbolic ways as opposition to affirmative action or sexual harassment policies, rather than directly or overtly, as in support for segregation. Although they reject traditional racist beliefs, they displace their prejudicial feelings onto more rationalizable abstract social and political issues, such as "family values" and "school voucher systems." People who practice symbolic prejudice, like those who practice avoidance prejudice, are therefore relatively unaware of their prejudicial feelings.

They Scapegoat

Most societies seem to encourage, officially or unofficially, the open expression of hostility toward certain groups that serve as scapegoats or safety valves for anger and aggression. Scapegoating is a form of group projection that helps groups to remain ethnocentric by projecting members' shortcoming and failures upon outgroups, blaming them for the ingroup's problems. In addition, most nations have numerous chauvinistic devices that breed ethnocentrism. For example, virtually no history book ever teaches that one's country was ever in the wrong. Geography is usually taught with a nationalistic bias, and claims to achievements in science and the arts are often overblown.

SUMMARY

The third step in gaining multicultural skills is recognizing your own biases, the ways in which you stereotype, assume, judge, and discriminate. Stereotyping is prejudging or assuming certain traits and characteristics about people, based on their ethnic group or other category, and rigid stereotypes lead to prejudice. Prejudice is our tendency to view people who are different as being inferior, while ethnocentricity is the tendency to think your own cultural group is superior. When we discriminate, we act out our prejudice in ways that disadvantage people from disparaged groups.

Although most prejudice is called either *racism* or *sexism*, most anthropologists agree that race has little or no meaning as a practical concept. *Ethnic prejudice* is a more appropriate term. On the other hand, sexism is said by some to be the root of all prejudice because it begins in the home.

How do we become prejudiced? Virtually every aspect of our culture teaches us to be prejudiced, from the differential in mother's and father's status and other family beliefs to the media, schools, workplace, government, and religious organizations. As children grow up, they develop an ethnic identity. Euro-American children usually become aware of ethnic differences after some type of ethnic conflict. They may react by defending minorities or by avoiding future contact with them. Minority children usually identify first with the Euro-American majority until they encounter prejudice and begin searching for their own identity. They may develop resentment toward Euro-Americans or become ashamed of being a minority. Most eventually identify with their own cultural subgroup and later integrate aspects of both cultures.

Prejudice and ethnocentrism are related to the human tendency to form ingroups. A reference group is either your ingroup, if you're happy you belong to it, or another group you want to belong to. People who are most ethnocentric and prejudiced tend to also be most rigid and authoritarian.

The authoritarian person is the most-studied aspect of personality. Such persons believe in strict categories of right and wrong, good and bad, and other black/white opposites. They tend to be intolerant of weakness, highly punishing, suspicious, and extremely respectful of authority. People develop either a relatively authoritarian or relatively open, flexible personality in childhood but can choose to change at any age. The United States provides fertile ground for prejudice to grow because it is an increasingly diverse society, still relatively segregated, and in the midst of rapid change.

How do we express prejudice? Most people are unaware of their prejudices, and denying or justifying prejudice is a typical way of handling the inner conflict that prejudice often creates. People may act out their prejudice in varying degrees of hostility, from talking against others or avoiding them to discriminating against them, physically attacking them, or even participating in programs to exterminate them. People who are unaware of their prejudices may express them quite subtly. Liberals tend to use avoidance prejudice and avoid discriminating when there are clear policies and procedures prohibiting discrimination. Conservatives tend to resort to symbolic prejudice, supporting an indirect method of bringing about discriminatory results. For example, they might oppose affirmative action but not advocate a return to legal segregation. Disparaged groups are often used as scapegoats so the dominant group can retain its belief in its superiority.

Case Study 4.1: Matthew: Fired Before He Got Started

Matthew Cusick is a highly trained acrobat. His dream was to work with the unique and top-rated acrobatic circus show Cirque du Soleil. From time to time, he applied for a job with Cirque but never got to the point of a job interview. Finally, in 2002 he made it through the hiring hoops to the interview stage. He was thrilled, joyful, but a little anxious. Matthew had been diagnosed as HIV positive several years ago, but the medications were controlling the condition, and he led a reasonably normal life. He decided to be honest about his condition, if asked. The subject didn't come up during the interviews, and Matthew was hired. He got his dream assignment, the Las Vegas production Mystere, so he was definitely on Cloud Nine, but first he must undergo several months of intense training before joining the troupe.

When Matthew reported for training, Cirque's physiotherapy specialists asked him if there were any health conditions that might be a factor in the rigorous training he would be undergoing. At this point Matthew volunteered information about his HIV condition, and reassured them that it did not affect his strength and stamina. Cirque asked him to visit designated doctors so that they could assess his HIV; they in turn reported that he was a "healthy athlete."

Matthew completed the months of intense training, and was ready to take his place with the Mystere troupe. At this point, Cirque managers called him into their office. They told Matthew that after much agonizing, they had decided to let him go. "We are just afraid of the possibility that you might transmit HIV to others in the troupe. We must protect our other employees from the known safety hazards of this disease." Matthew was devastated. He tried to reason with the managers, but they refused to reconsider.

1. What are they key issues in this case?
2. What do you think of the Cirque decision to fire Matthew?
3. What do you think Matthew should do?

*Gorenberg, Hayley, "Confronting HIV Discrimination in the Workplace: A Case Study," *Human Rights* 31, 4, 16-19, Fall 2004.

REFERENCES

Allport, G.W. *The Nature of Prejudice*. Addison-Wesley, 1954.

Allport, G.W., and J.M. Ross. "Personal Religious Orientation and Prejudice." *Journal of Personality and Social Psychology* 5, 432–443, 1967.

Allport, G.W., and B.M. Kramer. "Some Roots of Prejudice," *Journal of Psychology* 22, 9–19, 27, 1946.

Associated Press, "Study Says White Families' Wealth Advantage Has Grown"

Barrick, M.R. and M.K. Mount, "The Big Five Personality Dimensions and Job Performance: A Meta-Analysis, *Personnel Psychology* 44, 1–26, 1991.

Baskerville, D.M., and S.H. Tucker. "A Blueprint for Success." *Black Enterprise*, 85–92, November, 1991.

Blanchard, F.A., and F. J. Crosby. *Affirmative Action in Perspective*. Springer-Verlag, 1989.

Brewer, M.B. "Ingroup Bias in the Minimal Intergroup Situation," *Psychological Bulletin* 86 307–24, 1979.

BLS, Bureau of Labor Statistics, "Injuries, Illnesses, and Fatalities," www.bls.gov/iif/home.htm, 2006.

Catalyst. *Women in Corporate Management*. Catalyst, 2004.

Chrobot-Mason, D. "Managing Racial Differences: The Role of Majority Managers," *Hispanic Journal of Behavioral Sciences* 26, 1, 36–59, 2004.

Clark, C.X. "Race, Life Style, and Rule Flexibility." *Organizational Behavior and Human Performance* 13, 433–443, 1975.

Cox, Taylor. *Cultural Diversity in Organizations*. Berrett-Koehler, 1993.

DNC Democratic Party Platform, (regarding AA) p.5, www.democrats.org/a/party/platform.html, 2008.

Ekehammar, B. et al, "What Matters Most to Prejudice: Big Five Personality, Social Dominance Orientation, or Right-Wing Authoritarianism? *European Journal of Personality* 18, 463–482, 2004

FBI, Federal Bureau of Investigation, "Behind the Numbers: Hate Crimes Task Force Nets Results," www.fbi.gov April 10, 2006.

FBI, Federal Bureau of Investigation, "Crime in the United States," www.fbi.gov, 2004

Feagin, Joe R., *Racist America: Roots, Current Realities and Future Reparations*, Routledge, 2001.

Feagin, Joe R., and Clairece Booher Feagin. *Discrimination American Style: Institutional Racism and Sexism*. Prentice-Hall, 1978.

Friedland, N., G. Keinan and T. Tytiun, "The Relationship between Basic Assumptions, Posttraumatic Growth," *Journal of Research in Personality* 25, 88–107, 1999.

Gadamer, Hans-Georg. *Truth and Methods*, rev. ed., Crossroad, 1989.

Greenhaus, J.H., and S. Parasuraman. "Job Performance Attributions and Career Advancement Prospects" in *Organizational Behavior and Human Decision Processes*. Academic Press, 1991.

Herek, G.M. "Assessing Heterosexuals' Attitudes" in *Lesbian and Gay Psychology*. Sage, 1994.

Herek, G.M. Ed. "The Hidden Costs of Hidden Stigma," in *The Social Psychology of Stigma*. Guilford Press 2000

Holmes, Robyn. *How Young Children Perceive Race*. Sage, 1995.

Hopson, Darlene and Derek. *Raising the Rainbow Generation*. Simon & Schuster, 1993.

Ijzendoorn, M.H. "Moral Judgement, Authoritarianism, and Ethnocentrism." *Journal of Social Psychology* 129, 1, 37–45, 1989.

Jackson, J.A., & Poulsen, J.R. "Contact experiences mediate the relationship between five-factor model personality traits and ethnic prejudice," *Journal of Applied Social Psychology*, 35, 667–685, 2005.

James, L.R. and M.D.Mazerolle, *Personality in Work Organizations*. Sage, 2002.

Lee, Evelyn. *Working with Asian Americans*. Guilford Press, 1997.

Levin, Brian and Sara-Ellen Amster, "Making Hate History: Hate Crime and Policing in America's Most Diverse City," *American Behavioral Scientist*, 51, 2, 319–348, 2007.

Loury, G.C. *The Anatomy of Racial Inequality*. Harvard University Press, 2002.

McIntosh, Peggy. *White Privilege and Male Privilege*. Working Paper 189. Wellesley, MA: Center for Research on Women, 1988.

Montagu, Ashley. *Man's Most Dangerous Myth*. AltaMira Press, 1997.

NORC, National Opinion Survey Center, University of Chicago, "How Do Americans View One Another? The Persistence of Racial/Ethnic Stereotypes," *Diversity Digest*. www.diversityweb.org, 2000.

Pew Hispanic Research Center. Report. 2005.

Ponterotto, Joseph G. et al. *Handbook of Multicultural Counseling*. Sage, 2001.

Ponterotto, Joseph G. and Paul B. Pederson. *Preventing Prejudice*. Sage, 1993.

"Race is Not A Biological Distinction," *San Francisco Chronicle*, A-1, 4, February 23, 1998.

Ridley, C.R. "Racism in Counseling as an Adverse Behavioral Process" in *Counseling Across Cultures*, 3rd ed. University of Hawaii Press, 1989.

RNC. Republican National Committee Platform (regarding AA), 51–52, http://platform.gop.com, 2008.

Rubenstein, William B., "The Real Story of U.S. Hate Crimes Statistics," *Tulane Law Review*, 78, 1213–1246, 2004.

Sidanius, James, F. Pratto and J.L. Rabinowitz, "Gender, ethnic status, and ideological asymmetry: A social dominance perspective," *Journal of Cross-Cultural Psychology*, 25, 194–216, 1994.

Smith, W.T. *Ethnic Images*. National Opinion Research Center, GSS Topical Report No. 19. University of Chicago, December, 1990.

Snyder, Mark, "The Self-Monitoring of Expressive Behavior," *Journal of Personality and Social Psychology* 30, 4, 526–537, 1974.

Takaki, Ronald. *A Different Mirror: A History of Multicultural America*. Little, Brown & Co., 1994.

Thomas, K.M., L.D. Phillips and S. Brown, "Redefining Race in the Workplace: Insights from Ethnic Identity Theory, *Journal of Black Psychology* 24, 76–92, 1998.

RESOURCES

Center for the Study of Hate & Extremism, Professor Brian Levin, Director, College of Social and Behavioral Sciences, Department of Criminal Justice, California State University, San Bernardino, 5500 University Parkway, San Bernardino, CA 92407

Hate Crimes Research Network, www.hatecrime.net

Southern Poverty Law Center, Teaching Tolerance materials for K-12 schools. www.splcenter.org

Feedback: Self–Awareness Activity 4.4

R = Rigid, authoritarian personality

O = Open, flexible personality

Instructions:

- To get your R score, add up all the R questions you answered true and all the O questions you answered false.

- To get your O score, add up all the O questions you answered true and all the R questions you answered false.
- Compare your R and O scores to assess your relative levels of openness and rigidity.

1.	R	I have little or no difficulty decided what's right and what's wrong.
2.	O	I thrive on variety and change.
3.	O	I often enjoy being with people that some would call strange or weird.
4.	R	I like my routines.
5.	R	I know how I feel about most situations and don't need to keep thinking about them.
6.	R	I need to know exactly where I'm going and when.
7.	O	I often ask myself why I did certain things, or why I think or feel as I do.
8.	R	I hate it when people change our plans.
9.	R	There is only one right way to do most things.
10.	O	Few actions are totally right or wrong; most actions stem from complex situations and have varying effects.
11.	R	I prefer to focus on a few simple things rather than a wide variety.
12.	O	I can feel comfortable with most situations, even if I'm not sure about what's going on.
13.	O	I don't always agree with people from other groups, but I usually understand why they might think and feel as they do.
14.	O	People basically create the life they have and the sooner they take responsibility for it, the better it will be.
15.	O	I think I know my own strengths and shortcomings pretty well.
16.	R	Most actions can be classified as either proper or improper.
17.	O	People have different ideas about what's proper and improper; that's fine with me.
18.	R	I don't start a job until I know exactly how to do it.
19.	O	I'm comfortable "feeling my way" through a task, if necessary.
20.	R	I need to know what's going on and what to expect at all times.

Workplace Discrimination: Its Effects and Remedies

Prejudiced persons' thinking patterns tend to block their own happiness and zest for life—holding onto prejudice creates a joy drain.
M.D. Kite, 1986

You're probably aware that to be a valuable employee or business associate, you must move beyond the stereotypes and prejudices that exclude whole groups of people. This involves learning how to bridge the divisive walls of prejudice—and showing others the way. Doing so can bring huge rewards—to you in building success skills and profitable workplace relationships and to your company as you work more productively with people from diverse backgrounds. In this chapter you'll learn about:

- How prejudice affects people generally and in the workplace
- How discrimination specifically affects employees' chances to be hired and promoted
- How handling workplace discrimination has changed over time
- How people can move beyond prejudice and discrimination to valuing differences and building relationships that promote profitable collaboration

Before you delve further into the complexities of prejudice, complete Self-Awareness Activity 5.1.

Self-Awareness Activity 5.1: What Do You Know About Discrimination?

Purpose: To see what you know about the issues covered in this chapter.
Instructions: Determine whether you think the following statements are basically true or false—and think about why. The answers will emerge in this chapter, and the summary at the end of the chapter focuses on these issues.

1. Being prejudiced affects the personality of the holder as well as the receiver of the prejudice.
2. Members of disparaged groups become resentful toward others.
3. The melting-pot approach to managing diversity is effective for overcoming discrimination.
4. Affirmative action programs normally include quotas for hiring minorities.

5.   Affirmative action has been much more powerful than equal employment opportunity for reducing discrimination.

6.   A major leadership challenge is realizing that if people simply have contact with one another on a regular basis, prejudice will be dramatically reduced.

HOW DOES PREJUDICE AFFECT PEOPLE?

Prejudice affects the personalities of the persons who hold the prejudice as well as those on the receiving end. You can work more effectively with people who are prejudiced if you understand the ways that prejudiced thinking influences their life views and their day-to-day actions. You can relate more constructively to people from groups that have traditionally been disparaged in the mainstream culture when you understand how their life experiences may be influencing their behavior patterns.

Effects of Rejecting Others

When you stereotype and reject others as not good enough, the immediate payoff is feeling "better-than," but it's a cheap thrill. After all, the more time you spend with stereotyped, prejudiced, and discriminatory thoughts, the more time you spend in a critical, blaming, judging state of mind. It follows that you'll spend less time in an appreciative, enthusiastic, or joyous state of mind.

   The more prejudiced you are, the more you view life through a negative lens. The more your thoughts focus on distaste, dislike, resentment, revulsion, anger, and similar feelings, the more likely you are to experience the anxiety and fear of being despised by others, because that way of thinking is prominent in your experience. Your world becomes more hierarchical, with everyone becoming categorized as better or worse, and people always judging and comparing. You have less space in your mind and less time for the beauty, the joy, the love, the wonder of other beings. As prejudice becomes a habit, you may become more and more critical, and therefore you become more and more isolated because there are fewer and fewer people you can enjoy. You block the possibility of knowing a large part of the world's people with their fascinating variety because you choose to judge so many of them as too strange or not good enough.

Effects of Being Rejected

Feeling rejected and inferior is difficult to deal with, even if you're a Euro-American male. It's more difficult if you're a woman because you're told in thousands of subtle or blatant ways throughout your life that you're inferior in most life areas—just because you were born a woman. If you're a minority, you're not only told that you're inferior, you're frequently rejected—just because you were born into an "inferior" subgroup. The message that you're inferior cannot be hammered into your head day after day without doing something to your character. It may cause you to examine who you really are, to accept yourself, and to become a stronger person for it. Or it may cause you to develop defensive coping behaviors. These persecution-produced traits are not all unpleasant. Some people, even when they're in reaction to rejection, are able to overcome the human tendency to lash out against the unfairness of a dominant majority and to choose responses that are constructive and socially agreeable (Ponteretto and Pedersen 1993; Allport 1954).

   Just which ego defenses people develop is largely an individual matter, often coming out of choices made at an unconscious level but sometimes decided upon consciously. At one extreme, you'll find minority group members who seem to handle their status easily, with little evidence that their outgroup affiliation is of any concern to them. At the other extreme, you'll find people so rebellious that they have developed many ugly defenses, so that they continually provoke the very snubs they resent. Most people you meet fall somewhere between these extremes, showing some mixture of acceptance and resistance to their status.

   Only to a slight extent can we say that certain types of ego defense will be more common in one outgroup than in another. Every form of ego defense may be found among people of every disparaged group. Allport developed the model shown in Figure 5.1, which distinguishes between ego defenses that cause us to strike out at other persons from those that we turn inward to punish ourselves.

FIGURE 5.1: Model of Responses to Discrimination

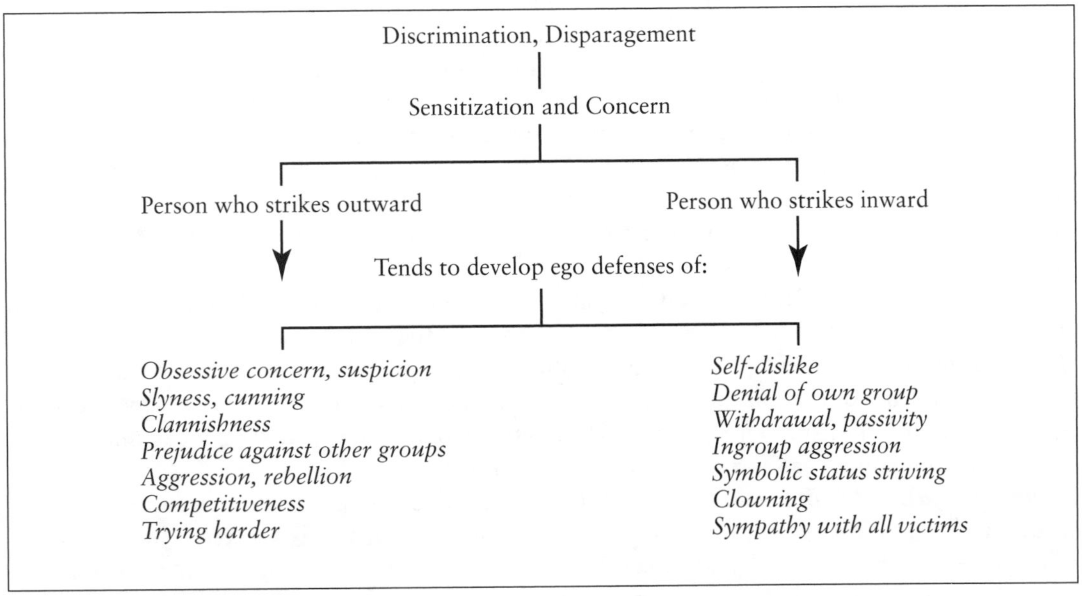

```
                    Discrimination, Disparagement
                                |
                      Sensitization and Concern
            ┌───────────────────┴───────────────────┐
   Person who strikes outward              Person who strikes inward
            │                                        │
            ▼       Tends to develop ego defenses of: ▼
            ┌───────────────────┴───────────────────┐

   Obsessive concern, suspicion          Self-dislike
   Slyness, cunning                      Denial of own group
   Clannishness                          Withdrawal, passivity
   Prejudice against other groups        Ingroup aggression
   Aggression, rebellion                 Symbolic status striving
   Competitiveness                       Clowning
   Trying harder                         Sympathy with all victims
```

Adapted from Allport, 1954.

Ego Defenses That Strike Outward

The basic feeling of members of disparaged groups is one of insecurity, which may lead to being on guard and hypersensitive. Minorities must make many more adjustments to their status than majority members. The latter interact mainly with their own kind and only occasionally with minority group members. The reverse is true for most minorities. In addition, they are more likely to be in a less-powerful position than each of the dominant group members they meet. Preoccupation with the strain of accommodation may become excessive, so that they come to view virtually all members of the dominant group with deep suspicion.

Obsessive concern and suspicion often result in a chip-on-the-shoulder attitude based on the belief, "I've been rejected so often that I've learned to protect myself in advance by not trusting any of you."

Slyness and cunning are responses of some people who are trying to survive or get ahead in a discriminatory environment. In really hostile environments "sneaky" traits may be a passive-aggressive way of gaining petty revenge against more powerful persecutors.

Clannishness, or clustering together with other minority group members, is a natural response to being excluded by the majority group. When people are excluded in work, play, and neighborhood settings, who else can they turn to but their own kind?

Prejudice against other outgroups, especially less-powerful groups, is one way to gain some sense of status and power. When we start with a foundation of inequality, a pecking order naturally develops, with the strong picking on the weaker, and they in turn picking on the still weaker.

Aggression and rebellion occur when people refuse to "take it lying down," and fight back whenever they can. Their frustration breeds aggression. This can be the source of criminal activity and riots. In contrast, some members see the futility of violence and join political or activist organizations that are dedicated to improving the existing situation.

Competing and trying harder are the responses of some minorities. Examples are attending evening classes, studying harder, and working harder than others, trying to make up for an uneven race. Dominant group members may respond with grudging admiration, but they also may accuse the minority of being *too* industrious and clever. Lower-class members of the dominant group may feel envious, resentful, or threatened.

Ego Defenses That Focus Inward

Some minorities turn their feelings and actions inward on themselves or their group. They tend to punish themselves for being inferior or "outcasts."

Self-dislike is related to a craving to be one of the dominant group and therefore to identify more with them than with your own group. Self-dislike is not merely pretending to agree with the dominant group; it involves actually seeing the world through their eyes. A person affected by self-dislike may be ashamed of belonging to a disparaged group. For example, self-dislike can cause women to identify more strongly with male viewpoints, with the patriarchal system, and with their limited roles as being positive and in their own best interests. Normally, they are not aware of this process and would probably deny it.

Withdrawal and passivity occurs in varying degrees when a disparaged minority person decides to retreat from life's more competitive activities and accept the status quo.

Ingroup aggression refers to attacking members of your own group because they possess the traits that you and the dominant group devalue. Aggression is sometimes related to self-dislike that extends to dislike for all disparaged persons. It sometimes occurs when two or more minority groups believe they're competing for scarce jobs and social services.

Symbolic status striving refers to attempts to gain status by pomp and circumstance, a flashy display of jewelry, cars, and clothes; pretentious use of language; obsessive interest in sexual conquests; and other ways of achieving marginal or symbolic status. It's self-punishing because it's not based on solid achievement and may include some elements of clowning.

Clowning is one way to receive good-natured, if patronizing, attention and to show that you are harmless, not threatening. Protective clowning extends into the subgroup itself. For example, some gay persons call themselves and each other *queers*, implying: "If we call ourselves 'queer,' it's no longer an epithet that you can use against us." Some African Americans call themselves "niggers," implying: "If we call ourselves 'niggers, we can harden ourselves to the sting of the insult. If we say it often enough, we'll become so hardened we won't ever feel its pain again."

Sympathy with all victims is considered the most positive of these inward-directed ego defenses. People who feel they've been victims of discrimination are usually either very high in prejudice or very low; they're seldom "average." Being a victim disposes you either to develop aggression toward or sympathy with other outgroups. Knowing all too well how it feels to be rejected, many minority persons reach out to other victims and offer support. Examples are Jesse Jackson's Rainbow Coalition and Jewish Americans who joined African Americans to put their lives on the line in the South during the Civil Rights era.

HOW DOES DISCRIMINATION AFFECT EMPLOYEES?

Discrimination against diverse employees not only affects their career progress, it also affects their trust, motivation, and productivity—their relationships with the rest of the workforce. It affects them in every phase and aspect of their work experience. Here are some ways companies exclude diverse employees (Cox 1993).

- recruitment practices
- screening practices
- terms and conditions of employment
- tracking and job segregation
- training and development decisions
- layoff, discharge, and seniority practices
- higher performance standards
- biased performance evaluations
- promotion practices
- glass ceiling barriers
- career alternatives

Recruitment Practices

Word of mouth is still the most common way that people learn about hiring and promotion opportunities. Up to 90 percent of workers find their jobs this way. Studies have concluded that the distribution of white-collar jobs to African Americans depends heavily upon informal networks of information, radiating outward from persons currently employed in upper rank slots. Does word-of-mouth recruiting in your company happen primarily among Euro-American men? What can you do to be sure that minorities and women find out about job opportunities?

Does your company place ads for all types of jobs in minority publications—or just ads for lower-level jobs? When the company makes plans for new facilities, are they ever located at sites that are convenient for minorities? A Civil Rights Commission study of housing (1973) found that "despite a variety of laws against job discrimination, lack of access to housing in close proximity to available jobs is an effective barrier to equal employment."

Screening Practices

Are the diplomas, degrees, and experience that your company requires of applicants really good predictors of whether those people will succeed on the job? If not, and if many minorities or women don't have them, they're discriminatory. Do the aptitude and intelligence tests that your company makes applicants pass really predict job success? The same principle applies here. Because minorities still tend to get an inferior education in the public schools, they're not as likely to do well on screening tests as Euro-Americans. Also, most people who make the tests are Euro-American men from middle-class backgrounds. People from minority subcultures obviously are at a cultural disadvantage in relating to the terminology, examples, cases, and other aspects of such tests. However, they may be quite intelligent, capable of learning how to do the job, and likely to succeed on the job.

Does your company have a strict requirement for applicants to have clean arrest and credit records? Do such screening practices really predict job success or failure? Police department practices often discriminate against minorities, especially African American men and to some extent Latino American men. Such men are more likely to have arrest records even though their behavior may have been as lawful as Euro-American fellow applicants. The same principle applies to credit records. Minorities tend to have lower incomes and to have more difficulty getting credit and maintaining good credit records.

How heavily does your company depend on cumulative employment records in making hiring decisions? Sometimes companies require women and minorities to have experience in areas where they previously have been excluded.

How does your company conduct background investigations of job applicants? If such reports include subjective, vague, and arbitrary assessments from prejudiced persons, they may be unfair to minorities and women.

Terms and Conditions of Employment

Are women and minority men earning approximately the same income as Euro-American men at all levels of the company? On average, they earn about 75 percent, even at the vice-presidential level. Above the "worker" level, they also tend to receive fewer benefits and perquisites.

Minorities must constantly deal with ethnic groups other than their own, primarily Euro-Americans. For example, most African Americans (72%) and Latino Americans (60%) have coworkers primarily from ethnic groups other than their own. In contrast, about half of Euro-Americans have coworkers who are all or nearly all Euro-American, and 17 percent say that about half their coworkers are Euro-Americans. In other words, nearly 70 percent of Euro-Americans work in predominantly Euro-American workplaces (Mazzuca 2004).

Tracking and Job Segregation

Does your company still have "women's jobs," "men's jobs," and "minority jobs," even though they're never called that? One example of tracking is the placement of well-educated women in clerical work. Do clerks, secretaries, and administrative assistants have chances to participate in training and development for better-paying jobs? Do they have the chance to get to know people in management? Are they groomed and recruited for higher-level jobs?

To some extent, discrimination in every job phase from recruitment to promotion results in a dual labor market in which women and minorities work disproportionately in occupations and industries with lower prestige, status, and compensation. Within organizations, they typically work in jobs and departments that are less influential and have lower status than those held by Euro-American men. Progress is being made, but we have a long way to go (U.S. Glass Ceiling 1995; Johnson 1987; Buono 1983).

Training and Development

Who makes the decisions about which employees will receive various types of training and development opportunities? Are these decisions open and equitable? Or are they colored by stereotypes about which types of persons have the potential and image to be groomed for certain jobs? For example, a study of who gets picked by corporations for mid-career programs at such universities as Harvard, Yale, and Stanford indicated those selected were virtually all Euro-American men. Such practices keep the glass ceiling in place for minorities and women (Carr-Ruffino 1991).

Layoff, Discharge, and Seniority Practices

What policies and practices does your company follow when they must lay-off or fire people? If they use seniority to protect workers who've been there the longest, does this mean that most of those laid off are minorities and women? If not, are older workers the ones who are most likely to lose their jobs? Employees have successfully sued employers for discrimination in both types of situations.

Seniority systems often affect women and minority members more adversely because they typically have less seniority than Euro-American men. The purpose of an organization-wide seniority system is to guarantee that employees with the greatest seniority will receive the greatest protection when cutbacks or layoffs take place. Such guarantees are usually part of a union contract. Yet seniority systems operating today often result in indirect discrimination. Where women and minority persons were barred from certain occupations in the past and therefore have been hired only in recent years, they will be the first to be laid off. This situation is common in organizations with a unionized workforce, such as manufacturing firms and local fire and police departments.

In most other organizations, older workers are more likely to be laid off because they are typically the highest-paid employees. In the process of reengineering, restructuring, and downsizing, companies are often looking for ways to decrease salary expense. Also, when a company computerizes a functional area, the experience and expertise of older workers in that area may become less valuable or even obsolete.

Unequal Treatment: Environment, Evaluations & Promotions

The workplace environment can be more stressful for minority employees due to informal exclusion, job bias, and harassment. Performance standards and evaluations that are different from those applied to mainstream employees can also constitute unequal and unfair treatment. As a result promotions decisions may be biased. Indirect discrimination can occur when Euro-American male supervisors fail to support and recommend their minority employees for promotion, even though company leaders rely on such subjective evaluations when they make promotion decisions.

Some studies indicate that reasons given for passing over diverse employees are "lack of initiative" or "not aggressive enough," when the real reason involves a misreading of cultural traits. Latino American and Asian American behavior is often interpreted as "too passive" when managers focus on style, not substance. African Americans' style may be seen as "too aggressive." In fact, some studies, such as those by Ann Morrison, have found that different standards of "getting along with others" have been required for African Americans than for others.

Informal Exclusion, Avoidance, and Social Distancing

Exclusion, avoidance, and social distancing are ways that individual employees may exhibit resistance to diversity in an organization. They represent informal discrimination—aspects of subtle and modern discrimination described in Chapter 4.

Formal discrimination refers to illegal behaviors that are overt and obvious, such as excluding persons from employment, advancement, resources, access, or other opportunities. Interpersonal, informal discrimination is more subtle and ambiguous; it is often nonverbal and may be unconscious. It may include differences in expectations, fewer informal ties, and negative facial expressions. Such discrimination can undermine the performance of target employees, in the same ways as overt harassment and hate crimes. Such subtle discrimination can be even more pernicious because of the difficulty of pinning it down and assessing it. Results for target employees can include decreased job satisfaction, affective commitment, and helping behaviors, and increased job stress and intentions to leave. (King et al 2006).

Stressful Pressures—Job Bias and Harassment

One of the best predictors of stressful outcomes at work is the fact of being a numerical minority (Gutierre1994). The effects of workplace harassment and hate crimes include psychological and physical problems for the targeted employees. For example, the targets tend to score poorer on global psychological assessments (Schneider et al 1997). They report increased feelings of anxiety, irritability, helplessness, and fear, along with lower self-esteem and self-confidence (Avina 2002), Physical responses include headaches, insomnia, gastrointestinal problems, ulcers, and increased blood pressure (Barlington 1999). Coping strategies may include increased alcohol consumption (Wisler et al 2002). Job-related consequences include withdrawal from tasks (the work) and withdrawal from the organization. Clearly, these can affect team members and organizational productivity, profitability, absenteeism, employee turnover, grievances, and lawsuits.

Why do women and minorities report higher stress levels in study after study? Here are some reasons:

- Having to perform to higher standards
- Needing to repress their natural attitudes and ways of functioning
- Coping with harassment, ethnic jokes, and more negative life events, such as job loss and physical abuse. (Diplacido 1998).
- Employees who belong to more than one "minority" group, such as African American women, tend to experience even greater stress (King 1988).

Another source of stress is AA (affirmative action) backlash. For example, studies indicate that the wages of Euro-American blue-collar workers have fallen significantly since the early 1970s. Some of these workers believe that AA has given minorities an unfair advantage, and they tend to resent African Americans the most (Swain 2002). Harassment intensified with these types of reported actions:

- Asking African Americans if they eat "monkey meat"
- Posting intimidating graffiti, such as Ku Klux Klan symbols, on workplace walls
- Wearing Ku Klux Klan-type robes
- Placing a noose or a cattle prod at a minority person's work site
- Hitting and poking African American salesmen with long sticks dangling tags with derogatory words.
- Attacking Euro-American coworkers who object to such harassment by such actions as threatening them directly, sending anonymous notes and phone calls, or breaking into their vehicles or homes

Poor Management Responses to Harassment Complaints

It is illegal for a company to retaliate against an employee for filing a complaint, but it frequently occurs anyway. In the 1990s the number of minorities who filed charges of retaliation with the EEOC doubled.

A mistake made by some corporate executives is to ignore or deny harassment and discrimination. Some are afraid that if they address the problem, it will be seen as an admission of guilt and lawsuits will be filed that perhaps could have been avoided. In fact, such negligence makes companies more vulnerable to lawsuits. The best defense is proof that management took preventive and corrective actions.

Many companies try to negotiate a money settlement with plaintiffs—on the condition that they keep quiet about all aspects of the case. Management hopes this strategy will avoid bad publicity, while not encouraging other employees to file complaints.

Higher Standards

How can minority persons succeed in a Euro-American male corporate culture?

- By performing to significantly higher standards than their Euro-American counterparts—because they must in order to be considered "as good" (Mainiero 1994 and Bell 1990).
- By adopting the attitudes and ways of the dominant group

Euro-American male managers feel less discomfort working with minority employees who think and act like they do (Morrison 1990, 1996; Thomas 1993; Bell 1993). And in fact, women who have attained top organizational positions, such as law partner, report that they had to change their behavior in order to gain acceptance from male peers (Ely 1995)

These peers tend to see women and minorities as basically deficient in workplace qualities and expect them to somehow compensate for their "inadequacies" (Stewart 1991) They are likely to:

- expect all "minority" employees to work harder
- expect women to use such sex-stereotyped behaviors as flirting, acquiescence, and indirectness
- expect gay persons to suppress their gayness

These stereotypes and expectations are hangovers from days when minority persons were not accepted in higher-level positions. Examples of such stereotypes include (Stone 1996):

- Women are seen as frivolous, demure, and passive
- Ethnic minorities are seen as incompetent and unfit for management
- Persons with disabilities are seen as potentially disruptive, unable to perform, threatening, or contagious (Heilman 1989, Stone 1996).

Biased Performance Evaluations

Are performance evaluation practices in your company free of bias? Research indicates that successful performance by women on tasks traditionally done by men tends to be attributed to luck, while Euro-American men's performance is more likely to be attributed to their ability. Compared to Euro-American managers, the performance of African American managers is less likely to be attributed to ability and effort and more likely to be attributed to help from others (Deaux 1974; Cash 1977; Greenhaus 1994).

Also, evaluations made by Euro-American men are often colored by their stereotyped expectations of the ways women and minorities act. As a result, Euro-American managers often hold women and minorities to tighter standards of behavior than the majority group members. Many women managers say they must "walk a tight rope," feeling their way through the narrow range of acceptable behavior. They see that the men can show more aggressiveness, ambition, competition, and similar traits without being criticized. African American men must show less anger and sexuality to avoid reinforcing stereotypes that cause discomfort. For diverse employees, it amounts to a double standard of acceptable behavior (Baack, Carr-Ruffino, and Pelletier 1993; Morrison 1987).

Biased Promotion Practices

How open and equitable are the promotion procedures in your company? In many companies, they're secretive and very difficult for outsiders to understand. Although formal promotion policies and procedures are spelled out in writing by large companies and government agencies, unwritten, informal rules or expectations usually have a much greater impact.

Many studies, past and present, indicate that Euro-American male executives and managers continue to harbor stereotyped views of women and minorities, views that shape the promotion decisions. A woman is disadvantaged if she's married ("We didn't promote her because she has children and her family responsibilities will interfere") and disadvantaged if she's not ("We didn't promote her because she's likely to quit and get married"). Another stereotype is that employees won't accept a woman or minority in a high position. Such subtle discrimination has kept the glass ceiling in place (Carr-Ruffino 1991; Morrison 1987).

Glass Ceiling Barriers

Several studies, such as those done by two separate U.S. Glass Ceiling Commissions, indicate that the major barrier to promotion up the ladder is the tendency for the men at the top to be more comfortable with their own kind. The reasons for this tendency are:

- They can better predict and understand another's behavior when that other is like them.
- It's easier to figure out why others in the group do what they do.
- It's easier to establish rapport and build a relationship.
- They're more likely to help others in the group, because people are generally more likely to help ingroup members than to help "strangers."

Limited Career Alternatives

Discrimination can even make it more difficult for minorities to choose alternatives to corporate careers when they can't get hired or when they hit the glass ceiling. For example, the Small Business Administration (SBA) did a study of its loans for 1990 through 1992 and declared that its loan guarantee program had been poorly serving minorities and women. The agency set a goal of at least doubling the number of loans to targeted groups during the coming year (WSJ 1994). The SBA reported in 2004 that 25 percent of loans granted in 2003 went to minorities and 20 percent went to women. Loan amounts by ethnic group were not given. The average general business loan was $165,000 and the average certified loan was $435,000 (SBA.com 2004).

Vignette: "Bid-With" and Unfair Standards

Rich was the first African American compensation manager ever hired by Juno Jeans. Because the compensation manager has access to information on salaries and benefits for every person in the company, top management considers it a very sensitive position calling for someone who is discreet, even secretive. Rich seemed to be a mature man with good judgment and the right kind of experience, so they were willing to give him a try.

Juno employees are given the choice of taking lunch at 12:00 or at 1:00 and many play cards or dominoes after lunch. Most of the clerks and hourly people take their lunch at 12:00, and virtually all the management and professional people take theirs at 1:00. Bridge was the game of choice of the 1 o'clock crowd, while games of the 12 o'clock bunch were as varied as their ethnic backgrounds. The African Americans regularly played Bid-With, a game similar to bridge and generally known only in their community. Rich was a wicked Bid-With player but had never mastered bridge. Because of this he usually joined the 12 o'clock bunch.

The Euro-American executives could not understand why Rich would hobnob with the clerks and maintenance people. To them, it is unwise to become too friendly with people from lower levels, especially when a manager works with sensitive information. It is too easy to relax, forget yourself, and let bits of information slip out. The executives mentioned their concern to Sandra, an African American lawyer in the legal department. She did not agree with their take on the situation. She explained to them that Rich probably just wanted to play Bid-With, and they should not worry about clustering, buddying, blabbing, or similar problems. But the executive's concerns did not go away. Within a few months they found an excuse to terminate Rich.

Sandra discussed the problem with her husband. "It's too bad, but these guys tend to get paranoid any time they see African American employees bonding—or women professionals talking together, for that matter. They'll make joking comments, such as 'Plotting a revolution?' or 'Ganging up on us?' But beneath the humor, I sense they feel threatened by us. Maybe it's a fear of giving up some power and privilege. Poor Rich, his love of Bid-With did him in. And the company lost a really loyal, talented guy, all because top management has these stereotypes about how managers must act."

THE MELTING POT APPROACH TO MANAGING DIVERSITY

Until the 1960s most corporate leaders adhered to the melting-pot approach to deal with workplace diversity. Because this didn't work for women and ethnic minorities, the Civil Rights laws of the 1960s ushered in the legal approach to managing discrimination. Now savvy leaders in forward-thinking companies are going beyond old approaches. Their focus is on valuing diverse employees for the unique contributions they can make to the company's success. They are crafting a multicultural approach to managing diversity—and a corporate culture that welcomes all types of employees to its doors and then appreciates and nurtures them. Let's look at the key myths and realities about the great American melting pot and how it has affected women and minorities.

Myths vs. Realities

People tend to avoid discussions of workplace discrimination. Many avoid even thinking about it. It should come as no surprise, therefore, that myths about this topic are more prevalent than the realities.

Myth #1: The American workplace is a melting pot.

Traditionally business has handled diversity by adopting the Melting Pot myth, but people of color and women never "melted in" because they don't look or act like the dominant majority, Euro-American men

Myth #2: The equal pay and equal opportunity laws have eliminate workplace inequities

In the 1960s Civil Rights laws began to open many doors of opportunity. However, the laws did not necessarily change the beliefs and attitudes, the thoughts and feelings that led to discrimination in the first place. Many of the people with the authority to make changes have found ways around these laws. And most employees who are discriminated against are unlikely to turn their employer in to a government agency.

Myth #3: If we ever needed Affirmative Action (AA), we no longer need it now

You learned in Chapter 1 that very few women or minorities have made it to the top of middle-to large-sized corporations—even after 40 years of affirmative action programs. On the other hand, large numbers have moved part-way up the ladder, and experts say that affirmative action is the most powerful career boost for them. Until women and minorities are adequately represented at all levels, corporate management still needs the guidance and motivation that affirmative action law provides.

Myth #4: AA imposes hiring and promotion quotas on companies

It's against the law for the federal government to set AA quotas for corporations, and it's against the spirit of the law to hire or promote unqualified people. More details later.

Myth #5: AA is really reverse discrimination

AA opponents often focus on the reverse discrimination myth. They say that because AA requires companies to fulfill quotas, they're forced to hire and promote women and minorities who are often less qualified than the white men who are being discriminated against.

Supporters of AA say it's ludicrous to believe that AA has the long-term general effect of discriminating against the most powerful, dominant group in the workplace. Supporting this conclusion is the fact that Euro-American males run the show in 95 percent of the corporations. Supporters also point out that Euro-American males have always had their own brand of AA—the old school ties, the old boys' network, and other ingroup privileges that few notice.

Myth #6: We can't afford to spend much time or money on diversity initiatives.

We must focus on bottom-line profits. Actually, companies that succeed in New Economy markets do it through talented employees. Inclusive, savvy corporate cultures are attracting and retaining the best talent—which translates into greater success and profits.

"But America has always handled its diversity so well," some say. "Why, we're the Great Melting Pot." But the melting pot has been a cruel myth for aspiring career women and for non-European minorities. Who has it worked for? In society in general, it has worked for all immigrants from European countries. In the workplace, it has worked for male immigrants from those countries. European immigrants were expected to learn the American ways so they could be assimilated and absorbed. The goal was to create a seamless American culture and workplace. This worked fairly well for European men because Western cultures have much in common and people from those cultures look much alike. Although the Jewish, Irish, Italian, and Eastern European immigrants experienced some distinct prejudice and discrimination, within a generation or two they blended in.

On the other hand, people of color actually lived in segmented and segregated subcultures and women grew up alongside men in parallel but different worlds. People of color and women simply don't look like Euro-American men, the dominant culture of the workplace, and they were never truly assimilated.

How to Recognize the Melting-Pot Myth at Work

How can you tell when a company is relying on the melting-pot myth to handle diversity? Look for the following kinds of messages:

- We (Euro-American men) are at the center of the universe here.
- Why should we bother to learn about newcomers? We're busy and we belong here.
- It's the newcomers' job to learn how to succeed here and how to fit in (become like us).
- They have to learn the ropes and speak the language correctly if they want to work here.
- If they learn to do it our way, they won't have any problems.
- Immigrants can be a nuisance to talk to because of their accent and grammar
- Women's culture is just a subset of whatever ethnic culture they belong to; Euro-American women live in the same cultural world we do.
- The best approach is to ignore cultural differences.
- Our goal is to eliminate cultural differences.
- Managers naturally have an adversarial relationship with workers.
- Managers must do the planning, then control and check on worker performance.

This set of beliefs logically leads to a belief that the a person from a different group is wrong or inferior. It causes you to rely on predominant stereotypes of people from other groups, often assuming they're stupid or lazy or stubborn or sneaky. It says to the newcomer, "Get rid of your unprofessional behavior, your odd language, your strange ways."

Problems Caused by the Melting-Pot Approach

Newcomers in the past have usually bought into the melting-pot belief system, which led them to new beliefs, such as

- I must become just like the dominant group.
- My native country is inferior; America is better.
- I must fit in, no matter what I have to do.
- I won't teach the children about the old country; let them be Americans.

The immigrants' children picked up on this attitude, and many grew up to be ashamed of their parents' "old country" ways (Simons et al 1993).

When assimilation was either a conscious or unconscious goal in dealing with diversity, the ideal was to ignore differences and treat everyone the same. The biblical Golden Rule was the ideal:

> *Do unto others as you would have them do unto you.*

This rule usually works in a homogeneous culture, but in a multicultural workplace life is not so simple, and a more appropriate Golden Rule would be,

> *Do unto others as they would have you do unto them*

People may prefer to be treated in ways you haven't even thought of—because they may have quite different values and habits than you. You must treat people differently when they are different, if you want to be fair. This is a much more complex and difficult task than treating everyone alike.

You can see that the melting-pot ideal has never been ideal for all. Here are some additional problems with this approach:

- Those who don't look the part can't blend in.
- Forcing everyone to take a similar approach leaves untapped potential that could blossom from different approaches.
- In a competitive environment, assimilation is stifling and deadly.
- When diverse newcomers are expected to fit in, they focus on doing the expected or accommodating the norm, on playing it safe, instead of making innovative suggestions.
- Newcomers avoid doing or saying things that might label them as "different."
- The more energy newcomers must expend on adapting, the less they have for developing innovative ideas and personal strengths.
- Talented newcomers tend to go (and grow) where they're appreciated for who they are—to companies with a more supportive multicultural approach.

Obviously, the more diverse the work force becomes, the more important it becomes for organizations to solve the problems presented by the melting-pot approach, to dismantle the traditional barriers to full productivity and contribution, and to develop an approach that's more inclusive.

Vignette: Growing Up Among Many "Pots"

A group of friends who grew up in a North Texas city during the 1940s was reminiscing about their "all-WASP" childhood. Ralph said, "You know, I never knew a Mexican American when I was growing up; never talked to one except for the man who sold tamales from a cart on the street. But I know there had to be a Mexican American community somewhere." Others agreed that this was a common experience. Andrea said, "I never had any African American friends either. Of course, that's easier to understand, with the severe segregation and all. The only African Americans I knew were the cleaning women who came to our home sometimes."

Many Pots: The Glue Is the American Dream

What about American unity? What glue holds Americans together as a nation? Certainly, two primary values that have pulled immigrants to these shores and kept them here are freedom and opportunity—the freedom to pursue one's own lifestyle and religion and the opportunity to make a decent living. A whole set of values formed around this American Dream, shaped the society, and is remarkably strong in holding it together. Americans have rallied round a common consumer market and media. Their political system lets them participate and have influence, and their political-legal system effectively sets the rules of the making-money game and referees conflicts. Their many interest groups get to have their say through members' votes and whatever influence they can wield within the system.

THE LEGAL APPROACH TO MANAGING DIVERSITY: EQUAL OPPORTUNITY AND AFFIRMATIVE ACTION

Because the melting pot approach did not provide equal opportunities for people of color and women, the legal approach was introduced by government in the late 1960s. First came the Civil Rights Act that established Equal Employment Opportunity (EEO). Later came an executive order establishing Affirmative Action (AA). EEO strengthens the individual employee's *rights* to equal opportunity and better jobs, but the employee must take action to complain about unfairness. AA requires employers to take action to bring in under-represented groups of people into better jobs. This increases the chances for a minority employee to *actually get* one of those jobs—without having to file a complaint.

Where people of color and women formerly faced brick walls, doors to opportunity appeared, so this legal approach has been more effective for their upward mobility than the melting pot approach. Although most business leaders agree that the equal opportunity approach has been generally beneficial, most people don't understand it well. Euro-American men tend to resent it, and many minorities and women don't know why they need it. How did it all come about and what does it mean?

Civil Rights Act of 1964: EEO—Good but Not Good Enough

A section of Title VII of the Civil Rights Act of 1964 (as amended in 1972) makes it unlawful for an employer with more than 15 employees to fail or refuse to hire or to discharge any individual, or otherwise to discriminate against any individual, with respect to his or her compensation, terms, conditions, or privileges of employment, because of such individual's race, color, religion, sex, or national origin—or to limit, segregate, or classify employees or applicants for employment in any way that would tend to deprive them of employment opportunities or otherwise adversely affect their status as an employee, because of such differences. This was a huge breakthrough for a whole range of diverse employees, but as we shall see, it was not good enough to open the doors of opportunity to all organizational levels.

Equal Employment Opportunity Commission

Title VII of the 1964 Civil Rights Act established the Equal Employment Opportunity Commission (EEOC) to define and enforce acceptable employment policies and practices, especially as they affect protected minorities and women. Businesses with more than 15 employees are subject to this law. EEO was an important step forward for people of color and women, because people who are discriminated against can complain to their employers, based on EEOC guidelines. If an employer doesn't satisfy such a complaint, the employee can go directly to a regional EEOC office and file a complaint there. If the employee can get other employees to join the complaint, it may become a class action. And if the EEOC cannot get the employer to resolve the discriminatory issue, the employees may be able to file a class action lawsuit. The courts then decide on the matter.

Defining Harassment and Hostile Work Environment

In the years following its establishment, the EEOC developed various guidelines and policies, including those concerning harassment of women and minority employees, whether consisting of blatant, direct attacks or more subtle actions that create a hostile work environment for such employees.

Harassment occurs when an individual in a protected class is subjected to unwelcome verbal or physical conduct that is "sufficiently severe, pervasive, or unreasonable" to 1) alter the conditions of employment; i.e. pay, promotion or other opportunities, and the like are affected, or 2) to create an abusive or offensive working environment (EEOC). Such behavior may be conducted by anyone in the workplace including a supervisor, coworker, or nonemployee (e.g. supplier or customer).

Harassment

The target of harassment can be anyone affected by the behavior, not just the individual to whom the behavior was directed. Thus, for an individual to make a legal claim of harassment, she or he must:

1. be a member of a protected class

2. demonstrate that she or he was subjected to unwelcome conduct related to her or his class membership

3. provide evidence that the conduct was sufficiently severe or pervasive to alter the conditions of employment or create an intimidating, hostile, or offensive work environment.

Harassment may consist of disproportionate criticism or monitoring behaviors toward a minority member compared to dominant members (Massengill 2004) such as:

- Intercepting phone calls
- Eavesdropping on conversations
- Physically hovering around the person as she or he works
- Checking their work more than others
- Openly criticizing them
- Actively searching for mistakes in order to "catch" poor performance or wrong doing

Hostile Work Environment

A hostile work climate is a form of psychological climate. This refers to individual perceptions of the work environment. A perceived hostile climate is one in which individuals believe that they are the target of conduct from others in the organization, whether verbal, physical, written, or graphic that:

- they perceive as offensive, abusive, hostile, exclusionary, discriminatory, and/or malicious
- creates significant negative emotional responses
- otherwise interferes with their individual well-being or job performance

Who determines whether a hostile climate exists? The target employee. How pervasive and severe? The severity should be judged from the perspective of a reasonable person in the complainant's position considering all of the same circumstances (Oncale 1998). Key questions to ask include:

- Is the behavior serious in terms of the degree of physical or psychological harm?
- How frequently did it occur?
- Would it unreasonably interfere with work performance or create a hostile environment for a "reasonable person"?

Objectionable Behavior

What are some types of behavior that have led to complaints or lawsuits? (Brown 2005) Objectionable behaviors based on ethnicity:

- Promoting negative stereotypes
- Using ethnically derogatory words
- Making comments about ones' skin color

- Having ethnically insensitive symbols (hangman's noose, Confederate insignia)

  Other behaviors that led to lawsuits:

- Using language that belittles, such as disparaging remarks, ethnic epithets, slurs, jokes
- Using profanity targeted toward specific persons
- Using inappropriate nicknames
- Cartoons posted on bulletin board, which ridicule older people
- Supervisor casually wondering if an employee "still has what it takes to do a job"
- Emails containing distasteful Helen Keller jokes
- Imitating others' speech patterns
- Imitating a disabled workers' posture or gait

Advantages and Disadvantages of EEO Law

One advantage of EEO law is that it gives an employee a direct way to deal with job discrimination. Another advantage is that employees can sue if a policy or practice has a "disparate impact" on employees of a particular ethnic, religious, or gender category—regardless of whether such impact was intended. Companies that wanted to protect themselves started categorizing employee records, which in turn has provided needed statistics on how people from each group are faring.

The disadvantage is that it is extremely difficult for an individual to prove discrimination. Those who go outside the company to complain are usually branded as troublemakers and blackballed throughout the industry. Although such retaliation is illegal, it is almost impossible to prove when it's handled by word of mouth and never put in writing. Individuals who pursue this route usually find their career progress put on hold for years. Often they must change occupations or industries and start over.

In 1991 an amendment to the Civil Rights Act increased the money damages that employees can receive if they can prove discrimination occurred. Before, they could only recover lost back pay with interest. Now they can receive money for compensatory and punitive damages—if they can prove that they were subjected to malicious, illegal behavior that resulted in undue stress. Still, the problem is in the proving.

Affirmative Action: A Major Impact

AA is a legal program, based on presidential Executive Orders, which is designed to end unfair workplace discrimination against certain groups of people who have historically experienced such discrimination. Research studies indicate that AA has had the most powerful impact of any law or program in opening doors of opportunity for such people (Leonard 1986, U.S. Glass Ceiling 1995).

Two Types of Discrimination

AA employment discrimination laws prohibit two types of discrimination.

1. *Disparate treatment.* The employer treats an employee from a protected group in a different way than it typically treats other employees. This employee may be singled out for such treatment, perhaps not given a privilege, advantage, benefit, or leniency that is given to co-workers. The focus of disparate treatment cases is to guarantee every worker gets equal opportunity, but not necessarily equal outcomes.

2. *Disparate impact.* The employer is using some employment practice that is not essential to the job and that acts in a way that systematically disadvantages a protected group. In other words, the impact or results of the practice is unfair to these employees. Such practices might include requiring diplomas or certificates that are not necessary for the job description, giving tests that are not valid in assessing the skills required for the job, and setting height or weight requirements that are not essential for the job. The focus of disparate impact cases is on equal outcomes.

Three Arenas for AA

In three distinct arenas we find the following categories of women and minorities who may seek protection from discrimination:

1. *Students* trying to get into public colleges and universities
2. *Contractors* trying to win bids from government agencies
3. *Employees* trying to get hired and promoted by corporations

Each arena has its own complexities. We will discuss each one briefly

AA for Student Admissions

The 2003 Supreme Court ruling on AA practices at the University of Michigan involved student admissions. However, the ruling has implications for AA in all types of organizations. The message is that ethnicity should be one factor that determines such decisions, but the entire process must be flexible and specific; i.e., applied to each individual's profile of background, achievements, and potential. Anything as rigid and general as a numerical system for assessing candidates would violate this principle—and a quota system would surely violate it.

AA for Small Minority Business Contractors

The Small Business Administrations 8a program is a "minority set-aside program" that "sets aside" a certain percentage of federal government contracts to go only to small "disadvantaged" business owners. To qualify, a minority contractor must prove that its business is owned by one or more minority persons and that the owners are also economically and socially disadvantaged. They can retain their special contract status for no longer than nine years.

Minority set-aside programs are also found at state and local levels, and have been bitterly criticized, primarily by EuroAmerican male business owners. Yet, the main problem with the programs has been that some of the companies that win minority contracts are merely fronts for Euro-American male businesses. The SBA 8a program sets aside only about 3 percent of all federal government contracts for minority bidders—a tiny proportion of the businesses that could qualify. About the same proportion is set aside in the various state and local programs. In the 1990s the Clinton Administration set a goal of giving 5 percent of federal government contracts to small, disadvantaged firms.

AA for Corporate Employees

Because EEO alone does not have a significant impact on the upward mobility of minorities and women, AA was stepped up. AA law is not so obvious as EEO to individual employees. The average employee will never meet with an AA official and never file an "AA complaint." That's because AA works in the background, normally with a human resources administrator, and at times with the top management team, developing an AA program that's approved by an officer from the Labor Department's Office of Federal Contract Compliance Programs (OFCCP). The compliance officer may periodically review the company's progress toward the diversity goals it has set in its AA program, as shown in Figure 5.2. Therefore, individual employees usually don't know that the higher-level job opportunities they found were open to them only because of the company's AA plans and goals.

But what exactly is AA and how does it work? Beginning in 1967 a series of executive orders signed by then-President Johnson empowered AA by

- requiring AA plans from firms doing business with the federal government
- randomly and periodically monitoring such firms for compliance to plans
- for firms that don't comply, cutting off their federal contracts

Specifically, all federal government contracts include provisions that prohibit employment discrimination because of race, color, religion, national origin, or sex. Any business that enters into federal contracts of more than $50,000 per year must develop an AA plan to hire and promote "under-utilized" minorities, setting goals and time targets, and periodically filing progress reports.

Adequate representation of minorities and women at all job levels usually relates to their proportions in the available workforce. This focus on overall numbers, proportions, and representations takes the pressure off the individual minority person who is not given an opportunity. The individual does not have to prove discrimination. Instead, discriminatory results are implied when, for example, 40 percent of the available work force and of actual employees are women but only 5 percent are managers. The employer would then be expected to set reasonable short- and long-term goals, over a period of several years, to increase the proportion of women in the better-paying managerial, professional, and technical jobs. Figure 5.2 shows how AA works.

FIGURE 5.2: How AA Works

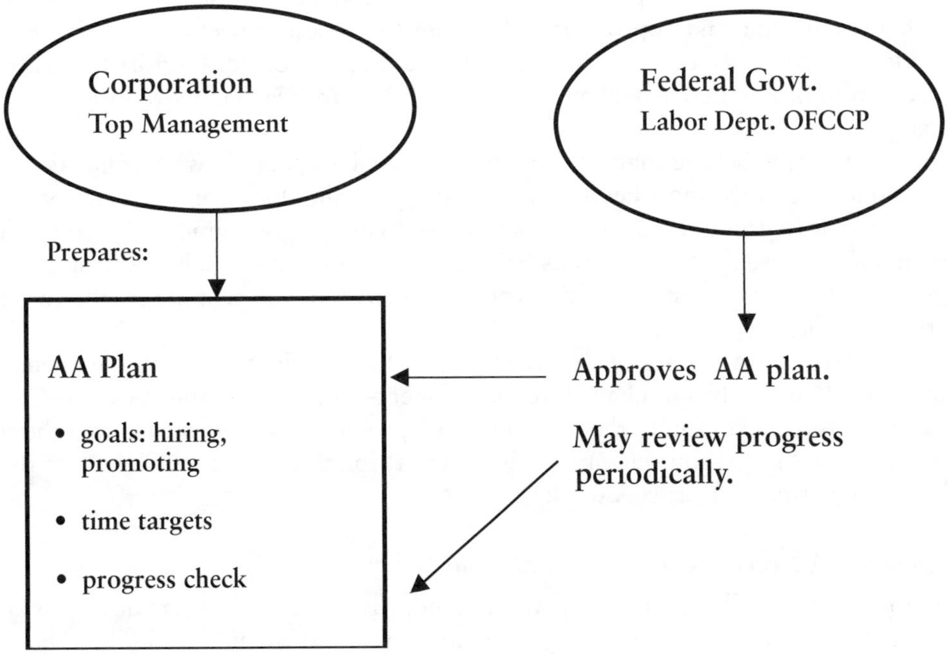

The Rationale for AA

AA provoked immediate controversy and backlash, but it was fairly well established during the 1970s. However, when President Reagan took office in 1981, he signaled a desire to dismantle the system. In response, the bipartisan government body, Commission on Civil Rights, issued the updated statement of principles, "Affirmative Action in the 1980s," which defined six AA principles.

Principle #1: Problem-Remedy Approach

The first AA principle is that discrimination is an entrenched problem that won't be resolved without the AA remedy. It is such a problem that prior to AA few women or persons of color pursued the education and training for higher-level occupations because they could see their investment would not pay off. There would be no jobs open to them, even if they became well qualified.

Principle #2: Color-blind Remedies Don't Work

The second principle is that discrimination is a self-perpetuating process that colorblind laws have not been able to change. Discrimination will never end without AA to break the cycle and to create new, more equitable processes when these factors are present:

- a history of widespread prejudice
- conditions of inequality with Euro-American males
- resulting barriers that have *not* been removed by measures that are color-blind and gender-neutral—that is, by measures that ignore ethnicity and gender.

The main point: Under such conditions as we still have in the United States, remedies for discrimination that insist on *color blindness* or *gender neutrality* are not sufficient. The only effective remedy to the problem is a type of AA that responds to discrimination as a self-sustaining process and sets specific hiring and promotion goals for dismantling it. The commission went on to respond to the major criticisms of AA concerning hiring quotas, lower standards, the stigma of AA hiring, and claims of reverse discrimination.

Principle #3: Hiring Quotas Are Illegal.

Quotas cannot be imposed on an employer by normal AA law. It is illegal for the government to demand hiring quotas of any private employer. This means that companies set their own numerical goals, which are then approved by a federal contract compliance officer. The goals are not quotas because they are flexible and approximate. If a company doesn't meet its diversity goals, it's not penalized, as long as management can show they're making a good-faith effort to create a diverse workforce. AA programs and goals will end when all groups are reasonably represented at all levels of the company.

Why do most people believe that AA imposes quotas? First, people who politically oppose AA love to refer to quotas because most people consider them unfair. Quotas imply a company must hire anyone from a minority group, even the unqualified—obviously poor practice, and unfair. Second, some companies *do* impose their own quotas because they've neglected their AA program and face a sudden urgency to make up for lost time. This is poor diversity management in the extreme, and courts have ruled that it is illegal.

Finally, in extremely rare cases of deeply entrenched discrimination that's completely impervious to change—such as the Birmingham Fire Department—minority employees may sue. A judge *may* rule that the nature and extent of the discriminatory problem is so entrenched that the court must set quotas in order to bring about change. This occurs through the court system, not the OFCCP, and is not how the normal AA process works.

Principle #4: AA Never Dictates Lower Standards

Nothing in the law calls for lowering valid standards. Companies that don't use long-range planning for recruiting, hiring, and training minorities may find themselves making little progress toward a diversified work force. Sometimes, when a federal review is looming, such companies voluntarily set their own quotas and then lower their hiring or promotion standards in order to meet their own quotas. But the government does not require this sort of crisis management, and does not condone it.

On the other hand, AA plans often require companies to examine their standards, and if standards cannot be shown to be related to successful performance, they must be discarded. Certain tests or requirements may be irrelevant to job success. They may simply measure the Euro-American male ways of thinking and performing. They may not even do that, but are simply some sort of screening device with little job relevance.

The use of such invalid tests and standards may deny opportunities to some people for reasons unrelated to merit. In situations where the use of valid standards serves to exclude women and minorities, civil rights law does *not* require the selection of unqualified minorities and women. It does, however, encourage

- the restructuring of jobs
- the development of new standards that are equally related to successful performance but do not exclude
- the development of training programs that prepare the excluded to meet valid standards.

Within a few years of the passage of the EEOC and AA laws, there was a significant increase in the enrollment of women and persons of color in college, university, and advanced vocational programs that would qualify them for the higher-level jobs that companies were now willing to offer them. Sometimes it took class action suits to get companies to open up their own advanced training programs, but gradually most large companies made some progress.

Principle #5: "AA Stigma" Is Manageable.

The Civil Rights Commission addressed the charge that AA further stigmatizes minorities and women when, for example, people adopt the attitude that an African American gained her position because of AA rather than because of merit. Such a woman has difficulty gaining respect and credibility. Often, the problem is actually faulty implementation of AA plans. For example, a woman may be placed as a "token" in a situation where she faces open hostility and/or lack of basic support. When the resulting isolation or failure causes her to quit or be removed, the employer may cite this as the reason for not promoting other women.

Company leaders set the tone by their attitudes toward diverse employees. When they signal respect, trust, and support, others are likely to value minority capabilities. Even when leadership support is grudging, many minorities and women say that an opportunity with stigma is better than no opportunity at all, which is what they had before AA. To them, throwing out AA means throwing out opportunity. They say that until some proven alternative to AA comes along, the stigmatization argument is invalid.

Principle #6: AA Is Not Reverse Discrimination.

The remedial use of goals, timetables, and setting aside a certain percentage of government contracts to go to minorities in order to bring about workplace equity for all ethnic groups has become part of international law. In 1969 the United Nations treaty called *Declaration of All Forms of Racial Discrimination* was passed and became international law. The treaty is clear about measures designed to bring ethnic groups into the mainstream.

> *Statement from the 1969 United Nations treaty*
> *Declaration of All Forms of Racial Discrimination:*
> *AA measures shall not be considered discrimination or reverse discrimination.*

The only qualification regarding such measures is that they be removed as soon as they are no longer required. By 1984, 107 nations had ratified it—more than for any other treaty that has emerged from the U.N., but the United States Senate has never seriously debated it nor ratified it.

A similar U.N. treaty calling for the same rights for women was passed in 1979. *The Convention on the Elimination of All Forms of Discrimination Against Women* calls for the same rights for women. It also calls for nations to "embody the principle of equality of men and women in their national constitution or other appropriate legislation." Because Congress also refuses to act on this U.N. treaty, the United States is the only industrialized democracy that has not ratified it (Carter 1995).

In 1999 the United Nations approved a protocol for enforcing the 1979 treaty. Women suffering any form of discrimination that's banned by the 1979 treaty, and who have tried all means of redress in their own countries, may appeal to a U.N. experts' committee. Women's organizations may also appeal on behalf of victimized women. The U.N. Committee may launch its own investigation into a member state's conduct if it receives reliable information indicating grave or systematic violations of the rights afforded women. The committee has no power to force a country's government to change. But if the committee finds a complaint justified, it must inform the country and make recommendations for correcting rights abuses.

AA Made a Difference in the 1970s

The track record of AA during the 1970s, when it was enforced with some consistency, indicates that it does open doors for minorities and women without harming business. Figures 5.3 and 5.4 depict the experiences of women and minorities before and after AA. At least four major studies concluded that the law was effective in boosting the careers and economic status of minorities and

FIGURE 5.3: Before Affirmative Action

Ladder of Opportunity

<u>High-Level Jobs:</u> *Euro-American Males Only*

Dead-End Drudge

<u>Low-Level Jobs:</u> *All Others, Qualified or Unqualified*

With EEO Only (no AA)
Employee discriminated against:
Must file company grievance
File complaint with EEOC
File a lawsuit
Informal blackballing—7 years limbo
Start a new career in different field

FIGURE 5.4: After Affirmative Action

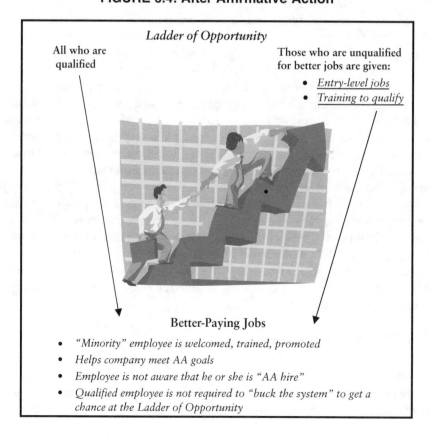

Ladder of Opportunity

All who are
qualified

Those who are unqualified
for better jobs are given:

- *Entry-level jobs*
- *Training to qualify*

Better-Paying Jobs

- *"Minority" employee is welcomed, trained, promoted*
- *Helps company meet AA goals*
- *Employee is not aware that he or she is "AA hire"*
- *Qualified employee is not required to "buck the system" to get a chance at the Ladder of Opportunity*

women. At the same time business suffered no loss in productivity and paid an average of $78 per employee per year for all EEO/AA related activities (Simpson 1984; U.S. Dept. of Labor 1984; Potomac Institute 1984; Leonard 1984a, b, 1985, 1986).

Bette Woody, Wellesley College, concluded that EEO/AA laws played a major role in allowing African American women, who were working predominantly as cleaning women, to make a dramatic shift to office positions. Clerical jobs were mostly off-limits for them before AA. In 1960 most worked as cleaning women. By 1980 only 6 percent worked as domestic maids, and 39 percent were in clerical jobs—up from 8.5 percent in 1960. The gap between African American and Euro-American women's earnings narrowed from 80 percent in 1967 to 90 percent in 1985 (Woody 1989).

Did AA lower productivity or raise costs? J. Leonard, U.C. Berkeley (1984a), compared national manufacturing figures for 1966 with those for 1977, when minority males and women had recently moved into jobs formerly held only by Euro-American men. Minority males were roughly 70 percent as productive as Euro-American males but earned only 70 percent the salary, so cost the company no more. Women were 1 percent more productive, but earned only 60 percent the salary, so cost the company 41 percent less on average. Costs overall fell by a fraction of a percent.

In summary, a review of the relative impact that AA, the EEOC, and class action lawsuits had during the 1970s indicates that AA had the greatest impact by far—because of its power to impose penalties that can affect the profits of so many large businesses (Carr-Ruffino 1991).

AA Was Undermined During the 1980s

From 1980 to 1992 successive Republican administrations chipped away at the foundation of AA from every angle. Several studies indicate that the noticeable, but not spectacular, progress minorities and women had previously experienced became generally stalled during the 1980s (Leonard 1988). In President Bush's administration Secretary of Labor Lynn Martin commissioned a study that found the glass ceiling was much lower than predicted, existing below midlevel positions for most minorities and women, and was generally lower for minorities than for Euro-American women (U.S. Dept. of Labor 1991).

Why Business Retained AA During the 1980s

While most analysts agree that the regulation and enforcement of AA and EEO laws were eroded during the 1980s, they also agree that most employers maintained a high level of interest in them, especially larger corporations that wanted to keep AA plans in place for four reasons:

1   As a practical matter, in corporate political terms, AA plans provide employers with a way to integrate work forces despite internal opposition from some Euro-American males.

2   AA fits with the long-term interests of some corporate human resource planners who want to streamline hiring systems, set and enforce valid standards, apply training requirements, and monitor progress of all workers.

3   Although executives generally resist government regulation, they also understand that government regulatory positions come and go, and that eventually the pendulum would swing back in favor of AA, leaving those employers who had dropped their plans at a disadvantage.

4   Many of the people who moved into positions formerly closed to them because of ethnic or gender discrimination were very productive and effective employees and were generally a bargain in salary terms, because companies still got away with paying them less for basically comparable, or superior, contributions.

AA Had Its Ups and Downs Since 1990

In 1996 California voters passed a ban on state-run AA programs via the indirectly-worded Proposition 209, which bans state officials from considering race or gender in state hiring, contracting, and college admissions. This language implies that the Proposition will ban racial and gender discrimination, when actually it results in banning AA. The drive was led by African American businessman Ward Connerly, who says that AA is a crutch, not an enabler for minorities. He went on to lead the passage of similar propositions in Florida, Michigan, Texas, Washington—and in 2008 Nebraska.

By 2000, only about 12 percent of California's Latino Americans and African Americans had college degrees, compared to 33 percent of Euro-Americans and 52 percent of Asian Americans (U.S. Census). This education gap is increasingly important; by 2007 nearly half of California's public school students, kindergarten to 12th grade were Latino Americans (California Dept. of Education). In 2001 California made an effort to offset the decline in minority enrollments at state universities by enacting a new plan that allows the top 12.5 percent of high school students to enter the top-tier UC system, either for all four years or after two years outside the system. The law guarantees the top 4 percent of all high school seniors admission into the UC system. This plan is similar to plans enacted by Florida and Texas.

In 2000 President Clinton's Department of Labor, to promote equal pay, made new AA regulations that include an Equal Opportunity Survey of all federal contractors. They must report hiring, termination, promotion, and compensation data by minority status and gender. This marked the first time in history that employers are required to report information on compensation by gender and minority status to the federal equal employment agencies.

The Department of Transportation in the late 1990s began a revised federal contracting program called Disadvantaged Business Enterprise. In 2000 the 10th Circuit Court issued an opinion that it was constitutional because it served a compelling government interest and was narrowly tailored to achieve that interest. The Supreme Court in effect supported the ruling.

In 2003 the Bush administration joined in a case against AA at Michigan State University. The Supreme Court, however, held that the University of Michigan's use of race among other factors in its law school admissions program was constitutional because the program furthered a compelling interest in obtaining "an educational benefit that flows from student body diversity". The Court also found that the law school's program was narrowly tailored; it was flexible, and provided for a "holistic" review of each applicant. On the other hand, the Court rejected a program in another part of the university that granted points based on race and ethnicity and did not provide for a review of each applicant's entire file (In Motion 2003).

Problems with Implementing AA

Problems include poor Human Resource planning by companies and too few penalties for failure to achieve AA goals.

Poor HR Planning

Too many organizations have focused on barely meeting requirements, often flying by the seat of their pants, rather than focusing on valuing diversity and gradually shaping a corporate culture that reflects that value. Many companies have fallen into a frustrating AA cycle that views the workforce as a pipeline and try to fill it with minorities that "fit in," as follows:

- Recognize an AA problem, such as failure to meet targets for hiring or promoting women and minorities, or excessive turnover of these employees, their inadequate upward mobility, or their low morale.

- Respond by recruiting the kinds of minorities who will fit in with the corporate culture, rather than making the corporate culture more flexible and inclusive and establishing practices that meet the needs of these minorities.

After a period of high expectations that the AA problem is being resolved, disappointment sets in when the problem remains or new related problems arise, such as:

- The new recruit doesn't progress as expected.
- Co-workers complain about reverse discrimination or preferential treatment.
- The new recruits sense that others resent them.
- Employees don't give management credit for a good faith effort.

Discouraged, management quits trying and AA efforts are given less attention. After a period, a new human resource crisis appears.

Weak, Infrequent Penalties

Another problem is that few companies are penalized for poor performance in hiring and promoting women and minorities. In fact, since AA began about 30 years ago, the OFCCP has debarred only 41 companies in all types of industries. The agency cannot fine firms unless it finds workers who were denied jobs that they were qualified for. In such cases the workers could get back pay for the period of unemployment. But few workers know of this option and even fewer pursue it.

Bottom Line: AA Is Still Essential

We've mentioned the other major problems of AA, such as the glass ceiling, backlash, and stigma. The bottom line: AA has been the most powerful tool society has ever used to open doors of opportunity where formerly there were brick walls blocking the entry of people of color and women into upwardly mobile career paths. Because of it, the United States has more women managers than any country in the world—and people no longer believe that an African American man or a Latino American woman could not possible work out as a manager in a Fortune 500 company. Yet in 2000, only four Euro-American women, and no minorities had worked their way up to CEO of such a company. About 95 percent of top managers are still Euro-American men and they're paid 25 percent more than minorities and women at every level, including vice presidents. That means we still need AA. If we as a culture want to complete our path toward equal opportunity for all, we must retain the best of AA and build on it by creating multicultural company climates that are welcoming to minorities and women.

But isn't blatant discrimination fading away? Apparently not. During the 1990s racial harassment charges doubled, while minorities in the workplace increased by 36 percent (Bernstein 2001). Job bias lawsuits filed in U.S. District Courts more than tripled and civil rights complaints of all types more than doubled. One causal factor is probably the 1991 Civil Rights Act, which amended five older laws. It broadened the scope of employment practices that are considered discriminatory and made it possible for plaintiffs to receive larger money damages to compensate for their mistreatment and to punish companies that allow such practices (Sixel 1998)

In the 13 years from 1992 to 2005, the amount of money employers reported paying to litigate and settle federal discrimination claims more than doubled to $379.3 million (Employee 2007). Still, this is less than $30 million a year. In 2005 the most common bias claims were in the following categories

- 22% race
- 19% retaliation (because employee supported the bias claim of a coworker)
- 19% gender
- 14% disability
- 13% age
- 8% national origin
- 2% religion
- 2% other

In 2005 more claims were filed over back pain and other orthopedic impairments (2,405) than over religion (2,349) or equal pay (1,044)

Hate Crimes Are Still a Problem

In the past few years, since 2000, reported hate crimes have remained fairly stable at 7,000 to 8,000 per year, normally increasing slightly each year (FBI.gov).

In 1969 a federal hate crimes law stated that federal agencies may prosecute hate crimes that are committed on the basis of the victim's race, color, religion, or nation origin when the victim is engaged in federal activities. Stronger penalties may be applied to hate crimes. In 1993, the U.S. Supreme

Court ruled unanimously that hate crimes laws, and enhanced sentences based upon intent, are constitutional (Wisconsin v Mitchell). Chief Justice William Rehnquist specifically noted that judges have traditionally been allowed to consider the motivation of defendants when imposing sentences. He also noted that hate crimes inflict distinct emotional harm on their victims and can trigger greater social instability.

Hate crimes send a message of terror to an entire group and are therefore unlike a random act of violence. For example, the brutal murder of African American James Byrd, who was chained to the bumper of a truck and dragged down a street in Texas, sent a chilling message to African-Americans that racial violence and murder remain continued threats. Likewise, gay persons wonder whether they will be the next Matthew Shepard. Hate crime laws recognize the particular social threat of bias-motivated violence

State Hate Crime Laws

Hate crime laws have passed in 45 states; the exceptions are Arkansas, Georgia, Indiana, South Carolina, and Wyoming. All of these statutes criminalize various types of bias-motivated violence or intimidation, on the basis of race, religion, or ethnicity. In addition, 32 of the statutes cover sexual orientation; 32 cover disability; 28 cover gender; 13 cover age; 11 cover transgender or gender-identity; and 5 cover political affiliation (State 2006). Statutes requiring the state to collect hate crime statistics have passed in 27 states; 16 of these cover sexual orientation.

Hate Crime Statistics

The U.S. Department of Justice and the Federal Bureau of Investigation (FBI), as well as campus security authorities, are required to collect and publish hate crime statistics This law is considered incomplete because it covers victims only when they are engaged in federal activities and it does not cover all disadvantaged groups, such as gay persons. State hate crime laws are intended to fill that gap. The Department of Justice and the FBI have kept statistics on hate crimes since 1992, which indicate that (Hate 2204):

- 70% were motivated by racial or ethnic bias
- 15% by religious bias
- 14% by sexual orientation bias
- 1% by disability bias

Which groups have the most members charged with such crimes? In 2007 the statistics were (FBI.gov):

- 64% Euro-American
- 21% African American
- 10% Other ethnicities
- 6% unknown

Intolerant Groups Still Exist

As a result of increased resentment of minorities, intolerant organizations and activities have been increasing, according to Carol Swain's research. Specific groups she investigated include:

- Creativity Movement, formerly World Church of the Creator, with perhaps 100,000 members, is now the largest group in the United States devoted to intolerance. They recruit on campuses and elsewhere. See their website CreativityMovement.net, which states that they are "Dedicated to the survival, expansion, and advancement of the white race." See also what other websites have to say about them, including ReligiousTolerance.org and adl.org (Anti-Defamation League).

- National Association for the Advancement of White People, whose mission seems obvious; www.naawp.com.
- Institute for Historical Review denies the Jewish holocaust and objects to the existence of the modern state of Israel. Their website is www.irh.org.

Fortunately, several organizations exist to counter the influence of intolerant groups.

- National Association for the Advancement of Colored People, www.naacp.org
- Anti-Defamation League and the Simon Weisenthal Center both were organized primarily to counter anti-Semitism, but they address abuses against all groups; www.adl.org
- ReligiousTolerance.org is a website sponsored by the Ontario Consultants on Religious Tolerance, whose purpose is to serve the people of the United States and Canada in disseminating accurate religious information; exposing religious fraud, hatred, and misinformation; and promote religious tolerance.
- Southern Poverty Law Center began with the mission of protecting African Americans. It managed to bankrupt the KKK and Aryan Nations groups. As a result many such groups now focus on "leaderless resistance," so it's hard to take them to court. They organize into small cells that people attend as individuals rather than a formal organization that can be attacked. The Southern Poverty Law Center is also well-known for its Teaching Tolerance programs; www.splCenter.org.

AN INCLUSIVE MULTICULTURAL APPROACH TO MANAGING DIVERSITY

During the hey-day of the legal approach, which is still an active and necessary aspect of managing diversity, something called the "valuing diversity approach" emerged. During the 1970s, when companies were opening new doors to diverse persons in order to meet EEO/AA requirements, most of them were still using the melting pot approach, expecting everyone to adapt to their Euro-American male corporate cultures. Minorities and women had difficulty fitting in. Even those who seemed to fit in didn't like the price it exacted, that is, giving up important aspects of their own culture and personality. Company leaders, human resource executives, and corporate consultants looked for ways to encourage productive work relationships and to stem turnover rates of diverse employees. Meeting these needs led to the valuing diversity approach.

Valuing diversity is based on moving beyond tolerance of diverse others to appreciation of what they have to offer. It means appreciating each person's unique spectrum of attributes, such as gender, ethnic and cultural heritage, sexual orientation, physical ability and appearance, age cohort, religious or spiritual beliefs, socioeconomic circumstances, life experiences, and personal style. Valuing diversity involves seeing a diverse work force as a treasure trove of valuable opportunities for innovation, networking, marketing savvy, and similar assets. The approach primarily involves a shift in beliefs and attitudes away from "we're all alike (or should be)" to "we're each unique and that's the source of our greatness. The valuing diversity approach focuses primarily on educating people through experiential and informational seminars to make appropriate attitude shifts. It emerged in the 1980s and is still a part of managing diversity.

Beyond the melting pot myth, the legal approach, and even the valuing diversity approach is a more action-oriented approach often called the inclusive multicultural approach. It is based on valuing diversity and goes further to find ways to shift the corporate culture itself, to make it more inclusive and therefore multicultural. The goal is to create a corporate culture that supports and nurtures all types of employees. We'll explore this multicultural approach in detail in the last chapter. To grasp this evolution of management approaches to diversity, examine Figure 5.5.

FIGURE 5.5: Evolution of Approaches to Workplace Diversity

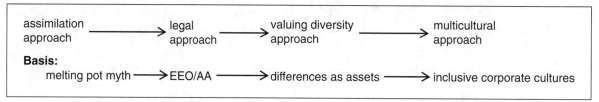

LEADERSHIP CHALLENGE: MOVING BEYOND STEREOTYPING TO PROFITABLE COLLABORATION

You can take a leadership role in helping people in your organization move beyond stereotyping and prejudice by simply being a role model, whether you're the new entry-level employee or the CEO. If you do as Mary Englebreitt suggests and *bloom where you're planted*, you can begin to experience the power of one. It's contagious. And one plus one plus one can soon become a critical mass for change.

You can start by understanding the negative effects of stereotypes on people's performance and the type of contact that tends to heal prejudice. You can then learn powerful action strategies for moving beyond the stereotypes.

Challenge #1: Understand the Effects of Prejudice on Performance

Prejudice and discrimination have a great impact on employee performance. At the deepest level, they undermine employee trust. They also undermine employee motivation and productivity.

Effects on Trust

Prejudice and discrimination sabotage trust. Given our history of intergroup prejudice, trust is more difficult to build across cultural groups than it is within them. "Don't trust Whitey" has long been a motto in many African American families and communities. Minorities tend to feel less free to spontaneously express their opinions and ideas in the workplace. They tend to engage in much more internal prescreening or self-censorship in order to fit into the work group. Euro-American men tend to be unaware that this kind of self-censorship is occurring. Losses to the group generally go unnoticed.

Effects on Employee Motivation

Minorities generally find it more difficult than Euro-American men do to determine the cause of their events and life experiences, often asking themselves, "Was this event caused by discrimination or by other factors?" This can be a major problem when they attempt to process feedback and to stay motivated: "Is my boss criticizing me because my work is not up to standards or because I'm African American?" Expectancy theory holds that the motivation to perform on a job is a function of three factors:

1. If I put forth enough effort, will it produce the performance level the boss wants?
2. If I achieve the performance level the boss wants, will I get what I want (praise, raise, promotion, etc.)?
3. Is it worth it to me?

Discrimination can interfere with factors 1 and 2. Even if the boss is not influenced by an employee's group identity when he evaluates performance, if the employee believes he is, then that employee's motivational level will almost certainly drop.

Effects on Employee Productivity

We've mentioned Jane Elliott's study of the effects of prejudice on productivity, which is described in the documentary film *A Class Divided*. Elliott separated students into blue-eyed and brown-eyed groups. On the first day, the instructor told the class that the brown-eyed "outgroup" was inferior (they wore collars for clear identification of their status). She reinforced this by various actions, such as giving certain privileges to the "ingroup." On the second day, the roles were reversed. On both days the superior ingroup discriminated against the inferiors, calling them names and ostracizing them in many ways.

The work performance of the so-called inferior group declined significantly after just a few hours of the discriminatory treatment. Test scores of the students went up on the day they were in the advantaged group and down on the day the same students were in the disadvantaged group. The change in behavior of the instructor and fellow students had an immediate impact on the performance of the students. The study highlights, among other things, the effect of leader expectations on performance.

Leader expectations are communicated to employees in several ways:

- The amount of output the leader wants signals expectations (How challenging and desirable are the goals? To what extent does the leader believe the employee can achieve high goals? How supportive is the leader?).

- The overall climate (favorable tone, positive responses, etc.) that leaders set communicates their expectations.

- The amount of input (information relevant to getting the job done) that leaders give employees signals their expectations.

- The amount of feedback (information about how well the employee is doing) that leaders give communicates or implies their expectations.

Leaders have more influence than anyone in the work group in setting an inclusive tone. If we want top performance, there must be no outgroups. Everyone must be a member of the ingroup.

Challenge #2: Understand the Life Experiences of Diverse Employees

If you can meet the leadership challenge of truly understanding what makes women and minority employees tick, you'll then be able to design policies, systems, and practices that are sensitive to their life experiences. You can use approaches that help them overcome such internal barriers as lack of organizational savvy and conflict in balancing career and family demands.

Typical Life Experiences

These may include:

- a history of oppression
- being excluded from mainstream business (and society, for minorities)
- feelings that differ, in a negative way, from those of Euro-American men
- when moving into new roles, low self-concept, self-esteem, and self-confidence
- being positioned in a one-down status
- being prohibited from, and not encouraged to seek, a better position and status in business, and, perhaps, in society and in life
- being denied equal opportunities

The experience of being in a subordinate position typically leads to certain attitudes and behaviors that become internal barriers to workplace effectiveness. Kanter (1979, 1997) concluded from her study of corporations that many of the behaviors attributed to women were actually behaviors typical of powerless employees stuck in dead-end positions. Examples are excessive focus on detail, over-concern with rules and procedures, and excessive interest in gossip about personal lives.

Typical Internal Barriers

These internal barriers may include lack of organizational savvy. Because of their very different backgrounds, some women and minority employees may be less likely than their Euro-American male peers to be aware of some corporate rules for getting ahead. They may lack mentors who can show them the ropes and help them understand office politics and the agendas of bosses and peers. They may need guidance in learning how to be strategic about their own career development.

- How can you mentor women and minorities in your area?

Women typically may have been reared to support men and seek their approval. Asian Americans and Latino Americans have been raised to respect authority to a greater degree and in a different way than Euro-American men. When these employees don't assert themselves and their views, as the Euro-American male leaders do, these men may see them as subservient or passive, not willing to take a stand. At the other end of this scale, African Americans are sometimes seen by people from other cultures as too aggressive, vocal, confrontational, or defensive, although other African Americans wouldn't interpret their behavior that way.

- How can you help people bridge these cultural gaps?

Women who are balancing responsibilities for children with a career can also be misunderstood. Leaders need to understand that a slow-down or time-out phase for a woman to have a child doesn't necessarily mean that she's not a candidate for rapid career development later. Companies that are flexible enough to support women in this phase are likely to win their loyalty and commitment.

- How can you help your organization identify and support such high-potential women?

Challenge #3: Understand the Type of Contact that Heals Prejudice

Segregation of the African American community was for hundreds of years legally enforced in the South and was a way of life in the rest of the country. Informal or de facto segregation was generally the rule for Latino American and Asian American communities until recently. We still have a great deal of de facto segregation in our cities, and even where integration has occurred, it has often been accompanied by misunderstanding, conflict, violence, and crime. Some psychologists have described the peaceful progression of contact between diverse groups as a four-step process (Ponteretto and Pedersen 1993):

1. initial contact, leading to
2. competition, which in turn gives way to
3. accommodation, and finally to
4. collaboration.

Whether or not this peaceful progression occurs depends on the nature of the contact that is established, whether it is casual contact, making acquaintances, simply living or working near each other, or working together to achieve common goals. The types of contact diverse groups typically experience range from conflict and superficial contact to true acquaintance and collaboration.

Type #1: Conflict

Clashes of interests and values do occur between groups, and these conflicts are not in themselves necessarily an expression of prejudice. Also some conflicts grow out of economic competition that is not necessarily rooted in prejudice but, again, tends to aggravate any prejudice that exists.

Type #2: Superficial Contact

This has traditionally been the most common type of contact between ethnic groups. Where segregation is the custom, most contacts are superficial, either because they're very casual or because they're firmly fixed into superior-subordinate relationships. Such contact is more likely to increase prejudice than to decrease it because we tend to selectively notice behavior that will confirm our stereotypes. Therefore, each contact may serve to "prove" that our stereotypes are true. Research indicates that superficial contact often reinforces prejudiced beliefs about the following aspects of outgroup members:

- their physical appearance
- their ability to communicate clearly
- the traits and qualities we assume they have (stereotypes and prejudice)

Reinforces Physical Appearance Stereotypes

Visibility serves as a central symbol of group differences (Allport 1954). The two most visible differences are skin color and sexual characteristics. Such differences can serve as a lightning rod for all kinds of thoughts and feelings about certain ethnic groups or about the other half of the human race. Such a lightening rod enables us to pull together and condense these thoughts and feelings and therefore to think of the outgroup as a cohesive unit. Remember, we tend to toss all we can into a category, for efficiency's sake.

For most of us, our view of others, whether favorable or unfavorable, is influenced by how we perceive their physical attractiveness. We assume that physically attractive people have more social skills, intelligence, and competence, so we're more likely to hire them. Various cultures have somewhat different views of physical attractiveness, which may change with the times, and our preferences reflect those views.

Physical distinctiveness can be a double-edged sword. If being different is viewed positively, it can be an asset that makes one stand out and be remembered. However, being too different or inappropriately different from the majority group will trigger prejudiced responses. For example, the token female sales rep in a male-dominated industry may be more successful because she's "different" and therefore remembered. But if she's "too different," she'll lose customers. Many studies illustrate the importance often placed on physical appearance in the workplace, and the dangers to career success of deviating too far from the majority norm (Cox 1993).

Reinforces Communication Stereotypes

Negative attitudes toward people who are difficult to understand has been linked with discomfort and frustration experienced by the persons who are trying to communicate with them. This applies to people who do not know the dominant language well, people who use "street language," and people with speech disabilities. As a result, others may avoid them or shorten their contact time with them (Cox 1993).

Type #3: True Acquaintance

In contrast, most studies show that true acquaintance lessens prejudice. Specifically, contacts that bring knowledge and acquaintance are likely to engender sounder beliefs concerning minority groups, and, therefore, contribute to the reduction of prejudice. But true acquaintance normally happens only where both parties view each other as basically equal human beings. And conversation must delve deeper into basic values, beliefs, and ways of functioning in the world.

Type #4: Collaboration: Contact that Reduces Prejudice

Collaboration is the type of contact that reduces stereotyped thinking and prejudice toward outgroup persons. The concept first introduced by Harvard psychologist G.W. Allport (1954) has been supported by numerous research studies including a meta-analysis of 513 intergroup and prejudice studies (Pettigrew and Tropp 2005). The four-point framework of contact that reduces prejudice is

1. Both parties perceive they have equal status as human beings.
2. They have a common goal that is
3. Very important to each of them, and
4. They must work together (collaborate) in order to achieve that goal

Think, for example, of times when you were involved in teamwork over an extended period with a person(s) from another culture—a team situation where success was important to everyone and all had to cooperate to make it? Didn't you get to know what kind of people those team mates really were? This was contact at the deeper, collaborative level—the type most likely to move beyond stereotyping and prejudice.

Research indicates that Euro-Americans who live side by side with African Americans of the same general economic class in public housing projects are on the whole more friendly, less fearful, and have less-stereotyped views than those who live in segregated arrangements. Merely living together is not the decisive factor. Whether people are jointly active in community enterprises is what counts. The form of the resulting communication is different and makes all the difference in the relationship that develops (Ponteretto and Pedersen 1993).

For example, a public housing project in Los Angeles was converted to private condominiums, which low-income families were able to purchase. Owners established a homeowners association that met regularly for the purpose of making the neighborhood as livable and vital as possible. During the Los Angeles riots of 1992 homeowners took a united stand against any invasion of their neighborhood, and it was spared from vandalism. Residents who were interviewed credited the friendships built by people from various subcultures for the solidarity they displayed during the crisis (*L.A. Times* 1992).

This pattern holds true for contact in the workplace. Only the type of contact that leads people to do things together is likely to result in healing prejudiced beliefs and attitudes. Common goals are all-important. It's the cooperative striving for a goal that engenders solidarity. Participation and common interests are more effective than mere equal-status contact. Self-managing work teams hold tremendous challenge and opportunity to finally break down prejudiced belief systems and establish the unity we so need. But we must meet the challenge of overcoming the barriers to effective collaboration.

> *The key to moving beyond prejudice is working together toward common goals that are highly valued, in situations where people need each other to achieve their goals.*

LEADERSHIP OPPORTUNITY: HOW CAN I PROMOTE COLLABORATION?

If you want to be a leader in your organization, develop the people skills that will enable you to promote collaboration, synergy, and creativity among people. These skills will help you lead people beyond prejudice and discrimination toward profitable ways of working together. Then adopt these seven leadership strategies to accomplish this type of change.

Strategy #1: Promote Tolerance

Work toward openness and acceptance of others, respect their right to have different beliefs and viewpoints, lifestyles and business images, and work styles and job behaviors.

Strategy #2: Be a Role Model of Respect and Appreciation

Be willing to listen to and learn about diverse people and groups, to examine your own ego needs, beliefs, and viewpoints that block your ability to respect and appreciate others, to work collaboratively with others to produce more creative, high-quality results. Be willing to change false beliefs.

Strategy #3: Value Empathy

Be willing to relax into your intuition and listen to its messages as you tune into others, allowing yourself to see things from their viewpoint.

Strategy #4: Promote Trust and Goodwill

Educate yourself and others about the key differences among diverse groups. Value those differences—see them as individual, colorful facets of the kaleidoscope of humanity. Expect everyone to build trust and goodwill in all their interactions—with all team members, business associates, and contacts in other countries.

Strategy #5: Encourage Collaboration

Encourage everyone to work toward common goals for the good of the whole organization, the whole industry, the whole nation, and the world. Value unity, which is not uniformity but individuated integration. See that in unity there can be great diversity. Understand that each part is vital to the integrity of an emerging whole.

Strategy #6: Work Toward Synthesis

Share a vision of people gathering together the separate elements that form the whole project, work team, organization, and industry. See them bringing the whole into active expression. Envision them acting as one to create a new reality—including new projects, processes, products, relationships, and corporate culture. Understand that synthesis is *not* assimilation.

Strategy #7: Create Synergy

Recognize that extra creative spark, that increment of information, knowledge, goodwill, or other benefit that is the by-product of collaboration and synthesis. Use it to carry the team and the organization to new heights of excellence and innovation. Celebrate that added gift, which is more than the sum of what each person brings to the group.

LEADERSHIP OPPORTUNITY: HOW CAN I IMPLEMENT COLLABORATIVE STRATEGIES?

A key diversity skill that you as a leader can bring to the diverse workplace is to recognize your own ethnocentricity, the ways in which you stereotype, judge, and discriminate, and your emotional reactions to conflicting cultural values. Now that you've raised your awareness about the nature of prejudice and ethnocentricity, you're ready to take specific action steps that will move you beyond it. The following are nine action steps that serve to implement the collaborative strategies. Once you, as a leader, work through the action steps yourself, you can serve as a role model and coach for helping others work through them. These action are listed below and then discussed in some detail.

1. Uncover your personal prejudices. Become aware of the ego needs and beliefs that support them and the feelings tied to them.

2. Open your mind. Be willing to listen and seriously consider other viewpoints.

3. Support civil rights measures and inclusive company policies and practices that bring about fairness and equity for disadvantaged groups.

4. Work on your capacity to respect and appreciate diverse people and groups.

5. Explore the ways that respecting diverse people and groups serves your self-interest as well as theirs.

6. Be open to developing your intuition and your capacity for empathy.

7. Learn ways to build trust and make it your top priority.

8. Learn about diverse groups. Pursue multicultural and diversity education.

9. Seek opportunities to collaborate with diverse people and groups and to work toward important common goals.

Action #1: Get in Touch with Prejudiced Beliefs and Feelings

The first step toward becoming more open and accepting of diverse persons is to decide you want to. Then you can begin to notice thoughts that occur when you see certain people, judgmental thoughts that lead to feelings of aversion, dislike, suspicion, and similar feelings that prevent good interaction and block collaborative relationships. Self-awareness activities and skill builders throughout this book are designed to help you in this process. We often hide prejudiced beliefs from ourselves, so uncovering them can be challenging, but it's a challenge worth pursuing.

Action #2: Open Your Mind to Other Viewpoints and Listen

Open-minded persons are relatively rare. They tend to look beyond labels, categories, and sweeping statements. They usually insist on knowing the evidence for broad generalizations before accepting them as true. They are open to new evidence that might lead them to modify a category. Good listeners are just as rare. Most of us take turns talking instead of listening to get another's ideas that we might incorporate into our own. Be willing to listen with an open mind to other viewpoints and to new information that might change your prejudiced beliefs.

Action #3: Support Equal Opportunity Measures

In 1954 Allport stated the belief that legal action can have only an indirect bearing upon reducing personal prejudice. It cannot coerce thoughts or instill personal tolerance. Legal restraints merely say, in effect, "You can have whatever prejudices you like, but you may not act them out to a point where they endanger the lives, livelihood, or peace of mind, of groups of American citizens." Law is intended only to control the outward expression of intolerance. Even so, outward actions have an eventual effect on inner habits of thought and feeling and inclusive actions can result in our opening up our views of limited, stereotyped roles for certain groups. For example, before AA you may have assumed that Latino American women generally didn't have the qualities to be managers. Now you have worked with several of these women who are competent managers, and your earlier stereotyped belief had to shift. Because this process is quite typical, legal action has been one of the major methods of reducing private prejudice as well as public discrimination.

Have you really become informed about the major civil rights laws that affect the workplace and the related policies of companies you've worked for? Or have you settled for basing your opinions on 30-second media sound bites or the glib opinions of co-workers? If you're serious about moving beyond prejudice, you owe it to yourself to become informed about civil rights issues, as well as diversity policies and practices.

Action #4: Express Respect and Appreciation

Once you've opened your mind, the next step is to become comfortable and imaginative in expressing respect and appreciation, primarily through your actions but also through your conversations. Every time you choose to focus on goodwill and trust instead of focusing on fear and mistrust, you automatically move to respecting and appreciating instead of judging and belittling.

Action #5: See Mutual Respect As Mutual Self–Interest

You stand to benefit greatly from moving beyond prejudice, as does your career, your organization, and the planet for that matter. And staying stuck in prejudice, no matter how hidden or subtle, has great costs. You may have learned from bitter failure in a relationship that your stereotypes were in error or that your friends or business associates disapproved of your prejudged categories. You're fortunate if you get such a "change message," for it can help you see clearly that it's in your own interest to change your prejudiced thinking.

Even when you're not confronted by others with your prejudices, and even when you're not consciously aware of them or the effects they have, you probably believe at some level that prejudice conflicts with your deepest beliefs about human value and equality. Most of us, when we catch ourselves in prejudice, don't feel good about it, and if you stop to take a good, hard look at it, you probably don't particularly like yourself when you think and act this way. Except for making you temporarily feel "better than," it's not nearly as satisfying to dislike people and look down on them as it is to appreciate them, collaborate with them, and have fun together. Further, prejudice sets in motion a negative cycle of action and reaction that divides and separates and throws up barriers to building trust. It prevents people from having the productive and harmonious workplace and society that would benefit us all.

Action #6: Open Up to Intuition and Empathy

Clearly, the ability to feel empathy for others can help you to move beyond tolerance to appreciation, and beyond prejudice to collaboration. When you empathize, you intuit how another person sees and feels about a situation; therefore, you're able to experience empathy when you're in touch with your intuitive side. With empathy and intuitiveness, you're better able to understand others and therefore have less need to feel apprehensive and insecure. You tend to gain confidence that you can sidestep unpleasant involvement if the need arises. Accurate perception of how others think and feel gives you the ability to avoid friction and to conduct successful relationships. In contrast, people who cannot empathize are forced to be on guard, to put strangers into categories, and to react to them as a group rather than as individuals. Lacking subtle powers of differentiation, they must resort to stereotyping.

Intuition is never wrong, else it wouldn't be intuition. To come in touch with intuition is similar to listening to your body when it's letting you know it's time to eat, to rest, to exercise. First, give yourself permission to be intuitive. Then, realize that you're most likely to contact your intuition when you're relaxed. So find a time to relax, ask your inner self for intuitive insight, and allow whatever wants to come into your awareness to come in. If you're sincere, answers will come. However, the moment that you set up expectations about *how* the event may occur and *when*, you're immediately limiting your possibilities. So put forth the desire, give yourself permission to ask for it, then be watchful. Intuition is not linear and rational; answers may come in unexpected ways and times. They often come as little flashes or "glimmers" of thought or feeling. Learn to recognize them and to use the power of insight.

Action #7: Build Trust

You build trust by building authentic relationships, in which you respect and appreciate others and show it through words and actions. When you're consistent in your actions and words, keep your commitments, and show respect and appreciation, time after time, then people begin to trust you. Where there is a long legacy of mistrust, it may take years to build trust. It can be destroyed in a moment of betrayal, and the healing process may be difficult or impossible. The best preventive is to consistently choose an attitude of goodwill and trust toward other people.

Action #8: Pursue Multicultural and Diversity Education

Once you begin to understand the typical stereotypes, biases, and barriers that persons from disparaged groups must cope with every day, you can begin to understand more about what their lives are like. Once you become aware of how cultural do's and don'ts affect such persons' self-image, self-esteem, and emotions, you have a better chance of anticipating how your own actions may affect them. The goal of cultural understanding is to be able to walk in another person's shoes for a while, to see the world as that person sees it, and feel what he or she feels. Or to step into a little slice of that person's life and look out at the world from that vantage point.

We've inherited the legacy of prejudice, but we've also inherited the legacy of equality, and we've recently grown to accept more and more people as qualified to be equal. We're approaching the time when Euro-Americans may become a minority in some states, and we face some confusion about our national identity and our future as one people. Euro-Americans, as the dominant majority, can insist on holding onto the past. That would mean continuing to ignore or discount all American cultures except the Euro-American. For many, it would probably mean hunkering down in separate enclaves.

Alternatively, the American culture can welcome its expansion into a multifaceted culture that acknowledges and values all its ethnic groups. As a nation that has thrived on the concept of expansion, it seems more constructive to expand our notion of cultural literacy to reflect the multicultural heritage of all our people, not just the Euro-American portion. If we take this inclusive approach, there will be no need to hide out in exclusive segregated communities or to cluster into ethnic groups in the workplace.

Action #9: Work With Diverse People toward Common Goals

You've learned that superficial contact does not help people to overcome stereotypes and prejudices toward a subgroup. What has worked to change prejudiced beliefs and attitudes is working with diverse others on projects that help all participants to achieve common goals. So continually seek opportunities to work together toward common goals—in alliances, teams, partnerships, and other joint efforts.

SUMMARY

What are some effects of prejudice? It causes the prejudiced to live a more limited life than is necessary. In fact, studies indicate they have less zest for life. They block many of the possibilities for exploring diversity in the world, and the sense of curiosity and adventure that goes with it. On the other hand, prejudice causes minorities to distrust the majority because they've felt hurt, betrayed, and rejected time after time. It affects the personality of those who are targets of prejudice in many ways. Some develop ego defenses that strike out at the majority, such as suspicion, slyness, clannishness, aggression, and competitiveness. Others develop ego defenses that are self-punishing, such as self-dislike, attacking or disliking their own group, putting on a superficial show of success, and clowning. And some are motivated to succeed in spite of discriminatory barriers and to sympathize with all victims.

Discrimination affects minorities' career paths at every step, from employment recruitment, screening and hiring practices to terms and conditions of employment, tracking and job segregation, training and development. It affects layoff, discharge, and seniority practices. It can result in biased performance standards and evaluations and promotion decisions—resulting in glass ceiling barriers. It even affects the career alternatives that are available to minorities.

Discrimination in the workplace was ignored in the past. The melting-pot approach to managing diversity has traditionally assumed that all employees would assimilate into a common corporate culture, but people who don't look like the dominant workplace group, Euro-American men, have never "melted in."

To overcome the discrimination and workplace barriers that minority employees experienced under the melting-pot approach, civil rights laws were enacted in the late 1960s. EEO allows employees to directly complain about discrimination, but individuals find this a difficult path that usually entails severe career setbacks. AA works in the background for most employees but has proven much more powerful than EEO in opening career doors. It requires that employers who obtain large federal government contracts to develop and implement AA plans for hiring and promoting minorities. Backlash and resistance to AA have been reflected in claims of reverse discrimination and beliefs that unqualified minorities are hired or promoted into good jobs only to fill "quotas." In reality AA does not condone any of this. The way leaders can prevent these problems is to make a commitment to diversity, to value diversity, and to create inclusive corporate cultures that support employees from all groups.

Religious diversity is protected by the First Amendment right to freedom of religion and by separation of church and state. Employees' religious practices that affect the workplace can be an issue. Federal law states that employers must accommodate such practices if possible, but in practice most do not.

Beyond the legal approach is the valuing diversity approach, the basis for the current inclusive multicultural approach to managing diversity. The key to success in this approach is expanding the organizational culture to embrace and include all major groups.

To move beyond stereotyping, recognize the effects of prejudice on performance, from trust to motivation to productivity. Understand how the life experiences of diverse employees may create certain internal barriers to career success, barriers that can definitely be overcome.

A major leadership challenge is understanding that superficial contact with people from disparaged groups may actually reinforce stereotypes and prejudices. The type of contact that reduces prejudice is based on getting to know people in depth and collaborating with them to achieve meaningful goals together. Work teams provide an ideal type of contact for moving beyond prejudice.

Leadership opportunities include adopting and implementing collaborative strategies that enable employees to move beyond prejudice to synergy, creativity, and productivity. As a leader, you can take action steps to heal your own prejudice, to become more intuitive and empathic in relationships, and to become a trustworthy ally and role model.

Self-Awareness Activity 5.2: Opening Up to New Experiences

Purpose: To help you open up to all types of people. Especially helpful for people who score above average on the authoritarian personality scale.

Barriers	*Motivators*
I don't know what to expect.	It may be fun.
I don't feel comfortable.	It may be interesting.
Maybe they won't like me.	I may learn something.
Maybe I won't like them.	They may like me.
Maybe they won't treat me well.	I may like them.
I may look end up looking foolish.	I may end up feeling better about myself.
I don't know what to say.	I may gain experience, perspective,
I don't know how to act.	understanding, empathy, compassion.
Others:	Others:

The barriers relate to some type of discomfort and ultimately to some type of fear. They cause us to mentally separate ourselves from others, to contract, withdraw. The motivators relate to an outgoing tendency and ultimately to some type of goodwill. They cause us to mentally reach out, to include, and to expand. They often involve curiosity, courage, and sense of adventure.

Step 1. Think of a situation where you did *not* say yes to an opportunity to experience a new situation with people you didn't know well. What were some of the barriers that held you back? Check off the barriers that apply in the list shown here. Add others that you experienced.

Step 2. Think of a situation where you *did* say yes to such an opportunity. What motivated you? Check off the motivators that apply in the list shown here. Add others that you experienced.

Step 3. What happened in the situation you said yes to? Was the experience more positive or negative in your opinion? If more negative, what lessons can you draw from this experience?

Step 4. What might have happened if you had said yes to the situation in step 1? What experiences, opportunities, advantages, lessons might you have missed? What lessons can you learn from this?

Self-Awareness Activity 5.3: Picturing Exclusion and Inclusion in Your Organization

Purpose: To use the power of symbols and pictures to help you better understand your thoughts and feelings about prejudice and exclusion.

Step 1. Draw a picture of prejudice and exclusion in your company. Draw anything you like, but do not use words in the picture. Use colors and symbols to express how people relate to one another, which groups have power, how they use power, and similar aspects.

Step 2. Look at your completed picture and respond to the following:

- What immediate feelings do you experience?
- What thoughts come to mind?
- What does your drawing say about exclusion in the organization?

Step 3. Draw a new picture. Show symbolically how people could relate to each other in ways that express respect, appreciation, and inclusion. Show how personal power, group power, and organizational power might relate, how it might change, how things would look.

Step 4. Look at your completed picture and respond to the following.

- What immediate feelings do you experience?
- What thoughts come to mind?
- What does your drawing say about how inclusion might change the organization?

Self-Awareness Activity 5.4: Process for Changing Beliefs

Purpose: For leaders who are ready for advanced personal development work.

Be open to the idea that your hostile feelings, or feelings that separate, might be reflections of your judgments about yourself—that what you dislike in others is what you dislike in yourself. In describing this process, we'll use the term *judgment* to mean categorizing people, things, or situations, as right or wrong, good or bad, blaming or praising others, or making them wrong, bad, or evil on the one hand or right or good on the other. *Discernment* is the term we'll use for making choices.

Step 1: Find the bottom-line belief.
  a. **Situation**

Think of a problem situation involving someone from a "different" group, a situation that you suspect involves prejudice on your part. Describe the situation in a few brief words. Then write in answer to the following questions.

  b. **Feelings**

- How do I feel about the situation?
- How do I feel about the diverse other(s)?
- Why do I feel this way?

For each response, again ask, "Why do I feel this way?" until you sense that you are at the root feeling.

  c. **Judgments**

- How am I judging the person(s)?
- How am I judging the situation?
- How am I making the person(s) wrong or bad?

  d. **Beliefs**

- Why am I making this judgment(s)?
- What belief causes me to make this judgment(s)?

Keep asking "Why? What belief?" until you sense you have found the bottom-line belief underneath the judgment.

Step 2: Take responsibility for the judgmental belief and its results

Acknowledge that you have created this reality through your beliefs. You have co-created the situation with the other person(s) in that situation. It takes two to create a relationship problem. Allow that idea to permeate your being. Be willing to accept full responsibility for your beliefs and the actions that flowed out from those beliefs.

Step 3: Acknowledge and embrace your judgmental belief

In your mind, you've been making the person(s) or situation(s) wrong or bad. You've been judging. That's part of being human. To create harmony, you must release your judgment, release the experience of making things good/bad, right/wrong, and move into the experience of accepting what is.

If you want to change what is, you must first acknowledge and accept it. The only way to release judgment is to first recognize and acknowledge that you are judging. If you make yourself wrong for judging, you're still into the experience of judging, only now you're judging yourself. The change process requires you to accept the humanness of your judgment, to embrace it.

Embracing the judgmental belief. By embracing your judgmental belief, you create the freedom to change. Intellectualizing the change process usually will not change a belief, but it is the first step. The change process is to say to yourself, "It's okay to believe this, but now it's time for a change." Then very gently allow the change to occur. Gather the judgmental belief from that judgmental part of yourself into your whole self, your greater self, with love and compassion. A metaphor that is powerful for some people is, "gather it into your light."

Releasing the resistance to painful feelings. A judgmental belief usually fits in with your bottom-line fear, and the belief is often hidden because the fear is hidden, covered with layers of rationalizations, defenses, and other, less-painful fears. When you have great pain, you tend to handle it an extreme way. At one extreme, you express the pain with rage, tears, or anger. At the other extreme, you suppress the pain, ignore it, pretend it's not there until you don't consciously feel it. So you'll normally have a great deal of repressed pain connected to the judgmental belief, and a great deal of resistance to feeling that pain, which for many people wants to be felt in the "pit of the stomach."

Step 4: Feel the feelings

The process of mentally embracing the judgmental belief with love and compassion lets you relax and let go of the "resistance to feeling pain." Allow yourself to feel any painful emotion that comes up. Don't intellectualize at this point, but move your consciousness out of your head into your stomach area. Go fully into this emotion and then let your consciousness go deeper into other underlying emotions if it wants to.

When you sense these painful emotions have run their course, be willing for your emotional consciousness to move into your heart area. The painful feelings can now give way to feelings of harmony, serenity, peace, and joy. These feelings come up when you truly acknowledge and embrace your judgment and move beyond beliefs that hold your separateness in place. You may experience a sense of oneness. Hang out there for a while so you can fully experience these expansive feelings.

REFERENCES

Allport, G.W. *The Person in Psychology.* Beacon, 1968.

Allport, G.W., and B.M. Kramer. "Some Roots of Prejudice," *Journal of Psychology* 22, 9–19, 27, 1946.

Allport, G.W., and J.M. Ross. "Personal Religious Orientation and Prejudice." *Journal of Personality and Social Psychology* 5, 432–443, 1967.

Allport. G. W. *The Nature of Prejudice.* Addison-Wesley, 1955.

Avina, C. and W. O'Donohue, "Sexual Harassment and PTSD: Is Sexual Harassment Diagnosable Trauma?" *Journal of Traumatic Stress* 15, 69–75, 2002

Baack, J., N. Carr-Ruffino, and M. Pelletier. "Making It to the Top: Specific Leadership Skills." *Women in Management Review* 8, 2. 1993.

Barlington, J. "The Prediction, Experience, and Consequences of Workplace Violence," in G. VandenBos and E. Bulatao, eds, *Violence on the Job: Identifying Risks and Developing Solutions,* 29–49, American Psychological Association, 1999

Bell, E.L, T.C. Denton and S. Nkomo, "Women of Color in Management," in E.A. Fagenson, ed. *Women in Management*: 105–130. Sage, 1993.

Bernstein, Aaron, "Racism in the Workplace," *Business Week*, 64–66, July 30, 2001.

Buono, A.F., and J.B. Kamm. "Marginality and the Organizational Socialization of Female Managers." *Human Relations* 36, 12, 112–1140, 1983.

Canby, Nicholas. "The Ideology of English Colonization: From Ireland to America." *William and Mary Quarterly*, 3rd series, 30, 4, October 1973.

Carr-Ruffino, Norma et al. "Legal Aspects of Women's Advancement" in U. Sekaran and F. Leong eds., *Womanpower: Managing in Times of Demographic Turbulence*. Sage 1992.

Carr-Ruffino, Norma. "U.S. Women: Breaking Through the Glass Ceiling." *Women in Management Review* 6, 5, 1991.

Carter, Jimmy. "Keeping Faith with the World's Women." *The Atlanta Constitution* A-11, March 8, 1995.

Cash, T.F., B. Gillen and D.S. Burns, "Sexism and 'Beautyism' in Personnel Consultant Decision Making." *Journal of Applied Psychology* 62, 301–310, 1977.

Deaux, K., and T. Emswiller. "Explanations of Successful Performance in Sex-Linked Tasks." *Journal of Personality and Social Psychology* 29, 80–85, 1974.

Diplacido, J., "Minority Stress Among Lesbians, Gay Men, and Bisexuals," 138–159 in G.M. Herek, ed. *Stigma and Sexual Orientation*. Sage., 1998.

EEOC. www.eeoc.gov

Elliott, Jane. *A Class Divided* (documentary videotape). Public Broadcasting Ssystem (PBS) Video.

Ely, R.J., "The Power in Demography: Women's Social Constructions of Gender Identity at Work," *Academy of Management Journal* 38,589–634, 1995.

Employee Bias Claims, by the Numbers, *Inc. Magazine*, 26, February 2007.

Erez, Miriam and P.C. Earley. *Culture, Self-Identity, and Work*. Oxford University Press, 1993.

Faludi, Susan. *Backlash*. New York: Doubleday, 1991.

"FBI Releases 2007 Hate Crime Statistics," www.FBI.gov, October 27, 2008.

Gates, Henry L., Jr. *Loose Canons*. Oxford University Press, 1992.

Greene, Kathanne. *Affirmative Action and Principles of Justice*. Greenwood, 1989.

Greenhaus, J.H., and S. Parasuraman. "Job Performance Attributions and Career Advancement Prospects" in *Organizational Behavior and Human Decision Processes*. Academic Press, 1991.

Grof, Stanislav, and Christina Grof. *The Stormy Search for the Self*. Jeremy P. Tarcher, 1990.

Gudykunst, W.B. *Bridging Differences: Effective Intergroup Communication*. Sage, 1995.

Gutierres, M., D.S. Saenz, and B.L. Green, "Job Stress and Health Outcomes among White and Hispanic Employees," 107–125 in G.P. Keize and J.J. Hurrell Jr., eds, *Job Stress in a Changing Workforce: Investigating Gender, Diversity, and Family*. American Psychological Assn., 1994.

Hate Crimes, www.thetaskforce.org, 2008.

Heilman, M.E., C.J. Block, R.F. Martell and M.C. Simon, "Has Anything Changed? Current Characterizations of Men, Women, Managers," *Journal of Applied Psychology*, 74, 935–942, 1989.

In Motion Magazine, www.InMotionMagazine.com, October 2003

Johnson, A. "Women Managers: Old Stereotypes Die Hard." *Management Review*, 76, 31–43, 1987.

Kanter, Rosabeth Moss. *Men and Women of the Corporation*. Basic Books, 1979.

Kanter, Rosabeth Moss. *Rosabeth Moss Kanter on the Frontiers of Management*. Harvard U. Press, 1997.

King, D.K., "Multiple Jeopardy, Multiple Consciousness: the Context of a Black Feminist Ideology," *Journal of Women in Culture and Society* 14, 43–72, 1988.

King, T. et al, "Weight and place: a multilevel cross-sectional survey of area-level social disadvantage and overweight/obesity in Australia," *International Journal of Obesity* 30, 2, 281–287, 2006.

Leonard, J. "The Impact of Affirmative Action on Employment." Cambridge, MA: National Bureau of Economics Research, reprint 535, 1984b

Leonard, J. *Antidiscrimination or Reverse Discrimination?* Berkeley, CA: Institute of Industrial Relations, Reprint no. 457, 1984a.

Leonard, J. "Affirmative Action as Earnings Redistribution." *Journal of Labor Economics* 3, 363–5, 1985.

Leonard, J. "What Was Affirmative Action?" *American Economic Review*, 359–363, May, 1986.

Leonard, J. *Women and Affirmative Action in the 1980's.* Paper presented at the Annual Meeting of the American Economic Association, 1988.

Locke, Don. *Increasing Multicultural Understanding.* Sage, 1995.

Los Angeles Times "Neighbors Stick Together," June 2, 1992.

Lynem, Julie N. reporting on 2002 survey by Society for Human Resource Management, *San Francisco Chronicle*, J-1,2, December 9, 2002.

Massengill, Douglas, "Adding Insult to Injury: Disability-Based Hostile Environment under the ADA," *Employee Relations Law Journal*, 30, 2, 74–88, 2004

Mazzuca, J. and L. Lyons, "Few Americans Feel Day-to-Day Racial Tension," Gallup Poll, Aug 31, 2004

Morrison, A.M., R.P. White, "Women and Minorities in Management," *American Psychologist* 45, 200–208, 1990.

Morrison, Ann, ed. The *New Leaders: Guidelines on Leadership Diversity in America.* Jossey-Bass, 1996.

Morrison, Ann, R.P. White, and E. Van Velsor. *Breaking the Glass Ceiling.* Addison-Wesley, 1987.

Oncale v. Sundowner Offshore Services, 1998.

Ponterotto, Joseph G. and Paul B. Pederson. *Preventing Prejudice.* Sage, 1993.

Ponterotto, Joseph G. et al. *Handbook of Multicultural Counseling.* Sage, 2001.

Potomac Institute. *A Decade of New Opportunity: Affirmative Action in the 1970s.* 1985.

SBA. Small Business Administration. www.sba.com, 2004.

Schneider, K.T., S. Swan, and L.F. Fitzgeral, "Job-related and Psychological Effects of Sexual Harassment in the Workplace: Empirical Evidence, *Journal of Applied Psychology*, 83, 3, 401–415, June 1997.

Simpson, Peggy A. "Affirmative Action in Action," *Working Woman* 105, March, 1984.

Simpson, Peggy A. Covering the Women's Movement. Harvard University, Nieman Foundation, 1999.

Sixel, L.M. "Retaliation Complaints Are On the Rise," *Houston Chronicle*, Oct. 11, 1998.

State Hate Crime Laws, Anti-Defamation League, June 2006.

Stewart, L.P., "How Many Gays Are There?" *Fortune* 19, 43, December 1991.

Stone, D.L. and A. Colella, "A Model of Factors Affecting the Treatment of Disabled Individuals in Organization," *Academy of Management Review* 21, 351–402, 1996.

Swain, Carol M. *The New White Nationalism in America.* Cambridge University Press, 2002.

Thomas, D.A., "The Dynamics of Managing Racial Diversity in Developmental Relationships," *Administrative Science Quarterly* 38, 169–194, 1993.

U.S. Commission on Civil Rights. "Affirmative Action in the 1980s: Dismantling the Process of Discrimination." Clearinghouse Publication 70, 1981.

U.S. Commission on Civil Rights. "Understanding Fair Housing." Washington DC: U.S. GPO, 1973.

U.S. Dept. of Labor, Employment Standards Administration. "Employment of Minorities and Women in Federal Contractor and Noncontractor Establishments, 1975.1980, " unpublished final draft (The Crump Report), 1985.

U.S. Glass Ceiling Commission. *Good for Business.* U. S. Department of Labor, 1995.

U.S. Glass Ceiling Commission. *A Report on the Glass Ceiling Initiative.* U. S. Department of Labor, 1991.

Wisconsin v. Mitchell, 508 U.S. 476 (1993)

Wisler, J.S. et al, "Sexual Harassment, Generalized Workplace Abuse and Drinking Outcomes: The Role of Personal Vulnerability," *Journal of Drug Issues*, 32, 1071–1088, 2002

Woody, Bette. "Black Women in the New Service Economy," working paper no. 196. Wellesley College Center for Research on Women, 1989.

WSJ. *Wall Street Journal*, B-1. "SBA Sets New Goals," June 16, 1994.

RESOURCES

Anti-Defamation League, 823 United Nations Plaza, New York, NY 10017–3560. www.adl.org

Simon Wiesenthal Center, 1399 South Roxbury Drive, Los Angeles, CA 90035 www.wiesenthal.net

Southern Poverty Law Center, 400 Washington Ave., Montgomery, AL 36104. www.splcenter.org

CHAPTER 6

Men and Women: Parallel Cultures

Men and women literally live in parallel, but different, worlds.
Deborah Tannen

Men make up about 55 percent of the U.S. workplace, while women are 45 percent. Researcher Deborah Tannen has spent much of her career exploring how men and women can communicate better with each other. She concluded that men and women communicate differently because they view the world differently—to the extent of actually living in different, parallel worlds. Gender differences are the most basic and pervasive of all differences, a good place to start working on the last two steps for gaining multicultural skills. We'll continue to work on these steps in the remaining chapters.

Step 4. Learning about other cultures you encounter in the workplace, so you can recognize when cultural differences may be at the root of problems and so you can appreciate the contributions people from diverse cultures can make to the work situation.
Step 5. Building interaction skills and practicing new behaviors through self-awareness activities and skill builder case studies.

You're about to deepen your understanding of what it's like to be a woman or man in today's society and workplace and how this experience can affect relationships with the opposite sex in the workplace. You'll learn about the following:

- How stereotypes about men and women compare with reality.
- How culture affects male-female traits and status
- How gender roles have evolved and are changing
- How the communication styles of men and women differ
- The resulting differences in worldviews of men and women
- Women's cultural barriers to workplace success
- Men's responses to new roles and expectations
- How men are responding to new expectations in the workplace

- Understanding sexual harassment
- How assertiveness helps to create win-win successes
- Handling the leadership challenges of meeting the needs of women and men
- Rising to the leadership opportunities for building a more gender-balanced work force and corporate culture.

People who have taken the time and effort to learn about our gender differences and similarities say they have boosted their ability to work productively with both men and women. Most of us are not fully aware of our beliefs, attitudes, thoughts, and feelings about these issues. To get in touch with your opinions, beliefs, stereotypes and biases concerning gender and to play with new beliefs, complete Self-Awareness Activities 6.1 and 6.2. Then, to test your current knowledge of gender issues, complete Self-Awareness Activity 6.3. After you've finished this chapter, briefly review these activities to see if any of your responses and insights have changed.

Man

Courtesy of Chris Carroll/Corbis Images.

Woman

Courtesy of Ken Kaminesky/Corbis Images.

Self-Awareness Activity 6.1: Traits of Men and Women

Purpose: To become aware of your beliefs about gender traits and roles

1 What are the traits or qualities that you like to see in men, traits and actions that you admire or feel comfortable with? List them.
2 What are the traits or qualities that you like to see in women, traits and actions that you admire or feel comfortable with? List them.

Self-Awareness Activity 6.2: What Do You Believe About Women and Men?

Purpose:

- to get in touch with your beliefs and stereotypes about this group of people
- to experience how judgmental beliefs affect your thinking and feeling processes
- to experience the ways in which your beliefs create your reality regarding other persons, even before you have any interaction with them.

Part I. What Do You Believe About Women?

Step 1. Associations

- *Relax as deeply as you can.*
- *Close your eyes for a moment and take a few deep breaths.*
- Now focus on the picture that symbolizes "woman"
- Imagine that you are this woman. Be woman.
- Notice any resistance to being this person—and any willingness.
- Notice words, images, thoughts, and feelings that come to mind as you are "seeing and being this woman."

Step 2. Negative Associations

- Next, as you focus on the picture, allow negative opinions to come up, perhaps some that you typically hold about women.
- Notice your *thoughts* as you see the person in this negative way. What *feelings*?

Step 3. Positive Associations

- Now, still focusing, allow positive opinions to come up, perhaps some that you typically hold about women.
- Notice your *thoughts* as you see the person in this negative way. What *feelings*?

Step 4. Insights and Write-up

- Now review this experience and write about it.
- When you first saw the picture, what thoughts and feelings came up? These may reflect your deepest responses to people from this group.
- Think about the differences in your thoughts and feelings when you consciously held a positive opinion versus a negative opinion.
- Write a few sentences about your feelings, thoughts, and insights.

Part II. What Do You Believe About Men?

- Repeat the phases and steps in part I, this time focusing on the image of a man.

Self-Awareness Activity 6.3: What Do You Know About Gender Issues?

Determine whether you think the following statements are basically true or false—and think about why.

1. The American culture is considered patriarchal because women are gaining equal rights.
2. Most American mothers of small children are not in the workplace; their husbands are.
3. Men focus on reporting information, while women focus on establishing rapport.
4. Balancing masculine and feminine strengths refers to hiring approximately equal proportions of male and female employees.
5. Few men are fazed by the increase in numbers of women holding degrees and higher positions in business and government.
6. Sexual harassment is rare and refers to bosses giving favors in exchange for a sexual relationship.
7. The best women leaders become just as aggressive as the men.

Our patriarchal culture provides us with an array of gender stereotypes, such as "women stay home and raise the kids while men go out and earn a living." Most of us adopt these beliefs as children and then forget we ever learned them. Meanwhile, megatrends that affect all aspects of American society, such as new workplace opportunities for women, are changing our culture. For example, nearly half of all employees are women, and 40 percent of all managers are women. Still, less than 5 percent of top managers are women, and women make an average of 25 percent less than men at all levels.

And boys and girls still grow up in two worlds, overlapping but different. These differences cause major misunderstandings at times; for example, when the man focuses on giving and getting information in a conversation while the woman is focusing on giving and getting emotional support. We'll discuss how female activists view these changes; we'll compare this with male activists' views, and we'll look at how gender issues affect both women and men.

What's In a Name? Sex is normally defined as the physical aspects we use to classify organisms according to their reproductive functions, while *gender* originated as a grammatical term referring to a category that includes masculine, feminine, and neuter. For our purposes here, we'll use *gender* to discuss workplace or social issues that stem from the fact that one is a man or a woman, and *sex* to discuss situations that stem more directly from one's sexuality.

STEREOTYPES AND REALITIES

Stereotypes about the roles that men and women should play are as limiting and challenging as the stereotypes about their traits.

Stereotype #1: The Typical American Family is a Working Husband with and a Wife who Stays Home to Take Care of the Two Children.

This stereotype reflects traditional male/female roles. The woman belongs at home doing housework and raising children, and the man belongs in the workplace earning a living for the family. This pattern was typical from about 1900 to 1960. Now, only about 15 percent of U.S. families fit that description—and even then only temporarily while the children are very young—making the roles more myth than reality.

Stereotype #2: There Are Only Two Types of Women: Good and Bad.

In the past "good women" were placed on a pedestal, called ladies and treated like little madonnas or dolls, while "bad women" were called sluts or whores. There was not much gray area in between. Women who had ever had sex outside of marriage were bad and the others were good. Men, on the other hand, were expected to have sex before marriage, and extramarital sex for them was covertly condoned and even admired. This stereotype tends to define women primarily by their sexual relationship to men. Its vestiges are definitely still in evidence, more in some subcultures and regions than in others.

Stereotype #3: Women's Status in Society Is Equal to Men's.

The stereotype is that since women got voting rights, equal opportunity, and affirmative action, they've gained equal status. However, we know that less than 5 percent of the top decision makers in business are women. And women at all levels average 25 percent less pay than men.

If the media reflects what's going on in society, women are still seen first as sex objects—at least while they're young. Later they're seen as wives and mothers. The media frequently portrays young women as little more than dimwitted bimbos hanging onto a powerful man's arm, or sex objects that help sell cars, liquor, cosmetics, and most anything else. The idea is that buying the product will help a man to attract a young, sexy woman or help a woman to become young-looking and sexy. A 1972 study showed that the role of women in 32 percent of TV commercials was sex object/decoration and in 20 percent it was wife/mother. A 1990 survey of women's opinions of advertising indicates that things haven't changed much (Dominick 1972; Crane 1992). Most say the few ads that feature career women tend to show them as superwomen who do it all, and that advertising generally:

- shows women mainly as sex objects
- does not show women as they really are
- suggests that women don't make important decisions

Stereotype #4: Real Men Are in Control of the Situation.

In our patriarchal culture, being in control has had high value. Men have typically been told by men in authority, "You're letting things get out of control," "Control your wife," "You've got to take charge." This stereotype implies that men are superior. At home they should be master of the house, and in the workplace they should be the managers. More and more American women are expecting to have equal relationships at home and in the workplace. Relationship styles and management styles are changing. The trend is that people are expected to control themselves and to take control of their own lives, then come together as basic equals to collaborate on joint projects. Trying to control others is becoming frustrating and counterproductive for men.

Stereotype #5: Real Men Don't Cry.

People in our culture typically tell little boys that "Big boys don't cry." Neither are they afraid. They are brave and confident. They may get angry and fight back, but they don't whimper or snivel. In hundreds of little ways men get the message that they should not be emotional nor show their feelings. Most boys learn to hide their feelings. By the time they grow up, many have denied their feelings for so long that they're numb to them, out of touch with them.

Once they're men, it's generally all right to show anger in certain situations, such as to get things done or to defend one's honor. And it's acceptable to show some feelings with one's mate in romantic settings. Otherwise, feelings are to be buttoned up, locked in, and kept contained. And that's the major problem with this stereotype. Unacknowledged and unexpressed feelings don't go away. They build and fester, contributing to stress and its related illnesses.

Stereotype #6: Women Are Too Emotional and Soft to Be Real Leaders.

Many stereotypes that are devastating for career women are based on the "too emotional and soft" belief. According to the Glass Ceiling Commission of the U.S. Labor Department, these stereotypes are the ones that create the greatest barriers:

- Women are too emotional.
- Women are too passive, too aggressive, not aggressive enough.
- Women aren't tough enough to fill some positions.
- Women can't or won't work long or unusual hours—or relocate.
- Women can't or won't make tough decisions
- Women can't crunch numbers.
- Women don't want to work.
- Women aren't as committed to careers as men.

These traits are primarily learned traits. They are a matter of style rather than substance. The impact of this stereotype is still strong. A Gallup Poll done in 2001 indicates that nearly half of Americans would prefer to work for a male boss, while 22 percent would choose a female boss, and

28 percent have no preference. The good news for women is the dramatic change in attitudes since the 1950s, when two-thirds said they preferred a male boss and only 5 percent preferred a woman.

DOES CULTURE DETERMINE MALE-FEMALE TRAITS AND STATUS?

While some traits may have a genetic component, we know that culture plays a large role. In patriarchal cultures, men and women have different status and different roles. Different traits provide a rationale for this and so are emphasized.

Stereotyped Traits

Almost from the moment we're born, we begin learning gender stereotypes and myths. Most of us also begin learning about inequality in relationships from the patriarchal system of family, church, and culture. Although the patriarchal system is beginning to change in the U.S., boys and girls are still socialized in very different ways. And boys and girls still grow up in two worlds, overlapping but different.

People generally expect men and women to express different traits, and the traits they admire in men are often traits they don't admire in women and don't expect women to express. Men's traits—such as aggressive, strong, and independent—are those traditionally expected of business leaders. That's why business women report they must walk a fine line between being considered too feminine and too masculine. The traits they need for business success are *not* the traits people expect or admire in women, as Table 6.1 indicates.

TABLE 6.1: Typical Masculine and Feminine Traits

Feminine Traits	Masculine Traits
emotional	aggressive
talkative	strong
sensitive	proud
affectionate	confident
moody	independent
patient	courageous
romantic	disorganized
cautious	ambitious
thrifty	
(Men also said *manipulative*. Women said *creative*.)	

Adapted from Gallup polls, 2000.

This "traits disadvantage" that business women have dealt with is beginning to recede as companies recognize the increasing importance of some of women's typical traits—such as a focus on personal connections, interpersonal relationships, and nurturing leadership—for managing today's participative workplace, which is increasingly peopled by well-educated employees working in self-managing teams. Men who are very aggressive and ambitious may need to develop more sensitivity and patience. All of us can benefit by becoming more well rounded and balanced, allowing the best of our personalities to emerge from both sides, the feminine and the masculine.

Developing this balance is becoming important for effective modern marriages, too. In the old survival times, men and women needed each other for a balance. Today's power couples, where both partners balance important careers with a fruitful family life, tend to develop themselves as whole persons first, then to form partnerships from preference rather than need.

Traits and Power Differentials

Not only are traits learned, they are affected by the power the culture accords to each group. When we are socialized at home in ways that establish and reinforce a power differential between men and women, male-female interactions in the workplace reflect interactions between the more powerful and the less powerful. For example, why do some women use tears to influence men, while men tend to use logical arguments to influence both men and women? Yes, through socialization, women have been allowed to express emotions and men have not. But also, men usually have more power in male-female relationships and therefore have the upper hand. It may be that women's logic would be ignored and they feel they must resort to tears in order to have effect. Research has led to two major conclusions about gender and power tactics (Peplau, 1991): 1) gender affects power tactics, 2) power, not gender, is the issue.

Gender affects power tactics.

Women are more likely to withdraw or express negative emotions, while men are more likely to use bargaining or reasoning. However, in a partnership between gay men, if one partner perceives himself as less powerful, he is likely to use withdrawal or expressions of negative emotions, and the more powerful partner is likely to use bargaining or reasoning. The same dynamics were found between two women in a lesbian partnership.

Power, not gender, is the issue.

Regardless of gender or sexual orientation, people who see themselves as relatively more powerful in a relationship tend to use persuasion and bargaining, while those who feel they are lower in power tend to use withdrawal and emotion.

As Rosabeth Kanter found in her studies of men and women in organizations, behaviors believed to be typical of women are actually behaviors that are typical of the powerless. Regardless of sexual orientation, a partner with relatively less power tends to use "weak" strategies, such as manipulation and pleading. Those in more powerful positions are more likely to use autocratic and bullying tactics. Signs of conversational dominance, such as interrupting, were linked also to the balance of power. Interruption is not so much a male behavior as a tactic of the powerful. Many studies provide support for the dominance interpretation of sex differences in male-female interaction (Peplau 1991; Howard, 1986; Kollock 1985).

Gender Differences as a Prototype of Group Differences

All cultures differentiate between male and female behavior, and usually when a given behavior pattern becomes associated with one gender, it will be dropped by the other, according to G.P. Murdock's work. Recently many sociologists and anthropologists have begun to see gender differences primarily as cultural differences and have started applying cross-cultural techniques to solving gender problems. Some researchers, such as Richard Brislin and Tomoko Yoshida, say that gender is not just one of many cultural differences, but *the* most important cultural difference, the root paradigm of difference, just as the inequality of patriarchy is the paradigm of all inequality among groups.

Instead of seeing women's culture as a subculture within each ethnic culture, they declare that the two most basic cultural groups are women and men. Between these two groups we find the prototypical cultural distinctions, after which all other cultural distinctions are modeled. If organizations can learn to accept and deal with gender differences, all other differences can be handled in due course. On the other hand, a great deal of diversity work remains superficial when gender issues are not first recognized and managed. This is because beliefs about gender influence us in the most fundamental ways about how to be with others and make choices in life.

HOW HAVE GENDER ROLES EVOLVED AND CHANGED?

Women in Western cultures have traditionally been viewed as a wholly different species from men, invariably an inferior species. Those primary and secondary sex differences that exist are greatly exaggerated and are inflated into imaginary distinctions that justify discrimination. In the past most men felt an in-group solidarity with half the humans on earth, other men, and with the other half, an irreconcilable conflict. Lord Chesterfield described the way women were traditionally viewed by men in the eighteenth century (Allport 1954):

> (Women are) *"children grown large, with little reasoning ability. They are to be trifled with, played with, humored, and flattered, as with a sprightly, forward child. Few men ever consult them or trust them with serious matters, though they often make women believe that they do both, which is the source of women's greatest pride. They are mainly concerned with matters of vanity and of love.*

The Patriarchal System

Patriarchy refers to the rule of a family or tribe by men, and a social system in which descent and succession are traced through the male line. It began by brute force and muscle power. Once established, men's superiority and advantage were institutionalized into every sphere of life. It's being undermined because brain power and relationship power are becoming true power. As men's superiority is undermined, some are resorting to extreme measures to hold onto it, even to physical abuse and rape, according to Robert Bly, Sam Keen, and other men's movement leaders.

Men's movement author Walter Farrell defines a patriarchy as the male areas of dominance, responsibility, and subservience in a culture, reinforced by both genders for the purpose of serving survival needs of both. Patriarchy has given men the authority, privileges, and responsibility that come with being in charge. Women's privileges involved being provided for and protected, if they picked the right man and all went well. Both men and women have been rewarded with "identity" when they followed the rules and punished with invisibility when they failed—or sometimes even death if they rebelled against them. Leaders were picked from the men who best followed the rules (Farrell 1993, 2005).

Feminist Movements

Women's groups have arisen from time to time to protest the limitations and unfairness to women and to men that patriarchy imposes. The most recent feminist movement began in the 1960s and has made significantly more progress than any previous movement. Perhaps gender equality is an ideal whose time has come. Feminists come in many political shades and stripes. For our purposes we'll use this simple definition.

> A *feminist* is someone who believes in equal rights for women.

Most feminists believe that the inequality inherent in patriarchy does not serve women's best interests, and that equality in the workplace will lead to equality in the family. They focus on eliminating all discriminatory barriers to women's moving up in the work world as the key to the overall liberation of women. They believe that changes in labor market conditions that women face will force changes in family dynamics. Economic power is a prerequisite to a balance of power in family relationships.

From Patriarchy to Equality

As we've moved from an agricultural economy through an industrial to a post- industrial economy, cultural values have shifted dramatically. The women's movement is a reflection of that basic shift. Marriage relationships are the most influential in a society, because children learn about life and relationships by observing their parents. Leaders of both the men's and women's movements propose that we move beyond patriarchy or matriarchy—beyond hierarchy—to a system that relies on leadership that arises spontaneously from those who are willing and able to lead in particular situations. See Table 6.2.

TABLE 6.2: Traditional and New Male-Female Relationships

	Traditional Marriage Relationships	*New Relationships*
Major goal	Survival	Fulfillment
Relationship focus	Role mates, to create a whole	Soul mates, whole persons, to create synergy
Effect on roles	Segregated roles	Common roles
Family obligations	Must have children Woman raises children, man makes money. Woman risks life in childbirth; man risks life in war.	Children are a choice Both raise children and both make money Childbirth relatively risk-free; ideally no more war
Partner choice	Parental influence primary; women try to marry "up"	Parental influence secondary; both marry for love
The contract	Lifetime; no divorce	As long as both parties want to stay together
Status of parties	Neither party can end contract Woman is property of man; man expected to provide and protect Both are subservient to needs of family	Either party can end contract Each equally responsible for self and other Both balance needs of family with needs of self
Emotional expectation	Love emerges from mutual dependence I'll stay no matter what	Love is based on choice I'll stay unless you abuse me or we grow in different directions

Megatrends That Opened Doors

Beginning in the 1960s a series of megatrends combined to accelerate the pace at which women moved into managerial, professional, technical, and leadership roles that had been almost exclusively Euro-American male territory.

Social Change

The 1960s brought major social upheavals. Those that most affected gender issues were greater acceptance of divorce, greater sexual freedom, and greater acceptance of equal opportunity for women and minorities. Such social changes allowed women more freedom of choice. During the 1970s women began moving into many fields of study, preparing for the occupations that were closed to them before AA.

Economic Change

As blue collar jobs moved offshore, growing number of husbands no longer earned an income that would support a family, and their wives went to work. As divorce became more economically feasible for women, an increasing percentage of women became heads of households. For all these reasons, middle-class working mothers, once a sign of liberation, became an economic necessity during the 1980s. As the average worker's take-home pay went down, family income grew an average of less than 1 percent per year, even with many wives working. Buying a home became more expensive and took a larger share of family income, and renters found it more difficult to save up a down payment. An ever-greater proportion of women will continue to enter the workforce and stay there, even when they have small children. This means that working mothers will be the largest potential source of qualified workers for the next decade.

Emphasis on Ethical Values

The excesses of the 1980s—such as the grand larceny of Wall Street dealers and savings and loan officers—brought a new respect for ethical principles. The recent Enron collapse and other major accounting scandals have reinforced this concern. Also, biotechnology companies say they are poised to solve many of our health and poverty problems, but people are realizing a corresponding need to define ethical values in order to regulate the industry. Several recent surveys indicate that people believe women can bring special talents to dealing with and cleaning up ethical issues, and that people tend to trust women's ethical standards and level of honesty. This applies to both the business and political worlds. Women represent a "fresh face" without the backroom connections and long years of deal making (Naisbett 1990).

Management Style Change

The underlying theme of all the megatrends is the individual (Naisbett 1982, 1990). While people are working together in more dynamic ways than ever, the trend is for power in work groups to stem from the power of individuals within the groups. Leaders who know how to empower others have an edge. This megatrend makes the natural management style of most women a plus because:

- Women are usually socialized to win commitment from people rather than to give orders and apply controls

- Women tend to adapt more naturally to the role of teacher/facilitator/coach than they do to the role of director/overseer.

- Women have historically been trained to focus on helping others achieve success, usually husbands and children.

Impact of Change: Current Socioeconomic Profile

The current socioeconomic profile of American women and men indicates that young women are bridging the gaps—educational, occupational, entrepreneurial, and pay gaps. But they face challenges, including the biological time clock.

Young Women Bridging the Gap

Younger women are bridging the gender gap in education, pay, and position. Older women have similar expectations toward work as their older male counterparts. However, younger women seem more focused on career success than the younger men, many of whom seem less ambitious than in the past. OTC Research surveyed 2,000 U.S. men and 600 women aged 18 to 54 to explore men's attitudes toward work, play, and relationships. Respondents aged 18 to 24 made the following responses (Garcia 2008).

Career Issue	Women 18–24	Men 18–24
I feel that my prospects will improve greatly in the next 5 years.	45%	35%
I have already met or exceeded my career expectations.	28%	46%
My future is looking brighter; I am on the move.	52%	41%

Women, 51 percent of the U.S. population, now earn 60 percent of all degrees. In the past decade women have made significant progress in educational attainment, while men have not moved forward (Pell 2008). And while overall women still experience a 25 percent pay gap, the trend has reversed in major U.S. cities such as Boston, Chicago, Dallas, Los Angeles, and New York, where women's incomes have soared as men's have stalled or declined (U.S. Census). There has been no growth in the average hourly wages of men in 25 years.

Some researchers believe that women's innate skills have helped them to thrive in today's corporate world, skills such as communication, multitasking, and collaboration. Women's tendency toward nurturing, caring, egalitarianism, and consensus-building often gives them an edge in today's increasingly feminine global markets. Mean are advised to lean toward less hierarchy and more networking, less aggression and more consensus.

The increase of wives in the workforce has raised family income by one-third on average. Women with dependent children are more likely to work than women with adult children. Nearly 80 percent of mothers with school-age children work, as do 60 percent of those with infants younger than one year. And women are increasingly likely to delay marriage and children in order to finish college and establish themselves in a career.

Are we making satisfactory progress? When it comes to workplace equality, most men (54 percent) say that women have equal job opportunities with men, but 61 percent of women say they don't. In a Gallup poll, 41 percent of women said they felt discriminated against at work at least a few times a year, and 19 percent said at least once a month. When it comes to how women are treated in the broader society, 82 percent of women are dissatisfied with the status quo, and 66 percent of men agree (Brooks 2002).

Education

Although there has traditionally been a male-female education gap, with more men getting degrees, the gap closed for graduates in 2000, with women baccalaureates slightly outnumbering men by 28 to 25 percent. Among younger persons, ages 25 to 29, women are now better educated than men, as follows:

- High school diplomas are held by 88 percent of young women, 85 percent of young men
- Bachelor's degrees are held by 32 percent of these women, 27 percent of the men

The fields where women graduates have increased the most dramatically are business and science, as shown in Table 6.3

TABLE 6.3: Men and Women—Occupations and Education

Relative proportions of men and women:	*Male*	*Female*
In total population (1995)	48%	52%
In the workforce	54	46
Managers	58	43
Professionals	46	53
Technical	46	64
Sales	51	50
Clerical	23	80
Service	37	63
Production, craft (electrician, plumber, etc.)	90	9
Machine operators	60	24
Laborers	80	20
Received bachelor's degrees (2000)	25%	28%
Psychology	29	71
Life sciences	49	51
Business degree	53	47
Social sciences	56	44
Physical sciences	69	31
Engineering	86	14
Working on Advanced Professional Degrees (2002)		
Law	51%	49%
Medicine	55	45

Source: *U.S. Bureau of Labor Statistics, 1997, 2002.*

Gender Segregation in the Workplace: By Industry and by Occupation

The male-female occupational imbalance is called "gender segregation" or "occupational segregation," where women and men hold very distinct occupations—such as nurse or teacher versus electrician or engineer. It can occur between occupations i.e. by industry (construction versus elementary education) and within particular occupations where it takes the form of "clusters" in staff and line functions (human resources versus plant operations), Either way, it leads to poor consequences for women's earning and career mobility (Maume 2001).

Women's wages are lower because female-dominated professions pay less; for example, according to the 2000 U.S. Census:

- Women were over 90% of clerical workers and only 11% of engineers.
- The lowest paid occupation is dishwasher followed by child care worker, housekeeper, cafeteria counter attendant, and teacher assistant, occupations heavily dominated by women.
- The highest paid occupations are physician and surgeon followed by dentist, lawyer and petroleum engineer, occupations with relatively few women.

Women who enter higher-paid, male-dominated fields are at higher risk of leaving their jobs and less likely to be promoted due to the challenges of social isolation and stereotyping (Glick 2007; Maume 2001.)

Gender-segregated workplaces tend to perpetuate gender stereotypes. When it's rampant, attitudes will not change, even with good training. Gender segregation is a form of resistance to diversity because it limits women's access to more powerful job positions. It is associated with differences between men's and women's job and promotional opportunities, wages and benefits, and other workplace features (Guthrie 1999; Maume 2001). It can motivate women to search for alternative lifestyles or job opportunities. But the connection is lost if people interpret mothers' decisions to stay home or work part-time as a "choice" made independent of the system of constraints around the decision (Stone 2004; Williams 2004). Gender segregation helps to erect a glass ceiling to the top, which we discuss later, and contributes to the pay gap.

The Pay Gap

In 2001 women's median earnings were 74 percent of men's—for full-time year-round employees, with men making $39,000 compared to women's $28,800. All ethnic groups experience some pay gap, and Euro-Americans have the greatest gender gap (U.S. Census Bureau 2002).

- Euro-American men earned $42,200, compared to women's $30,800
- African American men earned $31,000, compared to women's $25,700
- Latino American men earned $25,000, compared to women's $21,000

The fact that certain occupations are considered "women's work" is the largest contributor to the gender wage gap, according to the Bureau of Labor Statistics. (Gender segregation is discussed later.) But the data also showed that the gap between men and women's earnings increased with higher incomes. For example, the difference between men and women's earnings as dishwashers differed by only $2,000. But male physicians earned $140,000, while female physicians earned $88,000. Salaries increased in fields dominated by men, such as the technology sector, when there were employee shortages. But the same did not happen in women-dominated fields with shortages, such as nursing.

The Census report states that several factors—such as location, educational opportunities, marriage, unions, and work history—help explain the pay gap. An in-depth study (Blau 2007) addressed the question, What contributes to wage differential between men and women who are employed full time? Following are some answers.

- Occupational category   27.4%
- Industry category   21.9

- Labor force experience   10.5
- Union status   3.5
- Race   2.4
- Educational attainment   -6.7
- Unexplained   41.1 (discrimination?)

    Total   100%

    Wage differential   20.3%

The largest category of difference, 41 percent, is "unexplained," which researchers tend to attribute to some level of discrimination. The first two categories—occupational and industry categories—are aspects of gender segregation in the workplace. For example, men are more likely to be in blue-collar jobs and to work in mining, construction, or durable manufacturing; they are also more likely to be in unionized employment. Women are more likely to be in clerical or professional jobs (nurses, teachers, etc.) and to work in the service industry. Taken together these two aspects of gender segregation explain 49.3%t of the gender wage gap and when combined with "unexplained" accounts for 90.4% of the gap.

Men's greater labor force experience had narrowed to 3.5 years by 1998, and accounts for about 10.5% of the pay gap. Women actually have higher educational attainment than men these days, which works to lower the gender wage gap by nearly 7 percent.

The pay gap is especially tough for single mothers. And more families than ever were headed by single women—28 percent in 2000, compared to 17 percent in 1990 and 11 percent in 1970. Among "minority" households, the proportion of single mothers is even higher: for African Americans the figure is 44 percent and for Latino Americans, 32 percent, versus 12 percent for Asian American and Euro-American households. On average, these women had to survive on about one-third the median income of married-couple families. Therefore, they were nearly six times as likely to live in poverty. In fact, at all ages, more women than men live in poverty. For example, women over 65 are twice as likely as older men to live in poverty. And they live longer—by about 7 years on average.

Interestingly, the gender pay gap is less in some countries than in the United States; for example, according to one analysis from the late 1990s, women's proportion of men's average income was 80% in Hungary, 77% in China, and 74% in the U.K. compared to 72% in the U.S. Faring worse than U.S. women were women who earned 70% in Russia, 56% in South Korea, 55% in Australia, 45% in India, South Africa, Brazil, and Egypt, and only 35% in Costa Rica (Seager 2003).

Business Ownership

Women-owned businesses accounted for 40 percent of all privately-held firms in 2008—and 20 percent of all U.S. firms with revenues of $1 million or more (Center 2005). In fact, 10.1 million women-owned firms hired 13 million employees and generated $1.9 trillion in sales. Looking at the larger firms with revenues of $1 million or more, 3 percent of all women-owned firms were in this category, compared with 6 percent of all men-owned firms.

Women of color have also been starting their own businesses in great numbers. In 2008 they owned 2.3 million U.S. businesses with 1.2 million employees and $165 billion in revenues. Between 2002 and 2008 these firms grew three times as fast—35% versus 15%—as all privately held U.S. firms (Center 2009).

Women-owned businesses have been doing better than average. For example

- Their startup rate has doubled that of men-owned firms for over a decade.
- Revenues are growing faster than the overall average—5.6 percent a year since 1997, compared to 4.8 percent overall.
- Their workforce is growing twice as fast as the overall average—24 percent compared to 12 percent from 1997 to 2004.

Why do women start their own business? Here are the answers they gave the Center for Women's Business Research (Center 2005).

- Wanted to control my own schedule   46%
- Frustration with the glass ceiling at a big company   23
- Saw a lucrative market niche and decided to fill it   24
- Other reasons   7

Clearly corporate America is not meeting the needs of many high-powered women, so they create situations where they can meet their own needs—businesses where they call the shots. But we also see that about a fourth of these women are simply risk-taking entrepreneurs who see a market opportunity and rise to the occasion.

Women are increasingly better prepared to start a business than they were a few decades ago. They now hold 45 percent of all professional degrees, up from 4 percent in 1965, and more women than men are enrolled in college. They have better business experience than in the past—with 40 percent of all managerial positions held by women, compared to almost none in 1965. In fact, 65 percent of the women who have started businesses in the past decade learned the ropes as managers in big corporations.

Why are women-owned businesses more successful than most? When women owners are surveyed, they give a wide range of reasons. The one mentioned most frequently is their skill at building relationships—with clients, suppliers, and each other. Now that woman-owned businesses are so numerous and so robust, female entrepreneurs are helping one another the way men always have (Fisher 2005).

Biological Clock: The Baby Gap

As a result of all these changes, more and more women are delaying marriage and more and more couples are delaying the time when they have their first child. Most couples think that they have until their late thirties to get started, maybe even their early forties. That's understandable because it's been only recently that doctors discovered how dramatically a woman's fertility can decline after age 27. While at age 20, her risk of miscarriage is about 9 percent, it doubles by 35, then doubles again by 40. In fact, 90 percent of a woman's eggs are likely to be abnormal by age 42, and she has less than an 8 percent chance of having a normal baby using her own eggs (Hewlett 2002).

Many couples are shocked by this news. Some spend tens of thousands of dollars at fertility clinics before they have their first child. Some adopt, and others simply give up the idea of having children. Yet 86 percent of Americans between 18 and 40 who don't have children say they want children. This age group represents two-thirds of all Americans without children. The other one-third are over 40, and most say they wish they had at least one child. Only 4% of adult Americans say they're satisfied to have no children (Newport 2003). Women may want to revise their career-family sequencing pattern in order to accommodate such realities.

In fact, women who want career success need to face some facts. Half the women over 40 who make at least $100,000 don't have children. Half of women MBAs over 40 have no children, compared to 25 percent of men (Hewlett 2002).

MEN AND WOMEN: GROWING UP IN TWO DIFFERENT WORLDS

Women and men are much more alike than not. Most differences are probably more cultural than genetic, and individual men and women vary greatly as to their degree of typically masculine or feminine traits. Still, even though girls and boys grow up side by side, they live in two different experiential worlds. Because we as a culture and as individuals treat boys and girls, men and women, so differently, their experiences and worldviews are dramatically different.

Cultural Socialization of Girls and Boys

We raise boys and girls differently in our culture. They play differently as children. They have different values and experiences as teenagers. Since we are a patriarchal culture, boys gain more respect as they grow into men. As girls grow into women, they have more difficulty being perceived as competent leaders.

Some differences in the ways boys and girls are socialized in the American culture are shown in Table 6.4. Read the table from the top down, by column, since the each column represents a socialization process, by gender, not a comparison of types of experiences.

Teenage Differences

Many of the old stereotypes and socialization patterns are still in place for teenagers. Peggy Orenstein's research (Carroll 1994) indicates that girls routinely report feeling:

- resignation about the greater power that society grants boys
- resignation about society's acceptance of boys' greater assertiveness and power to disrupt
- pressure to emphasize appearance and minimize brains to win favor
- pressure to acquiesce in second-rate status
- fear of failure in science and math

Boys and Men: More Respect

As boys grow into men, their time and activities gain respect and tend to be viewed as important, while girls' time and activities are seen as less important. This tendency is tied to the fact that beginning with the Industrial Revolution, men went off to work they got paid for, while women stayed home and did not get paid. In our society income is seen as an indicator of a person's importance and value. Women are expected to be respectful of men's more important responsibilities. As little boys become adults, they take on the parent role with women, serving as their protectors. Men are thus seen as competent and tend to indulge women. On the other hand, as little girls become women, they retain much of the child role, needing to be protected and indulged, and thus they are seen as less competent than men.

TABLE 6.4: Process of Growing Up, by Gender

Note: *read each column separately.*

Girls and Women	Boys and Men
Girls experience a less active childhood than boys.	Boys lead a more active childhood, controlling their world with physical actions.
Girls are taught to be reactive more often than proactive.	Boys are taught to be self-sufficient, autonomous, a closed system.
Girls learn to experience lines of power going from women to men; power is gained through men.	Boys learn to ignore their needs to be dependent.
Girls learn to think ahead about how people might respond, to "psych out" situations, to be "schemers."	Eventually, males begin to deny they even have dependency needs.
Girls are encouraged to believe that a man's approval is more valuable than a woman's.	Males lose touch with the feelings that accompany dependency needs, then with other feelings.
Teenage girls begin competing with each other for male attention.	Boys and men become task-oriented, compartmentalized, mechanical, and highly rational.
Girls and women learn they're expected to be selfless helpers, not have needs for great space, territorial or psychological.	As a result men become quite dependent on women as the emotional, nurturant "translators" or bridges between men and family members, men and others.
Women learn to live for and through others, to define themselves in terms of their relationships with others.	

Based on the work of Warren Farrell and Julie Matthaei, 1993.

Girls and Women: Lower Status

Many studies, such as those by Alice and Rosalind Loring, have shown that males are considered more competent than females, at least outside the home. In one study (Kohn 1988) people were asked to evaluate an article, some copies with a woman's byline and identical copies with a man's byline. The article with the male byline was rated as better by 98 percent of the evaluators.

In another study of mixed-group conversations, 97 percent of interruptions were made by men. There were fewer interruptions when women were speaking with women or when men were speaking with men. In mixed-group studies of who does most of the talking, men talk from 58 percent to 92 percent of the time. Most women are unaware of this type of domination, perceiving that they did a fair share of the talking in 75 percent of the situations (Eisen 1984).

Men are allowed to take the lead and dominate in many subtle ways, as Deborah Tannen's research confirmed. For example, both men and women tend to regard topics introduced by women as tentative, whereas topics introduced by men are treated as material to be pursued. Men use humor to take the lead. They tend to remember and repeat jokes, using the opportunity to take center stage and gain control. Most women tend to forget jokes, rarely try to repeat them, and serve as supportive audience, laughing at the jokes men tell.

The many ways that males and females have learned to behave differently are summarized in Table 6.5, which is based on dozens of research studies.

TABLE 6.5: Male and Female Tendencies

	Men's Tendencies	*Women's Tendencies*
Relationships	*Self-focused*	*Other-focused*
	Focus on individuals	Focus on group
	More impersonal	More personal
	Need more distance	Need more closeness
	Fear engulfment	Fear abandonment
	Over-identify with work	Over-identify with people
	Do what I please	Do what others approve
	More independent	Dependent/interdependent
	Like group activities more	Have more intimate friends
	More aggressive toward others	Trust each other more
	Make war	Make peace
	Define self by job	Define self by relationships
	Seek the spotlight	Prefer the sidelines
	More competitive	More cooperative
	Money a measure of masculinity	Money a tool
	Want respect for achievements	Want to be liked
	Love sports and games more	Love shopping more
How to Support	*Challenge others*	*Agree with others*
How to Disagree	*Confront others*	*Comply with others*
Thinking-Feeling	*More rational*	*More emotional*
	Express feeling less	Express feelings more
	Worry less	Worry more
	Express anger	Repress anger
	Thinking more linear, narrow	Thinking more global
	Less cross-brain ability	More cross-brain ability
	Focus more on facts	Focus more on intuition
	Greater visual-spatial ability	Greater verbal ability
	Less depression	Handle stress better
	Like the way they look	More concerned about looks
	Take more risks	Tend to avoid risks

Communication:	*Initiate more*	*Listen more*
	Talk about things	Talk about people
	Talk more in public	Talk more in private
	Take words at face value	Search for hidden meaning
	Direct language	Circumspect language
	Interrupt women	Let men interrupt
	Decide now, on their own	Decide after group input
	Gossip about work lives	Gossip about personal lives
	Give advice for problems	Give sympathy for problems
	Make direct put-downs	Make backbiting put-downs
	Tell jokes more	Apologize more
	Figure it out themselves	Seek assistance
	Toot their own horn more	Nag more
	Intimidate more	Avoid confrontation more
	Being right is more important	Being liked is more important
	Comfortable giving orders	Uncomfortable giving orders
	Comfortable with hierarchy	Don't like hierarchy
	Don't talk about ailments	Discuss ailments more

Based on the work of Paul Okami 2001, Linda Mealey 2000, Bobbi Law 1999, David Geary 1998, Chris Evatt 1992, Alice Eagly 1987.

MALE-FEMALE COMMUNICATION STYLES: HOW THEY DIFFER

As a result of their different socialization patterns, men and women interpret and relate to their environments differently. Men tend to take more initiative, which results in their being more self-protective and assertive (Gove 1985). They tend to be more focused, future-oriented, and objective, with a greater urge to master. Other major differences in viewpoint and focus, according to Deborah Tannen's ground-breaking research, are:

Women's Focus	*Men's Focus*
• Connection	• Status
• Establish rapport	• Report information
• Cooperate	• Compete
• Play down my expertise	• Display my expertise

An awareness of these tendencies can help us to understand why men and women often see things so differently. Awareness also helps us to foresee possible misunderstandings and communication breakdowns and in turn helps us to improve male-female relationships and to communicate more effectively. Let's explore Tannen's findings in more detail.

Connection or Status?

Women live in a world of intimacy and men in a world of status concerns. Women, in their world, focus on connecting with others via networks of supportive friends. Much of their communication is aimed at minimizing differences and building on commonalties and agreements. The ultimate goal is to attain maximum consensus and to function in relationships where people are interdependent. Men certainly have their old boy networks, but their world of status places higher priority on independence, where the purpose of much communication is on giving or taking orders. The ultimate goal is to attain more personal freedom.

Rapport Talk or Report Talk?

Women like "rapport talk" because it establishes or maintains connections with others. The focus is on feelings and includes personal thoughts, reactions to the day's events, and the details of her life.

Men prefer "report talk," because it provides factual information that the listener needs to know and what's going on in the world. Women's major aim in listening is to communicate interest and caring; men's major interest is to get information. Women will frequently reveal their weaknesses, especially when the other person is feeling discouraged. The rationale: Sharing such personal information will make the other feel equal, and thus closer. Men nearly always feel that revealing a weakness would just lower their status in the other person's eyes.

Cooperative or Competitive?

Women's words and actions often revolve around giving understanding, while men's are more likely to revolve around giving advice. These tendencies are probably based on the different ways men and women measure power. Women view helping, nurturing, and supporting as measures of their power. The activities they engage in include giving praise, speaking one-on-one, and private conversations. The main arenas for these activities are the telephone, social situations, and the home. Men perceive different measures of their power, such as having information, expertise, and skills. The activities they engage in include giving information, speaking more and longer, and speaking to groups. The main arenas for these activities are the workplace and public places.

In the work arena, women tend to approach decision making in a participative way: "I cannot and should not act alone when it comes to important decisions." Men tend to feel they must act alone and must find their way without help. Women focus on mastering their jobs and increasing their skills, consulting and involving others in the process, and developing positive relationships with their peers. Men tend to focus on competition and power, hierarchy and status. Women may not stand up for their rights because they want to avoid conflict. Men are less likely to be afraid of conflict and more willing to confront issues in order to clear the air. Men are more likely to be intimidating to others, while women are more often perceived as approachable.

Women are more likely to be uncomfortable in taking the initiative. Because women tend to be more accommodating and self-sacrificing, they are also more likely to allow frustration to build. To overcome problems arising from these tendencies, women can develop assertiveness skills and habits. Men need clear facts in the communication process. They experience more difficulty in coping with unclear situations and expressing mixed feelings. To overcome these difficulties, they can get in touch with their emotions and intuitive side.

Expertise: Play It Up or Down?

A major source of power for managers, professionals, and other leaders is their expertise. Women tend to downplay their expertise, act as if they know less than they really do, and operate as one of the group or audience. Men are more apt to display their expertise and act as if they know more about their area than others in the group know. They're more likely to be comfortable taking center stage.

The male expert's main goal is to persuade, and he often firmly states his opinions as facts. In contrast, when female experts speak with males, their approach tends to be assenting, supporting, agreeing, listening, and going along. They want to emphasize similarities between themselves and listeners and to avoid showing off. Their concerns: "Have I been helpful? Do you like me?" The male experts' approach tends to be dominating, talking more, interrupting, and controlling the topic, whether they are speaking with males or females. They want to emphasize their superiority and display their expertise. Their concerns: "Have I won? Do you respect me?"

The typical female response to male experts' communication is to either agree or disagree. On the other hand, male listeners usually don't understand that the female expert's main concern is to not offend, so the males often conclude that she is either indecisive, incompetent, insecure, or all of the above. They respond by offering their own opinions and information and by setting the agenda themselves; that is, they incorrectly perceive a power vacuum and try to take over.

Support by Agreeing or Disagreeing?

Women tend to show support by agreeing with others, while men help out by disagreeing to reveal problems and provide alternatives. Women's feedback style tends to be more positive and plentiful.

They keep a running feedback loop going with such responses as "mmmm, uh huh, yes, yeah." They ask questions, take turns, and give and want full attention. They usually agree, and they laugh at humorous comments. They focus on the meta-message even more than the literal message. Men give fewer listener responses. They are more silent and listen less. They are more likely to challenge statements and to focus on the literal message.

Because women listen so attentively, they may think a man's silence implies concentration on their meta-message, when in fact he may not be listening. Later she says, "But I told you all about that yesterday!" Most men challenge any statement they disagree with, so a man tends to interpret a woman's silence as consent or agreement. Later, when her actions are incompatible with her "agreement," he concludes that she is insincere or changeable: "Women!" As we begin to understand the different worlds that men and women live in, we can begin to find ways to bridge such communication gaps.

Communication Style: Tentative or Assertive?

With their focus on rapport, connection, intimacy, and playing down their expertise, women's communication styles tend to be more tentative than men's. Because the business world is accustomed to an assertive male approach to communication, women's credibility is undermined by a tentative, overly polite, uncertain, or indecisive approach. Several studies indicate that women perpetuate the lower-credibility stereotype with the following types of behavior:

- *Women ask more questions*, about three times as many as men on average.
- *Women make more statements in a questioning tone*, with a rising inflection at the end of a statement.
- *Women use more tag questions*; that is, brief questions added at the end of a sentence: ". . . don't you think?" ". . . okay?" ". . . you know?"
- *Women lead off with a question more frequently.* "You know what?" "Would you believe this?"
- *Women use more qualifiers and intensifiers.* Qualifiers or "hedges" include "kind of, sort of, a little bit, maybe, could be, if." Such qualifiers soften an assertive statement, but also undermine its assertiveness. Intensifiers include *really, very, incredible, fantastic, amazing*, especially when those words are emphasized. The meta-message is: "Because what I say, by itself, is not likely to convince you, I must use double force to make sure you see what I mean."

Researchers Alice H. Eagly and Chris Evatt have noted striking similarities between the conversation of women with men and the conversations of children with adults. They conclude that women tend to express their thoughts more tentatively and work harder to get someone's attention, which may in turn reflect basic power differences.

On the other hand, it's not unusual for men to carry assertiveness too far and to be perceived as overbearing or authoritarian. The most effective conversational approach for leaders is usually one that conveys *both* their sensitivity as well as commitment to their beliefs and statements. Both women and men become more effective when they communicate assertively, expressing their thoughts and feelings clearly but with respect for the thoughts, feelings, and rights of others.

MALE-FEMALE LEADERSHIP STYLES: HOW THEY DIFFER

Men and women in general tend to have distinctly different leadership styles. In the old chain-of-command, authoritarian organizations, men's styles were preferred because women's styles were seen as too soft. But organizations have changed, and this has significance for both men and women leaders.

Changes: Toward the Networked Organization

Management writers since the late 1980s have increasingly talked about the changing workplace and how the roles of workers and their managers are changing. Management experts have been saying that leaders must respond effectively to these changes if their organizations are to remain competitive.

Business organizations globally are becoming increasingly networked and virtual, and thus more open, fluid, flexible.

Successful companies have transformed into continuously learning and improving organizations that empower teams and employees to become self-managing. These transformations rely on leadership styles that are interactional, relational, and participative. Here are typical comments (Fondas 1997):

- Workers must work more independently, contribute to problem solving and cost reduction, be more customer oriented and vendor minded, and do what's needed rather than merely follow job descriptions.

- As workers become self-managing, managers must reorient themselves toward new roles of coordinating, facilitating, coaching, supporting, and nurturing.

- Managers must be teachers, mentors, and resource developers of human potential.

- Managers must serve those they lead.

- Manager's principal aim must be the workers' fulfillment.

- Manager's main job is helping the efforts of others come to fruition.

- Managers must energize people to do new things they previously had not thought important.

- Managing is an emotional process at least as much as a rational one.

- Any managerial analysis must be tempered by intuition.

Women's Leadership Styles

So how do typical leadership styles of women fit into this picture? Studies of women managers (Shipman 2009) show they tend to be

- More interactional, relational, and participative than men

- Express more empathy, helpfulness, caring, nurturing

- Show more interpersonal sensitivity, attentiveness to and acceptance of others

- Are more responsive to others' needs and motivations

- Oriented toward the collective interest and toward integrative goals, such as group cohesiveness and stability

- Show a preference for open, egalitarian and cooperative relationships rather than hierarchical ones

- Have more interest in actualizing values and relationships of great importance to the community

The seminal work on women's leadership style, as distinctive from men's, was done by Judy B. Rosener (1995). She labels women's style as "interactive," summarized as follows:

- Collaborative—as opposed to men's top-down style

- Reward system that values group and individual contributions

- Empowering—of workers at all levels

- Feedback and performance evaluation—from employee to leader and vice versa

- Interpersonal and technical skills—strong emphasis

- Ambiguity—comfortable with it

- Multi-tasking—good at it

Rosener concludes that the female temperament is better suited than the male's for these leadership functions:

- concluding "win-win" negotiations

- resolving conflicts

- reaching consensus
- preferring to cooperate and collaborate rather than compete
- keeping an open mind
- asking direct and relevant but not insulting questions.

She describes the female temperament in terms of "consensus building, power sharing, and comfort with ambiguity." She believes that a major barrier to the advancement of women leaders is that most corporations believe in "one best model," which too often is the command-and-control style used by most Euro-American men. However, leading-edge corporations are becoming more flexible about style. They can embrace a style that focuses on individual growth, group self-direction, and comfort with sharing of power and information. That's the approach most women prefer.

Men's Leadership Styles

And how do typical leadership styles of men fit in? Well, some traits culturally ascribed to men are (Shipman 2009):

- Ability to be impersonal, self-interested, efficient, hierarchical, tough minded, assertive
- An interest in taking charge, control and domination
- A capacity to ignore personal, emotional considerations in order to succeed
- A proclivity to rely on standardized or "objective" codes for judgment and evaluation of others
- A heroic orientation toward task accomplishment
- A continual effort to act on the world and become something new or other

These management experts are not calling for the feminization of leadership or management, nor do they connect the new workers in new workplaces and the resulting need for new leadership style with women's ways of leading. However, serious students of leadership style are concluding that being socialized a woman is no longer a disadvantage that women must overcome as much as an advantage that male leaders must find ways to access.

Differences in Skills, Traits, and Management

Focusing on skills as well as style, Robert L. Kabacoss (1998) studied thousands of male and female managers. Ratings were made by bosses, peers, direct reports, and the managers themselves. Women were generally rated better than men on overall skills, people skills, and five categories of leadership traits and management style. Male managers were rated higher in the business skills and on six aspects of leadership traits and management style. Women rated higher on overall managerial skills and people-oriented skills, while men rated higher on business-oriented skills. On leadership traits and management style, women managers were rated higher on productivity orientation and getting results, while male managers scored higher on organization vision and strategic planning. Table 6.6 compares styles by gender.

TABLE 6.6: Leadership Style Differences by Gender

Men's Command-and-Control Style	Women's Interactive Style
Top-down decision making	Shared decision making
Use of structural power	Use of personal power
Focus on self-interest of followers	Focus on achievement of organization goals
Control by reward for specific tasks	Control by generating empowerment
Stress on individual contributions	Stress on shared power and information
Emphasis on rational decision making	Nontraditional forms of decision-making
Competition in negotiations	Collaboration in negotiations
Resolving conflicts through direction	Resolving conflicts through consensus process

CULTURAL BARRIERS TO WOMEN'S CAREER SUCCESS

Most career women must overcome both internal barriers and external barriers to workplace success that are rooted in the American culture. Internal barriers include self-limiting beliefs about women's abilities and roles. External barriers include the glass ceiling, inflexible work arrangements, and pay disparity.

Women's Self-Limiting Beliefs

Traditions from the past affect today's career woman in two basic ways: (1) how she pictures herself and, therefore, the roles and behaviors she's comfortable with, and (2) what others expect of her—their preconceived notions of her abilities, traits, strengths, and weaknesses and their resulting beliefs about proper roles and behaviors. These traditional beliefs and expectations often lead to problems with self-limiting and conflicting beliefs. Leaders who understand how such beliefs create internal barriers are in a better position to help women overcome them. Self-limiting beliefs many women still hold include:

- I should not be ambitious.
- I should wait to be asked.
- I should never parade my achievements and expertise, nor "toot my own horn."
- Women aren't supposed to be good in math, finance, computer, mechanical, technical, engineering, decision-making and other male fields.
- I should stay out of office politics.
- I don't need to nose around in the inner workings of the company (the hierarchy, chain of command, sources of power, career paths).
- It's best to just let others have their way rather than cause a scene.
- I need to steer clear of risky ventures.
- Criticism of my work or ideas is a criticism of me.
- All I need to get ahead is to improve myself and work hard.
- If I do good work, my boss will notice and promote me.

Some women have beliefs that cause them to personalize events, criticism, and messages of others, to react emotionally, and to act out such emotions. These are beliefs typical of the powerless, regardless of gender, and usually are picked up from the women in the family and community.

Some women have difficulty understanding how upward mobility works. If they've rarely worked on teams, they may have beliefs about self-development that prevent them from recognizing the necessity of networking and teamwork. They may neglect developing a power base, and they may not see how they can meet personal goals through helping the team achieve organizational goals.

Related to self-liming beliefs are certain conflicting beliefs that can lead to fear of success tend to be unique to women and may include:

- I want a successful career *BUT* Men don't want relationships with strong, achieving career women.
- I want a successful career *BUT* Prince Charming may come along, sweep me off my feet, and carry me away to live happily ever after.
- I want a successful career *BUT* Good wives and mothers stay home and take care of the home and kids.

The beliefs that limit women and cause conflict all stem from cultural beliefs, values, and stereotypes about women. Therefore, even when women move beyond such beliefs, they must daily cope with people who still hold similar beliefs. Building a network of supportive friends and co-workers can help career women retain a sense of balance and self-confidence as they juggle career demands with home demands. An understanding, supportive manager can make all the difference. Sometimes the manager can take the lead in helping a woman employee recognize the beliefs that may be holding her back.

Pay Inequity

Information in the current profile section of this chapter indicates that although the United States leads the world in proportion of women managers, we are not as advanced in providing pay equity and we have made little or no progress in the past decade. Median income for full-time women workers was only 75 percent of male workers' income in 1998 and remained at about that same level through 2007. Some argue that women generally have less training, experience, and job commitment than men, and that this accounts for the pay gap. However the 75 percent figure represents every management level.

> *Women vice-presidents earn only 75 percent of male vice-presidents' income.*

It's highly unlikely that women who have made it to the vice-presidential level have less training, experience, and job commitment than their male peers. In fact, some studies indicate that most women who make it this far must have higher qualifications than their male peers (U.S. Census Bureau 1993; Russell 1991). And, in 2002 men were almost 95 percent of the top-earning corporate officers in the Fortune 500, compared to only 5 percent of women top earners, still an increase from 2 percent in 1996 (Catalyst 2002).

Some analysts believe that in general women are less committed to careers than men because women take primary responsibility for raising children, which requires them to interrupt their careers. A Census Bureau study indicates that the earnings were the same for women with no work interruption as those who had at least one work interruption of six months or more since age twenty-one. The Census Bureau concludes that structural factors and discrimination, rather than discontinuous employment, explain the earnings gap. And much of the female "gain" reported in some studies actually reflects declining median male wages during the 1980s. Other studies indicate that perhaps 90 percent of the gap is due to occupational segregation and other aspects of gender discrimination, as described earlier. On the other hand, the pay gap for younger women is less than that for older women, and it is less for women in rapidly growing, high-tech industries.

The Glass Ceiling

Women, like other diverse persons, face a "glass ceiling" to higher-level positions. This is a barrier that corporations generally don't discuss and that most women don't see. Women have recently made clear progress into certain corporate officer positions, but the real "clout positions" of greatest power and wealth are not so accessible. Recently women have made some progress but they still face occupational segregation (the pink ghetto).

The Good News: More Top Positions and "Clout Titles"

Women in top positions of some of the biggest U.S. corporations recently doubled their proportions—from about 5 percent to 10 percent, according to the research organization Catalyst (2002). It's not clear why the Catalyst study indicates nearly twice the proportion of women at the top as all other studies.

The real power positions are often called "clout titles," those that wield the most corporate influence and policy-making power. These are limited to Chairman, Chief Executive Officer, Vice Chairman, President, Chief Operating Officer, Senior Executive Vice President, and Executive Vice President. Catalyst reports that women holding clout titles increased from 7 percent in 2000 to 10 percent in 2002. The most noticeable women CEOs included Anne Mulcahy of Xerox, Meg Whitman, founder and CEO of e-Bay, and Carly Fiorina of Hewlett-Packard, later fired by the Board.

When Catalyst included all types of corporate officers, the proportion increased to 16 percent. These officers include an array of "vice-presidents-of-this-and-that," plus such titles as Legal Counsel and Chief Financial Officer. In 2002 women from all ethnic groups represented 16 percent of corporate officers in 500 large companies, up from 12 percent in 2000 and 9 percent in 1995, when Catalyst began counting. Women-of-color corporate officers are less than 2 percent. Of these, two-thirds are African American, and about one-sixth each are Asian American and Latino American women.

Not-So-Good News: Still a Pink Ghetto

Women are 52 percent of the U.S. population and 47 percent of the workforce but only 42 percent of all managers and 5 to 10 percent of top managers (fewer in the largest corporations). Euro-American men are 35 percent of the population and 39 percent of the workforce; yet they are:

- 95 percent of top-earning corporate officers in Fortune 500 companies.
- 80 percent of corporate officers in the 500 largest U.S. companies (16 percent are women and 4 percent are minority men)
- 92 percent of senior managers in mid- to large-sized corporations (5% are women; 3% are men of all other ethnic groups)
- 82.5 percent of the Forbes 400 persons worth at least 265 million dollars
- 80 percent of Congress (90% of the Senate, 78% of the House)
- 92 percent of state governors
- 70 percent of tenured college faculty
- 90 percent of daily newspaper editors
- 77 percent of TV news directors

According to the Glass Ceiling Commission, they "dominate just about everything but NOW and the NAACP." It is clear that they hold the most powerful positions in the economic and political arenas. Still, women's numbers are increasing in the better-paying occupations. For example, in 2000, 19 percent of dentists were women, compared to 9 percent in 1990, and they were 30 percent of lawyers and judges, compared to 21 percent in 1990.

Fortune magazine's recent survey found only 19 women among 4,012 directors and highest-paid executives, 0.5 percent, not much better than in 1978 (0.16 percent). Although the United States leads the world in percentage of women managers, the 40 percent figure can be very deceptive for the following reasons:

- Most women managers are at the lowest managerial levels—lower paying, entry levels, such as working supervisor and first-line supervisor.
- Only 25% of managers were women in the 200 largest companies.
- Only 5% of vice presidents are women.
- Only four Fortune 500 companies were headed by women in 2000, up from none a few years earlier. That's less than 1%.
- Only 7.5% of all women employees work as managers, compared to 15% of all male employees.
- Women are likely to hit a glass ceiling to top-level, and even middle-level, positions. Therefore, few women are making it beyond lower-level management (U.S. Labor Department).
- An examination of Equal Employment Opportunity data, primarily from 2002 reports, provides further insights into the status of women as officials and managers in the private sector (EEOC 2008).
- The percent of women officials and managers in the private sector has increased from just over 29 percent in 1990 to 36 percent in 2002.
- Women represent 48 percent of all private sector employment, but represent only 36 percent of officials and managers.

Indications that occupational segregation of women still exists, sometimes called the pink ghetto, include:

- Women make up 80 percent of office and clerical workers.
- When women move into an occupation in significant numbers, the occupation goes down in status and pay, and men tend to move out of it. Conversely, if an occupation loses status and pay for other reasons, women are more likely to be hired into it.
- Interestingly, women exceed men's overall employment rates as professionals (which includes nurses and teachers) and sales workers and are quite close to their overall employment rate in technical jobs.
- Industries from the health care sector are the most likely to employ women as officials and managers, and manufacturing industries are the least likely.
- Comparisons between officials/managers and white collar jobs (professionals, technicians and sales workers) indicate that women have the highest odds of being managers in the industries of Legal Services, Scheduled Air Transportation, Services to Buildings and Dwellings; and Offices of Physicians.
- Women have the lowest odds of being managers in Nursing Care Facilities; Full-Service Restaurants; Pulp, Paper and Paperboard Mills; and Animal Slaughtering and Processing industries.

My survey (Carr-Ruffino 1991) of women managers revealed that 90 percent think the glass ceiling is the most important issue facing women managers. Virtually all who did not head their companies (80 percent) said women were underrepresented at the top in their firms. The major reason given was the reluctance of the men at the top to include women. The following barriers to the top were considered the most important ones to overcome, in the order listed:

- Top management harbors stereotypes about women, especially regarding ability to gain acceptance in a top role, level of career commitment, and decision-making ability.
- Women are often excluded from key informal gatherings where information and opinions are exchanged, deals made, etc.
- Women's contributions and abilities are not taken as seriously as men's.
- Women have more difficulty finding mentors
- Women don't get equal opportunities to serve on important committees and project teams

Leaders who want to attract and retain the best-qualified women must eliminate the stereotypes, attitudes, and practices that create a glass ceiling. Even those women who don't aspire to the top prefer to stay in companies that have opened all the doors to qualified women and have helped them move up.

Two recent surveys of male and female managers of large American companies found that although women expressed a much higher probability of leaving their current employer than men, and had higher actual turnover rates, their major reason for leaving was lack of career growth opportunity or dissatisfaction with rates of progress. To be an effective leader, you must be sensitive to career women's needs and are open to helping them meet those needs.

Glass Walls

Corporate glass walls refers to the clustering and segregation, along gender lines, of many key jobs, especially those that form a pool from which senior management positions are filled. A study of nine Fortune 500 companies found that most women managers are clustered in such areas as human resources, research, and administrative support (Sugawa 1991). Fast track positions are "line" positions that directly contribute to the bottom-line profit of the organization (sales, production) or represent the core technology, products, and/or services that the company sells (such as engineering or information technology).

Subtle Barriers

Barriers to the top today are more subtle and therefore harder to overcome. Most managers believe that women have it made and therefore there is no problem to discuss, but many metrics indicate that women's progress has slowed or slipped since 2000. For example, in 2007 there were only 12 female CEOs of Fortune 500 companies, or 2.4%, with none on Wall Street; of course that is up from 1996 when there were none. The *Wall Street Journal* publishes annually "50 Women to Watch." The CFO job has been a glass ceiling for women in finance and is rarely a path to the CEO suite for anyone. Even so, in 2007, only 38 of the Fortune 500 CFOs were female, 7.6%. In 1995 there were 10, or 2%. The pace is certainly slow, and at this rate it may take 100 years for women executives to achieve full equity.

An example of a subtle barrier: Women don't get as much feedback on their performance as men do (in Wall Street firms, for example). It is easier to give honest feedback to someone who looks like you. Women need to learn to ask for feedback constantly, and ask in a way that reassures a male boss that he will not get an emotional reaction.

Researchers have studied the effects of subtle gender biases in hiring and promotion decisions that have reduced and limited the proportion of women who make it to senior management (Cabrera 2007). Drawing upon a substantial body of empirical research, they argue that in hiring decisions:

- At a given objective level of competence, men will be deemed more competent than women. As the result of pervasive gender stereotypes, women are given fewer opportunities than men to demonstrate their abilities; their actual performance is evaluated less favorably then men's; they are held to a higher standard for proving their competence such that the same level of competence that proves ability for a man may not prove ability for a woman; and their success is more likely to be attributed to unstable or external factors such as luck and ease of task.

- Women will be perceived as less congruent with industry or job type, with subordinates, and with decision makers than men in male-dominated industries, resulting in a lower assessment of fit.

- Female candidates will be perceived as less committed to their work than male candidates.

- Because of the gender bias in evaluations of competence, congruence and commitment, men will often be deemed more credible than women. While there are avenues for women to overcome this credibility problem, such as by receiving support from a high-status organizational sponsor or having previously occupied a position comparable to the one being sought, women are less likely to have access to powerful social networks and less likely to hold positions of seniority.

- The combined effect of even small doubts about women's competence, congruence, commitment, and credibility often results in conclusions that women are simply less qualified, causing female candidates to be perceived as riskier hires (or candidates for promotion) than male candidates, and in turn, making them less likely to be hired or promoted than male candidates.

Courtroom Battles

These glass ceiling barriers—and gender discrimination in general—have led to numerous courtroom battles in recent years. Since 2000 there have been more than $787 million in settlements (Rubin 2008). These include Morgan Stanly $54 million, with one plaintiff getting $12 million and 340 employees sharing the rest. Other corporations making settlements included Verizon $49 million, Boeing $73 million, Lawrence Livermore Labs $18 million, American Express $31 million, U.S. Information Agency $508 million, and CBS $8 million. Pending are lawsuits against Wal-Mart, Novartis, Costco, Smith Barney, GE, and Bloomberg.

Blocked Entrepreneurial Talents

Women are starting their own businesses at twice the rate of men (Lowrey 2006). Most of them gained experience in large corporations and hit some sort of glass ceiling. Clearly their entrepreneurial and leaderships talents were not adequately appreciated. When asked what companies can do to retain such high-powered women, they gave these suggestions (Delaney 2003):

- Increase flexibility. Realize that many women are not willing to accept childlessness as the price for career success.
- Increase the opportunities for women to use entrepreneurial skills within the company. Companies that are trying to thrive in the global marketplace certainly need the risk-taking, innovation, and leadership skills that these women use to launch their own businesses.
- Find ways to identify these women early in their careers, and hold their managers accountable for developing and promoting their talent.
- Recognize and reward women's bottom-line contributions.
- Recruit entrepreneurial women to senior line positions and the corporate board.

Inflexible Working Arrangements

Women become frustrated when the demands of work and demand for blind corporate loyalty conflict with other valuable parts of their lives and prevent their full participation in the organization. Some corporate systems and practices are designed for men whose wives handle most family responsibilities. Some are designed by men who are workaholics and expect others to be. Such expectations are unreasonable for women who can't ignore family responsibilities but are committed career professionals.

Capitol One Financial surveyed their women employees, who overwhelmingly said that flexibility was was their most critical need. The more senior the woman, the greater the need. Then Capital surveyed the male employees and found the same type of response. (Shipman 2009). The facts for nearly 80 percent of couples: both partners work, and two-thirds say they need more time for each other. In addition over one-third are helping to care for an older relative.

As a result about half of married employees want to work fewer hours and would change their schedules. About three-fourths want flexible work options, such as flextime, compact work weeks, job sharing, part-time arrangements, contract work, sabbaticals, and telecommuting from home offices.

Flexible work arrangements provide significant benefits to both employees and employers, according to a national study of the changing American workforce (Bond 2002). Workers who have more access to flexible work arrangements report significantly better mental health than other employees, are more likely to be committed to their employers and to plan on staying at their current company. They are less likely to suffer burnout and more likely to contribute to generally higher morale and productivity.

Lack of Support during Child-Rearing Years

Good employees can be retained through the child-bearing years if leaders are flexible, accepting, and supportive of family needs.

Recent studies indicate that the optimal plan for children is having Mom at home, working no more than part time, for the first three years. At that age, the child begins spending a few hours a day in a high-quality preschool program—with Mom at home, working part time, or in a flexible telecommute job. At age 6 when the child starts to school, Mom may increase her work hours away from home. Children who get high-quality child care in a preschool program beginning at age 3 generally fare better when they start to school than those who stayed at home (Howe 2000). This means that ideally mothers need flexible alternatives for the first six years of a child's life, and especially for the first three years.

Asking for flexible alternatives or family benefits should not be the kiss of death to career ambitions, but it is in many companies. For example, women who take maternity leave are 10 times more likely to lose their jobs than employees on other kinds of medical leave. In addition pregnant women are often transferred, demoted, harassed, or fired. On the other hand, many new mothers don't return at the end of their leaves because leaves are unrealistically brief; they need more time with the baby. "Mommy-track" and part-time work are usually the boring, low-level grunt work that blocks chances of gaining the skills required to advance professionally. All these practices and attitudes must change if a firm wants to attract and retain career women who also become mothers.

If women are to have uninterrupted careers, rather than just jobs, they need these kinds of advantages:

- Adequate maternity and family medical leave, more than three months of unpaid leave required by law
- Help in obtaining affordable, quality child care, such as day-care on the job site.
- Flexible job work arrangements and benefits
- Comparable pay and benefits
- Equal opportunity to advance
- Other work/life measures such as eldercare resource and referral and supportive managers.

Working Mother magazine notes that companies offering such benefits are the best ones for fathers as well as mothers. The magazine has been citing the "Best Companies for Working Mothers" since 1986, beginning with only 30 companies, now 100. Companies are getting it; for example, those with on-site child care numbered 60 in 1999, up from only 4 in 1986. The main reason? They need to attract and retain talented women, as well as fathers who are determined to balance a career with home life.

Rather than lose competent women who go through a phase of needing more time for their small children, some companies are giving them whatever they need to do part or all of their work in a home office—fax machines, computers, cell phones. Some women can pack the work into three or four days instead of five. Some need to come into the office once or twice a week for meetings. Some women hire a sitter to help out while they work at home. The major advantages: They're near their children, they can handle crises and illnesses themselves, and they don't spend time and energy commuting every day.

Legal Requirements: Family & Medical Leave Act

For decades virtually all Western countries required employers to protect new mothers' jobs through maternity leaves, while the United States had no such law. Most of these countries designate paid leaves—from 60 to 100 percent of the employee's salary for leaves of 12 to 40 weeks. In 1993 the U.S. Congress finally passed the Family and Medical Leave Act requiring 12 weeks' leave time with no pay requirements.

MEN'S RESPONSES TO NEW ROLES AND EXPECTATIONS

Surveys by David Gates and Robert Speer give insight into men's reactions to new gender roles and expectations. About half of Euro-American men think they're losing influence and job advantage, while only a third of other respondents think that.

Losing Power: Personal vs. Collective

Recent surveys indicate that the major dilemma men are wrestling with is the power problem—the profound difference between personal and collective power. Most men do not feel very powerful; they report that they are:

- having a harder time making a living than their fathers did
- dealing with a boss telling them what to do

- trying to figure out how to be what women want: sensitive as well as strong; soft and cuddly as well as firm and "manly."

As a result, many men feel they've failed in their gender role. Men's movement leaders say the women's movement has triggered changes for men in every life area, and many are still trying to adjust. Men look around them and see that they're in danger because men are 83 percent of the homeless, 90 percent of AIDS deaths, and 94 percent of prison inmates. They're three times as likely as women to be murdered, likely to live seven years less than women, and much more likely to die of alcoholism, heart attack, or suicide, according to Warren Farrell.

In fact men live in a more violent world than women. The more violent the crime, the more likely the victim is a man. Yet men aren't allowed to see themselves as victims. After all, collectively they hold the power in the United States. And if a man is Euro-American, his complicity in maintaining the patriarchy is even greater, for the simple reason that Euro-American men continue to dominate in business, government, and the professions.

Yet, because so many men feel personally powerless, some are threatened by feminism and resist changes designed to give women more collective power. Men also live with the knowledge that many women are afraid of men. Decent, protective men still know that it's men who make it dangerous for women to walk city streets alone at night, men who rape and assault and beat them so that they are forever frightened. These are some of the contradictions that men must live with; there are many others.

Feeling Pressure to Perform and Pressure to Change

When men were asked "What are the biggest pressures on men today?" answers indicated that men are feeling much pressure these days, and it's coming at them from all directions. Traditional pressures remain: to succeed in careers, to provide for families, to be strong and courageous and protective. Men also seem to feel a great deal of pressure from women to change their ways, their very natures, and they don't fully understand what's expected of them. Many don't know how to be sensitive or vulnerable and still be the strong protector, the man in control. Adding to these pressures is their sense that it's becoming harder to make a good living, the planet is being destroyed, and politics is a mess.

When males were asked "Have men been helped or hurt by feminism?" the researchers got emphatic responses from both sides. The majority felt that feminism has generally helped both genders by allowing us to see beyond traditional roles and stereotypes. About 25 percent were vehemently anti-feminist, blaming the movement for promoting anti-male and anti-family attitudes. Still others held that change is always a double-edged sword, and the full impact of feminism is yet to be felt.

When the researchers asked men, "What are the best and worst things about women?" their replies focused on empathy, support, warmth, and nice bodies. But many revealed a deep hurt and resentment for the changing roles women have assumed. And for some, women's emotionalism is a drawback.

Unemployed men commit suicide at twice the rate of employed men. Among women, suicide has no correlation to employment status. Men's self-worth is more tied to their jobs. They often feel humiliated, violated, helpless, angry, and guilty over job loss. At all ages men's higher suicide rates are likely to be tied to lack of emotional support systems. Men often bond by giving each other criticism, women by giving each other support.

Being Groomed for Violence

Men are more likely to be subjected to violence throughout their lives. In fact, they're trained from childhood to endure and aspire to situations that include violence. Men's advocates suggest some ways in which we subject men to violence and reward them for being violent:

- unnecessary circumcision (without anesthesia) of baby boys
- violent sports (for school boys), such as football, hockey, and boxing
- approval by girls and parents when boys excel at violent sports

- government money to schools to support violent sports and military ROTC
- the draft of young men into military service
- entertainment dollars to adult males for violent activities such as rodeos, car racing, football, boxing, ice hockey, and violent films and television programs
- media glorification of men who use guns and easy access to guns in society

Historically, the "killer male" was essential to survival, marriage, and the family. In the future the communicative male will be essential. Men's movement author Walter Farrell says, "For the first time in human history, what it takes to survive as a species is compatible with what it takes to love." Some men's movement leaders say it's time for us to ask, How do we want our future to be and how do we adapt? All of us have the potential for killer-protector and for nurturer-connector. What will encourage males to develop the nurturer-connector within them? A good start is for each of us to notice when men and boys express nurturing-connecting attitudes, to openly appreciate men and boys who act in nurturing-connecting ways, and to reward them appropriately.

Experiencing Barren Father–Son Relationships

More and more men are becoming aware that the way they were raised affects their leadership style and therefore their careers, as well as every other aspect of their lives. For example, some men are beginning to talk about the lack of loving, touching, even liking in their experiences with their fathers.

Some express a very deep sadness and quite a bit of anger that their fathers had never told them that they loved them, were rarely around, and never hugged or kissed them, even when they were little kids. Along with feelings of emptiness and inadequacy because fathers didn't think their sons were "good enough" to justify their love, there was also a loss of role models: "These men just didn't know what men do. Sometimes they learned the most exaggerated male tendencies, such as adopting strict macho behavior. But they certainly didn't learn about father-child tenderness and love," says men's movement leader Bernie Zilbergeld. The upside? These men want to avoid the same mistakes with their sons. They are trying to learn comfortable ways to express love to their own children. And they're becoming more appreciative of women's style of relating to others and its empowering aspects.

Being Denied Emotional Skills

When boy babies are born and for the first few months of life, they are more emotionally expressive than girl babies, according to Harvard Psychiatrist William Pollack (1998). But by the time they're 5 or 6, much of that expressiveness has been lost or repressed.

Male Behavior Models

As a result of cultural norms, boys quickly begin adopting one or more of the four basic male behavior models, according to researchers Deborah Davis and Robert Brannon (Pollack 1998.

Sturdy Oak. Boys who learn this mode believe they must be stoic and independent, never show weakness, don't share pain or grieve openly. As a result they're constantly acting, pretending to be confident even when they feel afraid, sturdy even when they feel shaky, independent even when they're desperate for love, attention, and support.

Give 'Em Hell. These boys believe the must be daring, show bravado, be a macho, high-energy superman, be violent in conquering foes. Their heroes are guys like Sylvester Stallone, Jean-Claude Van Damme, Bruce Willis, and similar "action" or "adventure" stars. This mode relies on a false self based on the false belief that real men are biologically wired to act this way.

The Big Wheel. Boys who adhere to this mode believe they must achieve status and power, wear the mask of coolness, act as though all is under control, even if it isn't. As a result, many males push themselves too far in school, sports, or career, often to repress feelings of failure or unhappiness.

No Sissy Stuff. These boys believe they must never express feelings or urges that are "feminine," never express dependence, warmth, empathy, ridicule and shame boys who do. As a result, these boys can't allow themselves to explore these emotional states and feel forced to shut them out. If they start to break under the strain, they'll probably be greeted with taunts, ridicule, and threats that shame them for not acting like a real man. This is probably the most traumatizing and dangerous model of all. It's a gender straitjacket that blocks males from exploring and expressing normal human feelings, those that are basic to people skills.

The one emotion that boys are allowed to express, even admired for expressing, is anger. This is the one emotion that girls are rejected for expressing. Parents are likely to speak more about sadness with daughters and more about anger with sons, according to the research of Professor Esther Grief of Boston University. As a result, boys feel encouraged to use their rage to express the full range of their emotional experience because they don't feel permission to express the other emotions.

Mother Love Myths

Researchers stress that mother love is essential for developing "real men" who are whole and mentally healthy. There are many myths around mothers doting on their sons.

Myth #1: Mother love makes boys weaker. Reality: It makes them stronger, emotionally and psychologically

Myth #2: Mother love makes boys dependent. Reality: The base of psychological safety it provides gives boys the courage to explore the outside world.

Myth #3: Mother love makes boys act in "girl-like" ways. Reality: It helps them develop their masculinity—the self-esteem and strength of character they need to feel confident in their own masculine selves.

Experts in this field recommend that parents openly express their love and empathy for boy children as well as girls. They can't get too much. Experts stress being there for children, taking time to give them undivided attention and listening fully. Parents could look behind a boy's anger, aggression, and rowdiness to see how he is indirectly asking for help. They can try to read between the lines and create a space where he can talk to them openly. Fathers and older males can create a model of masculinity for boys—a model that's broad and inclusive with a wide range of behaviors and emotional expression. Finally, parents and teachers can value boys as people, not as little men. Expose them to many types of activities and careers that men can choose.

Not Asking for Emotional Support

Father-son arm's-length relationships are just one aspect of the lack of emotional support men typically give and get from one another. Most lack the powerful tool most women use to heal women friends—emotional support for one another. For men, stress is more likely to build, sometimes leading to depression and even suicide.

From adolescence to old age, men are more likely than women to commit suicide. During adolescence, boys' suicide rates go from slightly less than girls' to four times as great. Psychologists speculate that during puberty boys begin to feel intense pressure to perform, pursue, and pay—to be daring and take risks. Boys also sense it isn't acceptable to discuss fears, anxieties, and self-doubt. In 1970 young men aged 25 to 34 committed suicide at twice the rate of young women. In 2000 it was four times the rate. Young men's suicide rate increased 26 percent, while women's decreased 33 percent.

Men older than 65 are 14.5 times more likely than women to commit suicide directly. They're also more likely to skip needed medication and to get inadequate nutrition and thus die through self-neglect. A husband whose wife dies is about ten times more likely to commit suicide than a wife whose husband dies. Men tend to have fewer intimate friends and family than women, so for men, the loss of intimacy is more devastating.

Roots of Depression and Violence

The roots of adult male depression lie in the way boys and girls are raised, according to Dr. Terrence Real (1997). He cites the violence boys are immersed in and the relentless denial of emotions that constitutes masculinity—which come back to haunt men in many ways. Male depression is often a kind of mourning for what a man was forced to give up along the way. Even the depression tends to be hidden and denied, like the feelings underneath it. As for the violence, Real believes that "those who don't turn to face their pain are prone to impose it on others." Only by rooting out painful emotions and working through them can depression be lifted and potential violence quelled.

Depression in women, on the other hand, often stems from the swallowing of ambition and aggression in order to be "a good girl," and later "a good wife and mother."

The Men's Movement

Many men are confused about what's expected of them now, where the boundary lines are drawn, and how they want to be in this new era. Strong women won't put up with a dominating, dictatorial, or brutal man—but they don't want a weak man either. In the 1990s men's movement leaders began filling the void with ideas about what men need and with meetings to explore the meaning of being a modern man. Most participants were heterosexual, middle-class, midlife Euro-American men (Harding 1992).

Robert Bly, a founder of the men's movement, says the women's movement has been wonderful because it speaks of the pain women feel. Men feel a different kind of pain that the men's movement speaks to. Bly (1992) doesn't want to bring back the patriarchy, but prefers a new society, where male-female status is more equitable rather than the "ruling father, subservient mother" hierarchy.

Long before the industrial revolution, fathers nurtured sons and taught them intimacy and emotional resilience through a community of tribal elders. When men began leaving home every day for the workplace, their sons lost this bonding. The price men have paid for running the country is to "stop feeling, stop talking, and continue swallowing our pain and our hurt and keep dying younger than we need to," according to Bly. He focuses on men's need for a father figure, especially during puberty. He speaks of the importance of male initiation rites, the warrior aspect of the male personality, and the wild man inside. Men must get in touch with their emotions, with how to express caring and nurturing, and with how to ask for it. Some methods of doing that include group processes, retreats, chanting, drumming, body work, and storytelling.

The men's movement is helping some men move into equitable male-female relationships by giving them permission to be vulnerable and intimate. Men who never learned to share their fear are allowed to do so. Talking about feelings is healing, and when the talk is heard compassionately, even more healing takes place. When men have their men's movement weekends to get in touch with the wild man and warrior parts of themselves, they acknowledge the past with its structure, discipline, and ritual that helped men overcome obstacles, protected women, and sustained human survival. The men's movement also helps men move on to the modern age. It encourages men to give themselves permission to ask, "Who do I really want to become? How do I want to get there?" By doing this, they can reach a deeper level of personal power (Keen 1991).

MEN'S RESPONSES TO CHANGES IN THE WORKPLACE

In the past it was extremely unlikely that a man would ever work under a woman manager or be expected to take equal responsibility with his wife for housework or child care—as many do today. On the other hand, men say they were and are expected to do the most dangerous jobs of the society.

Dealing with Women Managers

Recent surveys (Working Woman) have asked men what they thought of women managers. Here are some typical comments:

- They obsess on getting one small thing right, and it's blown out of proportion.
- Some are detail-oriented, not conceptual—no sense of corporate mission, the big picture.

- They're too sensitive, take things too personally.
- Some don't get down to business fast enough. First you have to spend time with them on a personal level.
- They're harder on other women. There's more pettiness or jealousy.
- When two women are at each other's throats, it ruins team spirit.
- When women bond together against men, it's demoralizing.
- Unmarried women bosses can make men nervous, especially if their work is their life, and they can work 14-hour days because they have no home life.
- They don't conceal anger or bitterness as well as men.
- We'd rather work for men. Getting a performance review from a woman is like being lectured by mother; it's very castrating.

Studies indicate that men in predominantly male workplaces are more loyal to their companies than men who work with lots of women. It's largely a matter of comfort. Men think they can be themselves around other men, so it's easier to bond. It's also a matter of status because men attach less prestige to professions that attract a large number of women. Men in traditionally male work environments, such as manufacturing plants, are more upset at the prospect of women invading their turf than are men in hospitals, where women have long been a presence (WSJ 1991).

Workplace changes tend to be more traumatic for men than for women because their sense of self-worth is more tied to their work. Changes such as downsizings and layoffs, and the resulting demands to do more work without added pay and the loss of job security add to a sense of powerlessness and betrayal. American men want to feel needed and useful, especially for qualities and abilities that are masculine in nature. They love joint efforts, especially with other men, that result in meaningful productivity. Quiet industry and caretaking are a part of the masculine ethos that baby boomers inherited from their fathers. But the sweeping changes of a global economy run by huge multinational corporations is undermining the sense of mastery, self-confidence, and control that is the other part of the masculine ethos (Faludi 1999).

Meeting Career Demands

A major source of male frustration, and for some resentment and envy, is that they are trapped in the provider role. A married woman with an employed husband has some choice about work—when, whether, and how much to work. If she has children, the family may need or want the money she can earn, but her decision to stay home with the children or to work part time will normally be admired by friends and neighbors. It will almost never be considered lazy, selfish, or inappropriate. Men say they don't have that luxury.

When men are asked if they would like to take six-month paternity leave to be with their newborn child, nearly 80 percent say yes, if it wouldn't hurt the family economically and if their wife approved (Farrell 1993).

Men are more likely than women workers to agree to relocate to undesirable locations and to work less desirable hours. Full-time working men work 9 hours per week more in the workplace than full-time working women, but the women work about 17 hours per week more in the home. Therefore women typically work 8 hours more per week than men.

Doing the Most Stressful and "Worst" Jobs

Of the 25 jobs rated worst in *The American Almanac of Jobs and Salaries* 24 are 95 to 100 percent male-occupied. Ratings are based on a combination of salary, stress, work environment, outlook, security, and physical demands. Worst jobs include truck driver, sheet-metal worker, roofer, boilermaker, lumberjack, carpenter, construction worker, football player, welder, coal miner, and ironworker. Men are expected to brave the hazards and do the dangerous, tough jobs.

- 94 percent of workers who die on the job are men.
- We have one job safety inspector for every 6 fish and game inspectors.

- Every workday hour a U.S. construction worker loses his life.
- Only men are subject to military draft and combat requirements

Closely related are the most stressful occupations identified by a Wall Street Journal study (WSJ 1997). Weighing hundreds of factors, from deadlines and late nights to competitiveness and physical demands, researchers evaluated 250 jobs. They concluded that men have traditionally held either all or the large majority of such jobs, which include firefighter, senior corporate executive, race car driver, taxi driver, surgeon, astronaut, police officer, football player, and air traffic controller.

Holding the "Protector" Jobs

Men protect the innocent and helpless, women and children, and the ability to protect generates respect. But men must cope with the dark side of the world in order to protect, and the price is a loss of innocence. Men suffer the price of war more than women. The aftermath of war is devastating. After World War I, it was called shell shock; after Vietnam, post-traumatic stress disorder. There's also chemical warfare aftermath, such as Agent Orange and the Gulf War Syndrome. Other results cited by men's movement author Walter Farrell are:

- More Vietnam veterans have committed suicide since the war ended than were killed in the Vietnam War itself.
- About 20 percent of all Vietnam veterans, and 60 percent of combat veterans, were psychiatric casualties.
- In 1978 more than 400,000 Vietnam veterans were either in prison, on parole, on probation, or awaiting trial.
- In 1990 more than 20,000 Vietnam veterans were homeless in Los Angeles alone.

In cultures where men must be protectors, weakness is ridiculed. Young boys search out those with weaknesses, taunting and picking on them. Valuing men as protectors gives us police brutality, the military mentality, and gangs (Farrell 1993).

Men are expected to repress their feelings. The most widely respected cancer research cited by the National Cancer Society finds that cancer is six times more likely to occur among people who repress their feelings than among cigarette smokers (Fischman 1988).

Needing Career–Family Balance

Married men with working wives and children are spending more time on housework and on the care of children—and both men and women are spending much less time on themselves over the past decade (Bond 2003). Most employees use computers at work and at home in completing their tasks and achieving their goals. Employees who experience the most spillover from their jobs into their home lives rely most heavily on technology to stay in touch with families and friends.

These changes in the workplace don't appear to offset the conflicts that employees face, such as longer work hours, more demanding jobs, and technology that blurs the lines between work and family.

TABLE 6.7: Career-Family Aspects, 1997 and 2005

Employee Information	1997	2006
Dual-earner couples, proportion of married employees	55%	78%
Couples w/children, combined hours at work per week	82 hours	91 hours
Couples w/children, combined hours spent with children	5 hours	6 hours
Mothers, time for self	1½ hours	1 hour
Fathers, time for self	2 hours	1 hour
Significant interference, job and family tasks	34%	45%
Use computers in jobs on daily basis		65%
Use computers at home for job-related work		20%
Use computer at home for personal reasons		55%

Source: *Family and Work Institute*

Men need flexibility about relocating, just as women do. The days may be over when companies can insist that moving up the ladder means moving around the country. In 1994 surveyed companies reported that 45 percent of employees turned down requests to relocate, citing family ties or spouse's employment as key reasons, *up from 30 percent in 1986. Companies who are retaining good employees are adapting to their needs.*

SEXUAL HARASSMENT:
UNDERSTAND IT AND PREVENT IT

Sexual harassment has been a workplace factor since time immemorial, but only in recent decades has it become a legal issue. Guidelines were established by the Equal Employment Opportunity Commission in the late 1960s, but it wasn't until the 1991 Clarence Thomas-Anita Hill controversy that the term "sexual harassment" became understood by most Americans. Thomas was being examined by the U.S. Senate regarding his appointment to the Supreme Court when word leaked out that he had sexually harassed a former employee Anita Hill. The Senators felt compelled to call Hill to testify at the nationally televised hearings. Some viewers later felt that Hill was slandered more than Thomas, who was in fact appointed to the Supreme Court. The EEOC reported five years later that sexual harassment complaints doubled after those hearings.

As a manager you need to know the definition of sexual harassment, the two legal categories of harassment, how to recognize it, how prevalent it is, why it occurs, how women and men feel about it, what they can do about it, and what organizations and managers should do to prevent it and to handle complaints.

Before we discuss these aspects of sexual harassment, test your current viewpoint by completing Self-Awareness Activity 6.4.

Self-Awareness Activity 6.4: What Do You Know About Sexual Harassment?

Purpose: To see what you know about sexual harassment.
Instructions: Determine whether you think the following statements are basically true or false—and think about why. Answers are discussed in the following paragraph.

1. Sexual harassment is always about men harassing women.
2. When a manager has an affair with one of his employees, that's sexual harassment.
3. A group of men telling each other sexual jokes is not sexual harassment.
4. If both parties agree to have a sexual relationship, it's not sexual harassment.
5. Sexual harassment is just a misunderstanding about sexual attraction and flattery.

What is Sexual Harassment?

Wherever men and women work, there is a certain amount of sexual interaction on the job. When does it become harassment?

> *When the behavior is unwanted, unsolicited, and nonreciprocal,*
> *when it asserts a person's sex role over her or his function as a worker,*
> *or when it creates an environment that seems hostile to the employee.*

Sexual harassment can be about anyone of any gender or sexual orientation harassing an employee. It is pervasive in the workplace. Most surveys indicate that more that half of women employees have experienced it. The Equal Employment Opportunities Commission has identified two types of sexual harassment: quid pro quo and hostile environment.

Quid prod quo

"I'll give you job favors for sexual favors or "I'll take away job favors unless you give me sexual favors." These are the types of messages that occur in quid pro quo harassment, meaning "I'll do something for you if you do what I want," or "I'll withhold what you want if you refuse to do what I want." This type of harassment is usually more obvious and blatant than the "hostile environment" type. However, the degree of intensity can range from subtle hints to physical attack.

Hostile environment

A hostile environment is a workplace where sexuality is discussed, displayed, or used in a way that poisons the workplace for one or more employees. The cause may be workplace porn or a boss who has consensual sex with a subordinate, causing an unfair situation for the subordinate's co-workers.

During the1990s, about 75 percent of court cases on sexual harassment were based on the hostile environment form alone, with only about 6 percent based on quid pro quo alone, and 19 percent based on both forms. Examples of sexual harassment from court cases include:

- physical contact such as patting, stroking, hugging, kissing
- comments on a woman's clothing, body, or appearance
- swearing, or "dirty" jokes, pinups, pictures, graffiti, and other visual depictions that are embarrassing or degrading to most women
- indirect harassment caused by being subjected to an environment where sexual harassment occurs even though you are not a target
- isolated incidents of touching or innuendo do not constitute sexual harassment.
- favoritism that constitutes a hostile environment; for example, when one employee submits to sexual favors and is rewarded while others who refuse are denied promotions or benefits.

Courts have ruled that the standards of a reasonable woman (instead of the traditional "reasonable man") must be used to determine sexually offensive conduct in organizations, when the plaintiff is a woman.

The Civil Rights Act amendment of 1991 gives employees the right to jury trials and to limited punitive damages for sexual harassment—In addition to the reinstatement and back pay formerly provided. About 90 percent of sexual harassment complaints are filed by women, and in most cases the male harasser has power over the female harassee.

Sexual harassment is pervasive in the workplace. Most surveys indicate that more that half of women employees have experienced it. Sexual harassment is more about power, domination, and hostility than flirting or sexual attraction. A person who is attracted to you in a positive, respectful sense does not harass you.

Why Does Sexual Harassment Occur?

The most common causes of sexual harassment stem from people who:

- abuse power in trying to obtain sexual favors
- try to use sex to gain power
- use power to decrease the power of a victim by reference to her or his sexuality and gender identity
- are reacting to a personal crisis
- won't accept that an affair is over
- have a psychological or substance abuse disorder
- are confused about dealing with new gender roles in the workplace

Sexual harassment is more about power, domination, and hostility than flirting or sexual attraction. A person who is attracted to you in a positive, respectful sense does not harass you.

Genuine workplace attractions are certainly not unusual. In fact, a 2001 survey by Vault Inc. indicated that 44 percent of American workers say they have had an office romance and 78 percent think that dating co-workers is fair game. A key word here is "co-worker," meaning not your boss or someone who reports directly to you. That's because having workplace power over someone you are dating inevitably leads to harassment issues. Co-workers will suspect and resent the favoritism, the "reportee" may feel abused when the romance ends, and accusations of unfair evaluations are just a few of the typical problems.

How Do Men Feel about Sexual Harassment?

Men and women view harassment differently. Men have traditionally thought that women who complain of men's sexual advances have somehow asked for it. They have attempted to label such women as a seductress, trouble-maker, bimbo, fantasizer, frustrated wallflower, voluntary martyr, or nut case. Most women have some sense of the wide disparity between how men and women view sexual harassment and the stereotyped labels that may be pinned on them if they file a complaint. Understandably, most women have refused to file claims, believing that doing so would only make a bad situation worse.

Most men feel confusion and concern over sexual harassment. They also object when they think women get away with flirting and men get punished for responding.

Confusion and Concern

Most men are confused about just where the behavioral boundaries are drawn now, and at a deeper level there is an anxiety about changing norms. Some men's movement leaders say the workplace is an easy extension of male adolescence, where boys win attention and other rewards for performing and pursuing. Many are confused by the sudden switch in rules, and some are concerned about the possibility of a woman with some ulterior motive falsely accusing them of sexual harassment.

Many men don't understand how their girlie calendars and pinups in the office constitute harassment. Some assume they merely make women feel inferior by comparison, and that's why they object to them. Women's advocates disagree, saying that pinups signal that sexiness is what counts in the workplace and everywhere else. Such symbols imply that women co-workers are viewed primarily as sex objects rather than fellow human beings and professionals.

The major concern men have is that women can now threaten men with a sexual harassment charge, and they could theoretically victimize men with false accusations of harassment. Companies can certainly set up procedures for investigating and handling sexual harassment complaints that would make it very difficult for men to be victimized and yet provide protection and fairness for women. Conservatives advocate throwing out sexual harassment laws. Liberals say that would be throwing out the baby (women's legitimate problems with men's sexual dominance) with the bath water (women's potential misuse of the laws). Studies indicate that 99 percent of complaints prove to be valid.

Objections

Men's specific objections to sexual harassment policies include:

- Women still play their old sexual games, without being penalized.
- Women still buy the romance formula of the man pursuing and persisting, the women attracting and resisting, until the man overcomes her resistance.
- Women still send mixed messages, saying "no, no" when they mean "yes, yes" or "maybe."
- Women still dress and behave seductively in the office. Miniskirts, slit skirts, thin blouses, plunging necklines, heavy perfume, and flirting are all provocative. These traditional indirect female initiatives are signals to most men to take direct initiative.

- Sexual harassment laws often create a hostile environment for men, where the females are like children who must be protected by law.

Some men say that if women would communicate honestly and directly, there wouldn't be a problem. One said, "If a woman tells a man directly, with no mixed messages, that she thinks he's sexually harassing her, at least 99 percent of men will stop in that case." Actually, this is difficult for many women because they consider it direct confrontation, which they take great pains to avoid.

Men's advocates say that sexual harassment education needs to focus on the fact that for men to pursue and persist has been functional throughout history. Today, when we are struggling toward equality, it's no longer functional, at least in the workplace. Women need to understand that to attract and resist is natural because it's also been functional throughout history, but it is no longer functional in the workplace.

What Can Men Do to Avoid Problems?

Let's assume men are the ones who worry about being the harasser, although in a small percentage of cases women are the harassers. If you're a man, you can avoid being accused of sexual harassment by using these strategies.

Raise your awareness. Sexual harassment is a rather complex issue, but you can learn enough to stay out of trouble.

Respect the word "No." When you're at work, it's best to forget the old idea that a woman's "no" may not really mean "no" or that it merely makes the conquest more challenging and exciting.

Align your attitude. Are you still harboring the belief that women are inferior? That men should be in control? If so, work on shifting your beliefs to align with current reality.

Support clear policies and training that spell out what harassment is and how the organization will handle it. If you understand sexual harassment, and your company has clear policies about its definition and consequences, you can relax and be yourself (assuming your attitude is in line).

Be a role model. Now that you're savvy about sexual harassment, help other men get it by treating coworkers with respect. For example, don't refer to women as women, not as "girls," "chicks," "ladies," or similar names. Don't participate in story-telling and jokes that demean women as a group. Let others know you don't want to hear or see women being referred to as sex objects.

What Can Women Do to Avoid Problems?

Women can help ease the situation by becoming aware of men's confusion and complaints and, through a greater awareness, sending clear, straight messages. Some specific recommendations for women are:

Avoid the sexual stereotype trap. Women don't need to automatically and unthinkingly fall into others' expectations about their role. *Sex object* is one of the age-old stereotypes that women can avoid by dressing and acting in a businesslike, professional way. Check flirtatious or femme fatale tendencies at the office door.

Avoid sexual liaisons at work. The objective of the office sex game is to increase the man's status with other men. This is one of the ways a man becomes "one of the boys" who make decisions about promotions and salaries. A woman may therefore increase the status of any man she has sex with and at the same time decrease her own status.

Say no tactfully but clearly. Women can let men know if they don't like being called "honey," "babe," and similar names. Women can send I-messages when they say no to requests for a drink, lunch, dinner, or date: "I like you but I don't go out socially with business friends," "I like you but I never go out with married men," "I value our relationship but my husband would be hurt if he couldn't share the occasion," "I like you but I'm not comfortable with going beyond a business relationship." The underlying message is you're not interested in sexual involvement and will always say no to such overtures.

What Can Organizations and Leaders Do?

The fact that top management is unaware of harassment events does not excuse them from responsibility, according to 1998 Supreme Court rulings. So it is up to management to establish preventive policies, to publicize them, and to enforce them. Management is responsible for making a good faith effort to become aware of sexual harassment that is occurring in their workplace and to remedy it.

Publicize and Enforce Good Policies

The rulings indicate that employers can protect the company by demonstrating a commitment to enforcing a good sexual harassment policy. Proof of good intentions and good-faith efforts can make a big difference in decisions made by judges and juries. These include

- Management establishes and publicizes a strong policy that specifically describes the kinds of actions that constitute sexual harassment and sets out the consequences for offenders.
- Management suggests that if a manager-subordinate relationship becomes "serious," one party should change jobs, out of fairness to other subordinates.
- Management regularly signals that it is committed to fighting harassment.
- The firm provides training seminars designed to sensitize employees to the issue.
- The firm sets up complaint procedures and mechanisms that encourage private complaints of harassment and that bypass immediate supervisors, who are often the source of the problem.
- When complaints are filed, investigations are professional, thorough, complete, and fair to all parties.

A 1998 survey of 900 companies indicated that complaints have dropped significantly in companies that take these actions.

Ban Boss–Subordinate Romances?

Office romances are fairly common. One survey found that nearly half of employees had been involved at one time or another. Most (58 percent) said there were no repercussions at work, and 30 percent said it led to a long-term relationship (Vault.com 2001). Should companies have the right to institute a policy that disallows office romances? Most don't. However, 13 percent do have a written policy against dating between boss and subordinate, which is a very good practice (HR 1998). Banning of all office romances would certainly be seen as an invasion of privacy. The problem is the romance between boss and subordinate, which in a sense is a de facto form of sexual harassment and therefore illegal. So banning that type of romance makes sense, even though EEO regulations do not require such bans.

What Should a Harassed Employee Do?

Let's pretend the recipient of the harassment is a woman, since that's the typical pattern. A woman in business cannot afford to allow any man to persist in actions that constitute sexual harassment. To do so would signal to other men that such behavior may be condoned and would set a poor example for the entire work team. A woman need not accept such a victim role. Here are some specific steps to take.

Be clear. Say no to overtures, tactfully but clearly. Mean it; give no mixed messages. Object to sexually inappropriate behavior, communication, or symbolism—again tactfully but clearly and directly.

Confront. If objectionable behavior continues, tell your harasser that this behavior must stop immediately. Follow up with a memo documenting what you said and hand it to him in the presence of a witness.

Document. Keep notes of what happened, when, and where. Note who, if anyone, witnessed it. Discuss the incident with any witnesses, to nail it down in their minds. Ask them to make a note about it, with a date.

Confide. If you wish to keep the matter officially confidential while you try to put a stop to the behavior, tell only trusted work associates. Ask them to keep brief notes. These people can later testify on your behalf.

Look for a pattern. Chances are very good that he has harassed other women. Seek out women who have worked with him. Engage in discreet, probing conversations to learn if they have been harassed. If you can establish that he has a pattern of harassment, your case is greatly strengthened.

Report. If the harassment continues, find out who you should report it to, often someone in the human resources department. If you need further emotional support and advice, look for a local women's organization that provides such services.

Consider alternative steps. If you don't like the way your organization handles your complaint, you can carry it further—to the EEOC or to court. Consider consulting an attorney who specializes in such cases. Local women's organizations and bar associations may recommend someone. Some courts have recently allowed class action suits where sexual harassment is common in an organization. Carefully weigh the pros and cons.

Be timely. Determine the statute of limitations for reporting sexual harassment in your state. In most states you must file a claim within six months of the last occurrence.

How Should Management Resolve Complaints?

Guidelines for resolving sexual harassment complaints include:

- Take sexual harassment complaints as seriously as other grievances; investigate them as thoroughly.
- Keep such matters entirely confidential.
- Find out what the complainant wants and try to accommodate her.
- Carefully investigate. Appoint an investigative team: one man, one woman, preferably objective outsiders. Look for documentation, witnesses, confidants, observers.

If the team cannot substantiate that sexual harassment has occurred (she says it did; he says it didn't), tell the complainant why the firm cannot take definitive action and to report any further occurrences or any instances of retaliation. Tell the accused: The organization had a duty to investigate; he is cleared; but if another complaint is filed, it will have more serious implications.

If the team substantiates that sexual harassment has occurred, use disciplinary procedures that are similar to those used in cases of nonperformance of job duties. Normally, the first offense calls for a warning and some sensitivity training. The second offense calls for some form of punishment: no bonus, no promotion, a demotion, docked pay, temporary suspension. The third offense calls for dismissal. Extreme and blatant violations that are substantiated can result in immediate dismissal. Insure that no one retaliates against the complainant, no matter what the outcome.

ASSERTIVENESS: IMPROVING
MALE-FEMALE INTERACTIONS

Women often behave nonassertively and thus are viewed as weak or manipulative. Men often carry assertiveness too far and are seen as overbearing, demanding, or dominating. As a leader in a diverse workplace, you need to understand the basics of assertiveness. Relating to others assertively will improve your own people skills, and you can in turn help others to improve theirs. Women and minorities often need the encouragement to act assertively. Anyone who has been made relatively powerless in society tends to become passive. Making a habit of tactfully asserting yourself is one of the keys to preventing a buildup of frustration, resentment, and stress. It gives you more control over your life and builds self-esteem. It also lets others know what is going on with you.

Test your assertiveness knowledge by completing Self-Awareness Activity 6.5 now.

Self-Awareness Activity 6.5: What Do You Know About Assertiveness?

Purpose: To see what you know about assertiveness.

Instructions: Determine whether you think the following statements are basically true or false—and think about why. The answers are given in the paragraph that follows.

1. Assertion is getting your way.
2. Nonassertion is being willing to compromise.
3. Aggression is taking the initiative to get things done.
4. I-messages are self-centered messages that often violate others' rights.
5. Not asserting yourself is often desirable because it respects others' feelings.

First, we'll discuss brief definitions of assertion, nonassertion and aggression. Then we'll discuss them in more detail, with some examples.

Assertion is speaking up honestly and directly about what you think, feel, or believe, in ways that respect the rights and feeling of others. It's standing up for your rights, while being considerate of others' rights.

Nonassertion is not speaking up about what you think, feel, or believe, especially when your inaction bothers you when you later reflect upon it. It's allowing others to violate your rights, with no challenge from you. It's letting someone push you around, walk all over you, or not consider your feelings or rights—or to intimidate, demean, or devalue you.

Aggression is carrying assertion too far. It's going after what you want in ways that violate the rights of another— or expressing yourself in ways that intimidate, demean, or degrade another person. It's pushing other people around, using them as a doormat, or not considering their rights or feelings.

As you can see, all the statements made in Self-Awareness Activity 6.5 are essentially false (I-messages are discussed later).

Respecting Your Rights and Others' Rights

The key to assertion is being clear about your rights and then standing up for them. Since people's perceptions of who has what rights in a situation can vary, what happens when rights overlap? The assertive person is willing to listen, discuss the problem, and negotiate a solution that both parties can live with.

> *Your prime assertive right might be:*
> *You have the right to judge your own behavior, thoughts, and emotions.*
> *You have the right to decide whether and how to express yourself.*
> *You have the responsibility to be totally accountable for the results of these actions.*

What are some basic rights that you believe in and that most people in our culture believe in? The Bill of Rights is probably the best expression of our common beliefs about human rights. However, it was basically intended as a list of rights of Euro-American men. Women and minorities have had to fight to be included among the people entitled to these basic rights. What rights do women have that are often violated? Within organizations, managers have certain rights and employees have rights. Think of management and employee rights that you believe in. When you have clear, firm beliefs in the rights of individuals, you have the conviction to assert yourself when your rights are violated. You also have the basis for recognizing and respecting other people's rights.

For example, what do you do when another person tries to break in line in front of you? Do you automatically give way? Do you automatically resist? Or does it depend? Maybe the person previously waited in the line, had to leave for a moment, and just returned. Maybe he or she is in the midst of a minor crisis. Sometimes it's not clear who got there first or why the person is breaking in. Therefore, the two of you have different viewpoints about who is right, and your rights may overlap or be in conflict.

People who tend to be nonassertive rarely see situations as an issue of rights, and they don't know how to stand up for their rights anyway. They may have a compulsive need to "be nice," not cause a "scene," be a martyr, and their actions imply, "my rights, thoughts, or feelings aren't as important as yours." People who tend to be aggressive just want their own way and aren't about to be pushed around. They rarely think in terms of others' rights. Their actions imply, "my thoughts, feelings, and rights are more important than yours."

People who are assertive recognize their own rights and the rights of others and are willing to negotiate, and perhaps compromise, to settle situations where rights conflict or overlap. Such compromises respect the basic integrity of both people, and both get some of their wishes satisfied. This approach helps to avoid the temptation to use assertion to manipulate others in order to get what you want. It often leads to both people getting what they want because people are most likely to become cooperative when they're approached in a respectful way.

Being Assertive

You assert yourself when you stand up for your personal rights and express your thoughts, feelings, and beliefs in direct, honest, and appropriate ways. You do this in ways that don't manipulate, dominate, humiliate, or degrade the other person. Assertion is based on respect for yourself and respect for the other person. You express your preferences and defend your rights in ways that also respect other people's needs and rights. The goal of assertion is to get and give respect, to ask for fairness, and to leave room for compromise when your needs and rights conflict with another person's.

You can assert with empathy to soften the message. "Maybe you have a good reason for wanting to break in, but I was here first." You may need to assert with increasing firmness in those relatively rare cases when people ignore your assertive message. "I mentioned that I was here first. I must insist that you wait your turn." You can use I-messages that express your inner reality without judging, blaming, or interpreting someone else's behavior. Here are some examples of I-messages, in which you take responsibility for your thoughts and feelings. Compare them to the you-messages, which tend to blame and judge the other person.

I-Messages	*You-Messages*
I have sensitive hearing.	You talk too loudly.
I'm not comfortable talking about sex.	You have a dirty mouth.
I'd like to meet beforehand and make plans.	You shouldn't wait till the last minute.
I'd like to go over what we want to get done this week.	You need to manage your time better.
I'd like to prepare for the meeting.	You should send out an agenda.

Your nonverbal messages nearly always convey what you really feel or think. When you're not clear and honest in what you *say*, people receive a mixed message. For example, your voice tone, facial expression, and body language might say, "I'm upset," while your words say, "Oh, it's okay; I don't mind." When you are clear about your rights and say what you really think or feel, using I-messages and other effective assertion techniques, your verbal and nonverbal expressions are in harmony. Your message comes through confidently and congruently. You can be assertive in ways that actually build stronger relationships.

Being Nonassertive

When you don't express your honest feelings, thoughts, and beliefs, or when you express them in such an apologetic, unsure, or self-effacing way that others can easily disregard them, then you're allowing your rights to be violated by your nonassertiveness. By such actions you tell others: *You can take advantage of me. My feelings aren't very important; yours are. My thoughts aren't important; yours are the only ones really worth listening to. I'm nothing; you're superior.*

Nonassertion reflects a lack of respect for your own preferences. In an indirect way it reflects a lack of respect for the other person's ability to take disappointments, to assume some responsibility, or to handle problems. For example, a typical reason people give for not asserting themselves is, "I didn't want to hurt her feelings"—or embarrass him, or upset them. The goal of nonassertion is to please others and to avoid conflict at any cost. When you're being nonassertive, you're often being a victim.

Most experts believe that nonassertion is always accompanied by some degree of resentment that is experienced at some level, whether conscious or not. You resent situations where you don't assume control for your own experience. In other words, you resent your lack of self-control. You store these resentments, small or large, inside yourself. If you don't express them in some way, they build up and you become a pressure cooker of resentful energy. Then an unfortunate person comes along who hands you the final indignity, and you blow up, out of control for all to see. Your explosive reaction is probably as much a surprise to you as it is to others. When you begin to consistently assert yourself, you gain self-control.

Being Passive–Aggressive

Passive-aggressive behavior is a variation of nonassertion. For example, in organizations there are usually some people who smile and agree with the managers, but who undermine them in subtle or sneaky ways. They find ways to quietly sabotage a manager's efforts or projects, usually by not doing their part. They always have a good reason "why not," but meanwhile nothing got done. Passive-aggressive attitudes always result in some type of hostile action.

People who are consistently nonassertive may resort to passive-aggressive behavior because they won't want to face the consequences of speaking up. It may be their way of resisting someone whom they think is trying to dominate them. They may see themselves as the victim of a persecutor. Worst of all, they may secretly stew, fret, boil, or pout—all the while being "nice" and trying to hide their real feelings.

Being Aggressive

Being aggressive is going too far. It's standing up for your personal rights and expressing your thoughts and feelings in ways that belittle the other person or violate his or her rights. Such actions and words are usually inappropriate and often dishonest. Aggressive behavior carries such messages as: *This is what I think; you're stupid for thinking differently. This is what I want; what you want isn't important. Here's what I feel;; I haven't considered your feelings.*

The goal is getting your way, getting things done, prevailing, winning, or dominating—regardless of the effect on the other person. It's a win-lose approach. You win by taking needed action without consideration of others, by overpowering, intimidating, belittling, degrading, or humiliating. The result is that other people find it difficult or impossible to express their preferences and defend their rights. You don't really like yourself when you act this way, consciously or not, and others resent it.

Complete Skill Builder 6.5 to test your understanding of assertiveness, nonassertiveness, and aggressiveness.

LEADERSHIP CHALLENGES: BREAKING THROUGH GENDER BARRIERS

Barriers to career success that are often related to gender issues include lack of career planning, pay inequity, glass ceiling issues, lack of proper training, communication blocks, unequal relationships, gender stereotyping, sexual harassment, and career-family conflicts. You can personally help to overcome these barriers by being aware, becoming a role model, and helping co-workers become aware. In the process you and your co-workers will be changing the corporate culture.

Challenge #1: Support Career Planning

Support women and men in developing and implementing their career plans by treating all as valued individuals. Don't assume women are not as career committed as men. Encourage people to answer these questions:

- what do you want from your career?
- what goals do you want to set?
- what contributions do you want to make?
- what events might limit your career efforts in the foreseeable future?
- what sort of work life-personal life balance do you want?
- what can the company do to help?

Career planning may be blocked by self-limiting beliefs. Encourage people, especially women, to overcome self-limiting cultural beliefs. Suggest alternative self-empowering beliefs.

Challenge #2: End Pay Inequity

Pay inequity is endemic in our workforce, a huge problem that no leader could solve alone. However, you can become aware of the ways women have been discriminated against when it comes to pay. You can analyze the compensation packages of all the employees under your influence. And you can use your influence to eliminate inequities and to make sure that women and men receive fair compensation.

Challenge #3: Break the Glass Ceiling

Do your share to end or overcome all the ways—including those many small, hidden, or subtle ways—that the company discriminates against women.

Challenge #4: Give Training

Women need training geared to their particular needs. They may need encouragement to acquire math, computer, technological, and other typically male skills the firm needs. Some women thrive best in all-women classes. Studies indicate that women achieve higher levels of mastery when they take such classes without men around. Women often don't get equal opportunities to attend higher-level management training programs that prepare managers for promotion.

Men need training in people skills and in those aspects of management style that studies indicate need improvement., such as enthusiasm, communication, and feedback.

Challenge #5: Bridge the Communication Gap

Recognize the different ways women and men view the world and communicate about it. Use your knowledge to bridge the gaps. Recognize when a misunderstanding or a miscommunication is rooted in an assertiveness problem. Help to understand and resolve such problems. Relate to others in an assertive manner yourself and teach this approach to others.

Challenge #6: Value Equal Relationships

As a role model and coach you can help men understand the dramatic shifts in male-female relationships at work and at home. Help them to see the advantages of equality in relationships; for example:

- *Shared responsibility*, resulting in less stress for men because they now have help in making the decisions, earning the family income, and other responsibilities that can become burdensome and stressful.

- *More authentic communication* is a natural result of equality in relationships, as Madelyn Burley-Allen's research on assertiveness training indicates.
- *Better relationships with women* can be built as aggressive tactics are replaced with assertive ones, since women are less likely to resort to passive-aggressive responses.
- *More freedom* to develop and express all facets of the self grows from going beyond the limited confines of stereotyped gender traits and roles.

Challenge #7: End Gender Stereotypes

Many men feel a loss of power, are concerned about reverse discrimination, and express difficulties in accepting a woman as their manager. Help men and women drop the old role stereotypes about men's place and women's place. Take the lead in raising awareness of how such stereotypes limit men and unfairly block women. Speak up when you see people acting out the old myths and assumptions about men's and women's traits, their "place," and their limitations.

Challenge #8: Stop Sexual Harassment

Support clear, effective company policies regarding sexual harassment. Make sure that everyone on your team understands the issues and the policies. Be a role model in the way you treat people. If complaints occur, resolve them fairly, and firmly.

Challenge #9: Resolve Conflicts in Career and Family Demands

The core gender issues, both social and professional, can only be addressed when women and men explore and create a partnership where professional and social relationships are managed out of respect for individual talents and needs and aligned with a common vision that includes more than profit making. Such a partnership balances care-taking and bread-winning and views social, emotional, and spiritual needs on a par with economic responsibility. Key areas that we can bring into balance in organizations include:

- men and women having the freedom to strike a balance between work and home
- an ability to move beyond woman as sex object and man as success object
- a balance of men and women taking paternity leaves and maternity leaves without the company stigmatizing them
- organizations that provide more flexible systems and benefits for both men and women, without stigmatizing those who take advantage of them.

Most companies must make significant changes to provide the type of flexibility dual career families need. For example, in 1990 only 10 percent of firms with 10 or more employees provided such direct benefits as day care or financial assistance with child care.

LEADERSHIP OPPORTUNITIES: PROMOTING GENDER EQUITY IN THE CORPORATE CULTURE

The differences in worldviews of men and women suggest some possible difficulties for women in most organizations. They are likely to feel pressured to change their work style and leadership style and to experience conflict between leadership and gender roles. If they do become more directive, they are more likely than men to receive negative reactions. Actually, a variety of styles can be effective if the corporate culture values and embraces gender differences.

You can recognize ways in which the corporate culture fails to reflect women's values as well as men's. Help to resolve conflicts and disadvantages this poses for women and to start changing the culture accordingly.

Opportunity #1: Value Gender Differences

For many years women minimized their differences from men and stressed equality, in order to show that they could work as effectively as men and deserve equal treatment and rewards. The men who supported them tried not to notice this most noticeable of differences. Admitting one's differences in the American workplace has traditionally meant accepting inferiority. That's because we tend to jump to the conclusion that differences are either good or bad, rather than a source of interesting possibilities. Those who are different are commonly relegated to the edge of a work group. They may be devalued personally and their contributions ignored.

Opportunity #2: Value Female and Male Traits and Skills

Today's organizations, and those of the future, need a different mix of values, not only because women are present in larger numbers, but because of the ways work itself is changing in the age of the smart machine. Jobs require less muscle and motor skills and more information and people skills. While women continue to acquire many traditional male workplace skills, men must also now master things women have been taught to do well. What these are becomes clearer when we look at organizations run largely by women.

Opportunity #3: Value Female and Male Beliefs and Customs

When women create their own corporate cultures by starting their own companies, researcher J.B. Rosener found that the style that emerges is more democratic and less hierarchical, reflecting these beliefs and customs:

- the basic belief that allowing everyone to contribute and to feel powerful and important is good for employees and the organization
- the tendency to share power and information
- more emphasis on collaborative decision making
- more democratic, participative, consultative management
- more decentralization of decision making and responsibility
- greater concern with process and fairness
- more concern with quality of outcomes, while retaining a pragmatic concern for quantitative outcomes
- less autocratic, domineering, ego-involved management
- less concern with titles and formal authority, more concern with responsibility and responsiveness
- less concern for empire building, power and domination and less consciousness about one's turf

Opportunity #4: Value Female and Male Leadership Styles

Typical male leadership styles have stressed tasks and achievements first. Women's leadership style focuses on people first, tasks second and so is more indirect. Rosener's studies show women leaders achieve higher quality and productivity through these strategies:

- a greater responsiveness and concern for individual feelings, ideas, opinions, ambitions, and on- and off-the-job satisfactions
- skill at enhancing other people's self-worth
- desire to get others excited about their work
- more emphasis on skills as a listener and conversationalist
- high value placed on loyalty, longevity, and interpersonal skills

This represents a balance of masculine and feminine strengths, which would work nicely in today's workplace.

Opportunity #5: Remove Glass Ceiling Barriers

Management experts Alice Eagley and Linda Carli (2007) note that the bird's-eye view of the corporate path to the top reveals a labyrinth. But on the ground, you step through an inviting doorway, perhaps not aware that you are entering a maze. Three doorways later, you realize that you are confused and unclear about how to proceed. At every turn in this corporate maze, women face more barriers than men and more women veer off the fast track because of the maze and finally the glass ceiling. Therefore, fewer high-potential women make it to the top. Effective leaders are removing these glass ceiling barriers and helping talented women to navigate the path to the top. Eagley and Carli suggest the following interventions.

1. Increase awareness of the psychological drivers of prejudice toward women leaders, and work to dispel those perceptions.

2. Use open-recruitment tools, such as ads and employment agencies, rather than relying on informal social networks and referrals (the old boys' network) to fill positions.

3. Change the long-hours requirement for moving up the ladder to a more reasonable, practical norm.

4. Reduce the subjectivity of performance evaluations by such tactics as focusing on the achievement of mutually agreed-upon objectives.

5. Avoid having a sole female member of any team—the higher the level, the fewer the women on teams, which leads to their becoming seriously marginalized.

6. Work toward accruing a critical mass of women in executive positions—not just one or two token women—to head off the problems that come with tokenism.

7. Prepare women for line management positions, such as operations or sales, by offering challenging assignments. When women are in school or in training, teach them to insist on line jobs when they enter the workforce.

8. Establish family-friendly human resource practices and encourage male participation in family-friendly benefits. Change the culture if it penalizes women or men who accept such programs as maternity leave or flexible work arrangements.

9. Allow employees who have significant parental responsibilities more time to prove themselves worthy of promotion –they may need a few years more— instead of an up-or-out career progression policy.

10. Welcome women back into the firm after they complete sabbaticals to care for family.

Opportunity #6: Use Women's Marketplace Savvy

Women controlled about $5 trillion in U.S. business and consumer spending in 2004, and women influence about 80 percent of all such spending nationally (Arora 2005). Is your firm taking advantage of women's marketplace savvy and connections? While men can do their best to get inside women's heads and think like a woman, let's face it. No one does that quite as well as women themselves. Effective companies are using women's understanding of women, as well as their skill at building relationships with women—to boost revenues and profits.

The Bottom Line

Companies need a balance of male and female executives because it's good for business, according to three recent studies (Shipman 2009). Catalyst (2004) found that the greater the proportion of women in senior management of Fortune 500 companies, the more profitable the company—by more than one-third. Women and men need to work in holistic, balanced organizations that reflect the values and customs of both genders—including flexible work arrangements for everyone. Such organizations allow and encourage people to develop more of their talents and potentials and to use those talents to achieve personal and team goals.

SUMMARY

Women and men have traditionally been limited by stereotyped roles and traits that culture imposes upon them. In our patriarchal system, babies learn from the cradle that people have unequal power and privilege. However, marriage and family relationships are now moving toward greater equality.

Since the 1960s a number of megatrends have resulted in major changes in women's roles. Most women now work, even those with small children, and they have greater opportunities in the workplace. Women now hold about 40 percent of management positions but less than 5 percent of top executive posts. Their pay at all levels tends to be about 25 percent less than men's pay. Younger women are bridging the gender gap in education, pay, and position. Women owned 40 percent of all privately held businesses in 2008, which were increasingly above average in success.

The cultural socialization of girls and boys has traditionally been distinctly different, so they grow into men and women who often have difficulty understanding each other's worlds and viewpoints. Research indicates that women tend to be relationship oriented, somewhat tentative, and cooperative, while men tend to be status oriented, assertive, factual, and competitive. Changes in employee expectations and workplace cultures have favored leadership styles that come more naturally to women than to men; i.e., interactional, relational, and participative styles. Women managers generally have better people skills, while male managers have better traditional business skills. Women's leadership style is more enthusiastic, communicative and production-oriented, while men's is more conservative, yet innovative and strategic.

Cultural barriers to women's success include women's self-limiting or conflicting beliefs, pay inequity, the glass ceiling. The glass ceiling to top management causes many related barriers, such as glass walls, subtle barriers, blocked entrepreneurial talents, inflexible working arrangements, and lack of support during child-rearing years

Many men are having difficulty adjusting to the major changes in virtually every area of their lives, from wives to children to work. Nearly half think they're losing power as a group. Many are no longer sure what "real men" are expected to do, They may feel pressure to perform and to change. Men's issues include being groomed for violence, experiencing barren father-son relationships, and being denied emotional skills. The culture expects men to be strong, daring, successful, and unemotional. False myths imply that too much mother love makes boys weak, dependent, and feminine. As a result of such myths, many men do not ask for emotional support and may become depressed or violent. The men's movement attempts to deal with these issues, helping men to establish a healthy balance between their masculine and feminine aspects.

In the workplace men face an increase in women's position and power, and often must deal with a women manager. Men generally must meet higher career demands and expectations. They are expected to do the most stressful and worst jobs, as well as the dangerous "protector" jobs. Many experience a need for better career-family balance.

Sexual harassment primarily affects women, but men deal with concerns about being unfairly accused of harassment. Managers should know what it is, the types of harassment, how to recognize it, how to prevent it and manage it, and how to deal with complaints. They should know how to set up effective sexual harassment policies and procedures and to resolve complaints that are filed. Boss-subordinate sexual affairs have a harassment effect on co-workers and should be banned by the organization. Both men and women need to know how to avoid and manage sexual harassment—as well as what to do if it occurs.

Assertiveness training can help both women and men to interact with each other authentically. Many men tend to come across to women as overly aggressive in the workplace. Many women appear overly passive. Such training is based on respecting rights—one's own as well as others and negotiating a compromise when rights conflict.

The concept of each person strengthening both masculine and feminine aspects of their personality can be very powerful in the workplace. Leaders can encourage men and women employees to achieve this balance and to move into an attitude of equality. As this occurs, a new holistic corporate culture can emerge, and in turn a better balanced society. Leaders can also focus on supporting men in adapting to gender changes in the workplace, supporting women in breaking stereotyped molds and achieving career success, and providing both with support to meet emerging family demands.

Case Study 6.1: New Mother Jessica

Jessica is the mother of an 18-month-old child. She is a loan officer with Trust Bank. Jessica had resigned from her previous job because the maternity leave was inadequate for her to make the adjustment to a new baby. When she went to work for Trust Bank, it was with the understanding that it would not be a high-pressure position—no expectation that she would work overtime or make business trips. However, Jessica is beginning to feel pressure to do just that.

Jessica approaches you, her manager, to tell you that she has decided she must resign in order to find a part-time job, about three days a week. She says, "My son needs more of my time and attention just now. I need to work, and I want to work, but I have decided to give his needs top priority for the next year or two."
If you were Jessica, would you have offered to quit the job?

1. What are the root problems?
2. As Jessica's manager, what should you do?

Case Study 6.2: Alicia Ruiz, Legal Assistant

Alicia Ruiz has been employed at Appleby Associates law firm for nearly a year. She's just been promoted from secretarial assistant to legal research assistant, and she loves her work. She gets along well with the lawyers and other assistants. The only ongoing problem she must cope with is her relationship with *Jake Barnes*, one of the law partners. Lately it's been pretty rough. Jake manages to find more and more opportunities to catch her alone and lean on her—at the water fountain, in the coffee room, and, worst of all, at the elevator in the evening. A couple of times Jake has really given Alicia a hard time, insisting that she come with him for a drink at the bar around the corner.

As a full partner, Jake is one of the most powerful men in the office, and Alicia doesn't want to turn him against her. Her way of dealing with it lately is to ask her friend *Joe* to wait for her so they can leave together, since they park in the same parking garage. She hopes that if she can avoid Jake for long enough, he'll give up.

Alicia's managing attorney, *Dale Hutchison*, is looking for a file of legal papers and remembers that he gave the file to Alicia. It's urgent that he get some information from the file at once, and Alicia's out of the office. Dale goes to her desk and finds the file on top. He can't avoid seeing a note that Alicia has written on the top sheet of her notepad: *Hi, Could you wait for me again this evening? I'll leave at 5 and just take the work home with me. I don't want "you-know-who" to catch me alone again. Yesterday when I was in the research library, he closed the door and started making disgusting remarks about "heaven between the sheets." Yuk!*

Dale is stunned. Who can Alicia be talking about? And why hasn't she told him she's having a problem with one of the guys? Back in his office, he can't get the incident off his mind. About 30 minutes later he arrives for a previously-scheduled meeting with one of the partners, *Tom Drake*. Since Dale is the first to arrive, he takes the opportunity to discuss the incident with Tom. They both agree that Alicia must file an internal complaint against her harasser.

Later that day, Dale finds time to speak privately with Alicia. "I don't mean to pry, Alicia, but when I was looking for the file on your desk, your note about being harassed was just there. The words just jumped out at me. You know, you don't have to put up with this kind of harassment—and you shouldn't. I'm just so sorry this is happening to you. Tom and I think you should file an internal complaint." Alicia is upset and angry. "Dale, you had no right to discuss this with management, especially without talking to me first. I don't want to bring a complaint. All I would do is make an enemy. It would be his word against mine, and I know who has the power around here!" She stopped, sorry that she had said as much as she had.

"Look, I'll stand behind you. You need to take action to stop this problem."

"I won't have my privacy invaded," said Alicia, "and that's that."

"But the company has to maintain an office that's free of sexual harassment, and as your manager, I'm supposed to report this. It's company policy.

"And I have too much at stake," said Alicia. "I like my job and I want to keep it. Stay out of it, Dale. Let me take care of it."

1. What are the major issues (root problems) here?
2. What should Dale do?
3. What should Alicia do?

Case Study 6.3: Supervisor Jay and Employee Marion

As a top-level manager of Omni Inc., you have not been aware that Supervisor Jay has been sexually harassing one of his employees, Marian. Marian has not been fired or demoted, her pay and tangible benefits haven't been affected, and she hasn't formally notified higher management of any harassment.

Question #1: What can happen if Marion sues?

a. Supervisor Jay can be held liable for the harassment

b. Omni Inc. can be held liable for the harassment

c. Given that a formal complaint wasn't filed, Employee Marion has no case.

Question #2: You're investigating Employee Marion's claim of sexual harassment by Supervisor Jay. All five of the witnesses you have interviewed so far have supported her claim of sexual harassment. You should

a. Stop the investigation; call legal counsel, and issue a report on the investigation

b. Continue the investigation; interview everyone else who might have witnessed the harassment

c. Continue the investigation but stop the interview process—it's not necessary to drag other workers in for interviews at this stage

Question #3: After conducting a thorough investigation, you conclude that sexual harassment has not taken place. What do you do now?

a. Report back to the accuser, Employee Marion, and the accused, Supervisor Jay

b. Conduct a company-wide seminar on sexual harassment policy and procedure

c. Redistribute your company policy on sexual harassment

d. All of the above

Case Study 6.4: Jill, a New Professor

Jill is a Euro-American woman hired as associate professor at San Jose State University. She has been teaching at a relatively low-paying private university, teaching 3 different courses on 3 different days at 2 different campuses. Because of her experience, she came in at the higher rank of associate professor rather than the more typical (and slightly lower paying) rank of assistant professor. On the other hand, instead of having 6 years to achieve the teaching and publishing track record necessary for tenure, she will have only 3 years. Therefore, she has her work cut out for her.

Virtually all the current faculty (tenured and on the tenure track, 80 percent male) have schedules requiring them to come to campus one or two days a week to teach 3 sections of one or two courses, meaning one or two preparations. However, Jill finds that her tentative schedule for next semester will require her to come to campus 3 days a week to teach 3 different courses, meaning 3 different preparations.

Scheduling is done by the department chair, Jake Barnes, in consultation with the associate dean Spencer Graham. Jill makes an appointment to meet with these administrators to request a more amenable teaching schedule. She tells them that she is concerned about doing the necessary research and publishing as well as doing a good job of teaching in a new environment—in order to be qualified for tenure in 3 years. After all, a university teacher either a) receives tenure, b) is terminated, or 3) may be offered a part-time, insecure lecturer assignment.

The message that Jill picks up from Jake and Spencer may be summarized as: "You have been accustomed to this type of schedule at Private U, where you were making less income and had more administrative duties. You should be able to handle any schedule we give you like a pro. When we granted you associate professor status, we expected you to hit the ground running. We need for you to teach these classes at these times." Reading between the lines, Jill suspects they are viewing her as a whiner, complainer, even trouble maker, who is not adequately grateful, cooperative, and professional. When the schedule is published, she sees that her request for change has not been granted.

1. What are the root problems?
2. How do you interpret the actions of Jill? Of Jake and Spencer?
3. If you were Jake and Spencer, what actions would you take?
4. If you were Jill, what would you do now?

Skill Builder 6.1: Minicases: Is This Sexual Harassment?

Do you think the actions in these four cases constitute sexual harassment? If so, what would you recommend to each party involved?

1. **A male supervisor** occasionally compliments his young assistant with remarks such as "You ought to wear short skirts more often" and "Sit and talk to me a little longer; I'm enjoying the view."

2. **A female doctor** is discharged from a medical residency program. She tries to understand what went wrong. She remembers that she did not react favorably to a supervising professor's invitation to go out for drinks, compliments about her hair and legs, questions about her romantic life. He made comments that seemed to imply that he'd like to help her get through the program, but she sensed that going out with him would be part of the relationship. At first she tried to smile her way through these incidents. Later she gave disapproving looks or turned away. When he kept on, she finally told him one day that she was busy and abruptly walked away.

3. **A male journalist** willingly enters into a love affair with his female supervising editor. She has always rated his work performance as excellent. After a few months he breaks off the affair At his next performance review, the journalist receives a less-than-satisfactory rating from her.

4. **Rosita, an advertising copy writer,** has been passed over for promotion. A colleague, Hazel, got the job. Rosita is sure Hazel is having an affair with the boss. Several times in the past year, the boss has gone on business trips which called for a copy writer to go along. Each time he took Hazel instead of Rosita, even though in at least one instance Rosita was the one who had done most of the work on the account he was calling on. Rosita has heard talk from other employees. Rumor has it this is not the first affair the boss has had, nor the first time he has promoted a girl friend.

5. **One day, as you sit at your desk,** two colleagues walk by you as one delivers the punch line to a very dirty joke. You haven't heard them speak like this before, and you feel it's very inappropriate.

Skill Builder 6.2: Recognizing Assertiveness

Purpose: To apply your knowledge of assertiveness training.

Instructions: Indicate whether you think each response to each of the following situations is assertive, aggressive, or nonassertive.

1. At a meeting, someone interrupts when you're speaking. You say,

   a. Excuse me. I'd like to finish my statement.

   b. Oh, excuse me.

   c. You know, it's rude to interrupt like that.

2. You enjoyed a coworker's presentation. You say,

   a. See you back at the salt mine.

   b. Thanks for your presentation; it gave me a lot of new ideas.

   c. Well, *that's* over!

3. **Your women's advocacy group has been trying to get better maternity benefits. A coworker says, "What do you women want anyway?" You answer,**

   a. To put chauvinists like you in their place.

   b. I don't get involved in these things.

   c. Fairness and equality.

4. **You've been called several times by the same salesperson trying to sell you magazines. This time you say**

   a. Would you please not call me again?

   b. You're a disgusting jackass. Why don't you take a flying leap.

   c. This is the third time I've been disturbed, and each time I've told you that I'm not interested. If you call again, you leave me no choice but to report this to the authorities.

5. Asking your boss for a raise, you begin,

   a. Aaah, do you think that you could see your way clear to giving me a raise?

   b. I've been overworked around here for too long, and I'm overdue for a raise.

   c. I'd like to go over this list of extra projects I've completed and work I've reorganized to produce more with less time and money. . . .

REFERENCES

AAUW. *The AAUW Report: How Schools Shortchange Girls.* Washington DC: American Association of University Women, 1992.

Adler, Nancy, and D.N. Izraeli, eds. *Women in Management Worldwide.* M.E. Sharpe, Inc, 1988.

Allport, G.W. *The Nature of Prejudice.* Addison-Wesley, 1954.

Arora, Raksha and Lydia Saad, "Profiling America's Affluent Women," Gallup.com, March 29, 2005

Ballentine, Susan and Jessica Inclan. *Diverse Voices of Women.* Mayfield, 1996.

Blau, Francine D. and Lawrence M. Kahn, "The Gender Pay Gap: Have Women Gone as Far as They Can?" *Academy of Management Perspectives,* July 2007.

Blinder, Martin. *Choosing Lovers.* Avon, 1987.

Bly, Robert. *Iron John: A Book About Men.* Random House, 1992.

Bond, James T., et al. "Highlights of the 2002 National Study of the Changing Workforce" Families and Work Institute, *www.familiesandwork.org* 2003.

Brooks, Deborah Jordan, "Job Equality Views," Gallup Poll, August 27, 2002.

Burley-Allen, Madelyn. *Managing Assertively*, 2d ed. John Wiley & Sons, Inc., 1996.

Cabrera, Susan and Melissa Thomas-Hung, "Risky Business: A Theoretical Model Applied in the Advancement of Executive Women," Johnson School, Cornell University, 2007.

Carroll, Jerry. "The Secrets of Young Girls." *San Francisco Chronicle*, E-1, August 31, 1994..

Carr-Ruffino, Norma. "U.S. Women: Breaking Through the Glass Ceiling." *Women in Management Review* 6, 5, 1991.

Carr-Ruffino, Norma. *The Promotable Woman*. Career Press, 1997.

Catalyst, "More Women in Top Management," *www.CatalystWomen.Org* , November 19, 2002.

Catalyst, "The Bottom Line: Connecting Corporate Performance and Gender Diversity" catalyst.org, 2004.

Center for Women's Business Research, "Key Facts about Women-Owned Businesses," *www.NFWBO.org*, 2008, 2009.

Center for Women's Business Research, report, 2005.

Cherry, Robert. Discrimination: Its Economic Impact on Blacks, Women, and Jews. Lexington Books, 1989.

Chin, Steven. "50,000 at Oakland Rally Just for Men," *San Francisco Chronicle*, October 1, 1996.

Crane, F.G. and Susan DeYoung. "Attitudes to Portrayal of Women in Advertising." *International Journal of Advertising*, 251, 1992.

Delaney, Laurel, "Escape from Corporate American," *Across the Board*, March 2002.

Dominick, Joseph, and Gail Rauch. "The Image of Women in Network TV Commercials." *Journal of Broadcasting*, 259, Summer 1972.

Eagly, Alice H. *Sex Differences in Social Behavior*. Lawrence Erlbaum Associates, 1987.

Eagly, Alice H. and Linda L. Carli, "Labyrinth of Leadership," *Harvard Business Review*, 63–71, September 2007.

EEOC. "Glass Ceilings: The Status of Women as Officials and Managers in the Private Sector, Executive Summary." U.S. Equal Employment Opportunity Commission. *www.eeoc.gov,* 2008.

Eisen, Jerry. *Powertalk!* Simon & Schuster, 1984.

Evatt, Chris. *He & She*. Conari Press, 1992.

Faludi, Susan. *Backlash: The Undeclared War against American Women*. Crown, 1991.

Faludi, Susan. *Stiffed: The Betrayal of the American Man*. Wm. Morrow, 1999.

Farrell, Warren. *The Myth of Male Power*. Simon & Schuster, 1993.

Farrell, Warren. *Why Men Earn More*. AMACOM, 2005.

Fausto-Sterling, Anne. *Myths of Gender*. Basic Books, 1986.

Female Executive. Report on sexual harassment survey, 1992.

Ferguson, Andrew. "America's New Man," *The American Spectator*, 26–33, January, 1992.

Fischman, J. "The Character of Controversy," *Psychology Today*, December 1988.

Fisher, Anne, "Why Women Rule," *Female Entrepreneurs*, April 2005.

Fondas, Nanette, "Feminization Unveiled: Mgmt Qualities in Contemporary Writings," *Academy of Management Review* 22, 1, 254–282, 1997.

Garcia, Guy. *Decline of Men: How the American Male Is Tuning Out, Giving Up, and Flipping Off His Future*. Harper, 2008.

Gates, David. "White Male Paranoia." *Newsweek*, 48–54, March 29, 1993.

Geary, David C. *Male, Female: The Evolution of Human Sex Differences*. American Psychological Association, 1998.

Glick, P. and S.T. Fiske, "Sex Discrimination: The Psychological Approach" 155–187 in F.J. Crosby et al, eds., *Sex Discrimination in the Workplace*. Blackwell, 2007.

Gove, Walter R. *A Biopsychosocial Perspective.* Vanderbilt University, 1986.

Guthrie, D. and L.M. Roth, "The State, Courts, and Equal Opportunities for Female CEOs in U.S. Organiztions: Specifying Institutional Mechanisms," *Social Forces,* 78, 511–542, 1999.

H.R. Society for Human Resource Management, "Survey on Sexual Harassment," 1998.

Halpern, D.F. "Psychology at the Intersection of Work and Family: Recommendations for Employers, Working Families, and Policymakers, *American Psycholog*ist, 50, 97–409, 2005.

Hamilton, A. and P.A. Veglahn, " Sexual Harassment: The Hostile Work Environment." *Cornell HRA Quarterly,* 33, 88–92, 1992.

Hewlett, Sylvia Ann. *Creating a Life: Professional Women and the Quest for Children.* Talk Miramax Books, 2002.

Howard, J., P. Blumstein, and Pepper Schwartz. "Sex, Power, and Influence Tactics in Intimate Relationships." *Journal of Personality and Social Psychology,* 51, 102–109, July 1986.

Howe, Neil and Wm. Strauss. Millennials Rising: The Next Great Generation. Random House, 2000

ILO, "Women in Management: It's Still Lonely at the Top," *World of Work,* 23, 1998.

Jacobs, M.A. "Men's Club." *Wall Street Journal,* A-1, June 9, 1994.

Kabacoss, Robert I., "Gender Differences in Organizational Leadership: A Large Sample Study," American Psychological Association Annual Convention, San Francisco, CA, August 1998.

Kanter, R.M. *Men and Women of the Corporation.* Basic Books, 1979.

Keen, Sam. *Fire in the Belly.* Bantam Books, 1991.

Kohn, A. 1988.

L.A. Times. "Orange Juice War Against Bad Ideas." *Los Angeles Times,* M-6, August 14, 1994.

Lester, Joan S. *The Future of White Men.* Conari Press, 1994.

Low, Bobbi. *Why Sex Matters.* Princeton University Press, 1999.

Lowrey, Ying. Office of Economic Research, Office of Advocacy, U.S. Small Business Administration 2006.

Maume, D.F. and P. Huston, "Job Segregation and Gender Differences in Work-Family Spillover Among White-Collar Workers, *Journal of Family and Economic Issues,* 22, 171–189, 2001.

Mealey, Linda. *Sex Differences: Developmental and Evolutionary Strategies.* Academic Press, 2000.

Morrison, Ann, R.P. White, and E. Van Velsor. *Breaking the Glass Ceiling.* Addison-Wesley, 1987.

Naisbett, John, and P. Aburdene. *Megatrends 2000.* Wm. Morrow, 1990.

Naisbett, John. *Megatrends.* Warner Books, 1982.

Newport, Frank,"Desire to Have Children Alive and Well in America," Gallup Poll, August 19, 2003.

Okami, Paul, "Review of Male, Female," *Journal of Sex Rese*arch, February 1, 2001.

Orenstein, Peggy. *Schoolgirls: Young Women, Self-esteem, and the Confidence Gap.* Doubleday, 1994.

Patriarchy: What Is It? *Men's Council Journal,* special issue, 17, May 1993.

Peplau, L.A. "Lesbian and Gay Relationships" in *Homosexuality: Research Implications for Public Policy.* ed. J. C. Gonsiorek and J. D. Weinrich. Thousand Oaks, CA: Sage, 1991.

Pollack, William. *Real Boys.* New York: Random House Inc. 1998. Wm. Pollack, Ph.D, is Clinical Professor of Psychiatry, Harvard Medical School, clinical psychologist, and co-director of Center for Men, McLean Hospital, Harvard Medical School.

Real, Terrence. *I Don't Want to Talk About It.* Scribner, 1997.

Rosener, J.B.,"Ways Women Lead," *Harvard Business Review,* 199-226, Nov–Dec, 1990.

Rosener, Judy B. *American's Competition Secret: Women Managers.* Oxford University Press, 1995.

Rossman, Marlene L. *The International Businesswoman of the 1990s.* Greenwood Press, 1990.

Rubin, Harriet, "Sexism," *Portfolio,* 93–97, April 8, 2008.

Russell, A. M. "Women Vs. Men: Where We Stand Today," *Working Woman,* 66, January, 1991.

Seager, Joni. *The Atlas of Women: An Economic, Social and Political Survey.* The Women's Press, New Internationalist, 2003.

Shipman, Claire and Katty Kay. *Womenomics: Write Your Own Rules for Success.* Harper Business, 2009.

Speer, Robert. "What's New with Men?" *Chico News & Review*, April 16, 1993.

Stone, P. and M. Lovejoy, "Fast-Track Women and the 'Choice' to Stay Home," *Annals of the American Academy*, 596, 62–83, 2004

Sugawa, S. "Firms Holding Back Women, Minorities," *Washington Post*, 9, August 1991.

Sugawa, S. "Firms Holding Back Women, Minorities," *Washington Post*, 9, August 1991.

Tannen, Deborah. *You Just Don't Understand.* Wm. Morrow, 1990.

Tanner, M. Scot. Expert on Chinese politics in *Business Week*, 1994.

Time. "Indecent Exposure: The Navy Takes a Heavy Rap in the Tailhook Report on Sexual Harassment." *Time*, 141, 20–21, May 3, 1993.

Trost, C., "Firms Heed Women Employees' Needs, *Wall Street Journal*, B-1, November 22, 1990.

U.S. Census Bureau. "We the American Women." U.S. Department of Commerce, 1993, 2001.

U.S. Bureau of Labor Statistics, "Monthly Labor Review," April 1997, 2000.

U.S. Census Bureau. "Current Population Reports, Average Earnings of Year-Round Fulltime Workers by Sex and Educational Attainment." Department of Commerce, 1991, 2002.

U.S. Census Bureau. "Current Population Reports, Male-Female Differences." Department of Commerce, 1987, 2002.

U.S. Glass Ceiling Commission. *Better for Business*, Department of Labor, 1996.

U.S. Glass Ceiling Commission. *The Glass Ceiling Initiative.* Department of Labor, 1991.

U.S. Women's Bureau, Department of Labor. "Facts on Working Women." 1990, 1992, 1993, 1998.

Vanneman, Reeve, L.W. Cannon. *The American Perception of Class.* Temple University Press, 1987.

Vault.com survey, "Survey on Sexual Harassment," 2001.

Williams, J. *Unbending Gender: Why Family and Work Conflict and What to Do About It*, Oxford University Press, 2000.

Wilson, William Julius. *The Declining Significance of Race.* University of Chicago Press, 1978.

Wilson, William Julius. *The Truly Disadvantaged.* University of Chicago Press, 1987.

Wirth, L. *Breaking Through the Glass Ceiling: Women in Management.* Geneva: International Labour Office, 2001.

Working Mother, "100 Best Companies for Working Mothers," *www.workingmother.com*, annual October issue.

Working Woman, "How the Men in Your Office Really See You," 101–103, November 1991.

WSJ, *The Wall Street Journal Almanac.* Research firm Facts That Matter, 1997.

WSJ. Report on how men are dealing with women managers, *Wall Street Journal*, 1991.

Zilbergeld, Bernie. Statement by Berkeley psychologist, expert on men's groups, in interview, April 6, 1993.

Working with African Americans

*Negroes not only raised doubts about the white man's value system
but aroused the troubling suspicion that whatever else the true
American is,he is also somehow black.*
Ralph Ellison

About 12 percent of the people in the American workplace are African Americans, which accounts for about one in eight employees. People who have taken the time and effort to learn about the African American community and its values and customs, say they've boosted their ability to work productively with African Americans. Those who belong to the African American culture say studying it has helped them to better understand their own heritage and their strengths.

It's important in today's workplace to develop the level of understanding needed to build good relationships when associates are from another culture–whether you are a new entry-level employee or a top executive. A major key is to learn about an associate's culture and get a feel for his or her background. The more skilled you become at interpreting an individual's actions against the backdrop of his or her culture, the greater success both of you can achieve through working together.

The African American community is made up of many elements, and of course no one person expresses all the values and customs discussed here. You may be tempted to use this cultural information to form new rigid categories. To be fair, stay open and flexible as you interact with individual African Americans. Deal with the unique individual, bringing into play your understanding of his or her cultural background.

You're about to get a little taste of what it's like to be an African American in the American society and workplace and how this experience can affect interactions in the workplace. Specifically, you'll learn about these issues:

- How typical stereotypes and myths about African Americans compare with reality
- How the current situation is connected to certain historical events
- Key cultural values and customs that are important to people in this community
- Barriers to career success for African Americans and how to break through these barriers, a leadership challenge

- Assets African Americans may bring to your company and how to use those assets to create win-win successes, a leadership opportunity

First, check your attitudes and knowledge by completing Self-Awareness Activities 7.1 and 7.2.

African American Man

Courtesy of Chris Carroll/Corbis Images.

African American Woman

Courtesy of Chris Carroll/Corbis Images.

Self-Awareness Activity 7.1: What Do You Believe About African Americans?

Purpose:

- to get in touch with your beliefs and stereotypes about this group of people
- to experience how judgmental beliefs affect your thinking and feeling processes
- to experience the ways in which your beliefs create your reality regarding other persons, even before you have any interaction with them.

Part I. What Do You Believe About African American Women?

Step 1. Associations

- Relax as deeply as you can.
- Close your eyes for a moment and take a few deep breaths.
- Now focus on the picture that symbolizes "African American woman"
- Imagine that you are this woman. Be African American woman.
- Notice any resistance to being this person—and any willingness.
- Notice words, images, thoughts, and feelings that come to mind as you are "seeing and being this woman."

Step 2. Negative Associations

- Next, as you focus on the picture, allow negative opinions to come up, perhaps some that you typically hold about African American women.
- Notice your *thoughts* as you see the person in this negative way. What *feelings?*

Step 3. Positive Associations

- Now, still focusing, allow positive opinions to come up, perhaps some that you typically hold about African American women.
- Notice your *thoughts* as you see the person in this negative way. What *feelings?*

Step 4. Insights

Now review this experience and write about it.

- When you first saw the picture, what thoughts and feelings came up? These may reflect your deepest responses to people from this group.
- Think about the differences in your thoughts and feelings when you consciously held a positive opinion versus a negative opinion.
- Write a few sentences about your feelings, thoughts, and insights.

Part II. Experimenting with Opinions About African American Men

Repeat the phases and steps in part I, this time focusing on the image of an African American man.

Self-Awareness Activity 7.2: What Do You Know About African Americans?

Purpose: To see what you know about the issues covered in this chapter.

Instructions: Determine whether you think the following statements are basically true or false—and why. The answers will emerge in this chapter, and the summary at the end of the chapter focuses on these issues.

1. The Civil Rights Act of 1964 was a result of liberal Democrats' demands, led by Kennedy and Johnson.
2. Since the civil rights measures have been in force, African Americans have dramatically increased their status.
3. The best predictor of both school grades and SAT scores is ethnicity.
4. Significant numbers of African American managers and professionals leave corporate jobs due to the glass ceiling that prevents their advancement.
5. African Americans focus primarily on group expression rather than individual expression.
6. African American communication style tends to be more impersonal and cool than Euro-American style.
7. Many African Americans need assertiveness training to be most effective in American corporate cultures.
8. The leadership challenge of helping African Americans break out of lowered expectations is especially difficult because managers typically have little impact on African Americans' success cycles.

STEREOTYPES AND REALITIES

Most of the stereotypes African Americans must deal with stem from the legacy of slavery and segregation that is unique to this American subculture. In order to justify slavery, a practice so incompatible with the American ideals of human freedom and equality, some Euro-Americans created degrading stereotypes of Africans. Such beliefs are passed along from generation to generation and die hard.

Although the proportion of Euro-Americans that hold the more extreme stereotypes is continually declining, responses to a 1992 survey indicate the following beliefs may still be prevalent (Thornton), as confirmed by a later survey (NORC 2000).

- Are Blacks more violent than Whites? Yes, 63 percent
- Are they less intelligent? Yes, 53 percent
- Are they more likely to prefer to live off welfare? Yes, 78 percent
- Do they blame everyone but themselves for their problems? Yes, 57 percent
- Do they tend to be resentful troublemakers? Yes, 51 percent
- Bottom line: We have some work to do on changing these beliefs and attitudes.

Stereotypes are rigid, exaggerated, irrational beliefs, each associated with a mental category, such as a particular group of people. Although stereotypes aren't identical to prejudice, rigid stereotypes about people usually lead to prejudice. For example, in the past perhaps a Euro-American observed an abused slave whose rage finally consumed him and who lashed out violently. The Euro-American began saying to others, "African American men are violent." This became a convenient stereotype, a good excuse for keeping African American men under tight rein. Euro-Americans who accepted the violent stereotype didn't notice that most African American men were not violent, even when degraded and abused. But they noted every time one was violent, and each incident confirmed their belief. This is how stereotyping works.

Most Euro-Americans believe that blatant discrimination against African Americans is a thing of the past. But African American leaders consider racial profiling by police a major issue. And within the last few years, many major organizations were found guilty of blatant discrimination, including Texaco, Denny's, American Airlines, Coca Cola, United Parcel Service, Circuit City, Avis, and the U.S. Department of Agriculture.

To get to know what it's like to be an African American, you must understand the stereotypes they deal with every time they leave the family or community circle, or turn on the television, for that matter. To bridge the divisive walls these stereotypes hold in place, you must know what they are, know other realities that balance or refute them, and move beyond stereotypes to a more realistic view of the African American community. The goal here is to appreciate each cultural group's unique value and to strengthen our unity as one culture.

Stereotype #1: African Americans Are More Violent Than Others

A cultural custom that may perpetuate this stereotype is African Americans' preference for using direct confrontation to resolve a conflict. Most Euro-Americans, Asian Americans and Latino Americans prefer more indirect methods. African American behavior is therefore often seen as hostile and militant when it's not. This is reinforced by—and reinforces—the stereotype of African Americans as prone to violence (Foeman 1987; Kitano 1976; Hall 1976).

The reality is that certain behavior that is considered assertive and truthful by African Americans is often interpreted by others as anger or rage about to erupt into violence. What feeds this interpretation is:

- cultural differences about how to express concerns and emotions
- the "violent" stereotype itself. We see what we expect to see and ignore actions that don't fit our stereotypes.

While we can prove that African American men have higher criminal arrest and conviction rates, we cannot prove that they are more violent. For one thing, violence is a subjective term. For another, many studies indicate that African American men are more likely than others to be arrested and convicted for the same type of activity, according to Marc Mauer's research (1989).

Mauer also concluded that the United States is one of the more violent cultures of the world. More productive than using African Americans as the scapegoats who create violence in society would be addressing violence in the media and society at large.

Stereotype #2: African Americans Are Less Intelligent Than Others

In the workplace and elsewhere, Euro-Americans tend to assume that even highly intelligent African Americans are less competent. Some studies indicate that when it comes to Euro-American men helping each other, the other man's *ability* is the determining factor, not the fact that the man is Euro-American. But when it comes to helping African American men, their *ethnicity*, not their ability, is the major determining factor, according to studies by F. A. Blanchard and F. J. Crosby (1989). In a subsequent study using Euro-American women rather than African American men as the partners, researchers found identical patterns.

The reality is that school grades and grades on the SAT exam depend more on socioeconomic status than any other factor, including ethnicity, according to the meta-study done by the American Association of University Women. Children from low-income households, often with no father around, and whose parents have low educational achievement, tend to make lower grades. As socioeconomic status goes up, so do grades—for African Americans, Euro-Americans, boys, girls, and all others.

Learning style is different for many African Americans, according to psychologist James M. Jones. They tend to focus more on rhythms and patterns and recognize patterns better than people from other cultures. They are usually better at oral than written expression, and they tend toward improvisation and creative responses to the world and to the moment. Therefore, they tend to do better on tests where there are clear patterns as well as opportunities for creativity and oral responses.

Many people assume that African Americans value education less than Euro-Americans, since fewer complete high school and college. However, D.G. Solorzano's study indicates that African American high school students, and their parents, have significantly higher aspirations to achieve a college degree than Euro-Americans at the same socioeconomic level. In both groups, the higher the socioeconomic level, the higher the educational aspirations tend to be.

Stereotype #3: African Americans Are Lazy and Irresponsible

As a matter of fact, about the same proportion of African Americans as Euro-Americans hold jobs, but African American men receive only about 70 percent the pay of Euro-American men. African American women receive 62 percent as much. In spite of this wage gap, African Americans are industrious and responsible enough to get and keep jobs in down-sized mean-and-lean corporations that must be globally competitive and productive. Historically, they have done much of the hard labor that helped establish the U.S. economy. This stereotype goes back to the time when most slaves were treated as subhuman children, denied an education, expected to do exactly as the overseer ordered, and offered little or no reward for working harder and smarter. When some didn't act eager and committed, all were branded lazy and irresponsible.

For well-educated African Americans in corporate America, "lazy" and "incompetent" are two of the most frustrating stereotypes. Many who respond to surveys say they're permitted a much narrower range of behavioral styles to achieve their goals than their Euro-American peers. They also become quite frustrated when they perceive they must work twice as hard and must stay in a position longer than necessary—just to prove they're *not* lazy and incompetent and that they *can* handle the next assignment. See the Glass Ceiling section later in this chapter. This stereotype extends to the assumption by Euro-American colleagues that nearly all African Americans are incompetent to handle higher-level responsibilities, as indicated by research studies. Another result: African American professionals are often assumed to be sales clerks, waiters, or other entry-level or menial workers. Social interactions that they enjoy with their colleagues at work may disappear outside the office, where co-workers often literally don't recognize them on the street when they're not in "corporate uniform."

Stereotype #4: They Blame Everyone Else for Their Problems

African Americans have been struggling for hundreds of years to rise up from the massive burdens of the past, including 200 years of slavery, and another 100 years of legal segregation that included barriers to well-paying corporate or government jobs. They understand that this history is still affecting their chances to build a successful career and life. While virtually all community leaders focus on self-help programs, most believe the government should help the inner-city underclass to break out of this prison that was not of their own making. This has led to the stereotype of blaming others and expecting "government handouts."

The reality is that African American progress since the civil rights laws of the 1960s has taken two distinct directions: about one-third have made fairly good progress and are part of the hard-working, tax-paying, responsible middle class. These African Americans are not stuck in a victim mentality that blames others for their difficulties. Not all have been so fortunate, however. About one-third are actually worse-off, if anything—mired down in inner-city, underclass poverty and crime—and in dire need of help. The other third are hovering somewhere between underclass and middle class status, most of them struggling to make it on their own.

Most community leaders credit the progress that has been made to the people's own bootstrap efforts—including community efforts that are often church-based—in combination with civil rights laws and certain successful government programs.

Stereotype #5: Many African Americans Are Resentful Troublemakers

This stereotype is related to the violent and blaming stereotypes. It's connected to cultural differences in confronting issues and expressing concerns, and to a history of trying to break out of imprisoning discrimination. It's also connected to inner city underclass crime.

The reality is that most people in the African American community believe in speaking up assertively, especially about perceived injustices. Being genuine, expressing the feelings you are feeling, and directly confronting issues are all highly valued and typical patterns in the African American community. During the days of legal and open discrimination and oppression, African Americans did not dare to express these values outside the community. Now that they have more political freedom to do so, younger members are especially likely to feel it's important to be genuine and speak up in such situations. The point is that expressions interpreted as resentful troublemaking by persons outside the community may not be meant that way nor seen that way by African Americans.

To put all this in perspective, these stereotypes are stereotyped beliefs that result in prejudice and discrimination. Euro-Americans and African Americans operate with different definitions of ethnic prejudice. Euro-Americans tend to define it narrowly as "explicit, consciously held beliefs in ethnic superiority." African Americans authors define it more broadly as a "set of practices and institutions that result in the oppression of a group of people" (Lichtenberg 1992). African Americans say ethnic prejudice is still their principal challenge to moving up in the work world. They say management looks for "safe blacks" to develop and promote and are less willing to take the same risks with African Americans that they take with Euro-American males (Thomas 1991).

CONNECTIONS TO THE PAST

A unique legacy of slavery and legal segregation laid the groundwork for these diehard stereotypes and myths. Of all the ethnic groups in the United States, African Americans have traditionally faced the greatest obstacles, which are built on this foundation of entrenched prejudice and discrimination, usually called racism. The idea that African Americans are of another race is another myth.

The culturally devastating practice of slavery set the stage for the legal segregation in the South and de facto segregation in the North that followed the Civil War. The march toward true equality began the day slavery began, but major breakthroughs came on the heels of an intensified Civil Rights Movement in the 1950s and 1960s.

Slavery

During and just after America's colonial years, about four million Africans were brought over and made slaves. During the first 250 years of our nation, Africans were bought and sold as commodities on a slave market (from about 1615 until Emancipation around 1865). The founding fathers in 1776

The Myth of Race

The "one drop rule" (for one drop of blood) was used well into the 20th century to classify African Americans. But how many African Americans are of pure African stock? In 1930 less than 25 percent of African Americans were of unmixed descent, according to a respected anthropologist (Herskovitz 1930). The Census Bureau has concurred with that estimate. Prior to the 1960s it was illegal for African Americans and Euro-Americans to marry. Yet nearly 75 percent of African Americans had one or more Euro-American ancestors due to sexual unions outside marriage—primarily slave women submitting to sexual demands. Now that inter-marriage is legal, it's likely that the percentage of "unmixed" African Americans is much smaller.

What is the actual ancestry of the "average" African American? Studies show it's about 70 percent African, and 25 percent combined Euro-American and American Indian.

designated African Americans as three-fifths human. After the Civil War and Emancipation, during the legal segregation era, they were still seen by many Euro-Americans as subhuman, only a step above the apes but below humans.

The result was a caste system, with African Americans as the "untouchables." The women could wet-nurse babies of Euro-American women and prepare the family food, but could not drink from the same public water fountains nor eat at the same establishments. Euro-Americans who protested this treatment of African Americans were branded "nigger lovers" and ostracized or threatened in order to keep them in line.

Slavery had a deep and lasting effect that is clearly present today. Slavery was the culture of the great grandparents of today's African American adults, a culture that affected every aspect of their family life, beliefs about self and the world, hopes and expectations. The culture of slavery also affected everyone else in the United States at the time, and most Euro-American's great-grandparents inevitably handed down the interconnecting beliefs about privilege, inequality, and prejudice—by their attitudes and actions, if not by their verbal teachings. Slavery laid the foundation for the prejudice and discrimination that African Americans must cope with today—and for the resulting social problems many activists are working to overcome.

It began in Virginia, and by the time of the Civil War, 1860, about 92 percent of all African Americans lived in the South, and 95 percent of this group were slaves. In fact, African slaves made up 35 percent of the South's population, while slaveholders were only 5.5 percent of the total. Most slaves provided the essential labor for raising cotton, tobacco, rice, sugar, and hemp. Kept illiterate and ignorant, they were typically told they were incapable of caring for themselves. Most slaveholders liked to picture themselves as kind masters taking care of docile, happy slaves. In reality, many owners were harsh or cruel and most were terrified by the threat of slave rebellion. And many slaves wore masks of docility and deference in order to hide subversive plans (Harding 1980; Takaki 1993).

For African American women, slavery held special horrors. They worked in the fields and factories just as the men did, but many masters viewed them as "breeders" and the only legal source of more slaves after importation of slaves was outlawed in 1808. Their children were not even their own, for the laws allowed masters to separate slave children from their mothers and sell them. And many slave women were used to satisfy the sexual desires of their masters. If these rapes resulted in pregnancy, and the child resembled the master, the woman and her child were likely to be sold. The effect on the adult males in the slave group was to greatly undermine their self-esteem and confidence (Harding 1980; Takaki 1993).

The few slaves who managed to escape headed north toward freedom. But freedom in northern society was only a facade for the reality of caste. African Americans in the North faced segregation, prejudice, discrimination, and violence. They were excluded from the skilled and professional jobs and could find only menial labor. The North was certainly not the promised land of their dreams.

Because virtually every African American is still experiencing the aftermath of the slave experience (Handy 1995), it's important for all of us to understand the impact of being a slave. It included being:

- Uprooted from one's home
- Stripped of one's culture
- Separated from family
- Subjected to deprived and oppressive conditions
- Stripped of voice by enforced silence—required to speak only English, adopt English names, and forgo learning to read and write
- Told to think of self as a slave only
- Blocked from virtually all of life's opportunities
- Brutally punished—in front of other slaves, who had to remain silent—if you resisted

The psychological aftermath and feelings that result from the practice of slavery are far from positive and they tend to separate us. Here are the feelings Kenneth Handy (1995) discovered:

African American	Euro-American
Shame	Guilt
Humiliation	Shame/humiliation
Inferiority	Denial
Anguish	Rationalization
Rage	Anger

We as a culture must discuss and validate this experience before it will be healed. We cannot brush it under the rug, where it will continue to fester. We must go through the joint process of taking responsibility and forgiving before we can move on.

Vignette: A Slave Family's Ordeal

Sarah was a young slave woman who worked in the cotton fields on a plantation in Georgia. She was well aware that her master and any of his plantation bosses could force her to have sex with them. How could she refuse and still survive? She had somehow escaped this fate until recently when Mr. Jones caught her alone in the barn. Soon after, she realized she was pregnant. Her husband Jake knew something was wrong. When Sarah broke down and told him the story, he felt completely humiliated, so powerless in this situation. Sarah gave birth to a boy, Shane. Everyone noticed what light skin and European-like features he had. Mr. Jones frowned when he heard talk about the baby. The last thing he wanted was his wife noticing a slave child that looked suspiciously like her husband. Soon Sarah and Shane were taken to the slave market to be sold. She was torn apart from her husband, parents, and all the people she knew. She never saw them again.

Self-Awareness Activity 7.3: How Does It Feel to Be Trapped?

Purpose: To find common ground with the people who have the experience of being trapped.
Step 1. The situation. You've read about the experience of African slaves in the United States. They lived constantly with at least two major dilemmas: entrapment and degradation. They were

trapped in situations that provided no real personal freedom and almost no alternatives. They were told in many ways that they were inferior. Can you think of a situation in which you felt similarly trapped and/or degraded—physically, emotionally, or psychologically? Write a brief paragraph describing the situation.

Step 2. Thoughts and feelings. Go back to that time and place. Relive the situation. What were some of your thoughts at that time? How did you feel? Write a brief paragraph about your thoughts and feelings.

Step 3. Common ground. Now shift to the situations of African American slaves. Can you imagine what thoughts and feelings you might have had if you were a slave living on a southern plantation around 1800? Can you imagine how all this might affect the way you would raise your children? How even your grandchildren might be affected? Write a brief paragraph about thoughts and feelings that come to mind. If you are African American, do you have personal experiences of being affected by this past history?

After Slavery: Free but Segregated

Soon after the Civil War, African Americans' life in the South resembled their cousins' life in the North. The major difference was that segregation was de facto in the North and legal in the South. By the 1890s, laws provided for the "Negro's place" in neighborhoods, parks, schools, hotels, hospitals, restaurants, streetcars, theaters, and hospitals. In 1896 the Supreme Court said that such "separate but equal" segregation was constitutional. But African Americans knew that separate was never equal for them. When laws didn't keep African Americans in their "place," vigilantes did. Every year hundreds of African Americans who "stepped out of line" in some way were lynched. In 1909 the NAACP (National Association for the Advancement of Colored People) became the first African American organization with the ability to fight for justice in American courts, but its power was very limited.

During World War II there was a mass migration of African Americans from the farms and towns of the South to the cities of the North and West. Even though there was an acute worker shortage, African Americans initially were excluded from skilled jobs in the defense industry. African American labor leaders threatened to march on Washington, and President Roosevelt issued an executive order with the goal of "eliminating racial, ethnic, and religious discrimination in defense industries and in government." By 1945 more than 8 percent of all defense workers were African American. The war resulted in more industrial and occupational diversification for African Americans than had occurred in the 75 preceding years (McWilliams 1964).

Pulled by the employment opportunities in New York, Detroit, Los Angeles, San Francisco, and other urban areas, more than half a million African Americans left the South. At the outset of World War II, 75 percent of them lived in the South, and by 1970 only 50 percent were there. Over 80 percent of the ones who left went to urban areas, mainly to inner cities. This movement triggered violent backlashes, sometimes exploding into ethnic riots. When the war ended, author Maya Angelou wondered, "Can we make it through the peace?" But there would be no turning back to the old ethnic order (Takaki 1993).

The Euro–American Rationalizations

How did Euro-Americans make slavery, segregation, and discrimination compatible with the culture's basic belief that all persons are created equal? The most bigoted Euro-Americans rationalized their ethnic prejudice—and a history of slavery—by denying the humanness of African Americans, viewing them as subhuman and therefore not "persons who are created equal." The less bigoted rationalized prejudice by supporting the "separate but equal" doctrine that provided the basis for segregation through the first half of the twentieth century, ignoring the fact that *separate* for African Americans was far from *equal*. At a more personal, emotional level, many Euro-Americans simply ignored the issue, as if African Americans did not exist (Stewart 1972).

Pettigrew and Martin (1987) determined that Euro-Americans were generally against ethnic prejudice. The problem lies with the great majority who simply go along with the old myths and stereotypes. The specific proportions:

15 percent—extremely prejudiced toward African Americans
60 percent—conforming bigots, reflecting the ethnic ideology of the larger society
25 percent—against ethnic prejudice in ideology and behavior

Pettigrew and Martin concluded that persons in the extreme group were motivated largely by authoritarian personality needs. They found that persons in the anti-prejudice category consistently support rights for African Americans. More recent studies also indicate that most Euro-American adults increasingly reject ethnic injustice in principle but remain reluctant to accept and act on measures necessary to eliminate the injustice (Ponterotto 1993). African American leaders often refer to this as the majority's weak will to implement real change.

Robert Terry (1990) pointed out two ways that many Euro-Americans rationalize their ethnic prejudice.

- "We're all just people. I'm just a human being first and foremost." The hidden meaning is, "I don't have to take responsibility for what the dominant majority has done and is doing if I ignore my ethnicity and affirm my humanity."

- "I never even notice anyone's color or ethnicity. I believe we should be color-blind. I don't even think of you as Black," implying that if people mention someone's color, they're being racist.

The fact is that Euro-Americans have traditionally been privileged in this culture. And American culture is color conscious. Most people tend to sort others by color, to the advantage of some and detriment of others. African Americans don't have the luxury of ignoring color consciousness. Euro-Americans can choose to ignore what their ingroup has done and how they all continue to benefit from it, but that does nothing toward changing the facts.

When Euro-Americans feel the need to tell African Americans that they don't think about their color, they bring color into the picture. If color isn't important, why comment on it? Let's say Jane Doe makes such a comment to an African American co-worker. If Jane really means, "You're so white in color or in the way you act that I forget about your color," then she's not being color-blind but is absorbing blackness into whiteness. If she means, "I don't discriminate on the basis of color," then she's still not being color-blind but is trying to find a way to express her concern for racial justice.

The bottom line: Valuing diversity means acknowledging and appreciating *all* the differences, including skin color, and moving beyond using physical features as the measure of a person's worth.

The Movement Toward True Equality

Actual desegregation did not begin until the African American community began waging an open battle against oppression, now known as the Civil Rights movement. This nonviolent movement led directly to the civil rights laws of the 1960s, and the battle against oppression is still being waged today.

The Civil Rights Movement

The simple action that ignited and united an entire community, and beyond, occurred in 1955 in Montgomery, Alabama. Rosa Parks boarded a city bus and later refused to give up her seat to a "white man," as city law required and as the bus driver demanded. Such resistance was not new, but the nation's response to it was.

Her arrest led to an explosive protest and boycott of the bus system, led by Martin Luther King, Jr. One year later the court ordered the desegregation of the bus system. African Americans saw that they could transform their situation, and they felt a new sense of confidence.

In 1960 African American students declared a sit-in at a Woolworth's lunch counter, and in 1961 African American and Euro-American "freedom riders" rode together in buses throughout the South to protest segregation. Many were yanked from the buses and brutally beaten by mobs, sometimes before television cameras. In 1963 the conscience of the nation was galvanized by the famous March on Washington. Hundreds of thousands of marchers from all ethnic groups gathered in front of the Lincoln Memorial. As millions watched the event on television, Martin Luther King, Jr., gave his famous "I have a dream" speech.

Vignette: The Legacy of Slavery and Segregation

When we examine the institution of slavery and its power to diminish its victims, we can understand what a powerful impact it had on all Americans. What most people don't realize is the impact that slavery and, later, legal segregation still have on today's culture and workplace. In a 1994 television interview Marie Davis, an officer of the NAACP, said:

There's a perception among white Americans that time has erased slavery's effect. Many people think this was thousands of years ago, but it wasn't really that long ago. My grandfather was born into slavery and freed at the end of the Civil War, when he was still a toddler.

Slavery and the prejudice around it caused most Americans to accept the *stereotype that African Americans are inferior, almost another species. The prejudice that is the legacy of slavery affects virtually all of us today.

Recently my granddaughter came to me, crying because she is black. I never dreamed my granddaughter would be crying like that. Then I cried, too, because I knew what she was going through. I remembered the many times I had cried as a child—cried because I was so hurt.

Status Today

How are African Americans being treated since passage of the 1964 Civil Rights Act and affirmative action orders? As Table 7.1 shows, it depends on whom you ask. Euro-Americans generally see a rosier picture than African Americans.

Table 7.1: Gaps in African American and Euro-American Views

	African American %	*Euro- American %*	*GAP*
Only a few African Americans dislike Euro-Americans	54	52	+2
African-American/Euro-American relations are very good or somewhat good	59	69	–10
Only a few Euro-Americans dislike African Americans	51	62	–11
Civil rights have greatly improved in our lifetime	25	48	–23
The achievement gap is *not* due to discrimination	53	81	–28
Satisfied with treatment of African Americans	40	68	–28
New civil rights laws are *not* needed	41	77	–36
Euro-Americans have equal job opportunities	17	55	–38

Source: Saad, Gallup Poll, 2003.

A recent Harvard study found that 31 percent of African Americans say they have been denied a job because of their ethnicity (Lewis 2004). Another study of discrimination experienced by senior-level executives found more African Americans than any group reporting discrimination. Nearly 60 percent reported a double standard in the delegation of assignments, and 55 percent had received harsh or unfair treatment by Euro-Americans (Korn/Ferry 1998). Another study found that when pairs of workers from different ethnic groups applied for the same job, in 13 percent of cases, the Euro-American was offered the job and the equally qualified African American partner was not, while the reverse situation virtually never occurred (Urban Institute 1998).

Some studies verify that discrimination is alive and well. For example, one study tested employers' reactions to 5000 resumes that were doctored to make the applicants appear to be either African American or Euro-American. Job applicants with names like Emily and Neil were 50 percent more likely to get called for an interview that those with names like Lakisha and Tyrone. Having excellent credentials boosted chances for Euro-American resumes far more than it helped African American ones (Progress 2003).

What's in a Name? African American

Here are the typical terms for African Americans, in historical order:

Negro→Colored→AfroAmerican→Black→African American.

Negro was used from the time of slavery. Colored became the more "polite" term during the first half of the 20th century. AfroAmerican was used early in the Civil Rights era, followed by the "Black is Beautiful" era. By the 1990s most African Americans still preferred Black (39 percent) or Black American (10 percent), but African American (34 percent) was growing in favor and is probably predominant today. Those preferring Black tend to be the most conservative, those preferring African American the most liberal, with those preferring Black American somewhere in between (Larkey 1991)

CURRENT PROFILE

We'll discuss the relative proportions of African Americans in the population, where they live, the socioeconomic progress they are making, their career progress, educational progress, and political views of their status and progress.

Who They Are and Where They Live

The proportion of African Americans in the population, currently 12 percent, has been holding fairly steady at 10 to 12 percent for decades. Their growth rate is 15 percent, compared to the total growth rate of 13 percent and the Euro-American rate of 6 percent.

Over half the African Americans, 55 percent, live in the South. We know from history that most of their ancestors came to work on the plantations of the South. During World War II, when defense factories opened jobs to them, many migrated to industrial centers outside the South. Recently, many industries have moved their facilities to the Sun Belt, and many African Americans have also returned to the South. Nearly 20 percent make their home in the Midwest and nearly 20 percent in the Northeast, mainly in the largest cities. Relatively few, less than 10 percent, live in the West.

Two-thirds of Washington D.C. residents are African American. States where they comprise more than 25 percent of the population are Louisiana, South Carolina, Mississippi, Georgia, Maryland, and Alabama.

Three Tiers of Progress: Middle–Class, Under–Class, Struggling Between

Have African Americans made great progress since the Civil Rights laws of the 1960s were passed? Yes, to some extent. Actually, there has been a three-pronged progression. Nearly one-third of African Americans have made significant progress and live a middle class life. Nearly one-third have dropped into dire underclass poverty, with the other third somewhere in between. We'll look at African American progress in education, family income, occupations, and business ownership.

Changes Since The 1960s

Back in the 1960s, President Johnson appointed the Kerner Commission to probe the causes of rioting in the inner cities. The ensuing report said, "Our nation is moving toward two societies, one black, one white—separate and unequal." Thirty years later, a followup report by the Milton Eisenhower Institute (Fletcher 1998) noted that:

- The African American middle class has grown, with many living in the suburbs
- African American business has expanded.
- The number of African Americans elected to political office has increased.
- But some problems have become more deeply rooted, exemplified by the growing inner-city underclass

A central feature of African American progress since the 1960s is the simultaneous growth of the middle class and an underclass. Civil rights measures led to distinct improvement and upward mobility for many African Americans. The middle class began growing dramatically. They moved up and to the suburbs, earning more, sending their children to college, and living better

Poverty Patterns

The really poor tended to get poorer. This underclass began sinking further into intergenerational poverty, with increasing unemployment rates for young men and a dramatic rise in female-headed families. In 1990:
27 percent of African Americans lived in the suburbs
57 percent lived in central cities
Perhaps half of those in central cities live in poverty. These are some poverty patterns of 1990.
27 percent of all African American families lived in poverty
11 percent of married couples
45 percent of female-headed (single mother) families
In 1980 the official poverty rate for all African American families was just under 26 percent, almost the same as in the 1990s, but it was 50 percent for small children, 40 percent for all children and 32 percent for the elderly, a pattern that still continues.

In 2001 the poverty rate was at an all-time low of 21 percent, but still twice as high as the overall U.S. poverty rate of 12 percent (U.S. Census).

Income Gaps

In 2000 median income patterns reflected the continued poverty of African American women:

- $27,910 for African American households
- $20,600 for African American men
- $14,800 for African American women
- Overall income was 63 percent of Euro-American family income, a 37 percent gap
- African American men earn 74 percent of Euro-American male earnings, a 26 percent gap
- Average net worth for Euro-American families is 5 times that of African American

The pay gap for African Americans continues at all levels in all occupations. In 2002 African American male executives and managers earned 23 percent less than Euro-American peers. Analysts say that only about one-fourth of this pay gap is based on such factors as experience and education. The pay gap exists in every occupational category—from police officers to accountants. Those in security-services jobs got 16 percent less, and professionals make 19 percent less. The pay gap for those with advanced degrees actually increased, from 16 percent in 1992 to 25 percent in 2001 (Progress 2003).

The Growing Middle Class

Nearly one-third of African Americans are considered middle class. The emergence of a distinct African American middle class was reported in *Time* magazine in 1989. About one-third of all African American households had incomes of $35,000 or more (compared with 70 percent of all Euro-American households) in 1988. African American families living in the suburbs doubled from 13 percent in 1967 to 27 percent in 1990. Some of these people had parents and grandparents who achieved some success as entrepreneurs and professionals serving the African American community. Others somehow broke out of the poverty cycle to go through doors of opportunity opened by civil rights programs.

Closely related to socioeconomic status is home ownership. African American families who get "out of the projects" and foster "pride of ownership" in their children tend to escape the vicious cycle of drugs and crime that plague the ghetto. By 2004, 49 percent of African American families owned their homes, compared with 71 percent of Euro-Americans. The home ownership gap of 30 percent has remained fairly stable since 1990. Relative value has also remained stable. In 2000 African American median home value was $81,000, about 65 percent of Euro-American home value of $123,000 (U.S. Census).

Since the 1970s more and more industries have left the cities for the suburbs, and so did more and more Euro-American families, followed by some of the new middle-class African American families. This combination of societal forces has been a major factor in the expansion of the underclass neighborhoods in the central cities. The suburban rings around cities are symbols not only of post-industrialism but also of ethnic and class exclusiveness in a traditionally segmented society. "White flight" refers to the Euro-American tendency to get away from the problems of urban living, including desegregation and other diversity issues, by moving to the exclusive "white" suburbs. (Billlingsley 1992).

By 2000 over 25 percent of African American workers were in management or professional occupations and 27 percent were in sales and office positions, which represents a huge shift out of less desirable occupations. These successful middle-class families tend to have a reverence for learning second only to their reverence for the spiritual, according to African American author Andrew Billingsley (1992). Most of them came from the working class of the previous generation, so are first-generation middle class with relatively little accumulated wealth. As Billingsley says, the African American middle class is "a major achievement sustained by education, two earners, extended families, religion, and service to others." *New York Times* reporter Isabel Wilkerson (1990) said, "Two main things tend to distinguish black middle-class people from middle-class whites. One is the likelihood that many more of their relatives will come to them for help. The other is that they tend to lack the resources of people who started life in the middle class."

A Growing Underclass

Back in the inner city, at the other end of the scale, are increasing numbers of African Americans who are still trapped in poverty. In fact, 23 percent of these households had incomes below the poverty line, second only to American Indians. By comparison only 8 percent of Euro-American households lived in poverty and 10 percent of all American households (U.S. Census 2000).

The followup on the Kerner Commission report (Fletcher 1998, Mauer 2003) revealed the following: In assets, the top-ranking 1 percent of Americans have more wealth than the bottom 90 percent put together.

During an average week in the inner city, most adults do not work.

About 40 percent of minority children attend an urban school where more than half the students are poor and don't reach minimal academic achievement levels.

The United States has the largest proportion of prisoners of any nation. One-third of African American men ages 20-40, who do not have a high school education, are behind bars. Even more are on parole or on probation. In fact, far more are in prison than are in college, and it costs much more to keep them there than it would to pay for a private university education. Normally the prison experience does *not* lead to improvement.

The gap between the number of African Americans versus Euro-Americans who die in infancy has been rising steadily for the last 30 years. In 2000, it was at its widest point since 1900, with twice as many African American infants dying (Coy 2000).

Major Causes

The report gave the major causes of the underclass problem as:

- The 1980s political policies of supply-side, trickle-down economics, which expanded the gap between rich and poor
- Increasing hostility toward affirmative action
- The failure of some social programs, such as enterprise zones and the Job Training Partnership Act.

For African American women, the problem of welfare dependency was tied to the increase in single-mother families and gender inequality in the labor market. Nearly all women were crowded into female-dominated occupations, such as low-wage clerical and sales jobs, making it difficult or impossible for mothers to eke out living expenses *and* child care costs from their meager salaries.

Intensifying the middle-class/underclass disparity, the movement of plants and offices to the suburbs since the 1960s has isolated African American workers from many places of employment. African Americans have also been suffering from the effects of the "de-industrialization of America," with plants relocating to low-wage countries, such as Mexico and China. The loss of blue-collar jobs hit African American men especially hard, because they were concentrated in the smokestack industries, such as automobile, rubber, and steel.

Media Focus and Racial Profiling

The news media and politicians are doing an impressive job of highlighting the problems of the African American underclass, such as male drug pushers and welfare mothers. The public is quite aware of these issues. However, to focus so heavily on the problems tends to obscure the incredible successes of fully one-third of African Americans who have overcome the most onerous and entrenched barriers in American society to secure a place in the middle class. A focus on the African American strengths behind this major achievement would be productive.

Racial profiling, where the legal system treats African Americans differently, is also a contributor to the underclass phenomenon. Studies indicate that every facet of the system discriminates against African Americans, from who gets stopped by the police to who gets charged and convicted of crimes, to the types of sentences they get. For example, in 1998, of the 3500 people in 38 states who sat on death row, 48 percent were African American, 48 percent were Euro-American, and 2 percent were "other." And 85 percent of those on death row had killed a Euro-American, reflecting this pattern:

- 1 in 5 who kill a Euro-American are tried under the death penalty
- 1 in 19 who kill an African American are tried under the death penalty

The Best Remedies

What has worked best to remedy the underclass problem, according to the report, are the following initiatives:

- Head Start
- certain after-school programs

- targeted job training
- community-sensitive police strategies

Other reports add to that list the following remedies (Progress 2003):

- better education with smaller classes and better resources
- affirmative action in college admissions and in company hiring and promotion practices
- better anti-bias enforcement by the EEOC and Labor Department

Education for Careers

Educational progress has been good and is a key to breaking out of the poverty cycle. Recent educational statistics for people born in the United States who are 25 or older are shown in Table 7.2.

TABLE 7.2: Educational Achievement

Education	African American	Euro-American
High School	80%	90%
Some college	44	56
Bachelors degree	25	38

Source: U.S. Census, 2004.

The proportion of African Americans who have completed high school rose from 51 percent in 1980 to 80 percent in 2003. High school dropout rate went down, from 16 percent to 14 percent, and college enrollment increased by one and one-half times. Educational attainment is about the same for males and females.

Intellectual Achievement Depends on Income

School achievement depends heavily on family economic status, according to a breakthrough study. Table 7.3 shows the correlation between family income and student performance on SAT tests. The authors (AAUW 1992) conclude that

- Socioeconomic status—not ethnicity or gender—is the best predictor of both grades and test scores.
- Public schools must do more to provide educational opportunity for children of low socioeconomic status, who do less well in school regardless of ethnicity or gender.

TABLE 7.3: Family Income Affects School Performance

Average Family Income	Average SAT score
$22,000	750-800
$18,000	550-599
$14,000	350-399
$8,000	200-249

Source: American Association of University Women, 1992 Report.
Selected pairs are used, but missing pairs are consistent with these results.

It would appear that once an African American family is able to break the cycle of poverty and get good jobs, the cycle tends to stay broken for that family. The children do well in school and are therefore likely to get good jobs and earn good incomes when they grow up, which in turn increases the likelihood that their children will do well in school.

Still Segregated

Studies indicate that racially integrated classrooms tend to have positive effects for minorities. Yet in 1990 most African American students were still in classrooms with few, if any, Euro-Americans. And by the late 1990s judges had ended desegregation orders in many school districts. For those who have the advantage of integrated schools, classroom studies of teacher-student relationships have indicated that minority students receive biased treatment. For example, Euro-American teachers tend to give more praise and encouragement to Euro-American students and to accept and acknowledge their contributions to class discussions. Such subtle exclusion can do long-term damage to children's confidence, class performance, and educational aspirations. Although much attention has been paid to problems in the educational system that impact African Americans, the problems have not yet been solved.

A promising approach might be to study success factors. What if researchers were to focus on African Americans who have broken out of the poverty cycle and find patterns of factors that worked well for them? For example, are there external factors in family, school, or community that affected these members' success patterns? What kinds of internal beliefs and attitudes, thinking and feeling, decisions and choices, are common among the successful? How did successful African Americans use their imagination, desire, and expectations to avoid underclass pitfalls and move up to a better life? Community leaders can use success patterns to help those who are still stuck.

African Americans are increasingly moving into better-paying occupations, but there is still a significant pay gap, as well as glass ceiling obstacles. The changes in career opportunities and social status have been somewhat different for women than for men.

Employment Rates and Pay Gaps

About the same proportion of the African American and Euro-American populations hold jobs, as Table 7.4 shows, but African Americans on average make 25 percent less than Euro-American men.

TABLE 7.4: Employment Rates, 2000

	All	*Male*	*Female*
African American	60%	72%	66%
Euro-American	67%	77%	60%

African American men's average income was 80 percent of Euro-American men's, and the women's was only 62 percent (U.S. Census Bureau 2002). Median family income for African Americans as compared to Euro-Americans rose during the late 1960s and early 1970s, decreased during the 1980s, but is rising again, as shown in Table 7.5.

TABLE 7.5: Median Family Income Ratios, 1960–1997

Median Family Income	*1960*	*1970*	*1980*	*1990*	*2000*
Ratio: African American to Euro-American	55%	65%	58%	56%	64%

Source: U.S. Bureau of the census, 2002.

Movement into Better Paying Occupations

Since 1960 an increasing proportion of African Americans have moved into the higher-status, better-paying occupations of manager, professional, technical, sales, and administrative support. Table 7.6 shows the percentage of African Americans in each type of occupation and compares it with the Euro-American distribution. Part of this trend reflects changes in the economy as a whole, away from manufacturing and toward service and information. The decline in proportion of African Americans in service occupations generally reflects a shift out of cleaning and janitorial work into higher-status white-collar and blue-collar jobs. Still, African Americans tend to be at the lowest-paid levels of each job category. Since the census combines sales and other occupations, Table 7.8 does not show that only 3 to 4 percent of non-retail salespersons are African American. "African Americans may confront stereotypes that make it difficult for them to sell to customers and build rapport with colleagues . . . This is not a colorless society," according to Allison Lucas (1996).

TABLE 7.6: Occupations: African American, Euro-American, 1960–2000

Occupation	1960		1970		1980		1990		2000	
	Af	Euro	Af	Euro	Af	Euro	Af	Euro	Af	Euro
Manager, Professional	7.4%	23.8%	14.6%	27.2%	17.9%	28.5%	17.3%	27.2%	17.8%	29.7%
Technical, Sales, Admin. Support	8.5	22.7	15.3	24.7	21.3	27.4	28.0	31.3	n/c	
Service	31.7	9.9	27.0	10.7	23.1	12.1	21.9	12.1		
Farming, Forestry	1.0	7.4	3.9	4.0	1.8	2.9	1.6	3.1		
Precision production, Craft, Repairs	7.0	13.8	8.2	13.5	9.6	13.3	8.3	12.0		
Operators, Fabricators, Laborers	20.4	17.9	23.7	17.0	19.4	13.5	21.5	14.4		

Source: U.S. Census Bureau, Statistical Abstract of the United States, 1981, 1991, 2002. n/c = not comparable.

Changes in Women's Status

African American women have moved from being primarily agricultural or domestic workers to being office workers. AA opened the doors of America's offices to African American women, and huge numbers of them traded their maid's aprons for pink collars (Carr-Ruffino 1992). However, some researchers say the myth of the double-minority AA advantage is offset by the reality of double discrimination by gender and ethnicity, and sometimes by class. For example, African American women still tend to be:

- placed into training programs for traditionally female occupations
- discouraged from attempting innovative careers
- dependent upon the public sector for employment
- kept out of better private-sector jobs by rigid ethnic barriers

While Euro-American marriage rates have changed very little, rates for African Americans have dramatically dropped. Historically, 90 percent of African American women were married by the age of 44. That rate dropped to 55 percent by 1990. Moreover, the remarriage rate six years after a divorce was only 40 percent for African American women, compared to 60 percent for Euro-American women. African American women are getting married later. For example, the proportion of women in their late twenties who had never married rose from 11 percent in 1970 to 31 percent in 1990.

Changes in Men's Status

In the 1970s a significant proportion of African American men began moving out of blue-collar and service jobs into better paying jobs (Feagin 1991). But the unemployment rate for young African

American men, those from ages 20 to 24 has remained high, and the unemployment rate for African American men of all ages tends to be about twice that for Euro-American men, and three times as high for those with college degrees.

Glass Ceiling Obstacles

African American reaction to the corporate glass ceiling was reported in 1992 (WSJ), when so many managers and professionals were leaving that it signaled a trend. It was confirmed by a study in 2003 (Daniels 2004). The reasons they give include:

- hitting the Glass Ceiling, lack of opportunity, and upward mobility
- feeling pressured to undermine or drop their African American identity
- having to prove themselves, over and over again, due to being African American
- dealing with the stigma of co-workers assuming they are an affirmative action hire
- coping with ethnic stereotypes

While learning the language and customs of corporate America may seem like a necessary part of playing the game for Euro-American men and women, for African Americans it can smack of selling out to get ahead. Many report feeling pressured to become "almost white" in order to be accepted, or at best to become "neutral" or to be viewed as an exception to the typical African American type (Bell 1990). They feel the need to change their speech, their dress, their hair in order to fit into the corporate culture. If they go along, they begin to feel some degree of isolation from the African-American community. They don't really belong anywhere and feel "marginal" to all groups (WSJ 1992; Executive Female, 1992).

More recent studies (Daniels 2004) indicate that the current generation of African American executives are less patient than their parents were. Turnover rates in 2003 were 40 percent higher for African American executives than their Euro-American peers. African American men in the 25 to 35 age group with some graduate school experience are starting their own businesses more frequently than any group in the country on a per capita basis. Overall, African Americans are 50 percent more likely than Euro-Americans to start a business.

Breakthroughs to the Top

African American men have been making it to the top position, CEO, of Fortune 500 companies since 1995 as follows:

- 1999 Fannie Mae, Franklin Raines, till 2004
- 2001 American Express, Kenneth Chenault
- 2001 CNBC, Pamela Thomas-Graham
- 2002 Time Warner, Richard Parsons, till 2008
- 2002 Merrill Lynch, Stanley O'Neal, until 2007
- 2003 Young & Rubicam Brands, Ann M. Fudge
- 2004 Darden Restaurants, Clarence Otis (Olive Garden, Red Lobster, etc.)
- 2005 Sears Holding, Aylwin Lewis, till 2008
- 2006 Aetna, Ronald Williams

Networking organizations, such as Executive Leadership Conference, have undoubtedly played a role. Two of these CEOs are members and the other two are supporters. In fact, ELC comprises 300 of the most senior African-American corporate executives in Fortune 500 companies. Members have worked in corporate America an average of 23 years directing more than 1,500 employees. ELC's mission is to expand the pipeline of African-Americans at all leadership levels of corporate America. ELC is committed to offering executives access to leadership networks and career coaching that addresses personal comfort-level issues related to diversity (Stevens 2003).

African American women now hold about 1.5 percent of corporate officer positions in America's 500 largest companies (Catalyst 2002).

Boards of Directors

The 2004 Census of African Americans on Corporate Boards (Executive 2005) examines African American representation on boards of directors of Fortune 500 companies. Findings for 2004 (ELC 2005):

- 8% of the 5,572 board seats (or 449 seats) were held by African Americans.
- Of these "African American seats," 77% were held by men and 23% by women
- 67% of the Fortune 500 had one or more African Americans on the board
- 33% had none.
- Tobacco industry had the most, an average of 17% on each board
- Beverage industry, 14%
- 4 industries had no African American board members: wholesaler/diversified, pipeline, transportation and logistics, toys and sporting goods

Business Ownership

Within the African American community is a large and growing entrepreneurial class. Because private business ownership was prohibited during slavery, and greatly limited during legal segregation, it's less well developed in the African American community than in the nation as a whole, but it's growing. For example, African-American-owned businesses increased significantly in the five years from 1997 to 2002 (Census Bureau 2003). As shown in Table 7.7, the number of companies increased 51 percent and earnings increased 54 percent. The Census Bureau found that 38 percent of African-American-owned companies were involved in the industries of healthcare, retail trade, or other service sectors.

TABLE 7.7: African-American-Owned Businesses, 2002

Number of businesses	1.2 million
Total sales revenue	$92.7 billion
Firms with no paid workers	1.1 million
Firms with paid workers	100,000
Earning, firms w/no paid workers	$23 billion
Earning, firms w/paid workers	$70 billion

Source: U.S. Census.

Looking deeper into the Top 100 African American Industrial & Service Companies and the Top 100 Auto Dealers, they racked up nearly $23 billion in 2004 sales revenues (Black Enterprise 2005)

- The Top 100 Industrial & Service Companies had sales of over $14 billion, with nearly 65,000 employees.
- Technology was the largest industry, nearly 20 percent of total revenues
- Manufacturing 15 percent, food and beverage 14 percent, media 13 percent.
- Top 100 Auto Dealers had sales of nearly $9 billion with nearly 12,000 employees
- The top 25 banks had assets of over $5 billion, with over 2,000 employees
- States with the most Top 100 businesses: Michigan 25, Texas 20, Georgia 17, California 16

Political Views of African American Status

It is clear that many African Americans are achieving success in the workplace and marketplace. On the other hand, why are so many still caught in underclass poverty? Opinions vary widely about the causes and solutions for this continuing problem.

Conservatives tend to believe that more accurate measures of jobs and income would indicate that the problem isn't very serious. To the extent that problems exist, they reflect the personal inadequacies of African American youths, compounded by the adverse effects of government antipoverty policies, including welfare and minimum wage laws. Any inequity that exists is rooted in African American laziness and disregard for law and order. The conservative prescription is for government to stay out of it because attempts to help amount to handouts, which make the poor dependent on government and are a burden on taxpayers. Poor African Americans who want to will pull themselves up by their bootstraps, and those who don't can suffer the consequences.

Liberals emphasize external causes of the problem, such as declining employment opportunities due to a weakening of economic growth and labor market imbalances. They cite the movement of jobs away from the inner cities to suburbs, Sun Belt states, and low-wage countries. The movement of middle-class African Americans to the suburbs intensifies inner city problems. It reduces the youths' access to role models and to middle-class cultural values. Liberals say that discrimination also continues to be a barrier, and as a result some African Americans naturally become discouraged and demoralized. The problems are too great for African Americans to solve on their own, and it's up to government to help bring an end to inequity.

Black nationalists tend to see the problem as pervasive prejudice. Their concern is for recognition as free human beings. They do not call for integration but rather for true equality that values diversity.

Political differences are said to create difference in perceptions about the status and progress of African Americans (Issues 1999). When asked if they believe job differences, income differences and housing differences between African Americans and Euro-Americans are due to discrimination:

- 70 to 80 percent of African Americans agree
- 30 percent of Euro-Americans agree

When asked if there had been no real improvement in the position of African Americans in the United States:

- 73 percent African Americans agree
- 44 percent Euro-Americans agree

About 73 percent of African Americans agreed with the statement, "It makes me mad that affirmative action policies are *needed* in this country because that means that I'm not judged on my merits alone."

THE AFRICAN AMERICAN COMMUNITY: KEY VALUES

When we compare African American culture with other major world cultures, using the 11 major types of cultural difference, we see that the African American culture is generally perceived as follows:

1. Basic worldview: I'm controlled (because of past slavery, but changing)
2. Relationship priorities: us-first
3. Social fabric: tight ties (but family breakup due to slavery, then welfare rules)
4. Moderately feminine
5. Equality/Status: democratic
6. Risk Orientation: play-it-safe (but changing)
7. Decision Orientation: Short term re business planning, long-term re nature

8. Time Orientation: focus on present

9. Space: moderate, arm's length

10. Communication: direct

11. Economic: shifted from agricultural in past few decades

This culture is in a great state of flux because of winning more and more freedom and opportunity since the 1950s.

The African American culture is unique among American subcultures in that it evolved alongside the Euro-American culture. African Americans generally have been here as long as Euro-Americans. Because of their history they've been subjected more rigidly to Euro-Americans ways than have the other subcultures. The others consist primarily of more recent immigrants whose homeland cultural ways are still quite strong. Rather than trying to compare the African American culture by the yardstick of the 11 major cultural differences, let's look directly at what the scholars have learned about this community.

Seven typical core values affect how African Americans view themselves, the world, and others, based on work of several African American researchers, including Andrew Billingsley, M.L. Hecht, Thomas Kochman, J.L. White, and James M. Jones, Professor of Social Psychology at University of Delaware. Some values are rooted in African tribal values. Others are rooted in the need to bond together and to find inner strength and savvy in order to survive the circumstances of slavery and segregation. Here are seven core values typical in most African American communities:

1. *Sharing*, interrelating, interdependence, collectivism, spirituality

2. *Expressing personal style*, individuality, improvisation, and creative response with a special focus on rhythms and patterns—but in a sharing mode

3. *Being real and genuine*, tellin' it like it is; learning the truth from direct experience; being real; seeing the good as well as the bad

4. *Being assertive*, speaking up, standing up

5. *Expressing feelings* openly, very verbal

6. *Bouncing back*, maintaining vitality and resilience, and a positive attitude

7. *Not trusting* the mainstream establishment

Value #1: Sharing and Interrelating

Interconnectedness, interrelatedness, sharing, and interdependence are seen as central and unifying values in the African American community. This is a prominent theme in African American life and language with respect to

- interactive dynamics between speaker and listener
- the power of words to control
- ways of thinking
- timing
- communication skill.

Sharing knowledge and endorsing the group are related to collectivism, which means putting family and community relationships above one's own aspirations. It's acted out in the sharing of self and material possessions within the family. It's also expressed in the call-response pattern found in meetings of church members ("Amen! Praise God!") and other groups ("Right on, Brother!"). Interconnectedness is a vital part of spirituality (Halberstadt 1985; Hammer 1987; Hecht 1984).

Value #2: Expressing Personal Style and Uniqueness

Personal style is important in the way African Americans talk, walk, dress, work—in every aspect of life. They are especially aware of rhythm and patterns and tend to recognize patterns better than people from other cultures. In fact, they're likely to do better on tests where there are clear patterns.

Improvisation and creative responses to the world and to the moment are typical ways they express their individual take on things. This uniqueness in personal style and expression celebrates the individual. But the response of family, friends, and community is crucial to the expression. It's meaningless unless done in sync with others. For example, they may develop their own style of dancing, singing, or strutting by using both some known forms and their own improvisations. But all this is done with others. Jazz improvisation began with this custom. Musicians play a tune together, but one by one the individual musicians take the spotlight and improvise on the theme in their own way.

In contrast, American individualism refers to a more autonomous expression through personal achievement and self-reliance. It does not rely on the group in the immediate way that African American "personal style" expression does (Rose 1983; Kochman 1981; Donohue 1985).

Value #3: Being Real and Genuine

At church and at home, African Americans are taught to face up to their circumstances, admit who they really are, and deal with life as it is. Being real and genuine is rooted in a core belief about life: The natural facts, eternal truths, wisdom of the ages, and basic precepts of survival emerge from the experiences of life. Some related common teachings, discussed in L. F. Rose's work, are:

- You can't escape nothing. You got to pay your dues. If you've been through tragedy, it must be you needed it (for personal growth).
- You cannot lie to life.
- You might as well be who you really are, and tell it like it is.
- You learn the truth through direct experience.

Older people, because of their accumulated experiences, are the reservoirs of wisdom. Realness and genuineness are tied to the values of personal style, assertiveness, and open emotional expression. It means African Americans tend to confront problems they care about in a direct, loud, and passionate way. This is respected when it conveys sincerity and conviction (Rose 1983; Kochman 1981).

Value #4: Being Assertive

African Americans value standing up for personal rights and trying to achieve them without harming others. Assertiveness is a key symbol of standing up for yourself in the face of oppression and of taking charge of your own life. Coping with prejudice and discrimination often results in an assertive, determined, confrontational style.

Assertiveness is often expressed in a style that is intense, outspoken, challenging, and forward. It may be done with a loud strong voice, angry verbal arguments, threats, insults, a certain way of dressing, or the use of slang. It can range from calm debates to persuasion to intense expressions of anger.

Actions based on this value often cause misunderstandings outside the community. Others often misinterpret mere assertiveness as a form of violence, blaming, or troublemaking, linking it to those stereotypes. This assertiveness value is related to genuineness and tellin' it like it is, but others may see it as being over-aggressive, coming on too strong, being too argumentative, or stirring up trouble. The most disturbing interpretation is, "Uh-oh, he's about to get violent" (Johnson 2004, Kochman 1981).

Value #5: Expressing Feelings

African American style is more self-conspicuous, expressive, expansive, colorful, intense, assertive, aggressive, and more focused on the individual than the style of most other cultures. Studies indicate that African American use more:

- expressive communication patterns
- direct questions
- public debate and argument
- active nonverbal expression
- emotional intensity
- self-presentation through boasting and bragging

They tend to be quite verbal, and most will perform better with oral than written responses.

Debates, Arguments, Confrontations

African Americans tend to negotiate more loudly and intensely than others. When African Americans engage in public debate of any kind, their style is often high-key, that is, animated, interpersonal, and confrontational with the effect of expressing and generating emotion. African Americans see their style as natural and sincere expressions of their thoughts and feelings. Since they're accustomed to such expression in their communities, they accept others' passionate style in the spirit in which it's intended: honest engagement, participation, and expression that helps people know each other and ultimately contributes to unity. In general, African American culture allows members much greater freedom to assert and express themselves than do most other cultures (Kochman 1981).

For example the Euro-American culture has standards of quiet "good taste and decorum" as the chief restraining factors—at least in middle-class and upper-class environments. Euro-American style therefore tends to be more low-key; that is, relatively dispassionate, impersonal, non-challenging, and less likely to express or generate as much emotion. Asian Americans are even more averse to open confrontations. Latino Americans are likely to see confrontation as a violation of the need to be "sympatico," which is a style that smooths over differences in order to get along smoothly.

People from these other cultures often interpret African American expressions of anger and their verbal aggressiveness as more threatening and provocative than it's intended. The type of angry verbal disputes, even involving insults and threats, that often occur among African Americans without necessarily leading to violence, would in fact almost always be precursors to violence within the Euro-American, Asian, and Latino cultures.

Boasting and Bragging

Most African Americans distinguish between boasting and bragging. Boasting is typically done with some sense of humor; it's usually exaggerated; and it's not intended to be taken seriously. It's done as a form of play and entertainment used to gain recognition within a group. Bragging is a serious form of self-aggrandizement, and people are expected to back up their claims. Bragging about your ability is okay, but bragging about your possessions or social status is not.

Eye Contact Differences

Have you ever felt that you and an acquaintance were avoiding looking at each other in a conversation? Or staring each other down? Maybe it was unmatched eye contact. When African Americans speak, they tend to look at their partner more than they do while listening, while for Euro-Americans the pattern is reversed.

African American: Speak—keep looking. Listen—glance away
Euro-American: Listen—keep looking. Speak—glance away

You can see that when an African American is speaking to a Euro-American, there's too much looking going on. And when the Euro-American is speaking, there's not enough looking going on.

For African Americans, the meaning of this ritual may be: When I speak, I keep close watch to see how you're responding; when I listen, I glance away as I think about what you're saying. For Euro-Americans, the meaning may be: When I speak, I glance away to gather my thoughts; when I listen, I maintain eye contact to show you that I'm really listening.

Of course, when either party has spent a great deal of time with members of the other culture, they've probably learned to adjust their eye contact ritual. Certainly, once you become conscious of the differences, you can learn to adjust.

Value #6: Bouncing Back

Resilience and revitalization are admired and have been a key to survival. Older members are respected because they have

- been through the experiences that can only come with age.
- been "down the line," seen the comings and goings of life.
- survived the cycles of oppression, struggle, survival, backlash, and renewed struggle.
- stood the test of time and adversity, paid their dues, and transcended tragedy
- most, important, learned to "keep on keepin' on."

A lively sense of humor and spiritual beliefs support the bouncing back value.

Value #7: The Dual Culture—Not Trusting the Establishment

The burden of inequality placed upon African Americans is a major contradiction of American ideals. African Americans grow up a part of, yet apart from, American society—in it but not of it, included at some levels and excluded at others. This duality is at the heart of their identity struggle and often generates powerful feelings of frustration, anger, and indignation. It is further complicated by their bicultural value systems, worldviews, and historical legacies. They must try to set up a workable balance between African American and Euro-American values within their lives. Completely denying either one will restrict their life choices. If they focus only on individualism, competition, emotional insulation, power, dominance, and control, they may achieve success but they'll pay a huge price. If they focus only on genuineness, mutual aid, the collective good, and emotional closeness, they'll enjoy inclusion in the African American community but are unlikely to achieve economic success in the workplace. (Baldwin 1992). W.E.B. DuBois (1965, 215) described this dual cultural background as: . . . *this double consciousness, this sense of always looking at one's self through the eyes of others, of measuring one's soul by the tape of a world that looks on in amused contempt and pity. One ever feels his twoness—an American, a Negro; two souls, two thoughts, two unreconciled strivings; two warring ideals in one dark body, whose dogged strength alone keeps it from being torn asunder.*

History has taught African Americans to distrust the establishment, to keep their own counsel, and to use caution when communicating outside the community. One result was the use of "code talk" among themselves (White 1990). For example, "a bad nigger" in African American semantics has traditionally referred to a hero, someone they admire for his or her courage and guts to stand up to "white folks."

Today, the trust gap still shows up in work relationships when African Americans use protective hesitation before they speak up or take action around Euro-Americans. They take time to think about how their words or actions might reinforce negative stereotypes or how they might make themselves vulnerable to betrayal or attack. Where they have a choice, they may avoid working with Euro-Americans. Trust can be built, but it may be a relative slow and difficult process. One action perceived as betrayal can break the delicate new structure.

Vignette: Seeing Anew Through Informed Eyes

People who have studied the African American culture learn to look for accurate inter-pretations of behavior. Bill tells about his experience. "I overheard an African American having a telephone conversation the other day. He got so loud and vehement that I became very uncomfortable, even though I wasn't involved. Then I remembered what I had learned about the African American culture. I looked and listened more closely. I saw that he was smiling part of the time and his body was fairly relaxed. Then I shifted my perception, opening up the possibility that he wasn't really angry and about to explode. I began to hear a very different conversation, one in which the guy was just being real and genuine, asserting his thoughts and feelings, and tellin' it like it is."

THE AFRICAN AMERICAN COMMUNITY: TYPICAL CUSTOMS

The core values of the African American community are reflected in typical customs in three major life areas: community life, family life, and personal relationships

Customs in Community Life

The church took on a major role in advocating social change throughout the twentieth century, with ministers becoming leaders in the Civil Rights movement. The church still plays a central role in virtually every aspect of African American life, including major efforts to help the underclass break out of the shackles that keep them in poverty. Most offer an array of self-help programs.

Customs in Family Life

The sharing value is expressed in the practice of seeing relatives and close friends as an extended family, while the distrust factor results in "tough" child-rearing practices.

Extended Families

Among African Americans, the term *parents* often refers to natural parents, grandparents, and others who assume parental roles and responsibilities from time to time. Relationships with key people who are not blood relatives are considered essential to the maintenance of the family. This custom is rooted both in the African American tribal heritage and in the need to withstand the stress spawned by the slavery system and the survival struggles that are still prevalent (Mann 1981).

Child-Rearing Practices

The strict, no-nonsense discipline used by many African American parents, sometimes seen as harsh or rigid to some Euro-Americans, is actually functional and appropriate discipline by caring parents. They see it as preparation for survival in a hostile environment, one that is prejudiced and discriminatory against them (Allen 1981; Willie 1976; Young 1977).

Customs in Personal Relationships

The sharing value means that most African Americans place especially high value on trusting and helping one another. Most have one style for relating to acquaintances and a somewhat different style for relating to friends. And they may appear indifferent or uninvolved in their interactions with persons outside the community (Smith 1980; Ickes 1984).

African American Style with Acquaintances

African Americans are guided in their communication with other African American acquaintances, such as co-workers and casual friends, by the following four types of guidelines (Collier 1988).

1. *Follow role prescriptions.* African Americans generally pay more attention to this than Euro-Americans. Still, they place even more emphasis on individual roles that express each person's style than on conventional roles. This reflects their value for expressing personal uniqueness, but within group settings for the purpose of group appreciation.

2. *Be polite.* Politeness is viewed as more an individual than societal trait, and deciding your own rules for politeness is more important to African Americans than it is to other American subcultures.

3. *Watch your words.* African Americans tend to be much more cautious about what they say to people outside the community.

4. *Support "brothers and sisters."* African Americans especially value conversations within the community that are supportive, relevant, and assertive, reflecting the cultural values of sharing and being positive.

African American Style with Friends

African Americans are likely to develop closer, more intimate friendships than do Euro-Americans. They're likely to be more intimate in discussions of school, work, religion, interests, hobbies, and physical condition. On the other hand, Euro-Americans are likely to be more revealing and intimate in discussions of love, dating, sex, and feelings about these issues. African American stress on intimacy may fall into these four types of action. (Collier 1992)

1. *Acknowledge the individual.* Allow others to express themselves through assertiveness and individual style and accomplishment. Appreciate their uniqueness and their individual expressions of who they are.

2. *Develop intimacy.* The value of sharing is achieved through talking about family and other personal topics. It includes these kinds of actions:

   - giving and receiving friendly advice, leading to positive feelings
   - taking specific actions to establish trust as the most crucial element of relationships
   - expressing sensitivity, support, affirmation, honesty, and brotherhood or sisterhood.
   - accepting criticisms and requests without compromising the friendship

3. *Be supportive.* Do such things as:

   - offer solutions for a problems or advice on personal issues
   - seek mutual understanding
   - express individuality
   - affirm the other person or the culture
   - establish trust and intimacy.

4. *Appreciate the culture.* Focus on the similarities in our beliefs, attitudes, and interests. Express pride in our common roots and the cultural background itself.

Male-Female Relationships

African American culture presumes that all women have a general sexual interest in men and are sexually assertive, so they aren't considered less respectable or more available when they express these traits. African American men are more direct in their expression of sexual interest, and the women aren't insulted by this but generally feel confident about how to reject or accept such overtures. The men are normally not offended by a rejection if it's done in good humor, only by being ignored or rejected in a degrading way.

INTEGRATING AFRICAN VALUES:
THE NEW URBAN VILLAGE

A growing movement is afoot in the African American community, a movement that emphasizes African heritage and values and integrates them with American values and the American dream. A comparison of the Eurocentric and Afrocentric views, based on African tribal worldviews, as developed by African American community leaders, is shown in Table 7.8 to help explain the idea. Compare the two by entire viewpoint, not belief by belief.

TABLE 7.8: Comparison of Eurocentric and Afrocentric Viewpoints

Eurocentric Viewpoint	*Afrocentric Viewpoint*
• Survival of the fittest is central theme; the "fit" pull themselves up by their own boot straps; if you're a winner, it's because you're the "fittest." • Competition is a major theme in interactions with other humans and nature. • Humans devise the battlefields where life is played out. • Those who accumulate the most of what costs the most are the winners, the best. • War is the ultimate form of competition: Cold War, Star Wars, war on crime, war on drugs • Ultimate goal: to be #1, the symbol of achievement and worth.	• Humans are one with nature. • All entities experience cyclical, periodic, and inevitable changes. • In humans these changes are seen as life crises, which are disruptive but can be eased by group rituals of passages from one life phase to the next. • The death-rebirth cycle reflects the law of regeneration and applies to all of nature: systems become spent and must be regenerated. When one life phase ends, a new one begins. • Rites of passage reflect nature's cycle: separation from the old, transition to the new, and integration of old and new.

Based on the work of George Fraser, reflecting African tribal worldviews.

Regarding the Eurocentric ultimate goal, many African Americans say the ultimate illusion of the American Dream is that anyone who is focused, educated, and persistent can fight his or her way to the top and enjoy the distinction of being Number One. If being number one means others are number two, and so forth, then obviously everyone cannot make it. The "survival of the fittest theme" ignores situations where the rules are made by a dominant group in ways that exclude and disadvantage minority groups. The most successful thus tend to be the most privileged rather than "survivors" or the "fittest."

The Urban Village Concept

The urban village concept is a recent African American approach. It's grounded in the Afrocentric view but also recognizes that the Eurocentric view sets the rules of the American marketplace. A key principle is of the urban village is:

> *It takes a village to raise a child.*

The keys to success, from this urban village viewpoint, include networking, mentoring, and cooperative economics. The motto is economic empowerment. Virtually every African American church and community organization now operates some sort of economic program, from economic literacy and job training classes to community loan funds. Weekend mentoring programs focus on bringing together urban youth and business persons and other role models.

The urban village concept incorporates Afrocentric rites of passage, especially important for inner city youth, as well as the principles of Kwanzaa.

Kwanzaa

This is a way of life that honors the African heritage for the purpose of encouraging a greater sense of unity, identity, and purpose among African Americans. The seven Kwanzaa principles focus on unity, self-determination, collective work and responsibility, cooperative economics, purpose, creativity, and faith. Many of its symbols and terms come from African tradition, but it's a creation of African Americans that goes back to 1966. Special Kwanzaa celebrations occur from December 26 through January 1.

Kwanzaa and the urban village model are approaches that recognize the realities of African American life in the American society. They are seen by many African Americans as positive, empowering, practical approaches that are grounded in the interdependence and spirituality of an Afrocentric worldview. See *www.melanet.com/kwanzaa.*

ISSUES IMPORTANT TO THE AFRICAN AMERICAN COMMUNITY

Here is a summary of problems that African Americans ranked most important from a list offered by Princeton Survey Research Associates (Cose 1999, 2002).

1. Teenage mothers
2. Lack of jobs that pay a decent wage
3. Decline in moral and religious values
4. Welfare dependency
5. Crime in the neighborhood
6. Racism in society in general
7. Public school education—difficulty getting a good education
8. Social programs—the government should provide more funds for programs with a proven track record, such as Head Start
9. Unmarried parents
10. Racism in the workplace
11. Lack of role models for young people—too few successes in the workplace

LEADERSHIP CHALLENGE:
BREAKING THROUGH THE BARRIERS TO SUCCESS

You can play a role in helping African American associates overcome the "less-intelligent" stereotype that leads to lowered expectations for their skill development, promotability, and corporate success. You can also play a role in helping them break through the glass ceiling to better jobs. And, by understanding the typical career phases African Americans experience, you can learn how to support them in overcoming typical personal barriers and corporate-culture barriers at each phase.

Challenge #1: Breaking Out of Lowered Expectations—Success Cycles

A real barrier for many African Americans is the stereotype that they are less intelligent. Many have internalized this belief. All must deal with Euro-Americans in the workplace who hold this stereotype and therefore expect African Americans to be less competent learners and achievers.

You've learned that the higher the socioeconomic status of a family, the higher the grades and SAT scores of their children. Once an African American family is able to break the cycle of poverty and get good jobs, the cycle tends to stay broken for that family. The children do well in school and are therefore likely to get good jobs and earn good incomes when they grow up, which in turn increases the likelihood that *their* children will do well in school. Some predominantly African American schools have identified differences in the failure and success cycles (Howard 1988). They've adopted success cycle teaching and learning strategies to help children boost their academic achievement.

Some corporations have adopted these same strategies to help all employees, including African Americans, break out of failure cycles and establish success cycles.

What You Expect Is What You Get

Failure and success cycles are affected by what people expect. Here's what expectancy theory is all about: You, in your manager role, communicate in words and actions your beliefs and expectations about what a worker can achieve. If that worker values your opinion, then your expectations have a powerful impact on that person's skill development and performance. If you believe the co-worker will do well, she's more likely to believe she'll do well, she's more likely to actually do well, and she's more likely to credit her success to her own ability. Belief leads to performance.

If a worker thinks you're an important person, that you have knowledge or you can make a difference, then what you expect can affect the following aspects of her performance:

- how fully she believes she can succeed
- how hard she tries
- how intensely she concentrates
- how willing she is to take reasonable risks, which is a key factor in developing self-confidence and new skills
- how she interprets her success or failure

Failure Cycle

Here's how the failure cycle works: When you believe a worker has inferior abilities and therefore you have lower expectations for him than for others, you set up a failure cycle as follows:

- You assume that he is intellectually inferior, which leads to
- His internalized belief that he is intellectually inferior, which leads to
- Low self-confidence about succeeding at intellectual tasks, which leads to
- Poor performance on intellectual tasks, which leads to
- Avoidance of intellectual tasks

We can therefore conclude that avoidance of intellectual challenge is affected by fears and self-doubt, which are rooted in a history of strong negative stereotypes that Euro-Americans hold about African American's intellectual capabilities.

When a worker expects to fail, or assumes he can't succeed, or believes "I don't have what it takes," here's what's likely to occur:

- He takes a dim view of trying again.
- He loses his motivation and often gives up trying to learn.
- He blames the failure on his own lack of ability (or aptitude and potential) rather than on inadequate or erroneous effort, which is correctable.
- By this process he, in effect, internalizes the low opinion originally held by you (or others).

What makes African Americans unique in this regard is that they are singled out for the stigma of genetic intellectual inferiority. This negative stereotype suggests to African Americans that they should understand any failure in intellectual activity as confirmation of genetic inferiority. No wonder many African Americans shy away from any situation where the rumor of inferiority might be proved true.

FIGURE 7.1: Failure Cycle

Other's assumption that I'm intellectually inferior →
My internalized belief that I'm intellectually inferior →
Low self-confidence regarding intellectual tasks →
Poor performance on intellectual tasks →
Avoidance of such tasks →

Success Cycle

African Americans tend to experience greater success when they engage in sports, socializing, and entertaining others because of assumptions and stereotypes that they are "innately" gifted in these areas. Many of them have established success cycles in these areas. But suppose you are an important person in an African American worker's life. Here's how you would set up a success cycle.

- You assume that she can master a job task, which leads to
- her internalized belief that she can master the job task, which leads to
- self-confidence in her ability to master the job task, which leads to
- willingness to put forth effort on the job task, which leads to
- development of job skills

If she has a failure during this process, her self-confidence allows her to see it as merely an error, not a sign of incompetence. Failure is just an opportunity to find out what doesn't work and correct it, a lesson for how to succeed next time.

Your positive beliefs and resulting expectations for her success helps her to build self-confidence. She becomes inspired and willing to put forth the effort necessary to achieve specific job goals, which leads to learning, achievement, and growth in that job area. This achievement becomes the foundation for increased self-confidence in the next cycle, as summarized in Figure 7.2.

FIGURE 7.2: Success Cycle

Assumption by leader that I can master intellectual tasks →
Internalized belief that I can master intellectual tasks →
Self-confidence in my ability to master intellectual tasks →
Willingness to put forth effort on intellectual tasks →
Development of intellectual skills →

The success cycle is a process in which success increases self-confidence and effort, leading to even more success, over and over in the upward spiral. It's circular and feeds back on itself, moving upward in a geometrically expanding spiral, as shown in Figure 7.3, Skill Development Cycle.

FIGURE 7.3: Skill Development Cycle

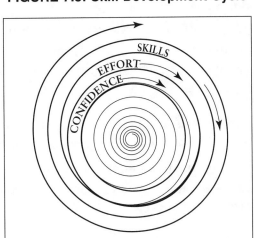

What You Can Do

Here's how you can encourage a success cycle during the various learning phases:

1. *During the confidence phase.* Begin with your own stereotyped beliefs, assumptions, and expectations. Get them straight. When you're sure you have a "you can" attitude, you'll know your verbal and nonverbal messages are likely to convey positive expectations.

2. *During the effort phase.* Take a positive attitude toward performance evaluation. Encourage African Americans to attribute their successes to ability, boosting their confidence level. Help them to see their failures as either a lack of effort or some correctable error—as a learning tool for creating success the next time around. The key question is, how can I do it differently next time?

3. *During the skill development phase.* Help African American employees to assume responsibility for their own performance and development, and let them know you are there as a resource person. Pay special attention to training and development, bringing in appropriate new opportunities as skills are built. Keep the cycle going.

Challenge #2: Breaking Through the Glass Ceiling

Corporate America cannot yet claim a diverse workplace that looks like America as a whole. African Americans have moved into better-paying occupations but most still hit a glass ceiling at middle management levels or even below, according to government reports.

In American society traditional prejudice and discrimination toward diverse groups results in a package of feelings and experiences that most members of these groups bring to the workplace. As a leader, you need to be aware of these factors that affect African Americans in a wide range of ways. Some have managed to ignore or rise above most of them. Others may have a problem in one area and none in the others. Knowing what to look for can help you give the right kind of support.

Whether your role is that of manager, team leader, or responsible co-worker, you can identify ways to support African Americans in leaving stereotypes behind and focusing on developing themselves for the next job promotion. The focus may be on increasing their flexibility, networking ability, bottom-line influence, computer literacy, skill in highlighting their own strengths, and other areas relevant to their career plan.

History's Impact

The barriers that most African Americans face in the workplace consist of a mixture of the burdens society has imposed upon them and how that has affected them personally. Most African Americans come to the workplace with some combination of these experiences:

- a history of oppression and exclusion from the mainstream activities of society
- a sense that they're seen as different (in a negative way) from Euro-Americans
- being positioned in a one-down status
- being barred or discouraged from seeking a better position in society—or in life
- lack of equal opportunities
- as a result: lower self-concept, self-esteem, and self-confidence

Career Issues

These problems, and sometimes their solution attempts, have led to other problems, mentioned in surveys of African Americans who have chosen to leave their corporations:

- Hitting the glass ceiling and lack of opportunity and upward mobility
- Feeling pressured to "act white" and to repress their ethnic identity in order to fit in, make others feel comfortable, and succeed.

- Feeling misplaced in a corporate culture where work life and social life focus only on Euro-American customs
- Having to prove themselves, over and over again, due to being African American
- Dealing with the assumption, and resulting stigma, that they are an "affirmative action hire"
- Coping with ethnic stereotypes

Coaching Needs and Strategies

To succeed in most corporate cultures, African Americans must learn to:

- Pay as much attention to building relationships and to monitoring and developing their career strategies as they do to achieving specific job goals
- Market themselves within the company and outside of it
- Network and establish relationships with other people in other divisions
- Tap into the grapevine and keep up with what's going on.

You have an opportunity as a leader is to encourage and support them in doing all this. Ellis Cose (2002) has studied African American managers and compiled a list of success strategies that mentors and coaches can encourage them to adopt, as follows:

1. As an African American, play the race card carefully, and at your own peril.
2. Complain all you like about the raw deal you have gotten in life, but don't expect those complaints to get you anywhere.
3. Expect to do better than the world expects of you; expect to live in a bigger world than the one you see. Dream big dreams, and prepare yourself to pursue them, instead of settling for fantasies of a wonderful existence forever beyond your reach.
4. Don't expect support for your dreams from those who have not accomplished very much in their own lives.
5. If someone typically brings out your most self-destructive tendencies, recognize that person as a nonfriend.
6. Ask for help, especially from those who are wiser and older.
7. Recognize that being true to yourself is not the same as being true to a stupid stereotype.
8. Don't expect competence and hard work alone to get you the recognition or rewards you deserve. Organizations are essentially political arenas that reward those fully engaged in the game. Learn the rules of the game.
9. You must make the most of your time, for it's already later than you think. Many African Americans are running late in getting their credentials and experience.
10. Even if you have to fake it, show some faith in yourself. Show confidence.

Challenge #3: Breaking Through Blocks at Each Career Phase

You can help African Americans break through career blocks by understanding the career phases typical for African Americans and by giving support at each phase. According to African American managers Jacqueline and Floyd Dickens (1982), African Americans who enter the corporate world typically move through several phases that might be described as:

- *Entry-level* phase—dealing with organizational and personal prejudice
- *Adjustment and frustration* phase—dealing with their own anger and frustration

- *Career development* phase—developing skills in conflict management and management of prejudice
- *Mastery* phase—refining
- protective hesitation and integrating core skills

Entry-Level and Adjustment Phases

Many African American applicants come to the organization with a positive but naive attitude. They usually encounter personal as well as organizational prejudice and may become angry, hostile, and culturally paranoid. If they decide to stay, they then adjust and plan their growth rather than allow anger and resentment to stifle it. They find ways to recapture their earlier positive attitude, so that negative attitudes cease to be a barrier to learning. Successful African American employees somehow retain a positive attitude even in the midst of prejudiced behaviors.

To succeed in corporate America, managers who are African American, as compared to Euro-Americans, must pay more attention to building and maintaining relationships. They must put Euro-Americans at ease, for example. Successful African American managers suggest making the first move in building workplace relationships, saying "If you don't reach out, you'll never be a part of important after-hours get-togethers" (Lancaster 1997).

Some Euro-Americans employees will think African American managers got their job just because they're African American. Nipping this perception in the bud may be best—by bringing it up in a meeting and dealing with the issue of adequate qualifications. About any real problem, it's usually best to speak up, point out the problem, and take issues to higher-level management, if necessary.

African American managers must walk a fine line between accommodating the Euro-Americans corporate culture and maintaining their identity, expressing it in ways that don't create backlash. African American role models and mentors are a great help, though managers may have to go outside their own company to find one.

- Do you think of African Americans first and foremost as human beings, as individuals, or as African Americans?
- Does your small talk with them cover the whole gamut of topics? Or is it normally confined primarily to African American news items, celebrities, and events?

In the early phases, many African Americans have great difficulty seeing themselves in a leadership position because they've been taught that Euro-American men lead, African Americans follow. They often apologize in various ways for taking leadership or initiative or for being put in even a temporary leadership position. They may have difficulty directing Euro-American males and therefore not be as self-confident as the norm because of discomfort with empowerment. Before they become comfortable with having and using power, their walk may be less assured, their voice tone may lack authority, and their attitude may be more *May I?* than *This is what we can do.* Keep in mind that typically African Americans are required to demonstrate competence at the next level before they are promoted, whereas Euro-American males are typically promoted on the basis of their potential. Ask yourself periodically

- Am I doing my share to see that people are treated equally? That everyone gets a fair chance at plum assignments and promotions?

Even when African Americans achieve the desired results, they typically must devote extra energy to ensure that the results are properly seen by the right people. This is because decision makers often harbor negative stereotypes that prevent them from seeing such achievements.

- Are you open to seeing everyone's achievements and potential?
- Are you helping others to see clearly?

Career Development Phase

Overcoming African American mistrust of the input from Euro-Americans is still an issue for most African American employees, even at the career development stage. They may establish one-to-one relationship with their manager, but they rarely expand this to a generalized attitude toward all Euro-Americans. During this phase African American employees usually keep their misgivings to themselves, choosing instead to behave in a manner of trust. They need to identify and access one or more mentors.

These employees must develop and use a network of supporters, whether the members are prejudiced or not. A commitment to succeed becomes the prime goal of successful employees. By now they should understand that waiting to be adopted by a Euro-American mentor is risky, so they may need to take the initiative to locate potential people in the organization and find a mentor.

- Are you willing to be a supporter or mentor?
- Are you encouraging others to support African American colleagues?

In this phase, two of the most important job skills to be acquired are *conflict management* and the *management of prejudice.*

If African Americans can't deal with conflict constructively, they're likely to be blamed as a *cause* of any conflict they become embroiled in. African Americans tend as a group to be more open and straightforward in their interactions than do Euro-Americans. They typically want to confront conflict directly and solve the problem quickly. In many organizations however, the norm is conflict avoidance. If so, the African American's style will be seen as inappropriate. African Americans are more likely to confront the other person as soon as they're aware of a conflict situation. If that's inappropriate, they'll do it later in private. Euro-Americans in many corporate cultures will discuss the situation with the other person's boss, and may talk about it with others, before they'll openly confront the person involved in the conflict.

- Are you willing to accept an open, direct style of conflict resolution?

Management of prejudice involves a range of skills most African Americans must develop in order to counteract and neutralize Euro-Americans' demeaning, prejudicial actions. For example, *protective hesitation* is a common African American strategy for dealing with prejudice and the hostile situations it engenders. It's based on the value of distrust of the establishment. The strategy consists of deliberately hesitating before interacting or preparing to interact with Euro-Americans, in order to think about how to protect oneself from possible psychological assault or to avoid reinforcing negative stereotypes about African Americans. Such preventive hesitation involves using caution and pre-planning. This behavior has been handed down from parents to children through generations and so comes naturally to many African Americans by the time they're adults. It can be especially helpful at the career development phase when the employee is being assessed for promotion potential.

- Are you willing to understand protective hesitation and to discover the underlying dynamics of prejudice and defense?

The Mastery Phase: Mutual Support

One of the key insights successful African Americans say they used in the mastery phase is that making mistakes or failing is not an option for African American managers. When they fail, they fail for the entire group of African American employees. Most have made protective hesitation a way of life in the corporation. Key to their style is preplanning, careful thought, and caution in relying on Euro-Americans as resources. Through trial and error, they take their rage and use its energy to help them achieve productive results.

- Are you willing to build trusting relationships by consistently being honest, direct, and supportive?

LEADERSHIP OPPORTUNITIES: BUILDING ON AFRICAN AMERICAN STRENGTHS

As a leader, you need to recognize the strengths that each of your team members brings to the organization and to build on those strengths. African Americans bring many assets to the workplace that can be used in numerous ways. They can contribute to team processes, to the development of networks and business relationships that are especially valuable for the organization, and to connections with the African American marketplace.

Opportunity #1: Planning, Creating, Problem Solving

Work teams must deal with fast-paced change—by recognizing niches, developing profitable products and services, moving in on the right opportunities at the right time, solving problems, and optimizing total quality. The best work teams develop a high level of skill in generating ideas, planning, and problem solving—and they do this through synergy, creativity, and innovation as well as by discipline and application.

You can help team leaders and members recognize the value of African American strengths, such as expressing personal style for the appreciation of the group, being assertive in expressing feelings and ideas, and not giving up. These traits can add to the team's strengths. Some of these traits may seem foreign to those accustomed to typical business traits and approaches.

- You can help your team realize that a different approach can sometimes score winning points, that "differentness" can be an asset.

Opportunity #2: Building Relationships

Relationships are the name of the game in the marketplace. Business is built upon networks of relationships among team members, customers, suppliers, other departments, the community, professional organizations, regulating agencies, and others. African Americans have a special advantage when they apply their tendencies toward: *a people focus, sharing, nonverbal communication skills, and expression of feelings*, as detailed in the earlier values discussion.

For example, in team relationships, African American members can set a tone that could help the team avoid game playing and hidden agendas through focusing on the values of *directness, emotional expressiveness, and sense of justice*. To be most effective, expression of these values may need to be stepped down to an intensity that other team members can accept.

- You can help African Americans members develop appropriate expressions of their strengths.
- You can also provide guidance about expressing the justice and distrust values in ways that avoid the stereotype of the resentful African American or the troublemaker.
- You can include African Americans in informal get-togethers both inside and outside the workplace. You can help them build relationships that are deeper than the superficial contact level.
- You can look for opportunities to create diverse teams that include African Americans, an excellent opportunity for building deeper relationships.

Opportunity #3: Connecting with the African American Marketplace

African Americans obviously have an inside edge in understanding other African Americans, the community, and the marketplace. They can contribute great strength to the organization in gaining African American market share. African Americans now represent over $500 billion a year in spending power, and the market is growing. So are global markets that include many African nations.

These customers and business persons like to do business with companies that "look like America" or that "look like us."

African American team members can provide an obvious advantage in those markets. They are naturals for recognizing opportunities to provide new products or services. For example, in a "Hallmark-type" company, they realized that African Americans would buy distinctive Kwanzaa season's greetings. The success of the greeting cards evolved into consumer demand for specially designed gift items, crafts, toys, clothing, and music with African motifs, which they provided for sale in a variety of venues. Eager crowds of shoppers at Kwanzaa festivals and expos walk away happy, and the sellers are pleased by their sales expansion.

- You can recognize the connections and the related opportunities to use African American employees' understanding of their own cultures and related cultures.

- You can make others aware of these connections and opportunities and use you influence to help African Americans make valuable contributions to the success of your team and your organization.

SUMMARY

The 12 percent of employees who are African American must deal with myths and stereotypes about violence, anger, intelligence, initiative, and style, all part of a heritage of slavery, segregation, and discrimination. African Americans led the Civil Rights movement that opened doors for all disadvantaged groups in the U.S. workplace. As a result, there is a growing affluent African American middle class, about one-third of African Americans, but also a growing underclass of about one-third, with another third struggling in between. African American educational achievement tends to be lower than that of Euro-Americans. Studies indicate that higher socioeconomic status is the best predictor of school grades and SAT scores, so the solution to this problem lies in finding ways to help more African Americans reach middle-class status. Meanwhile, for those who have achieved such status, there's still a glass ceiling to advancement for African Americans in corporate America, and many who hit it are leaving to form their own businesses.

The core values of the African American community are sharing, personal style, being genuine, being assertive, expressing feelings, bouncing back, dealing with a dual culture, and not trusting the establishment. The community is close-knit, and their ways of confronting one another assertively are part of being genuine. This trait is often misunderstood by Euro-Americans as being combative and even a prelude to violence. But it can be a strength, just as vitality and resilience are strengths, that African American employees bring to the workplace and marketplace. These strengths can be especially helpful in team projects and in building networks of relationships.

Leaders can communicate their positive expectations and support for African American employees in order to set up a success cycle. A managers' expectations have a strong impact on what the African American employee can achieve. Managers can also help to break the glass ceiling caused by traditional stereotypes if they understand African American's career issues, coach them, and suggest career strategies they might adopt. Leaders can help African Americans negotiate the typical career phases they experience in mainstream organizations: the phases of entry-level, adjustment, career development, and mastery. Leaders must be especially sensitive to the value of distrust of the establishment, and special care must be taken to build trust. Leaders can also help African American employees build on their strengths, such as a people focus, sharing, nonverbal communication skills, expression of feelings, directness, emotional expressiveness, and a sense of justice—helping them to find appropriate expression of such strengths in a workplace setting. Opportunities include helping African Americans to contribute to team innovation and productivity, and marketing more effectively to African American customers and African clients.

Case Study 7.1 Jason, African American Manager

Jason has applied for an assistant manager's position at Drysdale Corporation. He's looking for opportunities to learn and grow in his career and wants to leave his current job because such opportunities are lacking. His ultimate career goal is to become CEO of a large corporation. With his degree in business administration and plans to complete an MBA, he thinks he has a chance—if he can find the right firm—even though he's an African American. When Jason is escorted around the Drysdale offices, he sees no African Americans, a few Asian Americans, and one Latino American. Nearly everyone is Euro-American, and they mostly seem too busy to pay much attention to Jason or spend time with him. But Jason really believes in the Drysdale Corporation and decides to accept their job offer.

Soon after he begins work, he notices that ethnic jokes and comments are common at Drysdale. Jason doesn't look like a typical African American because his mother is Euro-American. He speaks up several times, saying he doesn't appreciate jokes and comments that belittle people from any ethnic group. Most of the comments stop, but so does the already-sparse friendliness of Jason's coworkers. While the environment is not particularly warm at Drysdale, Jason still believes he can achieve career success here because he loves the work itself.

Jason knows he's a rapid learner and a responsible person, one who works effectively and efficiently. His performance evaluations during the next year and a half are all excellent and his manager *Ken* seems to be encouraging.

In fact, Jason believes he is one of the most productive workers in the company. He meets his time targets and maintains high work quality. But Jason is getting restless. His work is becoming routine to him and therefore boring. He has asked Ken several times about a promotion and expanded job responsibilities. Ken has been vague, telling Jason to "hang in there and I'll keep an eye out for job opportunities for you." In the meantime, several management positions have opened up at Drysdale and been filled by others.

1. What are the root problems?
2. If you were Jason, what would you do?

Case Study 7.2 Karla, African American Salesperson

Karla is a salesperson at Ellison's Furniture, the only African American on the small sales force of 20 persons. She has been very successful in selling furniture, makes a good salary plus commission, and during the year she has been at Ellison's has made top salesperson of the month three times. Karla enjoys her work but feels isolated from most of her coworkers. Most of them are Euro-American men, and five are Euro-American women. The manager *Daniel* is Euro-American and has been very supportive of Karla's training, development, and sales work. He often praises her work and encourages her to "keep it up."

Rachel is the only salesperson who has seemed willing to spend much time with Karla during coffee breaks or at lunch. While Karla doesn't think of Rachel as a close personal friend, she does view her as more than just a business colleague. She's also a friend.

From time to time Karla has overheard comments of her coworkers about the good times they've had together at various parties and outings that they plan. She can't help thinking about the fact that she is never included. Last week as Karla approached the employees' lounge, she heard someone saying, ". . . at Rachel's party last Saturday. . . ." Karla stopped dead in her tracks. She felt as if someone had punched her in the stomach. What a blow to discover that even her friend, her only "real work friend," had thrown a party and had excluded her.

Daniel has noticed that during the past week Karla has seemed quieter and more withdrawn than usual. He is concerned because he believes that Karla's success as a salesperson is largely due to her outgoing, cheerful personality. When he gets a chance to talk privately with Karla, he says, "Is everything okay, Karla? You've been awfully quiet the past few days."

1. If you were Karla, what would you do?
2. If you were Daniel, what would you do?

Case Study 7.3 Karla Gets Promoted

Continuing the story of Karla, African American salesperson, fast forward one year. Daniel was promoted to an executive position at the headquarters office and recommended Karla as his replacement. Karla has mixed emotions about taking the job, feeling that the employees still do not accept her as a social equal but they do seem to respect her sales ability. She is hoping that they will accept her as manager and that she will be able to win their respect for her leadership ability.

During her first six months as manager, Karla sensed a degree of resistance from the employees. She has seen them joking and laughing, glancing over at her as though she were the butt of the joke. Sometimes they seem to be dragging in their heels in responding to her requests. Sometimes she must follow up and repeat the request a time or two.

During the past month, Karla has noticed some distinct changes. Employees suddenly seem more cooperative, amiable, and respectful. A couple of them have even invited her to social events after work. Karla realizes that it is time for her to conduct yearly performance reviews of all employees. She feels somewhat conflicted about how to rate the employees. She is really enjoying their changed attitudes and behaviors and does not want to jeopardize the improved relationships.

1. What are the root problems?
2. Should Karla base the performance reviews more on current behaviors or on previous behaviors?
3. If you were Karla, what would you do?

Case Study 7.4. Assistant Manager Doug

Doug is assistant manager of the Nashville branch of Angelo Shipping Company. He's been an employee there for 12 years, since he was 23, and he was promoted to assistant manager a year ago. Last month Doug learned of an upcoming opening in the Atlanta headquarters and applied for it. He believes he has all the necessary qualifications for the position as well as an exemplary performance record. Although there are many African American men working as manual laborers for the company, none are full managers or executives.

John, an executive in the headquarters office, is interviewing a applicants for the management position and will make a recommendation to the executive team. Of the four qualified applicants, all but Doug are Euro-American men. John, also a Euro-American, has never worked with an African American manager.

When Doug arrives for his interview with John, he's left waiting in the lobby for an hour. Then a secretary comes in and tells him that John is still interviewing another candidate and will be with him in a while. About 45 minutes later, John appears in the lobby with *Mike* of the Memphis branch. John is talking warmly with Mike, then thanks him and shakes his hand before turning to welcome Doug. They walk to John's office, where John waves toward a chair across from his desk, and Doug seats himself. John and Doug talk for about 10 to 15 minutes, mainly about how Doug feels about his current job and the company. The phone rings. John takes the call, puts his hand over the receiver, and says to Doug, "Thank you for coming in. Could you show yourself out? I must take this call." Doug was shocked, but he found his way out.

A few days later, Doug receives a telephone call from John, who tells him the executive team has selected Mike for the job. He says the executive team felt the position called for someone with Mike's experience. Later, Doug says to his friend Jan, "I know I've been with the company at least as long as Mike, and I've been employee-of-the-month here eight different times. I heard Mike has only won it twice. I don't understand how his experience could be any better than mine. What would make it better?"

1. What is your opinion of John's actions and the executive team's decision? i.e. what are the key issues (root problems)?
2. What do you think Doug should do?

Case Study 7.5 Sales Rep Evelyn

Evelyn has been one of the outstanding sales representatives for McCord Foods' West Coast region for the past three years. Her immediate supervisor *Rosalie* is in a quandary about what to do. The Houston office needs a sales supervisor with just the kind of experience and qualities that Evelyn has. However, the last time an African American was transferred into a management position at the Houston office, he faced many problems. The major issue was that key customers didn't accept him and he lost a number of accounts. These accounts were with large, traditional food processing and manufacturing firms.

McCord sells spices, flavorings, and other additives to the food industry. The field is very competitive, and accounts are often won and lost on the basis of the personal relationships between sales manager, sales rep, and purchasing agent. The sales manager periodically travels with sales reps to call on major accounts and potential accounts. The sales manager also enters the picture when thorny customer problems arise.

Louis, who is head of the Houston office, was enthusiastic about Evelyn's resume until he heard that she was African American. He called Rosalie and talked over the touchy situation with her. "Maybe it wouldn't be fair to Evelyn to ask her to move all the way down here and then be faced with a no-win situation," he said.

Now Rosalie must make a decision. She knows that two other well-qualified candidates are being recommended for the position, but actually Evelyn is better suited to the job than the others. Shall she recommend Evelyn for the position? Evelyn has a child in the fourth grade, who would have to adapt to a new school and the Houston environment. If it didn't work out, Rosalie would feel responsible

1. What are the key issues (root problems)?
2. What do you think Rosalie should do?

Case Study 7.6 Cuba, Junior Consultant

Cuba, a 23-year-old African American, is a senior at Stanford University. Initially he was an art history major but is now majoring in economics with an emphasis in "California technology." This is a special major supervised by a team of professors. Cuba is also gaining experience in Silicon Valley through an internship with Green Charts, a local consulting firm of 70 employees consisting of 60 Euro-Americans, 6 Asian Americans, 4 African Americans and one Latino American. Cuba is accumulating an extensive network of contacts through his research and his consulting work.

At Green Charts Cuba works closely with Bradbury, a Euro-American consultant with whom he has developed a very friendly relationship. Cuba believes that he will be hired to work full time with Green Charts when he graduates and is eagerly looking forward to taking on challenging assignments as a full-time employee.

Fast forward to six months after graduation. As a junior executive at Green Charts, Cuba is working with Bradbury's clients. He's getting somewhat restless with the assignments Bradbury has been giving him because they seem too clerical and very similar to the work he was doing as an intern. He hasn't complained, though, believing that greater opportunities are around the corner.

Fast forward again: Now, Cuba has been a junior consultant for 13 months. Green Charts announces a restructuring of the organization; they will terminate the "bottom 5 percent of performers" and promote some top performers. Cuba has been wondering why Bradbury still doesn't seem to trust him to take on his own clients—and he is excited about the restructuring, assuming that this will be his chance to get his own client accounts to manage.

Today Green Charts management makes the announcement: four employees are to be laid off and six will be promoted. Cuba was not laid off but neither was he promoted. He is angry and puzzled, not knowing where to turn. He overhears some employees discussing the reorganization: "Bradbury likes the work that Cuba is doing. . . . but, well, Cuba really belongs as a junior consultant; he's not ready to take on his own clients."

1. What might be happening behind the scenes here? Key issues? Root problems?
2. What do you think Cuba should do?

REFERENCES

AAUW. *The AAUW Report: How Schools Shortchange Girls*. American Assn. University Women, 1992.

Abrahams, R.D. *Deep Down in the Jungle*. Aldine Press, 1963.

Allen, W.R. "Moms, Dads, and Boys," in *Black Men*. Sage, 1981.

Baldwin, J.A. "The Role of Black Psychologists in Black Liberation," in *African American Psychology*. Sage, 1992.

Beaty, Paul. *The White Boy Shuffle*. Houghton Mifflin, 1996.

Bell, E.L., "The Bicultural Life Experience of Career-Oriented Black Women," *Journal of Organizational Behavior* 11, 459–477, 1990.

Billingsley, Andrew. *Climbing Jacob's Ladder: The Enduring Legacy of African American Families*. Simon & Schuster, 1992.

Black Enterprise. www.blackenterprise.com June 2005.

Blackwell, J.E. *The Black Community: Diversity and Unity*. Harper & Row, 1985.

Blanchard, F.A., and F.J. Crosby. *Affirmative Action in Perspective*. Springer-Verlag, 1989.

Burman, Stephen. *The Black Progress Question*. Sage, 1995.

Carr-Ruffino, "Legislative Measures for Women's Advancement" in *Womanpower*. Sage, 1992.

Carr-Ruffino, Norma. "U.S. Women: Breaking Through the Glass Ceiling," *Women in Management Review*, 6, 5, 1991.

Collier, M.J. "A Comparison of Intracultural and Intercultural Communication Among Acquaintances," *Communication Quarterly*, 36, 122–144, 1988.

Collier, M.J. "Communication Competence Problematics in Ethnic Friendships," *Communication Monographs* 63, 4, 314–336, 1998.

Comer, J.P. and A.F. Poussaint. *Raising Black Children*. Penguin, 1992.

Cose, Ellis. *The Envy of the World*. Washington Square Press, 2002.

Cose, Ellis, "The Good News About Black America," *Newsweek*, 29–40, June 7, 1999.

Coy, Peter, "Troubling Trends in Gaps between Blacks and Whites in America," Business Week Online, www.businessweek.com/bwdaily. January 10, 2000.

Cross, Wm. E. Jr. *Shades of Black: Diversity in African American Identity*. Temple University Press, 1991.

Daniels, Cora. *Black Power Inc*. John Wiley, 2004.

Dickens, Floyd, Jr., and Jacqueline B. Dickens. *The Black Manager: Making It in the Corporate World*. Amacom, 1982.

Donohue, W. A. *The Politics of the American Civil Liberties Union*. Transaction Books, 1985.

Dovidio, J.F. and S.L. Gaertner, eds. *Prejudice, Discrimination, and Racism*. Academic Press, 1986.

DuBois, W.E.B. *The Souls of Black Folk*, reprinted in *Three Negro Classics*. Avon Books, 1965.

ELC, Executive Leadership Council, www.elcinfo.com, 2005.

Executive Female. A survey on the glass ceiling, women and African Americans, 1991.

Feagin Joe, "The Continuing Significance of Race: Anti-black Discrimination in Public Places," *American Sociological Review*, 56,101–116, February 1991.

Fletcher, Michael A. "Kerner follow-up sees wide race gap," *Washington Post*, syndicated in the *San Francisco Examiner*, p. A-6, March 1, 1998.

Foeman, A.K. and G. Pressley, "Ethnic Culture and Corporate Culture: Using Black Styles in Organizations," *Communications Quarterly*, 35, 293–307, 1987.

Franklin, John Hope. From Slavery to Freedom: A History of African Americans, 8th ed., 2000.

Fraser, George. *Success Runs in Our Race*. Wm. Morrow, 1994.

Garner, T.E. "Playing the Dozens," *Quarterly Journal of Speech*, 69, 47–57, 1983

Glaser, D. "Dynamics of Ethnic Identification," *American Sociological Review*, 23, 31–40, 1958.

Graham, Stedman. *You Can Make It Happen*. Simon & Schuster, 1997.

Graves, Earl G. *How to Succeed in Business Without Being White*. HarperBusiness, 1997.

Halberstad, A.G. "Race, Socioeconomic Status, and Nonverbal Behavior," in *Multichannel Integrations of Nonverbal Behavior*. Lawrence Erlbaum, 1985.

Hall. E.T. *Beyond Culture*. Doubleday, 1976.

Hammer, M.R. and W.B. Gundykunst. "The Influence of Ethnicity and Sex on Social Penetration in Close Friendships" *Journal of Black Studies* 17, 418–437, 1987.

Handy, Kenneth. *The Psychological Residuals of Slavery*. Guilford Press, 1995.

Harding, Vincent. *The Other American Revolution*. Institute of the Black World, 1980.

Hecht, M.L., and S. Ribeau. "Ethnic Communication: A Comparative Analysis of Satisfying Communication," *International Journal of Intercultural Relations* 8, 135–151, 1984.

Hecht, M.L., M.J. Collier, S.A. Ribeau. *African American Communication*. Sage, 1993.

Herskovitz, M.J. *The Myth of the Negro Past*. Beacon, 1958.

Herskovitz, M.J. *Anthropometry of the American Negro*. Columbia University Press, 1930

Hom, Peter, "Women and Minorities' High Quit Rate," www.knowledge.wpcarey.asu.edu, *Knowledge @ W.P. Carey*, 2007.

Howard, Jeff, and Ray Hammond. "Rumors of Inferiority: The Hidden Obstacles to Black Success." *The New Republic*, September 9, 1988.

Ickes, W. "Composition in Black and White." *Journal of Personality and Social Psychology* 47, 1206–1217, 1984.

Issues of Public Policy, www.cnbl.org/html/appendices.html, 1999.

Johnson, Michelle. *Working While Black: The Black Person's Guide to Success in the White Workplace*. Lawrence Hill Books, 2004.

Jones, J. M. *Prejudice and Racism*, 2nd ed. McGraw-Hill, 1997.

Kanter, R.M. *Men and Women of the Corporation*. Basic Books, 1979.

Kenton, S.B. and D. Valentine. *CrossTalk*. South-Western, 1996.

Kitano, H. *Japanese-Americans*. Prentice-Hall, 1976.

Kochman, Thomas. *Black & White Styles in Conflict*. University of Chicago Press, 1981.

Korn-Ferry 1998 study reported by Todd Datz, "Workplace Diversity: Equity?" *CIO Magazine*, www.cio.com, January 15, 2000.

Lancaster, Hal, "Black Managers Often Must Emphasize Building Relationships," *Wall Street Journal*, A-1, February 4, 1997.

Larkey, L.K., and M.L. Hecht. "A Comparative Study of African American and Euro-American Ethnic Identity." Paper presented at the International Conference for Language and Social Psychology, Santa Barbara, CA, August 1991.

Lewis, Diane, "Equity Found Lacking in Hub Workforce: Despite Population Growth, Minorities Unrepresented," *Boston Globe*, December 31, 2004.

Lichtenberg, J. "Racism in the Head, Racism in the World." *Report from the Institute for Philosophy and Public Policy* 12, 1, 3–5, 1992.

Lynch, F.R. *Invisible Victims: White Males and the Crisis of Affirmative Action*. Praeger, 1989.

Mann, W. "Support Systems of Significant Others in Black Families." in *Black Families*. Sage, 1981.

Mark, "Facts about Prison and Prisoners," www.SentencingProject.org, 2003.

McWilliams, Carey. *Brothers Under the Skin*. Little, Brown & Co., 1964.

Myers, Samuel L., ed. *Economic Issues and Black Colleges*. Follett Press 1986.

NAEOHE, National Association for Equal Opportunity in Higher Education, 1990.

NORC, National Opinion Survey Center, University of Chicago, "HowDo Americans View One Another? The Persistence of Racial/Ethnic Stereotypes," *Diversity Digest*. www.diversityweb.org, 2000.

Pettigrew, Thomas F., and Joanne Martin. "Shaping the Organizational Context for Black American Inclusion." *Journal of Social Issues* 43, 1, 41–78, 1987.

Pinkney, Alphonso. *The Myth of Black Progress*. Cambridge University Press, 1984.

Ponterotto, Joseph G., and Paul B. Pedersen. *Preventing Prejudice*. Sage, 1993.

"Progress Without Parity," *Business Week*, 101–103, July 14, 2003.

Rose, L.F. "Theoretical & Methodological Issues in the Study of Black Culture and Personality. *Humboldt Journal of Social Relations* 10, 320–338, 1982-1983.

Saad, Lydia, "Black Dissatisfaction Simmers Beneath Good Race Relations," Gallup Poll, August 22, 2003.

Smith, D.E., F.N. Willis, and J.A. Gier. "Success and Interpersonal Touch in a Competitive Setting." *Journal of Nonverbal Behavior* 5, 26–34, 1980.

Smitherman, G. *Talkin' and Testifyin': The Language of Black America*. Houghton Mifflin, 1977.

Solorzano, Daniel G. "Mobility Aspirations Among Racial Minorities, Controlling for SES. *Social Science Review* 75, 182–188, July 1991.

Stanbeck, M., and W.B. Pearce. "Talking to 'the man.'" *Quarterly Journal of Speech* 67, 21–30, 1981.

Stevens, Joann, "The Power of Diversity in Corporate America," www.Linkage-Inc.com, March 15, 2003.

Stewart, Edward C. *American Cultural Patterns: A Cross Cultural Perspective*. Intercultural Network, Inc., 1972.

Stienstra, Tom, A Dramatic Turnaround for State Parks. *San Francisco Examiner*, D-12, January 22, 1995.

Takaki, Ronald. *A Different Mirror: A History of Multicultural America*. Little, Brown & Co., 1993.

Terry, Robert W. (Detroit Industrial Mission). *For Whites Only*. William B. Eerdmans Publishing Company, 1970, 1990.

Thomas, Roosevelt. *Beyond Race & Gender*. AMACOM, 1991.

Thornton, Jeanne, and Davis Whitman, "Whites' Myths about Blacks," *U.S. News & World Report*, 41–44, November 9, 1992.

Urban Institute study reported by Association of American Colleges and Universities, "The Knowledge We Need about Race and Racism," *Diversity Digest*, www.diversityweb.org, Winter 1998.

U.S. BLS, Bureau of Labor Statistics, http://stats.bls.gov, 1999, 2002.

U.S. Census Bureau, "Census 2000," www.census.gov, 2000.

U.S. Census Bureau, Current Population Reports. "Average Earnings of Year-Round Fulltime Workers by Sex and Educational Attainment." 1991, 2001, 2003.

U.S. Census Bureau, Department of Commerce, *We the American Children*, 1993.

U.S. Department of Labor. *A Report on the Glass Ceiling Initiative*, 1991.

U.S. Women's Bureau, Department of Labor, http://www.dol.gov/dol/wb, 1999.

Vas, Kim Marie, Ed., *Black Women in America*. Sage, 1995.

West, Cornell. *Keeping Faith*. Routledge, 1993.

West, Cornell. *Race Matters*. Beacon Press, 1993.

Whitaker, Mark, "White & Black Lies." *Newsweek*, 53–63, November 15, 1993.

White, J L., and T.A. Parham. *The Psychology of Blacks: An African American Perspective*, 2d ed. Prentice-Hall, 1990.

Wilkerson, Isabel of the *New York Times*, reported in November 1990.

Williams, Gregory H. *Life on the Color Line*: The True Story of a White Boy Who Discovered He Was Black. Penguin Books, 1996

Williams, Walter. "Career and Opportunities." *Black Enterprise*, February 1992.

Willie, C.V. *A New Look at Black Families*. General Hall, 1976.

Woodson, C.G. *The African Background Outlined*. Negro Universities Press, 1968.

Woody, Bette. "Black Women in the New Service Economy." Working paper no. 196. Wellesley College Center for Research on Women, 1989

WSJ. "Black Managers Leaving the Fold," *Wall Street Journal*, 1A, May 6, 1992.

Young, V. "Family and Childhood in a Southern Negro Community." American Anthropologist 72, 269–299, 1977.

Online African American Culture

History. Library of Congress. This research resource includes exploration of the African American experience from colonization, slavery and abolition to the explosion of black arts in the 20ᵗʰ century: www.loc.giv/exhibits/african/intro.html

Civil Rights. Historic places of the Civil Rights Movement. A national register of historic sites relating to the civil rights movement, including an extensive history of the movement and the people and strategies behind it. Part of the National Park Service. www.cr.nps.gov/nr/travel/civilrights

African. American Joint Center for Political and Economic Policy. This organization's mission is to improve the lives of African Americans and other communities by expanding their participation in politics and public policy. ww.jointcenter.org.

Dates. Deeper Shade of Black. This website includes a search engine allowing you to investigate historical dates of interest: www.ai.mit.edu/people/isbell/HFh/black/bhist.html A timeline beginning in 1527 with events leading up to African colonization and slavery to 1997's Million Women March.: www.wanonline.com/blackhistory/1999/

Culture. A variety of subjects from film and music articles to news and career resources, chats and Web events: www.blackplanet.com

Business. A business-to-business site for minority businesses: www.minority.net

A minority-owned site that helps students prepare for exams: www.cyberstudy101.com AALI African American Leadership Institute, UCLA Anderson School of Management. www.anderson.ucla.edu/EEPaali.xml.

CHAPTER 8

Working with American Indians

We did not inherit the Earth from our ancestors.
We are borrowing it from our children.
Chief Seattle

What's it like to be an American Indian in the United States today? Is it possible for you to "walk around in their moccasins" for awhile? Just as American Indians are the source of that powerful adage that we use so often, their ancestral culture is the source of many powerful concepts rooted in the American culture today.

While American Indians represent only about 1 percent of people in the United States, they are one of the most important groups in terms of their cultural contributions. About half of them live on Indian lands, and the other half live and work in towns and cities. The American Indians you are likely to meet in the workplace have adapted to modern American urban living. And they also retain strong elements of their native culture. They are likely to participate in one or more American Indian organizations in the city, and to return to the Indian lands they call "home" for regular visits and ceremonies.

American Indian Man

Courtesy of Kevin Peterson/Photodisc/Getty Images.

American Indian Woman

Courtesy of Ranald Mackechnie/Photonica/Getty Images.

SELF-AWARENESS ACTIVITY 8.1: WHAT DO YOU BELIEVE ABOUT AMERICAN INDIANS?

Purpose: The purpose of this activity is to get in touch with your beliefs and stereotypes about this group of people to experience how judgmental beliefs affect your thinking and feeling processes to experience the ways in which your beliefs create your reality regarding other persons, even before you have any interaction with them.

Part I. What Do You Believe about American Indian Women?

Step 1. Associations

- Relax as deeply as you can.
- Close your eyes for a moment and take a few deep breaths.
- Now focus on the picture that symbolizes "American Indian woman"
- Imagine that you are this woman. Be American Indian woman.
- Notice any resistance to being this person—and any willingness.
- Notice words, images, thoughts, and feelings that come to mind as you are "seeing and being this woman."

Step 2. Negative Associations

- Next, as you focus on the picture, allow negative opinions to come up, perhaps some that you typically hold about American Indian women.
- Notice your *thoughts* as you see the person in this negative way. What *feelings*?

Step 3. Positive Associations

- Now, still focusing, allow positive opinions to come up, perhaps some that you typically hold about American Indian women.
- Notice your *thoughts* as you see the person in this negative way. What *feelings*?

Step 4. Insights and Writeup

- Now review this experience and write about it.
- When you first saw the picture, what thoughts and feelings came up? These may reflect your deepest responses to people from this group.
- Think about the differences in your thoughts and feelings when you consciously held a positive opinion versus a negative opinion.
- Write a few sentences about your feelings, thoughts, and insights.

Part II. Experimenting with Opinions about American Indian Men

Repeat the phases and steps in part I, this time focusing on the image of an American Indian man.

SELF-AWARENESS ACTIVITY 8.2: WHAT DO YOU KNOW ABOUT AMERICAN INDIANS?

Purpose: To see what you know about the issues covered in this chapter.

Instructions: Determine whether you think the following statements are basically true or false—and why. The answers will emerge in this chapter, and the summary at the end of the chapter focuses on these issues.

Sports-team mascots and logos pay tribute to American Indians' place in American history.

1. A monthly check comes from the government to all American Indians who enroll in the program.
2. The American Indian population is decreasing rapidly.
3. American Indians have been on this continent nearly 5,000 years.
4. American Indian political theories provided inspiration for key aspects of the United States government.
5. American Indian nations have always been accorded the sovereignty and rights of independent nations.
6. When Europeans arrived, American Indian tribal systems were run by warrior-chiefs.
7. A basic American Indian worldview is that all things in the natural world are connected.
8. American Indian planning tends to be short-range and in-the-moment.
9. A key American Indian value is maintaining lifelong relationships.

MYTHS AND STEREOTYPES VS REALITY

How do American Indians experience today's dominant American culture, and especially the workplace? First, they face a unique array of myths and stereotypes, either direct or implied by the people, organizations, and media that they encounter.

Overview of Myths and Stereotypes

Typical myths held by mainstream society about American Indians tell us they're vanishing relics of the past, but we honor the noble redskin savage with their chiefs, braves and squaws through our using them as team mascots, product logos, and themes for youth programs. Myths also say that they're lazy, getting welfare checks and gambling-casino money. Not only that, but if we run into an American Indian, he or she should be able to answer most of our questions about Indian history and lore.

Before we get into a detailed discussion of myths and stereotypes, check out this overview of attitudes and actions that American Indians tend to see as disrespectful or stereotypical. Compare it with the list that follows citing attitudes and actions they consider respectful and appropriate.

Attitudes and Actions Considered Disrespectful or Stereotypical

The following attitudes and actions are problematic:

- ABC books that have "I is for Indian" or "E is for Eskimo," counting books that count "Indians," the song "Ten Little Indians"
- Story books with characters like "Indian Two Feet" or "Little Chief"
- Media that shows American Indians as savages, primitive craftspersons, or simple tribal people, now extinct
- Dressing up as "Indians," with paper-bag costumes or paper-feather headdresses, and shouting out "Indian war whoops"
- Making "Indian crafts" using inauthentic methods and materials
- Manipulating words like "victory," "conquest," or "massacre" to distort the history of American Indian and Euro-American interactions
- Viewing as heroes only those American Indians who in the past aided Europeans or Euro-Americans
- Thinking that "the Indians" were here only for the benefit of the colonists
- Stressing the superiority of European ways and the inevitability of European conquest.
- Referring to American Indian spirituality as "superstition"

- Using insulting terms, such as "brave," "squaw," "papoose," "Indian givers," "wild Indians," "blanket Indians," or "wagon burners"
- Media showing American Indians speaking in either "early jawbreaker" or in the oratorical style of the "noble savage."
- Media that portrays Native women and elders as subservient to tribal warriors

Attitudes and Actions Considered Respectful and Appropriate

These kinds of attitudes and actions are appreciated:

- Finding out what it's like to be an American Indian by referring to books and materials written and illustrated by American Indians
- Honoring American Indian culture—including dress, dance, and ceremony—by avoiding arts and crafts that trivialize this culture.
- Recognizing American Indian heroes who fought to defend their own people.
- Exploring both sides of the historical relationship between American Indians and the colonists and what went wrong with it.
- Respecting and understanding the sophistication and complexities of American Indian societies and their continuity—with traditional values and spiritual beliefs connected to the present.
- Recognizing how American Indian societies coexist with nature in a delicate balance.
- Realizing that American Indian speeches, songs, poems, and writings show the linguistic skill of people who come from an oral tradition.
- Recognizing that American Indian women, elders, and children are integral and important to their societies
- Talking about the lives of American Indians in the present.
- Realizing that most American Indian adults are appropriate role models with whom American Indian children can identify.

Myth #1. American Indian cultures are vanishing relics of the past—with their redskin savages, chiefs, warriors, and squaws

This myth involves a cluster of false assumptions that tend to equate American Indians with relics of the past. They include some of the most disturbing and offensive stereotypes that American Indians must deal with—on a daily basis if they work in mainstream America.

Vanishing Myth

Urban American Indians are, in the minds of most Euro-Americans, an invisible population. This is partly due to the abstract and scattered nature of the community. A greater factor may be the stereotype of American Indians as a vanishing population fading away on remote reservations. In reality, American Indians are an expanding population. For decades they have been significantly younger and growing at a faster rate than the American population as a whole (Miller 2001).

Most urban members still have close ties with their tribe and make frequent visits to the reservation. American Indian culture is *not* synonymous with rural tribal culture. Nor is it true that urban American Indians are somehow not genuinely Indian. While there are certainly differences in the two types of settings, establishing rural versus urban as a defining characteristic of identity is not realistic for most. It serves to further "officially" alienate American Indian people from their homelands.

Offensive Terms

The terms we use are important. For example, "squaw" is a term many American Indians find offensive because they consider it an obscene reference to women. In the 19th century it came to mean "Indian woman available for sexual purposes." On the other hand, when Euro-American settlers used the term "squaw" to name places, they often had a milder definition in mind, primarily "Indian woman." Examples are Squaw Valley, the ski resort in California, and Squaw Peak, the mountain in Phoenix, Arizona.

Regardless of intent, places with names that offend large groups of people should be renamed. As of 2002, six states had banned the word "squaw" as an official geographic name. These states—California, Idaho, Maine, Nebraska, Oregon, and South Dakota—are in the process of renaming such sites (Osnos 2002).

For decades, some American Indians have also objected to satanic labels for lands they hold sacred, such as Devils Tower in Wyoming and Devils Lake in North Dakota (Osnos 2002).

Media Images

In the past, media images of fierce Indian warriors hellbent on bloody massacre were often found in Western movies. These alternated with images of the happy or noble savage, typified by the cigar store Indian "dummy" and romantic art prints of the early 20th century. (Salamando 2001). Today's media images tend toward the bronze muscular Indian warrior seen on the covers of popular romance novels, wearing only a breechcloth and feathered headband. The female version is Disney's doe-eyed "Indian Princess" Pocahontas. The media has appropriated these images, using them as commodities for selling their products and fulfilling various political agendas. (Gonzales 2001)

Myth #2. Sports-team mascots and logos honor American Indians' place in American history

Early in the 20th century, many U.S. sports teams began to adopt American Indian symbols, logos, and icons—using them as the names of their teams, stadiums, and mascots. These symbols are incorporated into uniforms, school songs, cheers, and other related items. Many American Indian groups have stated that they consider this practice to be generally disparaging or offensive. Examples include such team names as Braves, Cherokees, Chiefs, Fighting Sioux, Indians, Mohawks, Redskins, Savages, Tomahawks, and Warriors.

The Problem

Because many teams have chosen wild animals as mascots (Bears, Eagles, Panthers, Tigers), a less-than-human association is implied. Conversely, most of the team sponsors who adopted these names may have viewed American Indians as a noble and admirable group that they wanted to emulate. But the real issue is how American Indians feel about it. Group leaders complain about this practice for the following reasons:

They mock and trivialize American Indian culture.

They are not accurate representations of American Indians.

Even those that seem to be positive are romantic stereotypes that give a distorted view of the past. These false portrayals prevent people from understanding the true historical and cultural experiences of American Indians. They also encourage biases and prejudices that have a negative effect on contemporary American Indians. These references may encourage interest in mythical "Indians" created by the dominant culture, but they block genuine understanding of today's American Indians as fellow Americans (U.S. Civil Rights Commission 2001).

The American Psychological Association (APA 2005) has stated that the continued use of such symbols creates the following types of problems (based on numerous cited research studies)

- Undermines the ability of American Indian Nations to portray accurate and respectful images of their culture, spirituality, and traditions

- May be a violation of the civil rights of American Indian people
- Is a form of discrimination against Indigenous Nations that can lead to negative relations between groups
- Is a detrimental manner of illustrating the cultural identity of American Indian people through negative displays and/or interpretations of spiritual and traditional practices
- Is disrespectful of spiritual beliefs and values of American Indian Nations
- Is an offensive and intolerable practice to American Indian Nations that must be eradicated
- Has a negative impact on other communities by allowing the perpetuation of stereotypes and stigmatization of another cultural group.

The Solution

The APA has announced that it supports and recommends the immediate retirement of American Indian mascots, symbols, images, and personalities by schools, colleges, universities, athletic teams, and organizations. The APA also encourages the development of programs for the public, psychologists, and students to increase awareness of the psychological effects that American Indian mascots, symbols, images, and personalities have on American Indian communities.

About 1,500 high schools and nearly 100 colleges and junior colleges nationwide have Indian or Indian-related nicknames and mascots. Since 1969 more than 600 schools and minor-league teams have dropped nicknames deemed offensive by American Indian groups, according to a study by *Sports Illustrated*. However, officials of most major league teams have no plans to change their nicknames, including baseball's Atlanta Braves and Cleveland Indians, the National Hockey League's Chicago Blackhawks, the National Football League's Washington Redskins and Kansas City Chiefs, and National Basketball League's Golden State Warriors.

California lawmakers considered a bill in 2002 that would make it the first state to ban public schools that use American Indian mascots from purchasing athletic uniforms, equipment, or stationery that feature such mascots (Rizo 2002). The bill did not pass.

Myth #3. Indian theme programs pay homage to American Indian traditions

The YMCA Indian Guide Program uses American Indian themes to foster bonds between parents and preteen children. Up to a dozen parent-child pairs organize into neighborhood tribes that gather for such activities as crafts and storytelling. The tribes are organized into nations under the auspices of a local YMCA chapter and meet annually at camp-outs.

YMCA officials say about one-fourth of the 2,400 chapters nationwide have Y-Indian Guide programs, with a total enrollment of around 200,000. The program was founded in 1926, so the practices are deemed traditional by many members.

The Problem

Some American Indian leaders say these practices demean and trivialize their culture. They object to the use of cherished American Indian customs like wearing feather headdresses and using face paint—as well as the practice of some groups of using the burlesque "How-How" as a form of greeting during meetings (Yi 2001). Two points are crucial, according to American Indian objectors:

- The issue is about power: Who controls how a culture is displayed and perceived?
- The practice distills a complicated and diverse culture into superficial images that encourage stereotypes.

The issue of sensitivity toward American Indian cultures has proved a great challenge. "Sometimes, culture can be reduced so all that is left is the image and no content," said Paul Apodaca, a professor of American Indian history at Chapman University. "That is what the Native Americans are complaining about. They are saying, 'We are still here.' American Indians have the lowest per capita income. They have the lowest life expectancy. . . . It is not legitimate to entertain yourself with people who are socially disenfranchised and powerless."

Acting out Indian roles is seen in many types of Euro-American organizations, from fraternal orders, to the Boy Scouts and YMCA, to athletic teams and their fans. Philip Deloria says, "Indians are like no other group of people in this country. They are associated with the land and nature and reality and authenticity. Indians are the people who possess the ultimate meanings and the ultimate truths on what America is about" (Rave 2001). Deloria (1998) believes that American Indians have been both empowered and villainized as a result of such Euro-American co-opting of culture.

Results for American Indians

Pam Colorado, scholar from the Oneida tribe, gets to the root of the problem: "This process of taking our pride, our history, our spiritual traditions is ultimately intended to supplant American Indians, even in areas of our own culture and spirituality." She fears that in the end Euro-Americans will have complete power to define what is and what is not American Indian, even for American Indians. "We are talking here about a complete ideological and conceptual subordination" of the American Indian people in addition to the total physical subordination they already experience. Colorado believes that when this happens, the last vestiges of real American Indian society and rights will disappear. Euro-Americans will then claim "to 'own' our heritage and ideas as thoroughly as they now claim to own our land and resources" (Churchill 1999b).

Results for Euro–Americans

When Euro-Americans know only the "Indians" they see in movies and television, they tend to look upon the most profound and sacrificial efforts of contemporary American Indians and find them wanting, Confrontation on the level of ideas becomes impossible, and misunderstandings abound. Vine Deloria (1999) says the real need is to understand the nature of the deep gulf separating Indians and Euro-Americans—our great differences in how we understand and treat the land and creation.

Myth #4: American Indians are lazy and won't work

The myth is that American Indians sit around collecting government welfare checks—or they're getting rich because their tribe owns gambling casinos. In fact, American Indians do not receive welfare checks from any U.S. government agency. Not only that, they pay every kind of tax that immigration brought to them—personal property, income, sales, excise, etc. And less than 5 percent of tribes receive any casino money, an issue discussed later.

Some American Indians hold title to allotted lands and their own private land holdings, and on those lands they pay property taxes just like everyone else. American Indians do not pay property taxes on reservation trust lands because they do not own these lands, which are held in trust by the federal government. American Indians only have rights to use and occupy these lands, but they have no rights to ownership or conveyance of title. The U.S. government, through the Bureau of Indian Affairs, has a trusteeship relationship with American Indian tribes that centers around the protection of administration of Indian lands.

Myth #5: My American Indian coworker is an expert on Indian lore

Americans have a tendency to assume that just because certain people are members of a particular ethnic group, they therefore must be experts on every aspect of the culture of that group. Given the fact that there are about 500 active American Indian tribes, this assumption is obviously unrealistic. In addition, American Indians are increasingly raised in urban rather than rural tribal environments. Even though most urban members have tribal ties, they may not have extensive experiential information about even their own tribe, much less all the others.

CONNECTIONS TO THE PAST

American Indians have a long history. In fact, they lived in the Americas for perhaps 30,000 years before Europeans "discovered" them. Josephy (1998) notes that although radio carbon dates are not always infallible, enough have been accumulated to place these peoples unshakably in America much more than 10,000 years ago, probably more than 20,000 years ago, and perhaps more than 30,000 years ago.

Achievements

It's not easy for technologically-dependent Americans to grasp the achievements of early American Indians; for example (Weatherford 1988):

- Their architecture was unexcelled, especially in what is now Mexico, Central America, and Peru.
- The Mayan calendar was extremely accurate, based on their understanding of the stars.
- They used the zero in mathematics before it was discovered by the Arabs.
- They spoke a greater variety of languages than in all the Old World put together—between 500 and 1,000 in North America alone.
- Their medical system was far superior to European systems, including use of natural pharmaceuticals, sanitation, surgery, and other healing modalities.
- Their political system served as the primary model for the U.S. political system and affected political and economic thinking worldwide in coming centuries.

In almost every North American tribe, clan, or nation that we know about, the supreme authority rested in a group rather than in an individual (as in the European system). The League of the Iroquois is reflected in modern political systems throughout all of North America and much of Central and South America. The Iroquois League united five Indian nations that controlled the territory from New England to the Mississippi. It endured for centuries (Weatherford 1988). Examples of concepts borrowed from the Iroquois League are shown here, with U.S. counterparts in parentheses:

- Each nation (state) retains power over internal affairs and the League (federal government) regulates affairs common to all.
- The council (Congress) is composed of elected delegates from each nation (state).
- Warriors (military) may not serve as elected delegates.
- The council (Congress) can expand if new tribes or nations (population, states) are added.
- Only one delegate can speak at a time during deliberations.
- The "caucus" (Algonquin word) was used for informal discussion of issues.

When Europeans arrived in the Americas, the Indians were living in a fairly democratic condition. They were egalitarian, and they lived in greater harmony with nature. Modern ideas of democracy based on egalitarian principles and a federated government of overlapping powers arose from the unique blend of European and Indian political ideas and institutions between 1607 and 1776 (Weatherford 1988). The Iroquois and the Algonquians played an especially important role. This small spark of democracy leapt from nation to nation in the ensuing years (Paine 1791). Its concepts were adopted by the League of Nations in an attempt to move toward world peace after World War I, and the United Nations when it formed after World War II.

These concepts also inspired the peaceful resistance philosophy of Henry David Thoreau, and in turn those of Mahatma Ghandi and Martin Luther King. In this way, an egalitarian spark led to the end of colonialism throughout the world and the end of legal racism in the United States.

Important Events in American Indian History

Certain important events in American Indian history give us a sense of the dramatic impact that European exploration, colonialism, and expansion had upon American Indians. We see the decline and decimation of tribes and nations that had ruled their territories for millennia (NCAI)

1492	**Columbus.** "Discovers" America.
1500	**Sixty million Natives** in North America. Begin decline to about one million by 1900
1565	**First permanent European settlement.** St. Augustine, Florida
1607	**First permanent English colony.** Jamestown, Virginia.
1616	**Smallpox epidemic.** Ravages Natives along New England coast.
1619	**First slaves.** Arrive in Virginia from Africa
1620	**First New England Colony.** Mayflower arrives at Plymouth, MA
1636-37	**Pequot War.** With Puritans near New Haven, CT
1638	**First Reservations.** Established by Puritans near New Haven, CT
1769	**Spanish occupy California.** Establish the first missions that enslave Indians
1778	**First Indian Treaty.** Continental Congress with Delaware Indians
1789	**United States Constitution.** Ratified by the states; Indian rights are reaffirmed.
1790	**First Indian Law.** Regulating trade and land sales with Indians
1803	**Louisiana Purchase.** Lewis and Clark expedition. U.S. expansion westward.
1819	**First Federal Funds for Indians.** $10,000 to "civilize" the Indians
1824	**Bureau of Indian Affairs.** Established in War Department.
1827	**Cherokee Republic formed.** An attempt to avoid forced removal
1830	**Indian Removal Act.** Legalized removal of all Indians east of Mississippi River to lands west of the river, leading to "The Trail of Tears" of the 1830s
1837	**Smallpox epidemic.** Plains Indians succumb; foul play is suspected
1860s	**Education.** American Indian children taken away from parents, placed in far-away boarding schools to "kill the Indian in them" (through the 1930s). Learned about racial hierarchy and the work ethic, given industrial vocational training. In summer boys interned on farms or businesses, girls worked as maids
1868	**Sioux Treaty.** Agreement by Sioux to live within Black Hills reservation in return for U.S. agreement to set this land aside for the Sioux's exclusive use
1876	**"Custer's Last Stand."** U.S. troops decimated by Sioux warriors led by Sitting Bull and Crazy Horse at Little Bighorn, Montana, over incursion by gold seekers into Black Hills reservation
1886	**Apache defeat.** The last of the Arizona Apache warriors were captured, those led by Cochise in 1874 and those led by Geronimo in 1886
1887	**Allotment Act.** The buying and selling of Indian lands, leading to extensive land loss for American Indians
1890	**Sioux defeat.** Massacre at Wounded Knee in South Dakota, of a Sioux tribe led by the ailing Sitting Bull
1924	**Citizenship.** American Indians were "declared" citizens of the United States, without their requesting it or even knowing it
1934	**Indian Reorganization Act.** To restore to American Indians the management of their assets and to return to local self-government on a tribal basis. Some question its supposed purpose of gradual assimilation into the dominant society
1952-68	**Relocation and Termination Acts.** Designed to "terminate" tribes and treaty rights, break up the reservation system, and "relocate" tribal members from reservation land to jobs in urban centers.
1970s	**American Indian occupation of Alcatraz and Wounded Knee.** Sovereignty rights finally acknowledged in federal courts and by government action.
1978	**American Indian Religious Freedom Act.** To protect traditional religions and practices
1978	**Indian Child Welfare Act.** To protect families from removal of children by courts and welfare departments, and to re-establish parental rights.
1988	**Indian Gaming Regulatory Act.** The jurisdictional framework for gambling casinos.
1990	**Native American Graves Protection & Repatriation Act.** To return bones and cultural artifacts to the tribes.

Decimation: Virulent Epidemics and Buffalo Slaughter

Despite the sophistication of their medicine at the time the Europeans arrived, American Indians had neither the immune system nor remedies for European virulent diseases. "Never in human history have so many new and virulent diseases hit any one people all at the same time" (Weatherford 1988, p.195). Not only smallpox but bubonic plague, tuberculosis, malaria, yellow fever, influenza, and other major killers swept quickly through the land. European childhood diseases, such as measles, mumps, and whooping cough, decimated whole Indian villages. Because these germs were new to them, their immune systems were completely vulnerable. "Probably 90 percent of the American Indian population died within the first century after the European arrival . . . Both continents were left decimated again and again by wave after wave of the new diseases" (Weatherford 1988, p.195). Some of the tribes were also decimated by starvation. The Plains Indians depended on the meat and hide of the abundant buffalo for their economic survival. The Euro-Americans soon realized this, and some said very pragmatically, "Every buffalo killed is an Indian gone." So the slaughter of buffalo went on until the Indian economy was decimated.

Covenant Versus Contract

A major historical issue, and still an issue among American Indian tribes and nations, is the breaking of treaty after treaty by the U.S. government. Wambdi Wacasa (Deloria 1974) believes the problem stems from the fact that the Euro-Americans viewed the treaties as "contracts," while the American Indians viewed them as "covenants." In this context, a "contract" is an agreement made in suspicion, where the parties do not trust each other, and it sets "limits" to their own responsibility. A "covenant," however, is an agreement made in trust. The parties love each other and put no limits on their own responsibility.

Wacasa says the American Indian leaders made "Treaties with the Great White Father" and called them "covenants," sealing them with the smoke of the Sacred Pipe. The trouble began when the Great White Father, his lieutenants and merchants, looked on the treaties and called them "contracts." Thus began the conflict between cultures, based on legal and religious differences in worldviews. Conflict continued until the 1970s when the social climate was ripe for dramatic change. American Indian occupation of Alcatraz, 1969-71) and Wounded Knee (1973) provided the impetus needed for the U.S. courts and government to acknowledge the sovereign rights of American Indian nations and the individual rights of their members.

World War II: Comanche Messengers and Navajo Code Talkers

During World War II many American Indians joined the military and entered the defense industry (about 10,000 just from the Navajo tribe). Especially crucial were the Comanche messenger runners in the European theatre and the Navajo code talkers in the Pacific theatre.

About 400 Navajo enlisted men served as code talkers. They helped to devise a secret code for relaying top-secret messages. The code was based on the Navajo language. To begin with, they devised a coded alphabet that equated each letter of the English alphabet with a Navajo word, such as "A = ant = Navajo word for ant." They also developed an English-Navajo dictionary that used translations such as "hand grenade = potato = Navajo word for potato". Teams of talkers-translators were sent to crucial war zones to send and receive coded messages that gave accurate pictures of current reality and could be translated almost instantly.

The Japanese never broke the code, and it is credited with saving many lives and winning key battles, such as Iwo Jima. At the end of the war, the code talkers were still only privates. They were discharged with no awards or medals and no special recognition. For 23 years their work has a top-secret classification. They later formed the Navajo Code Talkers Association, and in 2000 the film *Windtalkers* starring Nicholas Cage finally recognized the invaluable contributions of these heroes. According to Major Howard M. Connor, communications officer for the Fifth Marine Division, "Without the Navajos, the Marines would never have taken Iwo Jima." They played a vital role in the war with Japan, from Guadalcanal to Iwo Jima to Okinawa (Southwest 2008).

CURRENT PROFILE: WHO ARE THE AMERICAN INDIANS?

Between 1 and 2 percent of all Americans are American Indians. Over 4.1 million people designated themselves as all or part "American Indian or Alaska Native" in the 2000 census. In the 1990 census nearly 2 million people checked off that designation. At first glance it appears that the population has nearly doubled in ten years. However, these figures are not directly comparable because of differences in the way race and ethnicity were tallied in the two counts. For the first time in history, people responding to the 2000 census had the option to choose more than one race (AP 2000).

Still, we know that the American Indian population is growing because census figures for 1980 and 1990 are comparable. In that period the American Indian population grew by 35 percent (Bureau of Indian Affairs). Carol Miller (2000) notes that for decades the American Indian population has been significantly younger and growing more rapidly than that of the nation as a whole.

An American Indian or Alaska Native is a person having origins in any of the original peoples of North or South America (including Central America), and who maintain tribal affiliation or community attachment (U.S. Census 2000). Here are some key population figures from the 2000 Census:

- Total U.S. population: 281,421,906
- American Indian (mainland) population: 2,475,956 = .9 or almost 1 percent
- American Indian and Alaskan Native population: 4,119,301 = 1.5 percent
- The Indian population is one of the youngest in the United States.
- Over 60 percent of American Indians are under 19 years of age—with a median age of 28, compared to 39 for Euro-Americans
- Household income is $32,100, compared to $42,200 for all Americans.
- 56 percent own their own homes, median value $81,000
- Poverty rate is 26 percent, compared to 10 percent for all Americans

Cherokee and Navajo are by far the most populous of the 558 tribes. About 730,000 people claim Cherokee affiliation, while nearly 300,000 claim to be Navajo. These are total figures that include members who do not live on tribal land.

Where Do They Live? From Rural to Urban

More American Indians live in California than any other state, according to the 2000 census, about twice as many as in Oklahoma and Arizona, the next most populous states. In fact, one-third of American Indians live in these three states, as indicated in Table 8.1. Population density is greatest in the Four Corners area, the junction of Arizona, Colorado, New Mexico, and Utah—site of many reservations.

TABLE 8.1: Where American Indians Live

Percent of American Indian Population	Number of American Indians	State of Residence
15%	628,000	California
10%	392,000	Oklahoma
7%	293,000	Arizona

About 45 percent live on reservations, while about half live in urban settings, so the rural-urban mix is roughly half-and-half. This is a dramatic change from the situation in 1900, when nearly all (over 90 percent) lived on reservations.

In popular culture, images of American Indians are still associated with Indian Lands. They are seldom associated with urban settings. Yet for many, those spaces are where they live out their lives—as they have done for several generations. They are frequently motivated to move off the reservation by the poverty there and the promise of greater economic opportunity in the city. This trend has been growing, especially since World War II (Miller 2001).

On tribal homelands a major source of identity is embodied in the land, and often in the old stories and songs that tie personal reality to time and place. In the urban context, American Indian organizations have come to powerfully represent "a place that is Indian" and are intimately tied to identity. Members are widely scattered and the network of relationships is frequently shifting (Lobos 2001). Still the network represents a distinct community that may be characterized as a social group in which:

- Community members recognize a shared identity
- Members have shared values, symbols, and history
- They have created and sustained basic institutions
- Consistent features of social organization are present, such as those related to social control and specialized gender- and age-related roles.
- Activities may include competitions, music festivals, and pow-wows.

The community is linked in many ways to people and places in American Indian homelands. Medicine people frequently come out to the city for ceremonies, and urban residents return to their homeland for ceremonies. They may go to attend funerals, see relatives, or to take children there for the summer. Many people return home for personal and spiritual renewal. Some older people decide to retire back home.

Demographic Problems

Since the 1970s Indian Nations have been treated by the federal government as "sovereign governments," recognized in the U.S. Constitution and in hundreds of treaties signed by U. S. Presidents. Tribal governments are responsible for providing a broad range of governmental services on tribal lands throughout the United States, including law enforcement, environmental protection, emergency response, education, health care, and basic infrastructure. This sounds impressive. The other side of that coin is that states do not always recognize federal policies, and the harsh realities of life in Indian country include poverty, violence, and health problems.

Poverty

The average household income of American Indians is $29,500, much lower than the $46,300 income of Euro-Americans, yet comparable to that of African American and Latino American families. The average poverty rate of 26 percent is the highest of all groups. Still, averages do not reflect the dramatic differences between incomes of urban and reservation Indians. Nearly 40 percent of all American Indian children live in poverty. The highest rate of unemployment is reported for American Indians. Here are some other indicators (Mann 2000):

- Poverty ranging from 50 percent to 67 percent on some reservations, versus the national average of 12 percent
- Unemployment rates as high as 75 percent on some reservations
- Many houses on reservations with no indoor plumbing, electricity or telephones
- Schools on reservations with outdoor toilets and no insulation in some of the coldest parts of the country
- Crime rates that are more than twice as high as the rest of the population.

Looking specifically at residents of the Navajo reservation, the largest in the United States, the 2000 Census indicates that the average income per person is $6,200, meaning that well over half the residents live in poverty and 43 percent are unemployed. Over two-thirds have no high school diploma; in fact one-fourth went no further than eighth grade and only 5 percent have a college degree. Their housing is generally without the typical utilities; For example, half the homes have no sewer or septic system, one-third have no plumbing at all, and about 15 percent have no regular source of water. Nearly half the homes consist of one or two rooms and half burn wood exclusively for heat. About 60 percent have no telephone, which implies not only lack of communication but the inability to install computer modems in homes. On some reservations, computers have been put into Boys and Girls Clubs, along with computer training, which is a beginning step. There is a long way to go.

Solutions can be difficult because of the endemic poverty. For example, since only 30 to 50 percent of people on reservations have telephones, donating computers that need telephone modems is problematic.

Casino Gambling Wealth?

Casino gambling is the answer to poverty on the reservation, according to the mainstream media. However, it is a source of important revenue for only 5 percent of the 558 federally recognized tribes. It is working for groups with reservations near urban or tourist centers, but not for tribes located in isolated places.

Violence

American Indians, both males and females, are victims of violent crime at more than twice the rate of the general population, and more than 4 times the rate of the Euro-Americans. And they are more likely to experience interracial violence. These shocking statistics were released by the Bureau of Justice Statistics (BJS 1999) in its first-ever study of American Indians and violence. The most common type of violence is "simple assaults," 56 percent, followed by "aggravated assaults," 28 percent, then robberies, 10 percent, and rapes, 6 percent. When American Indians are arrested for violent acts, about 70 percent had been drinking at the time.

A similar study that focused on American Indians living in South Dakota found that:

- The women experience 122 percent more violent incidents than the general population.

In rape cases, the offender was found to be Euro-American in 82 percent of cases.

Health Problems

The health of American Indians in general is much poorer than that of the average American, due in part to chronically under-funded health services. For example:

- Nearly half of them have a problem with alcohol and drugs.
- Youths are more likely to die from accidents and suicide than young people of other groups.
- Babies born with Fetal Alcohol Syndrome: 1 in every 99
- They suffer from diabetes at three times the rate of the rest of the population, and it is their sixth leading cause of death.
- They are more than twice as likely to lose a child to Sudden Infant Death Syndrome as the average American.
- Women have the worst survival statistics from breast cancer of any ethnic group, because of late detection.

Life Expectancy

Life expectancy of American Indians living on reservations rivals that of Third World countries, like so many other factors in their lives. For example, it is 56.6 years for Oglala Sioux men living on the Pine Ridge Reservation in South Dakota. For the women it is 66 years.

American Indians have higher death rates attributable to accidents, suicides, and homicides than the American population as a whole. Compared to the total American population, American Indians are:

- 578% more likely to die from alcoholism,
- 475% more likely to die from tuberculosis
- 231% more likely to die from diabetes

The second leading cause of death for young adults is directly linked to the effects of alcoholism.

COMMON THREADS: AMERICAN INDIAN WORLDVIEWS

There are between 500 and 600 American Indian tribes and nearly 300 distinct Indian Nations. Each has its own unique culture, language, history, dress, spiritual beliefs, and its own sacred places and rituals. Each is rooted in and part of the land out of which it grew.

During the 19th century mainstream attempts at religious persecution and cultural assimilation drove American Indian culture underground. Although it seemed to almost vanish from sight, many tribes were merely wrapping their practices in a veil of secrecy. Now these practices are more out in the open because there is new acceptance of them by the dominant society.

New communities, art, poetry and other cultural expressions are burgeoning. One reason for this is their unity in portraying a general "Pan-Indian" viewpoint, especially when talking with the media (Trosper 1995). This Pan-Indian viewpoint reflects the common threads among the various tribes regarding worldview, values, and customs. It does not deny the cultural diversity found among the American Indian tribes and nations.

The Cultural Differences Comparison

First, let's compare American Indian cultures with other major world cultures, using the 11 major types of cultural difference. We see that common threads of these cultures are generally perceived as follows:

1. Basic worldview: primarily I control
2. Relationship priorities: us-first, with respect for individual views
3. Social fabric: tight ties, earthy
4. Masculinity: moderately feminine (cooperating, connecting)
5. Equality/Status: egalitarian
6. Risk Orientation: moderately risk-taking
7. Decision Orientation: very long-term
8. Time Orientation: dive-right-in; cyclical, like the seasons; time is not money
9. Space: fairly close
10. Communication: direct
11. Economic: from agricultural dependent on reservations to industrialist independent and post industrial interdependent for urban populations

As you explore these common cultural threads of worldview, values, customs, and issues, keep in mind that within this tapestry there lies great diversity as well.

Spirit, Nature, and The Land in Everyday Life

Spiritual belief was and is part of every aspect of American Indian life. It is based on the sacred landscape that surrounds the tribe and therefore cannot easily be transported to other locations. For this reason, American Indian religion or spirituality is as diverse as the landscape of the tribes where it originated. It's not about abstractions, a set of beliefs, or a genetic tendency. It is an attitude toward the world, coming out of many experiences (Deloria 1999).

American Indian traditions of a holistic view of life include a constant relationship with the spiritual forces that govern the lives of humans. They traditionally viewed "religion as life" and lived in the presence of the holy through a cooperative partnership with nature and perceiving time through nature's cycles.

Vine Deloria (1999) believes that when American Indians were given a Western education, this spiritual awareness was greatly undermined. And when they lack a compatible religion, many American Indian young people turn to dependence on chemicals and drugs, an issue discussed later.

Worldview #1. Holistic View vs. Scientific View

The holistic thought system of American Indian tradition and the dominant Euro-American thought system are exclusive of each other. When either system of thought is confronted with the other, it must begin to adopt the characteristics of the other or reject it. Many American Indians have shattered the circle of their existence and have become linear and fragmented individuals, says Deloria (1999). And in recent years many Euro-Americans have begun to bring the linear dimensions of their existence into a circle of relationships. The interaction of these two trends is extremely important.

Holistic View

The American Indian holistic viewpoint centers around their land, the animals they share it with, and the living world in general, seen as the Great Circle of Life.

The Land. The essence of the Indian attitude towards peoples, lands, and other life forms is one of kinship relations in which no element of life can go unattached from human society. Lands are therefore given special status because they are Mother Earth for the peoples who live on them. Like a mother, the land shapes and teaches the people and, area by area, produces certain basic forms of personality and social identity which could not be produced in any other way

The Animals. "Kinship" cycles of responsibility exist between humans and the other species. The responsibility of the human species is to perform certain tasks with respect to each form of life we encounter, learning from them the basic structure of the universe, and ensuring that they receive in return the respect and dignity they deserve.

The essences or spirits of animals are used to inspire and inform human life. Also, many legends focus on animals, such as the mythical man who can transform into a "boogie bear," similar to "boogie man" legends of many cultures. Parents may employ this legend to convince children to be obedient. As young adults, the children may see the "boogie man-bear" as representing human duality, sometimes kind, other times vicious.

The Living World—Waking and Dream. Honoring the dignity of other life forms underlies the American Indian attitude toward the entire organic world. Humans are allowed to use them for food, but in return we must ensure that their sacrifice becomes a means of fulfillment. The struggle for dignity dominates American Indian spirituality, but the struggle is one of conferring dignity, not seizing it. The dream world is made part of the waking world. Dream catchers, shaped like spider webs, are used to help a person receive and remember an insightful dream. These insights are often used in making decisions.

The Great Circle of Life. The circle of these concepts forms a network of beliefs in which nothing derives from a cause-and-effect chain of circumstances. Everything becomes an aspect of everything else, distinguishable only by unique situations in which persons are called upon to respond to new conditions.

Holistic Knowledge and Relative Truths. American Indians not only view nature as the web of life, they see the entire world as highly interconnected. On the other hand, how that world was created, and other basic truths, depends on the experience of individuals and the collective experience of their communities. Knowledge is multifaceted and holistic, not dual or two-dimensional, as in the "true-false, right-wrong, them-us" worldview of most Euro-Americans (Trosper 1995). Truth is relative, emerging from ever-changing experiences. There are many possible truths, depending upon a person's tribal heritage and personal experiences. Also, new truths may emerge as human experiences evolve. Euro-Americans tend to believe in one set of absolute truths, found in the writings of accepted authorities, such as the Bible and scholarly journals.

Reflection. The fundamental distinctions between the American Indian holistic view and the Euro-American scientific view flow from the American Indian attitude of reflection. This is a special art that requires maturity of personality and identity—and a feeling of equality with the other life forms in the world. It consists of allowing wisdom to approach you, rather than seeking answers to self-generated questions. Reflection, then, is not viewed as a unique intellectual ability that leads to correct beliefs. Instead, reflection is how people grow and mature; it's a way of life that leads to a consistency in admirable behavior (Deloria 1999).

Scientific View

The implications of the Western scientific view are immense. Euro-Americans tend to assume that an objective knowledge of something totally describes it. They also assume that nothing really important has happened until it is reported in the media, or until they "discover" it.

If you see the world around you as a collection of objects for you to manipulate and exploit, you will inevitably destroy the world while attempting to control it, according to Deloria (1999). Not only that, but by perceiving the world as lifeless, you rob yourself of the richness, beauty, and wisdom to be found by participating in its larger design.

In order to maintain the Newtonian fiction that the world is dead—and the related belief that people who believe the world is alive have succumbed to primitive superstition—science must reject any interpretation of the natural world that implies that nonhumans can feel or communicate. Science insists, at a great price in understanding that observers must be as detached as possible from the events they are observing. Such "pure science" establishes the knowledge needed for technological advances.

Deloria notes that in a capitalist economic system, whoever supplies the money determines the technology. This means that science, as it's applied, is never really for the good of humankind, but instead for the good of the financial elite or the military.

The Contrast

The scientific view contrasts sharply with American Indian views—for example, that humans must participate in events and not isolate themselves. American Indians obtain knowledge from birds, animals, rivers, and mountains that is inaccessible to modern science. Being attuned to their environment, they traditionally could find food, locate trails, protect themselves from inclement weather, anticipate coming events, and keep themselves healthy. This is because they understood how all things are related. This knowledge is available to anyone who lives primarily in the natural world, is reasonably intelligent, and respects other life-forms for their intelligence. A comparison of Euro-American and American Indian medicine is shown in Table 8.2, which is a good example of the contrast between Western scientific method and the American Indian holistic natural method.

Perhaps the recent intense interest that many Euro-Americans show in American Indian spirituality reflects their intense longing for a sense of reality that is grounded in their inner experience Deloria (1997, 1999).

Table 8.2: Comparison of Euro-American and American Indian Medicine

Euro-American Medicine	American Indian Medicine
Focus on pathology and curing disease.	Focus on health—healing person and community.
"How can we destroy this disease?" An adversarial approach.	"What can the disease teach the patient? Is there a message or story in the disease?"
Investigate disease with "divide and conquer" strategy, looking for microscopic causes.	Looks at big picture—causes and effects of disease in physical, emotional, social, spiritual areas.
Intellect is primary—medical practice based on scientific theory found in books.	Intuition is primary—healing based on spiritual truths from nature, elders, spiritual vision.
Fosters dependence on medication, technology, the medical system.	Empowers patients with confidence, awareness, tools to take charge of own health.
Emphasizes expertise of the individual physician.	Therapy often involves participation of family and community.
Health history focuses on patient and family: "Did your mother have cancer?"	Health history includes the environment. "Are the salmon in your rivers ill?"

Source: Kenneth Cohen. *Honoring the Medicine,* 2003

Worldview #2. Cooperative Harmony with Nature

Most tribes share the idea that humans should live in harmony with their surroundings. American Indian spirituality demands respect for the natural world. Failure to preserve balance in human interactions with nature can be dangerous. Conversely, Christian spirituality has generally allowed humans to dominate the natural world. The Garden of Eden origin myth has been used politically to justify this domination (although some Christians believe that "dominion" implies harmonious stewardship). The practical consequences of these two different mindsets can be seen in the environmental preservation practiced by pre-Colombian societies, compared with the environmental destruction inflicted by Euro-American society ever since. (Trosper 1995)

Worldview #3. Time as Cycles

American Indians view time as polychromic and cyclical. This means their focus is often multifaceted, and their primary framework consists of nature's cycles and processes. The rhythms of night and day, the lunar month, the seasons of the year, and the growth phases of plants and animals form the time framework most important to them.

- They tend to relax into the flow of the natural rhythms around them, living in "Indian time."
- They may give attention to many things at once.
- They may be easily distracted from activities, which are therefore subject to interruptions.
- They are much more committed to people and human relationship than to tasks.
- They may change plans often and easily.
- How prompt they are for appointments depends on the situation and the personal relationships involved.

This contrasts with the Euro-American sense of monochronic linear time. The tendency here is a single focus on one task or item at a time, breaking time up into distinct minutes, hours, days, years, and similar components, which make up a timeline that moves forward from past to present to future.

- They focus on doing one thing at a time.
- They concentrate on the task.
- They are committed to the task.
- They tend to adhere to plans and take time commitments seriously. In business, at least, "Time is money."

A summary and comparison of American Indian and Euro-American worldviews and values is shown in Table. 8.3.

COMMON THREADS: AMERICAN INDIAN VALUES

The common threads of American Indian values stem from their holistic, harmonious cooperation-with-nature worldview. They believe that people are basically good, communities should be close-knit, putting the group first while respecting individual views, lifelong personal relationship based on sharing and helping, a focus on action, and long-range planning that considers the impact of today's decisions on at least the seventh generation of the future.

Value #1. People Are Basically Good

Tribal religions have traditionally emphasized hospitality, inclusiveness, and even adoption of people needing and wanting shelter within the tribe. This value has carried over to present times. The traditional

Table 8.3: American Indian and Euro-American Worldviews and Values

American Indian Worldview & Values	Euro-American Worldview & Values
Nature:	**Nature:**
Humans must live in harmony with nature, preserve human-nature balance.	God gave humans dominion over the natural world. Use the land and all resources
Who We Are	**Who We Are**
A stable people; build home; identify with land	A very nomadic people; leave home; use land
Role of Tradition	**Role of Tradition**
Conservative; remember the past	"Progressive," break with the past
Knowledge–Holistic	**Knowledge–Compartmental**
Focus on the whole, parts secondary; web of life means all is connected, related	Focus on establishing objective facts, repeatable processes, fit into a whole.
Truth–Relative	**Truth–Absolute**
Many possible truths, grounded in experience, which evolves, multi-dimensional	One truth (true-false) found in accepted written authority, personal experience not objective
Holistic View	**Scientific Rational View:**
Experience and relate to a living universe	Reduce all things to objects
Humans must participate in events	Observers must be detached from events
Holistic, integrated web of life	Linear step-by-step reasoning
Time	**Time**
Multi-focus, nature's cycles	Single-focus, linear timeline
Education	**Education**
For wisdom in the why of things	For skill in manipulating things
Planning	**Planning**
Consider decision's impact on 7th generation of descendants. Future, present of equal importance; both more important than past	Ideal: focus on future, long-range planning. Reality: focus on present gain, short-range performance and profitability
Expressing Self	**Expressing Self**
Doing first, then becoming, then being	Expression primarily through doing
Relationships: Collectivist	**Relationships: Individualist**
Sharing, helping relatives comes first; lifelong relationships are common	Individual success, acquisition comes first; short-term relationships are common
Use of Space	**Use of Space**
People more important than privacy	Follow rules of privacy and consideration Private property; seldom borrow or lend
Borrow and lend things often and easily	
Workplace Orientation	**Workplace Orientation**
Charismatic leader represents group consensus, group sets goals that value members' goals, individuals adjust their goals. Decision-making by group consensus	Authoritarian hierarchy: top management sets company goals, individuals accept, subordinate their personal goals. Decision-making by hierarchical authority

assumption is that people are not naturally malevolent and that they intend to deal honestly. This has been a highly valued belief within most tribes. Vine Deloria (1999) says that treaty documents clearly show that, while the United States was busy perpetrating frauds upon the tribes, American Indian spokesmen were clinging to the belief that Euro-Americans were only trying to help them.

Value #2. Close-Knit and Collectivist: The Group Comes First

High-context communities are the essence of American Indian culture. The communal experiences of the group form the collective reality they experience—their key source of knowledge and truth. They go into situations and relationships with much information about the common history, worldview, values, and customs they share. American Indians are generally more collectivist than individualist. It is difficult to make generalizations about how they view the group versus the individual or the "superior" in relation to the "subordinate." Tribes vary from elder-oriented societies among the Pueblos to the extremely individualistic Sioux. In the pan-Indian synthesis, however, the group orientation predominates.

The goals of the group have a greater pull on modern American Indians than do their own personal goals. However, respect for an individual's right to pursue his or her own course is also high. Individuals are expected to moderate their goals according to the goals of the group, which will have set its group goals with the individuals' personal goals as one of the factors (Trosper 1995).

The Euro-American orientation is something of a paradox to American Indians. Individualism is clearly the primary mode, but on the job, orientation to superiors in fact dominates. Most organizations are highly structured, with the presumption that the boss's orders are to be followed, often with little consultation with the workers. Individuals are expected to subordinate their goals to those set by the top managers of a hierarchy. The only option a worker has is to move to another organization, where the hierarchy will again dominate. The superior or hierarchical principle governs work relationships, while the individualistic mode governs personal life decisions (Trosper 1995).

Value #3. Personal Relationships: Sharing and Helping

American Indians believe that sharing and being helpful to one's relatives is a kind of divine command. They perceive that most Euro-Americans view as a divine command the competition for goods and the inheritance and accumulation of goods. This difference in thinking has made it difficult for American Indians to move into Euro-American society.

Lifetime Relationships

For American Indians, the importance of this group relationship value means that agreement in a group is by consensus and leadership of the charismatic sort is preferable in most cases to that of a bureaucracy. The relative-truth mindset means that they accept a diversity of ideas (truths) within an organization's subunits. Still, the holistic view means that the organization as a whole is responsible for outcomes. Group relationships are, therefore, very important. Unity is sought as well as community. For Euro-Americans, whose ties to family, clan and community are diminishing, it may be difficult to understand the importance of this value for American Indians (Trosper 1995).

At a personal level, lifetime relationships predominate. Therefore, personal boundaries tend to be loose and flexible. For example, most American Indians are less concerned with privacy than with maintaining good personal relationships with family, friends, and business associates. Personal property is for their own use, but also for sharing and helping, so they easily lend and borrow things.

Extended Family

American Indians view ethical relationships in a more structured manner than Euro-Americans, who tend to focus on an overall ideal of equality. American Indian societies allocate duties, privileges and respect according to a unique system of family relationships. All older people are grandfathers and grandmothers. All the men and women are brothers and sisters. Even strangers may occupy the place of cousins within the network of specific relatives who must show concern for one another.

Apart from participation in this network, American Indians believe a person simply does not exist. But within this network, attitudes and behaviors must be expressed in ways particular to each situation and relationship, not in general and often unfulfilled rules of conduct. (Deloria 1999).

Group Motivation

Following directly from this ethic is the American Indian understanding of human personality and the meaning of life. If we are required to show respect and create dignity for others around us, then this respect and dignity cannot be simply a surface admission of social status. Dignity can be given even to the unworthy with devastating irony—so that people within the community can see in the most precise fashion whether or not the honored person in fact deserves such praise. Such lavish but undeserved praise can be more damning than an insult.

Tribal members work hard to deserve the dignity that the community gives them. Nothing would be more embarrassing than to be praised and honored when you are failing to perform according to expectations. Giving dignity therefore encourages individuals to deserve the praise they receive (Deloria 1999).

The purpose of this type of group action is to motivate people to become better. For example, when group leaders admire a woman for being wise, she's encouraged to try to become wiser. When they salute the man who is brave, that motivates him to become braver. When they honor a couple as good parents, they work to become better parents.

Group Leadership

How do leaders emerge? It begins with intensely wanting to deserve the respect and dignity that their family and the society accord them. This produces an attitude of quiet reflection, which grows with the passage of years and the accumulation of experiences. And the group is always an intimate part of individual experiences. Each community has its collective memory of past events and its common knowledge of the behavior of people within that immediate history. Over decades of community life, a leader emerges as the community recognizes in his or her continual activities a sense of consistency, commitment to the community, and wise decision-making.

As people come to deserve the respect and dignity that they receive, the community forms around the time-tested people of substance. In most American Indian communities in the old days, the most respected person was the one who gave freely of physical wealth, who showed a concern for the unfortunate, and who allowed weaker members of the community to rely on him or her. There was also an emphasis on doing things for the good of the community. For example, in some California tribes a hunter was not allowed to eat from his kill, which showed that he was killing for the community and not for personal gain.

Value #4. Self-Expression Mode: Doing, Being or Becoming

Are people in a culture most likely to express themselves spontaneously as the mood strikes them (the *being* mode)? Or through accomplishments (the *doing* mode), with achievements being most important? Or is it most important to pursue self-development (the *being in becoming* mode)? Both American Indians and Euro-Americans tend to emphasize a *doing* orientation, ranking *doing* above *becoming*, and *becoming* above *being* (Trosper 1995).

Value #5. Decision-Planning Mode: Long-Range vs. Short-Range

Many tribes share the Iroquois idea that when making important decisions and plans, the impacts on the seventh generation of descendants must be taken into account. Tribal leaders are concerned with the opinions their great-grandchildren will have about the stewardship decisions that they, the elders, make today. The present and the future are therefore seen equally, and are more important than the past. (Trosper 1995)

Euro-Americans, in contrast, look to the future, but in action, they tend to be present oriented. For example, the modest savings and multiple debts of the typical family do not reflect great concern for the future. This individual tendency is reflected in the national debt. Long-term environmental consequences of decisions are usually ignored or given lip service, especially by managers and executives who stand to profit today. The idea of preparation for the future underlies the emphasis on the education of youth, on retirement programs, and on the organization of capital markets. This future orientation, however, refers in most cases only to one person's lifetime. Euro-Americans may care about their children's future, but later generations are rarely a major concern when actual decisions are made (Trosper 1995).

COMMON THREADS: CEREMONIES, RITUALS, AND CUSTOMS

Most American Indian ceremonies are religious rituals performed for specific purposes. Some, such as Pow Wows, are more social in nature. Others, such as healing ceremonies, incorporate spiritual beliefs with a medical system and techniques handed down through the ages.

Types of Ceremonies

Two aspects of American Indian life are important to remember when exploring their religious ceremonies. First, spirituality is an integral part of all aspects of an American Indian's life. Most tribes have medicine men and women, sweat lodges, and vision quests to help members follow a spiritual path. Second, while most tribes traditionally did hunting and gathering, many were also advanced farmers, cultivating corn, beans, squash, and other crops. In one region tobacco was raised. Many ceremonies focus on these economic activities.

Ceremonies by Medicine Men and Women

Also called rainmaker and healer, these members have much in common with native shamans throughout the world. Both men and women become such healers, although in most tribes women are not eligible until after menopause. The knowledge is handed down by family members and other spiritual leaders in a lifelong learning process.

Religious Ceremonies

Many ceremonies center around the supernatural and often last a day or more. In most regions, there are ceremonies for general well being, world renewal, and thanksgiving Specific ceremonies are for the hunt, the sacrifice, and personal spiritual growth. Today ceremonies are held for birthdays. baptisms, healings, and for welcoming the harvest.

Hunter–Gatherer and Sacrificial Ceremonies

Hunter-gatherer rituals involve envisioning success in the hunt, plentiful foods, and fertile game animals. Sacrifices are often offered to the spirits. Tobacco is by far the most common offering. American Indians smoke it in pipes or tubes, offer it loose, or give the smoke as a gift to supernatural beings. Food, clothing, and adornment are also sacrificed. Individual piles of first fruits dedicated to all types of spirits are quite typical. Warriors, before going on an expedition, throw food in the fire or blow tobacco smoke in the air. The Iroquois sacrificed a white dog.

Sacred site ceremonies

Among the duties which must be performed at the Holy Places are ceremonies the people have been commanded to perform in order that the earth itself and all its forms of life might survive. These rituals are performed so that the sun may continue to shine, the earth prosper, and the stars remain in the heavens. The rituals symbolize the importance of human participation in the web of life. The underlying theme is one of gratitude expressed by human beings, on behalf of all forms of life. They complete the largest possible cycle of life, ultimately representing the cosmos in its specific realizations becoming thankfully aware of itself.

The Sun Dance: A Religious Ceremony

The Sun Dance is once again celebrated by northern plains tribes, following many decades of prohibition by the federal government. The preparation of the lodge or tipi and ceremonial raising of it lasts one to four days. The ceremony itself lasts eight days. Dancers blow whistles in many performances. Voluntary self-laceration is common in some groups. Male dancers may fast and then during the dance tear their flesh against the tethers of a sun dance pole or tow a gang plow of bison skulls from pierced rods in their backs. They endure much pain. Women dance in support.

For many of the American Indians who participate, the ritual is all about learning principles of balance and living in harmony with an interrelated universe. To many people, these are especially attractive aspects of Indian spirituality. It speaks to the universal questions:

What am I meant to do on this earth?

What is the right behavior? How do I live here?

The sun dance is also seen as the point of entry into a source of power, energy and supernatural beauty. It's not meant to be a spectator sport. It draws people into it. It reflects a way of life, a way of thinking, a spirituality that is integral to the way the person lives. Life is holistic, seamless, and not divided into categories and compartments.

Because of its dramatically painful elements, the Sun Dance has attracted all kinds of sensation-seekers who come to the dance merely to view the unusual. The ensuing publicity can overshadow the sacredness of the ceremony. This has raised the issue of whether to allow outsiders to participate.

Each sun dance is carried out in accordance with the vision of the person conducting it; therefore, some groups prohibit non-Indians from participating, while others welcome them. Strict orthodox Lakota, Dakota and Nakota members say it should be attended by American Indians only because sharing it with other people would risk commercializing it. Others say, "We have to share it with the rest of the world to help them. It was given by the Creator to help all of us . . . This religion leaves room for individual truth." (Harriman 2000).

In some traditions, the red, white, black and yellow colors on the sun dance pole represent the "four races" of mankind. Because those colors are there, people can come to the sun dance if they come in a good-hearted, sincere way The kind of people they do *not* want are the ones who go home, set up a toll-free telephone line and a Website, and announce to all, "I've been trained as a Lakota spiritual leader."

The Pow Wow: A Uniting Renewal Ceremony

A Pow Wow was originally a spring event to celebrate the seasonal renewal of new life. People congregate to sing, dance, renew old friendships and form new ones. Pow Wows are also significant opportunities to honor people and traditions. The term "Pow Wow" is traced to the Algonquin language (Pow Wow 2000).

Pow Wows are still very much a part of the lives of many American Indians around the country and may be held at several locations during peak periods, from June to September. Many families "go on the circuit," camp out, and enjoy the traditional activities. Competitive singing and dancing, relatively recent changes, are often featured. The circle, an important symbol, is used extensively in Pow Wows. The dancers are in the center circle, the drums and the audience are encircled around them, and the concession stands surround the entire gathering. The Pow Wow brings the circle of people closer to family, friends and the comfort and vitality of their culture.

The Grand Entry is the parade of dancers that opens each session of Pow Wow dancing. The Eagle Staff is carried into the circle, followed by the national, state, and tribal flags. Title holders from tribal pageants and invited dignitaries come next. The men and women follow, with traditional dancers first, then grass dancers, fancy shawl dancers, and jingle dress dancers, followed by junior boys and girls, then the little boys and girls. Next comes a flag song, an invocation blessing the gathering, and the positioning of the flags. The dancing then begins.

Dancers perform clockwise or sun-wise around the arbor. Their outfits (the term "costume" is seen by some as derogatory) and their steps let the audience and other participants know who they are and what they can do.

Songs are created and performed for different events, such as grand entries, dance categories, and honoring ceremonies. While they differ in tempo, words and emotions, all Pow Wow songs follow a similar structure. There are songs for all occasions: honor songs, veteran songs and war party songs. Many pre-reservation songs have been put aside in favor of a flood of new ones. Some groups sing only their own songs, while others borrow songs and perform their own as well. The songs are tape recorded (not written) and then learned by singers and dancers.

Honor songs are requested to honor a person such as a returning son or a deceased relative or other person. Some people have their own honor songs while others use generic ones. A drum from the honored person's home or a favorite song may be requested.

Drums may be handed down in the family, or they may be donated to a group. The drum is more than a musical instrument to those who own and play it. It has a life of its own. Some drum groups have ceremonies for getting their drums blessed and named. The drum is regarded as having its own powerful spirit. Gifts are made to it and some have their own sacred medicine pipes. In some traditions the drum symbolizes the heartbeat; in others, the powerful medicine of thunder. The term "drum" also refers to the drum group itself.

The men's traditional dance began when war parties would return to the village and dance out the story of a battle and when hunters would dance their story of tracking prey. The dancers are often veterans and carry items that symbolize their status as warriors—shields, weapons, honor staffs and medicine wheels. Movements imitate the life journey of birds and animals.

The women's fancy shawl dance is similar in style to the men's, but may involve more movement, especially spinning. Footwork is the chief element. Dancers wear a fancy shawl over a simple dress with matching leggings and beaded moccasins

The jingle dress dance is said to come from a holy man's dream, where four women performed a graceful dance wearing dresses covered with hundreds of tiny cone-shaped metal "jingles." The dance spread to many tribes.

An intertribal dance is one where everyone, including tourists, is welcome to join in. No regalia is needed. This is not so much a particular kind of dance as it is a chance for everyone to dance.

The eagle feather is sacred to most American Indians. Therefore, when one falls from a dancer's outfit, the Pow Wow stops and a ceremony is performed to restore the feather's lost power for good. For example, four men, usually veterans, dance around the feather from four directions and usually attack four times to retrieve it. Four is a sacred number for all tribes.

The give-away is thought to be universal among American Indians. Unlike societies where one expects gifts for accomplishments, the American Indian society holds that a person being honored should provide gifts. It is said that the chief was the poorest man in the village. Charged with the welfare of his people, honored by them, the chief gave away blankets, horses, food and whatever else the people might need. Today, giveaways by people being honored, or in honor of someone else, are common at Pow Wows.

Social Customs

Important social customs determine the rules for such essentials as marriage and family, work roles, property rights, dispute resolution, decision making, and political organization.

Marriage

In the Plains and Northwest tribes, the man presents a gift to the parents of the bride, called bridewealth or brideprice. This gift represents acknowledgement that the parents are losing their daughter's services and should be compensated for loss and for their time and effort in raising her. This gift also establishes the rights of the man's kin line to the children of the union.

Patrilineal descent means that membership in a tribe or group is only through father-to-children. Matrilineal descent means it's only through mother-to-children.

Some tribes allowed polygamy, but monogamy predominated everywhere. Polyandry (women having more than one mate) was very rare, usually within a family.

Women's Status

Women hold a respected place in nearly all communities. Their opinions and suggestion are highly regarded, though they are usually not decision makers. In the Iroquois tribes, women nominate and depose the chiefs, which gives them much political power.

Education and Social Control

The family takes main responsibility for the raising of the young, their education and welfare. The most powerful control comes from the spirit world. The tribe might reward members with prestige, praise, or gifts. It might punish with ridicule, gossip, shame, and guilt. Traditionally, other penalties were to take away the transgressor's weapons, banish him from the hunt, or confine him to the camp or the tipi. Very rarely was the death penalty imposed—only for such extreme acts as premature hunting or stampeding of the buffalo that endangered the whole tribe's food supply. This was a crime against society.

Property rights

Tribal families can gather, hunt, and fish within the tribe's territory. Tribal leaders assign garden areas to individuals or groups of kinfolk for cultivation. Traditionally, land was almost never owned by individuals. Kin groups or communities had rights to use land, but there was no concept of private ownership of real estate. Individuals owned personal property, but no one could "own" Mother Earth.

Work Roles

Women traditionally grew the crops and carried the family possessions when moving to another camp. They gathered wild plant foods, cured hides, and raised the children. They were very self-reliant. The men were well aware of the women's contributions and considered them indispensable. Men did the hunting and protected tribal rights.

War

American Indians settled internal disputes according to a regular pattern most of the time. When it came to solving intertribal conflict, there was not a standard way used by all tribes. Hunting territory disputes could be a cause of battles and skirmishes. Wars were not waged for expansion or imperialism. Wars for territorial expansion were very rare north of Mexico. Some tribes became more warlike after they got horses from Europeans. Raiding for captives, horses, and glory was the source of most aggression. Nowhere were there fulltime soldiers or war-makers.

Political Organization

"Nation" is not really the most accurate term for North American Indian organization. Tribes were large groups of clans or villages speaking the same language, integrated by intermarriage and councils of representatives from each clan.

Tribes were the most common form of organization and had as many as 5,000 members. The leader is more democratic than authoritarian. The leader listens to the council. Members follow the leader by choice. The leader is chosen for wisdom.

Chiefdoms were found in a couple of instances, where the chief had more authority and there was some hierarchy among people and families.

Bands or villages, which were independent, also existed, especially in California.

AMERICAN INDIAN ISSUES

In the past, the fact that American Indians belonged to many tribes and nations that were scattered throughout North America made political consolidation practically impossible. In the 20th century, a political American Indian movement emerged to campaign on behalf of their issues. This pan-Indian movement emerged in urban areas, where people of different tribes came together for mutual help and support.

Here are some key American Indian issues listed on the website of National Congress of American Indians (NCAI). These apply especially to Indian lands and tribes: 1) means testing, 2) cultural resources and historic preservation—including religious freedom, protection of sacred sites, and selling of fake "Indian" products and services, 3) economic development, including hunting and fishing rights and tribal gaming, 4) digital divide (see www.Indiantech.org), 5) federal appropriations for Indian programs, 6) housing, 7) Indian education, 8) land into trust, 9) nuclear waste, 10) tribal sovereign immunity, and 11) anti-defamation and mascots. We'll focus on the first three of these issues plus the alcoholism problem.

An issue that concerns both rural and urban American Indians is the question of who is considered an American Indian for government purposes. Also important is the question of how to preserve their cultural heritage—including their sacred sites, religious practices, privacy, and authentic arts and crafts. Economic issues concern hunting and fishing rights and commercial development on Indian lands, including gambling casinos. Alcoholism is the major social-health issue.

Issue #1. Who Is American Indian? And Who Decides?

While tribes have the exclusive right to determine who their members are, the general question of whether a person is an American Indian or not is more complex. Who is legally entitled to decide which persons can identify themselves as American Indians? The issue has implications for determining who has access to government programs designed to assist American Indians. This is an emotionally charged topic anywhere in Indian Country. It includes questions about

- self-identity
- externally-imposed identity
- shifts in identity (which may occur over a lifetime and which urban American Indians view as situationally appropriate)

The Federal Government "Blood" Requirement

The federal emphasis is on ancestry as the outstanding defining criteria for recognition as an American Indian and qualification to receive government services. This is represented in a "blood quantum" model, which is a much narrower, limiting criteria than that found in urban American Indian communities. To prove that they are officially "Indian," applicants need a "Certificate of Degree of Indian Blood." The degree of Indian blood has usually been determined by whether persons or their ancestors were enrolled in a federally-recognized Indian tribe, though persons from terminated or state-recognized tribes have sometimes been approved. The federal government makes the determinations for purposes of issuing the certificates, with at least one-quarter blood being the traditional requirement. On the other hand, existing federally-recognized American Indian tribes make their own determinations of blood degree for membership in the tribe (Stockes 2000).

Fallacy of the "Blood" Requirement

Ward Churchill (1999a) points out that in 1920 nearly 57 percent of American Indians were classified as "full-blood," but by 1970 about two-thirds of the marriages of those on the tribal rolls were to non-Indians. As a result, only 60 percent of births were to parents registered as having any Indian blood at all. The number of "full-blood" births had dropped to almost none. In a sense, to adhere to quantum requirements in the face of such realities is to engage in a sort of statistical extermination of American Indians.

Urban Community: Fluid Membership Requirements

The view of American Indian urban communities is much more fluid than that found on tribal homelands that are structured by federally imposed criteria. Membership here is agreed upon through informal consensus. American Indians feel more comfortable with this consensus approach than with the written document approach. Members have a shared understanding of the social boundaries of the American Indian community, as well as membership within the community. These are fluid, however, and are regularly reviewed and negotiated. In essence these people are asserting, "I am Indian because I say I am. I am Indian because you know me and my family and see me participate in the community. I am Indian because I know what it is to be Indian: the customs, the humor, the shared history, the struggle that are a part of who we all are" (Lobo 2001). In urban areas, therefore, American Indian identity is defined through:

Ancestry: Does a person have American Indian relatives and ancestors, and function as a member of an American Indian extended family?

Cultural knowledge: Is the person knowledgeable of the culture of their people and of those values and social expectations shared within the urban American Indian community?

Indian community participation: Does the person attend Indian events and activities in the American Indian community and contribute to the community well-being?

Appearance: (to a lesser extent) Does a person look "Indian"?

American Indians want to identify themselves by their own standards. Many see this as the key to offsetting the stereotypes found in mainstream media, education, and literature. They marry outside of their ethnic group, but many remain connected to their communities in many different ways. They are diverse in their interests, level of tribal connection, and urban community connection, as are people of other ethnic groups. Bottom line: Urban members are still American Indian.

Stricter Membership Requirements

Federal officials, people who still live within the tribal homeland, and others often look to a stricter definition of who is American Indian. For example, they may add one or more of these criteria to those offered by the typical urban community (Gonzales 2001):

Residence: On an Indian reservation, either currently or previously

Enrollment: In a federally-recognized Indian tribe

Genetics: Documented Indian blood quantum—the higher the percentage, the greater one's "Indianness"

Appearance: Stereotypically identifiable Indian features or style of dress—long, straight black hair, dark eyes, brown skin, chiseled features, high cheek bones

Language: Ability to speak a tribal language or to demonstrate the use of Indian colloquialisms, such as "mother earth," "the great spirit," animals as "the two-legged, the four-legged, the winged"

Issue #2. Preservation of Cultural Heritage

The general issue of preserving cultural heritage lies at the heart of several other more specific issues, such as who decides who is Indian, and how to protect religious freedom, sacred sites, sacred lands, religious customs, and tribal art and lore. Let's begin with dilution and dispersion away from the tribal homelands. This is accelerated by intermarriage with non-Indians—and affects "who is American Indian."

Prior to 1500

Before Europeans arrived on American soil, "intertribal" marriages were fairly common. Occasionally even whole societies were merged. These processes, over time, wiped out any meaningful genetic distinctions between the tribes or nations. Therefore, the modern idea that someone is Cherokee or Lakota "by blood" is invalid. Tribes often adapted certain aspects of the newcomers' values and customs to their own needs, without becoming culturally diluted. The mainstay of this timeless equilibrium seemed to be the strong "cultural glue" of group orientation that held each group together, and their orientation to their own territory, the land (Stiffarm 1992). All of this changed when Europeans introduced the concept of race as the definitive dimension of cultural membership and obliterated the traditional relationship between the native peoples and the lands they occupied.

By 1700

At the beginning of the 1700s there were literally thousands of "white Indians," mostly English and French, who had either married into, been adopted by, or petitioned for naturalization as members of American Indian groups. In addition, when Indians took Europeans as prisoners, they often adopted them rather than killing them. Escaped African American slaves were typically accepted by the American Indian societies they encountered. They married and produced children who were fully integrated into these societies.

By 1830

Because of this ethnic openness, by 1830 the idea of defining "Indianness" by race or genetic strain had become absurd. About half of all American Indians who still lived east of the Mississippi River were genetically intermixed with one another and with Africans and Europeans. This pattern spread westward during the next 50 years (Ward1999).

Throughout the 20ᵗʰ century

During the 20th century the rate of intermarriage among American Indians and non-Indians increased. If this rate continues, the proportion of the currently recognized American Indian population with *one-quarter or less "degree of Indian blood"* may rise from 4 percent in 1980 to 60 percent by 2080. Both genetic dilution and geographic dispersion tend to threaten the survival of American Indian culture. This has recently been counter-balanced by the pan-Indian movement of urban communities.

Issue #3. Protection of Sacred Sites and Practices

Today a major crisis exists in Indian country regarding the protection of sacred lands and therefore religious freedom. When Europeans arrived in North America, almost every tribal religion was based on relationship with the land. Each tribe felt that its lands were specifically given to it to use. The proceedings of treaty councils are filled with protests and declarations by Indians to the effect that lands cannot be sold since no human has the power or right to own them. Some of the old chiefs felt that, because generations of their ancestors were buried on the lands and because the sacred events of their religion had taken place on the lands, they were obligated to protect the tribal lands from exploitation.

The protection of American Indian sacred sites and practices is based on the American principle of freedom of religion. It includes the protection and use of sacred sites, the protection of burial sites, the right to use sacred substances such as peyote, and the right to privacy during sacred ceremonies.

Freedom of Religion

For sixty years, from the 1880s to the 1940s, American Indian religious beliefs and practices were prohibited by the U.S. government. During this time Christian organizations were given a free hand in gathering converts on the reservations. Then in 1978 the federal government enacted the American Indian Religious Freedom Act, to protect their inherent right of freedom to believe, express, and exercise their traditional religions. It includes access to sites, use and possession of sacred objects, and practice of traditional ceremonies and rites. However, the law functions more as a policy statement for federal agencies. It has no real means of enforcement, and it does not offer protection from state agencies, private employers, or other parties. State policy, laws, and court rulings vary on this issue (Deloria 1999).

Types of Sacred Sites

Vine Deloria (1999) explains three types of sacred sites: places of overwhelming holiness, those with deep and profound meaning, and those with historical meaning.

1) Places of overwhelming holiness

These are sites where the Higher Powers, on their own initiative, have revealed themselves to human beings. They might be analogous to Mt. Sinai where Moses received the Ten Commandments. These places are sacred in and of themselves, sites where human beings have always gone to communicate and be with the higher spiritual powers. They include Bear Butte, Blue Lake, and Mount Shasta.

2) Sites with deep, profound meaning

An example is the place where the buffalo emerged each spring from the Black Hills of South Dakota to begin the ceremonial year of the Plains Indian. This is seen as the place of the "beginning of the Great Race which determined the primacy between the two-leggeds and the four-leggeds at the beginning of the world."

3) Sites with historical meaning

These are sites where something important took place, and thereafter the site was sanctified each time ceremonies were held and prayers offered. The concept of sacred lands thus evolved from the original conception of sites where religious revelation had taken place to sites of deep historic significance, sanctified by immediate past events.

Sacred Lands within National Parks and Forests

National park and forest lands generally get heavy tourist use, such as camping, fishing, back-packing, hiking, and rock climbing. Government officials have generally disregarded American Indian pleas for the restoration of their most sacred lands within these areas. Instead, the uses of sacred lands that are proposed by the Forest Service, the Bureau of Land Management, and the National Park Service amount to rapid exploitation of natural resources by a few favored private clients. American Indians see this as a wholly secular and destructive use of the lands.

Sacred Sites as "Churches"

In 1988, the U.S. Supreme Court heard a case in which four California tribes sued the U.S. Forest Service for its intent to install a logging road over a shrine on the top of a holy mountain. The Court ruled that the Forest Service can do what it wants to on its own land, and that destroying the shrine does not destroy the religion.

If a corporation attempted to destroy a Euro-American church in order to construct a tourist attraction on the site, it would have some real legal problems. For many American Indians, their "churches" have been sacred sites, such as Bear Butte. When tribes tried to stop development of this site as a tourist attraction, the state said, "No, you lost that land." Again, American Indian religion had no standing under the Constitution (Chamley 2002).

The National Historic Preservation Act, as amended in 2000, has a section that is now being used to protect American Indian sites. The law states that tribes must be consulted when federal agencies have an undertaking on land that may contain an important site. American Indians consider this protection a "stop-gap."

Graves and Old Bones

Until 1990, when Congress passed The Native American Graves Protection and Repatriation Act, American Indian remains were in the permanent collections of at least 700 museums across the United States The 1990 law requires federal agencies and museums to return these skeletons and many culturally vital artifacts to appropriate tribes. Then the tribes are to determine what to do with them. In most cases, tribes say the remains will be reburied (Lawson 2000).

Complicating the process is the fact that this law clashes with some traditional beliefs. For example, elders of some tribes don't want to handle the bones. They believe the disturbed spirits of the dead can wreak havoc on the living. They would rather have archaeologists or museum officials rebury the bones. Other American Indian communities don't want the remains returned to their land at all. The skeletons have been removed from a very sacred place that was never meant to be violated, and there is no ceremony for reburying the dead. In a perfect world, they would still be in the ground (Lawson 2000).

The Peyote Ritual

In 1918, the Native American Church was chartered. Its major ceremonies are of pre-Columbian origin. It incorporates certain Christian beliefs and practices as well as the ceremonial use of peyote, a cactus found in northern Mexico and Texas. The plant, which produces intense hallucinogenic effects, has been in use since before the 1500s, but the ceremony surrounding it was developed later, by the Kiowas and Comanches on their Oklahoma reservation in 1885. The ceremony lasts all night and includes prayer, song, and meditation. Soon after, the peyote ritual spread swiftly throughout the reservations. Today, with drug laws and drug testing all the rage, the use of peyote has become a hot issue. (Deloria 1999)

The Supreme Court, in *Employment Division v. Smith* (1990), decided that two men, active participants in the ceremonies of the Native American Church, which uses peyote in its rituals, were not eligible for unemployment compensation if they had been discharged from their jobs as individuals using a prohibited drug. Since then, the state of Oregon has passed a law that allows the defense of "sacramental use" for anyone caught in a similar situation in the future. At the federal level, President Clinton signed a public law in 1994 carving out an exemption for the sacramental use of peyote for federally recognized Indians engaging in bona fide religious ceremonies.

Privacy Vs Sharing of Religious Rituals

Another hot debate is the extent to which tribes should share their religious traditions with Euro-Americans. Of greatest concern are Euro-Americans who gain a little knowledge in order to market themselves as "native American spiritualists" who can teach powerful spiritual techniques.

Specific groups that have voiced such concerns are the Pueblos, probably the most consistent and persistent of American Indian groups in continuing their old ways. Also, the Navajos, Apaches, and Iroquois strongly hold to certain religious traditions (Deloria 1999).

The Pueblos allow outsiders—both Euro-American and American Indian—to view only those aspects of the Pueblo religion that can be known by people outside the Pueblo.

The Hopi stand on non-violence, which goes back many centuries, has recently attracted Euro-American pacifists. But when they arrive at Hopi villages, they are often rebuffed. The fact that a person understands the Hopi philosophical propositions does not mean they have anything else in common, according to the Hopi.

The Navajo religion is deeply philosophical and ceremonially complex, and medicine men still practice the ancient rites of healing for many members of the tribe.

The Apache people have a strong sense of solidarity. They don't share their songs, even with other American Indian groups, because they don't want the songs profaned by people who would not understand their meaning to the Apache.

The Iroquois ceremonies involve masks, sacred wampum belts, and the telling of tribal legends. Any intrusion of non-Indians into their religious practices is troubling.

Issue #4. Fake Indian Lore and Art

Related to the issue of abuse by non-Indians of American Indian rituals is the issue of Euro-Americans confiscating American Indian lore or art for quick profit.

Fake Indian Lore: Rituals, Healings

"Shake and bake shamans" and "wannabe Indian gurus" represent a troublesome issue. American Indian activists call it shameful—this epidemic of Euro-Americans appropriating Indian beliefs, ceremonies, and herbal remedies for their own profit. Some of these imposters take the astrological horoscope and turn it into a Native American horoscope. Others create Native American Tarot cards based on Lakota spirituality. Lakota Sweat Lodge Cards are another takeoff (Indianz.com).

Other examples of fake offerings include: channeling sessions with dead Indian chiefs, vision quests, "professional" shamans from nonexistent tribes, Native American herbs and medicines, gurus who claim to be a member of a tribe that doesn't exist, or of a tribe where members have never heard of the claimant, ritual items, sweat lodge experiences and purification ceremonies, Native American healing services, sacred ceremonies such as pipe ceremony, medicine man lessons

American Indians have characterized interlopers who sell such services as fraudulent, sacrilegious charlatans who desecrate native spirituality. According to Richard Allen, a spokesman for the Cherokee nation, "Cherokee medicine people and spiritual leaders are known to the Cherokee people and do not practice medicine for a fee nor sell 'shamanic' lessons to anyone . . . One may assume that anyone claiming to be a Cherokee shaman, spiritual healer, or pipe-carrier is equivalent to a modern day medicine show and snake-oil vendor" (Indianz.com 2000).

Fake Indian Arts & Crafts

The Indian arts and crafts market is a lucrative $1.2 billion business, growing by the year. But American Indian artists are losing the battle against fake arts and crafts. Nationwide, the Indian Arts and Crafts Board, an agency of the Department of Interior, says that 40 to 50 percent of the artwork on sale today is actually fake. These fakes usually come from other countries, such as China, Taiwan, or Mexico. The New Mexico Department of Indian Tourism estimates that profits to the real American Indian artists are down 40 percent because of the fakes. There are now federal laws that enable American Indian artists and tribes to sue those who promote fake art (Indianz.com 2000).

Issue #5. Hunting and Fishing Rights

The right to subsistence hunting and fishing on tribal lands has always been deemed a human right, guaranteed under various government treaties, and even international instruments. But controversy stemming from these rights is not unusual. For example, tribes in Alaska are concerned about the inability of the State of Alaska to resolve native hunting and fishing rights, and the issue has been at an impasse for years (UN 2002).

Tribes vary in their willingness to sell their hunting-fishing rights. For example, the White Mountain Apaches receive substantial income from commercial hunting of their wildlife. These hunts seem to fit comfortably with Apache concepts of proper resource use. They attach higher cultural value to particular places than to the things (wildlife) found in those places. The Yakima, on the other hand, have rejected the commercial hunting of big game on the reservation, in part because it does not fit with Yakima cultural beliefs about the proper use of the habitat where their harvestable game is found or of the treatment of the wildlife itself (Cornell 1995).

Related to hunting and fishing rights is the issue of infringement and takeover of tribal lands, which takes many forms. For example, southern Arizona tribes, whose lands overlay the United States-Mexico border, are concerned about the militarization of their lands by both the military and drug enforcement officers. Indigenous peoples want access to their traditional lands, as well as unrestricted freedom of movement across national borders that were established without their involvement (UN 2002).

Issue #6. Commercial Development: Intrusion or Opportunity?

Perhaps no development activity provokes as much controversy today as the commercial development of natural and cultural resources. This is true not only in Indian Country but outside it as well.

Attitude toward Commercialization

Changing the face of a mountain to build a ski resort, advertising to attract tourists, harvesting wildlife, strip-mining the reservation and diverting water from it—these kinds of development activities are controversial because they force the tribal society to confront trade-offs between economic development and cultural values.

Commercialization of one portion of a reservation's forest may be non-controversial, while logging activity in an adjacent area may be abhorrent to most of the population. It depends upon what most members see as the appropriate uses of its various resources. Sometimes a tribe may be deeply divided over what constitutes a culturally acceptable use of resources.

Is there an inherent conflict between economic development and tribal sovereignty? Although the hard data is scarce, field experience suggests that when a tribe strongly asserts its sovereignty—if such actions are supported by tribal government policies and institutions capable of backing up that sovereignty—this has reinvigorated tribal identities on the reservation. It even appears that, in some cases, tribally controlled development may be accompanied by such phenomena as a resurgence of indigenous language and reductions in reservation crime (Cornell and Kalt 1995).

Receptivity to Interaction with Non-Members

How receptive a tribe is to interaction with nonmembers is an important criterion for determining the type and extent of business activities that might work on a reservation. Members of one tribe may be reluctant to expose their religious or social practices to tourists. Another tribe may see this as a welcome economic opportunity (Cornell and Kalt 1995).

Tourism enterprises. Obviously, where many tribal members are fundamentally unreceptive to interactions with tourists or to tourist demands for access to ceremonial activities, tourism is not an appropriate enterprise.

Large-scale enterprises. Whether it's large-scale manufacturing or resource development, such as mining, large-scale business has rarely been the most effective type of enterprise on the reservation.

Problems can arise when highly-skilled workers and managers are brought onto a reservation to take the primary power positions in the enterprise. American Indian culture is primarily cooperative and participative and members tend to view traditional corporate cultures as hierarchical and authoritarian. Older members especially may have difficulty adapting to the authoritarian management style of nonmembers. The intrusion often has the effect of disrupting tribal relationships and disempowering members. A large business will typically become the primary income source for the members, intensifying its power over community members.

Bottom line. Small-scale, localized manufacturing, retail or service businesses, and perhaps tourism, tend to be better suited than large-scale enterprises to commercial development on reservations. Even then, these enterprises must be viewed by the large majority of members as opportunities, not intrusions.

The Role of Gambling Casinos

Since 1988 certain qualified American Indian "nations," because they are sovereign nations, not subject to state gambling prohibitions, are allowed to operate legalized gambling casinos on Indian lands. This type of enterprise has rescued some reservation tribes from dire poverty, while others have mired down in controversy over how to run the show and budget the profits. Some tribes believe they're using this opportunity to become more visible by interacting with mainstream customers in ways that members control. Others believe that since gambling is a "vice," the business carries a negative connotation and undermines their culture. Most tribes have felt no impact at all.

Americans spend nearly $400 billion a year on gambling—more than on all other forms of entertainment and self-education put together. However, 55 percent of this money is spent in non-Indian casinos, mainly in Las Vegas, 40 percent is spent in state lotteries, and only 5 percent is spent at Indian casinos. And only 5 percent of tribes receive significant casino revenues. Even so, the tribes face the constant threat of losing the little casino revenue they have to new nonIndian gambling schemes.

On the bright side, some tribes use the casinos for 1) jobs for tribal members that allow them the time and money to advance their educations, 2) better food and medical care for elders, 3) decent housing for on-reservation members, 4) buy-backs and restoration of tribal lands, 5) development of resorts, theatres and other tourist attractions, 6) sale of tribal arts and crafts, and 7) education of non-Indian visitors about the tribe's history, culture, and issues.

Issue #7: Alcohol Abuse

The "drunken Indian" stereotype implies that American Indians have either a fatal genetic flaw or inherent character weakness that renders them unable to handle their liquor. Research has not supported either of these implications. What some researchers are suggesting now is a study of the psycho-emotional impact on this ethnic group of such historical events as the attempted decimation of their culture, enforced removal from their traditional lands, and the resulting change of lifestyle and economic profile.

The Problem

Alcoholism is considered by American Indian tribes to be their most prevalent health problem. It is a major concern, but finding an adequate solution has not been easy because the problem is as complicated as it is diverse. American Indians have the highest alcoholism rate of any U.S. ethnic group, according to at least one international survey (Helzer 1992). Conversely, Chinese Americans have the lowest rate. American Indians' cultural history and current profile seem to play a key role in the alcohol problem. Two researchers, Dwight Heath (1983) and Joseph Westermeyer (1974), have examined American Indian drinking and point to the wide variations in problem drinking, not by ethnic group, but by cultural situation. They suggest research into the impact of cultural destruction and economic dependency on the tendency toward using alcohol as an escape mechanism.

Responses

Alcohol abuse and alcoholism contribute to many problems for American Indians and enters insidiously into the daily lives of virtually every tribe When individuals lose their ability to control alcohol consumption, they are likely to feel hopeless and desperate. The problems of individuals collectively create broader problems for the community and the larger society. Responses to these societal problems have been the development of costly social service programs of welfare, alcoholism counseling, rehabilitation, and family services. Other community responses include expansion of law enforcement and judicial programs.

LEADERSHIP CHALLENGES & OPPORTUNITIES

Now that you've started learning some facts about American Indians, you can use this information to manage challenges and opportunities for them to become an integral part of your team and organization.

Anticipate the Challenges

How can you influence your organization's environment in ways that help American Indians overcome barriers to career success? You will think of many ways. A few suggestions include 1) help people move beyond stereotypes, 2) avoid giving "undue" public praise, and 3) express respect and confer dignity in ways they appreciate.

Move Beyond Stereotypes

Managers and coworkers may have stereotyped images of what American Indians look like and act like. These stereotypes range from limited to distorted to completely false. We need to understand the unfairness of holding American Indians to unattainable standards for proving that they are Indian. If they say they are American Indian, that should be adequate.

Realize the implications of "undue" public praise

You have learned a little of how group motivation works in many American Indian communities. Before you give "public praise" to an American Indian employee, ask yourself, "Will this person consider the praise undeserved or exaggerated?" If so, then your praise may be perceived as an accusation and an insult. It may be safer to first speak one-on-one about your admiration and appreciation of the person's performance. See what reaction you get.

Express Respect and Confer Dignity

If you want to give public recognition of an American Indian employee's performance, explore with that person some ways of acknowledging the contributions. Get feedback and ideas. The other side of the "praise coin" is that people from this culture tend to work hard to deserve the dignity that the community gives them. If praise is perceived as conferring respect and dignity, then it motivates them to become even more deserving.

Find the Opportunities

Now you know something about the typical strengths of American Indians. Ask yourself, "How can I help each person contribute strengths to the team and organization?" Remember that the best contributions are those that also enhance the career of the contributor. Giving and receiving must be a two-way street. You'll think of ways on your own, but here are some suggestions to get you started. Begin by examining their strengths, such as 1) their relationship to the environment, 2) their value of sharing and helping in maintaining life-long relationships, 3) their "doing" orientation, and 4) their experience in consensus decision-making and participative leadership.

Strength: Understanding of Environmentalism and Sustainable Practices

Does your team or organization have a project that requires assessing the impact of the project on the environment? Teams and organizations that are sensitive to environmental issues can prevent future problems, deal more effectively with environmental agencies, project a favorable image to the public, and generally smooth the way to successful results. Think about including an American Indian colleague on these types of teams.

Strength: Maintaining Life-Long Relationships

A strong American Indian cultural value is maintaining life-long relationships. Think about the types of skills this practice requires: sharing, helping, understanding, patience, compassion, forgiveness, commitment, devotion, caring, loyalty. These are highly-valued traits of good team members. How can you help employees from this group contribute to team functioning? Just including them on key teams is a start. Finding ways to show appreciation of these traits and how they advance a team's agenda is another. Finding ways for others to view them as role models, appreciating but not resenting them, is a key. Can you think of other ways?

Strength: A "Doing" Orientation

Find out how "doing" is expressed by your American Indian employee or colleague. Clearly, effective teams need action-oriented members. Ask yourself how you can help this person best contribute his or her "doing" orientation to personal and team success.

Strength: Leadership Approach—Yours and Theirs

You have learned that most American Indian tribes select a charismatic leader who represents group consensus. Their chiefs are nothing like the dictators and kings so common in world history. Decision-making occurs primarily through group consensus, and leaders adapt to group goals that are reached by a consensus process. What opportunities are inherent in this information?

To begin with, you can express your leadership style in ways that American Indian employees and colleagues can understand and relate to. Include them in the decision-making process where possible. At least ask for their input and keep them informed of information that is relevant to the decisions that are being made. Help them to feel included, not excluded.

Many organizations are moving into a more participative leadership approach. Be aware that American Indian employees may be good candidates for leadership training and promotion. It's likely that they already have a background and framework for applying the participative approach.

Doing Business On or Near Indian Lands

Moving from an individual level to an organization level, is your company considering doing business on or near Indian lands? If so, chances are you will be dealing with the federal government. The trust relationship between the United States and Indian tribes will be a factor in most, if not all, transactions involving Indian tribes. Sometimes the government acts as a representative of tribal interests, sometimes as an arbiter of disputes, and occasionally both.

To prevent problems, the company must determine the scope and nature of the government's responsibilities as trustee. Often the federal agency itself is unclear on its duties. The first step is to refer to specific statutes or regulations—or to establish the lack of such laws. The next step is to understand how the nature of the federal government's supervision over Indian resources may affect the scope of its responsibilities. By clarifying responsibilities in this matter, companies doing business on Indian lands can assist federal agencies in identifying and applying appropriate standards of review.

SUMMARY

Typical myths held by mainstream society about American Indians tell us they're vanishing relics of the past, but we honor the noble redskin savage with their chiefs, braves and squaws through their use as team mascots, product logos, and themes for youth programs. Myths also say that they're lazy, getting welfare checks and gambling-casino money. Not only that, but if we run into an American Indian, he or she should be able to answer most of our questions about Indian history and lore. Their reality disputes these myths.

American Indians lived in the Americas for perhaps 30,000 years before Europeans arrived. Their achievements included various political systems that served as the primary model for the U.S. political includes systems and affected political and economic thinking worldwide in coming centuries. Example states belonging to a federation, with elected delegates from each state, which often meet to caucus, and with a growing number of delegates to represent a growing population.

American Indians and Alaskan Natives are about 1.5 percent of the American population. They are a young, growing group, with the lowest income and highest unemployment and poverty rates. About one-third of American Indians live in California, Arizona, and Oklahoma, with the Four Corners area having the densest population. About 45 percent live on reservations, while about half live in urban settings. The largest tribes are the Cheyenne and Navajo.

The American Indian worldview centers around a holistic view of life and a constant relationship with the spiritual forces that govern the lives of humans. They traditionally viewed "religion as life" and lived in the presence of the holy through a cooperative partnership with nature and perceiving time through nature's cycles. The values that stem from this worldview include beliefs that people are basically good, communities should be close-knit, good members put the group first while respecting individual views, personal relationships last for life and are based on sharing and helping, doing is more important than being, and long-range planning must consider the impact of today's decisions on at least seven generations into the future.

Most American Indian ceremonies, such as the Sun Dance and various sacrificial ceremonies, are religious rituals performed for specific purposes. Some, such as Pow Wows, are more social in nature. Others, such as healing ceremonies, incorporate spiritual beliefs with a medical system and techniques handed down through the ages.

Issues that concern both rural and urban American Indians include the question of who is considered an American Indian for government purposes. Also important is the question of how to preserve their cultural heritage—including their sacred sites, religious practices, privacy, and authentic arts and crafts. Economic issues concern hunting and fishing rights and commercial development on Indian lands, including gambling casinos. Alcoholism is the major social-health issue.

You can influence your organization's environment in ways that help American Indians overcome barriers to career success. For example, you can 1) help people move beyond stereotypes, 2) avoid giving "undue" public praise, and 3) express respect and confer dignity in ways they appreciate. You can also identify opportunities for helping American Indians contribute to the team and organization; for example, you can help them contribute their strengths, such as 1) their relationship to the environment, 2) their value of sharing and helping in maintaining life-long relationships, 3) their "doing" orientation, and 4) their experience in consensus decision-making and participative leadership.

Case Study 8.1 To Cut or Not to Cut

Wallace Baird, an employee for XYZ, a large corporation, learned about an opening for a supervisory position in the company. He applied, took the required test for the job and passed, but was told that in order to get the job, he had to cut his hair. Since Wallace considers himself an Apache, he wears long hair for religious reasons.

California employees are covered in the California Government Code, which prohibits employers from discriminating in the hiring or promotion of an employee based on their race, religious creed, or national origin. The definitions of "religion," "religious creed," and "religious belief" include observance, practice and all aspects of the religious belief. Denial of this right is a violation of the employee's civil rights. Legal relief may include but is not limited to: being reinstated into the company and receiving formerly denied promotions, back pay, and out-of-pocket expenses.

Out of concern for consistency in their corporation's dress code policy, XYZ supervisors said that there would be no exception to the hair-cutting policy (although the company has previously made exceptions for members of other religions). Wallace offers to put his hair up in a hat, but the supervisors do not budge. They tell Wallace that he may file a petition to top management, asking them to make an exception to the policy.

Wallace makes the petition, claiming American Indian religious and cultural reasons for not cutting his hair. Top management denies his request, informing him that they do not recognize the Native American religion as an **actual** religion. They say that they need written proof that shows that hair-cutting is forbidden in a text, such as the Bible . . . some prohibition akin to a "thou shalt not . . . "

1. What are the key issues (root problems) here?
2. What should Wallace do?
3. Did management make appropriate decisions? If not, what should they have done?

Source: an organization that advocates for American Indian rights.

Case Study 8.2 Matt, a Chippewa Clerk

Matt is in his twenties and a member of the local Chippewa tribe. He works as a stock clerk in the men's department of a large department store in the local mall.

George is the lead sales clerk in the department. He thinks Matt is a good worker and a pretty nice guy. One problem, though, is that Matt doesn't always restock merchandise ahead of time for George. However, when George asks for missing merchandise, Matt gladly finds what's needed with a smile. Matt's daily round of tasks are often up to 30 minutes behind schedule. But when Matt is available, he will help George with special projects until the job is done; for example, when seasonal displays need to be taken down and new ones put up. Also, a couple of months ago Matt gave George $10 when he overheard him say that he had forgotten his wallet and wouldn't be able to buy lunch.

Other people in the work area have sometimes made jokes or rude comments about Matt, calling him a "lazy Indian." At lunch the other day, one of the people at the table said, "I don't know why he works here when he gets all those government subsidies and that casino money. You know he gets his college education for free, don't you?" George, who was sitting at the table, felt uncomfortable.

1. What are the key issues (root problems) here?
2. If you were George, what would you do?

Source: Elaine Pogoncheff, Instructor, Lansing Community College.

Case Study 8.3 Nursing Home Incident

Billings is a nursing assistant employed at Horizons Nursing Home. One day she was trying to help a patient **Jared** out of bed. Jared started fighting her, and in the scuffle Billings struck Jared. He fell against a nearby table, causing him to scrape his arm against items on the table. A coworker Harriet observed the incident and reported it to **Carter**, the charge nurse. Carter conducted an investigation, examining the patient and going over his medical record. Billings did not deny she had hit Jared, but insisted that her striking the patient was not what caused a tear in the skin on his arm. As a result of this incident, Carter immediately fired Billings.

Later, Billings filed suit against Carter and Horizon Nursing Home. She stated that under Title VII of the **Civil Rights** Act she had been discriminated against and was fired because she was a woman over 40years of age and an American Indian. She claimed that other employees who had struck patients were not immediately discharged as she had been, and therefore hers was a case of discrimination.

The personnel manual of Horizon Nursing Home states that the first-offense penalty for abuse of a resident, use of obscene or abusive language, striking, threatening or harassing a resident, is immediate discharge. Billings' personnel file contains a signed receipt acknowledging that she had received a copy of the personnel manual, and had read and understood it.

1. What are the key issues (root problems) in this case?
2. Did Carter do the right thing by firing Billings?
3. Do you think that Billings has a valid case?

Source: Barefoot vs. Sundale Nursing Home, 457 S.E. 2d 152 (W.Va., 1995).

Case Study 8.4 English Only?

RD's Drive-In is a diner located in Page, Arizona, a town that is adjacent to the Navajo reservation. Nearly all of the employees at RD's Drive-in are American Indians who live on the reservation. They grew up speaking the Navajo language, but of course learned to speak English at school and in the nearby town of Page. RD's owner Tim announced in early 2000 that employees should not speak Navajo when they are on the job, even during breaks. The employees basically ignored this restriction.

Then in June 2000, Tim posted an "official policy of RD's Drive-In." It stated: "*The owner of this business can speak and understand only English. While the owner is paying you as an employee, you are required to use English at all times. The only exception is when the customer cannot understand English. If you feel unable to comply with this requirement, you may find another job.*"

Tim told the employees that he expected them to sign an agreement that they would abide by this English-only policy. Two employees, Roxanne and Freda, were especially upset by this policy. Roxanne said, "Tim is getting very formal and legal about this 'no Navajo being spoken around here.' Is that legal? It seems like employees should be allowed to speak their own language on their own break time." Freda agreed: "I think we should talk to Tim about this. I know I will slip up and speak Navajo, even if I don't intend to." Roxanne and Freda spoke with Tim about the policy, voicing their concerns to him. He said, "The policy says that if you can't comply, you can find another job and I suggest you do that. If you don't sign the agreement, you're fired."

Two other Navajo employees, Joy and Wanda, were upset by the firings and turned in their own resignations "before we get fired, because we cannot agree to this policy." The four of them later got together at Joy's house to talk about the situation. They decided to call the EEOC office at Phoenix and ask some questions about this type of English-only policy.

1. What are the root problems?
2. Do you think Tim can legally implement this policy?
3. Do the Navajo employees have a case?

Source: EEOC v RD's Drive In, CIV 02 1911 PHX LOA.

REFERENCES

ACA. American Counseling Association Resolution of December 2, 2001. http://earnestman.tripod.com, 2001

AP. "State's Indian Population Highest in U.S," Associated Press; printed in *Press Democra*t, February 15, 2002.

APA Resolution Recommending the Immediate Retirement of American Indian Mascots, Symbols, Images, and Personalities by Schools, Colleges, Universities, Athletic Teams, and Organizations, www.apa.org, 2005.

BJS, Bureau of Justice Statistics, "American Indians and Crime," www.ojp.usdoj.gov, February 14, 1999.

Brown, Dee. *Bury My Heart at Wounded Knee*. 1970 (30th anniversary ed. Holt 2001)

Census 2000 Informational Memorandum No. 37. Policy on Using Athletic Teams with American Indian or Alaska Native Names in Promoting Census 2000. U.S. Bureau of the Census.

Chamley, Lisa, "Speaker: Sacred Sites Need More Protection," Vermillion, SD: *Yankton Daily Press & Dakotan*, April 17, 2002.

Churchill, Ward, "The Crucible of American Indian Identity," in Duane Champagne, ed. *Contemporary Native American Issues*. AltaMira Press, 1999a.

Churchill, Ward. *Indians are Us?* Common Courage Press, 1999b.

See also www.bluecorncomics.com.

Cornell, Stephen and Joseph P. Kalt. "Reloading the Dice: Improving Chances for Economic Development on American Indian Reservations" in *What Can Tribes Do? Strategies and Institutions in American Indian Economic Development*. UCLA, 1995.

Deloria, Phillip. *Playing Indian*. University Press, 1998.

Deloria, Vine, Jr. An interview by Derrick Jensen. "How Science Ignores the Living World." 2002.

Note: See DeLoria entry in Resources Section below.

Deloria, Vine, Jr. *For This Land: Writings on Religion in America*. Routledge, 1999.

Deloria, Vine, Jr. *Red Earth, White Lies: Native Americans and the Myth of Scientific Fact* Fulcrum Publishing, 1977, 1997

Deloria, Vine, Jr. *God Is Red: A Native View of Religion*. North American Press, 1994.

Deloria, Vine, Jr. *Custer Died for Your Sins*. University of Oklahoma Press, 1969, reprint ed. 1988.

Deloria, Vine, Jr. and Clifford Lytle. *The Nations Within: The Past and Future of American Indian Sovereignty*. Pantheon Books, 1984.

Deloria, Vine, Jr. Religion and Revolution among American Indians. 1974

Garbarino, M.S. *Native American Heritage*. Little, Brown, 1976

Gonzales, Angela A. "Who Is American Indian? A Cacophony of Voices and Perspectives," in *American Indians and the Urban Experience*. Ed. Susan Lobo and Kurt Peters. AltaMira Press, 2001.

Gutner, Howard. *America's Secret Weapon: The Navajo Code Talkers of World War II*. Good Year Books, 2004.

Harriman, Peter. "Sun Dance Attendance Raises Concern about Protecting Culture," *Argus Leader*, July 23, 2000.

Heath, D.B. "Alcohol Use among North American Indians," in *Research Advances in Alcohol and Drug Problems*, 7. Plenum, 1983.

Helzer, John E. and Gloria J. Canino (Ed.) *Alcoholism in North America, Europe, and Asia*. Oxford University Press, 1992.

Indianz.com, "Fake arts still an issue," August 17, 2000.

Inter-Tribal Council of the Five Civilized Tribes, Resolution of July 2001. http://earnestman.tripod.com

Jackson, Helen H. *A Century of Dishonor: A Sketch of the U.S. Government's Dealings with Some of the Indian Tribes*, 1881. Reprint Minneapolis: Ross & Haines 1964.

Josephy, Alvin M. *500 Nations: An Illustrated History of North American Indians*. Alfred A. Knopf, Inc. 1998.

Josephy, Alvin M. in *American Heritage Book of Indians* ed. Wm. Brandon. Dell Publishing Co., reissue 1984.

Kawano, Kanji. *Warriors: Navajo Code Talkers*. Northland, 2002.

Lawson, Willow, "Thousands of Indian Skeletons May Never Return to Tribes," *ABC News*, August 9, 2000.

Lobo, Susan., Ed. and Kurt Peters. "Is Urban a Person or a Place?" in *American Indians and the Urban Experience*. Altamira Press, 2001.

Long, Daniel W. "Federal/Tribal Trust Relationship." www.modrall.com/articles, September 12, 2000.

Manny, Judy, "Native Americans Need Commitment," *The Washington Post*, C-13, August 2, 2000.

McClain, Sally. *Navajo Weapon: The Navajo Code Talkers*. Rio Nuevo Publishers, 2002.

McKenna, Francis R. "The Myth of Multiculturalism and the Reality of the American Indian in Contemporary America." *Journal of American Indian Education*, 21, 1-9, 1981.

Miller, Carol. "Telling the Indian Urban: Representations in American Indian Fiction," *American Indians and the Urban Experience*. Ed. Susan Lobo and Kurt Peters. AltaMira Press, 2001.

Mitchell, Wayne and Kenneth Patch, "Indian Alcoholism and Education," *Journal of American Indian Education*, 21, 1, 31-33, October 1981.

NCAI (National Congress of American Indians) www.ncai.org

NEA (National Education Association), 2000-2001 Resolutions, I-41, Use of Prejudicial Terms and Symbols, www.nea.org

NIEA. National Indian Education Association, 2675 University Ave., St. Paul, MN 55114. (Resolution on the use of American Indian names for sports teams and mascots), 2002.

O'Brien, Sharon. *American Indian Tribal Governments*. University Oklahoma Press, 1989.

Osnos, Evan. "Efforts to Eliminate 'Squaw' from Geographic Sites," *Chicago Tribune* www.chicagotribune.com/ March 24, 2002

Paine, Thomas. *Rights of Man*. Middlesex, England: Penguin, 1969. Originally published 1791.

Pow Wow Viewers' Guide, Aberdeen, SD: Native American Students' Association, Northern State University, 2000.

Rave, Jodi. "White Americans Play Indian, Professor Says," *Lincoln Journal Star*, November 2001.

See http://ishgooda.nativeweb.org.

Riso, Chris. "Bill Banning Indian Team Names Get Mixed Reviews," *CNS News*, May 4 2002.

Saldamando, Alberto, "Racial Discrimination Against Indigenous Peoples in the United States," *Indigenous Affairs*. January 2001. Note: Saldamando is General Council with the International Indian Treaty Council.

Sonneburn, Liz. *The Navajos* (Native American Histories). Lerner Publications, 2005.

Southwest Indian Foundation. Information about Navajo Code Talkers. www.southwestindian.com, 2008.

Stiffarm, Lenore A. and Phil Lane, Jr. "The Demography of Native North America: A Question of American Indian Survival." *The State of Native America: Genocide, Colonization, and Resistance*. ed. M. Annette Jaimes. South End Press, 1992.

Stockes, Brian. "Indian Country Today: Federal Indian Certification Regulations Raise Concerns," *New York Times*, August 23, 2000.

Trosper, Ronald L. "Mind Sets and Economic Development on Indian Reservations," *What Can Tribes Do? Strategies and Institutions in American Indian Economic Development*. UCLA 1995.

U.N. (United Nations) www.unitednations.org, May 21, 2002

U.S. Census Bureau. Memorandum prohibiting the use of American Indian names in sports teams for promotion of census participation. 2000.

U.S. Census Bureau. *Census 2000*. www.census.gov

U.S. Commission on Civil Rights. www.usccr.gov, April 13, 2001.

Utter, Jack. *America Indians: Answers to Today's Questions*, 2nd ed. University of Oklahoma Press, 2002

Weatherford, Jack: *Indian Givers: How the Indians of the Americas Transformed the World*. Fawcett Books, 1988.

Westermeyer, J.J., "The Drunken Indian: Myths and Realities," *Psychiatric Archives*, 4, 29, 1974.

RESOURCES

Alaska Native Governments: www.uaa.alaska.edu

American Indian Culture Research Center, Blue Cloud Abbey www.bluecloud.org/dakota.html. Address: P.O. Box 98, Marvin, SD 57251-0098, Phone: (605) 432-5528, Fax: (605) 432-4754, E-Mail: indian@bluecloud.org. Principal purpose: to inform the general public of the worldview, philosophy of life, and spiritual insight of Native Peoples.

American Indian Historical Society, 1415 Masonic Avenue, San Francisco, CA 94117

Association of American Indian Physicians, University of Oklahoma, Norman, OK 73069.

Bureau of Indian Affairs, Federal Building, Aberdeen, SD.

Bureau of Justice Statistics, www.ojp.usdoj.gov/bjs/

California American Indian Museum and Cultural Center, 5250 Aero Drive, Santa Rosa, CA 95403 http://cimcc.indian.com

Deloria, Rev. Phillip Joseph, son Vine Jr. (both deceased), and grandson Phillip. Rev. Philip Joseph Deloria, aka Tipi Sapa, was an Episcopal priest, a missionary, and a leader of the Yankton band of the Nakota Nation. His son Vine Jr., earned a master's degree in theology and a law degree and became a professor at the University of Colorado. He was Executive Director of the National Congress of American Indians 1964-1967. After he burst onto the national scene in 1969 with the publication of *Custer Died for Your Sins, Time* magazine named him one of the great religious thinkers of the 20th century. He died in 2005. Vine Jr.'s son Philip Deloria is Professor of History at University of Michigan. With a Ph.D. from Yale, Phillip Deloria was president of the American Studies Association 2008-2009, author of several books on American Indians, and winner of several awards for his research and writing. Both Vine Jr. and Phillip have fought tirelessly for Indian sovereignty and values.

Indian Country. www.indiancountry.com

Indian Organizations and Government Web Sites

In Search of History: Navajo Code Talkers, DVD, 50 min., ASIN: B000CSTK74, A&E Home Video, 2006.

Institute for Development of Indian Law, 927 15th St. NW, Suite 612, Washington, DC 20005

National Congress of American Indians, 1301 Connecticut Ave NW, Suite 200, Washington D.C. 20036, (202) 466-7767, (202) 466-7797 (fax). NCAI was founded in 1944 and is the oldest and largest tribal government organization in the United States. Members come from over 250 tribal governments and every region of the country. NCAI's mission is to inform the public and the federal government on tribal self-government, treaty rights, and a broad range of federal policy issues affecting tribal governments. NCAI website links:

NCAI Directory of Indian Nations

Alaska Native Governments

Links to Tribal Governments

Links to Indian Organizations and Government Web Sites

National Indian Education Association, 2675 University Ave., St. Paul, MN 55114.

Native American Rights Fund, 1605 Broadway, Boulder, CO 80302 www.narf.org

NativeNews: www.pdnewmedia.com

Navajo Code Talkers: The Epic Story, VHS, 55 min., Amazon ASIN: 0963969811 or www.southwestindian.com, 1994.

Navajo Code Talkers: Top Secret Mission, VHS Superior Productions Inc. Amazon ASIN B000069I43, 2002.

News from Native California, magazine

CHAPTER 9

Working with Asian Americans

I keep the harmony and pay honor and respect to the manager.
Why didn't he talk to me about the new supervisor job?
Asian American worker

You're likely to have many Asian American colleagues if you live on the East or West Coast or certain urban areas of the country. Only 4 percent of Americans are Asian Americans, but they're clustered in certain cities and regions. People who have taken the time and effort to learn something about Asian Americans, their values and issues, say they've boosted their ability to work productively with these associates.

To help you better understand what it's like to be an Asian American, and therefore to build more empathic relationships, you'll learn in this chapter:

- How typical myths and stereotypes about Asian Americans compare with current reality.
- How the current situation has evolved from past history
- The major Asian American communities and the key cultural values, customs, and issues that are important to them.
- How you can help Asian American employees overcome barriers to career success.
- How you can help your organization build upon Asian American strengths.

The best use of this information about Asian American cultural patterns is
1. To help you understand how they might view situations or what their actions might mean,
2. To figure out what questions you might ask in getting to know them better
3. To avoid forming rigid ideas and new stereotypes based on this information, and

4. To be open and flexible as you interact with individual Asian Americans.

First, explore your opinions and knowledge of Asian Americans by completing Self-Awareness Activities 9.1 and 9.2.

Asian American Man

Courtesy of Michael Prince/Corbis Images.

Asian American Woman

Courtesy of Chris Carroll/Corbis Images.

Self-Awareness Activity 9.1: What Do You Believe About Asian Americans?

Purpose:

- to get in touch with your beliefs and stereotypes about this group of people
- to experience how judgmental beliefs affect your thinking and feeling processes
- to experience the ways in which your beliefs create your reality regarding other persons, even before you have any interaction with them.

Part I. What Do You Believe About Asian American Women?

Step 1. Associations

- Relax as deeply as you can.
- Close your eyes for a moment and take a few deep breaths.
- Now focus on the picture that symbolizes "Asian American woman"
- Imagine that you are this woman. Be Asian American woman.
- Notice any resistance to being this person—and any willingness.
- Notice words, images, thoughts, and feelings that come to mind as you are "seeing and being this woman."

Step 2. Negative Associations
- Next, as you focus on the picture, allow negative opinions to come up, perhaps some that you typically hold about Asian American women.
- Notice your *thoughts* as you see the person in this negative way. What *feelings?*

Step 3. Positive Associations

- Now, still focusing, allow positive opinions to come up, perhaps some that you typically hold about Asian American women.
- Notice your *thoughts* as you see the person in this negative way. What *feelings?*

Step 4. Insights and Writeup

- Now review this experience and write about it.
- When you first saw the picture, what thoughts and feelings came up? These may reflect your deepest responses to people from this group.
- Think about the differences in your thoughts and feelings when you consciously held a positive opinion versus a negative opinion.
- Write a few sentences about your feelings, thoughts, and insights.

Part II. Experimenting with Opinions About Asian American Men

Repeat the phases and steps in part I, this time focusing on the image of an Asian American man.

Self-Awareness Activity 9.2: What Do You Know about Asian Americans?

Purpose: To see what you know about the issues covered in this chapter.
Instructions: Determine whether you think the following statements are basically true or false—and think about why. The answers will emerge in this chapter, and the summary at the end of the chapter focuses on these issues.

1. Asian Americans are too passive in temperament to be effective business leaders in American corporate cultures.
2. Most Asian Americans in the workplace are more Asian than American.
3. Asian Americans tend to be more unemotional than people from other groups.
4. Early Asian immigrants were considered nonwhite and had to cope with segregation and other forms of discrimination.
5. Most Asian Americans are from China.
6. Traditional Asian Americans expect the manager to be "one of the guys."
7. The "model minority" label reflects the idea that Asian Americans adapt to the American workplace better than African Americans or Latino Americans.

Let's examine some common threads among all Asian American groups. Asian Americans have been in America for over 150 years, before many European immigrant groups. But because they were "different," they were often stereotyped as heathen, exotic, and unassimilable. The Chinese were the first group to arrive in significant numbers, seeking gold, and what happened to them influenced the treatment of the Japanese, Koreans, Filipinos, and Asian Indians, as well as the Southeast Asian refugees who have come since the end of the Vietnam War. Most must cope with similar stereotypes and myths, experience generational differences as new generations become Americanized, hold some common cultural values and behavior patterns, and are affected by some common political issues, including the model minority myth.

STEREOTYPES AND REALITIES

We'll focus on a few of the most common stereotypes that Asian Americans must deal with. These stereotypes reflect some typical Asian stereotypes, and they contribute to the flavor of prejudice and discrimination that Asian Americans face. Although most Americans hold relatively positive attitudes toward Asian Americans, 25 percent have strong negative attitudes. These people say they would disapprove of a family member marrying an Asian American, and would not vote for an Asian American for U.S. President. About 32 percent believe Chinese Americans are more loyal to China than to the United States. Still, 90 percent believe Asian Americans have strong family values and are as honest in business dealings as other business people (Yi 2001).

Stereotype #1: Asian Americans Tend to Retain Their Foreign Ways so It's Difficult for Them to Fit In

Asian Americans have traditionally coped with the exotic, perpetual foreigner stereotype because Euro-Americans have seen them as:

* immigrants who represent a small segment of the American population.
* people of color who bear distinct physical differences
* people from a culture and lifestyle that is just too different for comfort
* people who can never be completely absorbed into American society and politics.

Discriminatory laws and practices have reinforced this separateness. But in fact, one-fourth to one-half of the members of most Asian American groups were born in this country. Many are even third- or fourth-generation Americans. Further, those bilingual Asian Americans who have recently learned English and still have heavy accents can usually be understood by people who are willing to listen for the rhythm and pattern of their speech. Asian cultures can offer much ancient wisdom to those who are open to different ways of viewing situations. Incorporating different ideas can lead to discovery of new business opportunities and problem solutions.

Stereotype #2: Asian Americans Are Unemotional and Inscrutable

Euro-Americans often complain that they can't tell what Asian Americans are thinking or feeling, so they're seen as unemotional and inscrutable. This and the "foreign" stereotype are closely related and stem from two sources. The first is the vast differences in English and Asian languages. The other source is the Asian cultural values that call for self-discipline in expressing emotions and for indirectness in communicating. When Asians disagree with you, say no, or convey unwelcome information, they often do it so indirectly and subtly that a Euro-American doesn't know they've done it. Later, if the Asian Americans' actions reflect a lack of agreement, Euro-Americans may conclude that the Asian Americans were evasive, sneaky, dishonest, or even corrupt, when perhaps they were merely being polite.

The reality is that Asian Americans experience the same emotions as other people. The Asian "Face" that Asian Americans present to the Euro-American world is often impassive and hard to read. However this is the Face that American history has taught Asian Americans to present. They have another Face—one that they show to their collective family. This is the Face that is presented most everywhere in their native country. It's more expressive and more understandable.

Stereotype #3: Asian Americans Are Too Passive and Polite to Be Good Managers

This is a career-bashing stereotype with hardly a kernel of truth. One implication is that they're polite and therefore lack the conviction and backbone to stand up to the heat a supervisor must take. Another implication is that they're compliant, therefore passive, which means they don't have the ambition it takes to move up the competitive corporate ladder. The behavior of Asian Americans is often misread by people who don't understand their cultural values and training.

In their own countries, Asians are obviously the business and political leaders. In the United States, Asian American small business owners have established an impressive success record, overcoming great odds. Even women who work on assembly lines can be surprisingly assertive and persistent beneath their "face" of compliance and cooperation, according to recent studies.

Stereotype #4: Asian Americans Have Learned How to Make It in American Society by Working Hard and Being Thrifty

Asians are seen as the "good" minority when they're polite, deferent, and technically superior. As the "model minority" they've been more successful than other ethnic groups in penetrating professional ranks. Even though most Asian American professionals have unusually high preparation, they have experienced significant barriers to promotion and upward mobility (Cabezas 1989).

The model minority stereotype is true, as far as it goes. On the up side, it makes Asian Americans more acceptable in business and in society in general. But it ignores the complexities and difficulties of their situation, according to Karen Hossfeld's [1994] research. The downside is:

- The "hard worker" image sets up unrealistic expectations that they'll gladly make major sacrifices for their work, work for less than Euro-Americans, work harder, and work longer hours.
- It's easy to assume that such a model minority group has no pressing social or political issues that we must address.
- It causes undue resentment from other minorities.

The reality is that Asian Americans pay a high price for "making it." As a family unit, they work harder and longer for less pay than Euro-Americans and they get less help from society.

Related to the model minority stereotype is the belief that Asian Americans just want to own their own businesses and acquire real estate—that they don't care about social problems or politics. In fact, Asian American have among the highest rates of political contributions per capita, but their voting rates in 2004 were lower than for any American subgroup. In California only 20 percent of Asian Americans voted. Lack of voter participation results in the government being less responsive to Asian American issues

On the other hand, Asian American responses to surveys indicate they attach far more importance to political freedom than to buying a home. They're as happy to work for a U.S. corporation as to be self-employed. And, as we'll see, Asian Americans have viewed the establishment of small family businesses as the only way to survive and get ahead, not necessarily as a choice that's preferable to working for a large corporation. One survey also indicated that Asian Americans *are* concerned about social problems, especially the plight of the homeless (Viviano 1990).

Stereotype #5: Asian Americans Have Communication Problems

Asian languages are about as different from English as languages can be. Therefore, becoming fluent and proficient is a long, arduous process for Asian American immigrants. Most work diligently and continually to improve their communication skills. In general, they believe in mastering English, and nearly all believe that English should be the only official U.S. language. The reality is that virtually all Asian Americans who were born in the United States are fluent in English and in fact may not be fluent in their ancestral Asian language.

Stereotype #6: Asian Americans Are Good in Technical Occupations, but They Don't Have Leadership Potential

This stereotype is a faulty distortion that creates a huge barrier to career mobility. It's related to the idea that Asian Americans are technical coolies, computer nerds, or memorization whizzes, great at crunching numbers but short on people skills and creativity. It stems from the tendency of immigrant students with some language deficiencies to focus on what they *can* do well, which often includes mastering quantitative tasks and usually includes diligently studying, practicing, and memorizing.

As a group, Asian Americans do score better than any other group on math tests—as discussed later in the section on common threads of culture. But as a matter of fact, Asian American students demonstrate a broad range of aptitudes and talents. Those who were born in the United States do not have the language problem and are likely to gravitate to a wider range of career areas.

Stereotype #7: Asian Americans Know About All Things Asian

Some Euro-American business persons tend to look upon the company's "token" Asian Americans as the resident experts on all things Asian American—and Asian, for that matter. This assumes they know everything about the country their parents or grandparents immigrated from, its culture, adaptation of its people to the American culture, and which local restaurants are the best sources of its cuisine. For some Asian Americans, this stereotype has become a pet peeve. The reality is that many of them were born in the United States, are more American than Asian, and may be no more of an expert on "things Asian" than the average American.

CONNECTIONS TO THE PAST

Americans have always valued the ideals of equal opportunity and fairness, but reality has not always matched that ideal. From the beginning, Asian immigrants have faced many obstacles to acceptance in America. Recent generations are more Americanized and face fewer barriers to success.

Understanding the Asian American experience requires understanding the processes of their acculturation, how overt and subtle prejudices have constrained their choices, and how each generation has changed the community. Although they become increasingly Americanized and acculturated, Asian Americans have also retained much of their Asian cultural heritage.

Acculturation Processes

Asian immigrants to America have experienced two major processes of acculturation:

- They've had to acquire the values and behavior of Euro-Americans.
- They've had to learn to accept their standing as ethnic minorities.

Many report that they've been seen as people who, because of the skin color and physical appearance, were not allowed to enjoy the rights and privileges given acculturated European immigrants and Euro-American native-born citizens. If they wanted to stay and survive in the United States, they had to learn to "stay in their place" and to act with deference toward those of higher ethnic status; that is, Euro-Americans. Therefore, many of the choices they have made, such as becoming small-business owners or majoring in accounting, have been made within those limits. To fully understand Asian Americans' background as a group, we must be aware of these constraints.

The Chinese: Gold, Railroads, and Exclusion

The first group of Asian Americans were men from China who came during the 1850s California gold rush. Instead of gold, most found work building railroads and doing laundry. There was overt prejudice from the beginning.

Chinese Exclusion Act of 1882

This Act was the first law that prohibited the entry of immigrants on the basis of nationality. The Chinese condemned this restriction as racist and tyrannical. The precedent later provided a basis for the restriction of European immigrant groups such as Italians, Russians, Poles, and Greeks.

Alien Land Acts

The western states, where most Asian Americans lived, passed Alien Land Acts in the early part of the twentieth century that barred them from owning land because they were "aliens ineligible to citizenship." Asians were legally classified as "nonwhite" for many purposes, catching them in the segregation net cast around African Americans. Restrictive covenants were written into many deeds making it illegal to sell the property to a "nonwhite."

Miscegenation Laws

State laws prohibited the marriage of people from two different "races," but the main concern was marriage of Euro-Americans to others.

Legal Segregation

School segregation was practiced in districts that had significant numbers of Asians, such as in San Francisco. Asians were usually required to sit in the balcony or on one side of theaters, and some public pools and beaches were off limits to them (Kitano 1988).

Racial Profiling

All the discriminatory laws have been repealed, and new laws are in place to prevent discrimination. Still Asian Americans face modern discrimination, such as racial profiling. For example, Wan Ho Lee, a U.S. Citizen and Los Alamos scientist who immigrated from Taiwan, was arrested in 2000 for suspicion of espionage. This regarded the leaking of sensitive weapons secrets to China, and the charges were later dropped. Many leaders in the Chinese American community claimed that racial profiling was a major factor, one that Lee's Euro-American colleagues didn't have to face.

The Japanese: Migration, War, and Concentration Camps

The Supreme Court ruled in 1934 that Japanese, Chinese, Filipinos, and Asian Indians were not "white" and therefore did not meet qualifications of the Naturalization Law and so could not become U.S. citizens. At the outbreak of World War II, however, the draft law was amended to allow nonwhites to join. An all-Japanese unit went on to become the most-decorated group in American history.

Meanwhile, their relatives at home were rounded up as "potential spies" and confined in concentration camps. They lost everything except what they carried with them, and of course they could not earn income during the two or three years they were imprisoned. To Japanese Americans, this wartime exile and incarceration was and still is the central event of their history, making it unique among Asian Americans. In 1988 the U.S. government formally apologized to these families and began paying reparations.

Civil Rights Laws of the 1960s

Most of the discriminatory laws were in force until the 1960s. The great changes initiated in the 1960s affected Asian Americans, as they did everyone else. The new Civil Rights laws had a great impact on Asian Americans' options. Higher education opened up to them, and streams of second-generation students poured in, most choosing safe majors in the professions, such as accounting, education, dentistry, or pharmacy. Employment patterns tend to be less discriminatory in professions, where credentials open doors and private practice can be lucrative, especially within one's minority community.

Many occupations previously closed to Asian Americans, such as public school teaching, began to open up, so the phenomenon of second-generation college graduates working at fruit stands began to disappear. College degrees began to mean something and career choices could be planned with some reasonable hope of fulfillment.

Laws forbidding intermarriage were overturned by the Supreme Court in 1967, and "mixed marriages" have become more common. However, most private social clubs were closed to the second-generation, and housing segregation was still a reality until recently.

Generation Gaps

To understand significant differences among the Asian Americans you meet, you must understand the different experiences and attitudes of various generations.

First Generation

Those who immigrated from China or Japan in the early years of the twentieth century are called First Generation. They were isolated in their ethnic communities, related primarily or exclusively to other Asian American families, and retained their old cultural ways.

Second Generation

Those born in the 1940s to 1960s are more Americanized but still strongly affected by their Asian cultural heritage. Now mature and aging adults, the second-generation is primarily a low-profile group.

By the end of World War II second-generation Chinese Americans and Japanese Americans finally outnumbered their immigrant parents. Two immigrant groups that were much smaller, Asian Indian Americans and Filipino Americans, often intermarried with other ethnic groups. Their second-generation children, many of bi-ethnic parentage, tried their best to fit into the mainstream.

Young and inexperienced though they were, members of the second generation began to find a voice of their own and to become distinct from their parents' generation. Second-generation members are of course more Americanized but still strongly affected by their Asian cultural heritage.

Third and Fourth Generation

Those born during or after the 1970s are even more Americanized than their parents and grandparents, but they're still distinctly Asian in some ways. Most are definitely more American than Asian. Some are entering occupations once considered closed to Asians, such as advertising, the performing arts, journalism, and broadcasting.

One survey indicates that 47 percent think it's more important to move their family into mainstream American life, while 42 percent think it's more important to maintain traditional Asian ways (Baldassare 1990). Many have never faced the overt discrimination that their parents and grandparents faced. A few have never had close ethnic ties or friendships with other Asian American families. Most go to the university and are eager for good jobs, especially in the professions, such as medicine, engineering, and law.

They're more likely to reflect the influence of their surrounding communities than a strictly ethnic one. Nearly all live in urban areas in the West, especially in California and Hawaii. Although these young people question the lifestyle and certain values of their parents, they're the beneficiaries of the material success of the second generation.

A recent trend is for parents and grandparents to focus on teaching the Chinese culture to the new generation. Wherever you find large Chinese American communities, such as Northern California, you find a growing number of Chinese schools. All teach Chinese language along with such cultural courses as history, abacus, and folk dancing.

Current Immigrants

The contemporary Asian immigration and the refugee influx have been shaped by changes in U.S. immigration laws and by the political, economic, and social agreements made between the countries of origin and the United States since the end of World War II. The United States has favored escapees from communism above all others, such as refugees from Vietnam, Laos, and Cambodia.

The Immigration Act of 1990 includes two visa lottery programs designed to favor immigrants of particular national origins. Because Asian American and Latin American immigration has dominated legal immigration since the 1960s, the U.S. government established a "diversity" lottery system for residents of other countries that had not significantly used the family and employment preference system. This program almost halted Asian immigration from China, India, South Korea, and the Philippines. This has become a major issue for Asian American families trying to bring family members into the United States.

Regardless of their reasons for coming, as soon as they arrive, most Asians have quickly made themselves productive. This ability to find niches for themselves is a double-edged sword. Their very success has resurrected some deeply ingrained prejudices and hostility. These contradictions that have characterized Asian American history continue to limit the lives of many Asian Americans today (Takaki 1992).

CURRENT PROFILE: WHO ARE THE ASIAN AMERICANS?

The seven major groups of Asian Americans have many common cultural threads. Many of their values and customs are similar, although each culture also has its unique aspects. Each group came to the United States under somewhat different circumstances and therefore each has faced different situations. Proportion of the U.S. population that is Asian American, and their subgroup proportions, are shown in Figure 9.1 (U.S. Census). A unique group, refugees from the Hmong hill tribes of Laos have a unique profile, which is described later in the section on various Asian cultures.

FIGURE 9.1: Proportions of Asian Americans, 2000

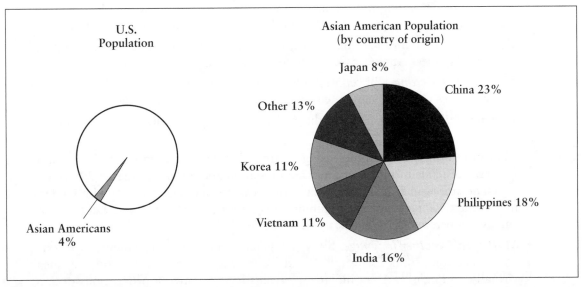

The following facts from the U.S. Census (2000) provide a general demographic picture of Asian Americans.

- *Half live in the West,* 49 percent, compared to 21 percent of the total population. The U.S. Census Bureau estimates that in 2000 Asian Americans were most populous in the following states:

State	% of Population	State	% of Population
Hawaii	56	New Jersey	4.5
California	13	Illinois	3.2
Washington	6	Texas	2.5
New York	5		

- *Most live in a dozen urban areas.* The largest Asian American populations in U.S. metropolitan areas, as estimated by the U.S. Census Bureau (1995b) are as follows:

+/– One Million		+/– 150,000 to ½ Million		+/– 100,000 to 150,000	
Los Angeles	1,340,000	Honolulu	526,000	Houston	132,000
S.F. Bay Area	924,000	Chicago	256.000	Philadelphia	121,000
New York	873,000	Washington DC	202,000	Sacramento	114,000
		San Diego	198,000	Dallas-Ft. Worth	98,000
		Seattle	164,000		

- *Greatest population density* is in Honolulu, where they are about two-thirds of all residents; Daly City, a suburb of San Francisco, where they're over one-half; and San Francisco, where they're nearly one-third.
- *Fast-growing.* They doubled in number between 1980 and 1990, due primarily to immigration, and increased again by 63 percent between 1990 and 2000.
- *Many are foreign born,* 66 percent, with Southeast Asian Americans having the highest percentage and Japanese Americans the lowest.
- *Some are recent immigrants.* Thirty-eight percent entered the United States during the 1980s, mostly refugees. Most live in the West, especially in California.
- *They live longer than Euro-Americans,* whose mean life expectancy is 76, compared to 80 for Japanese Americans and Chinese Americans.
- *They have less crime.* FBI reports indicate that arrest rates of Asian Americans for serious crimes are well below their proportion in the population (nicar.org).
- *They're relatively young.* Thirty is the median age, compared with the national median of 33.
- *Most groups have larger families,* on average 3.8 persons, compared to 3.2 for all U.S. families. Five members or more are present in about twice as many (23 percent) of Asian American families as in Euro-American families (13 percent). Hmong families average 6.6 persons, while Filipino, Vietnamese, Cambodian, and Laotian average over 4 persons per family. Japanese had 3.1.
- *Most speak another language.* Sixty-five percent speak another language at home, 56 percent don't speak English well, and 35 percent are linguistically isolated (speak virtually no English). Asian Indian Americans have the lowest proportion speaking another language at home, Hmong the highest.
- *They become citizens.* Nearly half of foreign-born Asian Americans have become citizens, even though 75 percent of them have been here less than 25 years. Only immigrants from Europe have a higher rate of naturalization.

Education: Higher Achievement than Most

The Asian American devotion to education results in the highest educational achievement of the major ethnic groups. They do better on quantitative exams than any other group. In 2003 (U.S. Census)

- 89 percent held high school diplomas, compared to 85 percent of all Americans
- 50 percent had bachelor's degrees or higher, compared to 27 percent of all Americans
- Highest SAT scores of any group (Bandon 1994)

Asian Indian Americans

Asian Indian Americans nearly all speak English, and few have language barriers, which is related to India's history as a British colony. Many are part of an Indian "brain drain" that occurred during the 1980s and was caused when India trained more professionals than its businesses could profitably employ.

- 67 percent of Asian Indian American men have degrees and 50 percent of women
- 72 percent have jobs, compared with 65 percent of all Americans.
- Nearly 50 percent of foreign-born Asian Indian workers are managers or professionals, compared to 24 percent of all Americans.
- They have the highest per capita income among all Americans after Japanese Americans.

University Studies

Asian American university students enter fields of study similar to the overall population, except there are about twice as many studying physical sciences and engineering, half as many study social science, and only one-third as many study education (National Center for Educational Statistics 1995)

Pay Doesn't Match Educational and Occupational Levels

Although Asian Americans have the highest educational levels, the greatest proportion of family members who work, and the highest concentration in managerial and professional jobs, their income does not reflect these achievements.

Asian American Households Have More Workers

About 67 percent of Asian Americans are employed, compared with 65 percent for all Americans. Groups with an employment rate higher than 70 percent are the Filipino Americans, Asian Indian Americans, and Thai Americans. Twenty percent of Asian American families contain three or more workers, compared with 13 percent nationally.

Self-Employment is High

Over 11 percent of Asian American workers are self-employed, double the rate of other minorities (U.S. Census 1995b).

More High-Status Jobs

Nearly 40 percent of Asian Americans work in managerial and professional specialty occupations, more than the 30 percent of the total population. Asian Americans are normally distributed across all types of jobs, except in "professional category," where there are twice as many Asian Americans (22.5 percent) as the overall population (11.7 percent). This is due primarily to their higher education levels and the tendency to start their own business or practice.

They work in all major industries, with a normal distribution pattern, except in the "electronic components" industry where there is nearly twice the proportion of Asian Americans (13.5 percent) as the overall population (8.8 percent). Asian Americans make up 2.4 percent of all the employees in the electronics industry.

High Pay Still Doesn't Match Educational Level

While median income *per family* looked good in 2000 at $46,200, Asian American families had 3.2 persons. Euro-American family income was $44,000, but only 2.5 persons per household. That means two things: 1) Asian American income must provide for more family members, and 2) more persons in their families go out to work than in Euro-American families.

Business Ownership Is Common

Asian Americans owned 1.1 million businesses in 2002, up 24 percent from 1997. Their receipts were $343 billion, up 13 percent from 1997, about 2 percent of total U.S. business revenues of $20 trillion. Only about 29 percent (320,000) of those companies had paid workers, with sales of about $308 billion. Asian American proprietors who have no workers have increased 30 percent since 1997, earning $36 billion, or 27 percent more than they earned in 1997.

About a third of Asian American business *revenues* come from wholesale trade, about a sixth from retail trade, and about a sixth from services. However, the proportionate *number* of businesses in the services sector is 44 percent, compared to 21 percent in retail and 6 percent in wholesale (U.S. Census).

Poverty Rate Is Average

The Asian American poverty rate is 11 percent, compared to 12 percent nationally. The poverty rate for the newest immigrant group, Southeast Asians, ranged from 35 to 64 percent in the 1990s but has declined dramatically. Hmong rates are down from 64 percent in 1990 to 38 percent in 2000, with Laotians at 19 percent and Vietnamese at 16 percent. Chinese American and Korean American rates are 14 percent, and rates for Filipino Americans, Japanese Americans, and Asian Indian Americans are under 10 percent.

Japanese Americans Are the Most Affluent

By 1990 Japanese Americans were the most successful of any Asian American group by most standards. Their educational attainment ran a close second to the top U.S. achievers, Asian Indian

Americans. They had the highest per capita income of any Asian American group, well above the national median. The poverty rate of 7 percent was near the lowest.

Home Ownership Rate Is Moderate

In 2004 nearly 60 percent of Asian Americans owned their own home, a slightly higher rate than most ethnic groups, but lower than the 75 percent for Euro-Americans (infoplease.com). Median home value was $200,000 compared to $123,000 for all Americans and $120,000 for Euro-Americans. Most Asian Americans live in areas where home prices are the highest in the nation (U.S. Census).

ASIAN AMERICAN CULTURES: COMMON THREADS AND CORE VALUES

There is not one Asian culture. There are at least six or seven major cultures and hundreds of sub-cultures. The extreme variations in Asian Americans' ways of life make it impossible to identify precise patterns for all. Still, many Asian cultures share a number of characteristics that help describe, but not define, them.

First, let's compare Asian cultures with other major world cultures, using the ten major types of cultural difference. We see that Asian cultures are generally perceived as follows:

- Basic worldview: I'm controlled
- Relationship priorities: us-first
- Social fabric: tight ties, stylized
- Masculinity: moderately feminine (cooperating, connecting)
- Equality/Status: rank-status
- Risk Orientation: play it safe
- Time Orientation: dive-right-in; cyclical, like the seasons; time is not money
- Decision Orientation: long-term
- Space: back-off (to a greater degree than any other major group)
- Communication: indirect
- Economic: varies from agricultural dependent through industrial independent to post-industrial interdependent

Common threads in the tapestries of Asian societies have been identified by such researchers as Philip Harris, Robert Moran, Ronald Takaki, William Wei, Esther Chow, Loraine Dong, Karen Hossfeld, and Nan Leaptrott. To begin with, of all the influences on Asian cultures, ancient China has had by far the greatest impact. Even today there are influential Chinese business minorities in many Asian countries outside China. So Chinese cultural values and practices provide most of the common threads.

The major deviations occur in those Asian countries with a Muslim religious majority, such as Indonesia and Malaysia, as well as the Philippines with its Catholic majority. There's also Japan, which was isolated for many years, during which time it developed some unique practices. And India, while in Asia, is actually a huge subcontinent that is quite complex. Still, many of the common threads are found there.

Five key values important in virtually all Asian cultures are:

1. Putting family and ingroup concerns before personal desires
2. Promoting group harmony
3. Accepting the hierarchy and status differences
4. Revering education, thrift, and hard work
5. Communicating vaguely, indirectly, and silently

First, we'll discuss some common threads of the general worldview that forms the foundation of these five key values.

A Collectivist Worldview

The worldview of most Asians is expressed in Confucianist principles. Some call this more a philosophy or social doctrine than a religion. For example, there is no belief in a separate, personified god. Reality is seen as an ongoing continuum that consists of everything in the universe, with all things being interrelated. The principles of harmony and continuity, as observed in the laws of nature, are the guiding principles of this worldview. The collective is the smallest unit that can survive, and people cannot survive on their own. A person really has no definition outside the group. People see themselves only as someone within a particular family, village, city, country, etc. Asians therefore put group concerns above their own desires and put family and group harmony above all else.

In a collectivist society each person is like a cell within a body. Some may be more important, as brain cells may be more important than finger cells, but all must work together to maintain a healthy whole. Asians tend to accept status differences within a social hierarchy, and they revere education. They can communicate without being explicit because they live in tight-knit cultures where people are on the same wavelength, and they often communicate indirectly in an effort to maintain harmony.

Research Comparing Asian and Euro–American Worldviews

Psychologist Richard Nisbett (2004) has conducted many research studies that attempt to compare American individualism and Asian collectivism. For example, Nisbett showed people a virtual aquarium on a computer screen. Most Euro-Americans focused on the biggest, brightest individual moving object and its features. Most Asians focused first on the context, the environment, and then the individual moving objects—putting the group context before individuals within the group setting.

In a memory experiment, Asians were more likely to recognize objects if they were presented each time on the same background or context, which by comparison had little effect on Euro-Americans' memory or recognition of objects. Again, group context was central to Asians' way of seeing things, while individual objects captured Euro-American attention.

In another experiment tracking the eyeball movements of persons, Nisbett found that Euro-Americans spend more time looking at the featured objects in an array, while Asians take in the entire scene, eyes darting between background and featured objects.

We know that symbols are powerful expressions of cultural values, such as individualism or collectivism. Savvy marketers know this, too. For example, Samsung ads for their cell phones are quite different for the American market—*I march to the beat of my own drum*—and the Korean market—*families staying connected.*

The Work Ethic

Rank and status are accepted as natural. But Asians believe that people, situations, and the collective can all be improved through education, thrift, and hard work. Collective cultures differ in this regard from the more fatalistic tribal cultures, such as the Arab culture. And Confucianism differs in this regard from the more fatalistic Catholicism that we find in Latino cultures. In this sense Asians are most like Protestant Europeans in their view of improvability through hard work, the well-known "Protestant Work Ethic."

Religions and Languages

Asian Americans have no common language or religion. Each major Asian ethnic group has its own language and dominant religion, philosophy, or social doctrine. Some groups have several languages and religions. Chinese, Japanese, and Koreans are physically and culturally very similar, stemming from a Confucianist focus on putting family, community, and patriotic duties above personal desires. Beliefs of other major Asian religions, such as Buddhism and Hinduism, tend to foster similar group values. India has its own culture, with major influences from the Hindu, Buddhist, and Islamic religions and the former rule of the British. The Philippine culture was influenced by the 300-year rule of Spain with its Catholicism. Even so, both India and the Philippines reflect many common Asian values and cultural patterns.

Value #1: Putting Group Concerns Before Individual Desires

All Asian cultures are collective, depending a great deal upon each other within close-knit families, extended families, and community groups. Members are expected to honor the group by:

- Seeing the group as the most important part of society
- Focusing on a group of people who are working toward a goal as more important than focusing on each one as individuals
- *Valuing group recognition and group reward above individual reward*
- Emphasizing a sense of belonging to the group and security within the group
- Extending tight, strong family ties to other relatives and close friends
- Placing central emphasis on a strong network of social relationships
- Making public service a moral responsibility
- Viewing personal saving and resource conservation as more important than consumption
- Placing fairness with the group and community above gaining wealth

Expressing Compassion

An important Confucian value involves compassion and benevolence for others, which seems similar to such Protestant values as "love your neighbor as yourself" and "do unto others as you would have them do unto you." However, a key difference is the relationship of the individual to the society as a whole. Euro-Americans believe that individuals should discover what they are good at, set their own standards, and go for it. Asians believe that individuals should use their talents to help the group develop and meet its goals. Success is joining an organization, and being part of a group that becomes successful.

Fitting In

The main point is to fit in with the group. To discourage young ones from going off on their own, parents cite such sayings as, "The nail that sticks up gets hammered down" and "The branch of the hedge that sticks out gets trimmed off."

Walking the Talk

Another difference is that Asians take these values more seriously in their daily lives. They are more constant in consciously reinforcing them throughout life with family altars, rituals, classes, and ceremonies. In Japan, for example, coming of age at 20 is a national holiday with ceremonies that focus on the responsibilities of adulthood.

Value #2: Promoting Group Harmony

Putting the group first naturally leads to the value of putting group harmony first. Customary ways of achieving this goal include the following beliefs and actions.

Disciplined Emotional Expression

Most Asians are taught that harsh words, scolding, temper flares, and similar emotional expressions will cause the other person to lose face and also to lose respect for the speaker. For example, to show your anger is seen as:

- the same as admitting loss of control
- a lapse in training and self-discipline
- a loss of face for you

As a result, in face-to-face relations, Asian Americans tend to maintain the amenities and cordialities, no matter how they are feeling. All this is true *unless* things have gone too far—and it's almost impossible for people outside the culture to estimate when things are about to go too far. Only insiders are likely to recognize these subtle signals.

Avoidance of Open Conflict

This includes avoiding personal confrontations, as well as not saying no, not giving others unpleasant messages, or doing this in a very indirect way.

Modesty

Everyone, especially females, is expected to show modesty by:

- Avoiding statements that can be perceived as boasting or self-congratulatory, as in overuse of the words "I," "me," and "mine."
- Being reticent to talk about themselves or their own accomplishments.
- Not drawing attention to themselves.
- Responding to compliments by belittling their abilities.

Self-Effacement or Humility

It's often appropriate for persons to act as if they are of lower status in order to show selfless humility and give honor to others. Highly respected people often assume an attitude of self-effacement in social and business contacts. Putting yourself forward is usually viewed as proud arrogance and invites scorn. To make a joke at someone else's expense and to cause embarrassment is highly resented In business. Also, "good" business persons place a higher value on allowing others in the group or community to save face and therefore preserve harmony than on achieving higher sales and profits.

Focusing on Others

The individual is expected to be extremely sensitive to others' feelings and wishes, giving second place to his or her own feelings and wishes.

Conforming

When persons are flexible, defer to others, or comply with the wishes of others in order to maintain harmony, they show maturity and self-discipline. Asian cultures expect people to conform to the wishes of those of higher status. This maintains harmony even when there is internal conflict between what persons want and what they think they should do. The key thing for you to remember: When an Asian American gives in to another person, it's not necessarily a passive or weak gesture, but is often a sign of tolerance, self-control, flexibility, and maturity.

Giving back

Mature persons are sensitive to the need to give to others who have given to them, to pay back devotion, generosity, and favors

Value #3: Accepting Status Differences—The Hierarchy

Protocol, rank, and status are important parts of all Asian cultures, ranging from the extremes of the former Hindu caste system to the Confucian system, which states:

- Everyone is expected to honor certain binding obligations to immediate family, relatives, clan, province, and state.
- Society should be structured to minimize deviations from these obligations.

- Women are subordinate to men, sons to fathers, younger brothers to older brothers, wives to husbands, and everyone to the state.
- Elders are especially respected, even revered, pampered, and appeased. Their every wish and desire is catered to whenever possible. Every home, no matter how poor, provides the best room for the honored grandparent

Across all religions and cultures, the Asian belief in hierarchy includes:

- Valuing a sense of order, propriety, and appropriate behavior between persons of varying status.
- Basing status on occupational position, education, wealth, and family background.

Typical Customs or Behaviors

Typical customs that reflect the status value include:

- When Asians meet someone, they quickly establish whether that person has higher status than they. If so, they show proper deference.
- They address people by their title and first name in all but informal or family situations.
- They respect seniority and the elderly
- Parents prefer sons to daughters. Daughters go to their husband's family and so lose the value they could bring to their own parents. As children are growing up, parents must protect daughters and can give sons more social freedom.
- Parents must arrange marriages for their children, aiming for partners with as high status as possible.

Respect for the Manager's Status

In the United States, it's appropriate at certain times for managers to roll up their sleeves and work alongside the people to get things done. Pitching in when there's an emergency is a sign you're a good sport, one of the guys. Many Asian Americans, especially the immigrants, would interpret it this way:

- This is an insult to me as a worker.
- You're implying that I can't get the work done the way I should.
- Such work is below your station as a manager
- I can't have the same respect for you now
- If you do this again, or do it insensitively, I'll really lose face. I may have to resign.

Value #4: Revering Education, Thrift, and Hard Work

Education is revered in Asian cultures, especially where there's a strong Confucian influence. Being educated is a high moral virtue and is a rigid prerequisite for moving up from lower to higher political and social standing. Scholars are given the greatest respect, have the highest rank, and are often among the most powerful and wealthy in society. Asian Americans therefore

- value education as a moral virtue
- value position in society and see education as the best way to achieve a good position and some financial security
- consider education an investment in family status

Asian Americans have tended to over-invest in education, given the fact that their income does not reflect as high a rate of return on education as the rate for Euro-Americans. Still, Asian Americans have seen education as one of their few tools for upward mobility in a hostile environment. Also, compared to most Asian countries, education in the United States is an incredible bargain, with tuition-free community colleges and low-tuition state colleges often available. Parents have been willing to make great sacrifices in order to provide a good education for their children.

Traditional methods of education involve learning the methods, skills, and facts. Everyone in a class is assumed to learn in the same way and to absorb the same information. Individual differences, imagination, and creativity are not a factor.

When young people from many nations are given the same set of math tests, the Americans score just below average. At the very top are students from Singapore, Hong Kong, Japan, South Korea, and Taiwan (Gladwell 2009). Some experts believe the reason has less to do with I.Q. and more to do with such Asian cultural traits as hard work and persistence. For example, when a random group of 8-year-old American and Japanese students are given a difficult math problem, most American students give up after 30 or 40 seconds. The Japanese students are still working on the problem after 15 minutes. Some researchers speculate that survival was more of a struggle for Asian peasant ancestors than for Europeans, resulting in a culture that highly rewards sacrifice, struggle, and persistence.

Psychologist Richard Nisbett (2009) asked, "Why do Asian American score higher on the SAT than other Americans? Why do students in Asian nations do much better on international math and science exams than U.S. students?" Achievement tests measure proficiency, the result of hard work, as much as innate skills. The Asian sense of obligation to family motivates them to work hard for academic excellence; collectivism is a strong factor. Also, Asian schools often have a student work out a math problem on the board as classmates join in. This collaboration is a sort of collectivism, a type of learning by induction that may be more effective than typical American methods of learning math and science.

The Asian attitude toward educational achievement is: Innate ability is not important; hard work is what counts. Beyond education, hard work and persistence in achieving long-term goals throughout life are highly valued. Gaining great wealth is not the goal. Rather, people are expected to fit in with the group and contribute to it by getting the best education and job position that they can, working hard, saving, and investing in order to achieve financial security within the community. This often involves sacrificing short-term pleasures for long-term benefits. Therefore, these work-save values are correlated with a planning and decision-making orientation that is long-term.

Value #5: Communicating Vaguely, Indirectly, Silently

Asian Americans may sometimes seem vague, indirect, or strangely silent, from the viewpoint of coworkers from other cultures.

Being Vague

In close-knit cultures, such as a collectivist region or an isolated nation (Japan), where everyone grew up in the same society, people can speak a sort of "shorthand" and be understood. In fact, being direct and making specific references may be seen as insulting. Being vague, indirect, or ambiguous is valued. As a result, people will often leave their sentences unfinished so listeners may mentally form the conclusion for themselves. After all, they know what the speaker is getting at—to "go on and on" might insult the listeners' intelligence. When these tendencies carry over into the U.S. workplace, coworkers can become quite confused.

Being Indirect

You've learned that being indirect is an Asian way of avoiding open conflict and preserving harmony. Pay special attention to situations in which an Asian American associate may need to say no, confront an issue, or deliver some other unpleasant message. For example, instead of telling you that your work is unacceptable, your colleague may simply refuse to discuss it, which for her means that she is signaling to you that the work needs revision and that you should ask how to improve it.

Remember that even when that person is trying to be direct in the Asian way, you may still consider it indirect. And their indirect message may be so subtle that you don't get it.

In Asian countries, pointing out errors as the cause of problems often results in denial and evasion. It's better to present the problem as a change that needs handling. On the other hand, real change is typically resisted, and managers typically need to show how it will benefit the collective, represent positive improvement or progress that is based on past traditions, or a similar reference to commonly-held values.

Saying No

To say no is an insult, could damage feelings and disrupt harmony, and is therefore bad manners. Asian Americans may say *yes*, meaning "I heard you," and then go about doing the opposite with little sense of breaking an agreement. Or, instead of saying, "No, I cannot have the report ready by Friday," your Asian American coworker may say, "Yes, I can try to complete the report by the time you need it." Thus, when an Asian American disagrees with you, says no, or conveys unwelcome information, he may do it so indirectly and subtly that you won't know it's been done. Later, if his actions reflect a lack of agreement, you may conclude that the he was not only unemotional and inscrutable, but perhaps evasive, sneaky, dishonest, or even corrupt. Probably, he was merely being polite.

- You can help by understanding these vague or indirect communication patterns and asking your Asian American associates to fill in the blanks.

Not Interrupting

If you were listening to a friend and didn't understand something she said, would you wait, expressionless, until she had finished a long explanation, expecting her to take responsibility for your understanding? Probably not. But if all the people you know believe that's the way to listen, then such behavior would be normal. For many Asian Americans, not interrupting is basic courtesy that is essential for conversations to proceed.

- You can help by encouraging Asian American associates to interrupt you in order to ask questions if they don't understand you

Keeping Longer Silences

When you finish speaking, how do you react when your listener is silent for a minute or more? Most Americans view such long silences as extremely uncomfortable and feel compelled to fill them in with comments or questions. For many Asian Americans, Japanese Americans for example, a few moments of quiet contemplation after listening may be essential, and comments are distracting.

- You can help by becoming comfortable with such silences and refraining from filling such moments with talk.

Other Customs

Other behavioral customs include:

- It's okay to call for someone to come to you by holding out your arm with your palm *down*, using a scratching movement. To turn your palm *up* and use the fingers to motion, which is typical in the United States, is considered rude.
- Meals are often more ritualistic, communal, and time consuming than in the United States The talk is considered more important than the food.
- Colors and numbers often have different meanings than they have in the United States For example, white may be used for mourning.

KEY ISSUES IMPORTANT TO ASIAN AMERICANS

Some key issues you should know about because they're important to many Asian Americans are 1) complications of the Model Minority myth, 2) changing male-female dynamics and differences, 3) educational concerns, and 4) discrimination and hate crimes.

Issue #1: Model Minority: A Mixed Blessing

In the 1960s, reporters began writing about the high education attainment, high median family income, low crime rates, and absence of juvenile delinquency and mental health problems among Asian Americans. Proponents of this model minority myth often ask, "Why can't African Americans succeed like this? (and not bother us)." This myth has been a mixed blessing for Asian Americans: it carries with it advantages and disadvantages.

Model Minority Advantages

The main advantages to Asian Americans of the Model Minority stereotype are that it showcases their cultural strengths, especially strengths connected with their success in running small family businesses.

Cultural Strengths

The Model Minority image eventually increased job opportunities for Asian Americans. Business managers say they favor hiring Asian Americans (Hossfeld 1994) because they:

- work hard and are productive
- invest in higher education, even at the cost of financial hardship
- are willing to work unusually long hours
- maintain a frugal lifestyle
- persevere in their goals and their work projects
- identify with the American Dream of hard work leading to a better life.
- save small amounts of money until they can invest in a small business
- use frugal strategies to keep their businesses going.

Small business ownership

A key aspect of the Model Minority image is Asian Americans' ability to start and hang onto small family businesses. Community credit associations and small family enterprises have traditionally been common in Asian countries. Immigrants who can't find work may use these strategies:

- Join mutual aid associations in the ethnic community provide needed financing and support, and members agree not to compete. Associations may loan capital, fix business locations and prices, locate employees, and help members in distress.
- Start businesses that are nonthreatening to the Euro-American majority because they're small and they specialize in limited areas.
- Work long hours for a certain minimum income.
- Give jobs first to family, then to extended family, neighborhood, and ethnic group members, in that order.
- Give employees as much job security as possible, with layoffs a last resort.
- Provide job flexibility to free employees to go to school or work at second jobs.
- Make the primary goal a long range one: to sustain the business over the long term.

Factors that may limit growth and expansion include:

- Owners' inadequate English skills
- Dependence on ethnic customers whose per capita wealth is lower.
- Reluctance to go outside the Asian American community to get money that would be needed for business expansion.

Small Business Success

During the 1990s Asian American businesses started up at twice the rate of all U.S. firms. They started with more capital than their Euro-American counterparts, and their owners were better educated, on average. Asian Americans more than doubled their share of contracts awarded under the Small Business Administrations 8a program between 1986 and 1996. One reason is their tendency toward high-tech firms. Although only about 3 percent of federal government contracts are in the SBA 8a program, Asian American firms got 24 percent of them in 1996, compared with 10 percent in 1986. By contrast African American contractors got 37 percent, compared to 50 percent in 1986, and the Latino-American share continued to hover around 30 percent (Sharpe 1997).

How Business Ownership Helped Create a Model Minority

Asian American families who have managed to build and hold onto at least a minimal level of business success have achieved the following advantages:

Protection from discrimination. For most of the twentieth century about half the Asian American male population worked for neighborhood small businesses, effectively shielding themselves from the open labor market with its discriminatory practices.

Higher educational attainment. Owners were able to accumulate money to send their children to college. Between 1940 and 1960 there was a dramatic increase in the percentage of Asian Americans who completed high school and went to college.

More opportunities. Small business success and higher educational attainment enhanced Euro-Americans' perception of Asian Americans as productive workers.

Disadvantages: Model Minority Costs

Several disadvantages offset the Asian American success story.

- They get less return on their educational investment than do Euro-Americans. Even though about twice as many have degrees, they average only 70 percent of Euro-American men's income.
- They are disadvantaged in getting the better-paying jobs. The percentage working as service workers, laborers, farm laborers, and private household workers is considerably higher than among Euro-Americans. They are under-represented in the professional ranks and in top management of mid- to large-size corporations.
- Most have a lower living standard than their income implies because 90 percent live in high-cost areas, such as San Francisco and Hawaii.
- More of the family members work than in Euro-American families (3.17 compared to 2.58 in 1997) and they work more hours on average.
- Underemployment is more common. Rather than be unemployed, most will accept low-paying, part-time, or seasonal jobs.
- It overlooks the fact that some recent immigrants, such as Hmong Americans, have major problems.

Political Viewpoints

Why do some scholars and reporters so eagerly focus on Asian American success, while others keep stressing discrimination? The debate is not just over economics but also over political viewpoint.

Those who depict Asian Americans as the model minority tend to be conservatives who believe that American society is indeed an egalitarian one. All people have the opportunity to succeed. Each person must make the necessary effort to achieve material well being. If an individual or group does not make it, it's their own fault.

Liberals, who focus on continued inequality, believe the problem lies primarily within the social, economic, and political system. Before the minority groups have equal opportunity to improve their status, some aspects of the system must change. But systemic change can occur only with a shift in the present balance of power between different groups. Therefore, those who perceive reality in this manner advocate greater political activism.

The answer probably encompasses both viewpoints. We each create our reality in a very important sense. Asian Americans who have certain attributes, and who do the right things and make the right moves, can indeed overcome all barriers and achieve the success they want. Andrea Jung became CEO of Avon, Elaine Chao became Secretary of Labor, and Norman Mineta became Secretary of Transportation. They discovered what it takes to break through the glass ceiling, but should it be so difficult and so rare for Asian Americans to do it?

Issue #2: Male–Female Dynamics and Differences

Most Asian cultures are extremely patriarchal and women are significantly more subjugated in these cultures than in the American culture.

Family Culture Clash

Culture clash often affects husband-wife dynamics, especially in families that have immigrated since the 1960s. That's when women's pay and work status began improving and traditional male jobs in manufacturing plants began deteriorating. Problems often arise over these events:

- The wife finds a better-paying job than the husband, upsetting the male status in a hierarchical family structure.
- The wife must learn to be assertive, decisive, and efficient on the job, which conflicts with her role as a shy, patient, and resilient wife and mother.
- Children at school learn they must speak up, express opinions, and ask why in order to succeed, but are expected to keep quiet and do as they're told at home.
- Girls must also speak up at school, but at home they're supposed to be even more reserved and compliant than boys.

Stereotypes of Asian Women Workers

Women who don't have the educational credentials to land better-paying jobs often take manufacturing assembly line jobs. They typically encounter myths, stereotypes, and other barriers to promotion and job satisfaction. For example, research indicates that the formula used by many hiring managers in California's Silicon Valley for entry level manufacturing assembly line operatives can be summarized as "small, foreign, and female" (Zinn 1994). This means they recruit and hire primarily Asian and Latina immigrant women. Reasons employers give for the hiring policy are based on stereotyped and prejudiced beliefs, especially about Asian American women, as follows:

- Immigrant women are more likely to be content with such jobs. (In fact, most want to advance.)
- They're unqualified for better-paying jobs. (In fact, they're trainable.)
- They have husbands who earn more than they do (in fact, about 80 percent are the main income earners in their families).
- Their patience and superior coordination better suits them to assembly line production involving tiny, intricate circuitry.

- Their small size makes it easier for them to sit quietly for long periods, doing small detail work.

- Their strong task orientation, high achievement motivation, and hard work qualify them as reliable production workers

- They're childlike, obedient, and submissive, good qualities for assembly-line work but not for managerial roles.

- Most U.S. citizens would not be content for long with such boring, low-paying jobs, but Asian American women are.

Reality: Beneath the Passive Surface, Active Achievement

Most Asian American women on assembly lines are actually active, goal-oriented doers, according to several studies. They're disadvantaged in at least three aspects of the social structure, that is, being an ethnic minority, a woman, and within a lower socioeconomic class.

The problems they experience with their supervisors (nearly all Euro-American) stem primarily from the following:

- supervisors' perception of their inabilities
- disrespect for Asian women
- unreasonable work assignments
- unfair performance evaluation
- accusation of job errors
- inappropriate decisions regarding promotion
- intolerance of language accents
- apparent discrimination

How do Asian American women handle the problems resulting from these stereotypes? Here are some facts from Esther Chow's (1994) research:

- About half have no difficulty challenging their supervisor about problems.

- Well over half have difficulty in expressing anger and in demanding their fair share from supervisors.

- Those of higher occupational status have more to lose and more difficulty demanding their fair share.

- Almost all attempt to establish congenial working relationships with people at all levels of the organization.

- Two-thirds have little difficulty in protesting unfair treatment by their Euro-American *co-workers* (as distinguished from their supervisors).

- Most had more difficulty protesting to Euro-American women than to the men, since they tend to consider the women as natural allies and hesitate to break that feeling of camaraderie.

- Only 6 percent said they choose to say nothing to offensive co-workers or to ignore incidents they think are unfair

A Range of Workplace Styles

Typical styles for dealing with workplace situations are avoidance or indirectness, affiliative, assertive, and confrontational. The style a woman uses depends primarily on how extreme or important the work problem is to her.

Adaptation and Indirectness

Adapting or being indirect seem to fit the passive stereotype. Silence is sometimes a temporary reaction in the process of coping. It may be part of a defensive stand in which they protect themselves from the hurt by pushing their tolerance to the limit. Variations of the approach include avoiding problem situations as much as possible, doing little about them, or hoping a problem will go away. They might write to a supervisor, talk to a supervisor about an offensive co-worker, or make an impersonal telephone call to a co-worker, all in hopes of finding a solution to the problem. Most don't carry this style to the extreme of quitting, which they would see as defeatist. A frequent pattern is to begin by adapting and later to shift to a more active strategy.

Congeniality

Being congenial is a style used sometimes to show willingness to cooperate in solving workplace problems. It involves personal consideration, friendliness, and candidness to achieve some kind of equity with coworkers. Women using this style may emphasize commonalties, such as being women or being Asian Americans, in order to establish rapport, to dispel issues of inequity, and to neutralize feelings of injustice. They are more apt to use this style with Euro-American women than with men.

Assertiveness

Asserting themselves is a direct style for claiming certain work rights and independence. It includes negotiating their time, effort, intellect, commitment, and personal involvement with other workers. About half the women use this style, and they're more likely to do so when they deal with Euro-American male workers than with females. It includes expressing their viewpoints and judgment of a situation, demanding explanations from offensive workers, and focusing their efforts on problem solving. This approach is active, goal-oriented, and a way of taking charge of their own lives. Women using this approach expect to negotiate a solution to a problem. For example, they may want some agreement about work hours that don't doesn't interfere with their family obligations.

Confrontation

Confronting the persons involved in the situation is a somewhat aggressive style of fighting prejudice and discrimination at work. The women directly protest against those co-workers they view as insensitive and threatening to their survival. They fight back in the face of apparently overwhelming odds in order to protect their work rights and to show they won't compromise themselves to what they see as others' unreasonable demands. Some even go as far as quitting their job rather than be pushed around, the ultimate form of resistance. They see it as affirming self-respect and human dignity, even above job security.

Issue #3: University Education

Educational issues important to many Asian Americans include getting into top universities and establishing Asian American studies programs.

Getting Into Top Universities

Many Asian American high school graduates with straight-As have been unable to get into the nation's top public and private universities. The admission *rate* of Asian American applicants to these universities was lower than that for any other ethnic group during the 1980s. No university has admitted any discriminatory intent, but officials at several have acknowledged that their affirmative action policies and practices may have had an unintentional adverse impact on Asian Americans.

Asian Americans have united to ensure that their educational rights will not be abridged, because access to quality higher education, perhaps more than any other issue, is something they feel very strongly about. Many Asians immigrate to the United States precisely to allow their children to receive such education. Most Filipino Americans, 56 percent, favor affirmative action programs that set quotas for minority admissions to college. Chinese Americans are almost evenly divided on the issue, with 41 percent favoring affirmative action and 43 percent opposing it. Interviews indicated that nearly all Chinese Americans are concerned about discrimination, but many are uncomfortable with using government regulation to alleviate the problem (Baldassare 1990).

Coping with the Model Minority Student Stereotype

Asian-Americans make up 10 percent or more of undergraduates at many of the most selective U.S. colleges—and considerably more than 10 percent in California—although they are only about 4 percent of the U.S. population. People tend to believe that Asian Americans focus almost exclusively on the STEM degrees—Science, Technology, Engineering, and Math—and in fact they did earn 32 percent of doctorates in those fields in 2003 (Lewin 2008). However, contrary to stereotype, most of the bachelor's degrees they earned were in business, management, social sciences, or humanities.

Most University of California and other top California campuses have student bodies that are over 40 percent Asian Americans—because they simply have much higher test scores than other groups. For example, in 2005 at University of Michigan the median test score for Asian American students who were offered admission was:

- 50 points higher than the median score for Euro-American students
- 140 points higher than for Latino American students
- 240 points higher than for African American students

The idea that Asian American "model minority" students are edging out all others is so widespread that common quips include "UCLA = United Caucasians Lost Among Asians" or "MIT = Made in Taiwan." Hmong Americans and Asian Pacific Islanders are most hurt by such model minority stereotypes because many come from the lowest income group and must select "Asian" when filling out university applications.

A recent report took aim at stereotyped beliefs (Lewin 2008), saying "Certainly there are many Asians doing well, at the top of the curve, and that's a point of pride, but there are just as many struggling at the bottom of the curve, so lumping together all Asian groups masks the poverty and academic difficulties of some subgroups." The SAT scores of Asian-Americans, like those of other Americans, tend to correlate with the income and educational level of their parents. "The notion of lumping all people into a single category and assuming they have no needs is wrong." The report also noted that more Asian-Americans are enrolled in community colleges than in four-year colleges.

Establishing Asian American Studies Programs

Many Asian American university students are asking for a more "relevant" education, meaning a multiethnic curriculum that includes the history of discrimination in the United States and an accurate portrayal of the contributions and struggles of people of color. This interest reflects a new cultural awakening among Asian American students, along with a rising political consciousness. Instead of choosing between their Asian heritage and the American culture, some young Asian Americans are forging a new culture of their own, one that goes beyond a simple blending of East and West. This culture directly reflects the historical experience and current life circumstances of Asians in America. In university courses about Asian Americans, they may get a glimpse of this emerging culture and even be encouraged to help create it.

In the late 1960s and early 1970s Asian American studies courses and programs were established at many West Coast universities. Those at San Francisco State University and at the University of California at Berkeley began as part of the settlement of two long and militant student strikes. What that generation of students, as well as succeeding generations who filled the classes, wanted was the more "relevant" education mentioned earlier. They also wanted practical training to enable graduates to bring about fundamental social change in their ethnic communities as well as in the society at large. Because of their radical agenda, the programs encountered stiff resistance from curriculum and personnel review committees. A number failed, while others managed to survive but did not grow.

In the late 1980s these programs took a new lease on life when students began demanding a more multiethnic curriculum. Dozens of campuses, including five of the eight University of California campuses, now have some version of an ethnic studies requirement. Students at some East Coast and Midwestern universities are also insisting that Asian American studies programs be set up.

Issue #4: Discrimination and Hate Crimes

Asian Americans closely watch trends in discrimination and the increase in hate crimes.

Discrimination

Most Asian Americans say that prejudice and discrimination is *not* a problem in their local area, with 64 percent of Filipino Americans and 51 percent of Chinese Americans saying it's not a problem. However, when asked if qualified members of their ethnic group can rise to the top in local companies, 56 percent of Filipino Americans and 37 percent of Chinese Americans said discrimination was a problem. When asked if the glass ceiling is a problem, about 70 percent of Filipino Americans and 66 percent of Chinese Americans said yes.

While they are not proportionately represented in corporate top management or elected political office, breakthroughs are occurring. For example, in 1996 the first Asian American state governor in U.S. history was elected—Gary Locke, a Chinese American, was elected governor of Washington. In 2001 Elaine Chao was appointed Secretary of Labor, the first Asian American woman to become a member of a U.S. President's Cabinet. And in 2007 Asian Indian American Bobbie Jindal was elected Governor of Louisiana, having served two terms as a U.S. Congressman from Louisiana.

Hate Crimes

Since 1980, increased instances of physical assault, harassment, vandalism, and anti-Asian racial slurs have been reported. The U.S. Civil Rights Commission has stated that "the issue of violence against Asian Americans is national in scope." Three subgroups are especially vulnerable: Southeast Asian Americans, immigrant entrepreneurs (especially Koreans), and various individuals. Many instances of hate crimes against Vietnamese are reported in Texas, California, and Massachusetts. Tensions have built between Korean merchants and residents of mostly African American or Spanish-speaking neighborhoods where many Koreans own stores. They have accused the Koreans of treating them rudely, even roughly. Some have responded with fire bombings and vandalism.

Next we'll explore some specifics of each major Asian American subculture.

CHINESE AMERICAN WORKERS

About one-fourth of all Asian Americans are Chinese Americans, the largest of the Asian groups. Because of their greater numbers and more extensive history in the United States than other Asian American groups, we'll spend a little more time on this group than the others. We'll review some background information about their immigration experiences, differences among generations, and facts from their current profile.

The First Immigrants: From Gold Mines to Laundries

The Chinese were the first sizable group of Asians to immigrate to America and most settled in the West. Most had been farm peasants in China. However, most who came after the 1940s were more affluent business and professional persons escaping from communism. The earliest immigrants came to California soon after the 1849 Gold Rush to work in the gold mines. Later they were the primary workers who built the railroads and the irrigation canals and levees of the river deltas, laying the groundwork for the agricultural industry.

For many years nearly all the Chinese immigrants were men, who came to earn a nest egg and return to China. But most stayed and since there were so few Chinese women, they formed a bachelor society. The workers were nearly always targets of Euro-American labor resentment, especially during hard times. Ethnic antagonism in the mines, factories, and fields forced thousands of Chinese to set up small stores, restaurants, and service shops, especially laundries, which took little start-up cash. By 1890 the Chinese represented nearly 70 percent of all laundry workers. The "Chinese laundryman" was an

American phenomenon. There were no laundries in China. The women there did the laundry, and men in China would have lost social status if they had done it (Ong 1983).

Euro-American workers often referred to the Chinese as "nagurs," and they were often stereotyped as oriental vampires with slanted eyes, a pigtail, dark skin, and thick lips. Like African Americans, they were perceived as heathen, morally inferior, savage, childlike, and lustful. The Chinese were seen as inferior colored people, along with African Americans and American Indians.

In 1880 Congress passed a Chinese Exclusion Act that prohibited further Chinese immigration, even though they represented only 0.002 percent of the total U.S. population. The exclusion act, which was extended indefinitely in 1904, also denied naturalized citizenship to the Chinese already here. Euro-American workers complained about competition from Chinese who would work for less. Many Chinese complained that the "cheap labor" cry was always a falsehood. They said that employers preferred Chinese workers because they were so much more honest, industrious, steady, sober, and painstaking. They said they were persecuted, not for their vices, but for their virtues (Chew 1906).

Subsequent Generations

By the 1920s and 1930s Chinese Americans had become more concerned than ever about their status because they were bringing up an increasing number of American-born children. The dominant Euro-American culture tended to grant more freedom and autonomy to children, as they grew into teenagers and young adults, than the Chinese culture. As in other immigrant families, a generational conflict existed in many Chinese American families over parental authority and the freedom of the American-born children coming of age. Many of them, especially females burdened with stricter limits than males, resented the restrictions on their social lives most of all (Chan 1991).

In the late 1940s to the mid 1960s relatively affluent and well-educated refugees from communism immigrated from China. In the 1990s, most immigrants were either wealthy investors from Hong Kong and Taiwan or poor political refugees from mainland China. Chinese Americans who immigrated as small children generally have no language problem, nor do any of the generations born in the United States More than half of this group attains at least some college education..

Identity Crisis

Chinese American children reared in America experienced an identity crisis that was intensified by the prejudice that permeated many areas of public life. They were barred from public recreational facilities, such as swimming pools, and forced to sit at the back of movie theaters. Those who participated in athletics usually had to join Chinese teams. One Chinese American gave a typical interview response, "At times I have been called a 'Chink' and I have resented it bitterly and would at times answer back, but recently I have not replied" (Chan 1991, 113). Most troubling, very few second-generation college graduates could find jobs appropriate to their education and training.

Distinct Socioeconomic Classes

By the 1960s Chinese Americans were drifting into two categories. One was educated, relatively affluent, and becoming acculturated to American society. The other was largely uneducated, not affluent, and still retained much of traditional Chinese culture. People in the Chinese American community tended to have either much education or none.

Given the number of well-educated adults, however, the incomes of Chinese Americans were quite low. Although well-trained Chinese Americans could find suitable employment with relative ease, it was still very difficult for them to gain promotion to supervisory and higher administrative positions. Many were clearly overqualified for the jobs they held, and the only conclusion was that employers were reluctant to place Chinese Americans in positions that gave them power over Euro-Americans (Kitano and Daniels 1988).

Since I960 the most notable developments have been the rapid growth of the Chinese American population, the degree to which it came to be seen as a model minority, and movement to the suburbs. The population increased four fold between 1960 and 1985, due primarily to expanded immigration quotas.

Movement to the Suburbs

A major development since 1980 is the movement of Chinese Americans out of Chinatowns into the suburbs. This move reflects their ongoing acculturation and Americanization. The so-called "miniature Chinatowns" sprouting up in suburban cities are actually small shopping malls, each usually anchored by a large American supermarket. These malls are often financed by Chinese Americans, who may also be some of the shop owners. The homes bought by Chinese Americans who frequent these malls tend to be scattered throughout the neighborhood, a different pattern than the dense homogeneous Chinatown pattern.

Current Profile

Chinese Americans are the largest group of Asian Americans; in fact, until recent decades they were the only large group of Asian Americans. Now they make up 23 percent of Asian Americans, with Filipino Americans running close behind at 18 percent. Nearly 70 percent of Chinese Americans are foreign born, so most are strongly influenced by Chinese cultural values and practices. Statistical averages of factors that purport to indicate Chinese socioeconomic status can be misleading due to the existence of the two distinct classes discussed earlier. When these two are averaged together, their profile is very similar to that of the average American.

One distinct difference however lies in educational attainment; nearly twice as many Chinese Americans hold bachelor's degrees as the national average, 47 percent of men and 35 percent of women. Such educational attainment is remarkable given the language problems. About 83 percent speak Chinese at home, 60 percent speak English "not very well." About 40 percent are linguistically isolated, meaning the language barrier minimizes their interactions with English-speaking persons.

Their per capita income does not reflect their higher educational attainment. At $14,900 it's only slightly higher than the $14,100 national median. Their family income is near the national average because more family members work. Nearly 20 percent of families have three or more members in the workforce compared to the national rate of 13 percent.

FILIPINO AMERICAN WORKERS

The earliest inhabitants of the Philippine Islands arrived from the Asian mainland about 30,000 years ago. In 1571 Spanish imperial rule began and lasted for 327 years until 1889, when the United States won possession in the Spanish-American War. U.S. rule lasted for 57 years until 1946 when Philippine independence was granted. The national language is Filipino and is based on Tagalog, but there are 111 dialects spoken in the country, and Spanish expressions are common. English is the language of commerce and law, and most educated immigrants speak English.

Immigration to the United States began early in the 20th century. A small group of male farm workers initially migrated to Hawaii and later to the United States. The second wave was mainly women who entered after World War II under the War Brides Act. The third wave has been entering under the Immigration Act of 1965 and includes many educated professionals.

Current Profile

Filipino Americans are 18 percent of all Asian Americans, with over two million people, the second largest Asian American subgroup after Chinese Americans. Most Filipino Americans are foreign born, well educated, hardworking, and relatively affluent.

Foreign born. Nearly 68 percent are foreign born immigrants, and about 25 percent have not yet become U.S. citizens. Therefore, Filipino values and practices are a strong part of their heritage. On the other hand, 75 percent are citizens and 32 percent were born in the United States. Language is not a problem for most. Only 13 percent are linguistically isolated, although 66 percent speak other than English at home.

Educated. Filipino Americans are the only Asian American group with more women holding degrees (42 percent) than men (36 percent). This is nearly double the rate of Euro-American men and more than two and one-half times the rate of Euro-American women. In 2000 most of them held management or professional jobs, 38 percent, with 25 percent in sales and office jobs, and 18 percent in service jobs. Many work in the medical field as nurses, therapists, lab technicians, and related jobs (Census 2000).

Hardworking & Affluent. Filipino Americans tend to be very industrious, having the highest percentage of employment of any ethnic group, 71 percent of men and 65 percent of women. They also have the highest percentage of families with three or more members working (30 percent), and the lowest rate of poverty (6 percent). Their families average 4 persons, more than the national average of 3.2.

In 2000 Filipino American per person income was $35,500 for men and $31,500 for women. Male earnings therefore were slightly below the U.S. male average of $37,000, but female earnings were above the U.S. female average of $27,000. Median family income was $65,000, well above the U.S. median of $50,000. (U.S. Census 2000).

Cultural Values and Practices

The Filipino culture itself encompasses a diverse, multi-layered mix of subcultures. Its complex, indigenous culture has strong Malay and other Asian influences. This is combined with Spanish and American colonial cultural influences, but since 1946 a clear Filipino cultural identity has been developing. Because of the historical Spanish influence, about 85 percent of Filipinos are Roman Catholic, and more than 90 percent have a Christian Malay heritage.

The most dominant cultural values are (Bautista 2002, Posadas 1999, Tanaka 1995, Pido 1992):

- putting family first, including extended family
- respecting authority and elders
- cooperating
- maintaining face and avoiding shame
- hospitality, repaying generosity, and meeting obligations

Other important cultural values include:

- Personalistic view of the universe and fatalistic view of the future
- "God will help," a fatalistic reliance on powers beyond self
- Good luck determines success.
- Sex and marriage are religious concerns; marriages are expected to last.

Let's discuss further the most dominant values.

Putting family first

Family needs and status are placed above individual needs, reflecting the interdependence among family members. Filipinos don't think in terms of accumulating wealth and prestige for themselves, but for their families. Education, which is highly valued, is seen as an investment, primarily to benefit the famiy—which may include aunts, uncles, cousins, and even close friends. Large extended families with many children are common in the Philippines, which has one of the highest birth rates in the world.

All important decisions that a person makes are first discussed with the family, especially the older members. Family obligations are more important than personal preferences or obligations to employers or the community. Given that, persons who are most admired are seen as understanding, unselfish with their time and help, and participating wholeheartedly in community activities.

Respecting authority and elders

Respect for authority and elders and obedience to authority are strong cultural values. They believe older people should be shown respect and allowed to take the lead. They generally seek out elders or other authority figures for approval and protection and for support or advice in making decisions.

Filipino American employees, in return for the respect, obedience, and politeness they give the boss, may expect protection and favors, due to the value of reciprocity. Also, they may expect the boss to have an authoritarian management style and may therefore interpret a participative style as evidence of weakness or indecision.

Cooperating

Filipinos value cooperation, the ability to get along with people, and are usually very receptive and willing to accept tasks on the job. They may cooperate with the work group at their own expense, and yet be too shy to make friends within the group. They tend to agree with those around them rather than express disagreement, to avoid confrontation, and to be cooperative and compliant. As a result

- Their true feelings may remain hidden from outsiders.
- They may use a go-between to bring up embarrassing or controversial matters.

Maintaining face and avoiding shame

From the Spanish comes a special sense of self-esteem called *amor propio,* meaning self-love. To maintain self-esteem, some Filipino Americans put great energy into displaying appropriate dress, modesty, and good manners. Shame, called *hiya,* is felt when self-esteem is damaged, and nothing is worse than being shamed. An adult worker may withdraw, becoming less cooperative. If questioned, he or she may feel frustrated and too embarrassed to respond. As a result, Euro-Americans may conclude that they're oversensitive and can't take criticism. Here are some behaviors that may result from *hiya:*

- An employee may not ask questions of a supervisor even if she is not sure what to do
- An employee who is laid off from his job may act violently
- A host may spend more than he can afford for an event
- A student may not disagree in a discussion, even when she feels strongly about the topic

Hospitality, Repaying Generosity, Meeting Obligations

Hospitality toward guests is highly valued and an important obligation. Guests are offered the best of everything that the family can offer—food and even clothing and shelter. When Filipinos are on the receiving end of someone's generosity, they feel obligated to repay it in some way. When Filipinos don't reciprocate and meet their obligations, they may be shamed. To be called shameless is a serious insult.

Communication Patterns

Although Tagalog is the major language, most speak English, reflecting the U.S. influence, Filipino Americans follow the pattern found in many Asian cultures of indirectness and the use of a mediator or go-between as a tool of indirectness. To get directly to the point with a supervisor might be seen as disrespectful. They also tend to use flowery language, based on the belief that an impressive command of language is the sign of a cultivated person and enhances one's image, which is similar to the Latino viewpoint.

On the other hand, most Filipino Americans readily adjust to the punctuality required in the U.S. workplace, as long as expectations are made clear. Their desire to cooperate, respect for authority, and fear of shame impel them to meet the supervisor's expectations regarding punctuality and meeting deadlines.

Expression of feelings

Filipino Americans place great emphasis on feelings or emotions, and generate warmth and friendliness. In this they're more like Latinos than other Asians. Supervisors must be especially careful in giving performance evaluations, critiques, and feedback. It's very difficult for most Filipinos to objectively separate the task at hand, the product, or their performance from themselves as subjective persons. They're likely to interpret a supervisor's objective analysis as a personal attack.

Use of time

Immigrants from the Philippines often must adjust to punctuality and use of time in the American workplace. In the Philippines, you are considered punctual if you arrive for an appointment within about 15 minutes after the scheduled time. Social events begin an hour or two after the appointed hour. According to Euro-Americans, Filipinos rarely complete things on time despite deadlines. They do get things done in their own time; many Euro-Americans say they do things "almost, but not quite."

View of nature

Traditional Filipino culture sees humans as part of nature, not dominating it as much as conforming to it and interpreting their experience of nature through religion, family, and other means.

Customs

Some typical Filipino customs include the followings (Andres 1999)

- *Gifts* are not opened in front of the giver, which might imply the receiver is materialistic and more concerned with the gift than the act of giving. Also, when multiple gifts are given, comparisons might be made that would embarrass some givers.

- *Home visiting* is often done on a drop-in basis. Guests remove their shoes and are not expected to walk into other rooms without asking for permission.

- *Affection* in public, displayed by couples, is minimal.

- *Handshakes* may be limp, which is socially acceptable.

- *Using the index finger* to beckon people is extremely rude.

- *Lips* may be used to point to things.

- *Nodding upwards* is a common form of greeting.

- *Eyebrows raised* in recognition means "yes."

- *Avoidance of eye contact* is implies dishonesty.

- *Smiling,* even for no reason, may be a sign of respect, showing deference and simpatia.

SOUTHEAST ASIAN AMERICAN WORKERS

About one-sixth of the Asian American group immigrated from Southeast Asian countries since the 1960s, most of them escaping the Vietnam War and communism. We'll discuss the unusual conditions of their emigration, their current profile, and the key issue, acculturation.

Background; Refugee Flight

About a million refugees have recently entered the United States from Southeast Asia as a result of the Vietnam War. The war created many political refugees from Vietnam, Cambodia, and Laos. The conditions of emigration may include

- a recent past marred by years of war, chaos, and political persecution

- panic, fear, crisis, distress

- evacuating under a state of emergency with inadequate time for planning

- problems in transit, perhaps even becoming a "boat person," attacked by pirates and turned away by various governments

- life in temporary centers for many, transition from a rural, agricultural society to a modern, industrial or post-industrial society

Because of U.S. involvement in the Vietnam War in the 1960s and early 1970s, the U.S. withdrawal in 1975, and the subsequent communist takeover of those countries, the United States has taken some responsibility for these political refugees, as well as children of American military men. Immigration legislation in 1975 and 1976 expanded Asian immigrant quotas, and the 1980 Refugee Assistance Act further expanded quotas and provided for federal aid to states during the refugees' first few years of residence.

Differences and Similarities among Groups

The first wave of refugees consisted primarily of middle and upper-class South Vietnamese who got out in the 1970s before the U.S. withdrawal, while the second wave contained many more Hmong, Cambodians, and Laotians. People of the first wave are generally more accustomed to Western ways, better educated, more affluent, and better equipped to enter the U.S. workforce than those of the second wave. By the mid-1980s they had a median income equal to that of the total population. Many among the second wave are have had a more difficult time, but are adapting.

Vietnamese

Vietnam is largely an agricultural country, but it has more large urban centers than Laos and Cambodia and more people, with a population of 55 million. Over 70 percent of Vietnamese Americans are refugees of the Vietnam War. Many were middle- and upper-class citizens, wealthy or well-connected, and were able to leave South Vietnam before the communist takeover. Most came as family groups, some with large bankrolls and others with only the clothes on their backs. Over half live on the West Coast. San Diego has the largest population and San Francisco the second largest (Vietnamese 2001).

Status in the Vietnamese culture is attained through age and education more than through wealth. The people are oriented more toward intuition than intellect. Their worldview and religious practices vary from Confucianism to Buddhism to Taoism. Stemming from the French colonial era, nearly 40 percent of Vietnamese Americans consider themselves Catholic. They've incorporated Asian traditions into their religious rituals. Here is a brief comparison of Vietnamese and Euro-American worldviews.

Vietnamese Worldview	*Euro-American Worldview*
Humans are basically good but corruptible	Human nature is evil but perfectible.
Humans should master Nature	Humans should master Nature.
Past orientation	Future orientation
Value attachment to a place, ancestral land	Value movement, migration, mobility.
Value accomplishment, individuality and self-reliance	Value the process of being or becoming, mutual dependence, connectedness.

Laotians

Laos is small, mountainous, rural, and undeveloped, with a sparse population. Many Laotians who lived near the Vietnamese border were swept up in the American-Vietnamese War of the 1960s-1970s. The infamous Ho Chi Minh Trail, the supply route from North Vietnam to South Vietnam, was extensively bombed by American forces. Meanwhile Laos had its own communist insurgency with fighting between the communists and the royal army. The end of the war and withdrawal of American troops forced about 384,000 Laotians to immigrate to the United States to avoid decimation when the communists took over the Laotian government.

Hmong Hill Tribes of Laos: A Unique Group

About half the Laotian refugees were members of Hmong hill tribes. They had lived as semi-nomadic farmers, clearing mountainous jungle areas to plant crops. The Hmong are generally described as industrious, independent, and peace-loving people. The culture is typically rural Asian—strong family-clan-tribe system, large families of 9 or 10 children who help with the work, male dominance, and veneration of elders. The household, not the individual, is the primary unit, with perhaps 5 to 10 households from a clan joining with 3 or 4 other clans to create a tribal mountain village of 20 to 30 households. The villages serve as mutual aid associations, and members typically marry within the tribe. They trust their local shaman more than modern medicine.

U.S. government policy was to scatter the Laotian refugees around the country to minimize their impact on any one area. This posed problems for the Hmong, who had no experience with cold weather or urban violence. As a result, during the early 1980s a third of all the Hmong migrated again in order to reunite into clans, form cohesive communities, and found mutual-assistance organizations (Fadiman 1998). About 50,000 settled in California, many in the Fresno area, 20,000 in Minnesota, and 15,000 in Wisconsin, with other clans in various states.

The Hmong had no experience with written language until 1953, when missionaries came into Laos. They introduced the Romanized Popular Alphabet to convert the Hmong oral language into written form (WPB 2008). Very few of the Hmong refugees spoke English. They had, and still have the lowest educational achievement of any U.S. group and have faced the greatest challenges to finding employment in the U.S. workplace. Imagine migrating from a hill tribe with no written language until very recently, to a post-industrial highly technological society. In 1990 only 29 percent of Hmong Americans had jobs, their average income was $2,600, and most depended on public assistance to survive. The 2000 Census reported the following demographic information about Hmong Americans:

- 170,000 current population in 2000, compared with 90,000 in 1990
- 60% had a high school diploma
- 7% had a college degree
- 40% lived below the poverty line
- 6.6 children per family, the highest birth rate of any U.S. group.

Adapting to a high-tech workplace that is based upon quite sophisticated uses of written information has presented a formidable challenge. Gaining facility with the English language was and still is the most crucial task. Although nearly 90 percent were on welfare in the 1980s, they have rapidly learned how to survive on their own.

However their children, and even grandchildren, many in California public schools, still face language difficulties. In 2003, about 85 percent of Hmong American students were classified as LEP (limited English proficiency). They are the group with the largest percentage in this category, by far. For example, although 1.3 million Latino American students are classified as LEP, that constitutes only 43 percent of the 3 million such students in the California school system (Vang 2005).

Cambodians

Cambodia is a small, primarily agricultural country, with a population of about 7 million. In 1979 Vietnamese communists invaded Cambodia, creating more than 3 million refugees. Cambodians who fled to the United States are mainly farmers, although some are skilled trade persons and a few are educated young people.

Current Profile of Southeast Asian Americans

Before 1970 there were about 20,000 Vietnamese in the United States and the number of other Southeast Asians was too small to count. In 1990 more than one million Southeast Asian Americans made up about 16 percent of the Asian American population. Although the U.S. government attempted to scatter them throughout the country, many migrated to the West, especially California.

Large families. They have the highest birth rates of any U.S. group; Hmong American families average 6.6 persons, while Filipino Americans, Vietnamese Americans, Cambodian Americans, and Laotian Americans average more than 4 persons per family, compared to the U.S. average of 3.2.

Less education. The Southeast Asian Americans have the lowest educational level of any U.S. cultural group. Causes probably include the chaos and disruption of years of war in the area they immigrated from, the rural agricultural background of many, language barriers, and their relatively destitute status as political refugees. The difference between educational level of men and women is significant, as indicated in Table 8.1.

Language Harriers. More than 90 percent speak their native language at home. In 1990 more than 70 percent of Hmong, Cambodians, and Laotians did not speak English very well, and more than half of them were linguistically isolated. About 65 percent of Vietnamese did not speak English very well and 44 percent were linguistically isolated.

TABLE 9.1: Educational Achievement of Southeast Asian Americans by Gender, 2000

Group	% Holding a High School Diploma or Higher	% Holding a Bachelor's Degree or Higher
Hmong	41	7
Cambodian	47	9
Laotian	51	8
Vietnamese	62	20
U.S. total	80	24

Low Incomes. Fewer refugees have jobs than the national average of 65 percent. In 1990 only 29 percent of Hmong had jobs, 46 percent of Laotians, 58 percent of Cambodians, and 65 percent of Vietnamese. They had dramatically lower per capita incomes than the national average of $14,000. The Hmong average only $2,700; Cambodians, $5,000; Laotians $5,600; and Vietnamese $9,000. It follows that a greater percentage lived in poverty: 64 percent of the Hmong reduced to 40 percent by 2000, 43 percent of Cambodians, 35 percent of Laotians, and 26 percent of Vietnamese. Surveys of Vietnamese indicate that 92 percent of families with two or more workers are above the poverty line. As recently arrived groups acquire job skills, become employed, and have two or more workers in a family, they too move out of the poverty category.

Cultural Patterns and Issues

Many Southeast Asian American values and practices are found in other Asian cultures. The primary religion is Buddhism, which is expressed more as a traditional philosophy of values and social relations than attendance at services or professions of belief. The following are general beliefs and behaviors that are especially emphasized by some Southeast Asian Americans, representing tendencies rather than rules (Van Do 2002, Do 1999):

- Having large, close-knit families, sometimes three generations in one house; it's very common for an extended refugee family to work together and pool resources to attain goals.

- Avoiding public displays of affection between men and women, especially between unmarried couples. Holding hands or touching among women and among men is a sign of close friendship. Greeting by hugging and kissing is not done. Sexual topics are not openly discussed, especially in mixed company,

- In Vietnam, people are introduced by their last name followed by their first name. A married woman retains her own last name, but is often called by her title and husband's last name.

- Being quiet around outsiders. Most Southeast Asian Americans are quite talkative, especially among themselves. The fact that they usually are perceived by Euro-Americans as unusually reserved probably reflects their unfamiliarity with the American culture and their natural reticence as "newcomers."

- Shaking hands upon meeting—for men, not women.

- Viewing a perceived unfairness or betrayal of trust as difficult to forgive or forget.

- Respecting teachers highly, even above parents. They are always referred to and addressed as teacher, never as he, she, or you.

Key Issue: Acculturation

Surveys taken a year after the first wave of refugees entered the United States indicate that major problems in adapting to the American culture were:

- breakup of the family and extended family units
- limits placed on the number of people who can live in one home
- lack of respect by Americans toward the elderly
- absence of friendly American people
- hectic pace in the American workplace
- dependence in America on the automobile and public transportation (difficult to walk or ride bikes from place to place)
- high value Americans place on work and achievement over interpersonal relationships

Factors that affect the acculturation of Southeast Asian refugees include the coercive aspects of their emigration, their need for a cohesive community, culture clashes that affect family cohesion, compatibility with American culture, reactions of other Americans, and occupational and educational fit.

Plans to Return or Stay

Because they were pushed out of their homes, many refugees hope to go back when conditions change. Those who plan to return have a strong incentive to retain their old cultural ways and less incentive to adopt American ways. Younger refugees are acculturating more rapidly than the older ones. Many want to become American citizens and are more hopeful about their future in the United States.

Need for a Cohesive Ethnic Community

U.S. policy was to scatter refugees to avoid backlash from American workers who compete for jobs. Another goal was to settle the refugees as quickly as possible so they could adapt and become self-sufficient. The scattering policy generally didn't work, and most moved to the warm climates they're accustomed to and to urban areas where they could network with other Asian groups. Since 1975 more than 500 mutual assistance associations have been created within refugee communities. They provide support, education, language development, job training, and cultural orientation. Some provide economic assistance in the form of business opportunities and jobs (Baldassare 1990).

Refugees who arrived in family units had the advantages of emotional support and multiple incomes. However, Vietnamese couples have experienced culture clashes that typically occur in families that recently immigrated from Asian cultures. Working wives' new status and children's Americanization can cause problems, reflected in the rapid rise in the divorce rate among Vietnamese couples in America.

Compatibility with the American Culture

The Vietnamese culture encourages responsibility, discipline, and hard work. Vietnamese value facing adversity with courage and stoicism, and they place a high value on education. Like other Asian cultures, they fit into a dominant society through conformity and avoiding confrontation and conflict. Most want a better life for their children and have a high degree of achievement motivation. The Hmong are most unlike Westerners and adaptation for them has been more difficult.

Reception by Other Americans

Some researchers have identified two groups that often feel threatened by new immigrants:

1. Downwardly mobile workers, those who once had more than they now have

2. Disadvantaged people, the unemployed or underemployed who have always lived on the fringes of society.

In this era of civil rights and valuing diversity, overt prejudice against Asians is relatively rare. However, in an era of de-industrialization and restructuring, job competition can be fierce. American fishermen have clashed with incoming Vietnamese fishermen, some minority farm workers and assembly line workers resent the competition for jobs, and some underclass minorities have complained about the special aid given to refugees. Some middle-class workers seem worried about further erosion of their take-home pay, saying refugees "must be getting a government handout," and therefore they, the taxpayers, must be supporting them.

Asian immigrants cannot merge into the dominant culture as easily as European immigrants. Because they're easily identifiable by their looks as Asians, they don't have the luxury of choosing whether or not to partake of the advantages and disadvantages of being of a distinct ethnic minority.

Refugees have many specific needs that are different from the typical immigrant's needs. However, the things they generally need from the dominant culture are similar to the needs of all minorities:

- sensitivity to their culture and life experiences
- recognition of both the similarities and differences among groups
- understanding that their communication patterns and feelings may not be expressed in the American way, so assumptions may be misleading
- the use of culturally relevant frames of reference for understanding each other
- competent people to process their papers and help them meet governmental requirements

Occupations and Education

The language barrier is the most immediate problem for the refugees, who need to gain the education and skills necessary for job success. Lack of child care has also been cited as a major problem. Because these cultures value hard work and education, most authorities think they will eventually overcome the barriers and become self-supporting citizens.

The most obvious goals for any migrating group are to find good jobs and get a good education for their children. Vietnamese have had the most success in finding jobs because of their urban background. Many are working as assembly line workers, technicians, machine operators, and office workers. Underemployment has been a real problem, as has a lack of Vietnamese in supervisory positions. When previously low-status employees in the home country are given higher job positions than former high-ranking army officers, or when women are in higher positions than men, conflicts occur, especially when directions and orders are given directly.

JAPANESE AMERICAN WORKERS

The Japanese were the second group of Asians to arrive in the United States in significant numbers. Their experiences have both similarities and differences to the Chinese experience.

Myths and Facts

Japanese Americans must cope with the myths and stereotypes that all Asian Americans face, which were discussed earlier, but they face at least two other myths that are specifically held about Japanese Americans.

Myth #1: Japanese Americans Are Greedy and Acquisitive

This is a variation on the myth that Asian Americans only care about starting their own businesses and buying real estate. The Japanese twist for this myth may reflect the fact that Japanese Americans are the most financially successful of Asian American groups. As mentioned earlier, results of a recent survey refutes this myth. Japan today is extremely competitive with the United States in several key industries, and the greedy, acquisitive stereotype is often applied to Japanese business persons. It may be projected onto Japanese Americans, most of whom have virtually no ties with Japanese business.

Myth #2: Japanese Americans Are Prejudiced toward African Americans

This myth apparently is based on reports that African Americans who go to Japan to do business report difficulties in dealing with Japanese discrimination. Japan is a very homogeneous society, and few persons of African heritage live there or do business there. Unfamiliarity seems to be part of the problem. More important, most Japanese Americans were born in the United States and do not necessarily have the same viewpoint toward African Americans that Japanese in Japan have.

Background; The Japanese American Experience

The first large group of Japanese that arrived in the United States first migrated to Hawaii as laborers in the late 1800s, later moving on to the U.S. West Coast. In 1900 about 25,000 Japanese lived on the West Coast, mostly men who came to get ahead and planned to return to Japan. By 1920 there were more than 100,000, about two-thirds of them in California. Like the Chinese immigrants, most were men working at physically strenuous, low-status, low-paying jobs, mainly in farming and building railroads.

Unlike the Chinese, the Japanese came from scattered rural areas all over Japan and Okinawa. As a group they were somewhat better educated and skilled than the Chinese immigrants. Some were quite skilled in intensive farming, such as truck gardening. Unlike China, Japan had begun the transition toward a modem industrial era. Although the Chinese presence in agriculture diminished after the 1880s, the Japanese became more heavily entrenched as farm owners and tenant farmers.

Community Growth

Due to pressure and negotiations of the Japanese government, immigrants' families were allowed to join them during the period from 1900 to 1924. This balanced the gender ratio and led to the establishment of families. By 1940 the nearly 80,000 second-generation Japanese Americans outnumbered the 47,000 immigrant parents. By 1940 Los Angeles had the largest Japanese American settlement, numbering 37,000, but San Francisco with only 5,000 was the headquarters for the major organizations of each generation.

War and Concentration Camps

The major issue for pre-1940 Japanese Americans was prejudice. Euro-Americans simply did not accept Asian Americans as equals. At the beginning of World War II President Roosevelt signed an executive order to classify Japanese Americans as "enemy aliens" and to intern those on the West Coast in detention camps. The apparent rationale was to protect the United States from Japanese spy and saboteur activity and a feared attack on the West Coast by Japanese submarines. At the same time he urged the men to volunteer in the all-Japanese American combat unit, which went on to become the most decorated U.S. military unit in history (Takaki 2000)

All persons of Japanese ethnicity living on the West Coast, were arrested, regardless of citizenship, age, or sex. They were forced to abandon all their possessions and assets, and allowed to take only what they could carry. In Northern California the first stop was a San Bruno racetrack-stable area called Tanforan, renamed Tanforan Assembly Center. (After the war it became Tanforan shopping mall.)

From there they were sent to one of 10 isolated camps: Gila River, Jerome, or Poston in Arizona; Tule Lake or Manzanar in southeast California; Heart Mountain in Wyoming; Topaz in Utah; Granada in Colorado; Minidoka in Idaho; and Rohwer in Arkansas. The camps were surrounded by barbed wire and were patrolled by armed soldiers, who shot and killed several of the Japanese they were guarding. While they were not death camps, they were concentration camps by most commonly accepted definitions.

Japanese Americans are the only group of U.S. residents ever to be deprived of their constitutional rights without a trial. Yet no individual Japanese American was ever found guilty of espionage nor were any so charged. Italian Americans and German Americans were not confined, even though their homelands were also our war enemies. More than 150,000 Japanese Americans living in Hawaii were left alone, as were the 10,000 who lived east of the Mississippi. Those who were sent to the camps lost virtually all their assets except those they could take with them. Their greatest economic loss was the income they weren't allowed to earn during their internment.

This wartime exile and incarceration was and still is the central event of Japanese American history, making their history unique among Asian Americans. The violation of Japanese American trust, and the extreme level of distrust expressed by the government of their homeland, the United States, was traumatic for those who lived through it. Every year the Japanese American community observes a Day of Remembrance with solemn ceremonies. In 1988 the U.S. government formally apologized to these families and set up a process for reparations.

Current Profile

Japanese emigration peaked around 1910, and by 1970 Japanese Americans were the largest Asian American group in the country. Thirty years later, in 2000, they were the fifth largest group, after those from China, the Philippines, India, Vietnam, and Korea. By then, few were first-generation immigrants. Originally they were heavily clustered in California but now are scattered rather widely.

By most measures of success, Japanese Americans are the most successful of any Asian American group. They have the fewest foreign born (32 percent) of any Asian American group, and the oldest average age, 36 compared to 30 for Asian Americans in general, and 33 for the total U.S. population.

Intermarriage with other ethnic groups, especially with Euro-Americans, has grown rapidly. In fact, 38 percent of the men and 52 percent of the women have married outside their group. The men are most likely to marry women from other Asian groups, while the women are likely to marry Euro-Americans. Since 1980 the number of babies born to a Japanese American and Euro-American parent actually exceeds the number born to two Japanese American parents.

Most speak English at home (57 percent) with only Asian Indian Americans at 85 percent having a greater percentage speaking English at home. However, 33 percent are still considered linguistically isolated.

Japanese American educational attainment is high. Nearly twice the percentage of men hold degrees as the average U.S. male. Only Asian Indian American men have a higher educational level. And a significantly greater proportion of Japanese women hold degrees than the average U.S. woman..

They have the highest per capita income of any Asian American group, at $19,400, well above the national median of $14,100. The poverty rate of 7 percent is just a step above the lowest for all Asian American groups, with the Filipino Americans at 6.4 percent. They have the smallest families, 3.1 compared to the Asian American average of 3.8 and the U.S. average of 3.2. And a relatively small percentage (15 percent) have three or more family members working, compared to the Asian American average of 20 percent and the U.S. average of 13 percent.

Cultural Values

Surveys indicate most Japanese American young people still believe in traditional Japanese cultural values, most of which are typical Asian cultural values. The following values seem to be especially meaningful in the Japanese American culture:

- self-confidence
- sympathy and compassion for others
- fun-loving approach
- craftsmanship, pride in work

KOREAN AMERICAN WORKERS

The Korean American population has increased significantly since 1965. During the Korean War in the early 1950s, millions of peasant refugees fled from their farms to South Korean cities. Many of their children who got professional degrees found inadequate opportunities in their developing economy.

When U.S. immigration law was liberalized for professionals in 1965, they flocked to the United States to escape political instability and high unemployment in Korea. They were one of the few immigrant groups in American history that was predominantly urban, educated, and from one generation. Most were Christian, a result of missionary efforts. Most also had some personal savings, military training, and a willingness to work hard.

Stereotypes & Myths

The demographic profile of most Korean Americans has naturally led to some stereotypes and myths about them.

Myth #1: Koreans Belong to Asian Religions

In fact, between 60 and 70 percent of Korean Americans attend Christian churches, preferably a church with many Korean American members. They report that such churches provide social and psychological support that helps them to adjust to the American culture (Lee 1997).

Myth #2: Most Korean Americans are Rich, Stingy, Suspicious Store Owners

While most Korean Americans are Christians, the Korean culture embraces Confucian principles of strong family ties, hard work, and self-discipline. For example, most of them would not buy products they do not really need, but would save their money to invest in the family business. Many of them have become owners of small retail stores, and they do try to protect their investment.

Current Profile

Over one million Korean Americans comprised about 10 percent of the Asian American population in 2000. About 73 percent were foreign born and the average age is 29. Nearly twice as many Korean Americans as Euro-Americans have degrees, 49 percent compared to 27 percent. About 63 percent hold jobs, compared to 65 percent of all Americans. About 20 percent are self-employed, the highest rate of all ethnic groups, including Euro-Americans. The median household income of $42,000 is the same as that of the U.S. population, somewhat less than other Asian American groups but more than the other ethnic minority groups (Census 2000).

Cultural Values and Practices

In Korea, the major religion is Buddhism, and there is a strong underlying ethic of Confucianism and Shamanism. Confucianism has especially affected cultural values and practices, and most of these are discussed under Asian American cultural patterns (Harris and Moran 1996). Some variations unique to Koreans include the concepts of inner feelings, nonpersons, use of names, flattery, and patience, as well as their version of status and hierarchy.

Inner Feelings, Mood

A concept that is important to understanding Korean Americans is that of *kibun,* literally "inner feelings," with the closest English translation probably being "mood." When the kibun is good, the person functions smoothly and easily and feels great. If the kibun is upset or bad, transactions may come to an abrupt stop, and the person feels depressed, awful. Part of the intention of business people is to enhance the kibun of all parties. To damage the kibun could end the relationship and even create enemies. Class or status is intimately involved in the nurturing of kibun.

Nonpersons

Koreans who fail to follow the basic rules of social interaction are considered by other Koreans to not even be a person—to be a nonperson. Foreigners in a certain sense and to a certain extent are considered by Koreans as nonpersons. Koreans show very little concern for nonpersons' feelings, their comfort, or whether they live or die. Nonpersons are simply not worthy of much consideration. Korean Americans obviously must modify this attitude in order to function effectively in a diverse society; however, some variation of it probably survives and affects relationships.

Use of Names

Newly arrived Korean Americans must adapt to the American use of first names in business situations. To the Confucian, a name is something to be honored and respected, not to be used casually. Therefore, to call someone directly by her or his name is an insult in most social circumstances. A Korean is addressed by her or his title, position, trade, profession, or some other honorary title.

Flattery and Patience

Flattery is a key aspect of doing business among Korean Americans. An important or delicate business matter is always approached gradually. To begin discussing it directly and immediately is considered mere stupidity and will almost always result in failure. A highly skilled business person moves with "deliberation, dignity, and studied motions, and senses the impressions and nuances" that others are signaling (Harris and Moran 1996).

Status–Hierarchy

Korea seems to have an especially strong sense of status-hierarchy and high power distance between persons in lower-higher groups. In other words, Koreans are especially obligated to be deferential toward their elders and superiors, Author Malcom Gladwell (2008) tells the story of Korean Air's extremely high rate of plane crashes during the late 1990s. A consultant started riding in the plane's cockpit to observe. He noticed that when the pilots ran into some bad weather, the pilot made an error, but the co-pilot said nothing. When questioned later, he said that to disagree with the pilot's decision would show disrespect, so he kept quiet. Korean Air executives finally concluded that the cultural power distance value was causing their plane crash problem.

ASIAN INDIAN AMERICANS

About one-eighth of Asian Americans are of Asian Indian heritage. They are the most highly educated U.S. group and nearly all speak English. We'll discuss the two waves of immigrants that came from India, their current profile, and some cultural values and practices.

Background: Sikhs and Professionals

Asian Indians came to the United States in two waves, the first around the turn of the twentieth century and the second after 1965. The first wave were Sikhs from rural areas, and the second wave were educated professionals from urban areas.

The First Wave

About 10,000 Asian Indians immigrated to the United States around 1900. Most were from one region of Punjab, a fertile, prosperous region in North India. Nearly all were Sikhs, a religion that combines aspects of the Hindu and Muslim religions. Highly visible religious customs for males include wearing a long turban, a dagger, and an iron bracelet, and never cutting their hair. About half the immigrants settled in eastern and Midwestern cities, especially New York, and worked as merchants and middle-class professionals.

The other half settled in the fertile valleys of California. Following a typically Asian pattern, most were married men who left their wives in India, planning to make money to send back home to buy land. A few of the men took wives after arriving, mostly women from Mexican American farm worker families. Because of cultural differences, these marriages tended to be conflict ridden, and at least 20 percent ended in divorce. They generally experienced the same kind of discrimination as other Asians. For example, the alien land laws made it impossible to own farmland.

From 1914 o 1946 few Asian Indians entered the United States, due to tight immigration laws, and the Asian Indian population in California declined from a high of more than 5,000 to about 1500. About 7,000 immigrants arrived between 1948 and 1965, mostly close relatives of American citizens. They did not establish new ethnic communities but rejuvenated those in existence.

The Second Wave

Since 1965 a much larger wave has established new communities with few connections with the old ones. Most are not Sikhs, are not farmers, and do not live in the Far West. The 1980 population of nearly 400,000 doubled by 1990 to more than 800,000. Asian American Indians are now dispersed around the country. About a third live in the Northeast, a fourth in the South, a fourth in the Midwest, and a fifth in the West.

Current Profile

Asian Indians comprise about 12 percent of all Asian Americans. About 75 percent are foreign born, and the average age is 30. They are the most highly educated U.S. ethnic group, with over 65 percent of the men and 50 percent of the women holding bachelor's degrees or higher, compared to the total population figures of 27 percent respectively.

Because of India's history as a British colony prior to 1950, most immigrants from India speak English. It's the major linking language in a nation of many languages and dialects. They have the least language difficulties of any Asian American group.

Asian Indian Americans are industrious and are heavily represented in high-status occupations. More than 72 percent of them have jobs, compared with 65 percent of all Americans, and 18 percent have three or more family members working, compared with 13 percent nationally. Nearly half of all foreign-born Asian Indian workers are managers and professionals. This is twice the proportion for all Americans, which is 24 percent, and significantly higher than any other Asian American group.

It follows that Asian Indian Americans have relatively high incomes and few live in poverty. Per capita income was nearly $18,000, compared to about $14,000 for all Americans. Among Asian American groups, only Japanese Americans earned more. Asian Indian Americans had one of the lowest poverty rates, 10 percent compared with 14 percent nationally.

To summarize Asian Indian Americans tend to be:

- strongly committed to maintaining family connections
- highly educated
- concentrated in the professions
- well paid
- trained in India, many part of a "brain drain" during the 1980s, caused by India's training more professionals than its businesses could profitably employ.

Cultural Values and Practices

The predominant religion in India is Hinduism, followed by Buddhism and Islam. All of these strongly influence the values and practices of the people. In Hindu marriages, the woman is expected to show absolute dedication, submission, and obedience to her husband. Her traditional status in the household is low until she produces a male child. Other traits include:

- Family and friends are much more important than in the West.
- Extended family living is highly valued.
- Friends sense each other's needs and do something about them.
- Speaking your mind to a friend is a sign of friendship.
- People are expected to be on time.
- Most believe that there are no accidents, that all things are interrelated in a cosmic order.

Indian women do not expect to be spoken to by men who are strangers; nor is it appropriate for such men to help women out of a car, up steps, etc. Women who dare to dance do so only with their husbands. Public displays of affection are considered inappropriate.

People don't address others outside the extended family by first name. The equivalent of *Mr. Bill* or *Miss Linda* is appropriate, as are such titles as *Teacher* and *Doctor.*

While Asian Indian Americans have much in common with other Asian Americans, their culture is probably the most distinct because of the influence of Hinduism. There are also many Buddhists, as well as members of other religious groups. There is a strong Muslim influence, especially in Pakistan and Bangladesh, which affects the values and practices of immigrants from those countries.

PACIFIC ISLANDERS

Pacific Islanders who live in the U.S. mainland are a relatively small ethnic group, but still more than 1 percent of the U.S. population. Business people in the West are most likely to encounter Pacific Islanders, since most of them live there, especially in Hawaii and California. We'll review their current profile and some common issues. Then we'll explore the background of the largest population within this group, the Hawaiians.

Current Profile

In the 1990 census, for the first time Pacific Islanders were identified as a distinct group of about 365,000 people living in the U.S. mainland. Their islands of origin are as follows

Hawaii	58 percent
Samoa	17 percent
Guam	14 percent
Other	11 percent

Most live in the West and a few (13 percent) are foreign born. The median age is 25. Many came to the United States to pursue an education, and 76 percent are high school graduates, while only 11 percent are college graduates.

Most speak English, but 33 percent don't speak it very well, and 11 percent are linguistically isolated. The average family size is four. Most have jobs, but their income is significantly less than the national average and their poverty rate is significantly higher. More than 70 percent have jobs, with 18 percent holding managerial or professional jobs. Their per capita income averages $10,342 and their poverty rate is 17 percent.

Issues Common to Pacific Islanders

Some issues shared by many Pacific Islanders include:

- Education and skills gaps representing the major differences in surviving in their island culture and the high-tech U.S. culture
- Loss of status, rank, and prestige of people who were leaders in the islands
- Low wages and high expenses
- Role and identity problems—hierarchical roles of males are threatened, and identity closely tied to the family is weakened
- Stereotyped as islanders, who are exotic, romantic, heavy-drinking revelers
- Stereotyped as Asians, whose patterns are decidedly different in many ways

What is functional in a small island economy may not be helpful in an urban, technological society. Pacific Islanders' numbers are too small and their resources too slim to develop a separate community and that could develop opportunities for its members. Strong family ties and the belief in helping one another have been an asset for the immigrants.

The Hawaiians: A Multicultural Group

Two hundred years ago Hawaii was the home of a rich, distinct culture, but today it is more multicultural than Hawaiian.

From Distinct Culture to Multiculture

When Captain James Cook, the English explorer, came upon the Hawaiian islands in 1778, he found a thriving, highly stratified culture of more than 300,000 Hawaiians ruled by a class of chieftains. Other Europeans soon followed, including Christian missionaries from New England. By 1890 the great "white man's diseases" had decimated the population, leaving only about 35,000 Hawaiians.

The event that most dramatically changed the Hawaiian social system was the 1848 pact that permitted private persons to buy the land. Much of the land, formerly under the king and chiefs, ended up in the hands of a few Euro-American plantation owners who wanted to grow sugar, pineapple, and similar crops. The sugar and pineapple industries grew rapidly, and the demand for cheap labor changed forever the cultural mix of people on the islands. Most of the Hawaiians were dead, and those who were left generally did not make good laborers. The plantation owners brought in Chinese, Japanese, Korean, and Filipino laborers, many of whom stayed, creating a multicultural population. Today there are almost no "pure" Hawaiians left.

In 1898 the United States annexed Hawaii as a territorial possession. By that time Euro-Americans owned most of the land, were in control of the economy, and ran the political system. The cultural aspects of plantation life were primarily Asian: The languages, games, worship, and attitudes toward family, property, and authority reflected Asian cultural themes. Although Asians were the majority of the population, they were divided by ethnicity and were economically dependent on the plantation owners. What little remained of the native Hawaiian culture was found in the more remote villages.

Twentieth-Century Hawaii

Of all the groups found in twentieth-century Hawaii, the native Hawaiians had the most difficulty in adjusting to the competitive Euro-American culture, and a retreat to the past left them further behind. They began blaming the Asians for their plight and helped the Euro-Americans write land laws discriminating against the Chinese and Japanese, which of course further entrenched Euro-American dominance.

In 1959 Hawaii became a state. The actual numbers of immigrants since then has been difficult to assess. Most who come to the mainland are of mixed ancestry, and their experiences are as diverse as the cultural diversity that they represent. Because of this background, Hawaii is the most multicultural of all the states, and the culture has both Euro-American and Asian American themes.

LEADERSHIP CHALLENGES:
OVERCOMING BARRIERS TO CAREER SUCCESS

As a leader you have many opportunities and challenges in working effectively with Asian Americans, in supporting their ability to contribute to work teams, and in building mutual respect and trust. You can help by providing support in overcoming barriers, avoiding typical assumptions and stereotypes, determining the generational status and citizenship status of each Asian American associate, constantly questioning your other assumptions about them, and helping people get to know these valuable co-workers

Challenge #1: Provide Support in Overcoming Barriers

Some typical barriers to job success faced by Asian Americans include:

- Being typecast as technologists (technical coolies) and therefore not being considered for higher level positions

- Being discriminated against because Euro-Americans are uncomfortable with their cultural style, which is considered too "foreign and strange."
- Communicating and verbalizing, problems especially crucial with first-generation immigrants
- Being misunderstood because of their values and behaviors, such as humbleness and passiveness. Such behavior is not necessarily an indicator that they are not qualified for leadership roles.

Challenge #2: Avoid Typical Assumptions and Stereotypes

You've learned about the most typical myths, stereotypes, and assumptions that can hamper good working relationships. Here are a few reminders.

Remember, They're Americans, Not Foreigners

Non-Asian Americans have a tendency to look upon Asian Americans as foreigners because of their Asian appearance. Most Asian-appearing workers you'll encounter will be Asian Americans. They're Americanized in varying degrees and possess varying language skill levels. Keep in mind that they aren't foreigners.

Avoid Assumptions about Language Ability

Some leaders assume Asian Americans are fluent in an Asian language and have problems with English. When Euro-Americans make such comments as "You speak very good English" or "Where did you learn to speak English so well?" Asian Americans who were born and raised in the United States may be understandably taken aback. It's one more reminder that even though they consider themselves as American as anyone, others tend to see them as foreigners.

Asian Americans are often embarrassed or frustrated when others expect them to be bilingual. For example, a worker who is third-generation Chinese may speak little or no Chinese. Let multiple language skills emerge and be used as an asset after you establish the facts.

Most important, when discussing an Asian American employee's skills, qualifications, and career goals, you can help to identify any communication skills or problems that he or she has and try to get remedial training.

Don't Assume They Arc Cultural Ambassadors

Don't try to make an Asian American worker your token Asian expert. Asian Americans appreciate people who don't assume they're experts in their ancestors' culture, just as they appreciate those who don't assume they're bilingual. For example, Japanese Americans who were born and raised in the United States are not necessarily experts in Japanese cuisine, culture, or politics. They do not necessarily agree with economic or political developments in Japan. Again, it's better to ask about special bicultural expertise than to make assumptions.

Avoid Such Labels as "Oriental"

For many Asian Americans the term Oriental, meaning Easterner, conjures up old Hollywood stereotypes (such as Charlie Chan and Tokyo Rose) depicting mysterious, unknowable, exotic Asians. It brings up unpleasant memories for many. Also, some consider it Eurocentric, since it describes Asia as east of Europe. A case could be made that it is west of the Americas, and that the Americas are the East to Asians.

Remember, People with Spanish Surnames may be Filipinos

Many types of people may have Spanish-sounding names. For example, many Filipinos took Spanish surnames during the era of Spanish colonialism. They are not Latinos, although their values and practices probably reflect a Spanish influence.

Challenge #3: Determine Generational Status

There tend to be significant differences between first-generation immigrants and second-, third-, and fourth-generation Americans. By open, direct, but tactful conversations, you can share information about your background and learn about each associate's background. Be sure that your tone or manner is not in any way condescending or patronizing. Getting information can help you to understand the associates' values, viewpoints, and actions. Keep in mind that information you've absorbed about such groups as third-generation Japanese Americans or recently arrived Hmong Americans can only provide general guidelines. Keep an open mind, get to know each individual, and avoid the tendency to use such information to form rigid stereotypes about these people.

Challenge #4: Ascertain Citizenship Status

For workers who are not American citizens or permanent residents, find out about their status, which can help you better understand their background. For example, some initially come as foreign students, then get work visas. Their values and actions therefore tend to stem from Asian values and practices, and they are less Americanized. Companies must sign papers for Asians to keep their work visas, which frequently makes such workers feel dependent on the company. Such workers may be more submissive, obedient, and compliant, a situation some companies prefer and capitalize upon. Take the lead in respecting such workers.

Challenge #5: Question Your Assumptions about Behaviors

Periodically review the cultural values and customs discussed here. Do further research on your own. Question your knee-jerk reactions and assumptions about why an Asian American acts a certain way. For example, in the American business culture "silence is consent," and if someone doesn't speak up about a decision being made during a meeting, we assume he or she has no objections. But in Asian cultures "silence is golden," and "maintaining harmony is virtuous."

Remember, too, that Asian Americans in general are changing, especially the new generations born in the United States. They tend to be more assertive, vocal, and equipped with better communication skills than their parents or grandparents.

Check your assumptions, and then ask some tactful questions to learn what's really going on. Above all, can look beyond surface behaviors and get to know Asian American team members personally in order to help them develop their talents and make appropriate career plans.

Challenge #6: Help People Get to Know Asian American Co-workers

You can take a leadership rote and influence others in the workplace by providing information about Asian American myths and realities, their cultural patterns and strengths, and guidelines for building productive relationships with them. Occasionally review the Asian American values and practices you have just learned. Do further research on your own.

You can help others get to know Asian American associates by including them on team projects. This can provide for in-depth contact with other employees and increased comfort levels.

LEADERSHIP OPPORTUNITIES: BUILDING UPON ASIAN AMERICAN STRENGTHS

You can learn to recognize Asian Americans' potential contributions and respond by building on typical Asian American traits, recognizing Asian American values as strengths, applying some leadership strategies, and helping Asian Americans make marketplace connections.

Opportunity #1: Build on Typical Asian American Characteristics

Some Asian American characteristics that are especially important in business are that they generally

1. have an interest in long-range benefits.
2. are steadfast, once they decide upon who and what is the best choice
3. stick to their word.
4. are punctual.

What can you do to build on these characteristics?

5. You can identify situations in which these traits are an especially good fit.
6. You can point out the good fit to Asian American associates and to others.
7. You can help them verbalize to team members the value of developing these practices.

Opportunity #2: Recognize Asian American Values as Strengths

Nearly all values and behavior patterns represent a two-sided coin in the workplace. One side is the advantages these can bring to the career achievement and organizational contribution of the employee. The other side is the barriers they could erect. You can learn to recognize the cultural and individual values and behaviors of team members. You can figure out ways to enhance them and bring them into the work situation in constructive ways. Here are some ideas.

Obligation to Family

Work with the value of strong obligation to family. In most American corporate cultures, workaholics are rewarded and people who do not consistently put the company first are viewed as lacking commitment. While most Asian Americans place high value on hard work and perseverance, when family members need them, family obligations must come first.

*   You can understand and respect Asian American priorities regarding family and work.
    By doing so, you're likely to win the respect and loyalty of these employees.

Hard Work and Cooperation

Respect their values regarding hard work and cooperation. Some managers take advantage of the Asian American tendency to value hard work and cooperation by piling on the work. Asian Americans are patient, but not stupid. Eventually such exploitation will backfire.

Most Asian Americans emphasize trust and mutual connections, a major aspect of building cooperative business relationships.

*   You can help them put their value for trust and mutual connections to good use for
    the team, the organization, and for their own careers.

Modesty and Humility

Understand their values of modesty and humility. By American corporate culture standards, many Asian Americans may appear to be too passive and too lacking in self-confidence and ambition to be given tough assignments that call for traditional leadership skills. In Asia such qualities are seen as positive, and the American standards are likely to be seen as egocentric and arrogant, as pushing or imposing oneself on others. First- and second-generation Asian Americans tend to value modesty and humility more highly than later generations.

In Asian countries the typical American can-do attitude may be viewed as too bold or individualistic. People from Asian cultures are more likely to explain optimism in low-key ways. They may say, "This is a very difficult challenge, and I'm trying, even though I may not be able to do it." Euro-American managers who are sensitive to such differences will not jump to the conclusion that Asian

American employees lack self-confidence and motivation simply because they don't project the can-do attitude that's typical of Euro-Americans, men especially.

Properly used, such values as modesty and humility can be quite appropriate for facilitative team leaders. Further, such values do not mean that the worker lacks self-confidence, ambition, or assertiveness, qualities that vary among Asian Americans, just as they do among Euro-Americans. Asian Americans merely tend to express them in a more low-key, indirect manner. Similarly, Euro-American managers usually reward employees who tactfully question the status quo, speak up, take initiative, or find a better way of doing things. Asian Americans do not necessarily behave in this manner.

- You can help find ways to reward and motivate Asian American employees who are not as verbal or assertive as Euro-Americans.
- You can help show them when and how to be assertive .

Indirectness and Respect

Understand the values of indirectness and respect. Instead of assuming that that they are devious, uncommunicative, or dishonest, get to know them as individuals so you can reach a deeper understanding of the values of indirectness and respect in their communication patterns. Another aspect of respect involves the use of space and touching. Asian cultures like more space between persons when communicating and less touching than is typical in the United States

- Upon meeting, a slight bow or brief handshake is appropriate.
- Follow their lead about how far apart to stand or sit from each other.

Emotional Expression

Understand how they express emotions. You have learned that Asian Americans are less likely to express emotions than are people from other cultures. To maintain harmony they avoid openly expressing such emotions as anger, resentment, and jealousy. In addition, they may hide their emotions when they sense they're in a "hostile foreign environment" that causes them to feel vulnerable, intimidated, or threatened. People from all cultures are likely to show less emotion, as a protective device, when they feel like a foreigner or minority. You can help by

- seeing them first as Americans and as a part of the group you're working with
- helping them to explore and express feelings that need to come out and be dealt with in order to build honest, trusting, work relationships.

Opportunity #3: Apply Leadership Strategies

Here are some strategies that may be especially appropriate for Asian American workers.

Enhance Boss–Worker Relations

Explain deviations from traditional boss-worker practices. Asian cultures tend to be more hierarchical and status-oriented than current American corporate cultures. Most corporations have moved beyond the old authoritarian boss-obedient employee model that still fits the pattern of many Asian cultures..

If you're a supervisor, have a conversation with Asian American employees in which you share your ideas of the leader-worker relationship. Once you understand their expectations, you can help them to understand your own deviations from that expectation. For example

- If they expect the boss to make all decisions, you can explain why workers in this company participate in decision making.
- If they would be personally humiliated if you pitched in to help complete a task, you can explain how this is viewed in the corporate culture and what it means.

Use a Team Approach

Good teamwork integrates cultural differences. One way to bridge the gap between Euro-American emphasis on individual initiative and Asian American emphasis on obedience to authority is to structure tasks so they can be performed by teams. Gradually introduce independent decision making by doing it as a group. Working in teams can also help Asian Americans and co-workers get to know each other at deeper levels, which breaks down walls of prejudice. It can also take advantage of Asian Americans' group-oriented values and skills.

- You can suggest opportunities for working together in teams.
- You can encourage Asian Americans to contribute their group-oriented values and traits to help the team become more close-knit and productive.

Uncover Relationship Problems

Help bring problems to the surface. Harmony and compliance are two Asian American values that have upsides and downsides. A downside can be an unwillingness to confront relationship problems. Most Asian Americans are taught that in troublesome situations, they should act as though nothing has happened. If they acknowledge a relationship problem, then they must take action, and action may be extremely serious. As a result, they tend to be long-suffering and patient, but resentment may build. In team situations it's usually important to bring problems and troublesome feelings to the surface and to deal with them—if they're important enough to an individual to eventually create communication and relationship barriers.

- You can work with Asian Americans in developing such team-related skills.

Provide Assertiveness Training

You have learned that even minimally educated Asian American women can be assertive on the job when they believe it's necessary or desirable. But because Asian cultures focus on humbleness and subordinating personal desires for group interests, Asian American employees often need some training about the role of assertiveness in the American workplace. For more than 20 years, Euro-American women have benefited from such training. Asian American employees also respond well to assertiveness training and can reap similar benefits.

- Help provide assertiveness training by your own examples and explanations.
- Encourage your organization to provide formal training sessions
- Encourage Asian American associates to attend such training. If the situation is touchy, you may want to go yourself and ask them to come with you.
- Look for opportunities to encourage them to speak up in meetings.

Build Trust

Our history of prejudice and discrimination may have created some trust barriers in inter-cultural relationships. When Asian Americans perceive that a Euro-American is trying to "buddy up" to them, they may respond internally with some distrust and suspicion. If you're a Euro-American, you must find ways to overcome this barrier.

- Begin by raising your awareness of the ways in which messages can be misunderstood or misinterpreted, and give special attention to clear communication.
- Then be very consistent in your messages and positions, and always follow through on agreements. Trust is built through the experience of another person as honest, fair, consistent, and reliable. Letting someone down, even once, can shatter newly-built trust.

Show Concern

Express sincere personal concern. Cooperative relationships are normally personal ones. Get to know Asian American workers as people in order to understand their goals and needs, which are usually tied to family status and needs. In this way you show that you understand the value of cooperation and want to establish a cooperative relationship.

- Establish personal relationships with Asian American associates.
- Find out what's most important to them and make their priorities a major part of your discussions and of the relationship.
- Consider cultural demands, such as family expectations and holidays. For example, the Lunar New Year is very important to many Asian Americans, so allowing time off would be greatly appreciated.

Communicate Clearly

Cultural differences often cause misperceptions and misunderstandings. Therefore, you must find ways to send clear, unmixed messages that involve requests, assignments, expectations, or explanations. Then you must check for understanding in ways that uncover misperceptions.

- If in doubt, be very specific and factual in making requests and giving instructions. Don't say, "You might want to think about doing xyz." Ask, "Can you do xyz before you leave today? How does that fit your schedule?"
- Check for understanding. Don't ask questions that can be answered yes or no; for example, "Is that clear?" Ask questions that clearly establish whether the person understands, such as "How do you plan to go about doing that?"

Select Motivators and Rewards

Consider each employee's values when you choose the motivators and rewards you use. Rewards such as individual recognition may not be as effective for motivating Asian American employees as they are with Euro-Americans. The same is true for perks and benefits.

- You can talk with Asian Americans about their values, goals, and expectations.
- Together you can develop rewards that they value and that serve as effective motivators for them.

Opportunity #4: Make Marketplace Connections

Asian American buying power was about $250 billion in 2001 (Selig). Many companies are realizing the potential of the growing Asian American market, and nearly all U.S. companies are doing more and more business with Asian countries in the global marketplace. This increased trade has created interest in Chinese language courses, which are growing faster than for any foreign language. Chinese now ranks fifth in popularity, after French, Spanish, German, and Japanese.

Asian American employees tend to have a special touch with Asian clients due to cultural similarities. They are also an invaluable resource in developing strategies and action plans for doing business in such markets. Most Asian Americans welcome such opportunities to improve their job prospects.

Help Them Connect with the Asian American Marketplace

Asian Americans have greater buying power than their share of the total population. Companies such as Coca-Cola and AT&T have established Asian American marketing departments and have tried to reach Asian American communities with donations and advertisements. Companies are targeting the rapidly increasing Asian American clientele. They are putting more Asian American models in their television commercials and advertisements. Some are looking to Asian American culture—art, music, dance, clothing designs, movies, and food—for inspiration and to make connections with the Asian American markets (Min 1995).

Savvy cosmetics companies are targeting people of color with new hair and skin product lines to accommodate every possible skin tone. Asian Americans account for up to 50 percent of the sales of premium cosmetic lines in California alone, even though they are only 15% of the population of that state. The Crayola company met a need when it added Multicultural Fleshtone Crayons to its product line. (Halter 2000)

- Asian American employees are most likely to recognize such opportunities for new services and products. You may be able to help your organization to recognize and use these employees as a valuable resource and connection in such efforts.

Help Them Connect with Asian Countries

Virtually all economists expect Asian countries to play a more important role as American economic partners in the twenty-first century. Some locations that are emerging as economic tigers are Singapore, Taiwan, Hong Kong, and South Korea. New trade relations with China are opening up a market of over a billion people (Min 1995).

- You may be able to help your organization see that Asian Americans employees can provide insights into these global markets and can serve as valuable links.

SUMMARY

Asian Americans must deal with many stereotypes and myths, such as they're too passive to be good American leaders, they're unemotional and inscrutable, they're "foreign," good at math, and "technical coolies." Much is this is a matter of style rather than substance. Actually Asian Americans are assertive when it's important and acceptable to be assertive, and they respond well to assertiveness training. Asian Americans have the same emotions as other people, but their values and training determine how they express themselves. Consideration for others' feelings and concern for harmony cause them to limit their emotional expression. Many have focused on technical skills until they could overcome language difficulties, but third- and fourth-generation Asian Americans tend to have good language skills.

Asian Americans have dealt with overt prejudice since Chinese immigrants first came to the United States about 150 years ago. The segregation and discrimination imposed reinforced their tendency to retain tight-knit families and communities. They've therefore retained many of their cultural values and patterns. Still, third- and fourth-generation Asian Americans tend to be quite Americanized. As a group, they have higher educational achievement than average. Although they hold higher-status jobs than average, they make less than Euro-Americans in comparable jobs, which reflects some workplace barriers that still remain.

Common cultural themes of all Asian cultures are putting group concerns before individual desires, promoting group harmony, accepting the hierarchy and status differences, revering education as a moral virtue, and communicating vaguely, indirectly, and silently.

The model minority stereotype has been a double-edged sword for Asian Americans, creating a belief that they are productive workers but leading to unfair expectations that they'll work harder for less than other employees. The myth has been used to blame African Americans and Latino Americans for their lower socioeconomic achievement. The model minority image is misleading and complex. On average Asian Americans do have higher educational and income levels than other groups. However, more of their family members must work to achieve these levels, and their education does not give them payback in income at the same rate as Euro-Americans. Asian Americans' success in small business has helped them to achieve higher education and some financial security in spite of discrimination. Women are expected to be especially modest and compliant, but most are strong and will be assertive and even confrontational when necessary.

Chinese Americans are the largest of the Asian American groups and have been here the longest. In fact they were the only Asian American group of any size for 100 years. They established Chinatowns in several cities, with their own small businesses and mutual aid associations.

Filipino Americans are almost as large though they came later. They retain many Asian cultural patterns, as well as patterns similar to Latino Americans because of several hundred years of Spanish rule.

Most Southeast Asian Americans arrived since the 1960s as refugees of the Vietnam War. Their backgrounds range from Vietnamese urban professionals to Hmong hill people from Laos.

Japanese Americans began arriving just after the Chinese and are considered the most successful of the Asian American groups by most measures.

Korean Americans are from a predominantly Confucian culture but most are Christians. Most have come since 1965.

Asian Indian Americans are mainly urban professionals. They have the highest educational achievements of any U.S. group and most hold degrees.

Pacific Islanders are a relatively small group that live primarily on the West Coast.

Leadership challenges include helping Asian American employees overcome the traditional workplace barriers, especially the myths and stereotypes. Opportunities include recognizing their values as strengths, explaining corporate cultures that may be confusing to them, and helping them to bring their issues out in the open to discuss. Their understanding of Asian cultures can be invaluable in doing business in Asian marketplaces.

Case Study 9.1: Doug Fong, Asian American Manager

Doug Fong is a restaurant manager for Jollytime Corporation. Jollytime consists of a chain of over 250 fast food restaurants throughout the United States Its corporate mission is to provide quality fast food at competitive prices and quality service. One of its strategies for quality control is to send "mystery shoppers" to every restaurant at least twice a month. These employees check on quality of food, cleanliness of restaurant, and quickness of service. Two managers operate each restaurant, a day manager and a night manager. Restaurants are categorized as low-level, medium-level, or high-level based on the following criteria: gross sales, annual profit, percentage of increase in sales and in annual profit, and scores assigned by mystery shoppers.

Doug Fong is a first-generation Asian American who lives in the San Francisco area. He's been with Jollytime for ten years and is respected by the other managers. Seven years ago he was promoted to manager of a low-level restaurant in the East Bay suburb of Concord, whose residents are primarily Euro-American but are also somewhat multicultural.

After two years he was transferred to a medium-level restaurant in the Hunters Point area of San Francisco, an area dominated by African Americans. Restaurant profits increased 13 percent the first year and 15 percent the second year. The top executive team was impressed with Doug's ability to handle the challenging Hunter's Point location, and at the end of two years transferred him to a "less hectic" restaurant in the Sunset district, where he has been working for three years,. Doug told a colleague, "I was sad to leave the Hunter's Point location because 1 had built a trusting relationship with my employees and my customers. There were a few trouble makers around, but I really didn't have any problems."

Residents in the Sunset are primarily Euro-American but also multicultural with a significant Asian American population. During the following three years under Doug's leadership, the Sunset district restaurant is ranked third, then sixth, and then second on the top 50 list of all Jollytime restaurants. Profits increased in each of these three years, and mystery shopper ratings have been outstanding, Doug has done well in managing a diverse group of employees. They speak well of him. For example, Kevin, a Euro-American food server, says, "Doug is a great manager; he treats everyone fairly." And Ruben, a Latino American cook says, "I've worked with Doug for nearly three years and he knows how to motivate people."

Doug's career goals include moving up to district manager and then to division manager. He's become more and more devoted to his job, often working 12-hour days. This is rather ambitious given the fact that Doug's educational background includes only a high school diploma. However, he's a rapid and avid learner. For example, he does all the accounting for his restaurant, and the auditors have always approved his work and even praised it.

A district manager oversees 10 to 12 restaurants. In an average day, the district manager may go over current operations and improvement plans with several restaurant managers. The job requires good interpersonal communication skills and knowledge of accounting principles, including budgeting.

Doug has never asked for a promotion. He has operated on the belief that his hard work and excellence speak for themselves and that he'll be offered a promotion when the time is right. In the past two years, two district manager positions opened up, and the outgoing managers picked their successors. All the district managers that Doug has met are Euro-American men with college degrees.

Jim Davis was one of the outgoing district managers. His job had been to oversee restaurants in Oakland, which is predominantly African American. Doug decided to overcome his reticence and speak to Jim about the possibility of taking his place. Jim told Doug, "You're an extremely well-qualified manager-no doubt about that. But maybe the Oakland area is not the best place for you." Jim obviously doubted that Doug was assertive enough to handle the employees there. He said, "Let's wait for an opening in an area that's predominantly Asian American or Euro-American. That would be a better fit." A few weeks later *Jordan Jones*, a Euro-American, was named new district manager for the Oakland area.

Now, a year later, the buzz is that Jones has failed miserably in overseeing the Oakland restaurant managers and he'll be replaced soon. *Jack Barnes,* the division manager will name the replacement.

1. What are the key issues (root problems) in this case?

2. If you were Doug Fong, what would you do?

3. If you were Jack Barnes, what would you do?

Case Study 9.2: Linda Vuong, Asian American Cashier

Linda Vuong has been working for two years as cashier for Computer City, one of a chain of retail electronics stores. It is located in a neighborhood populated primarily by Chinese Americans. In fact, all of the 20 employees, including its managers, are Chinese American, except Linda, who is Vietnamese American. Most of the employees are in their early twenties, attend college, and help support their families. Linda is majoring in business administration and hopes the company will soon promote her to assistant manager. She takes her job seriously, is very customer oriented, and cooperates well with coworkers.

Wallace is one of the store's three assistant managers and is Linda's immediate supervisor. One of the assistant managers is leaving next month, and Wallace is recommending Linda for the job. In his written evaluation that he submits to *Guy,* the manager and co-owner of the franchised store, Wallace includes the following:

Linda has continuously demonstrated quickness and efficiency in performing job tasks, which include taking customer orders promptly, packaging smaller items properly, and maintaining a clean work environment

*   Linda has good customer skills

*   Customers praise her performance

*   Linda is a team player, helping her coworkers and offering advice on how to improve communications with difficult customers

Guy seldom interacts with Linda and in fact spends minimal time communicating with employees except to exchange greetings. The exception is that he loves to gossip about the local Chinese American community with a few "insider" employees who speak Cantonese. He rarely speaks English to people in the company except to those at an equal or higher level than he. Guy is a concerned employer, paying attention to salaries, work loads, work schedules, and career opportunities within the company, especially for those employees he feels closest to. However, Linda has never had a chance to discuss her career ambitions with Guy.

Linda has not received a pay increase in 16 months. Guy recently instructed Wallace to delegate more work duties to Linda in order to relieve some of the other employees from job tasks. Not only is Linda expected to do more work without an increase in hours worked, her schedule is often changed to accommodate the requests of other employees who want to attend to personal matters. Linda is hoping all these problems will be solved if she can just get an assistant manager position. This promotion would also allow her to expand her skills and abilities.

Max, one of Linda's coworkers, also wants the assistant manager job. He's definitely in the running even though Wallace has rarely given him high performance ratings. Wallace has had to talk with Max several times about excessive tardiness. However, Max gets along well with Guy, often chatting and gossiping with him in Cantonese about mutual friends and acquaintances.

Today, Guy calls Wallace to his office and says, "I know you've recommended Linda for the assistant manager position, but 1 don't think she's quite ready for it. You know, Max has great communication skills, and I think he's better equipped to supervise our employees. Max reads people well, he knows how to get close to people, and that's what we need."

1. What are the key issues (root problems) in this case?
2. If you were Guy, what would you do?
3. If you were Linda, what would you do?

Case Study 9.3: Office Whiz Connie

Connie has been working for six years for Crystal Fizz, a manufacturer of drink mixes. She is one of six employees in the plant office, the youngest at age 27 and the only Asian American. Connie has learned how to do most all the major functions in the office and likes her job. However, she's become disillusioned with the work environment. If it weren't for the good pay and benefits, she'd be gone. In fact, she's thinking about looking for a job elsewhere.

Bob, the owner and manager, a year ago hired *Jim,* who performs duties similar to the ones Connie does. Soon Jim was making comments that disturbed Connie, such as "I can't understand what you're saying half the time," and "Why don't you do things the American way—whatever the American way is?" Connie's response has been to ignore and avoid Jim as much as possible. However, Jim was soon being consulted by Bob about various company decisions. Bob sometimes takes Jim with him to important business meetings. Connie is never included in this way, and she recently discovered that Jim makes about 10 percent more than she.

Company employees get four weeks of vacation. Before Jim came, Connie never took all four weeks at one time because of office demands. It was typical for her to come into the office even when she could have taken some time off, simply because there was much important work to be done. Now she finds she doesn't care about that any more. She came back from a four-week vacation last month, and she plans to take all the time off she has coming to her. She feels that she is being treated unfairly and has no real chance of advancement,

1. What do you think are the key issues (root problems)?
2. What should Connie do?
3. What should Bob do?

REFERENCES

Andres, Tomas D. *Understanding Filipino Values: A Management Approach.* Cellar Book Shop, 1985.

Asian Nation website. *www.Asian-Nation.org*

Baldassare, Mark. "Ethnic Groups Slow to Assimilate." *San Francisco Chronicle*, A-1, March 27, 1990.

Baldwin, Beth C. *Patterns of Adjustment*. Immigrant and Refugee Planning Center, 1984.

Bandon, Alexandra. *Chinese Americans*. Maxwell Macmillan, 1994.

Bautista, Veltisezar. *The Filipino Americans: From 1763 to the Present*. Bookahus. 2002.

Blinder, David, and Catherine Lew. "Asian Americans: Exit Poll." *San Francisco Chronicle*, A-l, November 6, 1992.

Brannen, Christalyn and Tracey Wilen. *Doing Business with Japanese Men*. Stone Bridge Press, 1993.

Brislin, Richard W., and Tomoko Yoshida, eds. *Improving Intercultural Interactions*. Sage, 1994.

Cabezas, A., T.M. Tam, B.M. Lowe, A.S. Wong, and K. Turner, "Empirical Study of Barriers to Upward Mobility for Asian Americans in the San Francisco Bay Area," in G.M. Nomura et al, eds., *Frontiers of Asian American Studies*: 85–97. Washington State University Press, 1989.

Chan, Sucheng. Asian Americans: An Interpretive History. Twaync Publishers, 1991.

Chew, Lee (interview), "Life Story of a Chinaman," in *The Life Stories of Undistinguished Americans as Told by Themselves*. New York, 1906.

Chow, Esther Ngan-Ling. "Asian American Women at Work." in *Women of Color in U.S. Society*. Temple University Press, 1994.

Corporate 1000: A Directory of Who Runs the Top 1,000 U.S. Corporations. Washington D.C. Monitor, Inc., 1985.

Do, Hien Due. *The Vietnamese Americans*. Greenwood Press, 1999.

Dong, Lorraine. Professor of Asian American Studies, San Francisco State University, interview, 1992.

Fadiman, Anne, "Hmong Odyssey, *Via*: 70–74, March/April, 1998.

Gladwell, Malcom. *Outliers: The Story of Success*. Little Brown & Co. 2008.

Gudykunst, W.B. *Bridging Japanese/North American Differences*. Sage, 1994.

Halter, Marilyn. Shopping for Identity: *The Marketing of Ethnicity*, Schocken Books, 2000.

Harris, Philip R., and Robert T. Moran. *Managing Cultural Differences*, 4th ed. Gull" Publishing Co., 1996.

Hmong Cultural Center, www.hmongcenter.org

Hossfeld, Karen, "Hiring Immigrant Women: Silicon Valley's 'Simple Formula.'" in *Women of Color in U.S. Society*. Temple University Press, 1994.

Hurh, Won Moo, and Kwang Chung Kim. *Korean Immigrants in America*. Fairleigh Dickinson University Press, 1984.

Kitano, Harry H.L. and Roger Daniels. *Asian Americans: Emerging Minorities*. Prentice Hall, 1988.

Kristoff, N.D. and Sheryl Wudunn. *China Wakes*. Random House, 1994.

Kumagai, regarding emotional expression, 1981.

Lee, Evelyn. *Working with Asian Americans*. Guilfotd Press, 1997.

Lewin, Tamar, "Report Takes Aim at 'Model Minority' Stereotype of Asian American Students," *New York Times*, June 10, 2008.

Markus & Kitayama. Comments on emotional expression and values, 1991.

Miller, Stuart C. The Unwelcome Immigrant: The American Image of the Chinese, 1752–1882. University of California, Berkeley, 1969.

Min, Pyong Gap, ed. *Asian Americans: Contemporary Trends and Issues*. Sage, 1995.

Morrison, Ann. *The New Leaders*. Jossey-Bass, 1992.

National Center for Educational Statistics, *www.ed.gov/nces*, 1995.

Nguyen, Liem T. and Alan B. Henkin. "Refugees from Vietnam," *Journal of Ethnic Studies*, 9, 4, 101–116, 1982.

Nisbett, Richard. *Intelligence and How to Get it: Why Schools and Cultures Count*. WW Norton & Co., 2009.

Nisbett. Richard. *The Geography of Thought: How Asians and Westerners Think Differently... and Why.* Free. Press, 2004.

Ong, Paul. "Chinese Laundries as an Urban Occupation in Nineteenth Century California." in *The Annals of the Chinese Historical Society of the Pacific Northwest.* Seattle, 1983.

Pido, Anthony J. A. *The Pilipinas in America.* Center for Migration Studies, 1992.

Posados, Barbara. *The Filipino Americans.* Greenwood Press, 1999.

Reid, T.R. *Confucius Lives Next Door.* Vintage, 2000.

Russell, John. "Narratives of Denial: Racial Chauvinism and the Black Other in Japan." Japan *Quarterly,* 416–428, Oct.–Dec. 1991.

Selig Center for Economic Growth, *www.selig.ega.edu,* 2002.

Sharpe, Rochelle, "Asian Americans Gain Sharply in Big Program of Affirmative Action," *Wall Street Journal,* A-l, September 9, 1997.

Takaki, Ronald. *A Different Mirror: A History of Multicultural America.* Little, Brown Co., 1993.

Takaki, Ronald. *Double Victory: A Multicultural History of American World War II.* Little, Brown, 2000.

Tanaka, Ronald. *In the Heart of Filipino America.* Chelsea Heart Publishers, 1995.

Tannen, Deborah. *You Just Don't Understand.* Win. Morrow, 1990.

Tyson, James and Ann. *Chinese Awakenings.* Wcstview Press, 1995.

U.S. Census Bureau, Department of Commerce. *Current Population Reports*: 60–80, 1995b.

U.S. Census Bureau, Department of Commerce, www.census.gov, 1995a

U.S. Census Bureau, Department of Commerce. *We the American . . . Asians, and We the American . . . Pacific Islanders,* 1993.

Van Do, Peter. *Between Two Cultures: Struggles of Vietnamese Americans.* University of Maryland, 2002.

Vang, Christopher, "Hmong American K-12 Students and the Academic Skills Needed for a College Education," Hmong Studies Journal, 5, 1–31, 2004–5.

Vietnamese 2001: *www.ins.usdoj.gov/graphics/publicaffairs/newsrels/*

Viviano, Frank. "Poll Contradicts Stereotypes." *San Francisco Chronicle,* A-l, March 27, 1990.

Wang, Gungwu. *The Chineseness of China.* Oxford University Press, 1991.

Wei, William. *The Asian American Movement.* Temple University Press, 1993.

WPT. "Being Hmong Means Being Free," Wisconsin Public Television *www.wpt*.org 2008.

Yi, Malthcw and Ryan Kim, "Asian Americans Seen Negatively: Results of Landmark Survey Called Startling, Disheartening,¹' San Francisco Chronicle, April 27, 2001.

Young, Jared. *Discrimination, Income, Human Capital Investment, and Asian-Americans.* R & E Research Associates, Inc., 1978.

Zinn, MB., and B.T. Dill. *Women of Color in U.S. Society.* Temple University Press, 1994.

RESOURCES

Information Exchange for Korean American Scholoras. Duke University
Journal of Cross-Cultural Psychology. Sage Journals Online, http://jcc.sagepub.com
Korean American Coalition, Census Information Center. California State University Los Angeles

CHAPTER 10

Working with Arab Americans

Out beyond ideas of right and wrong, there is a field.
I'll meet you there. Rumi

About ½ of 1 percent of people in the American workplace are Arab Americans, estimated at 1.2 million people who responded to the 2000 U.S. Census. However, research by the respected Zogby International firm place the population at 3.5 million, or about 1 percent of Americans (AAI 2008).

What's it like to be an Arab American? Too often, they are defined in simplistic terms. Although the Arab culture is one of the oldest on Earth, it is misunderstood in many parts of the United States. There are no easy, one-size-fits-all answers. Language, culture, and religion are distinct qualities that act in different ways to connect Arabs, and to distinguish them from one another.

The differences that seem to separate Arab Americans from nonArabs can be much smaller than the variations that at times differentiate them from one another. It takes time to learn about their culture and the issues that concern them, but it is essential and rewarding for us to do that. Misunderstanding ultimately hurts each one of us.

You're about to get a little taste of what it's like to be an Arab American in the American society and workplace and how this experience can affect interactions in the workplace. Specifically, you'll learn about these issues:

- How typical stereotypes and myths about Arab Americans compare with reality
- Connections to the past: a brief history
- Current profile: who, where, how much
- Key cultural values, customs, and issues that are important to these people
- Leadership challenges and opportunities for working effectively with Arab Americans

First, check your attitudes and knowledge by completing these Self-Awareness Activities.

Arab American Man

Courtesy of Stephen Derr/The Image Bank/Getty Images.

Arab American Woman

Courtesy of Jon Feingersh/Blend Images/Getty Images.

Self-Awareness Activity 10.1: What Do You Believe about Arab Americans?

Purpose:

- to get in touch with your beliefs and stereotypes about this group of people
- to experience how judgmental beliefs affect your thinking and feeling processes
- to experience the ways in which your beliefs create your reality regarding other persons, even before you have any interaction with them.

Part I. What Do You Believe about Arab American women?

Step 1. Associations

- Relax as deeply as you can.
- Close your eyes for a moment and take a few deep breaths.
- Now focus on the picture that symbolizes "Arab American woman"
- Imagine that you are this woman. Be Arab American woman.
- Notice any resistance to being this person—and any willingness.
- Notice words, images, thoughts, and feelings that come to mind as you are "seeing and being this woman."

Step 2. Negative Associations

- Next, as you focus on the picture, allow negative opinions to come up, perhaps some that you typically hold about Arab American women.
- Notice your thoughts as you see the person in this negative way. What feelings?

Step 3. Positive Associations

- Now, still focusing, allow positive opinions to come up, perhaps some that you typically hold about Arab American women.
- Notice your thoughts as you see the person in this negative way. What feelings?

Step 4. Insights and Writeup

- Now review this experience and write about it.
- When you first saw the picture, what thoughts and feelings came up? These may reflect your deepest responses to people from this group.
- Think about the differences in your thoughts and feelings when you consciously held a positive opinion versus a negative opinion.
- Write a few sentences about your feelings, thoughts, and insights.

Part II. Experimenting with Opinions about Arab American Men

- Repeat the phases and steps in part I, this time focusing on the image of an Arab American man.

Self-Awareness Activity 10.2: What Do You Know About Arab Americans?

Purpose: To see what you know about the issues covered in this chapter.
Instructions: Determine whether you think the following statements are basically true or false—and why. The answers will emerge in this chapter, and the summary at the end of the chapter focuses on these issues.

1. Most Arab Americans were born in the Middle East.
2. Most Arab Americans are Muslims.
3. The main occupations of the men are taxi driver and convenience store operator, for the women, housewife.
4. Arab Americans as a group have significantly more education than the average American.
5. The most unifying factor in Arab culture is the Arabic language.
6. It is rare to find Arab Americans who are actively engaged in politics.

STEREOTYPES AND REALITIES

Arab Americans came to the United States for the freedom and equal opportunity that the country symbolizes. And although the first wave of immigrants did confront the ethnocentricity, ignorance, and anti-foreign sentiments of the prewar period, they were rarely singled out for abuse or exclusion. This changed with the development of the Arab-Israeli conflict, which created a highly-charged political arena in which the United States became a strategic player and a strong supporter of the state of Israel. Arab Americans began to experience significant stereotyping, harassment, defamation, and exclusion brought on by the widespread perception of Arabs as immigrants from hostile, enemy lands.

Since the 1970s, in both popular culture and government policy, anti-Arab stereotypes have placed a stigma on Arab ethnicity in America. In response, Arab American activists became determined to document and publicize the Arab American experience as a political imperative, a defensive tool against ignorance and hostility.

Prior to 1980 the U.S. Census Bureau did not gather information on Arab Americans as a group. Although Arab Americans are still not designated as a distinct category, the Bureau has been collecting information on them. Although some Arab Americans feel a stronger identity with other minorities (people of color) than with Euro-Americans, the Bureau still officially classifies them as part of the majority "white" group. Regardless of their classification, they may still face stereotyping and discrimination.

Stereotype #1: Arab Americans' families come from nomadic desert tribes

Let's start with this oldest stereotype that the media has portrayed: Arab sheiks in the desert with their harems and camels. It was not difficult for this cultural bias to deepen in direct proportion to U.S. interests in the Middle East.

In fact, most Arab families live in urban areas, but portrayals of Arabs as desert dwellers have distorted the picture. Bedouins, nomadic people depicted in movies, make up only about 2 percent of Arab people. Many Arabs live in metropolitan areas. For example, one of the largest cities in the world is Cairo, with a population of more than 6 million.

While most Arab countries are more hot and dry than cold and wet, they do have a range of climates. You will find coastal areas, river delta regions, plateaus, and mountains, including some that get snow.

Stereotype #2: Arab Americans come from oil–rich Middle Eastern countries

The rich oil sheik is a newer stereotype that has permeated advertising, television, and movies. These moguls are few and far between, and the rest of the population tends to be in the poverty-stricken category. How many Arab Americans are from oil-rich countries? Relatively few. The area around the Persian Gulf is one of several oil-producing areas in the world, but not all Arab countries produce oil, and very few Arabs are rich from oil. Arab Americans are teachers, lawyers, grocers, executives and students. If you think about them only in terms of stereotypes, other facets of their experience are ignored and your perception of them is one-dimensional.

Stereotype #3: Arab Americans may have terrorist connections

The broader Arab American community is usually invisible in the news—except when there are highly volatile political events. Then the most visible Arab Americans and their institutions can be vulnerable to scapegoating. One prominent example is the 1995 Oklahoma City bombing tragedy in which initial suspicions of a Middle-Eastern link prompted incidents of anti-Arab backlash. Scapegoating is a human failure of understanding and wisdom. Americans resent being made scapegoats by Muslim political extremists, who blame all the world's ills on Western decadence. Moving beyond stereotypes requires that we all recognize this tendency to scapegoat and avoid it.

A person from any ethnic group is just as likely to have connections with terrorists as an Arab American is. Many types of people have committed acts of terror. However, news accounts seem to more often stress Arab terrorists than they do other terrorists. A tiny handful of terrorists can have, and have had, a devastating impact on the world, as in the recent September 11 attacks. Yet so far no Arab Americans fall into the terrorist category.

What is a terrorist? Is he someone who will murder persons, based only on their national or religious affiliation? Consider the Americans who murdered strangers whom they thought looked like Arabs. At least two such murders occurred soon after the September 11 attacks. Such "terrorist" acts included the murder of a store owner who was actually from India and wore the turban and beard of the Sikh religion. He had donated $75 to a fund for 9-11 victims only a few hours before his death (Inside 2001). These were extremely rare incidents. Most Americans responded to 9-11 with maturity and wisdom and don't wish to be painted with the same brush as these rare terrorists in their midst.

Stereotype #4: Arab Americans may be members of a violent Islamic fundamentalist religion

The term fundamentalist, whether applied to Muslims or Christians, is a largely American term that indicates strict adherence to a traditional code of belief and behavior. Throughout history political groups and leaders have used religion to justify many political actions, including violence. This is an old, all-too-common story.

In recent years, certain Islamic individuals and groups have declared jihad, or holy war, on Americans and American interests. The term Islamic fundamentalist is often used in the media to refer to these people, who use Islam to justify political actions. This usage has blurred the distinction between religion and politics. Very few Islamic individuals and groups who are conservative and traditional (fundamentalist) condone terrorist acts. So while we may have religious differences with Muslims, and even political differences, that doesn't make them violent.

Fairness and accuracy mean attributing political actions to the group, government or party responsible, and not to a religion that has about 1.2 billion followers around the world.

Stereotype #5: Arab American women are subservient to the men

This stereotype stems from the image of Arab Americans as strict Muslims. While most Arab women of the world live in Islamic households, less than one-fourth of Arab Americans do. Actually, most live in Christian households. By American standards Arab women do lack personal freedom—from a little to a lot, but that refers primarily to Muslim women. Even then, the degree of freedom varies widely from country to country.

Stereotype #6: Arab Americans look different

The media often seems to prefer images of people who look different or exotic. In trying for a more interesting image, they may emphasize the difference between Arab Americans and nonArab Americans. Most Arab Americans do not wear traditional clothing. They dress like Americans generally dress. The media tends to ignore Arab Americans except when there is a national or international crisis and they want to get the Arab American "take" on it. This keeps Arab Americans out of sight except when they are associated with trouble. The solution is to cover Arab Americans consistently and continuously. This results in fuller and deeper knowledge of this community.

Arabs may have light skin and blue eyes or olive-to-dark skin and brown eyes. Hair textures differ. The United States has, at different times, classified Arab immigrants as African, Asian, European, white, or as belonging to a separate group. Most Arab Americans identify more closely with nationality than with ethnic group.

CONNECTIONS TO THE PAST: HISTORY

About half of today's Arab Americans descended from the first wave of immigrants around the turn of the century. The second wave has come since World War II.

First Wave

The first wave of Arab persons arrived in the United States between 1875 and 1920. Most were from Lebanon, Syria, and Palestine and about 90 percent were Christian. Most were fleeing the changing economic and political conditions in their home countries. For example, Japanese competition had hurt the Lebanese silk market and a plant disease had hurt Lebanese vineyards. The first wave consisted primarily of farmers or village artisans, who were relatively poor with little or no education. They came to seek opportunity, intending to return home when they amassed enough money. Most settled in Arab communities and learned enough English to get by. Many eventually brought their families over and became permanent residents.

The earliest Arab American communities were built around a network of peddlers and their suppliers. Many of the suppliers became the first community leaders and acted as representatives to the outside world. What also seems to have set the Arab American experience apart was the relative degree of affluence that they quickly achieved. In the early 1900s—when miners, factory workers and farm laborers earned around $600 per year—Arab American pack peddlers were earning about $1,000. Another strength that set them apart was the relative degree of ease with which they assimilated into the mainstream.

Syrians, both Muslim and Druze, made up much of the remaining 10 percent of the first wave. This group, which came at the end of the peddling era in the 1920s, and during the rise of the mass retail consumer market, flocked to the industrial cities of the heartland like Toledo, Ohio, and Detroit-Dearborn, Michigan.

Like most immigrant groups, they had to struggle with negative stereotyping, ethnic slurs, prejudice, and discrimination. They faced poor working conditions, long hours, low wages, and an antagonistic society. They struggled with identity, culture, and marginality, forming ethnic communities that helped them establish their identity.

Second Wave

Beginning in the late 1940s, the second wave of Arab immigrants came from a wide variety of countries. The 22 countries of the current Arab League of Arabian countries are:

Algeria	Lebanon	Saudi Arabia
Bahrain	Libya	Somalia
Comoros Islands	Mauritania	Sudan
Djibouti	Morocco	Syria
Egypt	Oman	Syria
Iraq	Palestine	United Arab Emirates
Jordan	Qatar	Yemen
Kuwait		

Most of these immigrants wanted to escape the civil wars, famines, and hardships that followed World War II. They were primarily educated, bilingual, politicized, and nationalistic, having come from Arab nations that had gained their independence from European colonial nations immediately after the War. They identified themselves as Arabs and planned to settle permanently in the United States. Many were students, and there were many more Muslims in this group than in the first wave.

Both waves were pushed out of their homeland by harsh political and economic conditions. They were pulled to the United States by work opportunities due to industrialization. They came to work primarily in factories, the travel industry, and as tradespersons.

CURRENT PROFILE: WHO ARE THE ARAB AMERICANS?

On average, Arab Americans are younger, better educated and more affluent than most Americans. Arab Americans are among the fastest growing ethnic groups in major metropolitan areas. First, let's identify some terms we'll use. Then we'll look at some well-known Arab Americans and some interesting information about Arab Americans as a group (Arab American Institute).

Terminology

Here are terms recommended by the Arab American Institute.

- Arab American. Do not hyphenate when referring to a person.
- Arab-American issues. Hyphenate when using Arab-American as an adjective.
- Arab or Arab country. Arab is used as a noun for a person and as an adjective.
- She speaks Arabic. Arabic is the name of the language and is not usually used as an adjective.
- Saudi Arabian citizen; Arabian Peninsula; Arabian horse. Arabian is an adjective that usually refers to Saudi Arabia.
- Irani American, Egyptian American, etc. When ethnicity or nationality are relevant, it is precise and accurate to specify the country of origin. Other terms are "of Iraqi heritage," or "of Jordanian descent," but only if ethnicity is relevant. Arab Americans come from many places, so use the relevant perspective.

- The Islam religion. Muslim worshippers. Mohammedanism and Mohammedan are incorrect usages. Islam is the religion. Muslims are the members.

Notable Arab Americans

Some well-known Arab Americans are:

- **Darell Issa**, U.S. Congressman, Republican from California, member Foreign Relations Committee.
- **Najeeb Halaby**, former head of the Federal Aeronautics Authority, was CEO of Pan-American Airlines.
- **Queen Noor** of Jordan, daughter of Najeeb Halaby, who married King Hussein and became the first Arab-American to be queen of a foreign country
- **Paul Anka**, Canadian-born Arab American and a famous singer and songwriter.
- **Danny Thomas**, the late comedian and actor who founded St. Jude's Children's Research Hospital
- **Marlo Thomas**, feminist actress, daughter of Danny Thomas, wife of TV talk show host Phil Donahue. Marlo was the first actress ever to play a single, independent young woman living apart from her parents in a TV series, "That Girl."
- **Kristy McNichol**, actress once picked by People magazine as one of the "50 most beautiful people in the U.S."
- **Dr. Michael DeBakey**, the Houston surgeon who invented the heart pump and went on to become chancellor of Baylor University's College of Medicine.
- **Bobby Rahal**, Indy 500 winner
- **Doug Fluti**, Heisman Trophy-winner who threw the "miracle touchdown" pass for Boston College; the first American college quarterback to pass for 10,000 yards.
- **Casey Kasem and Don Bustany**, creators of radio's American Top 40
- **Jacques Nasser**, president and chief executive officer of Ford Motor Co.
- **Helen Thomas**, former dean of the White House press corps

NonArab Middle Easterners

Many people who are perceived to be Arab Americans are not actually of Arab origin but are of Middle East origin. The Arab group is the largest in the Middle East in terms of population and land holdings, but there are a number of nonArab groups. From the Arab region are Assyrians, Berbers from Morocco, and Chaldeans and Kurds, who speak languages rooted in pre-Arabic times.

Assyrians are Semites, closer in culture to the Jews than to the Arabs. They practice a unique early form of Christianity.

Chaldeans are also Semite people, their religion is Catholic, and they speak the Chaldean language. While they foster a separate identity, they also have an Iraqi nationality and some shared concerns with Arabs. They are the largest of these types of groups in the United States, with some large communities in Michigan, California, and Arizona, with the largest in Detroit.

The Kurds are a large, unique minority who speak a very ancient language that is not part of the Arab language group. They have no national homeland and live in areas of Turkey, Iraq, Iran, and Syria. Some Kurds are Sunni Muslims, others are Shiite Muslims, and still others are Yazdis, who follow an ancient religion similar to Zoroastrianism.

Iran is not an Arab country. It is in the Middle East, between Iraq and India, and it is an Islamic country, so many of its issues are similar. Iran is descended from the Persian empire and has a different language and cultural history than the Arab countries. The dominant language in Iran is Farsi, although Arabic and other languages are spoken there as well. Persian is sometimes used to describe either the language or the ethnicity, but the terms Farsi and Iranian are not interchangeable

Population

Estimates of Arab Americans living in the United States, as mentioned earlier, range from 1/2 of 1 percent to over 1 percent of the U.S. population. Contrary to popular assumptions or stereotypes, nearly half of Arab Americans are native-born. Of the half that are foreign-born, over half of those have become citizens—meaning that at least 75 percent of Arab Americans are U.S. citizens. While Arab Americans come from all 22 of the Middle Eastern countries, the majority trace their roots to seven nations (Census 2000; Arab American Institute 2009):

Lebanon	39%	Morocco	3%
Egypt	12%	Iraq	3%
Syria	12%	Arab or Arabic	18%
Palestine	6%	Other Arab*	7%

• *Algeria, Bahrain, Comoros Islands, Kuwait, Libya, Oman, Qatar, Saudi Arabia, Tunisha, UAE, Yemen*

Lebanese and Syrians

Nearly 40 percent of Arab Americans are Christians who trace their heritage to Lebanon, which was part of Greater Syria in those "first-wave" days, and they were known as Syrians then. Most of them came in the first wave and settled primarily in New York and New England. Since 1965 nearly 100,000 new immigrants have come from Lebanon, many settling in Michigan, California, Texas, and Ohio, as well as in the older Lebanese communities

Arab Americans from Syria make up 12 percent of the population and are also predominantly Christian and part of the first wave. Syrians and Lebanese together forged the early Arab American identity. They founded such institutions as the Southern Federation of Syrian and Lebanese-American Clubs and the renowned fundraising arm of St. Jude Children's Research Hospital, ALSAC (Associated Lebanese and Syrian American Charities). Despite this history of blurred identities between Lebanese and Syrian origins, the population of Syrian Americans equals or surpasses that of Lebanese Americans in eastern Pennsylvania, Rhode Island, and New Jersey.

Egyptians

Egyptians are 12 percent of the Arab American population. Many came to the United States in the 1950s as students, professionals, and skilled workers. Most wanted to escape the chaos of Egypt's struggle for independence from European colonialism. The Arab-Israeli war of 1967 provided another push. Egyptian Americans, both Muslim and Coptic Christian, are known for their high educational and occupational levels. At least 60 percent hold a bachelor degree or higher, compared with 20 percent of the U.S. population as a whole. Most are business or professional persons—in medicine, research, education, technical and other professions.

Palestinians and Jordanians

Arab Americans from Palestine, 6 percent of the total, have been predominantly Christian immigrants from cities or from towns and villages of the West Bank. A refugee program in the mid-1950s provided visas for thousands of Palestinians displaced in the Arab-Israeli war of 1948. Since the 1960s an estimated 65,000 Palestinians, including those carrying Jordanian passports, have been admitted to the United States, most of them Christian. And while most Americans probably think of Palestinian residents as Muslims, a minority of Palestinians are Christian. The total number of immigrants who came with Jordanian passports make up about 4 percent of the Arab American population

Moroccans

Moroccans are about 3 percent of the Arab American population. Along with the Iraqis, they're the most recent immigrants, most arriving since 1990. As such, both groups are less affluent than other Arab Americans. They have a somewhat lower median family income, higher poverty rate, and lower home ownership rate.

Iraqis

Immigrants from Iraq make up about 3 percent of Arab Americans. The majority immigrated after 1990 and Christians, who identify themselves as Chaldean or Assyrian. Iraqis, like Egyptians, are educated and well represented in the professional and business sectors of the U.S. economy. Since the Persian Gulf War of 1990, thousands of refugees have been resettled in the United States, and thousands more immigrants have fled the deteriorating economic and health conditions in their homeland.

Geographical Aspects

Arab Americans live in all 50 states, but about a third are concentrated in California, Michigan and New York. Another third are in these seven states: Illinois, Maryland, Massachusetts, New Jersey, Ohio, Texas and Virginia. About half of Arab Americans live in 20 metropolitan areas. The top six are Los Angeles, Detroit-Dearborn, New York, Northeastern New Jersey, Chicago, and Washington, D.C.

As is the case with most immigrant groups, Arab immigrants have had a tendency to settle in U.S. cities rather than in the countryside. About 90 percent of Arab Americans are urban dwellers, compared to about 75 percent of Americans overall. Of even greater significance, about 97 percent of Arab immigrants settle in urban areas, compared with the 87 percent of U.S.-born Arab Americans who are urbanites. Major settlements of Arab Americans are found in the:

- Northeast - where Arab Americans are more likely to be found
- Midwest – in Detroit-Dearborn, Cleveland, Chicago, Toledo
- South – with large, influential Southern Federation of Syria-Lebanon Clubs
- West - in growing southern California and San Francisco Bay Area communities

Those in the Northeast are more likely to be U.S.-born, while in the West they are much more likely to be immigrants.

By far the most concentrated areas of Arab American settlements are in the distinctly Arabic neighborhoods in the city of Dearborn. Michigan's vibrant expanse of ethnic, civic, and religious institutions have made it the new cultural and political magnet for the Arab American community nationwide. Unlike anywhere else in the country, Arab Americans make up 20 percent of Dearborn's population and more than 40 percent of the students enrolled in public schools.

Other Demographics

Arab Americans are generally better educated than other Americans, with a wide range of occupations that provide them with the highest median income of any American group. Still, their family size is relatively small.

Educational Level

Arab Americans place great value on education, and many of the second wave immigrants came here already educated or specifically for the purpose of obtaining higher education. Arab Americans are, on average, better educated than non-Arab Americans. The proportion of Arab Americans who attend college is higher than the national average (Census 2000).

- 85% of Arab Americans have high school diplomas (compared to 80% for all Americans)
- 40% have a bachelor's degree or higher (compared to 24% of all Americans)
- 15% have graduate degrees (compared to 7% for all Americans)

Occupations

Certain images or pictures come to mind when people think of the Arab immigrants to the United States: a man driving a taxi, a housewife with a head scarf rounding up several children, the man behind the counter at the local convenience store. Actually, Arab Americans' occupational patterns generally mirror the national pattern of proportion of people who are working or who are unemployed, and the types of jobs they hold. Arab Americans work in all types of occupations (Census 2000):

- 42% work as managers and professionals, compared to 34% of all Americans.
- 30% hold sales and office jobs, compared to 27% of all Americans.
- 10% hold low-paying service jobs, compared to 9% of all Americans.
- 5% hold production jobs, compared to 15% of all Americans.

Only Moroccans have more workers than the national average in service jobs, and Iraqis in production jobs—primarily because these are the most recent groups of immigrants.

By region, Arab Americans are most likely to be executives in Washington D.C. and Los Angeles, sales people in Cleveland and Anaheim, and manufacturing workers in Detroit (Zogby 2009). Some surveys indicate they are more likely than average to be self-employed.

Bottom Line: Arab Americans are more likely than the average Americans to own their own business and/or hold a managerial or professional position, and less likely to work for local government.

Income

Arab Americans earn more than the average American. Average affluence for subgroups within the Arab American population varies by how long they've been here. Median earnings range from $49,000 for Lebanese men to $17,000 for Moroccan women. Poverty rates range from 11 percent for Lebanese to 26 percent for Iraqis. Home ownership ranges from 70 percent for Lebanese to 35 percent for Moroccans. Here are some averages for Arab Americans (Census 2000).

- 73% of men are employed, compared to 71% of all American men.
- 46% of women are employed, compared to 58% of all women.
- $42,000 median earnings for men, compared to $37,000 for all men.
- $31,800 median earnings for women, compared to $27,000 for all women.
- $52,300 median family income, compared to $50,000 for all American families.
- 17% poverty rate, compared to 12% for all Americans.
- 55% own their own homes, compared to 66% of all Americans.

Family size

Arab American families are, on average, larger than nonArab American families and smaller than families in Arab countries. Traditionally, more children meant more pride and economic contributors for the family. The cost of having large families in the United States, however, and adaptation to American customs, seems to encourage smaller families.

COMMON THREADS OF ARAB CULTURES

When we compare the common threads of Arab cultures with other major world cultures, using the ten major types of cultural difference, we see that this cultural group is generally perceived as follows:

- Basic worldview: I'm controlled
- Relationship priorities: us-first, tribal
- Social fabric: tight ties, earthy
- Masculinity: moderately feminine (people-first, cooperative within societal group; work to live, not live to work)
- Equality/Status: rank/status
- Risk Orientation: play it safe; change is resisted
- Decision Orientation: short term

- Time Orientation: dive-right-in time, time as flexible and nonlinear; schedules are flexible; plans are not detailed; no concept of wasting time; time is not a commodity
- Space: up close and personal; the closest, with the most touching, of any group
- Communication: indirect; negative feedback is often given through a go-between; fixing blame on the person is avoided
- Economic: agricultural-dependent to industrial-independent

Some common threads of countries of the Arab world include their worldviews, language, family values, and customs—with the Arabic language considered the most consistently unifying factor. Islam is the predominant religion in these countries and plays a central role in family, social, and political life. Therefore, many aspects of these cultures stem from Islam. Because other religions do exist in these countries, and because of individual differences in any group, Arab Americans vary in their adoption of these cultural values and customs. Most are affected to some extent, recent immigrants the most, and successive generations less and less.

Each choice to become "more American" can require a giving up of their cultural heritage, and therefore can create inner conflict; for example:

- Changing their names to common American names enhances acceptance in the mainstream culture but takes away some of their unique identity.
- Using English almost exclusively creates an erosion of their Arabic language skills.
- Becoming American means giving up certain advantages of communal life in their homeland, such as the close proximity of family members in the same neighborhood, economic support from close-knit extended families, and a collective identity.

Language

The Arabic language is one of the great unifying and distinguishing characteristics of the Arab people. However, second- and third-generation Arab Americans may not speak it at all. Those who do speak it usually know that there are at least four major Arabic dialects, and they can identify a speaker's region of origin by his or her accent. Modern Standard Arabic (MSA) is a pan-Arabic language used in formal letters, books and newspaper. It's also spoken at Middle East peace conferences and on television news. Arabic is one of several languages written from right to left instead of left to right, as English is written. Instead of Latin characters, Arabic is written in the 28-character Arabic alphabet. Arabic letters are connected like script, and fine writing is an art form.

Arab use of language is more poetic, spiritual, emotional, and sensuous than highly rational or precise. Scientific evidence is less important than religious faith. Decisions may not be based so much on the objective merits of a proposal as on how it fits human needs. Arabs are not nearly so goal-oriented as Euro-Americans are.

The four main language groups in the Middle East are Arabic, Hebrew, Persian (Farsi) and Turkish. Arabic and Hebrew are Semitic languages; Farsi is of Indo-European origin, and Turkish originated in Korea. Other languages are Kurdish, which comes from an ancient form of Farsi, and Berber.

It is much more common for Arab Americans to speak more than one language than it is for most Americans. People in many countries place more emphasis on learning languages than Americans do, so many immigrants come to the United States speaking two or three languages. Most Arab countries emphasize the importance of knowing a foreign language, and they are very familiar with Western media. While 76 percent of Arab Americans speak English fluently, 69 percent of those speak at least two languages at home, and the other 31 percent speak only English.

In recent years, there has been a resurgence in the study of Arabic in universities, as well as in community schools or classes. As greater numbers of Muslims have entered during the second wave, the importance of Arabic to the practice of Islam has helped promote the proliferation of classes. These first-generation Muslims are motivated by religious concerns. At the other end of the spectrum, fourth- and fifth-generation Arab Americans have developed a deeper interest in Arabic culture because of a growing concern about the crisis situation in the Middle East. The uniqueness of the political situation in the Arab World has stimulated their interest.

Worldviews and Religions

Worldviews are based on beliefs and values, which usually stem from adherence to, or resistance to, certain religious beliefs. In the Arab countries people are connected by culture, especially by language, and although most Arabs are Muslim, Islam is not the primary uniting factor. Therefore, you must distinguish religion from culture if you want to understand your Arab American colleagues. In the Arab countries, Islam is the predominant religion. But the Arab American population is skewed by fact that the first wave of immigrants was predominantly Christian. Until the second wave, which was predominantly Muslim, about 80 percent of Arab Americans were Christians. Today, most of them are Christian, but a growing proportion are Muslim, as follows:

Christian	63%	(Catholic 3%, Eastern Orthodox 18%, Protestant 10%)
Muslim	24%	
Other or none	13%	

Muslims

Back in the Islamic world of their homeland, Muslims generally believe that everything is up to Allah, or God. People have little or no control over what happens in the world. Allah's will, fate, destiny are primary concepts. People can control their good intentions, but they cannot control the outcomes. Clearly, the 75 percent of Arab Americans who are not Muslims will not necessarily adhere to such beliefs, especially if one reason for coming to America was to escape religious intolerance back home.

Muslim American identity tends to be a compromise between two cultures, which may conflict at times. Traditional values may include

- identity of the honor of family/clan/society with virginal morality of females, leading to a clear double standard for males and females
- reverence for past traditions
- conformity and stability
- high esteem for elders due to their life experience and wisdom.

While Muslim Americans in urban areas, especially younger ones, may not hold as tightly to these traditional cultural values, they are influenced by them. These values may conflict with an American worldview that is likely to value

- equality of females with males, leading to acceptance of greater autonomy and freedom for females than in the past
- more focus on the future than on past traditions
- more focus on change and innovation than on holding to tradition
- relatively greater admiration for youthful looks and ways than for elders' wisdom

See the chapter on religious differences for a more complete comparison of Islamic and American cultures.

Christians

Although Arab Americans are frequently stereotyped as Muslims, three-fourths adhere to Christian or other beliefs, having descended from the first wave of Christian immigrants. This fact made it relatively easy for them to fit into American society. It made it easier for them to intermarry with Euro-Americans Christians, further facilitating their cultural integration. Many Arab American Christians have kept their Orthodox and Eastern Rite church affiliations (Greek Catholic, Maronite, Coptic). This helped them retain their ethnic identity. Their religious practices are not that different from those of the mainstream Euro-American culture, and so have not interfered with their acceptance.

Family Values and Customs

Family is more important than the individual and more influential than nationality. People draw much of their identity from their role in the family. Historically, Arab nations have been tribal nations, so first comes family, then close friends, then the tribe. Muslim belief and tribal organization have resulted in a strong social power hierarchy, with men the unquestioned heads of all organizations, including the family. A person is born into a family and tribe of a particular rank and affluence within the society and accepts that status as the will of God. People in higher-ranking wealthy families are expected to never do any types of manual labor.

Arab families are, therefore, traditionally patriarchal and extended. Name and inheritance pass from father to sons. Family name is established and maintained through the actions of every family member. Actions of females must be guarded in order to protect the family name. Gender and religion are the primary aspects of Arab identity. Adolescents tend to talk mainly about gender, while their parents are more likely to identify themselves with religion. Religion represents the system of meaning that the parents rely on to justify the behaviors they expect from their children and to demonstrate the significance of their cultural identity, according to M.W. Suleiman (1999)

The extended family may include parents, children, grandparents, uncles, aunts, and cousins living in one household. They provide financial, social, and emotional support for one another. This custom has fostered a pattern in which members of an extended family or tribe help one another to immigrate. It also means that many Arab Americans maintain ties with relatives who remain in their home countries.

Friends

Back in Arab countries, people generally may pay little attention to strangers. Making friends normally requires an introduction by another friend. If you are accepted as a friend into an Arab home, you'll receive the best that the host family can possibly offer you. Arab hospitality is legendary. They consider it a privilege and a duty.

Becoming true friends normally requires not only an introduction but extended, ongoing pleasant encounters that include getting to know each others' families. This goes on until the parties reach the point of becoming truly committed to supporting and helping one another whenever and wherever possible. Casual friendships are not part of traditional Arab culture.

Gender Differences

Gender roles vary greatly by country of origin, whether the family came from a rural or urban area, and how long they have been in the United States. The principle of "manly honor" motivates most Arabs, as well as other peoples of the Middle East and those of Muslim countries. In Muslim households girls and women play an enormous role in that their modesty and chastity reflect on the honor of the men, the family, the clan or tribe, and the community. The roots of women's repression in these regions lie in authoritarian tribal practices and the overarching concern with protecting the "honor" of the patriarchal name and the identity of the clan or tribe. Some say that a primary concern of Arab families is, "What will the neighbors say?" (especially about what our girls are doing).

Accordingly, in Arab American Muslim households boys and girls may be raised in dramatically different ways. Girls are typically taught that the American girl is perceived as immoral, while the Muslim girl is respected. Great pressure is placed on girls to be "moral." The actions of girls is restricted and limited at home. They are closely monitored. There are dramatically different sexual standards for girls and boys, men and women (Ahmed 1992).

Muslim boys acquire more material objects than girls and have more freedom. They are expected to take increasing responsibility to uphold the family name by watching over their sisters' actions. If he hears rumors about his sister's behavior, he is expected to take immediate action to regulate her behavior. When other males are present, he feels even greater pressure to intervene.

Marriage Patterns

Arab Americans are likely to live in households where both partners are of Arab background. In fact, about 29 percent live in households headed by two Arabs. They typically get married at a younger age than non-Arab Americans, although this is changing. As women follow careers, they are not expected to marry so young. Since most Arab Americans were born in the United States, they frequently marry people from other cultures.

In the home countries, typical marriages may be arranged by parents. The woman's family may demand and receive a large dowry (money or other assets) from the man's family. Arab women might marry older men who can provide greater financial security. Recent immigrants may adhere to these customs, and even arrange a marriage with someone from the country of origin. For most Arab Americans, however, couples meet and ask their families' approval before getting engaged, or make their own decision and then tell their families.

Arab American men are more likely than women to be single, while women are more likely to be married. U.S.-born Arab American women are twice as likely to be single as Arab-born women, though at 18 percent, single-women immigrants are perhaps higher than might be expected. Not surprisingly, women are more likely than men to be widowed.

Using Physical Space

Arab cultures are known as preferring the closest physical proximity to one another of any major culture. When they are interacting, they tend to sit or stand so close that they can actually feel and smell the other's breath. They also tend to engage in more touching than other cultures.

Food

Middle-Eastern food is considered very tasty by most connoisseurs. It is varied, but has some staples. Wheat is used in bread, pastries, salads and main dishes. Rice is often cooked with vegetables, lamb, chicken or beef. Couscous, a rice-like grain, is often served alongside a meat dish. Lamb and mutton are more common than other meats. Arab recipes often call for beans and vegetables, including eggplant, zucchini, cauliflower, spinach, onions, parsley and chickpeas. Middle Eastern vegetarian food is among the world's most delicious.

ARAB AMERICAN ISSUES

Arab Americans are especially interested in Middle Eastern events because many of them have relatives there as well as cultural or religious commonalities with people who live there. Some issues that significantly affect the Arab American community are the Israel-Palestine conflict, U.S. oil policy in the Middle East, Muslim condemnation of American personal morality, fair treatment of Arab Americans, and Arab American representation in the U.S. political system.

Issue #1. Israel–Palestine Conflict

In addition to conflicts between Arab countries and Israel, there is also conflict between and within Arab countries. These conflicts are rooted in some of the world's oldest religions, ethnic differences, and boundaries drawn during 20th Century colonialism. One reason many Arab American families immigrated was to escape the very conflicts that continue today. Most have a keen interest in news from the Middle East—and Mideast issues can unify the Arab American vote.

By far the most crucial Middle East conflict is the struggle over territory and rights between Israel and Palestine. The most unifying viewpoint in the Arab world seems to be that the United States has acted with extreme favoritism toward Israel and with great disregard for the plight of Palestinian residents and refugees. Further igniting the smoldering resentment over this perceived unfair favoritism is the belief that the United States has the power and influence to end this conflict. General opinion is that the U.S. government lacks the will and determination to effect a fair and just resolution of this ongoing crisis. This is the smoldering fire of resentment that in Arab countries occasionally ignites into demonstrations and acts against American interests.

Issue #2. U.S. Mideast Oil Policy

The fact that the United States has become more and more dependent on oil and gasoline to fuel its huge energy consumption has led to continuing conflicts in the Middle East oil-producing region. These range from the 1970s gasoline shortage and Iranian hostage situation to the 1990 Gulf War with Iraq, to current struggles. The Gulf War was especially devastating in the minds of many Arabs, and its bad taste lingers on. The U.S. invasion of Iraq in 2004 clearly compounded this distaste for American power, intensifying the view of the United States as a big bully, throwing its weight around in order to take care of its own insatiable appetites. Also, many Arabs resent feeling powerless and left behind in the burgeoning global economy, which intensifies the problem.

Issue #3. Culture Clash

For those Arab Americans who are Muslims, adding a little more fuel to that "smoldering fire" of U.S. Mideast policy may be the culture clash rooted primarily in differences between certain Islamic and American values. Arab Americans are obviously concerned about these fundamental differences between East and West. Islamic cultures are generally governed by the rule of a king, religious leader, or strongman. Governmental and economic institutions are run by men, and family and community see their honor as dependent on the honor of the women. There is a huge poverty class, and diversity of beliefs and ideas is discouraged. More on the roots of culture clash in the Islam section of the chapter on religious differences.

Issue #4. Generation Gap

Second generation Arab Americans may be less aware of traditional customs that are based in tribal-like identities. They were born in the United States, so their identities are not as intertwined with religious, gender, ethnic, and class origin as the identity of their immigrant parents. The parents may want to postpone identity loss and curb the children's assimilation into the larger American culture. They may pressure daughters to marry within the ethnic group. Sons may not be as pressured as daughters because they can carry forward the family name even when they do marry outside the ethnic group.

Issue #5. Discriminatory Profiling

Because of these East-West conflicts, the fair treatment of Arab Americans has emerged as a concern. Long before any U.S. terrorist attacks, the Arab as villain was a favorite scapegoat of popular American culture. This set the stage for acts of discrimination and bigotry that have affected Arab Americans at home and resulted in a range of reactions.

Arab Americans of the second wave came from independent nation states and arrived in America with an Arab political consciousness unknown to earlier immigrants. Because they were highly aware of a region in conflict, they sought to establish an Arab American political community.

The Israeli defeat of the Arab nations in 1967, the continuing occupation of Arab lands by Israel, the oil boycott of the 1970s, and the negative stereotyping of Arabs in the American media—all have focused attention on the central role that the U.S. government and media play in the Middle East crisis. It is these second wave immigrants whose political consciousness and public pride played a key part in mobilizing the Arab American community and refocusing its energies on political and social issues.

Stereotypes seeped into public policy. Beginning in the 1970s a number of government investigations, executive orders, and legislative provisions aimed at combating terrorism violated the rights of some Arab Americans. An activist response emerged as Arab American intellectuals, students, and professionals coalesced to counter the bias they saw in American policy and culture. Organizations to educate and to advocate the Arab American point of view laid the groundwork for the first publicly engaged movement to represent the needs and issues of Arab Americans and to create a national sense of community and common purpose.

The second wave of immigrants inspired the establishment of the national Arab American organizations, which have served as an emerging political movement and have also created a cultural bond across the immigrant generations. Therefore, they founded organizations in the 1980s to respond to these political, civic, and cultural challenges. They include the National Association of Arab Americans, the Association of Arab-American University Graduates, the American-Arab Anti-Discrimination Committee, and the Arab American Institute.

Recent anti-terrorism policies of airline-passenger profiling and the use of secret evidence by immigration judges have disproportionately affected Arabs and Muslims and have raised concerns about selective prosecution. Arab Americans ask only for fairness and justice. As a group, they are at least as anxious as others about terrorist acts.

Work-related complaints by Muslims have been increasing even before the September 11 attacks. The EEOC reported a 42 percent increase in 1998 compared to 1994 (Durani 2002). The most common complaints by women concerned the right to wear the headscarf. Many companies have dress codes that forbid wearing headscarves, refuse to hire women who wear them, or fire those who persist. Many complaints by Muslim men concern wearing beards, which are a religious ritual for many.

Issue #6. Representation in U.S. Politics

Arab Americans tend to be politically active. For decades, they have voted, run for office and been elected. In 1998, for example, 12 Arab Americans campaigned for the U.S. Congress in 10 states. Prominent Arab-American politicians have included U.S. Senate Majority (Democratic) Leader George Mitchell, Energy Secretary Spencer Abraham, Secretary of Health and Human Services Donna Shalala; New Hampshire governor and White House Chief of Staff John Sununu, California congressman Darrell Issa, and perennial presidential candidate Ralph Nader.

Fully 86 percent of Arab American adults were registered voters during the 2000 campaign, the first in which both major presidential candidates addressed Arab Americans as a group. Several organizations lobby on behalf of issues that concern Arab Americans. One is the Arab American Institute, which supports presidential and congressional candidates who are receptive to Arab American concerns. Another is the American Arab Anti-Discrimination Committee, a civil rights group.

Various polls of Arab American voters indicate that they tend to favor Democratic candidates. A recent poll (AAI 2008) found that 45 percent claim to favor Democrats, while 20 percent favor Republicans.

LEADERSHIP CHALLENGES & OPPORTUNITIES

Arab Americans have great contributions to offer work teams and organizations. Helping them to meet the challenges that face them and to rise to emerging opportunities will have high payoffs for you as a workplace leader. Here are some major ways you can help.

#1. Don't Assume They Are Arab or Middle East Experts

If you have asked the right questions, you are unlikely to make the mistake of thinking your Arab American colleague is an expert about a language she doesn't speak, a country he never visited, or a religion he has never studied.

#2. Give Stereotyping Protection

You know the current issues and the tendency of some people to stereotype and scapegoat Arab Americans. As a workplace leader, you can offer protection by being sensitive to Arab Americans' viewpoints and experiences, by speaking up during tense situations, and by serving as a role model in your respect for Arab Americans. Find a way to get information about Arab Americans to your colleagues. Even better, campaign for one or more formal diversity training sessions.

#3. Get to Know Them as Individuals

The Arab American community is diverse itself. So always use the information in this chapter as background information that can help you to ask the right questions, and never use it to make assumptions about an Arab American colleague. Ask about key variables, tactfully in the right time and place; for example:

- What is your cultural heritage?
- How long has your family lived in the United States?
- Tell me about your family.
- What is your religious affiliation?
- Do you speak more than one language?
- What are your career goals? Your goals for this job? Your aspirations with this company?

#4. Recognize Their Personal Strengths and Potential

You've learned that Arab Americans as a group have a history of being independent, achieving, well-educated, hard working, and productive. As you get to know individual colleagues, determine if they fit this profile, other strengths they may have, and areas of potential that may be developed. Explore together ways their strengths can be used to achieve career goals that also help your team and your organization to thrive and succeed.

#5. Capitalize on Their Networking Skills

Arab Americans are known as masters of the network approach to doing business. Get to know those who work on your team. If they have these skills, explore ways to use this ability and the contacts it generates. As part of this approach, look for opportunities to integrate the contacts this colleague may have in the Arab American community, as well as opportunities for trade with Arab countries in the global marketplace.

SUMMARY

Typical stereotypes that Arab Americans must deal with include the belief that they come from nomadic desert tribes or from oil-rich countries, that they have terrorist connections, that they may be violent themselves as members of an extremist Islamic group, that the women are subservient to the men, and that they look different.

In fact, only 2 percent come from a nomadic desert background, virtually none are oil-rich and most come from countries that are not oil exporters. They are no more likely than any other American to have terrorist connections and virtually none belong to violent religious groups. About one-fourth are Muslim and over three-fourths are Christian, or other religions, which means that their views of women's equality are similar to those of other Christians. And though some are darker-skinned than most Americans, others have light complexions and blue eyes.

Estimates of the size of the Arab American population range from 1/2 of 1 percent to over 1 percent of the U.S. population. The largest group is from Lebanon, with significant numbers from Egypt, Syria, Palestine, Jordan, Morocco, and Iraq. The first wave, which came around the turn of the 20th century, settled primarily in New England and New York. These Lebanese and Syrians constitute about 40 percent of the current Arab American population. The second wave, which has been coming since the late 1940s, settled primarily in six metropolitan areas. The most recent immigrants are Moroccans and Iraqis, who arrived since 1990.

Arab Americans work in all occupations, but a large proportion are self-employed, managers and professionals, and sales and office persons. Arab Americans as a group have achieved higher educational levels than the average American and therefore earn higher incomes than average.

The most unifying factor in Arab culture is the Arabic language. Islam is the dominant religion in Arab nations, although there are other religions. Only 24 percent of Arab Americans are muslim, while 63 percent are Christian. Only 12 percent of Muslims worldwide live in the Arab countries—and huge numbers live in Indonesia. India, and other countries. Traditional values may include reverence for the past, conformity, stability, high esteem for elders, and viewing women's modesty, virginity, and monogamy as essential to the honor of family, clan, and tribe.

Most Arab Americans are interested in Middle East issues because they may have relatives in those countries, may have cultural or religious commonalities with people there, and may suffer stereotyping and discrimination because of conflicts there. Key issues are the Israel-Palestine conflict, U.S. Mideast oil policy, Islamic-American cultural differences, discriminatory profiling of Arab Americans, and their representation in U.S. politics. In fact, they have always been politically active as a group. And many have served in recent years at top levels of the U.S. government; for example Ralph Nader, John Sununu, George Mitchell, and Darrell Issa.

To work effectively with Arab Americans, don't assume that they are experts on the Middle East or Arab culture, speak up to protect them from unfair stereotyping, get to know them as individuals, recognize their personal strengths and potential, and capitalize on their networking skills and connections.

Case Study 10.1: Mona and Suspicions, Suspicions

Mona was raised in the Muslim faith in Lebanon and had become an American citizen several years after she married **Hank, an American Catholic**. During the early years of their marriage, Hank's job with the U.S. State Department sent them to several Middle Eastern countries. Mona was proud of representing American interests in this part of the world. Hank, who spoke Arabic fluently, considered Mona a great asset in his work because of her familiarity with the cultures he works with.

Now Mona and Hank have two school-aged children, Hank's assignment is in Washington D.C. Wanting to get out of the house, earn some money, and still be available when her children need her, Mona takes a job in the fine jewelry department of Windsor, a large upscale department store chain featuring clothing and accessories. This job fits Mona's needs. Windsor is located in the mall near her home, the job pays well, and store management has agreed to give her a 35-hour a week schedule that's compatible with her children's school schedules.

Mona has had the job about a year now. A few months ago, one of her coworkers, **Vickie**, was promoted to manager of fine jewelry. Since then, Mona has found the job environment increasingly unpleasant. This is because Vickie, a Euro-Americans, is continually making critical remarks about minority customers who come into the store and often seems suspicious of them. Mona notices that she treats minority customers and employees differently than Euro-Americans.

For example, when a Filipino American customer said he would pay cash for a $500 watch, Vickie pushed the security alarm, which causes a security person to telephone her. She reported the customer as suspicious because he was carrying a large amount of cash. Yet within a week, a Euro-Americans woman came in and paid cash for a $1,000 item and Vickie did not report her.

Another example: Vickie told Mona and **Ashton**, an African American coworker, to leave their purses in their employee lockers and carry their personal items to the worksite in clear plastic bags. This is normally required to prevent employee shoplifting. After Ashton quit, Vickie hired a Euro-Americans woman to replace her. Every day she carries her purse to the worksite. No plastic bags for her.

Soon after, Ashton takes some sick days, and then resigns. **Sultan**, a Pakistani coworker, quits next. Of the three minorities in the department, only Mona is left. In fact the department now consists of only Vickie, Mona, and **Pat**, the new Euro-Americans employee,

Mona talks with Hank about Vickie's attitude, saying, "She says things to me that are insulting in a subtle way. She seems to think that I'm so passive that I'll never talk back. She treats Ashton the same way. Come to think of it, she tried to treat Sultan that way too, but he fought back, and she treated him better after that."

After September 11, 2001, Mona notices that Vickie's attitude toward minorities becomes even more suspicious, especially toward Arabs and Arab Americans. A day or two after the attack, Vickie actually says to Mona, "You know, it would be better to prohibit Arab persons from living here in the United States. After all, any one of them could become a terrorist-in-waiting." Mona objects, saying that many Arab Americans are children. Vickie replies, "Even the children are terrorists-in-waiting, as far as I'm concerned." Mona is appalled. To make matters worse, Vickie repeats this type of comment a couple more times in front of other employees.

In early October, Windsor managers hold a Thursday meeting to discuss the drop in sales, part of the general economic slump since 9-11. They decide they must lay off some peripheral personnel, such as some cashiers, but no sales people yet. However, at this meeting Vickie volunteers to lay off Mona. Her **manager Jeffrey** doesn't comment. The next day, Friday, Mona feels Vickie's animosity under her sharp comments and actions. On Saturday Vickie tells Mona she will be laid off, saying, "you're only a part-time person and sales are off." She implies that Mona's sales are dropping and that customers have complained about her. This is not Mona's experience and it's the first time Vickie has made these accusations.

Mona goes to the **Jan, the Human Resources officer**, to complain about Vickie's discriminatory treatment of her and other minorities. Jan tells Mona there's nothing she can do because Vickie is the authority in this situation. On Monday Mona receives a letter telling her she is laid off. She goes to Human Resources and asks for a copy of her file. They put her off, saying they'll send it to her later. When she receives it, there's nothing in it but her original hiring papers. In the next few weeks, Mona calls Human Resources four times, trying to get her job back, but is unsuccessful.

1. What are the major issues (root problems) in this case?
2. Did Mona take the best action? What would you recommend?
3. What should Windsor management do?

Case Study 10.2: Omar and Accusations

Omar Abu Jassar was born in Amman, Jordan. His father had lived and worked in the United States, where he met Omar's mother, a Euro-Americans. They went to live in Jordan, so Omar is legally a citizen of both Jordan and the United States. Omar went to school and married in Jordan. Then, in 1990 when he was 23 years old, Omar and his wife came to the United States. He settled in Alameda in the Bay Area of California. Over time, he and his wife had two children, and his mother came to live with them. Omar held several jobs and eventually graduated from the electronics program of a trade school.

In February 2001 Omar went to work as an engineering technician for Celerity Systems, a high-tech defense contractor, in Cupertino, California. For the first seven months, Omar's work experience was pleasant and productive. He got along well with **Jim, his manager**, and with the other 55 employees at the Celerity facility. He and Jim had weekly Status Meetings to update each other on projects and tasks and to coordinate Omar's work. Jim never indicated that Omar had any problems. Jim has always held these meetings with each of the technicians who report to him. Omar's experience of these meetings was that they were practical ways of communicating.

In June Omar got approval to take four days of personal leave to move his family from Alameda to Stockton, where housing was significantly cheaper and the commute to Cupertino was faster. Also, Omar could carpool with his boss Jim, who lived nearby.

Omar was happy in his job and all seemed well until the day after the September 11 attack on the World Trade Center. On that day **Beverly, a Latino American lesbian**, started talking about the attack with four or five coworkers, including Omar. She said, "Those G . . . D. . . . Arabs, we ought to get rid of all of them. The f. . . . Muslims, get them out of here. We should go over and nuke them all." No one objected to Beverly's comments. All of a sudden Omar sensed a wave of hostility, as if he were in danger, perhaps even physical danger. Right then, he decided to lie low, keep quiet, and try to fade into the background.

About a week after Beverly's outburst, Jim called Omar to his office and told him he would have to lay him off. He mentioned budgetary problems, as well as certain "performance and attendance problems." He said, "Omar, when we've checked your desk several times, you weren't there. Also, lately you have not always been working a full eight-hour day. Apparently my weekly coaching sessions with you have not solved your performance problems."

Omar is amazed by all this. To begin with, Jim had suddenly converted the routine weekly Status Meetings to coaching sessions. Omar also found it incredible that Jim would expect him to be at his desk all the time. As he said he to his wife, "My job requires that I interact with people in the lab, with other team leaders, and so forth. If Jim found that I was away from my desk, why didn't he just page me? He could have found me in seconds that way." Finally, Omar couldn't believe that Jim would accuse him of not working an 8-hour day since they carpooled together. In fact, Omar had accrued 72 hours of paid time off because he had not taken all his sick and personal leave days.

1. What are the key issues (root problems)?
2. What should Omar do?
3. What should Celerity management do?

Case Study 10.3: Bob and the Player X Attack

During fall semester 2001 instructor Page Nelson held two teaching jobs at the campus of Holy Names College (HNC) in Oakland. He taught 30 hours per week in a non-college course, English As a Second Language (ESL), as an employee of English Language Services (ELS), a subsidiary of Berlitz. ELS has rented office, classroom and dormitory space on the HNC campus for 35 years. Their services come in handy for foreign students who attend the ELS program (separate from HNC's), but they accept all types of students.

Page also taught two regular college courses, an ESL Reading and Writing class and Professional Writing, as an employee of HNC, a college of about 1,000 to 1,400 students. Page received his masters degree in English Literature there a few years ago.

Two of the approximately 45 students in the ELS program were Arabs, a **Saudi Arabian, Ibrahim (Bob)**, who was 19 years old, and **Hamid**, a Catholic seminarian, who was about 30 years old. No Arab foreign students were enrolled at HNC. Bob had been studying English in the U.S. for about a year and had adapted quite well to American culture. He liked to be called Bob and was popular with other students.

A couple of days after 9-11, Bob was having dinner in the campus cafeteria. Player X, member of the basketball team, approached Bob and asked him what he thought about the World Trade Center attack. Bob replied that "it was a very bad thing." What happened next is unclear, but apparently Player X became enraged, called Bob a liar, attacked him with racial insults, and finally was pulled back by some of his teammates. No one came to Bob's defense or said anything to him, and although many students witnessed the encounter, no one officially reported it.

Bob's reaction was to withdraw to his room for the next three weeks. He became depressed and when outside was generally alone. His main support came from his friends among former ELS students now studying at Bay Area colleges. None of his American friends came forward. It took more than three weeks for him to arrange his return home to Saudi Arabia.

Hearing about the attack and not seeing Bob in the classroom area, Page became concerned. The assurances of the **ELS Center Director Steve Shinn** that Bob was feeling OK and everything was under control did not convince Page. He felt that Bob needed much more support, including the ability to discuss his feelings in Arabic. Page asked Hamid to talk with Bob. Hamid later reported that Bob said, "I can't stay here any more, when there are people who hate me just because I'm Arab. I feel alone and abandoned." Bob feared for his safety and his life.

Later Page encouraged Bob to report the incident, but Bob refused. As an Arab, he believed that it was the host's duty to see to the comfort and security of the guest. To suggest that the guest, Bob, should take the lead in securing justice for himself was a culturally impossible idea. He believed that it was up to the school authorities to do something about such situations. It should be noted that, even without the strong cultural element, male victims often dismiss the severity of their situations out of a misplaced sense of pride.

At an ELS staff meeting five days after Bob was attacked, Page asked the ELS Center Director, Steve Shinn, what was being doing about Bob's situation. Steve said, "I've been assured by HNC administrators that the matter will be handled to our satisfaction." Remembering how these very people had ignored a mini-crime wave of campus thefts and robberies a few years ago, Page responded that "such assurances from them are B.S"

Meanwhile Page was interviewed by the FBI, as were administrators of ELS and HNC, about another former student. The terrorist who piloted the plane that crashed into the Pentagon had been tentatively identified. Apparently, he had been one of Page's students in an ELS class four years earlier. In fact 18 months ago he had applied for a second round of ELS lessons but never showed up for classes. It was possible he had merely used the ELS application as a ruse to enter the United States again. So far, this information had not appeared in the news media. At the time, everyone who previously had any contact with any of the terrorists was under a cloud of suspicion.

Back to the Bob-Player X situation, Page Nelson was the only person who took any action to address it. Here are some actions that he took.

A week after the ELS staff meeting, the end of September, Page wrote a letter to the Chair of Board of Trustees of HNC. He mentioned the need to avoid "moral cowardice" and proposed that the administration take action to: a) identify Player X, b) counsel with him, c) arrange a meeting of Bob and Player X in the President's office to negotiate mutual understanding and healing, and d) formulate a non-hate, tolerance policy for the campus and distribute it to everyone.

With the College President's permission, Page wrote an open letter to the Player X, which a student passed on to him. Page offered to serve as an intermediary to heal the rift and to counsel with both parties. Page had his students write proposed non-hate and tolerance policies for the college Page created "hate-free zone" posters and put them around his office and class area.

1. What are the key issues (root problems) in this situation?

2. What could Page have done differently to be more effective?

3. What should the ESL and HNC officials have done?

Case Study 10.4: Dagany at FedEx

Loa Dagany immigrated to the United States from Kuwait several years ago. In 2003 he got a job as a driver in the FedEx ground package division in Wilmington, Massachusetts. Dagany was thrilled to have this opportunity, but he soon discovered that the workplace could be quite toxic.

For one thing, whenever his supervisor **David Goyette** was frustrated with Dagany, he muttered insults about him, such as "terrorist" or "fanatic." Once he asked Dagany, "Are you planning to send money to Al Qaeda or bin Laden?" Other times he threw packages at his head. Soon Dagany was given delivery routes that restricted the amount of salary he could earn. After Dagany complained about route changes, Goyette told him "That's it. Take it or leave it. And don't go berserk over it and blow up my car."

Dagany said the treatment made him so sick that he developed a rash that wouldn't go away. He talked with other drivers, attempting to learn if they were having similar experiences. He learned that at least three other Arab American drivers were also having humiliating experiences. Some of them reported to Goyette and others to Michael Melnyk. In fact, one of the drivers, Yasir, had been questioned by the FBI after his supervisor made a call to them.

1. What are the major issues (root problems) in this case?

2. If you were Dagany (and the other drivers), what would you do?

Source: David Abel, "Arab-American Drivers Accuse FedEx Bosses of Discrimination,: The Boston Globe, October 22, 2007.

REFERENCES

AAI. "Arab Americans: Demographics," Arab American Institute, *www.aaiusa.org 2008*.

AAI. "How Arab America Will Vote in 2008 and Why," Arab American Institute, *www.aaiusa.org,* 2008.

Abraham, Nabeel, and Andres Shryock. *Arab Detroit: From Margin to Mainstream*. Wayne State University Press, 2000.

Abu-Laban, Baha and Faith T. Zeady, eds. *Arabs in America: Myths and Realities*. Medina University Press International, 1975.

Abu-Laban, Baha and Michael W. Suleiman, eds. *Arab-Americans: Continuity and Change*. Association of Arab-American University Graduates, 1989.

Ahmed, Leila. *Women and Gender in Islam*. Yale University Press, 1992.

Altorki, Soraya. "Women and Islam: Role and Status of Women." The *Oxford Encyclopedia of the Modern Islamic World*. Oxford University Press, 1995.

Ameri, Anan and Dawn Ramey, eds. *Arab American Encyclopedia*. Arab Community Center for Economic and Social Service (ACCESS), 2000.

Arab American Discrimination Committee, *www.adc.org*

Arab American Institute, 1600 K Street, NW, Suite 601, Washington, DC 20006. *www.arab-aai.org, www.aaiusa.org*

Ashabranner, Brent. *An Ancient Heritage: The Arab-American Minority*. Harper Collins, 1991.

Association of Arab American University Graduates, *www.aaug.org*

Aswad, Barbara C., ed. *Arabic Speaking Communities in American Cities*. Center for Migration Studies, 1974.

Aswad, Barbara, and Barbara Bilgé. *Family and Gender Among American Muslims: Issues Facing Middle Eastern Immigrants and Their Descendants*. Temple University Press, 1996.

Barakat, Halim. *The Arab World: Society, Culture and State*. University of California Press, 1993.

Castronova, Frank V. *Reference Library of Arab America*. Four volumes. Farmington Hills, MI: Gale Group, Inc., 1999.

Detroit Free Press, "100 Questions About Arab Americans," *www.freep.com*, 2001.

Durani, Anayat, "American Muslims Confront Discrimination in the Workplace," *Arabia.com*, September 2002.

Eisler, Riane. *Sacred Pleasure: Sex, Myth, and the Politics of the Body*. Harper, 1996.

Eisler, Riane. *The Chalice and the Blade: Our History, Our Future*. Harper, 1988.

El Guindi, Fadwa. *Veil: Modesty, Privacy and Resistance*. Berg Publications, 1999.

El-Badry, Samia, "The Arab-American Market," *American Demographics*, January 1994.

Freedman, Robert O., ed. *The Middle East and the Peace Process: The Impact of the Oslo Accords*. University Press of Florida, 1998.

Goodwin, Jan. *Price of Honor: Muslim Women Lift the Veil of Silence on the Islamic World*. Penguin, 1994.

Hooglund, Eric. J., ed. *Crossing the Waters, Arabic-Speaking Immigrants to the United States before 1940*. Smithsonian Institution Press, 1987.

Inside Costco, November 2001.

Kadi, Joanna, ed. *Food for Our Grandmothers. Writings by Arab-Americans & Arab-Canadian Feminists*. South End Press, 1994

Kayal, Philip M. and Joseph M. Kayal. *The Syrian-Lebanese in America: A Study in Religion and Assimilation*. Twayne, 1975.

Leaptrott, Nan. *Rules of the Game: Global Business Protocol*. International Thomson Publishing, 1996.

McCarus. E. *The Development of Arab-American Identity*. University of Michigan Press, 1994.

Naff, Alixa, *The Arab Americans*. Chelsea House Publishers, 1988.

Orfalea, Gregory. *Before the Flames: A Quest for the History of Arab Americans.* University of Texas Press, 1988.

Samhan, Helen. *Grolier's Multimedia Encyclopedia.* www.grolier.com

Samhan, Helen. "Notes on Anti-Arab Racism," *President's Initiative on Race,* February 1998.

Sawaie, Mohammed, ed. *Arabic-Speaking Immigrants in the United States and Canada: A Bibliographical Guide with Annotation.* Mazda, 1985.

Shaheen, Jack G. *Reel Bad Arabs.* Olive Branch Press, 2001.

Shakir, Evelyn. *Arab and Arab American women in the United States.* Praeger, 1997.

Suleiman, Michael W. *Arabs in America: Building a New Future.* Temple University Press, 1999.

United Nations. "Women and Empowerment: Participation and Decision Making," *Women and World Development Series,* 1995

United Nations. "The World's Women 1995: Trends and Statistics," *Social Statistics,* 1995

U.S. Census Bureau, "We the People of Arab Ancestry in the United States," 2005.

Waugh, Earle H., Baha Abu-Laban, and Regula B. Qureshi, eds. *The Muslim Community in North America.* University of Alberta Press, 1983.

Wormser, Richard. *American Islam; Growing up Muslim in America.* Walker and Company, 1994

Younis, Adele L. *The Coming of Arabic-Speaking People to the U.S.* Center For Migration Studies, 1995

Zogby, John (founder of Arab American Institute). *Arab Americans Today: A Demographic Profile of Arab Americans.* Arab American Institute, arab-aai.org, 2009.

RESOURCES

American Muslim Alliance, Newark, www.amaweb.org

Arab American Discrimination Committee, www.adc.org

Arab American Institute, 1600 K Street, NW, Suite 601, Washington, DC 20006. www.arab-aai.org, www.aaiusa.org

Association of Arab American University Graduates, www.aaug.org

──────────────────────────────CHAPTER 11

Working with Latino Americans

Latino Americans love their Spanish language and value the warmth and romance of their culture, even as they aspire to the American dream.
Jack Forbes

About 14 percent of the employees in the workplace in 2000 were Latino Americans—about one in every seven people you'll meet. Latino American communities include people from many countries. While most of their values and customs are woven from common Latino threads, each country also has its own unique design. For example, you'll find distinct cultural differences among Latino Americans from Mexico as compared to those from Puerto Rico or Cuba or other origins. And of course no one person expresses all the values and customs discussed here. This information can give you a deeper, broader understanding of Latino Americans you may meet. However, you already know the necessity of dealing with each person as a unique individual from a particular cultural background.

As you explore the topics of this course, try to begin seeing the world as a Latino American might see it—according to information gleaned here from scholars of that community. Specifically you'll learn:

- How typical stereotypes and myths about Latino Americans compare with reality.

- How the current situation is connected to certain historical events.

- Major Latino American communities, such as Mexican American and Puerto Rican American, their differences and similarities.

- Worldview beliefs, values, and customs that are important to people in these communities.

- Values and customs for conducting personal relationships.

- Some key issues that are important to many Latino Americans.

- Barriers to career success for Latino Americans and how to overcome them by meeting cultural needs.

- How to use Latino American strengths as opportunities to create win-win successes

First, get in touch with your beliefs and knowledge about Latino Americans by completing Self-Awareness Activities 11.1 and 11.2.

Latino American Man

Courtesy of Michael Matisse/Photodisc/Getty Images.

Latino American Woman

Courtesy of Thomas Barwick/Photodisc/Getty Images.

Self-Awareness Activity 11.1: What Do You Believe About Latino Americans?

Purpose:

- to get in touch with your beliefs and stereotypes about this group of people
- to experience how judgmental beliefs affect your thinking and feeling processes
- to experience the ways in which your beliefs create your reality regarding other persons, even before you have any interaction with them.

Part I. What Do You Believe about Latino American women

- Relax as deeply as you can.
- Close your eyes for a moment and take a few deep breaths.
- Now focus on the picture that symbolizes "Latino American woman"
- Imagine that you are this woman. Be Latino American woman.
- Notice any resistance to being this person—and any willingness.
- Notice words, images, thoughts, feelings that come to mind as you are "seeing and being this woman."

Step 2. Negative Associations

- Next, as you focus on the picture, allow negative opinions to come up, perhaps some that you typically hold about Latino American women.
- Notice your *thoughts* as you see the person in this negative way. What *feelings?*

Step 3. Positive Associations

- Now, still focusing, allow positive opinions to come up, perhaps some that you typically hold about Latino American women.
- Notice your *thoughts* as you see the person in this negative way. What *feelings?*

Step 4. Insights and Writeup

- Now review this experience and write about it.
- When you first saw the picture, what thoughts and feelings came up? These may reflect your deepest responses to people from this group.
- Think about the differences in your thoughts and feelings when you consciously held a positive opinion versus a negative opinion.
- Write a few sentences about your feelings, thoughts, and insights.

Part II. Experimenting with Opinions about Latino American Men

- Repeat the phases and steps in part I, this time focusing on the image of a Latino American man.

Self-Awareness Activity 11.2: What Do You Know About Latino Americans?

Purpose: To see what you know about the issues covered in this chapter.

Instructions: Determine whether you think the following statements are basically true or false— and think about why. The answers will emerge in this chapter, and the summary at the end of the chapter focuses on these issues.

1. Most Latino Americans are too emotional and excitable to be leaders in American corporations.
2. Most Latino Americans are originally from Mexico.
3. The largest Latino American population is found in New Mexico.
4. The value that's most important to Mexican Americans is achievement.
5. *Machismo* refers to being the boss.
6. *Simpatico* refers to giving sympathy to poor persons.
7. When communicating, Latino Americans tend to speak indirectly.
8. Latino American workers tend to buddy up to the boss.

STEREOTYPES AND REALITIES

Some typical stereotypes about Latino Americans are:

- They're too passive, polite, and lacking in conviction to be good leaders
- They're too emotional and excitable to fill leadership positions
- The men are macho and the women easily intimidated
- They're qualified only for menial jobs

Most of these stereotypes and stereotypes are either false or they're distorted, partial truths. They often stem from misunderstandings about the ways certain cultural values and customs affect Latino Americans' attitudes and actions. Cultural style, such as passive politeness, is often misinterpreted as leadership inadequacy, such as inability to take initiative and be firm.

Although stereotypes aren't identical to prejudice, rigid stereotypes about people usually lead to prejudice. Latino Americans must deal with these stereotypes every time they leave the family or community circle. Understanding this aspect of their life can help you move beyond stereotypes to bridge the divisive walls they hold in place. The ultimate goal is to appreciate Latino Americans' unique value to the workplace and to strengthen workplace unity.

Stereotype #1: Latino Americans Are Too Passive, Polite, and Lacking in Conviction To Be Good Leaders in the Workplace

Let's look at some realities about style versus substance.

Reality. This stereotype focuses on style, not substance.

Reality. The dozens of Latino nations throughout the world function quite effectively with Latino leaders—as do their corporations and business enterprises.

Reality. Euro-Americans and others can learn what these behaviors really mean and how they can enhance team relationships and other workplace situations. For example, the values of harmony and positive interpersonal relationships that are so important to Latinos have always been important in the workplace and are increasingly crucial to business success.

Reality. Latino Americans do learn to adapt to American corporate cultures and to be appropriately assertive in that arena. Euro-American and other leaders can help them adapt.

Stereotype #2: Latino Americans Are Too Emotional and Excitable To Be Leaders

Latino Americans generally hold views about expressing emotions that are different from Euro-Americans' views. More on this later. The resulting behavior is a difference in style, not substance, and the same realities apply here as in the passive/polite stereotype.

Stereotype #3: Latino American Men Are Macho and the Women Easily Intimidated

Although Latinos generally are viewed as passive and polite, the men are often stereotyped as being macho with their women—and with each other in bars and similar settings. They're said to have a quick smile and quick knife and love to fight. The *machismo* stereotype is that the male is strong, in control, and provides for his family, while the woman is submissive and lacking in power and influence.

Reality: This stereotype has not been fully researched, and some studies indicate that male dominance in marital decision making is not the rule among Latino American couples. Also, machismo style is changing along with changing economic realities and new job opportunities for Latino American women.

Reality: Latino cultures have their own brand of patriarchy, as do all the world's cultures. The "quick knife" stereotype is mainly a phenomenon of youth gangs, found in every culture. They're a small minority of the population and rarely affect co-worker relationships.

Reality: Latino Americans, especially the largest group, Mexican Americans, tend to be one of the most cooperative, accepting groups in the United States, and getting along is one of their highest values. This is true for both the men and the women.

Stereotype #4: Latino American Workers Are Qualified Only for Menial Jobs

Related stereotypes are: *They can't speak English well. They have only the most menial-level skills. They're not productive. They have a "mañana" attitude.*

Reality: Latino Americans are a diverse group. Many of them have been in the United States for generations and are highly educated. Some groups, such as Cuban Americans, have business qualifications comparable to Euro-Americans. Recent immigrants frequently have language, education, and skill barriers to qualifying for better jobs. But companies operating in urban areas with large Latino immigrant populations have found that providing remedial education and job training results in a pool of skilled, loyal workers.

Reality: The "man?ana" ("tomorrow") stereotype is a misunderstanding of their viewpoint of time. "Tomorrow" does not mean that they procrastinate. To the contrary, most have a strong "get it done" work ethic. Studies indicate that most identify with the American dream of getting ahead, which means they're willing to learn the skills and approaches it takes—including how to be productive and meet time requirements. Also, when Latino Americans feel they are part of an ingroup, they tend to be extremely loyal.

What's in a Name?

Latin America refers to Mexico, the countries within Central and South America, and certain Caribbean countries. *Latin Americans* are the people from those countries.

Latino Americans are U.S. residents whose cultural heritage derives from a Latin American country. Until 1970, U.S. census records counted Latino Americans as "white." As a result, demographic information about them was virtually nonexistent and was needed for civil rights purposes such as statistics affecting equal employment opportunity and affirmative action laws.

Leaders of the Chicano (Mexican American) movement won the separate designation battle in 1970 but lost the terminology battle and had to settle for *Hispanic*. The difficulty with this term is its root word *Spain*, which for Latino activists brings up painful memories of colonial conquest and domination. Most prefer the term *Latino American*.

In 2000 the Census Bureau began using the multiple designation Spanish/Hispanic/Latino. In 2003 it began to use the term *Latino*. The change to *Latino* still fails to distinguish *Latino Americans* from Latin Americans and other Latinos of the world.

CURRENT PROFILE:
WHO ARE THE LATINO AMERICANS?

The Latino American population consists of three large groups—Mexican American, Puerto Rican American, and Cuban American—as well as smaller groups from many countries. Generally, it is relatively young, fast-growing, and concentrated in a few states, mostly in cities. Educational levels and language ability vary by group. Most have lower than average income, higher poverty rates, and face job discrimination, according to U. S. Census Bureau reports.

A Diverse Population of Many Subgroups

You already know that about 12 percent of all Americans are Latino Americans. However, they are most likely to think of themselves as Mexican American or some other name that indicates their country of origin. Major Latino American groups by relative size are shown in Figure 11.1. The "other" category includes about 100,000 descendants of Spanish settlers. Many of them have ancestors who lived in the West before it became part of the U.S. Their profile is different because they were never immigrants to the U.S. The largest group in the "other" category consists of persons from the Dominican Republic; they make up 3 percent of the total Latino American population. And the largest group in the Central America category consists of persons from El Salvador, who also make up 3 percent of the total Latino American population.

FIGURE 11.1: Proportions of Latino Americans, 2004

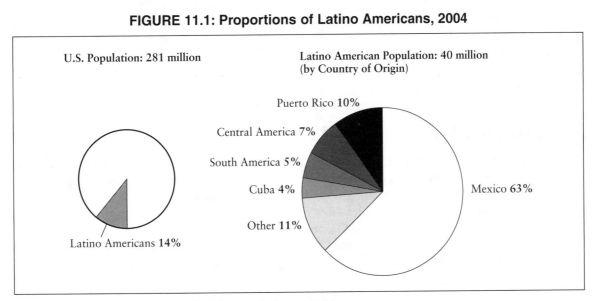

Sources: *U.S. Census Bureau, 2001, Pew Research Center, 2005.*

Employment Reflects Work Ethic

Many Latino Americans immigrate to the United States in order to escape from poverty in their native country. They are highly concentrated in such occupations as farm worker, yard men, cleaning woman, janitor, construction worker, and similar blue-collar jobs, as shown in Table 11.1. They occupy 40 percent of all U.S jobs in the low-paying farming-fishing-forestry sector, but only 5 percent of jobs in the highly-paid sciences sector. Many of them send part of their wages to families still living in their home country.

TABLE 11.1: Latino American Share of Employment in Selected U.S. Occupations

5 Occupations with Highest Share:	*Proportion Held by Latinos*
Farming, fishing, forestry	40%
Building/grounds cleaning/maintenance	30
Construction and extraction	24
Production	21
Food preparation and serving	18
5 Occupations with Lowest Share:	
Architecture, engineering	6%
Legal	6
Computer and math science	6
Healthcare practitioner, technical	6
Life, physical, social sciences	5

Source: *Pew Hispanic Center 2005*

Foreign-born Latino Americans have one of the lowest unemployment rates, as shown in Table 11.2, because many are willing to do farm and maintenance work.

TABLE 11.2: Unemployment Rates 2004

Ethnic Group	*Percent Unemployed*
Euro-Americans	5%
Foreign-born Latino Americans	6
U.S.-born Latino Americans	8
African Americans	11

Source: *Pew Hispanic Center 2005*

Fast-Growing and Young

Around 1900 there were less than 250,000 Latino Americans in the United States, fewer than the number of Swiss immigrants. By 2000, there were more than 35.3 million or 12 percent of the U.S. population, more than the entire U.S. population of 1850, which was about 22 million.

The Latino American population grew by 57 percent between 1970 and 1990, and again by 58 percent from 1990 to 2000—when the U.S. population total increased by only 13 percent, as shown in Table 11.3. This rapid growth is expected to continue because of the Latino American group's relative youth and higher birth rate.

Here are some facts from Census 2000:

- 35 percent were under age 18, compared to 26 percent of the U.S. population
- Their median age was 26, compared to 35 for the entire U.S. population.
- They produce nearly twice as many children as Euro-Americans, 3.3 compared to 1.9.
- Their numbers grew by 114 percent from 1970 to 1990, compared to 16 percent for all other Americans combined. From 1990 to 2000 they increased by 58 percent, compared to 13 percent for all others.
- While their growth *rate* is significantly less than that of Asian Americans, their increase in total population *numbers* was the largest of any group.

TABLE 11.3: Population Growth

	Population Growth	
Subgroup	**1970–1990**	**1990–2000**
Non-Latino population	16%	13%
Mexican Americans	147%	53%
Puerto Rican Americans	76%	25%
Total Latino American	114%	58%

Source: *Census 2000*

Concentrated in a Few Areas

How likely you are to work with a Latino American depends on where you live. Table 11.4 shows the regions where Latino Americans are most likely to live and the proportion of the total population in each of those regions.

TABLE 11.4: U.S. Regions with Large Latino American Populations

Region	Proportion of Latino American Population That Lives Here	Proportion of Total Population That Is Latino Americans
West	43%	25
South	33	12
Midwest	9	11
Northeast	15	2

Most Mexican Americans (55 percent) live in the West, especially in California and Texas, but nearly a third (32 percent) live in the South. Most Puerto Rican Americans (61 percent) live in New York, and most Cuban Americans (74 percent) live in the South, especially in Florida.

The tradition of most Latino immigrants has been that of rural peasant, mostly from Mexico. But by 1980, because of their migration to work in U.S. cities, most became urban dwellers. In America's 10 largest cities, an average of one in every four people is of Latino origin: about 60 percent in Miami and San Antonio, 46 percent in Los Angeles, and 27 percent in New York (U.S. Census Bureau 2000).

Wide–Ranging Educational Levels and Language Barriers

Language ability is related to educational level, which varies by subgroup. English language skills vary, depending primarily on whether a person was born and raised in a Spanish-speaking country or the United States. Most Latino Americans are foreign-born, but 88 percent of those younger than 18 were born in the United States, and virtually all of them speak English. So for language, the generation gap is huge (Pew 2005). Overall, Latino Americans are evenly divided between those who are fluent in English and those who aren't. All speak Spanish. About half still speak Spanish at home, although 75 percent also use English.

Educational levels are relatively low for the Latino American population as a whole, as follows:

- 57 percent hold high school diplomas, compared to 88 percent of Euro-Americans
- 27 percent have less than a ninth-grade education, compared to 4 percent of Euro-Americans
- 11 percent hold university degrees, compared to 28 percent of Euro-Americans

The least educated are those from Mexico, Central America, Dominica, and Puerto Rico. The best educated are Spanish Americans and South Americans, whose levels are almost as high as the national average, closely followed by Cuban Americans.

Latina American girls have been dropping out of school at a far greater rate than any other group of girls. About 26 percent are leaving high school without a diploma, compared with 13 percent of African American girls and 7 percent of Euro-American girls. The only group with a higher dropout rate is Latino American boys at 31 percent (Canedy 2005).

Job Discrimination, Lower Income, and Relative Poverty

Latino Americans are twice as likely as Euro-Americans to work as minimally skilled or skilled laborers. Conversely, Euro-Americans are twice as likely to hold managerial or professional positions. Here are some facts from the Census Bureau about Latino American workers:

- 20 percent work in service occupations, compared to 12 percent of Euro-Americans.
- 22 percent work as laborers and operators, compared to 12 percent of Euro-Americans.
- 14 percent work in managerial or professional occupations, compared to 33 percent of Euro-Americans.
- Management jobs in U.S. companies of more than 100 employees: Latino Americans hold less than one percent, though they are 12 percent of the U.S. workforce.
- Average household income in 2000 was $33,000, compared to $46,300 for Euro-Americans—a pay gap of $13,300 or 28 percent.
- 23 percent live in poverty, though they are only 12 percent of the population, while only 8 percent of Euro-Americans live in poverty.
- 75 percent of Latino American families fall in the middle to upper income category.

Causes of poverty include fewer job opportunities for the less skilled and educated—and lower wages for those who do have jobs. Single mothers have high poverty rates, and 30 percent of Latino American families are headed by single mothers, compared to 20 percent of Euro-American families. The earnings ratio of Latino Americans to Euro-Americans has been in a decline for several years, with the pay gap increasing by one-half percent per year.

LATINO CULTURES: COMMON WORLDVIEW VALUES

The most important values to most Latino Americans are the focus on family, ingroup loyalty, and getting along with family and ingroup persons. They love their culture, their language, and their tradition, so most have strong feelings about holding onto their ethnic heritage. In a 1980s survey, most Latino Americans expressed a deep desire to pass on to their children their cultural and religious traditions, especially the Spanish language and respect for elders. Passing on the tradition of commitment to the family ranked high, but not as high as passing on the language.

When we compare Latino American culture with other major world cultures, using the 11 major types of cultural difference, we see that the Latino American culture is generally perceived as follows:

1. Basic worldview: I'm controlled (sense of destiny, fatalism)
2. Relationship priorities: us-first (*familismo*)
3. Social fabric: tight ties (*simpatico, personalismo*)
4. Masculinity: moderately masculine (work ethic, differential gender roles)
5. Equality/Status: rank-status (*respeto, machismo*)
6. Risk Orientation: play it safe (reluctance to self-disclose)
7. Decision Orientation: moderately short-term
8. Time Orientation: dive-right-in; uncertain future; focus on now
9. Space: closer than arm's length; fairly high-touch (up close and personal)
10. Communication: indirect (high concern for feelings, sensitivity to criticism)
11. Economic: agricultural/dependent and industrial/independent

You'll better understand Latino personal values if you first understand their basic worldview—how they see reality. Basic to what Latino countries have in common is the influence of Spanish culture, which includes an aristocratic hierarchy based on a powerful patron who protects his subjects. They in turn serve him and owe him their loyalty. Therefore, the societies that developed in the Latino countries normally consisted of a small, privileged group of the served and a mass of underprivileged servers (Gann and Duignan 1986). Some common themes we'll explore are:

- *Worldview*: maintaining the status quo of the powerful and powerless and patriarchy, with a focus on the present moment; the future's up to God's will.
- *Relationships*: the highest values are family, ingroup loyalty, and getting along.
- *Spiritual life*: fatalism, destiny; a thin veil between physical world and spirit world.

Worldview Value #1: Closeness to the Spirit World

Latino spiritual beliefs are closely tied to the Catholic church, a belief in fate, and a unique attitude toward the relationship between life and death (Harris and Moran 1991; Gann and Duignan 1986).

The spirit world lives alongside Latino Americans, particularly Mexican Americans, in their everyday lives. They perceive less distinction between the living and the dead than do most Euro-Americans. They believe the dead are just beyond the veil of physical reality and there's nothing to fear from these spirits of relatives and friends.

They celebrate afterlife and death symbols—such as ghosts, skeletons, and skulls—in their holidays. They wear the symbols as costumes, similar to some of our Halloween costumes, and use them as themes in toys, confections, songs, and dances. Latino Americans tend to think of death as "passing on" and treat it as an old friend or special person. They frequently joke about death and include the theme in their play. This theme is related to their fatalistic sense of life and death, and draws on some aspects of a worldview that originated in their ancient Indian past.

The Mexican American relationship with death and the dead may be better understood by studying how they observe the Day of the Dead in early November as part of a three-day celebration. First, they observe Halloween, along with other Americans. The next day is known as All Saints Day, and they observe religious rites. The following day is the Day of the Dead, the most important of the three days. Rituals may include altars set up in churches, homes, and shop windows, an all-day picnic in the cemetery, a candlelit procession in costume, and an all-night vigil in the cemetery. Many Latino Americans believe that the spirits of family and friends who have passed on are present at these events and that their spirits in fact move in and out of the physical world all the time.

The Roman Catholic Church remains one of Latin America's major cultural institutions and has played a large role in shaping the various cultures of all Latin nations. Priests tend to be more involved in the family lives of Catholic churchgoers than are church leaders in other denominations. Most professing Christians in Latin America are Catholics. Their religious commitment varies widely, from indifferent to highly committed. Most are nonpracticing.

In the United States, adult Latino Americans who were asked about their religious affiliation indicated the following (ARIS 2001):

57%   Catholic
22%   Protestant
5%   other religious
12%   no religion.

Erosion of beliefs and practices increases with the second-generation Latino Americans. In recent years an increasing number are joining Protestant churches, primarily those of an evangelical, fundamentalist nature.

Worldview Value #2: A Sense of Destiny or Fatalism

Latinos are less likely than Euro-Americans to believe they're in control of their own destiny. This dependence on fate or destiny stems from ancient American Indian mysticism combined with a Latino interpretation of Roman Catholic church teachings. Many believe that outside forces govern their lives, for life follows a preordained course and human action is determined by the will of God. Those who hold this belief are therefore willing to resign themselves to the "inevitable," bow to fate, and take what comes. This is in direct contrast to the typically Euro-American belief that "God helps those who help themselves," or that people create their own reality to a great extent. Fatalism can result in an attitude that Americans often interpret as passivity, procrastination, or laziness and that they attribute to a *mañana* tendency (tomorrow's good enough for me). After all, if it's God's will, if it's written in the stars, why fight it? This belief is tied to the acceptance of unequal status we'll discuss next.

However, this belief—like other cultural values—depends on the degree of "Americanization" of the individual. The belief in fatalism is widespread in Latin America, especially among the poor. So most poor Latin American immigrants bring the belief with them. It tends to become weaker the longer they live in the United States, and is correlated with proficiency in speaking English. Pew Hispanic Center researchers (Pew 2005) phrased the fatalism value in these extreme terms: " …it doesn't do any good to plan for the future because you don't have any control over it." Sixty percent of Latino Americans who primarily speak Spanish agreed with the statement. Only 30 percent of bilinguals agreed, and 25 percent of those who primarily speak English. In comparison only 15 percent of Euro-Americans agree with the statement.

Worldview Value #3: Hierarchy and Status

A sense of hierarchy and status is a strong element in virtually all Latino countries. (Harris and Moran 1991; Hofstede 2001). People are born into an upper or lower class, and the middle class in most countries is small but growing. Traditionally the masses live in destitute poverty and the elite live with great wealth. The upper classes are more formal and elaborate than in the United States The work you do is directly related to your social class; therefore, to do manual labor, such as helping out as a house guest or pitching in to help an office worker would be undignified and inappropriate.

In recent years nearly all of the political unrest, upheaval and terrorism in Latino countries has centered around attempts to break down the hierarchy. Opposing groups try to break the hold of the rich aristocracy and multinational corporations on the wealth of the land.

Accepting One's Place

Latino Americans tend to accept their social status, even when it's extremely inferior to that of the ruling class. They tend to value the stability that comes with everyone knowing their place and staying in it, living up to societal expectations. Social climbing is frowned upon, and people who are seen as "trying to get ahead" are not admired. Such attempts, if successful, are seen as disturbing and disruptive, threatening the relative social position of many people. Climbing also appears as crass materialism and greed to many, and it shows disdain for sensitive human relationships.

Showing Respect or Respeto

People show respect for someone of superior status by their voice tone and manner. The traditional belief is that the reason people are poor or rich, have power or don't, is because of God's will. A patron is a man of power or wealth who receives loyalty from people of lesser status. He may be the boss, a politician, a landowner, or a businessman. The patron makes the decisions, and others don't question him. Where Americans attempt to minimize differences between persons due to status, age, sex, etc., Latino Americans tend to stress them.

Accepting the Powerful Superior

Those in positions of authority maintain their leadership by their ability to dole out resources to their followers and to help and protect them when they need it. The relationship is reminiscent of a parent-child relationship. The authority figures tend to set clear standards and boundaries for compliance with their policies and rules.

Patriarchal values may explain why Latino Americans tend to express less tolerance for gays and lesbians than do Euro-Americans in recent surveys. On the other hand, Latino Americans tend to be more tolerant regarding skin color. Social class is not tied to skin color in Latin American countries as it has been historically in the United States.

Power Distance

Where Euro-Americans attempt to minimize differences between persons due to status, age, or gender (sometimes called "power distance"), Latino Americans tend to stress these differences. Latino Americans tend to show greater deference and respect toward certain respected or powerful groups of people, such as the rich, the educated, the older, and toward certain professions, such as doctors, priests, teachers. They place a higher value on conformity and obedience, and they support autocratic and authoritarian attitudes from those in charge of organizations or institutions. People generally fear disagreeing with those in power. The less powerful try to meet all the expectations of the powerful.

Trusting the Government

The acceptance of social status, so traditional in Mexico and most other Latino cultures, is reflected in most Latino Americans' view of government's role. In a recent survey most Latino Americans agreed with most Euro-Americans that individuals are responsible for providing for their own needs. However, nearly twice as many Latino Americans as Euro-Americans felt the government should provide jobs, and significantly fewer Latino Americans expressed distrust of government.

Worldview Value #4: Expressing Emotions or the Passion Factor

Latino Americans highly value their emotions. The culture encourages them to fully experience their feelings and places fewer restrictions than Euro-American culture on expressing feelings—especially the ones that reflect caring and passion for life.

Several studies seem to confirm that this passionate tendency still exists in Latino Americans. For example, studies indicate that Latino Americans who respond to surveys are more likely to choose the extreme response categories (strongly agree, strongly disagree) than the middle categories, to a greater extent than Euro-Americans. Overall, the less time Latino Americans have spent in the United States, the more they prefer to make extreme choices. They see the use of the middle categories (somewhat agree) as a way of hiding a person's real feelings by presenting them in moderated terms. This indicates that Latino persons value their feelings, are encouraged to fully experience them, and have fewer restrictions about expressing them--especially the ones that reflect caring and passion for life— than Euro-Americans. The research results also imply that that the longer Latino Americans live in the United States, the more they tend to modify the way they express emotion.

Worldview Value #5: Space—Up Close and Personal

In general Latino Americans like to be physically closer to others than do Euro-Americans, and so they stand closer together when they converse. This preference is related to their close, mutually dependent relationships, and their frequent expression of warm feelings. They are a contact culture that feels comfortable when physically close to others. Therefore, when they brush close to another, moving into what Americans would consider personal body space, there would be no reason to say, "excuse me," as most Americans would. Latino Americans are also more likely to touch each other during a conversation.

Differences in personal space affect the emotional reactions of people in interactions. Latino Americans may seem too pushy as they close in on Euro-Americans, who in turn may seem cold and distant as they back away.

Worldview Value #6: Time—Who Knows What the Future Holds?

Mañana (literally, "tomorrow") doesn't refer to procrastination or laziness, but to the concept that the future is indefinite. In Latin countries it's not unusual for a business person to promise to give you a product or service by the deadline date you want even though they're unlikely to be able to meet the deadline. The main reason for agreeing is to make you happy in the moment. The backup reasoning is that the future is very uncertain, and some miracle may occur that will enable them to meet the deadline. Therefore, they know they can make you happy now, and they might be able to make you happy then.

Latino Americans typically focus more on the present moment than do Euro-Americans. Latino Americans spend less time thinking about the future and planning for it, partly because they see the future as too uncertain to do much planning. This view is related to their sense of fate. The typical Euro-American approach is to start with now and project thoughts into the future. The past is past; it doesn't need to get in the way. Latino-Americans are more concerned with tradition and more willing to continue with things as they have traditionally been. An example is the willingness of the poor masses in Latin American countries to accept their lot in life, although this view has been changing somewhat in recent years.

Meeting time deadlines and being on time for work and business appointments is generally the same for Latino Americans as for Euro-Americans. The main difference in attitudes toward promptness is in social situations, where it is typically less important for Latino Americans. The focus there is on relating to people in the moment, so the passage of time is not in immediate awareness.

The bottom line: Euro-Americans are considered to be generally future oriented because they stress planning for the future, being able to delay gratification, being on time, and making efficient use of time. Present-oriented Latino Americans put less emphasis on these traits and tend to have a more flexible attitude toward time. They feel they are on time even if they arrive 15 or 20 minutes after the appointed time. They place greater value on the quality of interpersonal relationships than on the length of time in which they take place. Highly efficient or time conscious people may be perceived as impolite or insulting. (Marin et al. 1991).

Worldview Value #7: Adopting the American Dream

Most Latino Americans buy into many aspects of the American Dream. They also express a deep desire to pass on to their children their cultural and religious traditions, especially the Spanish language and commitment to the family. First-generation Latino Americans are naturally less Americanized or acculturated than those of the second- and third-generation, for obvious reasons, but certain aspects of the Latino culture tend to be important across generations. This leads to a merging of the Latino and American cultures.

The Acculturation Process

Immigrants go through a stage of crisis or conflict due to culture shock, followed by finding a way to adapt to American culture, such as:

1. *assimilating* completely the American culture
2. *integrating* the American and Latino cultures

3. *rejecting* American cultural patterns

The ability to speak English has become a reliable shorthand measure for evaluating how successfully a Latino American has acculturated, such as:

- *assimilating* English, speaking it almost exclusively
- *integrating* the old and the new by becoming bilingual
- *rejecting* the new, continuing to speak Spanish almost exclusively

The higher the education level, the more successful the acculturation tends to be. Acculturation is important because it affects Latino Americans' mental health status, levels of social support, political and social attitudes, crime rate, and workplace skills. Integration generally works better than assimilation or rejection.

Integration: A Blend of Values

While Latino alienation, anger, and rage exist, most Latino Americans identify themselves with the United States. Only about a third of them identify themselves as Mexicans, Cubans, or Latinos first and Americans second. Most see their heritage as more European than Indian, just as Euro-Americans do. This raises the question: Are most Latinos predominantly Spanish, Indian, or a unique blend? Anthropologists seem to agree that approximately 95 percent are at least part Indian, but the Spanish cultural influence is strong. The cultural mixture of Indian and European elements that occurred in Latin American countries has further blended with the Euro-American in the United States to produce a value system within Latino American communities that is itself a blend.

The American Dream

Despite the prejudice and discrimination that have resulted in segregation and lower socioeconomic status than the mainstream, most Latino Americans believe they're better off in the United States than they would be in their country of origin. On the whole they tend to be law-abiding citizens. They love their Latino heritage but identify primarily with Euro-Americans and value the American Dream. Most parents work hard to send their children to school. They want them to learn a profession and become solid citizens.

LATINO AMERICAN WAYS: PERSONAL RELATIONSHIPS

Latino Americans place the highest priority on relationships, family, getting along, relating in a personal way, and protecting their honor, while machismo is still a factor in male-female relationships and among male peers. Communication patterns are often indirect and always sensitive to others' feelings.

Relationship Value #1—Familismo

The Latino culture is collective, so relationships are the most important value, and family obligations rate higher than individual aspirations. Family and group closeness is their most important priority. Family comes first, and extended family next. There's a much stronger sense of mutual dependence and undying loyalty than among most Euro-Americans, including greater respect for older members. And extended families are more common. (Triandis 1984a; Triandis 1982; Cohen 1979; Grebler 1970; Mannino 1976; Valle 1980).

Familismo includes three types of value orientations: (1) feeling obligated to provide material and emotional support to extended family members, (2) relying on relatives for help and support, and (3) constantly checking with relatives about the way they see various behaviors and attitudes and being influenced by their perceptions and feelings.

Family First

The family is the center of personal existence, more so than for most U.S. families. Latino Americans' identities are closely tied to that of their family and its members. The tight bonds of love and loyalty may exclude outsiders to a greater degree. The family may include many more members than most Euro-American families: Grandparents and great-grandparents stay close and aunts, uncles, and cousins may be almost as close; even some close friends may be included. Family business is considered private, and to discuss it with outsiders would be a betrayal. Families are inward-focused and members rely on these relationships for their emotional security. Within the family, members tend to be quite open, honest, and communicative. Parents exercise strong authority.

Mutual Dependence

Latino Americans typically have high levels of mutual personal dependence that includes these factors:

- relying on relatives for help and support
- feeling obligated to provide material and emotional support to relatives
- being highly sensitive to family relationships
- constantly checking with relatives about the way they see various behaviors and attitudes
- being influenced by relatives' perceptions and feelings.
- feeling what family members feel—mutual empathy
- conforming to relatives' beliefs and wishes
- sacrificing for the welfare of the family or ingroup members
- trusting the members of the ingroup.
- expecting that members will ask each other for assistance and that they'll give it when asked.

This value helps to protect each person against physical and emotional stress by providing natural support systems. As a result, Latino Americans place highest value on building interpersonal relationships in ingroups that are nurturing, loving, intimate, and respectful. While Euro-Americans value such relationships, they also value more confrontational and segmented relationships as an aid to independent growth (Hofstede 2001; Marin and Marin 1991).

Undying Loyalty

Latino Americans have incredibly strong ties and loyalties to family and friends. If an employee is asked to transfer to another location, many people in an extended family may be involved in the decision. If an employee loses his job or is transferred, the whole family may quit. If one is mistreated on the job, fellow employees who are also relatives will react as if they were personally being mistreated. As a result, disputes can have a more complex quality than Euro-Americans are accustomed to. The net effect may be for Latino Americans to hold back their true thoughts and feelings until they can stand it no longer. Then they may strike out in ways they later regret. Therefore, they may go to great lengths to avoid disputes or use a third party to intercede or to mediate a dispute.

Relationship Value #2—Simpatico: Getting Along

Getting along with others is extremely important to Latino Americans. They tend to acquiesce to the wishes of others and to agree with them in order to maintain *simpatico*, a Latin form of harmonious relationship. Most try to do what's expected by the culture and to be courteous. A potential problem for people from other cultures is figuring out what Latino Americans are *really* thinking and feeling before resentment builds to the breaking point and the relationship is severed.

Acquiescence

Getting along with the wishes of others, regardless of your own opinions and feelings, is important. It may include providing the answer you think another person wants to hear, whether you think it's factual or not. This is a rather extreme type of response frequently used by Latino Americans, especially by less-educated immigrants, men and women alike. They're more likely to acquiesce than the better educated, more acculturated ones (Landsberger and Saavedra 1967).

The willingness to conform to others' expectations is highly valued in Latino cultures, but so is the willingness to rebel at those rare times when too much has been too much for too long. Latino Americans conform because they want to please and support important others and because they want others to think well of them and accept them. In a high context culture a frequent concern is, "What will they say?"

Simpatico

The Latino cultural value of simpatico encourages acquiescence that promotes smooth, pleasant social relations. Simpatico(a) persons are

- pleasant, nice, likeable, congenial
- polite and respectful
- don't express criticism, confrontation, or assertiveness
- show a certain level of conformity and empathy for the feelings of other people
- try to behave with dignity and respect toward others
- value working toward harmony in interpersonal relations

Latino Americans therefore are more likely to give socially desirable responses, avoid face-to-face confrontations at all costs, and view assertiveness quite differently than Euro-Americans do. Small talk before and after discussing business is extremely important for building empathic relationships.

Latino Americans tend to report that they carry out socially desirable actions and avoid reporting less desirable attitudes and behaviors. They tend to provide the "correct" answer as they perceive it, independent of their actual experiences. Mexicans residing in Mexico are more likely to express socially desirable responses than are Mexican Americans. Also more likely to acquiesce are those in lower socioeconomic levels, indicating that acculturation may modify this tendency (Ross 1984; Triandis et al 1984b).

Courtesy

Latino Americans place great importance upon courtesy and therefore offer more profuse thanks, praise, and apologies than Euro-Americans are accustomed to. Elaborate courtesies are common and constant among the upper and middle classes. Lower class people may reserve such treatment for special occasions and for "superiors" and strangers.

Relationship Value #3—Personalismo: Relating in a Personal Way

To relate well to people from a Latino culture usually means relating everything to them on a personal level. Instead of talking in generalities, you would talk in terms of

- how situations relate to them personally
- their families
- their town
- most of all, their personal pride.

Especially for the male, the more the communication is personalized, the more successful it's likely to be. In fact, Latino Americans usually trust only those with whom they have a personal relationship, for only those persons can appreciate their soul. You may have to establish a personal relationship with any Latino American you want to do business with.

When doing business in Latino countries, Euro-Americans find they must spend more time building rapport than usual before they can move to discussing the business at hand. This tendency has some carryover, of course, to Latino Americans who immigrated to the United States Latino Americans tend to avoid at all costs having face-to-face confrontations or unpleasantness with business associates, coworkers or friends. (Cox 1993; Zurcher 1965).

Relationship Value #4—Reluctance to Self-Disclose

The value of *personalismo* does not mean that Latino Americans will say what they're really thinking and feeling to people outside their ingroup. The value of *simpatico* and power distance means they're less likely than Euro-Americans to self-disclose. When people reveal personal information, they become vulnerable to how the listener will use that information, and their *amor proprio*, or personal honor, could be damaged. Males are even less likely to self-disclose than females, especially with someone they're likely to interact with in the future, or in culturally unfamiliar situations. When Latino American males do self-disclose, it's usually with Latino American females, who pose the least threat of responding with scorn, rejection, or other blows to self-respect (LeVine 1981; Franco 1984; Constantino 1988).

Relationship Value #5—Machismo and Gender Roles

Most agree that gender roles are more strictly defined in Latin cultures than in the United States Men's higher status is more noticeable, they're more dominant, they're allowed more sexual freedom, and there are greater differences in men's and women's socially acceptable activities, attributes, roles, and occupations. The degree and importance of these values varies from one Latino culture to another. Also, women's inequality exists to some degree and in some form in virtually all the cultures of the world. It just happens that in Latino cultures, the inequality has a name—machismo—and people in those cultures are very aware of what it's all about.

Machismo

The machismo pattern of behavior represents male power and an attitude toward the world, especially toward women. While Latino men generally have a poetic, romantic side, the machismo aspect is aggressive and sometimes insensitive. This image consists of virility, courage, competitiveness, a readiness to fight, and a determination to conquer. Men are expected to be assertive, to be leaders, to be in control, and to earn the respect of other men by their masculinity. Machismo is basically about men impressing each other. In business this means that a man should be forceful, confident, unafraid, and take the lead among groups consisting of women and men of lower status. However, he should do this with a certain flair for personalismo and simpatico that reflects his higher socioeconomic status.

The *machismo* stereotype is that the male is strong, in control, and provides for his family, while the woman is submissive and lacking in power and influence. In Latino countries, both boys and girls are socialized to admire this image, and Latino husbands virtually always "wear the pants" in interactions with the outside world. It follows that men are less likely to participate in household and child care responsibilities than in Euro-American households. However, if the wife is a strong Latino woman, she may actually control the home, children, and husband. And Latino American women tend to be stronger than their counterparts in Latino countries.

The dark, extreme side of machismo involves wife-beating, excessive gambling, fighting, heavy drinking, and a tendency to have children with other women. Some form of spousal abuse and sexual promiscuousness is found in virtually every culture, but in Latino cultures, especially the Mexican culture, it is given a specific label, *machismo*. Some sociologists think the underlying roots of machismo lie in male-male relationships: how men "traffic in honor and how men negotiate status with one another, how men hammer out the measurements of their standing as a man" (Lancaster 1993). Tannen's work regarding the male focus on status seems to support this idea.

Domestic Abuse

A 1995 study concluded that domestic violence occurs in at least 30 percent of Mexican families as well as Mexican American immigrant families (WSJ 1999). In most Mexican states, domestic violence is not grounds for divorce, and there is no legal way for a wife to gain protection from an abusive husband. The divorce rate in Mexico is one-tenth the U.S. rate, and among recent Mexican immigrants the rate is scarcely higher than in Mexico. A strong Latino belief is that even physical and mental abuse should be borne in order to keep the family together. Family and friends reinforce pressure from the culture for the wife to stay in an abusive marriage. Many parents say, "Don't divorce. We would be ashamed to have you in this family if you did." Mexican women say that husbands are forever, no matter how badly behaved. Many mothers tell their daughters, "Your husband is your cross to bear for the rest of your life."

Women's Lot

Women are restricted by traditional views about their sexuality, assertiveness, and work roles. "Madonna or whore, no in-between, that's how we're seen" say liberated Latino women. The Madonna, or good woman, marries as a virgin and martyrs herself to her family. She accepts men as the dominant ones and experiences her lot as saintly suffering. Women are therefore expected to be reserved and modest with men outside the family. Assertive women are generally disliked.

Latino Americans are more likely than Euro-Americans to believe that mothers should not have outside jobs. In an extensive survey of Latino Americans, a little more than half said they didn't think married women with children should have the opportunity to pursue their own careers, even if they were able to look after their home and family while doing so. On the other hand, women who do work nearly always have a greater say in family decisions than those who don't. In Mexico and some other Latin American countries, a major shift seems to have begun in the late 1990s, a movement toward greater acceptance of women as administrators, managers, and business owners. This movement is reminiscent of women's progress in the United States in the 1970s.

Relationship Value #6—Communication Patterns

Latino Americans often speak indirectly out of concern for others' feelings and consideration for others' sensitivity to criticism. They may use speech to impress, follow some unique nonverbal patterns, and have clear expectations about how to say hello and good-bye.

Speaking Indirectly

Latino Americans are frequently indirect in their communication with strangers and outsiders. It may appear evasive, but it's intended to be courteous. It may be difficult to determine exactly what they are thinking and feeling. They may use a go-between in order to communicate unpleasant messages or to make requests.

High Concern for Feelings

Latino Americans may tell you what you want to hear, regardless of the "truth," out of great concern for your feelings. This reflects their belief that their own opinion doesn't matter as much as respecting your feelings and giving you the response you'd like to have. This conflicts with the American value of "telling it like it is."

High Sensitivity to Criticism

How Latino Americans take criticism is closely tied to the relative status of the people involved. Usually if criticism comes from a higher-status person, it's accepted sheepishly; if it comes from an equal it may be treated with humor; and if it comes from a lower-status person, it may not be tolerated since this would signal weakness and invite more criticism and even derision.

Saying Hello and Good-bye

If several people are in a group when you arrive, you're expected to go around and greet everyone, shaking hands, or if you know them well enough, embracing them. The "Hi, everyone" greeting would be considered rude. Likewise, upon leaving, you're expected to say good-bye to each person individually.

LATINO AMERICAN ISSUES

Many issues are important to Latino Americans, but four issues that will help you better understand your coworkers are: 1) how to overcome segregation and discrimination, 2) how to improve their knowledge and skills, 3) how to improve their workplace status, and 4) how to overcome recent immigration backlash. The causes of these socioeconomic disparities are related to their younger average age, inadequate schooling, larger families, the large percentage of immigrants, and the related language barrier. Although Latino American citizens have made impressive progress since the 1950s in educational attainment and occupational mobility, many Mexican Americans remain at a persistent, substantial disadvantage. These issues are discussed in books by such researchers as Clete Daniel, Gregory De Freitas, and Carey McWilliams and in U.S. Government reports.

Issue #1. Overcoming Segregation and Discrimination

The long history of discrimination against Latino Americans, together with the antagonism toward Latino cultures, especially the Mexican and Puerto Rican cultures, expressed by many Euro-Americans, has served to heighten their alienation from the dominant culture. While this discrimination has never been as formally overt as that against African Americans and American Indians, informal discrimination has yielded similar results. Three separate government studies conducted in 1942 found that Latino Americans were probably the most ignored and destitute U.S. group—economically, intellectually and socially.

Occupational Segregation

The huge differences in wage levels and worker expectations between the United States and most Latino countries, especially neighboring Mexico, has always motivated workers to migrate to the United States Discrimination against Mexican Americans has never been as formally overt as that against African Americans and American Indians. Informal discrimination, however, has often yielded very similar results.

The typical practice in the Southwest has been for an employer to hire Mexican Americans by the group—as work gangs, crews, or families—doing those menial jobs which are heavily manual, dirty, seasonal, and dead-end (McWilliams 1975). Where unions existed, they usually excluded them or established work rules that barred them from opportunities to compete with Euro-Americans. The better paying craft unions, in particular, were closed to Mexican American workers. These patterns became self-reinforcing over time. Because Mexican Americans were hired in large numbers for the worst jobs, they became stereotyped as being only good for those types of jobs.

During World War II, President Roosevelt's executive order regarding fair employment practices was mainly in response to African American demands,. However, Clete Daniel (1991) says that Latino Americans were actually facing the greatest potential for mistreatment on each of the four bases proscribed by the executive order—religion, color, national origin, and race. The three million Mexican Americans living in the United States during the 1940s were virtually all of Catholics, with Indian/Spanish skin coloring, and a Mexican national origin that had been disparaged by Euro-Americans for many years. To confuse the issue, the government couldn't decide whether Latino Americans were fellow "whites" or a race apart. Three separate government studies conducted in 1942 found that Mexican Americans were probably the "most submerged and destitute group in the United States—economically, intellectually and socially" (U.S. Government 1942).

Today Mexican Americans and Puerto Rican Americans remain disproportionately concentrated in blue-collar occupations and in such industries as manufacturing, mining, and agriculture, where employment opportunities are declining. Overt discrimination has decreased, but traditional business practices often result in discrimination that blocks upward mobility.

Residential Segregation

Occupational patterns determine residential patterns. For example, prior to 1950 most jobs available to Mexican Americans were in isolated rural areas of the Southwest. Latino Americans who resided in urban areas could only afford to live in camps or the worst parts of town. Occupational barriers meant they could hardly hope to ever afford much better. As a practical reality, therefore, most were segregated in barrios and barrio schools, just as African Americans were segregated in ghettos and ghetto schools. Since 1950 the Latino American population has rapidly urbanized, but segregation is still common.

The Unnoticed Minority

In 1940 about 90 percent of Mexican Americans lived in five Southwestern states, one of the most intense concentrations of any American subgroup—a pattern that continues in modified form to this day. People in the other forty-three states rarely encountered Mexican Americans and were hardly aware of their existence. Even in the Southwest, they were isolated from the mainstream of American life (Daniel 1991).

Difficulty in gaining access to adequate labor market statistics has been another barrier for Chicano advocates trying to get national attention and political action. To document the degree and nature of discrimination, they must be able to adequately assess both the present patterns and the trends over time. To make such assessments, they must have reliable statistics. Only since 1950 have relatively reliable census statistics been available for Latino Americans. Not until 1970 did the U.S. Department of Labor begin publishing statistics on its manpower programs with a Hispanic category.

Welfare benefits are rarely available to needy Mexican Americans because most of those who need it are either illegal immigrants or noncitizens (Aponte 1991). Recent immigrants tend to earn the lowest incomes and have the most barriers to upward mobility. Most are either speak virtually no English or don't speak it fluently. They tend to be from rural areas and have difficulty adapting to urban life. They rarely have the job skills needed to gain stable employment and make adequate wages. And many lack a high school diploma. Because of male underemployment and unemployment, an increasing percentage of immigrant mothers now work (Santiago and Wilder 1991).

Lack of Political Clout

Latino Americans have traditionally been wary of the U.S. government and have stayed quiet or underground, without political voice. Only 7 percent of registered Latino Americans voted in the 1996 general election (Paulette 2000). But 47 percent voted in the 2004 general election. In comparison, 67 percents of all Americans voted (U.S. Census Bureau 2005).

Inadequate education is a hurdle to exercising power in the American political system, the main arena for bringing about needed change. Despite their solidarity and pride of heritage, full participation is impossible as long as many of them lack adequate education, English literacy, citizenship papers, or clear legal status.

On the other hand, Latino Americans are now the largest ethnic group in Los Angeles, 47 percent. Relatively few were in the habit of voting when an anti-immigrant California proposition was passed. Such political passivity is changing, and voter turnout in 1998 was 52 percent for California Latino Americans, compared to 27 percent for Texas Latino Americans (Chronicle 1999). The community began speaking of electing a Latino American as mayor of Los Angeles, and in 2005 they elected Mexican American Antonio Villaraigosa.

After the 2000 elections, Latino Americans numbered 21 in the U.S. House of Representatives, about 5 percent, and none in the Senate. The unnoticed minority is gaining some visibility and political power.

Issue #2. Improving Knowledge and Skills

The language barrier and lower educational achievement of some Latino American workers accounts for a larger share of their earnings differential than is true for other groups. Continuing high dropout rates and low college enrollments indicate that Latino Americans will be the group most damaged by the shift to a better educated, highly skilled workforce (DeFreitas 1991).

Surveys of Latino Americans show they are deeply concerned about the U.S. public education system, with only 40 percent having a positive view of it. They say that drugs and violence are the biggest problems. As a solution, 64 percent support increased funding over a school voucher program, which only 32 percent support. Where bilingual education programs are offered, 74 percent believe they should focus on learning English, not on making sure they don't fall behind in other subjects. (Latino 2002).

When asked about barriers, they responded as follows:

- 30% cite language barriers and difficulties
- 20% cite lack of education—including deficient educational preparation in home country, poor achievement levels in segregated U.S. schools, and biased treatment in integrated U.S. schools
- 14% cite discrimination

Mentioned less often were recent immigration, poverty-level family incomes, higher unemployment in the family, early marriage, and early pregnancy

Latino Americans place a high value on education, even though they have the lowest educational level of any U.S. group. Studies indicate that Latino American high school students report significantly higher aspirations to get a college degree than Euro-American students whose families are at the same socioeconomic level. In both groups, the higher the socioeconomic level, the higher the educational aspirations tend to be. About the same percentage of Latino American and Euro-American parents want their children to attend college, again controlling for socioeconomic status (Solorzano 1991).

Issue #3. Improving Workplace Status

When we compare the workplace issues of Latino Americans to those of Euro-Americans, several major factors stand out: higher unemployment, lower economic status, problems of new immigrants, educational discrimination, the need for job skills, and employment discrimination.

Employment Barriers: Mexican Americans

Mexican Americans have made impressive progress since the 1950s in educational attainment and occupational mobility. However, many remain at a persistent, substantial disadvantage. Recent immigrants tend to earn the lowest incomes and have the most barriers to upward mobility. Most are either don't speak English well or speak almost no English. They tend to be from rural areas and have difficulty adapting to urban life. They rarely have the job skills needed to gain stable employment and make adequate wages. And many lack a high school diploma. Welfare benefits are rarely available to needy Mexican Americans because most of those who need it are either illegal immigrants or noncitizens. Due to male underemployment and unemployment, an increasing percentage of mothers now work.

Mexican Labor in United States and in Maquiladores

Today a sizable portion of the labor supply in the Southwest is Mexican American. In some areas, such as south Texas and southern California, Mexican Americans are a rapidly growing proportion of the labor force, and in some areas they are the largest segment. The huge disparities in wage levels and worker expectations between the United States and Mexico motivate Mexican workers to migrate to the United States

Such disparities also motivate U.S. manufacturers to build plants called *maquiladores* in special industrial zones in northern Mexico near the U.S. border. In return, U.S. firms agree to not compete with Mexican manufacturers by not selling these products in Mexico. The U.S. government cooperated initially by reducing tariffs on these products when they were brought into the United States. Now, through NAFTA (North America Fair Trade Agreement), it has eliminated import duties. Problems include lower wages, more dangerous work environment, and greater pollution than U.S. laws allow.

Language Barrier

Here are some examples of the language problem in the workplace (Latino 2002):

- A San Rafael, California, nursing home fired Latino immigrants for speaking Spanish at work. One employee was reprimanded for telling a housekeeper in Spanish to clean a room. Another was threatened with dismissal for using Spanish with a Spanish-speaking patient. In 1995 workers filed a discrimination complaint with the EEOC.

- At a Contra Costa, California, nursing home workers were fined $1 each time they spoke a language other than English.
- Dishwashers at a Santa Cruz, California, nursing home were ordered not to sing or whistle in Spanish.

On the other hand, some employers, such as Trimble Navigation in Sunnyvale, California, offer their workers free English language classes on company time. This employer focuses on team building as well. Production went up, and suspicions and rivalries among different ethnic groups went down. Ethnic "clustering" during breaks decreased. Latino employees had more opportunities to use English on the job every day, building language skill. A Trimble strategy is to increase the number of entry-level jobs filled by Latino immigrants with poor English skills but a strong work ethic. They believe it's easier to teach language skills than the work ethic.

The "English-Only Movement" is part of a backlash to increased immigration, as well as to the numbers of Latino Americans who do not speak English. Case law based on "The Spun Steak Case" established that under federal law, employers may demand that their employees speak only English, but this policy must be necessary for conducting business. This case also established that the EEOC rules assert that employers may not prohibit employees from speaking their native language in informal situations (Duncan 2000).

Systemic Employment Discrimination

Workplace discrimination persists because, even if employers do not themselves hold discriminatory attitudes, the practice of using stereotyped beliefs that minorities have lower-than-average productivity will result in employers ranking individual minority group members lower than other job applicants. Inside the company, employer discrimination usually involves the confinement of minorities to less skilled, more unstable job titles and slower promotional tracks, rather than differential treatment of minorities and Euro-Americans in the same jobs.

Health Care Concerns

Surveys indicate that 30 percent of Latino Americans have no health insurance, an issue that deeply disturbs them. A major cause is that jobs for many Latino Americans—farm worker, gardener, cleaning or maintenance person—are temporary or part-time and therefore offer no health care benefits. Because of the high cost of U.S. medical care, many Latino Americans must rely on Medicaid or charity programs. Many others fall between the cracks because they earn too much to qualify for such programs, yet can't afford adequate health care or insurance (Latino 2002).

Issue #4. Overcoming Immigration Backlash

Surveys of Latino Americans show they are deeply concerned about the U.S. immigration system, intensified by tightened policies and enforcement since September 11, 2001 (Latino 2002)

Nearly a third of Latino Americans are first-generation immigrants with limited English proficiency that significantly hinders their socioeconomic progress. Controversy rages over the cost to taxpayers of providing social services to these immigrants. People also worry about overpopulation straining the country's resources and illegal immigrants, who use many social services but don't pay into the income tax and property tax accounts that fund such services.

On the other hand, studies indicate that the long-run economic benefits these immigrants generate for the average U.S. taxpayer outweigh any short-run costs. "Immigration backlash" eases whenever the economy improves, but it remains a sensitive issue for many Latino Americans. More on this topic in the Mexican American segment.

MEXICAN AMERICANS

Mexican Americans are the largest of the Latino American groups, 58 percent, or nearly 21 million people. They are the largest minority group in the Southwest, where their influence on culture and society is quite visible. Today most Mexican Americans have immigrant roots; they or their parents or grandparents came from Mexico to *El Norte* in search of a better life. Los Angeles has more people of Mexican origin than any city in the world except Mexico City and Guadalajara (Chronicle 1999). Statistics used in the following discussion of Mexican Americans and other Latino Americans are based upon U.S. Census publications.

Background

After the Mexican-American War in the 1840s, the border between the two countries was moved, and many residents of northern Mexico were suddenly told they were living in the Southwest United States, foreigners in their own land (Weber 2004). They were caught in the path of the "manifest destiny" to expand U.S. territory to the Pacific Ocean. During the first decade of the 20th century, many Mexican farmers lost their land, leading to a civil war in Mexico that devastated the economy and triggered a migration of peasants to the United States. The Mexican population grew from about 175,000 to more than a million between 1900 and 1930. These immigrants were generally segregated and exploited as cheap labor by the Euro-Americans. During the Great Depression, Mexicans became the target of deportation programs designed to rid the country of illegal aliens. The purpose was to reduce the labor pool and preserve the few remaining jobs for legal citizens.

Current Profile

Mexican Americans are the fastest growing segment of the population, increasing by 147 percent between 1970 and 1990, compared with a 114 percent growth for all Latino Americans and 16 percent for non-Latinos. They increased by 53 percent from 1990 to 2000, about the same as other Latino American groups (Census 2000).

They have the lowest educational level: Only 44 percent hold high school diplomas and 6 percent hold degrees. About 25 percent of Mexican Americans and Puerto Rican Americans live below the poverty line, significantly more than other Latino American groups.

Compared to other Latino American groups, they have the largest proportion of native-born citizens (67 percent) except for the Spaniards (83 percent). About 7 percent are foreign born who became citizens, and 26 percent are foreign-born residents who are not citizens. About half speak English fluently. The longer they or their families have lived in the United States, the more acculturated they are, and the more likely they are to speak English fluently.

Cultural Themes

Mexican Americans have a strong cultural heritage. It's extremely important to them. They love their Spanish language and value the warmth and romance typical of their culture. But is it predominantly Spanish, Indian, or a unique blend? Anthropologists estimate that about 75 percent of Mexicans are mestizos, meaning of mixed European and American Indian descent. They have perhaps the strongest sense of national identity of all Latinos, although they occupy various levels of prosperity and social standing. The small percentage of citizens of purely European ancestry—about 10 percent of the population—were previously sometimes referred to as the Thousand Families. They controlled the country's political power and economic wealth, just as the Spanish did 300 years earlier. Here are estimates of the proportion of the three major ethnic groups in Mexico:

Mestizo (mixed European and American Indian)	75%
European ancestry	10%
American Indian ancestry	15%

Mexican Americans have nourished and sustained Mexican cultural characteristics to a greater extent than other American ethnic groups, keeping alive their language, identity, and values. This stems partially from the fact that the Southwest was the home of some before it was part of the United States. Another factor is the common border, over a thousand miles long, with continual flows of people back and forth. The most noticeable ethnic feature of Mexican Americans is the pervasive retention of the Spanish language.

Key Value Themes

One study found that the cultural values of Mexican Americans have been strongly influenced by a folk or rural culture in which organized and continuous striving for future monetary gains plays little part (Bullock 1971). This folk pattern of living, especially among the poor, promotes a mixture of individualism and family unity that leaves little room for an interest in the broader community. The welfare of the family is a key focus, along with the duty of older children to help support the family, even if it means dropping out of school. Mexican Americans generally focus less on involvement in the schools and other societal institutions than do Euro-Americans. Class has been a binding influence for the masses: "We're all the same—poor."

Mexican Americans' cultural values and patterns are virtually the same as the Latino American values discussed earlier. Special importance may be given the following values (Ramirez 1972).

- *Relationships* between individuals are more important than competitive, materialistic, or achievement goals. Latino Americans in the Southwest have a high context, highly involved culture, where people constantly monitor members' emotional states.

- *Family* ties are especially strong.

- *Machismo* and a patriarchal family and social structure are strong but they're changing along with changing economic demands and women's new job roles.

- *Ethnic loyalty*, a sense of solidarity and pride in their unique heritage, is strong.

Changing Male–Female Dynamics

Male dominance of the family traditionally emphasized physical occupations as opposed to intellectual endeavors. Women were discouraged from competing in male-dominated occupations. However, beginning in the 1970s some women began organizing and supporting one another in breaking out of some of these traditional limitations. And Mexican American wives are often able to find jobs more readily than the men, sometimes at higher pay. By the end of the 1990s, these efforts were paying off in the upward mobility of women in the business world.

Religion

Religion in Mexico is a unique blend of Catholicism and ancient beliefs handed down by the Mayans and Aztecs. God is deeply personal, caring for each person through specific saints. Home altars are decorated with *santitos*, images of saints dear to the family. Mexican Catholics believe that the Virgin Mary, Virgen de Guadalupe, has a particular concern for Mexicans and protects them.

Valuing the American Dream

Mexican Americans as a group tend to be law-abiding citizens who love their Latino heritage but identify primarily with Euro-Americans and value the American Dream. Despite the prejudice and discrimination that have resulted in segregation and lower socioeconomic status than the mainstream, most believe they're better off in the United States than they would be in Mexico.

The Chicano Movement

In the 1960s and 1970s Chicano activists confronted discrimination and its effects. The movement sparked a new interest in the Latino American culture, but it did not succeed in its original objective of converting the Mexican American masses. The early Chicano intellectuals had underestimated their own people's belief in the American system, identification with Euro-American values, and their conservatism. The average Latino American voter simply did not view U.S. society as one of the most repressive, intolerant, and prejudiced in the world.

Nor did most Mexican Americans identify themselves with the American Indian, and they had never done so in the past. The cultural mixture of Indian and European elements that occurred in Mexico also blended with the Euro-American in the United States to produce a value system within the Mexican American community that is itself a blend. The rejection of Euro-American values by the Chicanos, therefore, is seen by some Mexican Americans as a rejection of one element of their own culture (Gann and Duignan 2000).

Above all, Chicano activists didn't seem to understand the strength of the social conservatism that inspires the mass of ordinary people in the barrios. Most parents who work hard to send their children to college have no desire to see them become rebels. They want them to learn a profession and become solid citizens. In fact, just after the height of the movement, a 1983 *Los Angeles Times* poll showed that only a small percentage of Mexican Americans choose to identify themselves as Chicanos. While Latino alienation, anger, and rage exist, overall the Mexican Americans identify themselves with the United States. Only about a third of them identify themselves as Mexicans or Latinos first and Americans second. The poll showed that only about half of California Latino Americans were even aware of the Chicano movement, about the same rate of awareness as other citizens.

Immigrant Issues

What to do about Mexican immigrants to the United States—legal, illegal, temporary, or permanent—is an important issue for Latinos from Mexico particularly, and to a lesser extent to Latinos from Central America. Equally important is the issue of access to a good education for children of Mexican immigrants—both legal and illegal. We will review some major problems and recommended strategies for addressing them.

Immigrant Issue #1. Legal Guestworker Program

In 2005, 121,000 temporary H-2 guestworkers entered the United States from Mexico to work in agriculture (32,000) and in landscaping, construction, and similar industries (89,000). A recent report on the program concludes that these workers are frequently abused by employers (Bauer 2007). Some workers are forced to live in squalid conditions and denied medical benefits for injuries. Employers decide which workers may enter the United States, whether a worker can stay, where they will live and how they travel. Such workers are unable to change jobs if they are cheated or abused by their employer. If they complain, they may face deportation, blacklisting, and other retaliation.

"The mistreatment of temporary foreign workers in American today is one of the major civil rights issues of our time," according to Richard Cohen, President of Southern Poverty Law Center (Bauer 2007). He stated that Congress should eliminate the current H-2 system entirely or commit to making it a fair program with strong worker protections that are vigorously enforced.

Immigrant Issue #2. Illegal Mexican Immigrants

In 2006, 20 years after the last major reworking of U.S. immigration policy (the 1986 Immigration Reform and Contract Act), Congress began debating a new major immigration bill. Immigration talk began proliferating on the radio and television talk shows. Talk became animated—about "12 million undocumented immigrants, illegal-alien invasion, Mexican reconquest, and broken borders open to illegal Mexicans as well as Al Queda terrorists." By the end of May 2006 millions of people had taken to the streets of major U.S. cities, saying "enough" to immigrant bashing. Even illegal workers were standing up for the right to stay in the United States. The bill that eventually became law failed to systematically address immigration reform. It does not address the fate of undocumented workers already in the United States or the need for more visas and possibly a new guest worker program. Instead it called for the first 700 miles of a border fence, without allocating money for it (Surarez-Orozco 2008).

Proposed Immigrant Strategy: Try the European Approach as a Model

Undocumented workers flooding into the U.S. from Mexico became an increasingly troublesome political issue after the passage of North American Free Trade Agreement (NAFTA). In contrast, the

European Union (EU) has followed a dramatically different approach to working with local trade partners that are significantly less-developed, such as Spain, Portugal, Greece, and Ireland. They are currently working with 12 Eastern European countries, such as Poland and Romania. Douglas Massey, Professor of Sociology & Public Affairs at Princeton University and President of American Academy of Political and Social Science, suggests that the United States might do well to follow the EU model—building alliances rather than walls.

Contrast: Strategies of EU-Spain and US-Mexico

Using Spain as an example, the EU transferred $20 billion in structural adjustment subsidies to Spain in the decade leading up to Spain's joining the European Community (1976 to 1986). In contrast, the United States refused to discuss such subsidies with Mexico and instead embarked on a unilateral militarization of the Mexico-U.S. border, spending an additional $32 billion to block the inflow of migrant workers. Massey (2008) makes the point that if the U.S. devoted most of these billions to helping Mexico develop needed economic and social reforms, the flow of undocumented workers would likely slow to an insignificant trickle.

EU Goal: Full Economic Integration

In helping Spain to develop economically, before it became a member in 1995, the EU adopted full economic integration as the preferred goal. The equivalent of about 52 billion U.S. dollars was made available to modernize Spanish institutions and infrastructure so they would harmonize with conditions in the north. As a result Spanish out-migration of workers to the rest of Europe stopped. In contrast U.S. authorities negotiated NAFTA terms that were exploitative of Mexico and protective of U.S. corporations. As a result migration of workers from Mexico to the U.S., both documented and undocumented, has increased. And the north-south income gap grew in both relative and absolute terms from $17,700 in 1985 to $24,100 in 2004.

The EU had two central aims in working with Spain (Farrell 2001).

1. To integrate Spain's markets with those of northern Europe by specifying institutional, financial, and local changes that Spain would have to make.

2. To harmonize Spanish social systems with those in the north by requiring specific reforms in the administration of education, social welfare, criminal justice, and employment. The goal was not to make them identical to those in the northern nations but to move them toward convergence.

In the decade between Spain's EU application in 1976 and its final accession in 1986, the country's share of GDP devoted to international trade, continued to rise slowly. Following accession, it rose at a rapid pace. From 1986 to 2004 it more than doubled. The proportion of workers employed in agriculture fell by about two-thirds, while the proportion in services increased by more than 20 percent, and the proportion in industry held fairly steady. These paradigm shifts caused some disruption: an increase in unemployment from 4 percent when the dictator Franco died in 1975 to a peak at 24 percent in 1994, but then a slow decline to 10 percent in 2004 (Anderson 2003).

EU Result: Reversal of Immigration Pattern

In the years from 1967 to 1973, the net outflow of workers from Spain to other European nations ranged between 100,000 and 150,000 per year. After EU entry, in 1986, Spain received more Spanish workers than it lost, and the inflow has continued.

People migrate in response to relative incomes. The decision also appears to be driven more by a lack of access to markets for capital than by geographic differences in expected wages. For example, many Spanish workers migrated in order to finance the acquisition of a home, a business, or land because there were not viable lending markets in Spain. Also, the absence of well-developed social insurance and pension programs spurs migration (Huntoon 1995). Spain's entry into the EU reduced the various market and insurance failures that had been driving migrants outward for decades.

U.S. Approach: Build Walls Not Bridges

U.S. authorities led the NAFTA negotiations to secure "maximum U.S. access to Mexican resources and markets, while conceding as little as possible to Mexico" (Douglas 2008). U.S. firms gained access to Mexico's financial, agricultural, energy, textile, and manufacturing sectors. Mexican firms were blocked in their efforts to access the U.S. transport, agricultural, and textile sectors. Mexico was forced ultimately to dismantle its system of agricultural subsidies and tariffs, but the U.S. kept most of its own. NAFTA, enacted in 1994, calls for selective integration and unilateral action by the U.S., a dramatic contrast to the EU program of comprehensive integration of new member nations (Cameron 2000). U.S. authorities used the same approach in negotiating the Central American Free Trade Agreement (CAFTA) of 2004.

By 2002 Mexico's share of GDP devoted to international trade was at about the same level as Spain's, and total trade between Mexico and the U.S. stood at around eight times its 1986 level. But instead of working to integrate the labor markets of the two countries, the U.S. increased the number of Border Patrol officers from 4,200 in 1994 to 11,000 in 2002. The Immigration & Nationalization Service (INS) budget grew from $1.6 billion to $6.2 billion per year, a total increase of $32 billion since NAFTA.

Many authoritative studies of EU integration and NAFTA point to a clear lesson: If the money devoted to U.S. border enforcement were instead channeled into structural adjustment in Mexico, illegal migration would likely disappear as a political issue. Douglas Massey (2008) believes that all it takes is for U.S. leaders to view Latin and U.S. residents as "common citizens in a cooperative American union of equal and independent states."

Immigrant Issue #3. Children of Immigrants

Children of immigrants make up the largest-growing segment of the U.S. child population. They are 20 percent of American youth, projected to grow to one-third by 2040. Some experts say that "immigrant-origin youth are literally our future" (Suarez-Orozco 2008). Mexican immigrants are deeply family oriented. They want their children to learn English and have access to better jobs. In growing numbers they marry members of other ethnic groups; i.e., they integrate into American society.

A long-term immigrant student adaptation survey (LISA) concluded that very few schools have even given much thought to strategies that would ease immigrant students' path to college and the knowledge-intensive economies of the global era. Some questions that need attention include:

- How do we avoid the emergence of marginalized gangs?
- How do we minimize long family separations and foster faster family reunification and a more effective citizenship process?
- How do we support immigrant families as the reunite?
- How do we build on the optimism that motivates immigrants to search for a better life?
- How do we assure that their children have a good chance to become productive, engaged, and thoughtful citizens in the global societies of the 21st century?

The LISA study indicates that only 24 percent of immigrant youth thrive in U.S. schools. For over half of them, grades decline the longer they are here. Should we spend money educating children of undocumented workers? On the other hand, what are the long-term costs to society of failing to properly educate these young people? Strategies that are recommended by various scholars (Suarez-Orozco et al 2008; Duignan 2000) include addressing the unique problems of immigrant children, establishing schools that are engaging and relevant to them and that have realistic language policies, accepting dual cultural loyalties of these children, and building mentoring support and community supports.

Workplace Issues: Cultural Differences

Managers in the U.S. workplace who work with Mexican Americans, especially those who are first-generation immigrants, increase their effectiveness by understanding some basic cultural differences between Mexican and U.S. workplaces. Comparing workplace behaviors that reflect the cultural differences in power distance, collectivism, and masculinity can be especially informative.

Hierarchy—Status and Respeto

Hofstede (2001) defined power distance as the extent to which people accept unequal distributions of power; i.e. a distinct hierarchy with differences in status. Mexico and the United States differ greatly in this respect, with Mexicans being much more willing to accept power distance than are Americans. Mexico's score was 81, compared to 40 for the United States.

Mexican workers are likely to be accustomed to an autocratic yet paternalistic management style. Supervisors and subordinates in Mexico maintain a greater social and professional distance than do their counterparts in the United States. Mexican subordinates are more deferential and less likely to challenge or oppose a supervisor's ideas or directives, especially across hierarchical levels. While participatory styles are becoming more common in urban Mexican companies, many employees still hesitate to provide decision-making input or assume decision-making responsibilities and risks.

Management Style and Hierarchy

Some U.S. managers have a hard time developing an appropriate interpersonal style with Mexican American workers, especially in their dealings with unskilled, semi-skilled, or less well-educated employees. As in any authoritarian order, Mexicans value status and its observance. Americans regard status as undemocratic and try to minimize the differences by such behaviors as dressing casually and calling people by their first names. Most Mexicans accept the hierarchy and their "stations" in life. To them the issue is honor, not equality. Rather than resent their "rank," workers expect respectful recognition of their roles within the hierarchy. Even the janitor expects respect.

In some ways, Mexicans adapt more quickly to workplace change. This adaptability may be due, in part, to their acceptance of the supervisor's authoritarian role. When a manager says, "We are now going to do things this way," Mexican workers are more apt to accept the change without question.

Finally, Mexican workers tend to treat each other in a more respectful manner than one might find in many U.S. workplaces. "You can hurt the feelings of Mexican workers very easily," according to one expert (Stephens 1995). Mexican workers need more communication, more relationship building. They need more reassurance than American employees. U.S. managers who can adapt to such aspects of Mexico's "softer culture" tend to be more successful with Mexican American employees.

Paradox: Autocratic Paternalism

Mexican culture expects more autocratic behavior from managers—giving orders, expecting compliance, greater status, more rigid hierarchy, greater respect and power distance. At the same time the culture expects more paternalistic behavior from managers—a more benevolent, caring, personal relationship with employees and their families. The managers, being of a higher class, will at the same time they are being autocratic and authoritarian, also be patrician, noble, polished, polite, and caring. They will ask after the employee's family, be available for advice and counsel, and serve as a mentor.

Decision-Making Processes in the Hierarchy

U.S. managers tend to be more democratic in the making decision process than Mexican managers. In Mexican organizations, decision-making authority tends to be centralized, somewhat undemocratic, and retained among a few top-level managers. This is based on the accepted status differences between managers and subordinates and a clear separation of work roles. The boss says something and all employees have to follow that instruction. There is no room for discussion or for the expression of opinions. Workers typically think, "We cannot say something against the supervisor's opinion." In addition, workers learn that, "If I'm not told to do it, I don't do it."

Collectivism versus Individualism

In a collectivistic culture, people value social networks and relationships and expect group members to support and sustain one another. In more individualistic cultures, people are expected to be self-sustaining, and their responsibility for others rarely extends beyond the immediate family (Hofstede 2001). The United States is far more individualistic than Mexico, with a score of 91 compared to Mexico's 30. This means that personal relationships within groups are important in Mexico. Personal networks play a much bigger role in business success. In Mexico you have to know somebody to do business because the personal relationship carries into the business environment more than it does in the United States.

Us-First and Simpatico

A reluctance to challenge the manager's decisions also appears to stem in part from the greater respect and sensitivity employees offer to other workers of all ranks, both within and across hierarchical levels. Mexicans are far less tolerant of abrasiveness and insensitivity in the workplace than are Americans. An abrasive style would impede managers in gaining subordinates' support and compliance—and would impede an employee in getting co-workers' support (DeForest 1994).

Good workers show both respect and affection for their boss. For example, they may refer to him by a respectful nickname that is less formal than his usual title. Such behavior exemplifies the formal and informal duality of the Mexican style—*respecto* and *personalismo* at the same time.

Most Mexicans want to be seen as cooperative and simpatico, which can lead to counterproductive, face-saving behavior, a reluctance to admit failure or error, and a reluctance to relay bad news. They never want to tell you, "I don't know," or "I made a mistake," or "I have some bad news." Therefore, important information may not be relayed to the manager (DeForest 1994).

Teamwork in an Us-First Culture

Mexican culture may promote a quicker adaptation to teamwork than does U.S. culture. Mexicans care for and about each other. Team spirit is real; they will help co-workers in trouble. Some Mexican employees develop such strong allegiances to their team and/or company that they view it almost as family. On the other hand, Mexican power distance scores (hierarchy-status) suggest that Mexican team members may expect and require more direction from the manager than the self-managing teams now being implemented in many U.S. organizations. In such instances, the manager needs to convey a clear mission statement and set of goals, and some specific tactical directives, given with a personal touch (DeForest 1994).

Masculinity

In a masculine culture, assertiveness, achievement, and distinct and separate gender roles predominate (Hofstede 2001). Research indicates that Mexico and the United States both have relatively masculine cultures, with scores of 69 for Mexico and 62 for the United States. However, there are some important differences of degree, rather than content, in the masculine-oriented Mexican and U.S. workplaces. These include the typical work ethic and the treatment of women in the workplace.

The Mexican Work Ethic

One aspect of masculinity is a focus on achievement and thus the work ethic. Mexican and U.S. employees differ in their work ethic, and U.S. managers may be unprepared for this cultural difference. The "*mañana* syndrome" is still a factor for some low-level Mexican workers; i.e., they may appear to have little sense of urgency in completing their tasks. Conversely, many Mexican workers perform hard physical labor for long hours under difficult conditions—and the highly educated, professional class in Mexico exhibits a very strong work ethic (Stephens 1995).

Both lower-level and more highly-educated Mexican employees value a balance of work and non-work interests, placing a greater emphasis on non-work interests than most Americans. They typically assign higher priorities to family, relatives, personal relationships, religious activities, and leisure activities. Therefore, they are less likely to lose perspective and become obsessive about their work.

Women in the Workplace: Sexual Harassment and Discrimination

In Mexico laws against gender discrimination and sexual harassment are virtually nonexistent. Therefore these behaviors are more common than in the United States.

Sexual harassment. Sexual harassment is perfectly acceptable; in fact, it is almost considered a management privilege. Most young women would never think of complaining about sexual harassment., and some even think of it as positive interest. An ingrained custom in the workplace is for male managers to kiss their female secretaries good morning. In a way this is simply part of a warmer culture with more touching than in the United States. For example, it is also the custom for male colleagues to shake hands, hug, then shake hands again. Mexicans are more likely to emphasize communication through both physical and verbal contact.

What is changing is that there are more professional women entering the workforce, and sexual harassment occurs less often at professional levels where men and women have smaller power differentials. Even among women working at lower levels, although some women experience sexual harassment, it is usually not a significant issue for those who display professional behavior (Stephens 1995).

Gender Discrimination. The belief that married women should stay home is still a deeply rooted cultural expectation in Mexico. Once married, the wife is put on a pedestal (the saint), while the husband is out in the world having fun (the sinner). Women in general do not wish to have high-ranking positions, and are not found in them. This factor is consistent with the *marianismo* ethic (Mary, Madonna)—the female counterpart of the machismo ethic—in which Mexican women see their roles as fundamentally different from those of men. They are not only content to remain in these roles, but actively resist leaving them. This applies especially to women who are more traditional and/or older (Collier 1985, Stevens 1973, Stephens 1995).

Gender discrimination is not as significant a problem in the big cities as it is in the smaller cities and towns of Mexico. The problem is not being a woman, but rather being married. There are also generational differences in attitudes toward women. Younger women are more progressive, more proactive, and more career-oriented—and younger men are more likely to accept their ambitions.

An increasing number of Mexican women are, therefore, pursuing professional careers, although clearly to a lesser extent than in the United States. The International Labour Office estimates that Mexican women now make up more than 43 percent of the professional labor force, but less than 20 percent of the managerial labor force. According to the National Institute of Statistics, the percentage of women professionals with four or more years of college education increased from 19 to 34 percent between 1970 and 1990, although they are not yet well represented in nontraditional roles. The unemployment rate for women professionals is 17 percent, which is twice that of their male counterparts. Many Mexican employers continue to favor males in their hiring practices, hiring married men first, then single men, single women and finally (and rarely) married women.

Women generally have difficulty gaining respect in managerial jobs and seldom advance to high-level managerial posts. Among the glass ceiling barriers:

- The greater mix of personal relationships and business socializing. For example, managers often conduct business during lunch and would be reluctant to ask a female executive to lunch in order to negotiate a deal.
- Most firms would not send female employees on business trips alone.
- Women face greater difficulties when they must supervise the work of others

Despite these obstacles, some female Mexican managers have achieved significant career success.

PUERTO RICAN AMERICANS

Puerto Rican Americans are now the second largest Spanish-speaking community in the United States. They number nearly 3.4 million and constitute 10 percent of the Latino Americans on the U.S. mainland.

Past Connections

Puerto Rico was a Spanish colony for 400 years, and shortly after 1900 became an American affiliate, its citizens American citizens. The island is shifting from an agricultural to an industrial economy. Spanish is still by far the strongest cultural influence, which only slightly waned during the twentieth century. The island culture is a microcosm of Latin America, a culture in transition. Therefore, many Puerto Ricans "swing between extremes of apathy and frantic activity, hide hostility and frustration, and lean on fantasy" (Harris and Moran 1991, 86).

The migrations to the mainland began in the 1930s, most immigrants coming from the poverty level. They're primarily Catholic, from low-skill rural backgrounds, and many are dark skinned. On the island, about 20 percent of Puerto Ricans are considered African American and 16 percent "mixed blood." Those who emigrate to the United States tend to have better educational and employment credentials than the average African American on the island, but most experience downward mobility after they arrive in the United States.

In earlier decades nearly all Puerto Ricans landed in New York and stayed there. In 1950 about 80 percent lived in New York, but they've become more dispersed in the past two or three decades. In 1970 about 65 percent lived in New York and in 1980 only 50 percent. The others live primarily in New Jersey, California, Florida, and Illinois. When they moved out of New York, most moved up, both socially and economically.

Current Profile

Still, the majority of Puerto Rican adults in the mainland United States are first-generation immigrants who face considerable prejudice and discrimination. In 2000 there were over 2 million Latino Americans living in New York City, and 37 percent of these were Puerto Rican Americans.

The Puerto Rican American population has grown much faster than the non-Latino population but much slower than either the Mexican American or the total Latino American populations. The growth rates for all groups slowed after 1990.

Education and Income

Educational attainment was significantly above the Latino American average, with 64 percent holding diplomas and 10 percent holding degrees. After the Spaniard group, they have the largest proportion of members who speak English well (60 percent).

About 30 percent of Puerto Rican Americans earn more than $35,000, compared with 50 percent of Euro-Americans, and 20 percent of Mexican Americans. Yet they have the largest number of people, 26 percent, living in poverty, a few more than the Mexican American group (24 percent). The reason is likely linked to the 1990 census finding that Puerto Rican Americans had the smallest number of members living in family households (56 percent) with 37 percent living in female-headed households. And Puerto Rican women had the lowest median income of any Latino American group

Relatively high unemployment among Puerto Rican men is also a factor in the poverty picture. Puerto Ricans workers' concentration in declining manufacturing industries in the Northeast has been a factor. (De Frietas 1991).

Issue #1: Prejudice and Discrimination

On the surface, it appears that Puerto Rican immigrants would have an easier adjustment than the Europeans who immigrated to New York earlier. Puerto Ricans are U.S. citizens. They don't experience the traumatic shock of being illegals, like many Mexicans, or being "screened" at Ellis Island, as were Europeans in the past. (After screening, families were sometimes split up and the sick or "unsuitable" sent back home.)

Puerto Ricans seemed well adapted to fit into America's multicultural society because the Puerto Rican community contains persons of every possible color and complexion: people of European appearance, people with light-brown skin, and people with dark skin. The Puerto Rican upper and middle classes are generally more light skinned than the rest but by no means universally so. Most of the poverty-stricken people in the mountain towns are of European descent. There are no iron-bound distinctions, as is typically true in the United States. Intermarriage is common, class counts for more than color, and there is less concern over skin color than in the English-speaking world.

Once Puerto Rican immigrants arrive in the United States, all that changes. Discrimination based on skin color has encouraged dark-skinned Puerto Ricans to place special emphasis on their Spanish linguistic legacy in order to differentiate themselves from African Americans. There has often been rivalry between the two groups for jobs, between opposing neighborhood gangs, and between welfare recipients. They've had to cope with a cold climate dramatically different from their island warmth, and with a cold people, in contrast to the interpersonal warmth so common in their Latin culture. A common complaint is, "The weather is very cold here, just like the people."

Many Puerto Ricans, therefore, have great difficulty adjusting to New York, even when they're healthy and able to work. They often feel unwelcome and more discriminated against than Cubans and Mexicans. In New York City more than a million Puerto Ricans live in some of the city's most undesirable conditions. They are widely stereotyped as muggers and troublemakers and suffer from ethnic discrimination, especially those with darker skin tones.

Issue #2: Breaking Out of Poverty and Gaining Skills

Puerto Ricans often lack fluency in English, transferable skills, and formal education. Unskilled Puerto Ricans tend to benefit economically by leaving the island and settling in New York. But upwardly mobile Puerto Ricans often do better by returning home and many do after a while.

By 1960 half the Puerto Ricans families in New York were receiving welfare, and one-fourth of their children received some form of welfare assistance. Most didn't want to go on welfare when they arrived on the mainland. They have always preferred to work ,and they place high value on dignity, independence, and self-respect.

By 1970, whatever the stereotype, the bulk of Puerto Ricans in America did not belong to the underclass, and they neither shunned work nor broke the law. High fertility rates were concentrated among those who didn't finish high school. While the Puerto Rican Americans were one of the youngest and more poorly educated groups, they earned comparable incomes when compared with people of the same age and education. Those who did move up did it through education. Many second-generation Puerto Ricans went to college, then into various professions or public service. Many attained distinction in sports, entertainment, business, and academia. The proportion of semiskilled and unskilled workers declined significantly between 1950 and 1970, and the percentage in skilled and white collar occupations went up.

Beginning in the early 1980s, more and more professional people began to settle on the mainland. For example, more than half the engineering graduates on the island took jobs in the United States in 1983. As a result, the popular stereotype of the unskilled or semiskilled Puerto Rican immigrant has less and less relevance to the facts.

CUBAN AMERICANS

Cuban Americans are the smallest, 4 percent, of the three major Latino American groups. They are also the best educated and most affluent. Most Cubans in the United States arrived since 1960, when there were only about 30,000 here. Now there are one and a quarter million.

Current Profile

Cuban Americans are the Latino American group most likely to have at least a high school diploma, 73 percent as compared to 57 percent for the total Latino Americans. Still, 88 percent of all EuroAmericans over 25 have graduated high school. It follows that among Latino Americans, they have the most members working in managerial and professional occupations. Cuban Americans have the higher proportion (36 percent) earning over $35,000, as compared with 23 percent of all Latino Americans and 49 percent of EuroAmericans. They are generally an older group with smaller family households, and more likely to live in the suburbs than the inner city.

Most were born in Cuba and more than half of those have become citizens. Nearly half the Cuban-born members entered the United States during the 1960s to escape communism. Most settled in the Miami area. Many also moved to the eastern states, especially to western New York, Jersey City, Newark, and Bridgeport, and to a lesser extent to Los Angeles and Chicago.

Soon after Fidel Castro came to power in Cuba in 1959, people of the middle and upper classes began leaving. In fact, more than a million left, about 10 percent of Cuba's population. The overwhelming majority came to the United States

The early emigrants in the 1960s were from varied backgrounds but many were business or professional persons, and entrepreneurs. Those who left were far more likely to be relatively well-educated urban professionals than was the average island resident. They averaged three more years of schooling than Mexicans immigrating at the same time. About 11 percent were professionals or business owners, compared to 1 percent of Mexicans. Meanwhile 12 percent of Mexicans were farm workers compared to 2 percent of Cubans. There were many skilled blue-collar workers from both countries.

The first wave was soon joined by disillusioned members of the revolutionary regime as Castro became more aligned with the USSR. By the end of the 1970s there was a substantial Cuban American community, numbering more than legal immigrants from the whole of Latin America. Immigrants during the 1970s were primarily from the working class, including many skilled workers. Most had to settle for lesser jobs during their first two years. The Cuban American population swelled from about 30,000 in 1959 to about 600,000 by 1980 to 1,070,400 by 1990, and 1,242,000 by 2000. (U.S. Census Bureau).

Where Cuban Americans have created their own communities and established a middle-class or upper-class lifestyle, they've experienced little discrimination. However, Black Cuban Americans apparently believe that racial oppression in the United States is more severe than in communist Cuba. In the 1950s about 72 percent of Cuba's population consisted of people of European heritage. In the U.S. Census of 1970, almost 95 percent of Cuban Americans in the United States were of European heritage.

Cuban Success Story: Revitalizing Miami

Most Cuban Americans live in urban areas, and their capital is Miami, often called "Little Havana." By 1980 almost 60 percent of Miami's population was of Latin American origin. On average, Cuban Americans living outside Miami have a better formal education and higher income than those in Miami, which tend to include a higher proportion of the newer immigrants. But far from placing a burden on the city, the immigrants transformed its economy.

Before 1959 Miami depended mainly on tourism and money spent by retired persons who moved to Florida from the Northeast. The Cuban Americans used their enterprise and skills to turn Miami into the "new capital city of Latin America." Increasing numbers of tourists from Latin American nations fill the city's hotels. Latin American businessmen invested huge sums in real estate, about $1 billion a year by 1980. Miami became "the banking center" for investors from Central and South America. More than 100 multinationals doing business with Latin America have established headquarters in Miami. By 1982 international commerce was generating more than $4 billion a year in state incomes and had created 170,000 jobs.

By 1980 nearly half the Cubans in Miami worked for Cuban-owned firms and 21 percent were self-employed. Their wages were somewhat higher than those who worked in non-Cuban firms.

Cuban Professionals

In Miami and elsewhere educated Cuban Americans lost no time in moving up to the status they had enjoyed in their native land. By 1978, about 30 percent of Cubans worked in middle-class occupations as professionals, administrators, managers, and proprietors, as compared to 20 percent in 1970.

Cuban Americans are making an important contribution to American cultural life as artists, university professors, journalists, and other professionals. But they haven't tried to build a new Cuban American culture, comparable to Mexican American culture. Most consider themselves exiles who will return to their homeland after its liberation but are grateful for their freedom and prosperity in the United States. The mass emigration of these intellectuals became a cultural disaster for Cuba. Most of them are not right-wing conservatives but people of every shade of opinion, including many who had originally supported Castro. Most regard socialism as morally superior to capitalism, at least in the abstract, and continue to regard the United States as a bastion of reaction.

CENTRAL AMERICANS

About 7 percent of all Latino Americans are originally from Central America. Most are from El Salvador, Guatemala, Honduras, and Nicaragua, as shown in Table 11.5. These are among the smallest and poorest countries in Latin America.

Political Upheaval

The people of Central America are 65 percent Indian (primarily Mayan), 30 percent mestizo (a mixture of Indian and Spanish, and 4 percent of European descent. People of African descent are rare, especially in Guatemala and El Salvador, though they're about 9 percent of Nicaraguan people.

Guatemala has a Mayan majority that has been ruled for centuries by mestizo elites. Mayans have not integrated into Guatemalan society. During the 1980s much of the Mayan population organized to fight for land reform to end the theft and sale of their lands to foreign (primarily U.S.) businesses, such as United Fruit Company. Peasants in most other Central American nations have experienced similar political upheaval.

In El Salvador the Mayan indigenous population was decimated by those of European descent in the 1930s. Half the mestizo peasants are illiterate and most of the others attain only a fifth grade education—similar to the peasant situation in the other countries. All these countries went through decimating revolutions during the 1980s. The wars were a direct result of U.S. Cold War foreign policy, according to such researchers as J.K. Black (1998) and Juan Gonzales (2001). Policy favored repressive military juntas over democratically elected governments. Aid was given to the junta regimes, which in turn followed orders to fight any communist elements that might emerge from the rebels who fought for peasant rights.

Immigration

Those who could flee saw almost nowhere to go except the United States, and there was a large wave of immigrants during the 1980s. Since most had little education, they took jobs in the "informal sectors" as day laborers. Their major goal is to master the English language, and many of them attend community college English classes.

TABLE 11.5: Latino Americans from Central America

Country	Proportion of Central Americans in the U.S.
El Salvador	39%
Guatemala	22
Honduras	13
Nicaragua	5

Most of these immigrants are young men, married but traveling without their families, planning to work and save for a couple of years before returning. Most take minimum-wage blue-collar jobs, but these earnings are four times what they could earn at home. Nearly 90 percent work in crews composed of legal and illegal Latino aliens. Most say they intend to return again to work in an American city (Gann and Duignan 1998). However, as with virtually all immigrants to the United States, most actually stay and manage to bring their families in to join them.

Values for Central Americans are very similar to those of Mexican Americans, with a strong emphasis on family, religion, and the work ethic. Because of their homeland experiences, most see the police and military as the enemy. Helping extended family and community is highly valued.

OTHER LATINO AMERICANS

Other Latino Americans include those from the various countries of South America and from the Dominican Republic, as well as other Caribbean islands.

South Americans

Immigrants from South America are 4 percent of all Latino Americans living in the United States. Colombians are by far the largest group, about a third of South American immigrants. Those arriving in the United States appear to be heavily urban, with educational and occupational levels well above the Colombian average. Significant numbers of people have also emigrated from Ecuador, Peru, Argentina, and Chile.

Dominican Americans

In the "other Latino American" category are those from the Dominican Republic. They are the largest group of "others." The Dominican Republic is only 15 minutes by air from Puerto Rico, so these people have a close relationship with their Puerto Rican neighbors. Over half the current population of Dominican Americans entered during the 1980s due to political unrest on the island. Many were unskilled workers from rural areas, and they replaced the Puerto Ricans as the most disadvantaged group of Latino Americans. The elimination of many low-wage, manual U.S. manufacturing jobs created severe employment problems for these immigrants.

LEADERSHIP CHALLENGES:
MEETING CULTURAL NEEDS OF LATINO AMERICANS

Latino American barriers include trying to meet both job and family obligations, a communication style that may conflict with goal achievement and providing accurate information, unwillingness to confront conflict, and promotion anxiety.

Need #1. Meeting Family Obligations

Work is important to most Latino Americans. They want the American Dream. But family comes first. Therefore, when it comes to the following kinds of issues, the Latino American is more likely than the Euro-American worker to put family concerns first, which affects:

- job relocation that requires the family to move
- overtime work that conflicts with family obligations
- the need to be absent in order to deal with family problems, illnesses, or emergencies

Coworkers and managers must put this in perspective in order to understand the true dynamics of the situation.

Latino American workers will generally consult with the family when deciding to take a job, to seek or accept advancement, and whether to leave a job. For you to understand and work with Latino American employees, you must know about and understand their family concerns that impact work decisions and performance.

In Latino cultures people are hired and promoted based primarily on family and personal ties. Latino American employees may expect the company to give preferential treatment to their relatives and close friends. Managers may need to explain differences in company policy and in U.S. corporate cultures.

Need #2. Communicating Organizational Needs for Goal Achievement and Accurate Information

Latino cultures tend to value accurate data less highly than the American business culture. Most Latino business persons see nothing unusual or harmful in withholding information in order to gain or maintain power. While goals are important, the process of achieving the goals and the symbolic messages implied by various aspects of the process may be more important. In contrast, the success of U.S. corporations often hinges on effective and efficient goal achievement, doing what works, getting accurate data and passing it on to those who need it to do the best job. These values are so pivotal that Latino American employees may benefit from special training sessions on these topics.

Need #3. Seeing that Their Style Is Not Their Substance

Latino Americans can seem overly passive to some Euro-Americans because of the contrast in relationship styles. For example, when you combine the value of simpatico with that of power distance—the sense of status difference between supervisor and employee—you'll often find Latino Americans not speaking up in the same way her Euro-American peer does. Unless he's quite Americanized, a Latino American won't say anything that would imply criticism or contradiction of his supervisor—even if he knows the boss has probably made an uninformed and unwise decision. His supervisor might be tempted to label him as too passive for promotion, or even worse, too incompetent.

What this supervisor can do is communicate to the employee about such cultural differences and smooth the way to assertive contributions. Latino Americans have a deep understanding of family relationships. The supervisor, therefore, might compare the supervisor-employee relationship with the ways that brothers or cousins or sisters relate within the family—an equal relationship with one taking the lead.

Need #4. Turning Conflict Avoidance into Resolution with Sensitivity

The Latino value of simpatico compels most Latino Americans to avoid interpersonal conflict on the job. They try to emphasize positive behaviors in agreeable situations and de-emphasize negative behaviors in conflictive circumstances. This affects methods of conflict resolution and needs to be addressed in work team situations. Latino American employees need to understand why conflict is being addressed openly instead of ignored. They need to be reassured about the organization's need for openness, the expectation of openness, and why it is valued. Also, the team needs to respect Latino American members' sensitivities and find ways of resolving conflict that all can accept comfortably. Latino American workers may lead others in finding ways to combine openness with sensitivity and compassion.

Need #5. Dealing Constructively with Promotion Anxiety

Career development has some unique aspects for Latino American employees. For one thing, the employees, especially the men, may see more risk than Euro-Americans in applying for a promotion. If they don't get it, they not only experience a loss but their self-respect will suffer. Also, they may believe they'll be seen as competitive and too ambitious by their peers. Latino Americans tend to view competition as disruptive, leading to imbalance and disharmony. To overcome such barriers, leaders can begin working on career development with employees from the beginning. At periodic one-on-one meetings, career goals and ways of meeting them can be discussed. In this way, each step of development and advancement comes about naturally and the threats are diluted.

LEADERSHIP OPPORTUNITIES: BUILDING ON LATINO AMERICAN STRENGTHS

You can help Latino Americans use their love of group affiliation to enhance work teams and bring in their sense of honor, good name, and idealism to achieve at higher levels, You can relate to them in ways that show respect for Latino American values and issues, and you can help them make connections with Latino and Latino American marketplaces.

Opportunity #1. Enhance Work Team Relationships

Bring into play Latino Americans' cultural values of hard work, group loyalty, *personalismo*, and *simpatico*.

Highlight the Group Value.

The tradition of small group loyalty among Latino Americans offers a valuable opportunity for leaders to promote group values.

- Latino Americans place a very high value on belonging to a group and on cooperation and harmony within the group. Once they feel they are an accepted part of a work team, they are very comfortable functioning in this structure.
- For best results, Latino Americans need to feel personally close to the people in the group; otherwise, their first loyalty will lie elsewhere.
- Once they're committed to the team, motivational appeals and rewards geared to the team and the employee's contributions to the team can be the most powerful.
- Latino Americans tend to feel extreme loyalty to their ingroups. On the other hand, they may have difficulty adapting to an impersonal culture and to large groups in which personal recognition rarely occurs.

Remember, Latino Americans tend to give higher importance to relationships than to tasks. Keep the points in mind:

- Ask yourself, on a regular basis, how can I make the relationship value an asset?
- Ask, How can I create opportunities for them to work on tasks with others or to share projects?
- When delegating, coaching, and giving feedback, speak to them in terms of relationships where possible.

Promote Assertive Expression

Latino Americans' reluctance to self-disclose can pose a problem for optimal team functioning. Use *personalismo* to overcome it. Members often must know what's going on inside each others' heads in order to solve problems and keep operations flowing smoothly. When the corporate culture respects and values Latino Americans, their culture, history, and beliefs, then they are more likely to reveal their thinking and feeling to other team members.

Encourage Decision Making

In Latino cultures those in authority make the decisions, and subordinates don't pass judgment on leaders' ideas or question their decisions, as this would imply a lack of confidence in their judgment. Sometimes U.S. managers think they've communicated to Latino American workers that they can make certain decisions, only to find that the decisions are simply not made. In your manager role, you may need to appeal to Latino Americans' wish to be *simpatico*. You can explain in detail the decision-making process. You can reassure Latino American employees about when they can make certain decisions, when the team expects them to participate in making decisions, and when you expect their input, feedback, or questioning of ideas and decisions.

Opportunity #2. Appeal to Honor, Good Name, and Idealism

Coworkers and managers who offer feedback, evaluation, comments, or criticisms of Latino Americans' work would do well to understand and remember the importance of personal dignity, honor, and good name. If this is violated, the employee may feel compelled to leave. It may be futile to try to separate the person from the work or the end result. Latino Americans are likely to take criticism personally no matter how objective you try to be. Therefore, try these tips:

- Make the feedback personal but supportive and offered with great understanding and empathy
- Always give such feedback in private.
- Always offer it in a supportive, warm, concerned way.
- Always treat them as adults.

The idealist aspect of Latino culture can be an advantage when it motivates Latino American employees to support the organizational vision and mission, and to achieve the goals and standards set by the group or the company. Their idealism can inspire and energize other employees.

Opportunity #3. Show Respect for Their Values and Issues

Values around hierarchy and status, personalismo and simpatico, are important in work relationships. Also, women managers need to understand effective ways of interacting with Latino American men.

The Manager and Respeto–Status

Respect for status and authority runs deep in Latin cultures, but respect for the person, regardless of position, runs even deeper. Latino American employees generally expect that the boss will be demanding. They often expect the boss to tell them what to do and to exercise fairly close direction until it's done. On the other hand, they can be led to use their own initiative if the leader makes it clear what types of initiative are expected and that this does not conflict with the leader's authority. The combination of challenge and support can help them to be productive and feel comfortable on the job. Such an approach is likely to establish an effective working relationship and engage the Latino American's sense of strong loyalty.

Relationships with Personalismo

When a manager is generally warm, friendly, and encouraging with a Latino American employee, that deeper personal respect tends to develop. Otherwise, such employees may assume the manager is displeased with them. On the flip side, when the manager allows the employee to express his or her personality and share personal concerns, a greater rapport develops.

Since almost all relationships are more personalized in Latin America than in the United States, Euro-American leaders may have difficulty understanding the implications of simpatico. In American business cultures, people tend to value the separation of business matters from personal relationships and concerns. However, it's quite possible to balance the Latino Americans' need for their leaders to show personal understanding and warmth and the Euro-American leaders' need for some professional distance. The reverse is also true. Euro-American employees can understand that the Latino American manager's concern for their personal and family matters is not intended as a prying or controlling ploy. It's the leader's way of showing proper concern for each person.

Relationships and Simpatico

A certain charm is seen as crucial for dealing effectively with others and such *simpatico* is a quality that increases one's status. In fact, it's the surest form of acceptance in Latino culture. On the other hand, rudeness or insensitivity in a leader is shocking to Latino Americans. To them courtesy is synonymous with education, and they would wonder how such a rude person could ever be given a responsible position. Latino Americans greatly admire leaders who can get the job done while exercising smooth social skills that boost the employees' self-esteem and honor

The Woman Manager of Latino American Men

While machismo is often a misunderstood stereotype and is changing, it is still a factor to consider. Latino American men may have more difficulty than Euro-American men in dealing with a female manager. They are likely to react negatively to being corrected or criticized, especially where other men can hear, since this would be seen as a major attack on their honor. The more assertively the woman comes on, the more difficult it is for the employee. Therefore, women managers need to be especially sensitive to these feelings and to search for positive, tactful ways to achieve their purposes.

Occasionally a Latino American employee will make sexual overtures. It's important for the manager to keep in mind the implications of the Latino good woman-bad woman concept. She can nip such advances in the bud with clear I-messages, such as "I never get romantic with another employee; it wouldn't be fair to the others." She can continue to be warm and friendly, making sure she is also businesslike and professional, sending the clear nonverbal message, "I like you and respect you and I will not have a romantic or sexual relationship with you."

Opportunity #4. Help Make Connections to Latino Marketplaces

With about 75 percent of Latino American families in the middle- to upper-income brackets, Latino American spending power in 2003 was $575 billion and projected to be $925 billion by 2007 (Celent 2003). This offers huge opportunities to all types of businesses. However, this marketplace is complex, and capturing parts of it takes more than just providing information in Spanish. Companies need experts from the various Latino American market segments in order to best attract potential customers.

Latino Americans have been starting and growing their own companies. In 2002 they owned 1.6 million businesses, up 31 percent from 1997. Sales, which totaled $226 billion, were up 22 percent over five years ago. Federal researchers said most of these businesses—about 1.4 million—had no paid employees and earned a total of $42 billion, up 54 percent over 1997. According to the government, many of those companies were in administration and support, or waste management, healthcare or construction (Ownership 2005).

The U.S. media has responded dramatically to this market. Univision Communications is the largest Latino American media conglomerate. It reaches 98 percent of Latino Americans. Profits grew 73 percent from 1999 to 2004 (Business Week 2004). New Spanish-speaking television and radio stations are popping up, especially throughout the Southwest. Many established magazine publishers—such as Newsweek, People, Cosmopolitan, and Popular Mechanics—have launched Spanish versions. And the National Association of Hispanic Publishers estimated there were over 1,000 Latino American newspapers in 1997.

Fiesta Foods of Texas is a classic success story based on meeting the needs and wants of this demographic group. Other companies have capitalized on the "Roots Phenomenon," that is, people like to buy goods and services that reflect their distinctive cultural heritage. There are many lucrative marketing niches to fill here.

Even greater are the markets in all the other countries of Latin American. NAFTA and other trade agreements are opening up greater-than-ever trade opportunities with those nations. Latino Americans obviously understand Latino cultures better than anyone, and they're more likely than others to have key connections in Latino communities. They can be of invaluable help in dealing with those markets, customers, suppliers, and other associates. Corporate representatives who can speak the language and know the customs offer the company a valuable competitive edge.

SUMMARY

About one in eight Americans is a Latino American. This is the fastest growing minority group because of immigration and fertility rates. Myths and stereotypes center around traditional roles as menial workers, emotional temperaments, and the tendency to be perceived as passive or docile. The large majority are Mexican Americans who live primarily in the Southwest, followed by Puerto Rican Americans in the New York area, and Cuban Americans in Florida. New immigrants usually have a language barrier, are young, and often have low educational achievement. However 88 percent of those younger than 18 were born in the United States, speak English, and forego such barriers.

Traditional Latino American worldview values center around a closeness to the spirit world and a sense of destiny or fatalism. Only God knows, and death hovers around the other side of a thin veil, as do the spirits of those who have passed on. The Latin American worldview is built upon acceptance of a social hierarchy consisting of a few privileged elite and a mass of relatively powerless workers. Respect for superiors and a sense of distance between the elite and the masses is common. Emotions are honored and expressed, and the passion factor is important. The use of space is up close and personal in warm relationships with family, extended family, and business associates. Beliefs about time include the belief that the present moment is to be appreciated because the future is indefinite and unknown. Most Latino Americans immigrated because of their belief in the American Dream and are eager to integrate into the American culture while still honoring and preserving their core values and their love of the Spanish language.

Relationship values are the most important values for Latino Americans. Life centers around the family, including extended family; mutual dependence and undying loyalty are expected. *Simpatico* refers to getting along. Being agreeable, acquiescing to the wishes of others, especially those more powerful, and being courteous are all extremely important to promoting smooth social relations. Everything is translated into personal terms and personal relationships. In more formal relationships, Latino Americans tend to be reserved. Therefore, the idea that they're too emotional to hold leadership roles is mistaken. Machismo refers to male domination in male-female relationships, and the need for males to have a "manly" status with other men. This is changing along with changing work roles for men and women. In communicating, Latino Americans tend to speak indirectly, have a high concern for feelings, are highly sensitive to direct criticism, and make sure to acknowledge everyone when saying their hello's and goodbye's.

Current issues center around overcoming a tradition of segregation and discrimination—in workplaces, schools, and housing. Improving their educational opportunities and upgrading their knowledge and skill levels are crucial to achieving other goals. Improving their workplace status and overcoming employment discrimination is a critical issue. A recent issue is overcoming immigration backlash.

Mexican Americans are by far the largest Latino American group. Especially important to them are relationships, family ties, machismo, and ethnic loyalty. The Chicano movement brought attention to Mexican American issues, but most identify more with the American Dream than with the movement.

Many Mexican workers who enter the United States as temporary H-2 guestworkers are abused by employers. They may be forced to live in squalid conditions and denied medical benefits for injuries.

Employers have all the power over these workers. Some experts say this is one of the major civil rights issues of our time, and we need a fair program with strong worker protections that are vigorously enforced.

A burning issue since NAFTA concerns the millions of "illegal immigrants" who cross the Mexican border to find work in the United States. Equally important is the issue of access to a good education for children of Mexican immigrants—both legal and illegal. Using Spain as an example, Douglas Massey describes how the European Union transferred $20 billion in structural adjustment subsidies to Spain during the first decade that Spain prepared to join the European Community (1976 to 1986) and later spent $52 billion in helping Spain grow economically before becoming a EU member in 1995. In contrast, the United States refused to discuss such subsidies with Mexico and instead embarked on a unilateral militarization of the Mexico-U.S. border, spending an additional $32 billion to block the inflow of migrant workers. If the U.S. devoted most of these billions to helping Mexico develop needed economic and social reforms, the flow of undocumented workers would likely slow to an insignificant trickle.

The children of Mexican immigrants, legal and illegal, must be integrated into U.S. society by receiving educational support. Suggested strategies include addressing their unique problems, establishing schools that are engaging and relevant to them and that have realistic language policies, accepting dual cultural loyalties of these children, and building mentoring support and community supports.

U.S. managers can be more effective with first-generation Mexican American employees if they understand how the U.S. and Mexican workplace cultures differ. Based on the power difference value, Mexican managers have more power and status in a more distinct hierarchy. They are expected to be relatively autocratic as well as more paternalistic, serving as a mentor to employees. Based on the cultural value of collectivism, Mexican American employees value getting along with and helping coworkers and are less tolerant of an abrasive style. They tend to be better at teamwork but may need more direction than Euro-American employees. Based on the value of masculinity, most Mexican Americans have a strong work ethic but place more emphasis on non-work priorities than Euro-Americans. Gender roles are more pronounced in Mexican workplaces. Sexual harassment and gender discrimination are common, with no laws to protect women from such behaviors.

Puerto Rican Americans, the second largest Latino American group. Their growth rate slowed during the 1990s but still exceeds the total U.S. population. Educational attainment was significantly above the total Latino American figure, but poverty rates were the highest. Poverty is connected with the fact that one-third of Puerto Rican Americans live in female-headed households.

Cuban Americans, the third largest Latino American group, are a unique success story because were business owners and professionals who immigrated to Florida to escape Fidel Castro's communist regime. They revitalized Miami with their skills and Latin American business contacts.

Those from Central American countries are 4 percent, primarily from El Salvador, Guatemala, Honduras, and Nicaragua. Most were farm workers with relatively little education, escaping from political upheaval and very low living standards. Somewhat fewer, 5 percent are from South American countries. The largest group in the "other Latino American" category are immigrants from the Dominican Republic.

A major leadership challenge is meeting the cultural needs of Latino Americans, helping them to overcome workplace barriers to success. Needs include meeting family obligations, understanding the importance of sharing information and achieving job and company goals, learning how to turn conflict avoidance into conflict resolution, and learning how to deal with promotion anxiety.

Leadership opportunities include helping Latino Americans enhance work team relationships by building on their strengths of group loyalty, *personalismo* and *simpatico*. It includes helping them to express themselves assertively and to participate in group decision-making. Another opportunity is appealing to the honor, good name, and idealism of Latino Americans. Also important is showing respect for their values and issues. A major opportunity is encouraging Latino American employees to use their cultural knowledge and contacts to help the company capture new and expanding Latino markets—both in the United States and in Latino counties.

Case Study 11.1 New Manager Luis

Luis has been manager of the claims department for three months. He's on his way to the office of his immediate supervisor, *Gale*, for their monthly planning and evaluation session. Walking down the hall, his mind is filled with events of the past few months and what he wants to discuss with Gale.

When Luis applied for the management job, he had five years' experience with National Life Insurance. He had taken the screening exam for the new position and did well on both the written and oral portions. One of Luis' coworkers, *Richard*, also took the test and told Luis that he had done great on it.

Richard had come to National about a year before Luis and had trained Luis in some claims department procedures. Luis learned quickly and they soon had a friendly rivalry going. When their boss Gale was recruited from outside the company, Richard told Luis he heard it was because of pressure to place more women in higher positions. He said the company had recently gone through a government review of its affirmative action program and was found lacking. Richard said, "They brought Gale in mainly because she's a woman." Luis agreed with Richard at the time because he didn't really know the story and he didn't want to argue about it.

Four months ago, Richard told Luis that he really expected to get the claims department manager's job because he had such a good track record with the company and he also had more seniority than the other seven candidates. When Luis got the job, he became Richard's immediate supervisor. Luis felt uncomfortable giving Richard direction. He knew Richard was probably at least as well qualified as he to be boss. He worried about it quite a bit the first month. But he told himself that he must be the most qualified for the job; otherwise, he wouldn't have been selected.

During the second month, Luis noticed that Richard and several other employees seemed reluctant to follow his instructions. Luis attempted to meet them halfway by asking why they weren't doing certain things as he had directed, what they felt should be done, etc. Sometimes it seemed as if these few employees didn't take him seriously. He could see that efficiency and productivity were beginning to be affected by their resistance and balkiness. Time and time again Luis told himself that it would take time for his former coworkers to get used to him as their manager and for him to become adjusted to his new role and responsibilities.

Then just last week, Luis overheard a conversation in the lounge. Richard was talking with a coworker and didn't realize Luis was in the next room:

> *I don't know about this affirmative action. Why would anyone want to use the past as a reason why they haven't gotten ahead educationally or economically? I think it's time we all stood up for ourselves and accomplish or fail on our own merit, instead of some people falling back on excuses. Why should we American males be discriminated against just because of past history? If people want everyone to be treated equally, then they can't be given an extra advantage at the same time. I know my test scores were higher than some of these people who are being promoted, but they get promoted anyway—just so some job-climbing administrator can brag about his political correctness and make his track record look good. Worst of all, it just amazes me that Luis actually thinks he deserved that promotion.*

Luis was stunned at the time. He started thinking about the number of Latino Americans in company management. He could think of only one. Maybe Richard was right. Maybe he really wasn't qualified enough to handle the new job.

1. What do you think are the root problems in this situation?
2. If you were Luis, what would you do?
3. If you were Gale, what would you do?

Case Study 11.2 Evelyn Sanchez, Supervisor

Evelyn Sanchez is a Customer Services Supervisor for Buckman's, a large mail order house. Her duties include making sure that work is distributed and completed under strict deadlines, approving certain transactions, and reviewing employee's work. She is required to set quarterly goals for herself and to train employees to cross-sell to customers in ways that meet their needs.

Evelyn's team includes ten employees of diverse backgrounds, including African American, Euro-American, Latino American, and Asian American. Most of the employees are bilingual. *Rosita*, a Latina American, is hired as a new member of Evelyn's team. One day when Evelyn stops by to check on how Rosita is doing, they lapse into speaking their native Spanish. *Ophelia*, an African American team member, is working nearby. She feels uncomfortable because she doesn't know what the two were saying. It's no big thing, and she tries to forget her discomfort. However, Evelyn comes by almost every day and has a brief conversation in Spanish with Rosita. Finally, Ophelia mentions her discomfort to Evelyn. She says, "I feel really left out when you two speak on and on in Spanish—and it keeps happening. I wish we could all speak the same language around here."

Evelyn replies, "Lighten up, Ophelia, we're not talking about you nor are we sharing secrets. We're just chatting, and it's good for our heart and soul to be able to converse in our beautiful *Castellano* now and then."

Ophelia becomes more disturbed each day as Evelyn and Rosita have their little Spanish conversations. She decides to complain to *Gene*, the general manager.

1. What are the key issues (root problems) here?
2. If you were Gene, what would you do?
3. What do you think about Evelyn's actions?

Case Study 11.3 Gino George, Sales Rep

Gino George, is a sales rep for Delcor, a telecommunications company. Five years ago he completed a degree in business administration and went to work in the finance department of Delcor as a junior accountant. He was the only Latino American in his department, and he got along well with his coworkers. He earned good performance reviews and merit increases and two years ago applied for and got the sales rep job.

Gino likes being a sales rep. He especially likes getting a commission on every sale he makes. Because he's a good salesperson, his salary is significantly higher than it was as an accountant. Gino is proud of the fact that he can help his Euro-American coworkers when they must deal with Spanish-speaking clients. In fact, Spanish-speaking clients have learned to ask for Gino, making him a valuable asset to Delcor.

On the other hand, being the only Latino American makes Gino feel somewhat isolated. For example, coworkers frequently "forget" to inform him of meetings or to invite him to group events. Few of them talk with him about anything outside of business matters.

Recently Gino was going over some files in the office. A couple of sales reps entered the adjacent cubicle and Gino overheard their conversation. Jeff said, "I heard that Dave's raising our sales quotas for the spring quarter. Business is always slow in the spring. How are we going to sell more than last year? If we don't meet that quota, we won't get our bonus." Ralph replied, "I think it's Gino's fault. He just gives Dave ideas. If he weren't such an eager beaver, Dave wouldn't start thinking that the rest of us should do better." "Yeah," said Jeff, "Any ideas on how we can send Gino back to the accounting department? Let him count beans!"

Gino is very upset by the news that his coworkers view his achievements so negatively. He hates being viewed as a trouble maker and difficult person. He decides to pull back on his sales efforts and to be satisfied with barely meeting his quotas.

Today Dave receives the news that he's being promoted and that he should recommend a replacement to take over his job. As Dave goes through the performance evaluations of all his team members, he narrows the choice down to Gino or Jeff.

Jeff has a high school diploma, experience as a salesperson with one other company, and has been with Delcor for three years as a sales rep. He gets along well with coworkers and is well accepted as "one of the gang."

Gino is better qualified, with his bachelors degree that includes technical expertise in the telecommunications field. He has been building a better track record as a sales rep than Jeff has, but the coworkers don't seem to be as receptive to him as they are to Jeff.

Dave calls Gino and Jeff into his office. He tells them that they're both in the running for the job and sets up times to interview each of them separately. Gino is concerned. He really wants the promotion, but he's worried about being accepted in the managerial role. On the other hand, if Jeff gets the job, he'll probably offer Gino little or no support and encouragement. He'll probably make it tough for Gino.

1. What are the key issues (root problems) in this situation?
2. If you were Gino, what would you do?
3. If you were Dave, what would you do?

REFERENCES

Anderson, Sarah. "The Equity Factor and Free Trade: What the Europeans Can Teach Us," *World Policy Journal* 20, 45–51, 2003.

Aponte, Robert. "Urban Hispanic Poverty: Disaggregations and Explanations." *Social Problems* 38, 516–529, November 1991.

ARIS, American Religious Identification Survey, Graduate Center, City University of New York, 2001.

Bauer, Mary, "Close to Slavery: Guestworker Programs in the United States," *Southern Poverty Law Center*, www.splcenter.org, 2007.

Black, J.K. *Latin America: Its Problems and Its Promise*. Westview Press, 1998.

Bullock, Paul. "Employment Problems of the Mexican-American," in *Mexican Americans in the United States*. 1971.

Cameron, Maxwell A. and Brian W. Tomlin. *The Making of NAFTA: How the Deal Was Done*. Cornell University Press. 2000.

Canedy, Dana, "Latinas Fall Behind in Education," *New York Times*, April 25, 2005.

Chronicle, San Francisco, "California Century" series, p. A-1, August 31, 1999.

Cohen, R. *Culture, Disease and Stress Among Latino Immigrants*. Washington, DC: Smithsonian Institution, 1979.

Collier, Jane F. "From Mary to Modern Woman: The Material Basis of Marianismo and Its Transformation in a Spanish Village," *American Ethnologist*, 13, 100–107, 1986.

Condon, J. *Good Neighbors: Communicating with the Mexicans*. Intercultural Press, 1985.

Cox, Taylor. *Cultural Diversity in Organizations*. Berrett-Koehler, 1993.

Daniel, Clete. *Chicano Workers and the Politics of Fairness: The FEPC in the Southwest, 1941–1945*. Austin, TX: University of Texas Press, 1991.

De Forest, Mariah E. "Thinking of a Plant in Mexico?" *Academy of Management Executive*, 8, 1, 33–40, 1994.

De Freitas, Gregory. *Inequality at Work: Hispanics in the U.S. Labor Force*. Oxford University Press, 1991.

Duignan, Peter J. *Bilingual Education: A Critique*. Hoover Press, 1998.

Duignan, Peter J. and Lewis Gann, *The Spanish Speakers in the United States: A History*. University Press of America, 2000.

Duncan, Mary Cheatham, "Hispanics and the American Workplace," www.unc.edu/courses, 2000

Farrell, Mary. Spain in the EU: *The Road to Convergence*. London: Palgrave. 2001.

Forbes, Jack D. *The Chicano Worker*. University of Texas Press, 1977.

Gann, Lewis and Peter J. Duignan, *The Hispanics in the United States: A History*. Westview Press, 1986.

Gonzales, Juan. *Harvest of Empire*. Penguin, 2001.

Grebler, L., et al. *The Mexican American People*. Free Press, 1970.

Harris, Philip R., and Robert T. Moran. *Managing Cultural Differences*, 3d ed., and *Instructor's Guide*. Gulf, 1996.

Hero, Rodney. *Latinos and the U.S. Political System*. Temple University Press, 1992.

Heston, Alan et al. Penn World Table Version 6.2 Center for International Comparisons of Production, Income and Prices, University of Pennsylvania, www.pwt.econ.upenn.edu 2006.

Hofstede, Geert. *Culture's Consequences: International Differences in Work-Related Values*. Sage, 1980.

Hofstede, Geert. *Culture's Consequences: Comparing Values, Behavior, Institutions, and Organizations Across Nations*, 2d ed. Sage, 2001.

Humphreys, J. M. "Hispanic Buying Power by Place of Residence," The Selig Center, Terry College of Business, 58, 6, www.selig.uga.edu, Nov-Dec 1998.

Huntoon, Laura, "Return Migration When Savings Differ," *Journal of Urban Affairs* 17, 219–39, 1995.

Lancaster, Roger N. *Life is Hard*. Berkeley, CA: University of California Press, 1993.

Landsberger, H.A., and A. Saavedra, "Response Set in Developing Countries," *Public Opinion Quarterly* 31, 214–229, 1967.

Latino Coalition, The. "2002 National Hispanic Survey," www.TheLatinoCoalition.com, 2003.

LeVine, E., and J.N. Franco, "A Reassessment of Self-Disclosure Patterns Among Anglo Americans and Hispanics," *Journal of Counseling Psychology* 28, 522–524, 1981.

Mannino, F.V. and M.F. Shore, "Perceptions of Social Support by Spanish-Speaking Youth with Implications for Program Development." *Journal of School Health*. 46, 471–474, 1976.

Marin, G., et al. "The Role of Acculturation on the Attitudes, Norms, and Expectancies of Hispanic Smokers." *Journal of Cross-Cultural Psychology*, 20, 399–415, 1989.

Marin, Gerardo, and Barbara VanOss Marin. *Research with Hispanic Populations*. Sage 1991.

Massey, Douglas, "Caution: NAFTA at Work," Miller-McCune, 31–37, April 2008.

McWilliams, Carey. *North from Mexico*. 1975.

Morales, Rebecca, and Frank Bonilla. *Latinos in a Changing U.S. Economy*. Sage, 1993.

Morrison, Ann. *The New Leaders*. San Francisco: Jossey-Bass, 1992.

Orrenius, Pia, "The Effect of U.S. Border Enforcement on the Crossing Behavior of Mexican Migrants" in Jorge Durand and Douglas S. Massey, eds., *Crossing the Border: Research from the Mexican Migration Project*. Russell Sage Foundation, 2004.

"Ownership Business Creation Up for Women, Minorities," *Boston Globe*, August 14, 2005.

Padilla, A.M. "The Role of Cultural Awareness and Ethnic Loyalty in Acculturation," in *Acculturation*. Westview, 1980.

Padilla, A.M., ed. *Hispanic Psychology*. Sage, 1995.

Paternostro, Sylvana. *Land of God and Man: Confronting Our Sexual Culture*. Dutton, 1999.

Paulette, Thomas. "In the Land of Bratwurst, a New Hispanic Boom," *Wall Street Journal*, p. A-1, March 15, 2000.

Pew Hispanic Center, "Hispanics: A People in Motion," Pew Research Center, www.pewHispanic.org, January 2005.

Polls: Latino National Political Survey, 1993; *Wall Street Journal-NBC*, 1993.

Ramirez, Henry M. "America's Spanish Speaking: A Profile." *Manpower*, 33, September 1972.

Ross, C.E., and J. Mirowsky. "Socially-Desirable Response and Acquiescence in a Cross-Cultural Survey of Mental Health." *Journal of Health and Social Behavior* 25, 189–197, 1984.

Santiago, Anne M., and Margaret G. Wilder, "Residential Segregation and Links to Minority Poverty: The Case of Latinos in the U.S." *Social Problems* 38, 492–515, November 1991.

Shorris, Earl. *Latinos.* W.W. Norton Co., 1992.

Solorzano, Daniel G. "Mobility Aspirations Among Racial Minorities, Controlling for SES." *Social Science Review* 75, 182–189, July 1991.

Stevens, Evelyn P. "The Prospects for a Women's Liberation Movement in Latin America," *Journal of Marriage and the Family*, 35, 313–321, 1973.

Surarez-Orozco, C., M.M. Suarez-Orozco, I.Todorova. *Learning a New Land: Immigrant Students in American Society.* Harvard University Press, 2008.

Triandis, H.C. "Role Perceptions of Hispanic Young Adults" *Journal of Cross-Cultural Psychology* 15, 297–320, 1984a.

Triandis, H.C., et al. *Dimensions of Familism Among Hispanic and Mainstream Navy Recruits.* Chicago: University of Illinois, 1982.

Triandis, H.C., et al. "Simpatia as a Cultural Script of Hispanics." *Journal of Personality and Scoial Psychology* 47, 1363–1375, 1984b.

U.S. Bureau of Labor Statistics, http://stats.bls.gov, 1999.

U.S. Census, Department of Commerce. *The Hispanic Population in the U.S.,* 2000.

U.S. Census, Department of Commerce. *We the Hispanics* and *We the American Children,* 1993.

U.S. Department of Education. *The Condition of Education.* Washington, DC: GPO, 1989.

U.S. Government reports: (1) David J. Saposs, "Report on Rapid Survey of Resident Latin American Problems and Recommended Program," Office of the Coordinator of Inter-American Affairs," in Reel 28, HQ Files, FEPC Records 1, April 3, 1942. (2) "Spanish-Americans in the Southwest and the War Effort," in Reel 48, HQ Files, FEPC Records 1, June 1, 1941. (3) "Report on the Spanish-Speaking Peoples in the Southwest," in Reel 70, HQ Files, FEPC Records 13, Field Survey March 14 to April 7, 1942.

Valle, R., and C. Martinez, "Natural Networks Among Mexicano Elderly in the U.S." in *Chicano Aging and Mental Health.* Washington, DC: GPO, 1980.

Viviano, Frank. "Poll Contradicts Stereotypes." *San Francisco Chronicle*, p.A-1, March 27, 1990.

Weber, David (ed.). *Foreigners in Their Native Land: Historical Roots of the Mexican Americans*, Rev. Ed. University of New Mexico Press, 2004.

WSJ. Vargas, Alexia, "Split Decision," *Wall Street Journal*, p. A-1, November 19. 1999.

Zurcher, A.L., et al. "Value Orientation, Role Conflict, and Alienation from Work." *American Sociological Review* 30, 539–549, 1965.

Resources

Hispanic Center for Corporate Response, Washington D.C.

National Council of La Raza, a civil rights organization, www.nclr.org

Pew Hispanic Center www.PewHispanic.org

Mexican American Legal Defense and Education Fund of Los Angeles

CHAPTER 12
Working with Gay Persons

Gayness is not the illness; judgment is the illness.
Scott Stewart

Gay, lesbian, bisexual, and transgender persons (GLBT), referred to collectively as gay persons, are often called the invisible minority because they don't *look* different from others in their ethnic group. About one in every 50 persons you work with is a gay person—by best estimates of researcher R. T. Michael and associates, 2 percent, or almost 6 million, Americans. However, if you work in a major metropolitan area, as many as one in every 10 to 20 persons you meet may be gay.

To become comfortable with gay associates, and in turn to build good working relationships with them, you need get a feel for their lifestyle, community, and background. The more skilled you become at interpreting individual associates' actions against the backdrop of their background, the greater your chances of working well together. The goal of this chapter is to help you understand what it's like to grow up gay and be a gay person in today's workplace—according to scholars from that community. Keep an open mind and try to begin seeing situations as a gay person might view them. Specifically, you'll learn:

- How typical stereotypes about gay persons compare with reality
- How these stereotypes have come about and how they impact people
- What it's like to grow up gay
- Key aspects of the gay community
- Recent findings about why some people are gay
- How people manage a gay identity in the workplace
- Legal rights gay persons do and do not have
- Barriers to career success for gay persons and how to break through those barriers
- Assets gay persons may bring to your organization and how to use those assets to create win-win successes

First, test your opinions and knowledge by completing Self-Awareness Activities 12.1 and 12.2.

Gay Man
Courtesy of Chris Carroll/Corbis Images.

Gay Woman
Courtesy of Queerstock/Getty Images.

Self-Awareness Activity 12.1: What Do You Believe about Gay Persons?

Purpose:

- to get in touch with your beliefs and stereotypes about this group of people
- to experience how judgmental beliefs affect your thinking and feeling processes
- to experience the ways in which your beliefs create your reality regarding other persons, even before you have any interaction with them.

Part I. What Do You Believe about Lesbian Women?

Step 1. Associations

- Relax as deeply as you can.
- Close your eyes for a moment and take a few deep breaths.
- Now focus on the picture that symbolizes "gay woman"
- Imagine that you are this woman. Be gay woman.
- Notice any resistance to being this person—and any willingness.
- Notice words, images, thoughts, and feelings that come to mind as you are "seeing and being this woman."

Step 2. Negative Associations

- Next, as you focus on the picture, allow negative opinions to come up, perhaps some that you typically hold about gay women.
- Notice your *thoughts* as you see the person in this negative way. What *feelings?*

Step 3. Positive Associations

- Now, still focusing, allow positive opinions to come up, perhaps some that you typically hold about gay women.

- Notice your *thoughts* as you see the person in this negative way. What *feelings?*

Step 4. Insights and Writeup

- Now review this experience and write about it.

- When you first saw the picture, what thoughts and feelings came up? These may reflect your deepest responses to people from this group.

- Think about the differences in your thoughts and feelings when you consciously held a positive opinion versus a negative opinion.

- Write a few sentences about your feelings, thoughts, and insights.

Part II. Experimenting with Opinions About Gay Men

Repeat the phases and steps in part I, this time focusing on the image of a gay man.

Self-Awareness Activity 12.2: What Do You Know About Gay Persons?

Purpose: To see what you know about the issues covered in this chapter.

Instructions: Determine whether you think the following statements are basically true or false—and think about why. The answers will emerge in this chapter, and the summary at the end of the chapter focuses on these issues.

1. You can always tell gays by the way they act, dress, and talk.

2. Gay persons tend to influence young people to becoming gay.

3. The American Psychological Association takes the position that gays are mentally disturbed and need therapy.

4. With the proper therapy and motivation, gays can become heterosexual.

5. Most studies indicate that gay couples have difficulty raising normal children.

6. If a person has one or two sexual experiences with someone of the same sex, he or she is gay.

7. Most researchers conclude that gay persons are born with a gay orientation.

8. Gay persons are protected from workplace discrimination throughout the United States.

STEREOTYPES AND REALITIES

Gays must deal with some of the most vicious and degrading stereotypes and myths, and they probably suffer from more distorted or invalid stereotypes than any group. The effects are devastating, and antigay prejudice ranges from trivial snubs to violence. While most Americans still do not approve of a gay sexual orientation, they are against discrimination and for equal treatment in the workplace.

Many of the stereotypes reflect beliefs about outgroups in general, usually portraying outgroup members as both threatening and inferior to members of the dominant ingroup. Adam (1978) and others found that gays, African Americans, and Jews all are perceived as animalistic, hypersexual, over-visible, heretical, conspiratorial, and inclined to physical and mental disease.

Stereotype #1: Gays Cluster in Certain Occupations

Many people believe that gay men flock to the occupations of hair stylist, designer, dancer, and similar creative, "feminine" jobs. In fact, the gay men who happen to choose such occupations are more likely to come out for the simple reason that gays are more accepted in those jobs. Meanwhile, people are unaware of the gay men in the more masculine occupations because most stay in the closet in order to survive. Evidence suggests that gays and lesbians do not cluster in a few occupations but are found in a wide range of different occupations as diverse as the general population. A survey of 4000 gay persons found more gay men and women in science and engineering than in social services; 40 percent more in finance and insurance than in entertainment and arts, 10 times (1000%) more in computers than in fashion [Fortune 1992]. The true part of this myth is that some gay employees feel forced to cluster in certain jobs or departments because they feel safe there and unsafe in other, perhaps more appropriate, areas (McNaught 1993).

Stereotype #2: People Who Associate with Gays are Probably Gay Themselves

This belief is sometimes called "courtesy stigma" or stigma by association. When heterosexuals associate with gays, only to be suspected of being gay themselves, they may respond with anger or they may back off. Courtesy stigma, therefore, can create barriers to gays' establishing the support networks and mentor relationships they need for career success. It can block competent researchers from addressing gay issues because of the tendency of the general public to assume that heterosexuals would not be interested in these topics. Closet gays' reaction to courtesy stigma is frequently fear of disclosure and thus avoidance of association with other gays.

Stereotype #3: Gays in Sensitive or High-Level Jobs Are a Security Risk

This stereotype is downright vicious in its impact. No evidence has appeared to support the belief that gay persons represent an increased security risk. But the myth persists in this form: Gay employees try to keep their homosexuality a secret; therefore, they are easy blackmail targets for con artists and spies, which in turn makes them a security risk, so they shouldn't be hired or promoted into sensitive or high-level jobs. Author G. Herek reasons that if this were true, the fair solution would be to remove the stigma from homosexuality and protect them from discrimination, not to use the "potential blackmail target" rationale for inflicting further discrimination (Herek 1993). In 1995 President Clinton signed an executive order barring the use of this criterion for personnel decisions involving placement of federal employees.

Stereotype #4: Gay Persons Don't Have Normal, Lasting Relationships

This stereotype depicts gay persons as people drift from one sexual liaison to another, ending up alone when they're old. Studies indicate that most gay persons very much want to have enduring, close relationships and many do. Between 40 and 60 percent of gay men are currently involved in a steady relationship, and between 45 and 80 percent of gay women are so involved. In fact 75 percent of gay women are so involved according to most studies. The few studies that have included older gay persons have found that relationships lasting 20 years or more are not uncommon.

Research also indicates there are no significant differences between heterosexual and gay persons on any of the measures of relationship satisfaction. Further, when couples were asked the best things and worst things about their relationships, researchers found no significant differences in the responses of gay and heterosexual couples, all of whom reported a similar range of joys and problems. The point is not that all gay couples are happy and problem-free but that they are not any more prone to relationship dissatisfactions and difficulties than are heterosexual couples.

Another aspect of this stereotype is that gay persons don't have normal relationships with friends and therefore don't have strong support networks. While they do experience psychological stress from social rejection and stigma, most have made significant progress in overcoming these obstacles and creating rich, satisfying social networks. Overall levels of support received by gay men and women were similar to and slightly higher than those reported for heterosexual men and women. (Peplau 1991).

Stereotype #5: Gay Men Act Feminine and Lesbians Act Masculine

Most heterosexuals believe that gay persons possess the characteristics of their opposite sex. They also believe the reverse side of the coin, that men who act feminine are likely to be gay and women who act masculine are likely to be lesbian. In fact, gayness itself does not establish the types of sexual roles and behavior people will adopt. The expression of sexuality is diverse and functions along a continuum, rather than in an either/or manner. To refute the stereotype we can recall how the late film star Rock Hudson shocked the world when he came out, especially the women fans who idolized him as the essence of masculine attractiveness.

A conflicting stereotype is that gay partners take on clear husband and wife roles, which seems unlikely if both gay male partners act feminine, and likewise if both lesbian partners act masculine. In fact, masculine-feminine roles have sometimes been important in the past, but in recent years gender-linked roles have sharply declined. In fact, most gay couples today actively reject traditional husband-wife or masculine-feminine roles as a model for enduring relationships. Most are in dual-earner relationships, with neither member the exclusive breadwinner and each having some economic independence. Any specialization of activities is based on individual skills or interests rather than sex-role stereotyping. While many partners report that there is some sense of a masculine-feminine or husband-wife fit, it's subtle. The most common relationship pattern is the friendship model that emphasizes companionship, sharing, and equality.

Stereotype #6: Gay Sex Is Immoral and Gay Persons Are Promiscuous

This is a religious or philosophical belief and therefore cannot be rationally proved or disproved. Constitutional rights concerning the separation of church and state provide some protection in the legal system and in the workplace against discrimination based on such personal beliefs.

A percentage of the population engages in promiscuous sex, at least during a certain phase of their life, regardless of sexual orientation. The sexual behavior of gay persons who are in the closet, especially married persons, usually stems from their fear of discovery and the resulting need for secrecy and anonymity.

Related to the belief that gay sex is immoral is the belief that AIDS is God's punishment for gay persons. In fact, anyone can contract AIDS; it just happened to gain a foothold in the gay community first. Ignorance about the disease has led to the myth that people who come into contact with gay persons are exposing themselves to AIDS. However, AIDS can only be contracted through sexual intercourse or through the bloodstream. Therefore, casual contact in the workplace is not a threat.

Stereotype #7: Gay Persons Are a Bad Influence On Children

The extreme form of this belief is that gay persons are sexual perverts and therefore tend to be child molesters. Scientific studies have repeatedly disproven this stereotype. Each year a few straight and gay persons are convicted of child molestation, and sexual orientation is not a factor.

One aspect of this stereotype is the idea that gay men are looking for very young men and boys as partners. Research indicates that a majority of gay men aged 18 to 24 prefer a male partner who is older, a majority of those aged 25 to 34 prefer a same-age person, and of those older than 35 about half prefer a younger partner. It was found that the degree of emphasis on youthful partners varied with the social setting and reflected the diversity of the gay community. It also probably reflects the tendency of older men in the larger American culture to prefer younger partners (Harry and DeVall 1992).

Another fear is that gay persons will influence children and youth to become gay. This false fear is the basis for trying to bar gay persons from becoming teachers, counselors, and youth group leaders—and to deny gay parents their child custody rights. Since the preponderance of evidence suggests that sexual orientation is fixed by biology early in life, this stereotype has no basis in fact nor experience. No evidence exists that a gay teacher or parent could convert a child, even if he or she tried.

Related to the "bad influence" myth is the belief that gay persons shouldn't be allowed to raise children. Until recently courts routinely denied parental rights to gay persons. Some judges have based their decisions on the rationale that such children would be teased and stigmatized by other children and adults. Chief Justice Burger once said that the Constitution "cannot control such prejudices but neither can it tolerate them. Private biases may be outside the reach of the law, but the law cannot, directly or indirectly, give them effect" (Palmore 1985 p. 62).

Related stereotypes about lesbians as parents include:

- They don't care for children in maternal ways
- They hate men and deny their children access to positive male roles models
- Their lesbianism is a sort of illness that makes them unfit to be parents

New ideas about family life have opened up the idea of gay persons having an active family life that includes children. In fact, 20 percent of gay male couples have children, as do 34 percent of female couples. Research on gay parents clearly indicates that their lives are remarkably like those of heterosexual parents. Far more similarities than differences are found. Studies indicate that lesbian mothers do not differ significantly from heterosexual mothers in maternal attitude, self-concept as parents, attitude toward marital and maternal interests, current lifestyles, and child rearing practices. Lesbian mothers are more likely than heterosexual mothers to be child-centered (as compared to adult centered or task centered). There is no evidence that a lesbian mother is more likely to negatively influence her child's development, nor that the child is more likely to become gay.

What's in a Name? The American Psychological Association's (APA) Committee on Lesbian and Gay Concerns in 1991 adopted the following guidelines for terminology recommended to psychologists:

- *gay male* and *lesbian* rather than *homosexual*
- *gay persons* when referring to lesbians and gay men as a group
- *antigay prejudice* instead of *homophobia.*
- *bisexual* when referring to persons attracted to both same-sex and opposite-sex partners

Later, a couple of new designations developed.

- *transgender* when referring to persons who believe their physical gender doesn't match their emotional and psychological gender
- *GLBT* refers to the gay, lesbian, bisexual, transgender movement

The term *homophobia* is still used by many persons when referring to prejudice and discrimination against gay persons. Homophobia originally meant an irrational fear of same-sex eroticism, an appropriate use of the term. But in the 1970s it came to mean a fear or dread of gay persons, a prejudice against gay persons, or a general intolerance and disapproval of gay persons. The term *phobia* is not descriptive of such emotions.

PAST CONNECTIONS

During the past 50 years beliefs about gay persons have rapidly evolved from "They're mentally ill sexual deviants whose lifestyle is depraved and illegal" to "They have a right to express their sexual orientation and most are solid citizens." Antigay prejudice is more common among certain segments of the population than others, and it negatively impacts both the holders and receivers of the prejudice.

Milestones in History

Here are some key events in gay history.

- 1952 American Psychological Association (APA) classifies gayness as a mental illness rather than a choice to be "sexually perverted" and "depraved."
- 1969 Stonewall riots and first Gay Power meeting, New York.
- 1970 Gay pride parade in New York attracts 10,000 gay persons.
- 1973 APA announces that homosexuality is no longer considered a mental illness.
- 1990 APA states that gay persons cannot change their sexual orientation. They can choose to suppress it but pay a high price emotionally and psychologically. That choice is virtually always based on self-hate internalized from the culture.
- 1982 Gay Games are founded.
- 1992 President Clinton issues an executive order ending "gay security risk" as a rationale for personnel decisions and proposes removing the military's ban on gay persons.
- 1997 Ellen DeGeneres comes out.

Stonewall: A Turning Point

Stonewall refers to four days of gay riots that occurred in 1969 in New York in response to a routine police raid on a Greenwich Village gay bar called Stonewall Inn. Since then, Stonewall has become the symbol of gay resistance to oppression and gay empowerment around the world. To gay persons, it marks the birth of the modern gay political movement, "that moment in time when gays and lesbians recognized all at once their mistreatment and their solidarity," in Martin Duberman's words.

From Extremism to Reformism

Within months after Stonewall, a liberation movement emerged. Gay persons formed the Gay Activists Alliance, the Gay Liberation Front, and the Gay Academic Union—and other organizations sprang up later. Liberationists were political extremists who wanted to radically change American culture by changing or eliminating common concepts of gender and sexual orientation. They viewed "coming out of the closet," in which their sexual orientation had been hidden from public view, as an intermediate step in a process of releasing the ambi-sexual potential in everyone. They said that antigay prejudice is just heterosexuals' rejection of their own latent homosexuality or homosexual desires. Liberationists declared that for heterosexuals to move beyond such prejudice, they needed to confront their own sexuality. In summary, liberationists said to heterosexuals, All persons can go either way, gay or straight, and your rejection and fear of gayness are rooted in your denial that this is true for you. As a matter of fact, scientific research results since the 1970s have not supported the viewpoint that everyone is potentially bisexual.

Most gay persons came to see the liberationists as enraged persons lashing out at all straights, overreacting to the pain and rejection they had experienced as gay persons. Most gay persons were more attuned to the reformist movement. Reformists adopted a strategy of minority group politics that envisions gay persons as members of a subculture with its own needs, goals, and interests that deserve to be recognized and met within the larger culture. A major goal is protection from employment discrimination. Reformists view heterosexuals' antigay prejudice as a rejection of members of an outgroup, similar to ethnic prejudice. Change involves challenging heterosexuals' misconceptions about gay persons and prejudice toward them.

Cultural Breakthroughs

Gays have historically been rejected in all types of male competitive sports. The Gay Games was founded in 1982 in San Francisco as a gay alternative to the Olympics and has been held every four years since. By 1998, when the games were held in Amsterdam, over 15,000 competitors performed before 200,000 visitors (Associated Press 1998).

In 1997 Ellen DeGeneres, the girl-next-door comedian, came out as a lesbian and launched a sitcom television show in which she played the openly lesbian lead role. Gay rights groups hailed it as a turning point in American pop culture.

CURRENT PROFILE

In the past almost no one would admit to being gay, for obvious reasons, so accurate demographic information was impossible to gather. We know more now about how many gays there are and what their lives are like.

The 2 Percent Estimate

The Kinsey studies of sexuality in the 1950s indicated that gays were perhaps 10 percent of the population, but these statistics are now questioned. More recent extensive surveys (Laumann 1994) that are considered extensive and well-respected indicate that:

- 2.7 percent of men are gay
- 1.3 percent of women are gay
- 2 percent of all persons are gay

This proportion of gay persons holds true for all ethnic groups, economic categories, social classes, age groups, and other demographic categories.

Regarding gay couples, in 2000 less than 1 percent (0.6%) of U.S. households claimed to be gay households, 601,209 gay households of the total 105,500,000 American households (U.S. Census). Significantly more gay households occur in the major cities. For example, in San Francisco 7 percent of all couples are gay couples, and in the Castro neighborhood 32 percent, which is by far the greatest proportion of gay couples in the United States (San Francisco Examiner 2008).

Higher Educational Levels and Jobs

By the 1990s research by Beverly Green and G.M. Herek indicated that as a group, out-of-the-closet gays are highly educated and function effectively in responsible, well-paid occupations. They achieve significantly higher educational levels than the population at large. About 60 percent hold college degrees, compared with about 27 percent of the total population. Significantly more of them hold well-paying professional jobs and jobs that require creativity and innovation. The current centers of technological innovation in the United States—San Francisco Bay Area, Boston, and Austin, to name a few—are among the nation's most receptive places to gays (Editors 2008).

Lower Pay for Comparable Work

Researcher Dr. Lee Badgett reported on results of a nation-wide poll showing that gay men's wages were 27% lower than wages received by straight men of the same race and region who had comparable educational attainment and job positions. Badgett explored the pervasive notion that gay persons form an economic elite. After examining data from seven different surveys, she finds that none support this stereotype.

THE NATURE AND IMPACT OF ANTIGAY PREJUDICE

Antigay prejudice is the key barrier to gay persons being accepted in society. It affects every aspect of their lives. To understand antigay prejudice, you need to know why people prejudge gay persons, which people are likely to be most prejudiced, and the effects it has—on those who prejudge as well as on gay persons.

Why Are People Prejudiced?

People who hold antigay prejudice are likely to hold these beliefs:

- I believe in traditional gender and sex roles and feel threatened by gay couples
- A man should act like a real man, and a woman should act like a real woman.
- I feel uncomfortable with gay persons. I'm not sure what to say or how to act.
- Maybe they'll come on to me.
- Maybe they'll be jealous if I'm friends with a same-sex person they're attracted to.
- Maybe I'll get AIDS by being around them.
- I have to show disapproval of gays so people will know for sure I'm not one.
- Lesbians believe women don't need men. That really bothers me.

Who Is Likely to Be Prejudiced?

The people most likely to respond "yes" to questions about gay acceptability and gay rights have the characteristics shown in Table 12.1 as those most likely to approve of gay rights. They are compared with survey respondents least likely to approve. Gallup reports that age is a stronger differentiator than political party.

Table 12.1: Comparison of Attitudes toward Gay Rights

Survey Respondents Most Likely to Approve of Gay Rights	*Survey Respondents Least Likely to Approve of Gay Rights*
Liberal	Conservative
Seldom or never attend church	Strongly religious
Live in West	Live in Midwest or South
Urban areas	Rural areas
Younger	Older
Female	Male
College graduate	Less well educated
Democrat or independent	Republican
Unmarried	Don't personally know gay person
Good income	Males describe self as high in assertiveness, low in "feminine" traits

Gall pica up Polls 1978–2008.

G. M. Herek's research (1991) indicates that the major predictor of whether a church member will harbor antigay prejudice is whether or not the church has a fundamentalist orientation. A major aspect of fundamentalism is a literal interpretation of the Bible. For example, when discussing beliefs about gay persons, church leaders and members tend to focus on Bible passages that they believe condemn homosexuality. Critics argue that such interpretations ignore other core Biblical values, such as *"judge not that you be not judged," " love your neighbor as you love yourself,"* and *"do unto others as you would have them do unto you."* Others charge that Biblical interpretations vary widely, passages can be taken out of context, and almost anything can be proven by quoting the Bible. Also associated with antigay attitudes is how often people attend church services and the extent to which they say their religion is an important source of guidance (Fisher 1994, Loftus 2001, Scott 1998). As discussed in the chapter on Stereotyping & Prejudice, a person's primary motivation for religious affiliation may also impact one's antigay attitude.

Regarding male-female differences in attitudes toward gay persons, some researchers note that 1) women tend to express more favorable attitudes, 2) the most negative attitudes are those expressed by straight men toward gay men, and 3) overall, negative attitudes toward gay men tend to be more hostile than attitudes toward lesbians (Herek 2002; Kite 1994, 1996,1998). Another factor is that men are more likely than women to believe in traditional gender roles and to become concerned when people do not conform to those roles (Herek 1994, Jellison 2004, Kilianski 2003, Parrott 2002).

Finally, people who report having gay persons as friends or family members also report more favorable attitudes toward gay persons as a group. It seems that increased contact reduces prejudice, especially where such contact is seen in the context of "friends or family." It tends to increase a person's knowledge of gays in general, lead to greater empathy, and reduce anxieties about interacting with gay persons (Lewis 2006, 2007; Pettigrew 2006; Herek 2008)

What Does Antigay Prejudice Do to People?

The picture of prejudice is not pretty. When gay persons are excluded, ridiculed, or assaulted due to antigay prejudice, the impact on their lives can range from the mild to the devastating, from difficulty adapting to the workplace culture to deep psychological damage. The people who hold onto antigay prejudice are affected too. They typically experience more guilt, discomfort, and a draining away of joy than do less prejudiced people, according to research by M.D. Kite and K. Deaux. And they can cause conflict and discomfort for straight coworkers who view gayness as normal in a certain segment of the population.

> *Prejudiced person's thinking patterns tend to block their own happiness and zest for life—holding onto prejudice creates a joy drain.*

Is Antigay Prejudice Decreasing?

National opinion surveys suggest that people's attitudes toward civil rights for gay persons are often independent of moral judgments about homosexuality. While many people don't accept the gay lifestyle, most believe in equal treatment. Most, 62 percent, approve of policies that allow gay couples to have rights to partner health care, Social Security, and similar benefits. Most, 60 percent, are not ready for gay marriage, and they are about equally divided (49–49 percent) on the issue of legal civil unions Table 12.2 indicates how people's attitudes toward certain gay rights, including employment rights, are becoming more accepting.

One research study that tested people for level of prejudice and tolerance indicated that both tolerant and intolerant persons are usually willing to *meet* a gay person, though the intolerant ones were uncomfortable working with gay persons.

TABLE 12.2: Increasing Public Acceptance of Gay Rights

Issue	1977	1989	1998–9	2003	2008
Gay lifestyle is acceptable	34	47	38	54	57
Gay persons are born that way	13	—	—	38	
Upbringing, environment cause gayness	56	—	—	44	
Homosexuality should be legal	43	32	—	60	
For gay marraige	—	—	27	—	40
For guaranteed equal rights in jobs, housing	60	66	75	88	
For hiring gays as elementary teachers	27	42	75	56	
For allowing gays in the clergy	36	44	61	54	
For allowing gays in the military	51	60	70	72	
For allowing gays as doctors	44	56	75	78	

Gallup Polls 1977-2008.

Over 40 percent of gay employees in a Harris poll said they had been harassed, pressured to quit, or denied a promotion because of sexual orientation (Business Week 2003). But 85 percent of straight people don't even know that in 36 states an employer can legally fire a gay person based solely on sexual orientation.

Still, the increasing public acceptance of gay rights reflects a shift in social norms toward greater acceptance of homosexuality in general. More and more straight persons see antigay prejudice as incompatible with their personal value systems and are therefore uncomfortable with antigay thoughts, statements, and actions (Devine 1991, Ratcliff 2006). Because of this greater social acceptance of gay persons, more and more gays are coming out and even discussing gay issues with straight coworkers. As this occurs, more and more people have the opportunity to establish personal relationships with openly gay persons, a sort of virtuous circle.

WHAT'S IT LIKE TO GROW UP GAY?

Growing up gay usually involves a process of gradually becoming aware of gayness. In virtually all phases, gay persons must deal with the damage to self-esteem caused by rejection and prejudice.

Living through the Phases of Gay Awareness

Virtually all gay persons go through four distinct phases of dealing with their sexual orientation.

Stage #1—Identify Confusion and Denial

In the past most gay persons denied their gayness because of its devastating consequences. This involves blocking the recognition of same-sex feelings in a variety of ways. Some maintain these defensive strategies indefinitely and hold back their same-sex feelings, consuming huge amounts of psychological energy in the process. Those in denial usually marry and have children, making a valiant effort to fit into a straight world.

Stage #2—Identity Comparison and Recognition

The gay person pays more attention to same-gender attractions and to similarities they have with other gays. They begin to accept the possibility of being gay, but may feel alienation because of it.

Most gay persons say they first became aware of same-gender attraction before adolescence. In fact, nearly half of gay men say they were sexually attracted to males before they learned there were such sexual relations in the adult world. Gay adolescents who overcome denial will begin, by stages, to gradually tolerate the fact that they're having significant same-sex feelings.

Stage #3—Identity Tolerance and Experimentation

Next comes a phase of experimenting with same-sex feelings and activities. Some gay persons increasingly feel that same-sex feelings are normal for them. Obviously, parents and society don't socialize children to be gay, and gay youngsters are not prepared to deal with antigay prejudice and the wounding of self-esteem. At this stage the gay person may develop friendships with other gays and begin to establish a support network.

Stage #4—Identity Acceptance and Coming Out

The coming out process represents a shift in the person's core sexual identity and may trigger intense emotional distress. Denial of same-sex feelings may recur from time to time, but as gay persons begin to accept their same-sex feelings, they develop a sense of identity as gay persons. Ideally, this gay identity is successfully integrated and accepted as a positive aspect of who they are. Those who are able to accept their sexual orientation and "come out," usually join gay support networks and have access to healing acceptance within the gay community. Studies indicate that gay persons who are more open about their sexual orientation have higher levels of self-esteem and psychological well-being.

Dealing with Antigay Bias

A study of 4,159 high school students found that students who identified themselves as gay, lesbian, or bisexual are:

- More than four times as likely to have been threatened with a weapon at school.
- Nearly five times more likely to have been absent from school because of safety concerns.
- Three times more likely to have attempted suicide in the past year.
- Twice as likely to engage in risky behavior—such as having unsafe sex or using drugs before age 13. About 50 percent of gay students said they had engaged in more than five forms of risky behavior, compared to less than 25 percent of straight students.

The study was commissioned in 1998 by the National Centers for Disease Control and Prevention.

Gay rights organizations have been facing the issue of how to protect gay youth whose schoolmates attack them verbally or physically. Legal ground is being carved out to help gay students, using constitutional claims to equal protection as well as Title IX of the Civil Rights Act, which is the main law against sex discrimination and sexual harassment. Parents of abused gay youths are beginning to file lawsuits, and school districts that have not made a good faith effort to stem the problem are being held liable. Two states, Massachusetts and California, have passed specific laws to protect such students from harassment.

Dealing with the Damage to Self-Esteem

Most gay persons are socialized in a middle-class environment, yet the adoption of middle-class values traps them in antigay prejudice. Becoming aware of their gayness inevitably means their self-esteem is wounded. All around them, gay teenagers see their straight friends' sexuality being anticipated, embraced, and cultivated, while their own sexuality is not. Dating, becoming engaged, marrying, and having children hold joyous implications for others, but not for them. The result of this devaluation and neglect is often a sense of loss: loss of self-esteem, loss of initiative, and loss of the belief that they're entitled to a full life.

When gay persons use the closet as a long-term survival tool, they lose the spontaneity we all need for authenticity in relationships. The constant pressure to conceal parts of the self and the constant dread of being found out creates stress. Coming out is a great relief for gay persons, but the downside is facing direct antigay prejudice. This can lead to lower self-esteem, self-rejection, and new types of stressors. The major way most gay persons handle this is by joining the gay community and building support networks.

WHAT'S THE GAY COMMUNITY ALL ABOUT?

Gay persons who come out of the closet tend to migrate to gay communities in major metropolitan areas. Gay persons within this community have as wide a variety of lifestyles as the rest of the population. They have close friends in support networks that loosely form a gay community, as well as straight friends and associates outside the community. Singles may frequent a gay bar scene, while couples tend to focus on their relationships and sometimes on parenting roles.

The Gay Community

The gay community consists of many distinctive groups. Friendship binds the members of each group together in strong, ongoing relationships. Couple relationships may be stable and long-lasting. Noncouple members may be linked within the group and between groups by tenuous but repeated sexual contacts or by supportive friendships. As a result of these bonds and their relatively small numbers, gay persons within a city tend to know of each other. They have a number of common interests, values, and customs. Such communities have links to each other across the country and even internationally.

Most openly gay persons function in two cultures—the larger culture and the gay community—and may be considered bicultural. Most spend at least half their leisure time with other gay persons. A common pattern is to have two sets of friends, one straight and the other gay. Ethnic minorities who are gay have even more complexities to deal with.

Support Networks

Forming community with other gay persons is an important part of self-acceptance. For gay persons, it relieves their sense of being uniquely different and allows them to jointly form a set of beliefs about sexuality that counter the negative beliefs of the dominant culture. The main function of a gay community or group is psychological, to provide a social environment of acceptance and support, which gay persons cannot find elsewhere.

Gay Couples

A steady couples relationship is claimed by about half of gay men and three-fourths of lesbians, and many establish lifelong partnerships as they mature. Within the gay community, couple relationships are given a status similar to that of marriage. The two partners are sexually available to each other on a continuing basis, expect that the relationship will be relatively long-lasting, and present themselves as a social couple. Being out of the closet makes this possible. In fact, the gay promiscuity stereotype stems from the fact that being in the closet means one must indulge in secret sex whenever the opportunity presents itself.

Gay Parents

Many gay persons have married in hopes of overcoming or curing their gayness and having a "normal" life with children. Why would gay married persons later accept their gayness and come out of the closet? The most common reason is falling in love with a same-sex person. Once this happens, the married gay person tends to move from a covert, highly compartmentalized lifestyle, with all the surface appearances of suburban married life, toward an openly gay life. Divorce is a part of this movement, but most retain a commitment to their children and responsibility for them to the extent that the courts will allow.

In some states gay persons may adopt children. Regardless of how they become parents, almost all gay parents report that their children are straight and are typical for kids of their age and gender. Most have positive relationships with their children, try harder to create a stable home life and are more egalitarian, but otherwise are basically the same as straight parents, according to studies by T. S. Weisner, J. E. Wilson-Mitchell, and others.

Community Issues

Five issues that are especially important to the gay community:

1. Resolving the nature-nurture debate; i.e., are people born gay or do they choose to be gay?
2. Managing a gay identity in the workplace.
3. How to counter the myths and stereotypes that result in anti-gay prejudice
4. How to gain equal rights in the legal system—workplace rights, military rights, partnership rights, and parenting rights.
5. How to become accepted in the workplace, to come out of the closet
6. How to manage a gay identity in the workplace, once out of the closet

ISSUE #1: RESOLVING THE NATURE-NURTURE DEBATE: BORN GAY OR CHOOSE TO BE GAY?

Whether people are born gay or choose a gay lifestyle is perhaps the most crucial issue in the gay community's political struggle for equal legal rights. The major groups that are attempting to block gay political efforts use the rationale that homosexuality is learned and chosen. That belief supports their religious belief that homosexuality is a perversion and a sin against God and family values. They say gay persons therefore need counseling to help them become heterosexual or to abstain from sex altogether. The gay community vigorously refutes this viewpoint and sees it as their major barrier to achieving equal rights.

Recent scientific findings indicate that genes and hormonal events prior to birth are instrumental in establishing sexual orientation, though people can and do choose to experiment. You can better understand sexual orientation by seeing it as one of the layers of human sexuality, by seeing each sexual quality in terms of a continuum rather than in either-or terms. This will help you assess the arguments offered by nature theorists, who believe that genes and hormones are the primary determiners of sexual orientation, and compare them with arguments of nurture theorists, who believe people learn to be gay and/or choose that orientation. (Seligman 1994; Gonsiorek, Weinrich 1991; Gonsiorek, Rudolph 1991; Haldeman 1991).

Sexual Factors: Layers of Depth

Sexuality is most realistically viewed as having five layers of depth, the deeper layers being more innate, an unchanging part of us, and the superficial layers being potentially changeable, as shown in Figure 12.1.

Layer #1—Sexual Identity: Male to Female

The deepest, core layer refers to whether we identify ourselves as male, female, or transsexual. For nearly all persons, sexual identity, being male or female, is the least changeable aspect of their sexuality. All our forms and questionnaires offer only two gender choices: male or female. But we all know some people who seem extremely masculine or feminine and others who seem much less so.

Layer #2—Sexual Orientation: Gay to Straight

Wrapped around the core sexual identity layer is sexual orientation, meaning *who* turns us on—men, women, or both. A very small proportion are described as bisexual. Some bisexuals may be attracted to both men and women; others to either a man or a woman at any one time frame of their life.

Layer #3—Sexual Preferences: What Turns a Person On

Moving away from the core, we find the particular types of scenes, fantasies, or body parts that arouse a person. Sexual preferences can and do change more readily than the deeper layers of sexuality. For example, a woman, when she's 20, may be turned on sexually by men with dark hair, but when she's 30, men with red hair may be more attractive to her. A man, when he's 20, may be turned on by dependent women, but he may prefer more independent types when he's 30.

Layer #4—Sexual Roles

Even more superficial are sex roles, those ways of being and doing that are adopted primarily by males and those adopted by females. For example, a woman may shift from her professional career role to the wife and mother role as she returns home from the office each evening. A man may shift from football coach to family cook when he returns home.

Layer #5—Sexual Performance

At the most superficial layer we find the different ways that people behave when the time seems right for making love. Both men and women may choose from many behaviors that they think will

FIGURE 12.1: Layers of Depth in Sexuality

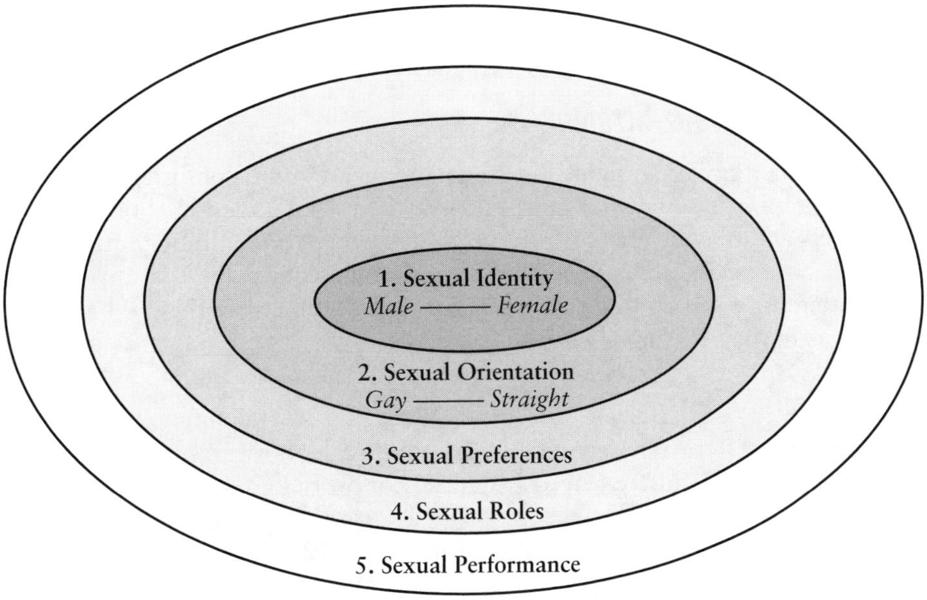

1. Sexual Identity
   Male ——— Female

2. Sexual Orientation
   Gay ——— Straight

3. Sexual Preferences

4. Sexual Roles

5. Sexual Performance

Based on the work of J.C. Gonsiorek and J.R. Rudolph, 1991.

make love-making more exciting or satisfying or comforting, for example. People can and do vary these behaviors regularly—from the way they flirt to the way they help their partner reach fulfillment.

Degrees of Sexuality: The Continuum Concept

All sexual factors can also be expressed in relative degrees on a continuum of intensity, from slightly-to-very male or female, slightly-to-very gay or straight, etc.

Sexual Identity: Male or Female?

We say a person is either male or female. But we all know some people who seem extremely masculine or feminine and other others who seem much less so. On the sexual identity continuum, people who are extremely masculine or feminine would fall at either end, with many people in between and transsexuals at the center, as shown in Figure 12.2. Being male or female, then, is not simply an either-or situation.

Transexuals

Scientists describe the miniscule proportion of persons who are transsexual as men or women who may or may not be physically indistinguishable from average men or women but who believe they're trapped in the body of the wrong sex. Some transsexuals act-out as cross dressers, drag queens, and female impersonators. Some choose to have sex-change operations and do in fact change their sexual identity from male to female or vice versa.

Hermaphrodites

A hermaphrodite is a person born with both male and female sexual organs, in varying forms or combinations. A "female pseudo hermaphrodite" is born with the XX female chromosome, with normal female internal organs but with "masculinized" genitalia. A "male pseudo hermaphrodite" is born an XY male with testes (usually in the abdominal cavity). External genitalia are usually female but can be ambiguous. (Sex 2003)

FIGURE 12.2: Continuum of Sexual Identity

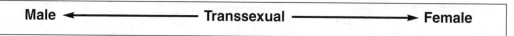

Sexual Orientation: Gay to Straight

We say a person is either gay or straight. But some people are more confirmed in their gayness than others. Sexual orientation is somewhat more flexible than sexual identity. Some straights are "less straight" than others and may be able to "choose" a gay orientation, although nearly all gay persons say that in retrospect they have always been gay and it's not a choice. Similarly, some gay persons are "less gay" than others and switch to a straight sexual orientation after they've had one or more gay relationships, although this is relatively rare.

The 7–Point Scale

The Institute for Sex Research devised a seven-point scale to represent the *continuum of homosexuality*, with 0 indicating exclusive heterosexuality, 4 or 5 predominant homosexuality, and 6 or 7 exclusive homosexuality.

On the sexual orientation continuum shown in Figure 12.3, the large majority of the population is at the straight end. At the gay end are 2.15 percent who are exclusively gay. In between are bisexuals and people who have had some gay experiences. For example, nearly one-third of all men, and about 10 percent of all women, report they have had overt same-sex experiences, most during their adolescent years.

FIGURE 12.3: Continuum of Sexual Orientation

Bisexuality

A small percentage of gay persons identify themselves as bisexual, being neither exclusively straight nor gay. Bisexual persons may well be born without strong tendencies toward heterosexuality or homosexuality. Some bisexual persons have both types of relationships during a given time of life. Others have only one sexual relationship at a time, and the sex of the potential partner could as easily be male as female.

Bisexual persons not only experience all the stresses and problems of gays, they may find themselves the objects of hostility from gays themselves. Gays may view them as people who are denying their true gayness. Straight persons may have the same negative stereotypes and judgments about bisexuals as they do about gays. In fact, bisexuals *seem* to choose their orientation, rather than be naturally pulled or driven by it and may therefore be denounced more harshly than gays. This may leave a bisexual person with no built-in supportive community except for other bisexuals, who may be scarce and difficult to identify.

Causes of Sexual Orientation: Genes, Hormones, Brain Differences

Back to the major issue of whether some people are born gay or chose to be gay: to begin with, how can we explain the fact that gays are found in every society, even though no known society socializes children into homosexual role? None has ever set up gay role models. For example, American parents, after years of teaching their little boys about male sex-ways and their little girls about female sex-ways, have traditionally been shocked and disappointed upon learning their child is gay.

If persons are not socialized into the role of homosexual, it doesn't seem likely that they *choose* their sexual orientation. If this is true, then persons who are predominantly gay can no more *will* themselves to become straight than straight persons can will themselves to become gay.

The idea that gayness is fixed before birth and is biologically based is the dominant belief among scholars today. Some research indicates a genetic basis for homosexuality. Other research points toward hormonal influences before birth.

Genes

Scientists have detected a "gay gene," as reported by Dean Hamer of the National Cancer Institute (Hamer and Copeland 1994). They do not claim that it is solely responsible for gayness, nor that any gene can dominate any behavior trait. They are saying that genes influence behavior through indirect and complex paths that require inputs from the physical body, the environment, and the culture.

Gayness in Identical Twins

Studies of the sexual orientation of identical twins point to a genetic basis for gayness, according to J.M. Bailey (1993). Since identical twins occur when the mother's egg divides after conception, twins begin life with identical genetic material. If gayness occurred only because of one or more "gay genes," then theoretically every twin who is gay would have a twin who is also gay.

Actually, about half of those who are gay have a twin who is also gay. This indicates that gayness is not entirely genetic. On the other hand, if genes played no part, we would expect that only 2 percent of gay twins would both be gay because that's the incidence of gay persons in the general population. The fact that about 50 percent of gay twins are both gay makes a strong case for the important role that genes must play in determining sexual orientation.

Hormones

Hormones secreted in the mother's womb during pregnancy affect the hormone balance of the child and whether that child will eventually be sexually attracted to opposite-sex or same-sex partners, according to researcher Martin Seligman (1994).

Brain Differences

Researchers are discovering striking differences between the brains of gays and straights in both men and women. Brain differences may be related to the increasingly convincing body of evidence that suggests sexual orientation results from fundamental developmental differences that are probably caused by hormonal exposures in the womb. Brain differences could be reflecting some genetic or hormonal factors that predetermine sexual orientation.

Size of Hypothalamus

In 1991 brain scientist Simon LeVay reported that the hypothalamus tends to be smaller in gay men. This part of the brain regulates the hormones, which in turn regulate sexuality, as well as such body functions as appetite, sleep, and body temperature.

Brain Responses to Sexual Odors

Other studies show brains of gay and straight people appear likely to respond differently to sexual images. They also seem to react differently to pheromones; i.e., odors thought to be involved in sexual arousal. However, these behaviors are not necessarily inborn; they could be the result of changes that occurred in response to experiences and behaviors.

Right-Left Brain Sizes

Ivanka Savic of Karolinska Institute in Stockholm and Per Lindstrom (2008) first used MRI (magnetic resonance imaging) to compare symmetry in the size of left and right brains of 25 straight men and 25 straight women with those of 20 gay men and 20 lesbians. Gay men's brains tend to be about the same size, like that of straight women. On the other hand, gay women's brains tend to be more like those of straight men, i.e., the right side is slightly larger than the left side.

Emotional vs Motor Brain Connections

Savic and Lindstrom then used PET scans (positron emission tomography) to examine how a part of the brain involved in processing emotions, the amygdala, was connected to other brain regions. They found that gay men tend to be more like straight women, with stronger links between the amygdala and regions involved in emotions. Gay women tend to be more like straight men, with stronger connections between the amygdala and motor functions rather than to emotions.

These findings need to be confirmed by more research, and it remains unclear how the differences might affect behavior. But the findings could help explain why gay men tend to respond to emotional situations more like women, and lesbians more like men and could even play a role in their sexual orientation. At the very least the findings support the nature argument of fundamental differences in brain structure, which would imply that sexual orientation is inborn. They suggest that something goes on during development that influences sexuality and the brain, which points to some early biological difference.

Other Clues

Scientists looking for physical clues to sexual orientation have examined everything from finger length to left-handedness to inner ear structure. Berkeley psychologist S. Marc Breedlove has concluded that differences in finger lengths are correlated to a prenatal basis for sexual orientation. Lesbians on average have a more masculine finger length pattern than straight women, reports Breedlove, indicating that they were exposed to more fetal androgen. Dr. Ray Blanchard of Toronto found a tendency toward left-handedness in gay subjects. Some scientists have found differences in the inner ears of lesbian and straight women.

Bottom Line: Human sexuality is complex, and scientists don't know yet how all the factors interact to produce a person's sexual orientation.

The Nature–Nurture Controversy

In 1998 President Clinton issued an executive order forbidding discrimination against gay persons in the federal workforce. Republican members of Congress began an immediate campaign to pass legislation that would undermine this order.

Full-page ads began running in newspapers throughout the country. They were sponsored by a dozen or so church and family organizations and quoted Republic Senate majority leader Trent Lott's statement that homosexuality is a sin. The ads urged gay persons to change their sexual orientation (Paid Ad 1998). The Ex-Gay Movement was born.

A *Newsweek* poll (Leland 1998) reveals that most people view gayness as much more flexible than do gay persons themselves, as shown in Table 12.3.

TABLE 12.3: Contrast in Gay-Straight Beliefs about Nature-Nurture

Agreed with the Statement:	*Overall Population*	*Gay Respondents*
Homosexuality is something people are born with, not the result of upbringing or environmental influences.	33%	75%
Gay men and lesbians can change their sexual orientation through therapy, willpower, or religious conviction.	45%	11%

Dr. Robert Spitzer, a Columbia University psychiatrist, conducted a telephone survey of 200 gay persons who claimed to have achieved a change to heterosexual attraction that had lasted at least five years. Asked why they wanted to change their sexual orientation, the large majority, 80 percent, cited both religious conflict and lack of emotional satisfaction from the gay lifestyle. Also, about two-thirds of the men and one-third of the women wanted to get or stay married.

Their main indication of success in the changeover was a lower frequency of looking at same-sex persons with desire. Still, nearly a third of the men said this still occurs at least a few times a month. About 66 percent of the men and 44 percent of the women said they had "good heterosexual functioning" in the past year (Spitzer 2001). Critics countered that these statistics do not reflect a change in sexual orientation. Changing one's behavior because of social pressure does not equal permanent change.

ISSUE #2: MANAGING A GAY IDENTITY IN THE WORKPLACE

A central career focus for gay persons is managing their sexual identity. Gays who are in the closet must deal with the stress of "living a lie," while gays who come out must deal with people's reactions, according to author R. Rich and others.

Gays in the Closet

Most gays stay in the closet. About 76 percent of gay men and 81 percent of lesbians who participated in a study said that they conceal their sexual orientation at work (Senate 1994). For those who haven't come out, vigilance is constant. They must devote great energy to pretending they have a lifestyle they don't or avoiding the lifestyle issue altogether. The fear of disclosure is ever present, resulting in anxiety and stress.

Counterfeiting a Straight Identity

How do gay persons manage to stay in the closet without raising suspicion? Many create fictitious spouses or opposite-sex lovers. Some complain about their status as a confirmed single, as someone unlucky in love, as a man with an old war wound, or as a woman with an inconsolable broken heart from an early tragic love affair.

Many corporate cultures make being straight and "coupled" a prerequisite for acceptance and involvement. Invitations to business-related events include mates or dates. If gays accept these invitations, they must make up an excuse for not having a mate, or they must bring an opposite-sex friend to keep up the pretense. If they shun such events to avoid the discomfort, important career opportunities can be lost.

Gay pretenders often complain that their social lives don't reflect their inner reality. Not surprisingly, they feel they're treated as if they are "someone else."

They pay the price of enormous wasted energy from the effort needed to keep up the pose and the anxiety over possible discovery. They also must cope with the ethical problems implicit in living a lie. Perhaps most crucial, they must deal with the feelings of isolation and detachment that result from not being "who you really are."

Dodging the Issue

Gay persons who evade the issue of gayness tend to avoid all discussions of sexuality and to insist that others respect their privacy. They withhold the sexual information that people usually exchange in conversations, information about wives and husbands, girlfriends and boyfriends. They try not to answer such personal questions without people *realizing* they're not answering. Strategies include changing the subject and asking the questioner a question, perhaps softening their evasions with humor.

They have no way of knowing what conclusions others have made about their avoidance of personal talk. They wonder, but never know, if others think they are gay. They may have no work-related social contact at all. Most eventually bump into a glass ceiling imposed by their social isolation. They just don't quite fit in with upper management.

Gays Who Come Out

Gays generally carefully calculate the risk before they come out at work. According to such authors as J.D. Woods and J.H. Lucas, when gay persons first come out, they experience great relief but must immediately deal with antigay prejudice. They do find strategies for coping, and virtually all say that coming out is worth it.

Calculating the Risk

Coming out is anxiety filled and liberating at the same time. Gay persons say that when their sexual orientation is disclosed (whether by choice or because someone guessed it or told others), their first response is apprehension and anxiety about their job and the workplace. They don't believe being gay affects their work performance but that prejudice against them does. Most believe their career progression will be slowed or blocked. In fact, about one in three gay persons who have come out say they have experienced some form of job discrimination.

As the awareness and coming-out process unfold, gay persons' natural tendency is to want to end the deception. They calculate the probable effects of coming out on their job security. Those who are most likely to come out have one or more of the following factors that provide some security. They:

- are self-employed
- have professional credentials
- work directly with customers, so their dependence is dispersed across many persons outside the company
- hold jobs that have concrete measures of success
- have unique, irreplaceable skills that are needed by the company or within the industry

Facing the Reactions

The most immediate reactions gay persons face when they come out can include:

- becoming the target of verbal abuse and nonverbal hostility
- increased stress levels stemming from harassment
- a backlash of negative attitudes
- being fired or demoted
- being heaped with effusive sympathy and support

Professionals may find their effectiveness compromised and their authority undercut. Teachers often feel that they must always be on guard. For example, they may think twice before giving a student a hug and saying "Great job," because it could be misinterpreted. Over 40 percent of gay persons who have come out report anti-gay discrimination from coworkers (Peeples 1985).

In the long run, they must still spend much energy managing their gay identity, and most of them must also deal with being a token gay in a straight work group. The most important strategy gays adopt is to build a support network, although being gay makes this more of a challenge. Strategies for managing the fact that they're admittedly gay include minimizing their gayness, making it seem normal, and offering it as an asset to the firm.

Minimizing Gayness

Some minimize the visibility of their sexuality with the goal of lessening their vulnerability. They fear that if they become too visible, or if gay persons in the organization appear too numerous, they will trigger hostility. They say there's a big difference for most heterosexuals in knowing about a gay's sexuality and actually engaging in conversations on the subject, seeing them with a gay partner, and especially seeing them touching, dancing, or embracing. Most gay persons feel safer behind veiled comments and insinuations.

Normalizing Gayness

Gayness *is* normal for more than 2 percent of the population, but most straight persons don't think of it as normal. Therefore, many gay persons use a strategy of subtly influencing others to see gayness as normal. They talk about their relationships and lifestyle in terms that highlight similarities to straight life, speaking of family, romance, civil rights. They speak of many of the same concerns as coworkers, such as making house payments, dealing with "in-laws," or finding a date.

Their purpose is to transform the unusual into the commonplace and acceptable and to give coworkers a framework for thinking about gay lifestyles. In doing this, they get away from the focus on their "different" sexual orientation so that others may see the similarities between gay and straight relationships and relate to them as people first. Just like straight persons, gays know that beneath their sexual self is a core self that is more essential and encompassing, a more complete and complex self. They have the strong belief: "Whether I'm gay or not, I'm still *me*."

Making Gayness an Asset.

A few gay persons are able to showcase their gayness as an advantage to the company. For example, they may highlight their multi-faceted connections with the gay community and marketplace and with talented professionals who might be recruited as employees, consultants, or suppliers.

Heaving a Sigh of Relief

Despite the hassles of discrimination virtually all gay males who have come out say they don't regret the decision. The most important result is an overwhelming sense of relief at being finally open, followed by reduced stress, enhanced self-image, and feelings of freedom. Gay persons who come out experience less anxiety and depression, have more positive self-concepts, and feel better able to fully experience their emotions and interests (Schmitt and Kurdek 1987; McDonald 1982).

ISSUE #3: GAINING LEGAL RIGHTS

Worldwide, there are at least eight nations that have national civil rights laws to protect all gay employees from workplace discrimination: Denmark, France, Israel, New Zealand, Norway, South Africa, Sweden, and Netherlands. In the United States gay persons are not included in federal Civil Rights laws that protect other groups from discrimination in employment, housing, parental matters, military service, and other areas.

Only a few states have laws that specifically protect gay persons from discrimination, and only six states provide for gay employees' partners to have access to the same benefits (such as health plans) that married partners enjoy. In most states they must face formidable barriers to parental rights. And gay sex was a crime in many states until a recent Supreme Court case deemed such laws unconstitutional.

Struggling for Equal Employment Rights

The most crucial issue, in the effect on gay persons' daily lives, is employment discrimination. The employment-at-will doctrine holds that employer and employee enter an agreement as legal equals because the employee can quit "at will" and the employer can fire "at will." In most states it remains a serious obstacle to worker protection from arbitrary and "at whim" personnel decisions. Table 12.4 gives a summary of current protections.

Federal Protection

In the past decade or so, Democratic lawmakers and Presidents have favored protection for gay persons, while Republicans have fought against it. Here are some highlights:

- In 1980, the federal government ruled that discrimination based on sexual orientation is prohibited under the 1978 Civil Service Reform Act, which covers all conduct that does not "adversely affect" work performance. However, this policy is not permanent "law," because in 2004 the Bush administration removed this type of discrimination from all federal websites and complaint forms.

- Congress has repeatedly refused to include sexual orientation in the anti-discrimination legislation of the Civil Rights Act

- Upon taking office in 1993, President Clinton signed executive orders banning federal government hiring barriers based on the old "security risk" stereotype.

- Clinton, at the same time, signed an order banning discrimination against gay persons in the military. Because of the controversy this order provoked, it was later reduced to a "don't ask, don't tell" policy.

- In 1998 President Clinton signed an executive order that banned discrimination against gay federal employees.

- Clinton also proposed the Employment Non-Discrimination Act (ENDA), which extends all the civil rights protections given other groups to gay persons and which must be passed by Congress before becoming law. The proposed law does not include the military, religious institutions, or small businesses with fewer than 15 employees. By 2008 Congress had not passed ENDA, even though 85 percent of Americans said they favored it (Gallup Poll 2003, LogCabin 2004).

- In 2004 the Bush administration removed information from government websites about sexual orientation in the workplace. Administration Special Counsel Scott Bloch announced that federal employees will "have no recourse if they are fired or demoted simply for being gay" (Barr 2004).

- President Obama is likely to reinstate the ban against gay discrimination in the federal workplace and has stated that he intends to change the military's "don't ask, don't tell" policy to make it more equitable and fair for gay persons.

State and Local Protection

Some state and local laws protect all gay employees, whether they work in private firms or for state or local government agencies. All-inclusive laws have been passed by 20 states. Nine other states have passed laws protecting only employees of state and local governments. Overall, then, government employees in 29 states are protected.

Protection in Private and Government Jobs

All gay and lesbian employees, whether working for private companies or state-local governments, were protected in only 20 states in 2008, as shown in Table 12.4. Those states were: California, Colorado, Connecticut, Hawaii, Illinois, Iowa, Maine, Maryland, Massachusetts, Minnesota, Nevada, New Hampshire, New Jersey, New Mexico, New York, Oregon, Rhode Island, Vermont, Washington, and Wisconsin, plus the District of Columbia. Some 50 additional cities and counties outside of these 20 states protect workers on the basis of their sexual orientation.

TABLE 12.4: Employment Discrimination Rights for Gay Persons, 2003

Type of Protection	Protection
Federal protection in all organizations	no
Federal protection for federal government workers	no
State protection in all organizations	20 states
In the other 30 states:	
State protection for state government workers	5 states
Cities and counties with laws to protect in all organizations	50
City or county protection for local government workers only	30
Civil unions	5
Protection for local and state government employees—Total	25 states

Source: National Gay & Lesbian Task Force, www.ngltf.org.

Protection in Government Jobs Only

Five states have laws protecting gay employees who work for state or local governments but not employees who work for private business: Alaska, Delaware, Indiana, Montana, and Pennsylvania. These states, along with the 20 that ban discrimination in both government and private business, bring to 25 the number of states that provide protection for gay employees in state and local government workplaces.

No Protection

In 36 states gay persons have no laws that specifically protect them from workplace discrimination. However, if they work for a Fortune 500 company, they are likely to find some protection because 95 percent had such policies in 2003 and 70 percent offered domestic partner benefits. The gay persons who are most vulnerable to discrimination may be those who work for small or medium size companies in these states (Business Week 2003; Human Rights Campaign 2005).

Pursuing Family Rights

Gay activists are fighting for basic equal rights for gay couples. They point out:

- Gay partners cannot file joint income tax returns.
- Gay employees usually cannot include their partners in their health plans
- When gay persons become seriously ill or die, their partners can't legitimately take time off to attend to the illness or funeral.
- When gays are hospitalized, their partners may be barred from their bedside by hospital staff because they're "not a family member."
- They are often denied custody, or even visitation rights, of their own children and are not allowed to adopt children in most states.

Domestic Partner, Civil Union, Same-Sex Marriage

At least three different types of laws are being used to address the family rights issues of same-sex partners: domestic partner, civil union, and same-sex marriage laws.

Domestic partnerships

Domestic partner laws usually extend certain employee benefit rights to unmarried couples; for example, health care and life insurance benefits. Most major U.S. corporations have adopted domestic partner laws. In addition some states, counties, and cities recognize domestic partnerships. However, domestic partners do not have access to most of the over-1,100 rights the state grants to married partners.

Civil unions

Civil union laws provide for same-sex unions. They usually give partners access to all of the legal rights and responsibilities that the state recognizes for married partners, but do not entail religious marriage rites. Such civil rights might include the probation of wills, state government programs such as workers' compensation and unemployment, state income taxes, and the laws covering parenting, separation, and divorce (Family 2000). They do not apply to federal law, such as Internal Revenue Service law. Five states recognized such civil unions in 2008: Connecticut, New Jersey, New Hampshire, Massachusetts, and Vermont.

Same-sex marriage

Same-sex marriage laws would be the same as other marriage laws. However, the United States has not taken the lead in passing civil union or same-sex marriage laws; in fact, the resistance and backlash to such laws are fierce. Most gay activist organizations believe that the best option for gay couples who want such commitment is legal marriage. They think that they should have exactly the same rights as straight couples and that any differentiation is a form of discrimination. While some states issue marriage licenses to same-sex couples, such licenses are not recognized by the U.S. government nor by many of the states. Such marriages are more accurately classified as civil unions.

Laws in 19 Nations

In the rest of the world, primarily Europe, at least 19 nations have legalized either same-sex marriages or civil unions. Belgium, Brazil, Canada, Croatia, Denmark, Finland, France, Germany, Hungary, Iceland, Israel, Netherlands, New Zealand, Norway, Portugal, South Africa, Spain, Sweden, and Switzerland. The Danish parliament, as pioneers, took the stand that you cannot make anyone homosexual who is not homosexual, and that gay marriage is not a threat to the community (Gay Rights Info 2005)

U.S. Laws—State by State

Regarding gay marriage, the issue of which states have legalized it is in constant flux—as local magistrates, such as San Francisco's Mayor Gavin Newsom make rulings, as state propositions pass or fail or appear again on ballots, and as state supreme court justices announce their decisions. In 2008, only two states sanctioned gay marriage: Connecticut and Massachusetts. The Connecticut decision by the state supreme court reversed the one-man one-woman limit formerly in place. Only two states had never passed a gay marriage ban: Massachusetts and Vermont. And 45 states had passed some type of gay marriage ban—29 states have bans that are part of the state constitution, and 19 have bans based on some version of "marriage is limited to one man and one woman." Three states have passed both types of ban through the years: Arizona, California, and Florida.

New York and Rhode Island recognize gay marriage ceremonies that have been legally performed elsewhere. They are among the five states that have never passed a gay marriage ban—along with Massachusetts, New Jersey, and New Mexico.

Domestic partner laws, which provide health benefits to partners, had been established for government employees in at least 18 states by 2005: California, Connecticut, Delaware, Hawaii, Illinois, Iowa, Maine, Massachusetts, Minnesota, Nevada, New Jersey, New Mexico, New York, Oregon, Pennsylvania, Rhode Island, Vermont, and Washington.

Regarding laws that sanction gay civil unions, Vermont was the first state to offer this option in 2000. This legal union gives gay partners access to all of the state-based rights and responsibilities of marriage. Since then, Vermont businesses have experienced a boost in tourist dollars because 80 percent of the licenses went to out-of-state gay couples. In 2005 Connecticut passed a similar law, followed by passage of a gay marriage law.

Backlash and Resistance

Alliances between certain religious groups and Republican politicians form the major backlash movement against various types of gay rights laws—ranging from family rights to employment discrimination, to gays in the military.

Family Rights Backlash

U.S. Roman Catholic bishops in 2006 advised gays to be celibate because the church considers their sexuality "disordered" (Gunther 2006). In 2008 various Mormon organizations, located mainly in Utah, contributed millions to support the California ban on gay marriage, which passed. The Southern Baptist Convention (SBC) not only condemns gay marriage but the entire gay lifestyle.

At its 2003 annual meeting SBC leaders called on its 16 million members and 42,000 churches to mount a massive campaign to convert gays into ex-gays by convincing them that they can become heterosexual if they accept Jesus Christ as their savior and reject their "sinful, destructive lifestyle." A pamphlet published by the church group states (Denominations 2008):

- The many Bible passages that are commonly quoted as condemning homosexuality are valid.
- Homosexual orientation is not "caused" by hormonal imbalance or genetic factors, but by an unhealthy relationship with one's parents.
- People can change their sexual orientation.
- Homosexuals can only lead moral lives by remaining celibate.
- Discrimination against gays in the workplace is proper in order to protect the family and society

Conservative religious beliefs about the gay orientation have become political fodder, complicating the "separation of church and state" principle based on the First Amendment of the U.S. Constitution. For example, the issue of gay marriage has been a key aspect of the "culture wars" that evolved during the presidential campaigns of 2000, 2004, and 2008. Backlash triggered the Federal Marriage Amendment, a proposal to amend the U.S. Constitution in 2003. The amendment would define marriage as the union of a man and a woman and could be used to overrule state or local protections for same-sex couples and their children. To become part of the U.S. Constitution, the amendment would need to be approved by two thirds of Congress and then ratified by three fourths of state legislatures (Human Rights Campaign 2005). This did not get adequate support, but religious conservatives flocked to the polls in recent years to support state bans on gay marriage (Gunther 2006).

Employment Anti-Discrimination Backlash

Laws making it illegal to discriminate against gay persons actually require certain religious employers to violate their personal moral standards. These employers would not hire or promote gay persons on moral grounds, but nondiscrimination laws would require them to do so on legal grounds. On this basis, antigay political groups have sprung up in many states with the purpose of blocking laws that establish civil rights for gay persons (Herek 1991; Paul 1982).

In 1992, for example, antigay groups persuaded Colorado voters to pass a controversial measure that prohibited local government from passing laws to protect gay employees from discrimination. This was a huge blow to the gay community because at least eight other states prepared similar initiatives. In response, gay rights activists got a court injunction against the law, and in 1994 the Colorado Supreme Court invalidated it. The Court said the measure singled out a class of people for denial of basic rights and thereby violated the equal protection clause of the Constitution. This marked the first time a state supreme court had validated gay rights—and the U.S. Supreme Court later upheld the ruling.

Coordinated Backlash

The Republican Party published a platform in 1995 that media analysts labeled "aggressively anti-gay" (Tuller 1996). The 2000 platform retained anti-gay language opposing civil rights protections based on sexual orientation and gay marriage. It also declared that "homosexuality is incompatible with military service" (Dunham 2000). To further their resistance to the Gay Rights Movement, some Republican politicians and religious groups joined forces to showcase the old idea that homosexuality is a sin and a perversion. They preach that people can choose to be gay or not, and they put great energy into urging gay persons to convert and join the Ex-Gay Movement.

Resisting Private Gay Sex as a Crime

In 2003, same-gender sexual conduct—private, adult, and consensual—was still a crime in 13 states, under sodomy laws. In many instances, sodomy was a felony punishable by up to 20 years in prison, but virtually never directly enforced As a practical matter, the laws have been used as the basis for legal bans on gay persons' rights in such areas as military service, marriage, child custody, employment, and similar areas.

The gay community was stunned when in 1986 the Supreme Court upheld Georgia's right to criminalize private gay sex by consenting adults. The Court relied on Judeo-Christian history and literature and characterized gay persons as a threat to the American family and not a legitimate alternative to traditional patriarchal family life. This in spite of the fact that opinion polls in the 1980s showed that most Americans believed that both gay and nongay persons have a fundamental right of privacy for adult, consensual sex.

In June 2003 the Supreme Court reversed that ruling, declaring that sodomy laws violate the constitutional right to privacy.

Supporting Anti–Hate Crime Laws

Reports of anti-gay violence were up 24 percent in 2006–2008, with reports of anti-gay assaults now averaging one each 36 hours. In New York City, for example anti-gay hate crimes were up by 32 percent in 2005 over 2004 even as other kinds of hate crime dropped, according to the New York City Gay and Lesbian Anti-Violence Project.

Speaking Out in the University

A tradition of academic freedom in public universities has provided gay students with more protection when they're on campus than most any other place. Gay persons on university campuses have a right to meet, create formal student groups, advocate gay rights, and socialize together. Federal and state courts have ruled that these are constitutionally protected free speech and free association rights. Courts have also required state universities and colleges to provide equal space and equal funding to gay student groups, as they do to other types of legitimate student groups. At least 100 universities have policies forbidding discrimination based on sexual orientation, and at least 46 schools have programs in gay and lesbian studies, according to the National Gay and Lesbian Task Force.

LEADERSHIP CHALLENGE: OVERCOMING SPECIFIC WORKPLACE BARRIERS

Your gay associates face many barriers in the workplace, most stemming from cultural myths and stereotypes. These barriers use up energy, drain productivity, and block profitable collaboration, so it is important for you to do your part in removing them.

Barrier #1: Prejudice and Discrimination That Drain Corporate Assets

Most gay persons remain in the closet at work. In fact 81 percent of lesbians and 76 percent of gay men fear they would be the victims of job discrimination if they came out at work. About one in three gay persons who have come out say they have experienced some form of job discrimination.

Talent Drain

Gay persons look for workplaces where it's safe to be themselves. They may move toward a "gay ghetto" within the company where they can socialize with others who are on the fringes rather than in the mainstream. Eventually most look to other companies that meet their needs and offer opportunities for growth. Gay employees are especially likely to leave companies that

- condone antigay prejudice, yet require extensive business-related socializing
- have vaguely defined managerial roles but stress social skills that assume everyone is straight.

Many gay employees leave such limiting corporate cultures to expand their careers in:

- smaller companies
- gay-run businesses

- their own business
- corporate cultures that treat gays fairly

This represents an important talent drain.

Energy Drain

Antigay prejudice creates an expensive diversion of human resources. Gay persons must learn to suppress ideas and actions that might invite suspicion, to monitor the way they dress and every word they say. Managing their identity at work consumes enormous amounts of energy, time, and personal resources. In prejudiced corporate cultures, closet gays must disguise their lifestyles or avoid the issue of sexuality altogether. Open gays must deal with various types of prejudice and discrimination. All must cope with high levels of stress that could be eliminated by a supportive work environment. The drain on energy and thus productivity is clear.

Productivity Drain

Prejudice also poisons work relationships and fosters misunderstanding. In its presence many gay employees feel forced to either deceive, disengage, or resign, taking with them whatever investment the company has made in their development. For straight persons, prejudice sets up limited behavioral boxes that may seem comfortable and safe but that stifle ways of thinking and behaving that might fall outside the boundaries. What a waste! The bottom-line result of antigay prejudice is to create walls of silence and mistrust, which in turn lowers productivity.

- Antigay prejudice stems primarily from lack of information about gay persons and the gay community. Everyone needs access to training that provides this information. You can help encourage your associates to pursue such training.

Barrier #2: Blocks to Spontaneity—Seeing Gays as Abnormal

Gay persons need to be seen as persons who are just as normal as straight persons. Sexuality is only one dimension of human beings. Although it is certainly a major dimension, time spent in actual sexual activity is very small in the whole scheme of things. Gay persons are as highly individualistic as the population at large, with the same variety of interests, abilities, and traits.

Gay persons' sexual orientation, by itself, is disruptive only when others despise them for it. When gayness is feared and despised, everyone may become fearful about actions might be viewed as symptoms of gayness. For example, when any type of same-sex affection and closeness may be viewed with suspicion, spontaneous collaboration among employees is inhibited. This is especially true for men, where standards of "manliness" compel them to remain relatively distant, competitive, and independent. Where men's tendencies to express their feelings or to nurture others might be devalued, men tend to be suppress them. Masculinity can become a burden when men perceive they must constantly take charge of situations, speak their minds, and view compromise and accommodation as signs of weakness.

- The solution is simple but not always easy to implement: *Accept gayness as a normal expression of human sexuality for some people* When gay persons are as valued as anyone else, people don't need to worry about appearing gay.

Barrier #3: The Sexual Double Standard

The Myth: The workplace is essentially asexual.

The Reality: Dating, engagements, weddings, mates, spouses, marriages, and children are discussed everywhere in the workplace, always from the straight person's viewpoint.

The Myth of the Asexual Workplace

Most people believe that ideally sex or sexual orientation should have nothing to do with the workplace, yet the symbols of straight sexuality are everywhere. In fact, personal and professional roles are not at all separate in most corporate cultures. The interactions there are colored by sexual possibilities, expectations, and constraints. Sexuality is often on display, explicitly or implicitly, in dress and image, jokes and gossip, looks and winks, fantasies and affairs. Sexuality is there in the range of persuasive behaviors we call flirtation or seduction and those coercive behaviors we call sexual harassment.

Actual sexual contact at work is rare. Yet we humans *are* sexual creatures, even though we're much more than that, and our interactions are always colored by sexual possibilities. We can't help but bring our sexuality to work. It often underlies such intangible assets as rapport, familiarity, charisma, and "chemistry." When we channel it constructively, it can be the source of intense feelings of personal commitment and loyalty to the work team.

The Sexual Double Standard

The myth of asexual workplace leads to a hidden double standard for expressing sexuality: it's generally okay for straight persons and not okay for gay persons. For example, it's okay for straight persons to discuss their sexual partners, such as husbands, wives, and lovers, and the children produced from such unions, but it is not acceptable for gay persons to do so. This is based on the belief that being straight is normal and desirable, but being gay is not.

Questions about marital status are a matter of course in professional circles, part of getting acquainted. When a man speaks of his wife at work, others interpret this as a statement about his social role as husband, not about his sexual performance as a straight man. People typically inquire about how he met his wife, how long they've been married, and similar facts. His sexual relationship is so socially acceptable, it's treated as asexual. When a gay man speaks of his male partner, the focus tends to be on "unnatural sex."

This double standard compels gay persons to remain silent while others talk about family life. Gay persons must mask and repress their sexuality while others do not. For example, many gay persons won't entertain coworkers at home because it's too risky, especially if they haven't come out. Some say, "I'd love to invite people from work to my home, but I can't because I don't know what their reaction to my partner would be."

One reason gay persons like working in San Francisco or New York is the tendency for people who live there to mind their own business. They simply view what others do outside of work as those persons' private business, which they may choose to discuss or not. Many gay persons say they love the indifference. It's so much better than judgment or pity. Because of their early experiences with censure and worse, their sexuality is always an issue with them, a perpetual threat in the straight world, something to be constantly monitored there.

Any kind of double standard is perceived as unfair by those it discriminates against. Gay employees, to feel as valued and accepted as others, must feel free to discuss their personal lives in the ways that other employees do. Everyone in the company needs information about the sexual double standard and how it affects gay employees.

- You can help set the tone by accepting gay associates' lifestyles. Your attitude will come through and will allow the gay person to feel at ease in discussing personal-life events as you and other co-workers do.

- When referring to employees' couple relationships in general, consider using the term "partner," which is inclusive, instead of "husband" or "wife."

Barrier #4: Walls of Silence That Deaden Creativity

Discomfort and avoidance of gay issues are typical in many corporate cultures. One danger is that people will get in the habit of not talking in order to avoid sensitive, sexual topics. This spills over to not talking about business topics. Such walls of silence tend to deaden relationships, and they deaden the synergy and creativity that can spring forth from lively interactions. They expand the productivity drain.

Like all forms of prejudice, antigay prejudice creates barriers between different groups of people, ensuring that they will have a distorted, insufficient understanding of one another's needs and talents. The bottom line result is an atmosphere of mistrust. Prejudice denies gay persons and co-workers the kind of trust and rapport that would enable them to discuss problems frankly. The result is a "spillover of silence."

- You can help to cure the prejudice and discrimination that builds these walls by being willing to openly discuss gay issues, by communicating regularly with gay associates, and by focusing on building rapport and trust.

Barrier #5: Treating Gay Persons as Tokens

Over half the gay persons in a recent survey said that a major reason they came out was their desire to educate others about gay lifestyles. Others refuse to come out precisely because they don't want to do "all that explaining." Some who come out find that being a symbol or token of the entire gay community means they can't quite be themselves after all, even though they're "out." They sense that co-workers are probing, testing their attitudes about gayness in general. Some token gays feel they're being dissected and examined, and that they're "on," performing, instead of just being themselves.

Token gays are likely to become lightning rods, targets for co-workers' attitudes toward the entire category of gay persons. Their mere presence may raise related issues beyond their immediate work performance. Whether gay persons are in the closet or out, fear of discrimination, together with impaired self-esteem, can motivate them to work harder and be better. Some suffer from double or triple stigma, such as also being a woman and an African American, and work even harder to compensate. But the pressure takes its toll, and burnout can be a result.

- You can help set a tone of acceptance. Treat gay persons as individuals whose achievements and failures reflect the person, not the gay community. Help educate others about the unfairness of viewing people as tokens.

Barrier #6: Hostile Corporate Cultures and Gay Ghettos

When gay persons perceive the corporate culture to be hostile, they may seek refuge in a safe job or position. They may find a protected niche in a large organization, stay out of the spotlight that goes along with high-visibility assignments, broad decision-making responsibilities, and major promotions. They may gravitate to departments that have a reputation for tolerance or in which other gay persons are clustered, sometimes called gay ghettos.

In ghetto-type jobs, the required skills are likely to be hands-on type with clear job duties, and performance can be measured more objectively in terms of sales figures or concrete tasks completed. Therefore, these jobs are safer, more secure and can provide a haven of tolerance in a larger, more biased organization. But comfortable niches nearly always have glass ceilings and walls all around them, in this case "lavender glass".

- You can help to eliminate gay ghettos by encouraging a corporate culture that values and welcomes gay persons—and people from all types of groups

Barrier #7: The Lavender Glass Ceiling

The "lavender" glass ceiling is what gay persons say blocks them when they reach a certain level of responsibility, so they never go higher. As managers and professionals move toward the top, reputation is everything. Careers are ruined by the perception that people are not "playing on the team" (are gay). Many say that the executives above them feel uncomfortable with bringing gay persons into the inner fold. Some executives rationalize that clients or employees won't accept a gay person at a high level, that relationships are more sensitive at that level, and that the company image might suffer.

Leading-edge companies don't fire people for being gay, but most gay persons are sure that gayness creates a lavender ceiling. And, knowing your job is safe is not the same as having a "warm, fuzzy environment" where people accept you as you are and therefore give you an equal chance.

LEADERSHIP OPPORTUNITIES: BUILDING ON GAY PERSONS' STRENGTHS

As a leader, you need to recognize the strengths that each of your team members brings to the organization and to build on those strengths. Gay persons bring many assets to the workplace that can be used in numerous ways. They can contribute to creative team projects, to the development of networks and business relationships that are especially valuable for the organization, and to connections with the gay community and marketplace.

Opportunity #1: Follow the Lead of Savvy Organizations

"Corporate America understands that fostering tolerance and diversity is important in order to recruit, retain, and motivate the best and the brightest," according to the editors of *Portfolio*. About two-thirds of Fortune 500 companies have policies that support workplace fairness for gay persons (Nolo 2004). By 2008 more than 80 percent of these companies offered health benefits and similar perks to employees' same-sex partners, compared to only 28 in 1996. Among the 10 largest U.S. companies, only Exxon, Mobil, and Wal-Mart did not provide domestic partner benefits (Editors 2008).

Along with health benefits for their families, many workers also get bereavement leave when their same-sex partner dies, adoption assistance or paid leave if they have children, and relocation assistance for their partners if they are transferred. "Corporate America is far ahead of America generally when it comes to the question of equality for GLBT people," says Joe Solmonese, president of the Human Rights Campaign (Gunther 2006). In fact, people who once were shunned, and then merely tolerated, are today being embraced by corporate America.

Big-name corporations were crucial in establishing the National Gay & Lesbian Chamber of Commerce in 2003. It began with IBM, followed by J.P. Morgan Wells Fargo, Motorola, Intel, American Airl and American Express. By 2008 the Chamber had 24,000 members. It certifies small businesses as gay-owned so that they can qualify for supplier-diversity programs at big companies.

Companies are also supporting state legislation to ban discrimination against gays. Microsoft CEO Steve Ballmer said, "Diversity in the workplace is such an important issue for our business that it should be included in our legislative agenda" (Gunther 2006). And companies as diverse as American Airlines and Chevron have programs to assist trans-gender employees.

Other companies, such as Proctor & Gamble, Kraft Foods, and Ernst & Young accounting firm have found new and creative ways to attract talented gay employees and to support them once on board.

At big companies, workplace changes regarding diversity often happen from the inside out. For example, gay and lesbian employees come out of the closet. They find one another. They organize. They enlist straight allies. And they take their concerns to top managers. Next, they establish a company-supported gay network, which typically meets in company facilities, uses the company intranet, and receives financial support. The first such network, called League, was formed by gay employees at AT&T in 1987. By 2008 more than 110 company-supported gay employee groups had registered with the national organization Out & Equal Workplace Advocates.

- Do you want to help your organization stem the talent drain? You can provide company leaders with examples of how other leading-edge companies are attracting and keeping talented gay employees.

Opportunity #2: Recognize That Gay Persons Have High-Value Skills

As a practical matter, nearly all companies must have business reasons for focusing attention on a problem and for spending time or money on solving it. Companies are most likely to combat prejudice when they have economic incentives for doing so.

Gay persons are over-represented in the pool of highly educated, well-qualified employees, possibly representing 5 to 10 percent of such workers, according to Robert T. Michael's survey. This is precisely the type of worker that's getting harder and harder to find and keep. Companies need a reputation for diversity in order to be able to hire and keep high-potential gay employees. So long as prejudice, and double standards block their career paths, the collective creativity, knowledge, and energy of millions will be lost to companies.

Gay employees have much to offer in business situations where a knowledge of the gay community is needed. They are likely to have an inside track on how to market products to gay customers, how to provide services to them, the implications of AIDS, and other business issues that involve gay persons. In addition, they can energize work teams. Most have experiences and insights that don't come with conventional lives—a cutting-edge sensibility, freedom from marital responsibilities, and a sensitivity and compassion for members of outgroups.

Opportunity #3: Encourage Company Benefits for Employees' Partners

To the gay or lesbian who is in a loving, long-term relationship, working for a company that provides benefits to state-recognized spouses but not to same-sex partners creates an atmosphere that devalues their couple relationship. Also, corporate antidiscrimination policies regarding gay and lesbian employees would almost certainly have a positive psychological impact on them. The change would probably trigger some negative backlash among certain straight employees in the short term. Top management support for an accepting, nonprejudiced environment, however, can produce positive results for all employees in the long run. Clearly, an accepting environment is likely to result in higher productivity for gay workers.

Opportunity #4: Promote Education about Gay Issues

Most employees base their opinion of gay persons on common stereotypes and myths. Leaders can provide educational seminars for all employees to inform them of the facts and to initiate discussions of concerns and of new attitudes. A frequent concern is AIDS anxiety, a key fear many people have regarding gay persons. The antidote is facts and figures. For example, AIDS is no longer a predominantly gay disease; it infects all segments of the population. It's not normally contagious and is spread only through very specific types of activities, almost none of which normally occur in the workplace. Savvy companies are building AIDS awareness into company policy, providing informative training sessions for all employees, and giving them written materials that explain the issue.

Opportunity #5: Help Create a Savvy Corporate Culture

A corporate culture is based on some basic beliefs and values of its founders and leaders that are accepted generally by most employees. These values are expressed in everyday rituals of communication and interaction, the stories that are passed around about the "big wheels," and the people who are allowed into the grapevines and inner circles. Values are also expressed in corporate policies and procedures and the ways they are carried out.

One example of changing the corporate culture is to change the belief that gayness is abnormal to the belief that it is normal for some persons. As a result, you and others in the company value gay employees as normal, contributing associates. In turn, you accept their family and community activities as normal and become comfortable with discussing them in the same ways you talk with others about their lives.

Gay persons most need to work in a corporate culture that accepts them as valuable persons, one that values nonjudgmental caring of one human being for another. They need to feel as welcome and included as straight persons feel.

Assess the Culture

All organizations benefit by looking squarely at the basic assumptions and beliefs that underlie their goals, values, and boundaries and questioning their fairness. You can use your influence to encourage such questioning and the adoption of needed changes in the corporate culture.

- You can encourage your associates to analyze the corporate culture to see how it encourages or allows antigay prejudice. You can jointly identify barriers gay persons encounter and ways to remove the barriers. You can find ways to make the culture safe for gay persons, and to open up new opportunities for profitable collaboration.

Heal Antigay Prejudice

Gay advocates say the workplace issue should not be one of denying sexual orientation but rather respecting all persons' rights to privacy and to a harassment-free environment. You can help your organization face the gay workplace rights issue. If your organization needs to move beyond antigay prejudice, you can help by encouraging specific company actions designed to reduce prejudice and eliminate discrimination.

- You can serve as a role model, setting the example of being as fair as possible in all your dealing with gay persons.
- If you're a supervisor, you can make personnel decisions based on individuals' work performance and potential, not sexual orientation, and encourage others to follow your example.
- Encourage company leaders to establish clear policies that ban antigay discrimination and specific procedures for implementing such policies.

Make it Safe for Gay Applicants

Gay persons need to "come out" at the time of hiring in order to be most productive within an organization. If they feel they must come in as closet gay persons, they may gain respect and credibility as straight persons in the organization, based on their skills, creativity, and competence. This credibility may be decimated if they later come out because coworkers may think they've been deceived all along and trust is shattered. The leading-edge companies that are attracting talented gay applicants have a reputation for accepting gay employees as normal, valuable contributors. They have created corporate cultures that reflect this belief.

- You can encourage your associates to adopt the belief that gay employees are as likely as straight employees to be normal, valuable contributors. This in turn will favorably impact the corporate culture.

Opportunity #6 Play to the Marketplace

Just as with the other diverse groups, the GLBT group buys goods and services. In fact, their disposable income is about 15 percent higher than average because nearly all of them work, most don't have children, their education level is higher than average and this boosts their income (Burford 2004). GLBT buying power for 2003 was estimated at $485 billion (Business Week 2003).

- You can identify gay employees who might be a source of creative ideas and contacts for marketing to this segment.

SUMMARY

Gay persons must cope with many stereotypes and myths, such as gay men act feminine and lesbian women act masculine, which is untrue. Gays don't cluster only in certain occupations, though they naturally gravitate to companies, businesses, and jobs where they feel most accepted. Gay persons tend to be better educated and to earn better incomes than average. People who associate with them are no more likely to be gay themselves than those who don't associate with gays.

Gay persons have a wide range of relationships, including long-term, committed ones, and ones in which gay couples raise children. Research indicates that children raised by gay parents have no major problems and are not more likely than other children to become gay adults. Gays are not more likely than heterosexuals to molest children.

The people most likely to accept gay persons are younger, well-education women who rarely or never attend church. Those most likely to express antigay prejudice are older, less well-educated men who are strongly involved with fundamentalist religious groups. Antigay prejudice has many negative effects on gay persons and on the persons who hold the prejudice, but there is increasing acceptance of gay persons in the workplace. In the 1950s gayness was considered a mental illness, which was an improvement over the criminal designation. But in 1973 the American Psychological Association took the position that gays are not mentally disturbed and in 1990 said they are not in need of therapy to change their sexual orientation.

Growing up gay is a confusing, painful process for most gay persons, and cultural prejudice creates self-esteem problems for them. Most initially deny the fact that they're sexually attracted to same-sex persons. However, those who come out are able to identify with the gay community, which is a healing and empowering process. The gay community is as diverse as the heterosexual community.

The core gay issue in American culture is, Why are some people gay? This brings into play the layers of sexuality, the continuum theory, the nurture theory, and the nature theory. The five layers of sexuality are sexual identity (male-female), sexual orientation (gay-straight), sexual preference (turn-ons), sexual roles, and sexual performance. According to the continuum theory, there are degrees of maleness or femaleness, degrees of heterosexuality or homosexuality, and degrees of every other layer of sexuality.

These aspects affect the question of whether some people are born gay or become that way as they grow up. People in the nurture theory camp think that people become gay primarily because of their environment, experiences, and role choices. Most conservative religious leaders adhere to the nurture theory, which, if correct, upholds their belief that the Bible condemns homosexuality. This means that it's a condition that can and should be prevented or cured.

Nature theory advocates think gay persons are probably born gay, even though they may not realize this until adolescence. Their gayness may be due to getting a "gay gene" at conception, hormone conditions in the womb, other unknown factors, and probably some combination of these elements. Most researchers tend toward the nature theory, which, if correct, means that it's perfectly normal and natural for about 2 percent of the population to be gay.

The struggle for acceptance in the workplace is a major issue. Gay workers must deal with prejudice and discrimination in every career aspect. They must cope with the sexual double standard that allows straight workers to discuss wives, children, and family events, while gay workers' personal lives are "off limits." This, combined with the "couples expectation," is especially difficult when advancement depends partly on social skills. Managing their gay identity is an ongoing issue for gay workers, whether they're in the closet or out. Pretending they're heterosexual or dodging the issue brings on the problems of "living a lie." Those who have come out often use such coping strategies as building a support network, minimizing their gayness, making it seem as normal as possible, and making their gay connections and insights a marketing asset to the company.

Struggling to gain equal rights is also an important issue. In 2008 there was still no federal protection from discrimination for gay employees who worked for private business, although gay federal government employees gained protection during the Clinton administration. Twenty states and the District of Columbia prohibited discrimination in both private and government jobs, Some cities and states required recognition of domestic partnerships and most large corporations now recognize them. Same-sex civil unions provide most of the rights and responsibilities that the states grant regular marriages; however, only 5 states recognized such unions in 2008. They were not recognized by the federal government nor most other states.

Case Study 12.1 Gay Rumors

You are a supervisor in the computer section of a large bank. One of your best computer technicians, *Diane*, has worked there for three years. She has been an excellent worker up to now. Lately, however, her productivity has fallen off and she has called in sick several times. The other day you noticed a cartoon about lesbians stuck on the wall near Diane's desk. You've also overheard some gossip in the restroom implying that Diane might be a lesbian.

1. What are the root problems?
2. What actions, if any, should you take and in what sequence (first, second, etc.)?
3. If you speak with Diane, what will be your strategy, approach, or attitude?

      a. If Diane mentions the cartoon and/or rumors, how will you respond?
      b. If Diane mentions only other problems, how will you respond?

Case Study 12.2 Clients' Comfort Zone

Carmen studies the file folder on her desk. As head of the Western Regional office of the Hartford Company, a lending and investment firm, she must decide how to handle a touchy situation. She's thinking about *Jayson*, one of her most productive employees. Jayson has been in the special customer department for two years, dealing with customers who have a net worth of $200,000 to $1 million. He has done an excellent job of handling these customers' needs to invest their available cash and to get loans for business or home-buying purposes.

Don, in the custom portfolio department, is being promoted and transferred, and Carmen has been considering who should take his position. Don deals only with customers who have a net worth of over $1 million. This is a different group, mostly older and more conservative than the customers Jayson has been working with. The only problem Carmen worries about is the fact that Jayson is a gay man. Carmen knows that at least one or two of Don's customers have made antigay comments. She's concerned not only with the possibility of losing some customers, she wonders if it's fair to Jayson to throw him into such a sensitive situation.

1. What are the root problems (key issues)?
2. If you were Carmen, what would you do?
3. If you were Jayson, how would you view this situation?

Case Study 12.3 Dale, a Gay Assistant

Dale Short is hired in November as an administrative assistant in public relations at Adobe Systems of Mountain View, California, a software firm. He considers it an excellent opportunity because the company has made a commitment to provide him with career development opportunities and to give him the backup resources he needs to carry out his projects. The resources include clerical help. Dale and his supervisor *Bradley* hit it off well, and Dale looks forward to a successful, rewarding career at Graphics Express.

    Dale makes no secret of the fact that he's a gay man—because he prefers to start off on an honest basis with his coworkers. Soon after he comes to work, however, one of his coworkers, *LaVon Peck*, begins making derogatory comments about gays to him. Dale tries to ignore these put-downs, but LaVon escalates them to direct insults about Dale's sexual orientation. The comments upset Dale. He discusses them with his partner, saying "It hurts to be treated this way in this day and age. I thought that in this city and this company I would be left alone."

Dale and his partner agree that the best response is to continue ignoring LaVon's negative comments and to focus on doing a good job.

The situation takes a turn for the worse, however, when *Katie,* who works closely with LaVon, brings some disturbing news to Dale. Katie says that LaVon frequently complains about Dale to others when she's in the employee dining room-lounge. Katie says, "Dale, I hate to be the one to tell you, but I think you should know. LaVon's saying you're unfit to represent the company to customers because you're gay. She says you tarnish the company and all of us with your perverse lifestyle."

This time Dale decides he must take action. It's one thing to put up with remarks directed solely at himself, but mudslinging in the presence of all his coworkers is more than he can take. He schedules a meeting with *Jeff,* the human resources director, and informs him of the situation. Jeff promises to look into it. This meeting takes place in early May.

In late May, Dale's supervisor Bradley is promoted. Dale shares Bradley's elation over the promotion, but when he hears who will take Bradley's place, his heart sinks. His nemesis LaVon will be his new supervisor. Dale decides to try to make the best of it, to ignore LaVon's hostility, and to do the best job possible.

By the end of June, Dale can see that his goals are becoming more and more difficult to achieve. LaVon is giving Dale more and more assignments, often menial and tedious ones, and makes it clear that Dale is expected to complete them by deadline without receiving additional clerical help or overtime. The final straw comes when LaVon tells Dale he can no longer depend on the help of Deborah, the clerk who has worked most closely with him in the past.

This occurs in late July, and Dale immediately goes to Jeff, the human resources director. Dale brings Jeff up to date on the situation, saying: "Jeff, you said you'd look into this problem of LaVon's hostility toward me. It was difficult enough when she was merely slandering me. Now she's in a position of direct power over me, and she's setting up impossible performance standards for me." Jeff promises to investigate.

In late September, Dale speaks to Jeff again, saying, "My work situation has become so stressful that I have great difficulty sleeping, and I've been putting in such long, hard, tension-filled days that I'm beginning to feel drained all the time. What can you do to relieve this situation?" Again, Jeff promises to look into the problem.

Now it's November. Dale has been at Adobe for a year. It's been months since he appealed to Jeff in H.R. for help and nothing has changed. Dale is trying to decide his next move. He feels exhausted, he's had a respiratory infection for six weeks, and his doctor tells him he must get more rest.

1. What are the key issues (root problems) in this situation?
2. If you were Dale, what would you do?
3. If you were Jeff, what would you do?

Case Study 12.4 Edna, Lesbian Employee

Edna has been working for Whizware, a Silicon Valley software company, for two years. She is 26 years old and for a long time refused to believe that she was a gay person. She married her high school sweetheart but the marriage ended in divorce after a year or so. Now Edna is living with her lesbian partner *Janice.* The relationship is good, and Edna finally feels comfortable about her sexuality. However, she has not told anyone about her sexual orientation except a few close lesbian friends.

Whizware has many liberal policies, including flextime, three-week vacations, and a relaxed dress code. Most of the employees are under age 40. Recently the company encouraged a gay support group to form. Edna was astonished that out of about 350 employees, 52 attended the first meeting. While this turn of events is heartening to Edna, the response of many coworkers is not. Most of what she hears is pretty nasty and hateful, with few accepting or supportive comments.

Having a divorced status has helped Edna to pass for a heterosexual. She says, "I don't deliberately lie, but when my colleagues talk about child care and how hard it is to find reliable help, I can safely murmur something about being glad I didn't have children when I was married. But at the same time I can be sympathetic to their problems, which of course I am."

The longer Edna is employed by Whizware, the more difficult it is for her to maintain her counterfeit identity. The workers tend to know a great deal about each other's lives outside the office. Edna knows, however, that most people are more interested in talking about themselves than hearing about other's lives, so she staves off friendly curiosity by showing more interest in the details of their lives than she actually feels. She says, "Most of my coworkers respect my privacy and assume I'm mourning my failed marriage."

Edna periodically travels to Vancouver and Dallas as part of her job of training clients in the use of Whizware products. Occasionally a colleague or executive will travel with her. Recently *David Southam*, Vice President, accompanied her to Vancouver. As Edna says, "He had a little too much to drink and definitely became too friendly. I had a tough time convincing him that 'no' means 'no.'"

Edna has never heard any office gossip about Southam being a womanizer, but she's concerned that he may seek revenge for her rejection of his overtures. If he does, and if her lesbian relationship with Janice becomes known to him, she would be especially vulnerable. Southam made several antigay remarks while under the influence and clearly was against the gay support program recently instituted at Whizware. After thoroughly bashing the program, he said, "*#* faggots, who needs 'em?" He also made several nasty cracks about *Jane Goodman*, one of the founders of the gay support program. Edna is terrified of the prospect of being regarded in the same devastating way by Southam. On the other hand, when Southam is sober and on the job in Silicon Valley, he's well respected. However, Edna wants to avoid traveling with him in the future.

Edna's partner Janice suggests that Edna could file a sexual harassment complaint against Southam, which could solve any future travel problems. This prospect horrifies Edna, who says, "I'm just gonna try to get out of traveling with him." She knows this might not be possible because one of Whizware's best clients is located in Dallas. The strategy for keeping this client satisfied depends on Edna's technical knowledge combined with Southam's customer relations skills.

1. What are the key issues (root problems) in this situation?
2. If you were Edna, what would you do?

REFERENCES

Achilles, Nancy. "The Development of the Homosexual Bar as an Institution." in *Sociology of Homosexuality*. Garland, 1992.

Adam, B.D. The *Survival of Domination: Inferiorization and Everyday Life*. Elsevier, 1978.

Allport, G.W., and J.M. Ross. "Personal Religious Orientation and Prejudice." *Journal of Personality and Social Psychology* 5, 432–443, 1967.

American Psychological Association. Minutes of the Council of Representatives. *American Psychologist* 30, 633, 1975.

Ashworth, A.E., and W.M. Walker. "Social Structure and Homosexuality: A Theoretical Appraisal." in *Sociology of Homosexuality*. Garland, 1992.

Badgett, Lee. *Industrial and Labor Relations Review*, July, 1995.

Badgett, Lee. Income Inflation: The Myth of Affluence Among Gay, Lesbian, and Bisexual Americans. National Gay & Lesbian Task Force, *www.ngltf.org*, 1998.

Bailey, J. Michael. Northwestern University, see *Archives of General Psychiatry*, March, 1993.

Barr, Steven, *Washington Post*, February 23, 2004.

Berrill, K.T. "Anti-Gay Violence and Victimization in the United States," *Journal of Interpersonal Violence 5,* 3, 274–294, 1990.

Berzon, Betty, Ed., *Positively Gay.* Berkeley CA: Celestial Arts, 1992.

Brause, Jay K. "Closed Doors" in *Identity Reports.* Anchorage: Identity Inc., 1982.

Buford, Howard, "The Gay Market: A Minimal Investment Can Reap Substantial Rewards," *The Gay Press Report,* 2004.

Business Week, "Coming Out in Corporate America," December 15, 2003.

Cahill, Sean. What's At Stake for the Gay, Lesbian, Bisexual, and Transgender Community in the 2000 Presidential Elections. *www.ngltf.org,* 2000.

Chronicle, The San Francisco, p. A-1, August 19, 1992.

Deaux, K., and L.L. Lewis. "Structure of Gender Stereotypes: Interrelationships Among Components and Gender Label." *Journal of Personality and Social Psychology* 46, 991-1004, 1984.

Denominations' Beliefs about Homosexuality: The Southern Baptist Convention and Homosexuality, *www.ReligiousTolerance.org* 2008.

Devine, P.R., M.J. Monteith, J.R. Zuwerink, and A.J. Elliot, "Prejudice with and without Compunction," *Journal of Personality and Social Psychology* 60, 817-830, 1991.

Duberman, Martin. *Stonewall.* Dutton, 1993.

Dunham, K.J. and R.E. Silverman, "Private Campaigner," *Wall Street Journal,* August 5, 2000.

Editors, *Conde Nast Portfolio,* "The Price of Prejudice,"10, July 2008.

Family, The. Human Rights Campaign, 13-14, *www.hrc.org,* 2002.

Firskopp, Annette and Sharon Silverstein. *Straight Jobs, Gay Lives.* Simon & Schuster, 1996.

Fisher, R.D., D. Derison, C.F. Polley, and J. Cadman, "Religiousness, Religious Orientation, and Attitudes towards Gays and Lesbians," *Journal of Applied Social Psychology* 24, 614-630, 1994.

Fortune, "Chicago Research Firm Surveys Gays," 45, December 16, 1992.

Gallup Poll, Homosexual Relationships: Gallup Pulse of Democracy. *www.Gallup.com/poll,* 2008.

Gay Rights Info, *www.actwin.com*

Gabhard, Paul H. "Incidence of Overt Homosexuality in the United States and Western Europe." in *Sociology of Homosexuality.* Garland, 1992.

Golden, C. "Diversity and Variability in Women's Sexual Identities" in *Lesbian Psychologies.* University of Illinois Press, 1987.

Gonsiorek, J.C. and J. D. Weinrich, eds. *Homosexuality: Research Implications for Public Policy.* Sage, 1991.

Gonsiorek, J.C., and J.R. Rudolph. "Homosexual Identity: Coming Out and Other Developmental Events," in *Homosexuality: Research Implications for Public Policy.* Sage, 1991.

Green, Beverly, and G. M. Herek, eds. *Lesbian and Gay Psychology.* Sage, 1994.

Green, R. "The Immutability of (homo)Sexual Orientation: Behavioral Science Implications for a Constitutional (legal) Analysis," *Journal of Psychiatry & Law* 16, 537-568, 1988.

Greenberg Research poll conducted for the Human Rights Campaign, November, 1996.

Gross, Larry, and S.K Aurand. *Discrimination and Violence Against Lesbian Women and Gay Men in Philadelphia and The Commonwealth of Pennsylvania.* Philadelphia Lesbian and Gay Task Force, 1992.

Gunther, Marc,"How Corporate America Fell in Love with Gays and Lesbians. It's a Movement," *Fortune,* November 2006.

Haldeman, D. "Sexual Orientation Conversion Therapy for Gay Men and Lesbians: A Scientific Examination" in J. Gonsiorek and J. Weinrich, eds. *Homosexuality: Research Implications for Public Policy.* Sage, 1991.

Hall, M. "The Lesbian Corporate Experience." *Journal of Homosexuality* 12, 9-75, 1989.

Hamer, Dean, and P. Copeland. *The Science of Desire: The Search for the Gay Gene and the Biology of Behavior.* Simon & Schuster, 1994.

Harry, Joseph, and Robert Lovely. "Gay Marriages and Communities of Sexual Orientation" in *Sociology of Homosexuality.* Garland, 1992.

Harry, Joseph, and William DeVall. "Age and Sexual Culture Among Homosexually Oriented Males." in *Sociology of Homosexuality.* Garland, 1992.

Herek, G. "Stigma, Prejudice, and Violence Against Lesbians and Gay Men" in *Homosexuality Research Implications for Public Policy.* Sage, 1991.

Herek, G. "Sexual Orientation and Military Service." *American Psychologist* 48, 538-5412, 1993.

Herek, G.M. "Assessing Heterosexuals' Attitudes toward Lesbians and Gay Men: A Review of Empirical Research with the ATLG Scale," in B. Greene and G.M. Herek, eds., *Lesbian and Gay Psychology: Theory, Research, and Clinical Applications* 205-228. Sage, 1994.

Herek, G.M. "Gender Gaps in Public Opinion about Lesbians and Gay Men," *Public Opinion Quarterly* 66, 40-66, 2002.

Herek, G.M. "Understanding Sexual Stigma and Sexual Prejudice in the U.S.: A Conceptual Framework," in D. Hope, ed., *Contemporary Perspectives on Lesbian, Gay and Bisexual Identities*: The 65th Nebraska Symposium on Motivation. Springer, 2008.

Hetherington, C. E., Hillerbrand and B.D. Etringer. "Career Counseling with Gay Men," *Journal of Counseling and Development* 67, 452-454, 1989.

Human Rights Campaign, *www.hrc.org*

Jellison, W.A., A.R. McConnell and S. Gabriel, "Implicit and Explicit Measures of Sexual Orientation Attitudes: Ingroup Preferences and Related Behaviors and Beliefs among Gay and Straight Men," *Personality and Social Psychology Bulletin* 30, 629-642, 2004.

Kennedy, E.L., and M.D. Davis. *Boots of Leather, Slippers of Gold: The History of a Lesbian Community.* Routledge, 1993.

Kilianski, S.E. "Explaining Heterosexual Men's Attitudes toward Women and Gay Men: The Theory of Exclusively Masculine Identity," *Psychology of Men and Masculinity* 4, 37-56.

Kite, M.E., and K. Deaux. "Attitudes Toward Homosexuality." *Basic and Applied Social Psychology* 7, 137-162, 1986.

Kite, M.E. "Age, Gender, and Employment," Paper presented at the meeting of the American Psychological Association, Boston, 1990.

Kite, M.E., "When Perceptions Meet Reality: Individual Differences in Reactions to Lesbians and Gay Men," in B. Greene and G.M. Herek, eds., *Lesbian and Gay Psychology: Theory, Research, and Clinical Applications*, 25-53. Sage, 1994.

Kite, M.E. and B.E. Whitley, Jr. "Sex Differences in Attitudes toward Homosexual Persons, Behaviors, and Civil Rights: A Meta-Analysis," *Personality and Social Psychology Bulletin* 22, 336-353, 1996.

Kite, M.E. and B.E. Whitley, Jr. "Do Heterosexual Women and Men Differ in Their Attitudes toward Homosexuality? A Conceptual and Methodological Analysis," in G.M. Herek, ed., *Stigma and Sexual Orientation: Understanding Prejudice against Lesbians, Gay Men, and Bisexuals*, 39-61. Sage 1998.

Laumann, Edward O., JH Gagnon, RT Michael, Stuart Michaels. *The Social organization of sexuality in the United States.* University of Chicago Press, 1994.

Leland, John and Mark Miller, "Convert?" *Newsweek*: 47-49, August 17, 1998.

LeVay, Simon, "A Difference in Hypothalmic Structure between Heterosexual and Homosexual Men," *Science*, 140, 9, 134, 1991.

Lewis, G.B. "Personal Relationships and Support for Gay Rights," paper at meeting of American Political Science Association, Philadelphia, 2006.

Lewis, G.B. "The Friends and Family Plan: Knowing LGBs and Supporting Gay Rights," paper at meeting of American Psychological Association, San Francisco, 2007.

Loftus, J. "America's Liberalization in Attitudes toward Homosexuality," *American Sociological Review* 66, 762-782, 2001.

LogCabin, "LCR Issues: Workplace Discrimination," *LogCabin.org*, March 2004.

Loznoff, Maurice, and W.A. Westley. "The Homosexual Community" *in Sociology of Homosexuality*. Garland, 1992.

Marcus, Eric. *Is It a Choice?* HarperCollins, 1993.

McDonald A.P., Jr., J. Huggins, S. Young, and R.A. Swanson. "Attitudes Toward Homosexuality." *Journal of Consulting and Clinical Psychology* 40, 161, 1973.

McDonald, G.J. "Individual Differences in the Coming Out Process for Gay Men." *Journal of Homosexuality* 3, 47-60, 1982.

McNaught, B. *Gay Issues in the Workplace*. St. Martin's Press, 1993.

McWhirter, D.P., and A.M. Mattison. *The Male Couple: How Relationships Develop*. Prentice-Hall, 1984.

Michael, Robert T., J.H. Gagnon, E.O. Laumann, and G. Kolata. *Sex in America: A Definitive Survey*. Little, Brown & Co., 1995.

National Gay & Lesbian Task Force, *www.ngltf.org*, 1999, 2000, 2003.

Newman, B.S. "The Relative Importance of Gender Role Attitudes to Male and Female Attidues toward Lesbians," *Sex Roles* 21, 451-465, 1989.

NOLO, "Sexual Orientation Discrimination in the Workplace," nolo.com, March 2004.

O'Leary, K.D., and R.E. Emery. "Marital Discord and Child Behavior Problems," in *Middle Childhood: Development and Dysfunction*. University Park Press, 1984.

Overlooked Opinions, a Chicago market research firm, in a 1991 study.

Paid Ad (see as an example), *San Francisco Examiner*, A-22, August 15, 1998.

Palmore, 466 U.S. at 433. For an application of Palmore in a lesbian mother case, see S.N.E. v. R.L.B. 699 P.2d 875 (Alaska, 1985).

Parrott, D.J., H.E. Adams and A. Zeichner, "Homophobia: Personality and Attitudinal Correlates," *Personality and Individual Differences* 32, 1269-1278.

Patterson, C.J. "Children of the Lesbian Baby Boom" in *Lesbian and Gay Psychology*. Sage, 1994.

Paul, W. "Minority Status for Gay People: Majority Reactions and Social Context," in *Homosexuality: Social, Psychological, and Biological Issues*. Sage, 1982.

Peeples, A Survey of Perceptions of Civil Opportunity Aming Gays & Lesbians in Richmond, Virginia (Research Task Force & Commission on Human Relations, City of Richmond, 1985) as cited in *Comstock*, p.53.

Peplau, L.A., and S.D. Cochran. "A Relational Perspective on Homosexuality" in *Homosexuality- Heterosexuality: Concepts of Sexual Orientation*. Oxford University Press, 1990.

Peplau, Letitia Anne. "Lesbian and Gay Relationships" in *Homosexuality: Research Implications for Public Policy*. Sage, 1991.

Pettigrew, T.F. and L.R. Tropp, "A Meta-Analytic Test of Intergroup Contact Theory," *Journal of Personality and Social Psychology* 90, 751=783, 2006.

Pollack, S., and J. Vaughn. *Politics of the Heart: A Lesbian Parenting Anthology*. Firebrand, 1987.

Ponse, B. *Identities in the Lesbian World*. Greenwood,1978.

Rafkin, L. *Different Mothers: Sons and Daughters of Lesbians Talk About Their Lives. Cleis*, 1990.

Ratcliff, J.J., G.D. Lassiter, K.D. Markman, and C.J. Snyder, "Gender Differences in Attitudes toward Gay Men and Lesbians: The Role of Motivation to Respond without Prejudice," *Personality and Social Psychology Bulletin* 32, 1325-1338, 2006.

Rich, R. "Compulsory Heterosexuality and Lesbian Existence." *Signs* 5, 1990, 631-660.

Rothblum, E.D. "Introduction: Lesbianism as a Model of a Positive Lifestyle for Women." *Women and Therapy* 8, 1-12, 1988.

Rutledge, Leigh W. *The Gay Decades*. Penguin Books, 1994.

Savic, Ivanka and Per Lindstrom, "Pet and MRI Show Differences in Cerebral Assemytry and Functional Connectivity between Homo- and Heterosexual Subjects," Proceedings of National Academy of Sciences 105:9403-9408, June 2008.

Scandura, T.A. "Mentorship and Career Mobility." *Journal of Organizational Behavior* 13, 169-174, 1992.

Schmitt, Patrick J., and L.A. Kurdek. "Personality Correlates of Positive Identity and Relationship Involvement in Gay Men." *Journal of Homosexuality* 13, 4, 1987.

Schneider, B.E. "Coming Out at Work," *Work and Occupations* 13, 463-487, 1987.

Scott, J. "Changing Attitudes to Sexual Morality: A Cross-National Comparison," *Sociology* 32, 815-845, 1998.

Seligman, Martin. *What You Can Change and What You Can't*. Knopf, 1994.

Senate ENDA hearing, 103rd Congress, Anthony Carnevale cited a 1992 study conducted in Philadelphia, 1994.

"Sex Differentiation Disorders," *Hermaphrodite Education and Listening Post*, www.jax-inter.net/~help/sexdiff.html, April 2003.

Signorile, Michelangelo. *Queer in America*. Doubleday, 1993.

Silverstein, C. "Psychological and Medical Treatments of Homosexuality" in *Homosexuality: Research Implications for Public Policy*. Sage, 1991.

Spitzer, Robert. Study of ex-gay persons, announced at the annual meeting of the American Psychiatric Association, May 9, 2001.

Stein, Rob, "Researchers Disagree on What 'Gay Brain' Study Results Mean," *San Francisco Chronicle*, June 24, 2008.

Tuller, Davis, "New Wave of Outings in Politics," *San Francisco Chronicle*, A-1, October 26, 1996.

Weisner, T.S., and J.E. Wilson-Mitchell. "Nonconventional Family Lifestyles and Sextyping in Six Year Olds." *Child Development*, 61, 1915-1933, 1990.

Whitam, Frederick L. "The Homosexual Role: A Reconsideration" in *Sociology of Homosexuality*. Garland, 1992.

Wishik, Heather and Carol Pierce. *Sexual Orientation and Identity*. New Dynamics, 1995

Woods, J.D., and J.H. Lucas. *The Corporate Closet*. The Free Press, 1993.

Yankelovich Partners. Income survey, 1994.

RESOURCES

Advocate, The, a national magazine

American Civil Liberties Union, www.aclu.org

American Psychological Association, www.apa.org/pi/lgbc/

Campus Pride – building future leaders and more gay-friendly campuses www.campupride.org

Center for Lesbian and Gay Studies, www.clag.org

Gay, Lesbian & Straight Education Network (about schools), www.glsen.org

Gay Rights Info, www.actwin.com

GLAAD, Gay & Lesbian Alliance Against Defamation, www.glaad.org

Human Rights Campaign www.hrc.org/work

National Gay & Lesbian Task Force, www.ngltf.org

Pride Agenda, www.prideagenda.org

Religious Tolerance www.religioustolerance.org

CHAPTER 13

Working with Persons with Disabilities

Persons with disabilities are in a different situation, not necessarily a less fortunate one—in the deeper, eternal sense.
Carolyn Vash

About one in every 19 persons you're likely to encounter in the workplace, 19 percent of Americans, is a person with a disability. In 2000 about 50 million Americans had disabilities that fall under the Americans with Disabilities Act (ADA) definition: "a physical or mental impairment that substantially limits one or more of the major life activities." About 33 million are considered severely disabled.

Strictly speaking, everyone has some type of impairment, perhaps a missing toe or finger, mild near-sightedness, or difficulty learning advanced mathematics. The people classified as disabled are impaired in a major life function. For some, the difference this makes in their lives is relatively minor; for others, such as quadriplegics, it's enormous.

A major key to building profitable relationships is to learn about an associate's community and get a feel for his or her background. The more skilled you become at interpreting an individual's actions against the backdrop of his or her background, the greater success both of you can achieve through working together. Keep in mind that there are many types disability and people deal with their disabilities in their own ways. Avoid the temptation to use this lifestyle information to form new rigid categories.

As you explore the following topics, designed to help you understand what it's like to be a person with a disability, try to begin seeing situations as you think a person with a disability would view them. Specifically, you learn:

- How typical myths about persons with disabilities compare with reality
- Major reasons why people devalue and exclude persons with disabilities
- How the current situation is connected to certain historical events
- What it is like to be a person with a disability
- Key facts about the Independent Living Movement
- What you should know about the Americans with Disabilities Act (ADA)

- Barriers to career success for persons with disabilities and how to break through these barriers.
- Assets that persons with disabilities bring to your company and how to use those assets to create win-win successes.

To raise your awareness about how you perceive persons with disabilities, and to determine what you already know about them, complete Self-Awareness Activities 13.1 and 13.2.

Man with a Disability
Courtesy of Warren Morgan/Corbis Images.

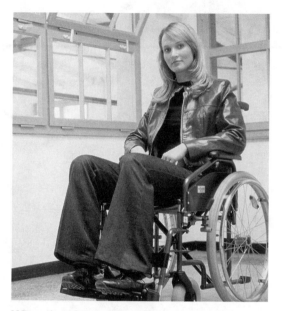

Woman with a Disability
Courtesy of A. Inden/zefa/Corbis Images.

Self-Awareness Activity 13.1: What Do You Believe about Persons with Disabilities?

Purpose:

- to get in touch with your beliefs and stereotypes about this group of people
- to experience how judgmental beliefs affect your thinking and feeling processes
- to experience the ways in which your beliefs create your reality regarding other persons, even before you have any interaction with them.

Part I. What Do You Believe about Women with Disabilities?
Step 1. Associations

Relax as deeply as you can.

- Close your eyes for a moment and take a few deep breaths.
- Now focus on the picture that symbolizes "woman with disability"
- Imagine that you are this woman. Be woman with disability.
- Notice any resistance to being this person—and any willingness.

- Notice words, images, thoughts, and feelings that come to mind as you are "seeing and being this woman."

Step 2. Negative Associations

- Next, as you focus on the picture, allow negative opinions to come up, perhaps some that you typically hold about women with disabilities.
- Notice your *thoughts* as you see the person in this negative way. What *feelings?*

Step 3. Positive Associations

- Now, still focusing, allow positive opinions to come up, perhaps some that you typically hold about women with disabilities.
- Notice your *thoughts* as you see the person in this negative way. What *feelings?*

Step 4. Insights and Writeup

- Now review this experience and write about it.
- When you first saw the picture, what thoughts and feelings came up? These may reflect your deepest responses to people from this group.
- Think about the differences in your thoughts and feelings when you consciously held a positive opinion versus a negative opinion.
- Write a few sentences about your feelings, thoughts, and insights.

Part II. Experimenting with Opinions Men with Disabilities

Repeat the phases and steps in part I, this time focusing on the image of a man with a disability.

Self-Awareness Activity 13.2: What Do You Know about Persons with Disabilities?

Purpose: To see what you know about the issues covered in this chapter.

Instructions: Determine whether you think the following statements are basically true or false—and think about why. The answers will emerge in this chapter, and the summary at the end of the chapter focuses on these issues.

1. The definition of a person with a disability is "anyone with a physical impairment that limits the range of tasks he or she can accomplish."
2. Employees with disabilities tend to have better records of punctuality, attendance, and turnover, but they're somewhat less productive than other employees.
3. Society has always attempted to rehabilitate and integrate persons with disabilities.
4. The large majority of persons with disabilities, even those with severe disabilities, can become independent and productive.
5. Only about 30 percent of persons with disabilities are currently employed.
6. The federal Americans with Disabilities Act requires employers to make special accommodation for the disabled, which is proving very costly for employers.
7. Job applicants with disabilities must provide a medical history to potential employers.
8. If you see that a person with a disability needs help, give it at once.

MYTHS AND REALITIES

Persons with disabilities say the limitations of their disability are not nearly as devastating as the myths, stereotypes, devaluation, and exclusion they experience from the people they encounter.

Myth #1: Persons with severe disabilities are childlike, dependent, and in need of charity or pity.

In fact, many persons with severe disabilities have a great deal to contribute and are able to work and to manage their own lives through the Independent Living Movement, which you'll learn about later.

A related myth is that a disability is a constantly frustrating tragedy. In fact, many persons with disabilities say that a disability need only be an inconvenience *if* it is dealt with as an inconvenience. Developing intelligent accommodations is one way to accomplish this. Although severe disabilities pose huge challenges, even they can be viewed primarily as a challenge to be overcome rather than a hopeless tragedy. For example, world-renowned physicist Stephen Hawking has stated that his disabling condition left him with not much to do but use his mind creatively and productively. Carolyn Vash, who has an impairment, suggests that we view her as being in a *different* situation, not necessarily a *less-fortunate* one—in the deeper, eternal sense.

Myth #2: Persons with disabilities are unable to lead normal lives.

Most persons with disabilities can live relatively normal lives and want to do so. Most are impaired in only one functional area. They tend to compensate for their impairment in numerous ways. They're able to do most things as well as anyone and usually can do some things better. Many people with disabilities view their limitations as a fact of life but go to work and participate as actively in society as they can. Persons with disabilities are increasingly better educated, with 75 percent completing high school in 1994, compared with 60 percent in 1986 (*Business Week* 1994).

Myth #3: Persons with disabilities can only do menial or entry–level jobs, and most don't want to work.

In fact, persons with disabilities are successfully employed at almost all levels in nearly every field. More than 90 percent of net new job openings are in information-intensive and service occupations, and at least 90 percent of persons with disabilities are capable of filling such jobs.

Among people between the ages of 16 and 64 who say they're able to work, about half of those with disabilities are employed, compared to 67 percent of the general population. (U.S. Census 2005, N.O.D. 2002). Of those who are not working, Harris Polls indicates that two-thirds say they want to work (Business Week 2000). In fact, most want to work, regardless of the extent of their impairment, and see work as a major route to self-fulfillment. They want to find work that draws on their skills and talents and helps them live a more abundant life. Dissatisfaction with life is reported by four times as many adults classified as having disabilities as other adults. This dissatisfaction is related to their desire to work and to live a normal life.

Myth #4: Employees with disabilities create safety risks, increase costs, and are less flexible and productive than other workers.

In fact, a review of 90 hands-on studies reveals that compared to other employees, persons with disabilities (Cox,1993; Green and Johnson 1987):

- have better safety records
- do not normally cause increased health care costs
- have equal or better turnover and absentee rates

- have equal or better job assignment flexibility
- are productive; more than 90 percent of 1,451 workers at DuPont rated as average or above average on overall job performance
- have better average attendance records than those of nondisabled employees.

Myth #5: Employees with disabilities are more difficult to work with.

Two large surveys of managers and coworkers of persons with disabilities indicate the following (Harris 1986, 1987):

- Eighty percent of managers say they are no more difficult to supervise than others.
- Fifty percent of managers rate the following qualities as *better than* those of other workers: willingness to work hard, reliability, punctuality, and attendance.
- Eighty percent of coworkers say they are just as productive as others.

WHAT'S IN A NAME?

Labels can hurt, especially when their effect is to isolate people from the rest of society. The terms we use to refer to persons with disabilities can be loaded with unintended meanings. Most activists prefer terms that are descriptive rather than euphemistic, emotionally neutral rather than charged, and words that don't elicit negative stereotypes (Longmore 1985a).

Preferred Terms	*Terms to Avoid*
• Persons with Disabilities	• Differently Abled
• The disabled (as a protected class)	• Physically Challenged
• Sight Impaired, Blind	• Handicapped
• Mobility Impaired	• Crippled, Lame, Gimpy
• Hearing Impaired, Deaf	• Deaf and Dumb
• Emotionally Impaired	• Insane, Crazy
• Neurologically Impaired	• Moron
• Mentally Impaired	• Retard

The term *persons with disabilities* is preferred when referring to the group as a whole because it focuses on them as persons first, rather than on their disability. The use of the term *the disabled* is acceptable when referring to them as a protected class. Such terms as *differently abled* and *physically challenged* are not descriptive and attempt to avoid the issue. They're politically correct in the worst sense.

Handicapped was considered acceptable for a time, but some people connect the term with the phrase *cap in hand*, which they mistakenly believe to refer to begging but which actually is derived from a game of chance. Now most persons with disabilities avoid the term *handicapped*.

The worst terms carry emotionally devastating stereotypes and tend to focus on the negative: deaf and dumb, crippled, limp, lame, gimpy. Replace them with more specific, descriptive terms, such as *hearing impaired*, *sight impaired*, and *mobility impaired*. They're often more accurate than *deaf* or *blind* because they refer to those with varying degrees of impairment, as well as those with total loss of an ability.

WHY ARE PERSONS WITH DISABILITIES EXCLUDED?

People tend to shun, be prejudiced against, or devalue people who are different. This is especially true when the persons are different because they have less of something than most people have. But people who have more than most others may also be devalued. People who are exceptionally rich, brilliant, beautiful, or even kind are suspected and punished by some people. Most every culture seems to display this tendency.

Most devaluation refers to regarding someone as inferior, a lesser being, not very capable, not very useful, possibly burdensome, not beautiful, and generally one down. Devaluation follows close behind outright oppression when it comes to psychologically damaging consequences. It is the most common and devastating attitude facing persons with disabilities. They consistently experience devaluation in the eyes of others, and therefore in their own eyes unless they can protect themselves from self-deprecation—whether their disability is physical, sensory, or mental in nature.

The form and degree of devaluation is heavily influenced by the surrounding culture. Devaluation can be blatant or subtle. The Nazis blatantly killed disabled people. Most societies are so subtle that their devaluative practices have gone unrecognized as such for many years until the new breed of activists began to call attention to them. The prevailing philosophical or religious beliefs of the culture have a distinct effect on how people view persons with disabilities (Vash 1981). In both the East and the West, for example, it has been common to segregate the disabled into their own schools and workplaces.

Western Viewpoint

Most Western religions and philosophies hold that we each have only one life to live. Therefore, being disabled has other implications, from "It's just God's will and we can't know why" to "It's God's punishment for something the victim did or something the victim's parents did" to "It's a tragedy because we're here to enjoy life."

Western cultures, such as the dominant culture of the United States, place a high value on standard modes of reasoning, a cultural model of physical beauty, and the physical, material world. Such values tend to create barriers to good relationships and to communicating with persons with certain impairments (Vash 1981; Althen 1988).

Many people in our culture view people as a personality inside a body. When one or both of those has been damaged "permanently," not much is left. Societies and individuals who are more spiritually oriented understand that the spirit is not damaged just because the body or personality is damaged.

Materialistic people are especially likely to believe that persons with disabilities continually mourn their misfortune, perhaps as long as they live. This is simply not the case for most persons with disabilities. Therefore, the implied belief that persons with disabilities are sad victims of terrible life circumstances erects a communication barrier between the believer and those persons.

Eastern Viewpoint

Some Eastern philosophies and religions include the idea of reincarnation into multiple lives. Many believe that before coming into a new lifetime, at a spiritual level we choose our parents, our body, and our total life situation. We do this in order to learn certain lessons and have certain experiences that deepen our awareness and understanding and promote our spiritual growth. Disability thus becomes a growth experience. This is not to say that all Asians view disability in this manner. It is to say that some persons with disabilities have found this viewpoint to be more constructive and empowering than the Western view.

When persons without disabilities believe they're more fortunate than persons with disabilities, they tend to feel pity, which implies superiority. People with this viewpoint may feel threatened when a coworker with disabilities excels, or they may assume that the coworker was excused from meeting the usual standards. On the other hand, some people view persons with disabilities as merely being in a *different* physical situation, not necessarily a less fortunate one—in the deeper, eternal sense. Such viewpoints allow us to relate to persons with disabilities as peers, colleagues, and equals.

Media Influences

In the past, films and television programs often presented persons with disabilities as villains, criminals, monsters, and tragic figures. All these stereotypes express the idea that disability involves the loss of an essential part of the person's humanity. The figures were often portrayed as almost subhuman. Think of Captain Hook, the hunchback of Notre Dame, mentally impaired Lennie in *Of Mice and Men*. Here disability implied the loss of moral self-control, often through bitterness and isolation that results from the fear and bigotry of others.

During the 1970s and 1980s we saw in increase in programs where persons with disabilities chose suicide as an escape from their "living death," or "vegetable existence," even though they retained many life functions. In many films disability implied total physical dependency and separation from the community, and the victims were unable to adjust to their disability. Death was presented as the only logical and humane solution to a horrible situation. Other dramas focused on bitter, self-pitying victims whose families eventually got tough in order to help the person with disability adjust and cope. The focus was usually on victims who worked courageously and achieved remarkable feats.

Both types of stories featured overcoming adversity, based on the concept of disability as primarily a problem that requires the person with the disability to accept the situation and find the emotional resources to cope and overcome. Social stigma and devaluation were not the issue and society was let off the hook.

A few recent productions have directly dealt with the issue of prejudice. Others have presented persons with disabilities as normal persons who happen to have some functional impairment. Deaf and paraplegic persons have been portrayed as attractive and sexual, entering relationships out of the strength of their own identities. Certain activist groups are trying to influence media decision makers to focus on these more realistic aspects of disability.

Fear of Becoming Disabled

People don't like to think about losing control of their destiny or that the hand of fate could strike them as well as the person with a disability whom they see before them. This fear can lead to extreme discomfort and distress upon even seeing persons with disabilities, much less spending time with them. What people fear, they tend to shun and stigmatize. Fear can also lead to blaming the disabled for their own predicament. Some people find comfort in believing that persons with disabilities must have brought it on themselves through sin, carelessness, or self-sabotage. In turn, they can tell themselves that they would never bring such a disaster upon themselves, and this makes them feel more in control and safer.

Unfamiliarity and Discomfort with Persons with Disabilities

When people have had little or no experience with persons with a certain type of disability, the unfamiliarity can be disconcerting. People are frequently confused and uncertain about how to act and what to do. Some avoid making eye contact with such persons because they got punished for "staring" when they were children. How many mothers have grabbed their child's arm and snapped, "Don't stare! It's rude." How many have said, "Shhh! Don't ask!" when their naturally curious child blurted out questions and concerns upon seeing a person with a disability? Parents' comments are well meaning, but they teach their children to ignore anyone with a disability.

Unfamiliarity can cause people to focus on the equipment surrounding some people—braces, crutches, wheelchair—and keep them from really seeing and tuning into the person. It can cause people to look at an interpreter, leaving out the hearing-impaired person, instead of viewing the translator as a mechanism for communication and focusing on the person they're communicating with. In all these cases, the person with the disability gets little or no eye contact and becomes something of a nonperson.

To help you imagine what it's like to have a disability, complete Self-Awareness Activity 13.3.

Self-Awareness Activity 13.3: What If You Became Impaired?

Purpose: To increase your awareness of the experiences of persons with disabilities.
Step 1. Various Activities. List some barriers you would face in a typical day if you lost your ability to walk, your vision or your hearing. Consider how you would manage the activities shown in the column to the left if you had each of the impairments shown on the right. What barriers would you have to overcome in each case?

	Mobility Impaired	*Visually Impaired*	*Hearing Impaired*
• getting up in the morning, getting ready			
• getting to work or school			
• doing your work, communicating, etc.			
• having lunch			
• using the restroom			
• other activities? (list)			

Step 2. Getting Dressed. Put on a tight blindfold, or close your eyes and don't peek. Go through the motions of getting dressed. What problems do you experience? Which are the most difficult?
Step 3. Sight and Sound. While watching a television drama, try the following experiments.

- Wear a blindfold for 5 or 10 minutes.
- Mute the sound for 5 or 10 minutes.

What are the key differences between no-sight and no-sound? What insights does this experience suggest to you about visual and hearing impairments?

EVOLUTION: FROM VICTIM TO ACTIVIST

Cultural attitudes and policies toward persons with disabilities have changed dramatically in this century (Longmore 1987). Persons with disabilities say that the most serious barriers to living reasonable lives and doing their work are not necessarily their own physical or psychological disabilities. The worst barriers are external: other people's stereotypes and attitudes and the buildings, vehicles, walks, steps, and restrooms they must negotiate. Some highlights of historical change include:

Before 1850	Traditional moral attitude: take care of the disabled.
1850s	Provide special schools for the trainable.
1880s	Institutionalize the disabled in large centers.
1880s–1920s	Involuntary confinement and sterilization.
1930s	Rehabilitation for some. Sight-impaired advocates fight for participation in society.
	F.D. Roosevelt, who uses a wheelchair, is elected U.S. president.
1940s	World War II opens doors to disabled workers because of manpower shortages; March of Dimes, Cerebral Palsy associations are formed.
1950s	Focus on rehabilitating and adapting to the environment.
1960s	Disabled-rights advocates organize to change their environment; Urban Mass Transportation Act, Architectural Barriers Act encourage access.
1970s	Federal law requires access and accommodation from some employers and organizations; some states pass similar laws; Independent Living approved by Congress and some states.
1980s	Independent Living Movement; Air Carriers Access Act.
1990s	Federal ADA requires access and accommodation from most employers and in nearly all buildings.

From Institutionalizing to Rehabilitating

The traditional moral attitude toward adults with disabilities was to take responsibility for their care. Social reform efforts of the 1850s sought to establish special schools for those children with disabilities who were considered trainable. In the 1880s there was a move to switch from small centers to large, more economical institutions that could accommodate more people, with the attitude that defective persons should be removed from the mainstream of society. Subsequent legislative drives from 1880 to 1925 focused on enforcing involuntary confinement and sterilization to prevent "defective" persons from having children.

Rehabilitating

The Rehabilitation Act of 1918 focused on World Ward I veterans with disabilities. Proponents of vocational rehabilitation assumed that people with disabilities could overcome them and become wage earners if given training. The major goal was to prepare people to work so they could pay back the government's investment; it did not seek to offer generalized assistance.

Rehabilitation became a part of the solution for persons with some types of disabilities, but after rehabilitation, they were given only the most menial jobs. During World War II, because of the extreme manpower shortage, workers with disabilities filled a variety of jobs. Studies indicated they incurred less absenteeism and tardiness than other workers and that their productivity was good. After the war, these work reports "got lost" and it was back to the old "moral" attitudes.

From Accepting Disability to Adapting

By the late 1950s it became unfashionable to talk about *accepting* disability. *Adapting* to or *coping with* became the preferred terminology. This thinking led in part to the disabled-advocates revolution. Some saw that counseling would not solve the problem if, in the end, people with disabilities still could not get from one point to another because there wasn't an accessible bus service or they couldn't get up the stairs. The world was not a very reasonable place to live for the disabled, so advocates began to shift the emphasis from modifying the disabled to modifying the world around them.

Adapting While Changing the Environment

"Persons with disabilities" became a movement in the 1960s. They also became a minority group with culture-like features, such as dominant values, cultural themes, and key issues. Emerging from their former victim roles, disability activists brought about important legislative changes. Looking to the future, their goal is to remove as many of the barriers to a normal life as they can.

Transformation: From Victims to an Activist Minority

A new day dawned for persons with disabilities in the late 1960s, as it did for many groups. Many of them began viewing themselves as part of a minority group that must manage its own brand of stereotypes and discrimination from others, develop and affirm its own values and issues, and take charge of its own destiny (Longmore 1985a, 1985b, 1987). Once the disabled started talking to each other, most of them concluded that:

- Other people with disabilities are valuable and worthwhile.
- They themselves weren't the only exceptions to those negative stereotypes that they had previously accepted.
- All persons with disabilities have valuable experience and information to share.
- In unity there is strength.

They began to fight in the civil rights mode of other minorities, to formulate their rights, and to demand protection for those rights. They campaigned for and won new laws during the 1970s. A 1973 federal law addressed the issue of making some public places accessible to persons with disabilities and eliminating discrimination, but it applied only to organizations receiving federal funds. It did not include most stores, restaurants, and theaters, nor did it include private corporations, except those involved in federal contracts. Soon after the 1973 law was passed, several states passed similar laws. California's law, considered an outstanding model, deals mainly with providing physical and program access to the disabled. School administrators began installing ramps and elevators instead of counseling people with disabilities to stop wanting to attend classes held upstairs. Managers began to remove discriminatory hiring practices instead of advising applicants with disabilities to start liking the few jobs they would be allowed to do.

Breakthrough: The Americans with Disabilities Act

The Americans with Disabilities Act (ADA), which was passed in 1990 and became fully effective in 1994, expanded accessibility to jobs and activities in virtually every major arena. It's an amendment to the Civil Rights Act, not a part of affirmative action law that stems from executive orders. It's therefore enforced by the EEOC. Complaints not resolved through the EEOC may be resolved in the courts through EEOC lawsuits.

Future Aspirations: To Bring Down Barriers

Now activists are clear that if the disability cannot be changed, then it must be accepted, as must any other reality, pleasant or unpleasant, if the person is to survive and grow. What they don't accept is the unnecessary handicapping imposed upon people with disabilities by a poorly designed or unaccommodating world or by their own failures to accept what is and go on from there. Nor do they want to be dependent from cradle to grave because this can severely limit their growth and contributions.

Activists have made significant progress toward reducing all types of barriers to a quality existence: barriers that existed in the legal, welfare, and educational systems, barriers created by modes of architecture, transportation, employment, housing, shopping, and recreation. Most important, activists initiated the Independent Living Movement (ILM), which we'll discuss later. The United States is the most highly individualistic of nations, so independence has the highest value here, and the ADA and the ILM reflect that.

WHO ARE THE DISABLED? CURRENT PROFILE

Virtually everyone has been or will be disabled at some point in their lives, as mentioned earlier. Virtually all persons with disabilities want to live as normal a life as possible. Most want to work, regardless of the extent of their impairment. When they do hold jobs, they tend to be productive and to have better-than-average attendance and turnover records (Myths & Facts 2002).

The Legal Definition

To be protected under the ADA, persons must fit one or more of these descriptions:

- They have a physical or mental impairment that substantially limits one or more of the major life activities, such as seeing, hearing, speaking, learning, walking, dressing, or feeding oneself.
- They have a record of such an impairment
- They are regarded as having such an impairment.

The ADA definition is broad and includes such chronic conditions as diabetes, heart disease, HIV, AIDS, past (but not present) drug addiction and alcoholism, and mental and emotional illnesses.

The Census Bureau reports that 18 percent of the population consists of persons with disabilities, 51 million people (Census Bureau 2000). The ADA is directed mainly to those who are hearing impaired, sight impaired and mobility impaired, which is about 1 percent of working-age adults (Minton 1994). However, the ADA is intended to protect anyone who encounters discrimination in the workplace because of a physical or mental disability, if that person could in fact do the job with some sort of reasonable accommodation.

Types of Disability

We may get some sense of the types of disabilities people experience at various ages by examining information regarding people who receive disability payments. Business leaders need to be aware that persons with disabilities who have been working all or much of their adult lives are not eligible for disability payments unless their disability becomes significantly worse. Managers should not assume that if they lay off persons with disabilities, they'll be able to collect disability payments.

The great majority of persons receiving disability payments suffer from one of four broad health conditions—mental disorders, musculoskeletal disease (primarily arthritis), and heart disease being the primary problems, with cancer less frequent. See Table 13.1. The ADA benefits older workers the most, since that group has the highest percentage of persons with disabilities. About 22 percent of people 55 to 64 years old receive disability payments, compared to 6 percent of people 25 to 34 years old.

The U.S. Census uses different categories for tabulating types of disability, as shown in Table 13.2. The most frequent problem is mobility impairment.

Table 13.1: Breakdown of Reasons People Receive Disability Payments

Types of Disability	All	Younger <50	Older 50–64
Mental disorders	28%	40%	17%
Arthritic disease	19	12	23
Heart disease	18	7	25
Cancer	3	3	4
All other	32	38	31

Source: *Mitchell, 1993.*

Table 13.2: Types of Disability, U.S. Population

Type of Disability (Some Persons Have Overlapping Types)	Total U.S. population	Ages 65–74
Mobility—walking, lifting, climbing, carrying	8%	21%
Inability to work	6	—
Mental—learning, remembering, concentrating	5	6
Mobility outside the home—shop, visit doctor	9	13
Sensory—sight, hearing	4	9
Self-care—dressing, bathing, mobility inside home	3	5

Source: *U.S. Census, 2005*

Variation by Ethnicity

The rate of disability varied by ethnic group: Asian American 17 percent, Euro-American 18 percent, Latino American 20 percent, African American and American Indian 24 percent.

Variation by Region

The rate of disability varied slightly by region: Midwest 18 percent, West and Northeast 19 percent, and South 21 percent. The higher rate in the South is affected by its large African American population.

The Mental Treatment Gap

Mental disorders are the most neglected of the major disabilities. Overall, in a given year, one out of four people meet the criteria for some type of mental disorder. This is huge, but the vast majority of those cases are mild. However, if they are not handled effectively, some will become severe, and nearly two-thirds of people with diagnosable mental disorders do no seek treatment (Pear 1999). Overall, about half of Americans will develop a mental disorder at some time in their lives. About half of these mental disorder cases start by age 14, and 75 percent by age 24 (Kessler 2005).

Mental disorders can be organized into four major groups

- *Anxiety Disorders* include panic, agoraphobia, social phobia, generalized anxiety, post-traumatic stress, obsessive-compulsive, and separation anxiety disorders.

- *Impulse-Control Disorders* include oppositional defiant conduct, attention-deficit/hyperactivity, and intermittent explosive disorders.

- *Mood Disorders* include mild chronic depression, major depression, and bipolar I-II (manic-depressive).

- *Substance Disorders* include alcohol abuse, alcohol dependence, drug abuse, and drug dependence.

These disorders may cause learning difficulties or behavior problems or both. Mental disorders are not character flaws. They are legitimate illnesses that respond to specific treatments. They appear in all types of families, of all social classes, and all backgrounds. The "cruel and unfair stigma attached to mental illness" is "inexcusably outmoded and must no longer be tolerated," according to Robert Pear (1999). He suggests that a major factor in such stigma is fear that people with mental disability will become violent. Yet there is "very little risk of violence or harm to a stranger from casual contact with an individual who has a mental disorder."

Some employers are reluctant to hire people with mental disabilities, citing concerns regarding their social skills and ability to function in teams. Supported-employment programs can be helpful, where a nonprofit agency sponsors mentally disabled employees and provides on-the-job training coaches. If such employees are unable to meet job standards, the agency will relocate them.

Other Demographics

Persons with disabilities experience a significant gap in income, poverty status, health care access, transportation, and social life. Are they satisfied with their lives? Most say no, but things are improving.

Employment

In 2000 about 56 percent of persons with disabilities were employed. This represents an increase of 10 percent since 1990 and probably attributable to the ADA.

Income

Persons with disabilities experience an income gap of about 35 percent—compared with the total population. Medical expenses and ability to work affect poverty rates, of course, which are double the rate of the general population ages 16 to 64—20 percent compared with 10 percent (Census 2000). These figures have improved over the past 15 years, thanks to the ADA.

Health Care and Transportation

People with disabilities are more than twice as likely to postpone needed health care because they can't afford it—28 percent compared with 12 percent. And they are three times as likely to say inadequate transportation is a problem—30 percent compared to 10 percent (N.O.D. 2002).

Education

In 2000 about 78 percent of the disabled had high school diplomas, compared to 91 percent of the total population, and 12 percent had college degrees, compared with 23 percent. This too is a significant improvement over 1990 figures (N.O.D. 2002).

Social Life and Satisfaction

Persons with disabilities generally report a 20 percent gap in activities that require discretionary income, such as eating out, going to movies and other events, and even socializing with friends and attending religious services. The gap exists even for those with similar incomes but practically disappears for those in their 20s.

About half as many persons with disabilities say they're very satisfied with their life as nondisabled persons—only 33 percent compared with 67 percent. This gap shrinks for those in their 20s— 44 percent are very satisfied compared with 57 percent of all people. Most disabled persons, 63 percent, say life has improved over the past decade. And 73 percent of those with slight disabilities agree.

WHAT'S IT LIKE TO BE A PERSON WITH A DISABILITY?

You've learned that 51.6 million Americans with disabilities fall under the ADA definition, about 26 million of whom are severely disabled (U.S. Census). About one-third are employed. This means that two-thirds of adults with disabilities are not working, which is the highest unemployment rate of any minority. About 80 percent of those who aren't working say they would rather have a job. Dissatisfaction with life is reported by four times as many adults classified as having disabilities as other adults (WSJ 1994).

Being a person with a disability is like being any other person, only with an impairment that prevents you from performing one or more major functions. For all severely disabled persons, it's having normal reactions to abnormal situations. Otherwise, your experience as a person with disability depends on the following types of factors:

- *Type of disability*: severity, stability
- *Inner resources*: temperament, self-image, self-esteem, gender, education, skills, creativity
- *Environment*: family support, access to a community of persons with disabilities, cultural attitudes, available technology, government funding

Facing Abnormal Situations

Human beings are more alike than different, regardless of variations in their physical bodies, sensory capacities, or intellectual abilities. Some abnormal situations are biological, such as having multiple sclerosis, which involves progressive nerve deterioration. Some are environmental, such as inaccessible entrances. Other abnormal situations are social, such as having a salesperson ask your companion, not you, what size you wear.

Not being able to get a job is an economic example. Some abnormal situations are obvious, such as a restroom door you can't get through. Others are subtle, such as people using or not using the word *cripple* when you're around. Some may be pleasant, such as being allowed to board the airplane first. Others are unpleasant, such as not being allowed to board at all. Persons with disabilities are continually perceiving and experiencing things that the majority of people around them cannot validate. Unless they are in regular contact with people who are similarly disabled, their sense of isolation and the lack of consensus for their ideas and feelings are added to the list of abnormal situations.

Type of Disability

The type of disability refers to the time and type of the onset of the illness or accident, which abilities are impaired and which are not, the severity and duration of the affliction, and the way society views it (Vash 1980, 1994).

Time and Type of Onset

Some persons are born with disabilities. They grow gradually to recognize that they are different from most other people in negatively evaluated ways. Others become disabled after a short or long lifetime of being "normal." The disability may occur in a catastrophic moment or over a period of illness.

To some, having been born disabled seems somehow less respectable than acquiring a disability later on. Such persons are more likely to be subjected to isolation, unusual child-rearing practices (such as overprotection or rejection), and separation from the mainstream in family life, play, and education.

Many become disabled after a close brush with death, which often has a powerful influence on their life. Some feel guilty for having survived to be a burden. Others feel an intensified faith and sense of purpose.

Functions Impaired

The extent to which the disability interferes with physical attractiveness is a key determiner of the disability experience. Sensitivity to its lack or loss can exceed the pain felt about the functional disability.

The functions impaired directly affect other experiences the person has. For example, deaf people describe the loneliness of being "left out" even when physically present in a group. Blind persons may speak of their terror of pitfalls they can't see, and wheelchair users of curbs they can't get up or down.

Severity, Duration, and Status

There is not a direct, consistent relationship between severity of disability and the intensity of reaction to it or quality of adjustment to it. One person can assimilate total paralysis with fair equanimity, while another is devastated by the loss of a finger. Varying degrees of severity do create different kinds of situations for people to respond to, somewhat independently of personal dynamics.

Some people are temporarily disabled, others are permanently disabled, and some fall into a gray area where some day their impairment may be reparable. For those people, the most depressing influence is often the not knowing. One spoke of living a "provisional existence of unknown limit," saying, "I was convinced that I would eventually walk, but the uncertainty of how long it would take was a most depressing factor."

Persons who are disabled perceive a status hierarchy of disabilities, with polio and spinal-cord injury at the top and mental retardation and cerebral palsy at the bottom. When a disability causes you to walk and talk like a drunk, you get a lot of rejection.

Inner Resources

To learn how inner resources affect the disability experience, we might ask such questions as:

- What kinds of temperaments do persons with disabilities have?
- What is the spiritual or philosophical base in their lives?
- What personality traits do they have that will influence the type and intensity of their reactions to being disabled?

The inner resources of persons with disabilities dramatically affect how they experience their disability. They include ability to adapt to the disability, self-confidence built in early childhood, personal interests and values, ability to express emotions, gender, and other personal variables.

Ability to Adapt

How well a person is able to adapt to the loss of abilities and to enjoy the abilities that remain is an important inner resource. Whether key activities can be continued obviously plays a big role in what inner resources can be tapped. What alternate activities are available is also an important factor. Inner strengths that help people to adapt may include high energy level, strong career motivations, life history of emotional stability, many artistic talents, social poise, and leadership ability or potential.

Psychological support

Inner resources and emotional stability are established early in life. Those who are disabled as children need more psychological support than most children. When they are taught to believe that they're "as good as anyone else and can do anything they want to do," they gain self-confidence to disregard the taunting of other children. The early years of confidence help them to combat the doubts and rejections they experience later on.

The hit movie *Forrest Gump* was an exposition of this idea. Forrest was mentally impaired, but his mother made sure that he joined mainstream society. She repeatedly told him that he was not inferior. One of the many mottoes she taught him was, "Stupid is as stupid does." She taught Forrest to do good deed because actions speak louder than words and to value the goodness of his inner self.

Interests, Values, and Goals

People tend to adjust more easily if they have a wide range of interests, such as physical interests, intellectual pursuits, vigorous activity, rigorous creativity, passive pastimes, and active involvements. For one thing, they're more likely to find some things they can still do that interest them. People who sustain spinal-cord injuries through adventurous, potentially dangerous activities are apt to be most intolerant of a physically inactive life. People from cultures that highly value physical or sexual prowess are more devastated by this disability than those whose traditions stress scholarly or other sedentary pursuits.

Ability to Express Emotions

What emotions do persons with disabilities tend to feel? Disability has the power to elicit the full range of human emotions, from fear, anger, and sorrow to relief and even joy. Chronic depression is the worst. Periodic fear, embarrassment, or righteous indignation are improvements over that.

Almost all persons with disabilities experience anxiety about survival as well as episodes of rage. Some rage against themselves, their own incompetence to do what others take for granted. They may rage against the universe for being unjust. Some turn their rage against other people for not helping or for helping inappropriately. Some of today's disabled peopled have been called an "angry generation," expecting change to come faster than it ever does and seething inside when it doesn't. Some say that even justified anger isn't good for them over the long term, but they feel they need its impetus to sustain their demands for change.

The ways of expressing and acting out emotions are unlimited. The specific trigger to feelings varies from one person to another. Because disability normally brings strong emotions, being able to express them is important for mental and physical health.

Being Male or Female

Being male or female does not imply better or worse reactions, only different ones. It's more acceptable for women to be helpless in our culture because of the greater social acceptance of a passive, dependent lifestyle for women than for men. Women also tend to have the advantage of being more in touch with their feelings and expressing them more freely. However, women's advantage is virtually destroyed by the far greater demand placed on women to be physically perfect specimens, beautiful in face and figure. By definition, women with physical disabilities cannot hope to meet this social ideal.

Other Personality variables

Such variables as flexibility, adaptability, maturity, and their opposites influence reaction to change generally, and this includes the changes imposed by disability. Personality variables will affect what meaning persons with disabilities give to the fact that they're disabled. The person who views disability as a punishment from God for past sins will feel differently about it than the person who views it as a test or an opportunity for spiritual development.

Reactions that people with disabilities have to their disability continue as long as the persons and the disability do. There is not some point in time when the person has "adjusted." Reactions simply change with each step in the learning process.

The Environment

At the most primitive level of existence, the ability to get around to find food and shelter is the basic requirement for independent survival. In civilization we must also be able to communicate with other people who are essential for our survival. We're dependent on our immediate environment as well as the greater cultural environment. Persons with disabilities are especially dependent on adequate funds, programs, laws, and technological developments to provide what their impairments prevent them from providing for themselves.

The Financial Environment

The financial assets of persons with disabilities make a crucial difference in the type of experience they have. Money can solve many disability problems. With enough money, persons with disabilities can buy all the equipment and gadgets available to help them do what they need to do. And they can pay other persons to do what's left. A major problem with disability is that it's often difficult to make money. A person's welfare and experiences are therefore greatly influenced by the family's social standing and power base in the community, parental acceptance of the person's disability, and their willingness and ability to offer practical and moral support.

The Disability Community

The larger community of persons with disabilities has been emerging as a subcultural group since the 1960s. It began with the activism of people such as Ed Roberts and Paul Longmore. It expanded with the Independent Living Movement. In every major metropolitan area, persons with a specific type of disability can probably find a small community of persons with a similar disability. Such communities can provide invaluable information, support, and inspiration.

The Culture

We've discussed the importance of cultural beliefs and attitudes toward the disabled. Predominant beliefs and attitudes are the direct cause of psychological and physical barriers on the one hand and their removal on the other.

The Physical Environment—Accessibility

The main issue for mobility-impaired people is accessibility, and safety is the main issue for the visually impaired. Inaccessibility has implications for survival. For example, if wheelchair users cannot get into a building, they can't get a job there. If they can't get over the curbs, up the stairs, or into the restrooms, they literally cannot function even though they have many other abilities.

The most typical ways people with disabilities cope with problems of inaccessible or unsafe facilities are by:

- minimizing their own disabilities by developing every possible adaptive skill
- keeping up the good fight to get remaining environmental barriers removed

Some wheelchair users are interested in the development of wheelchairs that climb steps. Most prefer to see ramps and elevators wherever steps are used. What do wheelchair users do if they're working in an upper floor of a skyscraper and fire breaks out, rendering all the elevators unusable? Some feasible plans do exist, but they're rare. When deaf passengers take an unknown bus route, how can they know when they reach their street destination? These are the crucial emergencies and everyday problems that disabled-rights advocates are trying to resolve.

Community and Regional Influences

The size and location of the community where the person lives are important. A small town may offer a quality of human support that is lost in the big city, but it may also lack the equipment and services that persons with disabilities need. Also important are the extent to which the community has been willing and able to eliminate mobility barriers, to mainstream children with disabilities into the public schools, and similar actions.

Other factors that affect the quality of life include the services that local voluntary organizations make available, television and telephone services available for the hearing impaired, the type of transportation that's available, and whether activist organizations are around. The climate and typical building styles also can have a significant impact on how persons with disabilities fare.

The Bureaucracies

The various bureaucracies that persons with disabilities must deal with may include live-in institutions and social service agencies.

Institutions

Living in an institution has a profound impact on the disabled person's experience. Few, if any, institutions, are ideal. By their very nature they tend to restrict residents' freedom and violate their privacy. Few people go there by choice. Giving up one's autonomy, even for a time, can have long-lasting, negative effects. In an institution, the staff tends to make most of the crucial decisions about the patients' lives. Those patients who are most willing to cooperate with the staff, therefore, may eventually be the least prepared to resume effective, assertive autonomy when they return to the outside world. Those who have been in institutions say it's the attendants who make the most difference in their quality of life while there (Vash 1980, 1994).

Social Service Agencies

The disabled must often interact with agencies that provide vitally important services. These interactions can be supportive, but they can also be stressful. According to disabled advocate Carolyn Vash, when dealing with agencies "in order to receive the benefits they need, disabled people must tell all, hand over the reins, and oftentimes swallow much, possibly for a very long time" (Vash 1980, 36).

Technological Support

How well the culture is able to provide the latest in technological tools, aids, therapies, cures, and other responses to the cause and aftermath of the disability makes a great difference in resolving functional problems. The U.S. culture provides a great deal of independence and convenience through motorized wheelchairs, powered lifts, electronic magnifiers, talking calculators, portable teletypewriters, computers, and similar aids.

Recent Technological Breakthroughs

Motorized wheelchairs have opened up dramatic new opportunities for the mobility impaired. For the sight impaired, Braille, audiotape, specialized computers, and other electronic or optical devices have greatly reduced the need for personal services, such as readers. Spare body parts are improved and more readily available—including parts for hands, eyes, and ears.

Hearing-impaired persons' communication problems are yielding more slowly to technological intervention than those of the blind. They continue to need interpreters to convey information that's presented orally. Signing is a tiring activity and is ideally done by one person for not more than an hour at a time. What's needed is a portable device that will decode speech and turn it into a visual readout. All televised information should be closed captioning for the hearing impaired.

Public transportation is making strides in assisting users with both short-distance and long-distance travel. The kneeling bus, which lowers a wheelchair-sized platform to curb level, has opened up many opportunities. Many housing functions are becoming computerized. In education, computers provide self-paced learning and easy access to libraries of information. Computers have also made employment more feasible, including home-based employment. Flexible work schedules, job sharing, and other programs to accommodate parents and older workers can also accommodate persons with disabilities.

Future Technological Probabilities

Technology holds enormous potential for easing and enriching the lives of persons with disabilities. For devices and equipment to be affordable under current business methods, they must be standardized, mass produced, and mass marketed. Individual needs often require unique technological solutions, and devices developed on a problem/solution basis cannot be standardized. Therefore, it's nearly impossible to mass produce and mass market such devices. However, under new business methods using computer-assisted design and manufacturing, customizing, or creating variations on a theme, is becoming economically feasible. New strategies to meet global competition by customizing can also be applied to the equipment or medical-device needs of persons with disabilities.

Technology will affect all aspects of a disabled person's life, such as education, health care, transportation, housing, occupations, and recreation. Some specific trends include:
Increased diversity among people, resulting from more individualized education and media

- easier access to all kinds of information
- decreased routine labor and physical labor
- less reliance on mass production of products and more access to custom-made products
- better communication devices, including computers with multimedia (screen, keyboard, and voice) input and output, resulting in a reduced need for physical transportation
- smaller work facilities that are easier to access and more use of the home as a place to learn and to work
- spare body parts for virtually every organ
- stem cells and gene therapy to regenerate and heal virtually every physical problem

Each of these trends will influence the future of persons with disabilities and their ability to live productive, independent lives.

WHAT'S THE INDEPENDENT LIVING MOVEMENT?

Throughout most of our history, people who were so severely disabled as to need an attendant had only two options:

- to be cared for by family or friends
- to live in a maintenance-care institution

SHOWCASE

Ed Roberts' Success Story

In 1962, when Ed Roberts, paralyzed from the neck down, applied for help from the California Department of Rehabilitation, they said no. The counselors argued that it was "infeasible" to think that Ed would ever be able to work. But Ed was persistent; he was accustomed to fighting such battles. At age 14 he had polio and heard the doctor tell his mother, "It would be better if Ed died because he's going to be a vegetable." Right then Ed decided that if he was going to be a vegetable, he'd be an artichoke: prickly on the outside, with a tender heart. His motto was "I'm paralyzed from the neck down, not from the neck up." He used his tough mind and soft heart to fight for disabled persons' rights and to change forever their place in society.

Ed had to persuade his high school principal at Burlingame High to give him his diploma even though he had not completed required classes in physical education and driver's education. He won that battle, and in 1962 he won the battle to get into the University of California at Berkeley, one of the top-ranking U.S. universities. On Ed's first day he was lifted out of his wheelchair and carried up the steps to Room 201 of Cal Hall. A local newspaper headline read, "Helpless Cripple Attends UC Classes."

Later, he organized a group of mobility-impaired students who called themselves the Rolling Quads. They in turn started the Physically Disabled Students' program at UC Berkeley, with the main goal of solving all problems that created barriers to academic achievement. They provided such services as finding attendants, accessible apartments, and 24-hour emergency wheelchair repair service. A broken wheelchair could mean weeks of missed class sessions.

When Ed graduated from UC Berkeley in 1972 he and fellow students founded the Center for Independent Living. It became the model for similar centers across the nation. Ed also founded the Independent Living Movement. In 1975, he became the head of the California Department of Rehabilitation, the very same state agency that had at first opposed helping him go to school. He held that position for seven years, until 1982.

In 1984 Ed Roberts was awarded a MacArthur Foundation "genius" award of $225,000, which he used to establish the World Institute on Disability, an influential policy and research center based in Oakland, California. When he died at age 56 in 1995, colleagues called him "the Gandhi of the disability rights movement."

The alternative of being provided with funds to live as an independent adult did not yet exist. By 1980 independent living was becoming the standard as a result of laws that recognized the human and monetary needs of the disabled.

Disability activists are owning their problem, saying they would rather take care of it themselves, and are demanding their rights. They have made their needs known to government entities at all levels. Their thesis is that people with disabilities, as the ones who share the needs, are uniquely qualified to plan ways of meeting those needs. They want to predominate in the advisory boards of professionally run agencies. They want to take over the key jobs of providing services to the disabled. The new type of service organization consists of independent living programs operated by and for the disabled (Crew and Zola 1983).

Self–Determination as Keystone

The independent living program is a community-based program with significant consumer involvement that provides services that persons with severe disabilities need in order to increase their self-determination and to minimize their dependence on others.

Persons with disabilities are now running many of the programs that offer a wide range of services never before offered to persons with all types of impairments. Some disability advocates, for example, help others find their way through bureaucratic red tape and regulatory obstacles. Others help severely disabled clients locate, select, and supervise personal attendants. Housing counselors help the disabled locate appropriate, accessible places to live. Transportation counselors, interpreter services, support groups, and peer counseling services are other types of programs that are found in some cities.

Other services include readers, advocacy or political action, financial counseling, training in independent living skills, equipment maintenance and repair, social or recreational opportunities, and information about other necessary services and products. The services are designed to serve the needs of persons in a particular community so that they need not move to a regional, state, or national facility. There are residential programs and transitional programs, as well as independent living centers. Persons with disabilities do most of the directing and managing and much of the staffing.

Independent Living Arrangements

The independent living setup can be as large and formal as an apartment complex of several hundred accessible, fully equipped units that offer extensive personal services and are planned along with adjacent accessible shopping and employment facilities. It can be as modest and informal as one person with a disability living in an ordinary apartment and having an agreement with a neighbor to provide needed morning and evening attendant care. Many in the disabled community believe that the full range of possibilities should be made available to allow for individual choice.

Individual choice is the keystone of independence. The independent living concept specifically includes the provision of needed assistance from other people that, when given, allows even very severely disabled people to live free from the control or determination of others. The goal is for persons with disabilities to take charge of their own lives and to allow them to contribute to an improved destiny for all people with disabilities.

Training for Assertive Communication

Assertiveness training offered by community organizations is becoming common for persons with disabilities. They are learning to speak up for their rights rather than leave the job to professional rehabilitators and other concerned advocates who are not themselves disabled. For example, they learn as patients how to interview physicians who say little or say it in technical jargon. They learn to get necessary information upon which to base their own decisions. They learn as students how to get helpful cooperation from teachers when they are physically unable to fulfill course requirements in the usual ways. As citizens, they learn to get the help that they're entitled to from agencies, without triggering resistance from agency workers. Persons with disabilities often rely on funds and services from public agencies, and failure to get what they need can mean poverty or institutionalization.

Training to Supervise Personal Service Employees

Supervisory training is essential for tactfully and assertively dealing with personal service employees, and community service organizations often provide this training. Many persons with disabilities must hire and supervise attendants, readers, drivers, or interpreters. Abuses are reported regularly, such as mistreatment, unreliability, exploitation, quitting without notice, and subtle cruelties of withholding help. This occurs when disabled employers don't know how to screen out poor risks during the hiring process or how to create a rewarding job for those they do hire. They must make the job intrinsically rewarding because the public funds provided often don't constitute a living wage. To survive, psychologically as well as physically, people using personal service providers must develop skill in their selection and supervision.

Education for Career Success

During the past few decades, public education for young people with disabilities has progressed from no education at all, to special education in segregated classrooms, to a concerted effort to integrate students with disabilities into mainstream schools. Major problems resulting from segregating disabled students from the mainstream include:

- Employers cannot imagine that job applicants with disabilities could function in their work settings because they never saw them functioning in school.
- Employees have trouble relating to coworkers with disabilities because they had no opportunities for contact from their earliest years.
- Students with disabilities do not get an equal education.
- Orientation toward college preparation is usually virtually absent.

The ILM recognizes that persons with disabilities must have access to optimal educational experiences in order to become self-sufficient.

Integration into Work and Community Life

The goal of the inner and outer struggles of the disabled is to break out of poverty and restrictive environments that offer nothing to do and no one to do it with. The goal is to stay out of institutions and back bedrooms and break into the mainstream of everything—school, work, politics, and love affairs. The ultimate goal is to live a more or less normal life in a fairly normal community. Integration into the workforce can be managed in a variety of ways, often in a gradual, step-by-step manner. An emerging trend is for employers to participate in this process by giving on-the-job training to the disabled. These trends are discussed in the last part of this chapter. A related goal is to change society's image of persons with disabilities—from that of pathetic victims to a more positive image of "people like you and me, who happen to have a disability." As such, they're entitled to basic human rights. The disabled have the right to participate, to give and receive, and to take risks like anyone else. The ADA, which we'll discuss next, is based on this belief.

To raise your awareness of how you react to wheel chair users and how you relate to them, complete Self-Awareness Activity 13.4.

Self-Awareness Activity 13.4: Relating to Wheelchair Users

Purpose: To raise your awareness of your reactions and attitudes toward persons who use wheelchairs.

Instructions: Have paper and pen handy. Follow the directions for each step and jot down brief answers to the questions.

Step 1. Person in a Wheelchair

a. Relax by closing your eyes and breathing deeply. Think of a person in a wheelchair and focus on this mental image. Notice the thoughts and feelings that come up.

b. Open your eyes and write a few brief sentences about the thoughts and feelings that came up, as well as your answer to this question:

- *What did you see first when you pictured a wheelchair user: A wheelchair? A person within a wheelchair? Or a person?*

Step 2. Person in a Lounge Chair

Repeat Step 1, but this time think of a person sitting in a lounge chair. When you write about your thoughts and feelings, answer this question

- *What did you see first when you pictured a lounge chair user: A lounge chair? A persons within a lounge chair? Or a person?*

Step 3. Person in a Wheelchair and Person in a Lounge Chair
Repeat step 1, but this time think first of a person in a wheelchair and then think of the same person in a lounge chair. Shift the mental image back and forth several times. When you write about your thoughts and feelings, answer this question:

- *How did shifting the mental image affect your thoughts and feelings about the person? How did it affect the way you position the person within your own mind and therefore how you're likely to relate to such a person?*

THE ADA—WHAT YOU NEED TO KNOW

The 1990 federal Americans with Disabilities Act (ADA) applies to virtually all government and private business operations. Its main provisions are set out in five sections or titles, as shown in Table 13.3.

TABLE 13.3: The Americans with Disabilities Act

Section	Purpose
Title I. Employment	Prohibits employment discrimination.
Title II. State and Local Governments	Requires accessibility and prohibits employment discrimination, similar to the 1973 law.
Title III. Public Accommodations	Requires accessibility to restaurants, theaters, stores, etc.
Title IV. Telecommunications	Requires accommodations, such as telephone relays for the deaf.
Title V: Miscellaneous	Catchall section with a variety of technical provisions.

The ADA definition of disability is broad and subject to interpretation by the courts. It is directed mainly to those who are hearing impaired, sight impaired and mobility impaired, all of whom comprise about 1 percent of working-age adults. However, it can include people with such chronic conditions as diabetes, heart disease, HIV, AIDS, past (but not present) drug addiction and alcoholism, and mental and emotional illnesses. It could potentially cover 25 percent of all workers.

Most large corporations have set up ADA task forces to ensure that all the provisions are met. Some smaller business owners have formed regional groups by type of business, such as restaurant, clothing store, or grocery store owner associations. Such associations plan their response to the ADA with the help of professionals, such as consultants and attorneys, and take the large-corporation viewpoint in handling the changes. For example, some send newsletters to employees to inform them of the provisions of the act, proper etiquette in dealing with persons with disabilities, hiring techniques, what the business is doing to adhere to the act, and other helpful information.

Keystone: Equal Opportunity and Reasonable Accommodation

The major stated goal of the ADA is for organizations to manage their affairs in a manner that includes all groups of applicants and workers with disabilities, where reasonable accommodation can make inclusion possible. The major factor that determines if an accommodation is reasonable is whether it imposes an undue hardship on the employer. Another ADA goal is to increase the employment rate of persons with disabilities in order to reduce the cost of government subsidies to them and to enable them to enjoy a more productive, satisfying lifestyle. The major provisions of the ADA are:

- to require employers to clearly state bona fide job requirements
- to provide equal opportunities for qualified persons with disabilities who have the bona fide job qualifications (BFOQs).

- to provide reasonable accommodations that will allow otherwise qualified persons with disabilities to do the job, as long as such accommodations don't cause undue hardship for the employer.

Clearly Stating Job Requirements

Job descriptions are a key factor in preventing unnecessary discrimination against the disabled. Essential job functions must be clearly spelled out. If physical ability is essential, the exact activities must be specified; for example, "lift a 5-pound packet 5 to 10 times a day." Requirements that are not truly necessary to do the job must be eliminated.

Providing Equal Opportunity

The ADA states that a job candidate may not be discriminated against on the basis of disability, history of disability, or perception of disability. In the past, most employers would not consider hiring candidates who have been in mental institutions, who have a history of epileptic seizures, who have attended classes or schools for the mentally retarded, or have similar indications of disability. The tendency was to see only the potential problems and ignore the positive contributions such persons can make.

The ADA bars discrimination in all aspects of employment, including hiring, compensation, training, and promotion. Employers also must give disabled employees equal access to employee benefits, including medical insurance. The law also protects family members from discrimination, such as an employer's assumption that caring for a disabled relative will be a job distraction.

Providing Reasonable Accommodation

Title I of the ADA focuses on "reasonable accommodation" by employers for disabled workers, where such reasonable accommodation will allow them to do the work. All employees must be given reasonable accommodation, whether they're new employees, have been with the company for some time, or become impaired after being hired.

Reasonable accommodation can occur during the recruiting and hiring phase and includes accommodation in job descriptions, medical tests, employment tests, job interviews, and all other pre-employment activities.

Human resource professionals must determine ways to make testing and interviewing procedures realistic and fair for all persons. Persons with disabilities who are fully competent to meet the demands of a job may have difficulties in completing the normal job-screening process successfully. Be sure that testing procedures actually measure those performance capabilities that are required by the target job and that tests are required for bona fide job requirements only.

Medical Screening

Companies cannot perform medical screening prior to hiring a person. That means they cannot require applicants to provide a medical history, nor can they require them to pass any sort of medical test. After hiring, medical screening and other types of screening are permitted only if all workers are included. Those who are thought to be disabled cannot be singled out.

Employment Tests

Reasonable accommodation must be provided for persons with disabilities to take employment tests. For example, reasonable accommodation for visually impaired persons might include reading the test to them or providing the test in large print or Braille. Tests must truly measure whether or not candidates have the ability or potential to be successful on the job.

Job Interviews

Interviewing procedures must protect persons with disabilities from discrimination. For example, interviewers cannot legally ask job applicants about such matters as physical or mental impairments, medical history, drinking habits, or phobias. What if an applicant voluntarily discloses a disability? The interviewer is not legally allowed to follow up with questions about the disability. It is *not* all right to ask directly about a disability, but it *is* all right to ask persons with disabilities whether they can and would do a particular type of work or job and how they would manage the job. There is a fine line between legal and illegal questions here, for *the interviewer cannot ask what kind of accommodation the applicant might need to perform the job until a conditional job offer is made*. After this point, applicants can be asked to demonstrate or describe how they would do the job. If applicants indicate the need for an accommodation, the employer must either provide reasonable accommodation for the demonstration or allow the applicants to merely describe how they would perform this function.

On-the-Job Accommodations

The key questions for employers are

- What are the one or two things I must do as an employer in order to give this person an opportunity to succeed?
- How can I level the playing field for this person?

Reasonable accommodation for some jobs, especially professional or technical positions, might be as easy as providing an amplified telephone receiver or larger computer screen. It is frequently an action as simple as providing flexible scheduling for work arrival and departure. It might include providing an interpreter for a hearing-impaired worker to attend a training session or reassigning job functions so that a wheelchair user handles telephone calls while another employee stores and retrieves folders in file cabinets.

Protection of Employers from Undue Hardship

The ADA states that employers are not required to make accommodations that would cause them undue hardship. This exemption applies when the measures necessary to allow a disabled person to do a job are unduly expensive or interfere with a business necessity. The major test is how the accommodation would affect the entire budget of the organization. Most cases of undue hardship occur in small businesses. Some don't have the profit margin, cash flow, or capital cushion to take such measures as remodeling a building or providing readers or interpreters. What constitutes undue hardship is decided on a case-by-case basis, since the range of disabilities and types of jobs are so vast that no set of legal formulas could begin to cover them. Some guidelines may eventually be worked out through precedents set in court cases.

Cost of Accommodations: 78 Percent Are Under $1,000

About two-thirds of accommodations cost under $500 and over three-fourths cost under $1,000; therefore, they are easily made by even the smallest businesses. Often it's as simple as rearranging a work area. Studies of costs (Shapiro 1993, Bennett-Alexander 2001; Office of Disability 2004) indicate the following

- 15% of all accommodations cost nothing at all
- 51% cost between $1 and $500, which means 66% cost less than $500
- 12% cost between $501 and $1,000, which means 78% cost under $1,000
- 22% cost over $1,000

Many companies are discovering that just by being flexible and opening up their attitudes toward persons with disabilities, they gain workers who are highly committed, productive, and loyal.

Protection of the Disabled: for the Few or for All?

Over 90 percent of plaintiffs who filed cases under the ADA during the 1990s lost, according to an American Bar Association study of 1,200 such lawsuits. Most involved the core issue the ADA was passed to address: people with medical conditions seeking some accommodation from an employer in order to continue working.

By the end of 1999 the U.S. Supreme Court had ruled on three of the five such cases on its docket. The verdict? If you have a disability that can be corrected by medicine or devices such as eyeglasses, you are not "disabled" within the meaning of the law, and you can't use the ADA.

One problem is court definitions of disability. According to Fordham University law professor Matther Diller (1999), many judges are not viewing the ADA as the civil rights law that Congress mandated, but as another piece of benefits legislation to which only a few are entitled—those who fall under some court definition of "disabled." Here are some examples of this interpretation problem:

- A law professor with a paralyzed left hand, arm and leg as the result of a stroke wasn't "disabled," since he continued to work: he wasn't entitled to use the ADA.

- A woman with breast cancer was not "disabled," said the court, since she managed to continue working. Thus she had no right to a "reasonable accommodation."

- An employee with AIDS wasn't allowed to bring an ADA lawsuit challenging his dismissal because he'd gotten Social Security disability benefits: that was tantamount to saying he "couldn't work," said the court. Thus he had no right to file an employment lawsuit. (Yet he and other plaintiffs are simply struggling to do exactly what in other contexts society demands that people do: look for a job, rather than sit at home collecting benefits.)

- A plaintiff with a spastic colon aggravated by multiple sclerosis wasn't entitled to an accommodation that would permit her to arrive at her clerical job 20 minutes late. The court said her condition did not qualify as a "disability."

- There are hundreds of other similar cases. Courts have decided that people with cancer, multiple sclerosis, strokes, hemophilia, carpal tunnel syndrome, brain damage and back and arm injuries aren't really "disabled." In making such decisions, they're falling prey to the stereotype that "being disabled means you can't work." This definition is a legacy of benefits laws and not at all the concept under civil rights law, which protects everyone, says

"The courts have seized upon the definition of disability as a way to stop cases and, in effect, shield an employer's conduct from scrutiny," says Diller. Making people prove they're disabled in order to get the benefit of the law—that's making it into a benefits law, not a civil rights law, says Professor Robert Burgdorf, Jr. (1999), who helped draft the ADA. What makes anyone eligible for protection under the ADA is the same thing that makes any of us eligible for protection under the laws against racial or age discrimination: We're eligible to use the law once we run into discrimination. Granted, the ADA was passed primarily to help people disabled in one or more major life function, just as the Civil Rights laws were passed primarily to help the plight of African Americans, but in all such cases these laws are meant to protect anyone who encounters the type of discrimination a particular law addresses.

What the ADA calls for—re-tooling the workplace so that the "essential functions of the job" are defined and that people are allowed to use a range of strategies and technologies to carry out those functions—is such a far-reaching, egalitarian idea that we aren't ready, it seems, to grasp its full implication: that the ADA is really the most egalitarian of laws. It's aimed at creating an accessible society for all of us. Many courts have not really accepted the premises of the ADA.

LEADERSHIP CHALLENGES: OVERCOMING BARRIERS TO CAREER SUCCESS

Persons with disabilities report that major barriers to their career success include making coworkers comfortable with their disability, finding adequate transportation to and from work, getting the technological support they need, and getting on-the-job training as well as the ongoing training and development that builds the skills they need.

Barrier #1: Making Coworkers Comfortable

The sensitivity and socializing issues are related to corporate culture and to level of employee awareness. Companies that have taken a leadership role in disability issues are providing training sessions for all employees in order to raise their awareness and provide skills for working effectively with this group. Influencing corporate culture change can open up many opportunities to utilize the talents of persons with disabilities—as well as other groups that are disadvantaged in the workplace.

Barrier #2: Finding Adequate Transportation

Transportation barriers are probably the simplest to overcome. Major cities now must modify their public transportation systems to provide lifts and ramps for persons with mobility impairments. Also, managers can work with these employees to solve transportation problems.

Barrier #3: Getting Technological Support

You know that technology can substitute for sensory and motor capacities, which opens up occupational options previously considered unavailable to those with certain disabilities. They are therefore able to engage in higher-level and more demanding kinds of work. With computer modems, fax machines, and similar technology, many computer-based types of work can be done at home, which eliminates the transportation barrier.

Barrier #4: Getting On-the-Job Training

Taking a broad view of how to integrate persons with disabilities in the mainstream workplace, leaders have identified five levels on an ascending scale of increasing integration:

Home-based or homebound employment, which is being upgraded with the advent of computer and telecommunications technology

- Sheltered workshops that hire predominantly workers with disabilities
- Semi-integrated units in mainstream industry that offer some disability-related accommodations and some shelter
- Fully integrated employment in mainstream industry with some disability-related accommodation
- Competitive employment with no disability-related accommodation

Sheltered workshops and semi-integrated work units can be provided by companies that need committed workers. The growing trend in such work preparation programs is to use mainstream industry as the setting for work training, evaluation, and adjustment, instead of using rehabilitation facilities. The trainees get acclimated to actual business situations, and employers and employees get to know the trainees through the relatively nonthreatening training process. Actual job performance sampling is also the best predictor of job success and the best way to identify problem areas and needs for further training.

These types of programs are used by the *crews* programs (Community Rehabilitative Employment Work Sites) This type of training program provides a gradual shift from rehabilitation training to on-the-job training to regular employment. About 70 percent of trainees in *crews* programs have mental disabilities, such as learning problems or retardation. They work in groups at workshops located in centers for persons with mental impairments. They are trained and supervised by trainers familiar with the skills needed by particular industries, such as assembling and packaging skills. Once trainees become productive, they are paid by the center to perform work for affiliated private businesses, who in turn pay the center (DDRCO website).

Barrier #5: Getting Ongoing Training and Development

Some studies, such as those by S. Stace, indicate that most organizations are less likely to provide training and development opportunities to employees with disabilities than to other employees. This reinforces a tendency for persons with disabilities to define their viable career options rather narrowly. Leaders can encourage broader definitions of career goals, help persons with disabilities to develop career plans, and provide appropriate training and development opportunities. Reasonable accommodation in the training function can pay off handsomely.

LEADERSHIP OPPORTUNITIES: BUILDING ON THE STRENGTHS OF PERSONS WITH DISABILITIES

It makes good business sense to accommodate persons with disabilities, for they usually make excellent employees who enrich the company talent pool. Highly qualified persons with disabilities are most likely to apply to companies that have corporate environments that are friendly to them. They're most likely to be productive in such companies and to stay with them. Corporate cultures are likely to change when leaders recognize the many benefits that employees with disabilities bring to the organization, from skills and commitment, to connection with a multi-billion-dollar marketplace.

A step in changing the culture is for employees to attend training sessions that provide information about persons with disabilities. Such training should set the stage for adopting positive attitudes toward persons with disabilities and using positive language when referring to them. You and your company can follow the lead of successful companies in changing the culture and help persons with disabilities to make marketplace connections.

Strategy #1: Provide Diversity Training for All Employees

Employee training should include exploring the beliefs, myths, and stereotypes that lead to devaluation of the disabled; giving accurate information about current facts, trends, issues, and profiles; and developing approaches that help coworkers appreciate all persons with disabilities and work effectively with them. Training should include positive attitudes and language as well as specific information on how to relate to and assist people with various specific disabilities (Massengill 2004).

As coworkers become better able to see beyond a person's abilities or disabilities and to form relationships with the "normal" core person within, the quality of work life is further enhanced. Training should include some guidelines for personal interactions with the disabled. For example, helpers should not rush in and take over when they think a person with disability needs help, such as finding the way or getting through a door. They should ask whether and what type of help is needed. The FAQs at the end of this chapter gives some suggestions for assisting persons with various types of impairment.

Strategy #2: Adopt Positive Attitudes toward Employees with Disabilities

The following are some constructive attitudes that business leaders can adopt for working with the disabled, attitudes that leaders can encourage among all employees.

Realize that people with disabilities are not all alike.

They have some common experiences and they are also highly diverse. On the one hand, many ask to be considered in the same vein as an ethnic minority. Most belong, in varying degrees, to a disabled community, with distinct cultural values, vocabulary, in-jokes, mutual support, and common issues. On the other hand, they ask that we also think in terms of diversity, for their disabilities and abilities range widely. Each person has his or her individual strengths, weaknesses, and peculiarities.

Focus on what people can do

The traditional tendency is to focus on the impairment. Cooperate with these employees in taking a can-do attitude. Focus also on what people, disabled and non-disabled, can do together. See persons with disabilities as basically normal people who happen to have lost some function. Recognize that this does not define their character. They are people first, and their disability is only something they must cope with; it's not who they are.

Move through fear of disablement

Be aware of the fear of many people, perhaps your own unconscious fear, of being around persons with disabilities. Others typically do not want to be reminded, "There but for the grace of God go I. This could happen to me." Almost everyone has fear around the issues of body image and brain power.

Accept persons with disabilities as normal persons

Don't think of them as sick, as patients, as victims, or as abnormal. Remember that we all have some disability; it's just a matter of degree. Most persons with disabilities can marry, have sex, have children, and live many aspects of a "normal" life. The key is that they must work in order to have a full life. Their resources must be used in order for them to gain the sense of purpose, meaning, and achievement that all people want in life.

Explore possibilities for persons with mental retardation

Even the mentally retarded can usually do some sort of meaningful work. Some are classified as "high functioning mentally retarded" or "high functioning Down's syndrome."

Never treat persons with disabilities as if they're childlike or childish

Some persons with disabilities, especially the mentally impaired, may appear childlike to some people because of certain mannerisms that go along with their impairment. Respect for them as adults is essential. So are realistic assessments of their capabilities and the tailoring of assignments, expectations, and guidance to fit their level of ability.

Focus on the benefits

Research reported by Taylor Cox indicates that employees with disabilities tend to be:

- very enthusiastic—because they're happy to have real employment
- eager to succeed—they're adaptable and cooperative
- absent and tardy less
- a terrific resource—one that has been wasted in the past

This adds up to highly committed, loyal employees.

Strategy #3: Use Positive Language

Certain language habits tend to support stereotypes and focus on a person's disabilities rather than on the person. Avoid such phrases as "John is a diabetic," and use instead "John has diabetes." When you say that someone *is* an alcoholic, arthritic, drug addict, or mental retardate, the implication is that he or she is nothing more than that. More realistic language is "Sue has a drinking problem" or "Jan has a learning impairment." Prefer the active to the passive, such as "person who uses a wheelchair" instead of "person confined to a wheelchair." Say "He is a wheelchair user" instead of "He is wheelchair bound."

Use tact in dealing with disabilities. In some cases, persons with disabilities do not want to deal with their disability. They don't want to talk about it or be reminded of it. This presents the greatest challenge for the manager. You can imply and communicate a complete acceptance of the disability, a willingness to work with it and to accommodate—without forcing the employee into unwanted discussions.

Strategy #4: Follow the Lead of Successful Companies

Hewlett Packard is on the top ten list of corporations that actively recruit from a pool of disabled workers. Their leaders say that the "HP Way" is to treat persons with disabilities with dignity and respect. It was among the first large corporations to set policies for a disability-sensitive workplace. This includes holding seminars to inform all employees about various types of disabilities, developing a mentorship program, and supporting an employee network for employees with disabilities. You can encourage people in your company to take similar actions.

Even small companies can afford to make reasonable accommodations, especially when tax credits and write-offs are available. The EEOC and Department of Labor list three types:

- Disabled Access Tax Credit—allows eligible small businesses credit for accommodations. Fifty percent of eligible access expenditures that fall between $250 and $10,500 each year may be written off.
- Tax Deduction to Remove Architectural and Transportation Barriers—allows a tax deduction of up to $15,000 a year.
- Work Opportunity Tax Credit—allows up to 40 percent of the first year's wages of disabled employees referred by certain government agencies.

Strategy #5: Make Marketplace Connections

Many companies overlook the U.S. disability market of nearly 52 million people, not to mention a global market estimated at 850 million people. Your company may find that employees with disabilities are a valuable resource for understanding this market arena. They can help the company create communication bridges for marketing to persons with disabilities. In 2001, disabled Americans' spending power was more than $1 trillion. Yet many companies have made no efforts to target this huge market. Those who do are likely to find some profitable niches.

Companies that design products and services for disability markets often find an even larger general market for the same or similar products and services. This principle is sometimes called universal design. Designs that work for persons with disabilities are also frequently more workable for the rest of the population. Examples include big-button telephones, voice-recognition and voice-output computers, safer bathtubs, easier-to-open boxes, and easy-to-grip tools. Special service designs can also apply to larger markets. For example, personal services targeted at disability markets, such as grocery shopping and home meal delivery, can also fill a need for working mothers and others.

Among the models featured in ads of leading companies are people who obviously have some disability. Studies indicate that 52 percent of households pay more attention to advertising messages featuring people with disabilities (Atlanta 1998). Nordstrom's uses disabled models in its catalogs. A Benetton ad campaign featured students from Institut St. Valentin, a school for the disabled in the Bavarian Alps. Allied Domecq in Europe hired a blind man for its campaign for Sauza tequila. General Motors, AT&T, IBM, Sears, and Kmart are also using models with disabilities. Meanwhile, some retail stores are catering to shoppers in wheelchairs by lowering the height of their counters.

All of this signals a real turning point in public attitudes. Gone are the days when people with disabilities were kept from public view, hidden away in institutions and private homes. In the past 25 years, that has changed in many parts of the world, as new laws and organizations work to help those with disabilities be welcomed into the mainstream for the many contributions they can make.

SUMMARY

Persons with disabilities are those who have a physical or mental impairment that substantially limits one or more of the major life activities, or a record of such impairment, or are regarded as having such an impairment. They're generally stereotyped as childlike, dependent, and in need of pity and not leading normal lives. At work they're often stereotyped as being capable of only menial jobs, a source of greater safety risks, costs, and other difficulties. The realities are that many do work and nearly all want to work and to lead lives that are as normal as possible. Their abilities and motivations to work are as wide-ranging as that of the general public with the exception of their having an impairment in one or more activities. Managers and coworkers report that they are just as productive and cooperative as other workers, and they tend to have better records of punctuality, attendance, and turnover.

Before the 1930s most persons with disabilities were confined to institutions. Disability activists have brought about a realization that when certain accommodations are made, most persons with disabilities can become relatively independent and productive.

About 18 percent of the population are persons with disabilities. At least 50 million Americans fall under the ADA definition, and about half are employed. Mobility impairment is the most frequent type of disability among those in the workplace, but mental disorders are the most dominant overall, especially among those under 50, and it's the most neglected impairment. Persons with disability experience a significant gap in income, health care, transportation, education, social life, and life satisfaction.

Leaders and coworkers need to understand what it's like to be a person with disabilities, to become aware that they are normal persons except for a specific impairment. They want to be viewed as a person, not as "a disabled." The ILM was founded to help persons with disabilities take charge of their own lives, to form their own subculture, and to remove barriers to living and working on their own. New technology, especially computer-based technology, is helping more and more persons with even severe disabilities to achieve these goals. Stem cells and gene therapy hold promise for future breakthroughs.

The ADA is intended to end discrimination against persons because of their disabilities when reasonable accommodation will allow them to function effectively on the job. The law protects employers from undue hardship in providing such accommodation. About 15 percent of accommodations cost nothing, two-thirds cost under $500, and three-fourths cost under $1,000.

During the job recruitment phase, companies can no longer do medical screening or require medical histories. After hiring, workers with disabilities cannot be singled out for medical tests and screening. Reasonable accommodation must be made for applicants taking employment tests, and such screening tests must truly predict the likelihood of job success.

The major challenge for leaders is finding ways to help employees with disabilities to eliminate and overcome barriers to their productivity and effectiveness. This includes training to help coworkers feel knowledgeable and comfortable, helping persons with disabilities find adequate transportation, and providing the technological support and on-the-job training they need. The major opportunity leaders have is building upon the strengths of persons with disabilities. This includes providing adequate diversity training for all employees, adopting positive attitudes and language, adopting successful policies and practices, and helping persons with disabilities make marketplace connections. The main thing to remember when you want to personally assist a person with disability is to first ask what kind of help they would like.

Case Study 13.1 Severely Disabled Judy

Judy was paralyzed from the neck down. She must have help getting out of bed, getting dressed, and getting into a motorized wheelchair. Judy says that she still has the greatest ability of all: her mind, which is as sound as ever. She says if she can find a way to attend the university, she will get a degree in public administration and she wants to have a career in that field. She has come to you, a vocational counselor at the state Department of Rehabilitation as the first step in getting the funding she needs from the state in order to pursue this educational and career goal. Your responsibilities are:

- *Regarding education:* to predict the possibility and probability that an applicant will actually complete the educational program he or she enters.
- *Regarding occupation:* to predict the possibility and probability that an applicant will actually get and retain a job in the proposed field.
- *Regarding funds:* to allocate scarce state funds for rehabilitation in a manner that produces the best results for persons with disabilities and for society.

Considering Judy's situation and your responsibilities,
1. What are the root problems?
2. What will your decision be?
3. What will you say to Judy?

Case Study 13.2 Paul, Who Becomes Disabled

Paul works for the San Francisco AIDS Foundation as a developmental system associate. He's been there for nearly three years and his work has become an asset to the foundation. He is solely responsible for overseeing the data base system, which he helped create. His responsibilities include tracking donations and generating the foundation's budget reports and income statements. Paul's performance evaluations have always been excellent.

A little over a year ago Paul was diagnosed with Aggressive Liver Disease. This disease eventually results in liver failure. Paul is waiting for a liver transplant and hopes a donor will make one available within the next three to five years. Last year Paul took a four-month medical leave of absence to get his disease under control. Since his return, he has managed to keep his performance up to par, even though he must miss work for his doctor's appointment each week. The main physical problems that Paul is currently experiencing are fatigue and the nausea caused by the drugs he must take.

Paul knows he cannot continue working forty-hour weeks, and the commute to and from work is an energy drain he'd like to avoid. Paul starts thinking that he could do most of his work at home. He would need a computer, modem, and dedicated telephone line. He researches this idea and determines that this would require an initial investment of $2,500 plus about $20 per month in telephone charges. Paul is thinking about asking for a meeting with his manager *Claudia* and requesting that the foundation provide him with the equipment for a home office. As far as he knows, no other employee has ever asked to do most of their work from a home office. However, Paul is concerned that if he doesn't make better use of his failing energy, he'll be required to go on disability leave until his liver transplant comes through.

1. What are the key issues (root problems) here?
2. If you were Paul, what would you do?
3. If you were Claudia, what would you do?

Case Study 13.3 Service Dog

Bret is manager of the Technical Service Department of FileNet, Inc. He's been interviewing all week for two customer service reps.

Amber appears to be the most qualified applicant in terms of education and work experience. She is blind and needs some special accommodations. For one thing, she needs a Braille computer screen and keyboard. And she needs to bring her dog to work with her. She uses a Labrador Retriever, Star, as a service animal for such activities as getting to and from the office and going to the restroom, break room, and lunch room.

Brad foresees no problem with the computer accommodations, but he's not sure about accommodating a dog. The company has a strict policy against pets in the workplace. Brad sees the possibility that some employees may have animal allergies or fears. He wonders how much of a distraction Star might be—both to employees who like dogs and to those who can't stand them. His experience with dogs is that they belong primarily outdoors, not in an office. He's known them to relieve themselves on the floor, chew on furniture legs and anything else in sight, bark at strangers, and generally create problems.

1. What are the root problems?
2. What questions should Bret ask Amber about her service dog?
3. What types of accommodation is FileNet Inc. required to provide?
4. What should Bret do if it turns out that a coworker is allergic or phobic?

Case Study 13.4 Alisa at Touch-Up

Touch-Up Inc. has just opened a new branch and is looking for a Human Resources Director. One of the requirements for the new position is the ability to work from 50 to 70 hours per week and to maintain a heavy workload at times.

Alisa has applied for the position because it would advance her career. She is a 31-year-old Euro-American woman who uses a wheelchair because of paralysis in her lower legs. She joined Touch-Up two years ago as a personnel assistant in the Human Resources Department. She has received several promotions for excellent job performance and has maintained a heavy workload.

Joe also applied for the position. He has been with the company for a year as a sales person and in this position has put in very long work hours. He worked in the human resources department of Actel Company a few years ago.

Ted, the CEO, interviewed both Alisa and Joe. Alisa noticed that Ted seemed uncomfortable during the interview, which was much briefer than she had expected. Ted really didn't give her an opportunity to discuss why she thinks she is an ideal person for the new position.

A few days later, Ted announced that Joe would fill the new position.

1. What are the key issues (root problems) here?
2. If you were Ted, would you have done anything differently?
3. If you were Alisa, would you have done anything differently? What would you do now?

BONUS: FREQUENTLY ASKED QUESTIONS (FAQS) ABOUT PERSONS WITH DISABILITIES

FAQs about persons with disabilities reflect the need to understand specifics of working effectively with such persons, according to disability advocates Chalda Maloff and Susan Macduff. Here you'll find answers to FAQs about persons with 1) mobility impairments, 2) visual impairments, 3) hearing or speaking impairments

FAQs About Persons With Mobility Impairments

Q: How do I offer help to a person with disability? Or should I?

*   Offer help; it's never the wrong thing to do. It can always be declined if not wanted, but always *ask first* if the person wants you to help and take *no* for an answer.
*   If help is wanted, ask specifically what you can do and how to do it, or suggest something and get agreement.
*   If you assist another helper, remember the person with the disability is in charge.
*   Handle the helping situation as unobtrusively as possible; avoid a "circus."

Q: How do I help persons using wheelchairs, crutches, etc.?

*   Never grab their appliances except in cases of obvious immediate physical danger
*   After helping, stay a moment and make sure matters are in hand before leaving. Let the person know you are leaving.

Q: Should I open doors for persons with mobility impairments?

*   Everyone can use help with doors at times.
*   Hold the door itself, rather than their arm or wheelchair—until the person is completely inside.

Q: How can I be considerate of people who use wheelchairs?

*   Avoid blocking aisles and other spaces that a wheelchair user needs to access—don't block them briefcases, wastebaskets, etc.; push chairs under tables or desks; be aware.
*   When having a conversation with a wheelchair user, try to seat yourself in front of the person, so you can talk eye to eye. If you must stand, step back so the person isn't required to look up to you.

- Reaching elevator buttons may be impossible for a wheelchair user; offer to help.
- Users of non-motorized wheelchairs may need help getting up inclines or around barriers, but never begin pushing a wheelchair without asking permission.
- Never release the chair without warning, so the wheelchair user is always in control.
- Be sure you know exactly where the person wants to go.
- Begin pushing a wheelchair cautiously if you are not familiar with it. Go slowly at first; wheelchairs can gain surprising momentum.
- Note the size and protrusions of the chair, such as protruding foot plates. Pay attention to the terrain, such as step-downs, and watch where you're going.
- When entering a crosswalk in a street, remember the wheelchair user's feet may be further out than you think and may be dangerously close to passing traffic.
- Going up steps, lean the chair back to raise the front wheels and push the chair up frontwards.
- Going down steps, ask if the person prefers going down frontwards or backwards. Either way, raise the front wheels and keep them up until the entire chair is down the step. The occupant should always be tilted toward the back against the backrest instead of toward the front where there is no support.

Q: How do I show consideration for persons who walk with difficulty?

- When approaching steps, walk alongside them and offer your arm, which they can grasp, giving them control and support. Grabbing their arm can upset their balance.
- If more help is needed, put your arm around their waist.
- Any time a person falls, ask how you can assist, or offer your arm for the fallen person to take if he or she needs it. Don't grab the person.

Q: What should I consider when I'm planning activities that require mobility-impaired persons to go to unfamiliar places?

- Mobility-impaired persons need to know in advance whether they will encounter a difficult barrier—such as inadequate parking places, ramps, and restrooms.
- Find out what kinds of parking arrangements they need.
- Wheelchair users need access to restrooms with hallways and doors wide enough for the chair, enough space inside the stall, and perhaps a handbar by the commode.
- Never insist on simply carrying a disabled person over, around, and through obstacles. They may find it demeaning, unpleasant, or even scary—and it could be dangerous for both of you. All of us prefer to be independent and self-possessed.
- When in doubt, ask the disabled person for some tips on places that are accessible and comfortable.

FAQs About Persons With Visual Impairments

Q: What should I consider when giving directions to visually impaired coworkers?

- The single most useful thing you may be able to do is to furnish relevant information about the immediate surroundings. Often just a few words will do.
- Furnish simple information without hesitation, anytime it seems appropriate.
- When giving directions, be sure you really know where the target location is.
- Find out what types of directions are most helpful; this will depend on what the person can see or not see. Use numbers, where possible. Ask yourself, How many blocks down the street? How many doors down the hall?

- Give directions that are as specific as possible. Describe turns or curves as *left, right, clockwise*, etc. Terms such as *north* or *south* will probably be irrelevant.
- Describe anything out of the ordinary along the way, such as possible safety hazards.
- Tell persons with some vision about large, noticeable landmarks.
- Be as complete as necessary without overloading the person with information.
- If you think the place is simply too hard to find, offer to take them there.

Q: What should I do when I'm walking with a visually impaired person?

- City streets pose one of the biggest hazards for visually impaired persons. Offer your arm, but do not clutch the person's arm. Be sure you understand which street the person wants to cross.
- Don't leave the person until she or he is safely up the opposite curb.
- If the person does not take your arm, walk closely enough for her or him to reach over and touch you. Avoid getting separated in crowds.
- If the person takes your arm, walk slightly ahead to guide the way and proceed normally. Never push the person ahead of you.
- Avoid sudden turns or jerky movements.
- Tell the person when it's time to step up, step down, or step around some obstacle.
- Watch for overhead obstacles, especially with a taller companion.
- When approaching steps, elevators, or other possible barriers, pause and briefly describe what's ahead.

Q: What should I know about helping persons who use canes?

- If a person touches your foot with a cane, step aside and let her or him pass.
- Don't touch a cane without permission.
- When walking with a person who uses a cane, offer your arm.

Q: What should I know about helping person with guide dogs:

- Guide dogs and service dogs are used by a minority of visually impaired persons to help them get around and by mobility impaired persons to perform certain tasks.
- A guide dog is on duty any time it's wearing a harness.
- Take care to do nothing that will interfere with the dog's performance. Have faith in the dog and do not interfere unless there is a genuine emergency.
- Don't disrupt the routine and training by touching, feeding, petting, playing with, speaking to or commanding the dog unless you're encouraged to do so.
- If you have a dog, keep it away from the guide dog.
- When walking with someone who is using a dog, offer your arm.

Q: What should I consider when I'm communicating with visually impaired persons?

- Be aware that they rely on sound and touch to know what's going on.
- When you first meet a visually impaired person, feel free to shake hands. You might say, "May I shake your hand?" to cue them that you're extending your hand.
- When you meet the person thereafter, identify yourself, and any others you are with.
- When you would normally hand a business associate a business card, brochure, or other written material, give the visually impaired person the option to accept. You might offer to stay a moment and help interpret the material.

- When you enter the presence of visually impaired persons, speak to them and let them know you're there. Otherwise they may be unduly jolted when they hear you make some noise. Also, let them know when you're leaving.

- When leaving in a public place, say how long you'll be gone. Consider whether you need to offer to guide the person to a place where he or she can wait comfortably.

- When visually impaired persons hear your voice, they may be unsure whether you are talking to them or to someone else. They may remain silent rather than respond to comments they think might be meant for someone else.

- Address them by name when you're in a group or in public. If you don't know their name, stand directly in front of them and begin speaking. You may also gently touch their arm or repeat yourself to be sure they understand.

- Don't yell.

- Offer to describe visual sights.

- Speak up tactfully when some aspect of their grooming seems unpremeditated.

Q: When making plans that include visually-impaired persons, what should I keep in mind?

- If you're planning to meet outside the office, the key issue is likely to be transportation. Give some advance notice so they can arrange for a ride.

- If you're not sure whether a visually impaired person would be able to attend an event, ask. Invite them and allow them to make the decision; then respect their wishes.

- At restaurants, remember to offer help in reading the menu and calling the server.

FAQs About Persons With Hearing or Speaking Impairments

Q: What do I need to know generally about working with persons with hearing or speaking impairments?

- Most people with speaking impairments have normal hearing, and many hearing-impaired persons have excellent speech skills, particularly those whose hearing impairment is not of long standing or is not severe.

- When you initiate a direct conversation with communication-impaired persons, begin by asking, orally or in writing, how best to communicate.

- When introducing communication-impaired persons to others, make every effort to introduce only one or two persons at a time. Try to find a quiet spot and pronounce names slowly and distinctly.

- If you're asked to make a telephone call for a communication-impaired person, get the key information first, perhaps asking the person write it.

- Before you hang up, check to be sure the message is complete, and after you hang up, give a complete report.

Q: What do I need to remember about lip-reading?

- When talking to persons who use lip-reading, position yourself about three or four feet directly in front of them with adequate light on your face so they can see your lips.

- Face them squarely without looking down or turning your head.

- Keep your hands away from your mouth and avoid eating, smoking, or chewing gum.

- Be aware that lip-reading is tiring, so avoid long monologues. Use a give-and-take format. Take a break during longer conversations.

Q: What do I need to remember about communicating nonverbally?

- Your eyes are especially expressive, so remove dark glasses, hats, etc. Maintain a natural and relaxed manner without straining to exaggerate.
- If nonverbal communication is inadequate, find other methods.
- When both speaking and using gestures, be sure the gestures correlate with the speech. Random motions throw the listener off balance, trying to sift them from the real clues.

Q: How about writing out messages?

Writing out messages is slow but is sometimes used. Be creative when you communicate in writing. Often a simple diagram, picture, or map is most effective.

Watch the person's face as he or she reads your message, just as you would do if you were speaking, so you can gauge the understanding and reaction.

When persons begin writing to you, don't talk or otherwise distract them until they finish. Allow them to finish writing before you try to read the message, and read the entire message before you begin to answer.

In a group, offer to read the person's written message aloud to others.

Q: How should I communicate when a professional interpreter is used?

- Professional interpreters who use sign language may be used by people with severe impairments. When you speak through an interpreter, your key goal should be to respect the dignity and autonomy of the impaired person who is the "listener." The interpreter is merely a device in this situation, a tool.
- Face the hearing-impaired person and speak as though no interpreter were present.
- Direct all your comments to the listener, the person with whom you have business, saying, for example, "Your project is being reviewed." The interpreter will relay these exact words to the person.
- Never direct comments intended for the listener to the interpreter, saying "His project is being reviewed." This has the effect of excluding the listener, implying that he is a helpless bystander.
- Remember to look at the listener, not the translator, and to speak to her or him in direct address, using *you*, not *he* or *she*.
- Avoid engaging an interpreter in side conversations that exclude the other person.
- Remember that with any translation process is difficult. Choose simple, specific words to be as clear and direct as possible, avoiding slang.

Q: How about communicating by telephone?

- A telecommunication device for the deaf (TDD) is used by many people with speaking or hearing impairments for communicating by telephone. If you don't have a TDD, you can still communicate through the device by going through a voice exchange system, available in most cities.
- Regular telephone communication with a hearing-impaired person is often possible without translator equipment, if the person has enough hearing ability.
- Organize your message ahead of time so you can convey it in a concise, direct manner.
- Try to quiet the noise at your end.
- Talk directly into the receiver clearly and firmly. Speak moderately slowly and pause at the end of a sentence.
- Be prepared to spell, rephrase, or use more creative ways to get your message across.

- If you have trouble hearing or understanding, ask for clarification as soon as you start getting lost.
- Keep the conversation short unless you are encouraged to extend it.

Q: How do I plan and conduct meetings that include communication-impaired persons?

- Select a room with good acoustics and a minimum of extraneous noise.
- Check ahead of time to determine what devices, such as interpreters, are needed.
- Offer the people with impairments preferential seating, where they will have a good view of speakers. Ask what they prefer.
- Ask speakers to stay in one spot rather than pacing the floor, for lip-readers.
- Pay special attention to the use of visual aids, handouts, charts, illustrations, and other communication aids.
- Write down new words or terms as you introduce them; it is almost impossible to lipread an unknown word.
- Write down important facts.
- Repeat all comments or questions from other people in the room before you respond to them.
- If you sit next to a hearing-impaired person in a meeting, be as quiet as possible. If you must communicate with the person during the meeting, write a brief note.
- Allow the hearing-impaired person to observe any notes you're taking
- Afterwards, offer to answer questions.
- Make occasional eye contact with speaking-impaired persons, to see if they have anything to contribute to the discussion.
- If they can't speak up quickly, you can create a break in the conversation and encourage them to participate.
- If you sit next to a speaking-impaired person, offer to ask questions for her or him during the meeting.

Q: How do I work effectively with persons with hearing impairments?

- The first step is getting their attention without startling them. Stand in front of them and say their name loudly, but don't shout. If you don't know their name, stand directly in front of them and begin speaking. You may also gently touch their arm or repeat yourself to be sure they understand.
- If they don't respond, tap them lightly on the arm or shoulder. If you're not in touching range, wave your hand and try to make visual contact. You may also get attention by knocking on the desk or rapping on a nearby wall, as many are sensitive to such vibrations. Flipping the light switch will get the attention of everyone in the room, so use this method with greater selectivity.
- Effort and concentration are needed by hearing impaired persons in order to understand the speech of others. Conversing at length while walking down a hall or street may be exhausting or impossible.
- You may be able to help as an interpreter when a hearing-impaired person is trying to understand someone with a foreign accent or a child with a high-pitched voice.
- Giving needed information is one of the most helpful things you can do—especially about any sound that may spell danger, such as honking horns, sirens, and alarms—but also information that comes over public address systems, radio, and other sources where lip-reading is impossible.

REFERENCES

Althen, Gary. *American Ways*. Intercultural Press, 1988.

Atlanta Paralympic Organizing Committee, as reported in "New Opportunities for Disabled People," *The Futurist*: 7, Dec 1998.

Bennett-Alexander, Dawn D. and Laura P. Hartman. *Employment Law for Business*, 3rd ed., McGraw-Hill 2001.

Brown, S.E. "Creating a Disability Mythology," *International Journal of Rehabilitation Research*, 15, 227–233, 1992.

Bureau of National Affairs, Inc. "The Americans with Disabilities Act: A Practical and Legal Guide to Impact, Enforcement, and Compliance," Washington, DC, 1990.

Burgdorf, Robert. L. "The ADA is a Civil Rights Law," *Electric Edge* magazine, www.ragged-edge-mag.com, September 1999.

Business Week, "The New Competitive Advantage." 63–93, May 30, 1994.

Business Week, "The New Workforce," March 20, 2000.

Census 2000, "Disability Status: 2000," Census 2000 Brief, U.S. Census Bureau.

Cox, Taylor, Jr. *Cultural Diversity in Organizations*. Berrett-Koehler Publishers, 1993.

Crew, Nancy M., and Irving Kenneth Zola. *Independent Living for Physically Disabled People*. Jossey-Bass, 1983.

Diller, Matthew, "Judges don't understand the ADA," *Electric Edge* magazine, *www.ragged-edge-mag.com* September 1999.

Green and Johnson 1987

Hopkins, Kevin, and Susan Nestleroth, supplement in *Business Week*, .24, October 28, 1991.

Kessler, Ronald C. et al, "The National Co-morbidity Survey Replication, *Archives of General Psychiatry* 62, archpsyc.ama-assn.org, June 2005.

Longmore, P.K. "A Note on Language and the Social Identity of Disabled People," *American Behavioral Scientist* 28, 3, 419–423, January/February 1985a.

Longmore, P.K. "Screening Stereotypes: Images of Disabled People." *Social Policy*, 32–37, Summer 1985b.

Longmore, P.K. "Uncovering the Hidden History of People with Disabilities," *Reviews in American History*, 355–364, September 1987.

Maloff, Chalda, and Susan Macduff. *Business and Social Etiquette With Disabled People*. Charles C. Thomas Publisher, 1988.

Massengill, D. "Adding Insult to Injury: Disability-Based Hostile Environment under the ADA," *Employee Relations Law Journal* 30, 74–99, 2004.

McDonough, Hugh H. "Hiring People with Disabilities." *Supervisory Management*, 11–12, February 1992.

McGovern, John. "Justice Department Publishes Final Rules on the ADA," *P&R*: 12–73, November 1991.

McKee, Bradford. "Achieving Access for the Disabled." *Nation's Business*, 31–34, June 1991.

Minton, Eric. "Implementing a Can-Do Attitude." *Hemisphere*, 31, July 1994.

"Myths & Facts: About People Who Have Disabilities." National Easter Seal Society, 2002.

Mitchell, Olivia S., ed. *As the Workforce Ages*. ILR Press, 1993.

N.O.D. National Organization on Disability, "2000 N.O.D./Harris Survey of Americans with Disabilities," *www.nod.org*. 2002.

Office of Disability Employment Policy, Job Accommodation Network, *dol.gov/odep/pubs/fact/mythfact*, 2004.

Pear, Robert, *New York Times*, as reported in *San Francisco Chronicle*, A-1, December 13, 1999.

Potter, Edward E. *A Compliance Guide to the Americans with Disabilities Act*. Washington, DC: Employment Policy Foundation, 1991.

Ragged Edge, The. "The Disability Experience from the Pages of the First Fifteen Years of the Disability Rag." ed. Barrett Shaw, www.ragged-edge-mag.com

Shapiro, Joseph. "The New Civil Rights." *Modern Maturity*, 28–35, November-December 1994.

Shapiro, Joseph. *No Pity: People with Disabilities Forging a New Civil Rights Movement*. Times Books, 1993.

Stace, S. "Vocational Rehabilitation for Women with Disabilities." *International Labour Review* 126, 3, 301–316, 1987.

Vash, Carolyn. "Sheltered Industrial Employment" in *Annual Review of Rehabilitation*. Springer, 1980.

Vash, Carolyn. *The Psychology of Disability*. Springer Publishing Co., 1981.

Vash, Carolyn L. *Personality and Adversity*. Springer Publishing Co., 1994.

WSJ. "Labor Letter" in *Wall Street Journal*, A-1, June 7, 1994. Resources

RESOURCES

Developmental Disability Resource Center, www.ddrcco.com

Disability History Website. www.disabilityhistory.org. Created by Patricia Chadwick and Stephen Dias of Oakland, CA.

Disability Rag & ReSource. *Ragged Edge* magazine, *Electric Edge*, online version, www.ragged-edge-mag.com.

Disability Rights Education & Defense Fund, national law and policy center, Berkeley, CA, www.dredf.org.

Disability Rights Advocates, national law center, Oakland, CA, www.draLegal.org.

National Organization on Disability, www.nod.org

Read Me a Book Website. www.readmeabook.com created by Dick Stein.

Society for Disability Studies, University of Illinois at Chicago, www.ulc.edu/orgs/sds

We magazine. 372 Central Park West, Suite 6B, New York, NY 10025, www.wemagazine.com, e-mail editors@wemagazine.com. A monthly magazine that focuses on issues of persons with disability.

World Institute on Disability, 510 16th Street, Suite 100, Oakland, California 94612, phone (510) 763–4100, www.wid.org

CHAPTER 14

Working with Older &
Younger Persons

*What if we began to value older persons as fountains of wisdom,
support, and vitality . . . and to expect that they would continue to
grow, develop, and unfold as they did earlier in life?*
Betty Friedan

*Generation X and Y want it all, and companies are starting to realize they need to listen.
Companies need to realize that work-life balance is not a problem to be solved; It's an
ongoing issue that needs to be managed.*
Jim Bird, CEO Work Life Balance

Americans are living longer and working longer these days, which means that all of us are working with a wider age range of people. Bridging generation gaps has become more important than ever. We will discuss all the generations that are now active in the workplace, with a special emphasis on older persons. "Ageism" is considered a significant workplace problem with legal implications, unlike "youth-ism".

Older Americans are the fastest-growing population group. Nearly half of all Americans are older than 40 and so are protected by the Age Discrimination Employment Act (ADEA). Nearly one-third are older than 50, and baby boomers, as they turn 50, are dramatically increasing the size of this group. Now that it's illegal to force persons to retire, and medical breakthroughs help people stay vital at every age, more people are working into their 70s and 80s. All of this means that more and more of your co-workers are likely to be persons older than 50.

Older workers who keep their skills and knowledge up to date are likely to have higher incomes than younger workers. But those who don't are more likely to lose their jobs. If they do, they then face more intense problems than their younger counterparts with unemployment, underemployment, and lowered wages. Those who keep their jobs may face age discrimination, management resistance to investing in training for older workers, and a resulting lack of new job skills. They must cope with the generation gap that can occur as new generations of younger workers enter the workforce. Older workers must also deal with retirement expectations—their own, their organization's, and the culture's—and decisions around retiring, not retiring, partially retiring, or starting a new career.

People who have taken the time and effort to learn some facts about older persons say they have boosted their ability to work productively with such persons. Supervisors say such information helps them understand how to help older employees to keep learning, stay motivated, and continue contributing to the organization. Co-workers, teams, and organizations gain a leading edge when they learn how to utilize the wealth of experience, knowledge, and talent that many older employees bring to the workplace.

In this chapter you'll explore what it's like to be an older person in the American workplace. You'll also learn about basic generational differences so that regardless of your age, you can bridge generation gaps. Remember, the more open you are to putting yourself in the place of others and seeing things the way they might see them, the better your ability to feel comfortable with people of all ages and to build productive work relationships. Specifically, you'll learn:

- How typical myths and stereotypes about older persons compare with reality
- How the current situation is connected to certain historical events
- How ageism in the workplace affects older persons and organizations
- What you should know about the Age Discrimination Employment Act
- How skills obsolescence affects older employees employment and wages
- When and why people retire and the need for more options
- Generation gaps and how to bridge them
- How to build on the strengths that older employees bring to the organization

Before we explore these fascinating aspects of working with people from other generations, complete Self-Awareness Activities 14.1 and 14.2.

Older Man

Courtesy of Gary Houlder/Corbis Images.

Older Woman

Courtesy of Chris Carroll/Corbis Images.

Self-Awareness Activity 14.1: What Do You Believe about Older Persons?

Purpose:

- to get in touch with your beliefs and stereotypes about this group of people
- to experience how judgmental beliefs affect your thinking and feeling processes
- to experience the ways in which your beliefs create your reality regarding other persons, even before you have any interaction with them.

Part I. What Do You Believe about Older Women?

Step 1. Associations

- Relax as deeply as you can.
- Close your eyes for a moment and take a few deep breaths.
- Now focus on the picture that symbolizes "older woman"
- Imagine that you are this woman. Be older woman.
- Notice any resistance to being this person—and any willingness.
- Notice words, images, thoughts, and feelings that come to mind as you are "seeing and being this woman."

Step 2. Negative Associations

- Next, as you focus on the picture, allow negative opinions to come up, perhaps some that you typically hold about older women.
- Notice your *thoughts* as you see the person in this negative way. What *feelings?*

Step 3. Positive Associations

- Now, still focusing, allow positive opinions to come up, perhaps some that you typically hold about older women.
- Notice your *thoughts* as you see the person in this negative way. What *feelings?*

Step 4. Insights and Write-up

- Now review this experience and write about it.
- When you first saw the picture, what thoughts and feelings came up? These may reflect your deepest responses to people from this group.
- Think about the differences in your thoughts and feelings when you consciously held a positive opinion versus a negative opinion.
- Write a few sentences about your feelings, thoughts, and insights.

Part II. What Do You Believe about Older Men?

- Repeat the steps in Part I, this time focusing on the image of an older man.

Self-Awareness Activity 14.2: What Do You Know about Older & Younger Persons?

Purpose: To see what you know about the issues covered in this chapter.
Instructions: Determine whether you think the following statements are basically true or false—and think about why. The answers will emerge in this chapter, and the summary at the end of the chapter focuses on these issues.

1. Older workers are no more forgetful than younger ones.
2. Older workers have more difficulty adapting to change.

3. Older workers are prone to frequent absences because of age-related conditions and illnesses.
4. Older workers have fewer work accidents than younger workers.
5. Extensive training for older workers doesn't pay off because they don't learn as well and they'll retire soon anyway.
6. The Age Discrimination Employment Act covers employees age 55 and older.
7. The Baby Boom generation is known for its focus on security and savings.
8. Generation X is one that's most dependent on parents, schools, and corporate America.

STEREOTYPED MYTHS AND REALITIES

Betty Friedan (1993) and Steven Sandell have surveyed a number of interesting studies of age discrimination. They found that most of the myths and stereotypes about older persons are either false or distorted, partial truths. In fact, most stem from the high value the American culture places on youth and appearance and the tendency to avoid facing one's own aging and eventual death.

Remember, although stereotypes aren't identical to prejudice, rigid stereotypes about people usually lead to prejudice. For example, you've heard that people lose their mental abilities after a certain age. When older co-worker Joe forgets an appointment, you think "Uh-oh, Joe's losing it." But when younger worker Janet forgets an appointment, you think "We all forget sometimes. She must be really busy." Each time a "Joe" forgets, your belief is reinforced, and soon you develop a rigid belief that all older persons lose their mental abilities and become forgetful. The ultimate goal in becoming aware of myths and stereotypes is to refute those that are false or rigid and to move beyond them to appreciating each generation's unique value and contribution to the workplace.

Myth #1: People Quit Learning When They Get Old

One of the most untrue and degrading myths is "You can't teach an old dog new tricks," closely related to the myth that "Anyone over 35 is a technological dinosaur." It's common and career-devastating for management to ignore training for older workers—and for older workers to believe training won't pay off for them. In fact, while the most rapid rate of learning occurs at very young ages, the capacity to learn remains high throughout life. They're not only trainable and retrainable, but also a unique resource.

Intellectual Performance

Intellectual performance remains robust throughout life for healthy people. From age 30 onward there is a slight mental slowdown in reaction time, but older workers compensate by increasing their speed on certain complex repetitive tasks. Other functions, such as vocabulary choice, get better with age, and the brain continues to develop throughout adult life. Some brain cells die each year, but connecting branches between them—pathways for the nerve impulses that create thought, feeling, and memory—keep sprouting and spreading, more than compensating for the loss of cells.

Forgetting names and poor concentration are not connected with normal aging. They're often connected with new priorities, more years of information, more names to sort through, and heavy work loads. Actually, 92 percent of persons older than 65 show no significant mental deterioration. Only about 8 percent have such symptoms as partial memory loss and slowing reaction time.

Research uncovered by author Betty Friedan indicates that age actually brings some positive changes in certain mental abilities. The type of intelligence that involves experience, meaning, knowledge, professional expertise, and wisdom continues to increase even though speed in completing IQ tests may decline. Older workers bring a lifetime of experience to the learning situation. That's why they tend to be better at problem solving, to draw on more information for decision making, and to be good mediators.

Further, people do *not* deteriorate in either basic mental competence or intelligence, even in their eighties, *if* they remain healthy and continue to be physically and mentally active and stimulated. For example, through mental activity, people can continue to develop vital new brain connections, and even reverse deterioration, until the end of life. Yet the false myths of older persons may keep them from seeking or getting continuing education and the right kind of health care.

Cyber Skills

Younger employees who grew up on computers and cell phones tend to assume that older employees avoid such technology. In fact, people over age 50 were the fastest-growing part of the U.S. internet users 1997–2000, doubling in size from 19 to 38 percent. People from 50 to 64 increased their usage by 15 percent, and those over 65 by 28 percent, according to a study by MediaLink.com (2001).

Alzheimer's and the Nun Study

Among people over age 65, only 8 percent have Alzheimer's, but the incidence rises to about half of those over age 85. A breakthrough long-term study of nearly 700 retired nuns is being conducted by researcher David Snowden (Lemonick 2001). He has linked the essays they wrote as young women entering the order to their emotional and intellectual capabilities and tendencies, which are in turn linked to the likelihood that they will develop Alzheimer's and similar brain disorders. Here are some preliminary suggestions about how to prevent the onset of these disorders:

> **Thinking.** Encourage rich density and complexity of ideas—to stimulate and exercise the brain's connections. Engage in an active intellectual life, if possible beginning with a college education, that values creative thinking.
>
> **Feeling.** Learn how to think and act in ways that trigger positive emotions, spending more and more time in ever more expansive emotional states such as joy and peace.
>
> **Acting.** Engage in active mental work and play. Choose interesting and challenging work that you like (better yet, that you love), hobbies that are engaging, absorbing, and fun such as crossword puzzles, card games, mind games and challenging craft and building projects.
>
> **Learning.** Continually learn new information and skills, such as new languages, vocations, hobbies, avocations, teaching, tutoring.
>
> **Relating.** Keep developing close relationships with family and friends and maintain close contact.
>
> **Protecting Head.** Avoid head trauma by using helmets, seatbelts, airbags, etc.
>
> **Preventing.** Check your family history for signs of Alzheimer's to determine if you must take more preventive measures than usual.

Myth #2: Older Workers Are More Rigid and Dogmatic

Evidence indicates that dogmatic behavior is unrelated to age. What is related to age is a tendency to become more caring, accepting, and mellow. This means that older persons tend to handle crises better than younger workers and to see the humor in life's slings and arrows.

Nurturing, Accepting

People are more likely to mentor others and become more accepting of life as they age. Carol Ryff's studies indicate that men and women tend to change their behavior during middle age to focus more on mentoring younger persons, showing more concern for guiding the next generation and feeling more of a sense of responsibility to younger persons. Beyond middle age, people tend to become more accepting of life, to adapt to the triumphs and disappointments of being human, and to view past events as inevitable, appropriate, and meaningful (Ryff 1985). While basic character traits tend to be stable, people's experiences and personal development become more varied with age.

Appreciative of Respect

An implication of the rigid stereotype is that older workers resent being told what to do by younger managers. In fact, no one really likes being told what to do, and younger workers are more apt to respond negatively. Older workers do appreciate receiving some respect for their years of experience. When managers get them on their side, they're less likely than younger workers to be vying for the manager's position, to quit, or to be disloyal. Their accumulated wisdom can be very helpful to managers and co-workers

Creative

Also implied in the rigid stereotype is that older workers are not very creative. In fact, creativity and intellectual activity are still vital in persons older than 100, according to a Social Security Administration survey of such people. When creativity is encouraged and rewarded, and when the environment is structured to enhance it, older workers bring a greater richness of ideas, stemming from their abundance of life experience (Friedan 1993).

Myth #3: Older Workers Are Less Productive, Just Coasting to Retirement

In 1998 over 100 leading image consultants were sent pictures of gray-haired men—along with pictures of the same men with darker hair. Their reaction? While they assumed that 49% of the dark-haired men would be "very capable," they gave only 27% of gray-haired men that rating. Scripps Howard News Service (1998) reported that researchers expected gray-haired women to fare even worse, due to gender bias.

Gray-haired persons, and those who otherwise look older, are seen as less capable and less productive than they were when they were younger, but research refutes this myth. There is no significant performance decline that's caused by aging in the case of engineers, scientists, blue-collar workers, clerical workers, and production workers. And several studies suggest that older paraprofessionals and clerical workers outperform younger workers.

U.S. Department of Labor studies reveal that age has little effect on manual-labor workers through age 50, and declines in productivity after age 50 never exceed 10 percent, on average. A study of 1,700 managers working in diverse organizations showed that when managerial performance is measured in terms of such bottom-line indicators as return on total capital, growth of stockholders' equity, earnings per share, and sales growth, no significant differences in performance could be related to the age of managers.

A similar myth is that older employees are less energetic and enthusiastic. For some older persons, but not all, some age-related decline may occur in speed and accuracy of movement, perception, hearing, vision, and certain types of problem-solving skills. However, researchers have concluded that these declines would affect performance in only a few jobs requiring extremely high levels of sensory or cognitive skills. Workers older than 60 are functionally able to excel in nearly all occupations, drawing on years of experience and good judgment. Overwhelming scientific evidence, reported in *Retirement Living* indicates that, compared to younger workers, older workers:

- enjoy higher morale
- have a greater sense of organization commitment
- are more involved in their jobs
- rate work as more important to their lives
- have the highest job satisfaction of any age group
- rate needs for job security as more important
- are less likely to report an intention to leave the organization
- are much less likely to leave the organization

Age stereotypes depict older people as frail and fragile, as having lost the vitality and energy necessary to make a full commitment to a career. Actually, large differences exist with respect to the health and well-being of persons in every age category. While some people remain very healthy in their eighties, and even in their nineties, others become mentally and physically old at 40. Recently, changes in lifestyles, dietary habits, and exercise patterns, along with the better medical interventions, have dramatically changed the health picture for older persons.

In summary, evidence on the performance of older workers and managers generally indicates that they perform as well as their younger counterparts on almost all criteria. Chronological age is a poor indicator of a person's mental and physical well-being and an inadequate basis for predicting vocational performance. Individual differences within age groups account for much more variation in performance than does age. Managers should carefully assess each employee's capabilities with an eye toward matching them to job requirements.

Myth #4: Older People Have Higher Absenteeism and Accident Rates

The accidents myth is totally false. Bureau of Labor Statistics data shows that occupational injuries occur at a lower rate for older workers. In many instances older workers are better risks than younger workers across a variety of jobs even when risk exposure is controlled. Some studies indicate that their accident rate is less than half that of younger workers. All managers agree that older workers tend to be more careful.

The absentee myth is essentially untrue. Older employees' overall attendance record is much better than that of younger workers. According to the American Council of Life Insurance, workers older than 45 call in sick an average of 3.1 days per year, compared to younger workers average of 3.8 days. For one thing, people older than 65 are less likely than those who are younger to suffer from the *acute* illnesses that require hospitalization and absenteeism. Also, younger workers are more likely to take days off for caring for family members, for dealing with love affairs, for going to the beach, and for other "mental health" reasons. Most older workers have outlived their responsibilities for dependent children and elderly parents and are free to concentrate on their careers.

The kernel of truth in the absentee myth is that older workers are more likely to be absent for unavoidable reasons such as illness. The older we get, the more likely we are to develop *chronic* diseases and to become disabled, primarily because of heart disease, arthritis, or cancer. However, medical breakthroughs are helping people to avoid and cope with these diseases. And nearly all older persons remain healthy until the last few months of their lives (Salzberg); for example:

- 95% of persons older than 65 live independent lives
- 95% of age-70 persons have no serious disabilities
- 80% of age-80 persons have no serious disabilities

The absentee myth is based on an image of age as inevitable decline and deterioration, which in turn is tied to a dread of aging and of dying. It causes people to deny that old age even exists for them. And the more age is denied, the more terrifying it becomes. Prejudice and discrimination toward the elderly are actually created by the American culture's obsession with and idealization of youth and by our refusal even to look at the reality of age on its own terms. Subconsciously, we think that if we can keep old people out of sight, we can keep the illusion of eternal youth and rarely have to face the fact that we all age and die.

Myth #5: Older Workers Are Not as Attractive to Clients

This myth contains the kernel of truth implied by our discussion of the American tendency to be obsessed with youth and fearful of old age. However, it overlooks the truth that beauty is in the eye of the beholder—and it's only skin deep.

Gender Differences

Since women's value is more firmly tied to looks than men's, women stand to lose the most as they age. If a man is old, ugly, and wise, he's a sage. If a woman is old, ugly, and wise, she's a hag, a witch, a crone. But in pre-patriarchal societies the elder women were generally considered founts of wisdom, law, healing skills, and moral leadership, according to Betty Friedan's study. Their wrinkles would have been badges of honor, not of shame. By contrast, our society regards elder women as relatively unattractive and useless.

When men are considered in their prime, in their fifties and sixties, women are considered to be over the hill. The aging woman is often surprised and hurt by the unexpected hostility she encounters as she slips into old age. The combination of sexism and ageism turns older women into invisible citizens of the modern world. We make them invisible by rarely featuring them in films or television programs, and generally passing them by as social and professional leaders.

Media and Advertising Stereotypes

Older people are generally pictured as "ugly, toothless, sexless, incontinent, senile, confused, and helpless," and old age is so negatively stereotyped that "it has become something to dread and feel threatened by." These were the conclusions of the Gray Panthers' nationwide volunteer force called Media Watch, reported in Advertising Age. The sales pitches for products that promise to stop or cover up aging send the message that age is acceptable only if it passes for or acts like youth. A multibillion-dollar beauty industry exploits women's well-founded fear of looking old. Many people proclaimed a real breakthrough in the 1980s when the female stars of the TV series *Dynasty* were considered still attractive and employable at age 50. A 1993 consumer survey, reported in Advertising Age, found that most consumers older than 35 now believe that a woman can be beautiful at 40, or 50, and *even* past 60. This was hailed as great progress, even though it implies that women past sixty-something have no chance (*Advertising Age* 1993).

Yet the U.S. population is about one-third older persons over age 50, one-third youngsters under age 20, and one-third adults in between. Assuming youngsters are not potential customers for many of the products and services that companies sell, people 50 and older represent nearly half the potential customers that most companies should target. Companies who project an image of older persons in a positive way, with attractive, natural older role models will hit pay dirt, especially with the me-generation of baby boomers, as discussed later.

Myth #6: One That's True—You're Only as Old as You Feel

A myth is a symbolic saying or story whose function is to bind together the thoughts of a group and promote coordinated social action. Some myths are essentially true, and this is one of them. Scientists are discovering that aging is mainly in the mind. The best ways to slow the mental aging process are (Wagster 2005):

- maintaining a positive attitude
- remaining mentally and physically active
- eating plenty of foods that are rich in anti-oxidants, such as fresh vegetables and fruits

These activities bring us to Myth #7.

Myth #7: One That's Very True—Use It or Lose It

This myth is not only true, it's a key to staying healthy and alert as we grow older. We can retain both our vitality and health by using our minds and bodies. Physical and mental exercise, along with a healthy diet, are the specific keys. Energy levels peak in the early thirties and normally drop about 7 percent per decade, primarily because people tend to become more sedentary. But physical exercise can dramatically slow the energy drop.

Aging decline has in fact been reversed with changes in diet, exercise, lifestyle, and environment. People who reached age 65 in the 1990s were more likely to be healthy, active, and financially self-sufficient than any previous generation as predicted by Alice Rossi (Campbell 1985). We must learn to view age as continued human development, a continuation of personal growth, not of decline and decay. Staying independent and connected to people in the workplace, community, and family are crucial to vital aging and longevity. The key is to move on to new growth in the last third of life, from age 60 to 90.

PAST AND PRESENT PROFILE

In 1860 people over age 65 were less than 3 percent of the population but they had great economic and political influence relative to their proportion. They dictated the behavior of younger family members because they owned the farm or family business and they knew more than anyone about making money from it. New generations adopted the occupations and lifestyles of parents and grandparents, so older people's knowledge and experience were indispensable. They were at the center of economic and social life, from trade and commerce to finance, political organization, and religious training. By the 1930s most who lived to old age faced poverty, loneliness, and ageism, according to J.C. Hushbeck's studies (1989). What happened in between?

Past: Separation of the Generations

Between 1860 and 1920 we moved from an agricultural to an industrial economy. Mass production led to the de-skilling of most workers. The rapid pace of work, need for stamina, and a rapid wearing-out of laborers led firms to prefer hiring younger applicants. This put older workers at a physical and technological disadvantage. As people moved to cities to get jobs, the nuclear family became the norm, housed in small quarters, and the older generation was separated from the younger.

Fewer and fewer older persons were able to be self-supporting or economically productive. Many were faced with no property, no job, and uncertain family support. Industrial pension plans were usually nonexistent or inadequate when it was time to retire. Social security and improved company pension plans have improved the retirement picture, but most retirees are still socially isolated, ghettoized, and ignored.

Current Profile: Who Are the "Older"?

Today, people are living longer, so what constitutes "old age" is changing, and the population of older persons is growing larger by the year. Now that childbirth is safer and less frequent, women are outliving men.

How Old is Old?

How old is old depends on who you ask and why you ask.

ADEA = 40. If you want to know who is protected by the ADEA, the answer is people 40 and older.

BLS = 55. If you want to know what information the Bureau of Labor Statistics (BLS) has on older employees, the answer is that older people are 55 and older. Research also shows this is the age when certain workplace problems become noticeable, such as skills obsolescence and difficulties in getting updated training and being rehired after job loss.

Census = 65. If you ask the U.S. Census Bureau for information on older persons, most publications deal with persons 65 and older, although some now use age 55 and older.

Gerontologists say that because people live longer and remain healthier than in the past, it's now more realistic to use two age categories:

- *young-old*, currently 65 to 75, soon to be 75 to 85
- *old-old*, now older than 75, soon to be older than 85.

Currently, persons who make it to age 55 without chronic illness will normally remain healthy to age 85.

How Many Are Old?

About 13 percent of Americans are currently older than 65, a huge increase during the 20th century, and the trend is expected to accelerate in the next 20 years, as shown in Table 14.1. By 2030 the proportion of over-65 persons will have grown to 1 in 4, compared to 1 in 25 back in 1900.

TABLE 14.1: Proportion of Americans Over Age 65

1900	1990	2000	2015 Projected	2030 Projected*
4%, 1 in 25	12.5%, 1 in 8	12.4%, 1 in 8	17%, 1 in 6	25%, 1 in 4
3 million	31 million	35 million	54 million	70 million

Source: *U.S. Census Bureau, 2003.*
A Profile of Older Americans: 2002, U.S. Dept. Health & Human Services

Ethnic Differences

The Average life span for all Americans in 2000 was 78 (U.S. Census Bureau). That's a big improvement over the past: in 1900 it was 47, and in the Middle Ages it was 31. How old you live to be is affected by your ethnic heritage. Here are percentages of people older than 65 in 2000, by ethnic subgroup:

- Euro-Americans   13 %
- Asian Americans   8
- Latino Americans   8
- African Americans   6
- American Indians   6

The Euro-American population had the highest proportion of elderly because they have the fewest recent immigrants, meaning fewer young persons, and lower birth rates.

- Who lives the longest? Euro-American women, who average age 80 at death.
- Who dies the youngest? African American men, average age 45 at death.

Women—Older and Poorer

About 60 percent of people older than 65 are women—because they live longer. The older they become, the less likely the women are to be married because their husbands die before they do. Therefore, older women are more likely to live alone, in contrast to older men, most of whom are married and living with their wives. And the women are more likely to live in poverty, with 12 percent classified as poor, compared with 7 percent of older men (Census 2000).

Working Longer

In recent years a higher proportion of persons 65 and older are remaining in the fulltime labor force, as shown in Table 14.2. Many more work on a part-time or temporary basis with a company or as a self-employed consultant or contractor.

TABLE 14.2: Older Persons Working Full Time

Gender	Age 55–59	Age 60–64	Age 65–74	Age 75–84
Men	77%	57%	25%	10%
Women	63	44	15	5

Source: *Census 2000.*

AGEISM: HOW IT WORKS, HOW TO MOVE BEYOND IT

Ageism means that as you progress from being perceived as a middle-aged employee in the prime of life to an older employee, you are likely to be increasingly devalued, avoided, and discriminated against. Such actions are usually subtle but occasionally blatant.

A study of over 12,000 cases of age discrimination (Roscigno 2007) revealed that workers around the age of 50 start to experience considerable age discrimination because of stereotypes about ability and competence. More Euro-American workers experienced age discrimination, and being an ethnic minority was not a significant factor. Women were more often discriminated against based on a combination of age and gender. Workers in the manufacturing and construction industries were most often subject to age discrimination. In 66 percent of cases the result was termination, in 12 percent it was harassment, and in 10 percent exclusion from hiring.

Typical cases included older salesmen whose hours were reduced because of alleged downturns in business, while younger salespersons' hours were increased. Or older employees' hours were reduced because they "lacked drive" or were told they were not "right" for the job because the business wanted to attract younger customers. Then the company hired younger people as replacements. Some companies used financial costs, personal liabilities, harassment, and "rightsizing" as the rationale for discriminating against older workers.

We need our older employees. They're the fastest-growing population group at the same time that the U.S. labor pool was shrinking. It's time for everyone in the workplace to reassess negative views of older workers. We all have a stake in how society will treat our future selves.

Impact of Ageism on Careers

The social impact of ageism can deflate your ego, but the career impact can deflate your bank account. Benson Rosen and Thomas Jerdee (1988) reported on a study sponsored by *Harvard Business Review* (HBR). Even though this study was done over 20 years ago, followup surveys indicate that the results are still valid. (Zoeckler 2003; Greenberg 2004) The researchers found that younger managers stereotype older workers as being rigid, too old to train, declining in competence, and less creative than younger workers. When the researchers compared the ways younger managers treat 30-year-olds and 60-year-olds, they found that:

> *Less Feedback and Guidance.* Managers perceive older employees to be relatively inflexible and resistant to change. They therefore make much less effort to give older persons feedback about needed changes in performance. As a result older employees get less information about where and how to improve their performance.

> *Less Training to Update Skills.* Managers provide very limited organization support for the career development and retraining of older employees. They implied that these workers were likely to retire soon and therefore the training would be wasted A major issue of older employees, obsolete skills, is therefore intensified.

> *Limited Promotion Opportunities.* The promotion opportunities for older people are somewhat restricted, especially when the new positions demand creativity, mental alertness, or the capacity to deal with crisis situations.

> *False Assumption: They Are Close to Retirement.* Some managers are reluctant to hire, train, or promote older employees because they assume they are likely to retire soon, meaning the effort would be largely wasted. Various research studies have established that many assumptions about older workers are false—from lack of competence, creativity, and flexibility—to the looming retirement myth. Many older workers in white collar jobs are postponing retirement, and many others have no plans to retire as long as they are healthy. Actually, younger workers are more likely to change jobs than the older ones, according to recent studies. In fact, the average younger workers will hold 10 different jobs over a lifetime, according to current projections—meaning a job change every five years. By contrast, employees in their 50s stay on the job an average of 15 years, and they are more likely than younger employees to complete training and stay on the job after training. (Prenda 2001, AARP 2008).

How to Move Beyond Ageism

Yes, the older you get, the more devaluation and discrimination you are likely to face. That's because we as Americans tend to view old age quite negatively, often equating it with loss of abilities, vitality, and attractiveness and with illness, nursing homes, and death. It's not surprising that many younger people prefer to avoid older people and the depressing thoughts their presence may trigger. But such pictures are increasingly false. To move beyond ageism, we must begin dealing with the new facts of life. We must adopt accurate, life-affirming beliefs.

The Third Age as Vital Age

We're entering an era when old age will be a full one-third of life for most people.

- Youth is the first 30 years of life.
- Middle age the second 30 years.
- Old age is the third 30 years, from age 60 to 90.

Many people today are retaining great vitality throughout the Third Age, embarking on a new adventure and finding new wholeness. They have a burning need to be part of an enterprise larger than self, whether in the workplace or the community at large, to contribute to humanity, and to pass on something to the next generation.

The Need for New Beliefs

What if we reexamine our devastating stereotypes of age as do-nothing retirement, deterioration, and decline and change our beliefs? What if we begin to value older persons as fountains of wisdom, support, and vitality—as slow-burning, steady energy, now past the flash fires of youth? What if we begin to allow and expect that they will continue to grow, develop, and unfold in the last third of life as they have during the first two-thirds? Won't we have much to gain and little to lose? Wouldn't such new beliefs lay the foundation for bridging the generation gap?

THE ADEA: WHAT YOU SHOULD KNOW

Before the Age Discrimination Employment Act (ADEA) was enacted in 1967, many large companies would not hire workers older than 40 and most required retirement at age 65. The act, designed to help overcome the effects of ageism on the careers of older persons, provides guidelines in the areas of recruiting, hiring, selection, promotion, and termination. The act has had a favorable impact on older workers, with minor negative side effects for others.

Major Provisions of the Act

The ADEA as amended, is intended to:

- Protect workers over age 40 (about half the workforce) from discrimination
- Promote employment opportunities for older workers capable of meeting job requirements
- Protect nearly all employees from forced retirement at any age

It covers private employers of 20 or more persons, labor organizations, employment agencies, and all government employees.

In 2005 the Supreme Court expanded the rights of older employees to sue employers for age bias. Previously employees had to show intentional discrimination. Now they only must show that a company policy, practice, test, rule, or role is having an adverse effect on older employees—even if such policies don't mention age. Companies can defend themselves against such claims if they can show good business reasons for adopting a policy.

Providing for Valid Assessments

The major exception to age requirements occurs when an age requirement is a bona fide occupation qualification (BFOQ), reasonably necessary to the normal operations of a business. Also, differential treatment of employees based on reasonable factors other than age, such as physical fitness, is permitted. The ADEA does not preclude the discharge or discipline of an older worker for good cause. For example, an employer might defend a personnel decision on the ground that the older employee could not meet performance standards or that his declining functional abilities represented a potential threat to the public safety. Careful documentation of such actions is critical if an age discrimination suit is filed. The EEOC is responsible for enforcing the ADEA.

Ending Recruiting Discrimination

An example of recruiting discrimination is the practice of focusing on college graduates. Since age tends to be highly correlated with college graduation, the policy of recruiting future managers only from the ranks of college seniors potentially discriminates against older employees with comparable credentials. A corporation would be especially vulnerable to charges of age discrimination if admission to its executive training programs were limited *exclusively* to recent college graduates.

Ending Selection Discrimination

Job application forms can no longer require applicants to state their age, nor can interviewers legally inquire about age. The issue is whether an applicant is capable of performing the job. An age limit is a BFOQ only when it can be shown that all, or almost all, persons over that age cannot meet the requirements of a specific job. A construction firm might be able to show that virtually no one over age 70 can meet the physical requirements for carrying 60-pound loads up a ladder. However, a restaurant chain or airline will have a difficult time showing that organization image, or even customer preferences for attractive young hostesses, is sufficient justification for rejecting an otherwise qualified over-40 job applicant.

Age limits are likely to be upheld as a BFOQ in jobs with stringent physical demands that also involve public safety. Accordingly, it is not uncommon to find age limits governing the selection and retirement of airline pilots, air traffic controllers, police officers, firefighters. These are jobs requiring strenuous physical exertion or work under stressful conditions, where even a slight decline in reaction time could endanger others' lives and where public safety is involved. Even in these instances, it is wise for companies to have statistical or medical data to back up decisions about physical incapacities associated with aging.

Ending Promotion Discrimination

Organizations most often get in trouble with age discrimination suits concerning promotion when they follow inconsistent promotion policies and then try to justify their decisions after an employee files a complaint. Personnel actions are more defensible when they are based on a systematic, objective, and job-related performance appraisal system.

Ending Termination Discrimination

Decisions to terminate older workers are almost always difficult because motivations for such termination can be subject to many interpretations. Perhaps the best defense against a charge of age bias is the ability to show that the decision was based on the employee's substandard performance or some similar legitimate business reason. Managers must be prepared to demonstrate that the employee's behavior was measured fairly and objectively and that the employee was given a reasonable opportunity to bring her performance up to standard. Managers should also be prepared to show that they didn't harass the employee in an attempt to "run her off."

Ending Mandatory Retirement

The ADEA includes protection of older workers from employers who want to make them retire just because they reach a certain age. The original Act stated that workers could not be required to retire before age 65, later extended to age 70. Effective in 1987 Congress eliminated mandatory retirement by striking all references to upper age limitations. The purpose was to ensure that people who are willing and competent to continue working are not denied the basic human right to earn a living.

People who opposed the elimination of mandatory retirement pointed to the possibility that retaining older workers would delay the promotion of some younger workers. It could also block the progress of women and minorities who entered promotion pipelines only after affirmative action programs were in place for several years. These workers are often just waiting for employees in higher positions to retire so they can move up and into their jobs. Researcher Benson Rosen (1988) found that ten years after passing laws to end mandatory retirement, only about 4 percent of these younger workers had been affected, so the concerns appear unfounded.

RETIREMENT: WHETHER, WHEN, AND HOW?

It's time to overcome the myth that everyone should retire by age 65. Currently 80 percent of employees have retired by age 70, but the retirement decision is a complex one that should not be based upon age alone. In fact, we could say the decision is a life-or-death one, and people should carefully consider the many key factors that affect retirement.

To begin with, people engaged in certain types of hard manual labor need to reduce the length and severity of their workdays as they age. Switching to work that's less physically stressful is even better. Men who work in coal mines or in heavy construction, for example, find that their bodies begin to wear out. That's why the expectation of retirement made sense in the past when many men held such jobs. Today, of course, the large majority of American workers hold relatively sedentary jobs.

Next, retirement often results in more losses than gains. People generally view retirement as a chance to finally be free from onerous responsibility and hard work. Yet many find that retirement can also mean loss, and therefore may lead to decline and deterioration. Typical concerns are:

- loss of the identity that comes from career roles
- loss of power—organizational power, earning power, prestige
- loss of challenge to keep developing abilities and potentials
- loss of inner fulfillment that is tied to work performance and achievement
- loss of the social ties and social status that are career-connected
- loss of involvement in the active mainstream

In our culture, prestige and self-worth are based largely on occupational status and income, especially for men. And women who haven't had careers of their own often bask in the reflected light of the husband's occupational status. For men and their wives, the sense of loss usually sets in a year or so into retirement. On the other hand, career women are less likely than men to be *defined* by their careers, but retirement can be just as traumatic for them.

Finally, surveys indicate that one-third of retirees would stay with the company and move on to some new type of work or different work pattern—if they could. About one-third of retired people look for second careers, according to a study by Putnam Investments. The ADEA and private 401(k) pension plans are allowing older employees to keep working or, even better, find a new work mode that suits them (Bureau of Labor Statistics).

Factors That Affect the Employee's Decision

The factors that have the strongest and most consistent influence on the timing of retirement are health considerations and financial well-being. Gender and educational level also appear to affect retirement intentions. The answers to the following questions will provide insight into the likelihood of an employee choosing to retire. The three most significant questions are:

1. Can the employee afford to retire?
2. Does disability or declining health make retirement desirable?
3. Is the employee male or female?

Boomers, now in their 50s and 60s, are beginning to retire, and research indicates that they have not saved as well for retirement as their parents did. Even the silent generation is piling on more debt. For example, credit card debt among persons older than 65 jumped 89 percent in the decade from 1992 to 2001, when balances averaged over $4,000. Debt for those aged 65 to 69 increased 217 percent (Keating 2008).

Disability rates among older Americans reduced dramatically between 1980 and 2000. The proportion of people over 65 with a disability serious enough to cause "a substantial limitation in major life activity" dropped from 26 percent in 1982 to 20 percent in 1999 (Keating 2008, Census Bureau 2005). The Census Bureau report predicted that the trend would continue.

Women tend to retire earlier than men, which may be related to the fact that women have been concentrated in lower-level jobs. Workers with less formal education tend to retire earlier, perhaps because they are clustered in more physically demanding and less intrinsically motivating jobs.

Another factor, which has a less significant impact on retirement plans is the issue of where on the occupational ladder a person is located. Over-65 men who continue to work are primarily at the bottom—or the top—of the occupational ladder. Most of those at the bottom are working from financial necessity. Those at the top work for the meaning, enjoyment, and vitality it gives them. They're more likely (than those who retire) to keep up with new developments and transmit and advance them. They also have a greater sense of their own identity and are better able to act contrary to public opinion and others' expectations.

Ethnicity has not been associated with patterns of early retirement.

On the other hand, an employee's attitude toward aging can have a dramatic impact on retirement plans. In his study of over 1,000 retiree households, Ken Dychtwalk (2006) found four distinct types of mature adults

1. **Ageless Explorer – 27%.** People in this group are becoming the new role models for retirement. They feel youthful, they are active, and they want to make a contribution to the world. They like to learn and make new friends. They feel very alive and want to keep working. They don't anticipate ever "feeling elderly." Most Boomers will probably go into this group.

2. **Comfortably Content – 19%.** They are living out the "golden years," yesterday's retirement dream. Their primary desire to simply relax, be free of worry and stress and obligation. They anticipate feeling elderly "soon."

3. **Live for Today – 22%.** They define themselves as fun and adventurous. They want to continue to grow as individuals but don't have enough money to feel comfortable. They report enormous worry and regret about how to make it through retirement financially.

4. **Sick and Tired – 32%.** People in this older group have the least amount of money and have done the least to prepare for retirement. Most tend to feel hopeless and unwilling to do much with their lives. They expect to suffer their way through to the end.

Work = a Longer Life

You may have heard that many men die soon after retirement. Does this mean people must keep working in order to keep living? Betty Friedan's studies indicate that if retirement doesn't lead to new purposes that involve continued work or a new line of work, it often ends in early death, or is experienced as a living death. While satisfying work tends to increase longevity, unsatisfying work tends to reduce it. Depression is a typical symptom of a retirement without satisfying work and often leads to reduced immunity to disease or to suicide.

In 2000, when persons 65 and older were 12.5 percent of the population, they committed 18 percent of all suicides. The male-to-female suicide rate goes from three-to-one for young men and women to ten-to-one among those 65 and older. The tendency of men to define themselves by their occupational roles—and the loss of those roles—is considered a major factor in post-retirement depression and suicide (Friedan 1993).

People who experience growth, change, and aliveness after age 60—those who don't complain of boredom, stagnation, or loneliness—have several things in common:

- They're passionately committed to a career or other vital activity that uses their mature qualities of broader perspective and greater wisdom and that motivates them to keep developing a variety of abilities.

- They don't expect their most valued qualities to decline with age—such traits as trust, risk-taking, adaptability, nonconformity, and ability to live in the present moment.

- They don't need to pretend to be young but they don't think of themselves as old.

- They refuse to conform to traditional old-age stereotypes in their choice of lifestyles and friends, and they have friends of all ages.

Baby boomers are aware of the role work plays in prolonging vitality. Eighty percent say they plan to work at lease part-time during their retirement. The Social Security Administration predicts that more than 7 million people aged 65 and over will be working in 2020 (Working Woman 1999).

LEADERSHIP CHALLENGE: PREVENTING OLDER EMPLOYEES' SKILLS OBSOLESCENCE

The most pressing problem for many of today's older workers is occupational obsolescence, which can lead to unemployment, underemployment and lower wages.

Savvy business persons see the benefits of helping older workers move into the twenty-first century, when physical strength and endurance will not be important factors in most jobs. Factory jobs will probably account for less than 10 percent of employment in this century. New jobs are being created in fields devoted to computerization, robotization, and human services, and these jobs require radically new skills.

How Skills Obsolescence Occurs

Several factors make up the job obsolescence picture:

- After age 50, age differences in years since schooling are associated with an appreciable skills disadvantage to older workers.

- Older workers tend to have less schooling than younger employees and are less likely to have degrees in business, computer, and similar high-demand fields.

- As we move from a manufacturing economy to an information and service economy, older workers' skills are too often industry-specific and not readily transferable.

- New jobs in high-tech fields call for specific kinds of education and training.

- Many companies are reluctant to invest in further training for older employees, and employees may be reluctant to invest in their own training.

Many managers hold stereotypes that older workers are harder to train and will soon retire anyway. They don't see older employees as part of a pool from which future leaders can be drawn. This may not be direct discrimination but it has the same effect. Managers assume that training for older workers has a shorter payback period. But let's look at reality

- Turnover rates are increasingly higher for employees of all ages.

- New technologies become obsolete in ever-shorter time spans.

- More people remain relatively healthy and vital well into their 70s and 80s.
- More older workers are planning to work for many more years—if companies offer a welcoming environment that meets their needs.

These facts suggest that the exclusion of older persons from training programs may be more a habit and a result of stereotyping than strict cost-benefit thinking.

Older workers internalize these stereotypes and many are less likely to invest in extensive retraining on their own. Rosen Benson's research indicates that younger workers are willing to make greater investments on the assumption that they have more time before expected retirement to pay back the costs and to reap the financial benefits of training. Since the younger ones earn less than the older, their time-out from work in order to attend school costs them less (in terms of wages they would have received if they had continued working).

Results: Unemployment, Underemployment, Lower Wages

Skills obsolescence often leads to unemployment for older persons. During downsizing phases prior to 2000, older workers were more likely to lose their jobs than their younger peers (and their skills were more likely to become obsolete) because they have usually worked up to a relatively high pay scale.

Once unemployed, older persons are likely to experience longer periods of joblessness than their younger counterparts due to obsolete job skills and age discrimination—and they're more likely to take a pay cut. Older women and minority men are likely to be hit the hardest. Most companies, however, found themselves short of experienced employees and suffered the consequences. Some executives remembered the problem and did not want to get themselves into that kind of situation again.

Older workers fared better during the recession of 2001. And during the dramatic layoffs of 2008, The Bureau of Labor Statistics found that the number of over-55 persons who were working actually increased by about 900,000. By comparison people aged 25 to 54 lost nearly 2.9 million jobs. Many companies now value their older employees, especially those who are most productive. They see these employees as those in whom the firm has invested the most training dollars. Some companies are even seeking older workers, saying "The good employees are in their prime in their 50s and 60s. We need their expertise, and they are good role models and mentors for younger employees." (Weber 2009).

How to Prevent Skills Obsolescence

Equal opportunity for older workers calls for companies to design policies that provide affordable and useful training to workers of all ages. Policies need to ensure equal access to this training, as well as to the more secure and better-paying jobs. When older workers find themselves with obsolete skills, in dead-end jobs or career ruts, their motivation and job performance are likely to decline. The potential is still there, but it's underutilized. Leaders can remedy this situation through career planning and appropriate training.

Career Planning

In these times of rapid technological change, the most important goal of career management programs may be to identify job categories where future organizational needs are likely to be low and to help employees in these jobs to plan a new career path. Organizations can prepare employees to move into high-demand career tracks compatible with their interests, skills, and aspirations.

Older employees can be encouraged to do ongoing career planning. This begins with a critical self-analysis of interests, skills, and potential. The employee should then develop short-term and long-term career goals, specific and in writing. Next comes written plans for achieving goals, including how to use strengths and overcome obstacles. Written plans help the employees and their managers to assess progress along the way. Finally, especially important for older employees, is making Plans B and C—backup plans to cover the possibility that their career progress may get seriously sidetracked.

Training to Prevent Skills Obsolescence

Technological change creates new opportunities for employees who are trained in business, technological, and scientific fields. It also leads to the displacement of middle managers and production workers, especially older workers with obsolete skills.

Preliminary evidence suggests that the training approaches most compatible with the cognitive strengths of older employees:

- Permit self-paced learning
- Focus on experiential learning rather than abstract learning, hands-on activities rather than theory alone

On the other hand, *most* people probably respond best to this type of training.

Some companies provide a tuition reimbursement plan designed to help retiring workers prepare for second careers. Senior employees begin to draw from their educational fund a few years before retirement and continue to draw from it for a few years after retirement. Employees who acquire skills in the company's "critical needs areas" may be offered post-retirement, part-time, or consulting positions.

LEADERSHIP OPPORTUNITY: BRIDGING GENERATION GAPS

Workers of all ages have many more commonalities than differences in their attitudes toward work, according to annual Gallup polls. Still, older and younger employees may experience communication gaps that are caused primarily by differences in their experiences and values. A generation is a society-wide peer groups, born over a period of about 20 years who collectively possess a common persona and ethos, which embodies attitudes about family life, gender roles, institutions, politics, religion, culture, lifestyle, and the future. Not every member will share the core generational ethos, but every member must deal with it over a lifetime. Understanding the key themes for each age group can build a base for understanding and can reduce stereotypes, prejudice, and discrimination.

The Generation Gap

Is there a "generation gap" in most workplaces? Over half of respondents to a survey on the generation gap issues (Deal 2007) said that there is a large gap in their workplace. Two-thirds agreed that the gap has a negative impact on the work. Nearly half said that people often get into conflicts over issues of which group should have more control, power, or authority.

The gap can affect career progress and opportunities. The HBR study mentioned earlier indicates that younger managers are less likely to support older employees' training. But managers in the over-50 age category are more likely to recommend financial support to enable an older employee to attend a technical seminar. In promotion decisions, older managers are much less likely to be influenced by the candidate's age. They are equally likely to promote both a younger and older man, and they would favor the creation of a new supervisory position for both a younger and an older woman. We might conclude that an older employee has a better chance of fair treatment from an older boss. We might also conclude that the older boss has lived long enough to begin seeing that age stereotypes are not necessarily true. We all need to be aware of these kinds of generation gaps. Including older managers on any decision-making panel can provide the balance needed for fair decisions.

Generational Values and Customs

How can you understand what makes each generation tick? Learn about their key values. Each generation internalizes the cultural ethos (essence of the key values) that are typical of the larger culture at the time that generation was coming of age. They incorporate that cultural ethos as they deal with the issues of the day, and as they respond to major historical events. Table 14.3 summarizes research on the ethos of various American generations of this century, based on studies by L.J. Gann and P.J. Duignan (1986) and S.E. Jackson (1992) and others (Howe 2000; Lancaster 2003; Zemke 1999).

Table 14.3: Generations and Their Cultural Ethos

Birth Years	Era	Key issues	Cultural Ethos
1925–1945	Silent (Senior)	Survival (Depression, WWII)	Security; savings Defending freedom; duty
1946–1964	Baby Boomers	TV "Me" Generation Self-Development	Rebuilding; demanding personal freedoms; individuality; seeking personal fulfillment
1965–1981	Generation Xers	Distrust institutions	Spanning the global village; cutting edge, fun, diversity
1982–2002	Generation Y Millennials	Protection, rules, achievement	Ethnic diversity, global concern, high tech, teamwork

While Table 14.3 can help you to identify which generation a coworker belongs to, Table 14.4 can help you to recognize certain traits that reflect a person's generation. The experiences, issues, and cultural beliefs of that generation tend to encourage certain values and personality traits.

TABLE 14.4: Typical Values and Traits by Generation

Silent	Boomers	Gen Xers	Gen Y Millennials
Loyal	Optimistic	Skeptical	Realistic
Pay dues	Highly competitive	"Show me the money"	Participate in decisions
Show up, on time	Affluence	Latchkey children	Expect diversity
Care about work	TV generation	Computer generation	Internet/cell phone
Strong, silent	Express self	Resourceful	Confident
Faith in institutions	Idealistic—rights	Distrust institutions	Collaborative
Hierarchy	Question status quo	Independent	Interdependent
Chain of command	Change of command	Self-command	"Don't command me"

The generations that now dominate the workplace are:

- 65 million Baby Boomers, who currently run the system and will be retiring over the next 25 years
- 46 million Gen Xers, a relatively small cohort of young to middle-age adults, who are gaining maturity and power, poised to take over as Boomers retire
- 81 million Gen Y Millennials, larger than the Boomer cohort, the older ones are the newest employees, and the younger ones are still in their teens.

Silent Generation

Born between 1925 and 1945, people in the Silent generation ranged in age from 64 to 84 in 2009. Less than 50 million strong to begin with, they are the smallest generation still in the workplace. In fact about 95 percent of these people have retired. They grew up in the 1930s to 1950s. Most share a strong work ethic and place a premium on job and financial security—and its flip side, employee loyalty, which they held onto long after younger generations had given up. Some, especially ethnic minorities, are first- or second-generation immigrants who still retain many customs from their home cultures, such as dress, music, principles of family life, respect for authority figures, and patriotism. Most hold to the traditional values that Americans are known for around the world. They tend to ask, "Why do young people think the world owes them a living?" They believe that "when the going gets tough, the tough get going" and generally keep a stiff upper lip in the face of adversity.

As their manager, assign them work that they consider meaningful and that reflects their skills and expertise. Let them know they are contributing to the long-term success of the organizations. Encourage them to document their best practices and to share them with other employees. They may make great mentors, especially for Gen Y employees, especially if the teaching-learning is a two-way street.

Baby Boomers

Over 70 million Baby Boomers were born between 1946 and 1964. Now about 65 million strong, they make up 23 percent of the U.S. population. Their impact on America is undeniable. Most Baby Boomers are now in their 50s and 60s. They grew up in the 1950s and 1960s and entered the work force in the 1970s and 1980s. Their large size has always given them significant social and economic clout. The defining events of their generation were the Kennedy assassination, the Vietnam War, the killing of Kent State University student protesters, the Woodstock music festival, the first man on the moon, and now the collapse of our Ponzi scheme financial system.

The Me Generation

In their youth they tended to be either quite traditional or radical. Some are former hippies or yippies, who were suspicious of big business and big government and rebelled against their parents and "the establishment." Yippies took to the streets to demonstrate against the Vietnam War and other political issues. Hippies experimented with drugs, and their slogan in the 1960s was "Don't trust anyone over 30." As they matured, most became more conservative (some always were), and many become yuppies (young urban professionals).

Having grown up in permissive homes, they placed great value on work that is self-actualizing. Some rejected their Silent Generation parents' focus on upward mobility and dedication to work. They insisted on finding and expressing their own individuality and pursuing a lifestyle that leaves ample time for the pursuit of leisure activities. Their focus on personal development led to the designation of "Me Generation" in the 1970s. In the 1980s, however, they encountered economic stagnation and disappointments in the workplace. Many, as yuppies, found that in order to succeed in careers, they had to sacrifice the kind of home life and personal life they desired.

Many yuppies settled down in large, luxurious look-alike suburban "McMansions." According to Kim Peterson (2008), "They raised overscheduled spoiled children, moved up the corporate ladder by pushing paper rather than making things, lived above their means in order to keep up with their neighbors, bought whatever they wanted using debt, and never worried about the future. Over-optimism, unrealistic assumptions, selfishness and conspicuous consumption have been their defining characteristics." In fact U.S. household debt, which was about 60 percent of income in 1982 careened to 130 percent of income by 2007, the 25 years when Boomers took control.

Running the Show

For the past 20 years, Baby Boomers have run the show. They have occupied the White House since 1993. The majority of Congress is Baby Boomers. The CEOs and top executives of Wall Street firms are Baby Boomers. The media is dominated by Baby Boom executives and on-air stars. Baby Boomers had the time, power, and ability to change our course, to balance the national budget and build savings and infrastructure for the future. Some say they have chosen to leave the heavy lifting to future generations in order to live the good life today.

Many Baby Boomer employees are battling their own midlife crises and even at midlife are focusing on discovering the meaning of life. Others are about to enter the Third Age and retirement issues.

Management Tips

As a manager, show boomer employees that you respect their opinions, skills, and knowledge. Give them authority to try new ideas, and praise them for a job well done.

Generation Xers

Generation X members, born between 1965 and 1981, ranged from age 28 to 44 in 2009. At 46 million, 17 percent of the U.S. population, they are a much smaller group than the Boomers or Gen Y Millennials. Some are children of hippies and other counter-culture types. Typically, their mothers worked so they are familiar with day care and later self-care. They were sometimes called "latchkey children" because they came home from school to an empty house until dinner time. Thus they learned to fend for themselves at an early age and may be the most independent and resourceful of the generations.

The Generation X generation is more diverse than older generations. They accept diversity and even insist on it. Most tend to be less materialistic and more idealistic than their Yuppie predecessors. Many are from broken homes and so tend to want marriages that work and that last. Many have adopted their parents' values of personal growth and development.

Generation X workers want to avoid stress and burnout; they search for jobs that will let them have a personal life. They want stress-free fun and are attracted to anything they consider leading-edge but also like certain old things in new packages, such as the new retro automobiles. The younger ones may sport tattoos, piercings and cake-coloring hair.

Bruce Tulgan (1999) discovered five typical myths about Gen Xers that help create a generation gap.

Myth #1: Xers Are Disloyal

The reality is that they're wary but not disloyal. They've entered the workforce at a time following great corporate downsizings and reorganizations, so the old-fashioned employee loyalty makes no sense for them. This contrasts with older employees who tend to hold onto the ideal of loyalty until and unless betrayal experiences finally shake them loose from this attachment.

Myth #2: Xers Are Arrogant

They tend to be very self-confident but not arrogant. Their parents were more likely to be divorced, both working, or more permissive than parents of previous generations. They learned to do things for themselves and to handle problems alone. They learned over and over again that if they had to, they could fend for themselves.

Myth #3: Xers Have Short Attention Spans

They're the first generation to grow up within the information revolution, which has shaped the way they think, learn, and communicate. They prefer audio, visual, and computer over print media. They can quickly sift through, select, and assimilate information from simultaneous sources. This fast-and-loose style fits the emerging chaotic world.

Myth #4: Xers Want Instant Rewards

They're not willing to pay their dues. Their experience with corporate downsizing has shown that dues-paying doesn't pay off. The only source of security they believe in is themselves. Waiting to be rewarded poses problems for most X'ers because they've always lived in a world where everything changes faster than anyone can keep track. They do need constant feedback from employers in order to feel secure. They prefer to work in a way that produces tangible results each day.

The reality is that managers who make slight accommodations for Gen Xers' ways of doing things will find most to be hard-working, creative, and productive.

Their Learning Style

They like to learn on their own. Their independence and ability to assimilate information make them suited to self-study courses. Agree on the learning goals and time targets, then provide them with multiple sources of the information they need and let them go for it.

Their Achievement Style

Help them see the daily tangible results of the work. For example, break down a job into concrete, achievable parts with daily checklists so they can note what they've accomplished. Provide frequent feedback. Give specific feedback each time a task is completed, with concrete suggestions for improvement, if necessary.

Management Tips

Offer to be a mentor. Most welcome the chance to create long-term bonds of loyalty with teaching managers and mentors since long-term relationships with organizations are unavailable. Make sure they're learning marketable skills on the job. Give them creative challenges and opportunities to build proof of their value. Increase their level of responsibility to prove that you trust them. All this can help them to build the security from within that they've learned to rely on rather than on a corporation. Use techniques that address their short attention span.

The X and Y Generations have a strong work ethic, but they want work-life balance—a satisfying work and personal life. They have seen the economic turbulence of the past couple of decades: the dot-com boom and bust, waves of mergers with downsizings and layoffs, corporate greed scandals, and the credit collapse. They know they can be good and want to have impact. They do not look to corporations for their security, only as a vehicle to get what they want in life. Some experts predict they will become the most high-performing civic-minded workforce in the history of the world—and the most high-maintenance (Shipman 2009).

Generation Y Millennium Generation

Born between 1982 and 2002 the Millennium Generation ranged from 7 to 27 years old in 2009. Sometimes called Generation Y, they are the largest generational group ever at 81 million, 29 percent of the U.S. population. They are also the most diverse and most watched-over generation ever, and are evolving their own unique persona and ethos (Howe 2000; Sacks 2006; Tapscott 2006). The older ones may elaborate on the types of tattoos, piercings and cake-coloring hair that were adopted by earlier Gen Xers.

Most Diverse

Millenniums belong to the most diverse group in history, with 60 percent more non-Euro-Americans than in previous generations. About 30 percent are either African American, Latino American, or Asian American. Most are raised in cities with a majority of non-Euro-Americans (Chideya 1999). Although some states, such as South Dakota, are still 90 percent Euro-American, others such as California are extremely diverse.

Most Protected

Millenniums are the most watched over, cared for, and protected group of children in our history. Most are raised in small families with older, better-educated parents, at a time when divorce trends are decreasing. Most are either first-borns or only children. Those with two working parents find their days filled with after-school tutoring, lessons, sports, camps, and similar adult-supervised activities. They are therefore highly involved with their parents. As young adults, they tend to return home after college and/or to keep living at home until they marry in their late 20s.

There is a growing rich-poor gap between the most-protected and the children raised by single moms. Single parenthood is associated with double and triple the risk of arrests, drugs, school failure, and suicide.

More Confident and Optimistic

Compared to their Boomer or Gen X parents or grandparents, they are more confident and optimistic. Specifically, they:

- have been pumped up to believe they can achieve anything, thanks to very involved parents

- are therefore more optimistic about the future
- are confident, believing they are special and vital to the nation's future
- believe they will change things for the better
- think they will have new-found power to energize our institutions in the future
- are active in online politics and most supported Barack Obama for president

Value Education and Learn Differently

GenYs value intelligence and respond well to a high-tech style of education and training. Specifically, they:

- think intelligence is cool and therefore accept higher academic standards, feel pressure to study hard
- are better behaved and accept zero tolerance policies about rule breaking
- more likely to avoid personal risks that could damage future potential, and to maximize opportunities
- grew up immersed in PCs, video games, email, Internet, cell phones, so they have different thought patterns, maybe different brain patterns
- live more in the now—used to TV soundbites and want information in short available soundbites when they need it, not in traditional training sessions
- learn best from training that provides a multisensory, rapid-fire style of information consumption—brief, on demand, short sound bites
- like bite-size "edutainment" training podcasts that can be downloaded to cell phones, laptops, or iPods as needed
- are impatient with anything that doesn't lead to learning and advancement; busywork angers them because it wastes their time
- are highly educated and highly creative if given the opportunity

Have a Different Career Orientation

GenYs view their careers somewhat differently than the previous generations. They are not so interested in the financial success that drove Boomers nor the independence of Gen Xers. GenYs can be disruptive because 1) size of their group and 2) attitudes, according to Danielle Sacks (2006) and Don Tapscott (2008). Most of them have no interest in working 60 hours a week in an office. They want flexibility, variety, and time for a full personal life. They specifically:

- are permanently plugged in, networked, and juggling technology and tasks
- are team oriented, with power cliques that tend to adhere to group norms
- are reluctant to accept many workplace failings—from a perceived lack of collaboration to office bans on Facebook participation
- want careers that are personalized, custom made to fit what they want in life
- want a workplace that offers creativity, social connectivity, fun, freedom, speed, diversity
- are willing to move around until they find a place that suits them
- want to be loyal employees, but average only two years at a job
- want performance feedback daily, not annually
- treat the boss like the guys—not disrespectful, just see fear as a waste of energy
- are relatively fearless and blunt—will speak up to you, regardless of your status
- don't have time to be intimidated
- want a chance to pitch their ideas

Management Tips

Gen Y employees generally appreciate a manager who is personable and shows a sense of humor. They want to be treated as colleagues, not kids. They especially like it if you let them know when they have done a good job and provide constructive feedback when they haven't.

Mellowing With Age

Gen Xers and Ys, simply as part of being young, are more likely to see themselves as emotional, nervous, competitive, uncooperative, and not helpful or supportive of others. Having arguments that lead to physical blows occurs almost exclusively among the young men. They are much less likely to vote, to make charitable contributions regardless of income, or to participate in voluntary organizations. Spirituality plays a relatively minor role in the lives of most young people and takes on increasing significance as they age.

Older persons, regardless of generation, tend to grow mellow with age. Studies by Walter Gove of Vanderbilt University suggest that as we age, we become less self-absorbed, more cooperative and attentive to others. We function more effectively, becoming more serene and less emotional. We act in more socially accepted ways, are more community oriented, and are more likely to see others as friendly and considerate. Finally, we become more spiritual, having a stronger interest in spiritual activities and turning to spiritual beliefs that comfort us.

The Impact of Cross-Generational Work Teams

As corporate structures become more flexible and web-like, as layers of hierarchy are removed, previously segregated generations of employees find themselves working together and even rotating jobs among themselves. Another factor throwing the generations together is the entry and reentry into the workforce of middle-aged women, former retirees, and young student interns and apprentices. Four generations of workers may now find themselves working side by side. This provides rich opportunities for all of them.

Younger employees have much to learn from older ones, ranging from alternative philosophies of life to practical tips gained from life experiences. Older workers can gain much from younger ones, ranging from learning about what's new to absorbing a fresh, high-energy outlook. Since most Gen Xers and Ys cut their teeth on computers—and the Ys on cell phones—that expertise can be put to good use in the workplace.

Strategies for Bridging Generation Gaps

Bridging the generation gap at all levels is becoming more important in the workplace because networking and relationships are more central to job performance. Here are a few bridging strategies to start your thinking. You may come up with others on your own.

Use Diverse Teams

Except at work, many young employees may have few relationships with older persons other than their parents and grandparents. One remedy for this experiential gap is to make assignments to teams and committees so that employees of different ages will work together. Studies discussed in Chapter 4 indicate that meaningful contact among diverse employees can reduce prejudice. Contact that involves working together toward meaningful goals is most likely to bridge generational differences.

Open Up Communication Lines

Be aware of communication across the generation gap. People tend to communicate within their own age groups rather than between them because they seek perspectives similar to their own and support for their opinions. Also, younger workers may shun and thus isolate older workers, creating a communication gap. Part of diversity training can be helping younger people find ways to include older workers in communication lines and vice versa.

Use Diversity Training

Training should include information that makes younger workers more aware and sensitive of older workers' needs, strengths, and potential contributions—helping them replace myths and stereotypes with facts.

Training can also include information that makes older workers more aware of their own actions that foster the generation gap and can suggest alternate actions. For example, a person's image is a powerful communication tool. An image that promotes rapport usually includes dressing in style, maintaining good grooming, enjoying an active personal life, showing a warm sense of humor, *not* offering knee-jerk judgmental criticisms of fellow workers or repeating the same old comments, contributing new ideas, and giving credit to co-workers.

Diversity training should also focus on building relationship skills with older employees. Training can focus on utilizing varied generational strengths as well as individual strengths. It can also include information about the desirable traits of older employees, according to studies by Carol Ryff and others, that compare them with younger employees. For example, older workers are likely to be:

- more cheerful
- more committed to the organization and involved with their jobs
- more stable, reliable, and careful
- less likely to have accidents, be absent, or quit

Training seminars can start with a frank discussion of generational value differences and how these differences are reflected in supervisory styles and in expectations about worker loyalty, commitment, and career aspirations. Case studies that present typical specific problems in the relationships between younger and older workers can be analyzed and solutions explored. For example, problems may occur when a young woman is assigned to supervise a much older man—and in other situations where traditional status relationships are switched. Finally, training participants can develop ways to stress generational unity when working together to achieve common job goals.

See the Bigger Picture

Finally, to bridge the generation gap, managers should step back and see the bigger picture—noticing commonalities as well as differences. Findings from extensive research by Jennifer Deal (2006) might be summed up as follows:

- People from all generations hold more values in common than not.
- People want leaders who are credible and trustworthy, leaders who treat them with respect.
- Organizational politics is a problem—no matter how old or young you are.
- No one really likes change that could negatively affect them.
- Loyalty depends more on the situation than on the generation.
- Everyone wants to learn—more than just about anything else.
- Almost everyone appreciates good mentors and coaches.

Older employees have years of experience, have learned from their successes and failures, and therefore have much wisdom they can share in mentoring younger employees. But it must be a two-way street; if older employees want to bridge the gap, they must be open to new ideas from the younger ones. They can do their share of mentoring in such skills as informational technology, networking, acceptance of diversity, and creativity. Along these lines, if younger employees want to do their share of mentoring, they must first become accepted as "insiders" by the older ones. For example, they must show an appreciation of the processes and practices the older ones have established, which helps them to be seen as "one of us." Once that occurs, younger employees' ideas for change are more likely to be heard and adopted, and productive relationships are born.

As a manager, you can retain both younger and older employees—if you meet their needs. For example, communicate your willingness to listen and accept younger workers' ideas. Reassure older workers about your own experience and expertise and your respect for theirs. Mutual respect is the name of the game: your deserve respect as the manager and they deserve respect as team members.

LEADERSHIP OPPORTUNITIES:
BUILDING ON THE STRENGTHS OF ALL GENERATIONS

New generations with new strengths and skills are entering the workplace. Learning to motivate them is essential for the success of your organization and your own career. In addition, the older population is ballooning. Baby boomers are beginning to retire, and by 2020 about one in six Americans (16%) will be older than 65. Some business leaders are preparing for the changes this implies. Some sociologists are predicting that the Boomers won't be as accepting of age stereotyping and discrimination as recent generations have been. Businesses that treat them more positively will have a definite advantage.

To build on their strengths, you can begin by understanding their needs and helping them get what they need to do a good job. You can support strategies for keeping older employees on the payroll by such actions as offering flexible career options, making fair appraisals, and making the corporate culture more welcoming. You can help them make connections with the growing over-50 marketplace.

Opportunity #1: Motivate Younger Employees

Generations X and Y have much in common. The first Generation Xers have been in the workplace for some time, so they are the subjects of most research on young employees, but much of it applies also to Gen Y. These young employees are unlikely to be motivated by a deep sense of mission or loyalty to an organization. In fact, most of them disregard corporate politics and bureaucracy and distrust all institutions, so they do not respond well to pep talks about morale and company loyalty. They have no expectation of job security and tend to see every job as a stepping stone to something else. They are unlikely to put in long hours at what they term dead end jobs. On the other hand, Xers will work very hard for a job they believe in or for something that challenges them, illustrated by the fact that they are involved in startups at about three times the rate of other age groups. Here are some suggestions for providing what most young employees are looking for.

> **Value the Individual.** These younger generations want you to get to know them as individuals, not as part of a generational group.
>
> **Nurture Relationships:** As former latchkey kids, Gen Xers may be homesick for the home they never had. They tend focus on relationships. Bottom line: what may appeal to them is a workplace with a strong sense of community and supportive personal relationships.
>
> **Offer Challenging Work.** Xers want new challenges and the opportunity to build new skills. Offering training in areas that interest them is one of the best motivators. They have a capacity to process lots of information and concentrate on multiple tasks. Their work style: get in, do the work, and move on to the next thing. This means they get impatient spending too much time talking about things or sitting in meetings. They tend to have a short attention span and will not stick around for jobs that are very repetitive and offer little challenge.
>
> **Give Them Freedom to Manage Their Time and Work.** Xers don't want over-your-shoulder, in-your-face managers who constantly check what they're doing. Perhaps as a result of their latchkey childhood, these young workers are not used to being closely supervised and are very good at working on their own.
>
> **Give Frequent Feedback and Recognition.** Conversely, most Gen Xers seem to crave time with their bosses and want feedback on their performance—those things many parents didn't give enough of. Because of their short attention span, recognition and rewards must arrive quickly. Employee of the month doesn't do much for them, much less the annual bonus.

Bottom line: If you want an empowered work force, give Xers the ball and they will run with it. If you want a self-directed work force, they have been self-directed from a very young age. If you want computer literacy, they are the best. If you want flexible, adaptable workers, provide these young employees with what they need and they'll stick around (Nagle 2009).

Opportunity #2: Understand How Educational Level Affects Needs

Current changes in the nature of work can be threatening to older employees with limited skills, but they may be challenging and intriguing to other, better-educated older employees. You can help less-educated workers face their fears and make new plans. On the other hand, you can support better-educated workers in using and expanding their skills.

Recognize Fears of the Less-Educated

The employment picture, as seen by many older employees with limited education and skills, includes:

- Technological change is a threat.
- Retraining is scary or unacceptable.
- Unions are not much help because they're going along with management to eliminate the old jobs and retrain for the new jobs.
- Government is not much help because its programs are also geared toward retraining.

Help these co-workers face their worst fears and become comfortable with the worst-case scenario. Lead them in understanding that age is not necessarily a barrier to handling change and learning new technological skills. Help them to make career plans for gaining new skills and knowledge and to get support for the training they need.

Support Goals of the Better Educated

Better-educated, more highly skilled older employees tend to be more flexible and to see a brighter job picture:

- They often want a few minor adjustments in their work situation.
- They may desire to work a few less hours per week.
- They often want to be freed from the prison of the 5-day, 40-hour week or the arduous commute to the workplace.
- They may wish to be liberated from the controls on time and place of work implied by traditional employment contracts.

They may want more flexibility and discretion in their work. Many may want to work at home on a full- or part-time basis, perhaps for more than one employer.

You can help them develop arrangements for time and place of work that will allow them to continue making valuable contributions to the team and the company.

Opportunity #3: Understand Older Employees' Motivational Needs

A vicious cycle of declining motivation can affect older employees. Here are the factors:

- Managers who expect a decline in motivation among older workers might make age-based managerial decisions that in fact lead to decreased motivation for these employees.
- To the extent that an older employee perceives that his or her efforts no longer lead to promotion or other significant rewards, his or her motivation tends to gradually decline.

- Limited opportunities for development and lack of feedback about performance may further reduce the older worker's motivation.
- In today's relatively flat organizational structures, there are shorter ladders to climb and fewer promotions to give. Many ambitious employees reach career plateaus much earlier than in the past. Employees need to become aware of this fact and to be given opportunities for lateral moves to expand their career growth and development.

It's likely that lowered motivation may result, not from aging itself, but from managerial expectations and treatment of older employees. If this is so, then policy changes to eliminate discrimination against older employees represent only a first step. Additional efforts to help managers and co-workers identify age stereotypes and eliminate their effects on everyday decisions need to be made. These efforts must also deal with all the practices that tend to support and perpetuate the stereotypes.

Opportunity #4: Adopt Strategies for Meeting Needs

Some simple general strategies for understanding an older employee's concerns include listening with awareness, developing empathy for their situation in life, and helping them to manage the changes they encounter.

Listen

Listen to older workers and be a supportive sounding board. You'll learn a great deal about their strengths and problems that way, gain insights to solutions to problems, and gain from their knowledge and experience. Encourage small group meetings of older workers for the purpose of getting in touch with their interests, desires, talents, and needs and then communicating those to co-workers and management.

Develop Empathy

If you live long enough, you'll be an older person one day, if you're not already. Ask yourself, What will I do when I'm no longer "young and cute?" and then put yourself in the older person's shoes. Look for the individual personality inside the older body. Be open to many kinds of beauty. Focus on skills, experience, contribution, and performance rather than narrow ideas about physical appearance. This is a positive strategy for relating to persons of all ages.

Manage Change

Encourage older workers to stay current. Help them to respond positively to change, to develop the new skills and acquire the new information they need in the changing business environment. Many older employees need a little encouragement to help them overcome the limitations imposed by cultural myths.

In organizations where self-managing teams are replacing most of the hierarchy, help people bridge the generation gap. Help older employees to pace themselves and avoid burnout. Stamina may decrease for some, but they can still be productive workers. Learning time may take a little longer but will be mastered.

Respect Employees' Retirement Decisions

We know that companies can no longer force employees to retire, but they can and do offer them tempting rewards to retire. Failing that, they can resort to subtle pressure: lower performance evaluations, onerous job assignments, taking away responsibilities or perks, exclusion from desired projects or meetings. Finally the employee gets fed up, gives up, and retires.

Studies indicate that managers are less likely to pressure employees to retire if they view them as having some of the following traits and life situations: younger, financially troubled, likely to make a poor social adjustment to retirement, supported by the union, engaged in personal activities that are compatible with business interests, and still earning high performance ratings. Of these reasons, most experts agree that the only rational, valid reason for encouraging one employee to stay over another is higher performance ratings. This leads us to why and how an organization can hold onto its effective older employees.

Opportunity #5: Support Corporate Culture Changes

If business leaders want to retain productive older workers, they must bring about changes in corporate culture norms. For example, we know that managers who hold age stereotypes are normally less willing to approve promotions, offer training opportunities, and work out performance problems with older workers. In fact, studies indicate that managers age 40 and over tend to be rated significantly lower than younger managers on readiness for promotion, even when education, performance, and job tenure are comparable. Such age stereotypes contribute to an organizational climate that discourages continued employment opportunities for older employees. But when companies are able to develop supportive organizational norms that encourage older workers to stay on, all middle-aged and younger workers get a clear message: *The contributions of senior employees are recognized and welcomed here* (Cox and Nkomo 1992).

Clearly, the information economy will ease the transition to longer working lives. Working with computers in service-sector occupations such as medical diagnostics or insurance services is much less demanding physically than assembly line, construction, and other manual labor. It's unrealistic for us to expect people to spend almost a third of their lives in retirement. The challenge leaders in traditional organizations is how to tap the knowledge of their older workers while keeping promotion opportunities open for younger employees.

Adopt a Variety of Change Strategies

Here are just a few examples of the many specific actions organization leaders could take for the purpose of making the culture more welcoming to older employees:

- The achievements of older workers are recognized and publicized.
- There is a shift away from celebrating retirements and toward celebrating continued contributions.
- Managers and co-workers do *not* anticipate retirement simply because of an employee's age. After all, people may retire at 50 or 80 or any other age—and may leave for any reason at any age.
- All employees are trained to understand the ADEA and any other legal considerations governing the employment of older workers.
- All employees participate in training to overcome deep-rooted assumptions and expectations about what senior employees can and cannot do.
- Training also raises employees' awareness of the pervasive influence of age stereotypes on day-to-day interactions and decisions and helps them move beyond myths and stereotypes.
- Training provides all employees with skills to bridge communication gaps between young managers and senior employees.
- Training is designed to explore value differences and similarities between younger and older workers and to move to appreciation for the diversity of values, as well as the unity that common values provide.
- Leaders expect and encourage creative thinking and innovative results from employees of all ages.

Value Older Employees

If the corporate culture values and supports older workers who delay their retirement, they're likely to stay longer. Your attitude has its impact, just as every employee's attitude counts, so you can influence the value that people generally place on the contributions of older workers and the belief that effective workers should be retained as long as possible. Some organizations actually encourage direct group pressure on people to retire. Other organizations encourage a more subtle expression of norms calling for early retirement. Such pressures do have a strong influence on employees' retirement decisions.

Opportunity #6: Support Strategies for Retaining Older Workers

Currently about one-third of Americans are out of the workforce before age 63, and 80 percent are out by the time they're 70. The goal of a retention strategy is to retain older workers as long as feasible. Such a strategy can benefit the organization and society as well as older employees.

Benefits to the organization of an effective retention strategy are that it:

- lowers pension costs
- lowers turnover rates and resulting turnover costs
- provides longer and larger paybacks for investments in training
- contributes to high employee morale
- enhances the organization's reputation in the community

Benefits to society of an effective retention strategy are that it:

- lowers social security costs
- adds to U.S. productivity and the tax base
- contributes to the social integration of the older population

Benefits to older employees of an effective retention strategy are that it:

- keeps them physically and mentally active
- maintains or enhances their self-respect
- provides them with income
- satisfies their social needs by keeping them in daily touch with other active people at work

Opportunity #7: Support Flexible Career Options

When over 1,000 older people were asked, "What do you want in your "Golden Years?" they replied (Dychtwalk 2006):

- To reinvent myself
- To pursue some dreams that I put on the shelf earlier
- To adjust the balance between work, leisure, and family
- To live a long, healthy life without being any particular age at all
- Ageless aging - to feel and act young

Many companies have only two alternatives for older employees: keep working or fully retire. That means sudden, not phased retirement, is typical. Why is retirement usually sudden? Primarily because so few career options are available to older employees. While many employees say they would prefer modified work and schedules, flexible options are seldom available. When they are, the pay is often so low that workers choose sudden retirement.

Most companies don't yet offer flexible scheduling, retraining at mid-career, or other perks that might attract or retain 50-plus workers, according to a 2005 survey by the Society for Human Resource Management (SRHM.com) in Alexandria, Virginia. "The big issue for most business executives is what's going to happen in the next quarter," says SHRM president Susan Meisinger. "Long-term labor-force development issues are unlikely to be at the top of their minds." Companies that do offer such alternatives have a competitive edge in attracting the best older employees. Alternatives that could be offered include:

- flexible career options—above all else
- flexible scheduling
- part-time or seasonal work
- short-term projects
- job changes or restructuring
- job rotation
- job sharing
- retiree labor pools
- telecommuting
- tandem staffing
- temporary assignments
- contract consulting
- periodic sabbaticals
- various phased retirement options
- other creative career options

About 40 percent of Boomers say they would be interested in a phased retirement program. AARP (2005) surveyed people, age 50 and over, who had officially retired but were still working. When asked why they were working, some gave more than one reason, as follows:

- I need the money   61%
- I want to stay mentally active   54
- I need the health benefits   52
- I want to stay physically active   49
- I want to remain productive or useful   47

Most boomers, 80 percent, say they plan to work at least part-time past age 65 (AARP 2005) This generation believes they'll live longer than the previous one, but few have saved enough money to last for 20 to 30 years of full retirement. In fact at age 50 about 75 percent of Americans have less than $5,000 invested for retirement. At age 65, about 45 percent depend on relatives for financial aid, 30 percent depend on charities, 23 percent are still working fulltime or part-time, and only 2 percent are self-sustaining (Senior Job Bank 2005)

In small but growing numbers, companies are beginning to offer programs to keep older workers or to lure them back—usually called phased retirement. What kinds of programs are they offering? A Watson Wyatt survey (2005) of 600 employers found the types of plans shown in Table 14.5.

An example of a phased retirement option is to establish a company temporary employee pool. Retirees who wish to work on a part-time basis sign up. Where appropriate, the company provides refresher courses to employees who have been away from the job for some time. Retirees may be called on to fill in during vacation periods or to add their expertise to special projects. At higher levels they're hired as consultants and work on a project fee basis.

What managers personally can do to help is to be flexible, choose from the various strategies others have used, and create new ones that fit the situation.

TABLE 14.5: Phased Retirement Programs

Type of Phased Retirement	% Employers That Offer It
Retirees as part-time workers	75%
Reduced workday or workweek	60
Retirees as consultants	42
Job transfers	32
Extended leaves of absence	23
Job sharing	19

Opportunity #8: Make Fair Assessments and Performance Reviews

Leading-edge companies have clear policies for managers, teams, and co-workers: Leave myths and stereotypes behind and make realistic assessments of older persons' abilities. Be sure you are fair and objective in evaluations.

Realistically Assess Ability and Disability

Managers and co-workers are likely to misinterpret health information on older employees if they hold stereotypes regarding the declining health of older people. Identical health conditions may be perceived as more serious and disabling for older workers than for younger ones. One study indicated that when medical reports emphasize capacities or functions that an employee can successfully perform, managers recommended continued employment. When medical reports emphasized disabilities, managers recommended part-time assignments, phase-outs, and termination—even when the health problems were not likely to interfere with ability to do the job, in some cases.

Disability laws could come into play in these instances. A systematic and comprehensive approach to health evaluations might include the following:

- Current and complete job descriptions, with emphasis on physical and psychological demands

- Medical reports that emphasize both employee capacities and limitations associated with illness or injury and that focus on job-related implications of medical problems

- Training for managers in interpreting medical reports in order to make better decisions regarding further employability

- Job redesign as one strategy for meeting the needs of senior workers with health problems

Give Fair Performance Evaluations

Good performance appraisal systems provide the accurate, objective information that managers and team co-workers need in order to make important decisions about motivating, rewarding, promoting, training, transferring, and terminating employees. Appraisals should be based only on job-related behaviors and achievements that are related to a job analysis, behavior standards, and agreed-upon measures. A management-by-objectives process is considered the most legally acceptable.

The appraisal system should generate the documentation that would be required to prove that personnel decisions comply with the law. All employees should get periodic feedback that highlights their strengths and weaknesses and explores the implications of their present performance for future career moves. This feedback should help dispel any misconceptions and misunderstandings employees may have and should help them create realistic expectations about their future with the company. Effective two-way communication between employees and their managers can usually prevent costly age discrimination suits. The bottom line: think of the last third of life as a time of continuing growth and learning, a time when people deserve constructive performance feedback that can help them continue to improve.

Opportunity #9: Help Make Connections to the Over-50 Marketplace

The over-50 marketplace is exploding. People are living longer, and older consumers tend to have more spending power than in the past. In fact those over age 55 own 77 percent of all financial assets in the United States (AARP 2008).

The Baby Boom generation is beginning to turn 65. so older Americans will increasingly offer a booming market in financial services, from insurance to estate planning. They are still a relatively untapped market in housing, clothing, travel, and investment services. Just as women professionals have an edge in understanding women's issues and relating to women customers, so older professionals and employees have an edge in understanding elders' issues and relating to older customers. And many older persons appreciate seeing that older employees are valued in the companies they do business with.

It's good business to retain older employees, to seek their views in designing "senior-oriented" products and services, and to position them for customer contact in the over-50 marketplace—but certainly not to limit them to these roles. The contributions people can make to the organization are not limited by age. In fact, the experiences and insights that come with age normally enhance a person's contributions. However, we may need to create a new, true myth about valuing older persons, a myth that moves younger employees to see and appreciate those contributions.

SUMMARY

The longer we live, the more likely we are to be faced with cultural devaluation, for ageism accelerated in the twentieth century. Age myths picture older employees as an increasing problem in terms of productivity, attendance and accident rates, physical and mental ability, rigidity and dogmatism, commitment to work, and physical attractiveness. Actually, older workers are just as mentally alert and productive as others and have better attendance, accident, and turnover rates. Their physical and mental ability are retained well beyond age 70 as long as they remain in good health. In fact, people reach their mental prime at about age 60. Older workers are no more likely to be rigid and dogmatic than others, but tend to have much greater knowledge and wisdom. Healthy people retain their creativity even past the age of 100.

The ADEA provides guidelines for treating older employees with fairness and giving them equal opportunities. It's designed to end age discrimination in recruiting, selection, promotion, and termination practices—and to end mandatory retirement for most jobs.

Since older workers have usually progressed to higher pay than younger ones, this can make them a layoff target during downsizing. However, since 2000 more employers tend to value the experience, expertise, and wisdom of their older employees and are less likely to dismiss them. When employees older than 50 do lose their jobs, they have more difficulty finding another position. If their skills are in high demand, they may have more job security than younger workers, but often their skills are becoming obsolete.

Skills obsolescence and ongoing training are major issues for those past age 50. Younger managers are often unwilling to invest in their retraining, and they themselves may not be motivated. One reason is the assumption that they'll retire before the training investment pays off. Another is the myth that older people have difficulty learning and adapting to change, even though these traits are not necessarily affected by age.

The generation that an employee belongs to usually has a strong impact on his or her experiences, beliefs, values, and traits, as well as issues important to that person. Knowing a little about the silent, boomer, Gen X, and millennium generations can help to bridge generation gaps. So can such strategies as using age-diverse teams, finding ways to open up communication lines between older and younger employees, and providing good diversity training.

You as a business leader have many opportunities to appreciate and utilize the wealth of experience and talent that older and younger employees can offer your company. You can give younger employees the challenges, freedom and empowerment they need in order to stick around. You can understand how their educational level affects their needs and how managerial expectations can affect their motivation. You can adopt specific strategies, such as empathy, change management, and retirement alternatives to meet their needs. You can support corporate cultural changes that value and respect older employees' contributions. You can support strategies for retaining older workers and giving them flexible career options. You can give fair performance evaluations and utilize their ability to connect with the over-50 marketplace.

Case Study 14.1: Older Worker Wendy

You're in charge of Bache Investment's college recruiting. You cannot remember a more hectic time in your life. When you were promoted to this job, your boss told you that the job would test your energy and endurance. During the past two months, you visited 24 universities and interviewed more than 200 MBA students for entry-level investment advisor positions. The experience has been exhausting. Because of your reading schedule, you have relied heavily on your assistant **Wendy** to handle many duties that you usually attend to personally.

Since returning to the office from your recruiting trips, you have become increasingly aware of Wendy's aloofness. You sense that she is purposely avoiding you. You also noted that she quickly looks away when you question her about a late travel voucher or a missing file. A little investigating reveals that Wendy is behind in her routine responsibilities and is now over a week late with an important EEO/AA report. Wendy's failure to attend a monthly staff meeting was the last straw. You are determined to get Wendy back on track or to find someone else who is capable of managing the workload. You leave a note for Wendy, requesting that she meet you in your office at 8:45 Monday morning.

Now take the role of Wendy. You have been having doubts about your ability to manage the growing workload and about your future at Bache Investments. Returning to fulltime work four years ago at age 53 represented quite a change for you. Although you had worked as an executive secretary before your marriage, your previous positions had been much less demanding than this position.

At home, your husband has also noticed a recent change in your behavior. He tells you that you seem tense and short-tempered and asks if you're having problems at the office. You confide that you think your boss is subtly pressuring you to quit. You explain that he told you to complete several complex monthly EEO/AA reports without reducing your regular workload. You confess to your husband that the reports require many statistical calculations, some beyond anything you ever encountered. Completing the reports accurately seemed to take forever. You tell him how you have worked through lunch hours two and three times a week. You relate how you skipped staff meetings just to catch up on regular paperwork.

You have been feeling overwhelmed and incompetent. With only six more years to go before you plan to retire, you wonder why your boss wants to force you out. Perhaps your future with the company will be resolved at the Monday morning meeting with the boss.

1. What are the key issues (root problems)?
2. If you were Wendy's manager, what would you do?
3. If you were Wendy, what would you do?

Case Study 14.2: The Youthful Supervisor

Jose is 27 years old. From a Latino American family, his parents were strict and taught him that older people deserve great respect and are usually the ones in authority. His father was the undisputed head of the home, and his grandfather was the highly respected patriarch of a large clan. Jose has been transferred from a field assignment and promoted to team leader of a product promotions group. One of the team members, *Scott*, is in his fifties and has been with the company for nearly ten years. Scott reminds Jose of his father is some ways.

Jose must meet with Scott to make suggestions for improvements on his part of a current team project. Jose senses that Scott is somewhat defensive toward him and a little resistant to taking constructive criticism and suggestions from him. Jose asks you for advice.

1. What are the root problems?
2. What would you say to Jose?

Case Study 14.3: Stock Broker John

Leigh is Human Resources Director for Goldman Funds, an investment firm. Her job is to hire stock brokers who have the ability to create wealth for Goldman clients and for the company. Leigh has been in this field for 20 years and spent many of those years as a stock broker herself, so she knows how demanding the job can be. Most of the stock brokers are young, unmarried, and devote 60 to 70 hours a week to their jobs. Most of them also spend several hours a week maintaining their physical fitness in order to deal with the stress of the job.

Leigh is interviewing applicants for a stock broker position that just opened up. The most unusual applicant is *John*, unusual because he's 67 years old while the other applicants are in their twenties or thirties. John had a long career in the insurance industry, with many years as a salesman, a few years as a claims adjuster, and the remaining years as an executive. John retired when he was 62, and within a year, he was extremely bored with retirement activities. He enrolled in the local university and has just completed a master's degree in finance. He earned grades that ranked him in the top 10 percent of his class.

John comes across as very personable in the interview. He tells Leigh, "I've always loved to sell, I've always loved dealing with calculated risks, and it's very important to me to get to know the clients I serve and to make a contribution through my work." Leigh is impressed, but she's concerned about how many years they can reasonably expect John to work. Leigh is also concerned about the high turnover rate that seems to come with the stock broker position. One of her goals is to lower the employee turnover rate.

1.   What are the key issues (root problems)?
2.   If you were Leigh, what would you do?

Case Study 14.4: Maggie's Way

Maggie, age 55, has been an office manager with the Pillsbury-Mason law firm chain for the past 15 years. She is extremely dependable, loyal, and committed to her job and the firm. She has received performance awards and is highly valued and respected in the firm.

Jake was hired a few months ago as an administrative assistant. He just graduated with honors and holds a brand new degree in business administration with a concentration in management. His goal is to become an office manager very quickly. He knows he has what it takes. However, he had only a few months of actual office experience before taking this job, so he's having a little difficulty adapting to his coworkers and the office environment. Jake's main frustration is that he has many good ideas, and he wants to take action on them. He knows he could run this office in a minute, but he's blocked because "Maggie's ways" control the entire office.

As the other employees say, "Maggie's Way" is sometimes confusing, but Maggie is very competent and always on top of everything. The problem is that her ways are sometimes unique, so it's difficult for new employees to understand or to find things. Her procedures generally are very simple and to the point, but sometimes they're so simple that others tend to look right over them, especially in a hectic office. On the other hand, when it comes to many procedures, Maggie insists that employees take their time, go through the proper channels, and follow her office manual. In contrast, Jake believes in getting things done efficiently, finding short cuts, avoiding time-consuming over-cautiousness, and basically getting on with it.

Jake's experience is that he has difficulty understanding many of Maggie's requests. He frequently sees the best way to handle a procedure or task, but Maggie always wants him to do it her way. When he tries to explain how a procedure could be improved upon, Maggie listens politely, but it always ends up that the procedure is done her way.

Last week, Jake was under a great deal of pressure to complete a project. He took things into his own hands, did it his way, and got it out on time. When Maggie found out, she confronted him. Tempers flared and they exchanged some heated words about each other's management style. *Stan,* one of the law partners, walked by as this exchange was going on. He's concerned. Pillsbury-Mason is known for its quiet, calm, harmonious environment.

1.   What are the key issues (root problems)?
2.   If you were Stan, what would you do?

3. If you were Jake, what would you do?

4. If you were Maggie, what would you do?

REFERENCES

AARP, "Attitudes of Individuals 50 and Older Toward Planned Retirement," *Modern Maturity*, March 2005.

AARP Magazine, 51–53. AARPmagazine.org, Sept-Oct 2008.

Advertising Age, .S-2, "Door Ajar to Women of All Ages in Ads," October 4, 1993.

Aldisert, Lisa M. *Valuing People*. Dearborn Trade Publishing, 2002.

Campbell, R.T., J. Abolafia, and G. L. Maddox. "Life-Course Analysis in Social Gerontology" in *Gender and the Life Course*. Aldine, 1985.

Chideya, Farai., "Shade of the Future," *Time* February 1, 1999.

Chideya, Farai. *The Color of Our Future*. Wm. Morrow & Co., 1999.

Coupland, Douglas. *Generation X: Tales for an Accelerated Culture*. St. Martin's Griffin, 1992.

Cox, Taylor, Jr. and Stella M. Nkomo, "Candidate Age As a Factor in Promotability Ratings." *Public Personnel Management* 2, 197–210, Summer, 1992.

Deal, Jennifer. *Retiring the Generation Gap: How Employees Young and Old Can Find Common Ground*. Jossey Bass, 2006.

Deal, Jennifer J. *World Leadership Survey*. Center for Creative Leadership, San Diego, CA. 2006.

Dychtwald, Ken *Age Power: How the 21st Century Will Be Ruled by the New Old*. Tarcher, 2000.

Dychtwalk, Ken. *The Power Years*. Wiley, 2006.

Friedan, Betty. *The Fountain of Age*. Simon and Schuster, 1993.

Gamonal, P. and J. Williams. *Leading Generation X: Getting in Touch with the Energy. Ravenwerks*, 2002.

Gann, L.J. and P.J. Duignan. *The Hispanics of the United States: A History*. Westview Press, 1986.

Gove, Walter R. "The Effect of Age and Gender on Deviant Behavior: A Biopsychosocial Perspective." in *Gender and the Life Course*. Aldine, 1985,

Greenberg, David and Jeremy Pasternake, "Age Discrimination in the Workplace," *DiscriminationAttorney.com*, March 2004.

Howe, Neil and Wm. Strauss. *Millennials Rising: The Next Great Generation*. Random House, 2000.

Hushbeck, Judith C. *Old and Obsolete: Age Discrimination and the American Worker, 1860–1920*. Garland Publishing, Inc. 1989

Jackson, Susan E. *Diversity in the Workplace*. Guilford Press, 1992.

Keating, Peter, "The New Retirement," *Money*, August 2008.

Lancaster Lynne and C., D. Stillman. *When Generations Collide: Who They Are. Why They Clash. How to Solve the Generational Puzzle at Work*. Collins, 2003.

Lemonick, Michael D. and Alice Park Mankato, "The Nun Study," *TIME*, 54–65, May 14, 2001.

Mitchell, Olivia S., ed. *As the Workforce Ages*. ILR Press, 1993.

Modern Maturity, American Assn. of Retired Persons, October 2001.

Mayer, Ira. *Marketing to the 50+ Population*. EMP Communications, www.epmcom.com, 2008.

Nagle, Terri, "Coaching Generation X," *www.coachingandmentoring.com*, 2009.

Peterson, Peter G. *Gray Dawn: How the Coming Age Wave Will Transform American—and the World*. Random House, 1999.

Prenda, Kimberly and S.M. Stahl, "The Truth About Older Workers," *Business & Health*, 2001.

Retirement Living, April 1976, report of survey regarding older workers.

Roscigno, V.J. et al, "Age Discrimination, Social Closure, and Employment," *Social Forces*, 86, 1, 313–334, 2007.

Rosen, Benson and Thomas Jerdee. "Managing Older Workers' Careers." *Research in Personnel and Human Resources Management* 6, 37–74, 1988.

Rosen, Benson, and T. H. Jerdee. *Older Employees: New Roles for Valued Resources*. Homewood, IL: Dow Jones-Irwin, 1985.

Ryff, Carol D. "Subjective Experience of Life-Span Transitions" in *Gender and the Life Course*. Aldine, 1985.

Sacks, Danielle, "Scenes from the Culture Clash," *Fast Company*, 73–77, Jan–Feb 2006.

Salzberg Seminar on Health, Productivity and Aging, June, 1983, 2003.

Scripps Howard News Service, reported in *San Francisco Examiner*, D-1, May 10, 1998.

Shea, Gordon F. *Managing Older Employees*. Jossey Bass, 1991.

Shipman, Claire and Katty Kay. *Womenomics: Write Your Own Rules for Success*. Harper Business, 2009.

Senior Job Bank, www.SeniorJobBank.org, 2005.

Tapscott, Don. *Grown Up Digital*. McGraw-Hill, 2008.

Tapscott, Don and A.D. Williams. *Wikinomics*. Portfolio, 2006.

Time, 46–49, "Shade of the Future," Feb 1 1999.

Tulgan, Bruce. *Managing Generation X: How to Bring Out the Best in Young Talent*. Merritt Publishing, 1997.

U.S. Census Bureau, "We the People: Aging in the United States," a Census 2000 Report.

U.S. Census Bureau, "The Older Population in the United States: March 2002."

U.S. Department of Health and Human Services. *Profile of Older Americans: 2002*.

Wagster, Molly. National Institute on Aging report. *www.nia.nih.gov*, August 2005

Weber, Joseph, "This Time, Old Hands Keep Their Jobs," *Business Week*, 50, February 9, 2009

Working Woman. 54–57, "The Age of Work," October 1999.

Zemke, Ron, C. Raines, B. Filipczak. *Generations at Work: Managing the Clash of Veterans, Boomers, Xers, and Nexters in Your Workplace*. American Management Association, 1999.

Zoeckler, Eric, "Corporations Aren't Addressing the Needs of Aging Workforce," *The Herald*, Everett, WA, D2, November 3, 2003.

RESOURCES

Administration on Aging, www.aoa.gov See the atatistics and the report *A Profile of America's Older Americans*.

Aging, a journal.

American Association of Retired Persons (AARP), the largest older persons' organization, which engages in research and lobbying and publishes the magazine Modern Maturity.

Brain Connections, 745 Fifth Avenue, Suite 700, New York, NY 10151, a source guide to 160 organizations devoted to brain diseases and disorders.

Gray Panthers, an organization. www.GrayPanthers.org

McCabe, Jim. Consultant on Aging Workers, Technical Assistance Group, San Ramon, CA (510) 838–7277.

National Olders Workers Career Center Online, nowcc.org.

Older Women's League (OWL), an organization. www.Owl-National.org

Waters, Elinor B. and Jane Goodman. *Empowering Older Adults*, San Francisco: Jossey-Bass, 1990. This book includes examples of corporate programs for older workers.

CHAPTER 15

Working with Persons of All Sizes and Shapes

Pretty women wonder where my secret lies.
I'm not cute or built to suit a model's fashion size.
But when I start to tell them, they think I'm telling lies.
Maya Angelou

Appearance discrimination is rampant in our society—especially for those who are "overweight." If you gain as few as 20 or 30 pounds over your "ideal" weight, you may suddenly face new career problems and even a lower income—yet about 60 percent of all Americans have done just that. Weight discrimination affects women more than men, probably because it is related to the beauty myth and to appearance discrimination in general. Virtually all the publicized lawsuits have been filed by women, and the support groups and organizations are created and joined primarily by women.

The Terms We Use

Terms are very touchy for people who have experienced appearance bias, especially for people who are considered medically and legally "obese." Some activists prefer the term "fat" and don't like "overweight" as a label. But "fat" still offends many people, and "large" is not descriptive since it can include a tall or muscular man who may in fact have an appearance advantage. We'll use the terms "overweight, obese, and morbidly obese" because we'll be discussing medical and legal implications.

Get ready to learn what it's like to be an obese person in the workplace. As you do, imagine seeing situations the way an obese person might see them. You'll also learn about other types of appearance issues. Specifically, in this chapter you'll learn:

- How typical myths about obese persons compare with reality
- How fat prejudice affects obese persons
- What the Beauty Myth is and how it affects obese persons and others
- Rights that obese employees want
- Rights that most employers want to retain
- Emerging law concerning obese persons' workplace rights

Obese Man

Courtesy of Steve Prezant/Corbis Images.

Obese Woman

Courtesy of Darren Modricker/Corbis Images.

- How you can help obese employees overcome barriers and contribute their strengths to the organization

Before the we explore this topic, complete Self-Awareness Activities 15.1 and 15.2.

Self-Awareness Activity 15.1: What Do You Believe About Obese Persons?

Purpose:

- to get in touch with your beliefs and stereotypes about this group of people
- to experience how judgmental beliefs affect your thinking and feeling processes
- to experience the ways in which your beliefs create your reality regarding other persons, even before you have any interaction with them.

Part I. What Do You Believe About Obese Women?

Step 1. Associations

- Relax as deeply as you can.
- Close your eyes for a moment and take a few deep breaths.
- Now focus on the picture that symbolizes "obese woman"
- Imagine that you are this woman. Be obese woman.
- Notice any resistance to being this person—and any willingness.
- Notice words, images, thoughts, and feelings that come to mind as you are "seeing and being this woman."

Step 2. Negative Associations

- Next, as you focus on the picture, allow negative opinions to come up, perhaps some that you typically hold about obese women.
- Notice your *thoughts* as you see the person in this negative way. What *feelings*?

Step 3. Positive Associations

- Now, still focusing, allow positive opinions to come up, perhaps some that you typically hold about obese women.
- Notice your *thoughts* as you see the person in this negative way. What *feelings?*

Step 4. Insights and Write-up

- Now review this experience and write about it.
- When you first saw the picture, what thoughts and feelings came up? These may reflect your deepest responses to people from this group.
- Think about the differences in your thoughts and feelings when you consciously held a positive opinion versus a negative opinion.
- Write a few sentences about your feelings, thoughts, and insights.

Part II. Experimenting with Opinions about Obese Men

- Repeat the phases and steps in part I, this time focusing on the image of an obese man.

Next, determine your current knowledge about obese persons by completing Self-Awareness Activity 15.2. After you've completed this chapter, review your answers, determine whether your answers reflect cultural stereotypes and myths or personal biases, and make any corrections necessary,

Self-Awareness Activity 15.2: What Do You Know About Obese Americans?

Purpose: To see what you know about the issues covered in this chapter.
Instructions: Determine whether you think the following statements are basically true or false—and why. The answers are discussed in the following paragraph and throughout this chapter.

1. People become obese only because they overeat.
2. Anyone with sufficient willpower can lose excess weight.
3. People become excessively overweight because of personality problems.
4. Obese people have jolly personalities.
5. Obese employees are likely to cost employers more in health care and sick leave than employees who diet to keep their weight low.
6. Being overweight has no significant effect on career success.
7. Obese men suffer as much discrimination as obese women.
8. Obese persons are protected by law from workplace discrimination.
9. Extremely overweight people generally make poor workers.

STEREOTYPES AND REALITIES

Most of the myths and stereotypes about obese persons are either false or distorted, partial truths. In fact, most stem from people's discomfort with obesity based on their fear of becoming obese themselves. It's true that becoming overweight is usually a matter of eating too much of the wrong foods and not getting enough exercise—and overweight has become a major U.S. health problem in recent years. However, for persons who are obese—beyond mere overweight—the situation is usually more complex than the simple energy-in, energy-out ratio. Those who become obese early in life usually have genetic, hormonal, metabolic, or similar problems. In fact half the children who are obese after age 6 remain that way their entire lives, as do 75 percent of those who are obese as teenagers, according to the New England Journal of Medicine.

Regardless of the reasons why certain employees are overweight or obese, they all have the right to privacy, respect, fair treatment, and reasonable accommodation on the job. As their coworker or manager, your job is not to "cure" their weight problem.

Your job is to give them the support they need in order to perform their tasks effectively and contribute to the organization. This means you must get to know what it's like to be an obese person. The first step is to understand the stereotypes they deal with every day. To bridge the divisive walls these stereotypes hold in place, you must know what they are, know other realities that balance or refute them, and move beyond stereotypes to a more realistic view of obese persons. The goal here is to appreciate each person's unique value and to strengthen our unity as one cohesive team, organization, and culture.

Stereotype #1: People Get Overweight When They Overeat and Don't Exercise

This may be true for most people. However, obese people consume no more calories per day than other people, according to 19 out of 20 studies on this topic. To get down to normal weight range and stay there, an obese person must eat excruciatingly less than a normal-weight person, probably for life. In addition, greatly overweight people have a complex physical situation. Large size probably *causes* the inactivity of greatly overweight persons, and not the other way around. In 1993 a National Institutes of Health panel wrote that evidence increasingly indicates that overweight is not a simple disorder of willpower but a complex disorder of energy metabolism. The experts concluded that diets almost always are disasters, with dieters regaining the weight they had lost.

Stereotype #2: People Are Overweight Because They Lack Willpower

This very basic myth says that individuals should be able to control themselves, and there is something morally wrong with them if they keep giving in to fattening foods. It says that being overweight means being a weak-willed slob, leading to related stereotypes of "lazy" and "stupid." It also ignores the "obesity gene" factor.

Willpower Doesn't Work in the Long Run

Choice and "willpower" are certainly an element in weight gain prevention for the average person. Since we've seen plenty of people who decided to lose weight and then did it within a few weeks, we believe that willpower is the key. What we ignore is the fact for virtually everyone who is significantly overweight gains it all back within a few months or years. Dieting is hard on the body and the psyche—and it is ineffective 95 percent of the time (Martin 2007).

When Martin Seligman, director of clinical psychology at the University of Pennsylvania, reviewed the dieting studies, the best result he could find was one in which 13 percent of the dieters maintained their losses after three years. About 90 percent gain all or almost all their weight back within four or five years, many within a few months. It may be that the 10 percent who succeed over the long term 1) watch every bite they eat, 2) are more or less obsessed with watching their weight, and 3) were close to their natural weight anyway and would weigh only a few pounds more if they had never dieted.

The "Weight Gene" Can Mutate

Scientists at the Rockefeller Institute in New York have discovered a genetic mutation they think is responsible for at least some types of obesity (Friedman 1995). As a result of this "faulty" gene, the body's fat stores don't tell the brain how big or small they are, so the brain may not be able to properly regulate appetite, food intake, and/or food metabolism in ways that in turn regulate the body's fat stores.

Stereotype #3: Obese People Just Need to Get on the Right Diet

After years of reviewing the scientific literature on dieting and weight loss, Martin Seligman (1994) concluded that

- Dieting may make overweight worse, not better.
- Dieting can have negative side effects, such as repeated failure and hopelessness, depression, fatigue, bulimia, and anorexia.

Long-term change requires new eating and activity patterns that constitute a lifestyle, not a "diet." People who keep the weight off think of the new pattern as a lifelong one. Even then, obese persons may not be able to get it off or keep it off.

Stereotype #4: Being Obese Poses Health Risks; Being Thin Does Not

Seligman's review led to less-firm conclusions about the health risks of overweight, but he makes these suggestions:

- Underweight is clearly associated with substantially greater risk of death. Staying 20 percent or more underweight, as virtually all high-fashion models do, can over time greatly reduce stamina, impair the immune system, and lead to other types of health problems.
- Mild to moderate overweight, 10 to 30 percent over so-called ideal weight, may possibly be associated with a marginal increase in mortality, particularly for those at risk for diabetes.
- Substantial obesity of 30 to 100 percent overweight possibly causes health damage and may be associated with somewhat increased mortality.
- Morbid obesity, over 100 percent overweight, may well cause premature death.

Seligman suspects, but is not yet certain, that the weight fluctuation hazard may be larger than the hazard of staying mildly overweight. Gaining weight gradually during adulthood is normal and healthy, but going on diets dramatically increases the risk of heart attacks and strokes later on. Therefore, a new eating disorder might be called "being 20 percent over your so-called ideal weight and ruining your life and health by dieting." An example is the 5'6" medium-frame woman who weighs 165 pounds instead of 135, and repeatedly gains and loses weight through dieting.

Stereotype #5: People Who Diet are Healthier and Live Longer

The health risks of obesity have been grossly exaggerated, according to some researchers, who say that being fat is not equivalent to being unfit. Fitness, not weight, is the most accurate measure of a person's health and life expectancy (Oliver 2006). Center for Disease Control and Prevention researchers acknowledge that "evidence that weight loss improves survival is limited." On the other hand, the health risks of dieting are real. Over one-third of people who diet eventually yo-yo diet, and about one-fourth of those who diet develop partial- or full-syndrome eating disorders (Oliver 2006).

A study by researcher Lyn Dettmar of 466 flight attendants found that 25 percent of them weighed five pounds or more than the airline's top limit. Within this "overweight" group, half either made themselves vomit or used laxatives to lose weight. Dettmar (1990) concludes that such dieting creates more stress than the added weight would create, as well as eating disorders.

Behavior change and self-acceptance are far more effective in achieving long-term health improvements in obese women than dieting, according to a two-year study by nutrition researchers at UC Davis. It is clear that what *does* contribute to health is moderate exercise; wholesome natural foods; minimal intake of sugar, fat, and alcohol; eating only when hungry; and eating slowly and only until satisfied. For example, S. Blair reported on a couple of studies that revealed the importance of exercise. In a study of 13,000 people, the least-fit 20 percent had a much higher death risk than even the next-to-least-fit 20 percent. In another study using a large sample of men, the death rate of sedentary men was 30 percent higher than those who exercised moderately (Blair et al 1988).

Although people in the "normal" weight range of those insurance company weight charts *do* live longer than heavier ones, on average, how much longer is in great dispute (so is how many people are exceptions to the rule because of bone structure and muscle development). In fact, no study has compared the longevity of people who stay within their so-called ideal weight without dieting to people who maintain it with dieting. Those who constantly diet may in fact shorten their lives.

Stereotype #6: Obese People Are Less Productive Workers

Most jobs don't require much physical activity, and there's no reason obese persons can't be just as productive as others. Activists concede that obese people are not appropriate for all jobs, such as those performed in tight quarters or those requiring certain physical abilities. Airline attendants and ballet dancers are examples. But for most jobs obese persons should not be disqualified from applying. They should have a chance to take whatever physical tests are required. If the job requires running down a track every day, let *all* the applicants show that they can run the track. In addition, employers should consider making reasonable accommodation to obese persons, as they do to persons with disabilities.

Stereotype #7: Poor Persons Are More Likely to Be Obese

High protein, low fat meals generally cost more than high carbohydrate, high fat ones—whether the ingredients are purchased at a grocery store or the meal is bought at a fast food chain. The food budget obviously has an impact on diet.

Still, the idea that poor persons are more likely to be fat implies that they are less informed and less in control of their lives. In fact, it's more likely that obese persons make less money because they're obese than that being poor leads to a higher incidence of obesity. This is a major workplace issue that we'll discuss in detail later.

Whether the issue is weight, height, attractiveness, skin color, or other aspect of appearance, your goal is to learn more about experiences of various types of people. And the ultimate goal is to move beyond myths and stereotypes to working productively and profitably together.

HOW DOES FAT PREJUDICE AFFECT PEOPLE?

Perhaps the cruelest aspect of obesity prejudice is that people tend to believe the obese could become slender if they simply summoned adequate willpower and self-discipline, in other words, character. The devaluing of obese persons often has the effect of invading their privacy, as well as limiting their job opportunities. Obese persons, especially women, face workplace discrimination and prejudice across the entire employment spectrum—from getting hired, to getting paid, to holding onto the job, to being offered opportunities to get ahead, to getting promoted (Fikkan 2005, Rothblum 1990, Roehling 1999). More about this in the section on legal workplace rights.

Research indicates that obese job applicants and employees face the following types of discrimination as compared with leaner employees:

- Applicants are seen as having more negative work-related attributes (Polinko 2001).
- Trainees receive more negative expectations from trainers and more negative evaluations.
- Employees receive more negative evaluations and more limited opportunities (Jasper 1990).
- Salespeople are rated as being less punctual, enthusiastic, productive, competent, well-mannered, and trustworthy than average-sized salespeople (Jasper 1990; Larkin 1979; Zemank 1998).
- Salespeople are assigned to less important and desirable sales territories (Ballizi 1998).

- Managers are rated as less desirable and worthy of recognition (Decker 1987).
- Salary differences are significant, especially for women (Pagan 1997, Register 1990, Sargent 1994)

The Message: You're Inferior

Obese women say that little glances and comments they receive are often more damaging than overt discrimination, wearing away at their self-esteem and confidence, reinforcing the message most have heard since childhood: "You're inferior because you're fat." Some typical humiliations obese persons have reported include:

- Frances went to see a doctor to get treatment for what appeared to be strep throat. The doctor insisted that she weigh in, then focused more on her overweight than on her illness. He insisted that she must immediately begin to lose 75 pounds.
- Joan's companion was stopped by a policeman for speeding. He gave Joan a ticket for not wearing a seat belt, even though she explained that the belt in her friend's car wouldn't reach around her body.
- Bill was embarrassed at the grocery checkout when the women behind him commented about two items of "fattening foods" that he was buying.
- Stephanie was trying to find a job. Time after time, she would send a resume and cover letter and the phone response was enthusiastic. When she showed up for the interview, however, she often saw shocked faces and heard, "We think you're over-qualified," or "We've changed strategies."
- Karen applied for a job as a legal secretary. The attorney was impressed with her skills and told her he would hire her—if she could show a 10-pound-a-month weight loss when he weighed her in his office.
- When Jay walked into the staff meeting, two of the men jokingly grabbed their dough-nuts, implying that he might scarf them down.
- Rosita was enjoying lunch at a seafood restaurant with two co-workers. One said, "You know, Rosita, that butter you just put on your bread comes to over 100 calories." The other said, "Yes, and I noticed you ordered a salad with figs, which are loaded with calories."

One activist said, "We're the last safe prejudice. The fat person is the last person employers can safely kick around." That's changing.

When they leave their homes each day, nearly 9 million morbidly obese Americans find themselves in a world built for small people, a world in which they're continually reminded they don't fit. Some of the problems they encounter:

- sitting: finding chairs anywhere that will accommodate them
- flying: fitting into tiny airplane seats
- going to a theater: fitting into tiny theater seats
- traveling in cars: fitting into small cars, dealing with seat belts that won't reach

The Assumption: You Are Your Body

The modern culture of dieting is based on the idea that the personality becomes the body. A related belief is that our size *does* change when we diet, so we must be able to choose it and therefore control it. For many overweight people, the misery is not so much about how they look, but that they feel to blame, that they've been bad to allow their bodies to get fat. Their fat is seen as perverse bad manners, and they can't walk to the corner store without risking insult.

Naturally-thin Sally saw naturally-obese Janice eating a cookie at lunch and commented to Aretha, "How is she going to lose weight that way?" This assumes that Janice should diet all the time, and that she *can*. It pinpoints a whole category of food that should be denied to Janice. It views Janice's unwillingness to forgo cookies as an act of rebellion. And it assumes that what Janice eats is everyone else's business.

At times obese persons feel truly reduced to being just a body and nothing more. As damaging as "conventional wisdom" about overweight has been, the more recent psychological viewpoints may be even more damaging:

- Obese people put on weight as a defense mechanism.
- They're trying to hide inside of all that fat.
- They're trying to feed their hungry, empty hearts.
- They're seeking release from the loss of mother or father . . . and on and on.

One woman who was obsessed for years with keeping her weight far below its natural point said, "By fussing endlessly over my body, I ceased to live in it." She gave up dieting and entered her body again with a whole heart. She says that by letting go of dieting, she freed up mental and emotional energy and space in her life-space for more productive and joyful thoughts and activities. She will no longer pursue a thin elusive body that others say she should have. She says, "It was a terrible distraction, a sidetracking that might have lasted my whole life. By letting go, I go places"

Devaluation and Rejection

Devaluation and rejection are two of the biggest hurdles obese persons must overcome in achieving self-esteem and claiming a place in the world. To illustrate how extreme our culture is about thinness, consider a comment made in the film "The Money Pit" by reed-slim actress Shelly Long to her estranged husband Tom Hanks. "Well, I haven't been out of the house much lately; you know I put on a few pounds." The implicit message was that she felt so bad about her appearance that she had been hiding out at home, and certainly had not had any romantic encounters!

Marian Burros (1994) asked William Dietz, director of clinical nutrition at a Boston hospital, about obesity stereotypes and myths. He replied that because of these myths, neither the government nor the health industry in this country are committed to obesity as a public health problem. He said, "We've ignored it and blamed it on gluttony and sloth." Many people believe that gluttony is a sin, and most believe it reflects laziness, lack of willpower, food addiction, and lack of self-esteem. In fact, gluttony and sloth are two of the classical "seven deadly sins." What a heavy burden to lay on anyone! But "fat activists" point out that people naturally come in different shapes and sizes and that for most obese people, obesity is a relatively uncontrollable genetic condition.

A Cultural Obsession with Thinness

What does it mean when more than 80 percent of U.S. women say they dislike their bodies? Coincidentally, 85 percent of them weigh more than the average fashion model, who in turn weighs 20 percent less than the average woman. The pressure to be very thin starts quite early for little girls. Their role model since the 1960s has been the most popular American doll of all time, Barbie. It's estimated that about one in a million women would naturally have proportions similar to Barbie's, but little girls start trying at a very young age. In fact, by age 10, about 80 percent of them have been on a diet. Later we'll discuss the tyranny of the Beauty Myth, especially for women, and obese persons' right to challenge it.

Women: The Hardest-Hit

A survey reported by Esther Rothblum (1993) indicates that 90 percent of employees cite acceptable weight as essential for a successful career, ranking it fourth, ahead of attractiveness and youthfulness. Intelligence, job qualifications, and education were the first three essentials. Since the stereotype of the ideal woman makes her much thinner than that of the ideal man, more women than men are affected by weight discrimination.

Rothblum also found that men must be significantly heavier than women before they experience the same discrimination. As shown in Table 15.1, employers are slightly more likely to directly urge overweight men than women employees to lose weight. But even moderately overweight women are dramatically more likely than men to experience abuse by co-workers.

TABLE 15.1: Discrimination—Men and Women Employees

Type of Discrimination	Men (%)			Women (%)		
	Average	30–40% Overweight	300 lbs + Overweight	Average	30–40% Overweight	300 lbs + Overweight
Not being hired	–	–	42	–	31	62
Fired/pressured to resign	–	–	11	–	2	17
Urged to lose weight	15	27	69	11	33	60
Abused by co-workers	15	47	–	23	62	73
Abused by supervisors	3	13	52	2	39	45
Needed to conceal weight	–	–	17	–	10	25

Based on the research of Esther Rothblum, University of Vermont, 1993.

Alternative Beliefs

Our entire society suffers when people are forced to fit into one appearance mold. Film maker Frederico Fellini became legendary by filling his films with many colorful characters. Diverse people make films fascinating, and they also make life fascinating and rich for us, once we give up our ego judgments and relax into the diversity. When will we start accepting diversity in size and shape, all sizes and shapes, instead of believing that beauty comes in a very narrow range of acceptable packages?

You could find hundreds of positive beliefs to adopt about obese persons. Author Sally Tisdale (1993) shares her own belief:

When I really look at the people on the street, I see a jungle of bodies, growing every which way like lush plants, growing tall and short and slender and round, hairy and hairless, dark and pale and soft and hard and glorious. They are all loved and lovable.

THE BEAUTY MYTH AND ITS IMPACT

The Beauty Myth says that good-looking people, sexually attractive people, all look a certain way. The acceptable range of body sizes and shapes—including the sizes and shapes of key body parts, such as facial features, breasts, hips, and legs—is extremely narrow and limited. And it's becoming slimmer and younger all the time, especially for women. The myth implies that the ideal woman always looks and acts about 25. When they're 15, most girls are trying to look and act 25. When they're 35, 45, and 55, many women are still trying to look and act 25. When they finally give up the impossible task, many feel invisible and ignored.

Naomi Wolf (1991), author of the book *The Beauty Myth*, argues convincingly that people in our culture didn't hate fat until women began to join forces and reject their inferior status. She says that until women got the vote "fat rounded hips and thighs and bellies were perceived as desirable and sensual." Can it be that the more powerful women become, the more pressure we unconsciously place on them to be smaller and to get rid of the curves that make their bodies different from men's?

Author Kim Chernin (1982) theorizes that we do this to women as a way of diminishing "mother power"—to wipe out the memory of the "primordial mother who rules over our childhood with her inscrutable power over life and death." Wolf adds, "A man's right to confer judgment on any woman's beauty while remaining himself unjudged . . . is the last unexamined right remaining intact from the old list of masculine privilege."

Anyone has the right to challenge the beauty myth by asking such questions as, "Who says so? Who made that rule?" in response to fashion and beauty decrees—and by asserting their human rights to consideration and respect. It's not easy, however.

Cultural Conflicts

To begin with, the weight-loss industry has billions at stake in Americans' obsession with slimness and dissatisfaction with their bodies. It has on its payrolls some of the most prominent weight-loss scientists, who publish journal articles recommending new, improved diets and warning of the health risks of being overweight. Instead of carefully evaluating their claims, and investigating the credibility of the sources, Americans tend to jump on every new diet bandwagon, shelling out billions each year for the privilege of depriving themselves of the foods they want when they want them.

Our values set up eating conflicts; for example we love fattening foods and hate fat people. Consider these random but related facts:

- Kellogg's spent $32 million per year advertising Frosted Flakes in the early 1990s, while only $34 million per year was spent for *all* U.S. obesity research.

- Advertising and commercials for calorie-rich junk foods flood the media, consumption of fast foods is increasing, and so are the overweight.

- Fast food is usually junk food—it's seductively available, convenient, cheap, and tasty.

- Americans spent $40 billion a year on diet programs and diet products in the early 1990s, double the amount spent in the early 1980s; adding diet-related foods sold in food stores, the amount was $80 billion.

In magazines, television, the movies, and shopping malls, women are constantly urged to prepare or indulge in fattening foods—by tantalizing recipes for fudge cake, smells wafting from the Mrs. Fields' cookie counter, and such. In the same media, at the same time, they're bombarded with female role models of beauty and talent who are thinner than almost all the actual women in the population.

In 1980 the average Miss America contestant weighed 6 pounds less than 1960 contestants, and the average *Playboy* centerfold became noticeably thinner. Meanwhile the average woman weighed 6 pounds more. These trends have intensified ever since. As a people, the more obsessed we've become with diets, the more we weigh. Defining overweight as 20 percent or more above the "normal" range, we find the United States leads the industrialized nations in overweight people (Garner1980; Jeffrey 1991).

New Self–Affirming Patterns

Recognizing that size acceptance is an issue for all women—not just large women—is a first step toward solving our nationwide eating problems, according to psychotherapists Jane Hirschmann and Carol Munter (1995). After all, it's our cultural intolerance of certain body sizes that sends us to diets in the first place. And diets often turn us into compulsive eaters or into people obsessed with food, calories, weight, and body size. Hirschmann and Munter use the following process to empower the obese women they work with to stand up for their rights:

- Stop hating your body by challenging those thoughts that put your body down. When you think, "My stomach's too big," shift to, "Who says so? Who made that rule?"

- Make friends with your body and become its loving caretaker; give your body unconditional acceptance and love.

- Become aware of concerns and needs that "bad body thoughts" might mask.

- Reclaim your appetite, dump diets, and learn to eat in response to stomach hunger instead of "mouth hunger" triggered by unconscious needs.
- Assert yourself when people insult your body or intrude into your business.

This process of challenging cultural myths includes many strategies and tactics for dealing with the complexity of overweight. The goal is to give people a solid basis for changing the way they think about their bodies, food, and eating and to establish new, self-affirming patterns.

WHO ARE THE OVERWEIGHT AND OBESE?

The overweight and obese now refers to 65 percent of American adults over age 20! This two-thirds figure includes over one-third (35 percent) of us who are overweight and another 30 percent who are obese. And 3 percent of the obese are "morbidly obese," which is 1 percent of the population, as shown in Figure 15.1. The government agency, Center for Disease Control & Prevention (CDC) conducts ongoing studies in an attempt to cope with this rapidly escalating problem. While being overweight is not associated with early death, as is obesity, it is associated with conditions related to heart disease, cancer, and diabetes, which ultimately are become the major causes of death.

The Body Mass Index Measure

The CDC uses a common measure known as BMI, for Body Mass Index, to indicate the relationship (or ratio) of weight-to-height. BMI is a mathematical formula in which a person's body weight is divided by the square of his or her height (using kilograms and meters). The BMI is more highly correlated with body fat than any other indicator of height and weight. Here are some definitions of the terms used in Figure 15.1:

- "overweight" persons are those with a BMI of 25 to 29.9. For an average 5'4" woman this might mean 20 to 30 pounds too much, and 30 to 40 pounds for the average 5'10" man.
- "obese" persons are those with a BMI of 30 or more, perhaps meaning more than 35 pounds for the woman and more than 45 for the man.
- "morbidly obese" persons weigh at least twice as much as the top of the medically recommended "normal weight range" for persons of their height, build, and age. For adults this means people at least 100 pounds above the normal weight range

Obesity is further defined as an excessively high amount of body fat in relation to lean body mass. The amount of body fat includes concern for both the distribution of fat throughout the body and the size of the fat deposits. Body fat distribution can be estimated by skinfold measures, waist-to-hip circumference ratios, or techniques such as ultrasound, computed tomography, or magnetic resonance imaging.

A Growing Trend

From 1960 to 1980 about 25 percent of Americans were overweight and obese. It rose to 30 percent by 1990 and jumped to 65 percent by 2000. Obesity is increasing even faster among young people than among adults.

- About 16 percent of children and adolescents (ages 6-19) are now seriously overweight.
- The percentage of children and adolescents who are defined as overweight has more than doubled since the early 1970s.

Overweight varies by ethnic group but has been greater for African Americans and Latino Americans than for Euro-American women and is increasing in every group.

Figure 15.1 U.S. Weight Distribution, 2005

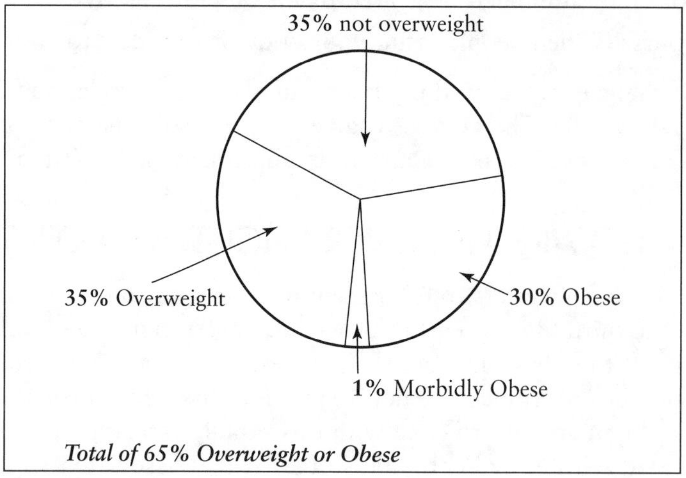

Source: Center for Disease Control

WHY DO PEOPLE BECOME OBESE?

No one simple explanation exists for why people become obese. The basics are: how many food calories you consume and how many you burn through physical activity in a given period. But other factors complicate this simple equation (Kassirer 1998). These factors include your environment, physical ability, genetic makeup, metabolism rate, and possibly exposure to certain viruses.

Environmental influences

A person's environment can discourage adequate activity, encourage fat-producing diets, and produce stress that can lead to the "comfort" of over-eating and being too tired to "get physical." Such environmental influences lead to obesity when you're genetically predisposed.

Physical Disability

Extreme obesity can be related to physical disability. Until 1995 such persons had no legal protection from discrimination; then state courts ruled that they were protected under the Americans with Disabilities Act. Obese persons are on average just as productive as other workers, but some accommodation may need to be made on account of their size.

Genetic causes

At least 75 genes and gene markers are associated with human obesity. The combinations and permutations of those 75 genes means there could be thousands of different kinds of obesity. Genes affect how quickly or slowly your stomach signals fullness. They affect metabolism—how much or how little food your muscles need as fuel to keep them going. They also affect how effectively your brain signals that you've had enough food for now and that you have enough body fat.

Metabolism

Metabolism rates vary so greatly that one person may burn off three times the food that another person can burn in a 24-hour period. Certain physical factors are involved. For example, the bigger you are, the more energy you use to keep all your cells running. Lean tissue burns about four times the energy at rest that fat tissue burns. Women, on average, burn off less food than men, and older people burn less than younger ones. Research indicates that even when all these factors are eliminated, metabolic rates still vary greatly from person to person because of genetic differences.

Viruses

Viruses can permanently damage the body's delicate weight maintenance apparatus. At least four viruses have been shown to cause obesity in animals. For example, researchers found a virus in mice and chickens that causes obesity in 15 percent of the animals it infects. The virus gets into the animals' brain areas that regulate eating and body weight, where it seems to cause permanent changes in the animals' ability to maintain a stable weight. Researchers examined human blood samples, looking for antibodies to similar viruses. About 15 percent of the obese people they tested had such antibodies, compared to none of the lean people. It is plausible that such viruses are a cause of obesity, but this has not yet been proven conclusively due to the difficulty of doing such research on humans.

Bottom Line

Until we have better data about the risks of being overweight and the benefits and risks of trying to lose weight, we should remember that the cure for obesity may be worse than the condition.

WHAT RIGHTS DO ACTIVISTS WANT?

Obesity activists say that everyone has a right to be accepted for the person within rather than the exterior physical appearance. In the workplace people have a right to be valued for their potential and actual performance.

Some Basic Rights

Obese people have begun organizing to fight one of the few remaining types of discrimination that has gone unchallenged. They see weight discrimination as one of the last frontiers in the civil rights struggle and hope to eventually expand the federal Civil Rights Act to cover obese people. However, for now they are relying on the Americans with Disabilities Act and its requirement for reasonable accommodation. This is judicial law based on court decisions. It's bolstered by administrative law in the form of legal briefs filed by the EEOC that support reasonable accommodation for obese persons.

The size acceptance movement has been active for about 20 years. An underlying principle is that by accepting yourself just as you are, you develop the strength, self-esteem, and confidence to fend off the insults, attacks, and discrimination the world heaps upon obese persons. Sally Tisdale states, "Rejection can't kill you. With the right attitude, rejection can make you stronger. Don't hide out at home. Go out in the world and risk rejection."

Critics say that social preference for thinness is too ingrained in the culture to be legislated away. Activists reply that these same arguments were used for other forms of discrimination. "It's the same as saying you can't hire black salespersons because the customers won't like it, or that you can't hire women because they can't handle male customers' resistance to buying from women," says Art Stine of Michigan's Department of Civil Rights. His department investigates 10 to 20 cases of weight discrimination each year. At least three national organizations have emerged in recent years to take up the cause of obese Americans. The activist group that's been most prominent in the media recently is the National Association to Advance Fat Acceptance (NAAFA). With 4,000 members in 75 chapters nationwide, NAAFA's goals include:

- improving the self-esteem of obese people
- ensuring their civil rights
- challenging our fat-rejecting culture through education, legislation, and the courts
- achieving equal access to employment

NAAFA leaders say they like the word *fat*. They don't like *overweight*, and they ask "Over whose weight?" They say *obesity* suggests a medical disorder. NAAFA has reclaimed the label *fat* much as some African Americans have reclaimed *nigger* and some gays the term *queer*—but these are still very controversial terms. Certainly not all obese persons agree that they want to be called fat, and most people in our culture have been conditioned to avoid calling people fat. For this reason, the most common term is the medical and legal term *obese*.

The International Size Acceptance Association (ISAA)is focusing on legal workplace rights by asking people to sign petitions to send to legislators. ISAA has attracted national news media and created some interest in this issue.

Legal Workplace Rights: Money Matters

Until recently overweight people had no legal rights for protection from employment discrimination based on weight. Those who are starting to fight back against such discrimination have been forced to resort to two related legal rights:

- protection under the ADA, which treats obesity as a disability in the workplace
- protection under the constitutional right to privacy, on the basis that personal eating habits should not affect how an employee is judged at work

Sally Smith, executive director of NAAFA, notes that one person may be 100 pounds over society's ideal, and others may be just 10. Talking to interviewer Jan Wahl, Smith said, "If employers can use it against the greatly overweight person today, what's to keep them from using it against the slightly overweight tomorrow?"

People who weigh more not only find it more difficult to get and keep jobs, they also make less money.

- One study found that businessmen sacrifice $1,000 in salary for every pound they are overweight. Obese women tend to earn less, too.
- Among women who earn more than $50,000, only 13 percent are obese, while among women in the poverty category, 30 percent are obese.
- In a study of women of all weights, Harvard sociologist Steven Gortmaker found that the overweight women, averaging 5¢ 3≤ and 200 pounds, had household incomes that averaged $6,710 below those of thinner women and that they were 10 percent more likely to live in poverty. Overweight apparently keeps people from becoming as affluent as they might otherwise become.
- Obese women are more likely than thin ones to lose socioeconomic status over the course of their adolescence and young adulthood, no matter how well they originally do on achievement tests or how affluent their families. The heavier the woman, the greater the job discrimination, according to a seven-year study of 5,000 women.

Even women of average size or only slightly heavy are often encouraged to lose weight and are more likely to be passed over for promotion than thinner women. This phenomenon is much more common for women than men.

To End Appearance Discrimination, Too

The workplace rights problem goes beyond weight discrimination to the Beauty Myth and the broader issue of appearance discrimination. Attractive people tend to earn about 5 percent more than those with average looks. And homely workers make about 7 percent less than those with average looks. That's a 12 percent pay gap between the homely and the attractive. Women considered to be unattractive are less likely to work than other women and tend to marry men with lower levels of education.

Attractive people are widely regarded as being more intelligent, friendly, honest, and confident than others, all traits that could influence employers and customers to discriminate in favor of them. Attractive children are rewarded with more praise from parents and teachers, influencing their self-esteem and confidence, both valued in the marketplace. Certain occupations cater to attractive employees more than others, but favoritism toward good looks and prejudice against homeliness is pervasive in most jobs. Even within any given occupation, good-looking people make more. When the appearance ratings of 700 MBA graduates were correlated with the salaries they were earning ten years after graduation, better-looking men made as much as $10,000 per year more (Hamermesh 1993).

WHAT RIGHTS DO EMPLOYERS WANT TO RETAIN?

Employee appearance and size can affect the success of certain businesses. Employers want to retain the right to achieve fair, reasonable business goals. In theory, activists in the fat acceptance movement do not disagree with this principle. In practice, the two groups may disagree about what is fair and reasonable.

Some employers who run airlines, fashion stores, restaurants, beauty salons, and real estate agencies say they have a right to establish an image and hire only employees who fit that image. Civil rights advocates counter that the only criterion should be performance. One who lost 40 pounds, said, "I did my job well before, and I do it well now. Weight has nothing to do with it." Another said, "Who are employers to play God, to judge what is acceptable or beautiful? Rubens painted large women who were beautiful. It seems clear to me that hiring and promotion ought to be based on your ability to do the job."

Some employers say that customers won't do business with obese persons and that coworkers won't respect them or work well with them. Activists reject the circular reasoning and the ethics of this argument, noting it was also used to resist equal rights for minorities and women. They say it's morally unacceptable for employers themselves to discriminate against obese persons just because prejudiced customers and coworkers might discriminate against them. Such actions signal that employers accept prejudice and encourage it. Just as it is the employers' responsibility to stop sexual harassment of women and ethnic discrimination toward African Americans, it's also their responsibility to stop harassment and discrimination toward obese persons.

Some employers claim that obese employees cost more in health care and sick time. Health professionals suggest that yo-yo dieting could make both obese and thinner persons less healthy. And some obese persons are reluctant to seek medical care because doctors often don't respect them, are condescending and patronizing about their weight, and harangue them to lose weight. Others don't have health care coverage. Nevertheless, there are no respectable studies showing that obese persons cost more because of health problems.

WHAT LAWS PROTECT OBESE WORKERS?

Persons who suffer weight discrimination by employers have only recently gained some legal protection. Laws take three forms.

1. *Legislation.* The most powerful and direct are laws specifically prohibiting discrimination based on weight, height, or other aspects of physical appearance. They follow in the tradition of civil rights laws prohibiting discrimination on the basis of race, creed, color, gender, and similar characteristics. Currently, these are rare.

2. *Court rulings.* Less direct are court rulings that equate obesity with disability and require employers to make reasonable accommodation for obese employees. This is currently the basis for protection from discrimination for obese persons.

3. *Administrative policy.* Government agencies can set policies and make rulings that have the effect of law in some instances. Currently the EEOC has filed legal briefs in court cases, supporting the idea that obese persons are entitled to the same reasonable accommodation as persons with disabilities.

Most activists agree that the best protection is to add weight discrimination to the other types of discrimination prohibited by the federal and state civil rights acts.

Legislation: Civil Rights & Privacy Rights

By the year 2000, Michigan was the only state in the country with a law that specifically protects the employment rights of overweight people. Weight and height were added to its civil rights statues. The cities of Santa Cruz, California, and Washington, D.C. are among the few local governments that have added such clauses to their civil rights laws.

Massachusetts and New York began considering legislation in 1994 that would add height and weight to civil rights statutes covering employment and housing. A similar bill failed in Texas. California's civil rights laws, while not specifically covering weight, were the basis for a million dollar court award to a 400-pound man. He had sued the automotive parts firm that had fired him after 10 years' employment. In September 1995, after a six-week trial, he was awarded back pay and reparation for emotional distress.

Another legal avenue is the right to privacy, based on the principle that one's personal eating or exercise habits should not affect how one is judged in the workplace. The American Civil Liberties Union has launched a national project to fight an employer trend to meddle in employees' private lives, such as their eating, drinking, and smoking habits.

Court Rulings: Disability

New Jersey law regards obesity as a disability that automatically triggers discrimination protection regardless of the cause of the obesity. In most of the states where obese employees have won their lawsuits, their cases were based on the ADA. Their attorneys claimed that obesity should be viewed as a physical disability. This is risky at best since some experts still claim that obese people could lose their excess weight if they really wanted to.

The disability argument did prevail in a federal appeals court in 1993. A woman sued the Rhode Island Department of Mental Health after she was denied a state job because at 5'2" she weighed 320 pounds. Lawyers for the state agency said the law should not be interpreted to cover obesity because obesity "is caused by voluntary conduct and is not immutable." They argued that the plaintiff could lose weight and rid herself of any disability arising from her obesity at any time. But the judge and jury ruled that there was credible evidence that the metabolic dysfunction causing weight gain in the morbidly obese lingers even after weight loss. Their decision was upheld in a federal appeals court, which said that discrimination against the obese could constitute a violation of the ADA. The court further stated that:

> In a society that all too often confuses "slim" with "beautiful or "good," morbid obesity can present formidable barriers to employment.

The court briefs and opinions don't indicate that obesity in itself is necessarily a disability. Instead, the reasoning is that when persons are discriminated against, either because their obesity limits their activities or because employers *perceive* obesity as a disability that limits their activities, then such persons can be protected under disability law.

Administrative Law: EEOC Policy

The Equal Employment Opportunities Commission (EEOC) filed a brief in federal appeals court in the Rhode Island case. EEOC lawyers urged the court to consider obesity just as it would view many other conditions not specifically mentioned in the ADA, based on how long the person has been affected by the condition and how difficult it would be to change. Noting that obesity isn't a "traditional" disability, the EEOC said that "although it's possible for an obese individual to lose weight, obesity is a chronic, lifelong condition." It further stated that a condition does not have to be involuntary or immutable to be covered. The EEOC did not indicate that a person must be "morbidly obese" in order to be protected from discrimination, and the ruling probably opens the door for claims from more moderately obese employees. Discrimination claims under the ADA must be filed first with the EEOC.

The idea behind the ruling is that the way persons look shouldn't affect their ability to get and keep a job.

In 2005 the federal Medicare program abandoned a long-standing policy that obesity is not a disease. This removed a major roadblock for people trying to get medical coverage for various weight-loss therapies. Representatives for some organizations praised the move, such as American Obesity Association and the North American Association for the Study of Obesity. Others, such as Dr. Paul Campos (2004), said "it's not a bad idea, just completely unscientific"

NAAFA activists say being fat doesn't necessarily mean poor health, and it's too bad that in most states their only recourse in fighting discrimination is through laws meant to protect the disabled. Several overweight persons interviewed by Jan Wahl said the predicament was offensive because most of them are not disabled and are in fact very healthy people.

LEADERSHIP CHALLENGE: MEETING WORKPLACE NEEDS

Your major challenge as a leader working with obese employees, and others that suffer from appearance discrimination, is to help them overcome the barriers they face to success in the workplace. Here's a summary of the basic needs of these employees.

- protection from discrimination and harassment by managers and employees
- respect for their privacy
- acceptance of them as they are
- appreciation of their value as human beings and of their contributions
- accommodation that will help them do their job
- fair and equal compensation

LEADERSHIP OPPORTUNITIES: BUILDING ON STRENGTHS

You have an opportunity to enlighten the corporate culture and to influence employees to move beyond the beauty myth to an appreciation of people for their inner qualities and contributions to the organization.

Opportunity #1: Look Below the Surface

You can move away from a focus on the superficial aspects of corporate employee image, such as size, shape, facial features, and other aspects of the Beauty Myth. An in-depth corporate image focuses on such inner strengths as being honest, respecting others, keeping agreements, honoring commitments, delivering the goods on time, providing top-quality service, being positive, focusing on others' strengths and contributions, seeing the humor, loving life, summoning courage, and on and on. These qualities seem old-fashioned in a way. Yet aren't they really the raw materials that leaders can skillfully draw on to create a highly motivated and committed world-class workforce?

Opportunity #2: Set Policies on Obesity Harassment and Discrimination

Employers and managers have a responsibility to stop the harassment of obese employees and to stop discriminatory actions against them. The first step is to develop policies and procedures designed to provide equal opportunity and fair treatment of obese persons. Affirmative action programs and equal opportunity policies already in place for minorities and women can be used for guidance in remedying discrimination. Company policies and procedures designed to prevent sexual harassment and to handle such cases can serve as a pattern for preventing and handling cases of obesity harassment.

Opportunity #3: Make Reasonable Accommodation

Although obese persons are not necessarily disabled, those who are greatly overweight usually need some type of accommodation. The best way to find out is to ask tactfully what can be done to help them to be as productive and successful as possible on the job. Comfortable, sturdy seating arrangements are nearly always needed and appreciated, not only at a work station or executive desk but also in meeting rooms, lounges, dining facilities, and any other place the employee frequents in the course of the job. If a company car or other transportation is provided, arrange for adequate size in seats and seat belts.

A few obese persons have difficulty getting around. The same provisions that are made for other mobility-impaired employees can be made for these employees—such as electric carts, ramps, elevators, and convenient parking.

Opportunity #4: Enlighten the Corporate Culture

Enlightening the corporate culture means encouraging all employees to establish productive relationships with obese employees—and with obese persons among customers, suppliers, and other stakeholders. Of course, this also applies to persons with other types of appearance issues.

Take customers. Research indicates that obese persons generally receive as much obvious acceptance—such as being greeted, being helped—as leaner customers. However, they experience more of the subtle forms discrimination, such as less eye contact and less friendliness (Martel 1996, Valian 1998). And this subtle discrimination has severe negative consequences. Such customers spend less money at the store than they intended to, they are less willing to recommend the store to others, and they are less likely to return for future shopping (King 2006). Clearly, it pays to help employees overcome negative stereotypes and attitudes toward obese persons.

You can encourage change in those company practices and habits that degrade and discriminate against obese persons through your own example, through appropriate storytelling, through making them heroines and heroes when they excel, through visibly supporting them in other ways, and through providing information and training for all employees about obesity issues. Corporate diversity training programs can include a segment on obese persons. Every employee needs to complete such a segment.

You can focus on the contributions of obese employees, and on their positive qualities. You can unfailingly respect their dignity and refuse to countenance disrespect in the form of wisecracks, jokes, put-downs, unsought advice, and similar behavior.

Opportunity #5: Consider New Marketing Opportunities

Some leaders are breaking the mold and giving talented obese persons job opportunities in such high-profile jobs as television news reporter, talk show hostess, and situation comedy star. Some say that such media personalities seem approachable, like a "next-door neighbor," and people feel comfortable with them. Business leaders need to examine this opportunity to relate to new types of customers and perhaps open up new markets. Since two-thirds of Americans are overweight or obese, marketing opportunities are almost unlimited.

SUMMARY

Myths and stereotypes about obese persons cause people to judge them negatively, to reject them as friends and employees, and even to invade their privacy by telling them how to lose weight. Most jobs are sedentary, and obese employees are just as productive as others. Because of appearance bias, however, obese persons are less likely to be hired and promoted, make less money on average, and are more likely to be poor than those considered attractive by cultural standards. These standards are more stringent for women than for men, primarily because of the Beauty Myth that appearance is more important as a way of judging women.

About 65 percent of Americans are considered overweight or obese, 35 percent of those being overweight and 30 percent obese. About 1 percent are morbidly obese. The causes of obesity are extremely complex. At least five factors play important roles: 1) environment, 2) physical ability, 3) genetics, with at least 75 genes and gene markers involved, 4) metabolism rates that vary greatly, and 5) viruses that may damage the body's delicate weight-control mechanisms.

Most studies indicate that obese persons eat no more than other people, and they often have difficulty exercising because of their size. Diets don't work for most people, especially the very obese, because nearly all dieters gain back the weight. Bottom line: obesity poses some health risks, but so does the dieting syndrome and so does being extremely underweight.

Obese employees have had no protection from job discrimination in the past, but that's changing. Nationally, the most significant development is a case won in a federal appeals court and supported by an EEOC brief that cites morbid obesity as a condition protected under the ADA. A size acceptance movement is emerging in which obese activists declare their rights to equal treatment, to equal pay, and to challenge the beauty myth. The major leadership challenge is meeting the needs of obese employees. Leadership opportunities include looking beneath surface appearances to career strengths and building upon them, setting policies the prohibit harassment and discrimination, making reasonable accommodation, enlightening the corporate culture, and considering new marketing opportunities in which persons of various sizes and shapes can be an asset.

Case Study 15.1: Chris, a Job Applicant

Chris is 35 years old, has two years of college, and weighs 350 pounds. In response to a newspaper ad, Chris applied and interviewed for a job at Kragen Auto Parts, an automotive supply store. He didn't get the job, but when he learned of another opening, he called the chain store's personnel coordinator, *Georgia*. Georgia told Chris the store wanted more experienced people. She also told him, "There is some concern about your weight and whether you can physically handle the accessing and lifting of some of the merchandise." Chris has 10 ten years' experience in retail selling although he has never worked in an automotive supply store.

1. What are the key issues (root problems)?
2. If you were Chris, what would you do?
3. If you were a top manager at Kragen's, how would you view this situation?

Case Study 15.2: Laura, Public Relations Manager

Laura was 40 years old and had successfully held several managerial positions in public relations. When she applied for a job at a major East Coast medical center, she was wearing a slenderizing dark suit and had been on a strict diet for two months. She got the job but didn't report for work until a month or so later. In the meantime, Laura relaxed her diet regime. As usual after such diets, she was starved and tired and quickly went back up to her usual 230 pounds. When she arrived for her first day on the new job, *Murray*, the director of public relations blurted out, "My God, you've put on a lot of weight since we interviewed you. I'm not sure this is the image we want for the hospital."

From that day on Laura was constantly pressured to diet and watched to see if she was slimming down. Laura felt demeaned, set apart from the others, and was subjected to humiliating comments. She had an expensive professional wardrobe, but *Jan*, her boss, told her to wear only black or navy. Laura knew that meant "camouflage your size." She says, "Every time I walked into the office, I got a quick once-over to see what I was wearing and whether I had lost weight." At a staff meeting Jan asked Laura to tell everyone about the liquid diet she was starting.

For the next year Laura was succesful in her job. She got national publicity for the hospital, raised large sums of money, and developed award-winning programs. Nevertheless, she was called into Jan's office one Friday afternoon and fired. Jan didn't mention her weight directly, but said, "Things that should have changed didn't change."

1. What are the root problems?
2. What is your opinion of the way Murray and Jan handled Laura's case?
3. Do you think Laura should have done anything differently?
4. What do you think she should do now?

Case Study 15.3: Louis' Career Goals

Louis has been working for Manko's, a privately-owned printing firm for about 5 years. The firm specializes in designing and printing forms used by automobile dealers. Louis' duties include taking phone orders and arranging for the shipping of the merchandise to clients. The shipping aspect requires lifting boxes of forms. His job calls for good customer relations skills, and over the years he has helped the firm develop and retain a loyal clientele.

Louis' doctor tells him that he's about 150 pounds over his ideal weight. This has been the case for nearly all his adult life, at least since his early twenties. Louis has dieted and lost weight several times in the past years, once even losing 125 pounds. As he says, "I've tried every dieting gimmick in the book, and I always end up at about the same weight in the long run." Louis has always been somewhat self-conscious about his weight, for he was a little "pudgy" even as a child. His mother frequently cautioned him about his eating patterns, saying, "Louis, you don't need to eat seconds; you've had enough to eat." Or, "No, Louis, you don't need to eat cookies; try an apple or an orange for a snack."

Louis' weight has not been a problem at the print shop. He gets along well with the employees, as well as the customers he relates to by phone. There are four employees: a printer, two outside salespersons, and Louis, who handles everything in the office. The owner, *Bill Manko*, relies on him to keep the office running, and the salespersons rely on him to do favors for their customers, such as shipping forms ASAP, providing information about the proper type of form a customer needs, and explaining to customers how to use certain forms.

Bill tells Louis that the firm has grown enough to need another outside salesperson. He's looking for a good person. Louis realizes that the job would be a good opportunity for him to expand his career, and he decides to apply. When Louis approaches Bill about the job, Bill seems quite surprised and says, "Well, let me think about it, Louis." A few days later, Bill says to Louis, "I think you're a better asset to the company in your present job. You don't quite fit the sales rep image, and we need your know-how and knowledge of the business and the customers to handle phone orders and shipping."

1. What are the key issues (root problems) in this case?
2. If you were Bill, what would you do?
3. If you were Louis, what would you do?

Case Study 15.4: Helen, Travel Agent

Helen has been working for World Points Travel Agency for about a year. World Point consists of a chain of 15 travel agencies with a total of about 100 employees. When Helen interviewed for the job, the office seemed perfectly suited to her style. People seemed to like their work and enjoy a little humor. *Franko*, the manager, was very flexible about allowing her to work only 25 hours a week and to schedule her hours around her daughter's needs. He hired her on the spot.

Helen was thrilled to get the job: all she wanted was to work part time so she could spend time with her three-year-old daughter Linda, whom she had just enrolled in a good nursery school. Helen figured that a nice part-time job at a travel agency would give her a chance to get out of the house and meet people and make enough money to pay Linda's school expenses.

Everyone was friendly from the beginning, and Helen was invited to join the employee's association even though part-time workers were technically not eligible for membership. The employee's association didn't negotiate contracts or require dues, but did consult with management in making policies for the agency and the employees. Little did Helen know that the actions of the group would eventually lead to her downfall.

A few weeks ago, the group suggested to management that the company's image needed to be improved. As one of them said, "We sell so many European vacation plans, we need to present a chic, updated European image." Most of the improvements involved changing the names of vacation packages and the office decor. The trouble arose when the group decided to adopt appearance standards for employees; for example: "Employees who deal directly with the public must look attractive and professional and wear outfits that reflect current European high-fashion. Employees must keep their weight within the optimal weight range for their height and bone structure."

Helen is 5'6" tall and weighs about 200 pounds. Last week, two of the women from the employee association committee that drafted the image policy met with Helen. They asked her if she would agree to bring her weight down to 160 pounds within the next six months, saying "That seems reasonable, don't you think." Helen said, "No, I don't think it's reasonable. I gained this weight three years ago when I was pregnant and then nursing my daughter. I've tried to lose it, and it's just not that easy. I'd like to lose it on my own terms and in my own time frame. To make this kind of agreement just puts too much pressure on me."

Marge, the committee chair said, "It was the employee association's idea to do this, and you are a member of our group, so you shouldn't view this as something the company is forcing on you." Helen replied, "Do you think I don't look good enough to sell European vacation plans? Don't I have a right to look the way I want to look, so long as it isn't outrageous or harmful to business?" Marge replied, "We all know you're a highly professional worker and an attractive representative of the company. But we think the rule should apply to everyone." The others seemed to agree with Marge.

The next day Franko approached Helen and suggested changing her job duties, saying, "Helen, let's try you out at the confirmation desk. You can keep your current salary and hours and it will probably be a better fit for you." Helen objected, "Franko, I love meeting with people and I'm good at it. I don't want a strictly telephone job behind the scenes. All I'll be doing is confirming hotel and flight reservations. It would be boring, and I would go nuts."

1. What are the key issues (root problems) in this case?
2. If you were Helen, what would you do?
3. If you were Franko, what would you do?

REFERENCES

Ballizzi, J.A. and R.W. Hasty, "Territory Assignment Decisions and Supervising Unethical Selling Behavior: The Effects of Obesity and Gender as Moderated by Job-Related Factors," *Journal of Personal Selling and Sales Management* 18, 35–49, 1998.

Blair, S., et al, "Physical Fitness and All-Cause Mortality"; J. Holloway, A. Beuter, and J. Duda, "Self-Efficacy and Training for Strength in Adolescent Girls"; Paffenbarger et al, "Physical Activity, All-Cause Mortality." *Journal of Applied Social Psychology* 18, 699–719, 1988.

Brown, Laura S. and Esther D. Rothblum, eds. *Overcoming Fear of Fat*. Harrington Park Press, 1989.

Burros, Marian. "More Americans Tipping the Scales." *New York Times*, July 15, 1994.

Campos, Paul. *The Obesity Myth*. Gotham, 2004.

CDC, Center for Disease Control & Prevention. "Defining Overweight and Obesity," *www.cdc.gov*, 2003.

Chernin, Kim. *The Obsession: Reflections on the Tyranny of Slenderness*. Harper & Row, 1982.

Decker, W.H. "Attributions Based on Managers' Self-Presentation, Sex, and Weight," *Psychological Reports* 61, 175–181, 1987.

Dettmar, Lyn. Chicago clinical psychologist, study conducted in 1990.

Fikkan, J. and E. Rothblum, "Weight Bias in Employment," in K.D. Brownell et al eds., *Weight Bias: Nature, Consequences, and Remedies*, 15–28. Guilford, 2005.

Fraser, Laura. "The Overweight Want Their Rights," *San Francisco Chronicle*, E-7, June 22, 1994.

Friedman, J. of Howard Hughes Medical Institute, Rockefeller Institute. See reports in *Nature* and *Discovery*, March, 1995.

Garner, D., P. Garfindek, D. Schwartz, and M. Thompson, "Cultural Expectations of Thinness in Women." *Psychological Reports* 47, 483–91, 1980.

Gortmaker, Steven, et al., "Social and Economic Consequences of Overweight in Adolescence and Young Adulthood," *New England Journal of Medicine* 329,14, 1036–1037, September 1993.

Grunwald, L. "Do I Look Fat to You?" *Discovery*, March 1995, 58–74.

Hamermesh, Daniel S. and Jeff Biddle. *Beauty and the Labour Market*. National Bureau of Economic Research, 1993.

Hirschmann, Jane and Carol Munter. *When Women Stop Hating Their Bodies*, Fawcett Columbine, 1995.

Jasper, C.R. and M.L. Klassen, "Perceptions of Salesperson' Appearance and Evaluation of Job Performance," *Perceptual and Motor Skills* 71, 563–455, 1990.

Jeffrey, R., S. Adlis, and J. Forster, "Prevalence of Dieting Among Working Men and Women." *Health Psychology* 10, 274–81, 1991.

Johnson, Carol A. *Self-Esteem Comes in All Sizes: How to Be Healthy and Happy at Your Natural Weight*. Doubleday, 1995.

Kano, Susan. *Making Peace With Food* (a step-by-step guide to self-help in freeing yourself from diet and weight obsession). Harper, 1989.

Kassirer, J. and M. Angell, eds. *New England Journal of Medicine*, January 1998.

King, E. et al, "The Stigma of Obesity in Customer Service: A Mechanism for Remediation and Bottom-Line Consequences of Interpersonal Discrimination," *Journal of Applied Psychology* 91, 579–593, 2006.

Larkin, J.E. and H.A. Pines, "No Fat Persons Need Apply," *Sociology of Work and Occupations* 6, 312–327, 1979.

Lyons, Pat and Debby Burgard. *Great Shape*. Bull Publishing Co., 1990.

Martel, R. D.M. Lane and C. Willis, "Male-Female Differences: A Computer Simulation," *American Psychologist* 51, 157–158, 1996.

Martin, Courtney E *Perfect Girls, Starving Daughters: The Frightening New Normalcy of Hating Your Body*. Free Press, 2007.

Olds, Ruthanne. *Big & Beautiful* (a book on overcoming fatphobia). Acropolis Books Ltd., 1992.

Oliver, J. Eric. *Fat Politics: The Real Story Behind America's Obesity Epidemic*. Oxford University Press, 2006.

Pagan, J.A. and A. Davila, "Obesity, Occupational Attainment, and Earnings," *Social Science Quarterly* 78, 756–770, 1997.

Polinko, N.K. and P.M. Popovich, "Evil Thoughts but Angelic Actions: Responses to Overweight Job Applicants," *Journal of Applied Social Psychology* 31, 909–917, 2001.

Polivy, Janet and Peter Herman. *Breaking the Diet Habit*. Basic Books, 1983.

Register, C.A. and D.R. Williams, "Wage Effects of Obesity among Young Workers," Social *Science Quarterly* 71, 130–141, 1990.

Roehling, M.V. "Weight-Based Discrimination in Employment: Psychological and Legal Aspects," *Personnel Psychology* 52 969–1016, 1999.

Rothblum C., R.A. Brand, C.T. Miller and H.A. Oetjen, "The Relationship Between Obesity, Employment Discrimination, and Employment-Related Victimization," *Journal of Vocational Behavior* 37, 251–266, 1990.

Rose, Laura, S. Brown and E.D. Rothblum, eds. *Life Isn't Weighed on the Bathroom Scale*. WRS Group, 1994.

Rothblum, Esther D. "Weight and Acceptance on the Job," in *Life Isn't Weighed on the Bathroom Scale*, ed. Laura Rose, S. Brown and E.D. Rothblum. WRS Group, 1994.

Sargent, J.D. and D.G. Blanchflower, "Obesity and Stature in Adolescence and Earning in Young Adulthood," *Archives of Pediatric Adolescent Medicine* 148, 681–687, 1994.

Seligman, Martin. *What You Can Change and What You Can't*. Knopf, 1994.

Tisdale, Sally. "A Weight That Women Carry." *Harpers*, May 1993.

Valian, V. *Why So Slow? The Advancement of Women*. The MIT Press, 1998.

Wahl, Jan. "Taking a Female Lead." *Radiance*, fall 1994.

Wolf, Naomi *The Beauty Myth: How Images of Beauty Are Used Against American Women*. Doubleday, 1991.

Zemank, J.E., R.P McIntyre and A. Zemanek, "Salespersons' Weight and Ratings of Characteristics Related to Effectiveness of Selling," *Psychological Reports* 82, 947–952, 1998.

Resources – Organizations and Workshops

AHELP, Association for the Health Enrichment of Large People. Annual conferences for health professionals. Joe McVoy, Ph.D., Director, AHELP, P.O. Drawer C, Radford, VA 24143.

American Obesity Association. *www.obesity.org*

Ample Opportunity. Organization, Portland, Oregon.

Annual Event: International No-Diet Day, May 5.

Boycott Anorexic Marketing, a Boston group founded by psychotherapist Dr. Mary Baures, who is concerned about a society that promotes eating disorders. In 1994 the group criticized the ultrathin models used by Coca-Cola and Calvin Klein and called for a boycott.

David Garner, Ph.D. Eating disorder specialist and antidiet activist.

Fed Up! Book, workshops, and support groups, by Terry Nicholetti Garrison, 233 Forest Home Drive, Ithaca, NY 14850.

Largely Positive. Workshops and support groups, manual on starting support groups, Carol Johnson, Milwaukee, Wisconsin, P.O. Box 17233, Glendale, WI 53217.

NAFAA, National Association to Advance Fat Acceptance, based in Sacramento, CA, with 4,000 members nationwide, *www.naafa.org*

National Council on Size and Weight Discrimination, *www.cswd.org*

North American Association for the Study of Obesity. *www.naaso.org*

Resources – Magazines and Films

Dimensions, the lifestyle magazine for men who prefer large, radiant women, and the women who want to learn about them. 7189 Capitol Station, Albany, NY 12224.

Extra! a magazine for large persons.

Fat Chance, a documentary film sponsored by the National Film Board of Canada, to be aired on public broadcasting systems.

Healthy Weight Journal (formerly *Obesity and Health*), published by Healthy Living Institute, 402 South 14 Street, Hettinger, ND.

Radiance, the magazine for large women, a sponsored project of the San Francisco Women's Center, P.O. Box 30246, Oakland, CA 9460.

CHAPTER 16

Working with Persons From Diverse Religions

My great hope is that we can enter this new millennium as the most successful multi-racial, multi-ethnic, multi-religious democracy the world has ever known.

President Bill Clinton, 1997

"Never discuss religion or politics at the dinner table," according to etiquette experts, if you want a pleasant, civil dinner party. People tend to have passionate, even dogmatic beliefs about God and country. Therefore, dealing with religious diversity in the workplace can be one of the most difficult aspects of managing diversity.

In this chapter you will explore some myths and realities about religion, including legal protections that employers must observe, and some basic information about seven major religions: Judaism, Christianity, Islam, Confucianism, Taoism, Hinduism, and Buddhism. While most Americans belong to a religious group, many are agnostics who view ultimate reality (God) as unknown or unknowable, or atheists who do not believe in the concept of God decreed by various religions.

We will also discuss leadership challenges and opportunities related to each religious group with suggestions for you in your role as manager. Our goal is to better understand the members of these various religions and to help you manage religious diversity in a fair and effective way in your workplace.

Self-Awareness Activity 16.1

What Do You Know About People from Various Religions?

Purpose: To see what you know about the topics covered in this chapter.
Instructions: Determine whether you think the following statements are basically true or false—and think about why. The answers will emerge in this chapter, and the summary at the end of the chapter focuses on these issues.

1. Religious observances and practices must be kept out of the workplace.

2. The religion that has the most followers in the world is Islam.

3. The religion that has the most followers in the United States is Catholic.

4. The Jewish Sabbath is on Friday.

5. Muslims follow the teachings in their holy book the Quran and do not recognize the holy books of any other religion.

6. The Confucian religion was influential in ancient China but has little influence in the world since China became a communist nation.

7. One of the three Taoist sects focuses on vital life energy.

8. Hinduism was the source of the caste system in India, and some political leaders are trying to make the system illegal.

9. Buddhists believe that ego is the cause of human suffering.

MYTHS & REALITIES

Many people believe that the founding fathers were Christian Protestants that came to this land to escape religious persecution; thus they founded a Christian Protestant nation. Others understand that the United States was founded upon separation of church and state, among other basic principles. They therefore assume that religious observances and practices must be kept out of the workplace. Let's look more closely at these assumptions.

Myth #1: The United States was founded by Christians as a Christian Nation

Reality: Many Founding Fathers Were Not Strong Believers in Christianity

The "Founding Fathers" did not struggle to establish a Christian nation but a nation where freedom of religion could prevail. Those leaders who signed the Declaration of Independence, led the American Revolution, and framed the United States Constitution (Ellis 2002)—either had no religious affiliation or were Protestants (mostly Episcopalian) except for three Catholics. Some of them expressed concerns about organized religion in their speeches and correspondence, including George Washington, John Adams, Thomas Jefferson, and Benjamin Franklin, although most recognized the role that religion could play in molding "national morality" and securing the rules of law. Some, such as Patrick Henry, were strong proponents of traditional religion. Several, such as Franklin, Jefferson, and Ethan Allen, held deist beliefs that a supreme god created the physical universe but does not intervene in its normal operations through such supernatural events as prophecy, miracles, divine revelation, or holy books (Lambert 2003).

Reality: A Basic Tenet of the U.S. Founders was Separation of Church and State

The concept of "separation of church and state" was not included in the Constitution in 1787, but after long and passionate debates about the need to designate freedom for individuals, including religious freedom, the first of ten amendments to the Constitution, later known as the Bill of Rights, was passed by Congress in 1789. It was ratified by the States in 1791. The First Amendment reads: "Congress shall make no law respecting an establishment of religion, or prohibiting the free exercise thereof; or abridging the freedom of speech, or of the press; or the right of the people peaceably to assemble, and to petition the government for a redress of grievances." The first segment of this amendment became known as the law establishing "separation of church and state," though "separation of religion and state" might be a more accurate term—and freedom of individuals to adopt any religion or no religion was the purpose (Gaustad 1987).

Freedom of religion, therefore, is a guaranteed right. This normally means that government cannot declare a state religion, require religious observance, or legislate dogma. People are free to join any religious group, or not. It does not guarantee unrestricted freedom of religious practice. Laws against bigamy, sex with children, human sacrifice, and similar practices are enforced even if such practices are part of a group's religious belief.

Reality: Christianity is the Dominant U.S. Religion But Diversity is Increasing

From the founding of the United States, the large majority of citizens have been Protestant Christians, but their dominance has lessened in recent decades as the country has become increasingly diverse. Most Protestants were from England, which had an official state religion, as did the other European nations at the time (Ahlstrom 1972). Jews have been coming to the United States since 1654, primarily from Central and Eastern European countries such as Germany and Russia. Most of the Catholics came from France and Ireland and later from Mexico. Waves of immigrants adhering to the other major religions came later in smaller proportions. Their numbers and religious diversity have been increasing significantly since the 1960s (U.S. Census Bureau). By 2005 the United States had a greater number of religious groups than any other country in the world, according to Encyclopedia Brittanica.

Myth #2: Religious Observances and Practices Must be Kept Out of the Workplace

Reality: The Federal Government has Guidelines for Freedom of Religion in All Federal Government Agencies

The federal government in 1997 adopted detailed guidelines for freedom of religion in the federal workplace. Because these guidelines incorporate, and elaborate upon, Title VII requirements, many private business firms have adopted similar guidelines. The following are some highlights of the federal workplace guidelines (Guidelines 1997).

Religious Expression

Religious expression in private work areas: Employees should be permitted to engage in private religious expression in personal work areas not regularly open to the public to the same extent that they may engage in nonreligious private expression.

Religious expression among fellow employees. Employees should be permitted to engage in religious expression with fellow employees, to the same extent that they may engage in comparable nonreligious private expression, subject to reasonable restrictions.

Religious expression directed at fellow employees. Employees are permitted to engage in expression directed at fellow employees, and may even attempt to persuade fellow employees of the correctness of their religious views. But employees must refrain from such expression when a fellow employee asks that it stop or otherwise demonstrates that it is unwelcome.

Religious Discrimination

Coercion of employee's participation or non-participation in religious activities. A person holding supervisory authority over an employee may not, explicitly or implicitly, insist that the employee participate in religious activities as a condition of continued employment, promotion, salary increases, preferred job assignments, or any other incidents of employment. Nor may a supervisor insist that an employee refrain from participating in religious activities outside the workplace.

Hostile workplace environment and harassment. The law against workplace discrimination protects federal employees from being subjected to a hostile environment, or religious harassment. Whether particular conduct gives rise to a hostile environment, or constitutes impermissible religious harassment, will usually depend upon its frequency or repetitiveness, as well as its severity.

Accommodation of religious exercise

Federal law requires all federal government agencies to accommodate employees' exercise of their religion unless such accommodation would impose an undue hardship on the conduct of the agency's operations.

Establishment of Religion

Supervisors and employees must not engage in activities or expression that a reasonable observer would interpret as government endorsement or denigration of religion or a particular religion.

Reality: Private Employers Must Not Discriminate on the Basis of Religion and Must Make Reasonable Accommodation for Religious Practices

As mentioned earlier, freedom of religion is a guaranteed right under the First Amendment to the U.S. Constitution. Further, a section of Title VII of the Civil Rights Act of 1964 (as amended in 1972) makes it unlawful for an employer with more than 15 employees to fail or refuse to hire or to discharge any individual, or otherwise to discriminate against any individual with respect to his compensation, terms, conditions, or privileges of employment, because of such individual's religion (as well as race, color, sex, or national origin)—or to limit, segregate, or classify employees or applicants for employment in any way that would tend to deprive them of employment opportunities or otherwise adversely affect their status as an employee, because of such individual's religion (et al). Religion is defined as including all aspects of religious observance and practice, as well as belief.

This federal law requires employers to reasonably accommodate an employee's religious observances, practices, and beliefs—unless the employer can show that accommodation would cause undue hardship on the conduct of the business. So far, however, court rulings indicate that if there's evidence the accommodation would impose even a minimal inconvenience or expense on the employer, it can be denied. Most large corporations have policies that attempt to make such accommodation; in fact, one-third of them have an official written policy on religious diversity.

Julie Lynem, reporting on a 2002 survey by the Society for Human Resource Management, noted the following types of religious accommodation in private workplaces.

Holidays. Most employers offer only the traditional Christian holidays, and only 28 percent allow employees to swap holidays. A few, like Intel, offer an additional paid holiday for religious observances, which can be taken when needed.

Dress Codes. Exemptions from dress codes for religious reasons are allowed by only 20 percent of employers. Such exemptions address issues like head coverings, beards, and hair length.

Religious Displays. Displaying religious materials in work areas is the least controversial aspect, with 75 percent of companies saying yes in 2002, compared to only 24 percent in 1997. Examples of displays include religious figurines, pictures, or sayings as well as beads, crosses, crystals, and similar artifacts.

Prayer Breaks. Least popular is providing a designated space for religious observances, such as the Muslim requirement for prayer breaks during the day—only 8 percent offer that accommodation.

Human Resources experts recommend that organizations develop and distribute effective policies regarding religion in the workplace, perhaps using guidelines for freedom of religion in the federal workplace as a reference source. Organizations should include their policies in diversity training seminars.

RELIGIONS OF THE WORLD

Over half the world's people belong to one of the three Abrahamic religions, those with a history going back to the biblical patriarch Abraham: Christianity, Islam, and Judaism. The largest of these is Christianity, 2.1 billion followers; next is Islam with 1.5 billion followers; then Judaism with 14 million adherents.

The religions shown in Table 16.1 are listed in order of number of followers. Abrahamic religions are the monotheistic faiths, such as Judaism, Christianity, and Islam, which are based on a spiritual tradition identified with the Biblical patriarch Abraham. Other religions that identify in this way, such as the Bahá'í Faith and Druze, are sometimes included. Abrahamic religions account for more than half of the world's total population, around 3.6 billion followers. Eastern religions form the other major religious group, encompassing the Dharmic religions of India and the major East Asian religions, together accounting for over 25 percent of the world population, nearly 2 billion people. Ethnic tribal religions account for most of the remainder.

TABLE 16.1: Religious Groups of the World, 2005

Name of Religion	No. of followers	Origin
ABRAHAMIC RELIGIONS	54%–3.6 BILLION	1300 BCE
Christianity	2.1 billion	1st century
Islam	1.5 billion	7th century
Judaism	14 million	1300 BCE
Bahai Faith	7 million	19th century
INDIAN RELIGIONS	20%–1.4 BILLION	1200-300 BCE
Hinduism	900 million	No known date or founder
Buddhism	376 million	1200-300 BCE
Sikhism	26 million	1400 CE
Jainism	4 million	1200-300 BCE
FAR EASTERN RELIGIONS	6.5%–500 MILLION	722-481 BCE
Taoism	Unknown	722-481 BCE
Confucianism	Unknown	722-481 BCE
Chinese folk religion	394 million	No known date or founder
Shinto	4 million	No known date or founder
Other	3.5 million	—
ETHNIC–TRIBAL RELIGIONS	400 MILLION	Unknown
Primal indigenous	300 million	No founder
African traditional and disasporic	100 million	No known founder

Source: Encyclopedia Brittanica

RELIGIONS IN THE UNITED STATES

Most Americans, 77 percent, identify with Christianity—52 percent with a Protestant church and 25 percent with Catholic—and 14 percent cite no religion.

The American Religious Identity Survey (ARIS) was conducted in 2001, with a sample size of 50,000 Americans. In 1990, about 90 percent of the adult population identified with one or another religious group. In 2001, such identification had dropped to 81 percent. This change may reflect the fact that young people are less likely to describe themselves as religious. As shown in Table 16.2, most Americans, 77 percent, identify with Christianity. About 3.5 percent affiliate with other religions, 14 percent cite no religion, and about 5 percent did not indicate a response.

Religious Beliefs and Practices

When 35,000 American adults were asked whether they were more religious or secular, they answered as follows (Pew 2007):

- 75% religious or somewhat religious
- 16% secular or somewhat secular
- 8% a little of both, unsure, or no answer

Looking at various demographic groups, Pew found:

- Women are more likely than men to describe their outlook as religious.
- Older Americans are more likely to describe their outlook as religious.
- African Americans are least likely to describe themselves as secular.
- Asian Americans are most likely to describe themselves as secular.

TABLE 16.2: Religions in the United States, 2001

Religious Category	*% of U.S. Population*	*Religious Category*	*% of U.S. Population*
CHRISTIAN	*77%*	*OTHER RELIGIONS*	*3.5%*
Catholic	25%	Jewish	1.3
Protestant:	52%	Islamic	0.5
		Buddhist	0.5
Baptist	16%	Hindu	0.4
Non-Denominational	7	American Indian	0.05
Methodist	7	Taoist	0.02
Lutheran	5	Other	0.73
Presbyterian	3		
Pentecostal	2	*NON RELIGIOUS*	*14%*
Episcopalian	2	No religion	13.1
Mormon	1	Agnostic	0.5
Other Christian	9	Atheist	0.4

Source: Teaching About Religion 2005; ARIS American Religious Identity Survey 2001

Note: In most instances, survey respondents designated which religious group they belong to; in a few instances, certain denominations provided their membership figures.

Increasing Diversity of Beliefs and Practices

The U.S. is one of the most religious countries in the world. The Pew survey (2007) indicates that while most Americans take religion seriously, most also tend to be flexible and tolerant in their beliefs.

- 92% of Americans believe in God
- 83% affiliate with some religion
- 6% say they are religious but have no specific affiliation

Americans view their own and others' religious identity through a much broader lens than previously understood. The survey reveals the great diversity of American religions, as well as the diversity of thought within them. For example, most do believe that there is more than one way to interpret the teachings of their religion and that if "salvation" is necessary, there is more than one way to achieve it." This openness to a range of religious viewpoints reflects the great diversity of religions and practices that exists in the United States.

- 70% of church members say multiple religions can lead a person to salvation—ranging from 16% of Jehovah's Witnesses to 51% of Muslims, 83% of Protestants, and 86% of Buddhists and Hindus.
- 68% of church members say teachings of their religion can be interpreted in more than one way—ranging from 18% Jehovah's Witnesses to 60% Muslims, 82% mainline churches, 90% Buddhists

- 57% of evangelicals say that multiple religions can lead to salvation
- 58% of Catholics believe society should accept gay persons (Catholic bishops disagree)
- 21% of people who identify as atheists also indicate that they do believe in some concept of "God"; i.e. what they actually reject is organized religion, not belief in God

American religious tradition is unique and diverse—with Christians alone claiming about 5,000 denominations. Religion has become more a matter of personal choice than the community one grew up in. Categories are not as strong as in the past, with many "cross-over" beliefs and practices. For example, the survey found Catholics who meditate and Protestants who pray to the Virgin Mary. In fact, the survey indicates that many believers know little about the official practices of their own faith, and even less about others. For them, the finding that most Americans are so open-minded may reflect the inexperience of such believers. However, some people are becoming more informed and appreciative of other religions and traditions; for them, the finding may reflect their true understanding.

Regional Aspects of Religious Affiliation

Despite the growing diversity nationally, some religious groups clearly occupy a dominant demographic position in particular states. For instance, Catholics are the majority of the population in Massachusetts and Maine as are Mormons in Utah and Baptists in Mississippi. Catholics comprise over 40 percent of Vermont, New Mexico, New York and New Jersey, while Baptists are over 40 percent in a number of southern states such as South Carolina, Tennessee, North Carolina, Alabama and Georgia.

Historical traces of the Bible belt in the South and an irreligious West are still evident. For example, the percentage of adults in the Pew Survey who identified as "no religion" is below 10 percent in Alabama, Mississippi, Tennessee, North and South Carolina, and North and South Dakota. Meanwhile, in Oregon, Washington, Idaho, and Wyoming more people responded "no religion" than in any other state or region.

Politics and Religious Affiliation

More than half of Americans report attending religious services regularly and praying daily. Most people in this group want their religion to preserve its traditional beliefs and practices. Significant minorities across nearly all religious traditions see a conflict between being a devout person and living in a modern society. And there is a close link between Americans' religious affiliation, beliefs and practices, on the one hand, and their social and political attitudes, on the other. In fact, the social and political fault lines in American society correlate with religious traditions.

The relationship between politics and religion is particularly strong with respect to political ideology and views on social issues such as abortion and homosexuality, with the more religiously committed adherents across several religious traditions expressing more conservative political views. On other issues included in the ARIS survey, such as environmental protection, foreign affairs, and the proper size and role of government, differences based on religion tend to be smaller. The most frequent answer to what influences political thinking is not "religion" but "personal experience," chosen by 34 percent of respondents. While only 14 percent of total respondents say that "religion" most influences their political thinking, twice as many (28 percent) of evangelical Christians cite religion.

Jews, Muslims, Buddhists and those with no religion have a greater preference for the Democratic Party. Mormons and Pentecostals (some call them Evangelical or Born-Again Christians; others call them fundamentalists) are the most apt to identify as Republicans and in fact have become an important part of the Republican "base" in recent years. Buddhists and those with no religion are most likely to be political independents. Jehovah's Witnesses disavow political involvement, in keeping with their theology.

Major Religions and U.S. Workplace Accommodations

We have seen that about 77 percent of Americans claim the Christian faith, and since its founding the large majority of the U.S. population has been Christian. Therefore, typical local and state laws, as well as typical organizational cultures, have accommodated Christian beliefs and practices. Because other religions represent relatively small minorities in the workplace, coworkers and managers may be unfamiliar with beliefs and practices that may need sensitivity and accommodation. We will explore the seven religions that have the most adherents in the United States, with more attention given to those religions that may be least familiar to managers and coworkers.

Our discussion begins with the Abrahamic religions—first with Judaism as the oldest of these, and then in chronological order Christianity and Islam. Asian Americans represent 4 percent of the U.S. population, the largest group that adheres to non-Abrahamic religions. We next discuss Confucianism, therefore, because of its pervasive influence throughout Asia and especially upon the largest Asian American group, Chinese Americans. We follow that with Taoism, prominent in China and Southeast Asia. Next is Hinduism, the ancient religion that is prominent in India. Finally, we explore Buddhism, a religion that reacted against the corruptions of Hinduism, strongly influenced it, and later proliferated in China and Southeast Asia.

JUDAISM: THE OLDEST ABRAHAMIC RELIGION

Globally, about 54 percent of people belong to one of the three major "Abrahamic" religions: Judaism, Christianity, or Islam. These religions are all based historically on beliefs that started with the patriarchs Abraham, Isaac, and Jacob. Judaism is the earliest of these religions, so we will explore it first.

About 14 million, or two-tenths of 1 percent of the world's 6.5 billion people, are Jewish. Where do most of them live these days? Either in the United States or in Israel, with about 40 percent living in each of these countries and the other 20 percent scattered around the world. That means there are about 5.3 million Jewish Americans, 1.3 percent of the American population.

This group is by far the most numerous of U.S. religious groups after Christianity. Yet most Americans know very little about it beyond the Holocaust and the new nation of Israel. Jewish coworkers and employees surely appreciate those who have a deeper understanding of the religion and the culture that is Judaism. Because of this, and the fact that it is the source of all Abrahamic religions, we will spend a little more time with Judaism than with the other religions.

A Brief History of Judaism

The Patriarchs Abraham, Isaac, and Jacob are the physical and spiritual ancestors of Judaism. Jewish history and beliefs are derived from the written Torah, Talmud, Midrash, and other sources. Some of these materials, such as that found in the Torah, are shared by Christians in the Old Testament of their Bible. (Seltzer 1980, Rich 2007).

The Patriarchs: Abraham, Isaac, Jacob (Israel)

Abraham was born in 1800 BCE, according to Jewish tradition. From his early childhood, he questioned his father's faith in numerous idols and sought the truth. Abraham came to believe that the entire universe was the work of a single Creator, and he began to teach this belief to others. Eventually, the one true Creator that Abraham had worshipped called to him, and made him an offer: if he would leave his home and his family, then God would make him the leader of a great nation and bless him. Abraham accepted this offer, and the covenant between God and what became the Jewish people was established, as set forth in the biblical book of Genesis.

Traditional Judaism believes the following: We have a contract (a covenant) with God, which involves rights and obligations on both sides. The terms of this covenant became the basis for the written law or Torah. Abraham was subjected to ten tests of faith to prove his worthiness for this covenant. Leaving his home was one of these trials.

Abraham, a city-dweller, adopted a nomadic lifestyle, traveling through what is now the land of Israel for many years. Jewish tradition holds that God promised this land to Abraham's descendants. Abraham and his wife Sarah had no children and were growing old. But Hagar, a daughter of the Pharaoh, was given to Abraham during his travels in Egypt. She and Abraham had a son, Ishmael, who, according to both Muslim and Jewish tradition, is the ancestor of the Arabs. Jews do not consider Ishmael to be their ancestor.

Isaac war born to Abraham and his wife Sarah, when he was 100 and she was 90, according to Jewish tradition. Isaac became the ancestor of the Jewish people, their second patriarch. Thus, the later conflict between Arabs and Jews could be traced to sibling rivalry between Isaac and Ishmael.

Jacob was born to Isaac and his wife Rebecca and became the third patriarch. He dreamed that an angel blessed him and gave him the name "Israel," meaning "God's Champion." The Jewish people are generally referred to as the Children of Israel, signifying their descent from Jacob. Jacob fathered 12 sons, who are the ancestors and namesakes of the tribes of Israel.

Joseph, Exodus from Egypt, Giving of the Torah

Joseph, Jacob's son, was the father of two of Israel's tribes, Manasseh and Ephraim. Joseph's jealous older brothers sold him into slavery, and he was taken to Egypt. Joseph's ability to interpret visions earned him a place in the Pharaoh's court, paving the way for his family's (Israel's) later settlement in Egypt. That is how the Jews came to be living in Egypt.

But over the centuries the descendants of Israel became slaves in Egypt and suffered greatly under the reign of later Pharaohs. Finally, a great leader Moses led the Children of Israel out of Egypt on a journey through the wilderness to Mount Sinai. There, it is said, God revealed Himself to Moses, and through him to the Children of Israel, offering them a new covenant. If they would listen to God and observe His covenant, then they would be the most beloved of nations, a kingdom of priests, a holy nation.

The new covenant is described in the written and oral versions of the Jewish holy book, the Torah, which is the core of Jewish law. The Torah, including the Ten Commandments, became the first five books of the Christian Bible. The entire nation agreed that "Everything that the Lord has spoken, we will do!" According to Jewish tradition, every Jewish soul that would ever be born was present at that moment and agreed to be bound to this covenant.

Judaic Beliefs

"What lifted the Jews from obscurity to permanent religious greatness was their passion for meaning," according to Huston Smith (1998, p. 272). Historically this quest for meaning was rooted in their understanding of God and the existential question, "Where did we come from?" Jews personified God in the sense that ultimate reality is more like a person than like a thing, and more like a mind than a machine. Where the Jews differed from their neighbors was in focusing this personalism in a single, supreme, nature-transcending will rather than focusing on multiple gods. In other words, the basic contribution of Judaism to the religious beliefs of the Middle East was monotheism—one god.

Jews believe that this one God is a beneficent God. Their creation story affirms the goodness of God and his world: In the beginning was the Word and the Word was God. God created the heavens and the earth and pronounced it to be good. God said of the people He created, "let them have dominion over all the earth." Here we see a focus on the Word, symbolizing mind and meaning. We see humans have dominion on earth, meaning freedom to use earth's resources to create an abundant life. The Jewish religion has never questioned human freedom (Heschel 1976).

The three outstanding aspects of Jewish culture are the Hebrew language, reverence for Jewish lore and for learning in general, and an affinity for the land of Israel. The Torah was followed by the Talmud, a vast collection of Jewish history, law, folklore, and commentary that is the basis of post-biblical Judaism. Supplementing this is the Midrashim, a large collection of legend, analysis, and teachings. All of this provides a treasure trove of scholarship, anecdote, and cultural identity. They speak to the Jewish passion for meaning and personal action.

The Modern Nation of Israel

Both the land of Israel and the Hebrew language are sacred because of their associations. The Jews were driven out of their homeland during the Roman occupation in 70 C.E. During the next 2,000 years Judaism crossed every national boundary and had no home but human minds and hearts, but the Jewish people retained their passion for Israel. Prayers for their return to the land were typically included in every public service and private prayer.

In 1948, for the first time since their dispersion, the United Nations restored to the Jews the land then called Palestine, and it became Israel once more. The reasons for this were many and complex, but four aspects stand out.

1. **Security argument.** After the Nazi Holocaust in which six million Jews (one-third of their world population) were killed, there was a growing conviction that the Jews must have a refuge from the persecution and genocide they had suffered in many nations over many centuries.

2. **Psychological argument.** It was considered psychologically unhealthy for the Jews to always be the minority, wherever they lived, because it was breeding a sense of submission and self-rejection.

3. **Social argument.** A nation dedicated to the historical realization of prophetic ideals and ethics would be a good thing in the world. Jews had been excluded by law from agriculture in the lands they left. They wanted to create a new community through a way of life built on the life of the land. Collective agriculture settlements were an expression of that idealism.

4. **Cultural argument.** Jews needed a land where Judaism was the dominant ethos.

The major problem with this development is that Palestinian natives were displaced from their homeland, which in turn upset the surrounding Arab nations. Hostilities have been an ongoing problem ever since. In recent years the "peace process" has had its ups and downs, and varying levels of hostility have prevailed.

Jewish Religious Observances

You should not assume that because you know a colleague is Jewish American, you can assume that she or he attends synagogue services each week or eats only kosher food. To begin with, fewer than half (46 percent) of American Jews belong to a synagogue, yet most of these non-members do have a strong affiliation with the Jewish culture. Also, the degree to which a synagogue member follows traditional religious observances varies in each of the three main branches of Judaism: 1) Orthodox, the most traditional; 2) Conservative, less traditional; and 3) Reform, the least traditional (Siegel et al 1975). Rituals vary, therefore, with some serving primarily to commemorate Jewish history, and others to help members think or act in ways consistent with Judaic beliefs (Rossel 2001).

Jewish Sabbath—Friday Sundown to Saturday Sundown

The Jewish Sabbath begins at sundown each Friday and ends the following day, at sundown on Saturday. A Biblical passage, Exodus 20:8-11, tells believers to "Remember the Sabbath day, to keep it holy. Six days you shall labor and do all your work, but the seventh day is the Sabbath of the Lord your God. In it you shall do no work . . . For in six days the Lord made the heavens and the earth, the sea, and all that is in them, and rested the seventh day. Therefore the Lord blessed the Sabbath day and hallowed it."

Most people know the Jewish Sabbath, Saturday, as the day of the week on which Jews are forbidden to work. As with all other aspects of Jewish law, different Jewish sects observe the Sabbath work prohibitions in varying degrees. Generally, Judaism regards the Sabbath as a day of joyful celebration and rest when Jews can relax, be with family, study, and reflect. In the Torah, the purpose of Sabbath observance is to remind the Hebrew people of two very important events in history: 1) the creation of the world and 2) the deliverance of the Jewish people from slavery in Egypt. Many

Jews also believe that God commanded the Sabbath to ensure that his people would stop every once in awhile to reflect on what it means to be human (Falcon 2001). During the 24-hour Sabbath play is encouraged and work is forbidden (Rich 2008).

Sabbath typically begins with the Friday evening family dinner, usually the most festive and tasty of the week. Synagogues of every Jewish denomination hold services on Friday night, the main prayer service of the week for Conservative and Reform Jews. Orthodox Jews tend to focus more on the Saturday morning service, and their Friday service is relatively short.

Kosher and Other Food Restrictions

As with many traditional Jewish practices, the large majority of Jewish Americans do not observe kosher restrictions. Most of the about 25 percent of American Jews who say they do are Orthodox and not often found in the workplace. To begin, there is no such thing as "kosher-style" food. Kosher is not a style of cooking, and any food can be kosher if it is prepared in accordance with Jewish law. Traditional Jewish foods, such as knishes, bagels, blintzes, and matzo ball soup, can all be non-kosher if not prepared in accordance with Jewish law. When a restaurant calls itself "kosher-style," it usually means that the restaurant serves these traditional Jewish foods, and it almost invariably means that the food is not actually kosher

Kosher describes food that meets Jewish law regarding standards for food to be eaten. Food can be kosher without a rabbi ever becoming involved with it; for example, the vegetables from a person's garden are kosher, if they have no bugs. Of the animals that might be found on most restaurant menus, pork, rabbit, and shellfish are never kosher; other meat must be properly processed and prepared.

In our modern world of processed foods, it is difficult to know what ingredients are in the food and how they were processed, so it is helpful to have a rabbi examine the food and its processing and assure kosher consumers that the food is kosher. The process of certification does not involve "blessing" the food; rather, it involves examining the ingredients used to make the food, examining the process by which the food is prepared, and periodically inspecting the processing facilities to make sure that kosher standards are maintained. The symbols of kosher certification are registered trademarks and cannot be placed on a food label without permission. About 75 percent of all prepackaged foods have some kind of kosher certification, and most major brands have reliable Orthodox certification. (Judaism 101).

Jewish Holidays

If you are a manager, your coworkers and employees may expect you to be familiar with the holidays most commonly observed by American Jews. They include 1) Passover in March or April, 2) Yom Kippur in September, 3) Rosh Hashanah in September or October, and 4) Channukkah in December (Rich 2008).

Two questions that arise about Jewish holidays: 1) Do they occur on the same date every year? 2) When does a holiday begin and end? Jewish holidays occur on the same day of the Jewish solar calendar, but not the same day on the Western lunar calendar. However, they always fall within the same month or two. A Jewish day starts at sunset, so holidays start the evening before the day on the secular calendar. For example, if the calendar says that Passover is on April 20, Jewish families will be getting together for Passover dinner on the night of April 19.

Passover – Exodus Memorial in March or April

This 7- or 8-day holiday commemorates the Exodus; that is, the time when Moses led the Jewish people out of slavery in Egypt. Almost all American Jews observe Passover to some extent, even if only to go to their parents' house for a ritual dinner called a seder (SAY-der) on the first night of the holiday. Strictly observant Jews do not work, go to school or carry out any business on the first two and last two days of Passover. This is a requirement of Jewish law; however, only about 10 percent of the American Jewish population strictly observes this rule (Rich 2008).

Jewish lore holds that the ancestors left Egypt in a hurry and didn't have time to wait for their bread to rise. To commemorate this sacrifice, most American Jews avoid "leavened bread" as well as non-kosher food, during this holiday. Leavened refers to yeast or other substances that cause bread or grain products to rise when baked. Employers might should keep this in mind when planning events that include food during this holiday, and to consult with Jews about travel because it may be hard for them to find suitable food away from home.

Rosh Hashanah – New Year in September

Rosh Hashanah (rah-sh hah SHAH nah) is Jewish New Year, usually occurring in September. Although it is a happy, festive holiday, it's somewhat more solemn than the American New Year. It is a time to look back at the past year and make resolutions for the following year. It is also a wake-up call, a time to begin mental preparations for the upcoming day of atonement, Yom Kippur. Like Christians who go to church only on Christmas and Easter, some Jews go to synagogue only on Rosh Hashanah and Yom Kippur. Therefore employers and teachers may want to avoid scheduling important events, meetings or tests on Rosh Hashanah, including the evening before. Even those Jews who do not go to synagogue and do not observe the holiday may be offended if such accommodations are not made. Their feelings might be similar to those of Christians who would be upset if such activities were scheduled at Christmas or Easter.

Yom Kippur – Atonement in September or October

Yom Kippur ("Yom" rhymes with "home"; Kippur = keyPOOR) occurs on the ninth day after the first day of Rosh Hashanah, the Jewish New Year, so it is usually in late September or early October. Yom Kippur is the Jewish day of atonement, a day of fasting and repentance to reconcile themselves with the Creator for the mistakes made in the last year. This is the busiest day of the year for synagogues. Most Jews take off from work or school on this day, even ones who are not religious at other times. Many Jewish employees will want to leave work early the night before, so they have time for a large, slow meal before this 25-hour fast. Most American Jews will be offended if their employer or teacher schedules important activities on Yom Kippur.

Chanukkah – Festival of Lights in December

Chanukkah (HAH na ka) is an 8-day holiday that begins between Thanksgiving and Christmas. Almost no Jew takes off from work or school for this holiday, but many may not want to work nights or travel because they want to light candles with the family, so employers should make accommodations for this.

Chanukkah is also known as the Festival of Lights that commemorates the rededication of the Temple in Jerusalem. Most Jews gather with their families in the evening to light candles on at least some nights of the holiday, so people like to be at home during this holiday. The Menorah is a special 8-branch candelabrum brought out for this event, with one candle being lit each night, after which the children may play a game with the dreidel, a four-sided spinning top.

The most important thing to remember about Chanukkah is that it is not Jewish Christmas, no matter what the card shops and toy stores want you to believe. In the Judaic world Chanukkah is a very minor holiday. While it is not about gift-giving, many Jewish American parents give their children gifts during Chanukkah—and even buy a "chanukkah bush" at the local Christmas tree lot—because they don't want their children to feel left out of Christmas. Gift-giving rarely extends much beyond one's own children, and it would be insensitive to assume that Chanukkah is like Christmas.

Jewish Rituals of Life

As with most religions and cultures, Jewish rituals include those connected with the life passages of birth, initiation, marriage, and death.

Birth Rituals: Circumcising and Naming the Baby

The first Jewish life-cycle celebration is circumcision for the male baby. Through this symbolic act, which, according to the Bible, began with Abraham and Isaac, Jewish males are brought into the community of Israel and given a Hebrew name. Girl babies may undergo a naming ceremony in the home or synagogue to welcome them to their new Jewish identities (Rossel 2001).

Initiation Rituals: Bar Mitzvah and Bat Mitzvah

Around the time of their thirteenth birthday, boys and girls are initiated into adulthood in the Jewish community. The ceremony is called *Bar Mitzvah* for boys and *Bat Mitzvah* for girl. Boys (and sometimes girls) lead the congregation in worship and read from scriptures, perhaps chanting them to an ancient melody. This elaborate ceremony marks the time when a Jewish child becomes responsible for keeping the commandments of Judaism and has a sufficient command of Judaism and of Hebrew to lead the congregation. It is a very important occasion for the family and close friends, who make special efforts to attend the worship service and the party held afterward.

The Jewish Wedding

According to Jewish tradition, marriage is the most holy of all human institutions. A person must be married and have children to properly fulfill his or her Jewish obligations. Jewish parents have traditionally urged their children to marry Jews. Rabbis or cantors officiate at the Jewish wedding ceremony on behalf of both the state and the Jewish people.

Funeral Ceremonies

Death of family members or friends is a sad time for Jews, even though Judaism teaches that the soul lives on after a person dies. Jewish belief does not require a final rite while a person is dying. There may be a brief confession, but no Jew feels that the soul of the deceased is endangered without it. The dead are buried as soon as possible; cremation is not acceptable. The body of the deceased is tended with great care and respect, which is considered an act of great value.

A time of intense mourning for family and friends follows the burial ceremony and lasts for about a week. The family remains at home, relatives and friends visit, and daily worship services are recited in the home. On the Sabbath the family leaves home and joins with the congregation at a synagogue or temple service.

During the first year after a death, the children of a dead parent and the dead person's sisters and brothers may attend synagogue regularly to recite a special prayer for the dead. Each year, on the anniversary of the death, Jews recite the prayer in memory of a dead family member and light a candle.

CHRISTIANITY: THE LARGEST ABRAHAMIC RELIGION

Christianity is the most widespread religion in the world with the largest number of adherents—about 2.1 billion, or nearly one-third of the world's 6.5 billion people, and about 77 percent of the U.S. population. It is basically a historical religion, not founded so much on abstract principles as in concrete events, actual historical happenings (Smith 1998).

Christian Beginnings

Christianity originated in Judea, now Israel, in the 1st century CE, as a radically reformed branch of Judaism. It spread to ancient Greece and Rome, and from there to most of Europe, the Americas, and most other parts of the world. Over the centuries, Christianity split into many separate churches and denominations. A major split was the East-West Schism in the 11th century, separating the Roman Catholic Church from the Eastern Orthodox Churches. Later, the Protestant Reformation of the 16th century gave birth to hundreds of independent Protestant denominations. Today the three main branches of Christianity are Roman Catholic, Eastern Orthodox, and Protestant.

The Christian Bible consists of the Old Testament and New Testament. The first five books of the Old Testament are also the basis of the Jewish Torah, and the remainder is a history of the Jewish people. Thus the Old Testament is considered a Holy book by adherents of Judaism and Christianity and is also respected in Islam. The New Testament is the story of Jesus' life and teachings. It is a Christian Holy book and also respected in Islam.

Moving from the Jesus of history to the Christ whom his adherents came to believe was God in human form, three aspects were most important to Jesus' followers: 1) what they saw Jesus do, 2) what they heard him say, and 3) what they sensed him to be (Crosson 1991, Smith 1998).

What Jesus Did and Said

Basically Jesus' followers perceived that he went about doing good. He circulated easily and without affectation among ordinary people and social misfits, healing them, counseling them, helping them pull out of the depths of despair. He did this with such effectiveness and focus that his disciples concluded that if divine goodness were to manifest itself in human form, this is how it would act (Smith 1998).

Jesus used vivid language to say simple things, such as:

- Love your neighbor as yourself
- Whatsoever you would that men should do unto you, do you also unto them (the Golden Rule)
- Come unto me, all you who labor and are heavy laden, and I will give you rest
- You shall know the truth, and the truth shall make you free

Mostly, though, Jesus told stories or parables—about reaping what you sow, about a good Samaritan who helped a stranger, about using God's gifts rather than burying them. He talked about turning the other cheek rather than retaliating. He spoke of loving your enemies and blessing those who curse you. At the time, these were shockingly different messages that represented a radically new worldview.

His stories focused the listeners' awareness on two key points: 1) God's overwhelming love of humanity, and 2) the need for people to accept that love and let it flow through them to others. He focused on a God that loves human beings absolutely, without pausing to calculate their worth or due.

Jesus apparently lived his own teachings. His followers came to see him as a man in whom the human ego had disappeared, leaving his life so completely under the will of God that it was transparent to that will. They believed that, as they looked at Jesus, they were looking at something resembling God in human form (Smith 1998).

Jesus' End: the Beginning of Christianity

Jesus' earthly ministry ended with his crucifixion. His followers reported that beginning Easter Sunday, three days after his death, he appeared to them as the same person they had known during his ministry but in a new way (Schillebeeck 1981). His resurrection was entry into another mode of being, a mode that was sometimes visible but usually was not. Jesus' followers began to experience him in a new way, as having the qualities of God, knowable from anywhere, heaven or earth. His "victory over death" was heralded as the Gospel, the Good News, which disciples began to spread around the Mediterranean world. His resurrection is a core belief of Christianity and basis for its most important religious observances.

These disciples became one of the most dynamic groups in human history (Borg 1988). They spread their message with such fervor that within a few years it took root in every major city in the Mediterranean region. His followers became people who seemed to be making a success of life itself. For one thing, they loved one another without regard to typical social barriers, such as race, gender, and status. They said that everyone was equal in the sight of God and they lived as though they meant it. In addition, they had an inner peace that found expression in a radiant joy, according to Christian historians.

Christianity's Three Major Branches

From the beginning, from the life and death of Jesus to 313 CE, Christianity struggled in the face of official Roman persecution. In 313 Christianity became legally recognized and enjoyed equal rights with other religions of the Roman world. In 380 it became the official religion of the Roman Empire and continued in this capacity until 1054, when it divided into the Roman Catholic Church in what is now Western Europe and the Eastern Orthodox Church in what is now Eastern Europe. In the 16th century, following the Protestant Reformation, the Roman Catholic Church divided when the Protestant branch arose (Bainton 1986). After that time, three major branches of Christianity have been prominent: Roman Catholic, Eastern Orthodox, and Protestant.

Roman Catholic Branch

Two of the most important concepts for understanding Catholicism are 1) the Church as teaching authority, and 2) the Church as sacramental agent (McBrien 1994)

The Church as Teaching Authority

God came to earth in the person of Jesus Christ to teach people the way to salvation—how they should live in this world so that they can achieve eternal life in the next world. This led to the concept of the Pope, in his capacity as God's spokesman on matters of faith and morals, being protected from error in these matters by the Holy Spirit. It resulted in a church hierarchy, including the Pope, cardinals, bishops, priests, and nuns. Members of this hierarchy are considered to be married to God and the Church. They vow not to marry and to abstain from sexual relations. Church members are expected to confess their wrong-doings to a priest in order to be forgiven by God.

The Church as Sacramental Agent

The sacraments empower followers to live according to Christ's teachings. The seven sacraments designed to do that are baptism of infants, confirmation of adolescents, holy matrimony, confession and reconciliation, last rites, and holy communion. More on this later.

Eastern Orthodox Branch

The Eastern church honors the same seven Sacraments as the Catholic Church and interprets them in the same way. There are two main differences, both relating to the Church as teaching authority. One difference has to do with the extent to which the Church initiates doctrine. The Catholic church stresses the development of Christian doctrine, while the Eastern Orthodox Church stresses its continuity, stating that there has been no need for the Church to exercise its teaching authority outside the Ecumenical Councils that were held before 787 CE.

The other difference on teaching authority relates to the means by which church dogmas are reached. The Catholic Church holds that in the end they come through the pope. The Eastern Church has no pope. Instead it holds that God's truth is disclosed through "the conscience of the Church," referring to the consensus of Christians generally.

In this and other ways the Eastern Church stands midway between Roman Catholicism and Protestantism. For them each Christian works out his or her salvation in conjunction with the rest of the Church—not individually to save a separate soul, as in the Protestant Church, and not through a priest as in the Catholic Church. The destiny of the individual is bound up with the entire Church, a corporate view, and the Church is responsible for helping to make holy the entire world of nature and history. The welfare of everything is affected to some extent by what each person contributes to or detracts from it. The Eastern Church grounds more of its decision in the members, while the Catholic Church relies more on the church hierarchy, from Pope to priest. Because officials of the Eastern hierarchy are not considered essential conduits from God to church members, they are not "married to the Church" and therefore may marry and have families.

Protestant Branch

The Protestant Reformation that occurred in the 16th century is, in a way, a further extension of the Eastern Orthodox viewpoint regarding church hierarchy. Martin Luther, who led the movement, objected to the hierarchy for many reasons. For one, Luther said that every person has access to God and does not need church hierarchy for that purpose and that God's grace alone can "save" individuals, having nothing to do with Popes and priests. Everyone must do his own believing, as he will have to do his own dying. From true faith, good works will flow naturally

Technology also played a role in the Protestant Reformation. Prior to the invention of the printing press in the 15th century (1440), only members of the church hierarchy had access to written materials or knew how to read them. Therefore the biblical scriptures had to be read and interpreted by priests for the church members. Later, as Bibles were printed and people learned to read, this translation process became less essential.

The Protestant Principle: No Other Gods before Me

Protestants came to believe that Scripture, rather than church tradition or interpretation of Scripture, is the only source of revealed truth. They concluded that neither the church hierarchy nor good works are essential to salvation. Only Christ, the Scriptures, faith, and God's grace are needed, and all glory should go to God, not to church hierarchy. This is expressed in the Protestant Principle as follows:

Allegiance belongs to God, the God of nature and history
that is also beyond nature and history.

The Protestant Principle protests idolatry, or making anything other than God as a focus of worship. Even making the Bible a focus of worship can be idolatrous when the believer forgets that in entering the world, God's word must speak through human minds (Bainton 1986).

Protestant theologians acknowledge that their perspective holds dangers; for example, the danger of uncertainty as individuals struggle inwardly to figure out whether they have heard God's will correctly. But they prefer precarious individual freedom to the security of church dogmas and doctrines, which may also be fallible.

Protestant Denominations

Through the centuries, many Protestant denominations have evolved. The major differences among today's Protestants are of relatively recent origin, but the denominations have multiplied rapidly, resulting in perhaps 33,000 denominations in 238 countries. Some researchers categorize the Protestant denominations as mainline, baptist-evangelical-pentecostal, and non-trinitarian (Bainton 1986, Pew 2007, Protestantism 2008, Murphy 2008).

Mainline Protestant. Methodists, Presbyterians, Lutherans, and Episcopalians, which are all large denominations with significant theologically liberal and conservative wings, have traditionally been the "mainline" U.S. Protestant denominations. All evolved from the traditions of Lutheranism. These groups historically were the largest in the United States but now represent only about 13 percent of U.S. adults (Methodists alone are 8 percent), compared to 26 percent for the next group. Members tend to be politically liberal, and the churches themselves are usually not active in political affairs.

Baptist-Evangelical-Pentecostal. This group, representing 26 percent of U.S. adults, has become the largest Protestant group and are still rapidly expanding. Charismatic and Born-Again groups also fit into this category. Baptists are by far the largest segment, 20 percent of U.S. adults. Members of these groups tend to be politically conservative, especially in social-cultural matters, active in politics, and have become a strong base of the Republican Party. They evolved from both the Lutheran movement and the Radical Reformation (Anabaptist) movement.

Anabaptists include the Amish, Mennonites, Hutterites, and Brethren. The Anabaptist movement developed from the Radical Reformation of the 16th century, differing from the Lutheran movement in the importance placed upon baptism. A central tenet is the individual's personal commitment to Christian belief, which is symbolized by baptism. Therefore they do not practice infant baptism. Pacifism is also a central belief, and they have historically been considered "Peace" churches. These groups have dwindled in size, especially those that have refused to accept new technologies, such as automobiles and electricity.

Baptists, Evangelicals, Pentecostals, and Adventists evolved from the Lutheran movement, and they adopted some Anabaptist (Radical Reformation) beliefs as well, along with strong evangelical, pentecostal, and charismatic components. They are not considered "peace" churches.

Non-Trinitarian. This group includes Mormon, Jehovah's Witness, Seventh-Day Adventist, Christadelphian, Christian Church (Disciples of Christ), Church of Christ, and some Quaker groups. Many evolved from the Restoration Movement, which was based on the belief that it was necessary to restore Christianity to its original teachings because it had gone terribly astray. Most of these groups reject the doctrine of the trinity; i.e. Father-Son-Holy Spirit as three aspects of the one God.

Christian Beliefs

Virtually all Christians adhere to the concepts of faith and allegiance to the one God. Faith is seen as a response of the entire self—of the mind, of the emotions of love and trust, and of the will and desire to be an instrument of God's love (Bainton 1986). Faith leads to release from inner burdens and to other basic Christian tenets.

Freedom from Three Inner Burdens

From those earliest days in the Mediterranean up until this day, many Christians say that their beliefs have lifted three huge burdens from them, inner burdens directly connected to the major tenets of Christianity:

1. **Fear.** They felt less fear, including fear of death. Jesus saying, "Fear not, for I am with you, always" they took to heart.
2. **Guilt.** They felt released from guilt, for Jesus constantly forgave them all wrongdoings that they confessed to him.
3. **Negative ego.** They felt released from the prison of their egos. They felt free to love others as they loved themselves.

Three Basic Tenets

A familiarity with three basic Christian tenets is helpful in understanding Christians and their religion. These tenets are the incarnation of God into the human body of Jesus Christ; the trinity of God-Jesus-Holy Spirit, and the atonement of humans with God (Smith 1998).

The Incarnation. The doctrine of incarnation holds that God assumed a human body in Jesus Christ, spirit incarnated into physical. It affirms that Christ was God-Man, both fully God and fully man at the same time. Christ is the bridge that joins humanity to God.

The Trinity. God the Father, Christ the Son, and the Holy Spirit—these are the three aspects of the divine, the Trinity of Christianity. God is fully one, and God is also three, just as H_2O is one element but it is also three—water, ice, steam—in its liquid form, solid form, and gaseous form.

The Atonement refers to reconciliation, the recovery of wholeness or at-one-ment, humans with God. In Christ, God was reconciling the world to himself. Christ released humanity from the bondage of sin, or estrangement from God. The bondage that imprisons humanity is attachment to self (ego), with the fear and guilt that this brings about; i.e. estrangement from full participation in the divine. Atonement bridges the gap and releases humans from their personal prisons.

Spreading the Gospel

Many Christians consider it their obligation to follow what is often termed the Great Commission of Jesus, recorded in Matthew: "Go to all the nations and make disciples. Baptize them and teach them my commands." The Acts of the Apostles and other sources contain several accounts of early Christians following this directive by engaging in individual conversations and mass sermons to spread the gospel, the "good news." Evangelical Christians often use the term "witnessing" to mean discussing one's faith with another person with the intent of proselytism, converting them to the

Christian faith. Most self-described Christian groups have organizations devoted to missionary work which in whole or in part includes proselytism of people of other faiths (Daily Mail 2007).

Christian Rituals, the Sacraments

Christians, especially Catholics, believe that God's saving power comes to believers through certain sacred rituals. What is now the Roman Catholic Church first established the Christian sacraments upon which most Christian rituals are not based. Not all sacraments are observed by all churches, though Baptism and Communion are accepted almost universally (Ahlstrom 1972). Some Christian rituals, such as communion and Catholic confession, are meant to help members in their daily practice of Christ's teachings. Other rituals recognize important life passages, such as birth, adolescence, marriage, and death.

Communion is considered the most important sacrament and the one most frequently performed. This ritual is based upon Christ's Last Supper with his disciples before his death by crucifixion. Several New Testament passages refer to this event; for example: "And when he had given thanks, he broke it (the bread) and said, 'This is my body, which is for you; do this in remembrance of me.' In the same way, after supper he took the cup (of wine), saying, 'This cup is the new covenant in my blood; do this, whenever you drink it, in remembrance of me.' For whenever you eat this bread and drink this cup, you proclaim the Lord's death until he comes" (1 Corinthians 11:24-26).

Church members consume bits of bread and wine as symbolic of the body and blood of Christ. The devout believe that they literally take spiritual nourishment from the elements themselves—and that it is as important for their spiritual life to feast upon this "bread and wine" as it is for their bodies to partake of food. Communion may also be called the Lord's Supper, Eucharist, Divine Liturgy, or Mass.

Baptism is the ritual by which a person becomes a member of the Christian community. The priest or minister either immerses the person in water or pours or splashes the head with water, symbolic of cleansing and new life. Denominations vary on the further meaning of baptism and on the age when it may occur. In the Catholic church, this ritual is done for infants and is part of the naming ceremony. In most Protestant churches baptism is reserved for adolescents or adults who profess their faith and a desire to join the church. In some Protestant churches there is a Christening ritual for infants, in which parents commit to a Christian upbringing for the infant, as well as baptism for adolescents and adults.

Confirmation of adolescents is a Catholic sacrament, recognizing their growth into adulthood and church membership as young adults. In most Protestant churches baptism serves this function.

Holy Matrimony is performed by priest or clergy, uniting two persons in marriage. This ritual is used in virtually all Christian denominations.

Ordination of clergy officially sanctions an individual as priest or pastor, another ritual that is used in virtually all Christian denominations.

Confession of sins to a priest is a Catholic sacrament regarding repentance and reconciliation with God when persons go astray.

Last Rites or Holy Unction is a Catholic sacrament performed for persons who are sick and/or dying. While church ministers of most Protestant churches are typically available to comfort persons who are near death, such service is not considered a necessary ritual.

Christian Religious Observances

The most frequent Christian observance is the Sabbath on Sunday of each week. Beyond that, the two most important Christian observances are Easter and Christmas. The Catholic and Eastern Orthodox branches observe more days and rituals surrounding these two major holidays than do Protestants (Ahlstrom 1972).

Sunday, The Sabbath

The Christian Old Testament includes the passage from Exodus, "Remember the Sabbath day, to keep it holy." Some Christians, especially in today's world, regard the Sabbath as a purely Jewish institution that is no longer binding on the New Testament church. However, most Christians traditionally observe this commandment on Sunday, as the "first day" of the week, "because on that day the Lord Jesus entered into the Redemption rest, even as the Father on the seventh day had entered into the Creation rest" (Hebrews 4: 10). In other words, Christ was crucified on Friday and on the third day, Sunday, he arose from the dead. Therefore, Sunday as the first day of the week became the Sabbath day of rest for most Christians.

A few Protestant groups observe the Sabbath on Saturday, the seventh day; for example, the Seventh Day Adventist Church and the Worldwide Church of God.

Christian observance of the Sabbath typically begins with church services in the morning followed by a family meal. The remainder of the day is devoted to rest and recreation. In some denominations, such as Baptist, the devout may also attend an evening church service.

Easter Observances – February–April

For all Christians, the most holy day of the Christian year is Easter Sunday, symbolizing the day that Christ arose from the dead. The exact date depends on the lunar cycle and occurs between March 22 and April 25. Dates for Easter-related observances are calculated slightly differently by the Western (Catholic and Protestant) and Eastern (Orthodox) branches of Christianity, so they are likely to fall on different dates each year, and Eastern days of fasting are different from those of the Catholic branch. Dates given here refer to the Western branch.

Carnival in February is a Catholic festival, also known as Mardi Gras, Shrove Tuesday, Fat Tuesday, or Fasching. For centuries Catholics and Eastern Orthodox Christians were expected to fast by abstaining from meat during the 40-day Catholic Lent (just as they were expected to abstain from meat every Friday). The term *carnivale* is Latin for "farewell to meat." Carnival is celebrated as a last fling before the solemn days of Lent.

Ash Wednesday in February marks the beginning of the 40-day season of Lent. Traditionally ashes are marked on worshippers' foreheads as a sign of penitence.

Lent occurs in February-March. It starts on Ash Wednesday, as early as February 12 or as late as March 16, and lasts for 40 days until Easter Sunday. Traditional Catholics and Eastern Orthodox Christians observe Lent, and Protestants typically do not. Observance of this 40-day period may include fasting and penitence, both in preparation for Easter and as a way of commemorating Jesus' 40 days of fasting and meditation in the wilderness. Fasting may mean taking just one meal a day, in the evening, with no meat, fish, eggs, or butter. Since 1966, Roman Catholics observe only Ash Wednesday and Good Friday as strict fasting days. Penance, however, is still observed by donating to charity and by devoting time to prayer and religious study.

Palm Sunday is the Sunday before Easter Sunday. It is the Christian celebration of the entry of Jesus into Jerusalem. This is the day that commences Holy Week. It is observed by worship celebrations and in Catholic communities by parades using palm branches.

Holy Week is the week before Easter, which Christians observe with solemn ceremonies based on events in Jesus' life, especially on Holy Thursday, commemorating the Last Supper of Jesus and his disciples, and Good Friday, commemorating Jesus' crucifixion.

Easter Sunday may occur as early as March 22 or as late as April 25. The most holy of Christian sacred days, it commemorates the resurrection of Jesus Christ from his death by crucifixion. Observances may include worship services, sometimes beginning at sunrise, special music, and feasting. In many denominations the wearing of new clothes to church services symbolizes Christ's resurrection to a new life.

Christmas Observances – December–January

Preparations for the Christmas Day celebration may begin as early as December 1. They last at least through December 25, and for some communities through January 6.

Advent, December 1-24, is the beginning of the season for observing the birth of Jesus Christ. Advent begins on the Sunday nearest November 30 and is observed with the daily lighting of advent candles, display of wreaths, and special ceremonies. The season continues through Christmas Eve.

Christmas Eve, December 24, is observed in many families with a family supper and attendance at evening church services, often with a focus on Christmas music.

Christmas Day, December 25, is the Christian celebration of the birth of Jesus Christ. This holiday is observed by a family dinner, prayers, and in most homes, the exchanging of gifts.

Three King's Day or Epiphany, January 6, is the Christian commemoration of the homage of the magi, the three kings, who came bearing gifts for the infant Jesus in recognition of his divine nature. Especially in Latino cultures, this day marks the end of the "Twelve Days of Christmas," that start on December 26. It is this day when gifts are exchanged, rather than December 25.

Because Christianity is the dominant religion in the United States, and has been since its founding, laws governing business practices have traditionally honored the major Christian religious observances. For example, Sunday is the traditional day of rest from work and Christmas Day is a national holiday.

ISLAM: ABRAHAMIC RELIGION OF A GROWING U.S. MINORITY

Historically, Islam is the third of the three Abrahamic religions. It is the second largest religion in the world after Christianity. About 1.5 billion people globally are Muslims, nearly one-fourth of the world population, but they comprise less than 1/2 of 1 percent of the U.S. population.

Beginnings of Islam

Islam originated in the 7th century in the Arabian cities of Mecca and Medina. Islam means "peace and surrender," and refers to the peace that comes when one's life is surrendered to God. Those who believe in Islam are known as Muslims. Islam is considered an Abrahamic religion because Muslims believe in a version of the Genesis story and in the lineal descent of the Arabs from Abraham through Ishmael, who was conceived through Abraham's servant Hagar (Smith 1998). For Muslims, Abraham was the first patriarch and Ismael the second.

Although Islam is not a dissident branch of either Judaism or Christianity, Muslims believe it to be a continuation of and replacement for them. The Quran (also Koran, both pronounced "Kuh RAN"), the holy book of Islam, holds itself to be the final word of God and its message is the message of *all* the prophets. They believe that Islam did not start with its founder Muhammad but was completed in his time. They say that Muhammad was the last of the great prophets, beginning with Abraham and coming down through Jesus.

In 622 Muhammad migrated from Mecca to Medina (Arabian peninsula), an event known as the Hijra (HEEJ ruh). Muslims view this journey as the turning point in world history, thus the date when their calendar begins (Danner 1988). Within a century after the founding of Islam, Muslims conquered vast regions radiating out from Arabia. They became the masters of an empire that ranged from Spain on the Atlantic Ocean, across North Africa and the Middle East, through Persia to the gates of China, an empire greater than Rome at its peak (Smith 1998).

Today, in the Middle East, most Arab countries are predominantly Muslim, but only about 12 percent of Muslims worldwide are Arabs. There are more Muslims in the southeast Asian island nation of Indonesia, for example, than in all Arab countries combined. Large populations of Muslims also live in India, Iran, Malaysia, Pakistan, Turkey, and Afghanistan as well as several former-USSR republics, such as Azerbaijan, Kazakhstan, Kyrgyzstan, Tajikistan, Turkmenistan, and Uzbekistan. Surveying the current Muslim world, we find:

- 23 percent of the world's people are Muslim, about 1.5 billion persons.
- 50 nations are predominantly Islamic, 25 percent of the world's 200 nations
- 40 percent of the world's natural resources are controlled by Islamic nations

We're speaking here of "Islam," not "Arab." Still, Islam has a strong Arab flavor because the religion's holiest places are in the Middle East, citizens of the 22 Arab nations are predominantly Muslim, and the Quran was originally written in Arabic, the unifying language of Arab nations.

Islamic Beliefs

Important beliefs of the Islam religions include their concept of God and creation, the human self, and judgment day, as set forth in their sacred book, the Quran. There are two main sects, Sunni and Shi'a, and both tend to favor Islamic law over separation of church and state (Hast 1966).

Concept of God

Muslims fear Allah (God) for his awesome power, but they also view him as a God of mercy, justice, and forgiveness. Many of the basic theological concepts of Islam are identical with those of Judaism and Christianity, the other "Abrahamic" religions. Islam honors Jesus as a prophet and accepts his virgin birth, but not the doctrine of the Incarnation nor the Trinity; i.e. they do not view Jesus as God in human form. Likewise, Muslims view Muhammad as an exceptional man but never view him as God or as the earthly center of their faith. That place is reserved for the Quran, the bible of Islam (Lings 1988).

The physical world is both real and important to Muslims. The physical world is the source of Islamic science, which prevailed during Europe's Dark Ages. Traditional Muslims believe that physical life consists of tests that qualify believers for the afterlife.

Concept of Human Self and God's Judgment

Foremost among God's creations is the human self. Muhammad's message insisted that in the sight of his Lord, all people are equal. Muslims believe that the fundamental nature of humans is good, and they are entitled to self-respect and a healthy self-image. Life is a gift from the Creator, and humans have two obligations in response: 1) to surrender to God's will and 2) to feel gratitude for the gift of life. Some people say that the term "infidel" was originally shaded more toward "one who has no gratitude" than "one who does not believe." (Smith 1998).

Islam celebrates the soul's individuality and freedom. However, human freedom stands in tension with God's omnipotence. The focus of the Quran is to proclaim the unity, omnipotence, omniscience, and mercy of God, as well as the total dependence of human life on God. On the Day of Judgment, there is a reckoning for every individual. The soul, depending on how it fares in its reckoning, goes either to the heavens or the hells, which the Quran describes in vivid, specific imagery. Most Muslims consider them to be actual places (Arberry 1955).

The Quran

Muslims believe the Quran contains the word of God as revealed to the prophet Muhammad in the seventh century. The Quran has many passages that are similar to those in the Bible, which Muslims also regard as a holy book. They view the Quran as the culmination of the Old and New Testaments of the Bible (Nast 1966). More importantly, they believe it is the direct pronouncement of God's laws. The Quran is intended to regulate every event in life, including the interpretation and evaluation of each event (Arberry 1955).

Islamic Sects

The two main branches of Islam are called Sunni and Shi'a. Most Muslims worldwide (85 percent) and in the United States are Sunni. Shias dominate in some countries, such as Iran, Iraq, Bahrain, and Lebanon. (Note: The African American religious group called Nation of Islam is closely related to Islam, but it evolved in the 20th Century and has some unique practices. Most African-American Muslims are not part of the Nation of Islam.)

Both Sunni and Shia Muslims share the most fundamental Islamic beliefs. The differences stem not from spiritual differences, but political ones. Over the centuries, however, these political differences have spawned a number of varying practices that have come to carry spiritual significance. The division between Shia and Sunni dates back to the death of the Prophet Muhammad, and the question of who was to take over the leadership of the Muslim nation.

Sunni Muslims

Sunni Muslims, the large majority, agree with what actually occurred when Muhammad died. The new leader was elected from among those capable of the job. Muhammad's close friend and advisor, Abu Bakr, became the first Caliph of the Islamic nation.

Sunni Muslims believe that there is no basis in Islam for a hereditary privileged class of spiritual leaders, and certainly no basis for the veneration or intercession of saints—as is practiced by the Shia. They contend that leadership of the community is not a birthright, but a trust that is earned and which may be given or taken away by the people themselves.

Shia Muslims

Shia Muslims, the minority, believe that upon Muhammad's death, leadership should have stayed within the Prophet's own family, or someone appointed by Muhammad or the Imams (priests). Thus, leadership should have passed directly to Muhammad's cousin/son-in-law, Ali. Throughout history, Shia Muslims have not recognized the authority of elected Muslim leaders, choosing instead to follow a line of Imams whom they believe have been appointed by the Prophet Muhammad or God.

Shia Muslims believe that the Imam is sinless by nature, and that his authority is infallible, as it comes directly from God. Therefore, they often venerate the Imams as saints and perform pilgrimages to their tombs and shrines in the hope of divine intercession. Shia Muslims also feel animosity towards some of the companions of the Prophet Muhammad, based on their positions and actions during the early years of discord about leadership in the community. Many of these companions (Abu Bakr, Umar, Aisha, etc.) have narrated traditions about the Prophet's life and spiritual practice. Shia Muslims reject these traditions (hadith) and do not base any of their religious practices on the testimony of these individuals. This naturally gives rise to some differences in religious practice between the two groups. These differences touch all detailed aspects of religious life: prayer, fasting, pilgrimage, etc.

Despite the differences in opinion and practice, Shia and Sunni Muslims share the main articles of Islamic belief and are considered by most to be brothers in faith. In fact, most Muslims do not distinguish themselves by claiming membership in either group, but prefer to call themselves simply, "Muslims."

Islamic Religious Observances

Islam does not have the same kind of hierarchy as some other religions. There is no top official or ruling board for Islam. Muslim mosques and associations are independent, and Muslims are not required to be members of a mosque. They do try to observe the Five Pillars of Islam, which set forth the most important beliefs and behaviors for Muslims. These are incorporated into their religious education and social customs (Danner 1988).

The Five Pillars of Islam

The Quran is a book that emphasizes deeds more than ideas (Iqbal 1979). The five pillars of Islam refer to the minimum sacred obligations of followers. They are:

1. Adherence to the belief, "There is no god but God, and Muhammad is his prophet."
2. Prayer five times a day
3. Giving to the poor
4. Fasting from sunrise to sunset during the holy month of Ramadan
5. Pilgrimage to the holy city of Mecca (in Saudi Arabia), once during a lifetime, for those who are able financially and physically

Prayer five times a day may require special consideration for Muslim employees. Prayer times are upon arising, mid day, mid afternoon, sunset, and bedtime. On Friday at noon prayer time, Muslims are expected to pray together in mosques if possible. Employees may want a modified version of group prayer by finding a place and time to pray together at the workplace.

Muslims refer to God as Allah (ah LAH). After Mecca, the other holiest cities are Medina in Saudi Arabia and Jerusalem in Israel. An imam (ee MAHM), sometimes called a sheik (SHAKE), is a leader of prayer at a mosque. He gives sermons on Friday, the holiest day of the typical Islamic week, usually during the noon prayer time.

Ramadan and Eid al–Fitr

The most important Muslim observance each year is Ramadan (RAH mah dahn), a month of fasting from dawn to dusk, symbolically burning away all sins, and a time of family togetherness. Ramadan is the month when the Quran is said to have been sent to earth, the month when the gates of Heaven are open and the gates of Hell are closed. The dates when Ramadan occurs depends on the lunar cycle, and each year it begins about eleven days earlier than in the previous year.

At the end of Ramadan, Muslims throughout the world observe a three-day celebration called *Eid al-Fitr*, which means the Festival of Fast-Breaking. It falls on the first day of the month that follows Ramadan in the Islamic calendar. In most Muslim countries, the entire 3-day period is an official government and school holiday. During the last few days of Ramadan, each Muslim family gives a determined amount of food as a donation to the poor so they can have a holiday meal and participate in the celebration. On the first day of Eid, Muslims gather early in the morning in outdoor locations or mosques for a sermon followed by a short congregational prayer. Then they typically visit various family and friends, give gifts especially to children, and make phone calls to distant relatives to give well-wishes for the holiday. Where U.S. employers give a "personal day" as a paid holiday, many Muslims choose to use it for Eid.

Integration of Church and State

In recent decades, a proliferation of "fundamentalist" Islamic groups has focused on (among other issues) the Quran's instructions to "fight against the rule of the infidel to bring about Allah's dominion on earth." Many Muslims interpret this Quranic instruction as a command to live an *inner* life according to God's law, but fundamentalists are more likely to interpret it as an encouragement toward social and political action, even militant aggression. "God's law" enforced by government is called the "Sharia,"(shah REE ah) meaning complete integration of church and state—the opposite of separation of church and state

Religious Education

When Muslim parents describe how they raise their children, they use religion as the underlying theme. Especially for immigrants living in non-Muslim countries, religion serves several purposes:

- It helps parents to maintain social rules and to instill expected behaviors.
- It provides the children with a sense of identity.
- It provides a moral code for children growing up.
- It reinforces their own fear of God, which they want to pass on to the children.

Muslim Social Customs

Muslims have a number of unique social customs, including physical proximity, shaking hands, and the defining of women's modesty, especially as it relates to their body coverings—all related to their religious beliefs. However, some researchers say that most of these customs, especially attitudes toward women, are based more on Arab desert cultures than on teachings of the Quran. They may also be more pronounced among fundamentalist groups and in rural regions (Ali 2008).

Using Physical Space

Muslim cultures are known as preferring the closest physical proximity to one another of any major culture. When they are interacting, they tend to sit or stand so close that they can actually feel and smell the other's breath. They also tend to engage in more touching than other cultures.

Handshaking

Americans typically offer to shake hands in greeting or when being introduced to someone. Most Muslims shake hands every time they meet you and leave you. Typical are long handshakes, grasped elbows, and two males walking hand in hand. Male close friends hug and kiss. However, men always wait for a woman to extend her hand first. When meeting Muslims, it's best to wait until they extend their hand before you extend your own. There are a couple of religious reasons for this. First, a traditional Muslim man observes "manly honor" by not invading a woman's space. He will not touch her or make direct eye contact if she is not a family member. This is a sign of respect and a part of his "gender separation duties." The other reason has to do with remaining untouched around prayer time.

Women's Modesty

Traditional Muslims place great importance on women's modesty and chastity and men's honor. The modesty and chastity of the females in the family reflect on the honor of the men, the family, the clan or tribe, and the community. Accordingly, there are significantly different sexual standards for girls as compared to boys, and for men as compared to women; therefore, boys and girls are raised in distinctly different ways. Boys have much more freedom, and brothers are charged with keeping their sisters' "morality" in line (Murata 1992).

Great pressure is placed on girls to be "moral, modest, and sexually inactive" before marriage. Their actions are restricted, limited, and closely monitored. Traditional Muslims disapprove of interfaith marriages, Western standards of dating, and the growing movement toward equal rights for males and females in the West. Girls may be taught that the typical Western girl is perceived as immoral.

Women's Body Covering

In countries where Islamic law (sharia) is basically the law of the land, such as Saudi Arabia, Iran, and Afghanistan, women's dress and behavior are more restricted than in countries where governments are more secular, such as Egypt, Iraq, Jordan, Palestine, and Turkey. Also, rural tribal communities in all the predominantly-Islamic countries tend to place more restrictions on women's freedom than do urban communities.

Some Muslim women wear head coverings that entirely cover their hair, and in countries ruled by Muslim authorities, this may be required and strictly enforced by law. The practice is rooted in Islamic teachings about women's modesty. Hair covering is not universally observed by Muslim women and varies by region and class.

Some church officials have declared that women's entire bodies and faces must be covered, and even the eye area is covered with netting; for example, the burqa in Afghanistan. Others require a long garment, a head covering, and a veil that covers all the face except the eyes. Still other rulings allow the face to show, so a long garment and a headscarf will do, and others require only a headscarf with any modest outfit. Usually, the headscarf must cover the woman's entire head of hair, with no hair showing.

In Saudi Arabia women are required to wear a long black garment, full head covering, and face veil, but underneath is a traditional dress, casual clothes, or a business suit. The cover garments come off when she moves from public to private space. In most predominantly-Muslim countries, women wear only the head covering along with a wide variety of outfits that satisfy the "modesty" requirement (AP 2006). Face veils are rarely worn these days except by women in Bedouin tribes and those from fundamentalist groups. Black garments may signify mourning, which might last from a few days to many years, depending on religious custom.

In a few of these countries, such as Tunisia, Indonesia, and Turkey, headscarves (and long cloaks and face veils) have been banned or discouraged. However, in most muslim of headscarves has increased since the 1990s. Such obviously Muslim symbols may have the effect of a religious-political statement in Western countries because they are perceived as signifying a more fundamentalist, militant, and extreme form of Islam. As such, headscarves worn in public have become especially controversial in European countries with significant populations of Muslim immigrants. Some European nations have either banned headscarves at work, school, and similar public places, or are debating such bans (France, Netherlands, UK). Face veils are even more controversial and more likely to be banned because of identification difficulties (AP 2006; BBC 2006).

Comparison of Islamic and American Cultures

Especially since the events of "9/11," concerns about the growth of fundamentalist extremism in the Islamic world and how it may clash with American culture have led to numerous books and articles analyzing this issue (Schmidt 2004, Gabriel 2007). Because of its impact in the U.S. workplace, we will spend some time exploring the question of culture clash.

A comparison of Islamic and American cultures is given in Table 16.3 showing differences in political systems, socioeconomic structure, laws, values, and views on diversity of beliefs and lifestyles. Islamic cultures are perceived by Americans as being neither democratic nor egalitarian, and lacking a large middle class that enjoys opportunities for advancement. The subordination of women bothers many Americans, as well as religious extremism with little or no appreciation of religious diversity.

TABLE 16.3: A Comparison of Islamic and American Cultures

Islamic Cultures	*American Culture*
Political System	
Monarchy, plutocracy, theocracy with laws often based on Islamic practices	Democracy based on separation of church and state
Socioeconomic Structure	
Pyramidal shape with huge poverty class	Diamond shape with huge middle class
Typical Laws that Affect Human Rights	
Polygamy for men; monogamy for women Sexual affairs legal for men, illegal for women Laws may require women to cover body and to get permission from a male for many life activities; laws may prohibit female activities, ranging from driving to working to getting an education	Monogamy Individual rights and freedom given top priority, as long as actions don't violate rights of others Movement toward equal rights and opportunities for men and women Movement toward balancing masculine strengths with feminine strengths
Typical Values	
Women's modesty as source of family and community honor Reverence for traditions of past Conformity and stability High esteem for elders	Women's roles changing, becoming more diverse Moving beyond traditions to future-focus Change and innovation Youth and a young orientation
Views on Diversity of Beliefs and Lifestyles	
Diversity seen as dire threat to the culture and the world	Diversity valued as source of creativity and power

These Americans see a large contrast with the American culture, which is based on the ideals of democracy, with a large middle class, relative gender equality, and appreciation for diversity (Gabriel 2007; Shepherd 1987).

Keep in mind that there is no one Muslim leader, nor a hierarchy of Muslim leaders, instructing adherents on how to be good Muslims. Because each mosque is relatively independent, groups range from the far right of fundamentalist extremism to the far left of modern interpretations of the Quran that adapt to 21st century realities (Manger 1999).

Political and Socioeconomic Systems

First, we'll compare political and socioeconomic systems in Islamic and American cultures.

Islamic System

Most nations where Islam is the dominant religion are generally governed by the rule of a king, religious leader, or strongman and virtually never have democratic governments. The Islamic governmental and economic institutions are typically run entirely by men, although there has been some progress recently. For example, the government of Morocco set up electoral quotas to insure that women win at least 10 percent of parliamentary seats, and Pakistan set a 20 percent quota for provincial and national seats. One purpose is to exert a moderating influence on religious fundamentalism (Coleman 2003).

The laws tend to uphold certain restrictions and beliefs of Islam as expressed by religious leaders. The extent and strictness of the restrictions are related to the degree of separation of church and state—less separation means less individual freedom. Some researchers state that oppressive rule breeds fundamentalism, violence, and even terrorism—meaning that a non-democratic system and religious extremism tend to feed into each other (Sharansky, 2004). A diversity of beliefs is generally seen as threatening and not well tolerated.

The resulting socioeconomic structure is pyramidal, as depicted in Figure 16.1. At the top is a tiny, very wealthy elite, which is supported by a small middle class and a huge lower class (Gerges 1999). A United Nations report "written by Arabs for Arabs" concludes that the Arab world is in economic decline (UN 2002). The core assumption of the report is that poverty is not merely a matter of income. It is also a matter of freedom and empowerment of both women and men, and access to knowledge. "By all these criteria, the Arab region—even some of its wealthiest corners—could only be described as impoverished." Although the Arab countries do not have the lowest level of *dire* poverty in the developing world, i.e. living on $1 a day, still 20 percent of people live on less than $2 a day or $700 per year. By comparison U.S. residents are considered to be living in poverty if they earn less than $10,000 per year.

In 2007, the combined Gross Domestic Product (GDP) of 19 Arab nations that reported (of the 22 Arab nations) was $1.3 trillion, which is less than the GDP of Spain, a single middle-size European country ranked eighth in the world at $1.4 trillion. To put this into perspective, GDP for the eight top-ranked nations (World Bank 2008) was:

- $13.8 trillion United States
- 4.4 trillion Japan
- 3.3 trillion Germany
- 3.3 trillion China
- 2.7 trillion United Kingdom
- 2.6 trillion France
- 2.1 trillion Italy
- 1.4 trillion Spain

Such figures highlight the relative dearth of economic activity in the Arab nations while highlighting the huge economic activity of the United States, which has a GDP greater than the next four wealthiest nations combined. Thus, the powerlessness felt by poverty-stricken Arab masses, who nevertheless have access to television programs that showcase Western affluence, may add fuel to the fire of frustration and resentment (Gabriel 2007).

American System

Americans value a democratic political system based on separation of church and state, a system that allows for maximum freedom for residents and a diversity of beliefs. This has led to a socioeconomic structure that is more diamond-shaped. A small wealthy elite is at the top, supported by a huge middle class that is relatively affluent, and a small lower class, 13 percent, that lives in relative poverty, an income of less than $10,000 a year for a one-person household or $13,000 for two persons (U.S. Census 2003).

Actually there is a huge and growing gap between the wealthy Americans at the top and the huge majority of Americans. The richest 1 percent owns 38 percent of all wealth; the richest 10 percent owns 85 percent of all financial assets and business equity (Wolff 2003). The closest rival in terms of economic inequity is Great Britain, where the top 1 percent owns 22 percent of all wealth. The key economic difference, however, between the U.S. and Arab nations is the huge U.S. middle class, which has a median income of nearly $50,000 a year (U.S. Census 2005).

Figure 16.1: Pyramid and Diamond Socioeconomic Symbols

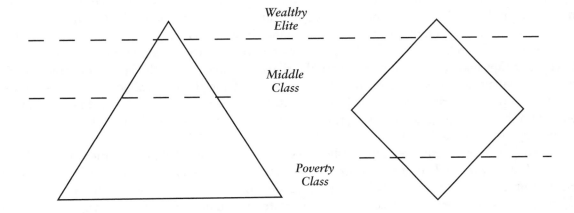

Values, Human Rights and the Role of Women

For many Americans, a difference in values that may be most troubling involves the human rights of women. In nations governed by Islamic law (sharia) or heavily influenced by it, boys and men are allowed much greater political, economic, and sexual freedom than girls and women. For example, males may have multiple wives and mistresses, while women may be cruelly punished for any deviation from premarital virginity and post-marital monogamy. Girls may be harshly punished (even killed by family) for talking or associating with a male friend of whom the father does not approve (Ali 2008; Murata 1992). Women may be expected to stay covered, silent, submissive, and obedient. Restrictions on personal freedom and growth can include laws that require all types of body coverings, from partial to complete. Some laws require the husband's permission for doing almost anything—and if there is no husband, then another male's permission. Others may forbid driving and even going to school (Ali 2008).

American girls and women may, therefore, be seen by some Muslims as having too much freedom and license to dress and behave as they please. American entertainment may be viewed as rife with immoral pornography and indecent role models.

Certainly not all Muslims agree that the subordination of women is a necessary part of the religion. Some historians (Ahmed 1992) say that early Islam actually opened up possibilities for gender egalitarianism, given customs in that time and place, but the male-centered teachings won out over these ethical teachings of Islam. This led to many laws and practices that restricted women, but not men. Some historians (Altorki 1995) therefore make a distinction between Islam as religion and Islam as culture. They say the religion actually places women and men as equals, in contrast to the cultural level of social relations, which has not. Neither does the Quran require veiling and seclusion. These experts are concerned that some Islamic groups are returning to these strict practices, claiming that such traditions represent a more "pure and true" Islam. Such groups feel especially threatened by a diversity of beliefs and lifestyles.

The United States has its own history of denial of women's rights, and there has been some return to fundamentalism that focuses on a return to traditional roles for women. Still, the large majority of Americans now see the repressive treatment of women as an immoral violation of basic human rights. A growing core of advanced thinkers (Eisler 1988, 1996) senses the need for individuals to embrace the traditional feminine strengths—of connection with people as equals, compassion, caring, and nurturing. These are needed to balance the masculine strengths—of achievement and competition for status. They believe we desperately need this balance of masculine-feminine within individuals, and within our institutions, in order to avoid the violence, wars, and Earth damage that threaten our very survival. In other words, emotional intelligence and intuitive intelligence of the feminine are needed to balance our focus on rational intelligence of the masculine. As individual leaders gain this balance, so will our nations and our world.

Diversity of Beliefs and Lifestyles

As certain Muslims groups become more traditional, fundamentalist, and extremist—focusing on the "one right way" to do all things according to their interpretation of the Quran—they naturally feel threatened by alternative beliefs, values, and lifestyles. These groups do not view cultural diversity, especially religious diversity as an asset or advantage to the community or society. Such extremist groups may live in countries where the sharia (Islamic law) is the law of the land; i.e. the Quran is the main source of all laws, and church officials administer the law. Some extremist groups who live in other countries (such as the Netherlands, France, and U.K.) have formed political movements with the long-term goal of making the sharia the law of their adopted land. They predict eventual victory in this moral battle.

Clearly this view clashes with the fairly widespread American belief in separation of church and state and the view that a diversity of worldviews, beliefs, and lifestyles is an asset to society and a business advantage. Most Americans believe that diversity contributes to greater creativity, innovation, and effectiveness in the marketplace and thus to greater abundance and a higher living standard for the population.

Bottom Line

Devout Muslims may find it more difficult to fit into U.S. society than most groups because of significant differences in religious beliefs that affect social practices. Many of their religious traditions and practices conflict with prevailing American culture and behavior. Muslims in the American workplace may also face difficulties because of some Americans' stereotypes and fears exacerbated by "9/11," as well as stereotypes about the powerlessness, and even abuse, of Muslim women. Managers can encourage employees to move beyond their stereotypes and fears and get to know Muslim coworkers on an individual basis.

CONFUCIANISM: A FOCUS ON ETHICS AND PUBLIC LIFE

About 4 percent of people in the U.S. workplace are Asian Americans. Understanding some of the basics of Confucianism is helpful in understanding Asian and Asian American cultures, especially the Chinese. For example, the opening segments of the 2008 Summer Olympics in Beijing consisted of performances symbolizing Confucianism, Taoism, and Buddhism, clearly seen by the Chinese as integral to who they are. Globally, the Far Eastern religions are followed by at least 500 million people, about 6.5 percent of the world's people. Confucianism has had its impact on all these religions.

It has been said that "though Confucius did not author Chinese culture, he was its supreme editor . . . he brought the culture to a focus that has remained remarkably distinct for 25 centuries" (Smith 1998, p. 154). He was always ready to champion the cause of common people against the oppressive nobility of his day. His influence was so great that until the Communist takeover in the late 1940s, observers still regarded Confucianism as "the greatest single intellectual force" among one-fourth of the world population.

Confucian Beliefs

Confucius is still considered one of the world's greatest teachers and in China "the first among teachers." Confucian beliefs are based upon valuing education for a harmonious society, maintaining ideal relationships, doing what is right, becoming a mature person, and using power properly (Waley 1958, Munro 1969).

Valuing Education for a Harmonious Society

Every device of education, both formal and informal, from birth to death, should be turned to seeing that the chosen values are universally internalized. Therefore, moral ideas are driven into the people by all possible means—temples, theaters, homes, toys, proverbs, schools, history, and stories—until they become habits in daily life. Festivals and parades became 'religious' in character. Thus even individualists who are inclined to rebel eventually come around to following social norms, even when authority figures are not looking (Molin 1947). All cultures use education to instill values and desired behavior; in China the Confucian tradition intensifies the focus on education to a reverence for it and great respect for teachers.

Education is revered in Confucian society—and the type of education that engenders a harmonious, flourishing society should focus on five key aspects: maintaining ideal relationships, doing what is right, becoming a mature person, understanding the power by which people are ruled, and practicing the arts of peace (Schwartz 1985).

Maintaining Ideal Relationships

A feeling of humanity toward others and respect for oneself are the basis of ideal relationships among people. In private life this is expressed in courtesy, unselfishness, and empathy.

Family is the basic unit of society. "The duty of children to their parents is the fountain from which all virtues spring."

Respect for Age is essential. Older persons deserve veneration by reason of their intrinsic worth. The years bring experience, seasoning, wisdom, and mellowing of spirit.

Important Relationships make up the fabric of social life and should be conducted as follows:

- *Parent-Child.* The parent is loving toward the child and the child reverential toward the parent; i.e. a loving-reverential relationship. Serve your parent as you would want your child to serve you.

- *Husband-wife.* The husband is good to the wife and the wife listening to the husband, a good-listening relationship.

- *Siblings.* The older sibling is gentle with the younger, and the younger respectful of the older, a gentle-respectful relationship. Serve your older siblings as you would expect your younger siblings to serve you.

- *Older-younger friend.* The older friend is considerate toward the younger, and the younger is deferential, a considerate-deferential relationship. Be the first to treat friends as you would expect them to treat you.

- *Ruler-subject.* The ruler is benevolent toward the subject, and the subject loyal to the ruler a benevolent—legal relationship. Serve your ruler as you would expect your ministers to serve you.

Doing What is Right

"What is right" involves actions based on belief in the primacy of family, respect for age, and basic duties in the important relationships, which we discussed. It also involves right language and the doctrine of the mean. Together they make a blueprint for the well-conducted life.

Right Language. A superior person sees that the words he uses are spoken appropriately, that what he speaks may be carried out appropriately, and that his words are correct.

Doctrine of the Mean. Search for the way that is in the middle between two unworkable extremes, with nothing in excess. This will be the way that works, the right way.

Becoming a Mature Person

Fully adequate and poised, the mature person is like the ideal hostess who is so comfortable in her home and so relaxed that she can turn her full attention to putting others at ease. She asks not, "What can I get from this person?" but "How can I accommodate this person?" Her expression is open, her speech free of coarseness and vulgarity. Holding always to her own standards, she does not push herself forward or display her superiority. Her head is not turned by success nor her temper soured by adversity.

Here is the philosophy: If there is righteousness in the heart, there will be beauty in the character, which will create harmony in the home, which collectively will create order in the nation, which will create peace in the world. Confucius saw life as a never-ending project of self-cultivation with the goal of becoming more fully human. The good person is always trying to become better. The self is a center of relationships, constructed through its interactions with others and is defined by the sum of its social roles. This is in contrast to the Western view of the person as an individual in her or his own right.

Using Power

Confucius' teachings about the use of power include those that describe how people gain prestige in the society, the essentials of a rulers' power, and the arts of peace.

The Power of Prestige

Every group has patterns of prestige that embody the values that the leaders of the group admire. Group members aspire to these patterns, trying to enact them to feel good about themselves and to win peer approval and prestige in the community. For example, teenage gangs may admire toughness and rebellion, while monks admire holiness and humility. The first sentence a Chinese child was taught to read was "Human beings are by nature good." From there, the huge body of Confucius' stories and sayings were designed to create the prototype of what the Chinese hoped the Chinese character would become and how prestige could be achieved. Confucian sayings teach about the power of prestige; for example:

- The true gentleman is friendly but not familiar; the inferior man is familiar but not friendly.
- The well-bred are dignified but not pompous; the ill-bred are pompous but not dignified.
- It is not sufficient that a person be liked by all his fellow townsmen; what is better is that the good among his fellow townsmen like him and the bad hate him.

The Power by which People Are Ruled

The three essentials of government are 1) attaining sufficiency in the economy, 2) maintaining an adequate military, and 3) earning popular trust. Of these, popular trust is by far the most important, for a government cannot stand if the people have no confidence in it. People must sense that their leaders are capable, sincerely devoted to the common good, with character that compels respect. The power of moral example is the real power to rule.

Practicing the Arts of Peace

Related to government and public life are Confucius' teaching on the arts of peace, which include music, art, poetry, and the sum of culture in its aesthetics and spirituality. Art has the power to transform human nature in the direction of virtue. By ennobling the heart, art makes it easy to feel a regard for others. In international relations, the victory ultimately goes to the state that develops the highest "arts of peace," the most exalted culture.

Confucianism: Religion or Ethic?

We can see that Confucius taught about how individuals should live a good life that has a positive impact on their family, community, and country. He did not speak of a "god." A question frequently asked therefore: Is Confucianism a religion or an ethic? If we define religion in its widest sense, as a way of life based on a people's ultimate concerns, then it qualifies as a religion. In the narrower sense of a concern to align humanity with the transcendental ground of its existence, or God, it qualifies in a muted way (Smith 1998). Confucius did shift the people's attention from Heaven to Earth, but he did not drop Heaven from the picture entirely. He taught that people should come first, though the spirits should not be neglected. He changed the emphasis of Chinese religion from ancestor worship to devotion to family. Confucius founded a class of scholars who became China's ruling elite. Confucianism became the equivalent of "China's state religion" for 2000 years (Smith 1998). In 130 B.C. the Confucian texts were made the basic discipline for training government officials, a pattern that continued until the Empire collapsed in 1905.

China reconciled her religions in a unique way. People were not expected to adhere to one religion exclusively, which leads to religions becoming competitive for adherents. Instead, every person was expected to become Confucian in ethics and public life, Taoist in hygiene and private life, and Buddhist in preparation for death, with a bit of shamanistic folk religion for good measure. When communism became the political system, religion was virtually banned and only recently has been making a comeback (Metzger 1977).

Japan, Korea, and much of Southeast Asia deliberately imported the Confucian ethic and adapted it to their local cultures. Therefore, understanding something of Confucianism enables a deeper understanding of most Asian cultures (Levenson 1968).

TAOISM: TAPPING VITAL LIFE ENERGY

Taoism (DOW ism) is a religion or practice whose adherents are found mainly in Asia. About two-tenths of 1 percent of Americans claim to be Taoists. The religion was founded by Lao Tze, who was born about 600 BCE and wrote the *Tao Te Ching*, meaning "The Way to Power," which speaks of humanity's place in the universe and ways of maximizing the life force that flows through it. It is still the basic text of Taoist thought. Taoism was adopted as the state religion of China in the fifth century CE. There is no governing body or hierarchy. Although there are Taoist ritual masters and teachers, most Taoists practice privately. They may worship in temples and at home altars. Taoism is a widespread and largely autonomous faith.

Taoist Beliefs

Taoism, or "The Way," is the natural order, or the force that flows through all living things, sometimes called the c'hi (KEE) or vital life energy. Tao is less a Deity than transcendent reality; however, as Taoism in China is inextricably bound up with folk traditions, there are also a variety of minor deities, which for Asians are generally considered aspects of the Tao.

In the Taoist worldview, violence is abhorrent, and they dream of transcending human error and limitation (Chan 1963). Taoists generally follow a sort of Golden Rule, but the principal Taoist ethic is "no-action," meaning to seek equilibrium and follow the natural order. Taoists value humility, naturalness, and the concept of equilibrium, meaning balance and relativity. The Taoist yin/yang symbol is central because it symbolizes the belief that all values are relative, with the two sides or aspects of each quality being in tension to the other but not totally opposed.

Taoists consider practice to be more important than creed. Although different sects do have established doctrines, none is universal. Taoists seek equilibrium above all else, and many traditional practices, such as acupuncture or other forms of "Chinese medicine" are founded on this principal. Meditation is also an important practice for many believers and helps them to attain equilibrium and maximize their vital life energy.

Humility and Naturalness

Taoists reject all forms of self-assertiveness and competition. They are almost reverent toward humility. They believe that people should avoid being strident and aggressive toward other people, and toward nature as well. In fact their attitude toward nature is the opposite of the Western attitude that nature is to be conquered, dominated, and controlled. The Taoist view is that nature is to be befriended.

This naturalism is combined with a love of naturalness, where the pomp and extravagance found in some religions are seen as silly. This preference for naturalness and simplicity most distinguishes the Taoist from the Confucianist. Taoists view dimly the Confucian formalism, show, and ceremony. Taoists believe that all calculated systems and attempts to arrange life in meticulous order are pointless.

Relativity versus Absolutes

Another important aspect of Taoism is belief in the relativity of all values and therefore the identity of opposites, symbolized by the traditional Chinese yin yang, as depicted in Figure 16.2. This polarity sums up all of life's basic oppositions: light-dark, male/female, positive/negative, etc. Each side is in tension with the other, but they are not totally opposed. In fact they balance and complement each other. Each invades the other's territory and exists in the deepest recess of its partner's space. They are both bounded by the circle that surrounds them, the Tao in its eternal wholeness. As such, the opposites seem no more than phases in an endless cycling process, with teach eventually turning into its opposite as they exchange places and then back again. Thus even good and evil are not exact opposites in the Taoist view. In fact, life and death are complementing cycles in the Tao rhythm.

Taoism Compared to Confucianism

Taoism and Confucianism symbolize two aspects of the Chinese character. Taoists are so averse to violence to humans or animals that their view verges on pacifism. They rank soldiers at the bottom of the social scale. Taoist philosophy is in many ways much more flexible than Confucianism. Taoist writers seek to avoid being "boxed in" by rules, definitions, and empty words. They encourage a sort of intuitive and non-logical way of seeking balance in the world by resisting the desire to interfere with normal processes of nature; i.e., by letting things be. Thus they tend toward spontaneous naturalness.

In contrast, Confucianism represents a more classical, practical view of humanity in the world and focuses more on rules, requirements, and social responsibility. Confucianists rank scholars at the top of the social scale. It has been said that Confucianism focuses on the human, Taoism on transcending the human. The Chinese say, "Confucius roams within society; Lao Tzu wanders beyond."

Figure 16.2: Yin Yang Symbol

Three Taoist Sects: All about Life Energy

In China there developed three sects or branches of Taoism, 1) philosophical Taoism, 2) Taoist hygiene and yoga, and 3) religious Taoism. All Taoist sects have the same concern—how to maximize c'hi, or life energy. This quest begins with how life's normal measure of life energy can be used in the best ways (Philosophical Taoism). It goes on to explore ways to increase that normal measure of ch'i (Taoist Hygiene and Yoga). It continues with learning how cosmic energies can be gathered into one person and beamed out to people who need help (Religious Taoism). These three types of Taoism are best viewed as currents in a river because most Taoists are involved in all three types to some extent (Saso 1978).

Sect 1: Philosophical Taoism

Philosophical Taoism is also called School Taoism in China. It focuses on living in a way that conserves life's vitality (ch'i) by not expending it in useless, draining ways, especially on friction and conflict. In the right way, friction is reduced to the minimum— in interpersonal relationships, in intrapsychic conflict, and in relation to nature. It involves managing life's normal quotient of c'hi efficiently.

Sect 2: Taoist Hygiene and Yoga

This cluster of Taoist outgrowths focuses on ch'i or vital energy in humans. It might be called Energizing Taoism because it seeks to boost the base supply of c'hi. The main object is to further its flow by working with matter, movement, and the mind (Kohn 1989).

Matter. Matter involves qigong or proper breathing, eating the right things, taking the right medicinal herbs, and performing the sexual act properly.

Movement. Programs of bodily movement include t'ai chi chuan and may include calisthenics, dance, meditation, yin/yang philosophy, and martial arts, such as kung fu or wushu, again to draw ch'i from the cosmos and remove blocks to its flow in the body. Acupuncture and acupressure are also used to remove blocks.

Mind. Taoist meditation involves shutting out distractions and emptying the mind so that the power of c'hi can bypass bodily blocks and enter the self directly. Taoist yogis sought to harness c'hi directly, drawing it first into their own heart-minds and then beaming it to others.

Sect 3: Religious Taoism

The religious branch of Taoism embraced the activities of traditional Chinese folk religion—soothsayers, psychics, shamans, and faith healers. Also influenced by Buddhism, this "Church Taoism" took shape about 100 to 200 C.E. The Taoist priesthood made cosmic life-power, or ch'i, available for ordinary villagers (Overmyer 1986). Rituals, if correctly performed, were promised to have magical effects.

HINDUISM: PATHS AND STEPS TO GOD

Nearly a billion of the world's 6.5 billion people are Hindus, and most live in India. In the United States about four-tenths of 1 percent of people claim the Hindu religion.

Hindu Beginnings

Some streams of Hinduism may go back as far as 35,000 BCE, and most experts agree that present-day Hinduism goes back to 1,000 BCE or earlier. Most also agree that Hinduism is beyond doubt the world's oldest living religion. The history of Hinduism is intricately associated with primitive cultures and pre-historic civilizations (Jayaran 2008). Because of this diversity of early Hinduism and the fact that it developed from various independent traditions, most Hindu scholars conclude that it is almost impossible to arrive at a precise date when Hinduism began. Hindu history is extensive and far-ranging.

The caste system is only a small part of Hinduism, but it is an important aspect that is crucial to understanding Hinduism and India. Sometime after 1.000 B.C. Hindu/Indian society became divided into four groups: seers, administrators, producers, and followers.

Seers. The Seers were society's intellectual and spiritual leaders. They were seen as reflective, with a passion to understand and an intuitive grasp of the values that matter most in human life. Their role was not to crack down but to counsel, not to drive others but to guide them. The Brahmin was to ascertain life's meaning and purpose and point the way to others, charting the way to the society's advancement.

Administrators. The administrators were managers who knew how to oversee people and projects in ways that make best use of human talent and physical resources.

Producers. People in the producer caste included artisans and farmers, people who were skillful in creating the material things the society needed.

Followers or Servants. Unskilled laborers made up this class. These people were perceived to have short attention spans, to be unwilling to sacrifice in the short run in order to achieve future gains. With proper supervision they could work hard and give devoted service. On their own they would not be able to achieve success in life.

During the long era of the caste system, the number of castes proliferated into over 3,000 subcastes, including the outcastes or untouchables.

Outcasts or Untouchables. To many outsiders, India was known for its caste system, especially the outcastes or untouchables. Although observers might have assumed that people in this class were slaves, that was not so.

Each caste was self-governed. If a member got in trouble, he would be tried by his peers. Within each caste there was equality, opportunity, and social insurance. The inequalities occurred between castes. Proscriptions against marrying or eating with someone of another caste developed, greatly complicating social life. Higher castes came to have great privileges, benefiting at the expense of the lower. And caste became hereditary so that the caste you were born into was the caste you kept for life.

Remnants of the Caste System

Many reformers attempted to remove the caste system—from Buddha forward. Finally, because of Mahatma Gandhi's leadership, in 1950 India's new constitution banned the caste system (Hopkins 1971). On the bright side, the man who became President of India in 1997 and the current Chief Justice of India belonged to castes that were formerly considered untouchable. Clearly, the caste barriers have mostly broken down in large cities (Bayly 1999).

On the darker side, the caste system is still very rigid in some rural areas and small towns. Caste is also a factor in the politics of India, much as racism and affirmative action are factors in U.S. politics. The government of India has officially documented through the census the various castes and subcastes, primarily to identify people who deserve "positive discrimination" in education and jobs. This is called the Indian reservation system, which relies entirely on quotas. The government lists consist of Scheduled Castes, Scheduled Tribes and Other Backward Classes. Scheduled castes generally consist of former "untouchables." The present population is 16% of the total population of India (Jaffrelot 2004).

Hindu Beliefs

"Hinduism is the first religion to conceive of an Absolute God, creator of not one but innumerable worlds in multiple dimensions and a time frame that stretches over billions of years, comparable to the modern scientific calculations of the universe," according to author V. Jayaran (2008).

In contrast with the materialism of Judaism and Christianity, in Hinduism the world of sense experience, the material world, is regarded as illusion. The religious person seeks release from the wheel of life in order to individually fade out into the World-Soul, the Brahma (Radhadkrishnan 1927).

The Hindu religion seems overwhelmingly complex to outsiders, with many god- and goddess-like beings. If we focus on the existential questions, however, we find that Hindus believe that spirit no more depends on the body it inhabits than body depends on the clothes it wears. When souls outgrow bodies, they exchange them for roomier ones; i.e., they die and reincarnate. Beings automatically pass through a series of increasingly complex bodies until they reach a human level. At this level spiritual growth is no longer automatic. The self-conscious human is capable of karma or work toward spiritual growth based on the law of cause and effect. Humans have free will to make their own decisions (Radhadkrishnan 1927).

Hindus believe in earth as the middle world between higher and lower worlds that some would equate with heaven and hell. They also believe in six cosmic worlds that might be translated as multiple world, moral world, middling world, tricky world, scholastic world, and world of cosmic dance.

Higher, Lower, and Middle Worlds

Hindus see the world as galaxies, each centering in an earth from which people make their way toward God. Around each earth are finer worlds above and coarser worlds below. Souls go to these worlds between incarnations according to what they have learned and earned. The world constantly swells out and is drawn back in, expanding and contracting (Klostermaier 1989).

Earth is a middle world, hanging midway between heavens above and hells below. Interwoven in this middle world, in about equal proportions, are good and evil, knowledge and ignorance, pleasure and pain, etc. The purpose of earthly life is to provide a school for the human spirit. What we do is important ultimately for the discipline it provides our individual character. This world of nature is grounded in God. Some Hindus see three modes of consciousness: 1) hallucinations that can be corrected by further perceptions; 2) the normal world of the human senses; 3) the super-consciousness of advanced yogis.

Hindus believe that what people really want—beyond pleasure and success—are well-being, knowledge, wisdom, and joy—and they always want these things. They want infinite being, infinite knowledge, and infinite bliss. In summary what they really want is liberation or release from the human limits that restrict them. Hinduism says that people already possess these qualities. The infinite center of every life is God. Body, personality and God (Atman-Brahman)—all three make up the human self. Generally the term "yoga" refers to a method of training designed to lead to union of the human spirit with God. A "yogi" is a person on the path to achieving such union (Zimmer 1969).

Higher Cosmic World

Hindus believe in a heavenly or cosmic world that is ultimately benign with no permanent hell. They view the entirety as a spell-binding dance of the cosmic magician, beyond which lies the boundless good that all humans will achieve in the end. This Hindu world has at least six aspects (Hopkins 1971, Smith 1998)

Multiple world is comprised of innumerable galaxies horizontally, innumerable tiers vertically, and innumerable time cycles.

Moral world is the one in which the law of karma is always in play.

Middling world exists between heaven and earth but will never replace paradise as the spirit's destination.

Tricky world passes off its multiplicity, materiality, and dualities as ultimate when they are actually provisional. It's all just a game we play.

Scholastic world is where humans learn and grow and play in their quest to keep expanding and developing themselves.

World of cosmic dance is a place where the play of the Divine is untiring, unending, resistless, and yet ultimately beneficent with a grace born of infinite vitality.

Hinduism is a religion that exists easily alongside other religions. Lord Shiva is quoted as saying, "I, by assuming this dual aspect, tried to convince you that all gods and goddesses are but various aspects of the one Absolute Brahman."

Hindu Religious Practices

Hinduism is distinctive among religions in the amount of attention the adherents devote to identifying basic spiritual personality types and the disciplines that are most likely to work for each type. The result is a recognition that there are many paths to God, each calling for its own journey. They believe in four broad paths that lead to realization of our total being and eight moral practices that are essential to success (Knipe 1991).

Four Paths

The great limitations of human life are physical pain, ignorance, and the restricted being who does not realize his whole self. The goal of life then is to achieve realization of our total being. The four paths to this goal are through:

1. knowledge, thinking, reflection
2. love, emotion, feeling (bhakti yoga)
3. doing, action, work (karma yoga)
4. psychophysical exercises (raja yoga)

The two major distractions are bodily cravings and mental noise. The yogi must follow some moral basics for overcoming these distraction (Ivengar 1965).

Eight Moral Practices

The eight steps of raja yoga, including the psychophysical exercises, for overcoming distractions and achieving wholeness are as follows (Zimmer 1969):

1. Practice the five abstentions from injury, lying, stealing, sensuality, and greed.
2. Practice the five observances of cleanliness, contentment, studiousness, self-control, and contemplation of the divine. (These first two steps are moral basics required of all yogis)
3. Use the five basic postures, including the lotus position.
4. Prevent disruptions through the mastery of breathing.
5. Close the doors of perception by controlled concentration on one thing that excludes all other things.

6. Relax the mind to allow thoughts to be released.

7. Deepen concentration into meditation to move beyond separate self and beyond time-space.

8. Perfect the paradox of seeing the invisible, filling the mind with that which is without form or name.

Rites of Passage

Hindu rites of passage are similar to those of the other religions we have discussed. These include

Rites concerning pregnancy, birth, infancy, and childhood

Ceremonies may be performed during pregnancy to ensure the health of the mother and growing child. At birth, before the umbilical cord is severed, the father may touch the baby's lips, whisper in his ear, and chant mantras to ensure a long life. Later rituals for the infant may include the first visit outside to a temple, the first feeding with solid food, the event of piercing its ears, and the first haircut, which often occurs at a temple or during a festival when the hair is offered to a deity.

Passage into adolescence

Some Hindu groups celebrate the passing of young boys into adulthood, which may occur as young as age 6 and as late as age 12. Some groups celebrate the onset of menses for girls, especially in South India.

Marriage ceremonies

For most Hindus in India, the betrothal of the young couple and the exact date and time of the wedding are matters decided by the parents in consultation with astrologers. At Hindu weddings, the bride and bridegroom represent the god and the goddess, although there is a parallel tradition that sees the groom as a prince coming to wed his princess. The groom, decked in all his finery, may travel to the wedding site on a white horse or in an open limousine, accompanied by a procession of relatives, musicians, and attendants carrying ornate electrified lamps. The actual ceremonies may range from extremely elaborate to quite simple. Orthodox Hindu marriages typically have at their center the recitation of mantras by priests. One central rite is for the new couple to walk seven steps northward from a sacred household fire, turn, and make offerings into the flames. Wide variations in ritual occur among various groups in regional languages.

Death and funeral rites

After the death of a family member, the relatives engage in ceremonies for preparation of the body and a procession to the burning or burial ground. For most Hindus, the body is cremated, although many practice burial; infants are buried rather than cremated. At the funeral site, the eldest son takes charge of the final rite and lights the funeral pyre. After cremation, ashes and fragments of bone are collected and eventually immersed in a holy river. After the funeral, everyone undergoes a purifying bath. The immediate family remains in a state of intense mourning for 10 to 13 days.

Festivals and Holidays

Hinduism is a vast, broad-ranging, and diverse religion. As a result, some scholars declare that Hindus have a holiday for every day of the year, but even that may be an understatement! Exactly how many Hindu festivals are celebrated is not known, but one scholar of Hinduism has listed more than a thousand different Hindu festivals (Bowker 2000). For that reason, and because the festivals are generally not held in the United States, Hindu employees are unlikely to request accommodation for them.

As in most ancient religions, many of the Hindu holidays are based on the cycle of nature. They mark the change of seasons, celebrate the harvest, and encourage fertility of the land. Others are dedicated to a particular deity or commemorate events in their lives. In general, Hindu festivals "are intended to purify, avert bad influences, renew society, bridge over critical moments, and stimulate or resuscitate the vital powers of nature." They include a wide variety of rituals, including worship, prayer, processions, magical acts, music, dancing, lovemaking, eating, drinking, and feeding the poor. Examples include: festival of colors and spring, as well as night sacred to Shiva in February-March, birthday of Lord Rama in April; birthday of Lord Krishna in July-August, and festival of lights in September-October.

BUDDHISM: BEYOND EGO AND SUFFERING

About 376 million people worldwide are adherents of Buddhism, most of them in Asia. In the United States only about 1/2 of 1 percent of people claim Buddhism as their religion. However, many Americans are affected and influenced by Buddhist ideas (Kohn 1989).

Buddhist Beginnings: Response to a "Corrupt" Hinduism

Buddhists are numerous in every Asian nation except India, the land of its birth. However, Buddhism did not so much disappear from India as it was incorporated back into Hinduism. Its contributions included a renewed emphasis on compassion, non-killing of animals, breaking down of caste barriers, and a generally strong ethical emphasis. Recently, after a thousand-year absence, Buddhism is reappearing in India. In fact, the Buddhist leader, Dalai Lama, now resides in northern India, having been exiled from Tibet, the traditional home of top Buddhist leaders. His migration was due to the takeover of Tibet by China (Conze 1950, Sri Rahula 1974, Ho 2009,)

The Buddha means "the enlightened one." Siddhartha Gautama was born to an affluent Indian family in 563 BCE. At age 29 he left his family in search of enlightenment, which he eventually found. Known as The Buddha, he then spent the remaining 45 years of his life preaching an ego-shattering, life-redeeming message that challenged the deadness of the current Hindu society. He founded an order of monks that carry on with his teachings (Thomas 1949).

Buddhism grew out of Hinduism, but in contrast to Hinduism's long-term development, Buddhism appeared almost instantly, fully formed. Some say it was to a great extent a reaction against Hindu perversions and corruptions. According to Huston Smith (1998), six aspects of religion appear so regularly as to suggest that their seeds are in the human makeup. In the Hinduism of the Buddha's day, all six of these aspects had become corrupted: 1) authority and power, 2) ritual, 3) answers to the existential questions, 4) tradition, 5) grace, and 6) mystery. We will explore how Buddhism began in reaction to each of these types of corruption of the Hindu religion of the day.

Reaction to Corrupt Authority and Power, including the Caste System

Some people will rise above the average in matters of spirit. Others will seek their advice and generally follow it. Also, when religion becomes organized, some people must administer it, thus occupying positions of authority. Their decisions carry weight. Buddha believed that authority in Hinduism had become hereditary and exploitative as Brahmin seers hoarded their religious secrets and charged huge sums for their services. He especially objected to the Hindu caste system.

Buddha preached a religion devoid of authority. Much of his reform involved making generally accessible to the many what Hinduism had made the possession of only a few. His teachings were open as contrasted with the secrecy of the Brahmins. Buddha challenged each person to do his or her own religious seeking. His reform also dealt with admonitions to eliminate the caste system.

Reaction to Corrupt Ritual

Religion arises out of celebration and its opposite, grief, both of which cry out for collective expression. Religious rituals provide the means for this expression. Buddha declared that Hindu rituals had become a mechanical means for attempting to achieve miraculous results, rituals that were actually ineffective in changing people's life situations. He often ridiculed Brahmanic rites as superstitious prayers to ineffectual gods, saying these trappings were irrelevant to the tough, challenging job of overcoming ego. He discounted Hinduism's forms and resisted every temptation to institute new ones of his own. Because of Buddha's avoidance of the usual trappings of religions—gods, prayers, rituals—some writers have characterized his teachings as an ethical way of living rather than a religion. Still, Buddhism is typically classified as one of the world's major religions.

Reaction to Existential Speculation

Even though religion may begin in ritual, adherents are soon searching for explanations of the existential questions: Where did humans come from? Why are we here? Where do we go when we die? People speculate about the answers. Buddha claimed that Hindu speculation had lost its experiential base and devolved into meaningless hair-splitting (similar to Catholicism's "how many angels can fit on the head of a pin?"). Buddha's teachings avoided existential speculation. His practical program for living was exacting, and he did not let his disciples become diverted from the hard road of practice into areas of futile speculation. Buddha focused on explaining human suffering, why humans suffer, and the path that leads to the end of suffering—"because that is what is useful" (Thomas 1935).

Reaction to Outmoded Traditions

For humans, tradition rather than instinct is what preserves the knowledge of past generations and offers it to future generations as patterns of action. Buddha said that Hindu tradition had turned into a dead weight. For example, Hindu leaders insisted that Sanskrit remain the language of religious discussion, although the people did not understand it.

Buddha's teachings were not based on tradition. In fact, he urged people to break free from Hinduism's traditional burdens, saying "Once you know yourselves, these teachings are not good. When followed and put into practice, they lead to loss and suffering. Reject them." (Woodward 1939, 283). Some say that the Buddha's most important break with tradition was his decision to quit Sanskrit and teach in the spoken language of the people of his time.

Reaction to Misinterpretation of God's Grace

People want to believe that reality is ultimately on their side, that the universe is basically friendly to humans, and that we can feel at home in it. Religion teaches that the best things are the more eternal things. Buddha said that in Hinduism God's grace was being misread in ways that undermined human responsibility. For example, Karma was confused with fatalism. Therefore, discouragement and defeat had settled over the India of Buddha's day. He saw the prevailing fatalism as extremely harmful and insidious, leading to a sense of powerlessness.

Here we move toward the core of Buddhism as self-awareness and self-empowerment. Buddha said that the source of all human suffering is ignorance of the natural laws of the universe. The deepest meaning of ignorance involves believing in the ego (the separate "I"), identifying with it, and clinging to it. Ego is an illusive mental phenomenon that denies the oneness of nature—our connection with all that is.

The solution to suffering is not faith in the supernatural but knowledge of the natural order of things, of causal relationships. We must see ourselves clearly as part of that order and become aware of what goes on in our own minds, in our life experiences, in society, and ultimately in the world around us. Once this system of causal relationship is understood on the inner level, we are then in a position to see the connections between these inner factors and the causal relationships in society and the natural environment.

Buddha taught that what happens to us in this life is the result of our own past and present actions. We ourselves are responsible for our own happiness. Buddha's teachings were, therefore, about internal self-awareness and external self-effort. He taught that there is a path to the end of suffering and every person can choose to follow it by arousing themselves and taking the initiative. He said, "Buddhas only point the way. Work out your (own) salvation with diligence." (Humphreys 1951, 120)

Reaction to a Focus on Mystery

The human mind is finite and therefore cannot begin to understand the infinite mind of God. Humans are drawn to this infinite mystery. Buddha said that Hindu practice had devolved into a perverse obsession with miracles, the occult, and the fantastic (Smith 1998).

Buddha's teachings do not include the supernatural. He condemned all forms of forecasting, soothsaying, and miracle-working as low arts. Although he concluded that the human mind is capable of paranormal powers, he forbade his monks from dabbling with such powers. He strongly discouraged the practice of mystic wonders because he perceived dangers in going down that path.

Buddhist Beliefs? Suffering & Ego

The Four Noble Truths refer to Buddha's "most considered convictions about life," which deal with release from the ego and therefore from human suffering. These four noble truths are: 1) life is suffering, 2) ego is the cause of suffering, 3) release from ego is the door to universal life, and 4) the eightfold path releases us from ego (Sri Rahula1974).

1. Life Is Suffering

Human life, as people typically live it, is dislocated. Something has gone wrong. It is out of joint. Because its basis is not true, friction and interpersonal conflict are excessive, movement toward creativity is blocked, and it hurts.

The Buddha was certain that these difficult conditions of human life can be improved. In fact, all is well, but people typically live in ways that are unfulfilling and wracked with insecurity. Buddha noted the conditions that highlight life's dislocation: the trauma of birth, the pathology of sickness, the fear of death, the condition of being tied to what you do not like or do not want, and the condition of being separated from what you do love and do want.

In fact the key life components can all be very painful: body, sensations, thoughts, feelings, and consciousness. Life can become estranged from reality, and this estrangement precludes true happiness until it is overcome.

2. Ego Is the Cause of Suffering

For the rift between suffering and happiness to be closed, we must know its cause. Today the concept probably closest to Buddha's description of the cause of suffering would be "negative ego." Seeking fulfillment in our egos, which ooze like secret sores, tends to continue or increase our sense of separateness. Ego refers to the desire for self at the expense, if necessary, of all other forms of life. Life being one, all that tends to separate one aspect from another must cause suffering to the unit, which even unconsciously works against natural law. Our duty to fellow beings is to understand them as extensions, other aspects of ourselves, fellow facets of the same Reality.

This is why we suffer: Instead of linking our faith, love, and destiny to the whole, we persist in tying these to our little separate selves, which are certain to stumble and eventually give up. Far from being the door to abundant life, the ego is a dead-end trap. The bigger it gets, the more it blocks the free flow of life and the more our pain increases.

3. Release from Ego is the Door to Universal Life

If the cause of life's dislocation is egotistical craving, its cure lies in overcoming such craving. Once we release ourselves from the narrow limits of egocentric concerns, we enter the vast expanse of universal life and are relieved of our torment.

4. The Eightfold Path Releases Us from Ego

The way out of our imprisonment in the bondage of negative ego is through following the Eightfold Path (Conze 1959). This leads us to Buddhist religious practices, which are based upon the eight-fold path.

Buddhist Religious Practices

The eight-fold path is the way to liberation from ego, alleviation of human suffering, and the attainment of happiness (Smith 1998). After reviewing the basic beliefs and practices of Buddhism, we can make some conclusions about the essence of Buddhism.

The Eightfold Path

The eightfold path to liberation from ego and attainment of true self consists of right views, right intent, right speech, right conduct, right livelihood, right effort, right mindfulness, and right concentration.

Right Views

Although a way of life involves more than beliefs or right views, we do need beliefs we can trust, in order to purposively direct our energies. The Four Noble Truths provide the basic beliefs; i.e., life is suffering, ego is the cause, release from ego is the solution, and the eightfold path releases us from ego.

Right Intent

What do you really want? Enlightenment? Or do your desires swing this way and that without stability? People who achieve greatness are passionately invested in a worthwhile purpose, a goal. When you seek liberation and enlightenment with such single-minded passion, you will make progress.

Right Speech

Become aware of your speech and what it reveals about your character. Notice how many times a day you deviate from the truth. Ask why you do so. Watch your speech to become aware of when it is unkind—and why. The motive is almost always fear of revealing your real self to others or to yourself, but each deceit strengthens the walls of your ego prison. Notice false witness, idle chatter, gossip, slander, and abuse, both the obvious and the subtle forms, such as belittling, accidental tactlessness, and barbed humor, often more vicious because of their covert nature. Noticing is the first step toward changing.

Right Conduct

The Five Precepts for right conduct might be seen as the Buddhist version of the second half of the Ten Commandments, the ethical half: 1) Do not kill. Strict Buddhists extend this ban to animals and are strict vegetarians). 2) Do not steal. 3) Do not lie. 4) Do not be unchaste; for the married, this means restraint in proportion to your interest in the Path, and your progress along it; for monks and the unmarried, it means no sexual intercourse. 5) Do not drink intoxicants.

First, understand your behavior more objectively before trying to improve it. Reflect on your actions, looking for the motives that prompted them. How much was motivated by ego? How much by generosity? Direct your change toward charity and compassion.

Right Livelihood

Spiritual progress is impossible if most of your activities pull against it. Engage in occupations that promote life instead of destroying it. Earning a living is the means to functioning in physical life, not life's purpose.

Right Effort

Reaching the goal of enlightenment takes right effort. You must develop virtues, direct your passion, and overcome destructive mind states, so that compassion and "letting go" can have a chance to work. Focusing on such thoughts as "he robbed me, he beat me, he abused me" entrenches hatred in the mind. You can escape misery only by earnestly and steadily thinking of the Way.

Right Mindfulness

"All we are is the result of what we have thought," according to a Buddhist text (*Dhammapada*), "and all things can be mastered by mindfulness." Freedom, meaning liberation from an unconscious, robot-like existence, is achieved through self-awareness. By maintaining a steady attention on your thoughts and feelings, you perceive that they swim in and out of your awareness and are not permanent parts of who you are. See them neutrally, neither holding onto nor condemning them. Fearful or disgusting sights or thoughts can be meditated on until you no longer experience aversion to them. The goal is to pervade the entire world with thoughts of loving-kindness.

Right Concentration

Using techniques similar to those in Taoist hygiene and yoga and Hinduism's raja yoga (such as breathing, postures, meditation), right concentration leads to substantially the same goal: experiencing the world in a new way. Moving beyond the three poisons—delusion, ego craving, and hostility—you see that things were not as you had supposed. In fact, suppositions have been replaced by direct perception, and the mind is at rest in its true condition.

The Essence of Buddhism

The essence of original Buddhism has been defined by Huston Smith (1998) as empirical (experiential), pragmatic (practical), therapeutic (healing), psychological (human), egalitarian (equality), and individualistic (personal).

Empirical. Followers are encouraged to apply direct validation of its teachings. On every question, personal experience is the final test of truth. What are the results?

Pragmatic. Buddha was concerned with problem solving. He refused to be sidetracked by speculative questions. He believed that unless his teachings were useful tools, they had no value. He likened them to boats that help people cross streams but are of no further value once the shore is reached.

Therapeutic. Buddha taught about suffering and the end of suffering. He said that it was just the "illness of ignorance and suffering" that he proclaimed, and how to cure this "illness."

Psychological. Rather than metaphysical, Buddhism is psychological. The Buddha invariably began with the human condition, its problems, and the process for coping with them.

Egalitarian. Buddha insisted that women were as capable of enlightenment as men. He rejected the caste system's assumption that aptitudes were hereditary.

Individualistic. While Buddha gave attention to the social side of human nature, his basic appeal was to the individual. Each person should proceed toward enlightenment by confronting his or her own situation and predicaments.

Buddhist Sects or Branches

The two earliest branches of Buddhism were 1) Theravada Buddhism, which does not focus on the supernatural, metaphysics, or ritual, and 2) Mahayana Buddhism, which does focus more on those aspects. Later came Zen Buddhism in Japan, which dramatically affected Japanese culture in many ways.

Theravada Buddhism

According to Buddhists of the Theravada branch, humans are freed by self effort, without supernatural aid. The key virtue is wisdom. Attaining enlightenment requires constant commitment and is primarily for monks and nuns. The ideal is the perfected disciple who remains in enlightenment after death. Buddha was a saint, supreme teacher, and inspirer. This sect minimizes metaphysics and ritual. Its practice centers on meditation (Sri Rahula 1974).

They focused on Buddha's vision of an entire society or civilization founded on the monarchy, the monastic community, and the people, each with responsibilities to the others and deserving services from them in return. South Asian countries are predominantly Theravadan, including Burma, Cambodia, Thailand, and Sri Lanka.

Mahayana Buddhism

Buddhists of the Mahayana branch believe that human aspirations are supported by divine powers and the grace that they bestow. The key virtue is compassion. Religious practice is relevant to life in the world, and therefore to lay people. The ideal is the bodhisattva, the person whose essence is perfected wisdom, such as Qwan Yin, the Chinese Goddess of Mercy. Having reached the brink of enlightenment, she returned to the world to make enlightenment available to others. Buddha was a savior. This sect elaborates on the supernatural or divine i.e. metaphysics, and emphasizes ritual, which includes prayers of petition to Buddha (Conze 1959)

King Asoka of India (c. 272-232 BCE) adopted Mahayana Buddhism and worked to extend it over three continents, making it a world religion. This is the branch that became predominant in China, Korea, Japan, and Tibet. China, especially, ignored the political aspects and adopted the psycho-spiritual components. This branch is by far the largest, and it eventually divided into a number of sects: The Pure Land Sect, Ti'en Tai sect, and the Zen sect.

The current Dalai Lama, considered the spiritual leader of this branch of Buddhism, has been in exile since 1959 from his former seat of government in Tibet. He speaks from Dharamsala India, saying, "The religion, culture, language and identity, which successive generations of Tibetans have considered more precious than their lives, are nearing extinction" referring to the Chinese occupation of Tibet (Ho 2009). On the other side, the Chinese Premier Wen Jiabao states that Tibet is an inalienable part of China's territory. He calls the Dalai Lama a political exile, not a religious figure, characterizing the former Tibetan government as theocratic and illegal (Wong 2009).

Zen Buddhism

Zen Buddhism evolved in Japan. Zen training consists of 1) seated meditation; 2) working with "koans," a type of riddle designed to lead to an intuitive breakthrough that bursts into awareness, throwing everything into a new perspective; and 3) "sanzen," the resulting mystical experience, which brings joy, at-one-ment, and a new sense of reality. The idea is to widen the doors of perception so that this magic floods the everyday world. Rather than removing adherents from the physical world, extensive Zen study returns them to the world, but a world bathed in new light. Newcomers may perceive Zen training as a blur of bewildering dialogues, obscure puzzles, stunning paradoxes, abrupt contradictions, and surprising non sequiturs—all delivered in a style that is elegant, jovial, and innocent (Abe 1985).

Zen's attitude toward dogma and creeds is that Zen is not founded on written words and is outside the established teachings. They say that signposts are not the destination, and maps are not the terrain. Life is too rich and textured to be categorized and labeled, let alone equated with such labels. An affirmation is no more than a finger pointing to the sun. Zen will point and then withdraw its finger at once to be sure that attention is not turned to the finger. Zen masters tell their followers to rip their scriptures to shreds, not with the intent to disrespect them but to break out of solutions that are only verbal. Zen is not interested in theories about enlightenment but only the real thing.

Zen trusts its future to a specific state of consciousness that is transmitted directly from one mind to another, Buddha-mind to Buddha-mind. This is the special transmission that is Zen's essence. On the other hand, Zen does not entirely ignore reason and words, which obviously help us make our way in the everyday world. Working in special ways, reason can actually help us move toward awareness.

Zen has had great influence on Japanese culture, especially the simple lives of Zen monks, living close to nature. Japanese art, especially black ink landscape painting, reflects this natural simplicity, as does Japanese flower arranging, landscape gardening, and the tea ceremony. We see beauty in the austerity, the slow, graceful ritual, and the spirit of tranquility, harmony, respect, and clarity.

LEADERSHIP CHALLENGES & OPPORTUNITIES: MANAGING RELIGIOUS FREEDOM IN THE WORKPLACE

As a workplace leader, you are now familiar with the fact that, by law, the people of the United States enjoy the freedom to choose any religious affiliation or no religious affiliation and are protected in the workplace from discrimination and harassment due to religion. You know that the First Amendment to the U.S. Constitution guarantees freedom of religion, and Title VII of the Civil Rights Act prohibits discrimination and harassment based upon religion and requires employers to make reasonable accommodations to allow employees to observe their religious practices. Employers cannot force someone to participate in a religious activity nor prohibit them from participating in a religious activity as a condition of employment. As a practical matter, an employee can be invited to participate in a religious activity but cannot be pressured to do so.

Religious Expression

The Equal Employment Opportunities Commission, EEOC, provides guidelines on religious exercise and expression in federal workplaces, as mentioned in the first section of this chapter. Many private employers have adopted similar guidelines for such issues as wearing religious jewelry, displaying religious materials at work, and inviting coworkers to religious events. The goal is to treat all employees with the same respect and consideration regardless of their beliefs.

Religious Accommodation

Employers are expected to make reasonable accommodation for employees' normal religious practices—as long such arrangements do not cause undue hardship for the employer. Accommodation might include modifying a workplace practice, providing flexible scheduling, and making job reassignments or lateral transfers. Many employers also have an anti-harassment policy that includes religious harassment and an effective procedure for reporting and responding to incidents of harassment.

We have discussed typical requirements and practices of the major religions of the world. Following is a recap of these practices that may call for work workplace accommodations by managers. The Western or Abrahamic religions tend to have specific dates and times for required rituals and practices. On the other hand, most Asian religions generally do not require observance of specific dates or times, and Asian cultural festivals and practices vary widely. Therefore managers often must rely on Asian American employees to make their own requests for religious accommodation. Let them know that the organization has a policy of granting reasonable requests. See Table 16.4 for a summary of dietary requirements of major religions.

Jewish: Workplace Considerations

Some basics of Judaism were explored earlier. Focusing now on Jewish Americans whom you might encounter in the workplace, a recent survey (ARIS 2001) indicates that there are over 5 million adults in the Jewish American population, about 1.3 percent of the American population. Of these:

- 53% (2.83 million) are adherents of Judaism
- 26% (1.36 million) are adherents of a religion other than Judaism
- 20% (1.08 million) are adherents of no religion

The Jewish adult population, therefore, falls into two categories:

1. The 53% who identify with Judaism as a religion.
2. The 47% who either are of Jewish parentage, were raised Jewish, or consider themselves Jewish on some other basis

Clearly, among American Jews the "Jewish identity" is an amalgam of religious, ethnic and cultural elements.

TABLE 16.4: Summary of Practices and Restrictions of Major Religions

Religion	Practice or restriction
JEWISH Orthodox	Pork, rabbit, shellfish prohibited Meat and dairy at same meal prohibited Grape products prepared only by Jews No bread during 7 days Passover Fasting, Yom Kippur
CHRISTIAN: Most Protestants	Virtually no restrictions of food No fasting Moderation in eating, drinking, exercise No alcohol in some denominations
CHRISTIAN: Seventh-day Adventist	Pork prohibited Meat and fish if kosher Vegetarian diet is encouraged Alcohol, coffee, and tea prohibited
CHRISTIAN: Mormon	Alcohol prohibited No caffeine Moderation in all foods Fasting practiced
CHRISTIAN: Roman Catholic	Meat restriction and fasting on certain days during the Lent season
CHRISTIAN: Eastern Orthodox	No meat, fish on certain Holy Days Fasting selectively
MUSLIM	Alcohol, pork, birds of prey prohibited Coffee/tea/stimulants avoided Fasting from all food and drink during specific periods, such as Ramadan
CONFUCIAN	No restrictions
TAOIST	No restrictions except avoid excess
HINDU	Beef prohibited Pork, fowl, duck, snail, crab avoided Alcohol avoided Numerous fasting days
BUDDHIST	No pork or added animal fat Vegetarian diet is desirable Moderation in all foods

Appreciating the Jewish Value of Intelligence

The large majority of Jewish Americans, about 85 percent, are descendants of Ashkenazim Jews who lived in the west of Germany during medieval times and over time migrated to other European countries. In those days Jewish cultural rules against marrying outside the group, coupled with external social pressures, resulted in a relatively closed genetic circle. The difficult conditions in Europe ensured a strong biological imperative for Jews to adapt and survive. European Jews were harshly persecuted and mostly locked out of land ownership. They developed survival skills that later were ideally suited when Europe moved from a primarily agricultural economy to a more urban manufacturing and service economy.

Without the legal ability to own large tracts of land, most Jews were relegated to villages and towns, which gave them a head start on urban life. The primary occupations available to Jews who settled in what later became urban centers were in the service trades that required literacy and arithmetic skills. The culture came to value abstract intelligence and reasoning skills more highly than manual labor skills. Over the centuries Jewish communities focused on developing quantitative intelligence rather than physical strength. The most highly valued trait was intelligence.

As a result, people of European Jewish descent, regardless of family background, perform better than average on IQ tests, and they are disproportionately well represented among lists of major math and science award winners. Although they account for less than 2 percent of the U.S. population, they account for 27 percent of U.S. Nobel Prize winners over that past two generations. They also comprise about 20 percent of CEOs and 22 percent of Ivy League students (Cochran 2009).

Recognizing Religious Practices

Surveys indicate that about 25 percent of American Jews observe such practices as eating only kosher food and observing the Sabbath and Jewish holidays. It may help to know whether a Jewish employee belongs to a congregation that is Orthodox, Conservative or Reform because the 10 percent of Jews who most strictly observe the Sabbath and all holidays typically belong to an Orthodox congregation.

Saturday is the Sabbath day, which begins at sundown on Friday with a special family dinner and a synagogue service. No work is to be done through sundown on Saturday. The holidays that are most commonly observed by American Jews are the ones that your Jewish employees and coworkers will expect you to be familiar with—Passover, Rosh Hashanah, and Channukah. Dates vary according to the Jewish calendar and may be found online at relevant website.

Passover occurs in April and the first night of the 7-or-8-day holiday is observed by most American Jews. They may avoid bread and grain products throughout this holiday. Strictly observant Jews do not work, go to school, or carry out any business on the first two and last two days of Passover. Employers should check with Jewish employees before scheduling work or travel at this time.

Rosh Hashanah is the two-day Jewish New Year, occurring in September. Many Jews who do not go to synagogue any other time of year will go on Rosh Hashanah. The holiday starts at sunset the night before the day shown on the calendar. Therefore employers and teachers may want to avoid scheduling important events, meetings, or tests on Rosh Hashanah.

Jewish rituals related to births, initiations, and weddings, may require no special accommodations by employers. However, the week after the funeral of a family member is a time of intense mourning when family members may need to remain at home.

Avoiding Stereotypical Jokes

Jewish Americans may be very sensitive to typical stereotypes and jokes about Jews. While members of any and all religious groups may experience such problems, the fact that Jewish Americans are by far the largest non-Christian group, which has been around from the beginning, makes this an important consideration for managers. Most of these jokes are based on stereotypes about money, banking, and occupations, which stem primarily from Jewish history (Singer 2000, Sowell 1981). Managers can take the lead in discouraging the use of stereotypical comments and jokes.

About 2,000 years ago, the Jewish dispersion to other lands occurred, with most Jewish refugees settling in Europe, where they were never fully accepted and experienced waves of persecution. They were barred from many occupations but usually allowed to perform banking and taxation tasks, which were considered morally inappropriate for Christians and in fact were scorned by them. For much of European history, dangers of popular resentment made it inadvisable for Jews to display any wealth or prosperity. In some situations, the possibility of needing to flee persecution made it sensible to invest in diamonds, gold or jewelry rather than real estate. It also made sense to become proficient in such professions as doctor, lawyer, or accountant, which could earn them a living wherever they landed. This history explains the origins of certain Jewish stereotypes and jokes. We can consider it ancient history and certainly not indicative of the Jewish experience and culture in current American society.

Christian: Workplace Considerations

Because Christianity is the dominant religion in the United States, and has been since its beginnings as a group of English colonies, the laws governing business practices have traditionally honored Christian religious observances, so special accommodation is normally not a factor. For example, Sunday is the traditional day of rest from work, and Christmas Day is a national holiday. However, some denominations observe the Sabbath on Saturday; for example, the Seventh Day Adventist Church and the Worldwide Church of God.

Catholics may observe fasting rituals on certain days during Lent, the 40 days preceding Easter, especially on Wednesday and Friday of Easter week. Fasting may mean eating only an evening meal with no meat or dairy. Members of Eastern Orthodox churches observe a different calendar and therefore different dates for Easter-related activities, including fasting. Such differences range from a few days to a month or so.

Muslim: Workplace Considerations

We will consider several aspects of Islam and its adherents, Muslims, who have become noticeable and sometimes controversial in the American workplace because of recent political and socio-economic developments. First we will review some religious considerations, then some cultural customs, and finally some political considerations.

Religious Considerations

For devout Muslim employees, prayer five times a day may require special consideration. Prayer times are upon arising, mid day, mid afternoon, sunset, and bedtime. On Friday at noon prayer time, Muslims are expected to pray together in mosques if possible. Employees may want a modified version of group prayer by finding a place and time to pray together at the workplace.

The most important Muslim observance each year is Ramadan, the entire ninth month of the Islamic calendar. Dates vary each year and can be found on various websites, such as About.com and eHow.com. The first day of the month following Ramadan is celebration time, Eid al-Fitr, which means the Festival of Breaking Fast. In the United States, Muslim employees of companies that provide a personal paid holiday typically will take Eid as their holiday.

As indicated in the Summary of Practices, devout Muslims do not eat pork, generally avoid over-indulgence in food as well as consumption of alcohol; coffee and tea are discouraged. In fact, alcohol is strictly forbidden in certain nations that incorporate Islamic law. Fasting may be practiced regularly on Mondays and Thursdays as well as during the entire ninth month of Ramadan, and for six days during the tenth month. Fasting on these occasions includes abstention from all food and drink from sunrise to sunset.

Cultural Customs

Arab Muslims are likely to follow the Arab cultural practice of sitting or standing so close together that they can actually feel and smell the other's breath. They also tend to engage in more touching than other cultures. However, when meeting Muslims, it's best to wait until they extend their hand for a handshake before you extend your own.

Much of Muslims' personal behavior comes directly from their religion, which makes them more visible than most religious minorities and often vulnerable to bigotry. Examples include women's head coverings and men's beards and turbans, as well as practices such as daily prayers and Friday noon prayer services, which may require accommodation at work, school, and the military.

Stereotypes about the powerlessness, and even abuse, of Muslim women tend to make some Americans uncomfortable around Muslims. Devout Muslims, likewise, may be uncomfortable with the perceived "freedoms" and behaviors of Americans, especially of young women. Acceptance, patience, and compassion are needed on both sides to avoid such culture clash and to promote workplace cooperation and collaboration.

Political Considerations

Because of recent political developments, globally and within the United States, interest in Islam and Muslims has increased dramatically. In the chapter concerning Arab American employees, we reviewed the myths and stereotypes that Arab Americans must deal with, and we saw in case studies the types of workplace problems that have resulted. Muslims in the American workplace may face difficulties because of stereotypes and fears exacerbated by the attack on the World Trade Center, referred to as "9/11." After that event, the EEOC issued statements encouraging employers and unions to be especially sensitive to discrimination against or harassment of persons who are, or are perceived to be, Muslim, Arab, Afghani, Middle Eastern, or South Asian (such as Pakistani or Indian).

Confucian: Workplace Considerations

We have reviewed some basics of Confucianism. This should be helpful in understanding the 4 percent of U.S. employees who are Asian Americans. Chinese American culture is the one most influenced by Confucianism, and it has also had significant impact on virtually all East Asian cultures. Historically China never expected people to adhere to one religion exclusively. Instead, every person was expected to become Confucian in ethics and public life, Taoist in hygiene and private life, and Buddhist in preparation for death, with a bit of shamanistic folk religion for good measure. When communism became the political system, religion was virtually banned and only recently has been making a comeback. We might conclude, therefore, that most Asian Americans in the workplace bring a mixture of beliefs and practices that might seem to most Westerners as more a set of ethical guidelines than a religion.

Managers need to communicate to Asian Americans the general policies about religious accommodation and encourage them to volunteer any special needs and requests they may have.

Taoist: Workplace Considerations

In working with people of the Taoist faith, remember that they highly value humility, naturalness and maintaining equilibrium. They abhor violence, whether to humans or animals. Modern-day Taoists typically have no food restrictions but they do avoid excess.

For devout Taoists, important days may include birthdays of certain gods, such as Kwan Yin, Goddess of Mercy and Compassion, and regular fast days throughout the month.

Hindu: Workplace Considerations

Managers may need to know a few facts about Hindu practices regarding food and fasting. As mentioned earlier, Hindus are unlikely to ask for accommodations regarding holidays. On the other hand, food and fasting may be a concern.

Hinduism's vast scriptures contain thousands of passages recommending vegetarianism based on the profound link between nonviolence and spirituality. Although not all Hindus are vegetarian. nearly all of them avoid beef since the cow is considered a sacred animal. Mahatma Gandhi took Hindu vegetarian observance one step further by declaring, "The greatness of a nation and its moral progress can be measured by the way in which its animals are treated."

Other foods that may be avoided by some are pork, fowl, eggs, crab, and snail. Alcohol may be avoided, though many drink beer. While beef is prohibited, dairy products from the cow, such as milk, yogurt, and butter, are considered innately pure and are thought to promote purity of the mind, spirit, and body. On special occasions a Hindu may fast with fruits and milk or juice. During occasions like bereavement, a combination of fruits, raw and steamed vegetables, and milk are taken once a day.

Many devout Hindus fast on the eighteen major Hindu holidays, as well as on numerous personal days, such as birthdays and anniversaries of deaths and marriages. Some also fast on Sundays and on days associated with various positions of the moon and the planets.

Buddhist: Workplace Considerations

Traditional Buddhism emphasizes compassion for humans and animals. Dietary restrictions may forbid eating of pork or added animal fat. Buddhists generally view a vegetarian diet as desirable as well as practicing moderation regarding all eating and drinking. Natural foods of the earth are preferred as the most pure of foods.

Most Buddhists in the American workplace do not take holidays from work for religious purposes. In Asian countries there may be many Buddhist festival days. People typically go to the local temple, offer food to the monks, and listen to a talk. In the afternoon, they distribute food to the poor, and in the evening perhaps join in a ceremony of walking around the temple, concluding with chanting of the Buddha's teachings and meditation.

Buddha Day. On the day of the full moon in May, Buddhists celebrate the birth, enlightenment and death of the Buddha over 2,500 years ago. This is the most significant Buddhist celebration.

Buddhist New Year. The date depends on the country of origin. In Theravadan countries—Thailand, Burma, Sri Lanka, Cambodia and Laos—the new year is celebrated for three days from the first full moon day in April. In Mahayana countries it starts on the first full moon day in January. Chinese, Koreans and Vietnamese celebrate in late January or early February according to the lunar calendar, and Tibetans usually celebrate about one month later.

Some of the many lesser holidays include the full moon day in March, recalling the Buddha's Four-Fold Assembly, and the full moon day in July that commemorates the Buddha's first teaching. Every month in Theravedan countries, four holy days fall on the new moon, full moon, and quarter moon days.

SUMMARY

While many people believe that the United States was founded by Christians as a Christian nation, the reality is that some founding fathers were not necessarily strong believers in Christianity and in fact had concerns about the role of organized religion. Therefore, a basic tenet of the United States founders was separation of church and state, as set forth in the first amendment to the Constitution. A section of Title VII of the Civil Rights Act of 1964 makes it unlawful for an employer to discriminate against or harass an employee based upon his or her religion. Federal workplace guidelines guarantee freedom of religious expression within certain limits. Employers must reasonably accommodate an employee's religious practice unless such accommodation would cause undue hardship for the employer's business.

Over half the world's people belong to one of the Abrahamic religions—the largest being Christian with 2.1 billion adherents, followed by Islam with 1.5 billion adherents, and Judaism with 14 million. The United States has a greater number of religious groups than any country in the world.

Judaism

About 14 million, or two-tenths of 1 percent of the world's 6.5 billion people, are Jewish. Their religion began over 3,000 years ago in the area now called Israel and Palestine. Beginning about 70 CE during the Roman era, Jews began dispersing throughout the Mediterranean area and Europe. In 1948 the United Nations restored to the Jews the land then called Palestine, and it became Israel once more. Currently most Jews live either in Israel (40 percent) or in the United States (40 percent), with the other 20 percent are scattered around the world. That means there are about 5.3 million Jewish Americans, 1.3 percent of the American population.

The Patriarchs Abraham, Isaac, and Jacob are the physical and spiritual ancestors of Judaism. Jewish history and beliefs are derived from the written Torah, Talmud, Midrash, and other sources. Some of these materials, such as that found in the Torah, are shared by Christians in the Old Testament of their Bible. Some experts state that ancient Jews' passion for meaning and questioning of where humans came from were what made their religion enduring. Also, Jews differed from neighboring groups in their belief in one God, not multiple gods.

Employers may need to accommodate Jewish employees, especially concerning the most widely observed holidays. Managers can discourage the use of typical stereotypes and jokes.

Christianity

Most Americans, 77 percent, identify with Christianity—52 percent with a Protestant church and 25 percent with Catholic—and 14 percent cite no religion. Christianity is basically a historical religion, not founded so much on abstract principles as in concrete events, actual historical happenings.

From the beginning of the life and death of Jesus to 313 CE, Christianity struggled in the face of official Roman persecution. In 380 it became the official religion of the Roman Empire and continued in this capacity until 1054, when it divided into the Roman Catholic Church in what is now Western Europe and the Eastern Orthodox Church in what is now Eastern Europe. In the 16th century, following the Protestant Reformation, the Roman Catholic Church divided when the Protestant branch arose. Through the centuries, many Protestant denominations have evolved. The major differences among today's Protestants are of relatively recent origin, but the denominations now total about 33,000 located in 238 countries.

Some researchers categorize the Protestant denominations as mainline, baptist-evangelical-pentecostal, and non-trinitarian. Mainline groups, such as Methodist, historically were the largest in the United States but now represent only about 13 percent of U.S. Members tend to be politically liberal, and the churches are usually not active in political affairs. Baptist-Evangelical-Pentecostal groups represent 26 percent of U.S. adults. This has become the largest Protestant group, rapidly expanding. Baptists are the largest segment, 20 percent: adults. A central tenet is the individual's personal commitment to Christian belief, which is symbolized by baptism. Members tend to be politically conservative and active as a group. Non-Trinitarian groups, such as Mormon, Jehovah's Witness, Seventh-Day Adventist, and Church of Christ, reject the doctrine of the trinity; i.e. Father-Son-Holy Spirit as three aspects of the one God.

A familiarity with three basic Christian tenets is helpful in understanding Christians and their religion. These tenets are the incarnation of God into the human body of Jesus Christ, the trinity of God-Jesus-Holy Spirit, and the atonement or reconciliation of humans with God through belief in Jesus Christ.

Rarely do special accommodations need to be made for Christian employees because laws have traditionally made accommodation for Christianity as the most populous U.S. religion. However, some denominations observe a Saturday Sabbath, devout Catholics may observe fasting before Easter, and Eastern Orthodox members observe fasting and other Easter observances according to a different calendar.

Islam

Islam is the second largest religion in the world after Christianity—about 1.5 billion people, nearly one-fourth of the world population. About 1/2 of 1 percent of Americans are Muslim. Muslims recognize the Old and New Testaments of Judaism and Christianity but see the Quran as the completion of the Abrahamic tradition. The Quran is the center of Islamic faith and the guide for virtually every aspect of human life.

Confucianism

Globally, the Far Eastern religions are followed by at least 500 million people, about 6.5 percent of the world's people. Confucianism, originating in China, has had its impact on all the Far Eastern religions. For example, Japan, Korea, and much of Southeast Asia deliberately imported the Confucian ethic and adapted it to their local cultures Understanding some of the basics of Confucianism is helpful in understanding Asian and Asian American cultures, especially the Chinese; i.e. the 4 percent of people in the U.S. workplace who are Asian American.

Confucius is still considered one of the world's greatest teachers and in China "the first among teachers." Confucian beliefs are based upon reverence of education for a harmonious society, maintaining ideal relationships, doing what is right, becoming a mature person, and using power properly. Family comes first, older persons must be respected, and specific instructions are given for conducting important relationships, such as parent-child, husband-wife, siblings, older-younger friends, and ruler-subject.

Confucius founded a class of scholars who became China's ruling elite. It became in effect China's state religion for 2000 years, and followers were free to also follow other religions. Actually, people were generally expected to become Confucian in ethics and public life, Taoist in hygiene and private life, and Buddhist in preparing for death, along with a bit of shamanistic folk religion. When communism became the political system, religion was virtually banned and only recently has been making a comeback.

Taoism

Taoism, or "The Way," is the natural order, or the force that flows through all living things, sometimes called the c'hi or vital life energy. Tao is less a Deity than transcendent reality; however, as Taoism in China is inextricably bound up with folk traditions, there are also a variety of minor deities (such as the goddess of compassion Kwan Yin) which for Asians are generally considered to be aspects of the Tao. In the Taoist worldview, violence is abhorrent, and they dream of transcending human error and limitation. Taoists generally follow a sort of Golden Rule, but the principal Taoist ethic is "no-action," meaning to seek equilibrium and follow the natural order. Taoists value humility, naturalness, and the concept of equilibrium, meaning balance and relativity. The Taoist yin/yang symbol is central because it symbolizes the belief that all values are relative, with the two sides or aspects of each quality being in tension with the other but not totally opposed.

Taoists consider practice to be more important than creed. Although different sects do have established doctrines, none is universal. Taoists seek equilibrium above all else, and many traditional practices, such as acupuncture or other forms of "Chinese medicine" are founded on this principal. Meditation is also an important practice for many believers and helps them to attain equilibrium and maximize their vital life energy.

In China there developed three branches of Taoism, 1) philosophical Taoism, 2) Taoist hygiene and yoga, and 3) religious Taoism. All Taoist sects have the same concern—how to maximize c'hi, or life energy. This quest begins with how life's normal measure of life energy can be used in the best ways (Philosophical Taoism). It goes on to explore ways to increase that normal measure of ch'i (Taoist Hygiene and Yoga). It continues with learning how cosmic energies can be gathered into one person and beamed out to people who need help (Religious Taoism). These three types of Taoism are best viewed as currents in a river because most Taoists are involved in all three types to some extent.

Hinduism

Nearly a billion of the world's 6.5 billion people are Hindus, and most live in India. In the United States about four-tenths of 1 percent of people claim the Hindu religion. In contrast with the materialism of Judaism and Christianity, in Hinduism the world of sense experience, the material world, is regarded as illusion. The religious person seeks release from the wheel of life in order to individually fade out into the World-Soul, the Brahma. What people really want—beyond pleasure and success—is liberation from the human limits that restrict them. Hinduism recognizes that there are many paths to liberation and God, each calling for its own way of travel. Hindus believe in four paths that lead to realization of our total being and eight steps that aid in overcoming distractions and achieving wholeness.

The ancient Indian caste system became hereditary, with proscriptions against marrying or eating with someone of another caste. Higher castes came to have great privileges, benefiting at the expense of the lower. Many reformers attempted to remove the caste system, from Buddha forward. Finally because of Mahatma Gandhi's leadership, India's modern constitution bans the caste system, but cultural remnants remain.

The Hindu worldview includes the belief that the human spirit no more depends on the body it inhabits than the body depends on the clothes it wears. When souls outgrow bodies, they exchange them for roomier ones; i.e., they die and reincarnate. The self-conscious human is capable of karma or work toward spiritual growth based on the law of cause and effect. Humans have free will to make their own decisions.

Hindus believe in earth as the middle world between higher and lower worlds that some would equate with heaven and hell. They also believe in six cosmic worlds that might be translated as multiple world, moral world, middling world, tricky world, scholastic world, and world of cosmic dance.

Buddhism

About 376 million people worldwide are adherents of Buddhism, most of them in Asia. In the United States only about 1/2 of 1 percent of people claim Buddhism as their religion. However, many Americans are affected and influenced by Buddhist ideas.

Buddhists are numerous in every Asian nation except India, the land of its birth. However, Buddhism did not so much disappear from India as it was incorporated back into Hinduism. Its contributions included a renewed emphasis on compassion, non-killing of animals, breaking down of caste barriers, and a generally strong ethical emphasis. Recently, after a thousand-year absence, Buddhism is reappearing in India. In fact, the Buddhist leader, Dalai Lama, now resides in northern India, having been exiled from Tibet, the traditional home of top Buddhist leaders. His migration was due to the takeover of Tibet by China

Buddhism grew out of Hinduism, but in contrast to Hinduism's long-term development, Buddhism appeared almost instantly, fully formed. Some say it was to a great extent a reaction against Hindu perversions and corruptions. Buddha called his most considered convictions about life the Four Noble Truths: 1) life is suffering, 2) ego is the cause of suffering, 3) release from ego is the door to universal life, and 4) the eightfold path releases us from ego. This path consists of right views, right intent, right speech, right conduct, right livelihood, right effort, right mindfulness, and right concentration.

The two earliest branches of Buddhism were 1) Theravada Buddhism, which does not focus on the supernatural, metaphysics, or ritual, and 2) Mahayana Buddhism, which does focus more on those aspects. Later came Zen Buddhism in Japan, which has dramatically affected Japanese culture; for example the striking simplicity and grace in such arts as black ink landscape painting, flower arranging, garden landscaping, and the tea ceremony

CASE STUDIES

Case Study 16.1: Ali's Headscarf

In August **Alamo Rental Car** hired **Zeinab Ali** as a management trainee. While on the job, she wore her uniform and a headscarf that covered all her hair, in accordance with her Islamic religious beliefs. In December **Scott Cooper** became Ali's new supervisor. Cooper told Ali that she would have to stop wearing the headscarf or be transferred to a position in which she would not be in frequent contact with customers. Ali refused to stop wearing the headscarf, and Cooper transferred her to a back office.

Ali was upset. She talked with a friend who is a human resources expert, who told her the following: A section of Title VII makes it an unlawful employment practice for an employer to fail or refuse to hire or to discharge any individual, or otherwise to discriminate against any individual with respect to his compensation, terms, conditions, or privileges of employment, because of such individual's religion; or to limit, segregate, or classify his employees or applicants for employment in any way which would tend to deprive any individual of employment opportunities or otherwise adversely affect his status as an employee, because of such individual's religion.

1. What are the major issues (root problems) in this case?
2. If you were Scott Cooper, what would you have done?
3. If you were Ali, what would you do?
4. If Ali goes to court, what do you predict would be the outcome?

Source: www.PublicPolicy.umd.edu

Case Study 16.2: Carol's Uniform: Pants or Skirt?

Carol Grotts, a practicing Pentecostal (a Protestant denomination) was hired by **Brink's, Inc.**, the armored car company, to work as a relief messenger at its Peoria, Illinois, facility. The relief messenger is one of the uniformed employees the nationwide security firm assigns to its armored car crews. Grotts, whose religious beliefs preclude her from wearing pants, requested a modification of the standard issue uniform. She asked to wear culottes of uniform material purchased at her own expense instead of pants. Brink's management refused her request and fired her.

1. What are the key issues (root problems) in this case?

2. If you were a Brinks' manager, how would you have responded to Grotts' request?

3. If you were Carol Grotts, what would you do?

4. If Carol goes to court, what would you predict as the outcome of this case?

Source: http://www.eeoc.gov

Case Study 16.3: Keith's Saturday Sabbath

Keith Balint is a member of the Worldwide Church of God, a Protestant denomination that strictly observes the Sabbath from sundown Friday to sundown Saturday. The Church proscribes all forms of secular work during the Sabbath observance. In February Balint was offered a position in the detention section of the **Carson City, Nevada, Sheriff's Department**. When he had completed the job application form, in the section entitled "check type(s) of work you will accept," Balint checked every box, indicating that he was willing to work swing-shift, graveyard, weekends and holidays. His application does not mention any religious or other objections to certain shifts.

In mid-March, Balint completed the requisite physical, psychological and drug testing and was told to report to work for a swing shift on Friday, March 31. At that time, he informed the Department that he could not work during his Saturday Sabbath and requested that his schedule be adjusted to accommodate his religious practice, On March 22 **Lieutenant Jake Dimit**, the head of the detention department, informed him that there could be no accommodation. Balint then withdrew his application with the Department.

Carson City deputy sheriffs are scheduled by a bid system. Every six months, the twelve or thirteen deputies assigned to the jail bid for shifts in order of seniority. A deputy cannot bid for the same shift he or she is currently working. Only one deputy can get both Saturday and Sunday off in any six-month period. This system is a longstanding practice of the Department, although not the subject of any written agreement. Similarly, although deputies are permitted to trade shifts on an ad hoc basis, there is an unwritten rule prohibiting deputies from trading shifts on a regular basis.

The Department notes that the system is designed to minimize the burden of weekend work in four ways. First, those employees with the least seniority can bid for the least burdensome shifts—including the one weekday-only shift. Second, each employee is required to change shifts every six months, thus no employee has an exclusive franchise on the best shift or is eternally relegated to the worst. Third, the shifts are designed to maximize the workforce during the weekends, when the Department is busiest, while ensuring that each officer has two consecutive days off for adequate rest. Finally, the shifts are designed to give as many officers as possible at least one weekend day off. The Department views the system as a neutral way of minimizing the number of occasions when employees must work on days they would prefer to have off.

1. What are the root problems?

2. Do you think the Department's system violates Title VII banning discrimination based on religion and requiring reasonable accommodation?

3. If you were Jake Dimit, what would you have done?

4. If you were Balint, what action if any would you take?

5. If Balint goes to court, what do you predict the outcome would be?

See http://jlaw.com/Briefs/Balint.html and http://caselaw.lp.findlaw.com

REFERENCES

Abe, Masao. *Zen and Western Thought.* University of Hawaii Press 1985.

Ahlstrom, Sidney. *Religious History of the American People.* Yale University Press 1972.

Ali, Ayaan Hirsi. *The Caged Virgin*. Free Press, 2008.

AP, "Muslim Women Protest Outside Dutch Parliament Against Burqa Ban. *International Herald Tribune*, November 30, 2006.

AP, *Associated Press*, "A Look at the Wearing of Veils, and Disputes on the Issue Across the Muslim World," October 31, 2006.

Arberry, A.J. *The Koran Interpreted: A Translation*. Macmillan, 1955.

ARIS, *American Religious Identification Survey*, Ariela Keysar, A. Barray A. Kosmin, Egon Mayer. *http://www.gc.cuny.edu/faculty/research_briefs/aris/aris_index.htm*. 1990, 2001.

Bainton, Roland. *Christianity*. American Heritage, 1986.

Bayly, Susan. *Caste, Society and Politics in India from the Eighteenth Century to the Modern Age*. Cambridge University Press, 1999.

BBC News, "'Remove Full Veils,' Urges Straw," October 6, 2006.

Borg, Marcus. *Jesus: A New Vision*. Harper & Row, 1988.

Chan, Wing-tsit, trans. *The Way of Lao Tzu*. Bobbs-Merrill Co., 1963.

Coleman, Isobel, "Women—A Moderating Influence on Islamic Fundamentalism," *The Printceton Independent*, February 2003.

Conze, Edward. *A Short History of Buddhism*. Bombay: Chetana, 1960.

Conze, Edward. *Buddhism: Its Essence and Development*. Harper & Brothers, 1959.

Cragg, Kenneth. *The House of Islam*. Wadsworth, 1975.

Crosson, John Dominic. *The Historical Jesus: The Life of a Mediterranean Jewish Peasant*. Harper, 1991.

Daily Mail, "Pope Insists on 'right and duty' of Catholic Church to Spread Its Message to Non-Believers," December 14, 2007.

Danner, Victor. *The Islamic Tradition*. Amity House, 1988.

Ellis, Joseph. *Founding Brothers: The Revolutionary Generation*. Knopf, 2002, Pulitzer Prize.

Falcon, Ted and David Blatner. *Judaism for Dummies*. For Dummies, 2001.

Gabriel, Mark A. *Culture Clash: Islam's War on the West*. Charisma House, 2007.

Gaustad, S. *Faith of Our Fathers: Religion and the New Nation*. Harper & Row, 1987.

Gerges, Fawaz A. *America and Political Islam: Clash of Cultures or Clash of Interests?* Cambridge University Press, 1999.

Guidelines on Religious Exercise and Religious Expression in the Federal Workplace at *www.whitehouse.gov*, 1997.

Heschel, Abraham J. *God in Search of Man: A Philosophy of Judaism*. Farrar, Straus and Giroux, 1976.

Ho, Stephani, "China Calls Dalai Lama 'Political Exile,'" *News.com* March13, 2009.

Hopkins, Thomas J. *The Hindu Religious Tradition*. Dickenson Publishing Co. 1971.

Humphreys, Christmas. *Buddhism*. Harmondsworth, England: Pelican Books, 1951.

Iqbal, Sir Muhammad. *The Secrets of the Self*. Lahore, India: Muhammad Ashraf, 1920, reprint 1979.

Ivengar, B.K.S. *Light on Yoga*. Reprint. Schocken Books, 1979.

Jaffrelot, Chrisophe. *Dr. Ambedkar and Untouchability: Fighting the Indian Caste System*. Columbia University Press, 2004.

Jayaran, V. "History, Antiquity, and Chronology of Hinduism," *www.HinduWebsite.com* (2008).

John Bowker, John, ed., "Festivals," *Oxford Concise Dictionary of World Religions*. Oxford University Publishing, 2000.

Judaism 101, *www.jewfaq.org*.

Klausner, Joseph. *The Messianic Idea in Israel*. Macmillan, 1955.

Klostermaier, Klaus K. *A Survey of Hinduism*. State University of New York Press, 1989.

Knipe, David M. *Hinduism: Experiments in the Sacred*. HarperSanFrancisco, 1991.

Kohn, Livia, ed. *Taoist Meditation and Longevity Techniques.* University of Michigan, 1989.

Lambert, Frank. *The Founding Fathers and the Place of Religion in America.* Princeton University Press, 2003.

Levenson, Joseph R. *Confucian China and Its Modern Fate: A Trilogy.* Berkeley: University of California Press, 1968.

Lings, M. *Muhammad: His Life Based on the Earliest Sources.* London: Islamic Text Society, Allen & Unwin, 1988.

Lynem, Julie N, reporting on 2002 survey by Society for Human Resource Management, *San Francisco Chronicle*, J-12, December 9, 2002.

Manger, Leif. *Muslim Diversity: Local Islam in Global Contexts.* RoutledgeCurzon, 1999.

McBrien, Richard P. *Catholicism: New Study Edition.* Harper One, 1994.

Metzger, Thomas. *Escape from Predicament: Neo-Confucianism and China's Evolving Political Culture.* Columbia University Press, 1977.

Molin, Chiang. *Tides from the West.* Yale University Press, 1947.

Murata, S. *The Tao of Islam.* State University of New York Press, 1992.

Murphy, Don. "Anabaptists Today," *www.anabaptistchurch.org*, 2008

Nast, S.H. *Ideals and Realities of Islam.* London: Allen & Unwin, 1966.

Overmyer, Daniel. *Religions of China.* Harper & Row 1986.

Pelosi, Alexandra, *Friends of God*, HBO-TV, November 2006.

Pew. *U.S. Religious Landscape Survey.* The Pew Forum on Religion and Public Life, *www.PewForum.org*, 2007.

Protestantism, *en.wikipedia.org*, 2008.

Rahadkrishnan, S. *The Hindu View of Life.* Macmillan, 1927.

Rich, Tracey R. *Judaism 101*, *www.jewfaq.org*, 2008.

Rossel, Seymour, *Basic Judaism*, *www.rossel.net*, 2001.

Said, E. *Covering Islam: How the Media and the Experts Determine How We See the Rest of the World.* Vintage, 1997.

Saso, Michael. *The Teachings of Taoist Master Chuang.* Yale University Press, 1978.

Schillebeeck, E. *Jesus.* Crossroad, 1981.

Schmidt, Garbi. *Islam in Urban America: Sunni Muslims in Chicago.* Temple University Press, 2004.

Schwartz, Benjamin I. *The World of Thought in Ancient China.* Harvard University Press, 1985.

Seltzer, Robert. *Jewish People, Jewish Thought: The Jewish Experience in History.* Macmillan and Collier, 1980.

Sharansky, Natan. *The Case for Democracy.* PublicAffairs, Perseus Books Group, 2004.

Shepard, W.E., "Islam and Ideology: Towards a Typology," *International Journal of Middle East Studies*, 19, 3, 307–26, 1987.

Siegel, Richard et al. *The Jewish Catalog.* Jewish Publication Society, 1975.

Singer, Jeffrey A. "Making Sense of Jewish Stereotypes," *Future of Freedom Foundation, fff.org*, April 2000.

Smith, Huston. *The World's Religions: Our Great Wisdom Traditions.* HarperSanFrancico, 1998.

Sowell, Thomas. *Ethnic America: A History.* Basic Books, 1981.

Sri Rahula, Walpola. *What the Buddha Taught*, rev. ed. Grove Press 1974.

Teaching About Religion with a View to Diversity. *www.teachingaboutreligion.org*, 2005.

Thomas, E.J. *The Life of Buddha as Legend and History.* London: Routledge & Kegan Paul, 1949.

Thomas, E.J., *Early Buddhist Scriptures.* Translation of Majhima Nikaya, Sutta 63. AMS Press, 1935.

U.S. Census reports *www.census.gov.*

UN, "Arab Human Development Report," United National Development Program, July 2, 2002.

Waley, Arthur. *The Way and Its Power.* Reprint, Grove Press, 1958.

Wolff, Edward, "The Wealth Divide: The Growing Gap in the United States between the Rich and the Rest," *Multinational Monitor* 24, 5, May 2003.

Wong, Edward, "Dalai Lama Says China Has Turned Tibet Into a 'Hell on Earth,'" *NYTimes.com*, March 10, 2009.

Woodward, F.L. *Some Sayings of the Buddha*. London: Gordon Press, 1939.

Zimmer, Heinrich. *The Philosophies of India*. Princeton University Press, 1969.

CHAPTER 17

Managing Diversity: Inclusive Corporate Cultures

A diverse company is better able to sell to a diverse world.
Microsoft executive

What does it take for you to fully commit to the mission and goals of an organization? What do you need in order to think of the organization as "my organization, one that I'll work hard for?" Don't you need to feel that what the organization stands for—its ethos and values—are basically in sync with your own? Don't you need to feel included as one of the people who count? And don't you need to believe that you're able to "go somewhere" in this organization—and get much of what you want from your worklife? This is true for all employees. And it means that successful corporate cultures must be broad enough, deep enough, and flexible enough to encompass the cultures of all the major groups that are part of the organization.

The best approach to managing diversity is one that includes all persons and excludes none. It provides a climate that supports all types of employees. Its goal is to include everyone in the inner circle of employees who are continuously learning to create continuous improvement—in activities that contribute to the bottom-line success of the organization.

While leaders of some companies still refer to their corporate culture as a melting pot and the company as one big happy family, a new breed of leaders is moving beyond the melting pot and legal approaches to an inclusive multicultural approach. This approach builds on the best affirmative action principles and a strong corporate culture, but it goes further. Its leaders value diversity. Just as important, they consciously improve the corporate culture by making it more multicultural and inclusive. Then they develop corporate strategies, systems, and action steps that reflect that core value. These leaders are change agents who learn how to inspire others to create the changes needed to build a productive, innovative, synergistic workforce.

Before you delve into the details of this inclusive approach to managing diversity, test your knowledge by completing Self-Awareness Activity 17.1.

Self-Awareness Activity 17.1:
What Do You Know about Managing Diversity?

Purpose: To see what you know about the issues covered in this chapter.

Instructions: Determine whether you think the following statements are basically true or false—and think about why. The answers will emerge in this chapter, and the summary at the end of the chapter focuses on these issues.

1. An inclusive multicultural approach to managing diversity focuses on minorities.

2. The most basic change that must take place in the organization is modifying its systems and practices to accommodate diverse employees.

3. Valuing diversity goes beyond tolerance to appreciation for all types of people.

4. The focus of employee training in the multicultural approach is on new minority employees learning about the corporate culture.

5. This inclusive approach builds upon equal opportunity principles and the current affirmative action program.

6. A key strategy for making this inclusive approach work is getting to know each individual employee.

7. The key to bringing about change is for top management to make a commitment.

Managing diversity is all about recognizing and responding effectively to the leadership challenges and opportunities you encounter in the workplace, such as the following:

- Meeting specific needs of all employees in your diverse workplace
- Creating an inclusive multicultural approach to managing diversity
- Creating an inclusive organization culture
- Including all employees in bottom-line efforts

LEADERSHIP CHALLENGES: MEET ALL EMPLOYEES' NEEDS

Your greatest diversity challenge as a leader in today's workplace is meeting the needs of all employees—people from all the diverse groups, including Euro-American men. You must understand the many barriers facing ethnic minorities and women in most American corporations and develop strategies for dismantling them. The most important barrier is the incompatible corporate culture and the resulting systems and practices that tend to exclude "minorities." Successful change requires that the dominant group, Euro-American men, buy into changes in the corporate culture and any new management approach. Specific barriers include networking barriers, conflict among subcultural groups, poor career development patterns, and the glass ceiling.

Challenge #1: Change an Incompatible Corporate Culture

The corporate culture is the heart and soul of the organization. The basic beliefs and values of the culture determine all other aspects, such as policies, systems, procedures, programs, and practices. To many diverse employees, the corporate culture seems unfriendly and stressful, often resulting in loneliness. At higher levels minorities, women, and employees from other diverse groups may be dramatically outnumbered by Euro-American men who treat them "differently," exclude them from social events and friendly camaraderie, and may view them as a curiosity. These newcomers sometimes report that the "insiders" watch them closely, over-scrutinize their work for mistakes, withhold information, and even sabotage their work. They say they must be better than the others just to keep up. They say that when they cluster with others from their own diversity group, they may be jokingly or seriously accused of plotting against the dominant group, being divisive, or excluding others. If they remain isolated, they may be seen as arrogant or resentful. If they try to join the insiders, they may be met with stereotyping or some degree of rejection. We'll discuss this basic aspect of managing diversity in more detail later.

Challenge #2: Restructure Unsuitable Organizational Systems

The most lasting and workable changes in the firm's systems and practices flow naturally from a commitment to corporate culture change. One reason AA programs have had such difficulty is that leaders rarely built them upon a commitment to corporate culture change. Once this commitment is made by a critical mass of employees, changing the systems and practices becomes relatively easy. Specific suggestions are discussed later in this chapter.

Challenge #3: End Historical Exclusion

Nontraditional employees have traditionally been kept out of the inner circle. The American culture has traditionally sent the message that Euro-American men take the lead role in all arenas of power. Studies indicate that a key barrier is their reluctance to share power and privilege and their natural tendency to associate with people like themselves (Carr-Ruffino 1991). Savvy leaders know it's time to break this cycle by giving everyone an equal chance.

Challenge #4: Raise the Comfort Levels of Euro-American Men

An effective multicultural approach respects the concerns of all, including Euro-American men. It focuses on the leadership benefits of gaining multicultural skills in order to meet diverse employees halfway in cultural understanding and collaboration. Diversity training is essential.

Resistance to change results in backlash, as we discussed in chapter 1 concerning affirmative action. In fact, backlash has become so prevalent that it now is the primary barrier to the diversity efforts of many major companies. When downsizing cuts job opportunities, people become especially resentful and fearful and more likely to resent any competition from diverse employees.

People tend to be most accepting and comfortable with others who are most like them. Virtually all the emotions that block goodwill toward others spring from fear, and fear in turn often springs from the unknown, from ignorance. Studying cultural differences makes people knowledgeable, diminishes their fear of the unknown, and increases their comfort level with diverse others. Learning about stereotypes and prejudice can help also, but the instructional approach must be respectful, not blaming. It must address such concerns as reverse discrimination, lowered standards and quality, erosion of income and job security, and loss of a traditional way of life.

Challenge #5: Remove Networking Barriers

For all nontraditional groups a major barrier is inability to create and manage networks. Individuals often can't get the information they need about industry trends and where the company is headed, nor handle company politics adequately. Understanding the organizational culture and the barriers it may have erected can be even more important than formal degrees, according to several surveys. In fact, courses and degrees may be less relevant to success in the executive suite than they once were because most omit these soft skills (Cox 1993; Carr-Ruffino 1991).

Challenge #6: Minimize Conflict among Subcultural Groups

When one underrepresented group competes with another for privileges, status, and power, infighting can occur and create a barrier for all. Managers have been known to use divide-and-conquer tactics to increase friction and infighting among diverse subgroups. The dramatic increase in hate crimes, at record levels now, indicates that backlash and infighting are problems in society at large, not just in organizations. The growing diversity in the population has increased interethnic tension. You can learn to apply the people skills you've learned here and elsewhere.

You can help to establish policies and practices that will minimize conflict. And you can lead conflict resolution efforts that bring seething problems out into the open and resolve them in ways that all can live with.

Challenge #7: Turn Around Poor Career Development Patterns

Euro-American men are often reluctant to assign nontraditional managers to those challenging, high-profile jobs that are needed to prepare people for senior management positions. They don't want people to fail, and they want the company to look good. Such assignments include leading a major start-up, troubleshooting (sometimes overseas,) serving on important task forces, taking a headquarters staff job, and taking line jobs of increasing responsibility. They involve autonomy, visibility, access to senior management, and control over significant resources. They are considered the fast track in many organizations and may be used as tests and rewards for high-potential candidates. Such career-enhancing assignments are often not available to diverse employees, who tend to be found in staff rather than line positions (Kotter 1990; U.S. Department of Labor 1991; Catalyst 1990; DiTomaso, Thompson, and Blake 1988).

You can use your influence and take the lead in showing confidence in the potential of diverse employee to handle such challenging assignments. Be willing to give those who are ready a chance, to support them every step of the way, and to give credit for their successes, achievements, and contributions.

Challenge #8: Break the Glass Ceiling

The U.S. Department of Labor reports that 30 percent of corporate middle management is made up of women, African Americans, and Latino Americans. These groups make up less than 5 percent of senior management, even though they're about 65 percent of the workforce. A major consulting firm surveyed nearly 1400 senior executives, and only 29 were women and 13 were people of color, meaning 97 percent were Euro-American males (U.S. Department of Labor 1991; Korn/Ferry 1999).

Universities such as Harvard, Yale, and Princeton, which are typically considered feeder institutions for high-paying management jobs, refused to admit women as undergraduates until the 1970s. Lack of education became a widely accepted explanation for the slow movement of nontraditional employees into and through management. It's still used today despite the fact that their educational achievement has soared. It's been over 40 years since the passage of the 1964 Civil Rights Act. It's been over 30 years since women and minorities entered leadership-oriented programs in significant numbers. Even if it takes 15 or 20 years to develop a general manager, more minorities and women should logically be reaching the middle- and top-level jobs. Clearly, lack of qualified candidates is not the only explanation for under-representation.

On the bright side, 1999 was a breakthrough year for women and African Americans—symbolically, at least. A woman and an African American man became the first to work their way up through the ranks and become CEO of a large corporation. Carly Fiorina of Hewlett-Packard (Fortune 100) and Lloyd Ward of Maytag (Fortune 1000).

LEADERSHIP OPPORTUNITIES

Leadership Opportunities for successfully managing a diverse workplace are all based on creating an inclusive organizational culture. The beliefs and values of an organization form its worldview and its mission in the world. These are the heart and soul of any organization. That's why change must start here. Organizations that ignore these basics—and start the change process with new programs or practices or even policies—cannot achieve optimal results. Real, sustainable change must come from the heart.

Once an inclusive corporate culture is underway, then a multicultural approach to business and to management can naturally evolve. These changes should build upon solid equal opportunity principles, not replace them. Then the company is ready to modify corporate systems and practices so they align with a multicultural approach. Systems should include all employees in bottom-line corporate efforts. Throughout all this change process, leaders must build consensus for change among all the employees.

The multicultural approach enhances success in virtually every area, including conflict resolution, negotiation, employee relationships, employee empowerment, leadership effectiveness, continuous learning, continuous improvement, innovation, productivity, total quality management, synergistic teams, and trust building. Given the potential payoffs, companies can't afford to be satisfied with outdated corporate cultures that exclude many potential contributors.

LEADERSHIP OPPORTUNITY #1: CREATE AN INCLUSIVE CULTURE

The beliefs and values at the heart of a culture are the place where any lasting change must start. Changing the corporate culture is most effective, of course, when top management makes a commitment to shifting the culture in ways that accommodate, motivate, and empower all employees. The ultimate goal is for everyone to grow and develop, to be effective and productive, to interact to create a synergy that sparks innovation and commitment. But any person anywhere in the organization can have an influence toward change. Wherever you are on your career path, you can accept a leadership role in this kind of change. The most powerful change starts in the basic cultural elements:

- *Beliefs* that form a worldview, beliefs about why the organization exists, what it primarily needs to do, who is included and recognized, how they are rewarded, etc.
- *Values* that are based on the beliefs, that build respect for all kinds of persons, and that build trust—a high value for diversity
- *Heroines and heroes*, role models of success from all the diverse groups
- *Stories*, myths, and legends about diverse heroes and heroines and new ways of succeeding in an inclusive organization
- *Rituals*, ways of doing things and ways of interacting with each other, that expand to include the ways typical of all groups
- *Ceremonies* that are meaningful to people of all groups, that incorporate the customs of all groups, that recognize people from all groups
- *Symbols* and slogans that touch people from all groups and that communicate an inclusive worldview.

Culture change is the basis for all other organizational change. Lasting change must come from inside the organization—and from the foundation of core beliefs and values. Role modeling and persuasion are the best methods of leading change, while coercion doesn't really work at all. When key leaders in all areas and at all levels become committed to change, this critical mass will bring along most other employees in its wake.

An inclusive culture gives people from all groups the freedom to be authentic, to express who they really are. It allows people from "minority" groups to adopt certain aspects of the dominant culture as appropriate and still retain those aspects of their own cultural identity as they see fit. It requires leaders who adopt traits necessary to function in a multicultural environment, and it requires appropriate diversity training for employees at all levels, from all groups.

Freedom to Be Authentic

The most effective organizational cultures allow people to retain key aspects of their cultural identity. Every person and every human culture needs to express who they are. The strong desire of many former communist countries and ethnic groups to claim a separate culture reflects this universal need. When groups unite to achieve certain common purposes, they can greatly increase their power. But when they can't find ways to accommodate cultural differences and blend them into a group strength, they lose their joint power. At the corporate level such groups may simply lose the opportunity to achieve greater goals, but at the societal level, they may deteriorate into anarchy and bloodshed, as happened in the Los Angeles riots and in Bosnia.

Whether in a national culture or a corporate culture, people are more productive and enthusiastic when they have the freedom to express their own values and determine their own lifestyle. The most effective organizations learn how to combine and balance the drive for individual freedom and achievement with the drive for belongingness and group affiliation. And they focus on building and maintaining trust, the essential ingredient.

Beyond the Melting Pot: Free Choice and Cultural Enrichment

Successful organizations allow minority members a great deal of freedom in their acculturation process. They can adopt new ways to succeed and still retain their essential cultural identity.

The most positively powerful aspects of American socio-economic acculturation patterns have been described by Nathan Glazer (1970) and Stephen Burman (1995) as our willingness to informally recognize that diverse members have a desire and a right to self-development, acculturation, or integration at their own chosen rate. Diverse groups have a right to an integrated or independent economic base; to social, religious and political institutions; and to political recognition as part of a united country. This has been the American genius for embracing diversity within a common unity.

Enduring Cultural Values

Creating an inclusive corporate culture means dealing with these cultural realities. The evidence on acculturation patterns among Asians and Latinos in the United States indicates that substantial identity with the root national cultures remains even after three or more generations of citizenship. The least effective policy an organization can pursue is to insist that members of any group give up cherished beliefs and practices. People always resist such pressure—usually by going underground and then engaging in passive aggressive behavior. Of course covert behavior is much more difficult to deal with than open, direct behavior (Deshpande et al 1986; Allport 1954).

Two-Way Accommodation

Since cultural accommodation is a two-way street, the process is subtle and complex and trying to force it on any of the parties may create as many problems as it solves. The best approach is to allow people the freedom to assimilate into the mainstream culture and the corporate culture to the extent they desire and to retain their cultural heritage as they see fit. This approach must rest on appreciating differences and respecting each person's cultural heritage and their decisions about what to retain. Cultural change takes time, and a relaxed, accepting attitude allows the shifts to occur with minimal friction.

When ethnic groups retain those distinctive and colorful ways that they treasure, the organization is enriched. Each individual decides those aspects of their ethnic cuisine, art, the philosophical and spiritual beliefs, myths and stories that they want to hold dear and to express. When people are allowed and encouraged to preserve these treasures, they become more interesting and valuable to the whole organization and to the nation. They "prevent drab standardization in a culture dominated by advertising, brand names, malls, and sedative television" (Cox 1993, p. 84).

Leadership Traits

Leaders in a multicultural workplace must demonstrate certain traits. Unlike people who stereotype, leaders who value differences tend to:

- base beliefs about characteristics of culture groups on a systematic study of reliable sources of data

- acknowledge that people within an ethnic group vary and that they have many voices and many individual styles and patterns
- resist the tendency to evaluate differences as inherently good or bad
- accept difference as interesting and potentially valuable
- avoid negative connotations

A multicultural approach enhances acceptance, tolerance, and understanding of differences.

Education for All

The inclusive multicultural approach is a relatively new concept for many employees. Training is normally needed at all levels of the organization for positive change to occur. Training usually begins at the top, since top management must thoroughly understand the concept and apply it consistently in their own thinking and acting. Training sessions tend to focus on the ways that people are both alike and different in values, attitudes, behavior styles, ways of thinking, and cultural background. Common goals of the educational programs are for participants to:

- expand their awareness and acceptance of cultural and individual commonalities and differences
- understand the nature and dynamics of cultural and individual differences
- explore their own feelings and attitudes about people they view as "different"
- identify ways that differences might be tapped as workplace assets
- build better work relations with people from all societal groups

This approach leads people to appreciate the value, richness, and creativity that can flow from a diverse workforce. It focuses on helping everyone to better understand some key commonalities and differences among employees from various groups and how differences can be valuable to the organization. It exhibits real concern and commitment to providing a corporate culture where people from all groups can thrive. When employees thrive, the company tends to thrive, as Microsoft has shown.

SHOWCASE: MICROSOFT
A VALUING DIVERSITY CULTURE

Microsoft focuses on valuing diversity and creating a corporate culture that reflects that value. This view has been productive and profitable for the firm, which grew from a start-up to the largest software firm in the world in a few short years. Microsoft has a diversity program that is proactive. Program leaders want to know when people feel unwelcome at work, when they're worried about things outside of work, or anything else that could stand in the way of top performance. A diversity staff implements diversity training programs, updates benefits policies, and investigates cases of discrimination and harassment.

The company's Diversity Advisory Council includes representatives from employee groups of gay persons, women, persons with disabilities, Jewish Americans, African Americans, Latino Americans, American Indians, and Asian Indian Americans, and it expands as new groups form. The council helps formulate policy, identify problems, and create the best possible working environment for all employees. Microsoft's diversity manager says the council helps to boost productivity and to stem turnover, adding millions to company profits.

Microsoft's management also understands that it takes more than a nondiscrimination clause and diversity groups to achieve a supportive environment for all groups. Some people are intolerant, and the company needs specific training programs to help people become more aware of the nature of prejudice, the facts about various groups, and of alternative ways of believing and interacting.

Microsoft wants to tap into the different needs and backgrounds of employees to use their talents, to use the various perspectives they bring, based on who they are. For example, a Microsoft marketing goal is to put a computer on every desk in every home. To do that, the company needs to know who these consumers are and what they're like. The philosophy:

We must make our products accessible to all types of consumers, and therefore we must market them differently to each group. A diverse company is better able to sell to a diverse world.

LEADERSHIP OPPORTUNITY #2: ADOPT AN INCLUSIVE MULTICULTURAL APPROACH

Once an organization has assessed its culture, determined needed changes, and started the change process, it is ready to adopt an inclusive multicultural approach to business. The inclusive approach is a diversity-within-unity approach, as indicated in Figure 17.1. Unity is provided through a strong corporate culture that focuses on the best niche for the organization to fill and on the purpose of the

TABLE 17.1: Manage Inclusion at All Levels

Barriers to Inclusion	Inclusive Strategies
Personal Level	
Stereotypes, prejudices	Become aware of prejudice and other barriers to valuing diversity
Past experiences and influences	
Stereotyped expectations and perceptions	Learn about other cultures and groups.
Feelings that tend to separate, divide	Serve as an example, walk the talk
	Participate in managing diversity
Interpersonal Level	
Cultural differences	Facilitate communication and interactions in ways that value diversity
Group differences	
Myths	Encourage participation
Relationship patterns based on exclusion	Share your perspective
	Facilitate unique contributions
	Resolve conflicts in ways that value diversity
	Accept responsibility for developing common ground
Organizational Level	
Individuals who get away with discriminating and excluding	All employees take a proactive role in managing diversity and creating a more diverse workplace culture
A culture that values or allows exclusion	All employees are included in the Inner Circle that contributes to the bottom-line success of the company
Work structures, policies, and practices that discriminate and exclude	All employees give feedback to teams and management
	All employees are encouraged to contribute to change
	All employees have access to networks and focus groups

Figure 17.1: Diverse Groups within a Strong Corporate Culture: Diversity within Unity

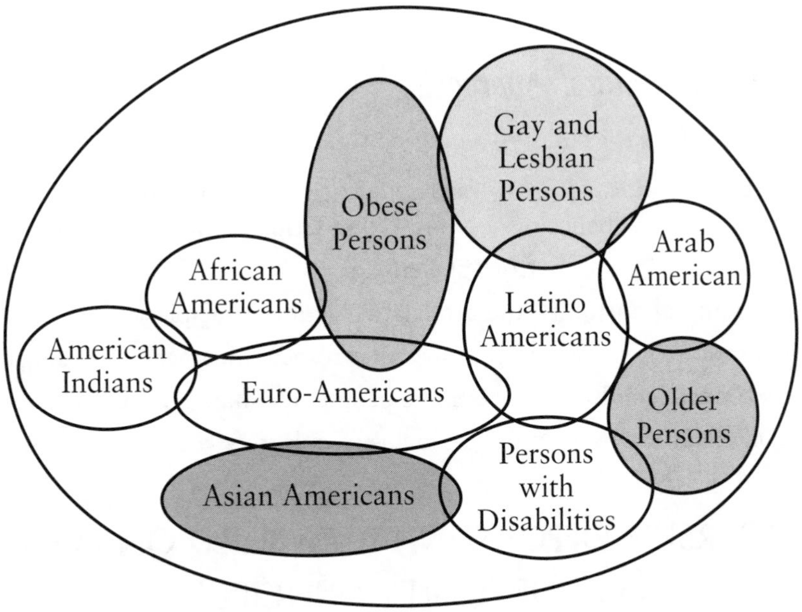

organization, as well as on valuing diversity. And diversity is provided for through a strong emphasis on appreciating each individual—respecting the uniqueness of every employee, including values, lifestyles, and cultural heritage. Above all, the multicultural approach is an inclusive approach. No one is excluded simply because he or she was not born a member of the ingroup—or has changed physically in ways that don't affect basic job performance.

Leaders encourage the organization to adapt in ways that support all types of employees, and they help all employees become oriented to the organization, a two-way street. Corporate leaders make certain the organization's values and norms accommodate a wide range of workers. They make sure that everyone has a chance to build multicultural skills and to update and refine them continually.

Include and Empower All Employees

This inclusive approach aims to support and empower all employees in learning, stretching, and moving up because leaders pay attention to this issue at the individual, interpersonal, and organizational levels. Leaders develop strategies to bring all employees into the "Inner Circle" and remove barriers to inclusion, as shown in Table 17.1. The multicultural approach is also about making sure that the systems and practices of the organization support employee empowerment, through natural evolvement so that stop-and-go types of AA programs are unnecessary. It's a comprehensive managerial process for developing an environment that works for all employees. Empowering the total workforce is achieved through such strategies as pushing decision making down to lower levels, organizing self-managing work teams, providing adequate education, and supporting career development.

This type of diversity management is not about Euro-American males managing women and minorities, nor is it about focusing on women and minorities to the exclusion of Euro-American men. It's about all managers empowering whomever is in their workforce. This inclusive approach focuses on understanding individuals and valuing the cultural background they came from. It's about respecting that heritage without assuming that a particular individual adheres to all aspects of the heritage. It's about asking questions in a sensitive, respectful manner based on your expanded knowledge and awareness of cultural differences. This approach views diverse employees as persons who can enrich the work team or organization, who can interact with others to create innovative sparks, entrepreneurial genius, and total-quality performance. It is symbolized in Figure 17.1.

Key Aspects of a Multicultural Approach

The most important activities for building a multicultural approach are:

- Modify the corporate culture toward a multi-culture that incorporates the values and customs of all the subcultures: essential foundation for all other changes.
- Include all employees in bottom-line efforts
- Build on equal opportunity and affirmative action principles
- Adapt corporate systems and practices that respect members of all subcultures
- Address concerns and resistances some people may have to this inclusive approach
- Build consensus for changing to an inclusive culture

LEADERSHIP OPPORTUNITY #3: BUILD ON EQUAL OPPORTUNITY PRINCIPLES

Now the organization is on the path of adopting a multicultural approach to business. While a multicultural approach goes beyond affirmative action programs, it does not ignore equal opportunity principles or abandon AA programs. It does build on lessons business leaders have learned about how to make AA work most effectively for all groups.

What are the most common diversity practices found in U.S. firms? Research indicates the following (Kravitz 2007):

- 63% Affirmative Action program
- 40% Diversity training
- 20% Diversity Committee
- 20% Networking program
- 20% Diversity evaluations (audits)

Consider establishing and implement these types of programs, beginning with the most important, the AA program.

Revitalize the Affirmative Action Program

The first step toward a multicultural approach is to review the company's AA program to see if it needs revitalizing. Is it comprehensive enough? Does it have widespread support among the workforce, or does it cause conflict and resentment? Is it being energetically implemented? Are all its elements up to par?

Gain Widespread Support

An effective AA program is one that has widespread support of the employees. Here are some suggestions for gaining support, based on research (Harrison 2006)

- Emphasize the opportunities that AA has provided to all workplace groups—opportunities to create a multicultural workforce, to expand the range of business skills and styles that diverse employees contribute to the organization, and to connect with a diverse marketplace.

- Explain the details of the AA program in terms of the opportunities. If the program is not adequately explained, people tend to jump to their own conclusions about it.
- Avoid the term "preferences," which some people interpret as "quota-like."
- Emphasize that the program is designed to promote the hiring, training, and promoting of qualified minority persons, especially those who have been discriminated against in the past.
- Avoid the term "under-represented groups," and prefer the concept of ending discrimination.

Emphasizing the fairness and opportunity aspects of AA is the key to gaining support for the program and minimizing conflict.

Ensure Implementation

On the other hand, leaders must communicate that the program is to be respected by everyone. Violation of AA policy should be treated as seriously as violation of other important corporate policies. Senior management needs to regularly monitor the organization to be sure diversity goals are being met. Employment data should be organized by gender and ethnic group status. It should show minority groups and women as a percentage of

- total employees in each job category
- total management pool
- each level of management

The organization's grievance process for handling individual cases of discrimination should be reviewed to make sure it's fair, effective, and credible. Management needs to systematically review grievance files to detect patterns of mistreatment or discrimination.

Every aspect of an employee's career path is affected by company policies and practices regarding equal opportunity and affirmative action. In chapter 5 we discussed some of the leadership challenges for eliminating discrimination from these practices. The following checklist can guide your efforts toward revitalizing your company's practices.

Recruiting

Focus on two key principles: (1) Go where diverse employees are to recruit applicants for all types and levels of jobs. (2) Make sure that word-of-mouth recruitment reaches all types of potential applicants. In order to find diverse applicants, do the following:

- Go to universities that have large numbers of minority students. Contact all types of minority student organizations, give them job postings, go to their job fairs, speak at their meetings.
- Get lists of various types of minority organizations—community, social, professional, business, etc. Make regular and systematic contact with the formal and informal leaders of these organizations.
- Ask qualified persons from minority groups to apply for open positions. As long as a 1992 ruling of the federal Sixth Circuit Court holds up, this is legal if it helps the firm to recruit minorities as a part of an effort to fairly balance their workforce. It's still illegal to take the next step and offer a job at that point (*HRM Ideas* 1992).
- Encourage your own minority employees to spread the word among their friends, family, and other contacts. Reward them for helping to recruit minority employees.
- Identify and solve applicants' transportation problems, where appropriate.

Screening

Be sure that all job criteria—such as experience, degrees, and certificates—are really good predictors of job success and don't unreasonably exclude certain groups whose members could succeed. Be sure all tests and exams are valid. Be sure that such barriers as arrest records, poor credit records, or subjective evaluations by prejudiced individuals do not unfairly discriminate against certain minorities.

Unbiased Pay, Staffing, and Evaluations

As people are hired and oriented, check the following guidelines:

- Set goals to achieve equitable salaries and perquisites across all cultural groups. Eliminate practices that lead to lower salaries and perquisites for some groups.

- Set goals to acquire a reasonably balanced staff in all corporate areas and at all levels, to eliminate "pink ghettoes," "gay ghettos," "minority jobs," etc.

- Find ways to eliminate performance evaluation that is colored by bias, stereotyping, or prejudice. For example, have a diverse panel of employees or managers perform important performance evaluations, especially those that affect promotions.

Training and Promoting

Avoid segregation by department. Be sure that minorities are not disproportionately clustered in certain departments with limited opportunities for interaction with Euro-American majority members. Occupational segregation does not enhance supportive relationships among employees (Dovidio 2003).

Monitor and track all employees' career paths and progress toward achieving their career goals. A diverse panel should make decisions about who will be offered training and development opportunities, especially those opportunities designed to prepare people for promotion.

A panel of diverse employees is more likely to make unbiased promotion decisions than is a homogeneous panel or an individual decision maker. Publicize the criteria for promotion, demystify the process. When everyone understands what it takes, those working toward promotion can better focus their attention and energy.

Dismissing

Laying off and firing are the most difficult aspects of dealing with employees. The difficult goal is to find procedures that don't unfairly discriminate against minorities who were unable to get better jobs until recently and therefore have little seniority, older workers who have been loyal to the company and have seniority, or any other group.

Learn from Past Lessons

Among the contributions AA has made to the workplace are the lessons it has taught us about what does and doesn't work in managing diversity. Even though it's important to consider common issues, patterns, and themes of each subcultural group, it's also important to deal with each person as an individual. Everything leaders do should encourage the minority person to take an achieving, team-oriented outlook, never a victim mentality.

Set High but Realistic AA Goals

Aim to move the organization steadily forward toward a workforce that is diverse at all levels. Progress in revitalizing AA is slow and incremental. Neither managers nor employees should expect a quick fix. Most AA programs have to be refined and refined, and some may be judged unsuccessful and terminated.

Identify Real Job Requirements and Standards.

Reexamine job standards but keep them high. Ensure that hiring and performance standards are as clear and job-related as possible. They must be common across groups to be perceived as fair. Instead of basing job requirements and standards on management's preferences, conveniences, or traditions, base them on specific needs for results.

Creating a diverse workforce is about enhancing the organization's capability to tap the potential of a diverse group of employees. Set the right goals for the AA program, and keep asking whether all systems and practices are helping to achieve those goals.

Management should test the assumptions underlying personnel policies and be able to support the claims they make about the effects of systems and programs.

Encourage an Achiever Self-Concept

Help diverse employees see themselves as achievers, rather than as victims. Every U.S. group, except for Euro-American men, has been disadvantaged in the workplace by stereotypes, prejudice, and discrimination. In that sense they have been and still are victims of the system, but the victim argument produces negative side effects. Victims must have persecutors, which implies that Euro-American men are collectively guilty of oppression. Resentment grows as victim and oppressor accuse each other of injustice in the pursuit of self-interest. Relying on the status of victim to obtain rights or favors is demeaning and self-destructive to the victims because it focuses on what they don't have instead of building on what they can and do have.

A more positive approach is for minorities to focus on setting personal career goals and then on developing the strengths, talents, initiative, and contacts needed to achieve those goals. The only way to become social and economic equals is to act like and demand treatment as equals. This means building skills, showing initiative, and persevering despite real and sometimes unfair obstacles. But just as Euro-American men need some support from the system, so do minorities. While there may be a few who can muster what it takes to overcome huge barriers and climb past the middle-management level, companies should not demand or expect such superhuman efforts. Organizations must also do their share in removing unnecessary barriers and providing reasonable support.

Use Leadership, Not Coercion

True leadership inspires positive change but doesn't force or coerce it. Coerced change usually leads to low morale, cynicism, and covert resistance. One leadership approach is to establish core groups for the purpose of bringing about change, for example to explore group differences and to promote effective communication and team building. Then management can encourage the formation of similar core groups through voluntary employee participation.

Focus on Individuals First, "Minority" Background Second

Stress each employee's uniqueness, while appreciating his or her cultural background. Be aware of the common group characteristics you're likely to encounter in different groups, but avoid a new type of stereotyping. Be open to the variance, or diversity, of individuals, and never automatically assume that a person is representative of his or her group. Be aware of the wide range of differences among individuals from a particular group.

Respect group differences in beliefs, skills, and so forth, but don't put them on a pedestal as more important than other differences among employees. An emphasis on group differences rather than individual differences can divide the workforce, invite blame and resentment, and risk the development of a we/them mentality. Group differences should be handled as factors in meeting business objectives, not as ends in themselves.

Focus on training and developing individuals, not groups, but at the same time address the particular characteristics or disadvantages found disproportionately in some ethnic or gender groups. Programs to assist and develop employees should not be conditioned on group status unless there is a compelling reason to do so. Target programs to the specific strengths and weaknesses, advantages and disadvantages of individuals. Special career tracks for African Americans or women can be demeaning to them and arouse resentment among others. Flexible jobs or benefits packages may be especially important to women but must be generally available to all employees. Compensatory treatment should be provided on the basis of individual, not group, characteristics. Basing rights on ethnicity or gender should be used only as a last resort.

Apply Success Strategies

Organizations can also learn diversity success strategies from each other. According to a Fortune survey (Rice 1998), the most effective corporate diversity programs function as follows; they:

1. Are backed by a CEO who is committed to diversity success
2. Tie diversity goals to manager's salaries and bonuses
3. Address the concerns of Euro-American men
4. Examine compensation and career tracking—to determine if these aspects are fair
5. Ask top executives and managers to experience what it's like to be a minority
6. Celebrate the differences that diverse employees bring to the organization
7. Improve the supply of diverse employees
8. Maintain diversity goals even when downsizing

Companies have gone from being examples of "worst-case diversity employers" to best-case examples by setting these kinds of goals:

- Change the perception that discrimination is an accepted part of the corporate culture—by promoting inclusiveness and diversity as part of the way of doing business.

- Give diversity training to every employee, from executive-level to entry-level, emphasizing respect for differences among people.

- Recruit minorities on the fast-track to managerial, professional, and highly-skilled technical positions

- Train managers to deal honestly with diversity problems instead of trying to explain them away.

LEADERSHIP OPPORTUNITY #4: MODIFY CORPORATE SYSTEMS AND PRACTICES

The organization begins by addressing needs for change in the corporate culture. Then leaders begin to adopt a multicultural approach to management. These basic changes will provide a solid foundation for the next step, modifying corporate systems and practices that align with new corporate culture values and the multicultural approach.

Top management controls the resources and has the decision-making authority to make the multicultural approach work. Top managers influence people whose prejudice is embedded in a set of beliefs and values that often includes respect for authority. They can favorably influence organization do's and don'ts that subtly guide egalitarian interpersonal behavior. All levels must support the multicultural approach, if it is to succeed. To manage the diversity, all leaders must be committed to creating unity among diverse employees. Management must include unity issues when they conduct a diversity audit to see what's needed. Then they have the basis for developing and implementing a plan that coordinates all major systems and practices (Thomas 1991; Cox 1993; Morrison 1992).

Address Unity Issues

Diverse organizations often have unity problems, and therefore a building a strong corporate culture is essential to overcoming these problems. Typical issues are finding common ground, maintaining group cohesiveness, and communicating through cultural barriers. Any diversity audit should address these issues.

Find Common Ground

Too much diversity in work teams, management groups, or any type of problem-solving group can be especially dysfunctional. When communication barriers, style conflicts, and points of view lack even a core of commonality, decision making may become impossible. Leaders can provide that core of commonality by fostering a corporate culture that's strong enough for all groups to feel connected to common values, heroes, myths, rituals, ceremonies, and other cultural anchors (Shephard 1964).

Maintain Group Cohesiveness

While group cohesiveness has many advantages, higher productivity is not necessarily one of them. Research has *not* shown that cohesiveness alone improves the work performance of groups. Highly cohesive groups are just as likely to have lower productivity as they are to be more productive. The best way to improve cohesiveness *and* productivity is to find common ground and work toward common goals. Leaders can encourage this through the ways they establish and lead work teams (Arnold and Feldman 1986).

Avoid Communication Breakdown

When a group becomes diverse, misunderstandings may increase, conflict and anxiety may rise, and members may feel less comfortable with being in the group. These effects may combine to make decision making more difficult and time-consuming. In these respects culturally diverse work groups are more difficult to manage effectively than homogeneous work groups. The challenge is to manage in such a way that you maximize the potential benefits of diversity while minimizing the potential difficulties.

Building a strong culture that focuses on corporate niche and also values diversity is a complex, ongoing effort. It means paying special attention to the values, norms, grapevine, heroes, rituals, and ceremonies that make up the culture. It means becoming a role model who vividly shows by actions and words what the company stands for. Two strategies that can be especially powerful in building a strong diversity culture are using self-managing teams and assigning managers as culture catalysts.

Use Diverse Self-Managing Teams

The multicultural approach leads to a new type of organization that better suits the needs of today's workers. People are more effective when they feel in control of their destinies. The strongest motivating force for today's workers is peer-group pressure, the primary control mechanism for teams. Strong cultures, which are necessary for bonding self-managing groups into a productive whole organization, are most easily built in smaller units. The electronic equipment that links teams is far cheaper than layers of middle management.

Make Managers Culture Catalysts

The role of managers will focus more and more on creating sparks in the corporate culture. They make culture change happen without forcing it. They build, enunciate, and promote a strong culture that bonds people together, giving people a core of common beliefs and values, a sense of common purpose.

Conduct a Diversity Audit

One of the first steps in developing a multicultural approach is to conduct a diversity audit to get feedback from employees about how they're affected by the systems and the culture. Interview questions can be based on the following types of general questions:

- Why do employees select and remain with the organization?
- What has determined their success?
- How do they assess the quality of work assignments and supervision they've received?
- What barriers hamper further upward mobility?
- How do they view the firm's overall success in managing diversity?
- Do the company's systems and practices work naturally for everyone? If not, why don't they? What must the organization do to make them work naturally for everyone?
- Will the cultural assumptions of this organization allow us to take the necessary corrective action? If not, what cultural changes must we encourage?

Leaders must examine each system in detail and identify patterns that hinder multiculturalism. They must:

- determine what is generating problem patterns
- determine what to do to eliminate the undesirable patterns and convert the system to a facilitating factor
- develop a plan for implementing the system changes

The multicultural approach calls for changing the systems and then encouraging the culture to naturally change as a result. For example, we know that since companies changed their hiring and promotion systems to allow women into management positions, corporate values and norms have changed so that people no longer are disturbed or upset when women are hired or promoted into those jobs—at least at the lower management levels.

As new people join the organization, informal customs and practices that have been comfortable for Euro-American men may need modifying in order to meet the needs of new employees. Formal practices may also need change: flexible work scheduling, working at home, family leave, child-care provisions. The recurring questions should be: How can we meet the needs and preferences of diverse employees? How can we enhance their strengths and elicit the unique contributions they might make?

Do some research on what has worked for other organizations. For example, a field experiment assessed the impact of flextime use on absentee rates and worker performance. Both short-term and long-term absences declined significantly. Three out of four worker efficiency measures increased significantly under flextime (Kim and Campagna 1981).

Develop a Diversity Plan

A diversity audit can provide the company with a profile of the organization's diversity. It can inform leaders about diverse employees' values and needs through information from surveys, focus groups, interviews, task forces, and similar sources. Leaders can then describe the future state they need to create in these areas:

- matching people and jobs
- managing reward and performance
- informing and involving people
- supporting lifestyles and life needs

The diversity audit provides information for analyzing the present state—where the company is now in each of these areas. The next step is to define the gap between this present state and desired future state. What needs to be done to bridge the gap? Leaders can then plan and manage transitions from the present state to the desired future state.

Suppose you were asked to recommend a plan for a multicultural approach to diversity for your organization. What would you include? Of course, you'd want to tailor the plan to fit your particular organization's needs, after conducting an audit. But there are certain actions that are typical of the most excellent companies for diversity. You'd want to seriously consider the following actions.

Set Diversity Goals

Set annual diversity goals for hiring and promotion in both staff and line jobs, for each division. To overcome the barriers inherent in being an isolated token minority, the goals should aim for a critical mass of each type of diverse worker in each area. To this end, management should consider clustering members of the same ethnic or gender group in particular work teams, departments, offices, or facilities—as a transitional procedure—in areas central to the mission of the organization, where jobs carry high status and wages. This can enhance the performance and retention of diverse employees.

The best way to ensure that diverse workers' needs and preferences are met is to promote enough members of each category up through all levels of the organization. When diverse managers gain power over significant arenas of decision making, substantive changes that meet the needs of other diverse workers will occur more naturally.

For example, the managers who understand best what Asian American employees value and need are the Asian American managers, and women managers have the greatest insight into needs of women employees.

Aim for a Diverse Board

Encourage the board of directors to include women and minorities in proportion to the workforce and customer base. Board decisions need to reflect a wide range of views.

Use diversity specialists

Make someone responsible for diversity issues. It may be an officer, a staff manager, or an entire department. In addition, establish a task force or committee that addresses diversity issues. Consider using a diversity consultant for specific needs.

Use Community Outreach

Connect with minority and women's organizations in the community. Establish a continuing dialogue for making job referrals, posting job openings, making charitable contributions, and similar activities.

Provide diversity training

Provide diversity training for every person, especially managers, every year. Incorporate appropriate diversity training into new employee orientation.

Develop for Promotability

Determine what must be done to retain and promote diverse employees. The organization must first discover and then create the conditions under which women and ethnic groups can thrive at all levels of the organization. Hire entry-level people who have enough skills and experience that they have a good chance to advance. Provide a basic level of support—that is, encouragement, training, resources—to all new employees. Encourage mentoring, career tracking, and other career development strategies. Rotate supervisors in order to expose new employees to different management styles and to expose supervisors to a range of employee skills and concerns. Systematically monitor all terminations, transfers, and promotions as part of an effort to retain and promote women and ethnic employees. Provide appropriate skills training to meet the needs of minority and women employees.

Provide Internships and Scholarships

Set up internship programs for minority and women students, to give them some training and exposure to the company, and to enhance recruiting efforts. Consider providing scholarship programs for members of targeted groups, both as an indirect recruiting device and as part of community outreach.

Reward Diversity Gains

When hiring and promoting Euro-American men, include criteria that predict their contribution to the organization's AA and multicultural goals. Before hiring, look for evidence that predicts their ability to function effectively in an organization that is achieving those goals. Examples of predictive experience include experience working in multicultural settings, being supervised by a woman or ethnic manager, collaborating on multicultural work teams, having resided in a racially integrated neighborhood, providing help with child care for employees, successfully balancing job and family responsibilities. Predictive educational experience might include attending equal status, interracial schools, studying with diverse teachers, belong to school groups with diverse members, attending courses or workshops on multicultural or non-Western cultural topics, and speaking another language.

Hold every manager responsible for the progress and success of their diverse employees. Performance in this area should be part of performance evaluation and rewards. Promotion criteria can be expanded to include success in helping diverse employees thrive in the organization. Examples of specific actions include finding, hiring, promoting, encouraging, and sponsoring diverse employees.

Encourage Support Groups

Help minorities and women to establish support groups for purposes of networking, mentoring, supporting, and influencing company decisions. Provide some company funds to these groups for bringing in speakers, holding events, and similar activities.

Set Diversity Contracting Goals

Create minority and women's vendor-supplier programs and use minority contractors, minority-owned banks, law firms, and other minority-owned business services for specified percentages of the annual purchasing budget.

Implement a Diversity Plan: Success Factors

Key success factors of the multicultural approach center around treating people as respected individuals and giving feedback in a culturally sensitive manner. It's important to get to know people as individuals, as well as part of a particular cultural group, to give feedback sensitively based on that knowledge, and to set the tone for creativity to occur (Thomas 1991; Gottfredson 1992; Morrison 1992).

Get to Know the Individual

Take time to get to know each employee, as well as his or her subcultural group. The more you learn about each person, the better you will be able to collaborate with that person as an individual and as part of a work team. What you don't know may keep you from doing your own job effectively. Here are some suggestions that may help.

- *Assess your own appearance stereotypes.* Don't assume race or ethnicity from appearance alone. Many Latinos have Asian features, and many Blacks have Latino, Jamaican, or other origins and strongly distinguish themselves from African Americans. Bi-ethnic persons' cultural backgrounds are not easy to determine from appearance only.

- *Assess your ethnic stereotypes.* Don't assume that all foreign or minority workers are impoverished or deprived. Get to know the background of each one.
- *Acknowledge cultural stereotypes.* Honestly acknowledge the stereotypes that exist and clarify that neither you nor the organization endorse them. Discuss strategies for reducing stereotype threat in the organization (Thomas 2001).
- *Put emotions in perspective.* Don't take emotional outbursts personally. Ask, are emotional outbursts a normal way of responding to the situation in that person's culture? Remember, also, that newcomers often experience a phase of frustration and anger during the adaptation phase.
- *Discover other people's values.* Watch how they behave. When someone behaves consistently in similar circumstances, it suggests a value at work.
- *Clarify which values apply in each situation.* Identify precisely which value or values are at play in a given situation. It is one thing to know that a person values family ties more than you do. It is more difficult to recognize that the family ties value is at stake when that person is absent from work for what would seem like a trivial family matter to you. Your tendency may be to judge by your standards for consistent attendance at work rather than by his standards of family loyalty.
- *Apply employee values to work enhancement.* Look for the positive side of the other person's values—not only how that value is positive in the other's culture, but also how that same value could be applied in ways that are consistent with organization values and objectives. Apply the value to the job at hand. How can you bring the person's value into play so that it help achieve job objectives? For example, when you need teamwork to accomplish something previously done by individuals, the person from a tightly woven culture is likely to rise to the occasion.
- *Apply relevant training.* Determine each new employee's knowledge of the system, and train each one accordingly. Has this employee faced the complexities of the U.S. corporate system before? You may need to train some employees in very basic ways.
- *Determine each employee's primary thinking pattern.* Determine their primary thinking pattern. If you see that abstract and hypothetical thinking is not familiar to them, try using examples, stories, and hands-on experience.
- *Determine each employee's primary learning pattern.* Be patient while employees are in the process of gaining necessary knowledge and experience. You may have to answer more questions, even very basic ones, than you would with Euro-American male employees.
- *Reinforce successful new behavior.* Choose reinforcers, recognition, and rewards that the recipients value as such. Give them in a way that is in line with that person's values.
- *Understand cultural style differences.* For example, learn to accept compliments gracefully and without suspicion; take them in stride. Some cultures use compliments and flattery as a normal, polite way of interacting.

Give Feedback Sensitively

People from tightly woven cultures often have some difficulty giving and getting feedback in the direct style used in most organizations and by most U.S. managers and workers. Many Asians and Middle Easterners have been taught never to confront others directly. And other European groups, such as the British, tend to be more subtle when communicating about performance. In the United States, feedback is a standard part of performance assessment and an integral part of management and creative collaboration. Your style can either respect or violate the values of harmony and consensus as practiced in some other cultures. Here are some suggestions for giving feedback sensitively.

- *Choose the right time and place.* What is culturally appropriate for giving feedback to this employee? Shall it be in a formal or informal session? Directly or using a third party? In private or in a group? Oral or written or both?

- *Clarify your commitment to the person receiving or giving feedback.* Stress the results you are working toward and the importance of the process of asking for, giving, and getting feedback.

- *Specifically describe behavior.* Tell the other person what you have seen or understand them to have said or done. Keep in mind possible cultural differences that may affect behavior.

- *Give positive acknowledgment.* Tell what stands out for you or excites you about what the other person did or said.

- *Give supporting information.* Share information, data, or facts that you have that pertain to what the other person has done.

- *Give an I-message.* Openly and frankly share your opinions and preferences as your own. Avoid talking in terms of absolute rights and wrongs.

- *Open up possibilities.* Share ideas and suggestions you have for the other's work or performance.

- *Share your experience.* Tell about your experience with activities or work similar to the recipient's.

- *Offer clear expectations.* Be clear about what you mutually agreed upon in the past or are now asking the other person to do.

- *Use creative questioning.* Raise questions that clarify the content or direction of the recipient's performance. Questioning can bring out cultural differences.

- *Give support.* Offer support, resources, and information to enable the other person to fulfill their agreements and meet your expectations.

- *Summarize.* Recognize what each of you has contributed during and after this feedback session.

- *Ask for feedback.* Get feedback on how the other has received your feedback. Listen for clues about cultural or individual differences that may affect the situation.

Giving feedback about job performance is crucial to employees' success and can help to build trust or destroy it. Therefore, becoming aware of cultural differences concerning evaluation, appraisal, and criticism is crucial to your success as a leader.

Set the Stage for Creativity

A key advantage of a diverse workforce is the increased potential for creativity and innovation. To tap this potential, leaders must set the stage for creativity to occur. Research indicates that the following factors foster creativity in diverse groups (Miller 1992).

- Create a nonjudgmental environment that encourages people to risk exploration without having to produce a "winner" every time.

- Avoid judgmental words such as good, bad, better, best, mistake—words that kill creativity.

- Cultivate an appreciation of bizarre questions and ideas without negatively labeling them as weird or crazy.

- Produce a noncompetitive atmosphere that focuses on performance and end results, rather than on the how-to's of creative discovery.

- Foster a cooperative spirit that encourages people to learn from each other and to delight in each others' success.

- Provide reasonable, organic structure and discipline to bring out creativity.
- Have fun! Encourage people to get carried away by the sheer fun of creating something.
- Support employees in ways that allow them to release their anxieties about whether their creation is good enough.

LEADERSHIP OPPORTUNITY #5: INCLUDE ALL EMPLOYEES IN BOTTOM-LINE EFFORTS

The company is beginning to modify systems and practices that are based on the multicultural approach. To be most effective, these practices should include all employees in bottom-line projects and efforts.

Continuous improvement is highly valued in most organizations these days. Although Americans tend to prefer dramatic breakthroughs, decisive victories, and clear "wins," leaders have learned that small incremental improvements are much easier to come by. They can also lead to comparable or greater success over time. One of the most powerful benefits of a continuous improvement approach and process is that it inevitably leads to continuous learning for the employees who are included in it. In fact many leaders are convinced that the successful organization these days must be a learning organization. Since organizations are people first and foremost, this means that successful organizations must be staffed by employees who are continuously learning.

We'll discuss three key ways to include all employees in bottom-line efforts:

- Every employee can become part of a continuous learning-productivity loop.
- All can work on important projects that bring them into the "inner circle."
- Employees can work on diverse teams toward important common goals, getting to know each other at deeper levels, beyond stereotypes.

Make an Inclusive Learning Loop

The cycle of continuous learning that leads to continuous improvement and that also results from efforts to continuously improve is sometimes called the learning loop because one process feeds into the other, as shown in Figure 17.3. Imagine ongoing learning loops leading to ever-higher levels of learning and improvement as an ongoing spiral.

Figure 17.3: Learning Loops

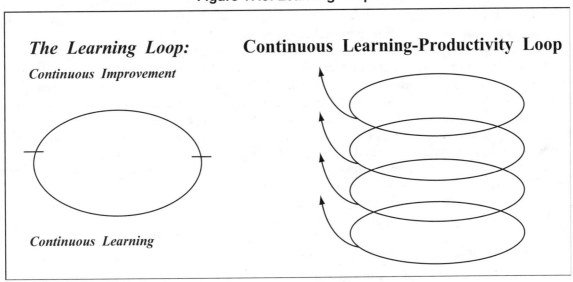

SHOWCASE: CONTINUOUS IMPROVEMENT

A Miami construction firm won a contract to "gut and rebuild the interior" of a 1930s hotel, to bring it up to modern standards but keep its Art Deco charm. The design and construction teams decided to complete one floor at a time, starting with the first floor of rooms, moving floor by floor to the tenth floor at the top, and finally to the lobby. When they finished the first floor, all were very proud of the results. The rooms looked great, and the work had been completed efficiently, effectively, and on time. It was so good they could have repeated exactly the same process for the other floors. Instead, they used the learning loop and engaged in a process of continuous improvement. They analyzed what could be done better, faster, more effectively, and more efficiently as well as how they could better coordinate tasks, combine them, reschedule them, and make similar improvements.

When they finished the second floor, it was even better in quality and appearance than the first floor and had been completed more efficiently. Continuing to learn from their experiences on each floor, the teams finally surveyed the completed tenth floor, which they had done in record time. Everyone agreed that this was the best floor yet.

The team leader had an idea: "Let's go back down to the first floor now and compare the results." The workers were amazed. The tenth floor was so superior to the first that they were actually a little embarrassed about the first floor.

One aspect of continuous learning might be called the ARC of improvement, standing for a process of analyzing, resolving, and changing as follows.

Analyze current process, practices, and results by asking: What happened that was effective or ineffective? Why did it happen? What needs to happen?

Resolve problems and find better ways of doing things by asking: How can we bring about what needs to happen? How can we prevent problems from recurring? How can the handle the situation differently in the future?

Change. Get agreement on what will change. Give support for the change.

The story in the showcase of continuous improvement that follows helps to illustrate the concept.

Make an Inclusive Inner Circle

All learning loops are not equally beneficial or productive. We all know people who become extremely efficient at filling out forms, filing papers, operating computer programs, and other activities—that are largely a waste of time. At best, these employees aren't contributing much to the bottom-line success of the organization, nor to their personal career success.

Employees who work on projects and tasks that *do* contribute directly to the quality of the organization's products and services are fortunate. The more improvement they create and the more they learn about doing the work elegantly, efficiently, and in line with customer needs and preferences, the more satisfying their jobs are. They make an important difference and they know it. That's more than fulfilling—it's exciting and motivating. It's like being a member of an inner circle.

For this reason, we'll use the Inner Circle as a metaphor for employees who are included in those learning loops directly connected to the bottom line success of the organization. Employees in the Inner Circle are in a position to grow, learn, and advance the goals of the organization. They're "where the action is," the important action, that is.

To get a clear picture of what the inner and outer circle looks like in your organization, complete Skill Builder 17.4 at the end of this chapter.

Bring All Employees into the Inner Circle

An important managing inclusion principle is to bring all the employees you can into the Inner Circle and its key learning loops. Think of the diagram in Skill Builder 17.4 as your organization. Who is a part of the inner circle and who is left out? If bottom-line success is your most important priority, it makes sense to get all the employees working toward it. Learning how to do this is a key managing diversity skill. Here are some suggestions:

- Specify the skills and capabilities that are required.
- Get to know all the employees, their weaknesses and strengths.
- Develop strategies to overcome the obstacles that stand in the way, to bridge the gaps between necessary skills and capabilities and those the employee now has.
- Provide them with required knowledge and skills

Give All Employees Quality Treatment

Savvy leaders must learn how to give quality treatment to all employees. This has become an important managing-diversity principle. Because each employee is unique, "quality treatment" will differ slightly for each person. The key is to find ways to connect with each person's humanity and individuality. Then help them figure out how they can use their unique talents to contribute to the team and to meet job goals. Here are some general actions and attitudes that constitute quality treatment:

- Believe in each employee and communicate that belief
- Explicitly communicate high standards and high expectations
- Promote a respect for diversity
- Show each person that he or she is important to you and the organization
- Provide support to *all* employees.
- Value people through your procedures and practices
- Teach people the basis of success in the organization, including the unwritten rules; be an effective mentor.
- Lead people to engage in learning loops and bring them into bottom-line learning loops

Create Diverse Teams—Beyond Superficial Contact

Look for opportunities to establish diverse teams. This is a great way to move beyond superficial contact among diverse employees—to working toward common goals that are important to all. People get to know one another on a personal level when they need each other to achieve important goals. This is the type of contact that breaks through walls of prejudice. Diverse teams have distinct advantages, and also some challenges to overcome (Ely 2001, Mannix, 2005, Hong 2004). Companies are discovering strategies for managing such teams. (Harstone 1995)

Advantages

Some advantages of culturally diverse teams are:

- Better understanding of people from other cultures—both in the United States and in other countries that the company does business with—including diverse employees, suppliers, customers, regulators
- More effective work relations with people from other cultures and countries
- Better ability to market to people from other cultures and countries
- More creative ideas produced over time. In equality-oriented cultures, such as the United States dominant culture, diverse teams tend to be more innovative than homogeneous teams (Van der Vegt 2005).
- Decisions that tend to stand the test of time and location

Challenges

A strong demographic-cultural difference, called a "faultline," may split a group into subgroups based on one or more attributes and provide an informal structure for intragroup conflict (Lau 2005). For example young Latino American women and older Euro-American men may be so different culturally that they have difficulty relating effectively to each other.

Competitive tendencies between subgroups can quickly emerge in groups. The development of an "us versus them" mentality within a team can undermine the idea of an effective, cohesive team. The faultline concept may help a manager to predict potentially divisive events. To overcome conflict, the leader must create integrative tasks with goals that require collaboration. When goal completion is crucial, then such issues as pressing deadlines, common threats, or competition can raise team members' awareness beyond subgroups and their faultlines to the level of the entire team.

When forming teams, pay attention to avoiding such faultlines—to take advantage of great diversity and to avoid potential conflict. Be aware of faultline dynamics of team members. Design tasks and task networks, and communication networks, to match current and future faultline dynamics.

The more diverse a group is, the more difficulty they have initially (Halter 2000). The reasons include more difficulty in 1) communicating, 2) working as a unit, and 3) setting up a useful way of doing things. Once they get an understanding and a pattern in place, the diverse group becomes more effective than the homogeneous group, especially when working on projects requiring creativity and problem solving. They are able to bring more to the group table, but they may have to work together over a longer time period (than homogeneous groups) in order to reach this higher level of productivity.

Degree of Diversity

For teams composed of Americans, those that are extensively diverse generally do better than those that are only moderately diverse (Elron 1997). For example, a manager creates of team of mostly Euro-Americans with one or two members from other ethnic groups. The "token(s)" tend to have little impact. Another manager creates a team of several Euro-Americans and several African Americans. Members are likely to cluster into two sub-groups and to function more as two teams than as a truly integrated team. Yet another manager creates an extensively diverse team of a couple of Euro-Americans, a couple of African Americans, and one or two Latino Americans and Asian Americans, There are not enough people in any one subgroup to form a sub-team, so everyone tends to integrate into one team, and the diverse members have significant impact.

Increasing the overall diversity of all-American teams by including Latino Americans, Asian Americans and others – not just Euro-Americans and African Americans—tends to enhance supportive relationships and to avoid intragroup conflict (Davidio 2003). African Americans become more supportive of Euro-American colleagues as the ratio of African Americans in the group increases. The opposite happens for Euro-Americans; they become *less* supportive of African American colleagues as the ratio of African Americans increases, according to one study (Bacharach 2005). Researchers concluded that managers must role model and reward supportive behavior among team members in order to increase a diverse team's performance.

On the other hand, teams with members from various nations (globally diverse) generally work best if they are moderately diverse rather than highly diverse. Many U.S. companies are building teams comprised of talents from around the world, at times in one location and at times working entirely as a distributed team. Whether they are in one place or spread around the world, the diversity in today's teams and organizations from different cultures, countries, religions, and languages can be at once stimulating and daunting, and presents unique challenges to today's leadership. One problem can be a lack of cohesion because of different values, norms, and customs.

A research group (Dahlin et al 2005) found that moderately diverse teams, in terms of national origin, tend to be most productive. They observed how teams use information to work on complex projects or issues, from 1) gathering information—where the range of information a team has access to is important, 2) analyzing the information, where the ability to go into depth on the connections, meanings, and significance of the information is important, and 3) integrating it into team action, implementing it, and putting it into use or action. Researchers concluded that if a team is too diverse, cohesion can break down, and if it is too homogeneous, it gets a narrower range of information and may engage in less in-depth analysis. Applying their findings to typical types of workplace teams, the researchers recommend as follows:

Top management teams need to make complex links between unique information categories. They need moderate to high global-diversity for richness of insight that cuts across areas of expertise.

Product development teams need greater depth of analysis. They benefit from moderate levels of global-diversity. They may be especially vulnerable to risks of very high diversity, which could make it difficult to develop a given perspective in depth and could create too many issues that compete for attention.

Market research and R&D teams are highly dependent on accessing a broad range of information. They can benefit from global-diversity in specific ways. Such diversity offers an opportunity to tap into multiple, unique perspectives on their tasks. Teams that work best are moderately diverse. Very high globally-diverse teams can interfere with cohesion.

Management Strategies

Some strategies for managing diverse teams are (Harstone 1995):

- Create teams that are extensively diverse
- Adopt a vision or mission and specific broad goals.
- Find ways to get everyone on the "same page," or "marching to the same drumbeat."
- Have open discussions about the strengths that each member may be able to contribute to the team project. Explore ways to identify these strengths and to integrate them most effectively.
- Promote equal status among team members.
- Encourage peer-based support. When you focus on encouraging peer support and on helping as a diversity management tool, supportive intergroup relationships are more likely to emerge than if you just increase the opportunities for intergroup contact (Dovidio 2003).
- Develop criteria for evaluating ideas, processes, projects, etc. Feedback should be frequent and should be based on how well the agreed-upon criteria would be met by adopting a particular suggestion.

LEADERSHIP OPPORTUNITY #6: BUILD CONSENSUS FOR CHANGE

Let's say the organization has addressed needs for corporate culture change, adopted a multicultural approach to management, built the new approach on solid equal opportunity principles, and is looking at changing systems and practices to align with the new approach, especially those that include all employees in bottom-line efforts. This represents a huge degree of change that must be implemented. So, not as a last step, but as an integral part of all these steps, leaders must build consensus for change throughout the organization.

Creating change is always a leadership challenge. First, build on current needs and desires for change within the organization. Second, work through your own issues around change and help others work through theirs. Third, recognize and avoid typical change traps. Finally, identify and develop conscious change agents who can in turn help you build a critical mass of people committed to making the needed changes.

Build on the Organizational Need and Desire to Change

Most organizations have many values and practices from the past, as well as current pressures and future concerns, that facilitate a multicultural approach. Among these are:

- a strong corporate culture that values diversity
- a well-planned and well-administered AA program
- Awareness of limitations of AA efforts, including backlash and stigma problems—managers are looking for a better way to create equal opportunity
- a prior substantial investment in managing diversity—management has a stake in making the investment pay off
- a good track record for diversity—the company already perceives itself as diverse
- the organization's pride in being a fair and equitable employer
- legal, moral, and social responsibility concerns
- intense competition that forces managers to examine all possibilities for enhancing productivity and effectiveness
- an increasingly diverse workforce with fewer available qualified recruits.
- employees' unwillingness to be assimilated and their comfort and pride with their diversity

These are the motivators that you can build on, the desires and needs for change that can help your multicultural approach become a winner.

Work through Change Issues

Building consensus requires networking with employees who are good candidates for becoming conscious change agents. Working through your own change issues can prepare you to help others open up to positive change. What if we could address the bottom-line concerns of all the major corporate players, or stakeholders, about changing the corporation? What if you could help them clear away all their reservations to supporting the changes? Answering the provocative questions that are posed in Skill Builder 17.2 may get your creative juices flowing. Even more important, you may come up with just the right questions for your organization to address.

Avoid Typical Change Traps

Change agents need specific skills. When you venture into new territory, from the known to the unknown, the going can be rough. Most of us need some guidance from people who've been there before. Here are some typical traps you'll want to avoid (Terry 1990).

- Believing there is one best way. Focus on the end result; the paths leading there may be many.
- Adopting a label, such as "diversity manager" or "change agent" but avoiding the real struggle. We must do the work.
- Not realizing that many people are unable to comprehend and/or accept these ideas. We must deal with people according to where they are in their own development and take it one step at a time.
- Focusing only on the *reasons* change is needed or only on change actions themselves. Both theory and action are needed.
- Holding Euro-American men responsible for solving the problem of prejudice. *All* stakeholders must be deeply involved in any solution.
- Becoming self-righteous, impressed by your own virtue. Remember to look at where you've been and where you're going.
- Believing we have a choice about whether to change or not.

This last trap deserves further comment. Our choice is not whether change will take place but whether we'll make it happen, watch it happen, or ask "What happened?" Savvy leaders take a proactive stance toward change, looking for opportunities and dealing with challenges. You as a leader can help people to understand that change is the constant in life. The world keeps changing whether we approve or not. An increasingly diverse workforce is a fact of life. Therefore, when we speak of creating organizational change and building consensus for change, we're talking about anticipating and recognizing changes that are already in motion and responding positively. We're speaking of making things happen in ways that build trust and cooperation rather than resisting the changing diversity of the workplace and proceeding as though it doesn't exist. A personal and organizational commitment to respect all types of employees and to support them in their career development is a proactive response to this change—one that's good for all employees and for the organization.

Develop Conscious Change Agents

To shift the corporate culture to one that is truly multicultural, inclusive, and increasing diverse at all levels, leaders must become change agents—and establish a network of change agents throughout the organization. The process for becoming a change agent is as follows:

- Become a conscious agent of change—recognize that new directions are possible.
- Seek ethical clarity—know what you want your organization, and America, to stand for and why.
- Identify the various forms and expressions of prejudice—know who we are and have been, and why.
- Get a clear vision of a multicultural, inclusive organization, how it would function.
- Develop long-range change strategies to eliminate and move beyond prejudice—to experience what a truly equitable organization might be.
- Discern the appropriate day-to-day tactics—assess your power for change.
- Experiment, test, and refine a personal lifestyle that expresses your newly affirmed values—experience who you might be.

*Making a personal commitment to bring about change is the first st*ep to becoming a conscious change agent. *The next step is becoming conscious of what needs changing.* To be conscious is to be always actively aware of ourselves in relation to other people and things around us. Skill Builder 17.3 focuses on becoming conscious of how changes in beliefs lead to changes in actions.

Core beliefs about a situation can either lock us into limited options or solutions or they can open the door to different ways of seeing the past and present, and a different guide for future action. For example, if we see African Americans as the problem, then both our attitudes and behaviors will flow from that belief about the situation. If we believe that the Euro-American culture and privileged Euro-Americans are the problem, then it becomes possible to explore new behavior and reevaluate earlier attitudes. We may see that people from both cultures need to take responsibility for bringing about change. The most important question for each person is actually *the next step, asking, "What can I do to bring about needed change?*

Once you've decided what you can do, *the last step is making a personal commitment to help bring about positive change*, as set out in Skill Builder 17.3. As a leader you have significant opportunities to take personal stands and to follow through with personal actions, no matter how small, toward creating positive change. You may need to go against the norms of the corporate culture, which is always challenging. But if your stands and your actions are consistently supportive of, for example, Latino American or gay employees as basically equal and valuable human beings, then your actions build a bridge over centuries of mistrust to the other side, to mutual respect and trust.

LEADERSHIP OPPORTUNITY #7: OVERCOME RESISTANCE TO DIVERSITY INITIATIVES

Growing a multicultural organization is challenging because the barriers are many, the guidelines are still being tested, and the barriers to a particular talented employee achieving his or her full potential are complex. But when we look at the changing face of organizations today and compare that with what we saw in the 1950s, we know that many barriers have already been overcome. If we want our organizations to change and are willing to devote the energy to it, we can make remarkable progress. Success is more likely if leaders are aware of typical resistances of top managers and employees, as well as typical managerial problems in implementing a multicultural approach. Then they can adopt strategies to overcome such resistance, including shock treatment, linking to resisters' values, and other strategies. They can introduce effective training for all employees—training that is ongoing in order to update and reinforce the basic training.

Recognize Resistance to Diversity Initiatives

The first step to overcoming resistance to diversity initiatives is to raise your awareness of typical types of resistance, so that you can recognize what is probably going on.

Typical Resistance from the Top

Typical reasons top managements give for not managing diversity are rooted in lack of information about diversity, short-range planning, and a lack of commitment:

- It costs too much.
- We can't find enough qualified minorities.
- We should hire the best person.
- We don't believe in reverse discrimination.
- Enough progress has been made.
- It's time to just be gender-neutral and color-blind.
- We have too many priorities that are more crucial than diversity.
- It's too much work to make the needed changes.
- Our organization is just too large to make the needed changes.
- A focus on diversity is divisive; we focus on being one big happy family.

This "divisive" rationalization is so common and erects such a rigid barrier to multiculturalism that it's worth pursuing. Here are some variations on that theme.

Divisive Rationale 1: We shouldn't focus on differences

Some people think that if we look at how cultures differ, we won't see how they're alike and therefore we won't find a common ground of unity. But learning about other cultures and valuing cultural differences need not be a barrier to unity. We can always connect with others for many reasons, including these.

- Anthropologists assure us that humans are more alike than they are different.
- Psychologists point out that we all have needs for survival, security, belonging, recognition, and self-actualization; we differ only in the ways we go about fulfilling these needs.

Therefore, we can value diversity and still find common ground almost everywhere, if that's our intent.

Divisive Rationale 2: We don't want to stereotype people

For an opinion to be a stereotype, it must be *rigid*, not taking into account individual differences within a group. Learning about cultural patterns and typical beliefs and values should provide *flexible general guidelines* to help us understand what makes people act they way they do—to know the right questions to ask people when problems arise. We must always keep in mind that general guidelines do not apply equally to every person from a culture, just as no one of us conforms to exactly the same beliefs and behaviors within our own culture.

Divisive Rationale 3: We don't want to be racist or sexist

Actually, not admitting differences is probably more ethnocentric than is exploring and respecting differences. After all, if we're all alike, who are we like, which culture? What culture represents the norm to which we all should conform? The unconscious assumption is that it's our own, of course. It's a way of saying, "People are basically alike—like me."

Divisive Rationale 4: Focusing on similarities is easier

Life seems easier, in the short run, if we assume that everyone is alike. Dealing with diverse people means dealing with complexity and uncertainty, and it may seem easier to settle for "we're all basically alike." But if misunderstandings are based on cultural differences, then ignoring differences keeps us from getting at the root of the problem, which in turn can build and fester.

Summarizing these tendencies to avoid the diversity issue, President Clinton's race advisory board chair, John Hope Franklin, said that stereotypes actually remain because Americans cling to the idea that it's best to try to ignore race. That, in turn, forces people to bury—and therefore harbor within— beliefs they form from stereotypes they heard at school, in the media, and from family members. Franklin, an African American leader, said: "The idea that we should aspire to a 'colorblind' society is an impediment to reducing racial stereotyping. Given that research has demonstrated that the best way to reduce racial stereotyping is to be conscious about racial differences, it is important to present a thoughtful alternative to the 'colorblind society' concept" (AP 1998). The bottom line: Companies that avoid addressing diversity adequately are short-sighted and in the long run will probably regret having fallen behind in the race to build and keep a staff of highly qualified people. Many just don't understand the advantages of managing diversity effectively.

Typical Implementation Problems

Some typical management problems in implementing a diversity plan include:

- top-down, directive management style, which doesn't provide for a two-way acculturation and adaptation, nor dialogue about what diverse employees need and want
- over-concern with getting tasks done and under-concern with the people doing them
- narrow view of diversity that focuses only on minorities and women rather than all employees, or only on increasing the numbers of minorities and women rather than taking a comprehensive multicultural approach
- short-term, results orientation: "We met our diversity goals for the year"
- lack of strategic perspective; a focus on daily operational concerns
- lack of leadership to develop the vision of an empowered diverse workforce, to articulate a strategy to gain competitive advantage, and to build and maintain systems and practices that support the vision and strategy

Typical Employee Resistance to Diversity Initiatives and Training

Exclusion, avoidance, and social distancing are ways that individuals may show resistance to diversity in organizations; they represent information discrimination. Formal discrimination refers to illegal behaviors that are overt and obvious, such as excluding persons from employment, advancement, resources, access, or other opportunities.

Interpersonal, information discrimination is more subtle and ambiguous; it is often nonverbal and may be unconscious. It may include differences in expectations, fewer informal ties, and negative facial expressions. Such discrimination can undermine the performance of targeted employees, in the same ways as overt harassment and hate crimes. Such subtle discrimination can be even more insidious because it is more difficult to recognize and assess. Results for the targeted persons may include decreased job satisfaction, emotional commitment, and helping behaviors as well as increased job stress and motivation to change jobs (Hebl 2008)

Typical reasons that employees resist managing-diversity initiatives and training are wide-ranging, from deeply psychological to mere inertia (Smither et al 1996). At the most basic level, employees may

- fail to see need for training or misunderstand why and how it will proceed
- fear their current reality will be threatened that they will lose status or economic security
- feel a threat to existing social relationships or to old routines, norms, and habits
- worry that existing power relationships will change, leading to uncertainty
- stereotype people in outgroups and feel prejudiced toward them
- dislike risk and be unwilling to experiment with the change that managing diversity requires

Some forms of resistance are more intellectual and/or political; for example employees may:

- believe in the melting pot, that people should adapt and be one big happy family
- not understand culture, and its potential as an effective tool for empowering employees
- not understand the business rationale for managing diversity, how it will affect the productivity and viability of their departments and the organization
- resist AA and suspect that any new diversity approach is an effort to sneak AA in through the back door
- think that the style or content of the initiative may clash with the corporate culture and way of doing things
- lack power, knowledge, or skills in managing diversity
- have too many responsibilities already and believe they don't have the time or energy for another initiative
- not see how managing diversity can help them achieve their goals, rather than being a distraction

Bottom Line: Resistance typically involves fear of losing the status quo, intergroup anxiety, and denial of the need for change. Knowing the resistances can help you plan for overcoming them. This knowledge can also help you analyze why the diversity efforts are not working as well as expected. The barriers list can become a checklist for figuring out why.

Adopt Strategies for Overcoming Resistance

The first, most basic strategy for preventing and overcoming resistance to diversity initiatives and training is to plan the process you will use for changing the culture and establishing diversity policies and practices. The goal is to promote a diverse workforce and inclusion of all diverse employees as part of the "inner circle." Also, anticipate likely sources of resistance to this change and plan strategies for overcoming resistance. To the extent that an organization does this, diverse persons perceive less discrimination and have more positive attitudes about their jobs (King et al 2006; Ragins and Cornwell, 2002).

Shock Treatment

You as leader have a key tactic for breaking firmly established types of resistance: you can try "external shock." You do this by initiating events and actions that upset the status quo of inequity by confronting dominants and subordinates with the profound costs of that status quo. Shock can loosen long-held beliefs and assumptions and open people to new information for rethinking their assumptions (Argyris 1993, Lewin 1951). Examples of external shock include

- New statements from leaders about organizational values and beliefs in diversity
- Clearly stated organization legal requirements regarding diversity
- Rediscovered memory of ancestors' beliefs regarding diversity and the need to face a new world order
- Explicit observations of inequity such as dominants unfairly getting resources and subordinates being unfairly blocked from resources.

Link Benefits of the Initiatives to Resisters' Values

Try to link the results of diversity initiatives to something that resisters value. Both leaders and trainers will find this helpful. For example,

- How do ideas about fairness, reverse discrimination, and job security impact their resistance?
- What value do they place on organizational performance and the bottom line—the overall success of the company?
- How important is learning and job effectiveness to them?

In each case, competing values might appear as diversity resistance. Leaders can introduce a broader story that incorporates competing values in ways that support a high-performing and inclusive organization (Thomas 1996).

Fairness: Diverse-Group Differences and Inclusion

Some resisters believe that any focus on diverse-group memberships is discriminatory and unfair. This viewpoint is based on an individualistic view of fairness (Ferdman 1997). These resisters believe we must reduce odious comparisons of group differences. They may think that a focus on diverse-group memberships means an examination of group differences and therefore is unfair or inappropriate. Their resistance to diversity is an expression of their commitment to what is good, fair, and just. Underlying this may be a competing commitment to security and the status quo.

An effective way to address this resistance is to expand the boundaries of this "fairness viewpoint" so that the "diverse-group viewpoint" is no longer seen as mutually exclusive with it. For example, the new "inclusion viewpoint" encompasses both. Management could focus on what members with this fairness viewpoint want to preserve—aspects that would also support inclusion. What do they want to preserve for themselves as individuals, for the group, and/or for the organization? How can they keep these aspects and still support inclusion of diverse employees?

Diversity as a valuable resource

Some resisters believe that a focus on diversity, or group differences, is harmful to the organization. An alternate perspective is that diversity is a valuable resource to be exploited for the good of the organization and its workforce. The goal is to make sure that all qualified people are able to enter and work in niches where their differences from others would be most useful to the organization.

For diversity to become a valuable resource, leaders and employees must attend to diverse-group memberships and to intra-group differences. This comes from a desire to be future-focused and to move on. Trainers and managers can address this type of resistance to diversity by identifying different ways people may frame the relationships. Help resisters to understand the different ways people view the present, from an individual to a group or cultural lens. Just noting the differences may enable resisters to honor and include others' perspectives.

Diversity as a learning process

Some resisters are open to situations and processes that increase people's learning and their effectiveness on the job. A "learning and effectiveness viewpoint" calls for a strategy of emphasizing the ways in which diverse-group differences can contribute to mutual learning, growth, and job effectiveness—both for employees and the organization as a whole. This viewpoint honors the bottom line and business success. Diversity is good as long as it enhances the bottom line. Note how diversity initiatives link employees to external markets.

Other Strategies for Overcoming Resistance

After the basics, and perhaps some shock treatment and linkage to resisters' values, other strategies leaders can use to overcome resistance might include:

- Articulate a new vision of the culture that incorporates the new polices and initiatives within the existing culture
- Make the case for diversity initiatives by articulating a clear business case for diversity. Address specific company needs
- Establish a broad umbrella for diversity that includes everyone within the organization, even advantaged groups. Inclusion becomes everyone's business
- Train senior managers in all key aspects of managing diversity and inclusion
- Senior managers give full support, model the new behaviors, and visually demonstrate support for the new initiatives

To keep the momentum going, leaders can use these types of strategies:
- Monitor the organization's culture and climate with respect to diversity inclusiveness versus diversity resistance—on a periodic, continuing basis
- Ensure that the representation of diverse members in management positions is equitable
- Educate employees on the entire range of diversity issues
- Make supervisors and managers accountable for setting and achieving goals for reducing diversity resistance by including criteria in their performance appraisals
- Establish mentoring programs to support the success of diverse persons
- Establish employee forums and networking opportunities for all diverse groups.
- Increase intergroup contact through teamwork and social functions. (This can reduce prejudice and lead to more network ties)
- Welcome same-sex partners at company social events

Some strategies for preventing recurrence of harassment and maintaining an inclusive environment include the following (Chrobot 2004):
- Identify and correct existing problems
- Facilitate or provide counseling services for perpetrators and targets
- Establish and publish a statement of organizational sanctions for perpetrators of harassment, violence, and hate crimes—what constitutes such violations and what their consequences will be.

Provide Diversity Training for All

Once a diversity audit has been conducted and a comprehensive diversity program has been developed, all employees must receive appropriate training in the multicultural approach to managing diversity in the organization. Training must be ongoing in order to update and reinforce the basic training.

The training approach can reduce resistance, both to diversity changes and to the training itself. It can help people to navigate the cycles of resistance.

Training Approaches that Reduce Resistance

Diversity training is a key, essential aspect of managing diversity and creating an inclusive corporate culture. Keep in mind the ways in which employees may resist such training. If employees perceive that the training content clashes with the organizational culture, they may view that as a signal that existing power relationships will change. That could mean their current reality will be threatened or that they will lose status or economic security. This in turn might threaten their existing social relationships and old routines, norms, and habits. The bottom line: fear of losing the status quo leading to intergroup anxiety, and resistance to change.

Here are some ways to reduce employee resistance to diversity initiatives and training (May 2005)

Have in place organizational support structures for managing diversity. The organizational culture, policies, structure, and practices—the more they support the goals of diversity training, the more successful it is likely to be. Diversity training is best seen as part of a comprehensive diversity strategy. Search for ways that the existing organization culture, policies, etc. may undermine or fail to support what is taught in diversity training and the incorporation of new means of fostering inclusion. Repair those gaps before commencing with diversity training.

Clarify the agenda, time, task, and space. Let trainees know when they are going to be doing what. Help them to understand the task of each part of the training. Meet in an appropriate physical environment where training will be uninterrupted. (Alderfer, 1980)

Provide clear interactive norms (rules of the game) and ongoing trainer support. Training sessions should include collaboration with trainees to establish norms that are supportive of constructive interaction and conflict resolution. Facilitators should be skilled in leading "in the moment" interactions.

Foster training readiness. Trainees should be ready to face such difficult topics as privilege and dominance. They should recognize the potential benefits of diversity and the existence of organizational discrimination and bias. Arousing feelings of empathic concern toward another group can reduce prejudice toward members of that group. Ask, What's it like to be you? (Vescio 2003, Dovidio 2004)

Deal with perceived threat. Reduce intergroup prejudice by dealing with the four types of threat that lead to prejudice against an outgroup: 1) realistic threat to power and well being, whether political, economic, or physical power; 2) symbolic threat to value or belief systems; 3) intergroup anxiety or fear about negative outcomes of interaction; 4) negative stereotypes that imply unpleasant interactions (Stephan and Stephan 2000). You can reduce prejudice by using Allport's four-point framework: 1) Both parties perceive they have equal status as human beings, 2) they have a common goal that is 3) very important to each of them, and 4) they must work together in order to achieve that goal.

Be sensitive to the framing and content of diversity training. How the purpose and aspects of diversity training are presented can decrease resistance. For example, framing it as "diversity management" rather than "affirmative action" decreases resistance (Kidder et al (2004). A meta-analysis of 126 studies of AA indicates that how a company defines and presents its AA program determines how well it is accepted by employees. Any hint of quota-like policies will cause resistance, while basing the program on fairness, merit, and equal opportunity will engender support (Harrison 2006). Provide a business reason for the training. Title the course to show a broad focus—for example a focus on gender, ethnicity or lifestyle—rather than a narrow racial focus (Holladay et al 2003).

Focus on a multicultural approach that values diversity and views difference as an asset toward achieving common goals—rather than an approach that ignores or "tolerates" differences (Cox 1991). Make trainees aware of difference, highlight the unique contributions of such differences within the organization, facilitate cross-group interaction, and help employees and groups to develop a larger, organizational identity.

Use skilled training facilitators, who are able to support learning despite trainee anxiety about change, identity, power, conflict, and similar issues. Use facilitators who have worked deeply on their own biases and prejudices. Trainers should be skilled at using small group work to implement training. This can foster deeper interpersonal interaction, less anxiety about taking a role, and more safety for learning

Training for Navigating the Cycles of Resistance

Diversity training can include processes to help employees navigate their cycles of resistance to diversity change. These processes involve some key principles for building relationships between dominants and subordinates to help them work together (Davidson 2008). The process includes the following steps.

Pausing. People need to respond to threats to identity with reflection first, rather than with habitual reaction. When confronted with a diversity problem or issue, people need to identify their emotional reactions and then consider how to act.

Connecting. If people can refocus their goals on a larger team goal or organizational objective, they may be able to create common ground and establish collaboration with the other—and to connect with the emotions of the other. The overarching goal is to cultivate a fair, empowering, and energizing inclusive organization.

Self-questioning. Encourage employees to ask such questions as "What am I missing in the way I'm seeing this situation? How might my desire to be right be distorting my view of reality or the other person?" Such questioning may lead to letting go of self-protective habits that block the employee from being receptive to others' views that are difficult to hear. Encourage them to see what they can learn from this process.

Soliciting genuine support. Now it is time for these employees to identify those who can help them to sort through their reactions, see a fuller picture of reality, and question their own assumptions about the situation.

Shifting the mindset. Finally, these employees may be able to radically shift their way of thinking about self in this situation, about the situation itself, and about other people. Perhaps they shift away from the mindset that says "you need to change" to one that asks "what can I change?"

Bottom line: Helping people to deal with their resistance to change and the possible threats they might perceive from increased diversity is the first step to overcoming resistance to a multicultural inclusive corporate culture. The follow-up is helping them to see the benefits and advantages to themselves as well as the organization.

SUMMARY

Leadership Opportunities for successfully managing a diverse workplace are all based on creating an inclusive organizational culture. The beliefs and values of an organization form its worldview and its mission in the world. These are the heart and soul of any organization. That's why change must start here. Organizations that ignore these basics—and start the change process with new programs or practices or even policies—cannot achieve optimal results. Real, sustainable change must come from the heart.

Once an inclusive corporate culture is underway, then a multicultural approach to business and to management can naturally evolve. A successful multicultural approach must be all-inclusive and must deal with employees as individuals, taking into account their cultural and experiential background against the backdrop of a diverse society. The inclusive approach is a diversity-within-unity approach.

While a multicultural approach goes beyond affirmative action programs, it does not ignore equal opportunity principles or abandon AA programs. It does build on lessons business leaders have learned about how to make AA work most effectively for all groups.

These basic changes will provide a solid foundation for the next step, modifying corporate systems and practices that align with new corporate culture values and the multicultural approach. Top management controls the resources and has the decision-making power to influence organization do's and don'ts that subtly guide egalitarian interpersonal behavior. All levels must support the multicultural approach, if it is to succeed. To manage the diversity, all leaders must be committed to creating unity among diverse employees. Management must include unity issues when they conduct a diversity audit to see what's needed. Then they have the basis for developing and implementing a plan that coordinates all major systems and practices.

Systems should include all employees in bottom-line corporate efforts. Every employee can become part of a continuous learning-productivity loop. All can work on important projects and efforts that bring them into the "inner circle." Employees can work on diverse teams toward important common goals, getting to know each other at deeper levels, beyond stereotypes.

Throughout all this change process, leaders must build consensus for change among all the employees. Building consensus for change is essential to successfully implementing the multicultural approach. While the commitment of top management is the first step, lasting change requires the consensus of a critical mass of employees. As a leader you can start the change process by building on those factors already at work within the organization that motivate people toward change. You can work through your own change issues and help others to do the same. You can anticipate some typical change traps in order to avoid them, and you must anticipate resistance and develop strategies to overcome it. Eventually you must develop others as conscious change agents who will in turn influence yet others toward positive change.

To shift the corporate culture to one that is truly multicultural, inclusive, and increasingly diverse at all levels, leaders must become change agents—and establish a network of change agents throughout the organization. The process includes the following steps: 1) Making a personal commitment to bring about change, 2) becoming conscious of what needs changing, 3) asking, "What can I do to bring about needed change? and 4) making a personal commitment to help bring about positive change,

Growing a multicultural organization is challenging because the barriers are many, the guidelines are still being tested, and the barriers to a particular talented employee achieving his or her full potential are complex. If leaders want their organizations to change and are willing to devote the energy to it, they can make remarkable progress. Success is more likely if leaders are aware of typical resistances of top managers and employees, as well as typical managerial problems in implementing a multicultural approach. Then they can adopt strategies to overcome such resistance, including shock treatment, linking to resisters' values, and other strategies. They can introduce effective training for all employees—training that is ongoing in order to update and reinforce the basic training. The training approach can reduce resistance, both to diversity changes and to the training itself. It can help people to navigate the cycles of resistance.

The multicultural approach enhances success in virtually every area, including conflict resolution, negotiation, employee relationships, employee empowerment, leadership effectiveness, continuous learning, continuous improvement, innovation, productivity, total quality management, synergistic teams, and trust building. Given the potential payoffs, companies can't afford to be satisfied with outdated corporate cultures that exclude many potential contributors.

Skill Builder 17.1: A Question of Change

Purpose: To stimulate thinking about ways to make your workplace more supportive of all employees.

Instructions: Record your responses and any additional insights, including further questions that could lead to creative solutions for your particular organization, perhaps for all organizations. If you don't work for a large organization now, think of past organizations you've worked for or have been a part of, such as a university or school.

Step 1. Consider the viewpoints of all stakeholders

Who are the stakeholders that have widely varying viewpoints in your organization? Examples might bet sales employees, women in the accounting department, African American employees, Euro-American managers. A) List the stakeholders, each on a separate page. B) Under each stakeholder, write a one-line statement that you think represents that group's general viewpoint. C) Under each one-liner, list the major corporate changes you think people in that group might want.

Step 2. Develop a concept of culture

Imagine that everyone in the organization agreed that the underlying problem of prejudice and inequity is rooted in the current corporate culture. What effect would this have?

Step 3. Identify barriers to mutual respect and trust

If you and other key people conducted a long, hard, critical examination of "why we haven't been able or willing to value and appreciate our diversity," what barriers do you think you would find?

Step 4. Take responsibility for personal growth

Imagine that most of the employees worked deeply with their beliefs and feelings about prejudice and diversity? Would this eliminate most of the barriers noted in step 3? What barriers would remain?

Step 5. Influence culture change

- Would this process be enough to begin some positive change in corporate values, norms, structures, and power? What specific changes might occur? What else would be needed?

- Is there any evidence of overt or subtle paternalism, threats, or punishment in the organization? Be specific.

- Would this process be enough to begin shifting this pattern? How might this evolve? What else would be needed?

- Could this process lead to collaboration based on mutual trust, as peers who are committed to solving a common problem within a common framework? How might this evolve? What else would be needed?

Skill Builder 17.2: Beliefs about What Needs Changing

Purpose: To become aware of the role and power of individuals changing their beliefs.

Step 1. How can we become conscious of what needs changing? We might start by examining some core beliefs, attitudes, thoughts, feelings, decisions and day-to-day action choices. Examine this core belief:

Belief #1: *America is the great melting pot. If African Americans can't succeed in business, it's not because Euro-American managers and coworkers don't welcome them. It's because they don't have what it takes to succeed.*

Based on this belief, what needs to be done in the workplace? In society in general? What ideas come to mind? Record them.

Step 2. Now think about this alternate core belief:

Belief #2: *American culture, systems, institutions, and beliefs are what block African Americans from succeeding in business The stereotypes, prejudice, institutionalized discrimination, and personal discrimination of Euro-Americans are the problem.*

Based on this alternate belief, what needs to be done in the workplace? In society in general? What ideas come to mind? Record them.

Step 3. Job down your insights regarding the difference a belief makes.

Skill Builder 17.3: Making a Commitment for Change

Purpose: To make a written commitment to help change the workplace toward valuing diversity and eliminating discrimination.

Step 1. List at least three personal stands you're committed to taking:

Step 2. List at least three personal actions you're committed to taking.

Skill Builder 17.4: Who's in the Inner Circle?

Purpose: To get a clear picture of insiders and outsiders in your organization.

Step 1. Think of the organization where you work. Think about which employees are involved in continuous improvement and continuous learning—in learning loops that directly affect the success of the organization, its bottom-line results. In other words, think about which employees are included in the Inner Circles?

Step 2. Place symbols, such as triangles or circles, inside the Inner Circle that represent employees you know. You might use a different symbol, incorporating colored ink or pencil, for each employee—or a different symbol for each work team, unit, or department that's in the Inner Circle.

Step 3. Which employees are not included in the Inner Circle? They may be in learning loops, but not those that make a real difference. Draw symbols for those employees in the area outside the Inner Circle below.

Step 4. What does this picture say to you about your organization?

- About its effectiveness in managing diversity?
- About its effectiveness in utilizing all its human resources
- About its effectiveness in developing all its employees' potential for contribution?

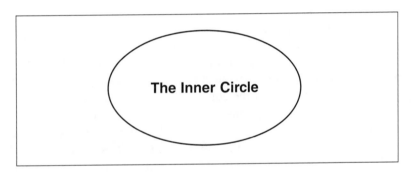

Case Study 17.1: Skills Gap at Lights Plus

Phyllis went to a Lights Plus store to buy some track lights she had seen advertised at a special reduced price. *Henry*, an African American salesperson, waited on her. Phyllis explained that the track lights were the only lighting in her home office and she needed lots of light throughout the room. Henry told her the sale track lights were very good lights, very popular. He went to the stock room to get the lights and tracks, couldn't find the tracks, and returned to tell Phyllis that they didn't have them in stock. Instead of giving up, Phyllis insisted on knowing if they could be obtained for her, so Henry asked the manager *Mark* about getting the tracks. Mark felt sure there were some tracks in the stock room and quickly found them. A sale was made. When Phyllis called in an electrician to install the lights, he pointed out that they gave small spots of very intense light and were not too effective for general lighting. In addition they were much more expensive that the general-lighting type. Phyllis decided to return them and wait for the general-lighting type to go on sale.

A month or so later Lights Plus advertised at half price the type of track lights Phyllis needed. She called the store near her to be sure they were still on sale and were in stock. When she walked into the store, Henry greeted her. He showed her the sale track lights, which were packaged in boxes, picked up a couple of boxes, and took them to the cash register. When he entered the transaction, Henry saw that the price displayed on the register was the regular price, not the sale price. Henry said, "Well, these lights are $59.99 a package." Phyllis was exasperated. She said, "Then I don't want them. I don't know why the woman who answered the phone here about an hour ago told me they were still on sale. If she had told me they were now regular price, I wouldn't have made the trip." Henry said nothing and Phyllis left the store, shaking her head.

Driving home, Phyllis recalled her last trip to Lights Plus. Henry had been uninformed about where to find merchandise in the stock room. "Maybe he's uninformed about prices too," she thought. She turned the corner, went back to the store, and asked to speak to the manager. When she explained the price problem, Mark replied, "Oh, yes, that's just one of those computer glitches. Somehow the sale information didn't get into the current computer file. No problem, you can have the track lights at the sale price." When Mark went to pick up the packets, he said, "Now some of these sets are black and some are white, even though the pictures on all the boxes show white lights." Phyllis thought, "Why didn't Henry tell me that? Without that information, I had a fifty-fifty chance of bringing home lights of the wrong color." (Note: The top management of Lights Plus has expressed the company's top-priority objective this way: "Customer satisfaction is the target.")

1. What are the root problems?

2. In what ways did Henry fail to meet the company's target?

3. Describe the gap between Henry's skills and capabilities and the required skills and capabilities. What do you think Henry should do?

4. Was Mark effective in managing inclusion? Giving quality treatment? Applying the ARC of improvement? What do you think Mark should do?

5. What cultural differences might explain the problems that occurred in this case?

Case Study 17.2: A "Diverse" Corporate Culture

Sharon is a 22 year old college student looking for a part-time job to help pay her school expenses. She interviews for a part-time receptionist job in a medical clinic. When *George*, the office manager, meets Sharon, he feels that she will "melt right into the company culture." The support staff is diverse, consisting of 11 Asian Americans, 6 African Americans, 4 Euro-Americans, and 8 Latino Americans. George believes that given her enthusiasm, Sharon will get along well with her coworkers, and given her educational background, he's sure she can perform the job duties. He offers her the job and she accepts.

Her first day on the job Sharon is introduced to all the staff members. She immediately feels as if she's part of the family. Her coworkers are very friendly, and each of them makes her feel welcome and comfortable. Sharon is assigned to report to *Tiffany*, an African American supervisor. From the first day Sharon notices that the staff in fact does not act like a family when it's time for coffee breaks and lunch. Actually the staff is pretty segregated. The African Americans sip and munch together, while the Asian Americans form their own group, speaking Cantonese. Meantime, the Latino Americans get together and speak Spanish. Tiffany leads Sharon straight to the African American group and they welcome her.

As Sharon and Tiffany get to know each other, Sharon reveals that her father is African American and her mother is Asian American. They divorced when Sharon was only three and Sharon has not seen much of her father since the divorce. Sharon doesn't have many African American friends. "Most of them seem to take the attitude that I'm not black enough," she says. "I think they're referring to the way I express myself rather than my skin color. I know I look more African American than Asian American. But I do speak Cantonese and of course my thinking is much like my mom's."

One day Sharon asks Tiffany, "Why do people go off into their own little ethnic groups all the time? They never seem to intermingle except on the job, only enough to get the work done." Tiffany replies, "Just human nature, I guess, We don't try to get people to intermingle. We just leave well enough alone. People get along pretty well now. If we try to get more interaction, they might start fighting, who knows?"

Now, a few weeks later, Sharon feels ignored by her African American coworkers and a little uncomfortable with them. She knows it's because she seems withdrawn and reserved to them, like she's holding back. But it's just the Asian way. Sharon tries a few times to join the Asian American group, even speaking Cantonese with them. At first they're surprised and interested in knowing more about her. But now they too tend to ignore her. Somehow she doesn't quite fit in with them either.

Sharon is feeling lonely. Every day she sits at the front desk, taking incoming calls, recording messages, and greeting patients. Sometimes Tiffany helps her out. But even when they're working side by side, they don't have many personal conversations any more. When her afternoon shift is over, Sharon goes home with few interesting stories to tell her mother—a few about patients, but none about coworkers. Sharon is thinking about looking for another job. Tiffany notices that Sharon is not as enthusiastic as she was when she first took the job. Even George has noticed a difference in Sharon's attitude.

1. What are the key issues (root problems) in this case?
2. If you were Sharon, what would you do?
3. If you were Tiffany, what would you do?
4. If you were George, what would you do?

A CONCLUDING ACKNOWLEDGMENT OF YOUR ACHIEVEMENT

Congratulations! If you've worked your way through this book, you now have a solid foundation for becoming a diversity leader and a conscious change agent. You've begun building a most valuable set of multicultural skills. In Chapter 1 you learned that you would proceed through five skill-building steps, and now you've completed those steps.

Steps You've Completed in Building Your Multicultural Skills

Step 1. You've become aware of culture and its pervasive influence.
Step 2. You've learned more about your own culture.
Step 3. You recognize your own biases, the ways in which you stereotype, assume, judge, and discriminate.
Step 4. You've learned about other cultures you encounter in the workplace so you can recognize when cultural differences may be at the root of problems and so you can appreciate the contributions people from diverse cultures can make to the work situation.
Step 5. You've started building your interaction skills and you've practiced some new behaviors, using self-awareness activities and skill builder case studies.

Being a diversity leader can be difficult and complex. You often must intuit your way into the murky unknown as change in the workplace accelerates. But the effort is so worthwhile, and success is so rewarding—and you now have some tools for doing it.

Managing diversity is the challenge of the new millennium—for our communities and our planet as well as for our workplaces. Do we want join a world of prejudice, bigotry, hatred, rage, riots, terrorism, and war? Or do we want to join in our common humanity and work through our differences so we can achieve great things together in peace and harmony? If we want harmony, then common sense tells us that workplace and community discrimination against whole groups of people must come to an end.

Managing diversity is also the opportunity for the new millennium. It offers opportunities to grow personally and collectively, to learn new ways of collaborating, to create a synergy that sparks innovation and accelerates human knowledge and achievement. Let's welcome these changes for the opportunities they open up and for the challenges that motivate us to keep sharpening our diversity skills.

REFERENCES

Alderfer, C.P. "Consulting to Underbounded Systems," in C.P. Alderfer and C.L. Cooper, eds. *Advances in Experiehntial Social Processes*, 2, 267–295, Wiley, 1980.

Allport, G. W. *The Nature of Prejudice.* Addison-Wesley Publishing Company, Inc., 1954.

AP, "Clinton Urged to Drop 'Colorblind' Concept," *Associated Press,* June 24, 1998.

Argyris, D. "Education for Leading-Learning," *Organizational Dynamics,* 21, 3, 5–17, 1993.

Arnold, H. and D. Feldman. *Organizational Behavior.* McGraw-Hill, 1986.

Bacharach, Samuel B., Peter A. Bamberger, and Dana Vashdi, "Diversity and Homophily at Work: Supportive Relations among Whites and African American Peers," *Academy of Management Journal,* 48, 4, 619–644, 2005.

Blanchard, F.A., and F.J. Crosby, eds. *Affirmative Action in Perspective.* Springer-Verlag, 1989.

Blank, Renee and Sandra Slipp, *Voices of Diversity.* Amacom, 1994.

Burman, Stephen. *The Black Progress Question.* Sage, 1995.

Carr-Ruffino, N., et al. "Legal Aspects of Women's Advancement" in *Woman Power.* Sage, 1991.

Carr-Ruffino, Norma. "U.S. Women: Breaking Through the Glass Ceiling." *Women in Management Review* 6, 5, 1991.

Catalyst. *Women in Corporate Management.* Catalyst, 1990.

Chrobot, D. and M.N. Ruderman, "Leadership in a Diverse Workplace, in M.S. Stockdale and F.J. Crosby, eds., *The Psychology and Management of Workplace Diversity,* 100–121. Blackwell Publishing, 2004.

Cox, Taylor, "The Multicultural Organization," *Academy of Management Executive* 5, 34–47, 1991.

Cox, Taylor. *Cultural Diversity in Organizations.* Berrett-Koehler, 1993.

Dahlin, Kristina B. et al, "Team Diversity and Information Use," *Academy of Management Journal* 48, 8, 1107–1123, 2005.

Davidson, M.N. and K. L Proudford, "Cycles of Resistance" in K.M. Thomas, ed., *Diversity Resistance in Organizations.* Lawrence Erlbaum Associates, 2008.

Deshpande, Hoyer, and J. Donthu. "The Study of Ethnic Affiliation." *Journal of Consumer Research* 13, 214–220, 1986.

DiTomaso, N., D.E. Thompson, and D.H. Blake. "Corporate Perspectives on the Advancement of Minority Managers" in *Ensuring Minority Success in Corporate Management.* Plenum, 1988.

Dovidio, J.F., S.L. Gaertner. and K. Kawakami, "Intergroup Contact: the Past, Present, and the Future." *Group Processes and Intergroup Relations,* 6: 5–21, 2003.

Elron, E. "Top Management Teams Within Multinational Corporations: Effects of Cultural Heterogeneity." *Leadership Quarterly,* 8, 292–412, 1997.

Ely, R.J. and D.A. Thomas, "Cultural Diversity at Work: The Moderating Effects of Work Group Perspectives on Diversity," *Administrative Science Quarterly* 46, 229–273, 2001.

Ferdman, B.M., "Values about Fairness in the Ethnically Diverse Workplace." [Special Issue: Managing in a Global Context: Diversity and Cross-Cultural Challenges.] *Business and the Contemporary World: An International Journal of Business, Economics, and Social Polity,* 9, 191–208, 1997.

Fernandez, J.P. *Managing a Diverse Work Force.* Simon & Schuster, 1991.

Gentile, Mary. *Managerial Excellence Through Diversity.* Irwin, 1996.

Glazer, Nathan and D.P. Moynihan, Eds., *Beyond the Melting Pot,* 2nd ed. MIT Press, 1970.

Gottfredson. "Dilemmas in Developing Diversity Programs" in *Diversity in the Workplace.* Guilford, 1992.

Graham, Lawrence. *The Best Companies for Minorities.* Penguin, 1993.

Halter, Marilyn. *Shopping for Identity: The Marketing of Ethnicity.* Schocken Books, 2000.

Harrison, David A., D.A. Kravitz, D.M. Mayer, L.M. Leslie, Dalit Lev-Arey, "Understanding Attitudes toward Affirmative Action Programs in Employment," *Journal of Applied Psychology,* 91, 5, 1013–1036, September 2006.

Harstone, M. and M. Augoustinos, The Minimal Group Paradigm: Categorization into Two Versus Three Groups," *European Journal of Social Psychology,* 25, 179–193, 1995.

Hebl, Mikke, J.M. Madera and Eden King, "Exclusion, Avoidance, and Social Distancing," in Decia M. Thomas ed., *Diversity Resistance in Organizations*, 127–150, 2008.

Helgeson, Sally. *The Web of Inclusion*. Doubleday, 1995.

Henderson, George. *Cultural Diversity in the Workplace*. Praeger, 1994.

Holladay, C.L. et al, "The Influence of Framing on Attitudes Toward Diversity Training," *Human Resource Development Quarterly* 14, 3, 245–263, 2003.

Hong, L. and S.E. Page, "Groups of Diverse Problem Solvers Can Outperform Groups of High-Ability Problem Solvers," *Proceedings of the National Academy of Sciences* 202, 46, 16385–16389, 2004.

HRM Ideas & Trends in Personnel, 272, 53. Commerce Clearing House, April 1992.

Jackson, Susan, Ed. *Diversity in the Workplace*. Gilford, 1992.

Kidder, D.L. et al, "Backlash Toward Diversity Initiatives: Examining the Impact of Diversity Program Justification, Personal, and Group Outcomes," *The International Journal of Conflict Management* 15, 77–102, 2004.

Kim, J.S., and A.F. Campagna. "Effects of Flextime on Employee Attendance and Performance." *Academy of Management Journal* 24, 729–741, 1981.

King, T., A. M. Kavanagh et al, 'Weight and place: a multilevel cross-sectional survey of area-level social disadvantage and overweight/obesity" *International Journal of Obesity*, 30, 2, 281–287, 2006.

Korn/Ferry International, "Diversity in the Executive Suites: Good News and Bad News," *www.kornferry.com/diversity*, 1999.

Kotter, J.P. "What Leaders Really Do," *Harvard Business Review*, 103-111, May-June 1990.

Kravitz, David A. "Can We Take the Guesswork Out of Diversity Practice Selection?" *Academy of Management Perspectives* 21, 2, May 2007.

Lau, Dora C. and J. Keith Murnighan, "Interactions within Groups and Subgroups: The Effects of Demographic Faultlines," *Academy of Management Journal* 48, 4, 645–659, 2005.

Levine, K. Field *Theory in Social Sciences*. Harper, 1951.

Mannix, E. and M. Neale, "What Differences Make a Difference? The Promise and Reality of Diverse Teams in Organizations," *Psychology in the Public Interest*, 2005.

May, M. and F. Cilliers. *Robben Island: A Container for Difference*. Montana Park, South Africa: ECT Educational Holdings, 2005.

Miller, Brian. "Adult Sexual Resocialization" *Sociology of Homosexuality*. Garland, 1992

Morrison, Ann, R.P. White, and E. Van Velsor. *Breaking the Glass Ceiling*. Addison-Wesley, 1987.

Morrison, Ann. *The New Leaders*. Jossey-Bass, 1992.

Ragins, B. R., and J.M. Cornwell, "Pink triangles: Antecedents and consequences of perceived workplace discrimination against gay and lesbian employees," *Journal of Applied Psychology*, 86, 1244–1261, 2002.

Shephard, C. R. *Small Groups*. Chandler Publishing, 1964.

Smither, R.D., J.M. Houston, and S.D. McIntire. *Organization Development: Strategies for Changing Environments*. Harper Collins, 1996.

Terry, Robert W. *For Whites Only*. William B. Eerdmans Publishing Company, 1970, 1990.

Thiederman, Sondra. *Bridging Cultural Barriers for Corporate Success*. Lexington Books, 1991.

Thomas, D.A. "The Truth about Mentoring Minorities: Race Matters," *Harvard Business Review* 79, 98–107, 2001.

Thomas, D.A. and R.J. Ely, "Making Differences Matter: A New Paradigm for Managing Diversity," *Harvard Business Review*, 74, 5, 790–792, 1996.

Thomas, Kecia M. ed. *Diversity Resistance in Organizations*. Lawrence Erlbaum Associates, 2008.

Thomas, Roosevelt. *Beyond Race & Gender*. AMACOM, 1991.

Thomas, Roosevelt. "From Affirmative Action to Affirming Diversity." *Harvard Business Review* 68, 2, 1990, 107–117.

U.S. Department of Labor. *A Report on the Glass Ceiling Initiative*. 1991.

Van der Vegt, G.S. et al, "Location-Level Links Between Diversity and Innovative Climate Depend on National Power Distance, *Academy of Management Journal* 48, 8, 1171–1182, 2005.

Vescio, T.K., G.B. Sechrist and M.P. Paolucci, "Perspective Taking and Prejudice Reduction: The Mediational Role of Empathy Arousal and Situational Attributions," *European Journal of Social Psychology* 33, 455–472, 2003.

Other Resources

The following materials address the political correctness issue:

Gates, H.L., Jr. *Loose Canons*. Oxford University Press, 1992.

Graff, Gerald. *Beyond the Culture Wars: How Teaching the Conflicts Can Revitalize American Education*. W.W. Norton, 1992.

The diversity training materials that follow are available from:

Managing Diversity, JALMC, P. O. Box 819, Jamestown, NY 14702

Banks, G. *The Human Diversity Workshop*.

Dickerson-Jones, Terri. *50 Activities for Diversity Training*.

Dickerson-Jones, Terri. *50 Activities for Managing Cultural Diversity*.

Directory of Diversity Recruitment

Fyock, C. *Cultural Diversity: Challenges and Opportunities*.

Gardenswartz, L. and A. Rowe. *Managing Diversity: A Complete Desk Reference and Planning Guide and The Diversity Tool Kit*.

Managing Diversity, a monthly newsletter.

Myers, S. and J. Lambert. *Diversity Icebreakers: A Trainer's Guide*.

Turkewych, C. and H. Guerreiro-Klinowski. *Intercultural Interviewing*.

Appendix

MANAGING DIVERSITY—RECOMMENDED FILMS

Stereotyping and Prejudice

Highly Recommended: *A Class Divided*—60 min – 1985 How stereotyping and prejudice were played out in a 3rd grade classroom. Originally a Frontline television sequel to a 1970 documentary *Eye of the Storm.* Currently a PBS video produced by Yale University Films. *http://diversity-dtg.com/store/*

Color of Fear—see African American films.

Racism 101—1988, 58 min. Discussion of racism on campuses.

Master Harold and the Boys—1985, 90 min. When Harold, a young Euro-American man, learns that his alcoholic, handicapped father is returning home, his frustration turns into racist viciousness against the two African American men who work for the family. *www.Amazon.com*

African American

Highly Recommended: *Color of Fear*—1994, 90 min. (can stop at 1hr.) Powerful interaction among men at a diversity retreat—includes African American, Asian American, Latino American and Gay issues. The African American segments are the most vivid, and therefore the film works well with the African American chapter. Source: StirFry Seminars & Consulting, *www.stirfry-seminars.com*

Are We Different?—1992, 28 min. African Americans discuss issues.

American Indians

500 Nations—2004, 45 min each, total 372 min. An 8-part documentary that explores the history of the indigenous peoples of North and Central America, from pre-Colombian times through the period of European contact and colonization, to the end of the 19th century and the subjugation of the Plains Indians of North America. Warner Studios, *http://whv.warnerbros.com*

American Indians—a series of films offered by *www.VisionMaker.org*

Indians of California—1991, 22 min. Yokuts made up the largest tribe inhabiting California. Known for their practical and resourceful ways, these Native Americans had a great respect for their bountiful food supply and for the land that provided it. *www.evnDirect.com*

Indians of the Southwest and Indians of the Plains—34 min. Gives some history, mostly from a cultural and spiritual viewpoint. Mentions crafts, beliefs, traditions.

Native American Indians—1994. About American Indian traditions, worldviews, and values. Parade.

Native American Indians—1994. Before Europeans set foot on these shores, Native Americans lived in harmony with all that surrounded them. Steeped in myth and tradition, they epitomize the extraordinary relationship between the people, the land and all living creatures. *www.Amazon.com*

Pow Wow Highway—1989, 88 min. A Cheyenne from Montana buys a '64 Buick and embarks on a cross country adventure with the reservation's political renegade. *www.Amazon.com*

Smoke Signals—1999. The first feature made by a Native American crew and creative team (Sundance Studios), the film concerns two young Idaho men with radically different memories of a former resident of the reservation who split years before and has just died in Phoenix. *www.Amazon.com*

The Mission—1994, 1 hr,. *Neighborhoods, the Hidden Cities of San Francisco* series, Public Broadcasting System, www.pbs.org Brief info on American Indians, mostly on Latino

The Native Americans—1994, 49 min. each for a series of 6 videos, based on geographical location: Northeast, Far West, Southeast, Southwest, Plains I and II. Turner Home Video, *http://video.abum.com/turner-home-video.html*

Asian American

Highly Recommended: *Chinatown*—1994, 1 hr, Using San Francisco's Chinatown as the venue, this film covers Chinese American history, culture, and issues from the beginning to recent times. *Neighborhoods, the Hidden Cities of San Francisco* series, Public Broadcasting System, *www.pbs.org*

A Small Happiness—1984, 58 min. Explores sexual politics in rural China with segments on love and marriage, foot-binding, child-bearing and birth control. *www.tsquare.tv/longbow/sh.html*

Fire—1996, 104 min. In New Delhi, India, Sita, a beautiful and intelligent young woman embarks on an arranged, loveless marriage to a faithless husband. *www.imdb.com*

Snow Falling on Cedars—2000, 128 min. A Japanese-American fisherman may have killed his neighbor at sea. In the 1950's, post-war anti-Japanese sentiments still run high in the ensuing trial. *www.Amazon.com*

Bi–ethnic

Just Black—1991, 59 min., interviews of bi-ethnic college students.

Disabled

Highly Recommended: *When Billy Broke His Head*—1994, 57 min—When Billy Golfus, an award-winning radio journalist, became brain injured in a motor scooter accident, he became one of 43 million Americans with disabilities—the nation's largest and most invisible minority. But this video, as he says, "ain't exactly your inspirational cripple story." It's a documentary with attitude, which will entertain, enlighten, and even enrage its viewers. *www.fanlight.com*

And Justice for All—1991, 57 min. Explanation of the Americans with Disability Act.

Different but the Same—1989, 13 min. Adults and children with physical, sensory, and intellectual disabilities introduce themselves, the tools that help them achieve independence, and the people who support them in reaching their goals. They share a desire to be seen as equal though different. Uses term *handicap* but otherwise makes some good points

Enabling Act (ADA, Is It Working?)—2001, 12 min. How lawsuits force companies to comply.

Vital Signs: Crip Culture Talks Back—48 min, 1997. Brings together influential voices in disability rights and disability studies to document an emerging disability culture. A mix of performances, interviews, dramatic readings, and activist footage. *www.fanlight.com*

Gender

Highly Recommended: *Men and Women Talking Talking Together*—1993, 60 min. Deborah Tannen and Robert Bly discuss gender issues. *www.MysticFire.com*

Annapurna: A Woman's Place—45 min. Inspiring story of 13 women who climbed the Himalayan mountain, Annapurna 1, in 1978 including the triumph of the summit and the tragic loss of two team members. *www.Amazon.com*

Mosaic Workplace—See #3 and #4 of this series, described in the Managing Diversity section.

Sexual Harassment at Work is not Play—1995, 57 min. Guide for small business owners and managers on the changing laws on sexual harassment in the workplace.

Sexual Harassment: A High Price to Pay A two part series that provides employees and management with a clear understanding of what legally constitutes sexual harassment; what to do if sexual harassment occurs; as well as the severe consequences if harassment is not dealt with swiftly and adequately. *www.mpcFilms.com*

Sexual Harassment: A Management Briefing Dramatically demonstrates how incidents of sexual harassment, including poorly handled or unresolved complaints, can translate into liability exposure and staggering monetary losses to the organization as well as to individual managers who fail to take immediate action. *www.mpcFilms.com*

Subtle Sexual Harassment—1992, two 30-min segments: "The Issues is Respect" for managers and employees; "Management's New Responsibilities for employees' view. *www.mpcFilms.com*

Gay

Highly Recommended: *The Castro*—1994, 1 hr. History of the gay community in San Francisco, culture, barriers, and issues. *Neighborhoods, the Hidden Cities of San Francisco* series, Public Broadcasting System. *www.pbs.org*

Homophobia in the Workplace—1995, 1 hr. Brian McNaught lectures employees on what it's like to be a gay employee in U.S. workplace. Covers most of the bases. *www.Amazon.com*

Before Stonewall: The Making of a Gay and Lesbian Community—1985, 97 min. Evolution of gay culture in the U.S. from the early 1920s to the 1969 riot at Stonewall bar in New York. The gay underground of the '20s and '30s, the rise of gay service in the military and workforce during WWII, the persecution of gays as "subversives" and "sexual perverts" by Senator Joseph McCarthy, the growth of the first grassroots political organizations for gay men and lesbians in the '50s, and the civil rights movement. *www.Amazon.com*

Priest—1998, 90+ min. A magnificent film that covers a lot of ground emotionally. The fact that the lead character happens to be a priest is secondary to the main point of the film—love (or the lack of it) and personal relationships. *www.Amazon.com*

Billy Elliot—2000. Dad, a miner, scrapes together money to send 11-year-old Billy to boxing lessons, but Billy loves ballet dancing. In this fiercely macho culture, admitting to such an activity is tantamount to holding up a sign reading "I Am Gay," so Billy keeps it quiet, supported by his sweet gay friend. *www.Amazon.com*

Better than Chocolate—1999, 90+ min. Two young lesbians meet, develop a passionate romance, and move in together. the well-meaning but naive mother of one of them gets divorced and decides to join the household. She is soon befriended by a transsexual about to undergo a sex-change operation. *www.Amazon.com*

Latino American

Highly Recommended: *The Mission*, 1994, 1 hr. *Neighborhoods, the Hidden Cities of San Francisco* series, Public Broadcasting System, *www.pbs.org*

Fruit of Dreams; The Mexican Cherry Pickers of Traverse City—1995, 27 min. Has rare film footage from 1926 to 1960, along with interviews with Mexicans cherry pickers. A first-hand look at the tribulations of these important workers who provided a major contribution to Michigan agriculture. *www.HillsdalePublishers.com*

Managing Diversity

Highly Recommended: #10 in the Mosaic Workplace series.

The Mosaic Workplace: Managing the Multicultural Workplace (video series)—1991, 10 films address the problem s and opportunities of diversity. *www.rctm.com*

Index